ELSEVIER'S
DICTIONARY OF
COMPUTER SCIENCE

ELSEVIER'S DICTIONARY OF COMPUTER SCIENCE

in

English, German, French and Russian

compiled by

B. DELIJSKA and P. MANOILOV
Sofia, Bulgaria

2001
ELSEVIER
Amsterdam – London – New York – Oxford – Paris – Shannon – Tokyo

ELSEVIER SCIENCE B.V.
Sara Burgerhartstraat 25
P.O. Box 211, 1000 AE Amsterdam, The Netherlands

First edition 2001

Library of Congress Cataloging in Publication Data
A catalog record from the Library of Congress has been applied for.

ISBN: 0-444-50339-0

⊗ The paper used in this publication meets the requirements of ANSI/NISO Z39.48-1992 (Permanence of Paper).
Printed in The Netherlands.

PREFACE

The dictionary contains 10,120 terms with about 4,000 cross-references that are commonly used in the theory and practice of computer science. The terms were selected according to their significance or frequency of use. We have tried to follow the latest developments in computer science and practice, including computer jargon, as well as classical terms. The terminology covers the areas of information technology, algorithmics, programming languages, system and application software, networking, communications, digital electronics, computer hardware, computer graphics, etc.

Most modern terms were extracted from Internet sites and from current publications in journals in the respective languages.

The dictionary consists of two parts. In the first part, the *Basic Table*, the English terms are listed alphabetically and numbered consecutively. The English term is followed by its German, French and Russian equivalents. The introduction of the English terms that are given as cross-references to the main entries is also alphabetical. The second part, *the Indexes,* contains separate alphabetical indexes of the German, French and Russian terms. The reference number(s) of every term stands for the number of the English equivalent in the basic table.

The authors hope that Elsevier's Dictionary of Computer Science will be a valuable tool for engineers, scientists and students and for everyone who takes interest in computer science and practice.

Dr. B. Delijska
Dr. P. Manoilov

CONTENTS

EXPLANATION OF SPECIAL SIGNS

1. The italics *d*, *f* and *r* in the basic table stand respectively for the German, French and Russian equivalents of the English terms.

2. The gender of nouns is indicated as follows:

f	feminine	*fpl*	feminine plural
m	masculine	*mpl*	masculine plural
n	neuter	*npl*	neuter plural
pl	plural	*m/f*	masculine or feminine

3. The symbol *v* designates a verb.

4. The symbol *adj* designates an adjective.

4. Synonyms and abbreviations are separated by semicolons.

5. Two kinds of brackets are used:

[ ] the information can be either included or left out;

( ) the information does not form an integral part of the expression, but helps to clarify it.

Basic Table

A

* abac → 1

1 abac[us]; calculating frame
d Abakus *m*; Rechenbrett *n*; Kugelbrett *n*
f abaque *m*; boulier *m*; table *f* à calculer
r абак *m*; счёты *pl*; счётная доска *f*

2 abbreviated; abridged; reduced
d abgekürzt; gekürzt
f abrégé; écourté
r сокращённый; укороченный

3 abbreviated addressing
d abgekürzte Adressierung *f*
f adressage *m* abrégé
r укороченная адресация *f*

* abbreviated code → 1176

* abbreviated division → 8

* abbreviated multiplication → 9 ·

* abbreviated subtraction → 11

4 abbreviation
d Abkürzung *f*; Kürzung *f*
f abrègement *m*; abréviation *f*; abréviature *f*
r сокращение *n*; аббревиатура *f*

* abend → 5

* ABIOS → 263

5 abnormal end; abend; abnormal termination; blow up
d Abnormalhalt *m*; fehlerbedingte Beendigung *f*; vorzeitige Beendigung
f arrêt *m* anormal; fin *f* anormale; fin précoce; fin imprévue
r аварийный останов *m*; аварийное завершение *n*; преждевременное прекращение *n*; авост *m*

6 abnormal system end; system crash
d Systemabsturz *m*; Systemzusammenbruch *m*
f effondrement *m* de système
r авария *f* в системе

* abnormal termination → 5

* abonent → 9007

* abort → 1171

7 abort sequence
d Abbruchfolge *f*
f séquence *f* d'abandon
r последовательность *f* [преждевременного] прекращения

* abridged → 2

8 abridged division; abbreviated division; shortcut division
d abgekürzte Division *f*
f division *f* abrégée; division courte; division accélérée
r сокращённое деление *n*; сокращённый способ *m* деления; ускоренное деление

9 abridged multiplication; abbreviated multiplication; short multiplication
d abgekürzte Multiplikation *f*
f multiplication *f* abrégée
r сокращённое умножение *n*; ускоренное умножение

10 abridged notation
d abgekürzte Bezeichnung *f*
f notation *f* abrégée
r сокращённое обозначение *n*

11 abridged subtraction; abbreviated subtraction; short subtraction
d abgekürzte Subtraktion *f*
f soustraction *f* abrégée
r сокращённое вычитание *n*; ускоренное вычитание

12 abridged symbolic notation
d Gleichungssymbolik *f*; abgekürzte symbolische Bezeichnung *f*
f notation *f* symbolique abrégée
r сокращённое символическое обозначение *n*

13 absence
d Fehlen *n*
f absence *f*
r отсутствие *n*

14 absence of failures
d Ausfallfreiheit *f*
f absence *f* de défaillances
r безотказность *f*

15 absentee-user job
d ohne Benutzer ausgeführter Job *m*
f travail *m* en absence d'utilisateur
r задание *n*, выполняемое в отсутствии пользователя

16 absolute address; direct address; physical address
d absolute Adresse f; direkte Adresse; physikalische Adresse; echte Adresse
f adresse f absolue; adresse directe; adresse physique
r абсолютный адрес m; прямой адрес; физический адрес

17 absolute assembler
d absoluter Assembler m
f assembleur m absolu
r абсолютный ассемблер m

* **absolute branch → 22**

18 absolute code; specific code
d absoluter Code m
f code m absolu
r абсолютный код m

* **absolute coding → 5544**

19 absolute error
d absoluter Fehler m
f erreur f absolue
r абсолютная ошибка f

20 absolute expression
d absoluter Ausdruck m
f expression f absolue
r абсолютное выражение n

21 absolute instruction
d absoluter Befehl m
f instruction f absolue
r абсолютная инструкция f

22 absolute jump; absolute branch; absolute skip
d absoluter Sprung m
f saut m absolu
r абсолютный переход m; переход к абсолютным адресам

23 absolute loader
d Absolutlader m
f chargeur m absolu
r абсолютный загрузчик m

* **absolute skip → 22**

24 absolute value
d Absolutbetrag m; Absolutwert m; absolute Größe f
f valeur f absolue
r абсолютная величина f; абсолютное значение n

25 absorbing barrier
d Absorptionsschirm m
f écran m absorbant
r поглощающий экран m

26 absorbing filter; absorption filter
d Absorptionsfilter m; absorbierender Filter m
f filtre m absorbant; filtre d'absorption
r поглощающий фильтр m

27 absorption
d Absorption f
f absorption f
r поглощение n

* **absorption filter → 26**

28 abstract v
d abstrahieren
f abstraire
r абстрагировать

29 abstract; summary
d Resümee n; Zusammenfassung f; Kurzfassung f; Kurzdarstellung f
f résumé m; abrégé m; raccourci m
r резюме n; извлечение n; реферат m

30 abstract alphabet
d abstraktes Alphabet n
f alphabet m abstrait
r абстрактный алфавит m

31 abstract code; pseudocode
d abstrakter Code m; Pseudocode m
f code m abstrait; pseudocode m
r абстрактный код m; псевдокод m

32 abstract [data] type
d abstrakter Datentyp m
f type m abstrait [de données]
r абстрактный тип m [данных]

33 abstract functional structure
d abstrakte funktionale Struktur f
f structure f abstraite fonctionnelle
r абстрактная функциональная структура f

34 abstraction
d Abstraktion f
f abstraction f
r абстракция f; абстрагирование n

35 abstract number
d abstrakte Zahl f
f nombre m abstrait
r абстрактное число n

* **abstract type → 32**

* **abundant → 7786**

36 abundant number
d überschießende Zahl *f*; abundante Zahl
f nombre *m* imparfait par excès; nombre abondant; nombre excédent
r избыточное число *n*

37 abuse
d Fehlbehandlung *f*
f violation *f*; erreur *f* d'exploitation
r неправильное обращение *n*; неправильная эксплуатация *f*

* **AC** → 348

* **ACB** → 67

* **accelerant** → 43

38 accelerate *v*
d beschleunigen
f accélérer
r ускорять

39 accelerated graphics port; AGP
d beschleunigter Grafikport *m*; AGP; beschleunigte Grafikschnittstelle *f*
f port *m* graphique accéléré; port AGP
r ускоренный графический порт *m*

40 acceleration
d Beschleunigung *f*; Akzeleration *f*
f accélération *f*
r ускорение *n*; разгон *m*

* **acceleration factor** → 1832

41 acceleration of tape
d Bandbeschleunigung *f*
f accélération *f* de bande
r разгон *m* ленты

42 acceleration time
d Beschleunigungszeit *f*
f temps *m* d'accélération
r время *n* ускорения

* **accelerator** → 8517

43 accelerator; accelerant
d Beschleuniger *m*
f accélérateur *m*; accélérant *m*
r ускоритель *m*; ускоряющее устройство *n*; акселератор *m*

44 accelerator card
d Beschleunigungskarte *f*; Beschleunigungsplatte *f*; Beschleunigungsplatine *f*
f carte *f* accélératrice
r ускоряющая плата *f*

* **accelerator key** → 8517

* **accelerator keyboard** → 5212

45 accent
d Akzent *m*; Gravis *m*
f accent *m*
r акцент *m*; акцент *m*; ударение *n*

46 accented character
d Akzentzeichen *n*; Akzentbuchstabe *f*; Buchstabe *f* mit Akzent
f caractère *m* accentué
r символ *m* с ударением; подчёркнутый символ

47 accentuate *v*; **emphasize** *v*
d betonen; hervorheben
f accentuer
r выделять

48 accept *v*
d annehmen; akzeptieren
f accepter; prendre
r воспринимать; принимать

49 acceptability
d Annehmbarkeit *f*
f acceptabilité *f*
r приемлемость *f*

50 acceptable
d annehmbar; akzeptabel
f acceptable
r приемлемый

51 acceptable program
d annehmbares Programm *n*
f programme *m* acceptable
r приемлемая программа *f*

52 acceptable use policy; AUP
d Gebrauch-Police *f*
f règles *mpl* de bon usage
r правила *npl* приемлемого использования (системы)

53 acceptance; recept[ion]
d Akzeptanz *f*; Annahme *f*; Empfang *m*; Aufnahme *f*
f acceptation *f*; acception *f*; réception *f*
r приём *m*; получение *n*

* **acceptance inspection** → 56

54 acceptance of data; data acceptance
d Übernahme *f* von Daten; Datenübernahme *f*
f acceptation *f* de données
r приём *m* данных

55 **acceptance sampling**
 d Annahmestichprobenverfahren *n*
 f échantillonnage *m* pour inspection
  d'acceptation
 r приёмочный контроль *m*; выборочный
  контроль

56 **acceptance test; acceptance inspection**
 d Abnahmeprüfung *f*; Übernahmeprüfung *f*
 f essai *m* de réception; contrôle *m* d'acceptation
 r приёмо-сдаточное испытание *n*

57 **acceptor**
 d Akzeptor *m*; Abnehmer *m*
 f accepteur *m*; acheteur *m*
 r акцептор *m*; приёмник *m*

58 **accept statement**
 d Annahmeanweisung *f*
 f instruction *f* d'acceptation
 r оператор *m* приёма

59 **access**
 d Zugriff *m*; Zugang *m*
 f accès *m*
 r доступ *m*; обращение *n*

60 **access address**
 d Zugriffsadresse *f*
 f adresse *f* d'accès
 r адрес *m* доступа; указатель *m*

61 **access arm**
  (of a disk head)
 d Zugriffsarm *m*
 f bras *m* de déplacement; bras de chargement
 r рычаг *m* крепления и перемещения; рычаг
  выборки

62 **access attribute**
 d Zugriffsattribut *n*
 f attribut *m* d'accès
 r атрибут *m* доступа; описание *n* обращения

63 **access authorization**
 d Zugriffsberechtigung *f*
 f autorisation *f* d'accès
 r разрешение *n* на доступ

64 **access by key; keyed access**
 d Schlüsselzugriff *m*; Zugriff *m* über
  Schlüsselfeld
 f accès *m* par clé; accès par parole
 r доступ *m* по ключу; доступ по паролю

65 **access code**
 d Zugangskennzahl *f*; Zugangskennziffer *f*
 f code *m* d'accès
 r код *m* доступа

66 **access control; access management**
 d Zugriffskontrolle *f*; Zugangskontrolle *f*
 f gestion *f* d'accès
 r управление *n* доступом

67 **access control block; ACB**
 d Zugriffsteuerblock *m*
 f bloc *m* de gestion d'accès
 r блок *m* управления доступом

68 **access control field**
 d Zugriffskontrollfeld *n*; Zugangskontrollfeld *n*
 f zone *f* de gestion d'accès
 r поле *n* управления доступом

69 **access control protocol**
 d Zugangskontrollprotokoll *n*
 f protocole *m* de gestion d'accès
 r протокол *m* управления доступом

70 **access cycle**
 d Zugriffszyklus *m*
 f cycle *m* d'accès
 r цикл *m* доступа; цикл обращения

71 **access denied**
 d Zugriff *m* verweigert
 f accès *m* dénié
 r отвергнутый доступ *m*

72 **access file attribute**
 d Zugriffsdateiattribut *n*
 f attribut *m* de fichier d'accès
 r атрибут *m* доступа к файлу; описание *n*
  обращения к файлу

73 **access hole**
  (on a diskette)
 d Zugriffsloch *n*; Zugriffsöffnung *f*
 f trou *m* d'accès
 r окно *n* доступа

74 **accessibility; reachability; attainability**
 d Erreichbarkeit *f*; Accessibility *f*
 f accessibilité *f*
 r достижимость *f*; доступность *f*

75 **accessible**
 d erreichbar; zugänglich; zugreifbar
 f accessible; loisible
 r доступный; достижимый

76 **accessible interface**
 d benutzbare Schnittstelle *f*
 f interface *f* accessible
 r достижимый интерфейс *m*

77 **access level**
 d Zugriff-Pegel *m*; Zugriffsebene *f*

f niveau *m* d'accès
r уровень *m* доступа

* **access limitation** → 86

* **access management** → 66

78 access mechanism
d Zugriffsmechanismus *m*
f mécanisme *m* d'accès
r механизм *m* доступа; механизм выборки

79 access method
d Zugriffsmethode *f*; Zugriffsverfahren *n*
f méthode *f* d'accès
r метод *m* доступа; метод обращения

80 accessories
d Zubehör *n*; Zubehörteil *f*
f accessoires *mpl*; outils *mpl*
r дополнительные части *fpl*;
   принадлежности *fpl*; вспомогательные
   сооружения *npl*; аксессуары *mpl*

81 accessory *adj*
d zusätzlich
f accessoire
r дополнительный; вспомагательный

82 access path
d Zugriffsweg *m*
f route *f* d'accès
r путь *m* доступа; путь обращения

83 access point
d Zugriffspunkt *m*
f point *m* d'accès
r пункт *m* доступа

84 access protocol
d Zugriffsprotokoll *n*
f protocole *m* d'accès
r протокол *m* доступа

85 access provider
d Zugangsanbieter *m*; Zugangsbereitsteller *m*
f fournisseur *m* d'accès; prestataire *m* d'accès
r поставщик *m* доступа; провайдер *m*
   доступа

86 access restriction; access limitation
d Zugriffseinschränkung *f*
f restriction *f* d'accès; limitation *f* d'accès
r ограничение *n* доступа

87 access right
d Zugriffsrecht *n*
f droit *m* d'accès
r право *n* доступа

88 access time; select time; request response time
d Zugriff[s]zeit *f*; Auswahlzeit *f*
f temps *m* d'accès; temps de sélection
r время *n* доступа; время выборки

* **accidental** → 7591

* **accidental error** → 7595

* **accordance** → 2120

89 accordion-folded paper; fanfold paper form
d Leporello-Papier *n*; zickzack gefaltetes
   Formularpapier *n*
f papier *m* en accordéon; papier plié en zig-zag
r бумага *f*, сфальцованная гармошкой;
   фальцованная бумага

* **account** → 9715

90 account; bill; invoice
d Abrechnung *f*; Rechnung *f*; Konto *n*
f décompte *m*; compte *m*
r расчёт *m*; смета *f*; учёт *m*

91 accounting
d Buchführung *f*; Rechnungsführung *f*
f comptabilité *f*
r отчётность *f*; учётность *f*

92 accounting file
d Abrechnungsdatei *f*
f fichier *m* barème; fichier de contrôle
r учётный файл *m*

* **accounting information** → 9715

* **accounting package** → 94

93 accounting problem
d Abrechnungsproblem *n*
f problème *m* de comptabilité
r задача *f* учёта и отчётности

94 accounting [software] package
d Buchhaltungssoftware *f*;
   Buchhaltungssoftwarepaket *n*
f logiciel *m* comptable; logiciel de comptabilité
r программное обеспечение *n* для учётности

95 accumulate *v*
d akkumulieren
f accumuler
r аккумулировать; накапливать

96 accumulated error; cumulative error; stored error
d akkumulierter Fehler *m*; kumulativer Fehler

f erreur *f* [ac]cumulée; erreur d'accumulation
r накопленная ошибка *f*; суммарная ошибка

97 accumulating register; A-register; accumulator
d Akkumulatorregister *n*; Akku[mulator] *m*
f registre *m* accumulateur; registre A; accumulateur *m*
r накапливающий регистр *m*; аккумулятор *m*

98 accumulation
d Akkumulation *f*; Aufhäufung *f*
f accumulation *f*
r аккумуляция *f*; накопление *n*

99 accumulation coefficient
d Akkumulationskoeffizient *m*
f coefficient *m* d'accumulation
r коэффициент *m* накопления

* **accumulator** → 97, 870

100 accumulator contents
d Akkumulatorinhalt *m*
f contenu *m* d'accumulateur
r содержание *n* аккумулятора

101 accumulator sign
d Akkumulatorvorzeichen *n*
f signe *m* d'accumulateur
r знак *m* числа в аккумуляторе

102 accumulator volume
d Akkumulatorvolumen *n*
f volume *m* d'accumulateur
r ёмкость *f* аккумулятора

103 accuracy; exactness; exactitude; precision
d Exaktheit *f*; Präzision *f*
f exactitude *f*; précision *f*
r точность *f*

104 accuracy of reading
d Ablesegenauigkeit *f*
f exactitude *f* de la lecture
r точность *f* отсчёта

105 accuracy rating
d Genauigkeitsgrenze *f*; Genauigkeitsklasse *f*
f classe *f* d'exactitude; classe de précision
r степень *f* точности; класс *m* точности

106 ac fault
d dynamischer Fehler *m*
f défaut *m* dynamique
r динамическая неисправность *f*

* **ACIA** → 597

* **ACK** → 109

* **acknowledge** → 109

* **acknowledge character** → 110

107 acknowledged interaction
d Dialog *n* mit Quittierung
f interaction *f* d'accusé de réception
r диалог *m* с подтверждением

108 acknowledged transmission
d quittierte Übermittlung *f*
f transmission *f* d'accusé de réception
r передача *f* с подтверждением

* **acknowledge identifier** → 111

109 acknowledge[ment]; ACK; answerback; quittance; handshake
d Rückmeldung *f*; Empfangsbestätigung *f*; Quittierung *f*; Handshake *n*
f annonce *f* en retour; acquittement *m*; quittance *f*; confirmation *f* de réception; accusé *m* de réception
r подтверждение *n* приёма; квитирование *n*; автоответ *m*

110 acknowledge[ment] character
d Erkennungszeichen *n*; Quittungszeichen *n*
f caractère *m* d'accusé de réception [positif]
r символ *m* подтверждения; знак *m* опознания; знак подтверждения приёма

111 acknowledge[ment] identifier
d Quittungsbezeichner *m*
f identificateur *m* d'accusé de réception [positif]
r идентификатор *m* подтверждения

112 acknowledgement priority
d Rückmeldepriorität *f*
f priorité *f* de quittance
r приоритет *m* подтверждения

113 acknowledge[ment] request
d Quittungsanforderung *f*; Quittungsaufforderung *f*; Quittieranforderung *f*
f demande *f* d'accusé de réception
r требование *n* подтверждения

* **acknowledge request** → 113

114 acoustic; sound; phonic; tone; audio
d akustisch; Ton-; Laut-; Schall-
f acoustique; sonore; son
r акустический; звуковой; тональный; аудио-

115 acoustic communications
d akustische Kommunikation *f*

f communication *f* acoustique
r звуковая связь *f*

116 acoustic coupler
(of a modem)
d Akustikkoppler *m*
f coupleur *m* acoustique
r акустичсский соединитель *m*

117 acoustic memory
d akustischer Speicher *m*; akustischer
Laufzeitspeicher *m*
f mémoire *f* acoustique
r акустическая память *f*

118 acoustic signal; audiosignal
d akustisches Signal *n*
f signal *m* acoustique
r звуковой сигнал *m*; аудиосигнал *m*

119 acoustic tablet
d akustisches Tablett *n*
f tablette *f* acoustique
r акустический планшет *m*

*   **acousto-optic → 120**

120 acousto-optic[al]
d akustooptisch
f acousto-optique
r акустооптический

121 acousto-optical effect
d akustooptischer Effekt *m*
f effet *m* acousto-optique
r акустооптический эффект *m*

122 acquisition; gathering; collection
d Erfassung *f*
f acquisition *f*; collection *f*
r сбор *m*; накопление *n*; получение *n*

123 acronym
d Akronym *n*
f acronyme *m*
r акроним *m*

*   **ACS → 502**

124 action
d Aktion *f*; Wirkung *f*; Bedienungsmaßnahme *f*
f action *f*
r действие *n*; воздействие *n*

125 action choice
d Aktion-Auswahl *f*
f option *f* d'action; commande *f* immédiate
r выбор *m* действия

126 action code

d Aktionscode *m*
f code *m* d'action
r код *m* [воз]действия

127 action redoing
d Aktionswiederherstellung *f*
f rétablissement *m* d'action
r переделывание *n* действия

128 activate *v*
d aktivieren; anregen
f activer; agir
r активи[зи]ровать; действовать;
воздействовать

129 activation
d Anschaltung *f*; Aktivierung *f*; Ansteuerung *f*
f activation *f*
r актив[из]ация *f*; пуск *m*; возбуждение *n*

130 active buffer address
d aktive Pufferadresse *f*
f adresse *f* intermédiaire active; adresse active
de tampon
r активный адрес *m* буфера

131 active desktop
d aktives Desktop *n*
f bureau *m* actif
r активный рабочий стол *m*

132 active document
d aktives Dokument *n*
f document *m* actif
r активный документ *m*

133 active-high signal
d high-aktives Signal *n*; Signal mit aktivem
H-Pegel
f signal *m* actif à niveau haut
r сигнал *m* с активным высоким уровнем

134 active link
d aktiver Zugangspfad *m*
f liaison *f* active
r активная связь *f*

135 active-low signal
d low-aktives Signal *n*; Signal mit aktivem
L-Pegel
f signal *m* actif à niveau bas
r сигнал *m* с активным низким уровнем

136 active matrix
d Aktivmatrix *f*
f matrice *f* active
r активная матрица *f*

137 active-matrix addressing
d aktive Matrixadressierung *f*

f adressage *m* par matrice active
r активная матричная адресация *f*

138 active-matrix color display
   d Aktivmatrix-Farbbildschirm *m*;
      Aktivmatrix-Farbdisplay *n*
   f écran *m* couleur à matrice active
   r цветной экран *m* на активной матрице

139 active-matrix display
   d Aktivmatrix-Display *n*
   f écran *m* à matrice active
   r экран *m* на активной матрице

140 active object
   d aktives Objekt *n*
   f objet *m* actif
   r активный объект *m*

   * **active return loss** → 3272

141 active selection
   d aktive Auswahl *f*
   f sélection *f* active
   r активный выбор *m*

142 active selection set
   d aktiver Auswahlsatz *m*
   f ensemble *m* de sélection active
   r активная совокупность *f* выбора

143 active sensor
   d aktiver Sensor *m*
   f senseur *m* actif
   r активный сенсор *m*

144 active status
   d aktiver Status *m*
   f état *m* actif
   r активное состояние *n*

145 active style
   d aktiver Stil *m*
   f style *m* actif
   r активный стиль *m*

146 active text style
   d aktiver Textstil *m*
   f style *m* de texte actif
   r активный текстовой стиль *m*

   * **active window** → 2423

147 ActiveX automation
   d ActiveX-Automation *f*
   f automation *f* ActiveX
   r ActiveX-автоматизация *f*

148 ActiveX event
   d ActiveX-Ereignis *n*

f évènement *m* ActiveX
r ActiveX-событие *n*

149 activity
   d Aktivität *f*
   f activité *f*
   r активность *f*

   * **actor** → 9131

   * **actual** *adj* → 2414

150 actual address; executive address; done address
   d aktuelle Adresse *f*; tatsächliche Adresse;
      Done-Adresse *f*
   f adresse *f* actuelle; adresse exécutive
   r актуальный адрес *m*; исполнительный
      адрес; адрес выполнения

   * **actual hardware** → 378

151 actual recipient
   d aktueller Empfänger *m*
   f destinataire *f* effectif
   r действительный получатель *m*;
      действительный приёмник *m*

152 actual value
   d Ist-Wert *m*
   f valeur *f* actuelle
   r фактическое значение *n*; действительное
      значение

153 actuate *v*
   d betätigen; erregen; antreiben
   f actionner; amorcer
   r запускать; задействовать; возбуждать

154 actuator; drive
   d Wirkungsglied *n*; Aktuator *m*; Antrieb *m*;
      Stellantrieb *m*
   f actionneur *m*; entraînement *m*
   r привод *m*; возбудитель *m*

155 acyclic; circuit-free; loopfree
   d azyklisch; kreisfrei; zyklusfrei; schlingenfrei;
      schleifenfrei
   f acyclique; sans circuits; sans cycles; sans
      boucles
   r ациклический; ацикличный; без циклов

156 acyclic graph; circuit-free graph; graph without loops
   d azyklischer Graph *m*; kreisfreier Graph;
      zyklusfreier Graph; Graph ohne Schleifen
   f graphe *m* acyclique; graphe sans circuits;
      graphe sans cycles; graphe sans boucles
   r ациклический граф *m*; граф без циклов;
      граф без контуров; граф без петель

157 **adapt** *v*
   d anpassen
   f adapter
   r адаптировать; приспосабливать

158 **adaptable; adaptive**
   d anpassungsfähig; adaptiv
   f adaptable; adaptatif
   r адаптивный; совместимый

159 **adaptation; adapting**
   d Anpassung *f*
   f adaptation *f*
   r адаптация *f*; согласование *n*

160 **adapted server**
   d adaptierter Server *m*
   f serveur *m* adapté
   r согласованный сервер *m*

161 **adapter**
   d Adapter *m*; Anpassungseinheit *f*;
       Anpassungsbaustein *m*; Zwischenstück *n*
   f adaptateur *m*
   r адаптер *m*; корректирующее звено *n*;
       согласующее устройство *n*

162 **adapter circuit**
   d Adapterschaltung *f*
   f circuit *m* d'adaptateur; circuit d'adaptation
   r схема *f* адаптера

163 **adapter for data channel**
   d Adapter *m* für Datenkanal
   f adaptateur *m* pour canal de données
   r адаптер *m* информационного канала;
       адаптер канала данных

164 **adapter plug**
   d Anpassstecker *m*; Zwischenstecker *m*
   f fiche *f* adaptative
   r согласующий разъём *m*; переходный
       разъём

   * **adapting → 159**

   * **adaptive → 158**

165 **adaptive algorithm**
   d adaptiver Algorithmus *m*
   f algorithme *m* adaptatif
   r адаптивный алгоритм *m*

166 **adaptive channel allocation**
   d adaptive Kanalzuweisung *f*
   f allocation *f* de canal adaptative
   r адаптивное назначение *n* канала

   * **adaptive meshing → 7578**

   * **ADC → 379**

   * **ADCCP → 264**

167 **add** *v*
   d addieren; hinzufügen
   f add[itionn]er; sommer; ajouter
   r складывать; суммировать; прибавлять;
       добавить; добавлять

168 **add** *v* **a noise**
   d Rauschen hinzufügen
   f ajouter un bruit
   r добавлять шума

169 **addend; summand**
   d Addend *m*; Summand *m*; Summenglied *n*
   f addenda *m*; sommant *m*; terme *m* d'une
       somme
   r слагаемое *n*

170 **addend register**
   d Addendregister *n*
   f registre *m* d'addenda
   r регистр *m* слагаемого

171 **adder; summator**
   d Add[ier]er *m*; Addierwerk *n*; Summierer *m*
   f addeur *m*; addit[ionn]eur *m*; sommateur *m*
   r сумматор *m*; суммирующее устройство *n*

172 **adder-accumulator**
   d Adder-Akkumulator *m*
   f add[itionn]eur-accumulateur *m*
   r накапливающий сумматор *m*

173 **adder-subtractor**
   d Adder-Subtraktor *m*;
       Addier-Subtrahier-Werk *n*
   f add[itionn]eur-soustracteur *m*
   r сумматор-вычитатель *m*

174 **add gate**
   d Addiergatter *n*
   f porte *f* d'addition
   r схема *f* сложения

   * **add-in → 177, 179**

175 **add-in manager**
   d Add-In-Manager *m*
   f gestionnaire *m* additionnel
   r добавляемый менажер *m*

176 **add-in module; add-on module; plug-in
     module**
   d Erweiterungsmodul *m*;
       Erweiterungsbaustein *m*; Zusatzmodul *m*;
       zusätzliche Hardware *f*
   f module *m* d'extension
   r модуль *m* расширения; приставка *f*

177 add-in [software]; add-on [software]
d Add-In *n*; Add-On *n*;
Erweiterung[ssoftware] *f*; Zusatz *m*
f logiciel *m* compagnon; compagnon *m*
r [программа-]надстройка *f*

178 addition; summation
d Addition *f*; Summierung *f*
f addition *f*; sommation *f*
r сложение *n*; суммирование *n*

179 additional; additive; add-in; add-on
d additiv; erweitert; zusätzlich; nachträglich;
Add-In-; Add-On-
f additionnel; additif
r аддитивный; добавляемый

180 additional addressing
d zusätzliche Adressierung *f*
f adressage *m* additionnel
r дополнительная адресация *f*

181 addition sign; plus [sign]; sign of addition
d Additionszeichen *n*; Plus[zeichen] *n*
f signe *m* d'addition; signe plus; plus *m*
r знак *m* сложения; знак плюс; плюс *m*

182 addition without carry; false add[ition]
d übertragslose Addition *f*
f addition *f* sans report; addition sans retenue
r сложение *n* без переноса

* **additive → 179**

183 additive code
d additiver Code *m*
f code *m* additif
r аддитивный код *m*

184 additivity
d Additivität *f*
f additivité *f*
r аддитивность *f*

185 additivity of luminance
d Luminanz-Additivität *f*
f additivité *f* de la luminance
r аддитивность *f* светового излучения

* **add-on → 177, 179**

186 add-on board
d Zusatzleiterplatte *f*; Erweiterungsplatine *f*
f plaque *f* supplémentaire
r дополнительная плата f[, расширяющая
функциональные возможности]

* **add-on conference → 9353**

187 add-on kit

d Nachrüstsatz *m*; Nachrüstbausatz *m*
f ensemble *m* de construction supplémentaire
r набор *m* [элементов] для расширения
функциональных возможностей

* **add-on memory → 3619**

* **add-on module → 176**

* **add-on software → 177**

188 add output; sum output
d Summenausgang *m*
f sortie *f* de somme
r выход *m* суммы

189 add overflow
d Überlauf *m* beim Addieren
f déplacement *m* à l'addition
r переполнение *n* при сложении

190 add *v* preset
d Voreinstellen hinzufügen
f ajouter une présélection
r добавлять предварительную установку

191 address
d Adresse *f*
f adresse *f*
r адрес *m*

192 address *v*
d adressieren
f adresser
r адресовать

193 addressability
d Adressierbarkeit *f*
f adressabilité *f*; possibilité *f* d'adressage;
capacité *f* d'adressage
r адресуемость *f*

194 addressable
d adressierbar
f adressable
r адресуемый

195 addressable cursor; addressing cursor
d adressierbarer Cursor *m*
f curseur *m* adressable
r адресуемый курсор *m*

196 addressable latch
d adressierbarer Zwischenspeicher *m*;
adressierbares Auffangregister *n*
f verrou *m* adressable
r адресуемый регистр-фиксатор *m*

197 addressable memory
d adressierbarer Speicher *m*

f mémoire f adressable
r адресуемая память f

198 address access time
d Adressenzugriffszeit f
f temps m d'accès d'adresse
r время n доступа по адресу

199 address administration
d Adressenverwaltung f
f administration f d'adresses
r администрирование n адресов

200 address arithmetic; address calculation
d Adressenarithmetik f; Adressrechnen n;
Adressrechnung f
f arithmétique f d'adresse; calcul m d'adresse
r адресная арифметика f; вычисление n
адресов

201 address array; address field
d Adressfeld n
f tableau m d'adresse; champ m d'adresse
r поле n адреса

202 address assignment
d Adressenzuordnung f
f assignation f d'adresse
r присваивание n адреса

* **address batch → 210**

203 address bit
d Adressenbit n
f bit m d'adresse
r двоичный разряд m адреса; бит m адреса

204 address book
d Adressbuch n
f carnet m d'adresses
r адресная книга f

205 address bus
d Adress[en]bus m
f bus m d'adresse
r адресная шина f

* **address calculation → 200**

206 address catcher; address trap
d Adress[en]trap m
f trappe f d'adresse
r адресная ловушка f

207 address change
d Adressenänderung f; Adressenmodifikation f
f changement m d'adresse
r изменение n адреса

208 address code selection

d Adresscodeauswahl f
f sélection f de code d'adresse
r выбор m кода адреса

209 address counter; location counter
d Adress[en]zähler m
f compteur m d'adresses
r счётчик m адресов

210 address cycle; address batch
d Adress[en]schub m
f cycle m d'adresse
r цикл m адреса

211 address decoder; address matrix
d Adressendecoder m; Adressenmatrix f;
Adressenentschlüsseler m
f décodeur m d'adresses; matrice f d'adresses
r дешифратор m адресов

212 address digit
d Adressziffer f
f chiffre m d'adresse; digit m d'adresse
r цифра f адреса; разряд m адреса

213 address driver
d Adress[leitungs]treiber m
f formateur m d'adresse
r адресный формирователь m

214 addressed field
d adressiertes Feld n
f champ m adressé
r адресованное поле n; вызванная зона f

* **address field → 201**

215 address generation
d Adressengenerierung f
f génération f d'adresse
r формирование n адреса

216 address information
d Adresseninformation f
f information f d'adresse
r адресная информация f

217 addressing
d Adressierung f
f adressage m
r адресация f; адресование n

* **addressing cursor → 195**

218 address[ing] mode
d Adressierungsart f; Adressiermodus m
f mode m d'adressage
r метод m адресации; способ m адресации

219 addressing signal
d Adressiersignal n

f signal *m* d'adressage
r сигнал *m* адресации

220 address latch
d Adressensignalspeicher *m*;
Adresshalteregister *n*
f verrou *m* d'adresse; registre *m* de maintien
d'adresse
r регистр-фиксатор *m* адреса; адресная
защёлка *f*

221 addressless
d adressenfrei; adress[en]los
f sans adresse
r безадресный

222 addressless programming
d symbolisches Programmieren *n*
f programmation *f* sans adresses
r безадресное программирование *n*

*   **address map → 223**

223 address map[ping]; allocation map[ping]
d Adressenabbildung *f*; Zuordnungstabelle *f*;
Belegungstabelle *f*
f image *f* d'adresses; tableau *m* d'allocation;
tableau d'assignation
r отображение *n* адресов; таблица *f*
распределения

*   **address matrix → 211**

*   **address mode → 218**

224 address mode byte
d Adressierungsmodusbyte *n*
f octet *m* de mode d'adressage
r байт *m* способа адресации

225 addressness
d Adresskapazität *f*
f nombre *m* d'adresses
r адресность *f*; число *n* адресов

226 address part; address section
d Adressteil *m*
f partie *f* d'adresse
r адресная часть *f*

*   **address pattern → 234**

227 address processing circuit
d Adressrechenschaltung *f*
f circuit *m* de traitement d'adresse
r схема *f* обработки адреса

228 address register
d Adress[en]register *n*
f registre *m* d'adresse

r регистр *m* адреса; адресный регистр

229 address-relative
d mit relativer Adresse
f à adresse relative
r с относительным адресом

230 address resolution protocol; ARP
d Adressauflösungsprotokoll *n*
f protocole *m* ARP
r протокол *m* определения адреса; протокол
ARP

*   **address section → 226**

231 address size
d Adresslänge *f*
f longueur *f* d'adresse; taille *f* d'adresse
r длина *f* адреса

232 address space
d Adressraum *m*; Adressbereich *m*
f espace *m* d'adresse
r адресное пространство *n*

*   **address spoofing → 5135**

233 address stop
d Adressenstopp *m*
f arrêt *m* sur adresse
r останов *m* по адресу

234 address structure; address pattern
d Adressstruktur *f*
f structure *f* d'adresse
r структура *f* адреса

235 address table
d Adressentafel *f*
f table *f* d'adresses
r таблица *f* адресов

*   **address trap → 206**

236 adhere *v*
d haften
f adhérer
r прилипнуть; прилипать; примыкать;
прилегать

237 ad hoc user
d Anwender *m* ad hoc
f utilisateur *m* ad hoc; utilisateur épisodique
r эпизодический пользователь *m*

238 adjacency
d Adjazenz *f*
f adjacence *f*; contiguïté *f*
r прилегание *n*; примыкание *n*; смежность *f*

239 **adjacent channel**
d Nachbarkanal *m*
f canal *m* voisin
r соседний канал *m*

240 **adjacent domains**
d benachbarte Bereiche *mpl*
f domaines *mpl* adjacents
r смежные домены *mpl*; соседние домены

241 **adjacent rows**
d nebeneinanderstehende Zeilen *fpl*
f lignes *fpl* adjacentes
r смежные строки *fpl*; соседние строки

242 **adjacent vertex**
(of a graph)
d adjazenter Knoten[punkt] *m*; benachbarter Knoten[punkt]
f sommet *m* adjacent
r смежная вершина *f*

243 **adjoint graph**
d adjungierter Graph *m*
f graphe *m* adjoint
r сопряжённый граф *m*; присоединённый граф

244 **adjoint operator**
d Adjungierte *f*; adjungierter Operator *m*
f opérateur *m* adjoint
r сопряжённый оператор *m*

245 **adjunction**
d Adjunktion *f*
f adjonction *f*
r сопряжение *n*

246 **adjust** *v*; **regulate** *v*
d justieren; einstellen; abstimmen
f ajuster; régler
r регулировать; настраивать; устанавливать

247 **adjustable parameter**
d Regelgröße *f*
f paramètre *m* ajustable
r регулируемый параметр *m*

* **adjusting** → 248

248 **adjustment; adjusting**
d Justierung *f*; Adjustierung *f*
f ajustement *m*; ajustage *m*; réglage *m*
r настраивание *n*; настройка *f*; юстировка *f*; регулирование *n*

* **ADMD** → 253

* **admin** → 255

249 **administration**
d Verwaltung *f*; Administration *f*
f administration *f*
r администрация *f*; администрирование *n*

250 **administration and data server; ADS**
d Betriebs- und Datenserver *m*
f serveur *m* d'administration et de données
r сервер *m* для администрации и данных

251 **administration call**
d Administrationsaufruf *m*
f appel *m* d'administration
r вызов *m* управления

252 **administration domain name; administrative domain name**
d Name *m* des öffentlichen Versorgungsbereiches
f nom *m* d'un domaine d'administration
r имя *n* административного домена

253 **administration management domain; administrative management domain; ADMD**
d öffentlicher Versorgungsbereich *m*
f domaine *m* de gestion d'administration; DGAD
r домен *m* административного управления

254 **administration program; administrator**
d Verwaltungsprogramm *n*; Verwalter *m*
f programme *m* d'administration; programme de gestion; administrateur *m*
r организующая программа *f*; администратор *m*

* **administrative domain name** → 252

* **administrative management domain** → 253

255 **administrator; admin; manager**
(a person)
d Administrator *m*; Verwalter *m*
f administrateur *m*; gestionnaire *m/f*
r администратор *m*; управляющий *m*; управитель *m*; менажер *m*; распорядитель *m*

* **administrator** → 254

256 **admissibility; permissibility**
d Zulässigkeit *f*
f admissibilité *f*
r допустимость *f*

257 **admissible error**
d zulässiger Fehler *m*
f erreur *f* admissible
r допустимая погрешность *f*

**258 admissible solution; permissible solution;
feasible solution**
d zulässige Lösung *f*
f solution *f* admissible; solution permissible
r допустимое решение *n*

259 admissible value; permissible value
d zulässiger Wert *m*
f valeur *f* admissible
r допустимое значение *n*

260 admission
d Zulassung *f*; Zutritt *m*; Eintritt *m*
f admission *f*; permission *f*
r позволение *n*; приём *m*

261 admittance
d Admittanz *f*; Scheinleitwert *m*
f admittance *f*
r [полная] проводимость *f*

* **ADP → 689**

* **ADS → 250**

* **advance → 3748**

262 advanced
d erweitert; modern; fortgeschritten;
fortschrittlich
f avancé; évolué
r продвинутый; развитый; прогрессивный;
современный; усовершенствованный

263 advanced BIOS; ABIOS
(an extension of BIOS for IBM PS/2
computers)
d erweitertes grundlegendes
Ein-/Ausgabesystem *n*; erweitertes
grundlegendes BIOS *n*
f BIOS *m* évolué
r усовершенствованный биос *m*;
продвинутый биос

**264 advanced data-communications control
procedure; ADCCP**
d modernes Datenübertragungssteuerfahren *n*
f procédure *f* de contrôle de communication de
données avancée
r процедура *f* управления передачей данных
с расширенными возможностями

**265 advanced facilities; comprehensive
facilities**
d erweiterte Möglichkeiten *fpl*
f facilités *fpl* avancées
r развитые возможности *fpl*

266 advanced language
d erweiterte Sprache *f*

f langage *m* évolue
r развитый язык *m*

**267 advanced power management; APM;
power management; power conservation;
power saving**
d modernste Leistungsverwaltung *f*;
fortgeschrittene Stromüberwachung *f*
f gestion *f* de la consommation; gestion de la
consommation d'énergie; gestion d'énergie
r усовершенствованное управление *n*
питанием; улучшённое управление
питанием

**268 Advanced Research Projects Agency
Network; ARPANet**
(the experimental network, established in the
1970s, where the theories and software on
which the Internet is based were tested)
d ARPA-Netz *n*
f réseau *m* ARPANet
r сеть *f* Агентства перспективных
исследовательских разработок
(министерства обороны США)

269 advanced settings
d erweiterte Einrichtungen *fpl*
f paramètres *mpl* avancés
r продвинутые установки *fpl* [параметров]

270 advanced setup wizard
d Assistent *m* der erweiterten Einrichtung
f assistant *m* d'établissement avancé
r советник *m* продвинутой установки

* **aerospace computer → 284**

271 afterglow screen; persistent screen
d Nachleuchtschirm *m*; nachleuchtender
Bildschirm *m*
f écran *m* à persistance; écran à
postluminescence; écran à rémanence
r экран *m* с послесвечением

272 after-image
d Nach[ab]bild *n*; Nachabbildung *f*
f post-image *f*; image consécutive
r остаточное изображение *n*;
последовательный образ *m*; последующий
образ

273 aged data
d Altdaten *pl*; veraltete Daten *pl*
f données *fpl* vieilles
r устаревшие данные *pl*

274 ag[e]ing
d Alterung *f*
f vieillissement *m*
r старение *n*

275 **agenda**
  d Agenda *npl*; Plan *m*
  f agenda *f*
  r план *m* решения; план основных операций

276 **agenda slide**
  d Agenda-Diapositiv *n*
  f diapositive *f* d'agenda
  r плановый слайд *m*

  * **agent** → 9716

277 **aggregate**
  (a structured collection of data objects
  forming a data type)
  d Aggregat *n*
  f agrégat *m*
  r агрегат *m*

278 **aggregated data; pooled data**
  d aggregierte Daten *pl*
  f données *fpl* agrégées
  r агрегированные данные *pl*; пул *m* данных

279 **aggregate function**
  d Aggregatfunktion *f*
  f fonction *f* d'agrégation
  r агрегатная функция *f*

280 **aggregation**
  d Aggregation *f*; Gesamtheit *f*
  f agrégation *f*
  r агрегация *f*; совокупность *f*

  * **aging** → 274

  * **AGP** → 39

281 **AGP configuration**
  d AGP-Konfiguration *f*
  f configuration *f* AGP
  r конфигурация *f* AGP

  * **AI** → 545

282 **aid; help**
  d Hilfe *f*; Mittel *n*
  f aide *f*
  r помощь *f*; подкрепление *n*

283 **aiming symbol**
  d Leitsymbol *n*
  f symbole *m* de guidage; symbole de
  positionnement
  r направляющий символ *m*

  * **AIR** → 619

284 **airborne computer; spaceborne computer;
  aerospace computer; trip computer**
  d Luftfahrtrechner *m*
  f ordinateur *m* [à bord] d'avion; ordinateur de
  navigation aérienne
  r авиационный компьютер *m*;
  аэрокосмический компьютер

  * **air-floating head** → 3902

  * **AI system** → 546

  * **alarm** → 286

285 **alarm message**
  d Gefahrenmeldung *f*
  f message *m* d'alarme
  r аварийное сообщение *n*

286 **alarm [signal]; alert [signal]; alerting tone**
  d Alarmsignal *n*; Alarm *m*;
  Alarm-Meldesignal *n*; Warnsignal *n*;
  Hinweiston *m*
  f alarme *f*; signal *m* d'alarme; signal d'alerte;
  alerte *f*
  r аварийный сигнал *m*; сигнал тревоги;
  сигнал предупреждения; сигнал
  извещения

  * **aleatory** → 7591

  * **aleatory variable** → 7604

  * **alert** → 286

287 **alert** *v*
  d alarmieren
  f alerter; alarmer
  r поднимать по тревоге

288 **alert box**
  d Alert-Kasten *m*
  f boîte *f* d'alerte
  r ящик *m* предупреждения; ящик извещения

289 **alerter; alert manager**
  (a program)
  d Alarmverwalter *m*
  f alerteur *m*; gestionnaire *m* d'alerte
  r обработчик *m* извещений; аварийный
  администратор *m*

  * **alerting tone** → 286

  * **alert manager** → 289

290 **alert routing**
  d Alarmanzeigelenkung *f*
  f routage *m* des alertes; acheminement *m* des
  alertes
  r маршрутизация *f* предупреждений;
  маршрутизация аварийных сигналов

algorithm 18

* **alert signal** → 286

291 algorithm
d Algorithmus m
f algorithme m
r алгоритм m

292 algorithm convergence; convergence of an algorithm
d Algorithmuskonvergenz f
f convergence f d'algorithme
r сходимость f алгоритма

293 algorithmic[al] language
d algorithmische Sprache f
f langage m algorithmique
r алгоритмический язык m

294 algorithmic animation
d algorithmische Animation f
f animation f algorithmique
r алгоритмическая анимация f

* **algorithmic language** → 293

295 algorithmics
d Algorithmik f
f algorithmique f; algorithmie f
r алгоритмика f

296 algorithmic undecidability
d algorithmische Unlösbarkeit f
f insolubilité f algorithmique
r алгоритмическая неразрешимость f

297 algorithmization
d Algorithmisierung f
f algorithmisation f
r алгоритмизирование n

298 algorithmize v
d algorithmisieren
f algorithmiser
r алгоритмизировать

* **algorithm of division** → 3061

299 algorithm theory; theory of algorithms
d Algorithmentheorie f
f théorie f des algorithmes
r теория f алгоритмов

* **alias** → 304

300 alias addressing
d Alias-Adressierung f
f adressage m par pseudonyme
r адресование n через псевдоимя

301 aliasing; desmoothing; stairstepping

(undesired visual effect by occasion of definition of bitmap image)
d Aliasing n; Desmoothing n
f crénelage m; repliement m
r неровность f; ступенчатость f

302 aliasing effect
d Aliasing-Effekt m
f effet m de crénelage
r эффект m ступенчатости; эффект неровности

303 aliasing noise
d Aliasing-Rauschen n
f distorsion f de repliement
r искажение n из-за неровности

304 alias [name]
d Aliasname m; Alias n; Pseudonym n; Parallelbezeichnung f
f alias m; pseudonyme m; pseudo m; nom m alternatif
r псевдоимя n; альтернативное имя n; псевдоним m

305 align v; justify v; equalize v
d ausrichten; abgleichen; ausgleichen
f aligner; justifier; égaliser; mettre au point
r выравнивать; подравнять; равнять; приравнивать; уравнивать

* **aligned** → 4868

* **aligner** → 307

306 aligner
d Justiergerät n
f dispositif m d'alignement
r эталонный прибор m; устройство n для точной регулировки

307 aligner [bar]
d Justierschiene f
f barre f d'alignement
r выравнивающая лента f

* **aligning** → 308

308 alignment; aligning; equalization; justifying; justification
d Ausrichtung f; Ausgleichen n; Ausgleich m; Abgleich m
f alignement m; égalisation f; justification f
r выравнивание n; налаживание n

309 alignment chart; nomogram
d Nomogramm n
f nomogramme m
r номограмма f

310 **all-channel decoder**
   d Mehrkanaldecodierer *m*
   f décodeur *m* de plusieurs canaux
   r многоканальный декодер *m*

311 **all-color; full-color**
   d Vollfarb-
   f de toutes couleurs; à plein couleur
   r полноцветный

312 **all-color copier**
   d Vollfarb-Kopierer *m*
   f copieur *m* à pleine couleur
   r полноцветное копирующее устройство *n*

313 **all-color mode**
   d Vollfarb-Modus *m*
   f mode *m* de toutes couleurs
   r полноцветный режим *m*

314 **all-color page**
   d Vollfarbseite *f*
   f page *f* de toutes couleurs
   r полноцветная страница *f*

315 **all-color printer**
   d Vollfarb-Drucker *m*
   f imprimante *f* à toutes couleurs
   r полноцветный принтер *m*

316 **all-color scanner**
   d Vollfarb-Scanner *m*
   f scanner *m* à toutes couleurs
   r полноцветный сканер *m*

   *   **all-digital display** → 2892

317 **alley**
   (the space between images or columns)
   d Gasse *f* [zwischen den Satzregeln]; Pfad *m*
   f ruelle *f*; venelle *f*
   r дорожка *f*; коридор *m*; аллея *f*

   *   **allocate** *v* → 3040

318 **allocation**
   d Zuordnung *f*; Zuweisung *f*
   f allocation *f*
   r размещение *n*; распределение *n*

   *   **allocation map** → 223

   *   **allocation mapping** → 223

319 **allocator**
   d Verteiler *m*; Zuordner *m*
   f allocateur *m*
   r распределитель *m*

   *   **allotter** → 1356

   *   **allowance** → 6917

320 **all-pass filter; universal filter**
   d Allpassfilter *m*
   f filtre *m* passe-tout
   r универсальный фильтр *m*

321 **all-point addressable; APA**
   d volladressierbar; punktadressierbar
   f à points [tous] adressables; adressable en tous
      points
   r полноадресуемый

   *   **all-purpose computer** → 5268

322 **all selection**
   d volle Auswahl *f*
   f sélection *f* totale
   r полный выбор *m*; полный отбор *m*

   *   **alpha** → 324

323 **alphabet**
   d Alphabet *n*
   f alphabet *m*
   r алфавит *m*

   *   **alphabetic** → 324

   *   **alphabetic addressing** → 325

324 **alphabetic[al]; alpha; lexicographic; literal**
   d alphabetisch; lexikographisch; buchstäblich;
      Buchstaben-
   f alphabétique; lexicographique; littéral
   r алфавитный; лексикографический;
      литеральный; буквенный

325 **alphabetic[al] addressing; symbol[ic]**
      addressing
   d alphabetische Adressierung *f*; symbolische
      Adressierung
   f adressage *m* alphabétique; adressage
      symbolique
   r символическая адресация *f*

   *   **alphabetical character** → 5339

   *   **alphabetical order** → 5346

326 **alphabetic-numeric; alpha[nu]meric**
   d alphabetisch-numerisch; alphanumerisch
   f alphabétique-numérique; alphanumérique
   r алфавитно-цифровой; буквенно-цифровой

   *   **alphabetic order** → 5346

327 **alphabetizing**
   d alphabetisches Ordnen *n*

f alphabétisation *f*
r упорядочение *n* по алфавиту

328 alpha blending
  d Alpha-Überblendung *f*; Alpha-Blending *n*
  f mélange *m* alpha
  r альфа-смешение *n* (механизм управления прозрачностью)

329 alpha-channel; mask channel
    (a temporary storage area for masks)
  d Alphakanal *m*
  f canal *m* alpha
  r альфа-канал *m*

330 alpha chip
  d Alpha-Chip *m*
  f puce *f* alpha
  r альфа-чип *m*

331 alphageometric graphics
  d alphageometrische Grafik *f*
  f graphique *m* alphagéométrique
  r буквенно-геометрическая графика *f*

  * **alphameric** → 326

  * **alphameric character story** → 334

  * **alphameric conversion** → 333

  * **alphameric data code** → 335

  * **alphameric generator** → 336

332 alphamosaic graphics
  d alphamosaische Grafik *f*
  f graphique *m* alphamosaïque
  r буквенно-мозаичная графика *f*

  * **alphanumeric** → 326

333 alpha[nu]meric[al] conversion
  d alphanumerische Umwandlung *f*
  f conversion *f* alphanumérique
  r буквенно-цифровое преобразование *n*

334 alpha[nu]meric character story
  d alphanumerischer Speicher *m*; Textspeicher *m*
  f mémoire *f* alphanumérique
  r память *f* буквенно-цифровых знаков

335 alpha[nu]meric data code
  d alphanumerischer Datencode *m*
  f code *m* de données alphanumérique
  r буквенно-цифровой код *m* данных

336 alpha[nu]meric generator
  d alphanumerischer Generator *m*

  f générateur *m* alphanumérique
  r генератор *m* буквенно-цифровых знаков

  * **alphanumeric mode** → 1619

  * **alpha processing** → 9313

337 alpha version
    (preliminary version of a software)
  d Alpha-Version *f*
  f version *f* alpha
  r альфа-версия *f*

338 alteration; altering; modification
  d Veränderung *f*; Alteration *f*; Modifizierung *f*
  f altération *f*; modification *f*
  r изменение *n*; модифицирование *n*

339 alter[ation] switch
  d Schalter *m* zur Informationseingabe in ein Computerprogramm
  f commutateur *m* à interrogation programmée
  r программно-опрашиваемый переключатель *m*

  * **altering** → 338

  * **alternate** → 347

340 alternate *v*
  d alternieren; [ab]wechseln
  f alterner
  r чередоваться; переменять; обменивать[ся]; менять; сменять

341 alternate channel; alternative channel
  d Ausweichkanal *m*; Alternativkanal *m*
  f canal *m* de déviation; canal alternatif
  r альтернативный канал *m*

342 alternate code
  d Austauschcode *m*
  f code *m* alternatif
  r переменный код *m*

  * **alternate instruction** → 5190

343 alternate mode
  d Alternativmodus *m*
  f mode *m* d'alternance; mode alternatif
  r режим *m* попеременного доступа

344 alternate recipient
  d anderer Empfänger *m*; Ersatzempfänger *m*
  f destinataire *m* suppléant; destinataire alternatif
  r альтернативный получатель *m*; альтернативный приёмник *m*

345 alternate track; backup track
  d Ersatzspur *f*

f piste *f* alternative; piste interchangeable
r запасная дорожка *f*; резервная дорожка

346 alternate track address
d Ersatzspuradresse *f*
f adresse *f* de piste alternative
r адрес *m* запасной дорожки

347 alternating; alternate; alternative
d alternierend; abwechselnd; veränderlich
f alterné; alternatif
r альтернирующий; альтернативный;
   чередующийся; обходной

348 alternating current; AC
d Wechselstrom *m*
f courant *m* alternatif
r переменный ток *m*

349 alternation
d Alternation *f*; Verschachtelung *f*
f alternance *f*
r чередование *n*; альтернирование *n*; смена *f*

* **alternative → 347**

* **alternative channel → 341**

350 alternative cylinder
d Ersatzzylinder *m*
f cylindre *m* alternatif
r альтернативный цилиндр *m*

351 alternative font file
d Datei *f* der alternierenden Schrift
f fichier *m* de police alternative
r файл *m* с альтернативным шрифтом

352 alternative index
d Alternativindex *m*
f indice *m* alternatif
r альтернативный индекс *m*

353 alternative index cluster
d Alternativindex-Datenmenge *f*;
   Alternativindexcluster *m*
f cluster *m* d'indices alternatifs
r кластер *m* альтернативных индексов

* **alter switch → 339**

354 Alt key
d Alt-Taste *f*
f touche *f* Alt
r клавиша *f* Alt

* **ALU → 517**

* **ambience → 3454**

355 ambiguity; vagueness
d Vagheit *f*; Ambiguität *f*; Mehrdeutigkeit *f*
f ambiguïté *f*
r неясность *f*; неоднозначность *f*

356 ambiguity diagram
d Mehrdeutigkeitsdiagramm *n*
f diagramme *m* d'ambiguïté
r диаграмма *f* неопределённости

357 amendment
d Berichtigung *f*; Verbesserung *f*; Korrektur *f*;
   Änderung *f*
f amendement *m*
r поправка *f*; исправление *n*

**358 American standard code of information
      interchange; ASCII**
d amerikanischer Standardcode *m* zum
   Informationsaustausch
f code *m* standard pour échange d'information;
   ASCII
r американский стандартный код *m* обмена
   информации

359 amount
d Betrag *m*; Gehalt *m*; Aufwand *m*
f montant *m*; teneur *f*
r количество *n*; сумма *f*

**360 amount of calculation; volume of
      computation**
d Rechenaufwand *m*
f volume *m* de calcul
r объём *m* вычисления

**361 amount of information; information
      content**
d Informationsgehalt *m*
f quantité *f* d'information; contenu *m*
   d'information
r количество *n* информации; объём *m*
   информации

362 ampersand
   (&)
d Ampersand *m*; Und-Zeichen *n*
f ampersand *m*
r амперсанд *m*

363 amplification
d Verstärkung *f*
f amplification *f*
r усиление *n*

* **amplification factor → 1833**

364 amplified signal
d verstärktes Signal *n*

ƒ signal *m* amplifié
r усиленный сигнал *m*

365 **amplifier; amplifying element**
d Verstärker *m*
ƒ amplificateur *m*
r усилитель *m*

366 **amplifier response**
d Verstärkerfrequenzgang *m*
ƒ réponse ƒ [harmonique] d'amplificateur
r характеристика ƒ усилителя

* **amplifying element** → 365

367 **amplitude**
d Amplitude ƒ
ƒ amplitude ƒ
r амплитуда ƒ

368 **amplitude factor; peak factor**
d Scheitelfaktor *m*
ƒ facteur *m* de crête; facteur pointe
r коэффициент *m* амплитуды

369 **amplitude fluctuation**
d Amplitudenschwankung ƒ
ƒ fluctuation ƒ d'amplitude
r амплитудное колебание *n*

370 **amplitude-frequency characteristics; gain-frequency characteristics**
d Amplitudenfrequenzcharakteristik ƒ; Amplitudengang *m*
ƒ caractéristique ƒ amplitude-fréquence
r амплитудно-частотная характеристика ƒ

* **analog** → 380, 381

* **analog computation** → 382

371 **analog computer**
d Analogrechner *m*; Analogierechenmaschine ƒ
ƒ ordinateur *m* analogique
r аналоговая вычислительная машина ƒ

372 **analog data**
d Analogdaten *pl*
ƒ données *fpl* analogiques
r аналоговые данные *pl*

373 **analog device**
d analoges Gerät *n*; analoge Vorrichtung ƒ
ƒ dispositif *m* analogique
r аналоговое устройство *n*

374 **analog-digital character recognition system**
d analog-digitales Zeichenerkennungssystem *n*
ƒ système *m* de reconnaissance des caractères

analogique-digital
r аналого-цифровая система ƒ распознавания знаков

* **analog-digital computer** → 4583

* **analog-digital converter** → 379

375 **analog display; analog monitor**
d Analogbidschirm *m*; Analogmonitor *m*
ƒ afficheur *m* analogique
r аналоговый дисплей *m*

376 **analog input/output**
d analoge Eingabe/Ausgabe ƒ
ƒ entrée/sortie ƒ analogique
r аналоговый ввод/вывод *m*

* **analog monitor** → 375

* **analogous** *adj* → 381

377 **analog plotter**
d Analogplotter *m*
ƒ traceur *m* analogique
r аналоговый графопостроитель *m*

378 **analog technique; actual hardware**
d Analogtechnik ƒ; analoge Gerätetechnik ƒ
ƒ technique ƒ analogique
r аналоговая техника ƒ

379 **analog-[to-]digital converter; ADC**
d Analog-Digital-Wandler *m*; Analog-Digital-Umsetzer *m*; Analog-Digital-Konverter *m*; ADU
ƒ traducteur *m* analogique-digital; convertisseur *m* analogique-numérique; CAN
r аналого-цифровой преобразователь *m*; АЦП

380 **analog[ue]**
d Analog *n*
ƒ analogue *m*
r аналог *m*

381 **analog[ue]; analogous** *adj*
d analog
ƒ analog[iq]ue
r аналоговый

382 **analog[ue] computation**
d analoge Rechnung ƒ; analoge Berechnung ƒ
ƒ calcul *m* analogue; simulation ƒ analogue
r аналоговое вычисление *n*

383 **analog video**
d Analogvideo *n*
ƒ vidéo *m* analog[iq]ue
r аналоговое видео *n*

384 analogy
 d Analogie *f*
 f analogie *f*
 r аналогия *f*; сходство *n*

385 analogy output module
 d analoges Ausgangsmodul *n*; analoges
    Ausgabemodul *n*
 f module *m* de sortie analog[iq]ue
 r модуль *m* аналогового выхода

386 analyse *v*; analyze *v*
 d analysieren
 f analyser
 r анализировать

387 analyser; analyzer
 d Analysator *m*
 f analyseur *m*
 r анализатор *m*

388 analysis
 d Analyse *f*
 f analyse *f*
 r анализ *m*

389 analysis of data; data analysis
 d Datenanalyse *f*
 f analyse *f* des données
 r анализ *m* данных

390 analyst
 d Analytiker *m*; Problemanalytiker *m*;
    Systemplaner *m*
 f analyste *m*; analyseur *m*
 r аналитик *m*; исследователь *m*;
    испытатель *m*

 * **analytic → 391**

391 analytic[al]
 d analytisch
 f analytique
 r аналитический

392 analytic[al] expression
 d analytischer Ausdruck *m*
 f expression *f* analytique
 r аналитическое выражение *n*

 * **analytic expression → 392**

 * **analyze *v* → 386**

 * **analyzer → 387**

393 anchor
 d Anker *m*
 f ancre *f*; signet *m*; pointeur *m* de lien
 r якорь *m*; опора *f*

394 anchorage
 d Verankerung *f*
 f accrochage *m*; ancrage *m*
 r закрепление *n*; анкераж *m*

395 anchorage zone
 d Verankerungszone *f*
 f zone *f* d'accrochage
 r зона *f* закрепления

396 anchor point
 d Ankerpunkt *m*
 f point *m* d'ancrage
 r якорная точка *f*; точка закрепления

397 AND circuit; AND gate
 d UND-Schaltung *f*; UND-Tor *n*;
    UND-Gatter *n*
 f circuit *m* ET; porte *f* ET
 r схема *f* И

 * **AND gate → 397**

 * **ANDing → 2166**

398 AND relay gate
 d UND-Relais-Gatter *n*
 f porte *f* à relais-ET
 r релейная схема *f* И

399 angle brackets; chevrons
    (< >)
 d spitze Klammern *fpl*; Winkelklammern *fpl*
 f parenthèses *fpl* anguleuses; chevrons *mpl*;
    équerres *mpl*
 r угловые скобки *fpl*

400 angled arrow
 d winkeliger Pfeil *m*
 f flèche *f* angulaire
 r угловатая стрелка *f*; изогнутая стрелка

401 angled text
 d winkeliger Text *m*
 f texte *m* angulaire
 r угловой текст *m*

402 angular
 d winkelig; Winkel-
 f angulaire
 r угловой; угловатый

403 angular acceleration
 d Winkelbeschleunigung *f*
 f accélération *f* angulaire
 r угловое ускорение *n*

404 angular frequency
 d Winkelfrequenz *f*

f fréquence *f* angulaire
r угловая частота *f*

405 angular velocity
d Winkelgeschwindigkeit *f*
f vitesse *f* angulaire
r угловая скорость *f*

406 animated bump map
d animiertes Bump-Map *n*
f texture *f* relief animée; bump-map *m* animé
r анимационное рельефное текстурирование *n*

407 animated button
d animierter Knopf *m*
f bouton *m* animé
r "живая" кнопка *f*

408 animated caption
d Trickuntertitel *m*
f caption *f* animée
r анимационная надпись *f*

409 animated characters
d animierte Zeichen *npl*
f caractères *mpl* animés
r оживлённые символы *mpl*

* **animated digital video** → 4109

* **animated GIF** → 410

410 animated GIF [image]
d animiertes GIF-Bild *n*
f image *f* GIF animée
r оживлённый GIF-рисунок *m*; анимационный формат *m* графического обмена

411 animated graphics
d animierte Grafik *f*
f graphique *m* animé
r оживлённая графика *f*

412 animated image
d Trickbild *n*; Animationsbild *n*
f image *f* animée
r движущееся изображение *n*; оживлённое изображение

413 animated texture
d animierte Textur *f*
f texture *f* animée
r анимационная текстура *f*; оживлённая текстура

414 animated video; motion video
d animiertes Video *n*
f vidéo *m* animé

r оживлённое видео *n*; движущееся видео

415 animation
d Animation *f*
f animation *f*
r мультипликация *f*; анимация *f*; оживление *n*

416 animation facility; animation option
d Animationmöglichkeit *f*
f possibilité *f* d'animation
r возможность *f* анимации

417 animation file
d Animationsdatei *f*
f fichier *m* d'animation
r анимационный файл *m*

418 animation frame
(a single image)
d Animationsaufnahme *f*
f cadre *m* d'animation
r анимационный кадр *m*

* **animation option** → 416

419 animation scene
d Animationszene *f*
f scène *f* d'animation; scène animée
r анимационная сцена *f*

420 animation scene manager
d Manager *m* der Animationszene
f gestionnaire *m* de scènes animées
r менеджер *m* анимационных сцен

421 animation sequence
d Animationfolge *f*
f séquence *f* d'animations
r анимационная последовательность *f*

422 animation software
d Animation-Software *f*; Programmierhilfen *fpl* für Animation
f logiciel *m* d'animation
r программное обеспечение *n* для анимации

* **anisochronous** → 596

* **anisochronous connection** → 599

423 anisotrope texture memory
d anisotroper Texturspeicher *m*
f mémoire *f* de textures anisotropes
r память *f* анизотропных текстур

* **annex** → 458

424 annotate *v*; **comment** *v*
d kommentieren

f annoter; commenter
r примечать; комментировать

425 annotation
d Annotation *f*
f annotation *f*
r аннотация *f*

426 announce *v*
d durchsagen
f annoncer
r объявлять; известить; сообщать;
передавать

427 announcement; notification
d Annonce *f*; Ankündigung *f*; Durchsage *f*;
Ansage *f*; Hinweisgabe *f*; Zuschreiben *n*
f annonce *f*; notification *f*
r объявление *f*; известие *n*; сообщение *n*;
уведомление *n*

* **annul** *v* → **10095**

428 annul *v*; **cancel** *v*; **reset** *v*
d annullieren; abbrechen; ausstreichen;
ungültig machen
f annuler; casser; rejeter; supprimer
r аннулировать; отменять; прекращать

* **annulus** → **1682**

429 anonymization
d Anonymisierung *f*
f anonymisation *f*
r анонимизация *f*

430 anonymous
d anonym
f anonyme
r анонимный

431 anonymous FTP
d anonymes Dateiübertragungsprotokoll *n*
f protocole *m* de transfert de fichiers anonyme
r анонимный протокол *m* переноса файлов

432 anonymous user
d anonymer Benutzer *m*
f utilisateur *m* anonyme
r анонимный пользователь *m*

* **answer** → **434, 435**

433 answer *v*
d abfragen; sich melden
f répliquer; répondre
r отвечать

* **answerback** → **109**

434 answer[ing]; response
d Antwort *f*; Ansprechen *n*;
Anrufbeantwortung *f*; Melden *n*; Reaktion *f*;
Wirkung *f*
f réponse *f*; réaction *f*
r ответ *m*; отклик *m*; реакция *f*

435 answer [signal]; response signal
d Antwortzeichen *n*; Bestätigungssignal *n*
f signal *m* de réponse; réponse *f*
r ответный сигнал *m*; сигнал ответа; ответ *m*

436 antialiased line
d geglättete Linie *f*
f ligne *f* anticrénelée; ligne *f* d'anticrénelage
r сглаженная линия *f*

437 antialiased text
d geglätteter Text *m*
f texte *m* anticrénelé
r сглаженный текст *m*

438 antialiased wireframe
d geglätteter Drahtrahmen *m*
f structure *f* filaire anticrénelée
r сглаженный каркас *m*

439 antialiasing; dejagging
(of a curve)
d Antialiasing *n*; Kantenglättung *f*
f anticrénelage *m*; lissage *m*
r сглаживание *n* [границ кривых, наклонных
линий и шрифтов]; плавное изменение *n*;
уменьшение *n* ступенчатости;
антиалиасинг *m*

**440 anti-blur mask; blur mask; unsharp[ed]
mask**
d Unscharfmaske *f*
f masque *m* anti-bué; masque non distinct
r маска *f* расплывания; нечёткая маска;
нерезкая маска

441 anticipate *v*
d vorwegnehmen; erwarten
f anticiper
r опережать; упреждать; предупреждать

442 anticipated carry adder
d Akkumulator *m* mit vorausermitteltem
Übertrag
f add[itionn]eur *m* à report anticipé
r сумматор *m* с ускоренным переносом

* **anticipator buffering** → **443**

443 anticipator[y] buffering
d Vorpufferung *f*
f tamponnage *m* anticipé; tamponnement *m*
anticipateur
r упреждающая буферизация *f*

**444 anticlockwise; counterclockwise;
sinistrorse; sinistrorsum**
 d dem Uhrzeigersinn entgegen; entgegengesetzt
    zum Uhrzeigersinn; linksgängig;
    linksgewunden; linkswendig
 f contre sens des aiguilles de la montre; en sens
    antihoraire; sinistrorsum
 r против часовой стрелки

445 antiglare filter; glare filter
 d Antireflexfilter *m*
 f filtre *m* d'anti-éblouissement
 r антибликовый фильтр *m*

446 antiglare panel
 d Entspiegelungstafel *f*
 f panneau *m* antireflet; panneau à suppression
    des reflets
 r бликоподавляющая панель *f*

* **antislash** → 772

* **antivirus** → 447

* **antivirus package** → 448

**447 antivirus [program]; virus-protection
program; virus-detection program**
 d Antivirusprogramm *n*; Antivirus *n*
 f programme *m* antivirus; programme antiviral;
    antivirus *m*
 r антивирусная программа *f*; антивирус *m*

**448 antivirus [software] package; antivirus
toolkit**
 d Antivirussoftware *f*
 f paquet *m* de logiciel antivirus; outil *m*
    antivirus
 r антивирусный софтуерный пакет *m*;
    антивирусный инструментальный набор *m*

* **antivirus toolkit** → 448

* **APA** → 321

449 APA display
 d volladressierbares Display *n*; Display mit
    voller Punktadressierung
 f afficheur *m* à points [tous] adressables;
    écran *m* à points [tous] adressables
 r полноадресуемый дисплей *m*;
    полноадресуемый экран *m*

450 APA graphics
 d volladressierbare Grafik *f*
 f graphique *m* adressable en tous points
 r полноадресуемая графика *f*

451 aperture
 d Apertur *f*; Öffnung *f*; Maskenöffnung *f*;

Bildpunktblende *f*
 f ouverture *f*; aperture *f*; embouchure *f*
 r апертура *f*; отверстие *n*; скважина *f*;
    открытие *n*

452 aperture box
 d Apertur-Kasten *m*
 f boîte *f* d'aperture
 r ящик *m* апертуры

* **aperture mask** → 8488

* **API** → 475

* **APM** → 267

**453 apostrophe; quotation mark
(')**
 d Apostroph *m*; Auslassungszeichen *n*;
    Hochkomma *n*
 f apostrophe *m*
 r апостроф *m*; кавычка *f*

454 apparent
 d scheinbar
 f apparent
 r явный; видимый

455 apparent storage
 d Scheinspeicher *m*
 f mémoire *f* apparente
 r видимая память *f*

456 appearance
 d Erscheinen *n*; Veröffentlichung *f*
 f apparence *f*; allure *f*; spectacle *m*
 r появление *n*; внешнее представление *n*

458 appendix; annex
 d Anhang *m*
 f appendice *m*; annexe *f*
 r приложение *n*

459 append mode
 d Nachschreibmodus *m*
 f mode *m* d'augmentation; mode d'ajout
 r режим *m* дозаписи

457 append *v*
 d anhängen; beifügen; anbringen
 f ajouter; lier
 r добавлять; присоединять;
    конкатенировать; пристраивать

460 applet
 d Applet *n*; Anwendchen *n*
 f applet *m*; appliquette *f*
 r апплет *m*; мини-приложение *n*;
    мини-программа *f*

461 applicability
d Anwendbarkeit *f*
f applicabilité *f*
r приложимость *f*; применимость *f*

462 applicable
d anwendbar
f applicable
r приложимый; применимый

* **application → 478**

463 application; employment
d Anwendung *f*; Verwendung *f*
f application *f*; usage *m*
r применение *n*; использование *n*;
приложение *n*

464 application development platform
d Anwendung-Entwicklungsplattform *f*
f plate-forme *f* de développement
d'applications
r платформа *f* развития приложений

465 application generator
d Anwendersoftwaregenerator *m*; Generator *m*
von Anwenderprogrammen
f générateur *m* de logiciel appliqué
r генератор *m* прикладных программ

466 application host
d Anwendungshost[computer] *m*
f hôte *m* d'application
r главный компьютер *m* прикладной
системы

467 application icon
d Anwendungssymbol *n*
f icône *f* d'application
r значок *m* приложения; значок прикладной
программы

468 application keypad
d Funktionstastenblock *m*
f bloc *m* de touches fonctionnelles; pavé *m*
fonctionnel
r функциональная клавиатура *f*; блок *m*
функциональных клавиш

469 application layer; utilization layer
(of a network protocol)
d Anwendungsschicht *f*
f couche *f* d'application
r приложный уровень *m*

470 application name
d Anwendungsname *m*
f nom *m* d'application
r имя *n* приложения

471 application object
d Anwendungsobjekt *n*
f objet *m* d'application
r объект *m* приложения

472 application package; package
d Anwendungspaket *n*
f package *m* d'application
r пакет *m* прикладных программ; ППП

* **application program interface → 475**

473 application programmer
d Anwendungsprogrammierer *m*
f programmeur *m* d'applications
r приложный программист *m*

474 application programming
d Anwendungsprogrammierung *f*
f programmation *f* d'application
r прикладное программирование *n*

475 application program[ming] interface; API
d Benutzungsschnittstelle *f*;
Anwendungsprogramm-Interface *n*
f interface *f* de programmation d'applications
r интерфейс *m* программирования
приложений; интерфейс прикладного
программирования

476 application protocol
d Verarbeitungsprotokoll *n*;
Anwendungsprotokoll *n*
f protocole *m* d'application
r прикладной протокол *m*

477 application screen; application window
d Anwendungsfenster *n*
f écran *m* d'application
r экран *m* приложения

* **application server → 2512**

478 application [software]
d Anwendungssoftware *f*; Anwendung *f*;
Applikation *f*; Aufgabe *f*
f logiciel *m* appliqué; progiciel *m*
r приложный софтуер *m*; приложение *n*

* **application window → 477**

479 applied informatics
d angewandte Informatik *f*
f informatique *f* appliquée
r приложная информатика *f*

480 apply *v*
d aufbringen; anlegen; anwenden
f appliquer; employer
r наносить; применять; прилагать;
приложить; прикладывать

481 apply *v* option
d Option anwenden
f appliquer l'option
r применять опцию

* **appraisal** → 3528

482 approach
d Vorgehen *n*; Herangehen *n*
f approche *f*
r подход *m*; приближение *n*

483 approach *v*
d nähern
f approcher; tendre
r приближать[ся]

484 approximability
d Approximierbarkeit *f*
f approximabilité *f*
r аппроксимируемость *f*

485 approximable
d approximierbar
f approchable; approximable
r аппроксимируемый

486 approximate *adj*
d annähernd; angenähert; Näherungs-;
approximativ
f approché; approximatif
r приближённый

487 approximate *v*; half-adjust *v*
d annähern
f approximer
r аппроксимировать

488 approximate calculation; approximate
computation; approximate computing
d Näherungsrechnung *f*; approximative
Berechnung *f*; Approximierungsrechnung *f*
f calcul *m* approché
r приближённое вычисление *n*

* **approximate computation** → 488

* **approximate computing** → 488

489 approximate solution
d Näherungslösung *f*; approximative Lösung *f*
f solution *f* approchée
r приближённое решение *n*

490 approximate value
d Näherungswert *m*; angenäherter Wert *m*
f valeur *f* approchée; valeur approximative
r приближённое значение *n*;
аппроксимирующее значение

491 approximation
d Approximation *f*; Annäherung *f*; Näherung *f*
f approximation *f*
r аппроксимация *f*; приближение *n*

492 approximation algorithms
d Approximation-Algorithmen *mpl*
f algorithmes *mpl* d'approximation
r алгоритмы *mpl* аппроксимации

493 approximation problem
d Approximationsproblem *n*
f problème *m* d'approximation
r задача *f* аппроксимации

494 approximation theory
d Approximationstheorie *f*
f théorie *f* d'approximation
r теория *f* приближений; теория
аппроксимации

* **Arabic digit** → 495

* **Arabic figure** → 495

495 Arabic numeral; Arabic digit; Arabic
figure
d arabische Zahl *f*; arabische Ziffer *f*
f chiffre *m* arabe
r арабская цифра *f*

496 arbiter; arbitrator; judge
d Arbiter *m*; Entscheider *m*; Zuteiler *m*
f arbitre *m*; arbitreur *m*; juge *m*
r арбитр *m*; схема *f* разрешения конфликтов

* **arbitrary** → 7591

497 arbitrary data; random data
d willkürliche Daten *pl*; Zufallsdaten *pl*
f données *fpl* arbitraires
r произвольные данные *pl*; случайные
данные

498 arbitration
d Arbitrierung *f*
f arbitrage *m*
r арбитраж *m*

499 arbitration logic
d Arbitrationslogik *f*; Arbitrierungslogik *f*
f logique *f* d'arbitrage
r арбитражная логика *f*

* **arbitrator** → 496

* **arc** → 3280

500 arcade games
d Videospiele *npl*

f jeux *mpl* d'arcade
r игры-аттракционы *fpl*; аркадные игры

501 architecture
d Architektur *f*
f architecture *f*
r архитектура *f*

502 architecture computer systems; ACS
d Architekten-Computersysteme *npl*;
Computersysteme *npl* im Bauwesen
f système *m* ordinateur d'architecture
r архитектурная компьютерная система *f*

503 archival option
d Archivierungsfunktion *f*
f option *f* d'archivage
r опция *f* архивирования

504 archival videodisk
d Archiv-Videodisk *f*
f vidéodisque *m* d'archivage
r архивный видеодиск *m*

* archive → 505

505 archive[s]
d Archiv *n*
f archives *fpl*
r архив *m*

506 archive server
d Archiv-Server *m*
f serveur *m* d'archives
r архивирующий сервер *m*

507 archive site
(a mechanism that renders access to a
collection of files across the Internet; also, a
computer on which such a collection is
stored)
d Archivstandort *m*
f site *m* archif
r архивный сайт *m*

508 archiving; filing
d Archivierung *f*
f archivage *m*
r архивное хранение *n*; архивирование *n*

* area → 10103

509 area-based zooming
d Fläche-basiertes Zoomen *n*
f zoom *m* axé sur la superficie
r масштабирование *n* взгляда, базированное
на площади

510 area erasing
(in computer graphics)

d Bereich-Löschung *f*
f effacement *m* de zones [d'image]
r стирание *n* [изображения] участками

511 area table
d Speicherbereichtafel *f*
f table *f* de zones [de mémoire]
r таблица *f* распределения областей
(памяти)

* **A-register** → 97

512 argument
d Argument *n*
f argument *m*
r аргумент *m*

513 argumentation; justification
d Beweisführung *f*
f argumentation *f*
r аргументация *f*; обоснование *n*

* **arithmetic** → 514

514 arithmetic[al] *adj*
d arithmetisch
f arithmétique
r арифметический

515 arithmetic[al] expression
d arithmetische Ausdruck *m*;
Rechenausdruck *m*
f expression *f* arithmétique
r арифметическое выражение *n*

516 arithmetic[al] operations
d Grundrechenarten *fpl*; Rechenoperationen *fpl*
f opérations *fpl* arithmétiques
r арифметические операции *fpl*; основные
действия *npl* арифметики

517 arithmetic [and logic] unit; ALU
d arithmetisch-logische Einheit *f*;
Verknüpfungseinheit *f*; Rechenwerk *n*; ALU
f unité *f* arithmétique[-logique]
r арифметико-логическое устройство *n*;
арифметическое устройство; АЛУ

518 arithmetic constant
d arithmetische Konstante *f*
f constante *f* arithmétique
r арифметическая константа *f*

* **arithmetic expression** → 515

* **arithmetic operations** → 516

519 arithmetic overflow
d arithmetischer Überlauf *m*

 f dépassement *m* arithmétique
 r арифметическое переполнение *n*

520 arithmetic processor
 d Arithmetik[zusatz]prozessor *m*;
  Rechenwerksprozessor *m*
 f processeur *m* arithmétique; processeur
  supplémentaire
 r арифметический процессор *m*

521 arithmetic shift
 d arithmetisches Schieben *n*
 f décalage *m* arithmétique
 r арифметический сдвиг *m*

 * **arithmetic unit** → 517

 * **arm** → 4378

522 arm
 d Zweig *m*
 f bras *m*; levier *m*
 r рычаг *m*

523 armed interrupt
 d zugelassene Unterbrechung *f*
 f interruption *f* activée
 r принятое прерывание *n*

 * **ARP** → 230

 * **ARPAnet** → 268

524 arrange *v*
 d anordnen
 f arranger
 r размещать; расставлять; раскладывать;
  располагать

525 arrange *v* **all**
 d alles anordnen
 f arranger tout
 r размещать все

526 arrangement
 d Anordnung *f*; Arrangement *n*
 f arrangement *m*; disposition *f*; agencement *m*
 r размещение *n*; расстановка *f*

 * **array** → 5683

527 array
 d Feld *n*
 f tableau *m*; champ *m*
 r массив *m*

528 array cell
 d Matrixzelle *f*
 f élément *m* matriciel
 r элемент *m* матрицы

529 array element
 d Feldelement *n*; Systemelement *n*
 f élément *m* de tableau; élément de champ
 r элемент *m* массива

530 array operation; array processing
 d Feldoperation *f*; Feldverarbeitung *f*
 f opération *f* sur un tableau; traitement *m* de
  champ
 r операция *f* над массивом; обработка *f*
  массива

 * **array pitch** → 8241

 * **array processing** → 530

 * **array processor** → 5690

531 array sensor
 d Matrixsensor *m*
 f senseur *m* matriciel
 r матричный датчик *m*

532 array ticket
 d Felddatenblatt *n*
 f ticket *m* de tableau
 r паспорт *m* массива

533 arrival
 d Ankunft *f*
 f arrivée *f*
 r прибытие *n*; поступление *n*; подача *f*

534 arrival rate
  (of data)
 d Ankunftsrate *f*
 f intensité *f* d'arrivées; flux *m* d'entrée
 r интенсивность *f* входного потока

535 arrow
 d Zählpfeil *m*; Pfeil *m*
 f flèche *f*
 r стрелка *f*; стрелочка *f*

536 arrow button
 d Pfeilknopf *m*
 f bouton *m* fléché
 r кнопка *f* стрелки

537 arrow key
 d Pfeiltaste *f*
 f touche *f* de flèche; touche avec flèche
 r клавиша *f* стрелки

538 arrow pointer
 d Zeigerpfeil *m*
 f pointeur *m* flèche
 r стрелочный указатель *m*;
  указатель-стрелка *m*

539 arrow-shaped; sagittal
 d Pfeil-; pfeilförmig
 f sagittal; en forme de flèche
 r стрельчатый; стрелочный

540 article
 d Artikel *m*
 f article *m*
 r статья *f*; параграф *m*; предмет *m*

541 articulation
 d Verständlichkeit *f*; Gliederung *f*
 f articulation *f*
 r артикуляция *f*; расчленение *n*;
    членораздельность *f*; разборчивость *f*

542 artificial
 d künstlich
 f artificiel
 r искусственный

543 artificial computer-generated world
 d durch Computer generierte künstliche Welt *f*
 f monde *m* artificiel, généré par ordinateur
 r искусственный мир *m*, генерированный
    компьютером

544 artificial form
 d Kunstform *f*
 f forme *f* artificielle
 r искусственная форма *f*

**545 artificial intelligence; AI; machine
    intelligence**
 d künstliche Intelligenz *f*; KI;
    Maschinenintelligenz *f*
 f intelligence *f* artificielle; IA
 r искусственный интеллект *m*; ИИ

546 artificial intelligence system; AI system
 d System *n* der künstlichen Intelligenz;
    KI-System *n*
 f système *m* d'intelligence artificielle; système
    d'IA
 r система *f* искусственного интеллекта

547 artificial neuron
 d artifizielles Neuron *n*; künstliches Neuron
 f neurone *m* formel
 r искусственный нейрон *m*

548 artificial reality
 d künstliche Realität *f*
 f réalité *f* artificielle
 r искусственная реальность *f*

* **artificial vision → 5552**

* **artificial white → 549**

549 artificial white [signal]; nominal white
 d Normalweißsignal *n*; Normalweiß *n*
 f signal *m* blanc artificiel; blanc *m* artificiel
 r искусственный белый сигнал *m*;
    нормальный белый сигнал

550 artwork
 d Druckvorlage *f*
 f modèle *m* imprimé
 r оригинал *m* печатного монтажа; оригинал
    фотошаблона

* **artwork → 5300**

551 artwork image; artwork layout drawing
 d Abbild *n* der Druckvorlage
 f image *f* imprimée
 r изображение *n* печатного монтажа;
    фототрафарет *m*

* **artwork layout drawing → 551**

552 artwork verifier
 d Vorlagenprüfer *m*; Zeichenvorlagenprüfer *m*
 f vérificateur *m* de schémas topologiques
 r верификатор *m* топологических схем

553 ascending; bottom-up; increasing
 d aufsteigend; hochsteigend; ansteigend;
    wachsend; zunehmend
 f ascendant; montant; levant; de bas en haut;
    croissant
 r возрастающий; восходящий

554 ascending key
 d aufsteigender Schlüssel *m*
 f clé *f* ascendante
 r возрастающий ключ *m*

555 ascending order
 d aufsteigende Anordnung *f*
 f ordre *m* ascendant
 r порядок *m* возрастания; возрастающий
    порядок

556 ascending ordering
 d aufsteigende Ordnung *f*
 f ordonnancement *m* ascendant
 r упорядочение *n* по возрастанию

* **ASCII → 358**

557 ASCII character set
 d ASCII-Zeichensatz *m*
 f ensemble *m* de caractères ASCII
 r ASCII-набор *m* знаков

**558 asleep process; sleeping process;
    hibernating process**
 d wartender Prozess *m*

f processus *m* attendant
r ждущий процесс *m*

559 aspatial data
d nichträumliche Daten *pl*
f données *fpl* non spatiaux
r непространственные данные *pl*

560 aspect
d Aspekt *m*
f aspect *m*
r вид *m*

561 aspect ratio
d Seitenverhältnis *n*
f rapport *m* largeur/hauteur; rapport caractéristique; rapport d'aspect
r отношение *n* широта/высота; характеристическое отношение

562 assemblage; assembling
(of a program)
d Assemblieren *n*; Assemblierung *f*
f assemblage *m*
r ассемблирование *m*

563 assemblage; assembling; assembly; setup
(of a device)
d Zusammenbau *m*; Montage *f*
f assemblage *m*; montage *m*
r сборка *f*; монтаж *m*; компоновка *f*

564 assemble *v*; **mount** *v*
d montieren; zusammensetzen; vereinigen; assemblieren; komponieren
f assembler; monter; mettre en place
r собирать; монтировать; компоновать; ассемблировать; устанавливать

* **assembler** → **566, 567**

565 assembler-emulator; assemulator
d Assembler-Emulator *m*; Assemulator *m*
f assembleur-émulateur *m*
r ассемблер-эмулятор *m*; ассемулятор *m*

566 assembler [language]
d Assembler *m*
f langage *m* assembleur
r ассемблерный язык *m*

567 assembler [program]; assembly program
d Assembl[ier]er *m*
f assembleur *m*
r ассемблер *m*

* **assembling** → **562, 563**

* **assembly** → **563**

568 assembly list
d Montageliste *f*
f liste *f* de montage
r список *m* сборки

* **assembly program** → **567**

569 assembly system
d Montagesystem *n*
f système *m* de montage
r система *f* компоновки

* **assembly unit** → **1238**

* **assemulator** → **565**

570 assertion; statement; sentence
d Behauptung *f*; Aussage *f*; Statement *n*
f assertion *f*; proposition *f*
r утверждение *n*; высказывание *n*

571 assertion box
d Behauptungskasten *m*; Versicherungskasten *m*; Beteurungsbox *f*
f pavé *m* d'organigramme
r ящик *m* утверждения

572 assertion sign
d Ergibt-Symbol *n*; Konsequenzzeichen *n*
f signe *m* de déductibilité
r турникет *m*; штопор *m*; знак *m* выводимости

* **assessment** → **3528**

573 assign *v*
d zuordnen; zuweisen
f assigner; attribuer
r сопоставлять; назначать; присваивать

574 assignation; assignment; assigning
d Zuordnung *f*; Zuweisung *f*; Festsetzung *f*
f assignation *f*; affectation *f*; attribution *f*
r присваивание *n*; приписывание *n*; назначение *n*

575 assigned address
d zugewiesene Adresse *f*
f adresse *f* assignée
r назначенный адрес *m*

576 assigned unit
d zugewiesenes Gerät *n*
f unité *f* assignée; unité affectée
r назначенное устройство *n*

577 assigned value
d zugeordneter Wert *m*
f valeur *f* assignée
r присваиваемое значение *n*

* assigning → 574

* assignment → 574

578 assignment-free language
d zuweisungsfreie Sprache *f*
f langage *m* sans affectations
r язык *m* без присваивания

579 assignment key
d Zuteiltaste *f*; Überweisungstaste *f*
f clé *f* de répartition
r вызывной ключ *m*

580 assignment sign
d Wertzuweisungszeichen *n*
f signe *m* d'assignation; signe d'affectation
r знак *m* присваивания

581 assignment statement
d Zuordnungsbeweis *m*; Ergibt-Anweisung *f*
f opérateur *m* d'assignation; opérateur d'affectation
r оператор *m* присваивания

582 assistance
d Unterstützung *f*
f assistance *f*
r поддержка *f*; помощь *f*

583 assistance request
d Platzanforderung *f*
f demande *f* d'assistance
r вспомогательный запрос *m*

584 assists
d Unterstützungen *fpl*
f assistances *fpl*
r средства *npl* поддержки

585 associate *v*; **join** *v*
d anschließen; vereinigen; verbinden
f associer; joindre
r ассоциировать; [при]соединять; привязать

586 associated [channel] signaling
d assoziierte Zeichengabe *f*
f signalisation *f* associée
r связанная передача *f* сигналов

* associated signaling → 586

587 association
d Assoziation *f*
f association *f*
r связывание *n*; ассоциация *f*

588 associative
d assoziativ
f associatif

r ассоциативный

589 associative link
d assoziativer Link *m*
f lien *m* associatif
r ассоциативная связь *f*

590 associative memory; content-addressable memory
d Assoziativspeicher *m*; inhaltsadressierbarer Speicher *m*
f mémoire *f* associative; mémoire adressée par contenu
r ассоциативная память *f*

591 associative operation
d assoziative Operation *f*
f opération *f* associative
r ассоциативная операция *f*

592 associative processor; content-addressable processor
d assoziativer Prozessor *m*; inhaltsadressierbarer Prozessor
f processeur *m* associatif; processeur à adressage par contenu
r ассоциативный процессор *m*

593 associativity
d Assoziativität *f*
f associativité *f*
r ассоциативность *f*

* assume *v* → 9062

* assumed → 4699

594 assumption
d Annahme *f*; Voraussetzung *f*; Vermutung *f*
f assomption *f*; supposition *f*
r предположение *n*; допущение *n*; предпосылка *f*

* astable → 4940

595 asterisk
d Stern *m*; Asterisk *n*
f astérisque *m*; étoile *f*
r звёздочка *f*

596 asynchronous; anisochronous
d asynchron; anisochron
f asynchrone; non synchrone; anisochrone
r асинхронный

597 asynchronous communications interface adapter; ACIA
d Asynchronübertragungs[schnittstellen-Anpassungs]baustein *m*; ACIA-Schaltkreis *m*

f module *m* d'adaptation d'interface à
transmission asynchrone; module ACIA
r асинхронный адаптер *m* связи

598 asynchronous compression
d asynchrone Kompression *f*
f compression *f* asynchrone
r асинхронная компрессия *f*

**599 asynchronous connection; anisochronous
connection**
d asynchrone Verbindung *f*; anisochrone
Verbindung
f connexion *f* asynchrone; connexion
anisochrone
r асинхронная связь *f*

600 asynchronous data transfer
d asynchrone Datenübertragung *f*
f transfert *m* de données asynchrone
r асинхронная передача *f* данных

601 asynchronous logic
d asynchrone Logikschaltung *f*
f montage *m* logique asynchrone
r асинхронная логическая схема *f*

602 asynchronous mode
d Asynchronmodus *m*
f mode *m* asynchrone
r асинхронный режим *m*

603 asynchronous modem
d asynchrones Modem *n*
f modem *m* asynchrone
r асинхронный модем *m*

604 asynchronous operation
d asynchrone Operation *f*; asynchroner
Betrieb *m*
f opération *f* asynchrone; fonctionnement *m*
asynchrone
r асинхронная операция *f*; асинхронная
работа *f*

605 asynchronous transfer mode; ATM
d asynchroner Übertragungsmodus *m*
f mode *m* de transfert asynchrone; mode ATM
r режим *m* асинхронной передачи

* **ATM → 605**

606 atomic operation
d atomare Operation *f*
f opération *f* atomique
r атомарная операция *f*

607 at sign; at symbol; @ sign
d @-Zeichen *n*; Klammeraffe *f*
f caractère *m* @; [caractère] a commercial;

arobas[e] *m*
r коммерческое at *n*; знак *m* "а" в кружочке;
собачка *f*; гадючка *f*

* **at symbol → 607**

608 attach *v*
d anschließen; anbringen; befestigen
f attacher; fixer
r присоединять; закреплять; пристраивать

609 attach *v* an option
d eine Option anschließen
f attacher une option
r присоединять опцию

610 attached device
d angeschlossenes Gerät *n*
f unité *f* attachée
r доступное устройство *n*; присоединённое
устройство

611 attached document
d angeschlossenes Dokument *n*; attachiertes
Dokument
f pièce *f* jointe
r приложенный документ *m*

612 attached file; attachment
(in e-mail)
d attachierte Datei *f*; angeschlossene Datei
f fichier *m* attaché; annexe *m*
r присоединённый файл *m*; прицепленный
файл

613 attached processor
d angeschlossener Prozessor *m*; integrierter
Prozessor
f processeur *m* attaché
r присоединённый процессор *m*

* **attaching → 614**

* **attachment → 612**

614 attachment; attaching; fastening
d Befestigung *f*; Anlage *f*
f attachement *m*; fixage *m*; fixation *f*
r присоединение *n*; закрепление *n*;
скрепление *n*; подключение *n*

615 attack
d Sturm *m*
f attaque *f*
r атака *f*; попытка *f* нарушения защиты;
пробой *m*

* **attainability → 74**

616 attempt; experiment; trial
d Versuch *m*; Probe *f*; Experiment *n*

f épreuve *f*; expérience *f*
r попытка *f*; опыт *m*; эксперимент *m*; проба *f*

* **attendance** → 5606

617 attention
  d Achtung *f*
  f attention *f*
  r внимание *n*

* **attention interrupt** → 618

618 attention interrupt[ion]
  d Achtungsunterbrechung *f*
  f interruption *f* d'attention
  r прерывание *n* по сигналу внимания

619 attention interrupt request; AIR
  d Anforderung *f* für Achtungsunterbrechung
  f interrogation *f* d'interruption d'attention
  r заявка *f* на прерывание по сигналу внимания

620 attenuate *v*
  d dämpfen
  f atténuer; amortir
  r затухать; ослаблять

621 attenuation; damping; falloff; drop-off
  d Dämpfung *f*; Abblendung *f*
  f atténuation *f*; amortissement *m*; affaiblissement *m*
  r затухание *n*; гашение *n*; успокоение *n*; ослабление *n*

622 attenuation characteristic
  d Dämpfungsverlauf *m*; Dämpfungscharakteristik *f*
  f caractéristique *f* d'affaiblissement; caractéristique d'atténuation
  r характеристика *f* затухания

623 attenuation coefficient
  d Dämpfungskoeffizient *m*; Dämpfungsbelag *m*
  f coefficient *m* d'affaiblissement; constante *f* d'affaiblissement
  r коэффициент *m* затухания

624 attenuator
  d Dämpfungsglied *n*
  f affaiblisseur *m*; atténuateur *m*
  r аттенюатор *m*; ослабитель *m*; демпфирующий элемент *m*

* **attraction power** → 625

625 attractiveness; attraction power
  d Attraktivität *f*; Anziehungskraft *f*
  f attractivité *f*; pouvoir *m* d'attraction; puissance *f* d'attraction

r привлекательность *f*; притягательная сила *f*

626 attractor
  d Attraktor *m*
  f attracteur *m*
  r аттрактор *m*

627 attribute
  d Attribut *n*
  f attribut *m*
  r атрибут *m*; признак *m*; описатель *m*

628 attribute attaching
  d Attributsbefestigung *f*
  f attachement *m* d'attribut
  r присоединение *n* атрибута

629 attribute byte
  d Attributbyte *n*
  f octet *m* d'attributs
  r байт *m* атрибутов

630 attribute class
  d Attributsklasse *f*
  f classe *f* d'attribut
  r класс *m* атрибута

631 attribute data
  d Attributdaten *pl*
  f données *fpl* d'attribut; données *fpl* descriptives
  r атрибутные данные *pl*

632 attribute definition
  d Attribut-Definition *f*
  f définition *f* d'attribut
  r атрибутная дефиниция *f*

633 attribute information
  d Attribut-Information *f*
  f information *f* d'attribut
  r атрибутная информация *f*

634 attribute object
  d Attribut-Objekt *m*
  f objet *m* attribut
  r объект-атрибут *m*

635 attribute option
  d Attributoption *f*
  f option *f* d'attribut
  r опция *f* атрибута

636 attribute prompt
  d Attributanzeige *f*
  f consigne *f* d'attribut
  r атрибутная подсказка *f*

637 attribute reference
  d Attributverweis *m*

f référence *f* d'attribut
r атрибутная ссылка *f*

638 attribute table
d Attributtabelle *f*
f table *f* d'attributs
r таблица *f* атрибутов

639 attribute tag
d Attributetikett *n*
f étiquette *f* d'attribut
r тег *m* атрибута; атрибутный тег

640 attribute tag field
d Feld *n* des Attributetiketts
f champ *m* d'étiquette d'attribut
r поле *n* атрибутного тега

641 attribute value
d Attributwert *m*
f valeur *f* d'attribut
r значение *n* атрибута

642 attributive grammar
d attributive Grammatik *f*
f grammaire *f* attributive
r атрибутивная грамматика *f*

* **audio** → **114**

643 audio capture
d Audiosammlung *f*
f enregistrement *m* audio
r цифровая звукозапись *f*; цифровая аудиозапись *f*

* **audionumeric** → **644**

644 audionumeric[al]
d audionumerisch
f audionumérique
r аудиоцифровой

645 audio response
d Audioantwort *f*
f réponse *f* audio
r звуковой ответ *m*

* **audiosignal** → **118**

646 audio stereo casque
d Audio-Stereo-Helm *m*
f casque *f* audio stéréo
r аудиостереонаушник *m*

* **audiovideo** → **648**

647 audiovideo interleaving; AVI
d Audio-Video-Abwechselung *f*
f entrelacement *m* d'audio et vidéo

r чередование *n* аудио и видео

648 audiovisual; audiovideo
d audiovisuell
f audiovisuel; audiovidéo
r аудиовизуальный

649 audiovisual library
d audiovisuelle Bibliothek *f*
f bibliothèque *f* audiovisuelle
r библиотека *f* аудиовизуальных файлов

650 audiovisual presentation
d audiovisuelle Präsentation *f*
f présentation *f* audiovisuelle
r аудиовизуальное представление *n*

651 audiovisual program; videogram
d audiovisuelles Programm *n*; Videogramm *n*
f programme *m* audiovisuel; vidéogramme *m*
r аудиовизуальная программа *f*; видеограмма *f*

* **audit** *v* → **1647**

652 auditing; revision; inspection
d Revision *f*; Inspektion *f*; Überwachung *f*
f révision *f*; inspection *f*
r ревизия *f*; инспектирование *n*

653 auditor
d Auditor *m*
f auditeur *m*
r ревизор *m*

654 audit report
d Auflagenprüfungsbericht *m*; Auflagenkontroll *n*; Prüfungsbericht *m*
f rapport *m* d'audit; rapport de révision; rapport d'enquête; rapport d'évaluation; apport *m* de contrôle
r отчёт *m* ревизии

655 audit trail
d Prüf[ungs]pfad *m*; Prüfungsweg *m*; Prüfbericht *m*; Prüfungsspur *f*
f trace *f* d'audit
r след *m* контроля

656 augend; first term of a sum
d Augend[us] *m*; erster Summand *m*
f augendum *m*; premier terme *m* d'addition; premier opérande *m* de somme
r первое слагаемое *n*

657 augend register
d Augendregister *n*
f registre *m* de premier opérande de somme
r регистр *m* первого слагаемого

658 augment *v*
d vermehren; zunehmen; zugeben; erweitern
f augmenter
r увеличивать[ся]; прибавлять; дополнять;
расширять

**659 augmentation; augmenting; magnification;
magnifying**
d Vergrößerung *f*; Zunahme *f*; Augmentation *f*
f augmentation *f*; croissance *f*; grossissement *m*
r увеличение *n*; расширение *n*

660 augmented grammar
d erweiterte Grammatik *f*
f grammaire *f* augmentée
r пополненная грамматика *f*

*   **augmenting** → 659

*   **AUP** → 52

661 authenticity
d Authentizität *f*
f authenticité *f*
r подлинность *f*

662 authentification
d Authentifizierung *f*; Beglaubigung *f*
f authentification *f*
r проверка *f* подлинности; подтверждение *n*
подлинности; установление *n* личности;
аутентификация *f*

663 author[ing] language
d Autorensprache *f*
f langage *m* d'auteur
r авторский язык *m*

664 authoring system; authoring tool
    (in computer education)
d Autorensystem *n*
f système *m* auteur
r авторская система *f*

*   **authoring tool** → 664

665 authority
d Befugnis *f*
f autorité *f*
r полномочие *n*

666 authorization; validation; enable
d Berechtigung[szuweisung] *f*; Ermächtigung *f*;
Gültigkeitsbestätigung *f*
f autorisation *f*; validation *f*
r разрешение *n*; санкция *f*; предоставление *n*
права доступа; уполномочивание *n*;
подтверждение *n* правильности;
аттестация *f*

667 authorization code
d Berechtigungszuweisung-Code *m*;
Benutzercode *m*
f code *m* d'autorisation
r код *m* санкции; код регистрирования

668 authorization signal
d Autorisierungssignal *n*
f signal *m* d'autorisation
r сигнал *m* санкции

669 authorization table
d Berechtigungsnachweis *m*
f table *f* d'autorisation
r таблица *f* разрешений

670 authorized access
d berechtigter Zugriff *m*; erlaubter Zugriff;
autorisierter Zugriff
f accès *m* autorisé
r санкционированный доступ *m*

671 authorized user
d autorisierter Benutzer *m*
f utilisateur *m* autorisé
r зарегистрированный пользователь *m*

672 authorizing rule
d Anweisungsregel *f*; autorisierende Regel *f*;
weisungsbefugte Regel
f instruction *f* d'autorisation
r правило *n* санкционирования;
инструкция *f* регистрации

*   **author language** → 663

*   **auto-adapting** → 8337

*   **auto-aligning** → 8339

673 auto-alignment; self-alignment
d Selbstausrichtung *f*; automatischer
Ausgleich *m*
f auto-alignement *m*
r автоматическое выравнивание *n*;
самовыравнивание *n*

*   **autoanswer** → 687

674 autoarrange
d automatische Anordnung *f*
f réorganisation *f* automatique
r автоматическая реорганизация *f*

675 autobackup
d automatisches Backup *n*
f archivage *m* automatique
r автоматическое архивирование *n*

676 autocall; self-call
d Autoabruf *m*; Selbstaufruf *m*

f appel *m* automatique; auto-appel *m*
r автоматический вызов *m*

* **auto-channeling** → 8340

* **auto-checking** → 8341

* **autocontrol** → 688

677 **autodial**
  d Automatikwahl *f*
  f numérotation *f* automatique
  r автоматический вызов *m*

* **autoformat** → 678

678 **autoformat[ting]**
  d Selbstformatierung *f*; Autoformatierung *f*
  f formatage *m* automatique; autoformatage *m*
  r автоматическое форматирование *n*

* **autoindexing** → 692

679 **auto-join**
  d automatische Teilnahme *f*; automatische
    Verbindung *f*
  f union *f* automatique
  r автоматическое соединение *n*

680 **auto-logon**
  d automatische Anmeldung *f*
  f ouverture *f* de session automatique; entrée *f*
    en communication automatique
  r автоматический вход *m* в систему;
    автоматическое начало *n* сеанса

681 **automated cartography**
  d automatische Kartografie *f*
  f cartographie *f* automatisée
  r автоматизированная картография *f*

* **automated data medium** → 5550

682 **automated design**
  d automatischer Entwurf *m*
  f études *fpl* automatisées; projet *m* automatisé
  r автоматизированное проектирование *n*

683 **automated digitizing**
  d automatische Digitalisierung *f*
  f digitalisation *f* automatique
  r автоматическое дигитализирование *n*

* **automated test** → 684

684 **automated test[ing]; automatic test[ing];
    automatic check[ing]; self-check[ing]**
  d automatische Prüfung *f*; Autoprüfung *f*;
    Autotest *m*; Selbstprüfung *f*; Eigendiagnose *f*
  f essai *m* automatique; autovérification *f*;

autotest *m*
  r автоматическое тестирование *n*;
    автоматическое испытание *n*;
    автоматический тест *m*; автотест *m*

685 **automatic; self-acting**
  d automatisch; selbstwirkend; selbsttätig
  f automatique
  r автоматический; самодействующий

686 **automatic activation; unattended
    activation**
  d Selbstanlauf *m*; automatische Anschaltung *f*
  f autodéclenchement *m*
  r автоматический запуск *m*

687 **automatic answer; autoanswer**
  d automatische Anrufbeantwortung *f*
  f réponse *f* automatique; autoréponse *f*
  r автоматический ответ *m*

* **automatic check** → 684

* **automatic checking** → 684

688 **automatic control; autocontrol; automatic
    regulation; autoregulation; self-regulation**
  d automatische Steuerung *f*; Selbstregelung *f*
  f contrôle *m* automatique; autocontrôle *m*;
    autoréglage *m*
  r автоматическое управление *n*;
    автоматическое регулирование *n*

689 **automatic data processing; ADP**
  d automatische Datenverarbeitung *f*
  f traitement *m* automatique des données;
    traitement automatique de l'information
  r автоматическая обработка *f* данных

690 **automatic dictionary; electronic
    dictionary; computerized dictionary**
  d automatisches Wörterbuch *n*;
    Computerwörterbuch *n*
  f dictionnaire *m* automatique; dictionnaire
    guidé par ordinateur
  r автоматический словарь *m*; компьютерный
    словарь *m*; автоматизированный словарь

691 **automatic framing; autositing**
  d automatische Rahmung *f*
  f cadrage *m* automatique; autocadrage *m*
  r автоматическое кадрирование *n*

692 **automatic indexing; autoindexing**
  d automatische Indizierung *f*;
    Selbstindizierung *f*
  f indexage *m* automatique; auto-indexage *m*
  r автоматическое индексирование *n*

693 **automatic language analysis**
  d automatische Sprachanalyse *f*

f analyse *f* automatique du langage
r автоматический языковый анализ *m*

694 automatic language translation; machine translation
d maschinelle Sprachübersetzung *f*; maschinelle Übersetzung *f*
f translation *f* par ordinateur; translation [par] machine
r автоматический перевод *m*; машинный перевод

695 automatic message
d automatisch generierte Nachricht *f*
f message *m* automatique
r автоматическое сообщение *n*

696 automatic message playback; autoplay
d automatische Wiedergabe *f* [der Nachrichten]
f écoute *f* automatique [des messages]
r автоматическое воспроизведение *n* [сообщений]

697 automatic plotter; autoplotter
d automatischer Plotter *m*; Autoplotter *m*
f traceur *m* automatique; autotraceur *m*
r автоматический графопостроитель *m*

698 automatic programming; autoprogramming; self-programming
d Autoprogrammation *f*
f programmation *f* automatique; autoprogrammation *f*
r автоматическое программирование *n*

699 automatic reduction; auto-reduction
d automatische Verkleinerung *f*
f réduction *f* automatique; auto-réduction *f*
r автоматическое уменьшение *n*

700 automatic regeneration
d automatische Regenerierung *f*
f régénération *f* automatique
r автоматическое регенерирование *n*

* **automatic regulation** → 688

701 automatic restart; autorestart
d automatischer Wiederanlauf *m*; selbständiger Wiederanlauf
f redémarrage *m* automatique; reprise *f* automatique; autorépétition *f*
r автоматический рестарт *m*

702 automatic save; autosave
d Autospeichern *n*; automatisches Sichern *n*
f enregistrement *m* automatique
r автоматическое сохранение *n*

703 automatic selection

d automatische Auswahl *f*
f sélection *f* automatique
r автоматическая выборка *f*

704 automatic stacking
d automatische Stapelung *f*
f empilage *m* automatique
r автоматическая запись *f* в стек

705 automatic start; autostart; unattended startup
d automatischer Anlauf *m*
f démarrage *m* automatique; autodémarrage *m*
r автоматический старт *m*

* **automatic test** → 684

* **automatic testing** → 684

706 automatic wiretapping
d automatisches Anzapfen *n* von Übertragungsleitungen
f interception *f* automatique de ligne
r автоматический перехват *m* линии

* **automation** → 707

707 automati[zati]on
d Automati[sati]on *f*; Automatisierung *f*
f automati[sati]on *f*
r автоматизация *f*

708 automatize *v*
d automatisieren
f automatiser
r автоматизировать

* **autonomous** → 6393

709 autonomous system
d autonomes System *n*
f système *m* autonome
r автономная система *f*

710 autonomy
d Autonomie *f*
f autonomie *f*
r автономия *f*

711 auto-panning
d automatisches Schwenken *n*
f panoramique *m* automatique
r автоматическое панорамирование *n*

712 autopark
(of a hard drive)
d automatisches Parken *n*
f blocage *m* automatique
r автоматическое паркование *n*

* **autoplay** → 696

713 autoplot
d automatisches Plottern *n*; automatische
grafische Darstellung *f*
f tracement *m* automatique
r автоматическое вычерчивание *n*

* **autoplotter** → 697

* **autoprogramming** → 698

714 auto-reduce *v*
d autoreduzieren
f auto-réduire
r автоматически уменьшать

* **auto-reduction** → 699

* **autoregulation** → 688

* **autorestart** → 701

* **autosave** → 702

715 autoscroll
d automatisches Rollen *n*
f défilement *m* automatique
r автопрокрутка *f*

* **autositing** → 691

* **autospool** → 716

716 autospool[ing]
d Autospulung *f*
f autospoulage *m*
r автоматический спулинг *m*

* **autostart** → 705

717 autoswitch
d Wählvermittlungseinrichtung *f*
f autocommutateur *m*
r автоматический переключатель *m*

* **auto-testing** *adj* → 8341

* **autotrace** → 719

718 autotrace function
d Autotrace-Funktion *f*
f fonction *f* de trace automatique
r функция *f* автотрассировки

* **autotracing** → 719

719 autotrac[k]ing; autotrace
d Auto-Tracing *n*; automatisches Spurlagen *n*;
Autospur *f*

f trace *f* automatique; poursuite *f* automatique
r автоматическое прослеживание *n*;
автотрассировка *f*

720 autowrap
d Autoumhüllung *f*; Autoumbruch *m*
f auto-habillage *m*
r автоматическое окутывание *n*;
автоматическое завёртывание *n*

721 auxiliary
d Hilfs-
f auxiliaire
r вспомогательный

722 auxiliary alphabet
d Hilfsalphabet *n*
f alphabet *m* auxiliaire
r вспомогательный алфавит *m*

723 auxiliary carry
d Hilfsübertrag *m*
f retenue *f* auxiliaire
r дополнительный перенос *m*

* **auxiliary memory** → 3639

724 availability
d Verfügbarkeit *f*
f disponibilité *f*
r готовность *f*; наличность *f*; доступность *f*

725 available address
d verfügbare Adresse *f*
f adresse *f* accessible
r доступный адрес *m*

726 available data
d verfügbare Daten *pl*
f données *fpl* accessibles
r доступные данные *pl*

727 available machine time
d nutzbare Maschinenzeit *f*; verfügbare
Rechnerzeit *f*
f temps *m* [de] machine disponible
r доступное машинное время *n*

728 available queue
d verfügbare Warteschlange *f*
f queue *f* disponible
r доступная очередь *f*

* **available time** → 3313

729 available unit queue
d Freigerätewarteschlange *f*
f queue *f* effective des appareils
r очередь *f* к доступному устройству

730 avalanche
  d Lawine *f*; Stoßentladung *f*
  f avalanche *f*
  r лавина *f*; лавинный разряд *m*

731 avalanche breakdown
  d Lawinendurchbruch *m*
  f panne *f* d'avalanche; décharge *f* d'avalanche
  r лавинный пробой *m*

732 avatar
  d Avatar *m*
  f avatar *m*
  r аватар *m*

733 avatar's owner
  d Avatar-Besitzer *m*
  f propriétaire *m* d'avatar
  r собственник *m* аватара

  * **average → 5700, 5703**

734 average access time
  d mittlere Zugriffszeit *f*
  f temps *m* moyen d'accès
  r среднее время *n* выборки

735 average calculating speed
  d mittlere Rechengeschwindigkeit *f*
  f vitesse *f* de calcul moyenne
  r средняя скорость *f* вычисления

736 average error; mean error
  d mittlerer Fehler *m*; durchschnittlicher Fehler
  f erreur *f* moyenne
  r средняя ошибка *f*; средняя погрешность *f*

737 average life; mean life
  d mittlere Lebensdauer *f*
  f durée *f* de vie moyenne
  r средний срок *m* службы

738 average operation
  d Durchschnittsbildung *f*
  f opération *f* de prise en moyenne
  r операция *f* усреднения

  * **average value → 5703**

739 average waiting time
  d mittlere Wartezeit *f*
  f temps *m* d'attente moyen
  r среднее время *n* ожидания

740 averaging
  d Mittel[wert]bildung *f*; Mittelung *f*
  f prise *f* en moyenne
  r усреднение *n*

741 averaging method
  d Mittelungsverfahren *n*; Mittelungsmethode *f*
  f méthode *f* du centrage; méthode des moyennes
  r метод *m* усреднения; способ *m* усреднения

  * **AVI → 647**

742 AVI format
  (of audiovisual files)
  d AVI-Format *n*
  f format *m* AVI
  r формат *m* AVI

743 awake process
  d aktiver Prozess *m*
  f processus *m* actif
  r активный процесс *m*

744 azerty keyboard
  d Azerty-Tastatur *f*
  f clavier *m* azerty
  r клавиатура *f* [типа] azerty; клавиатура с европейским расположением клавиш

B

* **backassembler** → 2975

745 **back bias; reverse bias**
d Sperrvorspannung *f*
f tension *f* de polarisation inverse
r обратное смещение *n*

* **backboard** → 765

* **backbone** → 746, 747, 748

746 **backbone [cable]**
d Backbone-Kabel *n*
f épine *m* dorsal; dorsale *m*
r магистральный кабель *m*

747 **backbone [line]**
d Hauptleitung *f*; Rückenlinie *f*
f raie *f* de dos
r магистраль *f*; магистральная линия *f*

748 **backbone [network]**
(the top level in a hierarchical network)
d Hauptnetz *n*; Backbone-Netz *n*
f réseau *m* principal; réseau général; réseau fédérateur; réseau dorsal; réseau national d'interconnexion
r базовая сеть *f*; основная сеть

749 **backbone node; backbone site**
d Rückgrat *n*
f nœud *m* fédérateur
r базовый узел *m*; узел базовой сети; магистральный узел

* **backbone site** → 749

750 **backbone switch**
d Backbone-Schlüssel *m*
f commutateur *m* fédérateur
r магистральный коммутатор *m* [сети]

* **backdown** → 764

751 **backdrop**
(of a scene)
d Hintergrund[vorgang] *m*; Kulisse *f*
f arrière-plan *m*
r фон *m*; фоновая плоскость *f*

752 **back edge; trailing edge**
d Rückflanke *f*; Hinterflanke *f*; Hinterkante *f*
f flanc *m* arrière

r задний фронт *m*

* **backend** → 753

* **backend processor** → 7169

753 **backend [program]**
d Nachschaltprogramm *n*
f programme *m* interface
r интерфейсная программа *f*

754 **background; foil**
(of a screen)
d Hintergrund *m*; Untergrund *m*
f fond *m*; arrière-plan *m*; plan *m* d'arrière; background *m*
r фон *m*; задний план *m*

755 **background color**
d Hintergrundfarbe *f*; Grundfarbe *f*
f couleur *f* de fond; couleur d'arrière-plan
r цвет *m* фона

756 **background frames**
d Hintergrundsaufnahmen *fpl*
f cadres *mpl* d'arrière-plan; cadres de fond
r фоновые кадры *mpl*

757 **background image**
d Hintergrundbild *n*
f image *f* de fond
r фоновое изображение *n*

* **backgrounding** → 760

758 **background pattern**
d Hintergrundmuster *n*
f motif *m* de fond; modèle *m* de fond
r модель *f* фона

759 **background printing**
d Drucken *n* im Hintergrundmodus
f impression *f* en arrière-plan
r печать *f* в фоновом режиме; фоновая печать

760 **background processing; backgrounding**
d Hintergrundverarbeitung *f*; nachrangige Verarbeitung *f*
f traitement *m* de fond; gestion *f* de traitement d'arrière-plan
r фоновая обработка *f*; организация *f* фоновой обработки

761 **background subtraction**
d Subtrahieren *n* des Hintergrunds
f soustraction *f* d'arrière-plan
r вычитание *n* фона

* **backing memory** → 3639

* **backlight** → 762

762 **backlight[ing]**
  d Hintergrundbeleuchtung *f*
  f rétroéclairage *m*
  r подсветка *f*

763 **backlit display**
  d von hinten beleuchteter Bildschirm *m*
  f écran *m* rétroéclairé; écran éclairé par l'arrière
  r дисплей *m* с подсветкой

764 **back-off; backdown**
  d Unteraussteuerung *f*
  f retraite *f*; refus *m*
  r отход *m*; отступление *n*; отказывание *n*

* **backout** → 8037

* **back out** *v* → 7988

* **backpanel** → 765

765 **backplane; backboard; backpanel**
  d Rückwandplatine *f*; Rückverdrahtungsplatte *f*
  f plaque *f* arrière; plaque de connexion; fond *m* de panier
  r задняя плата *f*; задняя панель *f*

766 **backplane bus**
  d Bus *m* auf der Rückwandplatine; Rückverdrahtungsbus *m*
  f bus *m* de face soudure
  r монтажная шина *f*

767 **back propagation**
  d Rückpropagierung *f*
  f rétropropagation *f*
  r обратное распространение *n*

768 **back propagation algorithm**
  d Rückpropagierungsalgorithmus *m*; Rückwärts-Fehlerkorrektur-Algorithmus *m*
  f algorithme *m* de rétropropagation
  r алгоритм *m* обратного распространения

* **backscatter** → 769

769 **backscatter[ing]**
  d Rückstreuung *f*
  f rétrodiffusion *f*; diffusion *f* en arrière
  r обратное рассеяние *n*

770 **backscattering signal**
  d Rückstreusignal *n*; rückgestreutes Signal *n*
  f signal *m* rétrodiffusé
  r сигнал *m* обратного рассеяния

771 **backscattering technique**
  d Rückstreumethode *f*
  f méthode *f* de rétrodiffusion
  r метод *m* обратного рассеяния

* **backslash** → 772

772 **backslash [character]; antislash** (\ )
  d Backslash *n*; umgekehrter Schrägstrich *m*; inverser Schrägstrich
  f barre *f* oblique inversée; barre de haut en bas; antislash *m*
  r обратная косая черта *f*

773 **backspace; backspacing**
  d Rückwärtsschritt *m*; Rücksetzen *n* um eine Position
  f espace[ment] *m* [d']arrière; rappel *m* [arrière]; retour *m* à une position
  r обратное перемещение *n*; возврат *m* на одну позицию

774 **backspace character**
  d Rückwärtsschrittzeichen *n*; Rückkehrzeichen *n*
  f caractère *m* d'espace [d']arrière; caractère de retour à une position
  r знак *m* возврата на одну позицию

775 **backspace instruction; return instruction**
  d Rücksetzanweisung *f*; Rückkehrbefehl *m*; Rücksprungbefehl *m*
  f instruction *f* de rappel; instruction de retour
  r инструкция *f* возврата

776 **backspace key**
  d Rückwärtsschritt-Taste *f*
  f touche *f* d'espace [d']arrière; touche d'espacement arrière; touche de retour à une position
  r клавиша *f* возврата на одну позицию

* **backspacing** → 773

777 **back-to-back connection**
  d Antiparallelschaltung *f*; gegensinnige Parallelschaltung *f*
  f couplage *m* antiparallèle
  r встречное соединение *n*

778 **backtracking**
  d Rückverzweigung *f*
  f recherche *f* arrière; retour *m* arrière
  r поиск *m* с возвратом; обратное слежение *n*

779 **back transfer; back transmission**
  d Rückübertragung *f*
  f transmission *f* en arrière
  r обратная передача *f*

* **back transmission** → 779

780 backup; reserve; standby
d Sicherung *f*; Reserve *f*; Backup *n*
f réserve *f*; sauvegarde *m*; secours *m* informatique
r резерв *m*; архив *m*

781 backup copy
d Sicherungskopie *f*; Backup-Kopie *f*; Hilfs-Kopie *f*; Stütz-Kopie *f*
f copie *f* de réserve; copie d'archives
r резервная копия *f*; архивная копия

782 backup device
d Backup-Einrichtung *f*; Reservegerät *n*; Reserveeinheit *f*
f dispositif *m* de réserve; unité *f* de réserve; appareil *m* de secours; unité de sauvegarde
r резервное устройство *n*

783 backup file
d Sicher[stell]ungsdatei *f*
f fichier *m* doubleur; fichier de secours
r дублирующий файл *m*; архивный файл

* backup memory → 3639

* backup plan → 2232

* backup track → 345

784 backward branching
d Rückkehrssprung *m*
f branchement *m* [en] arrière
r переход *m* назад; ветвление *n* назад; обратный переход

785 backward channel; return channel; reverse channel
d Rückkanal *m*; Hilfskanal *m*
f canal *m* arrière; canal inverse
r обратный канал *m*

786 backward glossary
d rückläufiges Glossar *n*
f glossaire *m* inverse
r обратный глоссарий *m*

787 backward pointer
d Rückwärtszeiger *m*
f pointeur *m* arrière
r указатель *m* возврата

788 backward signal
d Rückwärtszeichen *n*; Hinteransicht *f*; rückwärtiges Signal *n*
f signal *m* de retour; signal inverse l'arrière
r обратный сигнал *m*; возвратный сигнал

789 backward transfer characteristic
d Rückkopplungscharakteristik *f*
f caractéristique *f* de la réaction
r характеристика *f* обратной связи

790 bad data
d falsche Daten *pl*
f données *fpl* mauvaises; données erronées
r неправильные данные *pl*

* badge → 4615

791 bad sector
(of a disk or a diskette)
d fehlerhafter Sektor *m*; falscher Sektor
f secteur *m* défectueux
r дефектный сектор *m*

792 bad track
d defekte Spur *f*; fehlerhafte Spur
f piste *f* défectueuse; piste mauvaise
r дефектная дорожка *f*

793 balance; equilibrium
d Gleichgewicht *n*; Balance *f*
f balance *f*; équilibre *m*
r равновесие *n*; баланс *m*

794 balanced input
d symmetrischer Eingang *m*
f entrée *f* symétrique
r симметричный вход *m*

795 balanced pulses
d symmetrische Impulse *mpl*
f impulsions *fpl* symétriques
r симметричные импульсы *mpl*

* balance equalization → 796

796 balancing; balance equalization; compensation
d Ausgleich *m*; Auswuchtung *f*; Auswuchten *n*; Kompensation *f*; Entzerrung *f*
f équilibrage *m*; balancement *m*; égalisation *f*; compensation *f*
r уравнение *n*; компенсация *f*; выравнивание *n* [искажений]

797 balancing network; equivalent circuit; equivalent network
d äquivalente Schaltung *f*; Nachbildnetz *n*; künstliche Leitung *f*; Kunstschaltung *f*; Anpassungsschaltung *f*; Ersatzschaltung *f*
f circuit *m* équivalent; schéma *m* équivalent; équilibreur *m*; circuit artificiel
r балансный контур *m*; эквивалентная схема *f*; искусственная схема

* ball → 800

798 balloon; bubble
d Ballon *m*; Sprechblase *f*; Blase *f*

f ballon m; bulle f
r кружок m; шар m; пузырёк m

799 ball-point pen
d Kugelschreiber m
f crayon m à bulle
r шариковый элемент m

800 ball [terminal]; teardrop
d Kugel f
f boule f
r шар m; каплевидный элемент m

* BAM → 846

* ban v → 4834

801 banana problem
d Bananenproblem n
f problème m de banane
r "банановая проблема" f

* band → 5582

802 band; ribbon
d Band n
f bande f; ruban m
r лента f; полоса f

803 band gap
d Bandabstand m
f largeur f de bande interdite
r расстояние n между зонами

804 banding
(defect of halftone screens or screen tints
output by laser printers or imagesetters)
d Bandeinpassen n; Siebkettung f
f effet m de bande; étirement m
r нанесение n полос; обозначение n
полосами; полошение n

* band-limited → 809

* band-limited optical channel → 811

* bandpass → 806

805 bandpass
d Bandpass m
f passe-bande f
r полоса f пропускания; лента f пропускания

806 bandpass [filter]
d Bandpassfilter m
f filtre m passe-bande; filtre à bande
r полосовой фильтр m;
полосопропускающий фильтр

807 bandpass response

d Bandpassverhalten n; Bandresonanzkurve f
f réponse f passe-bande; courbe f de réponse
[d'un filtre] passe-bande
r полосовая характеристика f

* band plotter → 896

* band printer → 1554

808 bandwidth
d Bandbreite f
f largeur f de bande; bande f passante
r ширина f полосы [ленты]

809 band[width]-limited
d bandbreitebegrenzt; mit begrenzter
Bandbreite
f limité par largeur de bande; à largeur de
bande limitée
r ограничиваемый шириной полосы; с
ограниченной шириной полосы

810 bandwidth-limited operation
d bandbreitebegrenzter Betrieb m
f fonctionnement m limité par largeur de bande
r работа f, ограничиваемая шириной полосы

811 band[width]-limited optical channel
d bandbegrenzter optischer Kanal m
f voie f [de transmission] optique à largeur de
bande limitée
r оптический канал m, ограничиваемый
шириной полосы

812 bank
(of data)
d Bank f
f banque f
r банк m

813 bank address register
d Bankadressenregister n;
Speicherblockadressregister n;
Speicherbankzeiger m
f registre m d'adresse de banque; registre
d'adresse de bloc de mémoire
r регистр m адреса банка памяти; регистр
адреса блока памяти

814 bank carte
d Bankkarte f
f carte f bancaire
r банковская карта f

* bank phasing → 5036

815 bank switching
(between two memory blocs)
d Bankschaltung f; Blockumschaltung f

f commutation *f* de banques; commutation de blocs

r переключение *n* банков; переключение блоков

816 banner
(large headline, usually across the full width of a page)
d Banner *n*; Balkenüberschrift *f*; Werbeband *n*; Spruchband *n*
f bandeau *m*; bannière *m*
r баннер *m*; фантик *m*; шапка *f*; объявление *n*; реклама *f*

817 banner block
d Bannerblock *m*
f bloc *m* de bannière
r блок *m* баннера

* **bar** → 1276, 8950

818 bar
d Streifen *m*; Balken *m*; Leiste *f*
f barre *f*; tige *f*
r полоса *f*

819 bar code; strip code
d Strichcode *m*; Balkencode *m*; Barcode *m*
f code *m* à barres
r штриховой код *m*; штрих-код *m*

820 bar-code reader; bar-code scanner
d Strichcodeleser *m*; Balkencodeleser *m*
f lecteur *m* de code à barres
r устройство *n* считывания штрихового кода

* **bar-code scanner** → 820

821 bare chip; unpacked chip
d ungekapselter Chip *m*; gehäuseloser Chip *m*
f chip *m* sans corpus; puce *f* sans boîtier
r бескорпусный кристалл *m*

822 bare conductor
d nackter Leiter *m*
f conducteur *m* nu
r провод *m* без покрытия

823 bare machine
d ohne Software lieferbarer Rechner *m*
f machine *f* vierge; machine sans logiciel
r машина *f* без программного обеспечения

824 bar menu
d Menüzeile *f*
f menu *m* barre
r лента-меню *f*

825 barrel shifter
d Multipositionsverschieber *m*

f décaleur *m* multiple
r схема *f* сдвига на произвольное число позиций

826 barrier; shield
d Schranke *f*; Schirm *m*
f barrière *f*; barrage *m*
r барьер *m*; экран *m*

827 barrier capacitance; junction capacitance; depletion-layer capacitance
d Sperrschichtkapazität *f*
f capacité *f* de couche de barrage; capacité de jonction
r барьерная ёмкость *f*; ёмкость запирающего слоя; ёмкость перехода

828 barrier layer; depletion layer
d Randschicht *f*; Sperrschicht *f*
f couche *f* de barrage; couche barrière
r граничный слой *m*; запирающий слой

* **base** → 845, 7581

829 base; basis
d Basis *f*; Grund *m*
f base *f*
r база *f*; базис *m*; основа *f*

830 base address; presumptive address; reference address
d Basisadresse *f*; Grundadresse *f*; Bezugsadresse *f*
f adresse *f* de base; adresse de référence
r базовый адрес *m*; опорный адрес

831 base address register
d Basisadressregister *n*; Bezugsregister *n*
f registre *m* d'adresse de base
r регистр *m* базовых адресов

832 baseband
d Basisband *n*
f bande *f* de base
r базисная полоса *f*; основная лента *f*

833 baseband LAN
d Basisbandnetz *n*
f réseau *m* local en bande de base
r локальная сеть *f* базисной полосы

834 baseband modem
d Baseband-Modem *m*
f modem *m* en bande de base
r модем *m* базисной полосы

835 baseband-transfer function
d Basisband-Übertragungsfunktion *f*
f fonction *f* de transfert en bande de base
r передаточная функция *f* базисной полосы

836 **baseband transmission**
d Basisbandübertragung *f*
f transmission *f* en bande de base
r передача *f* базисной полосы

837 **baseband videosignal**
d Basisband-Videosignal *n*
f signal *m* vidéo en bande de base
r видеосигнал *m* базисной полосы

838 **based indexed addressing**
d indizierte Basisadressierung *f*
f adressage *m* basé indexé
r относительная индексная адресация *f*

* **base directory** → 4537

839 **based variable**
d basisbezogene Variable *f*
f variable *f* basée
r базируемая переменная *f*

* **base field** → 5199

* **base memory** → 2280

840 **base menu**
d Grundmenü *n*
f menu *m* de base
r базовое меню *n*

* **base notation** → 7584

* **base number** → 7581

841 **base of knowledge; knowledge base;
experience base**
d Wissenbasis *f*; Erfahrungsbasis *f*
f base *f* de savoirs; base de connaissances; base
d'expériences
r база *f* знаний

842 **base-page addressing**
d Basisleitenadressierung *f*
f adressage *m* par la page de base
r адресация *f* по базовой странице

843 **base pattern**
d Grundmotiv *n*
f motif *m* de base
r основной мотив *m*

* **base register** → 4772

844 **base table**
d Basistabelle *f*
f table *f* de base
r базовая таблица *f*

845 **basic; base; fundamental**

d Basis-; fundamental; Grund-; grundsätzlich
f de base; basique; fondamental
r основной; базисный; фундаментальный

846 **basic access method; BAM**
d Basiszugriffsmethode *f*; einfache
Zugriffsmethode
f méthode *f* d'accès de base
r базовый метод *m* доступа

847 **basic block**
d Grundbaustein *m*; Standardbaustein *m*
f bloc *m* de base; bloc standard
r стандартный блок *m*

848 **basic cable; basic unit**
d Bündelader *f*; Grundbündel *n*
f toron *m* [élémentaire]; assemblé *m*
élémentaire
r основной пучок *m* [кабеля]

849 **basic component**
d Basiskomponente *f*
f composante *f* basique
r базисный компонент *m*; основной
градивный элемент *m*

850 **basic hardware**
d Grundausrüstung *f*
f matériel *m* de base
r базовые аппаратные средства *npl*;
минимальные аппаратные средства

851 **basic input/output system; BIOS**
d grundlegendes Ein-/Ausgabesystem *n*; BIOS
f système *m* base d'entrée/sortie; BIOS
r базовая система *f* ввода/вывода

852 **basic interface multiplexer**
d Basisanschluss-Multiplexgerät *n*;
Basisanschlussmultiplexer *m*
f multiplexeur *m* d'interface de base
r базисный интерфейсный мультиплексор *m*

853 **basic noise**
d Eigenrauschen *n*; Eigengeräusch *n*
f bruit *m* propre
r собственный шум *m*

854 **basic record**
d Originaleintrag *m*
f enregistrement *m* de base
r основная запись *f*

855 **basic representation**
d Basisdarstellung *f*
f représentation *f* de base
r базисное представление *n*

856 **basic sequential access method; BSAM**
d sequentielle Basiszugriffsmethode *f*; einfache

sequentielle Zugriffsart *f*
f méthode *f* d'accès séquentielle simple
r базисный последовательный метод *m* доступа

857 basic symbol
d Grundzeichen *n*; Grundsymbol *n*
f symbole *m* de base; symbole fondamental
r базисный символ *m*; основной знак *m*

858 basic telecommunication access method; BTAM
d Basis-Fernzugriffsmethode *f*
f méthode *f* d'accès fondamentale télécommunicative
r базисный телекоммуникационный метод *m* доступа

859 basic timing signal
d Grundtakt *m*
f signal *m* d'horloge de base
r основной синхронизирующий сигнал *m*

* **basic unit → 848**

860 basic variable
d Basisvariable *f*
f variable *f* de base
r базисная переменная *f*

* **basis → 829**

861 basis of the cycle
d Zyklenbasis *f*
f base *f* de cycle
r база *f* цикла

862 batch
d Schub *m*; Batch *m*
f lot *m*
r группа *f*; серия *f*

* **batch → 6670**

* **batch communication → 6688**

* **batch computing → 867**

863 batch connection process
d serienweise Verarbeitung *f* der Verbunden
f processus *m* de connexion par lots
r процесс *m* пакетной связи

864 batch counter
d Paketzähler *m*
f compteur *m* de paquets
r счётчик *m* пакетов

865 batch file
d Stapeldatei *f*; Batch-Datei *f*

f fichier *m* de commandes groupées; fichier batch
r командный файл *m*

* **batching → 867, 6689**

866 batch plotting
d Batchplottern *n*; Stapelplottern *n*
f tracé *m* par lots
r пакетное вычерчивание *n*

867 batch processing; stacked data processing; batch computing; batching
d Batch-Verarbeitung *f*; Stapel[daten]verarbeitung *f*; blockweise Verarbeitung *f*
f traitement *m* [de données] en groupes; traitement échelonné; traitement par lots
r пакетная обработка *f*; групповая обработка [данных]; групповая операция *f*

868 batch trailer
d Pakettrailer *m*
f fin *f* arrière de paquets
r завершитель *m* пакетов

869 baton; token; buck
d Token *n*; Marke *f*; Markierer *m*; Buck *n*
f bâton *m*; jeton *m*; marqueur *m*
r жезл *m*; маркер *m*

870 battery; accumulator
d Batterie *f*; Akkumulator *m*
f batterie *f*; pile *f*; accumulateur *m*
r [аккумуляторная] батарея *f*; аккумулятор *m*

871 battery backup
d Batteriereserve *f*; Batteriestützung *f*
f maintien *m* par batteries; soutien *m* par batteries
r резервное батарейное питание *n*

872 baud
d Baud *n*
f baud *m*
r бод *m*

873 Baudot code
d Baudot-Code *m*
f code *m* de Baudot
r код *m* Бодо

874 baud rate
d Baudrate *f*; Baud-Zahl *f*
f débit *m* en bauds
r скорость *f* [передачи данных] в бод

875 bay
(of a selector or repeater)

d Bucht *f*
f baie *f*
r открытая ячейка *f*

876 bay; frame; stand; rack; cradle; crate; horse
d Bay *f*; Gestell *n*; Ständer *m*; Gestellrahmen *m*; Einschubschrank *m*
f support *m* [de modules]; panier *m*; cadre *m* [du bâti]; bâti *m*; râtelier *m*
r панель *f*; рама *f*; штатив *m*; корпус *m*; стойка *f*

877 bay-mounted
d gestellmontiert
f monté en châssis
r смонтированный на раме

* **B-box** → 4772

* **BBS** → 1250

* **BCA** → 1226

* **BCC** → 1052, 1062

* **BCD** → 928

878 beam; ray
d Strahl *m*
f rayon *m*; faisceau *m*; jet *m*
r луч *m*; пучок *m* [лучей]

* **beam pen** → 5361

* **beat** → 881

879 beat frequency
d Schwebungsfrequenz *f*
f fréquence *f* de battement; fréquence de flottement
r частота *f* биения

880 beat [frequency] oscillator
d Schwebungsoszillator *m*
f oscillateur *m* de battement
r осциллятор *m* биения

881 beat[ing]; pulsing; pulsation
d Schlagen *n*; Schwebung *f*; Impulsgabe *f*; Pulsen *n*; Pulsation *f*
f battement *m*; pulsation *f*; flottement *m*
r биение *n*; пульсация *f*

* **beat oscillator** → 880

882 beeper
d Tonsignalanlage *f*
f bippeur *m*; avertisseur *m* sonore
r устройство *n* звуковой сигнализации

* **before-image** → 7212

883 before-image block
d Vorabbildblock *m*
f bloc *m* de pré-image
r блок *m* предварительного изображения

884 begin
d Beginn *m*; Anfang *m*
f début *m*
r начинание *n*; начало *n*

* **begin** *v* → 6590

* **beginning mark** → 885

* **beginning of file** → 9446

885 beginning[-of-information] mark[er]; BIM
d Anfangsmarke *f*
f marqueur *m* de début [d'information]
r маркер *m* начала [информации]

886 beginning of tape; BOT; leading end; leader
d Bandanfang *m*; Streifenanfang *m*; Vorspann *m*
f début *m* de bande; amorçage *m* de bande
r начало *n* [магнитной] ленты; начальный отрезок *m* ленты; заправочный конец *m* ленты

887 beginning-of-tape marker; BOT marker; load mark
d Bandanfangsmarke *f*; Vorspannbandmarke *f*
f marqueur *m* de début de bande; marque d'amorce de bande
r маркер *m* начала [магнитной] ленты; метка *f* начала [заправочного конца] ленты

888 beginning of transmission
d Übertragungsbeginn *m*
f début *m* de transmission
r начало *n* передачи

889 behavioral controller
d Verhaltenkontroller *m*
f contrôleur *m* de comportement
r контроллер *m* поведения

890 behavioral simulation
d Verhaltenssimulierung *f*
f simulation *f* comportementale
r поведенческая симуляция *f*

891 behaviour
d Verhalten *n*
f conduite *f*; comportement *m*
r поведение *n*

* **BEL** → 894

892 believability
d Glaubwürdigkeit *f*
f véridicité *f*; droiture *f*; vraisemblance *f*
r достоверность *f*; правдоподобие *n*

893 believable approximation
d glaubwürdige Approximation *f*
f approximation *f* vraisemblable
r правдоподобная аппроксимация *f*

* **bell** → 895

894 bell character; BEL
d Warnzeichen *n*
f caractère *m* de sonnerie; caractère d'appel
r знак *m* звукового сигнала

895 bell [signal]
d Klingel *f*; Tonsignal *n*; Glockenzeichen *n*
f signal de cloche; sonnerie *f*
r звонок *m*; сигнал *m* звонка; звонковый
сигнал

* **belt-bed plotter** → 3188

896 belted plotter; band plotter
d Bandplotter *m*
f traceur *m* à bande
r ленточный графопостроитель *m*

* **benchmark** → 899

897 benchmark problem
d Bewertungsaufgabe *f*; Benchmark-Problem *n*
f problème *m* d'évaluation
r задача *f* оценки характеристик

898 benchmark program
d Bewertungsprogramm *n*;
Benchmark-Programm *n*
f programme *m* d'évaluation; programme
d'estimation
r программа *f* оценки производительности

899 benchmark [test]
d Benchmark *n*
f test *m* de performance
r эталонный тест *m*

* **BER** → 988

900 beta site
d Beta-Standort *m*; Beta-Site *f*
f site *m* bêta
r бета-сайт *m*

901 beta test
d Beta-Test *m*; Beta-Prüfung *f*

f bêta test *m*
r бета-тестирование *n*

902 beta version
(of a software)
d Betaversion *f*
f version *f* bêta
r бета-версия *f*

* **betweening** → 5890

* **bias** → 904

* **bias check** → 903

**903 bias check[ing]; marginal check[ing];
marginal test**
d Grenzwertprüfung *f*; Randwertkontrolle *f*;
Toleranzgrenzentest *m*
f test *m* aux marges
r проверка *f* при граничных условиях;
граничные испытания *npl*

904 bias[ing]
d Vorspannung *f*; Verschiebung *f*
f biais *m*; déplacement *m*; écart *m*
r смещение *n*; перекос *m*

905 bias one input
d Bias-One-Eingang *m*
f entrée *f* unité
r единичный вход *m*

906 bias zero input
d Bias-Zero-Eingang *m*
f entrée *f* zéro
r нулевой вход *m*

907 bibliographic database
d bibliographische Datenbasis *f*
f base *f* de données bibliographique
r библиографическая база *f* данных

908 bibliography
d Literaturverzeichnis *n*
f bibliographie *f*
r библиография *f*

**909 bibliography method; review article
method**
d bibliographische Methode *f*
f méthode *f* bibliographique; méthode de revue
des articles
r библиографический метод *m*; метод
рефератов

* **biconditional** → 910

910 biconditional [implication]
d [logische] Äquivalenz *f*; Gleichwertigkeit *f*;

Bijunktion *f*
f biconditionnel *m*; implication *f*
biconditionnée
r двусторонняя импликация *f*; логическая
эквивалентность *f*; равнозначность *f*

* **bidecimal** → 929

* **bidimensional** → 9590

911 bidimensional image; 2D image
d zweidimensionales Bild *n*
f image *f* bidimensionnelle
r двумерное изображение *n*; 2D
изображение; плоское изображение

**912 bidirectional; bothway; two-directional;
two-way**
d bidirektional; Zweirichtungs-;
doppelgerichtet; Zweiweg-
f bidirectionnel
r двунаправленный; в двух направлениях

913 bidirectional bus
d bidirektionaler Bus *m*; Zweirichtungsbus *m*
f bus *m* bidirectionnel
r двунаправленная шина *f*

**914 bidirectional counter; forward-backward
counter; reversible counter**
d Zweirichtungszähler *m*;
Vorwärts-Rückwärts-Zähler *m*
f compteur *m* bidirectionnel; compteur
réversible; compteur avant-arrière
r реверсивный счётчик *m*

915 bidirectional coupler
d bidirektionaler Koppler *m*
f coupleur *m* bidirectionnel
r двунаправленный соединитель *m*

916 bidirectional data transfer
d bidirektionale Datenübertragung *f*;
Datenübertragung auf
Zweirichtungsverbindung
f transfert *m* de données bidirectionnel
r двунаправленная передача *f* данных

917 bidirectional printing
d bidirektionales Drucken *n*
f impression *f* bidirectionnelle; impression à
deux directions
r печать *f* в двух направлениях;
двунаправленная печать

* **bidirectional simultaneous communication**
→ 3221

918 bifurcation
d Bifurkation *f*

f bifurcation *f*
r бифуркация *f*; раздвоение *n*

919 big font
d große Schrift *f*
f police *f* grosse
r большой шрифт *m*

920 bilateral; two-sided; double-side[d]
d bilateral; doppelseitig
f bilatéral; bilatère
r двусторонний

921 bilinear filtering
d bilineare Filterung *f*
f filtrage *m* bilinéaire
r билинейное фильтрование *n*

922 bilinear pixel interpolation
d bilineare Pixel-Interpolation *f*
f interpolation *f* bilinéaire de pixels
r билинейная интерполяция *f* пикселов

* **bill** → 90

923 billibit
d Kilo-Megabit *n*
f kilo-mégabit *m*
r киломегабит *m*; миллиард *m* битов

* **BIM** → 885

924 binary
d binär
f binaire
r двоичный; бинарный

925 binary adder
d Dualadder *m*; binärer Adder *m*
f add[itionn]eur *m* binaire
r двоичный сумматор *m*

926 binary arithmetic
d binäre Arithmetik *f*
f arithmétique *f* binaire
r бинарная арифметика *f*

927 binary code
d Binärcode *m*
f code *m* binaire
r двоичный код *m*

928 binary-coded decimal; BCD
d binär verschlüsselte Dezimalzahl *f*
f nombre *m* décimal codifié binaire; décimal *m*
codé binaire
r двоично-[кодированное] десятичное
число *n*

929 binary-decimal; bidecimal
d binär-dezimal

f binaire-décimal
r двоично-десятичный

* **binary-decimal conversion** → 954

930 **binary digit**
    d Binärziffer *f*; Dualstelle *f*
    f digit *m* binaire; chiffre *m* binaire
    r двоичная цифра *f*; двоичный разряд *m*

931 **binary DXF file format**
    d binäres DXF-Dateiformat *n*
    f format *m* binaire DXF de fichier
    r двоичный файловый формат *m* DXF

932 **binary element**
    d binäres Element *n*
    f élément *m* binaire
    r двоичный элемент *m*

933 **binary error-correcting code**
    d binärer Fehlerkorrekturcode *m*
    f code *m* autocorrecteur binaire; code
      autorectifiable binaire
    r двоичный код *m* с коррекцией ошибок

934 **binary error-detecting code**
    d binärer Fehlererkennungscode *m*
    f code *m* à détection d'erreurs binaire
    r двоичный код *m* с обнаружением ошибок

935 **binary file**
    d binäre Datei *f*
    f fichier *m* binaire
    r двоичный файл *m*

936 **binary function; Boolean function; logic[al] function**
    d binäre Funktion *f*; Boolesche Funktion;
      logische Funktion; Schaltfunktion *f*
    f fonction *f* binaire; fonction booléenne;
      fonction logique
    r двоичная функция *f*; булевая функция;
      логическая функция

* **binary-hexadecimal** → 937

937 **binary-hexadecimal [conversion]; binhex**
    (in e-mail)
    d binär-hexadezimale Konversion *f*
    f conversion *f* binaire-hexadécimale
    r двоично-шестнадцатеричное
      преобразование *n*

* **binary image** → 944

938 **binary large object; BLOB**
    (of data)
    d großes binäres Objekt *n*; Blob *n*
    f grand objet *m* binaire

    r большой двоичный объект *m*; "блоб" *m*

939 **binary notation; binary [re]presentation**
    d binäre Schreibweise *f*; binäre Darstellung *f*
    f notation *f* binaire; [re]présentation *f* binaire
    r двоичное представление *n*

940 **binary number**
    d binäre Zahl *f*
    f nombre *m* binaire
    r двоичное число *n*

941 **binary [number] system**
    d Binärsystem *n*; Dualsystem *n*;
      Zweiersystem *n*
    f système *m* binaire; système de nombres
      binaires
    r бинарная система *f*; двоичная система
      [счисления]

942 **binary operation**
    d binäre Verknüpfung *f*; binäre Operation *f*
    f opération *f* binaire
    r бинарная операция *f*

943 **binary operator; dyadic operator**
    d Binäroperator *m*
    f opérateur *m* binaire
    r бинарный оператор *m*

944 **binary picture; binary image**
    d Binärbild *n*
    f image *f* binaire
    r бинарное изображение *n*

945 **binary point**
    d Binärkomma *n*; Kommastelle *f* einer
      Binärzahl
    f virgule *f* binaire
    r двоичная запятая *f*; точка *f* в двоичном
      числе

* **binary presentation** → 939

946 **binary relation; dyadic relation**
    d binäre Relation *f*; zweistellige Relation
    f relation *f* binaire
    r бинарное отношение *n*; двучленное
      отношение

* **binary representation** → 939

947 **binary scale; two scale**
    d binäre Skale *f*
    f échelle *f* binaire
    r двоичная шкала *f*

948 **binary search; bisection search; dichotomizing search**
    d binäre Suche *f*

f recherche *f* binaire
r двоичный поиск *m*; дихотомический
   поиск; поиск делением пополам

* **binary search method** → 950

949 **binary search tree; binary selector tree**
d Binärsuchbaum *m*; binärer Selektorbaum *m*
f arbre *m* de recherche binaire; arbre binaire
   sélecteur
r дерево *n* двоичного поиска

950 **binary section method; binary search**
   method
d Bisektionsverfahren *n*
f méthode *f* de [la] bissection; méthode de
   recherche binaire
r метод *m* бисекций; метод двоичного
   поиска

* **binary selector tree** → 949

951 **binary sequence**
d Binärzeichenfolge *f*
f séquence *f* binaire
r последовательность *f* двоичных символов

952 **binary signal**
d Binärsignal *n*
f signal *m* binaire
r двоичный сигнал *m*

953 **binary symmetric channel**
d symmetrischer Binärkanal *m*; binärer
   symmetrischer Kanal *m*
f canal *m* symétrique binaire
r двоичный симметричный канал *m*

* **binary system** → 941

954 **binary-[to-]decimal conversion**
d Binär-Dezimalkonvertierung *f*;
   Binär-Dezimal-Umwandlung *f*
f conversion *f* binaire-décimale
r двоично-десятичное преобразование *n*

955 **binary tree**
d binärer Baum *m*
f arbre *m* binaire
r двоичное дерево *n*

* **binary variable** → 1120

* **bind** → 5401

956 **bind** *v*; **link** *v*
d binden; verbinden; verknüpfen
f joindre; lier
r связывать

* **binding** → 5401

* **binhex** → 937

957 **binocular; bi-ocular**
d binokular
f binoculaire
r биокулярный

958 **binocular stereo**
d Binokularstereo *n*
f stéréo *m* binoculaire
r биокулярное стерео *n*

959 **binocular vision**
d binokulares Sehen *n*
f vision *f* binoculaire
r биокулярное зрение *n*

960 **biochip**
d Biochip *m*
f biopuce *f*
r биокристалл *m*

* **biocomputer** → 961

* **bi-ocular** → 957

961 **biological computer; biocomputer**
d Biocomputer *m*
f ordinateur *m* biologique
r биокомпьютер *m*

962 **biometric identification systems**
d biometrische Identifizierungssysteme *npl*
f systèmes *mpl* d'identification biométriques
r биометрические идентификационные
   системы *fpl*

963 **bionet**
d Bionetz *n*
f bioréseau *m*
r бионическая сеть *f*

* **BIOS** → 851

964 **BIOS enumerator**
d BIOS-Zähler *m*
f énumérateur *m* du BIOS
r перечислитель *m* биоса

965 **bipartitioning**
d Zweiteilung *f*
f partition *f* en deux
r [последовательное] деление *n* пополам;
   [последовательное] разбиение *n* на две
   части

966 **biphase code**
d Zweiphasencode *m*

f code *m* biphase
r двухфазовый код *m*

* **biphase coding** → 968

967 **biphase decoding**
   d Zweiphasendecodierung *f*
   f décodage *m* biphase
   r двухфазовое декодирование *n*

968 **biphase [en]coding**
   d Zweiphasencodierung *f*
   f codage *m* biphase
   r двухфазовое кодирование *n*

969 **bipolar**
   d bipolar; zweipolig
   f bipolaire
   r биполярный; двухполюсный

970 **bipolar microprocessor**
   d bipolarer Mikroprozessor *m*
   f microprocesseur *m* bipolaire
   r биполярный микропроцессор *m*

971 **biprocessor system**
   d Doppelrechnersystem *n*
   f système *m* biprocesseur
   r двупроцессорная система *f*

972 **biquinary**
   d biquinär
   f biquinaire
   r двупятеричный; двоично-пятеричный

973 **biquinary code**
   d Biquinärcode *m*
   f code *m* biquinaire
   r двоично-пятеричный код *m*

974 **biquinary number notation**
   d biquinäre Zahlendarstellung *f*
   f notation *f* biquinaire des nombres
   r представление *n* чисел в
   двоично-пятеричной системе

* **bisection search** → 948

975 **bistability**
   d Bistabilität *f*
   f bistabilité *f*
   r бистабильность *f*

976 **bistable**
   d bistabil
   f bistable
   r бистабильный

977 **bistable liquid crystal**

   d bistabiler Flüssigkristall *m*
   f cristal *m* liquide bistable
   r бистабильный жидкий кристалл *m*

* **bistable multivibrator** → 9550

978 **bistable writing**
   d bistabiles Schreiben *n*; Schreiben in zwei
   Schichten
   f enregistrement *m* à deux niveaux
   r запись *f* по двум уровням

979 **bit**
   d Bit *n*
   f bit *m*
   r бит *m*

980 **bit addressing**
   d Bitadressierung *f*
   f adressage *m* de bit
   r побитовая адресация *f*

981 **bit blit; BLT**
   (a family of algorithms for moving and
   copying of bit arrays between main and
   display memory)
   d Transfer *m* der Bitblöcke
   f transfert *m* de blocs de bits
   r перекачка *f* битовых блоков

982 **bit capacity**
   d Bitkapazität *f*
   f capacité *f* en bits
   r ёмкость *f* в битах

983 **bit chain; bit string**
   d Bitkette *f*
   f chaîne *f* de bits
   r битовая строка *f*; цепочка *f* битов; строка
   битов; последовательность *f* двоичных
   разрядов

984 **bit compression**
   d Bitkompression *f*
   f compression *f* de bits
   r сжатие *n* битов

985 **bit decoder**
   d Bitdecoder *m*
   f décodeur *m* de bits
   r разрядный дешифратор *m*

986 **bit depth**
   (of color images)
   d Bittiefe *f*
   f profondeur *f* en bits
   r битовая глубина *f*; глубина в битах

987 **bit error**
   d Bitfehler *m*

f erreur *f* sur le bit
r ошибка *f* двоичного разряда

988 bit error rate; bit error ratio; BER
  d Bitfehlerhäufigkeit *f*; Bitfehlerquote *f*;
   Bitfehlerrate *f*
  f taux *m* d'erreurs sur le bits; TEB; rapport *m*
   d'erreurs sur le bits
  r коэффициент *m* ошибок двоичных
   разрядов; число *n* ошибок двоичных
   последовательностей

  * **bit error ratio** → 988

989 bitgroup; envelope
  d Bitgruppe *f*; Enveloppe *f*
  f groupe *m* de bits
  r группа *f* битов

990 bit-interleaved multiplexer
  d bitverschachtelter Multiplexer *m*
  f multiplexeur *m* entrelacé par bits
  r мультиплексор *m* с чередованием битов

991 bit interleaving
  d Bitverschachtelung *f*
  f entrelaçage *m* de bits
  r чередование *n* битов

992 bit line; digit line
  d Bitleitung *f*; Digitleitung *f*
  f ligne *f* de bit; ligne *f* de digit
  r разрядная линия *f*

**993 bit manipulating operation; bit
   manipulation; bit processing**
  d Bit[manipulations]operation *f*;
   Bitmanipulation *f*; Bitverarbeitung *f*
  f opération *f* de manipulation de bits;
   modification *f* de configuration binaire;
   traitement *m* de bits
  r операция *f* поразрядной обработки;
   операция побитовой обработки; побитовая
   обработка *f*

  * **bit manipulation** → 993

  * **bitmap** → 7626

994 bitmap autotrace function
  d Bitmap-Autotrace-Funktion *f*
  f fonction *f* de trace automatique du bitmap
  r функция *f* автотрассировки растрового
   отображения

995 bitmap background
  d Bitmap-Hintergrund *m*
  f arrière-plan *m* bitmap; fond *m* bitmap
  r растровый фон *m*

996 bitmap-based program
  d Bitmap-basiertes Programm *n*
  f programme *m* orienté bitmap
  r программа *f*, базированная на растровых
   изображениях

997 bitmap color mask
  d Bitmap-Farbmaske *f*
  f masque *m* couleur bitmap
  r растровая цветовая маска *f*

998 bitmap copy
  d Bitmap-Kopie *f*
  f copie *f* bitmap
  r растровая копия *f*

  * **bitmap data** → 1005

  * **bitmap display** → 1006

999 bitmap file
  d Bitmap-Datei *f*
  f fichier *m* bitmap
  r файл *m* растровой графики; файл
   растрового изображения; файл текстуры

  * **bitmap font** → 7622

1000 bitmap font mapping
  d Bitmap-Schriftabbildung *f*
  f image *f* de police bitmap
  r отображение *n* растрового шрифта

1001 bitmap format
  d Bitmap-Format *n*
  f format *m* bitmap; format image-point
  r формат *m* растрового отображения

  * **bitmap graphics** → 7623

  * **bitmap image** → 7626

1002 bitmap importing
  d Bitmap-Importieren *n*
  f importation *f* d'image pixélisée; importation
   de bitmap
  r внесение *n* растрового отображения;
   импортирование *n* растрового
   изображения

1003 bitmap mode
  d Bitmap-Modus *m*
  f mode *m* bitmap
  r режим *m* побитового отображения; режим
   растрового отображения

1004 bitmap pattern
  d Bitmap-Muster *n*
  f motif *m* bitmap
  r растровый узор *m*; растровый рисунок *m*

1005 bitmap[ped] data; raster data
  d Bitmap-Daten *pl*
  f données *fpl* bitmap
  r данные *pl* побитового отображения

1006 bitmap[ped] display; bitmap[ped] screen
  d Bitmap-Bildschirm *m*; Bitmap-Display *n*
  f écran *m* bitmap; écran [graphique] par points;
       écran pixel; écran pixélisé
  r растровый экран *m*

  * **bitmapped graphics** → 7623

  * **bitmapped screen** → 1006

1007 bitmap print
  d Bitmap-Druck *m*
  f impression *f* bitmap
  r растровая печать *f*; печать точками

1008 bitmap resolution
  d Bitmap-Auflösungsvermögen *n*
  f résolution *f* bitmap
  r разрешающая способность *f* растровой
       графики

1009 bitmap rotator
  d Bitmap-Rotator *m*
  f rotateur *m* bitmap
  r растровый вращатель *m*

  * **bitmap screen** → 1006

1010 bitmap selecting
  d Bitmap-Selektion *f*
  f sélection *f* de bitmap
  r выбор *m* растрового отображения

1011 bitmap size
  d Bitmap-Größe *f*
  f taille *f* de bitmap
  r размер *m* растрового изображения

1012 bitmaps tracing
  d Bitmap-Tracing *n*
  f traçage *m* de bitmaps
  r трассировка *f* растровых изображений

1013 bit mutilation
  d Bitverfälschung *f*
  f mutilation *f* de bits
  r искажение *n* битов

1014 bit padding
  d Bitauffüllen *n*; Auffüllen *n* von Bits
  f garnissage *m* de bits; remplissage *m* de bits
  r заполнение *n* двоичного кода незначащей
       информацией

1015 bit-parallel character-serial transmission

  d bitparallele zeichenweise Übertragung *f*;
       bitparallele zeichenserielle Übertragung
  f transmission *f* en parallèle par bits;
       transmission en série par caractère
  r последовательная передача *f* знаков при
       параллельной передаче битов

**1016 bit-parallel interface; parallel-by-bit
        interface**
  d bitparalleles Interface *n*; bitparallele
       Schnittstelle *f*
  f interface *f* parallèle par bit
  r интерфейс *m* для параллельного двоичного
       кода

1017 bit-parallel transmission
  d bitparallele Übertragung *f*
  f transmission *f* parallèle par bit
  r параллельная передача *f* битов

1018 bit pattern
  d Bitmuster *n*; Bitstruktur *f*
  f combinaison *f* de bits; dessin *m* de bits;
       structure *f* de bits
  r битовая комбинация *f*

1019 bit per inch; BPI
  d Bits *npl* pro Zoll
  f bits *mpl* par pouce
  r число *n* битов на дюйм

  * **bit processing** → 993

1020 bit rate
  d Bitgeschwindigkeit *f*; Bitfolgefrequenz *f*;
       Bitrate *f*
  f vitesse *f* [de transfert] de bits; vitesse de
       séquence de bits; débit *m* binaire
  r скорость *f* передачи битов

1021 bit-rate generator
  d Bitratengenerator *m*
  f générateur *m* de fréquence de bits
  r генератор *m* частоты следования битов

  * **bits by pixel** → 1029

1022 bit sequence independence
  d Bitfolgeunabhängigkeit *f*; Codetransparenz *f*
  f indépendance *f* de la séquence des bits
  r независимость *f* следования двоичных
       битов

**1023 bit-serial asynchronous multipoint line
        protocol**
  d bitserielle asynchrone Mehrpunktprozedur *f*
  f protocole *m* de ligne multipointe asynchrone
       parallèle par bit
  r протокол *m* асинхронной многоточковой
       линии с параллельной передачей битов

1024 bit-serial highway
d bitserielle Ringleitung *f*
f jeu *m* de lignes bit-sériel
r шлюз *m* с последовательной передачей битов

1025 bit-serial interface; serial-by-bit interface
d bitserielles Interface *n*; bitserielle Schnittstelle *f*
f interface *f* sérielle par bit; interface bit-sérielle
r интерфейс *m* для последовательного двоичного кода

1026 bit-serial transmission
d bitserielle Übertragung *f*
f transmission *f* sérielle par bit
r последовательная передача *f* битов

1027 bit-slice
d bitscheibenstrukturiert
f structuré en tranches de bits
r разрядно-модульный; разрядно-секционированный

1028 bit-slice microprocessor
d bitscheibenstrukturierter Mikroprozessor *m*; kaskadierter Mikroprozessor
f microprocesseur *m* structuré en tranches de bits
r разрядно-модульный микропроцессор *m*; разрядно-секционированный микропроцессор

1029 bits per pixel; bits by pixel
d Bits *npl* pro Pixel; Pixel-Bit-Tiefe *f*
f bits *mpl* par pixel
r число *n* битов на пиксел

1030 bits per second; bps
d Bits *npl* je Sekunde; Bit/s
f bits *mpl* par seconde; bps
r бит[а/ов] *mpl* в секунду; бит/сек
* **bit string** → 983

1031 bit string data
d Bitkettendaten *pl*
f données *fpl* de chaînes de bits
r данные *pl*, представленные в виде двоичной последовательности

1032 bit stuffing
d Auffüllen *n* mit Bits
f insertion *f* de bits
r вставка *f* битов

1033 bit synchronization
d Bitsynchronisation *f*
f synchronisation *f* de bits
r побитовая синхронизация *f*

1034 bit-transparent through-connection
d bittransparente Durchschaltung *f*
f connexion *f* entière transparente par bit
r прозрачное для битов сквозное соединение *n*

1035 bitwise operation
d bitweise Operation *f*
f opération *f* sur bits
r побитовая операция *f*

1036 black[-and]-white copy
d Schwarzweißkopie *f*
f copie *f* [en] noir et blanc
r чёрно-белая копия *f*

1037 black-and-white display
d Schwarzweiß-Bildschirm *m*
f écran *m* noir et blanc
r чёрно-белый экран *m*

1038 black-and-white image
d Schwarzweiß-Bild *n*
f image *f* noire et blanche
r чёрно-белое изображение *n*

1039 black-and-white printer
d Schwarzweißdrucker *m*
f imprimante *f* noir et blanche
r чёрно-белый принтер *m*

* **black-and-white scan** → 1040

1040 black-and-white scan[ning]
d Schwarzweiß-Scannen *n*
f échantillonnage *m* en noir et blanc
r чёрно-белое сканирование *n*

1041 black screen
(of death)
d schwarzer Bildschirm *m*; Schwarzscreen *n*
f écran *m* noir
r чёрный экран *m*

1042 black signal
d Schwarzsignal *n*
f signal *m* noir
r чёрный сигнал *m*

* **black-white copy** → 1036

* **blade contact** → 1043

1043 blade contact [connector]; knife plug
d Messerstecker *m*; Messerstift *m*; Messerkontaktstecker *m*
f connecteur *m* [de contact] en couteau; fiche *f* de couteau
r ножевое контактное соединение *n*; рубящий контакт *m*; ножевой разъём *m*; контактный разъём

* **blank** → 8738

1044 blank; idle; vacant; empty; void
  d leer; frei[schalten]; unbenutzt; unbesetzt
  f blanc; vide; vacant; vierge; inutile; libre
  r пустой; незанятый; свободный; холостой;
     бездействующий

* **blank character** → 8738

* **blank cycle** → 4628

1045 blanking
  d Löschschaltung *f*; Austastung *f*;
     Dunkelsteuerung *f*; Dunkeltastung *f*
  f effacement *m*
  r запирание *n*; затемнение *n*;
     бланкирование *n*; гашение *n*

1046 blanking level
  d Austastwert *m*
  f niveau *m* de blocage; niveau d'effacement
  r уровень *m* гашения

1047 blanking pulse; quenching pulse
  d Austastimpuls *m*; Dunkelsteuerimpuls *m*;
     Löschimpuls *m*
  f impulsion *f* de suppression; impulsion
     d'annulation; impulsion de découpage
  r импульс *m* гашения

1048 blank tape; raw tape; clear band
  d leeres Band *n*; Leerband *n*; freies Band;
     ungelochter Lochstreifen *m*
  f bande *f* vide
  r пустая лента *f*

1049 blank transmission
  d Leerübertragung *f*
  f transmission *f* libre
  r свободная передача *f*

* **blaster** → 7426

* **blend** *v* → 5857

* **blend** → 1050, 5859

1050 blend[ing]
  d Überblendung *f*; Überblenden *n*
  f dégradé *m*; dégradation *f*
  r переливание *n*; слияние *n*

* **blending** → 5859

* **blind carbon copy** → 1052

1051 blind-copy recipient
  d Empfänger *m* einer Blindkopie

  f destinataire *m* en copie muette; destinataire
     en copie cachée; destinataire caché
  r получатель *m* слепой копии

**1052 blind courtesy copy; blind carbon copy;
     BCC**
  (in e-mail)
  d blinder Kohlepapierdurchschlag *m*; blinder
     Durchschlag *m*; Blindkopie *f*
  f envoi *m* en BCC; copie *f* muette; copie
     cachée
  r скрытая копия *f*; слепая копия

1053 blind keyboard
  d blinde Tastatur *f*; Schattentastatur *f*
  f clavier *m* sans fonctions; clavier mort
  r "слепая" клавиатура *f*

* **blinking** → 3881

1054 blinking bar
  d blinkender Strich *m*
  f barre *f* clignotante
  r мерцающая черта *f*

1055 blinking cursor
  d blinkender Kursor *m*
  f curseur *m* clignotant
  r мерцающий курсор *m*

1056 blinking rectangle
  (of a cursor)
  d blinkendes Rechteck *n*
  f rectangle *m* clignotant
  r мерцающий прямоугольник *m*

1057 blip
  (on the screen)
  d Echozeichen *n*; Leuchtzeichen *n*; Blip *n*
  f marque *f* de recherche; pavé *m* optique
  r отметка *f*; [оптическая поисковая] метка *f*

1058 blitter; raster blaster
  (a processor performing BLT operations,
  especially used for fast implementation of
  bitmap graphics)
  d Blitter *n*; Grafikchip *m*
  f blitter *m*
  r блиттер *m*; модуль *m* блитирования

* **bloatware** → 3717

* **BLOB** → 938

* **block** → 9668

1059 block *v*; **lock** *v*
  d blockieren; sperren
  f bloquer
  r блокировать

1060 block attribute variable
d Variable *f* des Blockattributs
f variable *f* d'attribut de bloc
r переменная *f* блокового атрибута

1061 block-by-block mode
d blockweiser Modus *m*
f mode *m* bloc [par bloc]
r поблочный режим *m*

* **block-by-block transmission** → 1079

1062 block check character; BCC
d Blockprüfzeichen *n*
f caractère *m* de contrôle de bloc
r символ *m* контроля блока

1063 block code
d Blockcode *m*
f code *m* de bloc
r блочный код *m*

1064 block counter
d Blockzähler *m*
f compteur *m* de blocs
r блочный счётчик *m*; счётчик блоков

1065 block design
d Blockaufbau *m*
f construction *f* en blocs
r блочная конструкция *f*

* **block diagram** → 3920

1066 blocked record
d blockierter Satz *m*; Bausteinsatz *m*
f enregistrement *m* bloqué
r сблокированная запись *f*

1067 block-end recognition
d Blockendeerkennung *f*; Erkennung *f* eines Blockendes
f reconnaissance *f* de fin de bloc
r распознавание *n* конца блока

1068 block-end signal
d Blockendesignal *n*; Blockendemeldung *f*
f signal *m* de fin de bloc
r сигнал *m* конца блока

* **blockette** → 8989

1069 block gap; interblock gap; interrecord gap; record gap; start-stop blockout
d Blocklücke *f*; Start-Stopp-Lücke *f*
f espace *m* interbloc; intervalle *m* interbloc; espace entre enregistrements
r зонный интервал *m*; интервал между блоками

* **block graphics** → 5893

1070 blocking
d Blockierung *f*; Zerlegung *f* in Blöcke
f blocage *m*; partage *m* en blocs
r разбиение *n* на блоки

* **blocking** → 5454

1071 blocking acknowledgement signal
d Sperrbestätigung-Kennzeichen *n*
f signal *m* d'acquittement de blocage
r сигнал *m* подтверждения блокировки

1072 blocking factor
d Blockungsfaktor *m*
f facteur *m* de blocage
r коэффициент *m* разбиения на блоки

1073 block loading
d Blockladen *n*
f chargement *m* par blocs
r поблочная загрузка *f*

* **block mark** → 1074

1074 block mark[er]
d Blockmarkierer *m*; Blockmarke *f*
f marqueur *m* du bloc
r маркер *m* блока

* **block move** → 1079

1075 block-multiplex
d blockmultiplex
f bloc-multiplex
r блок-мультиплексный

1076 block-multiplex channel
d Blockmultiplexkanal *m*
f canal *m* bloc-multiplex
r блок-мультиплексный канал *m*

* **block scheme** → 3920

1077 block size
d Blocklänge *f*; Blockgröße *f*
f longueur *f* de bloc; taille *f* de bloc
r длина *f* блока; размер *m* блока

* **block sort** → 1078

1078 block sort[ing]; bucket sort[ing]
d Blocksortieren *n*; blockweise Sortierung *f*; Datensammelsortierung *f*
f tri[age] *m* par blocs; tri[age] bouquet
r блочная сортировка *f*

1079 block transfer; block-by-block transmission; block move
d Blocktransfer *m*; blockweiser

Datentransfer *m*; Blockübertragung *f*;
blockweise Übertragung *f*
f transfert *m* par blocs; mouvement *m* par blocs
r поблочная передача *f*; групповая передача;
передача блоками

* **bloom** → 1080

1080 bloom[ing]
(of an image)
d Ausblühen *n*; Aufblasen *n* des Leuchtflecks;
Bildweichheit *f*
f éblouissement *m*; efflorescence *f*;
hyperluminosité *f* du spot
r помутнение *n*; расплывание *n*; ореол *m*

* **blower** → 2301

* **blow up** → 5

* **blow** *v* **up** → 1104

* **BLT** → 981

1081 blue screen
(of death)
d blauer Bildschirm *m*; Blue-Screen *n*
f écran *m* bleu
r синий экран *m*

1082 blue trace arrows
d blaue Tracing-Pfeile *mpl*
f flèches *fpl* bleus de traçage
r синие стрелки *f* трассировки

* **blur** → 1087, 1088

1083 blur *v*
d doppel drucken; verdoppeln
f double imprimer
r двойно печатать

1084 blur *v*
(an image)
d unschärfen; schmitzen
f embrumer
r размывать; расплывать; помутнять;
потемнять

1085 blur effect
d Unscharfeffekt *m*
f effet *m* d'embrumer; effet d'embuer; effet flou
r эффект *m* помутнения; эффект размывания

1086 blur filter
d Unscharffilter *m*
f filtre *m* d'embrumer
r фильтр *m* размывания

* **blur mask** → 440

* **blurred** → 4149

1087 blurred image
d Unscharfbild *n*
f image *f* floue
r расплывчатое изображение *n*; неясное
изображение

1088 blur[ring]
d Unschärfe *f*; Schmitz *m*
f flou *m*; adoucissement *m*
r размывание *n* [границ]; помутнение *n*

1089 blur[ring]
d Doppeldruck *m*; vermischter Druck *m*
f impression *f* double
r двойная печать *f*

1090 board; plate
d Platte *f*; Brett *n*
f platine *f*; plaque *f*
r плата *f*; панель *f*

1091 board computer; on-board computer
d Bordrechner *m*; Bordcomputer *m*
f ordinateur *m* de bord
r бортовой компьютер *m*

1092 board module
d Leiterplattenmodul *n*; Steckeinheitenmodul *n*
f module *m* à unité enfichable; module à circuit
imprimé
r сменный модуль *m*

1093 board set; card set
d Leiterplattensatz *m*
f ensemble *m* de plaques; ensemble de cartes;
jeu *m* de plaques
r комплект *m* плат

1094 body
d Körper *m*
f corps *m*
r тело *n*

1095 body of message; message body
d Nachrichtenkörper *m*
f corps *m* de message
r тело *n* сообщения

1096 bogus newsgroup
d falsche Newsgruppe *f*
f groupe *m* de discussion faux
r фальшивая группа *f* новостей

1097 bogus transaction
d falsches Scheingeschäft *n*; falsche
Transaktion *f*
f transaction *f* fausse
r ложная транзакция *f*; фиктивная
транзакция

1098 boilerplate
  d Standardtextbibliothek *f*; Bibliothek *f* für
     vorformulierte Texte
  f bibliothèque *f* de textes standardisés
  r библиотека *f* стандартных текстов

  * **bold → 1101**

1099 bold
  d Fett-; fett; halbfett
  f gras
  r [полу]жирный; толстый; получёрный

1100 bold character
  d Fettzeichen *n*
  f caractère *m* gras
  r получёрный символ *m*; жирный символ

1101 bold [face]; bold typeface
  d Fett-Schrifttyp *m*
  f type *m* de caractères gras
  r получёрный тип *m* шрифта

1102 bold [face] print[ing]
  d Fettdruck *m*
  f impression *f* en gras
  r печатание *n* жирным шрифтом

1103 bold format
  d Fettformat *n*
  f format *m* gras
  r жирный формат *m*

  * **bold print → 1102**

  * **bold typeface → 1101**

1104 bomb *v*; blow *v* up; lock *v* up; explode *v*
     (a program)
  d abschiessen; explodieren; zerknallen
  f bombarder; éclater
  r взрываться; отваливаться

  * **bond → 1106**

1105 bond *v*
  d verbinden; löten; verlöten; befestigen
  f bondériser; coupler
  r связывать; скреплять; сцеплять

1106 bond[ing]
  d Verbindung *f*; Mikrokontaktierung *f*
  f bondérisation *f*; cohésion *f*; soudure *f*
  r связь *f*; пайка *f*; металлизация *f*

1107 bonus tools
  d Extrahilfsmittel *npl*; Gratishilfsmittel *npl*;
     unbezahlte Hilfsmittel *npl*
  f outils *mpl* extra
  r бонус-инструменты *mpl*; премиальные

инструменты

1108 booking
  d Buchung *f*; Anmeldung *f*
  f enregistrement *m*; demande *f*
  r заказ *m*

  * **bookkeeping → 4574**

  * **bookkeeping operation → 4574**

1109 bookmark
  d Lesezeichen *n*; Bookmark *n*
  f signet *m*; onglet *m*; marque-page *f*;
     boucmat *m*
  r закладка *f*

1110 book message
  d Sammelanschriftnachricht *f*
  f message *m* à la demande
  r заказанное сообщение *n*

1111 Boolean; logic[al]
  d Boolesch; logisch
  f booléen; de Boole; logique
  r булев; логический

  * **Boolean → 7186**

1112 Boolean[-based] language
  d Boolesche Sprache *f*
  f langage *m* de Boole
  r язык *m* булевых операторов

1113 Boolean expression
  d Boolescher Ausdruck *m*
  f expression *f* de Boole
  r булево выражение *n*

  * **Boolean function → 936**

  * **Boolean language → 1112**

1114 Boolean matrix
  d Boolesche Matrix *f*
  f matrice *f* de Boole; matrice booléenne
  r булева матрица *f*

1115 Boolean method
  d Boolesche Methode *f*
  f méthode *f* booléenne
  r булев метод *m*

1116 Boolean modeling
  d Boolesche Modellierung *f*
  f modélisation *f* booléenne
  r булево моделирование *n*

1117 Boolean operation; logic[al] operation
  d Boolesche Operation *f*; logische Operation

f opération *f* booléenne; opération logique
r булева операция *f*; логическая операция

1118 Boolean operator
  d Boolescher Operator *m*
  f opérateur *m* de Boole
  r булев оператор *m*

1119 Boolean polynom
  d Boolesches Polynom *n*
  f polynôme *m* booléen
  r булев многочлен *m*

  * **Boolean sum** → 2997

1120 Boolean variable; binary variable
  d Boolesche Variable *f*; binäre Variable;
    zweiwertige Variable
  f variable *f* booléenne; variable binaire
  r булева переменная *f*; бинарная переменная

  * **boost** *v* → 1126

  * **boot** → 1126, 4851

1121 boot[able] partition
    (of a disk)
  d Boot-Zerlegung *f*; Boot-Partition *f*
  f partition *f* de démarrage
  r загрузочный раздел *m*

  * **boot disk** → 1122

1122 boot disk[ette]
  d Boot-Diskette *f*; Urladerdiskette *f*;
    Anfangsladediskette *f*
  f disquette *f* de démarrage
  r загрузочная дискета *f*

1123 boot drive
  d Boot-Laufwerk *n*
  f lecteur *m* de démarrage
  r загрузочный дисковод *m*

1124 boot failure
  d Startausfall *m*; Startfehler *m*
  f échec *m* au démarrage
  r сбой *m* загрузки

  * **BOOTP** → 1128

  * **boot partition** → 1121

  * **boot protocol** → 1128

1125 boot sector
  d urlader Sektor *m*; Bootsektor *m*; Startsektor *m*
  f secteur *f* amorçage
  r начальный сектор *m*; сектор самозагрузки

1126 boot[strap] *v*; **boost** *v*
  d aufladen; urladen; anheben; booten
  f autocharger; hausser; amorcer
  r загружать[ся] автоматически;
    самозагружаться

  * **bootstrap loader** → 4851

1127 bootstrap memory
  d Anfangsspeicher *m*
  f mémoire *f* d'autochargement
  r память *f* автоматического ввода

  * **bootstrapping** → 8350

  * **bootstrapping loader** → 4851

1128 boot[strap] protocol; BOOTP
  d Bootstrap-Protokoll *n*
  f protocole *m* d'autochargement
  r загрузочный протокол *m*; протокол
    начальной загрузки

1129 border
  d Kante *f*; Rahmen *m*
  f bordure *f*; bord *m*
  r рамка *f*; полоса *f*; кайма *f*

1130 borrow
  d Borgen *n*; geborgter Subtraktionsübertrag *m*;
    negativer Übertrag *m*
  f manque *m*; emprunt *m*; retenue *f* de
    soustraction; retenue négative
  r заём *m*; отрицательный перенос *m*

  * **BOT** → 886

  * **bot** → 9716

  * **bothway** → 912

1131 bothway communication
  d beiderseitige Datenübermittlung *f*
  f communication *f* bidirectionnelle
  r двунаправленная связь *f*

1132 bothway mode
  d Zweiwegbetriebsweise *f*; Zweiwegmodus *m*
  f mode *m* bidirectionnel
  r двунаправленный режим *m*

  * **BOT marker** → 887

1133 bottleneck
  d Engpass *m*; Flaschenhals *m*
  f goulot *m* d'étranglement; pertuis *m*
  r критический элемент *m*; критический
    параметр *m*

1134 bottleneck problem
  d Engpassproblem *n*

f problème *m* de goulot d'étranglement
r задача *f* на узкие места

* **bottom-up** → 553

1135 bottom-up design
d Entwurf *m* von unten nach oben;
Bottom-up-Entwurf *m*
f conception *f* de bas en haut
r восходящее проектирование *n*

1136 bounce
d Zurückprall *m*; Aufprall *m*
f rebond[issement] *m*
r электронная почта *f* из-за ошибки адреса

1137 bound; boundary; frontier
d Schranke *f*; Grenze *f*; Rand *m*
f borne *f*; bord *m*; frontière *f*; limite *f*
r грань *f*; граница *f*; край *m*

1138 boundary; frontier *adj*
d Grenz-; Rand-
f frontière; limite
r граничный; краевой

* **boundary** → 1137

1139 boundary condition
d Grenzbedingung *f*
f condition *f* aux limites
r граничное условие *n*

1140 boundary perturbation
d Grenzstörung *f*
f perturbation *f* aux limites
r предельная помеха *f*

1141 boundary point; frontier point
d Randpunkt *m*; Grenzpunkt *m*
f point *m* frontière; point limite
r граничная точка *f*; краевая точка

1142 bounded; limited; restricted
d beschränkt; begrenzt
f borné; limité
r ограниченный

**1143 bounded box; bounding box; bounding
rectangle**
d begrenztes Kästchen *n*; begrenztes
Rechteck *n*
f boîte *f* délimitée; case *f* délimitée
r ограничивающий ящик *m*; граничный
прямоугольник *m*

* **bounding box** → 1143

* **bounding rectangle** → 1143

1144 boundless; unbounded; unlimited; limitless
d unbeschränkt; unbegrenzt
f non borné; non limité
r неограниченный

1145 bound register
d Grenzregister *n*; Randregister *n*
f registre *m* de borne
r ограничительный регистр *m*; регистр
границы

1146 bound variable
d gebundene Variable *f*; Scheinvariable *f*
f variable *f* liée
r связанная переменная

1147 box
d Kasten *m*; Kästchen *n*; Box *f*; Dose *f*
f boîtier *m*; boîte *f*; box *m*; case *f*; corbeille *f*
r ящик *m*; коробка *f*

* **box** → 1479

1148 box *v*
d einrahmen; in Kasten setzen; einpacken
f boxer
r класть в ящик; помещать в коробку

1149 boxed comment; framed comment
d umrahmter Kommentar *m*
f commentaire *m* encadré
r блочный комментарий *m*; комментарий в
рамочке

1150 boxing; casing; packing into boxes
d in Kasten Setzung *f*
f découpage *m* en boîtes
r упаковка *f* в ящик

* **box plot** → 3920

* **BPI** → 1019

* **bps** → 1030

1151 braces; curly brackets
({ })
d geschweifte Klammern *fpl*
f accolades *fpl*
r фигурные скобки *fpl*

1152 bracket; clamp; clip[board]
d Halterung *f*; Trägerarm *m*; Konsole *f*;
Klammer *f*
f appui *m*; crampe *f*; crampon *m*
r крепление *n*; зажим *m*; фиксатор *m*;
клипса *f*

1153 bracketing
d Einklammern *n*

f mise *f* entre crochets
r заключение *n* в скобки

1154 brackets
(a sign)
d Klammern *fpl*
f crochets *mpl*
r скобки *fpl*

1155 branch
d Zweig *m*; Abzweig *m*
f branche *f*
r ветвь *f*; переход *m*

1156 branch address
d Verzweigungsadresse *f*
f adresse *f* de branchement; adresse d'aiguillage
r адрес *m* разветвления; адрес перехода

* **branch bus** → 5440

1157 branching; ramification
d Verzweigung *f*; Verzweigen *n*; Gabelung *f*
f [em]branchement *m*; ramification *f*
r [раз]ветвление *n*

1158 branching decision
d Verzweigungsentscheidung *f*;
Programmzweigauswahl *f*
f décision *f* de branchement; choix *m* de branche [d'un programme]
r выбор *m* [программной] ветви

1159 branching element
d Verzweiger *m*
f répartiteur *m*
r разветвитель *m*

1160 branch[ing] instruction
d Verzweigungsbefehl *m*
f instruction *f* de branchement; instruction d'aiguillage
r инструкция *f* ветвления; инструкция [условного] перехода

1161 branching process
d Verzweigungsprozess *m*
f processus *m* ramifié; processus d'embranchement
r ветвящийся процесс *m*

* **branch instruction** → 1160

1162 branch offset
d Verzweigungsdistanz *f*; Adressdifferenz *f*
f distance *f* de branchement d'adresse
r приращение *n* адреса

1163 branch point; ramification point
d Verzweigungspunkt *m*; Verzweigungsstelle *f*
f point *m* de branchement; point de

ramification
r точка *f* [раз]ветвления

1164 branch target
d Verzweigungsziel *n*
f but *m* de branchement
r метка *f* перехода

* **breadboard** → 1165

1165 breadboard [circuit]; prototyping board; evaluation board; layout
d Brettschaltung *f*; Versuchsaufbau *m* einer Schaltung; Auswertungsplatte *f*; Layout *n*
f maquette *f*; plaque *f* de maquette; platine *f* d'évaluation; croquis *m*
r макет *m* [платы]; макетная плата *f*; оценочная плата

1166 breadboarding
d Versuchsschaltungsaufbau *m*; Versuchsausführung *f*
f maquettage *m*
r макетирование *n*

* **break** → 1171

1167 break *v*; interrupt *v*
d unterbrechen
f interrompre
r прерывать; обрывать

1168 break contact; off-normal contact
d Öffnungskontakt *m*; normal geschlossener Kontakt *m*; Nullkontakt *m*; Kopfkontakt *m*
f contact *m* de repos; contact normalement fermé; contact fermé à repos; contact à fermeture
r нормально замкнутый контакт *m*; размыкающий контакт; контакт покоя

* **breakdown** → 3679

1169 breakdown voltage; disturbing voltage
d Durchbruchspannung *f*; Durchschlagspannung *f*
f tension *f* de claquage; tension disruptive
r пробивное напряжение *n*

1170 break flag
d Abbruchflag *n*
f drapeau *m* d'interruption
r флаг *m* прерывания

1171 break[ing]; interruption; abort
d Unterbrechung *f*; Interrupt *m*; Abbruch *m*
f interruption *f*; coupure *f*; rupture *f*
r прерывание *n*; обрывание *n*; прекращение *n*

1172 **break key**
d Unterbrechungstaste *f*
f touche *f* d'interruption
r клавиша *f* прерывания

1173 **breakpoint**
(of a process)
d Unterbrechungsstelle *f*; Haltepunkt *m*;
Bedarfsschaltepunkt *m*; Haltemarke *f*;
Brechpunkt *m*; Knickpunkt *m*
f point *m* d'interruption; point d'arrêt
r точка *f* прерывания; точка останова; точка
разрыва

* **breakpoint register** → 5096

1174 **breakpoint symbol**
d Fixpunktzeichen *n*
f symbole *m* [de point] d'arrêt
r знак *m* контрольного останова

1175 **break priority**
d Unterbrechungspriorität *f*
f priorité *f* d'interruption
r приоритет *m* прерывания

* **break signal** → 5091

* **B-register** → 4772

1176 **brevity code; abbreviated code**
d abgekürzter Code *m*
f code *m* abrégé
r сокращённый код *m*

1177 **bridge**
d Brücke *f*
f bridge *m*; pont *m*
r мост *m*

1178 **bridge circuit**
d Brückenschaltung *f*
f circuit *m* à pont
r мостовая схема *f*

1179 **bridge filter**
d Brückenfilter *m*
f filtre *m* de pont
r мостовой фильтр *m*

* **bridge-router** → 1181

* **bridgeware** → 1182

1180 **bridging; shunt**
d Überbrückung *f*; überbrückende Verbindung *f*
f retenue *f*; report *m* [des retenues]; pontage *m*;
shunt *m*; mise *f* en parallèle
r установка *f* перемычки; перемыкание *n*;
шунтирование *n*; замыкание *n*;
запараллеливание *n*

1181 **bridging router; bridge-router; brouter**
d Überbrückung-Router *m*
f routeur *m* pont; brouteur *m*
r мост-маршрутизатор *m*

1182 **bridging software; bridgeware**
d Überbrückungssoftware *f*;
Brückenprogramme *npl*
f logiciel *m* pont
r мостовое программное обеспечение *n*;
средства *npl* обеспечения совместимости

* **briefcase** → 1456

1183 **brightness; luminous intensity**
d Helligkeit *f*
f brillance *f*; clarté *f*; luminosité *f*
r яркость *f*; блеск *m*

1184 **bring** *v*; **fetch** *v*
d bringen; einbringen; einreichen; holen
f ramener; apporter
r приносить; доставлять; приводить;
довести

1185 **broadband; wideband**
d Breitband *n*
f large bande *f*
r широкая полоса *f* частот

1186 **broadband bus; wideband bus**
d Breitband-Bus *m*
f bus *m* à large bande
r широкополосная шина *f*

1187 **broadband cable**
d Breitbandkabel *n*; BK
f câble *m* à large bande
r широкополосный кабель *m*

1188 **broadband channel; wideband channel**
d Breitbandkanal *m*
f canal *m* à large bande
r широкополосный канал *m*

1189 **broadband characteristics; wideband
characteristics**
d Breitbandigkeit *f*
f caractéristiques *f* à large bande
r широкополосность *f*

1190 **broadband communication network;
wideband communication network**
d Breitbandkommunikationsnetz *n*
f réseau *m* de communication à large bande
r сеть *f* широкополосной связи

1191 **broadband information retrieval;
wideband information retrieval**
d Breitband-Informationsabruf *m*

    f recherche *f* d'information à large bande
    r широкополосный поиск *m* информации

1192 broadband LAN; wideband LAN; local area broadband network; local area wideband network
    d lokales Breitbandnetz *n*
    f réseau *m* local à large bande
    r местная широкополосная сеть *f*; локальная сеть на основе широкополосного канала

1193 broadband line; wideband line
    d Breitbandleitung *f*
    f ligne *f* à large bande
    r коаксиальная линия *f*

1194 broadband signal; wideband signal
    d Breitbandsignal *n*
    f signal *m* à large bande
    r широкополосный сигнал *m*

1195 broadband source; wideband source
    d Breitbandquelle *f*; breitbandige Quelle *f*
    f source *f* à large bande
    r широкополосный источник *m*

1196 broadband transmission; wideband transmission
    d Breitbandübertragung *f*
    f transmission *f* à large bande
    r широкополосная передача *f*

    * **broadcast → 1201**

1197 broadcast addressing
    d allgemeine Adressierung *f*
    f adressage *m* général
    r широковещательная адресация *f*

1198 broadcast bus
    d Rundsendungsbus *m*; Rundsendebus *m*
    f bus *m* de diffusion générale
    r шина *f* широковещательной рассылки

1199 broadcast channel
    d Rundsendekanal *m*
    f canal *m* à diffusion générale
    r широковещательный канал *m*; циркулярный канал

1200 broadcast code
    d Rundsendekennung *f*
    f code *m* de radiodiffusion
    r широковещательный код *m*; код транслирования

1201 broadcast[ing]
    d Rund[funk]sendung *f*; Rundstrahlverfahren *n*
    f translation *f*; diffusion *f* générale
    r широковещание *n*; рассылка *f*; транслирование *n*

1202 broadcast mail
    (electronic mail that is transmitted to all user terminals in a computer network)
    d Rundsendemeldung *f*
    f courrier *m* en multidiffusion
    r широковещательная почта *f*

    * **broadcast mailbox → 1251**

1203 broadcast protocol
    d Rundsendeprotokoll *n*
    f protocole *m* d'accès de diffusion multipoint
    r протокол *m* широковещательной адресации сообщений

1204 broadcast query
    d Rundsendeabfrage *f*
    f appel *m* diffusé
    r широковещательный запрос *m*

1205 broker
    d Verfrachter *m*; Makler *m*
    f courtier *m*
    r программа-брокер *f*; брокер *m*

    * **brouter → 1181**

1206 browse *v*
    d ansehen; durchsuchen
    f parcourir; feuilleter
    r пересмотреть; просматривать; разглядывать; пролистать

1207 browse dialog box
    d Browser-Dialogbox *f*
    f boîte *f* de dialogue de revue
    r диалоговый ящик *m* просмотра

1208 browser; viewer; navigator
    d Browser *m*; Suchprogramm *n*; Navigator *m*; Fernsehzuschauer *m*; Betrachter *m*
    f logiciel *m* de visualisation; visionneur *m*; visionneuse *f*; module *m* de revue; butineur *m*; navigateur *m*; fureteur *m*
    r программа *f* просмотра; визуализатор *m*; браузер *m*; бродилка *f*; вьювер *m*; навигатор *m*

1209 browser-based application
    d Browser-basierte Anwendung *f*
    f application *f* basée à butineur
    r приложение *n*, основанное браузером

1210 browser window
    d Browser-Fenster *n*
    f fenêtre *f* du butineur
    r окно *n* браузера

1211 browse *v* **the scrapbook**
  d das Skizzenbuch durchsuchen
  f parcourir le classeur
  r просматривать альбом

1212 browsing
  d Browsing *n*; Durchsicht *f*; Grobrecherche *f*
  f revue *f*; survol *m*; feuilletage *m*
  r просмотр *m*; пролистание *n*

1213 browsing window
  d Vorschaufenster *n*
  f fenêtre *f* de survol
  r окно *n* рассмотрения

1214 brush
  d Bürste *f*
  f brosse *f*; balai *m* [à contact]
  r [контактная] щётка *f*

  * **brush → 6739**

1215 brush selector
  d Bürstenwähler *m*
  f sélecteur *m* à balais
  r щёточный селектор *m*

  * **BSAM → 856**

  * **BTAM → 858**

  * **bubble → 798**

  * **bubble-jet printer → 4864**

1216 bubble sort; exchange selection
  d Bubblesort *n*
  f tri[age] *m* de bulle; tri[age] par pairs
  r пузырьковая сортировка *f*; выборка *f* с обменом

  * **buck → 869**

1217 buck delay
  d Buckübertragungsverzögerung *f*
  f délai *m* de transmission du marqueur
  r запаздывание *n* передачи маркера

1218 bucket
  d Datensammel-Speicherbereich *m*
  f champ *m* de collection de données; collecteur *m* de données; bouquet *m*
  r блок *m* [сбора] данных

  * **bucket sort → 1078**

  * **bucket sorting → 1078**

1219 buck-passing protocol
  d Buck-Passing-Protokoll *n*

  f protocole *m* de passage de jeton
  r маркерный протокол *m*

1220 budget
  d Budget *n*; Bilanz *f*
  f budget *m*; bilan *m*
  r бюджет *m*; баланс *m*; ресурс *m*

  * **buffer → 1230**

1221 buffer
  (of a cable)
  d Polsterung *f*
  f rembourrage *m*
  r обивка *f*

1222 buffer cell
  d Pufferzelle *f*
  f cellule *f* tampon
  r буферная ячейка *f*

1223 buffer clock inhibition; buffer timing inhibition
  d Puffertaktsperre *f*
  f inhibition *f* de synchronisation de tampon
  r запрещение *n* синхронизации буфера

1224 buffer clock pulse
  d Puffertakt *m*; Puffertaktsignal *n*
  f horloge *f* de tampon
  r импульс *m* синхронизации буфера

1225 buffered channel
  d gepufferter Kanal *m*
  f canal *m* tamponné; canal bufférisé
  r канал *m* с буферной памятью

1226 buffered communication adapter; BCA
  d Adapter *m* für gepufferte Übertragung
  f adaptateur *m* pour communication tamponnée
  r адаптер *m* связи с буферизацией

1227 buffered port
  d gepufferter Port *m*
  f port *m* à tampon; port tamponné
  r порт *m* с буфером

1228 buffered terminal
  d gepuffertes Terminal *n*
  f terminal *m* tamponné; terminal bufférisé
  r терминал *m* с буферной памятью

1229 buffering
  d Pufferung *f*
  f tamponnement *m*; tamponnage *m*
  r буферизация *f*; буферирование *n*

1230 buffer [memory]; intermediate memory; temporary memory; pool [memory]
  d Zwischenspeicher *m*; Pufferspeicher *m*; Puffer *m*

f mémoire *f* tampon; mémoire intermédiaire;
tampon *m*
r буфер *m*; буферная память *f*;
промежуточная память

1231 buffer register
d Pufferregister *n*; Zwischenspeicherregister *n*
f registre *m* tampon
r буферный регистр *m*

1232 buffer start address
d Pufferanfangsadresse *f*
f adresse *f* de début du tampon
r начальный адрес *m* буфера

* **buffer timing inhibition** → 1223

1233 buffer zone
d Pufferzone *f*
f zone *f* tampon; zone de transfert
r буферная зона *f*

1234 bug
d Entwurfsfehler *m*
f défaut *m* de conception; bogue *m*
r ошибка *f* при проектировании;
программная или аппаратная ошибка;
"вошь" *f*

1235 bug diary
d Fehlerjournal *n*
f cahier *m* d'erreurs; journal *m* d'erreurs
r дневник *m* ошибок

1236 bug patch; soft patch; patch
(in a software)
d Flicken *n*; Direktkorrektur *f*
f correctif *m*; rapiècement *m*; patch *m*
r заплата *f*; патч *m*; вставка *f*

1237 builder
d Bilder *m*
f bâtisseur *m*
r построитель *m*; компоновщик *m*

* **builder** → 2364

1238 building block; assembly unit; module
d Baustein *m*; Baukasten *m*; Bauelement *n*;
Modul *n*
f élément *m* constitutif; brique *f*; unité *f*
d'assemblage; module *m*
r компоновочный блок *m*; модуль *m*

* **building block library** → 8823

1239 building block principle
d Baukastenprinzip *m*; Bausteinprinzip *m*
f principe *m* de la construction par blocs
r блочный принцип *m*

* **building-out network** → 2325

* **building-up time** → 8478

1240 build-up *v*
d aufbauen
f établir; dresser
r наращивать

* **build-up time** → 8478

* **built-in** → 6067

1241 built-in check
d eingebaute Prüfung *f*; eingebaute Kontrolle *f*
f contrôle *m* incorporé; essai *m* incorporé
r встроенный контроль *m*; схемный
контроль

* **built-in modem** → 4965

1242 built-in redundancy
d eingebaute Redundanz *f*
f redondance *f* incorporée
r внутренняя избыточность *f*; встроенное
резервирование *n*

1243 built-up addressing
d aufgebaute Adressierung *f*
f adressage *m* composé
r составное адресование *n*

* **bulge** → 1256

* **bulk** → 9922

1244 bulk; mass
d massiv; Massen-
f massif; volumique
r массивный; объёмный; большого объёма

1245 bulk absorption
d Volumenabsorption *f*
f absorption *f* volumique
r объёмное поглощение *n*

**1246 bulk [data] processing; mass data
processing**
d Massen[daten]verarbeitung *f*; Verarbeitung *f*
großer Datenmengen
f traitement *m* de données en masses;
traitement de masses
r обработка *f* [больших] информационных
массивов; обработка больших массивов
данных

* **bulk mail** → 1247

1247 bulk mail[ing]; mass mail[ing]
d Massenpost *f*; Massensendung *f*;

Masseneinlieferung *f*; Massenaufgabe *f*
f envoi *m* en nombre; envoi de courrier en lots;
   multidiffusion *f*
r массовая почта *f*; сплошная почта;
   массовая рассылка *f*

* **bulk memory** → 5659

* **bulk processing** → 1246

1248 bulk sample
d massive Probe *f*
f échantillon *m* massif
r массивная проба *f*

**1249 bulk transmission of data; data bulk
   transmission**
d Übertragung *f* großer Datenmengen
f transmission *f* de grandes quantités de
   données
r передача *f* данных большого объёма;
   передача больших объёмов информации

* **bullet** → 1253

1250 bulletin board system; BBS
   (computers access by remote users via
   modems for discussion, file downloads, and
   other BBS services)
d elektronische Nachrichtentafel *f*;
   elektronische Tafel *f*; elektronisches
   schwarzes Brett *n*; schwarzes Brettsystem *n*
f [serveur m] BBS; "babillard" *m*
r электронная доска *f* объявлений

**1251 bulletin [broadcast] mailbox; broadcast
   mailbox**
d Nachrichtenbriefkasten *m*; Mailbox *f*
f boîte *f* de diffusion de communiqués; boîte de
   diffusion
r почтовой ящик *m* редколлегии бюллетеней

* **bulletin mailbox** → 1251

1252 bullet position
d Aufzählungszeichen *n*; Blickfangpunktstelle *f*
f position *f* de balle
r позиция *f* пульки

1253 bullet [sign]
d Blickfangpunkt *m*
f balle *f*; puce *f*; gros point *m*
r жирная точка *f*; пулька *f*; маркер *m* абзаца;
   буллит *m*

1254 bullet size
d Blickfangpunktgröße *f*
f taille *f* de balle
r размер *m* пульки

1255 bump
d Chipkontaktierungsfläche *f*;
   Chipkontaktflecken *m*
f surface *f* à contact de puce
r контактная поверхность *f* чипа

1256 bump; bulge
d Beule *f*; Vorsprung *f*; Wulst *m*
f bosse *f*; boursouflure *f*; renflement *m*;
   inégalité *f*; gibbosité *f*
r неровность *f*; выпуклость *f*

1257 bump map
d Bump-Map *n*
f texture *f* relief; bump-map *m*
r рельефная текстура *f*

1258 bump-map image
d Bump-Map-Bild *n*
f image *f* de texture relief
r изображение *n* рельефной текстурой

1259 bump-mapping
d Bump-Mapping *n*
f mise *f* au texture relief; bump-mapping *m*
r рельефное текстурирование *n*;
   отображение *n* неровностей поверхности

1260 bump-mapping processor
d Bump-Mapping-Prozessor *m*
f processeur *m* de bump-mapping
r процессор *m* рельефного текстурирования

1261 bump-mapping surface
d Bump-Mapping-Fläche *f*
f surface *f* de texture relief
r рельефно текстурированная поверхность *f*

* **bunch** → 6884

1262 bunched frame alignment signal
d gepacktes Rahmenerkennungssignal *n*
f signal *m* de verrouillage de trame concentré
r упакованный тактовый опознавательный
   сигнал *m*

1263 bunching
d Phasenfokussierung *f*
f groupement *m* de phases
r группирование *n* фаз; пучкование *n* фаз

1264 bundle *v*
d zusammenpacken
f grouper
r группировать

* **bundle** → 6670, 6884

1265 bundle cable
d Kabel *n* mit Bündelfasern; Bündelkabel *n*

f câble *m* en faisceau de fibres
r пучковый кабель *m*

1266 buried cable
  d Erdkabel *n*
  f câble *m* enfoui
  r скрытый кабель *m*

1267 burner
  d Brenner *m*
  f brûleur *m*
  r горелка *f*

1268 burst
  d Burst *m*
  f burste *m*
  r пакет *m*; пачка *f*

1269 burster
  d Burster *m*
  f bursteur *m*
  r устройство *n* разделения страниц

1270 burst error correcting code
  d Fehlerbündelkorrekturcode *m*
  f code *m* correcteur de paquets d'erreurs
  r код *m* с исправлением пакетов ошибок

1271 burst mode; stream mode
  d Burstmodus *m*; Zeitgetrenntlage-Verfahren *n*
  f mode *m* de burste; mode rafale; régime *m* à coups
  r групповой режим *m*; поточный режим

1272 burst of errors; error burst
  d Fehlerburst *m*; Fehlerbündel *n*; Fehlerpaket *n*
  f burste *m* d'erreurs; paquet *m* d'erreurs
  r пакет *m* ошибок

1273 bus
  d Bus *m*; Sammelleitung *f*; Schiene *f*
  f bus *m*; jeu *m* de lignes; jeu de barres
  r шина *f*

1274 bus address register
  d Busadressregister *n*
  f registre *m* d'adresse de bus
  r регистр *m* адреса шины

1275 bus arbiter
  d Busarbiter *m*; Buszuteiler *m*
  f arbitre *m* de bus
  r шинный арбитр *m*

1276 busbar; bar
  d Stromschiene *f*; Sammelschiene *f*
  f barre *f* électrique
  r [электрическая] шина *f*; фидер *m*

1277 bus conflict; bus contention

d Buskonflikt *m*
f conflit *m* de [accès à] bus; collision *f* de bus
r конфликт *m* на шине

* **bus contention → 1277**

1278 bus driver
  d Bustreiber *m*
  f basculeur *m* de bus; formateur *m* de signaux de bus
  r возбудитель *m* шины; драйвер *m* шины; шинный формирователь *m*

1279 bus enable
  d Busfreigabe
  f validation *f* de bus
  r разрешение *n* шины

1280 bus enumerator
  d Buszähler *m*; Sammelleitungszähler *m*
  f énumérateur *m* de bus
  r перечислитель *m* шины

1281 bus exchange
  d Busverkehr *m*; Busvermittlung *f*
  f échange *m* de bus
  r обмен *m* по шине; коммутация *f* шин

* **bush → 7004**

1282 business graphics; management graphics; presentation graphics
  d Geschäftsgrafik *f*; Präsentationsgrafik *f*
  f graphique *m* de gestion; graphique d'affaires; graphique de [re]présentation
  r деловая графика *f*; представительная графика

1283 business logo; logo[type]; emblem
  d Logo *n*; Firmenlogo *n*; Emblem *n*; Firmenzeichen *n*; Systemzeichen *n*
  f sigle *f*; mire *f*; logotype *m*; logo *m*
  r фирменный знак *m*; логотип *m*; лого *n*

1284 business software
  d Verwaltungssoftware *f*
  f logiciel *m* d'affaires
  r программное обеспечение *n* для коммерческих приложений

1285 bus interface
  d Businterface *n*; Busschnittstelle *f*
  f interface *f* de bus
  r шинный интерфейс *m*

1286 bus LAN
  d lokales Busnetz *n*
  f réseau *m* local à topologie de bus
  r местная сеть *f* с шинной топологией

1287 bus line
  d Busleitung *f*
  f ligne *f* de bus
  r линия *f* шины

  * **bus network → 1291**

1288 bus structure
  d Busstruktur *f*
  f structure *f* de bus
  r структура *f* шины; шинная структура

  * **bust → 4580**

1289 bus terminator
  d Busterminator *m*
  f terminateur *m* de bus
  r шинный терминатор *m*; оконечная
       нагрузка *f*

1290 bus topology
  d Bustopologie *f*
  f topologie *f* de bus
  r шинная топология *f*

1291 bus[-type] network
  d Netz *n* mit Busstruktur; Busnetz[werk] *n*
  f réseau *m* à topologie de bus; réseau en bus
  r сеть *f* с шинной топологией; шинная сеть *f*

1292 busy
  d besetzt; beschäftigt
  f occupé
  r занятый

1293 busy condition
  d Belegtzustand *m*; Besetzfall *m*
  f condition *f* occupée
  r состояние *n* занятости

1294 busy waiting
  d aktives Warten *n*
  f attente *f* active
  r активное ожидание *n*

1295 busy-wait loop
  d aktive Warteschleife *f*
  f boucle *f* d'attente d'occupation
  r цикл *m* ожидания освобождения

  * **butt → 2797**

  * **button → 5202**

1296 button; knob
  d Schaltfläche *f*; Knopf *m*
  f bouton *m*; case *f* de commande
  r кнопка *f*; бутон *m*

  * **button bar → 1297**

1297 button bar [menu]; button menu
  d Tastemenü *n*; Knopfmenü *n*;
       Schaltflächeleiste *f*
  f barre *f* d'onglets; barre de boutons
  r лента[-меню] *f* кнопок; кнопочное меню *n*

1298 button editor
  d Knopfeditor *m*
  f éditeur *m* par boutons
  r кнопочный редактор *m*

1299 button icon
  d Schaltflächensymbol *n*
  f icône *f* de bouton
  r икона *f* кнопки

  * **button menu → 1297**

1300 button property
  d Knopfeigenschaft *f*
  f propriété *f* de bouton
  r свойство *n* кнопки

1301 bypass *v*
  d beipassen; umgehen; übergehen
  f contourner; dépasser
  r обходить; шунтировать

1302 bypass; traversal
  d Bypass *m*; Umgehung *f*; Übergehen *n*;
       Umlauf *m*; Durchlauf *m*
  f détour *m*; dérivation *f*
  r обход *m*

1303 bypass channel
  d Bypasskanal *m*
  f canal *m* dépassé
  r обходной канал *m*

1304 byte
  d Byte *n*
  f octet *m*
  r байт *m*

1305 byte access
  d Bytezugriff *m*; byteweiser Zugriff *m*
  f accès *m* d'octet
  r побайтовый доступ *m*

1306 byte capacity
  d Bytekapazität *f*
  f capacité *f* en octets
  r ёмкость *f* в байтах

1307 byte[-interleave] mode
  d Bytemodus *m*; Bytebetrieb *m*
  f mode *m* d'octet; régime *m* d'octet
  r байтовый режим *m*

* **byte mode** → 1307

1308 byte-multiplex
d bytemultiplex
f octet-multiplex
r байт-мультиплексный

1309 byte-multiplex channel
d Bytemultiplexkanal *m*
f canal *m* octet-multiplex
r байт-мультиплексный канал *m*

1310 byte-parallel data; parallel-by-byte data
d byteparallele Daten *pl*
f données *fpl* parallèles par octet
r данные *pl*, передаваемые параллельно по байтам

1311 byte-serial
d byteseriell; byteweise
f séquentiel par octets; sériel par octet
r побайтово последовательный

1312 byte-serial data
d Byteseriendaten *pl*
f données *fpl* à représentation séquentielle par octets
r данные *pl* с последовательным представлением по байтам

1313 byte-serial data communication
d byteserielle Datenkommunikation *f*
f communication *f* sérielle par octet de données
r [по]байтовая последовательная коммуникация *f*

1314 byte-serial highway
d byteserielle Ringleitung *f*
f artère *f* sérielle par octet
r побайтовый шлюз *m*

1315 byte-serial transmission
d byteserielle Übertragung *f*
f transmission *f* sérielle par octet
r [по]байтовая последовательная передача *f*

1316 byte swapping
d Bytevertauschung *f*
f échange *m* d'octets
r побайтовая замена *f*

1317 byte-wide interface
d bytebreites Interface *n*; bytebreite Anschlussstelle *f*
f interface *f* à largeur d'octet
r интерфейс *m* с побайтовым обменом

C

1318 cable
 d Kabel *n*
 f câble *m*
 r кабель *m*

1319 cable accessories
 d Kabelgarnituren *fpl*
 f accessoires *mpl* de câble
 r кабельные арматуры *fpl*; кабельные
   принадлежности *fpl*

1320 cable balancing
 d Kabelausgleich *m*
 f équilibrage *m* de câble
 r настройка *f* кабеля

1321 cable concentrator; concentrator; hub
 d Kabelbuchse *f*; Nabe *f*; Konzentrator *m*
 f douille *f* de câble; concentrateur *m*
 r [кабельный] концентратор *m*

1322 cable design; construction of a cable
 d Kabelaufbau *m*
 f construction *f* de câble; constitution *f* de câble
 r конструкция *f* кабеля

1323 cable distribution system
 d Kabelverteilsystem *n*
 f réseau *m* de distribution par câble
 r кабельная распределительная система *f*

1324 cabled optical fiber
 d verkabelter Lichtwellenleiter *m*
 f fibre *f* optique câblée
 r световод *m* в виде кабеля

1325 cable form
 d Drahtkabel *n*; Kabelform *f*
 f forme *f* de câble
 r кабельный шаблон *m*; расшивка *f* кабеля;
   разделка *f* кабеля

1326 cable grip
 d Kabel[ein]ziehstrumpf *m*
 f grip *m* de câble
 r [сквозной] кабельный чулок *m*

1327 cable jacket; cable sheath[ing]
 d Kabelmantel *m*
 f gaine *f* de câble; gainage *m* [de câble];
   enveloppe *f* de câble
 r кабельная оболочка *f*

1328 cable junction box; cable sleeve
 d Kabel[anschluss]kasten *m*; Kabelabzweiger *m*
 f boîte *f* de jonction pour câbles; boîte de
   division; sous-répartiteur *m*; manchon *m*
 r кабельный шкаф *m*; кабельная муфта *f*

1329 cable laying; cable lining; cabling
 d Kabelverlegung *f*; Verkabelung *f*;
   Beschaltung *m*
 f pose *f* de câble; câblage *m*
 r прокладка *f* кабеля; прокладка кабельной
   сети; соединение *n* кабелем

1330 cable length
 d Kabellänge *f*
 f longueur *f* du câble
 r длина *f* кабеля

1331 cable line
 d Kabelleitung *f*
 f ligne *f* de câble
 r кабельная линия *f*

1332 cable plugging list
 d Kabelsteckliste *f*
 f liste *f* des connexions de câble
 r список *m* разъёмных соединений кабеля

**1333 cable termination; cable terminal; cable
   end; cable socket; cable lug; cable eye**
 d Kabelendverschluss *m*; Kabelende *n*;
   Kabelschuh *m*; Kabelöse *f*
 f terminaison *f* de câble; boîte *f* d'extrémité de

câble; tête *f* de câble; bouchon *m*; cosse *f* de câble

r кабельная концевая муфта *f*; кабельный наконечник *m*

1334 cable test
d Kabelprüfung *m*
f essai *m* des câbles
r испытание *n* кабелей

1335 cable transmission
d leitungsgebundene Übertragung *f*
f transmission *f* par câble
r передача *f* по кабелю; передача по проводам

* **cabling → 1329**

1336 cabling plan; cable layout; cable map
d Kabel[führungs]plan *m*; Kabellageplan *m*
f plan *m* de pose des câbles; plan de câblage
r план *m* расположения кабелей

* **cache → 1339**

1337 cached processor
d Prozessor *m* mit Cache
f processeur *m* à antémémoire
r кэшированный процессор *m*

1338 cache explorer
d Cache-Durchforster *m*
f explorateur *m* cache
r кэш-путеводитель *m*

1339 cache [memory]; cache storage
d Cachespeicher *m*; Cache *m*
f mémoire *f* cache; cache *f*; antémémoire *f*
r кэш-память *f*; сверхоперативная память *f*

* **cache storage → 1339**

1340 cache tag
d Cacheetikett *n*; Cachespeicherinhaltskennung *f*
f marque *f* de cache
r признак *m* слова, хранящегося в кэш-памяти

* **CAD → 2053**

1341 cadence
d Takt *m*
f cadence *f*; rythme *m*
r темп *m*; ритм *m*; такт *m*

1342 cadre; frame
d Frame *n*; Zeitfenster *n*; einzelnes Videobild *n*
f cadre *m* [d'image vidéo]
r кадр *m*

1343 cage
d Karkasse *f*; Käfig *m*
f cage *f*
r каркас *m*; клетка *f*

* **CAI → 2071**

* **CAL → 2071**

1344 calculability; computability
d Zähligkeit *f*; Berechenbarkeit *f*
f calculabilité *f*
r исчислимость *f*; вычислимость *f*

* **calculable → 2044**

1345 calculate *v*; compute *v*; reckon *v*
d ausrechnen; berechnen; rechnen
f calculer; compter
r вычислять; рассчитывать; подсчитывать

* **calculating frame → 1**

1346 calculating rule; computing rule
d Rechenregel *f*; Rechnungsregel *f*; Rechenvorschrift *f*
f règle *f* de calcul
r правило *n* вычисления

1347 calculation; computation; computing
d Berechnung *f*; Rechnen *n*
f calcul *m*; computation *f*; comptage *m*
r вычисление *n*; исчисление *n*; смета *f*; [pa]счёт *m*

1348 calculator
d Rechenmaschine *f*; Taschenrechner *m*
f calculatrice *f*; calculateur *m*
r калькулятор *m*; счётная машина *f*

1349 calendar
d Kalender *m*
f calendrier *m*
r календарь *m*

1350 calibrate *v*; gauge *v*; graduate *v*
d eichen; kalibrieren
f calibrer; étalonner; jauger; graduer
r калибровать; эталонировать; градуировать; тарировать

* **calibrating → 1351**

1351 calibration; calibrating
d Eichung *f*; Kalibrierung *f*
f calibrage *m*; étalonnage *m*; tarage *m*
r калибровка *f*

1352 calibration bar
d Kalibrierungsbalken *m*

f barre *f* de calibrage; barre d'étalonnage
r лента *f* калибровки; лента эталонирования

1353 calibrator
  d Kalibrator *m*; Eichgerät *n*
  f calibreur *m*
  r калибратор *m*

  * **call** → 1383

1354 call *v*; **invoke** *v*
  d aufrufen; rufen; anrufen
  f appeler
  r вызывать; обращаться

1355 call address
  d Aufrufadresse *f*
  f adresse *f* d'appel; adresse de référence
  r адрес *m* вызова; адрес обращения

1356 call allotter; allotter; call distributor
  d Anrufverteiler *m*; Anrufordner *m*
  f répartiteur *m* d'appels
  r распределитель *m* вызовов

1357 call attempt
  d Anrufversuch *m*
  f épreuve *f* d'appel
  r попытка *f* вызова

  * **callback** → 7719

1358 call block
  d Rufblock *m*
  f bloc *m* d'appel
  r блок *m* вызова

1359 call booking
  d Gesprächsanmeldung *f*
  f demande *f* déposée
  r заказ *m* на разговор

1360 call by name; name call
  d Namensaufruf *m*; Aufruf *m* über den Namen
  f appel *m* nominal; appel par nom
  r вызов по имени

1361 call by reference
  d Referenzaufruf *m*; Aufruf *m* über Zeiger oder Adresse
  f appel *m* par référence
  r вызов *m* по запросом

1362 call by value
  d Wertaufruf *m*; Aufruf *m* über den Wert
  f appel *m* par valeur
  r вызов *m* по значению

1363 call card
  d Rufkarte *f*

f carte *f* d'appel
r карта *f* вызова

1364 call chain
  d Anrufkette *f*
  f chaîne *f* d'appels
  r цепочка *f* вызовов

1365 call collision
  d Belegungszusammenstoß *m*; Verbindungszusammenstoß *m*; Rufzusammenstoß *m*
  f collision *f* d'appel
  r столкновение *n* вызова

1366 call confirmation protocol; CCP
  d Bestätigungsprotokoll *n*
  f protocole *m* de confirmation d'appels
  r протокол *m* подтверждения вызовов

1367 call counter; call[-counting] meter; subscriber's meter
  d Gesprächzähler *m*
  f compteur *m* de conversations; compteur d'abonné
  r счётчик *m* вызовов; счётчик разговоров [абонента]

  * **call-counting meter** → 1367

1368 call data
  d Verbindungsdaten *pl*; Rufdaten *pl*
  f données *fpl* d'appel
  r данные *pl* вызова

1369 call data record
  d Rufdatensatz *m*
  f enregistrement *m* de données d'appels
  r запись *f* данных о вызовах

1370 call detection
  d Anruferkennung *f*; Ruferkennung *f*
  f détection *f* d'appel
  r обнаружение *n* вызова

  * **call disconnect** → 2176

  * **call distributor** → 1356

1371 call duration
  d Verbindungsdauer *f*
  f durée *f* de l'appel
  r длительность *f* вызова

1372 called program
  d aufgerufenes Programm *n*
  f programme *m* appelé
  r вызываемая программа *f*

* **caller ID** → 1373

1373 caller identification number; caller ID
d Anruferkennnummer *f*
f numéro *m* d'identification d'abonné demandeur
r идентификационный номер *m* вызывающего абонента

1374 call for discussion; CFD
(in Usenet)
d Aufruf *m* zur Diskussion
f appel *m* au discussion
r вызов *m* на обсуждение

1375 call for opinion; CFO
(in Usenet)
d Aufruf *m* zu einer Meinungsumfrage
f appel *m* pour l'opinion
r вызов *m* мнения

1376 call for vote; CFV
d Aufruf *m* zur Abstimmung; Abstimmungsaufforderung *f*
f appel *m* au vote
r вызов *m* на голосование

1377 call forwarding; CFW; forwarding
d Aufruf-Weiterleitung *f*
f renvoi *m* [automatique] d'appels
r переадресация *f* вызовов

1378 call frequency
d Ruffrequenz *f*
f fréquence *f* d'appels
r частота *f* вызовов; частота обращений

1379 call identification
d Rufidentifizierung *f*
f identification *f* d'appel
r идентификация *f* вызова

1380 calligraphic
d kalligrafisch
f calligraphique
r каллиграфический

1381 calligraphic display
d kalligrafischer Bildschirm *m*; kalligrafisches Display *n*; Direktablenkungsbildschirm *m*
f affichage *m* à balayage cavalier
r дисплей *m* с программным управлением лучом; каллиграфический дисплей *m*

1382 call indicator
d Nummernanzeiger *m*; Anrufanzeiger *m*
f indicateur *m* d'appel; indicateur de numéro demandé
r указателъ *m* вызываемого номера; указатель вызова

1383 call[ing]
d Aufruf *m*; Ruf *m*
f appel *m*
r вызов *m*; обращение *n*

* **calling dial** → 2845

1384 call[ing] instruction
d Abrufbefehl *m*; Aufrufbefehl *m*
f instruction *f* d'appel
r инструкция *f* вызова

1385 call[ing] order; call[ing] sequence
d Abrufsequenz *f*; Ruffolge *f*
f séquence *f* d'appels
r последовательность *f* запросов; последовательность вызовов

1386 calling program
d Aufrufprogramm *n*
f programme *m* appelant; programme d'appel
r вызывающая программа *f*

1387 call[ing] register
d Verbindungsregister *n*; Abrufregister *n*; Aufrufregister *n*
f registre *m* d'appel
r регистр *m* запросов; регистр вызовов

1388 calling script; script
(a record of keystrokes and commands that can be played back in order to automate routing tasks, such as logging on to an online service)
d Aufrufskript *m*
f script *m* d'appel
r вызывающий скрипт *m*

* **calling sequence** → 1385

* **call instruction** → 1384

* **call meter** → 1367

* **call order** → 1385

* **callout** → 1428

1389 call pulse
d Abrufimpuls *m*
f impulsion *f* d'appel
r импульс *m* вызова

1390 call recognition time
d Ruferkennungszeit *f*
f temps *m* de reconnaissance d'appel
r время *n* распознавания вызова

* **call register** → 1387

*   **call request** → 1391

1391 **call request [signal]**
  d Rufanforderung *f*; Verbindungsanforderung *f*;
       Verbindungswunsch *m*; abgehender Ruf *m*
  f signal *m* de demande d'appel; demande *f*
       d'appel
  r сигнал *m* запроса вызова; запрос *m* вызова

1392 **calls file**
  d Verbindungsdatei *f*
  f fichier *m* d'appels
  r файл *m* вызовов

*   **call sequence** → 1385

*   **call sign** → 1393

1393 **call sign[al]**
  d Meldeanrufzeichen *n*; Rufzeichen *n*;
       Rufsignal *n*
  f signal *m* d'appel
  r сигнал *m* вызова

1394 **call tracing**
  d Verbindungsverfolgung *f*; Fangschaltung *f*;
       Anruffangschaltung *f*
  f traçage *m* d'appel
  r маршрутизация *f* вызова

1395 **call waiting; camp-on**
  d Anklopfen *n*; Aufrufvermittlung *f*;
       Camp-on *n*; Warten *n*
  f attente *f* d'appel; appui *m* d'appel; camp-on *m*
  r задержка *f* вызова; ожидание *n* [вызова]
       при занятости

*   **CAM** → 2059

1396 **camera**
  d Kamera *f*
  f caméra *f*
  r камера *f*; фотографический аппарат *m*

1397 **camera adjusting**
  d Kameraeinstellung *f*
  f régulation *f* de caméra; ajustage *m* de caméra
  r настраивание *n* камеры

1398 **camera calibration**
  d Kamerakalibration *f*
  f calibrage *m* de caméra
  r эталонирование *n* камеры; калибровка *f*
       камеры

1399 **camera calibration algorithm**
  d Kamerakalibration-Algorithmus *m*
  f algorithme *m* de calibrage de caméra
  r алгоритм *m* эталонирования камеры

1400 **camera-captured image**
  d durch Kamera gesammeltes Bild *n*
  f image *f* captée par caméra
  r изображение *n*, захваченное камерой

1401 **camera control; camera managing**
  d Kamerasteuereinheit *f*
  f contrôle *m* de caméra; gestion *f* de caméra
  r управление *n* камеры

1402 **camera controller**
  d Kamerasteuerung *f*
  f contrôleur *m* de caméra
  r контроллер *m* камеры

1403 **camera cue**
  d Aufnahmelichtmarke *f*
  f repère *m* de caméra
  r индикатор *m* камеры; маркер *m* камеры

*   **camera managing** → 1401

1404 **camera-ready copy**
  d für eine Fotografie fertige Kopie *f*
  f copie *f* prêt à photo
  r оригинал-макет *m*

1405 **camped-on call**
  d Gespräch *m* in Wartestellung
  f appel *m* suspendu
  r задержанный вызов *m*

*   **camp-on** → 1395

*   **cancel** → 1410

*   **cancel** *v* → 428, 8520

*   **cancelable operation** → 1409

1406 **cancel button**
  d Taste *f* "Abbrechen"
  f bouton *m* d'annulation
  r кнопка *f* отмены; кнопка прекращения

*   **cancel character** → 1412

1407 **cancel code**
  d Annullierungskennziffer *f*
  f code *m* d'annulation
  r код *m* сокращения

1408 **cancel delay**
  d Abbruchanforderung *f*
  f délai *m* d'annulation
  r запаздывание *n* прекращения

*   **canceling** → 1410

* **cancel key** → 1718

1409 cancel[l]able operation
   d kürzbare Operation *f*
   f opération *f* simplifiable; opération réductible
   r сократимая операция *f*

1410 cancel[lation]; canceling
   d Annullierung *f*; Abbruch *m*
   f annulation *f*; élimination *f*
   r уничтожение *n*; прекращение *n*

1411 cancel[lation] request
   d Abbruchanforderung *f*
   f requête *f* d'annulation; demande *f* d'annulation
   r запрос *m* отмены [задания]; запрос
      прекращения работы

1412 cancel[-out] character
   d Löschzeichen *n*; Aufhebungszeichen *n*
   f caractère *m* d'annulation; caractère de rejet
   r знак *m* аннулирования; символ *m*
      удаления; символ отмены

* **cancel request** → 1411

* **CAP** → 2060

* **cap** → 1437

1413 capability
   d Fähigkeit *f*; Möglichkeit *f*
   f capacité *f*; habileté *f*
   r возможность *f*; способность *f*

1414 capability-based addressing
   d möglichkeitsbezogene Adressierung *f*
   f adressage *m* de mandat
   r мандатная адресация *f*

1415 capability machine
   d Rechner *m* mit möglichkeitsbezogener
      Adressierung
   f machine *f* à adressage de mandat
   r компьютер *m* с мандатной адресацией

1416 capacitance; capacity
   (of a number or of a machine word)
   d Zählbereich *m*
   f capacité *f*; puissance *f*
   r разрядность *f*

1417 capacitance; capacity
   d Leistungsfähigkeit *f*; Kapazität *f*
   f capacité *f*; puissance *f*
   r ёмкость *f*; производительность *f*

1418 capacitive coupling; capacity coupling
   d kapazitive Kopplung *f*; kapazitive
      Ankopplung *f*

   f couplage *m* capacitif
   r ёмкостная связь *f*

1419 capacitor
   d Kondensator *m*
   f condensateur *m*
   r конденсатор *m*

1420 capacitor array
   d Kondensator-Array *n*;
      Kondensatoranordnung *f*
   f matrice *f* de condensateur
   r конденсаторная матрица *f*

* **capacity** → 1416, 1417

* **capacity coupling** → 1418

1421 capacity limit
   d Kapazitätsgrenze *f*
   f limite *f* de capacité
   r предел *m* ёмкости

**1422 capacity of connection; connection
      capacity**
   d Beschaltungsmöglichkeit *f*
   f capacité *f* de connexion
   r коэффициент *m* связывания

1423 capacity record
   d Kapazitätssatz *m*; Spurkapazitätssatz *m*
   f enregistrement *m* de capacité
   r запись *f* с данными по ёмкости

1424 capitalization
   (of text)
   d Großschreibung *f*; Kapitalisation *f*;
      Kapitalisierung *f*
   f mise *f* en lettres majuscules
   r выделение *n* заглавными буквами

* **capital letters** → 9709

1425 cap[ital]s mode
   d Großbuchstabenmodus *m*
   f mode *m* majuscule
   r режим *m* заглавных букв

* **caps** → 9709

* **caps mode** → 1425

1426 capsulate *v*
   d kapseln
   f capsuler
   r капсулировать

1427 capsulation; encapsulation
   d Kapsulation *f*; Kapselung *f*; Verkapselung *f*

f encapsulation *f*; [en]capsulage *m*; enrobage *m*
r капсулирование *n*; герметизация *f*;
инкапсуляция *f*

1428 caption; callout; image signature
(identifying or descriptive text accompanying
a photograph, illustration or other visual
element)
d Bildunterschrift *f*; Bilduntertitel *m*;
Bildtext *m*; Bildüberschrift *f*; Referenz *f*
f signature *f* d'image; caption *f*; référence *f*
r надпись *f*; метка-идентификатор *f*;
выноска *f*

1429 caption property
d Legendeigenschaft *f*
f propriété *f* de légende
r характеристика *f* легенды

1430 capture *v*; grip *v*; trap *v*
d erfassen; sammeln; einspringen;
verschließen; [ein]fangen
f capter; saisir; empoigner; intercepter
r ловить; хватать; захватывать;
перехватывать; улавливать; фиксировать
[динамическое изображение]

1431 capture; grabbing; lock-on
d Sammlung *f*; Sammeln *n*; Fangen *n*
f capture *f*; captage *m*
r захват *m*; улавливание *n*

1432 capture area
d Sammlungsbereich *m*
f domaine *m* de capture
r область *f* захвата; область улавливания

1433 capture device; capturer
d Sammler *m*
f capteur *m*
r уловитель *m*

1434 captured image
d gesammeltes Bild *n*
f image *f* captée
r захваченное изображение *n*

1435 capture process
d Sammlungsprozess *m*
f processus *m* de capture
r процесс *m* захвата

* **capturer** → 1433

* **CAQ** → 2061

1436 card
d Karte *f*; Platte *f*
f carte *f*; plaquette *f*
r карта *f*; малая [печатная] плата *f*

* **card set** → 1093

* **caret** → 1437

**1437 caret [character]; circumflex [accent]; hat;
cap; cover; top**
(^)
d Hut *m*; Dach *n*; Fehlzeichen *n*
f signe *m* d'insertion; accent *m* circonflexe
r знак *m* вставки; крышка *f*

1438 carriage
d Wagen *m*
f chariot *m*
r каретка *f*; тележка *f*; суппорт *m*

1439 carriage advance
d Wagenvorschub *m*
f mouvement *m* de chariot
r перемещение *n* каретки

1440 carriage detent; carriage locking
d Wagenverriegelung *f*
f verrouillage *m* de chariot
r запирание *n* [перемещения] каретки

* **carriage locking** → 1440

1441 carriage return; CR
d Wagenrücklauf *m*
f retour *m* [de] chariot
r возврат *m* каретки

1442 carried calls
d angenommene Belegungen *fpl*;
Tagsanmeldung *f*
f demandes *fpl* de communication déposée
r удовлетворённые заказы *mpl* на разговор

* **carrier** → 1449

1443 carrier; support
d Träger *m*; Carrier *m*
f porteur *m*; support *m*
r носитель *m*

1444 carrier channel
d Trägerkanal *m*
f canal *m* de porteuse
r канал *m* несущей

**1445 carrier chrominance signal; chrominance
signal; chroma signal**
d Farbartsignal *n*; Chrominanzsignal *n*;
Farbwertsignal *n*
f signal *m* de support de chrominance
r несущий сигнал *m* цветовой
интенсивности

1446 carrier counter
 d Trägerzähler *m*
 f compteur *m* de porteurs
 r счётчик *m* носителей

1447 carrier detect[or] signal; CD signal
 d Trägerdetektorsignal *n*
 f signal *m* de détection de porteurs
 r сигнал *m* обнаружения носителей

 * **carrier detect signal** → 1447

1448 carrier frame
 d Trägerrahmen *m*
 f cadre *m* d'une porteuse
 r кадр *m* несущей [частоты]

1449 carrier [frequency]
 d Trägerfrequenz *f*
 f fréquence *f* porteuse; porteuse *f*
 r несущая [частота] *f*

1450 carrier signal
 d Trägersignal *n*
 f signal *m* porteur
 r несущий сигнал *m*; сигнал несущей
  [частоты]

1451 carrier-to-noise ratio
 d Träger-Rausch-Verhältnis *n*
 f rapport *m* porteuse/bruit
 r отношение *n* сигнала несущей [частоты] к
  шуму

1452 carry
 d Übertrag *m*
 f report *m*; retenue *f*
 r перенос *m*

1453 carry bit
 d Übertragungsbit *n*
 f bit *m* de report
 r бит *m* переноса; двоичный разряд *m*
  переноса

1454 carry call
 d Übertragungsaufruf *m*
 f appel *m* de report; appel de retenue
 r возбуждение *n* переноса

1455 carry flag
 d Carryflag *n*; Übertragsflag *n*
 f drapeau *m* de retenue
 r флаг *m* переноса

 * **carry *v* in** → 3437

1456 carrying case; briefcase
 d Aktentasche *f*; Aktenmappe *f*; Büchermappe *f*
 f porte-documents *m*

 r портфель *f* (для портативного компьютера)

 * **carry *v* out** → 3650

1457 carry-out
 d auslaufender Übertrag *m*
 f retenue *f* déversée
 r выход *m* [сигнала] переноса

 * **carry over** → 2004

1458 carry pulse
 d Übertragimpuls *m*
 f impulsion *f* de report
 r импульс *m* переноса

1459 carry trigger
 d Übertragstrigger *m*; Übertrags-Flipflop *m*
 f basculeur *m* de report
 r триггер *m* переноса

1460 cartridge
 d Patrone *f*
 f cartouche *f*
 r патрон *m* [предохранителя]

 * **cartridge** → 5583

1461 cartridge disk drive
 d Plattenkassettenlaufwerk *n*
 f unité *f* de disques à cartouche
 r накопитель *m* на кассетных дисках

 * **cartridge tape driver** → 8938

1462 cascadable counter; modular counter
 d Kaskadenzähler *m*
 f compteur *m* cascade
 r каскадный счётчик *m*; модульный счётчик

1463 cascade *adj*
 d überlappend
 f cascade
 r каскадный

1464 cascade; stage
 d Kaskade *f*; Stufe *f*; Staffel *f*
 f cascade *f*; étage *m*
 r каскад *m*; ступень *f*

 * **cascade carry** → 1466

 * **cascade circuit** → 1467

1465 cascade code; factorable code
 d Kaskadencode *m*; faktorisierbarer Code *m*
 f code *m* cascade; code factorisable; code de
  diffusion générale
 r каскадный код *m*; факторизуемый код

1466 **cascade[d] carry; step-by-step carry**
  d Kaskadenübertrag *m*
  f report *m* en cascade
  r каскадный перенос *m*

1467 **cascade[d] circuit; tandem circuit**
  d Kaskadenschaltung *f*; Tandemschaltung *f*
  f circuit *m* en cascade; circuit tandem
  r каскадная схема *f*

1468 **cascaded gates**
  d hintereinandergeschaltete Gatter *npl*;
      kaskadenartig geschaltete Gatter
  f portes *fpl* en cascade
  r каскадно-включённые вентили *mpl*

1469 **cascade list**
  d überlappende Liste *f*
  f liste *f* en cascade
  r каскадный список *m*

  * **cascade noise factor → 1470**

1470 **cascade noise figure; cascade noise factor**
  d Kaskaden-Rauschzahl *f*
  f facteur *m* de bruit en cascade
  r каскадный коэффициент *m* искажения

1471 **cascade process**
  d Kaskadenprozess *m*
  f processus *m* en cascade
  r каскадный процесс *m*

1472 **cascading choice**
  d überlappende Auswahl *f*
  f option *f* en cascade
  r каскадный выбор *m*

1473 **cascading menu**
  d überlappendes Menü *n*
  f menu *m* [en] cascade
  r каскадное меню *n*; меню каскадов

  * **cascading sheets → 1474**

1474 **cascading[-style] sheets; CSS**
  d überlappende Blätter *npl*; kaskadierende
      Stilvorlagen *fpl*; ortgesetzte Stilvorlagen *fpl*
  f feuilles *fpl* en cascade
  r каскадно расположенные листы *mpl*;
      каскадные стилевые листы;
      спецификация *f* CSS

1475 **cascading windows**
  d Fensterkaskade *f*; Kaskadenanordnung *f* der
      Fenster; überlappende Fenster *npl*
  f fenêtres *fpl* en cascade
  r каскадно расположенные окна *npl*; окна
      каскадом

1476 **cascode**
  d Kaskode *f*
  f cascode *f*
  r каскодная схема *f*; каскод *m*

1477 **cascode optical receiver**
  d optischer Kaskodenempfänger *m*
  f récepteur *m* optique cascode
  r оптический каскодный приёмник *m*

1478 **case**
  d Fach *n*; Register *n*
  f case *f*; registre *m*
  r регистр *m*

  * **CASE → 2062**

1479 **case; box; cabinet**
  d Gehäuse *n*; Schrank *m*
  f tiroir *m*
  r корпус *m*; ячейка *f*; шкаф *m*

1480 **case sensitivity**
  d Register-Empfindlichkeit *f*
  f sensitivité *f* au case
  r учёт *m* регистра (клавиатуры)

  * **case statement → 8336**

1481 **case structure; choice structure**
  d Fachstruktur *f*
  f structure *f* de choix
  r выбирающая структура *f*; развилка *f*

1482 **case study**
  d Fallstudie *f*
  f étude *f* de cas
  r исследование *n* конкретных условий
      [применения]

1483 **cash register**
  d Registrierkasse *f*
  f caisse *f* d'enregistrement
  r кассовый аппарат *m*

  * **casing → 1150, 3451**

1484 **casque**
  d Helm *m*
  f casque *f*
  r каска *f*

1485 **cassette tape recorder**
  d Kassettenmagnetbandgerät *n*
  f appareil *m* à cassettes pour bande magnétique
  r кассетофон *m*; кассетный магнетофон *m*

  * **cast → 1486**

1486 cast[ing]; coercion
  (of the datatypes)
  d Abguss *m*; Guss *m*; Druckguss *m*
  f transtypage *m*
  r приведение *n*

  * **catalog → 2962**

1487 catalog area
  d Katalogbereich *m*
  f domaine *m* de catalogue
  r область *f* каталога

1488 catalog data
  d Katalogdaten *pl*
  f données *fpl* de catalogue
  r данные *pl* каталога

1489 catalog data record
  d Katalogdatensatz *m*
  f enregistrement *m* de catalogue de données
  r запись *f* в каталог

  * **cataloged file → 1491**

  * **cataloged procedure → 1492**

  * **cataloging → 1493**

1490 catalog of images; picture catalog
  d Bilderkatalog *m*; Bilderverzeichnis *n*
  f catalogue *m* d'images
  r каталог *m* изображений

  * **catalogue → 2962**

1491 catalog[u]ed file
  d katalogisierte Datei *f*
  f fichier *m* catalogué
  r каталогизированный файл *m*

1492 catalog[u]ed procedure
  d katalogisierte Prozedur *f*
  f procédure *f* cataloguée
  r каталожная процедура *f*; библиотечная процедура

1493 catalog[u]ing
  d Katalogisierung *f*
  f catalogage *m*
  r каталогизирование *n*; каталогизация *f*

1494 category
  d Kategorie *f*
  f catégorie *f*
  r категория *f*

1495 category of access
  d Zugangsart *f*
  f catégorie *f* d'accès
  r категория *f* доступа

1496 catenary
  d Kettenlinie *f*
  f caténaire *f*
  r цепная контактная линия *f*

  * **catenation → 1550**

1497 cathode
  d Kat[h]ode *f*
  f cathode *f*
  r катод *m*

1498 cathode-ray tube; CRT; electronic beam tube
  d Katodenstrahlröhre *f*; Elektronenstrahlröhre *f*
  f tube *f* cathodique; tube à rayons cathodiques
  r электронно-лучевая трубка *f*; ЭЛТ

  * **CAW → 1561**

  * **CBL → 1596**

  * **CCB → 2473**

  * **CCI → 1924**

  * **CCP → 1366**

  * **CCW → 1563**

  * **CD → 1855, 1964**

  * **CD-DA → 1961**

  * **CD-E → 1962**

  * **CDF → 1566, 1926**

  * **CD-I → 4998**

  * **CD player → 1500**

  * **CD-ROM → 1964**

1499 CD recorder
  d CD-Schreiber *m*
  f graveur *m*
  r записывающее устройство *n* компактных дисков

  * **CD-ROM → 1964**

1500 CD[-ROM] player; CD-ROM reader
  d CD-ROM-Lesegerät *n*;
      CD-ROM-Laufwerk *n*; CD-Spieler *m*
  f lecteur *m* de CD-ROM
  r проигрыватель *m* компактных дисков

* **CD-ROM reader** → 1500

* **CD-RW** → 1966

* **CD signal** → 1447

1501 CD video
  d CD-Video *n*
  f vidéo *m* CD
  r компактдисковое видео *n*

* **CD-WO** → 1967

* **CD-XA** → 1963

1502 cell
  d Zelle *f*
  f cellule *f*; alvéole *f*
  r ячейка *f*; клетка *f*

1503 cell
  (of a table)
  d Zelle *f*
  f cellule *f*; élément *m*
  r клетка *f*

* **cell array** → 1517

1504 cell border
  d Zellenrahmen *m*
  f bordure *f* de cellule
  r рамка *f* клетки; кайма *f* клетки

1505 cell boundary
  d Zellenrand *m*
  f bord *m* de cellule; frontière *f* de cellule
  r граница *f* ячейки

1506 cell color
  d Zellenfarbe *f*
  f couleur *f* de cellule
  r цвет *m* клетки

1507 cell content
  d Zelleninhalt *m*
  f contenu *m* de cellule
  r содержание *n* клетки

1508 cell filling
  d Zellenfüllung *f*
  f remplissage *m* de cellule
  r заливка *f* клетки; закрашивание *n* клетки

1509 cell formatting
  d Zellenformatierung *f*
  f formatage *m* de cellule
  r форматирование *n* клетки

1510 cell merging
  d Zellenverschmelzen *n*

  f fusionnement *m* de cellules
  r слияние *n* клеток

1511 cell name
  d Zellenname *m*
  f nom *m* de cellule
  r имя *n* клетки

1512 cell reference
  d Zellenverweis *m*
  f référence *m* de cellule
  r ссылка *f* клетки

1513 cell rotating
  d Zellendrehung *f*
  f rotation *f* de cellule
  r вращение *n* клетки; поворот *m* клетки

1514 cell size
  d Zellengröße *f*
  f grandeur *f* de cellule
  r размер *m* ячейки

1515 cell splitting
  d Zellenaufteilung *f*
  f séparation *f* de cellules
  r разделение *n* клеток; расщепление *n*
      клеток

1516 cellular
  d zellular; Zell-
  f cellulaire
  r клеточный

1517 cell[ular] array
  d reguläre Zellenanordnung *f*; Zellenfeld *n*;
      Zellenarray *n*
  f champ *m* de cellules; matrice *f* [en grille]
      cellulaire
  r регулярная структура *f* ячеек; матрица *f* с
      регулярной структурой

1518 cellular automaton; tessellation automaton
  d zellularer Automat *m*
  f automate *m* cellulaire
  r клеточный автомат *m*

1519 cellular circuit
  d Zellenkreis *m*; Zellenstruktur *f*
  f circuit *m* de cellule; circuit cellulaire;
      structure *f* de cellule
  r клеточная структура *f*

1520 cellular modem
  d Zellenmodem *n*; zellulares Modem *n*
  f modem *m* cellulaire
  r клеточный модем *m*

1521 cellular network structure
  d zellulare Netzstruktur *f*

f structure f de réseau cellulaire
r клеточная сетевая структура f

1522 cellular texture
d zellulare Textur f
f texture f cellulaire
r клеточная текстура f

1523 cell unlock
d Zellenentsperrung f
f déverrouillage m d'une cellule
r разблокирование n клетки

1524 cell width
d Zellenbreite f
f largeur f de cellule
r ширина f клетки

1525 centered text
d zentrierter Text m
f texte m centré
r центрированный текст m

1526 centered wallpaper
d zentriertes Hintergrundbild n
f fond m d'écran centré
r центрированный экранный фон m

1527 cent[e]ring
d Zentrierung f
f centrage m
r центрирование n

1528 central
d zentral; Zentral-; Mittel-
f central
r центральный

* **central acquisition** → 1530

* **central collecting** → 1530

1529 central communication unit
d zentrale Datenübertragungseinheit f
f unité f de communication centrale
r центральное коммуникационное
устройство n

**1530 central [data] acquisition; central
collecting**
d zentrale Datenerfassung f; zentrales
Erfassen n
f acquisition f centrale de données; saisie f
centrale
r централизованный сбор m [данных]

1531 centralization
d Zentralisation f
f centralisation f
r централизация f

1532 centralized data channel
d gemeinsamer Datenkanal m
f canal m de données centralisé
r централизованный канал m данных

1533 centralized network
d zentralisiertes Netzwerk n
f réseau m centralisé
r централизованная сеть f

1534 centralizer; commutant
d Zentralisator m; Kommutant m
f centralisateur m; commutant m
r централизатор m; коммутант m

1535 central node; master node
d Zentralknoten m
f nœud m central
r центральный узел m

* **central processor** → 1536

**1536 central processor [unit]; CP[U];
mainframe [processor]**
d Zentralprozessor m; Hauptprozessor m;
zentrale Verarbeitungseinheit f; ZVE;
Zentraleinheit f
f processeur m central; unité f centrale de
traitement; UCT
r центральный процессор m; ЦП

* **centring** → 1527

1537 certain data processing
d zuverlässige Datenverarbeitung f
f traitement m certain de données
r надёжная обработка f данных

1538 certainty factor
d Gewissfaktor m
f facteur m de certitude
r коэффициент m достоверности;
показатель m уверенности

1539 certificate
d Zeugnis n
f certificat m
r свидетельство n; удостоверение n

* **certification** → 2155

* **CFD** → 1374

* **CFO** → 1375

* **CFV** → 1376

* **CFW** → 1377

* **CGA** → 1872

* **CGI** → 1927, 2080

1540 CGI script
d CGI-Skript *m*
f script *m* CGI
r скрипт *m* CGI

1541 chain
d Kette *f*; Folge *f*; Kettenzug *m*
f chaîne *f*
r цепь *f*; простой список *m*; цепочка *f*

1542 chain code
d Kettencode *m*
f code *m* en chaîne
r цепной код *m*; симплексный код

1543 chain condition
d Kettenbedingung *f*
f condition *f* de chaîne
r условие *n* обрыва [цепочки]

1544 chain database
d Datenbasis *f* mit Kettenstruktur
f base *f* de données en chaîne
r база *f* данных с цепной структурой

1545 chain data flag
d Kennzeichen *n* für Datenkettung;
  Datenkettenanzeige *f*
f signe *m* d'enchaînement des données
r признак *m* последовательности данных

* **chain-dot screen** → 3354

1546 chained addressing
d gekettete Adressierung *f*
f adressage *m* enchaîné
r составная адресация *f*; цепная адресация

* **chained data** → 2111

1547 chained file
d gekettete Datei *f*
f fichier *m* chaîné
r цепной файл *m*

* **chained list** → 5396

1548 chain[ed] structure
d Kettenstruktur *f*
f structure *f* en chaîne
r цепная структура *f*

1549 chain index
d Kettenindex *m*
f indice *m* en chaîne
r цепочный индекс *m*

1550 chaining; catenation
d Kettenung *f*; Verkettung *f*
f chaînage *m*; enchaînement *m*; adhérence *f*
r цепное связывание *n*; сцепление *n*

1551 chaining address
d Folgeadresse *f*; Verweisadresse *f*;
  Anschlussadresse *f*; Verkettungsadresse *f*
f adresse *f* d'enchaînement
r адрес *m* сопряжения

1552 chaining search
d Suchen *n* in geketteter Liste; Suchen in
  verknüpfter Liste
f recherche *f* des chaînes
r цепной поиск *m*; связной поиск

1553 chain letter
d Kettenbrief *m*
f lettre *f* en chaîne
r письмо *n* по цепочке

1554 chain printer; band printer
d Kettendrucker *m*
f imprimante *f* à chaîne; imprimante à bande
r цепной принтер *m*; лентовый принтер;
  ленточное печатающее устройство *n*

* **chain structure** → 1548

* **chance event** → 7596

1555 change *v*
d ändern; wechseln
f changer
r [из]менять

1556 change
d Änderung *f*; Wechsel *m*
f change[ment] *m*
r перемена *f*; изменение *n*

1557 changeover; switchover
d Umschaltung *f*; Umschalten *n*
f commutation *f* [alternative]
r переключение *n*; смена *f*

* **changeover circuit** → 1558

1558 changeover switch; changeover circuit
d Umschalter *m*
f permutateur *m*; inverseur *m*
r переключатель *m*; коммутатор *m*

1559 change queue
d Wechselwarteschlange *f*
f queue *f* de changes
r очередь *f* замен

1560 channel
d Kanal *m*
f canal *m*
r канал *m*

* channel → 9464

1561 channel address word; CAW
d Kanaladresswort *n*
f mot *m* d'adresse de canal
r слово *n* адреса канала

* **channel amplifier** → 1580

* **channel bank** → 1569

* **channel capacity** → 1590

1562 channel coding
d Kanalcodierung *f*
f codage *m* de voie
r кодирование *n* канала

1563 channel command word; CCW
d Kanalbefehlswort *n*
f mot *m* de commande de canal
r управляющее слово *n* канала

1564 channel-coupled multiprocessor
d Multiprozessor *m* mit Verbindungskanälen
f multiprocesseur *m* aux canaux unifiés
r мультипроцессор *m* с объединёнными каналами

1565 channel data
d Kanaldaten *pl*
f données *fpl* de canal
r канальные данные *pl*

1566 channel definition format; CDF
d Kanaldefinitionsormat *n*
f format *m* de définition de canal
r формат *m* дефинирования канала

* **channel director** → 1578

1567 channel end
d Kanalende *n*
f fin *f* de canal
r конец *m* работы канала

1568 channel filter
d Kanalweiche *f*; Kanalfilter *m*
f filtre *m* de voie; filtre de canal
r канальный фильтр *m*

1569 channel group; channel bank; line group
d Kanalgruppe *f*; Kanalbündel *n*
f groupe *m* de canaux
r группа *f* каналов

1570 channel-guide structure
d kanalgeführte Struktur *f*
f structure *f* de guide sillonné de canaux
r каналоведущая структура *f*

* **channel hopping** → 1588

1571 channeling
d Kanalbildung *f*; Einteilung *f* in Kanäle
f canalisation *f*; répartition *f* en canaux
r образование *n* канала; разделение *n* на каналы

1572 channel interface; line interface
d Kanalschnittstelle *f*; Kanalinterface *n*; Leitungsschnittstelle *f*
f interface *f* de canal; interface de ligne
r канальный интерфейс *m*; интерфейс с каналом

1573 channel interface adapter
d Kanalinterfaceadapter *m*
f adaptateur *m* d'interface de canal
r адаптер *m* канального интерфейса

1574 channel loading
d Kanalbelegung *f*
f occupation *f* de canal; chargement *m* de canal
r загрузка *f* канала; занятие *n* канала

1575 channel mid[dle]-frequency
d Kanalmittelfrequenz *f*
f fréquence *f* intermédiaire de canal
r средняя частота *f* канала

* **channel mid-frequency** → 1575

* **channel op** → 1576

1576 channel op[erator]; chop
d Kanaloperator *m*
f administrateur *m* de groupe de discussion; opérateur *m* de canal IRC; opérateur de canal de bavardage
r оператор *m* каналов [эстафетного разговора]

1577 channel pair
d Kanalpaar *n*
f paire *f* de canaux
r пара *f* каналов; канальная пара

1578 channel processor; channel director
d Kanalprozessor *m*
f directeur *m* de canaux; processeur *m* de canaux
r процессор *m* [управления] каналов; канальный процессор

* **channel queue** → 1591

1579 channel recording
 d Spuraufreichung *f*
 f enregistrement *m* de piste
 r дорожечная запись *f*; запись на дорожке

1580 channel repeater; channel amplifier
 d Kanalverstärker *m*
 f répéteur *m* de voie; répéteur de canal
 r канальный [промежуточный] усилитель *m*

1581 channel scheduling
 d Kanalverwaltung *f*; Kanalzuordnung *f*
 f attribution *f* de canal
 r составление *n* расписания канала

* **channel selector** → 1587

1582 channel separation
 d Kanalabstand *m*
 f séparation *f* de canaux
 r интервал *m* между каналами

1583 channel splitter; line splitter
 d Kanalaufteiler *m*
 f diviseur *m* de canaux
 r устройство *n* разделения каналов

1584 channel status word; CSW
 d Kanalzustandswort *n*; Kanalstatuswort *n*
 f mot *m* d'état de canal
 r слово *n* состояния канала

1585 channel stop
 d Kanalsperre *f*
 f arrêt *m* de canal
 r перекрытие *n* канала

1586 channel subdivision
 d Kanalteilung *f*
 f subdivision *f* de canal
 r подразделение *n* канала

1587 channel switch; channel selector
 d Kanalwähler *m*; Kanalselektor *m*;
    Kanal[um]schalter *m*
 f sélecteur *m* de canaux; commutateur *m* de
    canaux
 r канальный переключатель *m*; селектор *m*
    каналов

**1588 channel switching; channel hopping; line
    switching; link switching; circuit switching**
 d Kanaldurchschaltung *f*; Kanalumschaltung *f*;
    Leitungsvermittlung *f*; Kanalhüpfen *n*
 f commutation *f* des canaux; commutation des
    lignes
 r переключение *n* каналов; коммутация *f*
    каналов; линейная коммутация

* **channel throughput** → 1590

1589 channel time response
 d Kanalzeitverhalten *n*
 f caractéristique *f* temporelle de canal
 r временная характеристика *f* канала

**1590 channel [transmission] capacity; channel
    throughput**
 d Kanal[transfer]kapazität *f*;
    Kanalübertragungskapazität *f*;
    Kanaldurchlässigkeit *f*
 f capacité *f* du canal; capacité de la voie;
    rendement *m* du canal
 r ёмкость *f* канала; пропускная
    способность *f* канала;
    производительность *f* канала

* **channel waiting line** → 1591

**1591 channel [waiting] queue; channel waiting
    line**
 d Kanalwarteschlange *f*
 f queue *f* de canal; file *f* d'attente de canal
 r очередь *f* к каналу; канальная очередь

1592 chapter
 d Kapitel *n*
 f chapitre *m*
 r глава *f*; секция *f*

* **char** → 1593

1593 character; char; symbol; sign
 d Zeichen *n*; Symbol *n*
 f caractère *m*; symbole *m*
 r знак *m*; символ *m*

1594 character attribute
 d Zeichensattribut *n*
 f attribut *m* de caractère
 r атрибут *m* знака

1595 character bar; symbol bar
 d Symbolleiste *f*
 f barre *f* de caractères
 r лента *f* символов

1596 character baseline; CBL
 d Zeichengrundlinie *f*
 f ligne *f* de base de caractère
 r знаковая эталонная линия *f*

1597 character blanking
 d Zeichenunterdrückung *f*
 f suppression *f* de caractères; annulation *f* de
    caractères
 r гашение *n* знаков

1598 character buffer
 d Zeichenpuffer *m*; Zeichensender *m*

f tampon *m* de caractères
r знаковый буфер *m*

1599 character cell; dot-matrix field
d Position *f* des Symbols
f position *f* de caractère
r знакоместо *n*; символьная ячейка *f*

1600 character code
d Zeichencode *m*
f code *m* de caractère
r код *m* символа; код знака

1601 character code register
d Zeichencoderegister *n*; Symbolcoderegister *n*
f registre *m* [de code] de caractère
r регистр *m* [кода] знака; знаковый регистр

1602 character [code] translation
d Zeichenumcodierung *f*; Zeichenumsetzung *f*
f translation *f* [de code] de caractère
r преобразование *n* кода знака

* **character contour** → 1621

1603 character coupling
d Zeichendurchschaltung *f*
f couplage *m* de caractères
r связывание *n* знаков

* **character crowding** → 1622

1604 character density
d Zeichendichte *f*
f densité *f* des caractères
r плотность *f* знаков

* **character design** → 1605

1605 character design[ing]
d Zeichendesign *n*
f dessin *m* de caractère
r символьный дизайн *m*

1606 character disassembly
d Zeichenzerlegung *f*
f décomposition *f* de caractère
r разложение *n* знака

* **character emitter** → 1612

1607 character expression
d Zeichenausdruck *m*
f expression *f* à caractères
r символьное выражение *n*

1608 character fade-in
d Zeichenaufblendung *f*
f apparition *f* graduelle de caractères
r постепенное возникновение *n* символов

1609 character fade-out
d Zeichen-Abblendung *f*
f disparition *f* graduelle de caractères
r постепенное исчезновение *n* символов

1610 character font; symbol font; font; type font; type [style]
d Zeichenschriftart *f*; Schrift[art] *f*; Font *n*
f police *f* [de caractères]; fonte *f*; style *m* de types
r шрифт *m*; литера *f*; комплект *m* шрифта; гарнитура *f* [шрифта]

1611 character formatting
d Zeichenformatierung *f*
f formatage *m* de caractère
r форматирование *n* символа

1612 character generator; character emitter; symbol generator
d Zeichen[impuls]geber *m*; Zeichengenerator *m*
f émetteur *m* d'impulsion de caractères; générateur *m* de caractères; générateur de symboles
r знаковый генератор *m*; генератор знаков; генератор символов

* **character graphics** → 7472

1613 character-height unit
d Einheit *f* der Zeichnenhöhe
f unité *f* de hauteur de caractère
r единица *f* высоты символа

* **characteristic** → 1614, 1616

1614 characteristic [curve]; response [curve]
d Kennlinie *f*; Charakteristik *f*
f courbe *f* caractéristique; caractéristique *f*
r характеристическая кривая *f*; характеристика *f*

1615 characteristic frequency
d Kennfrequenz *f*
f fréquence *f* caractéristique
r характеристическая частота *f*

1616 characteristic[s]
d Charakteristik *f*
f caractéristique *f*
r характеристика *f*; особенность *f*; свойство *n*

1617 characteristic string
d charakteristische Zeichenkette *f*
f chaîne *f* caractéristique
r характеристическая строка *f*

1618 character map; symbol table
d Zeichentabelle *f*; Symboltabelle *f*

  f table *f* de caractères; table de symboles
  r таблица *f* символов

1619 character mode; alphanumeric mode; text mode
  d Zeichenmodus *m*; zeichenweiser Betrieb *m*; Textmodus *m*
  f mode *m* des caractères; mode de texte
  r знаковый режим *m*; символьный режим; режим обработки знаков; текстовой режим

1620 character-oriented communication; character-oriented transmission
  d zeichenorientierte Kommunikation *f*; zeichenweise arbeitende Übertragung *f*
  f communication *f* par caractères; transmission *f* par caractères
  r познаковая связь *f*; посимвольная передача *f*

  * **character-oriented transmission** → 1620

1621 character outline; character contour; character shape
  d Zeichenumriss *m*; Zeichenkontur *f*
  f contour *m* de caractère; forme *f* de caractère
  r контур *m* знака; очертание *n* символа; форма *f* символа

1622 character packing; character crowding
  d Zeichenpackung *f*
  f compression *f* de caractères; compaction *f* de caractères
  r уплотнение *n* знаков; уплотнение символов

  * **character pitch** → 7270

1623 character reading; character sensing; character scanning
  d Zeichenlesung *f*; Zeichenabtastung *f*
  f lecture *f* de caractères; balayage *m* de caractères
  r считывание *n* символов; считывание знаков

1624 character recognition
  d Zeichenerkennung *f*; Schriftzeichenerkennung *f*
  f reconnaissance *f* de caractères; identification *f* de caractères
  r распознавание *n* знаков

  * **character repertoire** → 1627

1625 character request
  d Zeichenanforderung *f*
  f demande *f* de caractère
  r запрос *m* символа

  * **character scanning** → 1623

  * **character sensing** → 1623

1626 character sequence
  d Zeichenfolge *f*; Zeichenreihe *f*; Zeichensequenz *f*
  f séquence *f* de caractères; série *f* de caractères; suite *f* de caractères
  r последовательность *f* знаков; ряд *m* знаков

1627 character set; character repertoire
  d Zeichensatz *m*; Zeichenvorrat *m*; Zeichenmenge *f*
  f jeu *m* de caractères; répertoire *m* de caractères
  r набор *m* знаков; набор символов

  * **character shape** → 1621

  * **character signal** → 1825

1628 character size
  d Symbolgröße *f*
  f taille *f* de caractère
  r размер *m* символа

1629 character skew
  d Zeichenschräglauf *m*; Zeichenneigung *f*; Schrägstellung *f*
  f inclinaison *f* du caractère
  r наклон *m* символа

1630 character spacing; inter-character space
  d Zeichenabstand *m*; Abstand *m* zwischen Zeichen; Zeichenlücke *f*
  f espace *m* entre caractères; pas *m* horizontal des caractères
  r расстояние *n* между знаками; интервал *m* между знаками; межсимвольный интервал

1631 character string; string
  d String *m*; Kette *f*; Zeichenkette *f*
  f chaîne *f* [de caractères]; ordre *m* symbolique
  r [символьная] строка *f*; цепочка *f* символов

1632 character subscript
  d tiefgestelltes Zeichen *n*
  f indice *m* inférieur de caractère
  r символ-нижний индекс *m*; нижний индекс символа

1633 character subset
  d Zeichenvorratsuntermenge *f*; Zeichenteilmenge *f*; Zeichenteilvorrat *m*
  f sous-ensemble *m* de caractères
  r подмножество *m* знаков

1634 character superscript
  d hochgestelltes Zeichen *n*
  f indice *m* supérieur de caractère
  r символ-верхний индекс *m*; верхний индекс символа

1635 **character-to-background contrast**
    d Zeichen-Hintergrund-Kontrast *m*
    f contraste *m* caractère-fond
    r контраст *m* знак-фон

* **character translation** → 1602

1636 **character-type file**
    d zeichenorientierte Datei *f*; byteorientierte Datei
    f fichier *m* orienté caractère; fichier orienté octet
    r байт-ориентированный файл *m*

1637 **character weight**
    d Zeichengewicht *n*
    f poids *m* de caractère
    r толщина *f* символа

1638 **charge**
    (of a particle)
    d Ladung *f*
    f charge *f*
    r заряд *m*

* **charge** *v* → 3823

* **charge** → 5429

1639 **charge; fee; tax; rate**
    d Gebühr *f*
    f taxe *f*; taux *m*
    r такса *f*; налог *m*; плата *f*

* **charging** → 5435

* **charging equipment** → 1640

1640 **charging unit; charging equipment**
    d Gebühreneinheit *f*; Ladeeinrichtung *f*
    f chargeur *m*
    r зарядное устройство *n*

* **chart** *v* → 3158

* **chart** → 5635

1641 **chart; diagram; graph[ic]; plot; image curve**
    d Diagramm *n*; Schaubild *n*; Kurvenblatt *n*; Kurvenbild *n*; Grafik *f*
    f diagramme *m*; graphique *m*; courbe *f* représentative
    r диаграмма *f*; схема *f*; график *m*; лист *m* кривых

1642 **chart wizard**
    d Diagramm-Assistent *m*
    f assistant *m* de diagrammes
    r советчик *m* построения диаграммы

1643 **chassis; subrack**
    d Fahrgestell *n*; Chassis *n*; Geräteträger *m*
    f châssis *m*; armoire *f*; râtelier *m*
    r шасси *n*; каркас *m* корпуса

1644 **chat** *v*; **converse** *v*
    d sprechen; plaudern; chatten
    f converser
    r разговаривать

1645 **chat; conversation; talk**
    d [Online-]Gespräch *n*; Konversation *f*; Plausch *m*; Plauderei *f*
    f conversation *f*; causette *f*
    r разговор *m*; переговор *m*; болтовня *f*; трёп *m*; чат *m*

* **chat room** → 9970

1646 **check; checkout; test; verification; proof**
    d Prüfung *f*; Prüfen *n*; Test *m*
    f [é]preuve *f*; essai *m*; examen *m*; test *m*; vérification *f*
    r проверка *f*; испытание *n*; тест *m*; верификация *f*

1647 **check** *v*; **test** *v*; **verify** *v*; **audit** *v*
    d überprüfen; [nach]prüfen; verifizieren
    f essayer; examiner; vérifier
    r проверять; испытывать; верифицировать

1648 **check bit; test bit**
    d Prüfbit *n*; Kontrollbit *n*
    f bit *m* de contrôle
    r бит *m* проверки; контрольный бит

1649 **checkbox**
    d Kontrollkasten *m*; Kontrollkästchen *n*
    f case *f* à cocher; cocher *m*; boîte *f* d'essai; case d'option
    r тестовый ящик *m*; поле *n* для галочки; графа *f* для галочки; флажок *m*; триггерная кнопка *f*

* **checker** → 1658

* **check information** → 1650

1650 **check[ing] information**
    d Kontrollinformation *f*
    f information *f* de vérification; information de test
    r контрольная информация *f*

1651 **checklist**
    d Kontrollliste *f*; Prüfliste *f*
    f liste *f* de contrôle
    r контрольная таблица *f*

1652 **check mark; score**
    d Häkchen *n*

f coche *f*
r отметка *f*; галочка *f*

* **checkout** → 1646, 2631

1653 check *v* out
(a program)
d austesten
f vérifier; tester; essayer
r отлаживать

1654 checkout compiler
d Ausprüf-Compiler *m*
f compilateur *m* de mettre au point
r отладочный компилятор *m*

1655 checkpoint; testpoint
d Prüfpunkt *m*; Kontrollpunkt *m*; Testpunkt *m*
f point *m* de contrôle; point de vérification
r контрольная точка *f*

1656 checkpointing
d Testpunktkopieren *n*; Fixpunktkopieren *n*
f pointage *m*
r копирование *n* в контрольных точках

1657 checkpoint restart
d Testpunktwiederanlauf *m*;
Fixpunktwiederanlauf *m*
f redémarrage *m* à point de contrôle
r перезапуск *m* с контрольной точки

1658 check program; checker
d Prüfprogramm *n*
f programme *m* de contrôle
r программа *f* контроля

1659 checksum; control total; hash total
d Kontrollsumme *f*; Prüfsumme *f*
f somme *f* de contrôle; somme d'essai; total *m*
de contrôle
r контрольная сумма *f*

* **chevrons** → 399

* **chiffre** → 2874

* **child** → 1660

1660 child [record]
d Nachkommesatz *m*; Child *n*
f enregistrement *m* fils
r дочерняя запись *f*

* **Chinese binary code** → 1884

* **chip** → 5808

* **chip card** → 7112

1661 chip carrier
d Chip[träger]rahmen *m*
f cadre *m* à puces
r кристаллодержатель *m*;
кристаллоноситель *m*

1662 chip[-carrier] socket
d Chip[träger]sockel *m*
f socle *m* de chip; douille *f* de cadre à puces
r микросхемная панелька *f*; гнездо *n* для
кристаллодержателей

1663 chip designer
d Chipdesigner *m*
f concepteur *m* de puces
r проектировщик *m* чипов

1664 chipselect time
d Chipauswahlzeit *f*; Schaltkreisauswahlzeit *f*
f temps *m* de sélection de chip
r время *n* выбора микросхем

1665 chipset
d LSI-Schaltkreissatz *m*; Chipsatz *m*
f jeu *m* de circuits intégrés; jeu de composants;
circuit *m* microprogrammé
r комплект *m* микросхем

* **chip socket** → 1662

* **choice** → 8319

* **choice device** → 8332

1666 choice of style; style selection
d Stilwahl *f*
f sélection *f* de style
r выбор *m* стиля

* **choice structure** → 1481

* **choose *v*** → 8313

* **chop** → 1576

* **chroma signal** → 1445

1667 chromatic
d chromatisch
f chromatique
r цветной; хроматический

1668 chromaticity; chromaticness
d Farbart *f*; Farbvalenz *f*; Chromazität *f*
f chromaticité *f*
r цветность *f*; хроматизм *m*

* **chromaticness** → 1668

1669 **chromatic wheel; color wheel; color circle**
   d Farbkreis *m*
   f roue *f* chromatique; roue de couleurs
   r хроматическое колесо *n*

   * **chrominance signal** → 1445

   * **CIM** → 2059

   * **cipher** → 2874

   * **cipherer** → 1819

1670 **circuit; network**
   (as an electrical schema)
   d Schaltung *f*; Kreis *m*
   f circuit *m*
   r схема *f*; контур *m*

1671 **circuit alarm**
   d Stromkreiswecker *m*
   f avertisseur *m* de circuit
   r схемная аларма *f*

1672 **circuit board; circuit card**
   d Schaltungsplatte *f*; Leiterplatte *f*; Leiterkarte *f*
   f platine *f* de circuit
   r схемная плата *f*

   * **circuit card** → 1672

1673 **circuit diagram; circuit layout**
   d Schaltbild *n*; Schaltplan *m*; Stromlauf[plan] *m*
   f schéma *m* de circuit
   r принципиальная схема *f*; схема
      соединений

1674 **circuit drop-out**
   d Schaltungsunterbrechung *f*
   f dropout *m* de circuits
   r схемное прерывание *n*

   * **circuit-free** → 155

   * **circuit-free graph** → 156

   * **circuit layout** → 1673

1675 **circuitry; circuit technique**
   d Schaltungskomplex *m*; Schaltungstechnik *f*
   f circuiterie *f*; ensemble *m* de circuits;
      technique *f* de montage
   r сборка *f* схем; множество *n* схем;
      схемотехника *f*

   * **circuit switching** → 1588

   * **circuit technique** → 1675

1676 **circuit throughput**

1677 **circular**
   d Schaltkreisdurchsatz *m*
   f débit *m* de circuit
   r пропускная способность *f* схемы

1677 **circular**
   d Kreis-
   f circulaire
   r кольцевой; циклический; круговой

1678 **circular arrow**
   d Kreispfeil *m*
   f flèche *f* circulaire
   r круговая стрелка *f*

1679 **circularity**
   d Rundheit *f*
   f circularité *f*
   r цикличность *f*

1680 **circular list**
   d Kreisliste *f*
   f liste *f* circulaire
   r круговой список *m*; циркулярный список

1681 **circular reference**
   d Kreisreferenz *f*; Kreisbezug *m*
   f référence *f* circulaire
   r круговая ссылка *f*

1682 **circular ring; annulus; donut**
   d [ebener] Kreisring *m*
   f couronne *f* [circulaire]; anneau *m* [circulaire]
   r [плоское] круговое кольцо *n*

1683 **circular screen; round screen; round dots**
   d Kreisraster *m*
   f trame *f* circulaire
   r [концентрично-]круглый растр *m*

1684 **circular selection**
   d Kreisauswahl *f*
   f sélection *f* circulaire
   r круговая выборка *f*

1685 **circular shift; cycle shift; cyclic shift;**
      end-around shift; ring shift
   d zyklische Verschiebung *f*; Ringschiften *n*
   f décalage *m* circulaire; déplacement *m*
      cyclique
   r циклический сдвиг *m*; кольцевой сдвиг

1686 **circular visual selector**
   d rundes visuelles Auswahlfeld *n*
   f sélecteur *m* visuel circulaire
   r круговой селектор *m*

1687 **circulate** *v*; **rotate** *v*; **revolve** *v*
   d umlaufen; rotieren; kreisen; verschieben
   f circuler; tourner
   r циклировать; вращать[ся]

1688 circulating decimal fraction; periodic decimal fraction
d periodischer Dezimalbruch *m*
f fraction *f* décimale périodique
r периодическая десятичная дробь *f*

1689 circulating memory; cyclic stor[ag]e
d Umlaufspeicher *m*
f mémoire *f* circulante; mémoire cyclique
r циклическая память *f*

1690 circulating register
d Umlaufregister *n*
f registre *m* à circulation; registre cyclique
r циклический регистр *m*; кольцевой регистр

1691 circulating shift register; recirculating shift register
d Umlaufschieberegister *n*
f registre *m* de décalage circulaire
r кольцевой сдвиговый регистр *m*

1692 circulation; rotation; rotating
d Zirkulation *f*; Kreislauf *m*; Rotation *f*; Drehung *f*
f circulation *f*; rotation *f*
r циркуляция *f*; вращение *n*; периодическое повторение *n*

1693 circulator
d Zirkulator *m*
f circulateur *m*
r циркулятор *m*

* **circumflex** → 1437

* **circumflex accent** → 1437

1694 circumvention; encirclement; wraparound
d Umlauf *m*; zyklischer Arbeitsablauf *m*
f bouclage *m*; retour *m* en boucle; contournement *m*
r заворачивание *n*; циклический возврат *m*

* **CISC** → 2008

* **CIX** → 1916

* **cladding** → 1796

1695 clamp *v*
d klammern
f appuyer
r фиксировать; задерживать; ограничивать

* **clamp** → 1152

* **clamper** → 1696

1696 clamping circuit; clamper
d Klemmschaltung *f*; Blockierschaltung *f*; Randwertschaltung *f*
f circuit *m* de blocage; circuit de verrouillage
r фиксирующая схема *f*; фиксатор *m*

* **clamping connector** → 1738

1697 clamping roller; pinch roller
d Klemmrolle *f*; Andruckrolle *f*
f rouleau *m* presseur; galet *m* presseur
r прижимной ролик *m*

1698 class
d Klasse *f*
f classe *f*
r класс *m*

1699 class comparator
d Klassenvergleicher *m*
f comparateur *m* de classes
r компаратор *m* классов

1700 class counter
d Ordnungszähler *m*
f compteur *m* ordinal
r счётчик *m* порядкового номера

1701 classification; grading
d Klass[ifiz]ierung *f*; Klassifikation *f*
f classification *f*; classement *m*
r классификация *f*; классирование *n*

1702 classified data
d geheimzuhaltende Daten *pl*
f données *fpl* à accès restreint
r данные *pl* ограниченного доступа

1703 classifier
d Klassifikator *m*; Klassifizierer *m*
f class[ificat]eur *m*
r классификатор *m*

1704 classify *v*
d klassifizieren; klassieren
f classifier; classer
r классифицировать

1705 clause
d Klausel *f*
f clause *f*
r условие *n*; клауза *f*

* **clean** → 7512

* **clean** *v* → 1709

1706 clean boot
d reiner Start *m*

f démarrage *m* minimal
r чистая загрузка *f*

* **clean data** → 9744

1707 cleaner
   d Reinigungseinrichtung *f*; Reiniger *m*
   f nettoyeur *m*; épurateur *m*
   r устройство *n* очистки

* **cleaning** → 7512

1708 clean-up editing
   d endgültiges Editieren *n*; Reinaufbereitung *f*
   f édition *f* finale
   r окончательное редактирование *n*

* **clear** → 1715, 7512

* **clear** *v* → 10095

1709 clear *v*; **clean** *v*; **discard** *v*; **remove** *v*;
   scratch *v*; **erase** *v*; **nuke** *v*
   d löschen; reinigen; [ver]kratzen
   f balayer; effacer; détruire
   r очищать; стирать; удалять

1710 clear *v* **all**
   d alles löschen
   f tout effacer
   r стирать все

* **clearance** → 7512

1711 clear area
   (of a document)
   d freie Fläche *f*
   f champ *m* vide
   r чистое поле *n*

* **clear band** → 1048

1712 clear confirmation
   d Auslöschebestätigung *f*
   f confirmation *f* d'effaçage
   r подтверждение *n* стирания

1713 clear data
   d Klartextdaten *pl*
   f données *fpl* pures
   r незашифрованные данные *pl*

1714 cleardown
   d Abbau *m*; Auslöschung *f*
   f effaçage *m* en arrière
   r обратное гашение *n*

* **clearing** → 7512, 10096

1715 clear[ing]; erasing; erasure; deletion;

deleting; purging
   d Löschen *n*; Löschung *f*
   f effaçage *m*; effacement *m*
   r стирание *n*; отмена *f*

1716 clearing button
   d Auslöschertaste *f*
   f bouton *m* d'effaçage
   r кнопка *f* гашения; кнопка стирания

1717 clearing signal
   d Auslöscherzeichen *n*
   f signal *m* d'effaçage
   r сигнал *m* стирания; отбойный сигнал

1718 clear key; cancel key
   d Löschtaste *f*
   f touche *f* d'annulation
   r клавиша *f* гашения; клавиша отмены

1719 clear method
   d Löschungsmethode *f*
   f méthode *f* d'effaçage
   r метод *m* очищения

1720 clear *v* **screen**
   d Bildschirm löschen
   f effacer l'écran
   r очищать экран

1721 cleavage
   d Spalten *n*
   f clivage *m*
   r расщепление *n*

1722 click
   d Klick *m*; Klicken *n*
   f clic *m*; click *m*
   r клик *m*; щелчок *m*; нажатие *n* кнопки

* **clickable area** → 4573

* **clickable image** → 1723

1723 clickable image [map]; image map; hot
   image; interactive graphic
   d klickbare Imagemap *f*; Bildatlas *m*; klickbare
   Karte *f*
   f image *f* réactive; image cliquable; carte *f*
   sensible; carte-image *f*; carte imagée
   r адресуемое отображение *n*

1724 click *v* **and drag** *v*
   d klicken und ziehen
   f cliquer et glisser
   r нажать кнопку и переместить

1725 clickstream
   (of the Internet sites)
   d Klickstrom *m*

f parcours *m*
r история *f* посещений; перечень *m* сайтов; маршрут *m* перемещения (пользователя) по web-узлу

1726 click[-]through
d Klickdurchgang *m*
f clic *m* publicitaire
r выбор *m* рекламного объявления (в процессе перемещения пользователя по web-узлу)

* **client** → 1728

1727 client; customer
d Kunde *m*; Client *n*
f client *m*
r клиент *m*; заказчик *m*

1728 client [application]; client software; client program
d Kundenanwendung *f*
f application *f* d'acheteur; application d'acquéreur; logiciel *m* client
r заказное приложение *n*; [программа-]клиент *m*

* **client installation** → 2442

1729 client profile
d Kundenprofil *n*
f profil *m* de client
r профиль *m* клиента

* **client program** → 1728

1730 client/server area; client/server environment
d Client/Server-Bereich *m*
f environnement *m* client/serveur
r среда *f* клиент/сервер

* **client/server environment** → 1730

* **client software** → 1728

* **clinch** → 2621

* **clip** → 1152

1731 clip *v*
d schneiden; zerschneiden; kappen
f découper
r срезать; отсекать

1732 clip; fragment
d Clip *n*; Teil *m* in einem grafischen Dokument
f clip *m*; agrafe *f*
r клип *m*; вырезка *f*; фрагмент *m*

1733 clip algorithm
d Schneiden-Algorithmus *m*
f algorithme *m* de découpage
r алгоритм *m* отсекания

* **clipart** → 1735

1734 clipart collection
(ready-made images)
d Clipart-Sammlung *f*
f collection *f* de cliparts; bibliothèque *f* d'éléments graphiques
r коллекция *f* вырезок

1735 clipart [image]
d Clipart *f*; Clipart-Bild *n*
f clipart *m*; graphique *m* prédessiné
r иллюстративная вставка *f*; графический фрагмент *m*; вырезная иллюстрация *f*; аппликация *f*

1736 clipart scrapbook
d Clipart-Skizzenbuch *n*
f classeur *m* de cliparts
r альбом *m* вырезок

* **clipboard** → 1152

1737 clipboard
d Einfügungspuffer *m*; Klemmbrett *n*
f presse-papiers *m*
r буфер *m* обмена

* **clipboard computer** → 6300

* **clip connector** → 1738

1738 clip [contact] connector; clamping connector
d Andruckleiste *f*; Federleiste *f*; Federleistenstecker *m*
f connecteur *m* écrêteur; connecteur en forme de mâchoire
r пружинный зажим *m*; зажим типа "крокодил"

1739 clipdepth
d Schnitttiefe *f*
f profondeur *f* de coupe
r глубина *f* среза

1740 clip gallery
d Clipgalerie *f*
f galerie *f* de clips
r галерея *f* картинок

1741 clipper
d Klipper *m*
f écrêteur *m*
r ограничитель *m*; отсекатель *m*

*   **clipper** → 1743

1742 **clipping; scissoring; cutting**
   d Ausschnitt *m*; Schneiden *n*; Kappen *n*;
      Klippen *n*
   f [dé]coupage *m*; écrêtage *m*; détourage *m*
   r отсечение *n*; усечение *n*; срезание *n*;
      отсекание *n*

1743 **clipping circuit; clipper**
   d Begrenzerschaltung *f*; Begrenzkreis *m*;
      Impulsbegrenzer *m*; Begrenzer *m*
   f circuit *m* d'écrêtage; écrêteur *m*; circuit
      limiteur
   r схема *f* отсекания

1744 **clobber** *v*
      (e-slang)
   d verprügeln
   f écraser (généralement par inadvertance)
   r портить; стирать (случайно)

*   **clock** → 1755

1745 **clock cable**
   d Taktkabel *n*
   f câble *m* d'horloge
   r кабель *m* тактового импульса

*   **clock/calendar** → 1746

1746 **clock/calendar [circuit]; hardware clock;
      internal clock**
   d Uhren/Datum-Schaltung *f*
   f horloge/calendrier *m* [interne]
   r часы/календарь *m*; внутренные часы *pl*;
      встроенные часы; аппаратный таймер *m*

1747 **clock changeover; clock switchover**
   d Taktumschaltung *f*
   f transition *f* d'horloge
   r переключение *n* тактового канала

1748 **clock channel; timing channel**
   d Taktkanal *m*; Synchronisationskanal *m*
   f canal *m* d'horloge; canal de synchronisation
   r канал *m* синхронизации

1749 **clock cycle**
   d Taktzyklus *m*
   f cycle *m* d'horloge; cycle de synchronisation
   r цикл *m* синхронизации

*   **clocked** → 9387

*   **clock edge** → 1756

1750 **clocked latch**
   d getaktetes Latch *n*
   f verrou *m* synchronisé

   r синхронная защёлка *f*

*   **clock failure** → 1757

*   **clock frequency** → 1762

*   **clock generator** → 1758

*   **clocking** → 9420

1751 **clock interrupt**
   d Zeitgeberunterbrechung *f*
   f interruption *f* par horloge
   r прерывание *n* по таймеру; прерывание от
      таймера

1752 **clock interval**
   d Taktzeit *f*
   f intervalle *m* entre impulsions d'horloge
   r [между]тактовый интервал *m*

1753 **clock line**
   d Taktleitung *f*
   f ligne *f* d'horloge
   r линия *f* синхроимпульсов

1754 **clock marker track**
   d Steuerspur *f* für die Taktgabe; Taktspur *f*;
      Uhrspur *f*
   f piste *f* de rythme; piste de temps; piste de
      synchronisation
   r дорожка *f* тактовых импульсов;
      синхронизирующая дорожка

*   **clock offset** → 1759

*   **clock phase** → 1760

*   **clock phase synchronization** → 1761

1755 **clock [pulse]; timing pulse; tact; tick**
   d Takt *m*; Taktimpuls *m*
   f tact *m*; impulsion *f* d'horloge; horloge *f*;
      impulsion de temps
   r такт *m*; тактовый импульс *m*;
      синхроимпульс *m*

1756 **clock [pulse] edge; timing [pulse] edge**
   d Taktflanke *f*
   f flanc *m* d'impulsions d'horloge
   r фронт *m* тактового импульса

1757 **clock [pulse] failure; timing [pulse] failure**
   d Taktstörung *f*
   f défaut *m* d'impulsion d'horloge
   r ошибка *f* тактового импульса

1758 **clock [pulse] generator**
   d Taktgeber *m*; Taktgenerator *m*;
      Taktimpulsgenerator *m*;
      Synchronisiereinheit *f*

f générateur *m* d'impulsions de
synchronisation; générateur de rythme
[d'horloge]; générateur d'horloge
r тактовый генератор *m*; генератор тактовых
импульсов; датчик *m* тактовых импульсов

1759 clock [pulse] offset; clock skew
d Taktversatz *m*
f décalage *m* d'impulsions d'horloge
r смещение *n* тактовых импульсов;
расфазировка *f* тактовых сигналов

1760 clock [pulse] phase; timing phase
d Taktphase *f*
f phase *f* d'impulsion d'horloge
r фаза *f* тактового импульса

1761 clock [pulse] phase synchronization;
timing phase synchronization
d Taktphasensynchronisierung *f*
f synchronisation *f* par phase d'impulsion
d'horloge
r синхронизация *f* в соответствии с фазой
тактового импульса

1762 clock [pulse] rate; timing [pulse] rate;
clock frequency; clock speed
d Taktfolge *f*; Teilertakt *m*; Taktfrequenz *f*;
Taktrate *f*
f vitesse *f* d'horloge; fréquence *f* de base;
fréquence d'horloge
r частота *f* тактовых импульсов; тактовая
частота

1763 clock [pulse] retrieval; clock recovery
d Taktimpulsrückgewinnung *f*
f récupération *f* d'impulsions d'horloge
r восстановление *n* тактовых импульсов

1764 clock [pulse] train; timing [pulse] train
d Taktimpulsfolge *f*; Zeitsignalmäander *m*
f train *m* d'impulsions d'horloge
r последовательность *f* тактовых импульсов;
тактовая последовательность

*   **clock rate** → **1762**

*   **clock recovery** → **1763**

*   **clock retrieval** → **1763**

1765 clock selection switch; clock selector switch
d Taktwahlschalter *m*; Zeitgeberselektor *m*
f sélecteur *m* de minuterie
r переключатель *m* тактового генератора

*   **clock selector switch** → **1765**

1766 clock signal
d getaktetes Signal *n*

f signal *m* rythmé
r синхронизированный сигнал *m*

*   **clock skew** → **1759**

*   **clock speed** → **1762**

*   **clock switchover** → **1747**

1767 clock track
d Takt[geber]spur *f*; Zeitgeberspur *f*
f piste *f* d'horloge
r тактовая дорожка *f*

*   **clock train** → **1764**

1768 clock voltage
d Taktspannung *f*
f tension *f* d'horloge
r напряжение *n* тактового импульса

1769 clockwise
d im Uhrzeigersinn
f en sens des aiguilles d'une montre; en sens
horaire
r по часовой стрелке

1770 clone *v*
d klonen
f cloner
r клонировать

1771 clone; cloning
d Klonen *n*
f clone *m*; clonage *m*
r клонирование *n*

1772 clone frame
d Klonen-Frame *n*
f cadre-imitation *m*
r кадр-имитация *f*

*   **clone tool** → **1773**

*   **cloning** → **1771**

1773 cloning tool; clone tool
d Klonen-Hilfsmittel *n*
f outil *m* de clonage
r инструмент *m* клонирования

1774 close *v*
d abschließen; schließen
f fermer
r замыкать; закрывать

1775 close coupling; tight coupling
d Kurzkupplung *f*
f attelage *m* serré
r сильная связь *f*

1776 **closed**
  d geschlossen; abgeschlossen
  f fermé; clos
  r замкнутый; закрытый

1777 **closed circuit**
  d geschlossener Stromkreis *m*; geschlossenes Netzwerk *n*
  f circuit *m* bouclé
  r замкнутая цепь *f*

  * **closed cycle → 1779**

1778 **closed LAN**
  d geschlossenes lokales Netz *n*
  f réseau *m* local fermé
  r закрытая локальная сеть *f*

1779 **closed loop; closed cycle**
  d geschlossene Schleife *f*; geschlossener Wirkungskreis *m*
  f boucle *f* fermée; cycle *m* fermé
  r замкнутый контур *m*; замкнутый цикл *m*

1780 **closed user group; GUP**
  d geschlossene Benutzergruppe *f*; geschlossene Teilnehmerbetriebsklasse *f*
  f groupe *m* d'utilisateurs fermé
  r замкнутая группа *f* потребителей

1781 **close scanning**
  d Feinabtastung *f*
  f balayage *m* à haute définition
  r точное сканирование *n*

1782 **close texture**
  d geschlossene Textur *f*; feste Textur
  f texture *f* fermée
  r замкнутая текстура *f*

1783 **close-up view**
  d Nahaufnahme *f*
  f vue *f* [de plan] rapprochée
  r крупномасштабный вид *m*; вид крупным планом

  * **closing → 1785**

  * **closing duration → 1784**

1784 **closing time; closing duration**
  d Schließungszeit *f*; Schließungsdauer *f*
  f temps *m* de fermeture; durée *f* de fermeture
  r длительность *f* замыкания

1785 **closure; closing**
  d Abschließung *f*; Abschließen *n*
  f fermeture *f*; clôture *f*
  r замыкание *n*; закрытие *n*

1786 **cluster**
  d Cluster *m*; Klumpen *m*
  f grappe *f*; bouquet *m*; cluster *m*
  r кластер *m*; блок *m*; группа *f*

1787 **cluster analysis**
  d Cluster-Analysis *f*
  f analyse *f* de cluster
  r кластерный анализ *m*

1788 **cluster controller**
  d Cluster-Kontroller *m*; Gruppensteuereinheit *f*
  f contrôleur *m* de grappe
  r групповой контроллер *m*

1789 **clustered access**
  d Gruppenzugriff *m*
  f accès *m* groupé
  r групповой доступ *m*

  * **clustered structure → 1791**

1790 **clustering; clusterization**
  d Gruppierung *f*; Clusterbildung *f*
  f [re]groupement *m*; groupage *m*; coalescence *f*
  r группирование *n*; кластеризация *f*

  * **clusterization → 1790**

1791 **cluster[iz]ed structure**
  d gruppierte Struktur *f*
  f structure *f* en grappes
  r кластерная структура *f*

1792 **cluster sample**
  d Klumpen[stich]probe *f*
  f échantillon *m* en grappes
  r гнездовая выборка *f*

  * **CM → 2240**

  * **CMYK → 2455**

1793 **CMYK color**
  d CMYK-Farbe *f*
  f couleur *f* CMYK
  r цвет *m* CMYK

  * **CNA → 1948**

  * **coalitionless game → 6224**

1794 **coarse scanning**
  d Grobabtastung *f*
  f balayage *m* approximatif
  r грубое сканирование *n*

1795 **coarse time**
  d Grobzeit *f*
  f temps *m* approximatif

r приблизительное время *n*

1796 coating; cladding; covering; plating
d Beschichtung *f*; Bedeckung *f*; Mantel *m*; Plattierung *f*
f revêtement *m*; enrobage *m*; gaine *f*; placage *m*
r покрытие *n*; оболочка *f*; наружный слой *m*

* **coax → 1797**

1797 coaxial cable; coax; concentric cable
d Koaxialkabel *n*; konzentrisches Kabel *n*
f câble *m* coaxial
r коаксиальный кабель *m*

1798 coaxial transmission line
d konzentrische Übertragungsleitung *f*; Koaxial-Übertragungsleitung *f*
f ligne *f* de transmission coaxiale
r коаксиальная линия *f* связи

* **co-channel → 8289**

1799 code
d Code *m*
f code *m*
r код *m*

1800 code auditor
d Programmauditor *m*; Programmrevisor *m*
f réviseur *m* de programme
r программный ревизор *m*

* **code block → 7390**

* **codec → 1820**

1801 code chain
d Codekette *f*
f chaîne *f* de code
r кодовая цепочка *f*; последовательность *f* кодов

1802 code character
d Codezeichen *n*
f caractère *m* de code; signe *m* de code; symbole *m* de code
r кодовый знак *m*

1803 code chart; code list
d Codeschema *n*; Codeliste *f*
f schéma *m* des codes; liste *f* des codes
r кодовая таблица *f*; список *m* кодов

* **code chip → 1814**

1804 code compression
d Codekompression *f*
f compression *f* de codes
r свёртывание *n* кодов; сжатие *n* кодов

* **code conversion → 9484**

1805 code converter; transcoder
d Code[um]wandler *m*; Codeumsetzer *m*; Transcoder *m*
f convertisseur *m* de code; transcodeur *m*
r преобразователь *m* кода; кодопреобразователь *m*

* **coded → 3394**

1806 coded address
d codierte Adresse *f*
f adresse *f* cod[ifi]ée
r закодированный адрес *m*; зашифрованный адрес

1807 coded aperture imaging
d codierte Apertur-Abbildung *f*
f imagination *f* d'ouverture codée
r кодированное изображение *n* отверстия

1808 coded binary file
d codierte Binärdatei *f*
f fichier *m* binaire codé
r кодированный двоичный файл *m*

1809 code division
d Codeteilung *f*; Codevielfach *n*
f répartition *f* en code; division *f* de code
r кодовое деление *n*

1810 code-division multiple access
d Mehrfachzugriff *m* durch Codeteilung
f accès *m* multiple par répartition en code
r коллективный доступ *m* кодовым делением

1811 coded matrix
d Codiermatrix *f*
f matrice *f* codifiée
r кодированная матрица *f*

1812 code[d] signal
d Codesignal *n*; codiertes Signal *n*
f signal *m* codé
r кодированный сигнал *m*

* **coded TV-signal → 1813**

1813 code[d] videosignal; code[d] TV-signal
d codiertes Videosignal *n*
f vidéosignal *m* codé
r кодированный видеосигнал *m*; кодированный телевизионный сигнал *m*

1814 code element; code chip; code unit
d Codeelement *n*
f élément *m* de code; codet *m*
r элемент *m* кода; кодовый элемент

1815 code-for-code compatibility
  d Codekompatibilität *f*
  f compatibilité *f* des codes
  r кодосовместимость *f*

  * **code-independent** → 1823

  * **code list** → 1803

  * **code multiplex** → 1816

1816 code multiplex[ing]
  d Codemultiplex *m*
  f multiplexage *m* par répartition en code
  r кодовое уплотнение *n*

1817 code optimization
  d Programmoptimisation *f*; Codeoptimierung *f*
  f optimisation *f* de programme
  r оптимизация *f* программы

1818 code page
  d Codeseite *f*
  f page *f* code
  r кодовая страница *f*

1819 coder; coding device; cipherer; encoder
  d Encoder *m*; Codierer *m*; Verschlüssler *m*
  f codeur *m*; dispositif *m* de codification; chiffreur *m*
  r шифратор *m*; кодирующее устройство *n*; кодер *m*

1820 coder-decoder; codec
  d Codierer-Decodierer *m*; Codec *m*; Kodek *m*
  f codeur-décodeur *m*; codec *m*
  r шифратор-дешифратор *m*; кодер-декодер *m*

1821 code reader; code scanner
  d Codeleser *m*
  f lecteur *m* de code
  r устройство *n* для считывания кода

1822 code receiver
  d Codeempfänger *m*
  f récepteur *m* de code
  r приёмник *m* кода

  * **code scanner** → 1821

  * **code signal** → 1812

1823 code-transparent; code-independent
  d codetransparent
  f transparent au code
  r кодово-прозрачный

1824 code-transparent transmission
  d codetransparente Übertragung *f*

  f transmission *f* transparente au code; transmission par code transparent
  r кодово-прозрачная передача *f*; передача прозрачным кодом

  * **code TV-signal** → 1813

  * **code unit** → 1814

  * **code videosignal** → 1813

1825 code word; character signal
  d Codewort *n*; Schriftzeichensignal *n*
  f mot *m* de code; signal *m* de caractère
  r кодовое слово *n*

1826 coding; encoding
  d Codieren *n*; Verschlüsseln *n*; Codierung *f*; Chiffrieren *n*
  f codage *m*; codification *f*
  r кодирование *n*

  * **coding device** → 1819

1827 coding format
  d Codierformat *n*; Codier[ungs]blatt *n*
  f format *m* de codage
  r формат *m* кодирования

1828 coding law; encoding law
  d Codierungskennlinie *f*; Codierungsgesetz *n*
  f loi *f* de codage; loi de codification
  r формула *f* кодирования; кодовая характеристика *f*

1829 codirectional
  d kodirektional
  f codirectionnel
  r сонаправленный

1830 codirectional interface
  d kodirektionale Schnittstelle *f*
  f interface *f* codirectionnelle
  r сонаправленный интерфейс *m*

1831 coefficient; factor; rate
  d Koeffizient *m*; Faktor *m*
  f coefficient *m*; facteur *m*
  r коэффициент *m*; фактор *m*

1832 coefficient of acceleration; acceleration factor
  d Beschleunigungskoeffizient *m*
  f coefficient *m* d'accélération
  r коэффициент *m* ускорения

1833 coefficient of amplification; amplification factor; gain constant
  d Verstärkungskoeffizient *m*; Verstärkungsfaktor *m*

f coefficient *m* d'amplification; rapport *m*
d'amplification
r коэффициент *m* усиления

1834 coefficient of contraction
d Kontraktionskoeffizient *m*
f coefficient *m* de contraction
r коэффициент *m* сжатия

1835 coefficient of correction; correction factor
d Korrektionsfaktor *m*
f coefficient *m* de correction; facteur *m* de
correction
r поправочный коэффициент *m*;
коэффициент коррекции

1836 coefficient of excess
d Koeffizient *m* des Exzesses
f coefficient *m* d'excès
r коэффициент *m* эксцесса

* **coercion** → 1486

1837 coherence; coherency
d Kohärenz *f*
f cohérence *f*
r связанность *f*; когерентность *f*

1838 coherence of frequency
d Frequenzkohärenz *f*
f cohérence *f* de fréquence
r частотная когерентность *f*

1839 coherence of phase
d Phasenkohärenz *f*
f cohérence *f* de phase
r фазовая когерентность *f*

* **coherency** → 1837

1840 coherent processor
d kohärenter Prozessor *m*
f processeur *m* cohérent
r когерентный процессор *m*

1841 coherent signals
d kohärente Signale *npl*
f signaux *mpl* cohérents
r когерентные сигналы *mpl*

1842 coherent transmission
d kohärente Übertragung *f*
f transmission *f* cohérente
r когерентная передача *f*

1843 coincide *v*; match *v*
d koinzidieren; übereinstimmen
f coïncider
r совпадать

1844 coincidence; matching
d Koinzidenz *f*
f coïncidence *f*
r совпадение *n*

1845 coincidence error
d Koinzidenzfehler *m*
f erreur *f* de coïncidence
r погрешность *f* совпадения

* **coincidence gate** → 5675

1846 coincidental binding
d Koinzidenzbinde *f*
f association *f* par coïncidence
r объединительная связь *f*

* **cold boot** → 1847

* **cold link** → 2620

* **cold reboot** → 1847

1847 cold restart; cold [re]boot
d Kaltrestart *m*
f reprise *f* à froid; réamorçage *m* à froid
r холодный рестарт *m*

* **collaborative virtual environment** → 3048

1848 collate *v*
d vergleichen und sortieren
f collationner
r сопоставлять и упорядочивать

1849 collating sequence
d Sortierfolge *f*; Mischfolge *f*
f séquence *f* de collation
r последовательность *f* объединения;
сортирующая последовательность

* **collection** → 122

1850 collection
d Kollektion *f*; Sammlung *f*
f collection *f*
r коллекция *f*; набор *m*; комплект *m*

1851 collector
d Kollektor *m*
f collecteur *m*
r коллектор *m*

1852 collision
d Kollision *f*; Konfliktsituation *f*;
Zusammenstoß *m*
f collision *f*; situation *f* de conflit
r столкновение *n*; коллизия *f*; конфликтная
ситуация *f*

1853 collision avoidance; CA
 d Kollisionsverhinderung *f*
 f évitement *m* de collision
 r предотвращение *n* коллизии

1854 collision check
 d Kollisionsprüfung *f*
 f essai *m* de compatibilité; test *m* de compatibilité
 r проверка *f* на непротиворечивость; проверка на совместимость

1855 collision detection; CD
 d Kollisionserkennung *f*
 f détection *f* de collisions
 r обнаружение *n* конфликтов; детектирование *n* столкновений

1856 collision detection system
 d Kollisionsdetektion-System *n*
 f système *m* de détection de collisions
 r система *f* обнаруживания коллизий

1857 collision-free protocol
 d kollisionsfreies Protokoll *n*
 f protocole *m* sans collisions
 r протокол *m* без столкновений

1858 collision index procedure
 d Kollisionsindexverfahren *n*
 f méthode *f* d'indice de la collision
 r процедура *f* индекса столкновении

1859 collision probability
 d Kollisionswahrscheinlichkeit *f*
 f probabilité *f* de collisions
 r вероятность *f* столкновений

1860 collision resolution; CR
 d Kollisionsauflösung *f*
 f résolution *f* de collisions
 r разрешение *n* столкновений

1861 collision strategy
 d Kollisionsstrategie *f*
 f stratégie *f* de la collision
 r стратегия *f* коллизии

1862 colon
 (:)
 d Doppelpunkt *m*
 f caractère *m* deux points
 r двоеточие *n*

1863 color
 d Farbe *f*
 f couleur *f*
 r цвет *m*

 * **coloration → 1874**

 * **color circle → 1669**

1864 color code
 d Farbcode *m*
 f code *m* couleur
 r цветовой код *m*

1865 color code label
 d Farbcodiermarke *f*
 f étiquette *f* de code couleur
 r метка *f* цветового кода

1866 color code table
 d Farb[en]tabelle *f*
 f table *f* de code couleur
 r таблица *f* цветовых кодов

1867 color coding
 d farbige Kennzeichnung *f*; Farbcodierung *f*
 f repérage *m* coloré; codage *m* de couleurs
 r цветная маркировка *f*

1868 color cube
 d Farbwürfel
 f cube *m* en couleur
 r цветной куб *m*

1869 color data
 d Farbdaten *pl*
 f données *fpl* de couleur
 r цветовые данные *pl*

1870 color depth; pixel depth
 (number of bits of color information per pixel)
 d Farbtiefe *f*; Pixeltiefe *f*
 f profondeur *f* de couleur
 r глубина *f* цвета; разрядность *f* атрибутов пикселов

1871 color display; color monitor; color screen
 d Farbdisplay *n*; Farbbildschirm *m*; Farbmonitor *m*
 f écran *m* en couleurs; écran couleur; afficheur *m* en couleurs
 r цветной дисплей *m*; монитор *m* цветного изображения

1872 color graphics adapter; CGA
 d Farbgrafik-Bildschirmadapter *m*
 f adaptateur *m* de graphique en couleurs
 r адаптер *m* цветной графики

 * **coloring → 1874**

1873 coloring problem; problem of coloration
 d Färbungsproblem *n*
 f problème *m* de coloriage
 r задача *f* раскраски; задача о раскрашивании

1874 **color[iz]ation; coloring**
   d Färbung *f*, Kolorierung *f*
   f coloriage *m*; coloration *f*
   r раскраска *f*; раскрашивание *n*

1875 **color laser printer**
   d Farblaserdrucker *m*
   f imprimante *f* à laser couleur
   r цветной лазерный принтер *m*

1876 **color management software**
   d Farbverwaltungssoftware *f*
   f logiciel *m* de traitement de couleurs
   r программное обеспечение *n* для
      управления цветов

1877 **color manager**
   d Farbenmanager *m*
   f gestionnaire *m* de couleurs
   r менажер *m* цветов

   *   **color monitor** → 1871

   *   **color plotter** → 5937

1878 **color printer**
   d Farbdrucker *m*
   f imprimante *f* en couleurs
   r цветной принтер *m*

   *   **color print** → 1879

1879 **color print[ing]**
   d Farbendruck *m*
   f impression *f* en couleurs; impression couleur;
      impression polychrome
   r цветная печать *f*; многокрасочная печать

1880 **color scanner**
   d Farbscanner *m*
   f scanner *m* en couleurs
   r цветной сканер *m*

   *   **color screen** → 1871

1881 **color separation**
   d Farbauszug *m*
   f séparation *f* en couleurs
   r разделение *n* цветов

1882 **color video printer**
   d Color-Video-Drucker *m*
   f imprimante *f* vidéo en couleurs
   r цветной видеопринтер *m*

   *   **color wheel** → 1669

1883 **column**
   d Spalte *f*

   f colonne *f*
   r колонка *f*; столбец *m*; графа *f*

1884 **column-binary code; Chinese binary code**
   d binärer Spaltencode *m*; spaltenbinärer
      Code *m*
   f code *m* binaire de colonne; code colonne
      binaire
   r поколонный двоичный код *m*; двоичный
      код столбца

1885 **column decoder**
   d Kolonnendecoder *m*
   f décodeur *m* de colonne
   r поколонный дешифратор *m*

1886 **column heading; column title**
   d Spaltentitel *m*
   f en-tête *f* de colonne; titre *m* de colonne
   r колонтитул *m*; заголовок *m* колонки

1887 **column image**
   d Spaltenbild *n*
   f image *f* de colonne
   r изображение *n* колонки

1888 **column pattern**
   d Spaltenraster *m*
   f rastre *m* de colonne
   r растр *m* колонки

   *   **column pitch** → 1889

1889 **column spacing; column pitch**
   d Spaltenvorschub *m*; Spaltenschritt *m*;
      Spaltenabstand *m*
   f écart *m* des colonnes
   r интервал *m* между колонками;
      расстояние *n* между столбцами

   *   **column sum** → 9039

   *   **column title** → 1886

1890 **column width**
   d Spaltenbreite *f*
   f largeur *f* de colonne
   r ширина *f* колонки

1891 **combination**
   d Kombination *f*
   f combinaison *f*
   r комбинация *f*; сочетание *n*

1892 **combinational circuit; combinatorial
      circuit**
   d kombinatorische Schaltung *f*; Schaltnetz *n*
   f circuit *m* combinatoire
   r комбинационная схема *f*

1893 **combinational logic**
d Verknüpfungslogik *f*
f logique *f* combinatoire
r комбинационная логика *f*

* **combinatorial circuit** → **1892**

1894 **combine** *v*
d kombinieren
f combiner
r комбинировать

* **combined head** → **7679**

1895 **combiner**
d Kombinator *m*; Übersetzer *m*
f combinateur *m*
r групповой переключатель *m*;
комбинирующее устройство *n*

1896 **combo box**
d Kombinationsfeld *n*
f zone *f* de liste [déroulante]; boîte *f* combinée
r комбинированное окно *n*

1897 **comma**
d Komma *n*
f virgule *f*
r запятая *f*

* **command** → **4944**

1898 **command alias**
d Aliasname *m* des Befehls
f pseudonom *m* de commande
r псевдоимя *n* команды

1899 **command buffer; instruction buffer;**
instruction register
d Befehlspufferspeicher *m*;
Auftragspufferspeicher *m*; Befehlspuffer *m*;
Befehlspufferregister *n*;
Befehls[code]register *n*
f tampon *m* de commande; tampon
d'instruction; registre *m* d'instruction
r командный буфер *m*; буферный регистр *m*
команд; буфер команд; регистр [текущей]
инструкции

1900 **command button**
d Befehlsschaltfläche *f*
f bouton *m* de commande
r кнопка *f* команды

1901 **command control block**
d Befehlssteuereinheit *f*
f bloc *m* de commande
r блок *m* управления выборкой команд

1902 **command-driven interface**

d befehlsgesteuerte Schnittstelle *f*
f interface *f* à déclenchement par commande
r интерфейс *m* командного типа

1903 **command history**
d Chronologie *f* der Befehle
f historique *m* de commandes
r хронология *f* команд

1904 **command key**
d Befehlstaste *f*
f clé *f* de commande
r клавиша *f* команды

* **command language** → **5168**

* **command message** → **2272**

1905 **command mode**
d Kommandomodus *m*; Befehlsbetriebsart *f*;
Befehlsmodus *m*
f mode *m* de commande; mode d'ordre
r режим *m* [по]командного управления;
командный режим

1906 **command prefix**
d Befehlspräfix *n*
f préfixe *m* de commande
r префикс *m* команды

1907 **command prompt**
d Befehlsanzeige *f*
f invite *f* de commande
r подсказка *f* команды

1908 **command-rich interface**
d Schnittstelle *f* mit erweitertem Befehlssatz
f interface *f* à jeu de commandes étendu
r интерфейс *m* с расширенным набором
команд

1909 **command script; script**
d Skript *m*
f script *m*
r скрипт *m*; программа *f* на макроязыке;
сценарий *m*

* **command terminator** → **1910**

1910 **command terminator [symbol]**
d Befehlsendezeichen *n*
f terminateur *m* de commande
r оконечный символ *m* команды

1911 **command window**
d Befehlsfenster *n*
f fenêtre *f* de commande
r окно *n* команды

1912 **command word; verb**
d Befehlswort *n*

f mot *m* de commande
r слово *n* команды

1913 comma representation form
d Kommadarstellungsform *f*
f forme *f* de représentation de virgule
r форма *f* представления [чисел] с запятой

1914 comment
d Kommentar *m*; Erläuterung *f*
f commentaire *m*
r комментарий *m*

* comment *v* → 424

1915 comment statement
d Kommentaranweisung *f*
f opérateur *m* commentaire
r оператор *m* комментария

1916 commercial Internet exchange; CIX
(a pact between network providers that allows
them to do accounting for commercial traffic)
d Internet-Handelsaustausch *m*;
Austauschknoten *m* von Internet-Providern
f échange *m* commercial d'Internet
r коммерческий Интернет-обмен *m*

* commit → 1917

1917 commit[ment]
(a transaction)
d Verpflichtung *f*
f validation *f*
r фиксация *f*

1918 common
d gemeinsam
f commun
r общий

1919 common bus; unified bus; global bus
d gemeinsamer Bus *m*; Globalbus *m*; globaler
Bus
f bus *m* commun; bus global
r общая шина *f*

1920 common carrier
d gemeinsamer Träger *m*; Netzträger *m*
f porteur *m* commun; porteur uniforme
r стандартный носитель *m*

1921 common carrier frequency
d gemeinschaftliche Trägerfrequenz *f*
f fréquence *f* porteuse commune
r общая несущая частота *f*

1922 common channel
d gemeinsamer Zeichenkanal *m*
f canal *m* commun

r общий канал *m*

1923 common channel signaling
d Zeichengabe *f* mit gemeinsamem
Zeichenkanal; Zentralkanalzeichengabe *f*
f signalisation *f* par canal commun
r передача *f* сигналов общим каналом

1924 common client interface; CCI
d gemeinsame Client-Schnittstelle *f*
f interface *f* utilisateur standardisée
r общеклиентский интерфейс *m*; интерфейс
CCI

1925 common communication interface
d gemeinsame Kommunikationsschnittstelle *f*;
gemeinsamer Übertragungsanschluss *m*
f interface *f* de communication commune
r общий интерфейс *m* связи

1926 common data format; CDF
d gemeinsames Datenformat *n*
f format *m* de données communes
r формат *m* общих данных

1927 common gateway interface; CGI
(a Web server scripting standard)
d Programmierschnittstelle *f* zwischen
WWW-Server und Programmen
f interface *f* CGI; standard *m* CGI
r общий шлюзовый интерфейс *m*;
интерфейс CGI

1928 common hardware
d Kleinteile *mpl*; Verschleißersatzteile *mpl*
f petites pièces *fpl* de rechange
r мелкие запасные части *fpl* компьютера

1929 common input
d gemeinsame Eingabe *f*
f entrée *f* commune
r общий вход *m*

* common interface → 4187

1930 common transmission path
d gemeinsamer Übertragungsweg *m*
f voie *f* commune de transmission
r общий путь *m* передачи

1931 common user access; CUA
d allgemeiner Benutzeranschluss *m*;
allgemeiner Anwenderzugriff *m*
f interface *f* commune d'accès
r общий пользовательский доступ *m*

1932 communicate *v*
d übermitteln; verkehren
f communiquer
r связывать; сообщать; передавать

* communication → 1955

1933 communication access method
d Kommunikationszugriffsmethode *f*
f méthode *f* d'accès de communication
r коммуникационный метод *m* доступа

1934 communication area
d Kommunikationsbereich *m*;
Verständigungsbereich *m*
f région *f* de communication
r область *f* коммуникации

1935 communication break
d Kommunikationsunterbrechung *f*
f interruption *f* de communication
r прерывание *n* связи

1936 communication buffer
d Kommunikationspuffer *m*
f tampon *m* de communication
r коммуникационный буфер *m*

1937 communication cable
d Nachrichtenkabel *n*
f câble *m* de communication
r коммуникационный кабель *m*;
сообщительный кабель

1938 communication channel; link
d Kommunikationskanal *m*;
Übertragungsstrecke *f*;
Kommunikationsleitung *f*;
Nachrichten[übertragungs]kanal *m*
f canal *m* de communication; ligne *f* de
communication; voie *f* de communication
r коммуникационный канал *m*; канал связи

**1939 communication control; transmission
control**
d Übermittlungskontrolle *f*;
Übertragungssteuerung *f*
f contrôle *m* de communication; contrôle de
transmission
r коммуникационное управление *n*;
управление передачей

**1940 communication control character;
transmission control character**
d Übertragungssteuerzeichen *n*
f caractère *m* de commande de communication
r символ *m* управления передачей

1941 communication delay; transmission delay
d Übertragungsverzögerung *f*
f délai *m* de communication; délai de
transmission; retard *m* de transit
r задержка *f* на передачу [данных]; задержка
в цепи передачи

1942 communication flag
d Kommunikationsflag *n*;
Verständigungsanzeige *f*
f flag *m* de communication
r флаг *m* коммуникации

1943 communication form
d Kommunikationsform *f*
f forme *f* de communication
r вид *m* связи

1944 communication interface
d Kommunikationsschnittstelle *f*
f interface *f* de communication
r коммуникационный интерфейс *m*

1945 communication laser
d Fernmeldelaser *m*
f laser *m* de communication
r лазер *m* связи

1946 communication medium
d Kommunikationsmedium *n*
f médium *m* de communication; milieu *m* de
communication
r средство *n* связи

**1947 communication network;
telecommunication network**
d Nachrichtennetz *n*; Fernmeldenetz *n*;
Kommunikationsnetz *n*;
Telekommunikationsnetz *n*
f réseau *m* de [télé]communication
r сеть *f* связи; [теле]коммуникационная сеть

**1948 communication network architecture;
CNA**
d Netzwerkarchitektur *f* für Kommunikation
f architecture *f* de réseau de communication
r архитектура *f* коммуникационной сети

1949 communication network availability
d Verfügbarkeit *f* eines Nachrichtennetzes
f disponibilité *f* d'un réseau de communication
r готовность *f* сети связи к эксплуатации

1950 communication operating system
d Betriebssystem *n* für Kommunikation
f système *m* opérationnel de communication
r коммуникационная операционная
система *f*

**1951 communication outlet; communication
socket**
d Kommunikationssteckdose *f*;
Fernmeldeanschlussdose *f*
f sortie *f* de communication
r входная точка *f* в коммуникационной сети

1952 communication parameters
d Kommunikationsparameter *mpl*;

Fernmeldeparameter *mpl*
f paramètres *mpl* de communication
r параметры *mpl* коммуникации

1953 communication processor
d Kommunikationsprozessor *m*;
Datenübertragungsprozessor *m*
f processeur *m* de communications
r связной процессор *m*; коммуникационный
процессор

* **communication protocol** → **1957**

* **communication queue** → **5777**

1954 communication routing
d Kommunikationslenkung *f*
f routage *m* de communication
r маршрутизация *f* связи

1955 communication[s]
d Kommunikation *f*; Nachrichtenverkehr *m*;
Informationstausch *m*
f communication *f*
r коммуникация *f*; связь *f*

* **communication socket** → **1951**

* **communication software** → **1959**

1956 communications port; COM port
(a plug-in socket in back of the computer for
hooking up devices such as modems)
d Kommunikationsport *m*;
Kommunikationsstelle *f*
f port *m* de communication
r коммуникационный порт *m*

**1957 communication[s] protocol; transmission
protocol; transfer protocol**
d Kommunikationsprotokoll *n*;
Übertragungsprotokoll *n*
f protocole *m* de communication; protocole de
transmission; protocole de transfert
r протокол *m* связи; протокол передачи

1958 communications server
d Kommunikationsserver *m*;
Kommunikationsstation *f*
f serveur *m* de communication
r коммуникационный сервер *m*

1959 communication[s] software
d Kommunikationssoftware *f*
f logiciel *m* de communication
r коммуникационное программное
обеспечение *n*

* **commutant** → **1534**

* **commutation** → **9086**

* **commutator** → **9081**

1960 compact
d kompakt
f compact
r компактный

* **compact disk** → **1964**

1961 compact disk-digital audio; CD-DA
d Digital-Audio-Video-Disk *f*
f disque *m* compact audionumérique
r компакт-диск *m* с цифровой звукозаписью

**1962 compact disk erasable; CD-E; erasable
optical disk**
d löschbare Bildplatte *f*; löschbare optische
Speicherplatte *f*
f disque *m* compact effaçable; disque optique
effaçable
r стираемый компакт-диск *m*; стираемый
оптический диск

**1963 compact disk extended architecture;
CD-XA**
d erweiterte CD-Architektur *f*
f format *m* étendu de CD-ROM
r расширенная архитектура *f* компакт-диска

* **compact disk-interactive** → **4998**

**1964 compact disk [read-only memory];
CD[-ROM]; optical disk; laser disk**
d Kompaktplatte *f*; Bildplatte *f* [für optische
Speicherung]; optische Disk *f*;
Laserbildplatte *f*; CD[-ROM]
f disque *m* compact; compact *m*; mémoire *f* à
disque compact; cédérom *m*; disque optique;
disque laser; CD-[ROM]
r компактный диск *m*; компакт-диск *m*;
постоянная память *f* на компактном диске;
оптический диск *m*; лазерный диск

1965 compact disk recordable; CD-R
d beschreibbare Bildplatte *f*
f disc *m* compact enregistrable
r записываемый компакт-диск *m*

1966 compact disk rewritable; CD-RW
d wiederbeschreibbare Bildplatte *f*
f disque *m* compact réinscriptible
r перезаписываемый компакт-диск *m*

1967 compact disk write once; CD-WO
d Bildplatte *f* mit einmaligem Schreiben
f mémoire *f* optique inscriptible une seule fois
r компакт-диск *m* с однократной записью;
неперезаписываемый компакт-диск

* compaction → 2040

1968 compactness
d Kompaktheit *f*
f compacité *f*
r компактность *f*; плотность *f*; сжатость *f*

1969 compact presentation
d kompakte Darstellung *f*
f présentation *f* compacte
r компактное представление *n*; сжатое
представление

* companion processor → 2307

* comparator → 1970

**1970 comparator [circuit]; comparer;
comparison unit**
d Komparator *m*; Vergleicher *m*;
Vergleichseinheit *f*
f comparateur *m*; unité *f* de comparaison
r компаратор *m*; блок *m* сравнения;
устройство *n* сравнения

1971 comparator signal
d Vergleichermeldung *f*
f signal *m* de comparateur
r сигнал *m* компаратора

1972 compare *v*
d vergleichen
f comparer
r сравнивать

1973 compare operator; comparison operator
d Vergleichsoperator *m*
f opérateur *m* de comparaison
r оператор *m* сравнения

* comparer → 1970

1974 comparison
d Vergleich *m*; Komparation *f*; Vergleichung *f*
f comparaison *f*
r сравнение *n*

1975 comparison element
d Vergleichsstelle *f*; Vergleichselement *n*
f élément *m* de comparaison
r элемент *m* сравнения

**1976 comparison method; method of
comparison**
d Vergleichsmethode *f*
f méthode *f* de comparaison
r метод *m* сравнения

* comparison operator → 1973

* comparison unit → 1970

1977 compatibility
d Verträglichkeit *f*; Kompatibilität *f*;
Gleichbehandlung *f*
f compatibilité *f*
r совместимость *f*; совместность *f*

1978 compatibility condition
d Verträglichkeitsbedingung *f*
f condition *f* de compatibilité
r условие *n* совместимости; условие
совместности

1979 compatible; consistent
d kompatibel; verträglich; vereinbar;
konsistent; widerspruchsfrei
f compatible; consistant
r совместимый

**1980 compatible family of computers; family of
compatibles**
d Familie *f* von kompatiblen Rechnern;
kompatible Rechnerfamilie *f*
f famille *f* de machines compatibles
r ряд *m* совместимых машин

1981 compensate *v*
d kompensieren
f compenser
r компенсировать

1982 compensated character recognition
d kompensierte Zeichenerkennung *f*
f reconnaissance *f* de caractères compensée
r компенсационное распознавание *n* знаков

* compensating circuit → 1984

* compensation → 796

1983 compensation line
d Kompensationsleitung *f*; Ausgleichsleitung *f*
f ligne *f* de compensation; équilibreur *m*
r балансная линия *f*

**1984 compensator; compensating circuit;
equalizer; equalizing network**
d Kompensator *m*; Entzerrer *m*;
Ausgleichsglied *n*; Entzerrerschaltung *f*
f compensateur *m*; égalisateur *m*
r компенсатор *m*; компенсирующая схема *f*;
корректирущая цепь *f*; выравнитель *m*

1985 competition; concurrency
d Wettbewerb *m*; Konkurrenz *f*
f compétition *f*; concurrence *f*
r состязание *n*; конкуренция *f*

1986 competition principle
d Konkurrenzprinzip n
f principe m de concurrence
r стратегия f конкуренции

1987 compilation; compiling
d Kompilieren n; Kompilierung f
f compilation f
r компиляция f

1988 compile v
d kompilieren
f compiler
r компилировать

* **compiled language** → 1990

1989 compiler; compiling program
d Compiler m; Kompilierer m
f compilateur m
r компилятор m

1990 compiler language; compiled language
d Compilersprache f, Kompilierersprache f
f langage m compilé
r компилируемый язык m

* **compiling** → 1987

* **compiling program** → 1989

1991 complement
d Komplement n; Ergänzung f
f complément m
r дополнение n

1992 complementary
d komplementär; Komplement[är]-; ergänzend;
   Ergänzungs-
f complémentaire
r дополнительный

1993 complementary channel pair
d komplementäres Kanalpaar n
f paire f de canaux complémentaire
r дополнительная пара f каналов

1994 complementary event
d komplementäres Ereignis n
f événement m complémentaire
r противоположное событие n

1995 complementary operator
d komplementärer Operator m
f opérateur m complémentaire
r оператор m инвертирования

1996 complementary output
d Komplementausgang m
f sortie f de complément

r выход m дополнительного кода

1997 complementation; complementing
d Komplementbildung f; Komplementierung f
f établissement m de complément;
   complémentation f
r образование n дополнения; дополнение n

1998 complement code
d Komplementcode m
f code m de complément; code complémentaire
r дополнительный код m

1999 complementer; complementing circuit
d Komplementwerk n; Komplementschaltung f
f complémenteur m; circuit m de
   complémentation
r схема f образования дополнения; схема
   формирования дополнительного кода

* **complementing** → 1997

* **complementing circuit** → 1999

2000 complementing flip-flop
d Komplementflipflop m
f basculeur m complémenteur
r триггер m со счётным входом

2001 complementing input
d Zähleingang m
f entrée f de [signal de] basculement
r счётный вход m

* **complement on n** → 7582

* **complement on n-1** → 7583

* **complement on nine** → 6161

* **complement on one** → 6429

* **complement on two** → 9593

2002 complete v
d vollenden; beendigen; vervollständigen;
   ergänzen; fertigstellen
f achever; compléter
r завершать; пополнять; дополнять

2003 complete adj
d vollständig
f complet
r полный; завершённый

2004 complete carry; carry over
d vollständiger Übertrag m
f report m définitif; report complet; retenue f
   complète
r полный перенос m

2005 **complete code**
  d vollständiger Code *m*
  f code *m* complet
  r полный код *m*

2006 **completed transaction**
  d abgeschlossene Transaktion *f*
  f transaction *f* complète
  r завершённая транзакция *f*

2007 **complete flag; completion flag; terminate flag; terminator**
  d Beendigungskennzeichen *n*;
  Beendigungsanzeiger *m*; Beendigungsflag *n*
  f flag *m* d'achèvement; flag de terminaison
  r признак *m* окончания; флаг *m* завершения

2008 **complete instruction set computer; CISC**
  d Rechner *m* mit komplexem Befehlssatz;
  Computer *m* mit erweiterten Befehlsvorrat;
  CISC
  f ordinateur *m* à jeu d'instructions complet
  r компьютер *m* с полным набором команд

2009 **completeness**
  d Vollständigkeit *f*
  f complétude *f*; achèvement *m*
  r полнота *f*; завершённость *f*

2010 **complete packet sequence**
  d vollständige Paketfolge *f*
  f séquence *f* de paquets complets
  r последовательность *f* полных пакетов

2011 **completion**
  d Vervollständigung *f*; Komplettierung *f*
  f complétion *f*; complètement *m*
  r пополнение *n*

  * **completion** → 9269

2012 **completion code**
  d Beendigungscode *m*; Abschlusscode *m*
  abschließender Code *m*
  f code *m* achevant; code de terminaison; code d'achèvement
  r код *m* завершения; код окончания

  * **completion flag** → 2007

2013 **complex**
  d Komplex *m*
  f complexe *m*
  r комплекс *m*

2014 **complex** *adj*
  d komplex
  f complexe
  r комплексный; сложный; составной

2015 **complexity**
  d Komplexität *f*; Kompliziertheit *f*
  f complexité *f*
  r сложность *f*

2016 **complex network**
  d komplexes Netz *n*
  f réseau *m* complexe
  r комплексная сеть *f*

2017 **complex transfer**
  d komplexe Übertragung *f*
  f transfert *m* complexe
  r комплексная передача *f*

2018 **complex transfer function**
  d komplexe Übertragungsfunktion *f*
  f fonction *f* de transfert complexe
  r комплексная передаточная функция *f*

2019 **component**
  d Komponente *f*
  f composant *m*; composante *f*
  r компонент *m*; компонента *f*; [схемный] элемент *m*; составляющая *f*

2020 **component parts; componentry**
  d Bauteile *mpl*; Bauelemente *npl*
  f parties *fpl* constitutives; éléments *mpl* constitutifs
  r комплектующие изделия *npl*

  * **componentry** → 2020

  * **COM port** → 1956

2021 **compose** *v*; **set** *v*
  d zusammenstellen; anfertigen
  f composer; instaurer
  r составлять; формировать

  * **composer** → 2086

2022 **composite; compound**
  d zusammengesetzt; Komposit-
  f composé; composite
  r составной; сложный

2023 **composite data stream**
  d zusammengesetzter Datenstrom *m*
  f flot *m* de données composé
  r комбинированный поток *m* данных

2024 **composite lead; composite line**
  d Vielfachleitung *f*
  f conducteur *m* composite; ligne *f* composite
  r многоканальная магистраль *f*

  * **composite line** → 2024

2025 **composite printer**
  d Komposit-Drucker *m*
  f imprimante *f* composite
  r комбинированный принтер *m*

2026 **composite texture**
  d zusammengesetzte Textur *f*
  f texture *f* composite
  r составная текстура *f*; комбинированная текстура

2027 **composite video signal**
  d zusammengesetztes Videosignal *n*; Composite-Videosignal *n*
  f signal *m* vidéo composite
  r составной видеосигнал *m*

2028 **composition**
  d Zusammensetzung *f*; Komposition *f*
  f composition *f*
  r композиция *f*; состав *m*

  * **composition → 9294**

  * **composition computer → 2086**

  * **compound → 2022**

2029 **compound character**
  d Doppelzeichen *n*
  f caractère *m* composé
  r составной символ *m*

2030 **compound document**
  d Compound-Dokument *n*
  f document *m* composite
  r составной документ *n*

2031 **compound network**
  d Verbundnetz *n*
  f réseau *m* composé
  r сложная сеть *f*; многокомпонентная сеть

  * **comprehensive facilities → 265**

2032 **comprehensive keyboard**
  d Volltastatur *f*
  f clavier *m* compréhensif
  r полнонаборная клавиатура *f*

2033 **compress** *v*; **zip** *v*
  d kompressieren; komprimieren; verdichten
  f comprimer; compresser
  r сжать; уплотнять; компрессировать

2034 **compressed digital video**
  d kompressiertes Digitalvideo *n*
  f vidéo *m* numérique compressé
  r уплотнённое цифровое видео *n*

2035 **compressed drive**
  d kompressiertes Laufwerk *n*
  f lecteur *m* compressé
  r уплотнённый накопитель *m*; сжатый накопитель

2036 **compressed file; packed file; squeezed file; crunched file**
  d kompressierte Datei *f*; gepackte Datei
  f fichier *m* compressé; fichier paqueté
  r упакованный файл *m*; сжатый файл; сплющенный файл

2037 **compressed SLIP; CSLIP**
  d kompressiertes SLIP-Protokoll *n*
  f protocole *m* SLIP compressé
  r компрессированный межсетевой протокол *m* для последовательной линии; компрессированный протокол SLIP

2038 **compressibility**
  d Kompressibilität *f*; Zusammendrückbarkeit *f*
  f compressibilité *f*
  r сжимаемость *f*

2039 **compressing program; condensing program; cruncher**
  d Verdichtungsprogramm *n*
  f programme *m* de compression; logiciel *m* de compression
  r программа *f* уплотнения; программа сжатия

2040 **compression; compaction; condensation**
  d Kompression *f*; Kompaktion *f*; Komprimierung *f*
  f compression *f*; compaction *f*
  r сжатие *n*; уплотнение *n*; компрессия *f*

2041 **compression algorithm**
  d Kompression-Algorithmus *m*
  f algorithme *m* de compaction
  r алгоритм *m* сжатия; алгоритм компрессирования

2042 **compression coefficient; compression ratio** (of image coding)
  d Kompression-Verhältnis *n*; Kompressionsfaktor *m*
  f coefficient *m* de compression; taux *m* de compression
  r коэффициент *m* компрессии

2043 **compression options**
  d Kompression-Optionen *fpl*
  f options *fpl* de compression
  r опции *fpl* уплотнения

  * **compression ratio → 2042**

* **compunication** → 9233

* **computability** → 1344

2044 computable; calculable
  d berechenbar
  f calculable
  r вычислимый

* **computation** → 1347

2045 computational
  d Rechen-
  f computationnel
  r вычислительный

2046 computational cost
  d Rechnungskosten *npl*
  f dépenses *fpl* de [ressources de] calcul
  r затраты *fpl* вычислительных ресурсов

**2047 computational error; computing error;
      error of computation; miscalculation**
  d Rechnungsfehler *m*; Rechenfehler *m*
  f erreur *f* de calcul
  r вычислительная ошибка *f*; ошибка в
      вычислении; арифметическая ошибка

2048 computational linguistics
  d linguistische Datenverarbeitung *f*;
      Computerlinguistik *f*
  f linguistique *f* de calcul
  r вычислительная лингвистика *f*

2049 computational scheme
  d Rechenschema *n*
  f schéma *m* de calcul; plan *m* de calcul
  r схема *f* вычислений

* **computation centre** → 2068

* **compute** *v* → 1345

2050 computer
  d Computer *m*; Rechner *m*
  f ordinateur *m*
  r компьютер *m*

**2051 computer-aided; computer-assisted;
      computerized**
  d rechnergestützt; rechnerunterstützt;
      computergestützt
  f [assisté] par ordinateur
  r автоматизированный; компьютерный;
      компьютеризированный

2052 computer[-aided] animation
  d computerunterstützte Animation *f*
  f animatique *f*; dessin *m* animé par ordinateur
  r анимация *f* с помощью компьютера;

компьютерная анимация

2053 computer-aided design; CAD
  d computerunterstütztes Design *n*; CAD
  f conception *f* assistée par ordinateur; CAO
  r проектирование *n* с помощью компьютера;
      система *f* автоматизации проектирования;
      САПР

2054 computer-aided dodging
  d computergestützter Kontrastausgleich *m*
  f masquage *m* assisté par ordinateur
  r автоматизированное получение *n*
      комбинированного изображения

* **computer-aided drafting** → 2055

**2055 computer-aided drawing; computer-aided
      drafting**
  d computerunterstütztes Zeichnen *n*
  f dessin *m* assisté par ordinateur; DAO
  r черчение *n* с помощью компьютера

**2056 computer-aided engineering;
      computer-assisted engineering**
  d computergestütztes Engineering *n*;
      rechnergestützte Produktanalyse *f*
  f ingénierie *f* assistée par ordinateur; IAO
  r автоматизация *f* инженерного труда

2057 computer-aided geometric design
  d computerunterstütztes Geometriedesign *n*
  f conception *f* géométrique assistée par
      ordinateur
  r геометрическое проектирование *n* с
      помощью компьютера

2058 computer-aided graphic arts
  d computerunterstützte Grafikkunst *f*
  f arts *mpl* graphiques assistés par ordinateur
  r рисование *n* с помощью компьютера

**2059 computer-aided manufacturing; CAM;
      computer-integrated manufacturing; CIM**
  d computerunterstützte Fertigung *f*; CAM
  f production *f* assistée par ordinateur; PAO;
      fabrication *f* assistée par ordinateur; FAO;
      productique *m*
  r автоматизированное производство *n* с
      применением компьютера

**2060 computer-aided publishing;
      computer-assisted publishing; CAP;
      electronic publishing**
  d computergestütztes Publizieren *n*;
      rechnergestütztes Publizieren
  f publication *f* assistée par ordinateur; PAO;
      éditique *f*
  r автоматизированное издательство *n*

2061 computer-aided quality assurance; CAQ
- *d* rechnergestützte Qualitätssicherung *f*;
  computerunterstützte Qualitätskontrolle *f*
- *f* assurance *f* qualité assistée par ordinateur
- *r* автоматизированное обеспечение *n*
  качества; автоматизированный
  технический контроль *m*

**2062 computer-aided software engineering;
CASE**
- *d* rechnerunterstützte Softwaretechnik *f*
- *f* technique *f* de programmation à l'aide
  d'ordinateur; génie *m* logiciel assisté par
  ordinateur
- *r* автоматизированное программирование *n*

**2063 computer-aided text processing;
computer-assisted text processing**
- *d* rechnergestützte Textverarbeitung *f*
- *f* traitement *m* de texte par ordinateur
- *r* компьютерная текстообработка *f*

2064 computer-animated film
- *d* vom Computer erzeugter Film *m*
- *f* film *m* animé par ordinateur
- *r* фильм *m*, оживлённый с помощью
  компьютера; компьютерный
  мультипликационный фильм

*   **computer-animation → 2052**

*   **computer-assisted → 2051**

2065 computer-assisted cartography
- *d* computergestützte Kartografie *f*
- *f* cartographie *f* par ordinateur
- *r* компьютерная картография *f*

2066 computer-assisted diagnostics
- *d* computergestützte Diagnostik *f*
- *f* diagnostic *m* assisté par ordinateur
- *r* автоматизированная диагностика *f*;
  компьютерная диагностика

*   **computer-assisted engineering → 2056**

*   **computer-assisted instruction → 2071**

*   **computer-assisted learning → 2071**

2067 computer[-assisted] music
- *d* rechnergestützte Musik *f*
- *f* musique *f* assistée par ordinateur;
  informatique *f* musicale
- *r* компьютерная музыка *f*

*   **computer-assisted publishing → 2060**

*   **computer-assisted text processing → 2063**

**2068 computer centre; computation centre;
computing centre**
- *d* Rechenzentrum *n*;
  Datenverarbeitungszentrum *n*
- *f* centre *m* de calcul
- *r* вычислительный центр *m*

2069 computer communication
- *d* Rechnerkommunikation *f*
- *f* communication *f* par ordinateur
- *r* компьютерная связь *f*

2070 computer composition
- *d* Rechnersatzverarbeitung *f*
- *f* composition *f* par ordinateur
- *r* компьютерный набор *m*

*   **computer crime → 2099**

**2071 computer education; computer-assisted
instruction; CAI; computer-assisted
learning; CAL**
- *d* computerunterstützter Unterricht *m*;
  Ausbildung *f* mittels Rechner;
  Rechnerausbildung *f*; rechnergestützter
  Unterricht
- *f* enseignement *m* assisté par ordinateur; EAO;
  formation *f* assistée par ordinateur
- *r* обучение *n* при помощи компьютера

2072 computer fraud
- *d* Computerschwindel *m*; Computergaunerei *f*;
  Computerbetrug *m*
- *f* utilisation *f* d'ordinateur frauduleuse
- *r* злоумышленное использование *n*
  компьютера

2073 computer-generated characters
- *d* durch Computer generierte Zeichen *npl*
- *f* caractères *mpl* générés par ordinateur
- *r* символы *mpl*, генерированные
  компьютером

2074 computer-generated color
- *d* durch Computer generierte Farbe *f*
- *f* couleur *f* générée par ordinateur
- *r* цвет *m*, генерированный компьютером

2075 computer-generated diffraction pattern
- *d* durch Computer generiertes
  Diffraktionsbild *n*
- *f* image *f* de diffraction générée par ordinateur
- *r* дифракционная картина *f*, генерированная
  компьютером

2076 computer-generated hologram
- *d* durch Computer generiertes Hologramm *n*
- *f* hologramme *m* généré par ordinateur
- *r* голограмма *f*, генерированная
  компьютером

2077 **computer-generated image; synthetic image**
    d durch Computer generiertes Bild *n*
    f image *f* générée par ordinateur; image synthétique; image de synthèse
    r изображение *n*, генерированное компьютером

2078 **computer-generated imagery**
    d durch Computer generierte Abbildung *f*
    f imagerie *f* générée par ordinateur
    r изображения npl, генерированные компьютером

2079 **computer graphics; infography**
    d Computergrafik *f*; Rechnergrafik *f*
    f infographie *f*; graphique *m* d'ordinateur
    r компьютерная графика *f*; машинная графика

2080 **computer graphics interface; CGI**
    (for printers and plotters)
    d Computergrafik-Schnittstelle *f*
    f interface *f* d'infographie
    r интерфейс *m* машинной графики; стандарт *m* CGI

2081 **computer graphics metafile**
    d Computergrafik-Metadatei *f*
    f métafichier *m* d'infographie
    r графический метафайл *m*

2082 **computer graphics workstation; graphics [work]station**
    d grafische Arbeitsstation *f*
    f station *f* de travail graphique
    r графическая рабочая станция *f*

2083 **computer illustration program; illustration program; paint program**
    d Malprogramm *n*
    f programme *m* d'illustrations
    r программа *f* для иллюстраций

2084 **computer-independent language**
    d rechnerunabhängige Sprache *f*
    f langage *m* indépendant d'ordinateur
    r машиннонезависимый язык *m*

   * **computer-integrated manufacturing** → 2059

2085 **computer[-integrated] telephony**
    d rechnerintegrierte Telefonie *f*; computerintegrierte Telefonie
    f téléphonie *f* assistée par ordinateur
    r компьютерная телефония *f*; КТ

   * **computerized** → 2051

   * **computerized dictionary** → 690

2086 **computerized documentation system; composition computer; composer**
    d rechnergestütztes Dokumentationssystem *n*; Drucksatzaufbereitungsrechner *m*
    f système *m* de documentation par ordinateur; ordinateur *m* de composition
    r компьютер *m* для подготовки печатных документов

2087 **computerized document preparation**
    d rechnergesteuerte Erstellung *f* von Dokumenten
    f préparation *f* de documents par ordinateur
    r автоматизированная подготовка *f* документов

   * **computerized workstation** → 3339

2088 **computer jargon; computer slang; e-slang; cybercrud**
    d Computerjargon *m*
    f terme *m* argotique
    r компьютерный жаргон *m*; киберлслэнг *m*; компьютерный техноязык *m*

2089 **computer linguistics**
    d algorithmische Linguistik *f*
    f linguistique *f* d'ordinateur
    r компьютерная лингвистика *f*

2090 **computer literacy**
    d Computeralphabetismus *m*
    f instruction *f* informatique
    r компьютерная грамотность *f*

   * **computer mail** → 3330

2091 **computer-message system**
    d rechnergestütztes Nachrichtenverwaltungssystem *n*
    f système *m* de messages par ordinateur
    r система *f* компьютерных сообщений

2092 **computer micrographics**
    d rechnergestützte Mikrografik *f*
    f micrographique *m* d'ordinateur
    r автоматизированная micrographика *f*

   * **computer music** → 2067

2093 **computer network**
    d Rechnernetz[werk] *n*; Informatiknetz *n*
    f réseau *m* d'ordinateurs; réseau informatique
    r компьютерная сеть *f*

2094 **computer on a chip; one-chip computer**
    d Einchip-Computer *m*

f ordinateur *m* à une puce; ordinateur à puce
unique

r однокристаллический компьютер *m*

**2095 computer-oriented language;
machine-oriented language**
d rechnerorientierte Sprache *f*;
maschinenorientierte Sprache
f langage *m* orienté par ordinateur; langage
orienté [vers] l'ordinateur
r машинноориентированный язык *m*

2096 computer phobia
d Computerphobie *f*
f phobie *f* d'ordinateurs
r машинобоязнь *f*

2097 computer photocomposition
d elektronischer Lichtsatz *m*
f photocomposition *f* par ordinateur
r компьютерный фотонабор *m*

2098 computer pulse code
d Rechnerimpulscode *m*
f code *m* d'impulsion d'ordinateur
r импульсный код *m* компьютера

2099 computer[-related] crime
d Computerkriminalität *f*;
Computermissbrauch *m*
f délit *m* informatique
r компьютерное преступление *n*

2100 computer remote control
d Rechnerfernsteuerung *f*
f télécommande *f* par ordinateur
r дистанционное управление *n*
компьютером

2101 computer science
d Computerwissenschaft *f*
f science *f* d'ordinateur
r теория *f* и практика *f* вычислительных
машин и систем

2102 computer security
d Computersicherheit *f*
f sécurité *f* d'ordinateur
r защита *f* компьютера; безопасность *f*
компьютера

2103 computer simulation
d Computersimulation *f*
f simulation *f* [assistée] par ordinateur
r компьютерное моделирование *n*

* **computer slang** → 2088

* **computer telephony** → 2085

* **computer time** → 5551

2104 computer tomography; CT
d Computertomografie *f*
f tomographie *f* par ordinateur
r компьютерная томография *f*

2105 computer trespasser
d Computerpirat *m*
f pirate *m* d'ordinateur
r компьютерный "взломщик" *m*

2106 computer virus; virus
(a program)
d Computervirus *n*; Virus *n*
f virus *m* [d'ordinateur]; code *m* viral
r компьютерный вирус *m*

2107 computer vision
d Computersehen *n*; maschinelles Sehen *n*
f vision *f* d'ordinateur; visionnique *f*
r компьютерное зрение *n*

* **computing** → 1347

* **computing centre** → 2068

2108 computing check; computing test
d Rechenkontrolle *f*; Rechenprobe *f*
f contrôle *m* de calcul; preuve *f* de calcul
r контроль *m* вычислений; проверка *f*
вычислений

* **computing error** → 2047

* **computing result** → 6630

* **computing rule** → 1346

2109 computing table
d Rechentafel *f*
f tableau *m* de calcul
r счётная таблица *f*; вычислительная
таблица

* **computing test** → 2108

2110 computing time
d Rechenzeit *f*
f temps *m* de calcul
r время *n* вычисления

2111 concatenated data; chained data
d verkettete Daten *pl*; gekettete Daten
f données *fpl* en chaîne
r объединённые данные *pl*; сцеплённые
данные

2112 concatenation
d Konkatenation *f*

f concaténation f
r сцепление n; сочленение n; конкатенация f

2113 concatenation number
d Verkettungsnummer f
f numéro m d'enchaînement
r номер m цепочки; номер сцепления

2114 concealed wiring
d Unterputzverlegung f
f câblage m caché
r скрытый монтаж m

2115 concentration
d Konzentration f
f concentration f
r концентрация f; сосредоточение n

* **concentrator** → 1321

2116 concentrator network
d Konzentratornetz n
f réseau m concentrateur
r сеть-концентратор f

* **concentric cable** → 1797

2117 concept
d Begriff m; Konzeption f; Konzept n
f concept m
r понятие n; представление n; концепция f

2118 conceptually organized glossary
d begrifflich strukturiertes Fachwörterglossar n
f glossaire m organisé conceptuellement
r концептуально организованный глоссарий m

2119 conceptual model
d Konzeptualmodell n; konzeptionelles Modell n
f modèle m conceptuel
r концептуальная модель f

2120 concordance; accordance
d Übereinstimmung f
f concordance f
r согласованность f

* **concurrency** → 1985

2121 concurrent; simultaneous
d gleichzeitig; simultan
f concurrent; simultané
r одновременный; совместный

2122 concurrent channel maintenance
d simultanes Kanalunterhalten n
f maintenance f concurrente de canaux
r поддержка f звукового канала с блочным уплотнением

* **concurrent computer** → 6775

2123 concurrent mode
d Gleichzeitigkeitsarbeitsweise f
f mode m concurrent
r режим m параллельной работы

* **condensation** → 2040

* **condensing program** → 2039

2124 condition
d Kondition f; Bedingung f
f condition f
r условие n

* **conditional branch** → 2125

2125 conditional branch[ing]; conditional jump
d bedingter Zweig m; bedingte Verzweigung f; bedingter Sprung m
f branche f conditionnelle; branchement m conditionnel; saut m conditionnel
r условный переход m

* **conditional jump** → 2125

2126 conditional selection; conjugate selection
d bedingte Wegesuche f; weitspannende Wegesuche; konjugierte Wahl f
f sélection f conditionnelle; sélection conjuguée
r условный выбор m

2127 conditional transfer
d bedingte Übertragung f
f transfert m conditionnel
r условная передача f

* **condition code** → 8884

2128 conductance; conduction
d Konduktanz f; Leitwert m; Leitfähigkeit f
f conductance f; conductibilité f active
r [активная] проводимость f

2129 conducting paper
d leitfähiges Papier n
f papier m conducteur
r проводящая бумага f

* **conduction** → 2128

2130 conductive coupling
d konduktive Kopplung f
f couplage m conducteur
r кондуктивная связь f

2131 **conductive ink**
    d leitfähige Tinte *f*
    f encre *f* conductrice
    r проводящее чернило *n*

2132 **conductive strip**
    d Streifenleiter *m*
    f bande *f* conducteuse
    r печатный проводник *m*

2133 **conductivity; electrical conductance**
    d Leitfähigkeit *f*
    f conductivité *f*; conductance *f* électrique
    r электрическая проводимость *f*

2134 **conductor**
    d Leiter *m*
    f conducteur *m*
    r проводник *m*; провод *m*

2135 **conference**
    d Konferenz *f*
    f conférence *f*
    r конференция *f*

    * **conference call** → 2136

2136 **conference call [connection]; conference connection**
    d Konferenzverbindung *f*;
        Konferenzgespräch *n*;
        Rundgesprächverbindung *f*
    f communication *f* collective [pour conférence]
    r конферентная сообщительная связь *f*

2137 **conference circuit**
    d Konferenzschaltung *f*
    f circuit *m* de conférence; ligne *f* de conférence
    r конферентная линия *f*

    * **conference connection** → 2136

2138 **conference studio**
    d Konferenzstudio *n*
    f studio *m* de conférence
    r конферентная студия *f*

    * **conferencing** → 9232

2139 **confidence**
    d Konfidenz *f*; Vertrauen *n*
    f confidence *f*; confiance *f*
    r доверие *n*

2140 **confidence coefficient**
    d Konfidenzkoeffizient *m*;
        Vertrauenskoeffizient *m*
    f coefficient *m* de confiance
    r коэффициент *m* доверия

2141 **confidence interval**
    d Konfidenzintervall *n*; Vertrauensintervall *n*
    f intervalle *m* de confiance
    r доверительный интервал *m*

2142 **confidence level; confidential level**
    d Konfidenzpegel *m*; Konfidenzniveau *n*
    f niveau *m* de confidence; seuil *m* de confiance
    r доверительный уровень *m*; уровень доверия

2143 **confidence region**
    d Konfidenzbereich *m*; Vertrauensbereich *m*
    f région *f* de confiance; domaine *m* de confiance
    r доверительная область *f*

2144 **confidential**
    d geheim; konfidentiell
    f secret; confidentiel
    r секретный; доверительный; конфиденциальный

2145 **confidential data**
    d geheime Daten *pl*
    f données *fpl* secrètes
    r секретные данные *pl*; конфиденциальные данные

    * **confidential level** → 2142

2146 **configurability**
    d Konfigurierbarkeit *f*
    f configurabilité *f*
    r конфигурируемость *f*

2147 **configuration**
    d Konfiguration *f*
    f configuration *f*
    r конфигурация *f*

2148 **configuration file**
    d Konfigurationsdatei *f*
    f fichier *m* de configuration
    r конфигурационный файл *m*

2149 **configuration level**
    d Konfigurationsniveau *n*
    f niveau *m* de configuration
    r уровень *m* конфигурации

2150 **configuration profile**
    d Konfigurationsprofil *n*
    f profil *m* de configuration
    r профиль *m* конфигурации

2151 **configurator**
    d Konfigurator *m*
    f configurateur *m*
    r конфигуратор *m*

2152 configure *v*
　d konfigurieren; ausformen
　f configurer
　r конфигурировать; образовать

2153 configuring
　d Konfigurationsauswahl *f*
　f choix *m* de configuration
　r выбор *m* конфигурации

2154 confirm *v*; **validate** *v*
　d bestätigen
　f confirmer; valider
　r подтверждать

2155 confirmation; certification
　　(of the access right)
　d Bestätigung *f*
　f confirmation *f*; certification *f*
　r подтверждение *n*; удостоверение *n*

2156 confirmation report; positive delivery
　　notification
　d Bestätigungsansage *f*
　f avis *m* de livraison
　r обозначение *n* подтверждения

2157 confirmative answer
　d bestätigende Antwort *f*
　f réponse *f* affirmative
　r утвердительный ответ *m*

2158 conflict; contention
　d Konflikt *m*
　f conflit *m*
　r конфликт *m*

2159 conflicting event
　d gegenteiliges Ereignis *n*
　f événement *m* conflit
　r конфликтное событие *n*

2160 conflict resolution
　d Konfliktauflösung *f*
　f résolution *f* des conflits
　r разрешение *n* конфликтов

2161 conformability; similitude; similarity
　d Ähnlichkeit *f*
　f conformité *f*; similitude *f*; similarité *f*;
　　ressemblance *f*
　r подобность *f*; соответствие *n*; сходство *n*

2162 congestion
　d Stauung *f*
　f embouteillage *m*; encombrement *m*
　r затор *m*; пробка *f*; тесное место *n*

　* **congestion** → **6653**

2163 conjugate
　d konjugiert
　f conjugué
　r сопряжённый

2164 conjugate marking
　d weitspannende Markierung *f*
　f marquage *m* conjugué
　r сопряжённая маркировка *f*

　* **conjugate selection** → **2126**

2165 conjugation frequency
　d Verknüpfungsfrequenz *f*
　f fréquence *f* conjuguée
　r сопряжённая частота *f*

2166 conjunction; logical multiply; logical
　　product; ANDing
　d Konjunktion *f*; logische Multiplikation *f*;
　　logisches Produkt *n*; UND-Verknüpfung *f*
　f conjonction *f*; multiplication *f* logique;
　　produit *m* logique
　r конъюнкция *f*; логическое умножение *n*;
　　логическое произведение *n*

2167 conjunctive query
　d konjunktive Anfrage *f*
　f interrogation *f* conjonctive
　r конъюнктивный запрос *m*

2168 connected
　d verbunden; zusammenhängend
　f connexe; connecté
　r связной; связанный; соединённый

2169 connected graph
　d zusammenhängender Graph *m*; verbundener
　　Graph
　f graphe *m* connexe
　r связный граф *m*

2170 connected in Internet; online
　d verbunden; in der Leitung
　f enli; liau
　r связанный

　* **connectedness** → **2179**

　* **connecting area** → **2207**

2171 connecting cable
　d Verbindungskabel *n*
　f câble *m* de connexion
　r соединительный кабель *m*

2172 connecting line; connection line
　d Verbindungsleitung *f*
　f ligne *f* de connexion

   r соединительная линия *f*

2173 connecting pad; connection pad; pad
   d Kontaktstelle *f*; Kontaktierungsinsel *f*;
      Anschlussinsel *f*; Anschlusskontaktstelle *f*
   f galette *f* à contacts; plot *m* [de boîtier]
   r контактная площадка *f*

2174 connecting sequence
   d Einstellablauf *m*
   f séquence *f* de connexion
   r последовательность *f* подключения

2175 connection; tag
   d Konnektion *f*; Anschluss *m*
   f connexion *f*; raccordement *m*
   r [при]соединение *n*; связывание *n*;
      включение *n*; подключение *n*

   * **connection capacity** → **1422**

2176 connection cleardown; connection release;
      disconnect[ion]; call disconnect
   d Verbindungsabbau *m*;
      Verbindungsauslösung *f*
   f déconnexion *f* [d'appel]; effaçage *m* de
      connexion
   r разъединение *n* связи

2177 connectionless
   d verbindungslos
   f sans connexion
   r не требующий соединения

   * **connection line** → **2172**

   * **connection pad** → **2173**

   * **connection release** → **2176**

2178 connective
   d Satzband *n*; Anschluss *m*;
      Verbindungsglied *n*; Koppler *m*
   f copule *f*; pièce-raccord *m*
   r связка *f*; соединительный элемент *m*

2179 connectivity; connectedness
   d Konnektivität *f*; Verbundenheit *f*
   f connectivité *f*; connexité *f*; connectabilité *f*
   r связываемость *f*; связность *f*

   * **connectivity software** → **5824**

2180 connector; coupler; coupling element
   d Konnektor *m*; Koppler *m*;
      Verbindungsstecker *m*; Verbinder *m*
   f connecteur *m*; raccord *m*; coupleur *m*;
      serre-fil *m*
   r конъектор *m*; соединитель *m*;
      [штепсельный] разъём *m*; штеккер *m*

2181 connect time
   d Verbundzeit *f*
   f temps *m* de connexion
   r время *n* соединения; продолжительность *f*
      сеанса связи

2182 connect *v* to printer
   d zum Drucker verbinden
   f raccorder à l'imprimante
   r подключать к принтеру

2183 connect *v* user
   d Benutzer einschalten
   f connecter un utilisateur
   r соединять пользователя

   * **consecutive** → **8414**

   * **consecutive access** → **8407**

2184 consecutive writing
   d fortlaufendes Schreiben *n*
   f écriture *f* consécutive
   r последовательная запись *f*

2185 consequence
   d Folgerung *f*; Konsequenz *f*
   f conséquence *f*
   r следствие *n*

   * **consequent** → **9018**

2186 conservation
   d Einsparung *f*
   f conservation *f*
   r сохранение *n*

2187 conservation of energy; energy
      conservation
   d Energieeinsparung *f*
   f conservation *f* d'énergie
   r сохранение *n* энергии

2188 conserved information
   d konservierte Information *f*
   f information *f* conservée
   r законсервированная информация *f*

2189 considerable information
   d bedeutende Information *f*
   f information *f* considérable
   r значительная по объёму информация *f*

2190 consistency
   d Konsistenz *f*; Widerspruchsfreiheit *f*
   f consistance *f*
   r совместимость *f*; непротиворечивость *f*

   * **consistent** → **1979**

2191 **console**
d Pult *n*; Konsole *f*; Bedienungskonsole *f*;
Bedienungsplatz *m*
f console *f*; pupitre *m*
r консоль *f*; пульт *m*

2192 **console processor; service processor**
d Bedienprozessor *m*
f processeur *m* de pupitre
r сервисный процессор *m*

2193 **consolidation**
d Konsolidation *f*; Verfestigung *f*
f consolidation *f*
r консолидация *f*; укрупнение *n*

* **constant** → 3864

2194 **constant**
d Konstante *f*
f constante *f*
r константа *f*; постоянная *f*

2195 **constant area**
d Bereich *m* der Konstanten
f domaine *m* de constantes
r область *f* констант

2196 **constant offset indexed addressing**
d indizierte Konstantenversatzadressierung *f*
f adressage *m* indexé au déplacement constant
r индексная адресация *f* со смещением на
константу

2197 **constant of integration; integration
constant**
d Integrationskonstante *f*
f constante *f* d'intégration
r интеграционная константа *f*; постоянная *f*
интегрирования

* **constant-ratio code** → 3464

2198 **constant-spread playback**
d Wiedergabe *f* mit gleichbleibender
Geschwindigkeit
f reproduction *f* à vitesse constante
r воспроизведение *n* с постоянной
скоростью

2199 **constant sum game**
d Konstantsummenspiel *n*
f jeu *m* de somme constante
r игра *f* с постоянной суммой

2200 **constituent**
d Konstituente *f*; Schaltelement *n*
f constituant *m*
r конституэнт *m*

2201 **constituents of unity**
d Einsfunktion *f*
f constituants *mpl* d'unité
r конституэнты *mpl* единицы

2202 **constituents of zero**
d Nullfunktion *f*
f constituants *mpl* de zéro
r конституэнты *mpl* ноля

* **constraint** → 8027

2203 **construction**
d Konstruktion *f*
f construction *f*
r конструкция *f*

* **construction of a cable** → 1322

2204 **consultation**
d Konsultation *f*
f consultation *f*
r консультация *f*

* **consumer** → 9714

2205 **consumption**
d Verbrauch *m*
f consommation *f*
r потребление *n*; расход *m*

2206 **contact**
d Kontakt *m*
f contact *m*; plot *m*
r контакт *m*

2207 **contact area; contact surface; connecting
area**
d Kontaktfläche *f*; Kontaktierungsfläche *f*
f surface *f* de contact
r контактная поверхность *f*

2208 **contact arrangement; contact
configuration**
d Kontaktanordnung *f*
f arrangement *m* de contacts
r упорядочение *n* контактов;
конфигурирование *n* контактов

* **contact configuration** → 2208

2209 **contacting**
d Kontaktierung *f*
f formation *f* des contacts
r контактирование *n*

2210 **contactless**
d kontaktlos
f sans contact
r бесконтактный

* **contact surface** → 2207

2211 container
  d Container *m*; Behälter *m*
  f conteneur *m*; container *m*; contenant *m*;
  réceptacle *m*
  r контейнер *m*; сосуд *m*

2212 contamination
  d Kontamination *f*
  f contamination *f*
  r загрязнение *n*; заражение *n*

* **content** → 2217

* **content-addressable memory** → 590

* **content-addressable processor** → 592

2213 contention
  d Kontention *f*
  f contention *f*
  r состязание *n*; соревнование *n*

* **contention** → 2158

2214 contention bus
  d Konkurrenzbus *m*
  f bus *m* à l'encombrement
  r широковещательная шина *f*

2215 contention mode
  d konkurrienender Betrieb *m*
  f mode *m* à conflits
  r режим *m* конкуренции

2216 content provider
  d Inhaltsanbieter *m*
  f fournisseur *m* de contenu; fournisseur de
  données
  r поставщик *m* данных

2217 content[s]
  d Inhalt *m*
  f contenu *m*
  r содержание *n*; вместимость *f*

2218 contents supervision
  d Inhaltsüberwachung *f*
  f supervision *f* du contenu
  r контроль *m* содержания

2219 context
  d Kontext *m*; Zusammenhang *m*
  f contexte *m*
  r контекст *m*

2220 context-free
  d kontextfrei; kontextunabhängig
  f sans contexte; à contexte libre

  r бесконтекстный; контекстно-независимый

2221 context-free grammar
  d kontextfreie Grammatik *f*;
  kontextunabhängige Grammatik
  f grammaire *f* sans contexte; grammaire à
  contexte libre
  r бесконтекстная грамматика *f*;
  контекстно-свободная грамматика

2222 context-free language
  d kontextfreie Sprache *f*
  f langage *m* sans contexte
  r контекстно-свободный язык *m*;
  бесконтекстный язык

* **context help** → 2225

* **context menu** → 2227

2223 context-sensitive; contextual
  d kontextabhängig; textabhängig;
  kontextempfindlich
  f contexte-sensitif; à contexte; contextuel
  r контекстно-зависимый; контекстный;
  контекстуальный

2224 context-sensitive grammar
  d kontextempfindliche Grammatik *f*;
  kontextabhängige Grammatik
  f grammaire *f* contexte-sensitive; grammaire à
  contexte
  r контекстно-зависимая грамматика *f*;
  контекстная грамматика

2225 context[-sensitive] help
  d Kontexthilfe *f*
  f aide *f* contextuelle
  r контекстная помощь *f*

2226 context-sensitive language
  d Kontextsprache *f*; Kontextsensitivsprache *f*
  f langage *m* contexte[-sensitif]
  r контекстно-зависимый язык *m*;
  контекстный язык

2227 context[-sensitive] menu; shortcut menu
  d Kontextmenü *n*
  f menu *m* contextuel
  r контекстно-зависимое меню *n*;
  контекстное меню; сокращённое меню

2228 context-switching instruction
  d Kontextumschaltbefehl *m*;
  Programmzustandswechselbefehl *m*
  f instruction *f* de commutation de contexte
  r инструкция *f* замены информации о
  состоянии программы

* **contextual** → 2223

2229 **contextual declaration**
  d textabhängige Vereinbarung *f*
  f déclaration *f* contextuelle
  r контекстное определение *n*

2230 **contiguity**
  d Benachbarheit *f*
  f contiguïté *f*
  r смежность *f*

2231 **contiguous [data] item**
  d abhängiges Datenwort *n*
  f mot *m* contigu [de données]
  r смежный элемент *m*; зависимый элемент
     [данных]

  * **contiguous item** → **2231**

2232 **contingency plan; disaster plan;
     emergency plan; backup plan**
  d Sicherungsplan *m*
  f plan *m* de sauvegarde
  r план *m* сохранения (информации)

2233 **continuation**
  d Fortsetzung *f*
  f continuation *f*; suite *f*
  r продолжение *n*; следование *n*

2234 **continuation address**
  d Fortsetzungsadresse *f*
  f adresse *f* de continuation
  r адрес *m* продолжения; адрес следования

2235 **continuation coding**
  d Fortsetzungvorschrift *f*;
     Fortsetzungscodierung *f*
  f codage *m* de continuation
  r кодирование *n* продолжения

2236 **continuation line**
  d Folgezeile *f*; Fortsetzungszeile *f*
  f ligne *f* de continuation; ligne de suit
  r строка *f* продолжения

2237 **continuity**
  d Stetigkeit *f*; Kontinuität *f*
  f continuité *f*
  r непрерывность *f*

2238 **continuous**
  d stetig; kontinuierlich; Dauer-
  f continu; continuel
  r продолжительный; непрерывный

2239 **continuous[-form] paper; continuous
     stationery**
  d Endlospapier *n*; Endlosformular *n*;
     Rollenpapier *n*
  f papier *m* en continu; papier sans fin;

formulaire *m* sans fin
  r бесконечная бумага *f*; рулонная бумага;
     принтерная бумага

2240 **continuous mail; CM**
  d kontinuierliche Meldung *f*
  f poste *f* continue
  r беспрерывная почта *f*

  * **continuous mode** → **2241**

2241 **continuous [operation] mode**
  d kontinuierlicher Modus *m*; kontinuierliche
     Betriebsweise *f*
  f mode *m* continu
  r непрерывный режим *m* [работы]

  * **continuous paper** → **2239**

2242 **continuous random variable**
  d stetige Zufallsgröße *f*
  f variable *f* aléatoire continue
  r непрерывная случайная величина *f*

2243 **continuous request**
  d Daueranforderung *f*
  f interrogation *f* continue
  r непрерывный запрос *m*

  * **continuous stationery** → **2239**

2244 **continuous tone; contone; full tone**
  d kontinuierlicher Ton *m*
  f tonalité *f* continue; ton *m* continu
  r непрерывный оттенок *m*; безрастровый
     тон *m*

2245 **continuous-tone image; contone image**
     (all photographs and illustrations having a
     range of shades)
  d Bild *n* mit kontinuierlichem Ton
  f image *f* en dégradé; image à tonalité continue;
     image à ton continu
  r псевдополутоновое изображение *n*;
     безрастровое изображение; многотоновое
     изображение

2246 **continuous variable**
  d stetige Variable *f*; kontinuierliche Variable *f*
  f variable *f* continue
  r непрерывная переменная *f*

2247 **continuous zooming**
  d kontinuierliches Zoomen *n*
  f zoom *m* continu
  r непрерывное масштабирование *n*

  * **contone** → **2244**

2248 **contone chip**
  d Contone-Chip *m*

f chip *m* d'image en ton continu
r микросхема *f* формирования безрастрового
изображения

* **contone image** → 2245

2249 contour; outline
d Kontur *m*; Umriss *m*
f contour *m*
r контур *m*; очертание *n*

2250 contracted
d verengt; zusammenzogen; kontrahiert
f contracté
r свёрнутый; сжатый

2251 contracted graph
d kontrahierter Graph *m*
f graphe *m* contracté
r сжатый граф *m*

* **contraction** → 8529

2252 contradiction
d Widerspruch *m*; Kontradiktion *f*
f contradiction *f*
r противоречие *n*

2253 contradirectional
d kontradirektional
f contradirectionnel
r контранаправленный

2254 contradirectional interface
d kontradirektionale Schnittstelle *f*
f interface *f* contradirectionnelle
r контранаправленный интерфейс *m*

2255 contrast
d Kontrast *m*
f contraste *m*
r контраст *m*

2256 contrast image; hard image
d Kontrastbild *n*; hartes Bild *n*
f image *f* contraste
r контрастное изображение *n*

2257 contrast signal
d Kontrastsignal *n*
f signal *m* de contraste
r сигнал *m* контрастности

2258 contrast threshold
d Kontrastschwelle *f*
f seuil *m* de contraste
r порог *m* контраста

2259 control
d Kontrolle *f*; Steuerung *f*

f contrôle *m*; commande *f*
r управление *n*

2260 control *v*
d kontrollieren
f contrôler
r контролировать

2261 control action
d Regelwirkung *f*; Steuereinwirkung *f*
f action *f* de contrôle; action de commande
r управляющее воздействие *n*;
регулирующее воздействие

* **control ball** → 8109

2262 control bus
d Regelbus *m*; Steuerbus *m*
f bus *m* de contrôle; bus de commande
r управляющая шина *f*; шина управления

2263 control character
d Steuerzeichen *n*
f caractère *m* de contrôle
r управляющий символ *m*

2264 control circuit; steering circuit
d Steuerschaltung *f*
f circuit *m* de commande; circuit de contrôle;
circuit de réglage
r управляющая схема *f*; схема управления;
цепь *f* регулирования

* **control clock** → 2265

2265 control clock [pulse]
d Steuertakt *m*
f impulsion *f* d'horloge de commande; horloge *f*
de contrôle
r управляющий тактовый импульс *m*

2266 control code
d Steuercode *m*
f code *m* de commande
r управляющий код *m*

* **control data** → 2268

* **control device** → 2270

2267 control-flow computer
d Steuerflussrechner *m*
f ordinateur *m* à flux d'instructions
r компьютер *m*, управляемый потоком
команд

2268 control information; control data
d Steuerdaten *pl*; Steuerinformation *f*
f données *fpl* de commande; information *f* de
commande
r управляющие данные *pl*

*   **control input** → 2269

2269 control input [signal]
  d Steuereingang *m*; Steuereingangsignal *n*
  f signal *m* d'entrée de commande; entrée *f* de
    commande
  r управляющий вход *m*; управляющий
    входной сигнал *m*

2270 controller; control device; control unit
  d Kontroller *m*; Leitwerk *n*; Steuereinheit *f*;
    Regler *m*; Steuergerät *n*
  f contrôleur *m*; unité *f* de contrôle; unité de
    commande
  r контроллер *m*; управляющее устройство *n*

2271 controller card
  d Kontrollerkarte *f*
  f carte *f* contrôleur
  r карта *f* контроллера; плата *f* контроллера

*   **control memory** → 5819

2272 control message; command message
  d Steuernachricht *f*; Befehlsnachricht *f*
  f message *m* de commande
  r управляющее сообщение *n*; командное
    сообщение

2273 control panel
  d Controllfeld *n*; Bedienfeld *n*
  f panneau *m* de configuration; tableau *m* de
    commande
  r управляющая панель *f*; панель управления;
    окно *n* настройки компьютера

*   **control pulse** → 3175

2274 control register
  d Steuerregister *n*
  f registre *m* de commandes
  r управляющий регистр *m*

2275 control sequence
  d Steuerfolge *f*
  f séquence *f* de contrôle; séquence de
    commande
  r управляющая последовательность *f*

*   **control store** → 5819

2276 control theory
  d Regelungstheorie *f*; Kontrolltheorie *f*
  f théorie *f* de réglage; théorie de contrôle
  r теория *f* [автоматического] управления

*   **control total** → 1659

*   **control unit** → 2270

2277 convention
  d Konvention *f*; Vereinbarung *f*
  f convention *f*
  r соглашение *n*

2278 conventional
  d konventionell; herkömmlich
  f conventionnel
  r конвенциональный; обычный

2279 conventional component
  d konventionelles Bauelement *n*
  f composant *m* conventionnel
  r стандартный элемент *m*; стандартный
    компонент *m*

2280 conventional memory; base memory
  d konventioneller Speicher *m*
  f mémoire *f* conventionnelle
  r конвенциональная память *f*

2281 convergence
  d Konvergenz *f*
  f convergence *f*
  r сходимость *f*

2282 convergence algorithm
  d Konvergenzalgorithmus *m*
  f algorithme *m* convergent
  r сходящийся алгоритм *m*

*   **convergence of an algorithm** → 292

*   **conversation** → 1645

2283 conversational; interactive; online
  d interaktiv; Dialog-
  f conversationnel; de dialogue; interactif
  r диалоговый; интерактивный

2284 conversational communication
  d Dialogverkehr *m*
  f communication *f* à dialogue
  r передача *f* в режиме диалога

2285 conversational language; dialog language
  d Dialogsprache *f*
  f langage *m* conversationnel; langage de
    dialogue
  r диалоговый язык *m*

*   **conversational mode** → 2850

*   **converse** *v* → 1644

2286 conversion; converting
  d Konvertierung *f*; Umformung *f*;
    Umwandlung *f*
  f conversion *f*
  r преобразование *n*; превращение *n*;
    конверсия *f*

2287 conversion code
d Konvertierungscode *m*; Umwandlungscode *m*
f code *m* de conversion
r код *m* преобразования

2288 conversion coefficient
d Konvertierungskoeffizient *m*
f coefficient *m* de conversion
r коэффициент *m* конверсии

2289 conversion prohibition
d Konvertierungsverbot *n*
f interdiction *f* de conversion
r запрещение *n* преобразования

2290 conversion table
d Konvertierungstabelle *f*; Umsteigetabelle *f*;
   Umrechnungstabelle *f*; Umsetzungstabelle *f*
f table *f* de conversion
r таблица *f* преобразования; переводная
   таблица

2291 convert *v*
d konvertieren; umwandeln; verwandeln
f convertir
r преобразовывать; превращать

2292 converter
d Konverter *m*; Umwandler *m*; Wandler *m*
f convertisseur *m*; traducteur *m*
r конвертер *m*; преобразователь *m*

* **converting** → 2286

2293 convert *v* **to black-and-white**
d in Schwarzweiß konvertieren
f convertir en noir et blanc
r преобразовать в чёрно-белый

* **conveyance** → 9534

2294 convolution
d Faltung *f*; Konvolution *f*
f convolution *f*
r свёртка *f*; свёртывание *n*

2295 convolution code
d Faltungscode *m*
f code *m* convolutif
r свёрточный код *m*

2296 convolution processor
d Faltungsprozessor *m*
f processeur *m* de convolution
r процессор *m* свёртки

2297 convolve *v*
d zusammenrollen
f plier; envelopper
r скручиваться; свёртывать[ся]; сплетать[ся]

2298 cookie
   (e-slang - small bits of data that a Web page
   asks a browser to store on a user's computer,
   either in RAM or on the hard drive)
d Cookie *n*; Keks *m*
f cookie *m*; fichier *m* de témoin; témoin *m*;
   message *m* de qualification d'audience
r куки *n*

2299 cookie filtering tool
d Cookie-Filtrierungshilfsmittel *n*
f outil *m* de filtrage de cookies
r средство *n* фильтрации куки

* **cooler** → 7575

2300 cooling
d Kühlung *f*
f refroidissement *m*
r охлаждение *n*

**2301 cooling fan; fan; ventilation unit;
        ventilator; blower**
d Kühl[luftge]bläse *f*; Kühlventilator *m*;
   Lüfter *m*; Luftkasten *m*
f ventilateur *m* [de refroidissement]
r вентилятор *m* [охлаждения]

2302 cooperative processing; reach-through
d Verbundverarbeitung *f*
f traitement *m* coopératif; intertraitement *m*;
   traitement multienvironnement
r совместная обработка *f*; коллективная
   обработка

2303 coordinate display
d Koordinatendisplay *n*
f affichage *m* de coordonnées
r координатный дисплей *m*

**2304 coordinated universal time; universal time
        coordinated; UTC; Greenwich meantime**
d koordinierte Weltzeit *f*; mittlere
   Greenwich-Zeit *f*
f temps *m* universel coordonné; heure *f* de
   Greenwich
r универсальное координированное время *n*
   (по Гринвичу)

* **coordinate store** → 5689

2305 coordination
d Koordinierung *f*
f coordination *f*
r согласование *n*; координация *f*

2306 copier; copy[ing] device
d Kopierer *m*; Copier *m*; Copiergerät *n*
f copieur *m*; appareil *m* à copier
r копирный аппарат *m*; копировальное
   устройство *n*

2307 coprocessor; companion processor
d Coprozessor *m*; Koprozessor *m*
f coprocesseur *m*
r сопроцессор *m*

* copy → 2311

2308 copy
d Kopie *f*; Exemplar *n*
f copie *f*; exemplaire *m*
r копия *f*; экземпляр *m*

2309 copy *v*
d kopieren; abschreiben
f reproduire; copier
r копировать

2310 copy check
d Copy-Prüfung *f*
f essai *m* de copie
r контроль *m* копирования

* copy device → 2306

2311 copy[ing]
d Kopieren *n*; Vervielfältigen *n*
f copiage *m*
r копирование *n*

* copying device → 2306

2312 copy protection
d Kopierschutz *m*
f protection *f* contre copiage
r защита *f* от копирования

2313 copy recipient; secondary recipient
d Empfänger *m* von Kopien
f destinataire *m* en copie
r получатель *m* копии; приёмник *m* копии

2314 copyright
d Autorrecht *n*; Urheberrecht *n*; Copyright *n*
f droit *m* d'auteur; droit d'exploitation;
copyright *m*
r авторское право *n*; копирайт *m*

2315 copyrighted software
d Copyrightsoftware *f*
f logiciel *m* protégé par le droit d'auteur
r программное обеспечение *n*, защищённое
авторским правом

2316 copy special
d Spezialkopie *f*
f copie *f* spéciale
r специальная копия *f*

2317 copy speed

2318 cordless mouse
d drahtlose Maus *f*
f souris *f* sans fil
r беспроводная мышь *f*

2319 core
d Kern *m*
f cœur *m*; tore *m*; âme *f*
r сердцевина *f*; сердечник *m*

2320 core language
d Grundsprache *f*
f langage *m* hôte
r базовый язык *m*

2321 core memory
d Kernspeicher *m*
f mémoire *f* à tores [magnétiques]
r ферритовая память *f*

2322 corporate communications
d Unternehmenkommunikation *f*
f communication *f* corporative
r фирменная связь *f*; фирменные
сообщения *npl*

2323 corporate database
d Firmendatenbasis *f*
f base *f* de données de firme
r база *f* данных фирмы

* corporate network → 5110

2324 correct *v*
d korrigieren
f corriger
r корректировать; исправлять

**2325 correcting circuit; corrective network;
building-out network**
d Korrekturnetzwerk *m*; Korrekturkreis *m*;
Korrekturschaltung *f*
f réseau *m* correcteur; circuit de correction
r корректирующая схема *f*; корректирующая
цепь *f*; корректирующий контур *m*

2326 correction
d Korrektion *f*; Korrektur *f*
f correction *f*
r поправка *f*; коррекция *f*; исправление *n*

* correction factor → 1835

* corrective network → 2325

2327 corrective signal
d Stellsignal *n*

d Kopiergeschwindigkeit *f*
f vitesse *f* de reproduction
r скорость *f* копирования

f signal *m* correcteur
r корректирующий сигнал *m*

2328 correct operation; error-free operation
d richtiges Arbeiten *n*; fehlerfreies Arbeiten
f fonctionnement *m* correct; fonctionnement
sans erreurs
r безошибочная работа *f*; правильная работа

2329 corrector
d Korrektor *m*
f correcteur *m*
r корректор *m*

2330 correlation
d Korrelation *f*
f corrélation *f*
r корреляция *f*; взаимная зависимость *f*

2331 correspond *v*
d entsprechen
f correspondre
r соответствовать

2332 correspondence
(exchange of messages)
d Korrespondenz *f*
f correspondance *f*
r корреспонденция *f*

2333 correspondence; matching
d Korrespondenz *f*; Entsprechung *f*;
Übereinstimmung *f*
f correspondance *f*
r соответствие *n*

2334 correspondence code
d Korrespondenzcode *m*
f code *m* de correspondance
r код *m* корреспонденции

2335 corrupt *v*; damage *v*; destroy *v*
d zerstören; beschädigen
f endommager; corrompre; détruire
r разрушать; повреждать; портить

2336 corruption
d Korruption *f*; Verstümmelung *f*
f corruption *f*
r разрушение *n*

2337 cost/efficiency ratio
d Kosten-Effektivität-Verhältnis *n*
f rapport *m* prix-efficacité
r соотношение *n* стоимость-эффект

2338 count
d Zählung *f*; Zählen *n*; Zählvorgang *m*

f calcul *m*; compte *m*; comptage *m*
r счёт *m*; подсчёт *m*

* count → 9189

2339 count *v*
d abzählen; zählen
f compter; calculer
r считать; подсчитать

**2340 countability; denumerability;
enumerability**
d Abzählbarkeit *f*; Aufzählbarkeit *f*
f dénombrabilité *f*; énumérabilité *f*
r перечислимость *f*; счётность *f*

2341 countable; denumerable; enumerable
d abzählbar; numerierbar
f dénombrable; comptant
r счётный

* **count base** → 7581

2342 countdown
d Rückwärtszählen *n*
f compte *m* régressif; comptage *m* en arrière
r обратный счёт *m*; счёт в обратном
направлении

2343 counter
d Zähler *m*
f compteur *m*
r счётчик *m*

* **counterclockwise** → 444

2344 counter period
d Zählerperiode *f*
f période *f* de compteur
r счётный период *m*

2345 counter position
d Zählerstelle *f*
f position *f* de compteur
r разряд *m* счётчика

* **counter-timer** → 2346

* **counter-timer circuit** → 2346

**2346 counter-timer [unit]; counter-timer circuit;
timer-counter**
d Zähler-Zeitgeber-Einheit *f*;
Zeitgeber-Zähler *m*;
Zähler-Zeitgeber-Baustein *m*
f unité *f* compteur-rythmeur; circuit *m*
compteur-rythmeur; rythmeur-compteur *m*;
compteur *m* horaire
r устройство *n* задания [интервала] времени;
счётчик *m* времени; счётчик-таймер *m*

2347 count field
 d Zählenfeld *n*
 f champ *m* de comptage; zone *f* de comptage
 r поле *n* счёта

2348 counting chain; counting decade
 d Zählkette *f*, Abzählkette *f*
 f chaîne *f* à compter
 r счётная цепочка *f*

 * **counting decade → 2348**

 * **counting-down circuit → 4084**

2349 count[ing] pulse; metering pulse; count[ing] signal
 d Zählimpuls *m*; Gebührenimpuls *m*; Zähltakt *m*
 f impulsion *f* de comptage
 r счётный импульс *m*

 * **counting signal → 2349**

2350 counting stage
 d Additionsstelle *f*
 f étage *m* d'addition; étage de sommation
 r точка *f* сбора; ячейка *f* счёта

 * **count pulse → 2349**

2351 country code
 d Landeskennzahl *f*
 f code *m* national
 r национальный код *m*

 * **count signal → 2349**

2352 coup; stroke; impact
 d Anschlag *m*
 f coup *m*; frappe *f*; impact *m*
 r удар *m*; нажатие *n*

 * **couple → 6740**

 * **coupler → 2180**

2353 coupling
 d Kopplung *f*
 f couplage *m*; accouplement *m*
 r связывание *n*

 * **coupling element → 2180**

2354 courseware; teachware
 d Lehrsoftware *f*
 f logiciel *m* didactique; didacticiel *m*
 r программное обеспечение *n* [для] обучения

 * **cover → 1437**

 * **covering → 1796**

 * **covering of the plane with tiles → 9377**

 * **covert → 4458**

 * **CP → 1536**

 * **CPU → 1536**

 * **CR → 1441, 1860**

 * **crack → 2357**

2355 crack *v*
 d aufbrechen; einbrechen; zerbrechen; knacken
 f craquer
 r взламывать; пробивать

2356 cracker; intruder
 (someone who attempts to thwart computer security systems)
 d Reißer *m*; Cracker *m*; Aufbrecher *m*; Knacker *m*; Raubkopierer *m*
 f craqueur *m*; crackeur *m*; intrus *m*
 r кракер *m*; взломщик *m*; злоумышленник *m*

2357 crack[ing]
 (of a protection)
 d Aufbruch *m*; Einbruch *m*
 f fissure *f*
 r взлом *m*; пробив *m*

 * **cradle → 876**

 * **crash → 2359**

2358 crash
 d Havarie *f*; Absturz *m*; Bruch *m*
 f krach *m*; avarie *f*; incident *m*
 r аварийный отказ *m*; авария *f*

2359 crash [message]
 d Havarie-Meldung *f*
 f message *m* d'avarie
 r спешное сообщение *n*; высокоприоритетное сообщение

 * **crate → 876**

2360 crawler
 d Kriecher *m*
 f crawler *m*
 r программа *f* автоматического сбора информации; краулер *m*; "червяк" *m*; механизм *m* поиска в WWW

 * **CRC → 2478**

2361 create *v*
 d bilden; erstellen; entwerfen

f créer
r создать; создавать

2362 creation; formation
  d Erstellung *f*; Bildung *f*; Kreation *f*;
  Anfertigung *f*
  f création *f*; formation *f*
  r образование *n*; создание *n*

2363 creation of documents
  d Belegherstellung *f*; Beleganfertigung *f*
  f création *f* de documents
  r создание *n* документов; выписка *f*
  документов

2364 creator; builder
  d Hersteller *m*; Bauer *m*; Gründer *m*
  f créateur *m*
  r создатель *m*

2365 credit
  d Kredit *m*; Genehmigung *f*
  f crédit *m*
  r кредит *m*

2366 credit card
  d Kreditkarte *f*
  f carte *f* de crédit
  r кредитная карта *f*

2367 criterion
  d Kriterium *n*
  f critère *n*
  r критерий *m*; признак *m*

2368 crop *v*
  d abschneiden; stutzen
  f rogner
  r отсекать; кадрировать; отрезать

2369 cropping the screen in rendering
  d Bildschirm-Beschneiden *n* beim Rendern
  f découpage *m* de l'écran en temps de rendu
  r отсекание *n* экрана при тонировании

2370 crop tool
  d Beschneiden-Hilfsmittel *n*
  f outil *m* de découpage
  r инструмент *m* отсекания

  * **cross** → 9538

2371 cross assembler
  d Crossassembler *m*
  f cross-assembleur *m*
  r кросс-ассемблер *m*

2372 crossbar
  d Querstrich *m*; Crossbar *n*
  f barre *f* [transversale]; barre croisée

  r поперечная черта *f*; соединительный
  штрих *m*

2373 crossbar selector
  d Koordinatenselektor *m*
  f sélecteur *m* crossbar; sélecteur coordonné
  r координатный селектор *m*

2374 crossbar switch; cross switch
  d Koordinatenwähler *m*; Koordinatenschalter *m*
  f commutateur *m* à barres croisées
  r координатный коммутатор *m*

2375 cross-channel switching
  d Datenzugriff *m* über zwei Kanäle
  f commutation *f* de canaux croisée
  r перекрёстная коммутация *f* каналов

2376 cross compiler
  d Crosscompiler *m*
  f cross-compilateur *m*
  r кросс-компилятор *m*

  * **cross connecting** → 2377

2377 cross connection; cross connecting; hookup
  d Querverbindung *f*
  f connexion *f* transversale
  r перекрёстная связь *f*

2378 cross-correlation
  d Querkorrelation *f*; Kreuzkorrelation *f*
  f corrélation *f* croisée; corrélation avec retards;
  corrélation avec décalage; corrélation
  mutuelle
  r перекрёстное соотношение *n*; взаимная
  корреляция *f*; перекрёстная корреляция

  * **cross-cut** → 2390

2379 cross directory
  d Querverzeichnis *n*
  f index *m* multifichier
  r перекрёстный каталог *m*; кросс-каталог *m*

2380 crosshair
  d Fadenkreuz *n*
  f réticule *m* en croix; croisée *f* des fils; fils *mpl*
  croisés
  r крест *m* нитей; сетка *f* нитей;
  перекрестие *n*

  * **cross-haired cursor** → 2381

2381 crosshair pointer; cross-haired cursor
  d Fadenkreuz-Zeiger *m*
  f pointeur *m* en croix
  r указатель-прицел *m*

2382 cross index
  d Querindex *m*

f index *m* transversal
r поперечный индекс *m*

* **crossing** → 5103

2383 crossing windows
d Schnittfenster *npl*
f fenêtres *fpl* croisées
r пересекающиеся окна *npl*

* **cross interlacing** → 5033

2384 cross intersection
d Querdurchschnitt *m*
f intersection *f* transversale
r поперечное пересечение *n*

2385 cross multiplication
d verschränkte Multiplikation *f*; kreuzweise Multiplikation
f multiplication *f* croisée; multiplication en croix
r умножение *n* крест-накрест; скрещённое умножение

2386 crosspoint commutator; crosspoint switch
d Crossbar-Schaltmatrix *f*; Koppelpunktmatrix *f*
f commutateur *m* matriciel
r матричный переключатель *m*

* **crosspoint switch** → 2386

2387 cross posting; multiposting
d Streusendung *f*
f postage *m* croisé; multipostage *m*
r перекрёстная рассылка *f*

2388 cross-reference
d Crossreferenz *f*; Querverweis *m*
f référence *f* croisée
r перекрёстная ссылка *f*

* **cross-reference list** → 2389

2389 cross-reference table; cross-reference list
d Crossreferenztabelle *f*; Querbezugsliste *f*
f table *f* de références transversales
r таблица *f* перекрёстных ссылок; список *m* перекрёстных ссылок

2390 cross-section; cross-cut
d Querschnitt *m*
f section *f* transversale
r поперечное сечение *n*

* **cross switch** → 2374

* **CRT** → 1498

* **cruise** *v* → 9065

2391 crunch *v*
d zusammenpacken; verdichten
f compresser
r перемалывать; сильно снимать; спрессовывать (данные); уплотнять (дисковое пространство)

2392 crunch; hash [symbol]
(#)
d Rautenzeichen *n*
f dièse *m*
r знак *m* "решётка"

* **crunched file** → 2036

* **cruncher** → 2039, 6316

2393 cryogenic memory
d Kryogenspeicher *m*; Supraleitungsspeicher *m*
f mémoire *f* cryogène
r криогенная память *f*

2394 cryogenics
d Kryogenik *f*
f cryogénie *f*
r криогенная техника *f*

2395 crypted communication
d Kryptokommunikation *f*
f communication *f* cryptée
r криптосвязь *f*

2396 cryptoanalysis
d Kryptoanalyse *f*
f cryptoanalyse *f*
r криптоанализ *m*

2397 cryptoanalyst
d Kryptoanalytiker *m*
f cryptoanalyste *m*
r криптоаналитик *m*

* **cryptocenter** → 2398

2398 cryptocentre; cryptocenter
d Schlüsselzentrale *f*; Kryptozentrum *n*; Cryptocenter *n*
f cryptocentre *m*
r криптоцентр *m*

2399 cryptochannel
d Schlüsselkanal *m*; Kryptokanal *m*
f cryptocanal *m*
r криптоканал *m*

2400 cryptodata
d Chiffrierdaten *pl*
f cryptodonnées *fpl*
r криптоданные *pl*

* **cryptoequipment** → 2401

2401 cryptographic equipment;
      cryptoequipment
   d Schlüsselgerät *n*; Verschlüsselungsgerät *n*
   f équipement *m* cryptographique
   r криптографическое оборудование *n*

2402 cryptographic security; cryptosecurity
   d kryptografische Sicherheit *f*;
      Schlüsselsicherheit *f*
   f sécurité *f* cryptographique
   r криптографическая защита *f*

2403 cryptographic server
   d kryptografischer Server *m*
   f serveur *m* cryptographique
   r криптографический сервер *m*

2404 cryptographic system; cryptosystem
   d Schlüsselsystem *n*; kryptografisches System *n*
   f système *m* cryptographique; cryptosystème *m*
   r криптографическая система *f*;
      криптосистема *f*

2405 cryptography
   d Kryptografie *f*
   f cryptographie *f*
   r криптография *f*

2406 cryptologic equipment
   d kryptologische Ausrüstung *f*
   f équipement *m* cryptologique
   r криптологическое оборудование *n*

2407 cryptology
   d Kryptologie *f*
   f cryptologie *f*
   r криптология *f*

   *   **cryptosecurity → 2402**

   *   **cryptosystem → 2404**

2408 cryptotext
   d Schlüsseltext *m*; Kryptotext *m*
   f cryptotexte *m*
   r криптотекст *m*

   *   **crystal → 5808**

   *   **crystal oscillator → 7532**

   *   **crystal resonator → 7532**

   *   **CSLIP → 2037**

   *   **CSS → 1474**

   *   **CSW → 1584**

   *   **CT → 2104**

   *   **CUA → 1931**

2409 cue; reference mark
      (on the screen)
   d Strichmarke *f*; Cue *n*
   f caractère *m* indicateur; repère *m*
   r индикаторный знак *m*; репер *m*; относимая
      метка *f*

2410 culling; dropping
   d Pflücken *n*
   f écartement *m*
   r отстранение *n*; игнорирование *n*;
      отбрасывание *n*

   *   **cumulative error → 96**

2411 curl *v* a page
   d Seite aufrollen
   f coiffer une page; friser une page
   r завить страницы

   *   **curly brackets → 1151**

   *   **currency sign → 2412**

2412 currency symbol; currency sign
   d Währungssymbol *n*
   f symbole *m* de monnaie; symbole monétaire;
      signe *m* de monnaie
   r валютный символ *m*; символ валюты

2413 current
   d Strom *m*
   f courant *m*
   r электрический ток *m*

2414 current; actual *adj*
   d laufend; gegenwärtig; aktuell; eigentlich;
      tatsächlich; wirklich
   f courant; en cours; actuel
   r текущий; рабочий; действительный

   *   **current address counter → 4947**

   *   **current amplification → 2417**

2415 current amplifier
   d Stromverstärker *m*
   f amplificateur *m* de courant
   r усилитель *m* тока

2416 current driver
   d Stromtreiber *m*
   f circuit *m* formateur de courant
   r формирователь *m* тока

2417 current gain; current amplification
   d Stromverstärkung *f*

f gain *m* en courant; amplification *f* de courant
r усиление *n* тока; усиление по току

2418 current gain factor
  d Stromverstärkungsfaktor *m*
  f coefficient *m* de gain en courant
  r коэффициент *m* усиления тока

  * **current information → 3923**

2419 current loop
  d Stromschleife *f*
  f boucle *f* de courant
  r токовая петля *f*

2420 current page; working page
  d Arbeitsseite *f*
  f page *f* en cours; page de travail
  r рабочая страница *f*

2421 current position
  d aktuelle Position *f*
  f position *f* courante
  r текущая позиция *f*

2422 current pulse
  d Stromschritt *m*; Stromimpuls *m*
  f impulsion *f* de courant
  r токовый импульс *m*

2423 current window; active window
  d [derzeit] aktives Fenster *n*; aktuelles Fenster
  f fenêtre *f* courante; fenêtre active
  r текущее окно *n*; активное окно

2424 current write address
  d aktuelle Schreibadresse *f*
  f adresse *f* d'écriture actuelle
  r активный адрес *m* записи; текущий адрес записи

2425 cursor
  d Cursor *m*; Kursor *m*; Schreibmarke *f*; Lichtmarke *f*
  f curseur *m*
  r курсор *m*

2426 cursor arrow
  d Cursorpfeil *m*
  f flèche *f* du curseur
  r стрелочка *f* указателя курсора

2427 cursor blinking
  d Cursorblinken *n*
  f clignotement *m* de curseur
  r мерцание *n* курсора

  * **cursor indicator → 2429**

2428 cursor key

d Cursor[positionier]taste *f*; Cursorsteuertaste *f*
f touche *f* de curseur
r клавиша *f* [движения] курсора

2429 cursor mark; cursor indicator
  d Cursorindikator *m*
  f indicateur *m* de curseur
  r индикатор *m* курсора

2430 cursor menu
  d Cursormenü *n*
  f menu *m* de curseur
  r меню *n* курсора

2431 cursor movement
  d Cursorweg *m*
  f mouvement *m* de curseur
  r движение *n* курсора

2432 cursor position
  d Cursorposition *f*
  f position *f* de curseur
  r позиция *f* курсора

2433 cursor size
  d Cursorgröße *f*
  f taille *f* de curseur
  r размер *m* курсора

2434 cursor state
  d Cursorstatus *m*
  f état *m* de curseur
  r состояние *n* курсора

  * **custom → 2436**

2435 custom [adapting] element
  d Kundenanpassungsglied *n*
  f élément *m* d'adaptation pour clients; adaptateur *m* de clients
  r элемент *m* сопряжения с абонентом

2436 custom[-built]; customized; custom-made; custom-design[ed]
  d kundenspezifisch; Kunden-
  f personnalisable; personnalisé; demandé; à la demande; précaracterisé
  r изготовленный по заказу; клиентский; заказной

2437 custom chart format
  d angepaßtes Diagrammformat *n*
  f format *m* de diagramme personnalisé
  r заказной формат *m* диаграммы

  * **custom chip → 2446**

  * **custom-design → 2436**

  * **custom-designed → 2436**

2438 custom dialog box
  d angepaßte Dialogbox *f*
  f boîte *f* de dialogue personnalisée
  r заказной диалоговый ящик *m*

2439 custom dictionary
  d angepaßtes Wörterbuch *n*
  f dictionnaire *m* personnalisé
  r заказной словарь *m*

  * **custom element** → 2345

  * **customer** → 1727

2440 customer interface
  d Kundenschnittstelle *f*
  f interface *f* d'utilisateur; interface pour client
  r клиентский интерфейс *m*; интерфейс с нестандартными устройствами пользователя

2441 customer mail
  d Teilnehmermeldung *f*
  f poste *f* d'abonné
  r почта *f* клиента

2442 custom installation; client installation
  d angepaßte Anlage *f*
  f installation *f* personnalisée
  r заказная инсталляция *f*

2443 customization; customizing
  d Personalisierung *f*; kundenspezifische Produktgestaltung *f*; kundenspezifische Anpassung *f*; Anwenderanpassung *f*
  f adaptation *f*; personnalisation *f*; production *f* à la demande
  r разработка *f* заказного варианта

2444 customize v
  d kundenspezifisch herstellen
  f produire à la demande
  r изготовлять по заказу

  * **customized** → 2436

  * **customized chip** → 2446

2445 customized file
  d kundenspezifische Datei *f*
  f fichier *m* personnalisé
  r заказной файл *m*

2446 custom[ized] microcircuit; custom[ized] chip
  d kundenspezifischer [integrierter] Schaltkreis *m*; Kundenwunschchip *m*
  f microcircuit *m* à la demande; puce *f* précaractérisée
  r заказная микросхема *f*; заказной

кристалл *m*

  * **customizing** → 2443

  * **custom-made** → 2436

2447 custom-made software
  d kundenspezifische Software *f*
  f logiciel *m* à la demande; logiciel personnalisé
  r заказное программное обеспечение *n*

2448 custom menu
  d angepaßtes Menü *n*
  f menu *m* personnalisé
  r заказное меню *n*

  * **custom microcircuit** → 2446

2449 custom toolbar
  d angepaßter Hilfsmittelstreifen *m*
  f barre *f* d'outils personnalisé
  r заказная панель *f* инструментов

2450 cut v
  d ausschneiden
  f [dé]couper
  r вырезать

2451 cut v all
  d alles ausschneiden
  f [dé]couper tout
  r удалять все

2452 cut-in
  d Einschaltung *f*; Einschalten *n*
  f connexion *f*; enclenchement *m*
  r включение *n*; начало *n* работы

  * **cutoff** → 2979

2453 cutoff frequency
  d Grenzfrequenz *f*
  f fréquence *f* de coupure
  r предельная частота *f*

2454 cutout
  d Abschalter *m*
  f interrupteur *m*; disjoncteur *m*
  r выключатель *m*

  * **cutout** → 2979

  * **cutting** → 1742

  * **CVE** → 3048

2455 cyan, magenta, yellow and black; CMYK
  d Zyan, Magenta, Gelb und Schwarz

f cyan, magenta, jaune et noir

r зеленовато-голубой, фиолетовый, жёлтый
и чёрный; голубой, пурпурный, жёлтый,
чёрный

**2456 cyberaddiction; cyberholism; net
addiction; netaholism; pathological
Internet use**

d Cybersucht *f*

f cyberdépendance *f*; dépendance *f* à
l'ordinateur; dépendance à Internet

r пагубная привычка *f* к Интернету

2457 cyberart

d Cyberart *f*

f cyberart *m*

r компьютерное произведение *n* искусства

2458 cybercafe

(cyberspace for Internet problems)

d Internet-Café *n*

f cyber-café *m*

r киберкафе *n*; виртуальное кафе *n*

* **cybercash** → **3333**

* **cybercrud** → **2088**

* **cyber glove** → **2563**

* **cyberholism** → **2456**

* **cybernaut** → **2461**

2459 cybernetics

d Kybernetik *f*

f cybernétique *f*

r кибернетика *f*

* **cyberphone** → **5056**

2460 cyberspace

d Cyberspace *m*; künstlicher Raum *m*

f cyberespace *m*; espace *m* cybernétique

r киберпространство *n*

**2461 cybersurfer; network surfer; netsurfer;
surfer; spider; wanderer; cybernaut;
internaut; nethead; inforouter**

(e-slang for regular user of Internet)

d Wanderer *m*; Cybernaut *m*; Spinne *f*

f internaute *m*; consommateur *m* excessif de
l'Internet; personne *m* qui utilise
fréquemment le World Wide Web

r спайдер *m*; бродяга *m*; интернавт *m*;
кибернавт *m*; [сетевой] серфер *m*

* **cybersurfing** → **9980**

2462 cyberworld

d künstliche Welt *f*

f cybermonde *m*

r кибермир *m*

2463 cycle buffer

d Zykluspuffer *m*

f tampon *m* de cycle

r буфер *m* цикла

2464 cycle count

d Zählung *f* der Schleifendurchläufe;
Zykluszählung *f*

f comptage *m* de cycles

r счёт *m* циклов

2465 cycle counter

d Zykluszähler *m*

f compteur *m* de cycles

r счётчик *m* циклов

2466 cycle reset

d Zyklusrückstellung *f*

f remise *f* de cycle; remise de boucle

r восстановление *n* цикла

* **cycle shift** → **1685**

2467 cycle stealing

d Zyklusstehlen *n*

f vol *m* de cycle

r захват *m* цикла

2468 cycle time

d Zykluszeit *f*

f temps *m* de cycle

r время *n* [одного] цикла

2469 cyclic

d zyklisch

f cyclique

r циклический

2470 cyclic access

d zyklischer Zugriff *m*

f accès *m* circulaire

r циклический доступ *m*

2471 cyclic borrow; end-around borrow

d Ringborgen *n*

f emprunt *m* circulaire

r круговой заём *m*

2472 cyclic carry; end-around carry

d Rückübertrag *m*; Rücklaufübertrag *m*;
Endübertrag *m*

f retenue *f* circulaire; report *m* circulaire;
retenue en arrière; transfert *m* circulant

r циклический перенос *m*; круговой
перенос

2473 cyclic check byte; CCB
   d zyklisches Prüfbyte *n*; zyklisches
      Kontrollbyte *n*
   f octet *m* de contrôle cyclique
   r циклический контрольный байт *m*

2474 cyclic code
   d zyklischer Code *m*
   f code *m* cyclique
   r циклический код *m*

2475 cyclic group
   d zyklische Gruppe *f*
   f groupe *m* cyclique
   r циклическая группа *f*

2476 cyclic permuted [binary] code; reflected
     binary code
   d zyklisch vertauschter binärer Code *m*;
      reflektierter Binärcode *m*
   f code *m* binaire cyclique; code binaire réfléchi
   r циклический двоичный код *m*

   * **cyclic permuted code → 2476**

2477 cyclic readout
   d zyklisches Auslesen *n*
   f lecture *f* cyclique
   r циклическое считывание *n*

2478 cyclic redundancy check; CRC
   d zyklische Blockprüfung *f*; zyklische
      Redundanzprüfung *f*
   f contrôle *m* cyclique par redondance
   r проверка *f* цикличным избыточным кодом;
      циклический контроль *m* по избыточности

2479 cyclic redundant code
   d zyklisch redundanter Code *m*
   f code *m* redondant cyclique
   r цикличный код *m* избытком

   * **cyclic shift → 1685**

   * **cyclic storage → 1689**

   * **cyclic store → 1689**

2480 cycling
   d periodisches Durchlaufen *n*; Durchlaufen von
      periodischen Arbeitsgängen; zyklische
      Wiederholung *f*
   f [re]bouclage *m*
   r циклирование *n*; зацикливание *n*

2481 cycling frequency
   d Durchlaufhäufigkeit *f*
   f fréquence *f* d'itérations
   r частота *f* циклирования

2482 Cyrillic alphabet
   d kyrillisches Alphabet *n*
   f alphabet *m* cyrillique
   r кириллическая азбука *f*

D

* **2D** → 9590

* **3D** → 9351

* **DAC** → 2929

2483 2D acceleration
  d 2D-Beschleunigung *f*
  f accélération *f* 2D
  r 2D ускорение *n*

2484 3D acceleration
  d 3D-Beschleunigung *f*
  f accélération *f* 3D
  r 3D ускорение *n*

2485 3D accelerator
  d 3D-Beschleuniger *m*
  f accélérateur *m* 3D
  r 3D акселератор *m*

2486 d[a]emon
  (a resident program)
  d Dämon *n*
  f démon *m*; écouteur *m*; tâche *f* attentive
  r демон *m*

2487 daisy chain
  d Prioritätskette *f*; Daisy-Chain *n*
  f chaîne *f* à marguerite; connexion *f* en
    guirlande
  r последовательно-приоритетная цепочка *f*

2488 daisy-chain bus structure
  d verkettete Busstruktur *f*; Busstruktur mit
    Steuersignalkaskadierung
  f structure *f* de bus en guirlande
  r последовательно-приоритетная структура *f*
    шин

2489 daisy-chain terminals
  d im Daisy-Chain-Verfahren angeschlossene
    Terminals *npl*
  f terminaux *mpl* raccordés en guirlande
  r терминалы *mpl*, объединённые в
    последовательно-приоритетную цепочку

2490 daisy[-chain] topology
  (of LAN)
  d Verkettungstopologie *f*
  f topologie *f* en chaîne
  r цепочечная топология *f*; шлейфовая
    топология

* **daisy topology** → 2490

**2491 damage; deterioration; destruction;
    violation**
  d Schaden *n*; Beschädigung *f*; Verletzen *n*;
    Zerstörung *f*
  f dommage *m*; détérioration *f*; destruction *f*;
    violation *f*
  r порча *f*; повреждение *n*; разрушение *n*;
    нарушение *n*; износ *m*

* **damage** *v* → 2335

* **damping** → 621

2492 3D animated characters
  d animierte 3D-Zeichen *npl*
  f caractères *mpl* animés en 3D
  r трёхмерные оживлённые символы *mpl*

2493 3D animation
  d 3D-Animation *f*
  f animation *f* 3D
  r 3D анимация *f*

2494 2D array
  d 2D-Datenfeld *n*; zweidimensionales
    Datenfeld *n*
  f tableau *m* 2D; tableau à deux dimensions
  r 2D массив *m*; двумерный массив

2495 3D array
  d 3D-Datenfeld *n*
  f tableau *m* 3D
  r трёхмерный массив *m*; 3D массив

* **dash** → 8950

2496 dash marking; stroke marking
  d Strichmarkierung *f*
  f marquage *m* de trait
  r штриховая маркировка *f*

* **DAT** → 2876

2497 data
  d Daten *pl*
  f données *fpl*
  r данные *pl*

* **data acceptance** → 54

2498 data access
  d Datenzugriff *m*
  f accès *m* à données
  r доступ *m* к данным

**2499 data acquisition; data collection; data
    capture**
  d Datenerfassung *f*; Messwerterfassung *f*;
    Datensammeln *n*

f acquisition *f* de données; saisie *f* de données;
collection *f* de données
r сбор *m* данных; совокупность *f* данных

* **data administration** → 2576

* **data administrator** → 2577

2500 **data aggregate**
d Datenaggregat *n*
f agrégat *m* de données
r агрегат *m* данных

* **data analysis** → 389

* **data array** → 2557

2501 **databank**
d Datenbank *f*
f banque *f* de données
r банк *m* данных

2502 **databank register**
d Datenbankregister *n*
f registre *m* de banque de données
r регистр *m* банка данных

2503 **database**
d Datenbasis *f*
f base *f* de données
r база *f* данных

* **database administrator** → 2508

2504 **database engine; database mechanism**
d Datenbasismaschine *f*;
Datenbasismechanismus *m*
f machine *f* de base de données; moteur *m* de
base de données
r машина *f* [доступа до] баз данных;
процессор *m* баз данных

2505 **database file organization**
d Datenbasisdateiorganisation *f*
f organisation *f* de fichiers dans une base de
données
r организация *f* файлов базы данных

* **database handler** → 2508

2506 **database interface**
d Datenbasis-Schnittstelle *f*
f interface *f* de base de données
r интерфейс *m* базы данных

* **database management** → 2513

2507 **database management system; DBMS**
d Datenbasisverwaltungssystem *n*;
Datenbasis-Managementsystem *n*; DBMS

f système *m* de gestion de base de données;
SGBD
r система *f* управления баз данных

2508 **database manager; database
administrator; database handler**
d Datenbasisverwalter *m*
f gestionnaire *m* de base de données;
programme *m* de gestion de base de données
r администратор *m* баз данных

* **database mechanism** → 2504

2509 **database object**
d Datenbasis-Objekt *n*
f objet *m* de base de données
r объект *m* базы данных

2510 **database organization**
d Datenbasisorganisation *f*
f organisation *f* de la base de données
r организация *f* базы данных

2511 **database recovery**
d Datenbasiswiederherstellung *f*
f récupération *f* de base de données
r восстановление *n* базы данных

2512 **database server; application server**
d Datenbasis-Server *m*
f serveur *m* de bases de données
r сервер *m* баз данных

2513 **database service; database management**
d Datenbasisverwaltung *f*
f management *m* de base de données
r управление *n* базы данных

2514 **database synchronization; DBSYNC**
d Datenbasissynchronisation *f*
f uniformisation *f* des bases de données;
UNIBD
r синхронизация *f* баз данных

2515 **database table**
d Datenbasis-Tabelle *f*
f tableau *m* de base de données
r таблица *f* базы данных

2516 **database transaction**
d Datenbasistransaktion *f*
f transaction *f* de base de données
r транзакция *f* базы данных

2517 **data binding**
d Datenbindung *f*
f association *f* de données
r привязка *f* данных

* **data blocking** → 2586

2518 **data break**
d Datenunterbrechung *f*
f interruption *f* de données
r прерывание *n* для обмена данными

2519 **data buffer**
d Datenpuffer *m*
f tampon *m* de données
r буфер *m* данных

2520 **data bulk**
d Datenmassiv *n*; große Datenmenge *f*
f masse *f* d'information
r большой объём *m* данных; большой
   массив *m* данных

* **data bulk transmission → 1249**

2521 **data bus; data path**
d Datenbus *m*; Datenweg *m*; Datenpfad *m*
f bus *m* de données; voie *f* [omnibus] de
   données; trajet *m*
r шина *f* данных; информационная шина

* **data capture → 2499**

2522 **data capture station**
d Datenerfassungsstation *f*
f station *f* de collection de données
r станция *f* сбора данных

2523 **data capture system; data collection
       system; data gathering system**
d Datensammelnsystem *n*;
   Dattenerfassungssystem *n*
f système *m* de collection de données
r система *f* сбора данных

2524 **data carrier; data medium**
d Datenträger *m*
f porteur *m* de données; support *m* de données
r носитель *m* данных

2525 **data chaining**
d Datenkettung *f*
f chaînage *m* de données
r цепочная организация *f* данных

2526 **data channel; data line; data circuit;
       information channel**
d Datenkanal *m*; Datenleitung *f*;
   Informationskanal *m*
f voie *f* de données; canal *m* de données; ligne *f*
   de données; canal d'information
r канал *m* [связи] данных; линия *f*
   [передачи] данных; информационный
   канал

2527 **data channel selection**
d Datenkanalauswahl *f*

f sélection *f* de canal de données
r выбор *m* канала данных; подключение *n*
   канала данных

2528 **data channel switch**
d Datenkanalschalter *m*
f interrupteur *m* pour canal de données
r переключатель *m* каналов данных

* **data circuit → 2526**

2529 **data circuit transparency**
d Transparenz *f* der Datenverbindung
f transparence *f* de circuit de données
r прозрачность *f* канала передачи данных

2530 **data clause**
d Datenklausel *f*
f clause *f* de données
r предложение *n* описания данных

2531 **data coding; data encryption**
d Datencodierung *f*
f codage *m* de données; chiffrage *m* de
   données; cryptage *m* de données
r кодирование *n* данных; шифрование *n*
   данных

* **data collection → 2499**

* **data collection system → 2523**

2532 **data communication network; data
       [exchange] network; transmission data
       network**
d Daten[kommunikations]netz *n*;
   Datenübertragungsnetz *n*;
   Datenvermittlungsnetz *n*
f réseau *m* [de communication] de données;
   réseau de médiation de données; réseau de
   transmission de données
r сеть *f* обмена данными; сеть передачи
   данных; информационная сеть

2533 **data compaction; data compression; data
       condensation**
d Datenverdichtung *f*; Datenkomprimierung *f*
f compaction *f* de données; compression *f* de
   données; concentration *f* de données
r сжатие *n* данных; уплотнение *n* данных

* **data compression → 2533**

2534 **data concentrator**
d Datenkonzentrator *m*
f concentrateur *m* de données
r концентратор *m* данных

* **data condensation → 2533**

2535 **data consolidation**
 d Datenverfestigung *f*
 f consolidation *f* de données
 r консолидация *f* данных

2536 **data contamination; data corruption**
 d Datenbeschädigen *n*; Verletzung *f* [der
    Integrität] der Daten
 f contamination *f* de données
 r порча *f* данных; искажение *n* данных

2537 **data convention**
 d Datenformatvereinbarung *f*
 f convention *f* de données
 r соглашение *n* о данных

2538 **data conversion**
 d Datenkonvertierung *f*
 f conversion *f* de données
 r преобразование *n* данных

  * **data corruption** → 2536

  * **data definition language** → 2539

2539 **data description language; data definition
    language; DDL**
 d Datenbeschreibungssprache *f*;
    Datendefinitionssprache *f*
 f langage *m* de description de données; langage
    de définition de données
 r язык *m* описания данных; язык
    определения данных

2540 **data dictionary**
 d Datenverzeichnis *n*
 f vocabulaire *m* de données; dictionnaire *m* de
    données
 r словарь *m* [базы] данных

2541 **data direct register; DDR**
 d Datendirektregister *n*; DDR
 f registre *m* direct de données
 r регистр *m* прямого доступа к данным

  * **data element** → 2568

2542 **data encapsulation**
 d Datenverkapselung *f*
 f emballage *m* de données
 r скрытие *n* данных; инкапсуляция *f* данных

  * **data encryption** → 2531

2543 **data encryption standard; DES**
 d Standard *m* für Datenverschlüsselung
 f standard *m* de cryptage de données
 r стандарт *m* шифрования данных

2544 **data end device; data final device; data**

terminal
 d Datenendgerät *n*; Datenterminal *n*
 f poste *m* terminal; terminal *m* de données
 r оконечное устройство *n* [ввода-вывода]
    данных; терминал *m* данных

2545 **data entity**
 d Dateneinheit *f*
 f entité *f* de données
 r информационный объект *m*

2546 **data entry; data input; insertion of data**
 d Dateneingabe *f*; Dateneinführung *f*
 f introduction *f* de données; entrée *f* de
    données; insertion *f* de données
 r ввод *m* данных

2547 **data-entry administrator**
 d Datenerfassungsüberwacher *m*
 f administrateur *m* d'entrée de données
 r администратор *m* ввода данных

2548 **data-entry field; entry field**
 d Dateneingabefeld *n*
 f zone *f* de saisie; zone d'entrée
 r поле *n* ввода данных

2549 **data-entry station; data-entry terminal**
 d Betriebsdatenstation *f*;
    Dateneingabeterminal *n*
 f unité *f* de saisie enregistreur
 r терминал *m* для ввода данных

  * **data-entry terminal** → 2549

2550 **data escape signal**
 d Datenumschaltesignal *n*
 f signal *m* d'échappement de données
 r сигнал *m* переключения данных

2551 **data exchange; data interchange; DATEX**
 d Datenaustausch *m*; Datenvermittlung *f*
 f échange *m* de données
 r обмен *m* данными

2552 **data exchange interface**
 d Datenaustauschinterface *n*
 f interface *f* d'échange de données
 r интерфейс *m* обмена данными

  * **data exchange network** → 2532

2553 **data extrapolation**
 d Datenextrapolation *f*
 f extrapolation *f* de données
 r экстраполяция *f* данных

2554 **data/fax modem; fax-modem**
 d Faxmodem *n*

f modem *m* données/télécopieur; carte *f* de télécopie et modem; modem fax
r факс-модем *m*

2555 data feedback
  d Datenrückkopplung *f*
  f réaction *f* de données
  r информационная обратная связь *f*

2556 data fetch
  d Datenholen *n*; Datenbereitstellung *f*
  f mise *f* à disposition de données
  r выборка *f* данных

2557 data field; data array
  d Datenfeld *n*
  f champ *m* de données; tableau *m* de données
  r поле *n* данных; массив *m* данных

2558 data file
  d Datendatei *f*
  f fichier *m* de données
  r файл *m* данных

  *   **data final device** → 2544

2559 data flowchart
  d Datenflussplan *m*
  f organigramme *m* de traitement de données
  r блок-схема *f* обработки данных; функциональная схема *f*

2560 data-flow graph
  d Datenflussgraph *m*
  f graphe *m* de flux de données
  r информационный потоковый граф *m*

2561 data-flow program
  d datengesteuertes Programm *n*
  f programme *m* de flux de données
  r программа *f*, управляемая данными

  *   **data format**
2562 data format
  d Datenformat *n*
  f format *m* de données
  r формат *m* данных

  *   **data gathering system** → 2523

2563 data glove; sensor glove; wired glove; cyber glove
  d Datenhandschuh *m*
  f gant *m* sensitif; gant de données; gant détecteur
  r электронная перчатка *f*; сенсорная перчатка

2564 datagram
  d Datagramm *n*
  f datagramme *m*

r дейтаграмма *f*

  *   **data handling** → 2587

2565 data holding time
  d Datenhaltezeit *f*
  f temps *m* d'arrêt de données
  r время *n* [со]хранения данных; период *m* сохранения данных

2566 data importing
  d Datenimportieren *n*
  f importation *f* de données
  r внесение *n* данных

  *   **data input** → 2546

2567 data integrity
  d Datenintegrität *f*
  f intégrité *f* de données
  r целостность *f* данных

  *   **data interchange** → 2551

2568 data item; data element; datum
  d Dateneinzelheit *f*; Datenelement *n*; Datengrundeinheit *f*; Angabe *f*; Datum *n*
  f détail *m* de données; élément *m* de données; donnée *f*; datum *m*
  r элемент *m* данных; данная величина *f*; данное *n*

2569 data latching
  d Datenhalten *n*
  f verrouillage *m* de données; fixation *f* de données
  r фиксирование *n* данных

  *   **data line** → 2526

2570 data link
  d Datenverbindung *f*; Datenübertragung *f*; Datenübertragungsstrecke *f*; Datenübermittlungsabschnitt *m*
  f enchaînement *m* de données; liaison *f* de données; liaison informatique; raccord[ement] *m* de données
  r соединение *n* данных; связывание *n* данных; связь *f* данных; информационная связь

2571 data link control; DLC
  d Datenleitungssteuerung *f*; Datenverbindungssteuerung *f*
  f commande *f* de liaison de données
  r управление *n* каналом передачи данных

2572 data link escape
  d Datenübertragungumschaltung *f*

f échappement *m* de transmission de données
r переключение *n* канала передачи данных

2573 data link layer; DLL; link layer
d Datenleitungsschicht *f*;
Datensicherungsschicht *f*;
Verbindungssicherungsschicht *f*;
Sicherungssicht *f*
f couche *f* liaison de données
r канальный уровень *m* данных

2574 data link relay
d Datenverbindungsstation *f*
f commutation *f* liaison de données
r узел *m* сети передачи данных

2575 data logging
d Datenerfassung *f* und -aufzeichnung *f*;
Datenregistrierung *f*
f enregistrement *m* de données
r [сбор *m* и] регистрация *f* данных

2576 data management; data administration
d Datenmanagement *n*; Datenverwaltung *f*
f management *m* de données; gestion *f* de
données; administration *f* de données
r управление *n* данными;
администрирование *n* данных

2577 data manager; DM; data administrator
d Datenverwalter *m*
f gestionnaire *m* de données; administrateur *m*
de données
r администратор *m* данных

*   **data manipulation → 2587**

2578 data manipulation language
d Datenbehandlungssprache *f*
f langage *m* de manipulation de données
r язык *m* манипулирования данных

*   **data medium → 2524**

2579 data mining
d Datenschürfen *n*
f extraction *f* de données
r добывание *n* данных; извлечение *n* данных

2580 data mode
d Datenmodus *m*
f mode *m* de données
r режим *m* обработки данных

2581 data model
d Datenmodell *n*
f modèle *m* de données
r модель *f* данных

*   **data network → 2532**

2582 data network identification code; DNIC
d Datennetzkennzahl *f*
f code *m* d'identification de réseau de données
r код *m* идентификации сети данных

2583 data object
d Datenobjekt *m*
f objet *m* des données
r объект *m* данных

*   **data out → 2584**

*   **data out line → 2585**

2584 data out[put]
d Datenausgabe *f*
f sortie *f* de données; émission *f* de données
r вывод *m* данных

2585 data-out[put] line; DOUT
d Datenausgabeleitung *f*; DOUT-Leitung *f*
f ligne *f* de sortie de données
r линия *f* вывода данных

*   **data overrun → 6662**

2586 data packing; data blocking
d Datenpackung *f*
f assemblage *m* de données; groupage *m* de
données; condensation *f* de données
r упаковка *f* данных

*   **data path → 2521**

*   **data pooling → 7109**

*   **data preparation → 7214**

**2587 data processing; data manipulation; data
handling**
d Datenverarbeitung *f*
f traitement *m* de données
r обработка *f* данных

*   **data protection → 2593**

*   **data rate → 2599**

2588 data receiver
d Datenempfänger *m*
f récepteur *m* de données
r приёмник *m* данных

2589 data record; record
d Datensatz *m*; Satz *m*
f enregistrement *m* [de données]; article *m*
r запись *f* [данных]

2590 data record name
d Datensatzname *m*

  f nom *m* d'enregistrement de données
  r имя *n* записи данных

  * **data reduction** → 7780

2591 data refinement operation; refinement operation
  d Datenverfeinerungsoperation *f*; Verfeinerungsoperation *f*
  f opération *f* de raffinage [de données]
  r операция *f* уточнения [данных]

  * **data remote transfer** → 2597

2592 data-retention time
  d Datenaufbewahrungszeit *f*; Datenspeicherzeit *f*
  f temps *m* de rétention de données
  r время *n* сохранения информации

  * **data securing** → 2593

2593 data security; data securing; data protection
  d Datensicherung *f*; Datenschutz *m*; Datensicherheit *f*
  f sécurité *f* de données; protection *f* de données
  r защита *f* данных

2594 data sender
  d Datensender *m*
  f émetteur *m* de données
  r источник *m* данных

2595 data set
  d Datenmenge *f*
  f ensemble *m* de données
  r множество *n* данных

  * **data-set extent** → 3792

  * **data-set list** → 3805

2596 data sink
  d Datensenke *f*
  f dépression *f* de données
  r отход *m* данных

  * **data structure** → 4819

2597 data telecommunication; data remote transfer; remote data transmission
  d Datenfernübertragung *f*; DFÜ
  f télécommunication *f* de données; transfert *m* de données à distance; télétransmission *f* de données
  r дистанционная передача *f* данных

2598 data teleprocessing; remote data processing
  d Datenfernverarbeitung *f*
  f télétraitement *m* de données; traitement *m* éloigné de données
  r дистанционная обработка *f* данных

  * **data terminal** → 2544

2599 data [transfer] rate
  d Daten[übertragungs]rate *f*
  f débit *m* de données; vitesse *f* de transfert de données
  r скорость *f* передачи данных

2600 data triggering
  d datengesteuerte Triggerung *f*
  f déclenchement *m* par données
  r запуск *m* по данным

2601 data type
  d Datentyp *m*
  f type *m* de données
  r тип *m* данных

2602 dataware
  d Dataware *f*
  f produits *mpl* d'information; approvisionnement *m* d'information
  r информационное обеспечение *n*

2603 date
  (a period of time)
  d Frist *f*
  f délai *m*
  r срок *m*

2604 date
  (a fixed point of time)
  d Datum *n*; Tagesdatum *n*
  f date *f*
  r дата *f*

  * **DATEX** → 2551

  * **DATEX-P** → 6684

  * **DATEX-S** → 8181

2605 dating routine
  d Datumprogramm *n*
  f programme-dateur *m*
  r программа *f* датирования

2606 datum
  (in digital control)
  d Datum *n*; Null *f*; Bezugsgröße *f*
  f datum *m*; référence *f* de base
  r начало *n* отсчёта; нуль *m*

  * **datum** → 2568

* **DBCS** → 3123

2607 2D bitmap
  d 2D-Bitmap *n*
  f bitmap *m* 2D
  r двумерное растровое изображение *n*

* **DBMS** → 2507

2608 3D box
  d 3D-Kasten *m*
  f boîtier *m* 3D; boîte *f* 3D
  r 3D ящик *m*

* **DBSYNC** → 2514

* **DC** → 2953

* **3D character** → 3197

2609 3D chart
  d 3D-Diagramm *n*
  f diagramme *m* 3D
  r 3D диаграмма *f*

* **DCL** → 2848

2610 3D code system
  d 3D-Codesystem *n*
  f système *m* de code 3D
  r трёхмерная система *f* кодирования

2611 3D computing
  d 3D-Rechnen *n*
  f calcul *m* en 3D
  r 3D исчисление *n*

2612 3D data capture device
  d 3D-Daten-Sammlungsgerät *n*
  f dispositif *m* de capture de données 3D
  r устройство *n* захвата трёхмерных данных

* **DDC** → 3019

* **DDE** → 3247

2613 3D digital image
  d digitales 3D-Bild *n*
  f image *f* numérique en 3D
  r трёхмерное цифровое изображение *n*

2614 3D digitizing techniques
  d 3D-Diskretisierungstechnik *f*
  f technique *f* de digitalisation en 3D
  r метод *m* трёхмерного дигитализирования

* **DDL** → 2539

* **DDR** → 2541

2615 3D dynamic view
  d dynamische 3D-Ansicht *f*
  f vue *f* dynamique 3D
  r трёхмерный динамический вид *m*

2616 deactivation
  d Inaktivierung *f*; Entaktivierung *f*
  f déactivation *f*
  r деактивация *f*

2617 dead block
  d passiver Block *m*
  f bloc *m* passif
  r пассивный блок *m*

2618 dead letter queue
  d Warteschlange *f* von aufgehobenen Nachrichten
  f queue *f* de messages interdits
  r очередь *f* отвергаемых сообщений

2619 deadline
  d Gefahrengrenze *f*
  f échéance *f*
  r "мёртвая" линия *f*

2620 dead link; cold link
  d tote Verknüpfung *f*
  f lien *m* mort
  r оборванная связь *f*; холодная связь

2621 deadlock; deadly embrace; clinch; interlock[ing]; spin lock
  d gegenseitige Sperre *f*; gegenseitige Blockierung *f*; gegenseitige Verriegelung *f*; wechselseitige Blockierung *f*; Verklemmung *f*; Totalblockierung *f*
  f blocage *m* mutuel; interblocage *m*; embrassement *m* mort[el]; impasse *f*; étreinte *f* totale; verrouillage *m* mutuel [réciproque]
  r тупик *m*; взаимная блокировка *f*; взаимоблокировка *f*; тупиковая ситуация *f*

* **deadly embrace** → 2621

2622 dead reckoning; DR
  d Koppelnavigation *f*; Besteckrechnung *f*
  f navigation *f* à l'estime
  r расчёт *m* траектории движения; счисление *n* пути

2623 dead time; downtime; outage time
  d Ausfallzeit *f*; Störungszeit *f*; Totzeit *f*; Stillstandzeit *f*
  f temps *m* mort; temps d'arrêt; durée *f* d'interruption
  r мёртвое время *n*; простой *m*; длительность *f* отказа; время перерыва

2624 **dead zone; inert zone**
 d tote Zone *f*; Unempfindlichkeitszone *f*
 f zone *f* morte; zone d'inertie
 r мёртвая зона *f*; зона нечувствительности

2625 **deallocate** *v*
 d freigaben; aufheben
 f désallouer
 r освобождать (память); перемещать

2626 **deallocation**
 d Freigabe *f*; Aufhebung *f*
 f déallocation *f*
 r освобождение *n*; открепление *n*

2627 **debate; discussion**
 d Diskussion *f*
 f débat *m*; discussion *f*
 r дискуссия *f*; беседа *f*

2628 **debit**
 d Durchfluss *m*; Volumenstrom *m*;
 Ergiebigkeit *f*; Debit *m*
 f débit *m*
 r дебит *m*; расход *m*

2629 **debit sign**
 d Debitzeichen *n*
 f signe *m* de débit
 r символ *m* расхода

* **deblock** *v* → **9681**

2630 **debug** *v*
 d Fehler beheben; [Programm] von Fehlern
 bereinigen; austesten eines Programms
 f déboguer
 r отлаживать [программу]

* **debugger** → **2633**

2631 **debugging; checkout**
 d Debugging *n*; Fehlerverfolgung *f* und
 Fehlerbeseitigung *f*; Ausprüfen *n*;
 Ausprüfung *f*; Fehlerausmerzung *f*
 f débogage *m*; dépannage *m*
 r отладка *f*; наладка *f*; выверка *f*;
 устранение *n* ошибок; устранение
 неисправностей

2632 **debugging statement**
 d Ausprüfanweisung *f*; Testhilfeanweisung *f*
 f instruction *f* de débogage
 r отладочный оператор *m*

2633 **debug program; debugger**
 d Debugger *m*; Fehlersuchprogramm *n*
 f programme *m* de mise au point; programme
 de débogage; débogueur *m*
 r программа *f* отладки; отладчик *m*

2634 **decade**
 d Dekade *f*
 f décade *f*
 r декада *f*

* **decade** → **2645**

* **decade counter** → **2648**

2635 **decatenation**
 d Aufteilung *f*; Aufgliederung *f*
 f décaténation *f*; désenchaînement *m*
 r разъединение *n*; декатенация *f*

2636 **decay; extinction**
 d Abklingen *n*; Extinktion *f*
 f affaiblissement *m*; extinction *f*
 r ослабление *n*; угасание *n*; спад *m*;
 затухание *n*; экстинция *f*

* **decay time** → **3696**

2637 **deceleration; negative acceleration**
 d Dezeleration *f*; negative Beschleunigung *f*;
 Verzögerung *f*
 f décélération *f*; accélération *f* négative
 r замедление *n*; отрицательное ускорение *n*

* **deceleration time** → **2728**

2638 **decentralization**
 d Dezentralisierung *f*
 f décentralisation *f*
 r децентрализация *f*

2639 **decentralized control**
 d dezentralisierte Steuerung *f*
 f commande *f* décentralisée
 r децентрализованное управление *n*

2640 **decentralized data processing**
 d dezentralisierte Datenverarbeitung *f*
 f traitement *m* de données décentralisé
 r децентрализованная обработка *f* данных

2641 **decentralized operating system**
 d verteiltes Betriebssystem *n*; dezentralisiertes
 Betriebssystem
 f système *m* opérationnel décentralisé
 r децентрализованная операционная
 система *f*

2642 **decidability**
 d Entscheidbarkeit *f*
 f décidabilité *f*
 r разрешимость *f*

2643 **decidability problem; decision problem**
 d Entscheidungsproblem *n*

f problème m de décision
r проблема f разрешимости; проблема
разрешения; задача f принятия решения

2644 decidable
d lösbar; entscheidbar
f décidable
r разрешимый

2645 decimal; decade
d dezimal; Dezimal-; Zehner-; dekadisch
f décimal; décadique
r десятичный

2646 decimal address; dot address
d dezimale Adresse f
f adresse f décimale; adresse en notation
pointée
r точечный адрес m

2647 decimal-binary
d dezimal-binär; dezimal-dual
f décimal-binaire
r десятично-двоичный

* **decimal-binary conversion** → **2655**

2648 decimal counter; decade counter
d Dezimalzähler m; Dekadenzähler m
f compteur décimal; compteur m décadique;
compteur à décades
r десятичный счётчик; декадный счётчик m

2649 decimal form
d Dezimalform f
f forme f décimale
r десятичная форма f

2650 decimalize v
d in Dezimalsystem umwandeln
f décimaliser
r переводить в десятичную систему

2651 decimal number
d Dezimalzahl f; Zehnerzahl f
f nombre m décimal
r десятичное число n

2652 decimal [number] system
d Dezimalsystem n; dekadisches
Zahlensystem n
f système m décimal
r десятичная система f [счисления]

2653 decimal point
d Dezimalkomma n; Dezimalpunkt m
f point m décimal; virgule f décimale
r десятичная запятая f

2654 decimal pulsing

d dekadische Impulsgabe f;
Dezimalziffern-Impulsgabe f
f pulsation f décimale
r десятичная пульсация f

* **decimal system** → **2652**

2655 decimal-[to-]binary conversion
d Dezimal-Binär-Konvertierung f;
Decimal-Binär-Umwandlung f;
Decimal-Binär-Umsetzung f
f conversion f décimale-binaire; conversion de
décimale en binaire
r преобразование n из десятичной системы в
двоичную

2656 decimation
(in decimal signal processing)
d Decimation f
f décimation f
r децимация f; прореживание n

* **decipher** → **2670**

* **decipher** v → **2669**

* **decipherer** → **2670**

2657 decision; solution; resolution
d Lösung f; Entscheidung f
f décision f; solution f; résolution f
r решение n

2658 decision block; decision box; thinker
(in a block-schema)
d Entscheidungsblock m;
Entscheidungskästchen n; Lösungsblock m
f unité f de décision; bloc m de décision
r [логический] блок m ветвления; блок
решения

* **decision box** → **2658**

2659 decision circuit; decision unit
d Entscheiderschaltung f;
Entscheidungsschaltung f
f circuit m de décision; concepteur m
r решающая схема f

* **decision-help information system** → **2661**

2660 decision making
d Entscheidungstreffen n;
Entscheidungsfindung f;
Entscheidungsvorbereitung f;
Beschlussfassung f
f prise f de décision; procédé m de décision;
découverte f de décision
r принятие n решения; выбор m решения

2661 **decision-making information system;**
decision-help information system
d Entscheidungsfindung-Informationssystem *n*
f système *m* d'information décisionnel
r информационная система *f* принятия
решений

* **decision problem** → **2643**

2662 **decision procedure**
d Entscheidungsverfahren *n*
f méthode *f* de décision
r [раз]решающая процедура *f*

2663 **decision theory**
d Entscheidungstheorie *f*
f théorie *f* de la décision
r теория *f* решения

2664 **decision threshold**
d Entscheiderschwelle *f*
f seuil *m* de décision
r порог *m* решения

* **decision unit** → **2659**

2665 **decision value**
d Entscheidungswert *m*
f valeur *f* de décision; amplitude *f* de décision
r решающее значение *n*

2666 **declaration**
d Deklaration *f*; Beschreibung *f*; Erklärung *f*
f déclaration *f*; description *f*; convention *f*
r декларация *f*; описание *n*

* **declarative language** → **6257**

2667 **declarator; declarer**
d Deklarator *m*; Vereinbarungsanweisung *f*
f déclarateur *m*; instruction *f* de déclaration
r оператор *m* объявления; декларатор *m*

2668 **declare error**
(of a variable)
d Vereinbarungsfehler *m*; Deklarationsfehler *m*
f erreur *f* de déclaration
r ошибка *f* при объявлении

* **declarer** → **2667**

2669 **decode** *v*; **decipher** *v*; **decrypt** *v*
d decodieren; entziffern; entschlüsseln;
dechiffrieren
f décoder; déchiffrer; décodifier
r декодировать; дешифрировать;
раскодировать

2670 **decoder; decipher[er]; decode unit;**
decoding network; decoding circuit;

decryption circuit
d Decod[ier]er *m*; Decodierschaltung *f*;
Entschlüsseler *m*; Entzifferer *m*;
Entschlüsselungseinrichtung *f*
f décodeur *m*; déchiffreur *m*; circuit *m* de
décodage; circuit décodeur
r декодер *m*; дешифратор *m*; декодирующая
схема *f*; дешифрирующая схема

2671 **decoder matrix**
d Decodiermatrix *f*; Entschlüsselungsmatrix *f*
f matrice *f* de décodage
r дешифраторная матрица *f*

* **decode unit** → **2670**

* **decodification** → **2672**

2672 **decoding; decodification; decryption**
d Decodierung *f*; Decodieren *n*; Entschlüsseln *n*
f décodage *m*; déchiffrage *m*; décryptage *m*
r декодирование *n*; дешифрирование *n*;
расшифровка *f*

* **decoding circuit** → **2670**

* **decoding network** → **2670**

2673 **decoherence**
d Entfrittung *f*
f décohérence *f*
r декогерирование *n*; отстранение *n*
слипания

2674 **decollation; deleaving**
d Aussortieren *n*
f triage *m*; classification *f*
r рассортировка *f*; разделение *n* на части

* **decompact** *v* → **2679**

2675 **decompiler**
d Decompil[ier]er *m*; Umkehrcompiler *m*
f décompilateur *m*
r декомпилятор *m*

2676 **decompiling**
d Dekompilierung *f*
f décompilation *f*
r декомпиляция *f*

2677 **decompose** *v*
d zerlegen; zergliedern; [auf]spalten
f décomposer; développer
r разложить; разлагать

2678 **decomposition**
d Dekomposition *f*; Zerlegung *f*
f décomposition *f*
r разложение *n*; декомпозиция *f*

2679 **decompress** *v*; **decompact** *v*; **uncompress** *v*;
      unzip *v*
      d dekomprimieren; entkomprimieren
      f décompresser; décompacter; dézipper
      r декомпрессировать

2680 **decompression**
      (of an image)
      d Dekompression *f*
      f décompression *f*
      r декомпрессия *f*

2681 **deconcentration**
      d Dekonzentration *f*
      f déconcentration *f*
      r деконцентрация *f*

2682 **decorrelation**
      d Dekorrelation *f*
      f décorrélation *f*
      r декорреляция *f*

2683 **decoupler**
      d Entkoppler *m*
      f découpleur *m*
      r разъединитель *m*

2684 **decoupling**
      d Entkopplung *f*
      f découplage *m*
      r развязка *f*; разъединение *n*

2685 **decrease** *v*; **diminish** *v*
      d vermindern; verringern; verkleinern
      f décroître; diminuer
      r уменьшать; убывать

2686 **decrement**
      d Dekrement *n*
      f décrément *m*
      r декремент *m*; уменьшение *n*

   * **decrypt** *v* → 2669

   * **decryption** → 2672

   * **decryption circuit** → 2670

2687 **dedicated**
      d zugeordnet; zweckentsprechend;
        zweckbestimmt; spezialisiert; zweckorientiert
      f attribué; conforme; dédi[cac]é
      r выделенный; специализированный

   * **dedicated computer** → 8756

2688 **dedicated data network**
      d eigenständiges Datennetz *n*
      f réseau *m* de données dédi[cac]é
      r выделенная сеть *f* данных

2689 **dedicated device**
      d zweckorientiertes Gerät *n*
      f dispositif *m* dédi[cac]é
      r специализированное устройство *n*;
        выделенное устройство

2690 **dedicated line**
      d Standleitung *f*
      f ligne *f* dédi[cac]ée; ligne attribuée
      r выделенная линия *f* связи

2691 **dedicated network**
      d Standverbindungsnetz *n*
      f réseau *m* dédi[cac]é
      r выделенная сеть *f*

2692 **deduction**
      d Deduktion *f*
      f déduction *f*
      r дедукция *f*

   * **deepness** → 2762

2693 **default**
      d Standard *m*; Standardwert *m*
      f défaut *m*; standard *m*
      r умолчание *n*; стандарт *m*

2694 **default; standard** *adj*
      d Standard-
      f sous-entendu; standard
      r подразумеваемый; стандартный

2695 **default colors**
      d Standardfarben *fpl*
      f couleurs *fpl* par défaut
      r стандартные цвета *mpl*; цвета по
        умолчанию

2696 **default declaration**
      d Standardvereinbarung *f*
      f déclaration *f* par défaut; convention *f* standard
      r стандартное описание *n*; объявление *n* по
        умолчанию

2697 **default graphic style**
      d Standardgrafikstil *m*
      f style *m* graphique par défaut
      r стандартный графический стиль *m*

2698 **default option**
      d Standardoption *f*; Option *f* im Normalfall;
        Standardabnahme *f*
      f option *f* par défaut; option standard
      r выбор *m* по умолчанию; стандартный
        выбор

2699 **default paragraph text**
      d Standardabsatztext *m*

   f texte *m* courant standard
   r стандартный текст *m* параграфа

2700 default printer
   d Standarddrucker *m*
   f imprimante *f* par défaut
   r принтер *m* по умолчанию

2701 default setting
   d Standardeinrichtung *f*
   f établissement *m* standard; établissement par
      défaut
   r стандартная установка *f*

2702 default text style; standard text style
   d Standardtextstil *m*
   f style *m* de texte par défaut
   r стандартный текстовой стиль *m*

   * **defect → 3679**

2703 defects structure
   d Defektstruktur *f*
   f structure *f* des défauts
   r структура *f* дефектов

2704 deferred
   d verzögert; zurückgesetzt
   f différé; retardé; décalé
   r отсроченный; задержанный; отложенный

   * **deferred address → 4779**

   * **deferred addressing → 4780**

2705 deferred transmission
   d zeitversetztes Senden *n*
   f transmission *f* différée
   r отсроченная передача *f*, отложенная
      передача

2706 deferred update
   d zeitversetzte Fortschreibung *f*; zeitversetzte
      Aktualisierung *f*
   f actualisation *f* décalée
   r задержанное обновление *n*; задержанная
      корректировка *f*

2707 define *v*; determine *v*
   d definieren; bestimmen
   f définir; déterminer
   r определять; дефинировать

2708 defined; definite; determined
   d definiert; bestimmt; determiniert; erklärt;
      festlegegt
   f défini; déterminé
   r определённый; дефинированный

   * **definite → 2708**

2709 definition
   d Definition *f*
   f définition *f*
   r определение *n*; дефиниция *f*

   * **definition → 8497**

2710 definitive program
   d endgültiges Programm *n*
   f programme *m* définitif
   r окончательная программа *f*; отлаженная
      программа

2711 deformation
   d Deformation *f*
   f déformation *f*
   r деформация *f*

   * **defragger → 2714**

2712 defragment *v*
   d defragmentieren
   f tasser
   r дефрагментировать

2713 defragmentation
   d Defragmentieren *n*; Defragmentation *f*
   f defragmentation *f*; tassement *m*
   r дефрагментирование *n*

**2714 defragmenter; defragger; packing
      program**
   d Defragmentierer *m*
   f programme *m* de tassement
   r программа *f* дефрагментации (диска)

2715 degauss button
   d Degauss-Taste *f*; Entmagnetisierungstaste *f*
   f bouton *m* de démagnétisation
   r кнопка *f* размагничивания

   * **degaussing → 2740**

2716 degeneracy; degeneration
   d Ausartung *f*; Entartung *f*
   f dégénérescence *f*; dégénération *f*
   r вырождение *n*; дегенерация *f*

   * **degeneration → 2716**

   * **degenerative feedback → 6057**

2717 degradation
   d Degradation *f*
   f dégradation *f*
   r деградация *f*

2718 degree; order
   d Grad *m*; Potenz *f*

  f degré *m*
  r степень *f*

2719 degree of attenuation
  d Schwächungsgrad *m*
  f taux *m* d'atténuation
  r степень *f* ослабления

2720 degree of purity
  d Reinheitsgrad *m*
  f degré *m* de pureté
  r степень *f* чистоты

  * **dejagging** → **439**

2721 delay; lag[ging]; retardation
  d Verzögerung *f*; Verzug *m*; Nacheilung *f*
  f retard[ement] *m*; délai *m*
  r запаздывание *n*; замедление *n*; задержка *f*

2722 delay chain
  d Verzögerungskette *f*
  f chaîne *f* de délai
  r цепочка *f* замедления; цепочка задержки

2723 delay counter
  d Verzögerungszähler *m*
  f compteur *m* à retard
  r счётчик *m* интервалов задержки

2724 delay delivery
  d späteres Weitersenden *n*; verzögertes
     Zuschreiben *n*
  f livraison *f* retardée
  r замедленная передача *f*

2725 delay line
  d Verzögerungsleitung *f*; Verzögerungsstrecke *f*
  f ligne *f* à retard; ligne de délai; ligne de
     retardement
  r линия *f* задержки

2726 delay operator
  d Verzögerungsoperator *m*
  f opérateur *m* de retard
  r оператор *m* запаздывания

2727 delay-pulse latch
  d Verzögerungsimpulsschalter *m*
  f commutateur *m* d'impulsions de retardement
  r переключатель *m* импульса с задержкой

2728 delay time; deceleration time; lag time
  d Verzögerungszeit *f*; Verzugszeit *f*
  f temps *m* à retard
  r время *n* задержки; время запаздывания

  * **deleaving** → **2674**

2729 delegate *v*

  d delegieren
  f déléguer
  r делегировать

2730 delete *v* a page
  d eine Seite löschen
  f effacer une page
  r стирать страницы

2731 delete key; Del key
  d Löschtaste *f*
  f touche *f* d'effacement
  r клавиша *f* стирания; клавиша Del

2732 delete option
  d Löschen-Option *f*
  f option *f* d'effacement
  r опция *f* стирания

2733 delete *v*; erase *v*; expunge *v*; eliminate *v*
  d eliminieren
  f délimiter; éliminer
  r вычёркивать; уничтожать

  * **deleting** → **1715, 2734**

2734 deletion; deleting
  d Streichen *n*; Radieren *n*
  f suppression *f*
  r вычёркивание *n*

  * **deletion** → **1715**

2735 delimiter; limiter
  d Begrenzer *m*
  f [dé]limiteur *m*; séparateur *m*
  r разделитель *m*; ограничитель *m*

  * **delimiter sign** → **8395**

2736 delink *v*
  d entketten
  f déchaîner; détacher
  r разрывать; разъединять

2737 delivery
  d Übergabe *f*
  f livraison *f*; délivrance *f*
  r передача *f*; вручение *n*; выдача *f*

2738 delivery confirmation
  d Übergabebestätigung *f*
  f confirmation *f* de livraison
  r подтверждение *n* доставки; подтверждение
     поставки

2739 delivery length; supply length
  d Lieferlänge *f*
  f longueur *f* de livraison
  r поставляемая длина *f*

* **Del key** → 2731

2740 demagnetization; degaussing
 d Entmagnetisieren *n*
 f désaimantation *f*; démagnétisation *f*
 r размагничивание *n*; стирание *n* магнитной
 записи

* **demand** → 7963, 7972

2741 demand [data] processing; on-demand processing
 d Datenverarbeitung *f* auf Anfrage
 f traitement *m* [de données] à la demande
 r обработка *f* [данных] по запросам;
 обработка данных по требованию

2742 demand-paged memory
 d Speicher *m* mit Seitenumlagerung auf
 Anfrage
 f mémoire *f* à la demande de pages
 r память *f* с подкачкой страниц по
 требованию

* **demand processing** → 2741

* **demo** → 2747

2743 demodifier
 d Demodifizierer *m*
 f démodificateur *m*
 r демодификатор *m*

2744 demodulator
 d Demodulator *m*
 f démodulateur *m*
 r демодулятор *m*

2745 demo mode
 d Demomodus *m*
 f mode *m* démo
 r демо-режим *m*

* **demon** → 2486

2746 demonstration
 d Demonstration *f*
 f démonstration *f*
 r демонстрация *f*

* **demo package** → 2747

* **De Morgan formulae** → 5293

* **De Morgan laws** → 5293

* **De Morgan's formulae** → 5293

* **De Morgan's laws** → 5293

2747 demosoftware; demoware; demo package; demo
 d Demonstrationspaket *n*
 f logiciel *m* de démonstration; démo *m*
 r демонстрационный пакет *m*; демо *m*

* **demount** → 2749

2748 demountable connection; demountable coupling
 d lösbare Verbindung *f*
 f jonction *f* démontable; connexion *f*
 démontable
 r разъёмное соединение *n*

* **demountable coupling** → 2748

* **demountable disk** → 3564

2749 demount[ing]; dismount[ing]
 d Demontieren *n*; Abbau *m*
 f démontage *m*
 r демонтирование *n*; удаление *n*

* **demoware** → 2747

2750 demultiplexer
 d Demultiplexer *m*
 f démultiplexeur *m*
 r демультиплексор *m*

2751 demultiplexing
 d Demultiplexierung *f*; Entschachtelung *f*
 f démultiplexage *m*
 r демультиплексирование *n*

2752 denomination; naming
 d Namengebung *f*; Benennung *f*
 f dénomination *f*; désignation *f*; nommage *m*
 r наименование *n*

2753 denote *v*; notch *v*
 d kennzeichnen; bezeichnen
 f désigner; signifier; noter
 r означать; обозначать

2754 dense
 d dicht
 f dense
 r плотный; компактный

2755 dense code
 d dichter Code *m*
 f code *m* dense
 r уплотнённый код *m*

2756 dense packaging
 d dichte Packung *f*
 f [em]paquetage *m* compact
 r плотная упаковка *f*

2757 density
  d Dichte *f*
  f densité *f*
  r плотность *f*

  * **denumerability → 2340**

  * **denumerable → 2341**

  * **depackaging → 6677**

  * **depacketize** *v* **→ 9686**

2758 dependence
  d Abhängigkeit *f*
  f dépendance *f*
  r зависимость *f*

2759 dependent variable
  d abhängige Variable *f*
  f variable *f* dépendante
  r зависимая переменная *f*

  * **depletion layer → 828**

  * **depletion-layer capacitance → 827**

2760 deposit
  d Ablagerung *f*
  f dépose *f*
  r укладка *f*

2761 depot
  d Ablage *f*
  f dépôt *m*
  r склад *m*; устройство *n* хранения

2762 depth; deepness
  d Tiefe *f*
  f profondeur *f*
  r глубина *f*

  * **depth buffer → 10085**

2763 depth-first search
  d Tiefendurchlauf *m*
  f recherche *f* à profondeur
  r поиск *m* в глубину

2764 derivation
  d Ableitung *f*
  f dérivation *f*
  r отвод *m*; ответвление *n*; деривация *f*

2765 derived field
  d abgeleitetes Feld *n*
  f champ *m* dérivé
  r производное поле *n*

2766 derived font
  d abgeleitete Schrift *f*
  f police *f* dérivée
  r производный шрифт *m*

  * **DES → 2543**

  * **descend → 2767**

2767 descend[ing]
  d Abstieg *m*
  f descente *f*
  r спуск *m*; снижение *n*

2768 descending order
  d absteigende Anordnung *f*; fallende
      Anordnung
  f ordre *m* décroissant
  r порядок *m* убывания; нисходящий порядок

2769 descending sequence
  d absteigende Reihenfolge *f*
  f séquence *f* descendante
  r нисходящая последовательность *f*

2770 descending sort
  d absteigender Sort *m*
  f triage *m* descendant
  r нисходящее сортирование *n*

2771 descramber
  d Entwürfler *m*; Descramber *m*
  f désembrouilleur *m*
  r дескрэмблер *m*

2772 description
  d Deskription *f*; Beschreibung *f*
  f description *f*
  r описание *n*; дескрипция *f*

2773 descriptive knowledge
  d deklaratives Wissen *n*
  f connaissances *fpl* descriptives
  r знания *npl* в форме описаний

2774 descriptor
  d Deskriptor *m*; Vereinbarungssymbol *n*;
      Vereinbarungszeichen *n*
  f descripteur *m*
  r дескриптор *m*; описатель *m*

2775 descriptor field
  d Deskriptorfeld *n*
  f champ *m* de descripteurs
  r поле *n* дескрипторов

2776 desequencing
  d Ablauffolgestörung *f*
  f violation *f* de séquence
  r нарушение *n* последовательности

* **deserializer** → 8438

* **design** → 2780, 3161

2777 **design; project**
 d Entwurf *m*; Bauplan *m*
 f projet *m*; conception *f*
 r проект *m*

2778 **design** *v*; **project** *v*
 d entwerfen; anlegen; konstruieren
 f concevoir; projeter
 r проектировать

2779 **designation**
 d Bestimmung *f*
 f désignation *f*
 r назначение *n*; предназначение *n*

* **designation** → 6294

* **designer** → 3169

2780 **design[ing]**
 d Projektierung *f*
 f conception *f*; établissement *m* d'un projet
 r проектирование *n*

2781 **design knowledge base**
 d Entwurfswissensbasis *f*
 f base *f* de connaissances conceptuelles
 r база *f* проектных знаний

* **design software** → 3169

* **desired** → 7971

* **desk** → 2784

2782 **desk**
 d Tisch *m*
 f table *f*
 r пульт *m*; стенд *m*

2783 **desk application**
 d Tischanwendung *f*
 f application *f* bureautique; application de bureau
 r настольное приложение *n*

* **desk-mounted** → 2784

* **desk-size** → 2784

2784 **desk[top]; desk-mounted; desk-size; table-top**
 d Tisch-; Auftisch-; Desktop-
 f tabulaire; bureautique; dessus de bureau; à plat
 r настольный

2785 **desktop**
 d Desktop *n*; Benutzeroberfläche *f*; Schreibtisch *m*; Schreibtischoberfläche *f*
 f appareil *m* du bureau
 r рабочий стол *m* (метафорическое представление на экране)

2786 **desktop computer**
 d Desktop-Computer *m*
 f ordinateur *m* de table
 r настольный компьютер *m*

2787 **desktop copier**
 d Tischkopierer *m*
 f copieur *m* tabulaire
 r настольный копировальный аппарат *m*

2788 **desktop device**
 d Desktop-Gerät *n*
 f dispositif *m* bureautique
 r настольное устройство *n*

2789 **desktop model**
 d Tischmodell *n*
 f modèle *m* tabulaire
 r настольная модель *f*

* **desktop presentation** → 7230

2790 **desktop publishing; DTP**
 d Publizieren *n* vom Schreibtisch; Publizieren am Arbeitsplatz
 f publication *f* bureautique; microédition *f*
 r настольная издательская деятельность *f*

2791 **desktop radio**
 d Tischradio *n*
 f radiotique *f*
 r настольное радио *n*

2792 **desktop scanner**
 d Tischabtaster *m*; Tischscanner *m*; Desktopscanner *m*
 f scanner *m* tabulaire; scanner de table
 r настольный сканер *m*

2793 **desktop software**
 d Desktop-Software *f*
 f logiciel *m* bureautique
 r программные средства *npl* для настольных систем

2794 **desktop system**
 d Tischsystem *n*
 f système *m* bureautique; système tabulaire
 r настольная система *f*

2795 **desktop version**
 d Tischversion *f*

f version *f* tabulaire
r настольная версия *f*

2796 desktop video; DTV
   d Desktop-Video *n*
   f vidéotique *f*
   r настольная видеостудия *f*; компьютерное
     видео *n*

   * **desmoothing → 301**

2797 destination; butt; target
   d Verwendungszweck *m*; Ziel *n*
   f destination *f*; but *m*
   r [место]назначение *n*; цель *f*; адресат *m*

2798 destination address; target address
   d Zieladresse *f*
   f adresse *f* de destination
   r адрес *m* местоназначения; конечный адрес

2799 destination code
   d Bestimmungs[ort]kennzahl *f*; Zielcode *m*
   f code *m* de destination
   r код *m* [место]назначения

2800 destination register
   d Zielregister *n*
   f registre *m* de destination
   r выходной регистр *m* [пересылки данных]

   * **destroy** *v* **→ 2335**

   * **destroyed information → 2801**

2801 destructed information; destroyed information
   d zerstörte Information *f*
   f information *f* détruite
   r разрушенная информация *f*; стёртая
     информация

   * **destruction → 2491**

2802 destructive reading
   d zerstörendes Lesen *n*; löschendes Lesen
   f lecture *f* destructive
   r считывание *n* с разрушением
     [информации]

2803 destructive test
   d nicht zerstörungsfreie Prüfung *f*
   f essai *m* destructif
   r разрушающее испытание *n*

   * **detach** *v* **→ 2978**

2804 detachment
   d Trennung *f*; Abtrennung *f*
   f détachement *m*

r разъединение *n*; разделение *n*

2805 detach option
   d Trennungsoption *f*
   f option *f* de détachement
   r опция *f* разъединения

   * **detail file → 9480**

2806 detail management algorithm
   d Algorithmus *m* der Detailsbearbeitung
   f algorithme *m* de traitement de détails
   r алгоритм *m* обработки деталей

   * **detectability → 2810**

2807 detected information
   d aufgefundene Information *f*
   f information *f* détectée
   r обнаруженная информация *f*

2809 detection
   d Erkennen *n*; Kennung *f*; Erkennung *f*
   f détection *f*; reconnaissance *f*
   r обнаружение *n*; обнаруживание *n*;
     выявление *n*

2808 detection; rectification
   d Detektion *f*; Rektifikation *f*; Gleichrichtung *f*
   f détection *f*; rectification *f*; redressement *m*;
     redressage *m*
   r детектирование *n*; ректификация *f*;
     выпрямление *n*

2810 detectivity; detectability
   d Nachweisfähigkeit *f*; Nachweisvermögen *n*;
     Ansprechbarkeit *f*; Identifizierbarkeit *f*
   f détectivité *f*
   r обнаруживающая способность *f*;
     способность индикации

2811 detector; rectifier
   d Detektor *m*; Gleichrichter *m*
   f détecteur *m*; redresseur *m*
   r детектор *m*; выпрямитель *m*

   * **deterioration → 2491**

   * **determine** *v* **→ 2707**

   * **determined → 2708**

2812 determinism
   d Determinismus *m*
   f déterminisme *m*
   r детерминизм *m*

2813 developer
   d Entwickler *m*

f développeur *m*
r разработчик *m*

2814 development; extension
d Entwicklung *f*; Abwicklung *f*
f développement *m*; élaboration *f*
r развитие *n*; разложение *n*; разработка *f*

2815 development game
d Entwicklungsspiel *n*
f jeu *m* de développement
r развивающаяся игра *f*

2816 development system
d Entwicklungssystem *n*
f système *m* de développement
r система *f* развития; система проектирования

2817 development time
d Entwicklungszeit *f*
f temps *m* de développement
r время *n* разработки; время отладки

2818 deviation
d Abweichung *f*; Deviation *f*
f déviation *f*
r отклонение *n*; девиация *f*

2819 device
d Gerät *n*
f dispositif *m*; appareil *m*
r устройство *n*

2820 device channel controller
d Gerätekanalsteuereinheit *f*
f contrôleur *m* de dispositif canal
r контроллер *m* канального устройства

2821 device code
d Gerätecode *m*
f code *m* de dispositif
r код *m* устройства

2822 device driver
d Gerätetreiber *m*
f driver *m* de dispositif; pilote *m* de dispositif
r драйвер *m* устройства

2823 device end
d Geräteende *n*
f fin *f* de dispositif
r конец *m* [работы] устройства

2824 device identification
d Gerätebezeichnung *f*
f identification *f* de dispositif
r распознавание *n* устройства

2825 device identificator; device name

d Gerätekennzeichen *n*; Gerätename *m*
f identificateur *m* de dispositif; nom *m* de dispositif
r идентификатор *m* устройства; имя *n* устройства

2826 device independence
d Geräteunabhängigkeit *f*
f indépendance *f* d'unité
r независимость *f* от устройства

2827 device manager
d Geräteverwalter *m*; Gerätemanager *m*
f gestionnaire *m* de périphérique
r менажер *m* устройств; аппаратный менажер

* **device name** → 2825

2828 device queue
d Gerätewarteschlange *f*
f queue *f* de requêtes d'un dispositif
r очередь *f* запросов к устройству

2829 device selection
d Geräteauswahl *f*
f sélection *f* de dispositif
r выбор *m* устройства; обращение *n* к устройству

2830 device space
d Gerätekoordinatenraum *m*
f espace *m* d'appareil; espace périphérique
r пространство *n* устройства

2831 device takedown time
d Gerätefreigabezeit *f*
f temps *m* de libération d'un dispositif
r время *n* освобождения устройства

2832 device termination interrupt
d Geräteendeunterbrechung *f*
f interruption *f* de fin de dispositif
r прерывание *n* из-за конца работы устройства

* **3D figure** → 3193

2833 3D geometry processor
d 3D-Geometrie-Prozessor *m*
f processeur *m* de géométrie 3D
r процессор *m* 3D геометрии

2834 3D glasses
d 3D-Brille *f*
f lunettes *fpl* 3D
r 3D очки *npl*

2835 3D graphics
d dreidimensionale Grafik *f*; 3D-Grafik *f*

f infographie f tridimensionnelle; graphique m à trois dimensions; graphique 3D
r трёхмерная графика f; 3D графика

2836 3D graphics benchmark program
d 3D-Grafikbenchmark-Programm n
f test m d'évaluation de graphique 3D; programme m d'évaluation de graphique 3D
r эталонный тест m 3D графики

2837 3D graphics card
d 3D-Grafikkarte f
f carte f graphique 3D
r карта f 3D графики

2838 3D hardware
d 3D-Hardware f
f matériel m 3D
r аппаратные средства npl трёхмерной графики

2839 diagnostic bus
d Diagnosesammelleitung f; Diagnosebus m
f bus m de diagnostic
r диагностическая шина f

2840 diagnostic code
d Diagnosecode m
f code m de diagnostic
r код m диагноза

2841 diagnostic packet
d Diagnosepaket n
f paquet m diagnostique
r диагностический пакет m

2842 diagnostic program; diagnotor
d Diagnoseprogramm n
f programme m diagnostique
r диагностическая программа f

2843 diagnostics
d Diagnostik f
f diagnostic m
r диагностика f

* **diagnotor** → 2842

* **diagram** → 1641

* **dial** → 2845

* **dial code** → 2846

2844 dial[ed] line; dialup line; switched line
d Wählleitung f; kommutierbare Leitung f
f ligne f commutée; ligne commutable
r коммутируемая линия f

* **dialed network** → 9085

2845 dial[ing]; dialup; calling dial; selection
d Wählen n; Wahl f; Einwahl f
f appel m par numéro; numérotation f; sélection f
r вызов m по номеру; кодовый вызов; набор m номера

2846 dial[ing] code; office code; prefix code; selection code
d Amtsschlüssel m; Amtswählcode m
f code m d'office; code d'appel; code d'indicateurs
r код m вызова; избирательный код; станционный буквенный код

* **dial line** → 2844

* **dialog** → 2852

2847 dialog box
d Dialogbox f
f boîte f de dialogue; case-dialogue f; fenêtre f d'interface
r диалоговый ящик m

2848 dialog control language; DCL
d Sprache f der Dialogregelung
f langage m de réglage de dialogue
r диалоговый язык m управления

2849 dialog field
d Dialogfeld n
f champ m de dialogue
r диалоговое поле n

* **dialog language** → 2285

2850 dialog mode; conversational mode; interactive mode
d Dialogbetrieb m; Dialogarbeitsweise f
f mode m à dialogue; mode dialogué; mode interactif
r диалоговый режим m; интерактивный режим

2851 dialog structure
d Dialogstruktur f
f structure f de dialogue
r структура f диалога

2852 dialog[ue]
d Dialog m
f dialogue m
r диалог m

* **dialup** → 2845

2853 dialup connection
d Einwahlverbindung f

f connexion f commutée
r коммутируемая связь f

* **dialup line** → 2844

* **dialup network** → 9085

2854 diamond-shaped dot
d rhomboidaler Punkt m
f point m rhomboïdal
r ромбовидная точка f

* **diapositive** → 8655

2855 dibit
d Dibit n; Doppelbit n
f dibit m
r дибит m; двухбитовая конфигурация f

* **dichotomizing search** → 948

2856 dichotomous
d dichotomisch
f dichotomique
r дихотомический

2857 dichotomy
d Dichotomie f
f dichotomie f
r дихотомия f

2858 dictionary
d Wörterbuch n
f dictionnaire m
r словарь m

* **didot** → 2859

2859 didot [point]; French point
(=1,07 US points or 0,376 mm)
d Didotpunkt m
f point m didot; point typographique; point
français
r пункт m Дидо; французский пункт;
типографическая точка f

2860 dielectric
d dielektrisch
f diélectrique
r диэлектрический

2861 dielectric-coated
d dielektrisch beschichtet; mit dielektrischer
Beschichtung
f à revêtement diélectrique
r с диэлектрическим покрытием

2862 dielectric constant; permittivity
d Dielektrizitätskonstante f
f constante f diélectrique; permittivité f

r диэлектрическая постоянная f;
диэлектрическая проницаемость f

2863 dielectric scanning
d dielektrische Abtastung f
f exploration f diélectrique
r диэлектрическая развёртка f;
диэлектрическое сканирование n

2864 difference
d Differenz f
f différence f
r разность f

2865 differential
d differentiel
f différentiel
r дифференциальный; разностный

2866 differential amplifier
d Differenzverstärker m
f amplificateur m différentiel
r дифференциальный усилитель m

2867 differential group delay
d Gruppenlaufzeitdifferenz f
f temps m de propagation de groupe
différentiel
r разность f группового времени
распространения

2868 differential pulse
d Differentialimpuls m
f impulsion f différentielle
r дифференциальный импульс m

2869 differential transformer
d Differentialtransformator m
f transformateur m différentiel
r дифференциальный трансформатор m

2870 differentiating circuit
d differenzierende Schaltung f
f circuit m de différentiation
r дифференцирующая схема f

2871 diffraction pattern
d Beugungsmuster n; Beugungsbild n
f figure f de diffraction
r дифракционная картина f

2872 diffuse v; scatter v
d diffundieren; streuen; zerstreuen; ausstreuen
f diffuser; disséminer; disperser
r рассеивать; разбрасывать

2873 diffusion
d Diffusion f
f diffusion f
r диффузия f; рассеяние n

2874 **digit; chiffre; cipher; figure**
   d Ziffer *f*
   f chiffre *m*; digit *m*
   r цифра *f*

   * **digital** → 6330

   * **digital-analog computer** → 4583

   * **digital-analog converter** → 2929

2875 **digital animation**
   d Digitalanimation *f*
   f animation *f* numérique
   r цифровая анимация *f*

2876 **digital audio tape; DAT**
   d digitales Audioband *n*
   f bande *f* audionumérique
   r цифровая аудио-лента *f*

2877 **digital camera**
   d Digitalkamera *f*
   f caméra *f* numérique; appareil *m*
        photonumérique
   r цифровая камера *f*

   * **digital cash** → 3333

2878 **digital cinematography**
   d digitale Kinematografie *f*
   f cinématographie *f* numérique
   r цифровая кинематография *f*

2879 **digital circuit**
   d digitale Schaltung *f*; digitales Schaltwerk *n*;
        digitaler Stromkreis *m*
   f circuit *m* digital; circuit numérique
   r цифровая схема *f*

2880 **digital code; numerical code**
   d Digitalcode *m*; Zifferncode *m*; numerischer
        Code *m*
   f code *m* digital; code numérique
   r цифровой код *m*

2881 **digital color**
   d Digitalfarbe *f*
   f couleur *f* numérique
   r цифровой цвет *m*

2882 **digital color camera**
   d Digitalfarbkamera *f*
   f caméra *m* numérique en couleurs
   r цифровая цветная камера *f*

2883 **digital color copying**
   d digitales Farbkopieren *n*
   f copiage *m* numérique en couleurs
   r цифровое цветное копирование *n*

2884 **digital color image**
   d Digitalfarbbild *n*
   f image *f* numérique en couleurs
   r цифровое цветовое изображение *n*

2885 **digital communication network**
   d digitales Kommunikationsnetz *n*
   f réseau *m* de communication digital
   r цифровая коммуникационная сеть *f*

2886 **digital concentrator**
   d Digitalkonzentrator *m*
   f concentrateur *m* digital
   r цифровой концентратор *m*

2887 **digital copier**
   d digitaler Farbkopierer *m*
   f copieur *m* numérique
   r цифровое копировальное устройство *n*

2888 **digital cordless telephone**
   d digitale schnurlose Telefone *f*
   f téléphone *m* numérique sans fil
   r цифровой беспроводный телефон *m*

2889 **digital data; numerical data**
   d digitale Daten *pl*; Zahlenangaben *fpl*
   f données *fpl* digitaux; données numériques
   r цифровые данные *pl*; численные данные;
        числовые данные

2890 **digital design; logical design**
   d digitaler Entwurf *m*; logischer Entwurf
   f projet *m* digital; projet logique
   r цифровое проектирование *n*; логическое
        проектирование

2891 **digital device**
   d Digitalgerät *n*
   f dispositif *m* numérique
   r цифровое устройство *n*

2892 **digital display; numeric[al] display;
        all-digital display**
   d digitales Display *n*; numerisches Display;
        Digitalmonitor *m*
   f écran *m* digital; afficheur *m* numérique
   r цифровой дисплей *m*; цифровой экран *m*

2893 **digital echo suppressor**
   d digitaler Echosperrkreis *m*
   f suppresseur *m* d'échos digital
   r цифровой подавитель *m* отражённых
        сигналов

   * **digital end-to-end** → 2894

2894 **digital end-to-end [transmission]**
   d Digitalübertragung *f* von Endgerät zu
        Endgerät; Digitalübertragung von Teilnehmer
        zu Teilnehmer

f transmission *f* numérique de bout en bout;
transmission numérique intégrale
r цифровая сквозная передача *f*

2895 digital error
   d Digitalfehler *m*
   f erreur *f* numérique
   r цифровая погрешность *f*

2896 digital filter
   d Digitalfilter *m*
   f filtre *m* numérique
   r цифровой фильтр *m*

2897 digital filtering
   d digitale Filtrierung *f*
   f filtrage *m* numérique
   r цифровое фильтрирование *n*

2898 digital filter simulation
   d Simulierung *f* des Digitalfilters
   f simulation *f* de filtre numérique
   r симулирование *n* цифрового фильтра

   * **digital format** → 6342

2899 digital grid
   d Digitalnetz *n*
   f grille *f* digitale
   r разрядная решётка *f*; цифровая сетка *f*

2900 digital image; numeric[al] image
   d digitales Bild *n*; digitales Abbild *n*
   f image *f* numérique
   r цифровое изображение *n*

2901 digital image copyright
   d Digitalbild-Copyright *n*
   f copyright *m* d'image numérique
   r авторское право *n* цифрового
изображения; копирайт *m* цифрового
изображения

2902 digital image processing
   d digitale Bildverarbeitung *f*
   f traitement *m* d'images numériques
   r обработка *f* цифровых изображений

2903 digital image synthesis
   d Digitalbild-Synthese *f*
   f synthèse *f* d'image numérique
   r синтез *m* цифрового изображения

2904 digital imaging
   d digitale Abbildung *f*
   f imagerie *f* numérique
   r цифровое изображение *n*

2905 digital input; numeric input
   d Digitaleingabe *f*; Digitaleingang *m*;

Zahleneingabe *f*
   f entrée *f* numérique
   r цифровой вход *m*; цифровой ввод *m*; ввод
чисел

   * **digital integrator** → 4752

   * **digitalization** → 2993

2906 digit[al]ize *v*
   d digitalisieren
   f numériser; digitaliser
   r дигитализировать; преобразовывать в
цифровую форму

2907 digital line
   d digitale Leitung *f*; Digitalanschluss *m*
   f ligne *f* numérique
   r цифровая линия *f*

2908 digitally coded voice
   d digitalcodierte Sprache *f*
   f voix *f* codée numériquement
   r цифрово кодированный голос *m*

2909 digital model
   d numerisches Modell *n*
   f modèle *m* numérique; modèle digital
   r цифровая модель *f*; дигитальная модель

2910 digital multimedia standard
   d digitaler Multimediastandard *m*
   f norme *f* multimédia numérique
   r цифровой мультимедийный стандарт *m*

2911 digital network
   d digitales Netz *n*
   f réseau *m* numérique
   r цифровая сеть *f*

2912 digital noise
   d digitales Rauschen *n*
   f bruit *m* digital
   r цифровой шум *m*

2913 digital output; numeric output
   d Digitalausgabe *f*; Digitalausgang *m*;
Zahlenausgabe *f*
   f sortie *f* numérique
   r цифровой выход *m*; цифровой вывод *m*;
вывод чисел

**2914 digital photography; digitized
photography**
   d numerisches Foto *n*; digitalisierte
Fotografie *f*; digitales Foto
   f photo[graphie] *f* numérique; photo[graphie]
numérisée
   r цифровой снимок *m*; дискретизированная
фотография *f*; оцифрованный снимок

2915 digital photo memory
 d numerischer Fotospeicher *m*
 f photothèque *m* numérique
 r цифровая фотооптическая память *f*

2916 digital photomontage
 d numerische Fotomontage *f*
 f photomontage *m* numérique
 r цифровой фотомонтаж *m*

2917 digital plotter
 d numerischer Kurvenschreiber *m*
 f traceur *m* numérique
 r цифровой графопостроитель *m*

2918 digital probe
 d digitale Probe *f*
 f sonde *f* numérique
 r цифровой зонд *m*

2919 digital pulse; numeric[al] pulse
 d Zahlenimpuls *m*
 f impulsion *f* digitale; impulsion numérique
 r цифровой импульс *m*

2920 digital signal; discrete signal; numerical signal
 d digitales Signal *n*; numerisches Signal
 f signal *m* digital; signal numérique
 r цифровой сигнал *m*; дискретный сигнал

2921 digital signal analyzer
 d Digitalsignalanalysator *m*
 f analyseur *m* de signaux numériques
 r анализатор *m* цифровых сигналов

2922 digital signal processing
 d digitale Signalverarbeitung *f*
 f traitement *m* de signaux numériques
 r цифровая обработка *f* сигналов

2923 digital signature
 d digitale Unterschrift *f*; digitale Signatur *f*
 f signature *f* numérique
 r цифровая подпись *f*; цифровая сигнатура *f*;
 электронная подпись

2924 digital signature standard; DSS
 d digitaler Unterschrift-Standard *m*
 f norme *f* de signature numérique
 r стандарт *m* цифровой подписи

 * **digital sorting** → 7586

2925 digital space
 d digitaler Raum *m*
 f espace *m* numérique
 r цифровое пространство *n*

2926 digital speech channel; digital voice channel
 d Digitalsprachkanal *m*
 f canal *m* vocal digital
 r цифровой речевой канал *m*

2927 digital speech interpolation
 d digitale Sprachinterpolation *f*
 f interpolation *f* vocale numérique
 r цифровая интерполяция *f* речи

2928 digital subscriber line; DSL
 d digitale Abonnentenleitung *f*
 f ligne *f* d'abonné numérique
 r цифровая абонантская линия *f*

 * **digital tattoo** → 2935

2929 digital-[to-]analog converter; DAC
 d Digital-Analog-Konverter *m*;
 D/A-Umwandler *m*;
 Digital-Analog-Umsetzer *m*
 f convertisseur *m* numérique-analogique
 r цифрово-аналоговый преобразователь *m*;
 ЦАП

2930 digital video
 d numerisches Video *n*; Digitalvideo *n*
 f vidéo *m* numérique
 r цифровое видео *n*

2931 digital video compression
 d Digitalvideo-Kompression *f*
 f compression *f* de vidéo numérique
 r уплотнение *n* цифрового видео

2932 digital videodisk; DVD
 d digitale Videoplatte *f*
 f vidéodisque *m* numérique
 r цифровой видеодиск *m*

2933 digital video-interactive; DVI
 d interaktives Digitalvideo *n*
 f vidéo *m* numérique interactif
 r интерактивное цифровое видео *n*

2934 digital video service
 d digitaler Videodienst *m*
 f service *m* vidéo numérique
 r обслуживание *n* цифрового видео

 * **digital voice channel** → 2926

2935 digital watermark; digmark; digital tattoo
 d digitales Wasserzeichen *n*
 f filigrane *m* numérique; filigrane électronique
 r цифровой водяной знак *m*

 * **digitization** → 2993

 * **digitize** *v* → 2906

2936 digitized device; digitizer; quantifier
d Digitalgeber *m*; Digitalisierer *m*; Digitizer *m*; digitalisierendes Gerät *n*
f dispositif *m* digitalisé; digitaliseur *m*; capteur *m* digital; numériseur *m*
r устройство *n* оцифровки; дигитайзер *m*

2937 digitized image
d digitalisiertes Bild *n*
f image *f* numérisée
r оцифрованное изображение *n*; изображение, преобразованное в цифровую форму

* **digitized photography** → 2914

2938 digitized speech
d digitalisierte Sprache *f*
f parole *f* numérisée
r дискретизированная речь *f*

* **digitizer** → 2936

2939 digitizer configuration
d Digitizerkonfiguration *f*
f configuration *f* de digitaliseur
r конфигурация *f* дигитайзера

2940 digitizer driver
d Digitizer-Treiber *m*
f pilote *m* de digitaliseur
r драйвер *m* дигитайзера

2941 digitizer tablet; digitizing tablet; tablet
d Tablett *n*; Täfelchen *n*
f tablette *f* [à numériser]; planchette *f*
r планшет *m*; блокнот *m*

2942 digitizer template
d Digitalisierer-Schablone *f*
f modèle *m* de numériseur
r шаблон *m* дигитайзера

* **digitizing** → 2993

* **digitizing tablet** → 2941

* **digit line** → 992

2943 digit position
d Stelle *f* eines Codeelements
f position *f* d'un élément numérique; position d'un élément de signal
r позиция *f* кодового элемента

* **digmark** → 2935

* **2D image** → 911

2944 dimension
d Dimension *f*
f dimension *f*
r размерность *f*; размер *m*

* **diminish** *v* → 2685

* **diminished radix complement** → 7583

* **diminishing** → 3146

2945 diode
d Diode *f*
f diode *f*
r диод *m*

2946 diode logic; DL
d Diodenlogik *f*; DL
f logique *f* diode
r диодная логика *f*; ДЛ

2947 diode-transistor logic; DTL
d Dioden-Transistor-Logik *f*; DTL
f logique *f* diode-transistor
r диодно-транзисторная логика *f*; ДТЛ

* **DIP** → 3204

2948 direct
d direkt
f direct
r прямой; непосредственный

2949 direct access
d direkter Zugriff *m*
f accès *m* direct
r прямой доступ *m*

* **direct address** → 16

2950 direct code
d direkter Code *m*
f code *m* direct
r прямой код *m*

2951 direct coding
d Direktcodierung *f*
f codage *m* direct
r прямое кодирование *n*

2952 direct coupling
d direkte Kopplung *f*
f couplage *m* direct
r непосредственная связь *f*

2953 direct current; DC
d Gleichstrom *m*
f courant *m* continu
r постоянный ток *m*

2954 direct current amplifier
d Gleichstromverstärker *m*

f amplificateur *m* à courant continu
r усилитель *m* постоянного тока

* **directed → 6584**

2955 directed graph; oriented graph; orgraph
d gerichteter Graph *m*; orientierter Graph
f graphe *m* dirigé; graphe orienté
r направленный граф *m*; ориентированный граф; орграф *m*

2956 direction; sense; way
d Richtung *f*
f direction *f*; sens *m*
r направление *n* [связи]

2957 directional; directive
d leitend; führend; Richtungs-
f directionnel; directif; directeur
r направляющий; управляющий

2958 direction keys
d Richtungstasten *fpl*
f touches *fpl* de direction
r клавиши *fpl* направления

2959 directive; order
d Anweisung *f*; Auftrag *m*
f directive *f*; ordre *m*
r директива *f*; приказ *m*

* **directive → 2957**

2960 direct list database
d Datenbasis *f* mit direkter Listenstruktur
f base *f* de données à listes directes
r база *f* данных с простой списковой структурой

2961 direct memory access; DMA
d direkter Speicherzugriff *m*; DMA
f accès *m* direct [vers la] mémoire; DMA
r прямой доступ *m* к памяти; ПДП

2962 directory; catalog[ue]; repertory; roll
d Verzeichnis *n*; Directory *n*; Katalog *m*; Namenverzeichnis *n*
f catalogue *m*; répertoire *m*; directoire *f*; index *m*
r справочник *m*; каталог *m*; оглавление *n*

* **directory client agent → 2970**

2963 directory database
d Directory-Datenbasis *f*
f base *f* de données d'annuaire
r база *f* данных справочника

2964 directory index
d Verzeichnisindex *m*

f index *m* de répertoire
r справочный индекс *m*

2965 directory inquiries
d Verzeichnisauskünfte *fpl*
f demandes *fpl* au catalogue
r запросы *mpl* к каталогу

2966 directory name
d Katalogname *m*
f nom *m* de catalogue
r имя *n* каталога

2967 directory server agent
d Directory-Server-Agent *m*
f agent *m* de serveur d'annuaire
r агент *m* сервера-справочника

2968 directory system agent; DSA
d Verzeichnis-Systemteil *m*; Directory-System-Agent *m*
f agent de système d'annuaire; ASA
r системный агент *m* каталога

2969 directory tree
d Verzeichnisbaum *m*
f arbre *m* de répertoire
r дерево *n* каталога

2970 directory user agent; DUA; directory client agent
d Verzeichnis-End-Systemteil *m*; Verzeichnis-Client-Programm *n*
f agent *m* d'usager d'annuaire; AUA
r агент *m* пользователя справочника; агент клиента справочника

2971 direct scanning
d Direktabtastung *f*
f balayage *m* direct
r прямое сканирование *n*

* **disable → 4838**

* **disable** *v* → 4834

2972 disabled interrupt
d gesperrte Unterbrechung *f*
f interruption *f* inhibée
r блокированное прерывание *n*

* **disabling bit → 4835**

2973 disabling pulse
d Sperrimpuls *m*
f impulsion *f* de blocage
r запирающий импульс *m*

* **disarm** *v* → 4834

2974 disarray
d Unordnung f; Fehlordnung f
f désordre m
r неупорядоченность f

2975 disassembler; backassembler; reassembler
d Disassembler m; Reassembler m;
Rückassembler m
f désassembleur m
r обратный ассемблер m; дисассемблер m

* **disassembling** → 7715

* **disassociate** v → 2978

2976 disaster dump
d Katastrophenumspeicherung f
f vidage m de dépannage
r аварийный дамп m

* **disaster plan** → 2232

* **disc** → 3000

* **discard** v → 1709, 7854

* **discharge** → 9680

2977 discharge current
d Entladungsstrom m
f courant m de décharge
r разрядный ток m

* **disconnect** → 2176, 2979

2978 disconnect v; **detach** v; **disjoint** v;
disassociate v
d trennen; abtrennen
f déconnecter; disjoindre
r разъединять; размыкать; прерывать;
отделять

* **disconnecting** → 2979

* **disconnection** → 2176

**2979 disconnect[ion]; disconnecting;
switching-off; cutoff; cutout**
d Abschaltung f; Ausschaltung f; Ausschalten n
f déconnexion f; débranchement m; coupure f;
déclenchement m; disjonction f
r отключение n; выключение n;
прерывание n

2980 discontinuity
d Unstetigkeit f; Diskontinuität f;
Sprunghaftigkeit f
f discontinuité f
r разрыв m; разрывность f; прерывность f

2981 discontinuous
d unstetig; sprunghaft
f discontinu
r разрывный

**2982 discontinuous information; discrete
information**
d unstetige Information f; diskontinuierliche
Information; diskrete Information
f information f discontinue; information
discrète
r дискретная информация f

2983 discrete
d diskret
f discret
r дискретный

2984 discrete channel
d diskreter Kanal m
f canal m discret
r дискретный канал m

* **discrete information** → 2982

2985 discrete message
d diskrete Nachricht f; Einzelnachricht f
f message m discret
r дискретное сообщение n

2986 discrete mode
d diskreter Modus m
f mode m discret
r дискретный режим m

* **discrete optimization** → 2987

**2987 discrete programming; discrete
optimization**
d diskrete Programmierung f; diskrete
Optimierung f
f programmation f discrète; optimisation f
discrète
r дискретное программирование n;
дискретная оптимизация f

2988 discrete random variable
d diskrete Zufallsgröße f
f variable f aléatoire discrète
r дискретная случайная величина f

2989 discrete sampling pulse
d Einzelabtastimpuls m
f impulsion f d'échantillon discrète
r импульс m дискретной выборки

* **discrete signal** → 2920

2990 discrete structure
d diskrete Struktur f

f structure *f* discrète
r дискретная структура *f*

2991 discrete variable
d diskrete Variable *f*
f variable *f* discrète
r дискретная переменная *f*

2992 discretionary hyphen
d willkürliche Trennung *f*
f couplage *m* [de mot] discrétionnaire
r перенос *m* без соблюдения
  грамматических правил

**2993 discretization; digit[al]ization; digitizing;
  quantization; quantizing**
d Diskretisierung *f*; Quantisierung *f*;
  Quantelung *f*
f discrétisation *f*; digitalisation *f*;
  numérisation *f*; quantification *f*
r дискретизация *f*; дискретизирование *n*;
  дигитализирование *n*; оцифровка *f*;
  квантование *n*; преобразование *n* в
  цифровую форму

**2994 discriminating; discriminative;
  discriminatory**
d ausscheid; unterscheid
f discriminant; sélectif
r отличительный; дискриминирующий;
  избирательный

  * **discriminative** → **2994**

2995 discriminator
d Diskriminator *m*; Entscheider *m*
f discriminateur *m*
r дискриминатор *m*

  * **discriminatory** → **2994**

  * **discussion** → **2627**

  * **discussion forum** → **2996**

**2996 discussion group; newsgroup; N-group;
  [discussion] forum**
d Diskussionsgruppe *f*; Newsgruppe *f*;
  Nachrichtenbrett *n*; Nachrichtengruppe *f*;
  Diskussionsforum *n*; Forum *n*
f groupe *m* de discussion; newsgroup *m*;
  forum *m*; fordit *m*
r дискуссионная группа *f*; группа новостей;
  форум *m*; [сетевая теле]конференция *f*

  * **disjoint** *v* → **2978**

**2997 disjunction; logical add[ition]; logic[al]
  sum; Boolean sum; OR function**
d Disjunktion *f*; logische Addition *f*;

ODER-Funktion *f*
f disjonction *f*; addition *f* logique; sommation *f*
  logique; fonction *f* OU
r дизъюнкция *f*; логическое сложение *n*;
  функция *f* ИЛИ

2998 disjunctive data
d disjunktive Daten *pl*
f données *fpl* disjonctives
r разделительные данные *pl*

**2999 disjunctive normal form; standard sum of
  products; DNF**
d disjunktive Normalform *f*
f forme *f* normale disjonctive
r дизъюнктивная нормальная форма *f*

3000 disk; disc
d Speicherplatte *f*; Platte *f*; Disk *f*
f disque *m*
r диск *m*

3001 disk buffer
d Plattentreiber *m*
f tampon *m* de disque
r дисковой буфер *m*; буфер диска

3002 disk cartridge
d Plattenkassette *f*
f cassette *f* à disques; cartridge *m* à disque
r кассета *f* дискового запоминающего
  устройства

  * **disk duplexing** → **3005**

3003 diskette; flexible disk; floppy disk
d Diskette *f*; flexible Magnetplatte *f*;
  Floppy-Disk *f*
f disquette *f*; disque *m* flexible; disque floppy;
  disque souple
r дискет *m*; гибкий диск *m*

  * **diskette drive** → **3917**

3004 disk label
d Speicherplattenetikett *n*
f étiquette *f* de disque
r метка *f* диска

**3005 disk mirroring; disk shadowing; disk
  duplexing; shadow recording**
d Disk-Spiegeln *n*; Festplattenspiegelung *f*
f redondance *f* de disques; écriture *f* miroir
r отображение *n* диска; дублирование *n*
  диска; дуплексирование *n* диска

3006 disk operating system; DOS
d Plattenbetriebssystem *n*; PBS; DOS
f système *m* d'exploitation sur disque; DOS
r дисковая операционная система *f*; ДОС

3007 disk pack; pack
   d Plattenstapel *m*
   f chargeur *m* de disques
   r пакет *m* дисков

   * **disk shadowing** → 3005

3008 disk striping
   d Platten-Ringeleinrichtung *f*
   f répartition *f* de fichiers sur plusieurs disques
   r группирование *n* дисков;
   диск-страйпинг *m*

   * **dismount** → 2749

   * **dismounting** → 2749

   * **dispatch** → 9534

3009 dispatcher
   d Dispatcher *m*; Zuteiler *m*
   f dispatcher *m*
   r диспетчер *m*

3010 dispersion; scattering
   d Dispersion *f*; Streuung *f*
   f dispersion *f*
   r дисперсия *f*; рассеивание *n*; разброс *m*

   * **displacement** → 8507

3011 displacement address; offset address
   d Verschiebadresse *f*; Versatzadresse *f*
   f adresse *f* de décalage; adresse de déplacement
   r адрес *m* смещения

   * **displacement operator** → 8513

3012 display *v*
   d darstellen
   f afficher; visualiser
   r показывать; отображать

   * **display** → 3020, 3024, 4775

3013 displayable attribute
   d Darstellungsattribut *n*
   f attribut *m* affichable
   r воспроизводимый атрибут *m*

3014 display attribute
   d Displayattribut *n*
   f attribut *m* graphique; attribut visuel
   r атрибут *m* дисплея

3015 display buffer; screen buffer
   d Bildschirmpuffer *m*
   f tampon *m* d'afficheur
   r буфер *m* дисплея

   * **display card** → 9809

3016 display character generator
   d darstellbarer Zeichengenerator *m*
   f générateur *m* de caractères de display
   r генератор *m* символов дисплея

3017 display command; display instruction
   d Darstellungsbefehl *m*
   f commande *f* d'affichage; instruction *f* graphique
   r команда *f* визуализации

3018 display configuration
   d Displaykonfiguration *f*
   f configuration *f* d'afficheur
   r конфигурация *f* дисплея

3019 display data channel; DDC
   d Kanal *m* der Darstellungsdaten
   f canal *m* de données d'afficheur
   r канал *m* дисплейных данных

3020 display [device]; video display; monitor
   d Monitor *m*; Display *n*; Bildschirmgerät *n*; Anzeigegerät *n*
   f visuel *m*; visu *f*; afficheur *m*; display *m*; moniteur *m*
   r дисплей *m*; устройство *n* визуального изображения; монитор *m*

3021 display driver; screen driver
   d Bildschirmtreiber *m*
   f pilote *m* d'écran; pilote d'affichage; pilote d'afficheur; gestionnaire *m* d'écran
   r драйвер *m* дисплея; экранный драйвер

3022 display[ed] information
   d Displayinformation *f*
   f information *f* d'affichage
   r индицируемая информация *f*; информация, представляемая на экране

3023 display element
   d Darstellungselement *n*
   f élément *m* d'affichage
   r элемент *m* изображения

   * **display information** → 3022

3024 display[ing]
   d Bildschirmdarstellung *f*
   f affichage *m*
   r изображение *n* на экране

   * **display instruction** → 3017

3025 display mode
   d Darstellungsmodus *m*; Anzeigebetriebsart *f*; Darstellungsart *f*

f mode *m* d'affichage
r режим *m* изображения на экране

3026 display order
d Darstellungsordnung *f*
f ordre *m* d'affichage
r порядок *m* изображения

3027 display position
d Anzeigestelle *f*, Anzeigeposition *f*, Position *f* auf dem Bildschirm
f position *f* d'affichage
r позиция *f* на экране дисплея

3028 display preferences
d Bildschirm-Präferenzen *fpl*
f préférences *fpl* d'affichage
r предпочтительные параметры *mpl* дисплея

3029 display process
d Display-Prozess *m*
f processus *m* d'affichage
r процесс *m* изображения

* **display processor → 9811**

3030 display quality
d Darstellungsqualität *f*
f qualité *f* d'affichage
r качество *n* изображения на экране

* **display regeneration → 4673**

3031 display space
d Darstellungsbereich *m*
f espace *m* d'affichage
r пространство *n* изображения

3032 display standard
d Darstelungsstandard *m*
f standard *m* d'affichage
r стандарт *m* изображения

3033 display technique; display technology
d Darstellungstechnik *f*, Anzeigetechnik *f*, Anzeigeverfahren *n*
f technique *f* d'affichage; procédé *m* d'affichage
r техника *f* индикации; техника изображения

* **display technology → 3033**

3034 display update
d Bildschirmaktualisierung *f*
f mise *f* à jour d'afficheur
r регенерирование *n* дисплея; обновление *n* дисплея

3035 display variable
d Bildschirmvariable *f*

f variable *f* d'afficheur
r дисплейная переменная *f*

* **display view → 8258**

* **disregard *v* → 6065**

* **dissemination → 3036**

3036 dissipation; dissemination
d Dissipation *f*, Zerstreuung *f*
f dissipation *f*, dissémination *f*
r рассеяние *n*; диссипация *f*

* **dissociate *v* → 3605**

3037 distance
d Abstand *m*; Entfernung *f*, Distanz *f*
f distance *f*
r расстояние *n*

* **distance control → 7895**

3038 distortion
d Distorsion *f*, Verzerrung *f*
f distorsion *f*
r искажение *n*; дисторсия *f*

3039 distortion degree
d Verzerrungsstufe *f*
f degré *m* de distorsion
r степень *f* искажения

3040 distribute *v*; allocate *v*
d verteilen
f distribuer
r распределять

3041 distributed; distributive
d verteilt; distributiv
f distribué; distributif; réparti
r распределённый; дистрибутивный

3042 distributed database
d verteilte Datenbasis *f*
f base *f* de données distribuée; base de données répartie
r распределённая база *f* данных

3043 distributed data processing
d verteilte Datenverarbeitung *f*
f traitement *m* de données distribué
r распределённая обработка *f* данных

3044 distributed file system
d verteiltes Dateisystem *n*
f système *m* de fichiers distribué
r распределённая файловая система *f*

3045 distributed network; distribution network
d verteiltes Netz *n*

f réseau *m* distribué; réseau décentralisé
r распределённая сеть *f*

3046 distributed teleprocessing
d verteilte Fernverarbeitung *f*
f télétraitement *m* distribué
r распределённая дистанционная
обработка *f*

3047 distributed viewer
d verteiltes Suchprogramm *n*
f visionneur *m* distribué
r распределённая программа *f* просмотра

3048 distributed virtual environment;
collaborative virtual environment; CVE
d verteilte Virtualumgebung *f*
f environnement *m* virtuel distribué
r распределённое виртуальное
пространство *n*

3049 distribution
d Verteilung *f*
f distribution *f*; répartition *f*
r распределение *n*

3050 distribution code
d Verteilcode *m*
f code *m* de distribution
r код *m* распределения

* **distribution network** → 3045

* **distributive** → 3041

3051 distributor
(a person)
d Verteiler *m*
f distributeur *m*
r распространитель *m*

* **disturbance** → 3679

3052 disturbed one
d gestörte Eins *f*
f un *m* perturbé
r разрушенная единица *f*

* **disturbing voltage** → 1169

* **disturb pulse** → 6194

* **disturb signal** → 6198

* **ditch** → 4326

* **dither** → 3053

3053 dither[ing]; pixel shading
(representing a color by mixing dots of

closely related colors)
d Dithering *n*; Rastern *n*; Pixelschattierung *f*
f juxtaposition *f*; tramage *m*; ombrage *m* pixel
r [псевдо]смешение *n*; имитация *f*
полутонов; размывание *n* [погрешности];
размытие *n*; сжатие *n* палитры; пиксельное
оттенение *n*

3054 dither matrix
d Dithermatrix *f*
f matrice *f* de juxtaposition
r матрица *f* псевдосмешения; матрица
имитации полутонов

3055 divide *v*
d dividieren
f diviser
r делить

* **divided screen** → 8780

3056 dividend register
d Dividendregister *n*
f registre *m* de dividende
r регистр *m* делимого

3057 divide overflow
d Überlauf *m* beim Dividieren
f dépassement *m* à la division
r переполнение *n* при делении

3058 divider
(a circuit)
d Teiler *m*
f diviseur *m*
r делитель *m*; делительное устройство *n*

* **divider** → 8562

* **dividing** → 3060

3059 division
(as a section)
d Teil *m*
f division *f*
r раздел *m*

3060 division; dividing
(as an operation)
d Division *f*; Teilung *f*
f division *f*; partage *m*
r деление *n*

3061 division algorithm; algorithm of division
d Divisionsalgorithmus *m*
f algorithme *m* de division
r алгоритм *m* деления

3062 division by zero; zero division
d Nulldivision *f*; Division *f* durch Null

f division *f* par zéro
r деление *n* на нуль

* **division sign** → 8562

* **divisor** → 8562

* **DL** → 2946

* **DLC** → 2571

* **DLL** → 2573, 3244

* **DM** → 2577

* **DMA** → 2961

3063 3D metafile; 3DMF
d 3D-Metafile *m*
f métafichier *m* 3D
r 3D метафайл *m*

* **3DMF** → 3063

* **3D modeler** → 3065

3064 3D modeling
d 3D-Modellierung *f*
f modelage *m* en 3D
r 3D моделирование *n*

3065 3D modeling program; 3D modeler
d 3D-Modellierungsprogramm *n*;
3D-Modellierer *m*
f programme *m* de modelage en 3D;
modélisateur *m* 3D
r программа *f* для 3D моделирования

3066 3D mouse
d 3D-Maus *f*
f souris *f* 3D
r 3D мышь *f*

* **DNF** → 2999

* **DNIC** → 2582

* **DNS** → 3106

3067 DNS server
d DNS-Server *m*
f serveur *m* de système *m* noms de domaines
r сервер *m* системы именования доменов;
сервер DNS

3068 dock *v*
d andocken
f amarrer
r стыковать

3069 dockable template
d andockbare Schablone *f*
f modèle *m* amarré
r присоединённый шаблон *m*;
перетаскиваемый шаблон

3070 dockable toolbar; docked toolbar
d andockbarer Hilfsmittelstreifen *m*
f barre *f* d'outils amarrée
r присоединённая инструментальная
панель *f*; перетаскиваемая
инструментальная панель

* **docked toolbar** → 3070

3071 docked visible line
d angedockte sichtbare Linie *f*
f ligne *f* visible amarré
r присоединённая видимая линия *f*;
перетаскиваемая видимая линия

* **docker** → 3072

3072 docker [window]
d Andock-Fenster *n*
f fenêtre *f* fixe
r фиксированное окно *n*

3073 docking
d Ankern *n*
f amarrage *m*
r стыковка *f*

3074 document
d Dokument *n*; Beleg *m*
f document *m*
r документ *m*

3075 documentation
d Dokumentation *f*
f documentation *f*
r документация *f*

3076 documentation navigating
d Dokumentation-Navigation *f*
f navigation *f* de documentation
r навигация *f* по документу

3077 document components
d Bestandteile *mpl* des Dokuments
f composantes *fpl* de document
r компоненты *mpl* документа

3078 document counter
d Belegzähler *m*
f compteur *m* de documents
r счётчик *m* документов

3079 document delivery
d Dokumentenlieferung *f*; Lieferung *f* von
Dokumenten

f remise *f* de document
r доставка *f* документа

3080 document design
d Belegentwurf *m*
f dessin *m* des documents
r подготовка *f* документов;
проектирование *n* документов

3081 document dimensions
d Belegabmessungen *fpl*
f dimensions *fpl* du document
r размеры *mpl* документа

3082 document feeding
d Belegzuführung *f*
f avancement *m* de documents
r подача *f* документа

* **document handling** → 3087

3083 document icon
d Dokumentsymbol *n*
f icône *f* de document
r значок *m* документа

3084 document imaging
d Dokument-Abbildung *f*
f imagination *f* de document; présentation *f* de
document en image
r изображение *n* документа

3085 document interchange format
d Dokumentaustauschformat *n*
f format *m* d'échange de documents
r формат *m* обмена документов

3086 document length
d Beleglänge *f*
f longueur *f* de document
r длина *f* документа

3087 document processing; document handling
d Dokumentverarbeitung *f*
f traitement *m* de documents
r обработка *f* документов

3088 document reader
d Dokument[schrift]leser *m*
f lecteur *m* de documents
r считыватель *m* документов

3089 document server
d Dokument-Server *m*
f serveur *m* documentaire
r сервер *m* документов

3090 document setting
d Dokument-Einrichtung *f*
f établissement *m* de document

r установление *n* параметров документа

3091 document sorting
d Belegsortieren *n*
f triage *m* de documents
r сортировка *f* документов

3092 document stacker
d Belegablage *f*
f dépôt *m* de documents
r устройство *n* приёма-выдачи документов

3093 document structure
d Struktur *f* des Dokuments
f structure *f* de document
r структура *f* документа

3094 document transmission
d Dokumentübertragung *f*
f transmission *f* de documents
r передача *f* документов

3095 document type definition; DTD
d Dokumententypdefinition *f*
f définition *f* de type de document
r определение *n* типа документа

* **document view** → 3096

3096 document view[ing]
d Dokumentansicht *f*
f visualisation *f* de document
r визуализация *f* документа

3097 document width
d Belegbreite *f*
f largeur *f* du document
r ширина *f* документа

3098 document window
d Dokumentfenster *n*
f fenêtre *f* de document
r окно *n* документа

3099 domain
(the name and type of Internet site)
d Domäne *f*; Domain *f*
f domaine *m*
r домен *m*; область *f*

3100 domain addressing
d Domain-Adressierung *f*
f adressage *m* de domaine
r адресование *n* области

3101 domain constraint
d Bereichbeschränkung *f*
f contrainte *f* de domaine
r ограничения *npl* проблемной области

3102 **domain directory system**
  d Domain-Directory-System *n*
  f système *m* d'adressage par domaines
  r система *f* доменных каталогов

3103 **domain list**
  d Domain-Liste *f*
  f liste *f* de domaines
  r список *m* доменов

3104 **domain name**
  d Domain-Name *m*
  f nom *m* de domaine
  r имя *n* домена; название *n* домена;
  именование *n* домена

3105 **domain name server**
  d Domain-Name-Server *m*
  f serveur *m* de noms de domaines
  r сервер *m* доменных имён

3106 **domain name system; DNS**
  d Domain-Name-System *n*; System *n* von
  Domainbereichungen
  f système *m* de noms de domaines
  r система *f* имён доменов; система
  именования доменов

  *   **domestic** → 4531

  *   **done address** → 150

  *   **done flag** → 7682

  *   **do-nothing instruction** → 6283

  *   **donut** → 1682

  *   **DOS** → 3006

3107 **dossier databank**
  d personenbezogene Datenbank *f*
  f banque *f* dossier
  r анкетный банк *m* данных

3108 **dot**
  d Punkt *m*; Punktmarke *f*
  f marque *f* ponctuelle; index *m* ponctuel;
  point *m*
  r точка *f*

  *   **dot** → 8240

3109 **dot** *v*; **punctuate** *v*; **point** *v*
  d punktieren
  f pointiller; pointer
  r пунктировать; ставить точку; означать
  точками

  *   **dot address** → 2646

  *   **dot-chaining screen** → 3354

3110 **dot counter**
  (in display)
  d Punktzähler *m*
  f compteur *m* de points
  r счётчик *m* точек

3111 **dot gain; dot spread**
  d Punktverbreiterung *f*
  f grossissement *m* du points
  r расплывание *n* растровой точки;
  увеличение *n* размера растровой точки

3112 **dot grid**
  d Punktgitter *n*
  f grille *f* à points
  r точечная решётка *f*

3113 **dot interlace scanning**
  d Bildpunkt-verschachtelte Abtastung *f*
  f échantillonnage *m* point par point entrelacé
  r поточечное презредовое сканирование *n*

3114 **dot mask**
  d Punktmaske *f*
  f masque *m* en points
  r точечная маска *f*

3115 **dot matrix**
  d Punktmatrix *f*
  f matrice *f* de points
  r точечная матрица *f*

3116 **dot-matrix character**
  d Punktmatrixzeichen *n*; Punktrasterzeichen *n*
  f caractère *m* dans une matrice de points
  r точечный символ *m*

3117 **dot-matrix character generator**
  d Raster-Zeichengenerator *m*
  f générateur *m* de caractères dans une matrice
  de points
  r генератор *m* точечных символов

  *   **dot-matrix field** → 1599

  *   **dot pitch** → 8241

  *   **dots** → 3351

3118 **dot-scanning method**
  d Punktscannen-Verfahren *n*;
  Punktrasterverfahren *n*
  f méthode *f* d'échantillonnage par points
  r точечный метод *m* сканирования

3119 **dots per inch; dpi**
  d Punkte *mpl* pro Zoll

    f points *mpl* au pouce
    r точек *fpl* на дюйм

    * **dot spread** → 3111

3120 double
    d doppelt; Doppel-; zweifach
    f double
    r двойной; сдвоенный; удвоенный

3121 double buffering
    d Doppelpufferung *f*
    f tamponnage *m* double
    r двойное буферирование *n*; двойная
      буферизация *f*

3122 double-byte character set; DBCS
    d Doppel-Byte-Zeichensatz *m*
    f jeu *m* de caractères à deux octets
    r набор *m* двухбайтовых символов

3123 double channel; dual channel
    d Zweikanal *m*
    f canal *m* double; canal dual
    r дублированный канал *m*

3124 double click
    d Doppelklick *m*
    f double clic *m*
    r двойной клик *m*; двойной щелчок *m*;
      двойное нажатие *n* кнопки

3125 double-clocked microprocessor
    d doppelt-getakteter Mikroprozessor *m*
    f microprocesseur *m* à double fréquence
    r двойно синхронизированный
      микропроцессор *m*

3126 double coding
    d Doppelcodierung *f*
    f codage *m* double
    r двойное кодирование *n*

    * **double computer** → 9190

3127 double-density diskette
    d zweidichte Diskette *f*
    f disquette *f* double densité; disquette DD
    r дискет *m* с удвоенной плотностью

3128 double error
    d Doppelfehler *m*
    f erreur *f* double
    r двойная ошибка *f*

3129 double error-correcting code
    d Code *m* mit doppelter Fehlerkorrektur
    f code *m* à correction des erreurs doubles
    r код *m* с исправлением двойных ошибок

3130 double index
    d Doppelindex *m*
    f indice *m* double
    r двойной индекс *m*

3131 double-indexed sequence
    d zweifachindizierte Folge *f*
    f suite *f* à deux indices
    r последовательность *f* с двумя индексами

    * **double-length number** → 3138

3132 double[-length] word
    d doppelt langes Wort *n*; Wort mit doppelter
      Länge; Doppelwort *n*
    f mot *m* [à longueur] double
    r слово *n* двойной длины; двойное слово

3133 double-linked list; two-way linked list;
    symmetric list
    d verkettete Doppelliste *f*
    f liste *f* d'enchaînement double
    r двунаправленный список *m*; двойной
      связный список

3134 double loop
    d Doppelschleife *f*
    f double lacet *m*
    r двойная петля *f*

3135 double negation
    d doppelte Negation *f*
    f double négation *f*
    r двойное отрицание *n*

3136 double-picture plotter
    d Stereoauswertegerät *n*
    f appareil *m* de restitution stéréoscopique
    r стереообрабатывающий
      графопостроитель *m*

3137 double precision
    d doppelte Genauigkeit *f*
    f précision *f* double
    r двойная точность *f*

3138 double-precision number; double-length
    number
    d Doppelgenauigkeitszahl *f*; doppelt lange
      Zahl *f*; Zahl doppelter Länge
    f nombre *m* à double précision; nombre à
      double longueur
    r число *n* удвоенной точности; число
      двойной точности; число двойной длины

3139 double quotes; quotation marks; quote
    marks; quotes
    (")
    d Anführungszeichen *npl*

   f guillemets *mpl*
   r кавычки *fpl*

   * **double-side** → 920

   * **double-sided** → 920

3140 double underline *v*
   d doppelt unterstrichen; doppelt unterstreichen
   f souligner double
   r двойно подчёркивать

   * **double word** → 3132

3141 doubling; duplication; replication
   d Duplikation *f*; Verdoppelung *f*; Duplizierung *f*
   f duplication *f*
   r удвоение *n*; дублирование *n*

   * **DOUT** → 2585

3142 down counter
   d Abwärtszähler *m*
   f compteur *m* de soustraction; compteur descendant
   r вычитающий счётчик *m*; счётчик вычитания

3143 down-line loading; downloading; telecharging; remote load[ing]
   d Herunterladen *n*; Abwärtsladen *n*; Telebeschickung *f*; Fernladen *n*
   f chargement *m* en bas; téléchargement *m*
   r дистанционная разгрузка *f*; выгрузка *f*

3144 download *v*
   d nachladen
   f décharger
   r разгружать; выгружать (из главной системы); скачать (с Интернета)

3145 downloadable images
   d heruntergeladene Bilde *npl*
   f images *fpl* téléchargées
   r разгружаемые изображения *npl*

   * **downloading** → 3143

3146 downsizing; rightsizing; diminishing
   d Schrumpfen *n*
   f micromisation *f*; microtisation *f*; rétrécissement *m*
   r уменьшение *n* (сложности системы); уменьшение размеров

   * **downsizing** → 8089

   * **downtime** → 2623

3147 downward

   d absteigend
   f descendant
   r нисходящий

3148 downward compatibility
   d Abwärtskompatibilität *f*
   f compatibilité *f* descendante
   r совместимость *f* сверху вниз; нисходящая совместимость

3149 2D patch; planar patch
   d 2D-Oberflächenstück *n*
   f surface *f* paramétrique 2D; surface paramétrique plane
   r плоский кусок *m*; плоский фрагмент *m*

3150 3D patch
   d 3D-Oberflächenstück *n*
   f surface *f* paramétrique 3D
   r трёхмерный кусок *m*; 3D фрагмент *m*

   * **dpi** → 3119

   * **3D pixel** → 9923

3151 3D procedural texture
   d prozedurale 3D-Textur *f*
   f texture *f* procédurale 3D
   r трёхмерная процедурная текстура *f*

   * **DR** → 2622

   * **draft** *v* → 3158

   * **drafting** → 3161

   * **draft mode** → 3152

3152 draft [print] mode
   d Entwurfdruck *m*; Listendruckmodus *m*
   f mode *m* [d'impression] rapide
   r экономичный режим *m* печати

   * **drag** → 3157

   * **drag** *v* → 8654

3153 drag *v*; **draw** *v*
   d führen; ziehen
   f traîner; déposer
   r переместить; таскать; увлекать

3154 drag and drop; drag&drop
   d Ziehen *n* und Loslassen *n*; Z&L
   f glissement *m* et relâchement *m*
   r перемещение *n* и опускание *n*; таскание *n* и опускание

3155 drag-and-drop insertion of objects
   d Einfügung *f* der Objekte durch Ziehen und Loslassen

f insertion *f* d'objets par glissement et
relâchement
r вставка *f* объектов перемещением и
опусканием

* **drag&drop** → 3154

3156 dragged object
d gezogenes Objekt *n*
f objet *m* entraîné; objet lissé
r перемещаемый объект *m*

3157 drag[ging]
d Ziehen *n*; Nachziehen *n*
f [en]traînement *m*; traînage *m*
r перемещение *n*; таскание *n*; буксировка *f*

* **DRAM** → 3257

* **draw** → 3160

* **draw** *v* → 3153

3158 draw *v*; **chart** *v*; **draft** *v*; **trace** *v*
d zeichnen
f tracer; tirer; étirer; dessiner
r чертить

3159 drawer
d Zeichner *m*; Entwerfer *m*
f tiroir *m*
r выдвижной ящик *m*; выдвижная доска *f*

3160 draw[ing]
d Zeichnung *f*
f dessin *m*
r чертёж *m*; рисунок *m*

3161 drawing; design; drafting
d Zeichnung *f*; Zeichnen *n*
f tracement *m*; étirage *m*
r черчение *n*

3162 drawing browser
d Zeichnung-Browser *m*
f butineur *m* de dessins
r браузер *m* чертежей

3163 drawing database
d Zeichnungsdatenbasis *f*
f base *f* de données de dessin
r база *f* данных чертежа

* **drawing file** → 7056

3164 drawing file format
d Zeichnungsdatei-Format *n*
f format *m* de fichier de dessin
r формат *m* чертёжного файла

**3165 drawing interchange binary file format;
DXB file format**
d DXB-Dateiformat *n*
f format *m* de fichier DXB
r файловый формат *m* DXB

3166 drawing interchange format; DXF
d Zeichnungsaustausch-Format *n*;
DXF-Format *n*
f format *m* DXF
r формат *m* DXF

3167 drawing page
d Zeichnenseite *f*
f page *f* de dessin
r страница *f* рисунка

3168 drawing processor
d Zeichnung-Prozessor *m*;
Drawing-Prozessor *m*
f processeur *m* de dessin
r чертёжный процессор *m*

**3169 drawing software; graphics designer;
design software; designer**
(software for design and illustration)
d Zeichnen-Software *f*; Grafikdesigner *m*;
Konstruktionssoftware *f*
f logiciel *m* de dessin; dessineur *m*; logiciel *m*
de conception; concepteur *m*
r программное обеспечение *n* для
проектирования; графический
проектировщик *m*

3170 drawing Web format; DWF
d Zeichnung-WEB-Format *n*
f format *m* Web de dessin
r формат *m* DWF

3171 drawing window
d Zeichnenfenster *n*
f fenêtre *f* de tracement
r чертёжное окно *n*; чертёжный экран *m*

3172 draw menu
d Zeichnenmenü *n*
f menu *m* de tracement
r меню *n* черчения

3173 draw toolbar
d Zeichnungshilfsmittelstreifen *m*
f barre *f* d'outils de tracement
r инструментальная лента *f* черчения

3174 dribbleware
d Dribbleware *f*
f ajustagiciel *m*
r порционное программное обеспечение *n*

* **drive** → 154, 4394

3175 drive pulse; driving pulse; control pulse
   d Treiberimpuls *m*; Steuerimpuls *m*
   f impulsion *f* excitatrice; impulsion de
      commande
   r импульс *m* возбуждения; управляющий
      импульс

   * **driver** → 3177

3176 driver
     (a program)
   d Driver *m*; Treiber *m*
   f driver *m*; pilote *m*; gestionnaire *m* de
      périphérique
   r драйвер *m*

3177 driver [circuit]; driving circuit
   d Treiberschaltung *f*; Treiber *m*; Driver *m*
   f excitateur *m*; circuit *m* d'excitation; pilote *m*;
      driver *m*
   r формирователь *m*; буферная схема *f*;
      возбудитель *m*; возбуждающая схема

   * **driving circuit** → 3177

   * **driving pulse** → 3175

   * **drop** → 3185

3178 drop *v*; fall *v*
   d auslassen
   f lâcher
   r спускать; отпускать; опускать; падать

   * **drop cap** → 3186

3179 drop-down
   d Dropdown-
   f déroulant
   r выпадающий; ниспадающий;
      раскрывающийся

3180 drop-down box
   d Dropdown-Feld *n*
   f boîte *f* déroulante
   r ниспадающее окно *n*; выпадающее окно

3181 drop-down combo box
   d Dropdown-Kombinationsfeld *n*
   f zone *f* de liste déroulante fixe
   r раскрывающееся комбинированное окно *n*

3182 drop-down list box
   d Dropdown-Listenfeld *n*
   f zone *f* de liste déroulante modifiable; boîte *f*
      de liste déroulante modifiable
   r раскрывающееся окно *n* списка

   * **dropdown menu** → 7494

   * **drop-in** → 6198

   * **drop-in signal** → 6198

   * **drop-off** → 621

   * **drop-out** → 3183

3183 drop-out [signal]
   d Signalausfall *m*; Lesespannungsausfall *m*;
      Dropout *m*
   f manque *m* de signal; dropout *m*
   r пропадание *n* сигнала; исчезновение *n*
      сигнала; выпадание *n*

3184 dropped frames
   d herausgefallene Bilder *npl*
   f cadres *mpl* perdus
   r потерянные кадры *mpl*

3185 drop[ping]
   d Auslassen *n*; Auslassung *f*
   f lâchage *m*; troncation *f*
   r выпадание *n*; пропадание *n*

   * **dropping** → 2410

3186 dropping capital; drop cap
   d Initial *n*; verrutschter Buchstabe *m*
   f lettrine *f*
   r буквица *f*; большая стилизованная первая
      буква *f*

3187 drum
   d Trommel *f*; Walze *f*
   f tambour *m*
   r барабан *m*

3188 drum plotter; belt-bed plotter
   d Trommelplotter *m*; Walzenplotter *m*;
      Walzenschreiber *m*
   f traceur *m* à rouleau; traceur à tambour
   r барабанный графопостроитель *m*;
      рулонный графопостроитель

3189 drum scanner
   d Trommelscanner *m*
   f scanner *m* à tambour
   r барабанный сканер *m*

   * **dry run** → 3190

3190 dry run[ning]
   d Trockenlauf *m*
   f marche *f* à sec
   r формальный прогон *m* [программы]

   * **DSA** → 2968

3191 3D scanner
   d 3D-Scanner *m*

f scanner *m* 3D
r 3D сканер *m*

3192 3D scene
d 3D-Szene *f*
f scène *f* 3D
r 3D сцена *f*

3193 3D shape; 3D figure
d 3D-Figur *f*
f figure *f* 3D
r 3D фигура *f*

* **DSL** → 2928

3194 3D software
d 3D-Software *f*
f logiciel *m* 3D
r трёхмерное программное обеспечение *n*

3195 3D sound
d 3D-Schall *m*
f audio *m* 3D
r 3D звук *m*; 3D аудио *n*

3196 3D spreadsheet
d 3D-Rechenblatt *n*
f feuille *f* de calcul 3D
r трёхмерная электронная таблица *f*

* **DSS** → 2924

3197 3D symbol; 3D character
d 3D-Symbol *n*
f symbole *m* 3D
r 3D символ *m*

* **DTD** → 3095

3198 3D text
d 3D-Text *m*
f texte *m* 3D
r 3D текст *m*

* **DTL** → 2947

* **DTP** → 2790

* **DTV** → 2796

* **DUA** → 2970

3199 dual
d dual
f dual
r дуальный; двойственный

3200 dual access
d Doppelzugriff *m*
f accès *m* dual; accès double

r сдвоенная выборка *f*; двойное обращение *n*

* **dual-channel** → 3206

* **dual channel** → 3123

* **dual channel switch control** → 3201

3201 dual channel switch[ing] control
d Dualkanal-Schaltsteuerung *f*
f commande *f* de commutation de canal dual
r управление *n* переключением двойного канала

3202 dual circuit
d Dualschaltung *f*
f circuit *m* dual
r дуальная схема *f*

3203 dual element
d duales Element *n*
f élément *m* dual
r двойственный элемент *m*; дуальный элемент

3204 dual-in-line package; DIP
d Doppelreihengehäuse *n*; DIP-Gehäuse *n*
f boîtier *m* à deux rangées de broches
r корпус *m* с двухрядным расположением выводов

3205 duality; reciprocity; reciprocation
d Dualität *f*; Reziprozität *f*
f dualité *f*; réciprocité *f*
r двойственность *f*; взаимность *f*

* **dual-line** → 3206

3206 dual-link; dual-rail; dual-channel; dual-line
d Zweikanal-; Zweiport-
f à deux canaux; à deux ports; à deux voies; à deux lignes
r двухканальный; двухпортовый

* **dual-rail** → 3206

3207 dual-redundant bus
d Bus *m* mit zweifacher Redundanz
f bus *m* dual redondant
r дублированная шина *f*

3208 dual-scan display
d Doppelaufbau-Bildschirm *m*
f écran *m* à double balayage
r дисплей *m* с двойным сканированием

3209 dual screen
(DOS screen and high-resolution graphics screen appearing on two separate monitors)

d Zweischirm *m*
f écran *m* dual
r дуальный экран *m*

3210 dual-standard interface
d zweifache Normschnittstelle *f*
f interface *f* à standard dual
r интерфейс *m* двойного стандарта

3211 dumb terminal
(a terminal that doesn't contain an internal microprocessor)
d Dialogstation *f* ohne eigene Intelligenz
f terminal *m* léger
r глупый терминал *m*; простой терминал

3212 dummy; fictive; pseudo-
d blind; Schein-; Leer-; fiktiv; Pseudo-
f fictif; pseudo-; formel; factice; muet
r фиктивный; псевдо-; холостой

*   **dummy character → 4625**

*   **dummy index → 3213**

3213 dummy index [of summation]; sum index
d Summationsindex *m*
f indice *m* muet [de sommation]; indice de sommation
r немой индекс *m* [суммирования]; индекс суммирования

3214 dummy information
d belanglose Information *f*
f information *f* fictive
r фиктивная информация *f*

*   **dummy instruction → 6283**

3215 dummy statement
d Leeranweisung *f*
f ordonnancement *m* factice
r пустое утверждение *n*

3216 dummy tag
d leere Adressendefinition *f*
f étiquette *f* factice
r фиктивный этикет *m*

*   **dummy variable → 8643**

3217 dump *v*
d ausspeichern; abladen; abziehen; ausziehen; ausleeren
f vider; clicher
r делать дамп; выполнять дамп

*   **dump → 5726**

3218 duodecimal

d duodezimal
f duodécimal
r двенадцатиричный

3219 duplex; full duplex; FDX
d Duplex *n*; Vollduplex *n*
f duplex *m*
r дуплекс *m*

3220 duplex circuit; duplex line; two-party line
d Duplexleitung *f*; Gegenschreibleitung *f*
f circuit *m* [en] duplex; ligne *f* duplex
r линия *f* дуплексной связи

3221 duplex communication; two-way simultaneous communication; bidirectional simultaneous communication
d Duplexverbindung *f*; Gegenschreibverbindung *f*
f liaison *f* en duplex; communication *f* bidirectionnelle simultanée
r дуплексная связь *f*; двунаправленная параллельная связь

*   **duplex line → 3220**

3222 duplex method; FDX method
d Duplexverfahren *n*; Gegenschreibverfahren *n*
f méthode *f* duplex
r дуплексный метод *m*

3223 duplex mode; two-way mode
d Duplexbetriebsweise *f*
f mode *m* duplex
r дуплексный режим *m*; режим двухстороннего взаимодействия

3224 duplicate *v*
d verdoppeln; duplizieren
f doubler; dupliquer
r дублировать

3225 duplicate; redundant replica
d Duplikat *n*; Doppel *n*; Zweitexemplar *n*
f duplicata *m*; réplique *f*
r дубликат *m*

3226 duplicated system
d verdoppeltes System *n*
f système *m* doublé
r дублированная система *f*

3227 duplicate test
d verdoppelter Test *m*
f essai *m* doublé
r дублированный тест *m*; дублированная проверка *f*; двойная проверка

*   **duplication → 3141**

3228 **duration**
d Dauer *f*
f durée *f*
r продолжительность *f*

3229 **duty factor; load factor**
d Tastverhältnis *n*; Lastfaktor *m*;
Belastungsfaktor *m*
f facteur *m* de suit; facteur de réponse; facteur
de charge
r коэффициент *m* нагрузки

* **DVD** → 2932

* **DVI** → 2933

3230 **3D video-communication**
d 3D-Videokommunication *f*
f communication *f* vidéo 3D
r 3D видеокоммуникация *f*

3231 **3D videogame**
d 3D-Videospiel *n*
f jeu *m* vidéo 3D
r 3D видеоигра *f*

3232 **3D viewer**
d 3D-Suchprogramm *n*; dreidimensionales
Suchprogramm *n*
f visionneur *m* 3D
r трёхмерная программа *f* просмотра

3233 **3D viewing processor**
d 3D-Viewing-Prozessor *m*
f processeur *m* de visualisation 3D
r процессор *m* трёхмерной визуализации

3234 **2D virtual world**
d 2D-Virtualwelt *f*
f monde *m* virtuel 2D
r двумерный виртуальный мир *m*

3235 **3D virtual world**
d 3D-Virtualwelt *f*
f monde *m* virtuel 3D
r трёхмерный виртуальный мир *m*

3236 **3D visualization**
d 3D-Visualisierung *f*
f visualisation *f* en 3D
r 3D визуализация *f*

3237 **3D voxel data**
d 3D-Voxeldaten *pl*
f données *fpl* de voxels 3D
r 3D данные *pl* об элементах объёма

* **DWF** → 3170

3238 **DWF file**

d DWF-Datei *f*
f fichier *m* DWF
r файл *m* DWF

3239 **3D wireframe model**
d 3D-Drahtrahmenmodell *n*
f modèle *m* 3D fil de fer; modèle 3D filaire
r трёхмерная каркасная модель *f*

3240 **3D world**
d 3D-Welt *f*
f monde *m* 3D
r 3D мир *m*

* **DXB file format** → 3165

* **DXF** → 3166

* **dyadic operator** → 943

* **dyadic relation** → 946

3241 **dynamic**
d dynamisch
f dynamique
r динамический

3242 **dynamic address**
d dynamische Adresse *f*
f adresse *f* dynamique
r динамический адрес *m*

3243 **dynamic address translation**
d dynamische Adressenübersetzung *f*
f traduction *f* d'adresse dynamique
r динамическая трансляция *f* адреса

3244 **dynamically linked library; DLL**
d dynamisch verknüpfte Programmbibliothek *f*;
dynamische gelinkte Bibliothek *f*; DLL
f bibliothèque *f* chaînée dynamiquement;
bibliothèque de liens dynamiques
r динамически связанная библиотека *f*

3245 **dynamic binding; dynamic link[ing]**
d dynamische Verknüpfung *f*
f lien *m* dynamique; liaison *f* dynamique
r динамическая связка *f*; динамическая
связь *f*

3246 **dynamic branding**
d dynamische Veränderung *f*; dynamisches
Brennen *n*; dynamisches Brandmarken *n*
f marquage *m* dynamique
r динамическое маркирование *n*

3247 **dynamic data exchange; DDE**
d dynamischer Datenaustausch *m*
f échange *m* de données dynamiques
r динамический обмен *m* данными

* **dynamic display image** → 3962

3248 **dynamic dragging**
  d dynamisches Ziehen *n*
  f entraînement *m* dynamique
  r динамическое перемещение *n*

3249 **dynamic fonts**
  d dynamische Schriftarten *fpl*
  f polices *fpl* dynamiques
  r динамические шрифты *mpl*

3250 **dynamic information structure**
  d dynamische Informationsstruktur *f*
  f structure *f* dynamique d'information
  r динамическая информационная
     структура *f*

* **dynamic image** → 3962

3251 **dynamic IP**
  d dynamisches Internet-Protokoll *n*
  f protocole *m* Internet dynamique
  r динамический Интернет-протокол *m*

* **dynamicizer** → 6797

* **dynamic link** → 3245

* **dynamic linking** → 3245

3252 **dynamic memory; dynamic stor[ag]e**
  d dynamischer Speicher *m*
  f mémoire *f* dynamique
  r динамическая память *f*

3253 **dynamic model**
  d dynamisches Modell *n*
  f modèle *m* dynamique
  r динамическая модель *f*

3254 **dynamic optimization; dynamic
     programming**
  d dynamische Optimierung *f*; dynamische
     Programmierung *f*
  f optimisation *f* dynamique; programmation *f*
     dynamique
  r динамическое оптимирование *n*;
     динамическое программирование *n*

3255 **dynamic option**
  d dynamische Option *f*
  f option *f* dynamique
  r динамический выбор *m*

3256 **dynamic page**
  (HTML document containing animated GIF
  images)
  d dynamische Seite *f*
  f page *f* dynamique

  r динамическая страница *f*

* **dynamic programming** → 3254

3257 **dynamic RAM; DRAM**
  d dynamischer RAM-Speicher *m*; dynamischer
     Schreib-/Lesespeicher *m*
  f mémoire *f* vive dynamique; mémoire RAM
     dynamique
  r динамическая [оперативная] память *f*

3258 **dynamic range**
  d Dynamikbereich *m*; Aussteuerbereich *m*
  f gamme *f* dynamique
  r динамический диапазон *m*

3259 **dynamic routing**
  d dynamische Lenkung *f*; dynamische
     Routensteuerung *f*
  f routage *m* dynamique
  r динамическая маршрутизация *f*

3260 **dynamic simulation**
  d dynamische Simulation *f*
  f simulation *f* dynamique
  r динамическая симуляция *f*

* **dynamic storage** → 3252

* **dynamic store** → 3252

3261 **dynamic view**
  d dynamische Ansicht *f*
  f vue *f* dynamique
  r динамический вид *m*

3262 **dynamic Web page**
  d dynamische Webseite *f*
  f page *f* Web dynamique
  r динамическая Web-страница *f*

3263 **dynamic zooming**
  d dynamisches Zoomen *n*
  f zoom *m* dynamique
  r динамическое масштабирование *n*

E

* **EARN** → 3532

* **easy-to-use** → 9727

* **e-cash** → 3333

* **ECC** → 3485

3264 echo
d Echo n
f écho m
r эхо n

* **echo canceller** → 3269

3265 echo channel
d Echokanal m
f canal m écho
r эхо-канал m

* **echo check** → 3266

3266 echo check[ing]; echo test[ing]; read-back check
d Echoprüfung f; Echokontrolle f; Prüfung f durch Rückübertragung; Rücklesekontrolle f
f contrôle m par écho; essai m par lecture répétée; test m d'écho
r эхоконтроль m; проверка f обратным считыванием

3267 echo check register
d Spiegelregister n
f registre m de contrôle par écho
r регистр m эхоконтроля

3268 echo compensation; echo suppression; echo killing
d Echokompensation f; Echounterdrückung f
f compensation f d'écho; suppression f d'écho
r эхо-компенсация f; подавление n эха

3269 echo compensator; echo canceller; echo suppressor; echo equalizer; time equalizer
d Echokompensator m; Echoentzerrer m
f compensateur m écho; correcteur m d'écho
r эхо-компенсатор m

3270 echo correction
d Echokorrektur f
f correction f d'écho
r коррекция f эхо-сигнала; коррекция отражённого сигнала

* **echo equalizer** → 3269

3271 echo image
d Echobild n
f écho-image f
r эхо-изображение n

* **echo killing** → 3268

3272 echo loss; active return loss
d Echodämpfung f
f affaiblissement m d'écho
r эхо-потери fpl

3273 echomail
d Echomeldung f
f poste f écho; échomail m
r эхо-почта f

3274 echomail area
d Echomeldungsregion f
f domaine m de poste écho; aire f échomail
r область f эхо-почты

3275 echoplex
(echo-based protocol)
d Echoplex n
f échoplex m
r эхоплекс m

3276 echo replica
d künstliches Echosignal n
f écho-réplique f
r дубликат m эха; искусственное эхо n

* **echo suppression** → 3268

* **echo suppressor** → 3269

* **echo test** → 3266

* **echo testing** → 3266

* **ECL** → 3371

* **e-commerce** → 3324

3277 economic circuit
d Sparschaltung f
f circuit m économe
r экономичная схема f

3278 economic information
d ökonomische Information f
f information f économique
r экономическая информация f

3279 edge
d Rand m; Schranke f

ƒ tranche ƒ; côte ƒ; bord *m*
r граница ƒ [поверхностей]; грань ƒ; край *m*;
кромка ƒ

* **edge** → 7502

3280 edge; arc
(of a graph)
d Kante ƒ
ƒ côte ƒ; arête ƒ
r ребро *n*; дуга ƒ

3281 edge-assigned terminal
d Randanschluss *m*
ƒ terminaison ƒ de bord
r краевой вывод *m*

3282 edge board; edge card
d Kerblochkarte ƒ; randgekerbte Karte ƒ
ƒ carte ƒ à encoches marginales
r плата ƒ с печатным соединителем;
[перфо]карта ƒ с краевой перфорацией

* **edgeboard connector** → 3283

* **edge card** → 3282

**3283 edge connector; edgeboard connector; plug
connector**
d Steckverbinder *m*; Steckerleiste ƒ;
Randstecker *m*
ƒ connecteur *m* à fiches; connecteur *m* plat
r [торцевой] соединитель *m*; разъём *m*
[платы]

3284 edge processor
d Kantenprozessor *m*; Edge-Prozessor *m*
ƒ processeur *m* [de traitement] de côtes;
processeur d'arêtes
r процессор *m* обработки краев; процессор
обработки рёбер

* **edge sharpness** → 3286

3285 edge steepness
(of a pulse)
d Flankensteilheit ƒ
ƒ inclinaison ƒ de flanc
r крутизна ƒ фронта

3286 edge[-to-edge] sharpness
d Kantenschärfe ƒ
ƒ contraste *m* marginal
r резкость ƒ контуров

* **EDI** → 3323

* **edit** → 3290

3287 edit *v*

d bearbeiten
ƒ éditer
r редактировать

3288 edit code
d Aufbereitungscode *m*
ƒ code *m* d'édition
r редактирующий код *m*

**3289 edit-controlled data transmission;
edit-directed data transfer**
d editgesteuerte Datenübertragung ƒ
ƒ transmission de données commandée par
édition
r передача ƒ данных с редактированием

* **edit-directed data transfer** → 3289

3290 edit[ing]
d Bearbeitung ƒ; Aufbereitung ƒ; Editieren *n*
ƒ mise ƒ en forme; édition ƒ; rédaction ƒ
r редактирование *n*

3291 editing commands
d Bearbeitungsbefehle *mpl*
ƒ commandes *fpl* d'édition
r команды *fpl* редактирования

3292 editing function
d Editierfunktion ƒ
ƒ fonction ƒ d'édition
r функция ƒ редактирования

3293 editing keypad; editing keys
(including Ins, Del, End, Home, PageUp,
PageDown keys)
d Editiertasten *fpl*; Editiertastatur ƒ
ƒ bloc *m* [de touches] d'édition
r блок *m* клавиатуры редактирования

* **editing keys** → 3293

3294 editing program; editor
d Aufbereitungsprogramm *n*;
Editierprogramm *n*; Editor *m*
ƒ programme *m* d'édition; éditeur *m*
r редактирующая программа ƒ; редактор *m*

3295 editing time
d Editierzeit ƒ
ƒ temps *m* d'édition
r время *n* редактирования

3296 edit menu
d Bearbeitungsmenü *n*
ƒ menu *m* d'édition
r меню *n* редактирования

3297 edit mode
d Aufbereitungsbetrieb *m*

f mode *m* d'édition
r режим *m* редактирования

* **editor** → 3294

* **EDMS** → 3326

* **EDS** → 3325

* **education** → 5319

3298 educational multimedia software
  d Multimedia-Bildungssoftware *f*; multimediale Unterrichtssoftware *f*
  f ludiciel *m* éducatif
  r обучающее мультимедийное программное обеспечение *n*

3299 edutainment
  (artificial word in the multimedia composed by education + entertainment)
  d Edutainment *n*
  f ludo-éducatif *m*
  r развлекательное образование *n*; учение *n* с развлечением

* **EEPROM** → 3317

3300 effect
  d Effekt *m*
  f effet *m*
  r эффект *m*; воздействие *n*

3301 effect application
  d Effekt-Anwendung *f*
  f application *f* d'effet
  r применение *n* эффекта

3302 effective; efficient
  d effektiv; effizient
  f effectif; efficace
  r эффективный

3303 effective address
  d effektive Adresse *f*
  f adresse *f* effective
  r эффективный адрес *m*

3304 effective bit
  d Nutzbit *n*
  f bit *m* efficace
  r полезный бит *m*; рабочий бит

3305 effective byte
  d effektives Byte *n*
  f octet *m* effectif
  r рабочий байт *m*

3306 effective cycle
  d effektiver Zyklus *m*

f cycle *m* effectif
r эффективный цикл *m*

3307 effective data transfer rate
  d effektive Datentransferrate *f*
  f vitesse *f* de transfert de données effective
  r эффективная скорость *f* переноса данных

3308 effector
  d Effektor *m*
  f effecteur *m*
  r эффектор *m*; спецификатор *m*

3309 efferency
  d Efferenz *f*
  f efférence *f*
  r эфферентация *f*

3310 efferent branch
  d zentrifugaler Zweig *m*
  f branche *f* centrifuge; branche efférente
  r центробежная ветвь *f*

3311 efficiency
  d Effektivität *f*; Effizienz *f*; Wirkungsgrad *m*
  f efficacité *f*; efficience *f*
  r эффективность *f*

* **efficient** → 3302

* **e-form** → 3327

* **EGA** → 3431

* **EIS** → 3439

* **EISA** → 3617

* **EIT** → 3397

3312 eject *v*
  d ausstoßen; vorschieben
  f éjecter
  r выдавать; выбрасывать

* **ejection** → 6610

3313 elapsed time; uptime; available time
  d verbrauchte Zeit *f*; Benutzungszeit *f*
  f temps *m* écoulé; temps de fonctionnement
  r время *n* работы; полное время (работы системы)

3314 elapsed timer
  d Benutzungszeitzähler *m*
  f minuterie *f* à mesurer la durée totale de fonctionnement
  r часы *pl* использованного времени; счётчик *m* использованного времени

3315 elapsed-time recorder
d Benutzungszeitaufzeichner *m*
f enregistreur *m* du temps utilisé
r регистратор *m* использованного времени

* **electrical conductance** → 2133

3316 electrical conductivity
d elektrische Leitfähigkeit *f*
f conductibilité *f* électrique
r электропроводность *f*

3317 electrically erasable PROM; EEPROM
d elektrisch programmierbarer löschbarer
Festwertspeicher *m*; EEPROM
f mémoire *f* à lecture seule programmable et
effaçable électriquement
r электрически стираемая программируемая
постоянная память *f*

3318 electrographic printer
d elektrografischer Drucker *m*
f imprimante *f* électrographique
r электрографическое печатающее
устройство *n*

3319 electroluminescent matrix screen
d Elektrolumineszenz-Matrixschirm *m*
f écran *m* matriciel électroluminescent
r электролюминесцентный матричный
экран *m*

3320 electron
d Elektron *n*
f électron *m*
r электрон *m*

3321 electron beam
d Elektronenstrahl *m*
f faisceau *m* d'électrons
r электронный луч *m*

3322 electronic
d elektronisch
f électronique
r электронный

* **electronic beam tube** → 1498

**3323 electronic [business] data interchange;
electronic document interchange; EDI;
electronic document exchange**
d elektronischer Datenaustausch *m*
f échange *m* électronique de données; échange
de données informatisé; échange de
documents informatisés; EDI
r электронный обмен *m* данными;
электронный обмен документами

* **electronic cash** → 3333

**3324 electronic commerce; e-commerce;
e-shopping**
d E-Commerce *f*
f commerce *f* électronique
r электронная коммерция *f*; электронная
торговля *f*

* **electronic data interchange** → 3323

3325 electronic data switching system; EDS
d elektronisches Datenvermittlungssystem *n*
f système *m* de commutation de données
électronique
r электронная коммутируемая система *f*
данных

* **electronic dictionary** → 690

* **electronic document exchange** → 3323

* **electronic document interchange** → 3323

**3326 electronic document management system;
EDMS**
d elektronisches
Dokument-Managementsystem *n*;
elektronisches
Dokumentverwaltungssystem *n*
f système *m* de gestion électronique de
documents; SGED
r система *f* управления электронными
документами

3327 electronic form; e-form; form
d Formular *n*; Vordruck *m*; Formblatt *n*
f formulaire *m* [électronique]
r [электронная] форма *f*; формуляр *m*

3328 electronic journal
d elektronische Zeitschrift *f*
f journal *m* électronique
r электронный дневник *m*

**3329 electronic magazine; e-zine; Web
magazine; Webzine**
d elektronisches Magazin *n*; Magazin im Web
f Webzine *m*; ézine *m*
r электронный журнал *m*

3330 electronic mail; e-mail; computer mail
d elektronische Post *f*; E-Post *f*; E-Mail *f*;
Email *f*; E-Brief *m*
f courrier *m* électronique; messagerie *f*
électronique; poste *f* électronique
r электронная почта *f*

3331 electronic mailbox; mailbox
d elektronisches Postfach *n*; [elektronischer]
Briefkasten *m*; Mailbox *f*; Telebox *f*;
Postablagefach *n*

f boîte *f* aux lettres [électronique]; bal *f*
r электронный почтовый ящик *m*

3332 electronic mail system; e-mail system; EMS
d elektronisches Briefkastensystem *n*
f système *m* de poste électronique; système de courrier électronique
r электронная почтовая система *f*; система электронной почты

3333 electronic money; electronic cash; e-cash; cybercash; digital cash
d elektronisches Geld *n*
f monnaie *f* électronique
r электронные деньги *pl*

* **electronic pen** → 5361

* **electronic publishing** → 2060

3334 electronic pumping
d elektronisches Pumpen *n*
f pompage *m* électronique
r электронная накачка *f*

3335 electronics
d Elektronik *f*
f électronique *f*
r электроника *f*

3336 electronic software distribution; ESD (by Internet)
d elektronische Softwareverteilung *f*
f distribution *f* électronique de logiciel
r электронное распространение *n* программного обеспечения

* **electronic spreadsheet** → 3337

3337 electronic spreadsheet [program]; spreadsheet
d Tabellenkalkulationsprogramm *n*; Journalbogen *m*
f programme *m* tableur; tableur *m*
r программа *f* табличных вычислений

3338 electronic white pages
d elektronische weiße Seiten *fpl*
f pages *fpl* blanches électroniques
r электронные белые страницы *fpl*

3339 electronic workplace; computerized workstation
d elektronischer Arbeitsplatz *m*; rechnergestützter Arbeitsplatz; elektronische Arbeitsstelle *f*
f place *m* de travail automatisé; bureau *m* électronique
r автоматизированное рабочее место *n*

3340 electronic yellow pages
d elektronische gelbe Seiten *fpl*
f pages *fpl* jaunes électroniques
r электронные жёлтые страницы *fpl*

3341 electrophotographic printer
d elektrofotografischer Drucker *m*
f imprimante *f* électrophotographique
r электрофотографическое печатающее устройство *n*

3342 electrosensitive printer
d elektrosensitiver Drucker *m*
f imprimante *f* électrosensitive
r электрочувствительное печатающее устройство *n*

3343 electrostatic plotter
d elektrostatischer Plotter *m*
f traceur *m* électrostatique
r электростатический графопостроитель *m*

3344 electrostatic printer
d elektrostatischer Drucker *m*
f imprimante *f* électrostatique
r электростатическое печатающее устройство *n*

3345 electrothermal recording technique
d elektrothermische Registrierungstechnik *f*
f technique *f* électrothermique d'enregistrement
r электротермический метод *m* записи

* **electrothermic printer** → 9342

3346 element
d Element *n*; Glied *n*
f élément *m*
r элемент *m*

3347 elementary calculation
d elementare Rechnung *f*
f calcul *m* banal
r элементарное вычисление *n*

* **elementary logic** → 3857

3348 elementary logical connections
d elementare logische Verknüpfungen *fpl*
f connexions *fpl* logiques élémentaires
r основные логические операции *fpl*

* **element cursor** → 8320

* **elevator** → 8266

* **eliminate** *v* → 2733

3349 elimination
d Elimination *f*; Beseitigung *f*

f élimination *f*
r исключение *n*; элиминация *f*;
элиминирование *n*

3350 elimination algorithm
d Eliminationsalgorithmus *m*
f algorithme *m* d'élimination
r алгоритм *m* исключения

3351 ellipsis; dots
(wildcard character)
d Auslassungspunkte *mpl*;
Fortführungspunkte *mpl*
f points *mpl* de suspension
r многоточие *n*; эллипсис *m*

3352 elliptical
d elliptisch
f elliptique
r эллиптический

3353 elliptical dot
d elliptischer Rasterpunkt *m*; elliptischer
Punkt *m*
f point *m* de trame elliptique
r растровая точка *f* эллиптической формы

**3354 elliptical dot screen; dot-chaining screen;
chain-dot screen**
d Kettenpunktraster *m*
f trame *f* à points elliptiques; trame à points en
chaîne
r растр *m* с эллиптическими цепеобразными
элементами

3355 elongation; prolongation; lengthening
d Verlängerung *f*; Längsdehnung *f*
f allongement *m*; élongation *f*
r удлинение *n*

* **e-bomb** → 5340

* **e-mail** → 3330

3356 e-mail address
d E-Mail-Adresse *f*
f adresse *f* [de poste] électronique; adresse
e-mail
r адрес *m* электронной почты

* **e-mail-bomb** → 5340

* **e-mail system** → 3332

3357 embedded chart
d eingebettetes Diagramm *n*
f diagramme *m* incorporé
r встроенная диаграмма *f*

3358 embedded fonts

d eingebettete Schriften *fpl*
f polices *fpl* incorporées
r встроенные шрифты *mpl*

3359 embedded objects
d eingebettete Objekte *npl*
f objets *mpl* encastrés; objets incorporés
r встроенные объекты *mpl*

3360 embedded window
d eingebettetes Fenster *n*
f fenêtre *f* encastrée
r вложенное окно *n*

* **embedding** → 6072

* **emblem** → 1283

3361 emboss *v*
d prägen
f gaufrer; bosseler; estamper
r выдавливать выпуклый рисунок; чеканить;
гофрировать; лепить рельеф; украшать
рельефом

3362 emboss[ed] effect; relief effect
d Reliefeffekt *m*
f effet *m* relief
r эффект *m* рельефа

3363 embossed surface; surface in relief
d Relieffläche *f*
f surface *f* en relief
r рельефная поверхность *f*

* **emboss effect** → 3362

3364 embosser
d Reliefschreiber *m*
f imprimeur *m* en relief
r рельефно печатающее устройство *n*

3365 emergency
d Not *f*
f urgence *f*
r непредвиденный случай *m*

* **emergency plan** → 2232

3366 emergency power supply
d Notstromversorgung *f*; Notstromaggregat *n*
f alimentation *f* de secours
r аварийное питание *n*

3367 emission
d Emission *f*
f émission *f*
r эмиссия *f*; излучение *n*

3368 emissive display
d Bildschirm *m* mit Emission

f afficheur *m* à émission
r дисплей *m* с излучением

3369 emissivity
   d Emissionsvermögen *n*; Emissionsfähigkeit *f*;
     Strahlungsvermögen *n*
   f émissivité *f*; pouvoir *m* d'émission
   r эмиссионная способность *f*; способность
     излучения

3370 emitter
   d Emitter *m*
   f émetteur *m*
   r эмиттер *m*

3371 emitter-coupled logic; ECL
   d emittergekoppelte Logik *f*; ECL
   f logique *f* connectée par émetteurs; ECL
   r эмиттерно-связанная логика *f*; ЭСЛ

3372 emitting; radiant
   d strahlend
   f rayonnant
   r излучающий

   * **emoticon** → 8675

   * **emphasis** → 4496

   * **emphasize** *v* → 47, 4492, 9624

3373 empirical
   d Erfahrungs-; empirisch
   f empirique
   r эмпирический; опытный

3374 empirical data
   d empirische Daten *pl*
   f données *fpl* empiriques
   r эмпирические данные *pl*

   * **employment** → 463

   * **empty** → 1044

3375 empty cell
   d leere Zelle *f*
   f cellule *f* vide
   r пустая клетка *f*

3376 empty packet
   d leeres Datenpaket *n*; abgearbeitetes
     Datenpaket
   f paquet *m* vide
   r пустой пакет *m*

3377 empty socket
   d Leersockel *m*; Leerfassung *f*
   f prise *f* vide
   r незанятый разъём *m*; свободный разъём

3378 empty word
   d leeres Wort *n*
   f mot *m* vide
   r пустое слово *n*

   * **EMS** → 3332

3379 emulation
   d Emulation *f*; Nachbildung *f*
   f émulation *f*
   r эмуляция *f*

3380 emulator
   d Emulator *m*; Nachbilder *m*
   f émulateur *m*
   r эмулятор *m*

   * **enable** → 666, 7868

3381 enable *v*
   d wirksam machen; freigeben; befähigen
   f permettre; autoriser; résoudre
   r разрешать; позволять

3382 enable bit
   d Freigabebit *n*
   f bit *m* de validation
   r бит *m* разрешения

3383 enable command
   d Freigabebefehl *m*
   f commande *f* de validation
   r команда *f* разблокирования; команда
     разрешения

3384 enable decoding
   d Freigabedecodierung *f*
   f décodage *m* de validation
   r дешифрирование *n* разрешения

3385 enable function
   d Freigabefunktion *f*
   f activation *f* d'une fonction
   r функция *f* разрешения

   * **enable input** → 3386

   * **enable signal** → 3387

3386 enabling input; enable input
   d Freigabeeingang *m*
   f entrée *f* de validation; entrée d'autorisation
   r разрешающий вход *m*

3387 enabling signal; enable signal
   d Freigabesignal *n*
   f signal *m* de validation
   r сигнал разрешения

3388 encapsulate *v*
   d einkapseln; verkapseln

f [en]capsuler
r герметизировать

3389 encapsulated PostScript; EPS
d eingekapselter PostScript *m*
f PostScript *m* encapsulé
r капсулированный язык *m* описания
страниц

3390 encapsulated PostScript file; EPS file
d EPS-Datei *f*
f fichier *m* EPS
r EPS-файл *m*

3391 encapsulated type
(of data)
d eingekapselter Typ *m*
f type *m* encapsulé
r скрытый тип *m*

* **encapsulation** → 1427, 6689

* **encasement** → 3393

* **enciphered message** → 3398

* **encirclement** → 1694

3392 enclose *v*; **include** *v*
d umschließen; einschließen; [ein]kapseln;
enthalten
f enclore; inclure; contenir
r включать в себя; охватывать; заключать

3393 enclosure; encasement; package
d Gehäuse *n*; Bausteingehäuse *n*; Verkleidung *f*
f boîtier *m*; revêtement *m*; emballage *m*
r корпус *m*; упаковка *f*

3394 encoded; coded
d codiert
f codé
r кодированный

3395 encoded document
d verschlüsseltes Dokument *n*
f document *m* codé
r кодированный документ *m*

3396 encoded document collection
d Sammlung *f* der verschlüsselten Dokumente
f collection *f* de documents codés
r сбор *m* кодированных документов

3397 encoded information type; EIT
d codierte Informationsform *f*
f type *m* d'information codé
r зашифрованный тип *m* информации;
[за]кодированный тип информации

**3398 encoded message; encrypted message;
enciphered message**
d verschlüsselte Nachricht *f*
f message *m* chiffré
r зашифрованное сообщение *n*

* **encoder** → 1819

* **encoding** → 1826

* **encoding law** → 1828

* **encrypted message** → 3398

3399 encrypted virus; scrambled virus
d verschlüsseltes Virus *n*
f virus *m* crypté
r зашифрованный вирус *m*

3400 encryption
d Zeichenverschlüsselung *f*
f [en]cryptage *m*; chiffrage *m*; chiffrement *m*;
cryptoopération *f*
r шифрование *n*

3401 encryption technique
d Chiffriertechnik *f*; Verschlüsselungstechnik *f*
f technique *f* de cryptage
r способ *m* шифрования

3402 end
d Ende *n*
f fin *f*; bout *m*
r конец *m*

* **end** → 3831

3403 end address
d Endadresse *f*
f adresse *f* de fin
r конечный адрес *m*

* **end-around borrow** → 2471

* **end-around carry** → 2472

* **end-around shift** → 1685

* **end client** → 3422

3404 end connector
d Endsteckverbinder *m*; stirnseitiger
Steckverbinder *m*
f connecteur *m* de fin; connecteur frontal
r конечный разъём *m*

* **end device** → 9266

3405 end echo delay
d Endecholaufzeit *f*

f délai *m* d'écho final
r конечная эхо-пауза *f*

3406 End key
  d Ende-Taste *f*
  f touche *f* End
  r клавиша *f* End

  * **endless** → **4795**

3407 endless loop; infinite loop
  d unendliche Schleife *f*; Endlosschleife *f*
  f boucle *f* sans fin
  r бесконечный цикл *m*

  * **end mark** → **3408**

3408 end mark[er]
  d End[e]marke *f*; Endsteuerzeichen *n*
  f marque *f* de fin; marque finale
  r метка *f* конца; маркер *m* конца

3409 end marking
  d Endmarkierung *f*
  f marquage *m* de fin
  r маркировка *f* конца

3410 end of file; EOF
  d Dateiende *n*
  f fin *f* de fichier
  r конец *m* файла

3411 end of message
  d Nachrichtenende *n*
  f fin *f* de message
  r конец *m* сообщения

3412 end of paper
  d Papierende *n*
  f fin *f* de papier
  r конец *m* бумаги

3413 end of record
  d Satzende *n*
  f fin *f* d'enregistrement
  r конец *m* записи

3414 end of tape; EOT
  d Bandende *n*
  f fin *f* de bande
  r конец *m* ленты

3415 end-of-test message
  d Prüfendemeldung *f*
  f message *m* de fin d'essai
  r сообщение *n* о конце проверки

3416 end of text; ETX
  d Ende *n* des Textes; Textende *n*
  f fin *f* de texte

  r конец *m* текста

3417 end of transmission; transmission end
  d Ende *n* der Übertragung
  f fin *f* de transmission
  r конец *m* передачи

3418 end of volume label
  d Datenträgerendekennsatz *m*
  f étiquette *f* de fin de volume
  r метка *f* конца тома

3419 endpoint; terminal point
  d Endpunkt *m*
  f point *m* final; extrémité *f*
  r конечная точка *f*

3420 end sequence
  d begrenzte Folge *f*
  f séquence *f* finale
  r конечная последовательность *f*

3421 end-to-end encryption
  d Ende-zu-Ende-Verschlüsselung *f*;
    Übermittlungsverschlüsselung *f*;
    Verschlüsselung *f* von Daten von Endstelle zu
    Endstelle
  f encryption *f* entière
  r сквозное шифрование *n*

3422 end user; end client
  d Endbenutzer *m*; Endkunde *m*;
    Endverbraucher *m*
  f utilisateur *m* final; consommateur *m* final;
    client *m* final
  r конечный пользователь *m*; конечный
    клиент *m*

3423 end view
  d endgültige Ansicht *f*
  f vue *f* de derrière
  r конечный вид *m*

3424 energy
  d Energie *f*
  f énergie *f*
  r энергия *f*

  * **energy conservation** → **2187**

**3425 energy-dependent stor[ag]e; volatile
memory**
  d energieabhängiger Speicher *m*; flüchtiger
    Speicher
  f mémoire *f* dépendante d'énergie; mémoire
    volatile
  r энергозависимая память *f*

  * **energy-dependent store** → **3425**

3426 **energy-independent stor[ag]e; non-volatile**
memory
  d energieunabhängiger Speicher *m*
  f mémoire *f* indépendante d'énergie; mémoire
  non volatile
  r энергонезависимая память *f*

* **energy-independent store** → 3426

3427 **energy-saving technology**
  d Energiespar-Technologie *f*
  f technologie *f* de sauvegarde d'énergie
  r энергосберегающая технология *f*

* **engine** → 5538

3428 **engineering data; operating data**
  d technische Daten *pl*
  f données *fpl* techniques
  r технические данные *pl*

3429 **engineering design**
  d technischer Entwurf *m*
  f projet *m* technique; conception *f* technique
  r технический проект *m*; техническое
  проектирование *n*

3430 **engineering [design] graphics**
  d Ingenieurgrafik *f*
  f graphique *m* technique
  r инженерная графика *f*

* **engineering graphics** → 3430

3431 **enhanced graphics adapter; EGA**
  d EGA-Standard *m*
  f standard *m* EGA
  r улучшенный графический адаптер *m*;
  видеографический стандарт *m* EGA

3432 **enhanced LAN/WAN connectivity**
  d erweiterte LAN/WAN-Verbindung *f*;
  erweiterte LAN/WAN-Zusammenhang *m*
  f interconnexion *f* RL-RLD évoluée
  r улучшенная связь *f* LAN/WAN

3433 **enhanced view**
  d erweiterte Ansicht *f*
  f vue *f* améliorée
  r расширенное представление *n*

3434 **enhancement; improvement**
  d Verbesserung *f*; Anreicherung *f*
  f enrichissement *m*; amélioration *f*
  r улучшение *n*; обогащение *n*

3435 **enhancement of the contrast**
  d Verbesserung *f* des Kontrastes
  f amélioration *f* du contraste
  r улучшение *n* контраста

* **enlargement** → 3591

3436 **enqueue** *v*
  d anordnen in Reihenfolge
  f ordonner à la queue; prendre à la queue; se
  mettre à la queue
  r поставить в очередь

* **enquiry** → 7963

* **enquiry character** → 4921

* **ensemble** → 8466

3437 **enter** *v*; **introduce** *v*; **carry** *v* **in**
  d einführen; eintragen; einbringen
  f entrer; introduire
  r входить; вводить

3438 **Enter key**
  d Enter-Taste *f*
  f touche *f* Enter; touche de validation
  r клавиша *f* ввода; клавиша Enter

3439 **enterprise information system; EIS**
  d Enterprise-Informationssystem *n*
  f système *m* d'information d'entreprise; SIE
  r информационная система *f* предприятия

3440 **enterprise level**
  (of data)
  d Enterprise-Ebene *f*; Fachebene *f*
  f niveau *m* d'entreprise
  r предметный уровень *m*

* **entire** → 4962

3441 **entity**
  d Entität *f*; Wesen *n*
  f entité *f*
  r сущность *f*; категория *f*; целость *f*

3442 **entity; feature**
  (transformed graphic primitive with assigned
  nongeometric properties)
  d Einheit *f*
  f entité *f* [géométrique]
  r [геометрический] примитив *m*

* **entrance** → 3444

3443 **entropy**
  d Entropie *f*; mittlerer Informationsgehalt *m*
  f entropie *f*
  r энтропия *f*; содержательность *f* сообщения

3444 **entry; entrance**
  d Eintritt *m*; Einführung *f*
  f entrée *f*
  r вхождение *n*; введение *n*

   * entry → 4880

   * entry field → 2548

3445 entry hub
   d Eingangsbuchse *f*
   f jack *m* d'entrée
   r входное гнездо *n*; входная клемма *f*

3446 entry node
   (of a graph)
   d Eingabeknoten *m*
   f nœud *m* entrant
   r входящий узел *m*

   * entry page → 4542

   * enumerability → 2340

   * enumerable → 2341

3447 enumeration
   d Aufzählung *f*, Abzählung *f*
   f énumération *f*
   r перечисление *n*; пересчёт *m*

3448 enumeration data
   d Zählungsdaten *pl*
   f données *fpl* énumérées
   r перечисленные данные *pl*

3449 enumeration type
   (of data)
   d aufzählbarer Datentyp *m*; Aufzählungstyp *m*
   f type *m* d'énumération
   r перечислимый тип *m*

3450 enumerator
   d Zähler *m*
   f énumérateur *m*
   r перечислитель *m*

   * envelope → 989

3451 envelope; shell; sheet; hull; casing
   d Hülle *f*
   f enveloppe *f*
   r оболочка *f*

3452 envelope alignment
   d Bitgruppesynchronisation *f*
   f synchronisation *f* de groupe de bits
   r синхронизация *f* группы битов

   * envelope delay → 4339

3453 envelope density
   d Hülldichte *f*
   f densité *f* d'enveloppe
   r плотность *f* оболочки

3454 environment; ambience
   d Umgebung *f*, Einkreisung *f*
   f environnement *m*; ambiance *f*
   r среда *f*; окружение *n*; окрестность *f*

3455 environment[al] data
   d Umweltdaten *pl*
   f données *fpl* d'environnement
   r данные *pl* о внешней среде

3456 environmental design
   d Umgebungdesign *n*
   f dessin *m* d'environnement
   r проектирование *n* окружения;
      проектирование окрестности

   * environment data → 3455

3457 environment description
   d Umgebung-Beschreibung *f*
   f description *f* d'environnement
   r описание *n* окрестности

   * EOF → 3410

   * EOF label → 3458

3458 EOF mark; EOF label
   d Dateiendemarke *f*; Dateiendekennsatz *f*
   f marque *f* de fin de fichier; étiquette *f* de fin de
      fichier
   r метка *f* конца файла

   * EOT → 3414

   * EPROM → 3317, 3476

   * EPS → 3389

   * EPS file → 3390

   * EQ gate → 3469

3459 equality
   d Gleichheit *f*
   f égalité *f*
   r равенство *n*

   * equalization → 308

3460 equalization bit
   d Ausgleichsbit *n*
   f bit *m* d'égalisation
   r бит *m* выравнивания

3461 equalization register
   d Entzerrerregister *n*
   f registre *m* d'égalisation
   r компенсирующий регистр *m*

* **equalize** $v \rightarrow 305$

* **equalizer** $\rightarrow 1984$

3462 equalizing amplifier
   d Entzerrerverstärker *m*
   f amplificateur *m* d'égalisation
   r корректирующий усилитель *m*

* **equalizing network** $\rightarrow 1984$

3463 equal-ratio channel
   d Zeitvielfachkanal *m* mit gleichmäßiger
      Periodenverteilung
   f canal *m* à distribution égale de périodes
   r канал *m* равномерного распределения
      периодов

**3464 equal-ratio code; fixed-ratio code;
   equiweighted code; fixed-count code;
   constant-ratio code**
   d gleichgewichtiger Code *m*; Verhältniscode *m*
   f code *m* à rapport [fixe]
   r равновесомый код *m*; код с
      фиксированным кодовым расстоянием

* **equal sign** $\rightarrow 3465$

3465 equal symbol; equal sign
   (=)
   d Gleichheitszeichen *n*
   f signe *m* d'égalité; signe égal
   r знак *m* равенства

3466 equation
   d Gleichung *f*
   f équation *f*
   r уравнение *n*

* **equilibrium** $\rightarrow 793$

3467 equipment; facility
   d Ausrüstung *f*; Ausstattung *f*; Apparatur *f*;
      Einrichtung *f*
   f équipement *m*; appareillage *m*
   r оборудование *n*; аппаратура *f*;
      сооружения *npl*

3468 equivalence
   d Äquivalenz *f*
   f équivalence *f*
   r эквивалентность *f*

3469 equivalence gate; EQ gate; identity gate
   d Äquivalenzgatter *n*; Identitätsgatter *n*
   f porte *f* d'équivalence; porte d'identité
   r схема *f* [функции] эквивалентности; схема
      равнозначности

3470 equivalence sign; symbol of equivalence

   d Äquivalenzzeichen *n*; Bijugat *n*
   f signe *m* d'équivalence
   r знак *m* эквивалентности

3471 equivalent
   d äquivalent; gleichwertig; gleichbedeutend
   f équivalent
   r эквивалентный; равнозначный

3472 equivalent bit rate
   d äquivalente Bitrate *f*
   f débit *m* binaire équivalent
   r эквивалентная скорость *f* передачи битов

* **equivalent circuit** $\rightarrow 797$

* **equivalent network** $\rightarrow 797$

* **equiweighted code** $\rightarrow 3464$

3473 erasable disk
   d löschbare Platte *f*
   f disque *m* effaçable
   r стираемый диск *m*

3474 erasable information
   d löschbare Information *f*
   f information *f* effaçable
   r стираемая информация *f*

3475 erasable memory; erasable store
   d löschbarer Speicher *m*
   f mémoire *f* effaçable
   r стираемая память *f*

* **erasable optical disk** $\rightarrow 1962$

**3476 erasable programmable read-only
   memory; EPROM**
   d löschbarer programmierbarer
      Festwertspeicher *m*; EPROM
   f mémoire *f* permanente programmable et
      effaçable; EPROM
   r стираемая программируемая постоянная
      память *f*

* **erasable store** $\rightarrow 3475$

* **erase** $v \rightarrow 1709, 2733$

* **erase head** $\rightarrow 3478$

3477 erase message
   d Löschen *n* von Nachrichten
   f message *m* d'effacement
   r сообщение *n* о стирании

* **erasing** $\rightarrow 1715$

3478 erasing head; erase head
   d Löschkopf *m*

f tête *f* d'effacement
r головка *f* стирания; стирающая головка

* **erasure** → 1715

3479 erroneous bit
d fehlerhaftes Bit *n*
f bit *m* erroné
r искажённый бит *m*

3480 error
d Fehler *m*
f erreur *f*
r ошибка *f*; погрешность *f*

* **error burst** → 1272

3481 error character
d Fehlerzeichen *n*; Irrungszeichen *n*
f caractère *m* d'erreur
r знак *m* ошибки

* **error check** → 3484

3482 error check bit
d Fehlerprüfbit *n*; Fehlerkontrollbit *n*
f bit *m* de contrôle d'erreurs
r бит *m* контроля ошибок

3483 error check character
d Fehlerkontrollzeichen *n*; Fehlerprüfzeichen *n*
f caractère *m* de contrôle d'erreurs
r знак *m* контроля ошибок

3484 error check[ing]; fault checking; error control
d Fehlerprüfung *f*; Fehlerkontrolle *f*
f essai *m* des erreurs; essai des défauts; contrôle *m* des défauts; contrôle des erreurs
r проверка *f* ошибок; контроль *m* неисправностей; контроль ошибок

* **error-checking code** → 3491

* **error constant** → 9134

* **error control** → 3484

3485 error-correcting code; ECC
d Fehlerkorrekturcode *m*
f code *m* correcteur d'erreurs; code à correction d'erreurs
r код *m* с исправлением ошибок

3486 error correction
d Fehlerkorrektur *f*; Fehlerkorrektion *f*
f correction *f* d'erreurs
r коррекция *f* ошибок

3487 error correction circuit

d Fehlerkorrekturschaltung *f*
f circuit *m* de correction d'erreurs
r схема *f* исправления ошибок

3488 error counter
d Fehlerzähler *m*
f compteur *m* d'erreurs
r счётчик *m* ошибок

3489 error data collection
d Fehlerdatenerfassung *f*
f collection *f* de données d'erreurs
r сбор *m* данных об ошибках

3490 error-detecting and feedback system
d Fehlererkennungssystem *n* mit Wiederholung
f système *m* de rétroaction avec détection d'erreurs
r система *f* обратной связи и с обнаружением ошибок

3491 error-detecting code; error-checking code
d Fehlererkennungscode *m*; fehlererkennender Code *m*
f code *m* à détection d'erreurs; code détecteur d'erreurs
r код *m* с обнаружением ошибок

3492 error detection; failure detection; fault detection; error discovery
d Fehlerentdeckung *f*; Störungsentdeckung *f*
f détection *f* d'erreurs; détection de défauts
r обнаружение *n* погрешностей; обнаружение ошибок

3493 error detection circuit; failure detection circuit; fault detection circuit
d Fehlererkennungsschaltung *f*
f circuit *m* de détection d'erreurs; circuit de reconnaissance de défauts
r схема *f* обнаружения погрешностей; схема обнаружения отказов; схема обнаружения ошибок

3494 error diffusion
d Fehlerdiffusion *f*
f diffusion *f* d'erreurs
r рассеивание *n* ошибок

* **error discovery** → 3492

3495 error exit; failure exit; fault exit
d Schlechtausgang *m*
f sortie *f* d'erreur
r выход *m* ошибки

* **error-free operation** → 2328

3496 error handling; error processing; error treatment
d Fehlerbehandlung *f*; Fehlerbearbeitung *f*

f management *m* d'erreurs; traitement *m*
d'erreurs
r обработка *f* ошибок

3497 error indication; fault indication
d Fehleranzeige *f*
f indication *f* d'erreur; signalisation *f* de défaut
r индикация *f* ошибки

**3498 error indicator; fault indicator; trouble
indicator**
d Fehleranzeiger *m*
f indicateur *m* d'erreurs
r индикатор *m* ошибок

3499 error interrupt
d Fehlerunterbrechung *f*; fehlerbedingte
Unterbrechung *f*; Fehlerinterrupt *m*
f interruption *f* par erreur
r прерывание *n* при ошибке

* **error in the input data** → **4897**

3500 error level
d Fehlerebene *f*
f couche *f* d'erreur
r уровень *m* ошибки

3501 error logging
d Fehlerauflistung *f*; Fehlerregistrierung *f*
f enregistrement *m* d'erreurs; consignation *f*
d'erreurs
r регистрирация *f* ошибок

3502 error message
d Fehlermeldung *f*
f message *m* d'erreur
r сообщение *n* об ошибке

* **error message list** → **3504**

3503 error message processing
d Fehlermeldungsbearbeitung *f*
f traitement *m* des messages d'erreurs
r обработка *f* сообщений об ошибках

3504 error message table; error message list
d Fehlermeldeliste *f*
f table *f* de messages d'erreurs; liste *f* de
messages d'erreurs
r таблица *f* сообщений об ошибках;
список *m* сообщений об ошибках

3505 error of a procedure
d Verfahrensfehler *m*
f erreur *f* de la méthode
r погрешность *f* метода

* **error of computation** → **2047**

* **error of truncation** → **9573**

* **error processing** → **3496**

3506 error-propagation
d Fehlerfortpflanzung *f*
f propagation *f* d'erreurs
r распространение *n* ошибок

3507 error protection
d Fehlersicherung *f*; Fehlerschutz *m*
f protection *f* contre les erreurs
r защита *f* от ошибок

3508 error protocol
d Fehlerprotokoll *n*
f protocole *m* d'erreurs
r протокол *m* ошибок

3509 error range
d Störbereich *m*
f plage *f* d'erreurs
r диапазон *m* погрешностей; область *f*
рассогласования

* **error rate** → **3684**

3510 error register
d Fehlerregister *n*
f registre *m* d'erreur
r регистр *m* ошибки

3511 error register indicator
d Fehlerregisteranzeige *f*
f indicateur *m* de registre d'erreur
r индикатор *m* регистра ошибки

3512 error research; fault search
d Fehlersuche *f*
f recherche *f* d'erreurs
r поиск *m* ошибок

3513 error response table
d Fehlerrangiertabelle *f*
f table *f* des réponses d'erreurs
r таблица *f* характеристики ошибок

3514 error return
d fehlerbedingte Rückkehr *f*
f retour *m* par erreur
r возврат *m* из-за ошибки

3515 error signal
d Fehlersignal *n*
f signal *m* d'erreur
r сигнал *m* ошибки

3516 error source; source of error
d Fehlerquelle *f*

f source *f* d'erreur
r источник *m* ошибки; источник *m* погрешности

3517 error statistics field
d Fehlerstatistikfeld *n*
f champ *m* de statistique des erreurs
r поле *f* статистики ошибок

3518 error table
d Fehlerliste *f*
f table *f* d'erreurs
r таблица *f* ошибок

3519 error transfer function
d Fehlerübertragungsfunktion *f*
f fonction *f* de transfert d'erreur
r передаточная функция *f* по ошибке

* **error treatment** → 3496

3520 error word
d Fehlerwort *n*
f mot *m* d'erreurs
r слово *n* ошибки

* **ESC** → 3522

3521 escape
d Escape *n*; [Code-]Umschaltung *f*; Codewechsel *m*
f échappement *m*; changement *m* de code
r переключение *n*; смена *f* кода

3522 escape character; ESC
d Escape-Zeichen *n*; Umschalt[ungs]zeichen *n*; Code-Umschaltzeichen *n*
f caractère *m* d'échappement; caractère d'extraction; caractère de changement de code
r знак *m* перехода; символ *m* выхода; знак смены регистра

3523 escape language
d Escape-Sprache *f*
f langage *m* à échappements; langage à références externes
r язык *m*, допускающий внешние обращения

3524 ESC key
d ESC-Taste *f*
f touche *f* Echap
r клавиша *f* Esc

* **ESD** → 3336

* **e-shopping** → 3324

* **e-slang** → 2088

3525 essential data
d wesentliche Daten *pl*

f données *fpl* essentielles
r существенные данные *pl*

3526 establishing of availability
d Verfügbarkeitsbestimmung *f*
f établissement *m* d'accessibilité
r установление *n* доступности

* **establishment** → 8474

3527 estimate *v*; evaluate *v*
d schätzen; auswerten; bewerten
f estimer; évaluer
r оценивать

* **estimating function** → 3530

3528 estimation; assessment; evaluation; valuation; appraisal
d Abschätzung *f*; Schätzung *f*; Bewertung *f*; Auswertung *f*
f estimation *f*; appréciation *f*; évaluation *f*
r оценка *f*; оценивание *n*

3529 estimation problem
d Schätzungsproblem *n*; Estimationsaufgabe *f*
f problème *m* d'estimation
r задача *f* оценивания

* **estimation unit** → 3535

3530 estimator; estimating function
d Schätzfunktion *f*
f estimateur *m*; fonction *f* d'estimation
r функция *f* оценки

* **ETX** → 3416

3531 ETX character
d Textendezeichen *n*; Nachrichtenendezeichen *n*
f caractère *m* de fin du texte
r символ *m* конца текста

* **Eurocard** → 3533

* **Euroformat card** → 3533

3532 European Academic and Research Network; EARN
(the European equivalent to BITNET)
d europäisches Akademie- und Forschungsnetz *n*
f Réseau *m* européen pour l'échange de données dans le monde scientifique
r Европейская академическая сеть *f*

3533 European format printed circuit board; Euroformat card; Eurocard
d Karte *f* mit europäischem Format;

Europaformatkarte f; Eurokarte f
f carte f au format européen; Eurocarte f
r плата f европейского формата; евро-плата f

* **evaluate** v → 3527

* **evaluation** → 3528

* **evaluation board** → 1165

3534 evaluation circuit
d Auswerteschaltung f
f circuit m d'évaluation
r схема f оценки

3535 evaluation unit; estimation unit; evaluator
d Auswertegerät n; Auswerter m;
Auswerteeinheit f
f bloc d'estimation; organe m d'estimation
r блок m оценки

* **evaluator** → 3535

3536 even
d gerade
f pair
r чётный

* **even address** → 3538

3537 even index
d gerader Index m
f index m pair
r чётный индекс m

3538 even[-numbered] address
d gerade Adresse f; geradzahlige Adresse
f adresse f [à nombre] paire
r чётный адрес m

* **even-odd check** → 6377

3539 even parity
d gerade Parität f
f parité f paire
r чётный паритет m

* **even parity check** → 6807

3540 event
d Ereignis n; Vorgang m
f événement m
r событие n

3541 event data
d Ereignisdaten pl
f données fpl d'événement
r данные pl типа "событие"

3542 event flag
d Ereigniskennzeichen n

f marque f d'événement
r флажок m события

3543 event flag byte
d Ereigniskennungsbyte n
f octet m de marque d'événement
r байт m флажка события

3544 event log
d Ereignisjournal n; Ereignisprotokoll n
f journal m des événements
r журнал m регистрации событий

3545 event management
d Ereignisverwaltung f
f management m d'événements
r управление n событий

3546 event probability
d Ereigniswahrscheinlichkeit f
f probabilité f d'événement
r вероятность f [наступления] события

3547 event processing
d Ereignisverarbeitung f
f traitement m d'événements
r обработка f событий

3548 event processing logic
d Logik f für Ereignisverarbeitung
f logique f de traitement d'événements
r логика f обработки событий

3549 event synchronization
d Ereignissynchronisation f
f synchronisation f d'événements
r синхронизация f событий

3550 ever-faster computer
d Ultraschnellrechner m
f ordinateur m surpuissant
r сверхбыстродействующий компьютер m;
сверхбыстрый компьютер

* **exactitude** → 103

* **exactness** → 103

3551 exceed v
d überschreiten
f dépasser
r превышать

3552 exceeding
d Überschreitung f
f dépassement m
r превышение n

3553 exception; exclusion
d Ausnahme f; Exzeption f; Exklusion f

    f exception *f*; exclusion *f*
    r исключение *n*

3554 exceptional condition
    d Ausnahmebedingung *f*
    f condition *f* exceptionnelle
    r исключительное условие *n*

3555 exception[al condition] code
    d Ausnahmebedingungscode *m*
    f code *m* de condition des exceptions
    r код *m* исключительного условия

    * **exception code** → **3555**

3556 exception control
    d Ablaufunterbrechung *f*
    f contrôle *m* d'exception
    r управление *n* в исключительной ситуации

3557 exception handling
    d Bearbeitung *f* von Ausnahmebedingungen
    f traitement *m* d'exception
    r обработка *f* исключительной ситуации

3558 exception word dictionary
    d Ausnahmewörterbuch *n*
    f dictionnaire *m* des mots exceptionnels
    r словарь *m* исключений

3559 excess
    d Überschuss *m*; Exzess *m*
    f excès *m*
    r избыток *m*

    * **excessive** → **7786**

    * **excessiveness** → **7782**

3560 excess-three code; three-excess code
    d Drei-Überschuss-Code *m*;
    Drei-Excess-Code *m*; Stibitz-Code *m*;
    Plus-Drei-Code *m*
    f code *m* excès-trois; code *m* par excès de trois
    r код *m* с избытком три

3561 exchange; interchange
    d Austausch *m*; Umtausch *m*;
    Auswechs[e]lung *f*, Vertauschung *f*
    f échange *m*; interchange *m*
    r [взаимо]обмен *m*; перестановка *f*; замена *f*

3562 exchangeability; interchangeability
    d Austauschbarkeit *f*, Auswechselbarkeit *f*
    f échangeabilité *f*; interchangeabilité *f*
    r [взаимо]заменяемость *f*

3563 exchangeable; interchangeable
    d austauschbar; auswechselbar
    f échangeable; interchangeable

    r [взаимо]заменяемый; сменный

3564 exchangeable disk; removable disk; demountable disk
    d Wechselplatte *f*; auswechselbare Platte *f*,
    herausnehmbare Platte
    f disque *m* interchangeable; disque amovible;
    disque démontable
    r сменный диск *m*; съёмный диск;
    заменяемый диск

3565 exchange buffering
    d Austauschpufferung *f*
    f tamponnement *m* d'échange
    r обменная буферизация *f*

3566 exchange device
    d Datenaustauschgerät *n*
    f dispositif *m* d'échange
    r устройство *n* обмена [данными]

    * **exchange selection** → **1216**

    * **exclusion** → **3553**

3567 exclusive access
    d alleiniger Zugriff *m*
    f accès *m* exclusif
    r монопольный доступ *m*

3568 exclusive control
    d exklusive Steuerung *f*
    f commande *f* exclusive
    r монопольное управление *n*

3569 EXCLUSIVE-OR gate; non-equivalence gate; modulo 2 sum gate
    d EXKLUSIV-ODER-Gatter *n*;
    Inäquivalenzgatter *n*;
    Modulo-2-Addition-Gatter *n*
    f porte *f* OU EXCLUSIF; porte de
    non-équivalence; porte d'addition en
    module 2
    r схема *f* исключающее ИЛИ; схема
    неравнозначности; схема сложения по
    модулю 2

3570 EXCLUSIVE-OR operation; XOR
    d EXKLUSIV-ODER-Operation *f*; EXOR;
    XOR
    f opération *f* OU EXCLUSIF
    r операция *f* исключающее ИЛИ

3571 exclusive segment
    d exklusives Segment *n*
    f segment *m* exclusif
    r несовместный сегмент *m*; монопольный
    сегмент

3572 executable file
    d ausführbare Datei *f*

f fichier *m* exécutable
r исполняемый файл *m*

3573 execute *v*
d ausführen
f exécuter
r выполнять

3574 execution; run[ning]
d Ausführung *f*; Ablauf *m*; Run *m*
f exécution *f*
r исполнение *n*; выполнение *n*

3575 execution process
d Ausführungsprozess *m*
f processus *m* d'exécution
r процесс *m* выполнения

* **execution time** → 8162

* **executive** → 3578

* **executive address** → 150

3576 executive dump
d Speicherauszug *m* während der Ausführung
f vidage *m* exécutif
r рабочий дамп *m*

3577 executive mode
d Supervisormodus *m*
f mode *m* [de] superviseur
r режим *m* супервизора

3578 executive [program]; supervisor; monitor[ing] [program]
d Supervisor *m*; Monitorprogramm *n*; Überwachungsprogramm *n*; Überwacher *m*
f programme *m* exécutif; superviseur *m*; programme *m* moniteur; monitrice *f*; moniteur *m*
r супервизор *m*; программа-диспетчер *f*; программа-монитор *f*

3579 executive register
d Organisationsregister *n*
f registre *m* d'exécution; registre de service
r рабочий регистр *m*

3580 executive system
d Exekutivsystem *n*; Chefanlage *f*
f système *m* d'exécution
r исполнительная система *f*

3581 exercise *v*
d üben; trainieren
f exercer
r упражняться; тренировать[ся]

* **exercizer** → 9277

3582 exit; output; quit
d Ausgang *m*; Austritt *m*
f sortie *f*
r выход *m*

3583 exit code
d Ausgangscode *m*
f code *m* de sortie
r выходной код *m*

3584 exit connector
d Ausgangskonnektor *m*
f connecteur *m* de sortie
r выходной соединитель *m*

3585 exit event
d Ausgangsereignis *n*
f événement *m* de sortie
r событие *n* выхода

3586 exit flag
d Ausgangskennzeichen *n*
f flag *m* de sortie
r флаг *m* выхода

3587 exit losses
d Austrittsverluste *mpl*
f pertes *fpl* de sortie
r потери *fpl* на выходе

3588 exit node
(of a graph)
d Ausgangsknoten *m*
f nœud *m* sortant
r исходящий узел *m*

* **expand** *v* → 3615

3589 expandable; extensible
d erweitbar
f expansible; extensible
r расширяемый

3590 expander
d Erweiterungsschaltung *f*; Expander *m*
f expanseur *m*; extenseur *m*
r расширитель *m*; экспандер *m*

3591 expansion; extension; enlargement
d Erweiterung *f*; Expandierung *f*; Dehnung *f*; Extension *f*
f expansion *f*; extension *f*; élargissement *m*
r расширение *n*; развитие *n*; растяжение *n*

3592 expansion board; extended board
d Erweiterungsleiterplatte *f*; Erweiterungskarte *f*
f plaque *f* d'extension; plaque de rallonge
r расширительная плата *f*; плата расширения

3593 expansion connector
d Erweiterungskonnektor *m*
f connecteur *m* d'extension
r соединитель *m* расширения

3594 expansion slot
d Erweiterungsschlitz *m*;
Erweiterungssteckplatz *m*
f jack *m* d'extension; emplacement *m* libre
r разъём *m* расширения

3595 expansion stage
d Expansionsstufe *f*
f étage *m* d'extension
r ступень *f* расширения

* **expectation** → 9947

3596 expedition
d Expedition *f*
f expédition *f*
r отправление *n*

* **experience base** → 841

* **experiment** → 616

3597 expert system
d Expertensystem *n*; wissenbasiertes System *n*
f système *m* expert
r экспертная система *f*

3598 expire *v*
d fällig werden
f expirer
r оканчиваться; истекать (о сроке)

* **explainer** → 3600

3599 explanation generator
d Erklärungsgenerator *m*
f générateur *m* d'explications
r генератор *m* объяснений

3600 explanation module; explainer
d Erklärungsmodul *m*; Erklärungskomponente *f*
f module *m* d'explication; unité *f* d'explication
r модуль *m* объяснения; блок *m* объяснения

3601 explicit address
d explizite Adresse *f*
f adresse *f* explicite
r явный адрес *m*

3602 explicit conversion
d explizite Konvertierung *f*
f conversion *f* explicite
r явное преобразование *n*

3603 explicit language

d explizite Sprache *f*
f langage *m* explicite
r явно определённый язык *m*

3604 explicit representation
d explizite Darstellung *f*
f représentation *f* explicite
r явное представление *n*

* **explode** *v* → 1104

3605 explode *v*; **dissociate** *v*
d zerlegen; auflösen
f dissocier
r разъединять; развязывать; разбивать

3606 exploration
d Forschung *f*; Untersuchung *f*
f exploration *f*
r исследование *n*

* **exploration** → 8209

3607 explorer
(type of navigator)
d Explorer *m*; Durchforster *m*
f explorateur *m*
r путеводитель *m* (по системе каталогов)

3608 explorer
d Erforscher *m*; Forscher *m*
f programme *m* d'exploration
r программа *f* анализа

* **exploring** → 8209

3609 exponential
d exponential
f exponentiel
r экспоненциальный; показательный

3610 exponential time algorithm
d Algorithmus *m* mit exponentiellem
Zeitaufwand; Exponentialzeitalgorithmus *m*
f algorithme *m* à temps exponentiel
r экспоненциальный алгоритм *m*

* **export** → 3612

3611 export *v*
d exportieren
f exporter
r экспортировать

* **exportation** → 3612

3612 export[ing]; exportation
d Versand *m*; Export *m*
f exportation *f*
r экспортирование *n*; отправка *f*; отсылка *f*

3613 expression
d Ausdruck m
f expression f
r выражение n

3614 express message
d Expressnachricht f
f message m rapide
r быстрое сообщение n

* **expunge** v → 2733, 8941

3615 extend v; **expand** v
d erweitern; ausdehnen
f étendre; élargir; agrandir
r расширять

3616 extended addressing
d erweiterte Adressierung f
f adressage m étendu
r расширенная адресация f

* **extended board** → 3592

3617 extended industry standard architecture; EISA
d EISA-Norm f
f architecture f EISA
r расширенная промышленная стандартная архитектура f; стандарт m EISA

3618 extended markup language; extensible markup language; XML
d XML-Sprache f
f langage m à balises personnalisable; langage XML
r язык m XML

3619 extended memory; extension memory; add-on memory
d Erweiterungsspeicher m
f mémoire f étendue; mémoire d'extension
r увеличенная память f; память для расширения [системы]

3620 extended operation code
d Operationsteilerweiterungscode m
f code m d'opération élargi
r расширенный код m операции

3621 extended precision
d erweiterte Genauigkeit f
f précision f étendue
r повышенная точность f; увеличенная точность

3622 extended prompt
d erweiterter Hinweis m
f guide m parlé toutes fonctions
r расширенная подсказка f

3623 extended-time scale; slow-time scale
d gedehnte Zeitskala f
f échelle f de temps étendu; échelle de temps ralenti
r расширенный масштаб m времени

* **extensible** → 3589

3624 extensible addressing
d erweiterbare Adressierung f
f adressage m extensible
r адресация f переменной длиной адреса

3625 extensible language
d erweiterbare Sprache f
f langage m extensible
r расширяемый язык m

* **extensible markup language** → 3618

* **extension** → 2814, 3581, 3812

3626 extension bus
d Erweiterungsbus m
f bus m d'extension
r расширительная шина f

3627 extension code
d Erweiterungscode m
f code m d'extension
r код m расширения

* **extension memory** → 3619

3628 extent
d Extent m
f étendue f; zone f d'étendue
r экстент m; зона f расширения; расширение n

3629 exterior; external; outer; outside; outward adj
d Außen-; äußer
f extérieur; externe
r внешний; наружный

* **external** → 3629

* **external clocking** → 3647

3630 external connection; external lead
d Außenanschluss m; äußere Verbindung f
f connexion f externe
r внешнее соединение n

3631 external connector set
d Externverbindungssatz m
f ensemble m de connecteurs externes
r набор m внешних соединителей

3632 external data
d äußere Daten *pl*
f données *fpl* externes
r внешние данные *pl*

3633 external database
d äußeres Datenbasis *f*
f base *f* de données externe
r внешняя база *f* данных

3634 external database toolbar
d Hilfsmittelstreifen *m* der äußeren Datenbasis
f barre *f* d'outils de base de données externe
r инструментальная лента *f* внешней базы данных

3635 external data identification
(in CAD and GIS)
d Identifikation *f* der äußeren Daten
f identification *f* de données externes
r обозначение *n* внешних данных

3636 external document
d äußeres Dokument *n*
f document *m* externe
r внешний документ *m*

3637 external interrupt
d externe Unterbrechung *f*
f interruption *f* externe; interruption extérieure
r внешнее прерывание *n*

* **external lead** → 3630

3638 external line network
d Außenleitungsnetz *n*
f réseau *m* de lignes externes
r сеть *f* внешних линий

3639 external memory; backup memory; backing memory; auxiliary memory; extra memory
d Externspeicher *m*; Sicherungsspeicher *m*; zusätzlicher Speicher *m*; Reservespeicher *m*
f mémoire *f* externe; mémoire additionnelle; mémoire supplémentaire
r внешняя память *f*; вспомогательная память; дополнительная память

3640 external modem; Xmodem
(a file transfer protocol, predecessor to Ymodem and Zmodem)
d externes Modem *n*; X-Modem *n*
f modem *m* externe
r внешний модем *m*

3641 external query
d Außenabfrage *f*
f interrogation *f* externe
r внешний запрос *m*

3642 external reference
d Außenreferenz *f*
f référence *f* externe
r внешняя ссылка *f*

3643 external reference file
d Außenreferenz-Datei *f*
f fichier *m* de références externes
r файл *m* внешних ссылок

3644 external-reference listing
d Externverweisliste *f*
f liste *f* de références externes
r список *m* внешних ссылок

3645 external request
d externe Anforderung *f*
f requête *f* externe
r внешняя заявка *f*

3646 external terminal; X terminal
d externes Terminal *n*
f terminal *m* externe; terminal X; terminal sans marque; clone *m*
r внешний терминал *m*

3647 external timing; external clocking
d Fremdtakt *m*; externe Taktierung *f*
f rythme *m* externe
r внешняя синхронизация *f*

3648 external viewer
d Außensuchprogramm *n*
f visionneur *m* externe
r внешняя программа *f* просмотра

* **extinction** → 2636

* **extra bit** → 6641

3649 extra code
d Zusatzcode *m*
f code *m* supplémentaire
r экстракод *m*

3650 extract *v*; **fetch** *v*; **carry** *v* **out**
d extrahieren; ausziehen; ziehen; schleppen; abrufen
f extraire; prélever; apporter
r извлекать; выделять; выводить

* **extraction** → 3754

3651 extract *v* **the content**
d das Inhaltsverzeichnis extrahieren
f extraire le contenu
r извлекать содержание

* **extra memory** → 3639

3652 extranet
(an extended intranet connecting not only
internal personnel, but also selected
customers, suppliers, and strategic partners)
d Extranet *n*
f extranet *m*
r экстранет *m*; экстрасеть *f*

3653 extrapolate *v*
d extrapolieren
f extrapoler
r экстраполировать

3654 extrapolation
d Extrapolieren *n*; Extrapolierung *f*;
Extrapolation *f*
f extrapolation *f*
r экстраполяция *f*; экстраполирование *n*

3655 extra pulse
d Störimpuls *m*
f impulsion *f* extraordinaire
r импульс-выброс *m*

3656 extrude *v*
d extrudieren
f mettre en relief; étendre
r экструдировать

3657 extruded object
d extrudiertes Objekt *n*
f objet *m* extrudé; objet en relief
r экструдированный объект *m*

3658 extruded text
d extrudierter Text *m*
f texte *m* extrudé; texte en relief
r экструдированный текст *m*

3659 extruder
d Extruder *m*
f extrudeuse *f*
r экструдер *m*

3660 extrusion
d Extrusion *f*; Extrudierung *f*
f extrusion *f*; mise *f* en relief
r экструзия *f*

* **eye icon → 3661**

3661 eye-type icon; eye icon
d Augentyp-Symbol *n*; Augensymbol *n*
f icône *f* en forme d'œil
r икона *f* глаз

* **e-zine → 3329**

F

3662 face *v*
d verkleiden
f surfacer
r покрывать; облицовать

3663 face recognition software
d Gesichterkennung-Software *f*
f logiciel *m* de reconnaissance d'un visage
r программное обеспечение *n* распознавания лица

3664 facet analysis
d Facettenanalyse *f*
f analyse *f* par facettes
r фасетный анализ *m*

3665 faceting
d Facettierung *f*
f mise *f* à facettes
r фасетирование *n*

3666 facial animation
d Gesichtsanimation *f*
f animation *f* faciale
r оживление *n* лица

3667 facilities management
d Anlagenverwaltung *f*; Verwaltung *f* der Stätten
f gérance *f* informatique; infogérance *f*
r управление *n* ресурсами

3668 facility
d Fähigkeit *f*; Mittel *n*
f facilité *f*
r [вспомогательное] средство *n*; возможность *f*

* **facility** → 3467

3669 factbase
d Faktenbasis *f*
f base *f* de [données pour stocker de] faits
r база *f* [данных для хранения] фактов

* **factor** → 1831, 5995

* **factorable code** → 1465

3670 factual information
d Fakteninformation *f*
f information *f* de faits
r фактографическая информация *f*

3671 factual knowledge
d Wissen *n* in Form von Fakten; Faktwissen *n*
f connaissances *fpl* en forme de faits
r знания *npl* в форме фактов

3672 fade; fading
d Fading *n*; Schwund *m*
f fading *m*; décroissance *f*
r замирание *n*; затухание *n*; фединг *m*

3673 fade-in
(of an image)
d Aufblendung *f*
f apparition *f* graduelle; apparition progressive
r постепенное возникновение *n*

3674 fade-out; going to black
(of an image)
d Ausblendung *f*; Abblendung *f*; Abblende *f*; Verdunkelung *f*
f disparition *f* graduelle; disparition progressive
r постепенное исчезновение *n*

* **fading** → 3672

3675 fail *v*
d ausfallen; versagen
f tomber en panne
r отказывать; портиться

3676 failed state
d Ausfallzustand *m*
f état *m* de défaillance
r состояние *n* отказа

3677 failsafe; fault-tolerant
d ausfallunempfindlich; ausfallsicher; störsicher; fehlertolerant
f résistant aux défauts; tolérant aux fautes
r отказоустойчивый

3678 fail-soft; with graceful degradation
d mit schrittweisem Ausfall
f flexible contre perturbation; à dégradation graduelle
r с амортизацией отказов; с постепенным отказом

3679 failure; fault; defect; breakdown; outage; trouble; disturbance
d Ausfall *m*; Störung *f*; Mangel *m*; Panne *f*; Defekt *m*
f défaillance *f*; défaut *m*; faute *f*; panne *f*; dérangement *m*
r дефект *m*; отказ *m*; выпадение *n*; неисправность *f*

3680 failure bound
d Ausfallgrenze *f*

f limite *f* de panne; limite de défaut
r отказоопасная граница *f*

3681 failure clearance; fault clearance
d Entstörung *f*
f nettoyage *m* de défauts
r очистка *f* неисправностей

* **failure current** → 3682

* **failure detection** → 3492

* **failure detection circuit** → 3493

* **failure exit** → 3495

3682 failure flow; failure current; fault current
d Ausfallstrom *m*
f flot *m* de défauts
r поток *m* отказов

* **failure logging** → 3686

3683 failure message; fault message
d Störmeldung *f*
f message *m* de défaillance; message de défaut
r сообщение *n* об отказе

3684 failure rate; error rate; hazard rate
d Ausfallrate *f*; Ausfallhäufigkeit *f*; Fehlerrate *f*; Fehlerhäufigkeit *f*; Fehlerquote *f*
f taux *m* de défaillance; taux de pannes; taux d'erreurs; fréquence *f* d'erreurs; débit *m* d'erreurs; intensité *f* de défauts
r интенсивность *f* отказов; коэффициент *m* ошибок; частота *f* [повторения] ошибок

3685 failure rate prediction
d Vorausberechnung *f* der Ausfallrate
f prédiction *f* du taux de défaillances
r прогноз *m* интенсивности отказов

3686 failure recording; fault recording; failure logging
d Störungsregistrierung *f*; Störungsprotokollierung *f*
f enregistrement *m* des défauts
r регистрация *f* неисправностей

3687 failure signal; fault signal; trouble signal
d Ausfallsignal *n*
f signal *m* de défaillance; signal de défaut
r сигнал *m* отказа

3688 fair game
d gerechtes Spiel *n*; faires Spiel
f jeu *m* équitable; jeu juste
r справедливая игра *f*

3689 faithful representation; true
representation
d treue Darstellung *f*
f représentation *f* fidèle
r точное представление *n*

* **fall** *v* → 3178

3690 fallback *v*
d herunterschalten; zurückschalten
f repasser de défaut; récupérer de défaut
r повторно запускать после устранения неисправностей; переходить на аварийный режим

3691 fallback
d Ersatzfunktion *f*; Realisierung *f* die Ersatzfunktion; Prozesswiederanlauf *m* nach Fehlerkorrektur
f repassage *m* de défaut; récupération *f* de défaut
r повторный запуск *m* после устранения неисправностей; возврат *m* в исходный режим; переход *m* на аварийный режим

3692 fallback character
d Abfallzeichen *n*
f caractère *m* de reprise
r резервный знак *m*

3693 fallback recovery
d Notfallwiederherstellung *f*
f remise *f* en service après une panne
r аварийное восстановление *n*

3694 fallback system
d Bereitschaftssystem *n*; Standby-System *n*
f système *m* à reprise
r резервная система *f*

* **fall delay** → 3695

3695 fall[ing] delay
d Abfallverzögerung[szeit] *f*
f délai *m* de descente [de signal]
r задержка *f* спада [сигнала]

* **falloff** → 621

3696 fall time; decay time
d Abfallzeit *f*; Abklingzeit *f*; Abklingdauer *f*; Ausschwingzeit *f*
f temps *m* de descente; temps d'affaiblissement; période *f* d'extinction
r время *n* спада; время затухания; время угасания

3697 false *adj*
d falsch
f faux
r ложный; ошибочный

3698 **false**
(as logical zero)
d Lüge *f*; [logische] Null *f*
f faux *m*
r "ложь" *f*; логический нуль *m*

* **false add** → 182

* **false addition** → 182

* **false code** → 5118

3699 **false control input signal**
d falsches Steuereingangssignal *n*
f signal *m* faux d'entrée de commande
r ложный управляющий входной сигнал *m*

3700 **false drop**
d falsche Suchinformation *f*; falsche Informationssuche *f*
f recherche *f* fausse d'information
r ложный поиск *m* информации

3701 **false information input**
d falscher Informationseingang *m*
f entrée *f* fausse d'information
r ложный информационный вход *m*

3702 **false statement**
d falsche Aussage *f*
f assertion *f* fausse
r ложное утверждение *n*

3703 **family**
d Familie *f*
f famille *f*; série *f*
r семейство *n*; серия *f*

* **family of compatibles** → 1980

* **fan** → 2301

* **fanfold paper form** → 89

3704 **fan-in**
d Eingangslastfaktor *m*; Eingangs[auf]fächerung *f*
f charge *f* à l'entrée; déploiement *m* d'entrée; entrance *f*
r коэффициент *m* объединения по входу

3705 **fanning**
d Auffächern *n*
f aération *f*
r обдув *m*

3706 **fan-out**
d Ausgangslastfaktor *m*; Ausgangs[auf]fächerung *f*
f charge *f* à la sortie; déploiement *m* à la sortie;

sortance *f*
r коэффициент *m* разветвления по выходу

* **FAQ** → 4090

* **fast** → 4509

3707 **fast access**
d schneller Zugriff *m*
f accès *m* rapide
r быстрый доступ *m*

* **fast-acting** → 4509

3708 **fast animation**
d schnelle Animation *f*
f animation *f* rapide
r быстрая анимация *f*

* **fast computer** → 4511

* **fast data transmission** → 4513

* **fastening** → 614

3709 **fast information retrieval; highspeed information retrieval**
d schnelle Informationswiederauffindung *f*
f récupération *f* d'information rapide
r быстрый поиск *m* информации

3710 **fast mode**
d schneller Modus *m*
f mode *m* rapide
r быстрый режим *m*

3711 **fast-stop-go tape**
d Band *n* mit schnellem Stopp und schnellem Anlauf
f bande *f* à arrêt et lancement rapides
r лента *f* с быстрым остановом и разгоном

3712 **fast zoom**
d schnelles Zoomen *n*
f zoom *m* rapide
r быстрое изменение *n* масштаба

* **FAT** → 3785

3713 **fatal error**
d fataler Fehler *m*; schwerer Fehler
f erreur *f* fatale
r фатальная ошибка *f*

3714 **father file**
d Stammdatei *f*; Quell[en]datei *f*
f fichier *m* d'origine
r исходный файл *m*

3715 **father tape**
d Vaterband *n*

f bande *f* père; bande de deuxième génération
r лента *f* второго поколения

3716 fat server
  (e-slang)
  d fetter Server *m*
  f serveur *m* lourd
  r толстый сервер *m*

3717 fatware; bloatware
  (e-slang)
  d fette Software *f*
  f inflagiciel *m*; superlogiciel *m*
  r раздутое программное обеспечение *n*

  * **fault → 3679**

  * **fault checking → 3484**

  * **fault clearance → 3681**

  * **fault current → 3682**

  * **fault detection → 3492**

  * **fault detection circuit → 3493**

  * **fault exit → 3495**

  * **fault indication → 3497**

  * **fault indicator → 3498**

  * **fault message → 3683**

3718 fault recognition
  d Fehlererkennung *f*; Störungserkennung *f*
  f reconnaissance *f* de défaut
  r распознавание *n* неисправности;
    распознавание ошибки

  * **fault recording → 3686**

  * **fault search → 3512**

  * **fault signal → 3687**

3719 fault threshold
  d Fehlerschwelle *f*; Fehlerschwellwert *m*
  f seuil *m* des défauts
  r порог *m* ошибок

3720 fault tolerance
  d Fehlertoleranz *f*; Fehlerzulässigkeit *f*
  f tolérance *f* des défauts; tolérance aux pannes
  r нечувствительность *f* к отказам;
    отказоустойчивость *f*

  * **fault-tolerant → 3677**

3721 fault tree
  d Fehlerbaum *m*
  f arbre *m* des défaillances
  r дерево *n* отказов

3722 fault tree analysis
  d Fehlerbaumanalyse *f*
  f analyse *f* de l'arbre des défaillances
  r анализ *m* дерева отказов

3723 faulty circuit
  d fehlerhafter Schaltkreis *m*
  f circuit *m* défaillant; circuit défectueux
  r неисправная схема *f*

3724 favorite; preferred
  d vorzuziehen; verdrängend
  f favori; préemptif
  r предпочтительный; вытесняющий;
    преференциальный

  * **favorites → 3725**

3725 favorite Web sites; favorites
  (frequently used URLs)
  d Favoriten *mpl*
  f faveurs *fpl*
  r фавориты *mpl*

  * **fax adapter → 3726**

3726 fax board; fax adapter
  d Fax-Karte *f*
  f carte *f* de télécopie
  r плата *f* факсимильной связи; факс-плата *f*

  * **fax-modem → 2554**

3727 fax-modem-radio card
  d Faxmodem-Funkkarte *f*
  f carte *f* fax-modem-radio
  r факс-модем-радио-плата *f*

3728 fax server
  d Fax-Server *m*
  f serveur *m* de télécopie
  r факс-сервер *m*

3729 fax/voice modem
  d Fax-Sprach-Modem *n*
  f modem *m* fax-vocal
  r модем *m* голоса и факса

  * **FCS → 4038**

  * **FDD → 3917**

  * **FDM → 4086**

  * **FDX → 3219**

* **FDX method** → 3222

3730 feasibility; realizability
d Realisierbarkeit f
f faisabilité f
r выполнимость f; реализуемость f

3731 feasible program
d zulässiges Programm n; ausführbares
Programm
f programme m réalisable
r реализуемая программа f

* **feasible solution** → 258

3732 feature; property
d Merkmal n; Feature n; Eigenschaft f;
Besonderheit f
f propriété f; particularité f; signe m; moyen m
r признак m; свойство n; особенность f

* **feature** → 3442

3733 feature key; function[al] key
d Funktionstaste f
f touche f fonctionnelle
r функциональная клавиша f

**3734 feature VGA connector; VGA output
connector**
(for connecting expansion boards to a
graphics board using a flat cable)
d VGA-Ausgangsstecker m
f connecteur m de sortie VGA
r выходной соединитель m VGA

* **fee** → 1639

* **feed** → 3747

3735 feed v
d zuführen; vorschieben
f avancer; acheminer; alimenter; entraîner
r подавать; продвигать

3736 feedback
d Rückführung f; Rückkopplung f
f rétroaction f; rétrocouplage m; action f en
retour; contre-réaction f
r обратная связь f

3737 feedback channel; return path
d Rückkoplungskanal m; Rückführungsweg m
f canal m de réaction; voie f de retour
r канал m обратной связи; линия f обратной
связи

3738 feedback factor
d Rückführungskoeffizient m
f taux m de ré[tro]action; facteur m de réaction

r коэффициент m обратной связи

3739 feedback integrator
d Rückkopplungsintegrator m
f intégrateur m à réaction
r интегратор m с обратной связью

3740 feedback learning system
d Feedback-Lernsystem n,
Rückführungssystem n
f système m d'enseignement à réaction
r самообучающаяся система f с обратной
связью

3741 feedback noise
d Rückwirkungsrauschen n
f bruit m de contre-réaction
r шум m обратного действия

3742 feedback path
d Rückkopplungskreis m;
Rückführ[ungs]kreis m
f circuit m de réaction; voie f de réaction
r цепь f обратной связи

3743 feedback shift register
d rückgekoppeltes Schieberegister n
f registre m de décalage à rétroaction
r сдвиговый регистр m с обратной связью

3744 feedback signal
d Rückführungssignal n
f signal m de réaction
r сигнал m обратной связи

* **feed circuit** → 3749

3745 feedforward
d Vorwärtswirkung f
f devancement m; action f directe
r упреждение n; предварение n; прямая
подача f

3746 feedforward control
d Vorwärtsregelung f
f réglage m en avant; réglage direct
r прямое управление n

3747 feed[ing]
d Zuführung f
f alimentation f
r подача f; питание n

3748 feeding; advance
d Vorschub m; Fortschritt m
f avancement m; acheminement m
r подача f; движение n вперёд

3749 feed[ing] circuit
d Speise[brücken]schaltung f; Speisekreis m

f circuit *m* d'alimentation
r питающая схема *f*

3750 feed wheel
  d Vorschubrad *n*; Kettenrad *n*
  f roue *f* d'entraînement
  r лентопротяжное колесо *n*

  * **female connector** → 7004

  * **fenestration** → 9995

  * **FEP** → 4098

3751 ferroelectric liquid crystal display
  d ferroelektrisches Flüssigkristalldisplay *n*
  f afficheur *m* aux cristaux liquides
    ferro-électriques; afficheur CLF
  r дисплей *m* на ферроэлектрических жидких
    кристаллах

3752 ferromagnetic RAM; FRAM
  d ferromagnetischer Lese-Schreib-Speicher *m*
  f mémoire *f* vive ferromagnétique
  r ферромагнитная память *f*

  * **fetch** → 3754

  * **fetch** *v* → 1184, 3650

3753 fetch cycle
  d Abrufzyklus *m*; Holzyklus *m*
  f cycle *m* d'extraction
  r цикл *m* извлечения; цикл выборки

3754 fetch[ing]; extraction
  d Extraktion *f*; Auszug *m*; Bereitstellung *f*
  f extraction *f*; choix *m*; mise *f* à disposition
  r извлечение *n*; выделение *n*; выборка *f*

3755 fetch phase
  d Abholphase *f*; Bringephase *f*
  f phase *f* d'extraction; phase de recherche;
    phase d'appel
  r фаза *f* извлечения

  * **fetch protect** → 3756

3756 fetch protect[ion]
  d Lesesperre *f*; Abrufschutz *m*;
    Zugriffsschutz *m*
  f protection *f* d'extraction
  r защита *f* от несанкционированной выборки

  * **fibered product** → 7492

  * **fibered sum** → 7518

3757 fibering; fibration
  d Faserung *f*

f fibration *f*
r расслоение *n*

3758 fiber-optic cable
  d Faseroptikkabel *n*; faseroptisches Kabel *n*;
    Lichtleiterkabel *n*
  f câble *m* à fibre optique; câble fibroflex
  r волоконно-оптический кабель *m*

  * **fiber optic LAN** → 6543

3759 fiber optics; FO
  d Faseroptik *f*; Lichtleitertechnik *f*
  f optique *f* fibrillaire; optique à fibres
  r волоконная оптика *f*

**3760 fiber optic transmission; optical fiber
transmission**
  d Lichtwellenleiterübertragung *f*; faseroptische
    Übertragung *f*; Glasfaserübertragung *f*
  f transmission *f* sur fibres optiques
  r световодная передача *f*

  * **fibration** → 3757

3761 fiche
  d Fiche *n/m*
  f fiche *f*
  r фиша *f*

  * **fictive** → 3212

3762 fidelity
  d Genauigkeit *f*
  f fidélité *f*
  r верность *f*

3763 fidelity of information transmission
  d Genauigkeit *f* der Informationsübertragung
  f fidélité *f* de transmission d'information
  r достоверность *f* передачи информации

3764 fidelity of reproduction
  d Wiedergabetreue *f*; Genauigkeit *f* der
    Reproduktion
  f fidélité *f* de reproduction
  r точность *f* воспроизведения

3765 field
  (as unit of data record)
  d Feld *n*
  f champ *m*
  r поле *n*

3766 field attribute
  d Feldattribut *n*
  f attribut *m* du champ
  r атрибут *m* поля

3767 field code
  d Feldcode *m*; Feldschlüssel *m*

f code *m* du champ
r код *m* поля; ключ *m* [защиты] поля

3768 field conditions
d Feldbedingungen *fpl*;
Baustellenbedingungen *fpl*;
Baustellenverhältnisse *npl*
f conditions *fpl* sur chantier
r полевые условия *npl*

3769 field data
d Felderdaten *pl*
f données *fpl* d'exploitation; données à
application
r эксплуатационные данные *pl*; данные в
области памяти

3770 field description
d Feldbeschreibung *f*
f description *f* du champ
r описание *n* поля

3771 field length; field width
d Feldlänge *f*
f longueur *f* du champ
r длина *f* поля

3772 field location
d Feldposition *f*
f location *f* du champ
r местоположение *n* поля

3773 field lookup
d Feldverweis *m*
f revue *f* du champ
r просмотр *m* поля

3774 field-programmable
d im Einsatz programmierbar; vom Anwender
programmierbar
f programmable à l'application; programmable
par l'utilisateur
r программируемый в условиях
эксплуатации [пользователем]

3775 field separator
(a sign)
d Feldtrennzeichen *n*
f séparateur *m* de champs
r разделитель *m* полей

3776 field tag
d Feldkennung *f*
f étiquette *f* de zone
r признак *m* поля

* **field width** → 3771

* **FIF** → 4018

* **FIFO** → 3855

**3777 FIFO list; FIFO stack; pushup list; pushup
stack; queue**
d FIFO-Stapel *m*; FIFO-Liste *f*;
FIFO-Schlange *f*
f pile *f* inverse; liste *f* FIFO; queue *f*
r список *m* обратного магазинного типа;
обратный стек *m*; очередь *f*

* **FIFO stack** → 3777

3778 figurative
d figurativ
f figuratif
r фигуративный; фигуральный; образный;
символьный

3779 figurative constant
d vorgesehene Konstante *f*
f constante *f* figurative
r наименованная константа *f*

* **figure** → 2874, 3967

3780 figure case
d Ziffern- und Zeichenfeld *n*
f registre *m* de chiffres
r цифровой регистр *m*; клавишное поле *n*
цифр

3781 figure key
d Zahlentaste *f*
f touche *f* numérique
r цифровая кнопка *f*

3782 figure shift
d Ziffernumschaltung *f*; Zahlenumschaltung *f*
f décalage *m* de chiffres; changement *m* de
chiffres; inversion *f* de chiffres
r переключение *n* на цифровой регистр

3783 file *v*
d einordnen; sortieren
f ordonner; classer
r классировать; регистрировать

3784 file
d Datei *f*; File *n*
f fichier *m*
r файл *m*

3785 file allocation table; FAT
d Tabelle *f* der Dateizuweisungen;
Dateizuordnungstabelle *f*
f table *f* d'allocation de fichiers
r таблица *f* размещения файлов

3786 file attribute
d Dateiattribut *n*

ƒ attribut *m* de fichier
r атрибут *m* файла

3787 file compression
   d Dateikompression ƒ
   ƒ compression ƒ de fichier
   r сжатие *n* файла

   * **file control block** → 3791

3788 file conversion
   d Dateikonvertierung ƒ
   ƒ transformation ƒ de fichier
   r конверсия ƒ файла

3789 file date
   d Dateidatum *n*
   ƒ date ƒ de fichier
   r дата ƒ файла

3790 file description
   d Dateibeschreibung ƒ
   ƒ description ƒ de fichier
   r описание *n* файла

3791 file descriptor; file control block
   d Dateideskriptor *m*
   ƒ descripteur *m* de fichier
   r описатель *m* файла

   * **file extension** → 3812

3792 file extent; data-set extent
   d Dateibereich *m*
   ƒ étendue ƒ de fichier
   r зона ƒ файла

3793 file format
   d Dateiformat *n*
   ƒ format *m* de fichier
   r формат *m* файла

3794 file format converter
   d Dateiformat-Umwandler *m*
   ƒ convertisseur *m* de format de fichier
   r преобразователь *m* формата файлов

3795 file format for background images
   d Dateiformat *n* der Hintergrundbilder
   ƒ format *m* de fichier d'images de fond
   r файловый формат *m* для фоновых
     изображений

3796 file format for environment images
   d Dateiformat *n* der Umgebungsbilder
   ƒ format *m* de fichier d'images d'environnement
   r файловый формат *m* для изображений
     окрестности

3797 file format for exporting

d Dateiformat *n* des Exportierens
ƒ format *m* de fichier pour exportation
r файловый формат *m* экспортирования

3798 file format for extract attribute data
   d Dateiformat *n* der Attributdaten-Extraktion
   ƒ format *m* de fichier pour extraction des
     données d'attributs
   r файловый формат *m* извлечения
     атрибутных данных

3799 file format for import
   d Format *n* der importierenden Datei
   ƒ format *m* de fichier d'importation
   r формат *m* импортного файла

3800 file header label
   d Dateianfangskennsatz *m*
   ƒ étiquette ƒ de début de fichier
   r метка ƒ начала файла

   * **fileid** → 3801

3801 file identifier; fileid
   d Dateibezeichner *m*; Dateikennung ƒ
   ƒ identificateur *m* de fichier
   r идентификатор *m* файла

3802 file interchange format
   d Dateiaustausch-Format *n*
   ƒ format *m* d'échange de fichiers
   r формат *m* обмена файлов

3803 file layout
   d Dateiorganisation ƒ; Dateianordnung ƒ
   ƒ disposition ƒ de fichier; dessin *m* de fichier
   r размещение *n* файла; расположение *n*
     файла

3804 file library
   d Dateibibliothek ƒ
   ƒ bibliothèque ƒ de fichiers
   r библиотека ƒ файлов

3805 file list; data-set list
   d Dateiliste ƒ
   ƒ liste ƒ de fichiers
   r список *m* файлов

3806 file location
   d Dateiposition ƒ
   ƒ localisation ƒ de fichier
   r местоположение *n* файла

3807 file locking
   d Dateisperrung ƒ
   ƒ blocage *m* de fichier
   r запирание *n* файла

3808 file management
   d Dateiverwaltung ƒ

f gestion *f* de fichiers
r управление *n* файлами

* **file manager** → 3809

3809 file manager [program]
d Dateiverwalter *m*;
Dateiverwaltungsprogramm *n*
f gestionnaire *m* de fichiers; programme *m* de
gestion de fichiers
r программа *f* управления файлами

3810 file mark
d Dateimarke *f*
f marque *f* de fichier
r метка *f* файла

3811 file name
d Dateiname *m*
f nom *m* de fichier
r имя *n* файла

3812 file [name] extension; extension
d Datei[namen]erweiterung *f*
f extension *f* [de nom] de fichier
r расширение *n* [имени] файла

3813 file preview
d Dateivorschau *f*
f prévisualisation *f* de fichier
r предварительный просмотр *m* файла

3814 file protecting
d Dateischutz *m*
f protection *f* de fichier
r защита *f* файла

* **file scanning** → 3815

3815 file searching; file scanning
d Absuchen *n* einer Datei
f recherche *f* dans un fichier
r поиск *m* в файле

3816 file separator
d Dateiseparator *m*
f séparateur *m* de fichiers
r файловый разделитель *m*

3817 file server
d Dateiserver *m*
f serveur *m* de fichiers
r [служебный] файловый процессор *m*;
файловая станция *f*

3818 file system
d Dateisystem *n*
f système *m* de fichiers
r файловая система *f*

3819 file transfer
d Dateiübertragung *f*
f transfert *m* de fichiers
r перенос *m* файлов

3820 file transfer protocol; FTP
d Dateiübertragungsprotokoll *n*;
File-Transfer-Protokoll *n*
f protocole *m* de transfert de fichiers
r протокол *m* переноса файлов; протокол
передачи файлов

3821 file type
d Dateityp *m*; Dateiart *f*; Dateiform *f*
f type *m* de fichier
r тип *m* файла

3822 file updating
d Dateiaktualisierung *f*; laufende
Änderungen *fpl* einer Datei
f actualisation *f* de fichier; mise *f* au jour de
fichier
r обновление *n* файла; корректировка *f*
файла

* **filing** → 508

3823 fill *v*; **charge** *v*; **pad** *v*; **stuff** *v*
d füllen; vollbesetzen; ausfüllen; auffüllen;
vollstopfen
f remplir; compléter; garnir
r заполнять; вставить

* **fill character** → 3825

3824 fill command
d Füllungsbefehl *m*
f commande *f* de remplissage
r команда *f* заполнения

* **filler** → 3825

**3825 fill[er] character; filler; ignore character;
pad[ding] character; padding character**
d Füllzeichen *n*
f caractère *m* de remplissage; remplisseur *m*
r знак-заполнитель *m*; заполнитель *m*

* **filling** → 6691

3826 fill rate
d Füllrate *f*
f taux *m* de remplissage
r скорость *f* заполнения; скорость
закрашивания; филрейт *m*

* **film recorder** → 6953

3827 filter
d Filter *m*; Sieb *n*

f filtre *m*
r фильтр *m*

3828 filter cascade
d Filterkaskade *f*
f cascade *f* de filtre
r каскад *m* фильтра

3829 filtering; filtration
d Filterung *f*; Filtrierung *f*; Filtering *n*
f filtrage *m*; filtration *f*
r фильтрация *f*; фильтрование *n*

3830 filtering operator
d Filtrierungsoperator *m*
f opérateur *m* de filtrage
r оператор *m* фильтрования

* **filtration → 3829**

3831 final; end; terminal *adj*
d endlich; terminal
f final; terminal
r конечный; концевой; терминальный

3832 final bit
d letztes Bit *n*
f bit *m* final
r конечный бит *m*

3833 final stage
d Endstufe *f*
f étage *m* final
r конечный каскад *m*; выходной каскад

3834 final state
d Endzustand *m*
f état *m* final
r конечное состояние *n*

* **final total → 9450**

3835 find *v*
d finden; suchen
f trouver; découvrir; [re]chercher
r найти; искать

3836 finder
d Sucher *m*; Finder *m*
f viseur *m*; chercheur *m*
r визир *m*; [видо]искатель *m*

* **finder chain → 8285**

3837 finding
d Erforschung *f*
f localisation *f*
r отыскание *n*

3838 finger

d Fühler *m*
f palpeur *m*
r щуп *m*; датчик *m*

3839 finger
(a program used to find out if someone is online)
d Finger *m*
f finger *m*
r указатель *m*

3840 finger
d Hebel *m*; Griff *m*
f levier *m*; bras *m*
r рычаг *m*; гриф *m*

3841 fingerprint
d Fingerabdruck *m*
f empreinte *f* digitale
r отпечаток *m* пальца

3842 fingerprint identification
d Fingerabdruck-Identifikation *f*
f identification *f* d'empreintes digitales
r идентификация *f* отпечатка пальца

3843 fingertip access
d Zugriff *m* über Tastatur
f accès *m* par clavier
r доступ *m* с помощью клавиатуры

* **finishing → 9269**

* **finite automaton → 3848**

* **finite decomposition → 3846**

3844 finite game
d endliches Spiel *n*
f jeu *m* fini
r конечная игра *f*

3845 finite graph
d endlicher Graph *m*
f graphe *m* fini
r конечный граф *m*

3846 finite partition; finite decomposition
d endliche Zerlegung *f*
f partition *f* finie
r конечное разбиение *n*

3847 finite pulse width
d endliche Breite *f* des Impulses; endliche Impulsbreite *f*
f durée *f* d'impulsion terminale; largeur *f* d'impulsion terminale
r конечная длительность *f* импульса

3848 finite[-state] automaton; finite-state machine
 d endlicher Automat *m*
 f automate *m* fini
 r конечный автомат *m*

3849 finite-state grammar
 d von endlichem Automaten definierte Grammatik *f*
 f grammaire *f* à nombre fini d'états
 r автоматная грамматика *f*

3850 finite-state language
 d von endlichem Automaten akzeptierte Sprache *f*
 f langage *m* à nombre fini d'états
 r автоматный язык *m*

 * **finite-state machine** → **3848**

3851 firewall
 (special computer that is set up on a network to prevent intruders from stealing or destroying confidential files)
 d Feuerschutzwand *m*; Schutzwand *m*; Feuerwand *m*; Schutzwall *m*; Brandschutzmauer *m*; Brandmauer *m*
 f pare-feu *m*; coupe-feu *m*; garde-barrière *f*; guérit *m*
 r брандмауэр *m*; перегородка *f*; сетевой экран *m*

 * **firing pulse** → **9554**

3852 firmware
 d Firmware *f*
 f firmware *m*; programmes *mpl* encastrés; micrologie *f*
 r внутреннее программное обеспечение *n*; встроенные программы *fpl*

3853 first clock pulse
 d erster Taktimpuls *m*
 f première impulsion *f* d'horloge
 r первый тактовый импульс *m*

3854 first data multiplexer
 d erster Multiplexer *m*
 f multiplexeur *m* de données premier
 r ведущий мультиплексор *m* данных

 * **first in, first out** → **3855**

3855 first in[put], first out[put]; FIFO
 d FIFO
 f premier entré, premier sorti; premier arrivé, premier servi; FIFO
 r первым пришёл, первым вышел; первым пришёл, первым обслужен

3856 first-order language
 d Sprache *f* erster Stufe
 f langage *m* du premier ordre
 r язык *m* первого порядка

3857 first-order logic; elementary logic
 d Prädikatenkalkül *m* erster Stufe
 f calcul *m* logique du premier échelon; calcul des prédicats du premier ordre
 r исчисление *n* предикатов первого порядка

 * **first term of a sum** → **656**

 * **fit** → **3861**

3858 fit *v*
 d fitten; anpassen
 f ajuster; accoler
 r подходить; точно соответствовать; прилаживать; налаживать

3859 fit *v* **data**
 d Daten anpassen
 f ajuster les données
 r налаживать данные

3860 fit *v* **options**
 d Optionen anpassen
 f ajuster les options
 r налаживать опции

3861 fit[ting]
 d Anpassung *f*; Passung *f*; Fitten *n*; Ausrichtung *f*
 f ajustement *m*; ajustage *m*; calage *m*
 r наладка *f*; подгонка *f*; пригонка *f*; припасовка *f*

3862 fix *v*
 d befestigen; fixieren
 f fixer
 r фиксировать; закреплять

3863 fixation; locking
 d Fixieren *n*
 f fixation *f*
 r фиксация *f*; закрепление *n*

3864 fixed; constant; permanent; stuck-at
 d fest[stehend]; festgelegt; konstant; starr; permanent; dauernd
 f fixe; constant; permanent; invariable
 r установленный; постоянный; неподвижный; жёсткий; фиксированный

 * **fixed-count code** → **3464**

 * **fixed data** → **6912**

 * **fixed disk** → **4393**

* **fixed error** → 9134

3865 fixed format information
  d Festformatinformation *f*
  f information *f* en format fixe
  r информация *f* фиксированного формата

**3866 fixed-head disk; multihead disk;
head-per-track disk**
  d Magnetplatte *f* mit fixierten Köpfen;
  Festkopfplatte *f*
  f disque *m* à têtes fixes
  r диск *m* с фиксированными головками;
  диск с множеством головок; диск с
  головкой на каждом тракте

* **fixed image** → 8868

**3867 fixed-image communication; freeze-frame
[video]communication**
  d Festbildkommunikation *f*
  f communication *f* par images fixes
  r связь *f* фиксированными изображениями

3868 fixed-image teleconference
  d Festbild-Telekonferenz *f*
  f téléconférence *f* par images fixes
  r телеконференция *f* фиксированными
  изображениями

* **fixed joint** → 6915

3869 fixed-logic query
  d Anfrage *f* mit fester Logik
  f interrogation *f* à traitement fixe
  r запрос *m* с фиксированным порядком
  обработки

* **fixed memory** → 7671

3870 fixed-path protocol
  d Protokoll *n* mit fester Route
  f protocole *m* de chemin fixe
  r протокол *m* с фиксированным маршрутом

3871 fixed point
  (in calculation)
  d Festkomma *n*; Festpunkt *m*
  f virgule *f* fixe
  r фиксированная запятая *f*

3872 fixed-point calculation
  d Festkommarechnung *f*
  f calcul *m* en virgule fixe
  r вычисление *n* с фиксированной запятой

3873 fixed-point number
  d Festkommazahl *f*
  f nombre *m* à virgule fixe
  r число *n* [в форме] с фиксированной
  запятой

* **fixed-ratio code** → 3464

3874 fixed sample
  d feste Stichprobe *f*
  f échantillon *m* permanent
  r фиксированная выборка *f*

3875 flag; sentinel
  d Zustandsmarke *f*; Flag *n*
  f repérage *m*; drapeau *m*; flag *m*
  r флаг *m*; признак *m* состояния

3876 flag activation
  d Flagsetzen *n*
  f activation *f* de drapeau
  r выставление *n* флажка

* **flagging** → 5646

3877 flag indicator
  d Flaganzeiger *m*; Kennzeichenanzeiger *m*
  f indicateur *m* de condition; indicateur de
  drapeau
  r индикатор *m* условия

3878 flag portion
  d Kennzeichenteil *m*
  f part *f* du drapeau
  r часть *f* флага

3879 flame
  d Anmacherei *f*; Anpflaumerei *f*;
  Beschimpfung *f*
  f torpille *f* (message critique, voire injurieux
  envoyé à un internaute ou posté publiquement
  sur un groupe de discussion)
  r брань *f*; вызывающая речь *f*

3880 flamer
  d Flamer *m*
  f flingueur *m*
  r "скандалист" *m* (пользователь, известный
  своей скандальной репутацией)

* **flame war** → 4530

3881 flashing; flicker[ing]; blinking
  d Flackern *n*; Flimmer *n*; Blinken *n*
  f clignotement *m*; papillotement *m*;
  scintillement *m*
  r мигание *n*; мерцание *n*

**3882 flashing display; flashing screen; flickering
screen**
  d blinkender Bildschirm *m*; blinkendes
  Display *n*
  f afficheur *m* clignotant; écran *m* clignotant
  r мерцающий дисплей *m*; мерцающий
  экран *m*

* **flashing screen** → 3882

3883 flash[ing] symbol
 d blinkendes Symbol *n*
 f symbole *m* clignotant
 r мерцающий символ *m*

3884 flash memory; flash ROM
 (introduced by Intel)
 d Flash-Speicher *m*
 f mémoire *f* flash
 r память *f* с групповой перезаписью;
 флэш-память *f*

* **flash ROM** → 3884

* **flash symbol** → 3883

3885 flat-address architecture
 d Flachadressenarchitektur *f*
 f architecture *f* plane
 r архитектура *f* со сплошной адресацией

3886 flatbed plotter
 d Tischplotter *m*
 f table *f* traçante à plat; traceur *m* à plat
 r планшетный графопостроитель *m*;
 плоский графопостроитель

3887 flatbed scanner
 d Flachbettscanner *m*
 f scanner *m* à plat
 r плоскостный сканер *m*; планшетный
 сканер

3888 flat buttons
 (onto toolbar)
 d Schaltflächen *fpl*
 f boutons *m* plats; onglets *mpl*
 r иконки *fpl* бутонов

* **flat cable** → 3889

**3889 flat cable [conductor]; flat flexible cable;
 ribbon cable; tape cable; strip printed
 cable**
 d Flach[band]kabel *n*; Bandkabel *n*;
 Streifenkabel *n*
 f câble *m* [conducteur] plat; câble-ruban *m*;
 câble à bande imprimée; câble à [structure]
 ruban
 r плоский [гибкий] кабель *m*; ленточный
 кабель

* **flat display** → 3896

3890 flat file system
 d flaches Dateisystem *n*; nichthierarchisches
 Dateisystem
 f système *m* de fichiers [à] plat; système de

fichier non hiérarchique
 r плоская файловая система *f*;
 неиерархическая файловая система

* **flat flexible cable** → 3889

3891 flat keyboard; low-profile keyboard
 d flache Tastatur *f*; Flachtastatur *f*
 f clavier *m* plat
 r плоская клавиатура *f*

3892 flat LCD
 d flaches LC-Display *n*
 f afficheur *m* à cristaux liquides plat
 r плоский жидкокристаллический
 дисплей *m*

3893 flat memory; linear memory
 d flacher Speicher *m*
 f mémoire *f* linéaire
 r сплошная память *f*

3894 flat pack
 d Flachgehäuse *n*
 f boîtier *m* plat
 r плоский корпус *m*

* **flat-panel display** → 3896

3895 flat ring
 d flacher Ring *m*
 f anneau *m* plat
 r плоское кольцо *n*

3896 flat screen; flat[-panel] display
 d flacher Bildschirm *m*; Flachbildschirm *m*;
 Flachschirmanzeige *f*
 f écran *m* plat; écran en plan
 r плоский экран *m*; плоский дисплей *m*

3897 flexibility
 d Flexibilität *f*; Elastizität *f*
 f flexibilité *f*
 r гибкость *f*; упругость *f*

3898 flexible
 d flexibel; anpassungsfähig; biegsam
 f flexible
 r гибкий; огибаемый

* **flexible disk** → 3003

* **flexiplace** → 9230

* **flicker** → 3881

* **flickerfree display** → 3899

* **flickering** → 3881

* **flickering screen** → 3882

3899 **flickfree screen; nonflickering screen; flickerfree display**
  d flimmerfreier Bildschirm *m*; flimmerfreies Display *n*
  f écran *m* sans scintillement; écran sans clignotement
  r немерцающий экран *m*; немерцающий дисплей *m*

* **flip-flop** → 9550

3900 **flip-flop relay**
  d Relais *n* mit zwei festen Stellungen
  f relais *m* à deux positions stables
  r реле *n* с двумя устойчивыми положениями

* **floated** → 3901

3901 **floating; floated**
  d gleitend; schwimmend; fließend
  f flottant
  r плавающий; астатический

* **floating bar** → 3911

3902 **floating head; air-floating head; flying head**
  d fliegender Magnetkopf *m*; schwimmender Magnetkopf; gleitender Magnetkopf
  f tête *f* flottante
  r плавающая головка *f*; летучая головка

3903 **floating menu**
  d fließendes Menü *n*
  f menu *m* flottant
  r плавающее меню *n*

3904 **floating point**
  d Gleitkomma *n*; Gleitpunkt *m*
  f virgule *f* flottante
  r плавающая запятая *f*

3905 **floating point [arithmetic] unit; FPU**
  d Recheneinheit *f* für die Gleitkommaoperation
  f unité *f* exécutante des calculs en virgule flottante
  r устройство *n* с плавающей запятой

3906 **floating-point calculation**
  d Gleitkommarechnung *f*
  f calcul *m* en virgule flottante
  r вычисление *n* с плавающей запятой

3907 **floating-point notation; semilogarithmic representation**
  d Gleitkommadarstellung *f*; halblogarithmische Darstellung *f*
  f représentation *f* à virgule flottante; notation *f* semi-logarithmique
  r представление *n* чисел в виде с плавающей запятой; полулогарифмическое представление

3908 **floating-point number**
  d Gleitkommazahl *f*
  f nombre *m* à virgule flottante
  r число *n* с плавающей запятой

3909 **floating-point operations per seconds; FLOPS**
  d Gleitkommaoperationen *fpl* je Sekunde; Gleitpunktoperationen *fpl* je Sekunde
  f opérations *fpl* à virgule flottante par seconde
  r операции *fpl* с плавающей запятой [выполняемые] в секунду

* **floating-point unit** → 3905

3910 **floating rule**
  (usually between columns, whose ends do not touch other rules)
  d fließende Linie *f*
  f règle *f* flottante
  r плавающая линейка *f*

3911 **floating toolbar; floating bar**
  d fließender Werkzeugstreifen *m*
  f barre *f* [d'outils] flottante
  r плавающая инструментальная лента *f*; плавающая панель *f* инструментов

* **flooding** → 3914

3912 **flooding**
  d Lawinenlenkung *f*
  f raz *m* de marée (technique de piratage consistant à inonder un serveur en requêtes jusqu'à défaillance de celui-ci)
  r лавинная маршрутизация *f*

3913 **flooding; paint bucket**
  d Fluten *n*; Flutung *f*; Überflutung *f*; Flooding *n*
  f inondation *f*
  r заливка *f* [цветом]; закраска *f*

3914 **flooding [addressing]**
  d Lawinenadressierung *f*
  f adressage *m* sous forme avalanche
  r лавинная адресация *f*

3915 **flooding method**
  (of packet transmission)
  d Berieselungsverfahren *n*; Überflutungsmethode *f*
  f méthode *f* de ruissellement
  r волновой метод *m*

3916 **floodlight**
  d Flutlicht *n*; Scheinwerfer *m*

f projecteur *m* d'illumination
r прожектор *m* освещения; прожектор заливающего света

* **floppy disk** → 3003

3917 floppy disk drive; FDD; diskette drive
d Floppy-Disk-Laufwerk *n*; Diskettenlaufwerk *n*
f unité *f* de disques flexibles; dispositif *m* de disques floppy; unité de disquettes
r запоминающее устройство *n* на гибких дисках; накопитель *m* на гибких дисках

* **FLOPS** → 3909

3918 flow *v*
d fließen
f flotter; flouer
r вылить; выливать

3919 flow; flux; stream
d Fluss *m*; Strom *m*; Strömung *f*
f flux *m*; flot *m*
r поток *m*

3920 flowchart; flow diagram; block diagram; block scheme; organization chart; box plot
d Flussdiagramm *n*; Ablaufdiagramm *n*; Ablaufschema *n*; Blockdiagramm *n*; Block[schalt]bild *n*; Blockschema *n*; Organigramm *n*; Boxplot *n*
f diagramme *m* de flux; diagramme de blocs; schéma-bloc *m*; organigramme *m*; schéma *m* de principe
r блок-схема *f*; схема *f* последовательности; диаграмма *f* последовательности; структурная схема; органиграмма *f*

* **flow diagram** → 3920

3921 flow graph
d Flussgraph *m*
f graphe *m* de flux
r потоковый граф *m*; граф с потоками

3922 flowing
d fließend; zufließend
f courant; fluant; en écoulement
r текущий; гладкий; плавный; мягкий

3923 flowing information; current information
d fließende Information *f*; laufende Information
f information *f* courante
r текущая информация *f*

3924 flow line; flow row
d Ablauflinie *f*
f ligne *f* de flux
r плавающая строка *f*

* **flow of calls** → 3926

3925 flow-of-control programming
d Ablaufprogrammierung *f*
f programmation *f* de flux de commandes
r программирование *n* алгоритма

3926 flow of demands; flow of calls
d Forderungsstrom *m*
f flot *m* de demandes; flot d'appels
r поток *m* вызовов; поток требований

* **flow row** → 3924

3927 fluctuation
d Fluktuation *f*; Schwankung *f*
f fluctuation *f*
r флуктуация *f*; колебание *n*

3928 flush *v*
(the cache)
d leeren
f vider
r сбрасывать на диск; подавлять (ненужную информацию в памяти)

* **flutter** → 5161

* **flux** → 3919

3929 flyback; retrace
d Rücklauf *m*
f retour *m* du spot; retour de balayage
r обратный ход *m* [луча]

3930 flyback time
d Rücklaufzeit *f*
f temps *m* de retrait; temps "flyback"
r время *n* обратного хода

* **flying head** → 3902

3931 flying simulation
d Flugsimulation *f*; fliegende Simulation *f*
f simulation *f* au vol
r плавающая симуляция *f*

* **flying-spot scan** → 2845

3932 flying-spot scanner
d Lichtpunktabtaster *m*
f scanner *m* de spot flottant
r сканер *m* бегущего пятна

3933 flying-spot scan[ning]
d Flying-Spot-Abtastung *f*; Lichtpunktabtastung *f*
f balayage *m* de spot flottant; balayage au vol; balayage point par point
r сканирование *n* бегущего пятна; сканирование бегущего луча

* **flyout** → 3934

3934 flyout [icon]
(a set of icons nested under a single icon)
d Flyout *n*
f volet *m*
r множество *n* икон, объединённых в одну

* **FMP** → 3949

3935 FMP file
d FMP-Datei *f*
f fichier *m* FMP
r файл *m* FMP

* **FO** → 3759

* **focalization** → 3936

3936 focusing; focalization
d Fokussierung *f*
f focalisation *f*
r фокусировка *f*; фокусирование *n*

3937 fog background
d Schleierhintergrund *m*
f fond *m* de voile
r фон *m* вуали

3938 fog effect
(in 3D image)
d Nebeleffekt *m*
f effet *m* de voile; effet de brouillard
r эффект *m* вуали

* **foil** → 754

3939 folder
d Heftmappe *f*; Mappe *f*; Ordner *m*
f dossier *m*
r фольдер *m*; программная группа *f*; папка *f*

3940 folding
d Faltung *f*
f plissement *m*; pliage *m*; pliement *m*
r свёртка *f*; сгибание *n*; огибание *n*

* **folio** → 3942

3941 folio
(a page number)
d Seitenzahl *f*; Folio *n*; Folie *f*
f folio *m*
r колонцифра *f*

3942 folio [format]; folio size
(of a book)
d Folioformat *n*; Folio *n*
f format *m* folio; folio *m*
r фолио[-формат] *n*

* **folio size** → 3942

3943 follower
d Folge[r]stufe *f*
f suiveur *m*
r повторитель *m*; следящий элемент *m*

* **follow-up message** → 3944

3944 follow-up posting; follow-up message
d Folgepost *f*
f suivi *m* d'article
r рассылка *f* откликов; отклик *m*

3945 follow-up system; self-aligning system
d Folgeregelungssystem *n*; Folgesystem *n*;
Nachfolgesystem *n*
f système *m* de correspondance
r следящая система *f*; система с
самовыравниванием

3946 follow *v* up; imply *v*
d nachfolgen; folgen; implizieren
f diffuser; impliquer
r следовать; вытекать

* **font** → 1610

3947 font generator
d Baustein *m* zum Erzeugen von Zeichen
f générateur *m* de fonte
r генератор *m* шрифта

* **font map** → 3948

3948 font map[ping]
d Schriftabbildung *f*
f image *f* de police
r отображение *n* шрифта

3949 font mapping table; FMP
d Schrift-Abbildung-Tabelle *f*
f table *f* d'application de polices
r таблица *f* отображения шрифтов

3950 font name
d Schriftname *m*
f nom *m* de police
r имя *n* шрифта

3951 font options
d Schriftoptionen *fpl*
f options *fpl* de police
r опции *fpl* шрифта

3952 font size
d Schrifthöhe *f*; Schriftgröße *f*; Schriftgrad *m*
f taille *f* de police; dimension *f* de fonte
r кегль *m*; размер *m* шрифта

* **font style** → 9598

3953 foolproof guardian
 d Narrenschutz *m*; Narrensicherheit *f*
 f protection *f* contre une action imbécile
 r защита *f* "от дурака"

3954 footer
 d Fußzeile *f*
 f note *f* en bas de page
 r нижний колонтитул *m*

3955 forbidden character
 d Pseudozeichen *n*; leeres Zeichen *n*
 f caractère *m* interdit; caractère inadmissible
 r запрещённый символ *m*

3956 forbidden code
 d unzulässiger Code *m*
 f code interdit
 r запрещённый код *m*

3957 forbidden-code combination
 d unzulässige Codekombination *f*; verbotene Codekombination
 f combinaison *f* de code inadmissible
 r запрещённая кодовая комбинация *f*

* **forced disconnect** → 3958

3958 forced disconnect[ion]; forced release
 d zwangsweise Auslösung *f*;
 Zwangsauslösung *f*; Zwangsfreischaltung *f*
 f déconnexion *f* forcée
 r вынужденное разъединение *n*;
 принуждённое прерывание *n*

3959 forced-read cycle
 d Lesezwangszyklus *m*
 f cycle *m* de lecture forcée
 r цикл *m* вынужденного чтения

* **forced release** → 3958

* **forecasting** → 7199

3960 foreground *adj*
 d prioritätsgenießend
 f principal; prioritaire
 r [высоко]приоритетный

3961 foreground
 d Vordergrund *m*
 f premier plan *m*; avant plan
 r передний план *m*

3962 foreground [display] image; dynamic [display] image
 d Vordergrundbild *n*; dynamisches Bild *n*
 f image *f* principale; image de premier plan

r основное изображение *n*; накладываемое изображение

* **foreground image** → 3962

* **foregrounding** → 3964

3963 foreground initiation; foreground [program] start
 d F-Programmstart *m*;
 Vordergrundprogrammstart *m*
 f initiation *f* [de programme] du premier plan
 r инициирование *n* приоритетной программы

3964 foreground processing; foregrounding
 d Vordergrundverarbeitung *f*; vorrangiger Betrieb *m*
 f traitement *m* de premier plan; traitement de haute priorité
 r [высоко]приоритетная обработка *f*;
 приоритетное обслуживание *n*

* **foreground program start** → 3963

* **foreground start** → 3963

* **foreshortening** → 7778

* **fork** → 3966

3965 fork
 d Gabel *f*
 f fourche *f*; aiguillage *m*
 r [раз]вилка *f*

3966 fork[ing]
 d Mehrfachverzweigung *f*; Gabel[ung] *f*
 f branchement *m* multiple; fourche *f*;
 fourchure *f*
 r [многократное] разветвление *n*

3967 form; figure; shape
 d Form *f*; Figur *f*; Gestalt *f*
 f forme *f*; figure
 r форма *f*; фигура *f*

* **form** → 3327

3968 formal
 d formal
 f formel
 r формальный

3969 formalism
 d Formalismus *m*
 f formalisme *m*
 r формализм *m*

3970 formalization
 d Formalisierung *f*

f formalisation *f*
r формализация *f*

3971 formal language
   d formale Sprache *f*
   f langage *m* formel
   r формальный язык *m*

3972 formal logic; mathematical logic; symbolic logic
   d formale Logik *f*; mathematische Logik; symbolische Logik
   f logique *f* formelle; logique mathématique; logique symbolique
   r формальная логика *f*; математическая логика

3973 format
   d Format *n*
   f format *m*
   r формат *m*

3974 format check
   d Formatkontrolle *f*
   f essai *m* de format; vérification *f* de format
   r проверка *m* формата

3975 format code
   d Formatcode *m*
   f code *m* du format
   r код *m* формата

3976 format control
   d Druckbildsteuerung *f*; Druckerformatsteuerung *f*
   f commande *f* de format; commande d'édition; contrôle *m* de format
   r управление *n* форматом; управление форматированием

3977 format description
   d Formatbeschreibung *f*
   f description *f* de format
   r описание *n* формата

* **format effector** → 5299

3978 format file
   d Formatdatei *f*
   f fichier *m* de formats
   r файл *m* форматов

3979 format instruction
   d Formatbefehl *m*
   f instruction *f* de formatage
   r команда *f* форматирования

3980 format interpreter
   d Format-Interpreter *m*
   f interpréteur *m* de format

r интерпретатор *m* форматов

* **formation** → 2362

3981 formation rule
   d Bildungsregel *f*
   f règle *f* de formation
   r правило *n* образования

* **formative time** → 8480

3982 formatless input; form-free entry
   d formatfreie Eingabe *f*
   f entrée *f* sans format; entrée non formatée
   r бесформатный ввод *m*

3983 format library
   d Formatbibliothek *f*
   f bibliothèque *f* de formats
   r библиотека *f* форматов

3984 format manager
   d Formatverwalter *m*
   f gestionnaire *m* de format
   r управляющая программа *f* формата

3985 format request
   d Formatanforderung *f*
   f demande *f* de format
   r форматный запрос *m*

3986 format segment
   d Formatsegment *n*
   f segment *m* de format
   r сегмент *m* формата

3987 formatted disk
   d formatierte Platte *f*
   f disque *m* formaté
   r форматированный диск *m*

3988 form[atted] entry; form[atted] input
   d formatierte Eingabe *f*; formatgebundene Eingabe
   f entrée *f* formatée
   r форматированный ввод *m*

* **formatted input** → 3988

3989 formatted printout
   d formatgerechter Textausdruck *m*
   f impression *f* formatée
   r форматированная распечатка *f*

3990 formatter
   d Formatierer *m*
   f formateur *m*
   r форматер *m*

3991 formatting
   d Formatieren *n*; Formatierung *f*

f formatage *m*
r форматирование *n*; задание *n* формата

* **form entry** → 3988

3992 former
d Formierer *m*
f formeur *m*
r формирователь *m*

* **form feed** → 3993

3993 form feed[ing]
d Formularvorschub *m*
f avancement *m* de formulaires
r подача *f* бланков

* **form flash** → 3996

* **form-free entry** → 3982

* **form input** → 3988

3994 form overlay
d formatiertes Formular *n*
f formulaire *m* formaté
r форматированный бланк *m*

3995 forms editor
d Formulareditor *m*
f éditeur *m* de formulaires
r редактор *m* [экранных] форм

3996 form[s] flash
d Formulareinblendung *f*
f impression *f* d'un formulaire; cadre *m*
préimprimé
r накладывание *n* бланка; проецирование *n*
бланка; кадр *m* формуляра

3997 form size
d Formulargröße *f*; Formularformat *n*
f format *m* de formulaire
r размер *m* формуляра

3998 forms mode
d Formularmodus *m*; Betriebsart *f*
"Formularausfüllen"
f mode *m* de formes
r режим *m* заполнения форм

3999 form stop
d Formularstopp *m*; Anhalten *n* des Formulars
f arrêt *m* de fin de papier; arrêt de formulaires
r останов *m* при отсутствия бумаги;
прекращение *n* подачи формуляров

4000 form type
d Formularart *f*
f type *m* de format

r тип *m* формата

4001 formula
d Formel *f*
f formule *f*
r формула *f*

* **forum** → 2996

4002 forward *v*; **redirect** *v*
(e-mail)
d weiterleiten; umleiten; umadressieren
f faire suivre; redistribuer; rediriger
r перенаправлять; переадресовывать;
пересылать

* **forward-backward counter** → 914

4003 forward branching
d Vorwärtsverzweigung *f*
f saut *m* d'avant; branchement *m* en avant
r ветвление *n* [с переходом] вперёд

4004 forward channel; forward path
d Vorwärtskanal *m*; Vorwärtsweg *m*;
Vorwärtszweig *m*; Hinkanal *m*
f canal *m* d'action; chaîne *f* d'action; voie *f*
d'action
r канал *m* прямой связи

* **forward edge** → 7504

**4005 forward indication bit; forward indicator
bit**
d Vorwärtsindikatorbit *n*;
Vorwärtskennungsbit *n*
f bit *m* d'indication de renvoi
r бит *m* индикации перепосылки

* **forward indicator bit** → 4005

* **forwarding** → 1377, 5780

4006 forward-looking cache
d Forward-Looking-Cache *m*;
Cache-Speicher *m* mit vorausschauendem
Einholen
f antémémoire *f* à prélecture; mémoire *f* cache
à relecture
r кэш *m* с упреждающей выборкой

* **forward path** → 4004

* **forward slash** → 8644

4007 four-color; quadrichromatic; quadricolor
d vierfarbig; Vierfarben-; Vierfarb-
f quadrichromatique
r четырёхцветный

**4008 four-color print process; quadricolor print
process**
  d Vierfarbendruckverfahren *n*;
     Vierfarbendruck *m*
  f processus *m* d'impression en quatre couleurs
  r процесс *m* четырёхцветной печати

**4009 four-color problem; problem of coloring
maps in four colors**
  d Vierfarbenproblem *n*
  f problème *m* du coloriage des cartes; problème
     des quatre couleurs
  r задача *f* [о] четырёх красок

4010 four-element code
  d Vierercode *m*
  f code *m* à quatre éléments
  r четырёхэлементный код *m*

  * **fps → 4062**

  * **FPU → 3905**

4011 fractal
  d Fractal *n*
  f fractale *f*
  r фрактал *m*

4012 fractal attractor
  d fractaler Attraktor *m*
  f attracteur *m* fractal
  r фрактальный аттрактор *m*

4013 fractal compression
  d Kompression *f* des Fractals
  f compression *f* de fractale
  r сжатие *n* фрактала

4014 fractal curve
  d fractale Kurve *f*
  f courbe *f* fractale
  r фрактальная кривая *f*

4015 fractal dimension
  d Fractaldimension *f*
  f dimension *f* de fractale
  r размер *m* фрактала

4016 fractal formula
  d Fractalformel *f*
  f formule *f* de fractale
  r формула *f* фрактала; фрактальная формула

4017 fractal image; fractal pattern
  d fractales Bild *n*
  f image *f* fractale
  r фрактальное изображение *n*

4018 fractal image format; FIF
  d Fractalbildformat *n*

  f format *m* d'image fractale
  r формат *m* фрактального изображения

4019 fractal imaging
  d Fractalabbildung *f*
  f imagination *f* fractale
  r фрактальное изображение *n*

4020 fractal modeling
  d Fractalmodellierung *f*
  f modelage *m* de fractale
  r фрактальное моделирование *n*

  * **fractal pattern → 4017**

4021 fractal surface
  d fractale Fläche *f*; fractale Oberfläche *f*
  f surface *f* fractale
  r фрактальная поверхность *f*

4022 fractal trees
  d Fractalbäume *mpl*
  f arbres *mpl* fractals
  r фрактальные деревья *npl*

4023 fraction
  d Bruch *m*
  f fraction *f*
  r дробь *f*

4024 fragment
  d Fragment *n*
  f fragment *m*
  r фрагмент *m*

  * **fragment → 1732**

4025 fragment *v*
  d zerteilen; zertrennen
  f fragmenter
  r фрагментировать

4026 fragmentation
  d Fragmentierung *f*; Zerstückelung *f*
  f fragmentation *f*
  r фрагментирование *f*

  * **FRAM → 3752**

  * **frame → 876, 1342, 4045**

4027 frame
     (limits of design page)
  d Rahmen *m*
  f cadre *m*
  r рамка *f*

4028 frame
     (of data)
  d Frame *n*; Datenübertragungsblock *m*;
     DÜ-Block *m*; Datenblockrahmen *m*

ƒ trame ƒ; frame *m*; bloc *m* de données
r фрейм *m*; блок *m* данных

4029 frame address
d Rahmenadresse ƒ
ƒ adresse ƒ de trame
r адрес *m* фрейма; адрес кадра

4030 frame alignment; frame synchronism
d Rahmengleichlauf *m*;
Rahmensynchronismus *m*;
Rahmensynchronität ƒ
ƒ verrouillage *m* de trame; synchronisme *m* de
trame
r тактовый синхронный ход *m*

4031 frame alignment signal; framing signal
d Rahmenerkennungssignal *n*
ƒ signal *m* de verrouillage de trame
r тактовый сигнал *m* опознавания

4032 frame alignment word
d Rahmenkennungswort *n*
ƒ mot *m* de verrouillage de trame
r слово *n* опознавания кадра

4033 frame assignment
d Rahmenbelegung ƒ
ƒ assignation *m* de trame
r назначение *n* кадра

4034 frame-based
d framebasiert
ƒ de trame
r фреймовый; кадровый

4035 frame-based language
d framebasierte Sprache ƒ
ƒ langage *m* orienté trame
r фреймовый язык *m*

4036 frame bit; framing bit
d Rahmenbit *n*; Trennbit *n*
ƒ bit *m* de trame
r бит *m* кадра

**4037 frame buffer; frame store; frame memory;
image buffer; [off-]screen memory**
d Rahmenpuffer *m*; Frame-Buffer *m*;
Bild[schirm]speicher *m*
ƒ tampon *m* d'image; zone ƒ de mémoire
d'image; mémoire ƒ d'image; mémoire
[supplémentaire] d'écran
r дисплейный буфер *m*; кадровый буфер;
буферная память ƒ дисплея; память
[содержимого] экрана

4038 frame check sequence; FCS
d Blockprüfzeichenfolge ƒ;
Rahmenprüfzeichen *n*

ƒ séquence ƒ de contrôle de bloc
r последовательность ƒ проверки кадра

4039 frame conversion
d Rahmenumsetzung ƒ
ƒ conversion ƒ de trame
r преобразование *n* кадра

4040 frame [data] format
d Rahmen[daten]format *n*; Datenblockformat *n*
ƒ format *m* de bloc [de données]
r формат *m* фрейма; формат блока [данных]

* **framed comment** → 1149

4041 frame detection
d Rahmenerkennung ƒ
ƒ détection ƒ de trame
r обнаружение *n* кадра

4042 framed text
d gerahmter Text *m*
ƒ texte *m* encadré
r текст *m* в рамке

4043 frame duration; frame length
d Rahmendauer ƒ; Rahmenlänge ƒ
ƒ durée ƒ de trame; longueur ƒ de trame
r длительность ƒ кадра; длина ƒ кадра

* **frame format** → 4040

* **frame frequency** → 4053

* **frame length** → 4043

* **frame memory** → 4037

4044 frame number
d Rahmen[folge]nummer ƒ
ƒ numéro *m* de trame
r номер *m* кадра

4045 frame of reference; reference frame; frame
(a motionless body to which moving bodies
are attached)
d Bezugsrahmen *m*; Basisrahmen *m*
ƒ repère *m*
r репер *m*

4046 frame out[put] signal
d Rahmenausgabesignal *n*
ƒ signal *m* de sortie de trame
r выходной сигнал *m* фрейма

* **frame out signal** → 4046

4047 frame pattern; framing pattern
d Rahmenmuster *n*

f modèle *m* de trame
r модель *f* кадра; модель фрейма

4048 frame pointer
d Bereichszeiger *m*; Sprossenzeiger *m*
f pointeur *m* de champ
r указатель *m* области

4049 frame position
d Rahmenposition *f*
f position *f* de trame
r расположение *n* кадра

4050 frame procedure
d Rahmenprozedur *f*
f procédure *f* d'images
r фреймовая процедура *f*

4051 frame pulse
d Rahmenimpuls *m*; Bildimpuls *m*
f impulsion *f* d'image
r кадровый импульс *m*

4052 framer
d Gestalter *m*
f système *m* de cadrage; encadreur *m*
r система *f* кадрирования

4053 frame rate; frame frequency
d Rahmenfrequenz *f*
f fréquence *f* de cadres
r частота *f* [смены] кадров

4054 frame rate analysis
d Analyse *f* der Bildergeschwindigkeit
f analyse *f* de fréquence de cadres
r анализ *m* скорости пакетов

4055 frame reject
d Blockrückweisung *f*
f rejet *m* de trame
r отбрасывание *n* кадра

* **frame relay → 4056**

4056 frame relay[ing]
d Frame-Relay *n*; Rahmenrelais *n*;
Frame-Weitergabe *f*; Rahmenweiterleitung *f*
f relais *m* de trames; relayage *m* de trames
r ретрансляция *f* пакетов; ретрансляция
кадров

4057 frame relaying technology
d Rahmenweiterleitungstechnologie *f*
f technologie *f* de relayage de trames
r технология *f* ретрансляции пакетов

4058 frame relay network
d Netz *n* für Rahmenrelais
f réseau *m* [à] relais de trames

r сеть *f* с ретрансляцией пакетов

4059 frame size
d Rahmengröße *f*
f taille *f* de trame
r размер *m* пакета

4060 frame size
d Bildgröße *f*
f taille *f* de cadre
r размер *m* кадра изображения

4061 frame slip; picture slip
d Pulsrahmenschlupf *m*; Bildschlupf *m*;
Rahmenverschiebung *f*
f glissement *m* de trame
r скольжение *n* кадра

4062 frames per second; fps
d Bilder *npl* pro Sekunde
f cadres *mpl* par seconde
r кадры *mpl* в секунде

* **frame start → 8849**

* **frame store → 4037**

4063 frame structure
d Rahmenstruktur *f*; Aufbau *m* des
Datenübertragungsblocks
f structure *f* de trame
r структура *f* пакета

* **frame switch → 4064**

4064 frame switch[ing]
d Bilder-Durchschaltung *f*
f commutation *f* de cadres
r переключение *n* кадров

* **frame synchronism → 4030**

4065 frame synchronization; frame timing
d Rahmensynchronisation *f*
f synchronisation *f* de trames
r синхронизация *f* кадров

4066 frame synchronizer; phaser
d Rahmensynchronisationseinrichtung *f*;
Bildsynchronisationseinrichtung *f*
f synchroniseur *m* de trames; cadreur *m*;
circuit *m* de synchronisation verticale
r устройство *n* кадровой синхронизации;
кадровый синхронизатор *m*

* **frame timing → 4065**

4067 framework; scaffold
d Gerüst *n*

    f échafaudage *m*
    r каркас *m*; конструкция *f*; "скелет" *m*

4068 framing; phasing
    d Framing *n*; Rahmung *f*; Einrahmung *f*;
       Umrahmung *f*; Bildlageeinstellung *f*
    f tramage *m*; cadrage *m*
    r формирование *n* кадра; кадрирование *n*

    * **framing bit** → **4036**

    * **framing pattern** → **4047**

    * **framing signal** → **4031**

4069 free bit
    d freies Bit *n*
    f bit *m* libre
    r свободный бит *m*

4070 free box
    d freier Kasten *m*
    f boîte *f* libre
    r незанятая коробка *f*

    * **free channel** → **4622**

    * **free-channels list** → **4071**

4071 free-channels table; free-channels list
    d Freiliste *f* für Kanäle
    f table *f* de canaux libres
    r таблица *f* незанятых каналов; список *m*
       незанятых каналов

4072 free index
    d Laufindex *m*
    f indice *m* libre; indice franc
    r свободный индекс *m*

4073 freeing of store
    d Speicher[platz]freigabe *f*
    f libération *f* de l'emplacement de mémoire
    r освобождение *n* памяти

4074 free language
    d freie Sprache *f*
    f langage *m* libre
    r свободный язык *m*

4075 freenet
    d Freinetz *n*
    f réseau *m* libre; libertel *m*
    r бесплатная сеть *f*; сеть с бесплатным
       доступом

4076 free-running mode
    d Freizugriffmode *f*
    f mode *m* d'accès libre
    r режим *m* свободного доступа

4077 free software; freeware
    d Freeware *f*
    f logiciel *m* gratuit; gratuiciel *m*; freeware *m*;
       logiciel *m* [du domaine] public
    r бесплатный софтуер *m*; софтуер без
       перепродажи

    * **free variable** → **4763**

    * **freeware** → **4077**

4078 freeze *v*
    d einfrieren; gefrieren
    f figer; geler; congeler
    r замораживать

4079 freeze frame; frozen frame
    d Freeze-Frame *n*
    f cadre *m* figé; cadre fixe
    r замороженный кадр *m*; фиксированный
       кадр

    * **freeze-frame communication** → **3867**

    * **freeze-frame image** → **8868**

    * **freeze-frame videocommunication** → **3867**

4080 freeze image; frozen image
    d gefrorenes Bild *n*
    f image *f* gelée; image figée
    r замороженное изображение *n*

4081 freezing
    d Gefrierung *f*
    f congélation *f*
    r замораживание *n*

    * **freezing frame** → **8868**

4082 freezing of layer
    d Schichtgefrierung *f*
    f congélation *f* du plan
    r замораживание *n* слоя

    * **French point** → **2859**

4083 frequency
    d Frequenz *f*
    f fréquence *f*
    r частота *f*

4084 frequency divider; counting-down circuit
    d Frequenzteiler *m*; Frequenzteilerstufe *f*
    f diviseur *m* de fréquence; circuit *m* de division
       de fréquence
    r частотный делитель *m*

4085 frequency divider chain
    d Frequenzteilerkette *f*

f chaîne *f* de diviseurs de fréquence
r цепочка *f* частотных делителей

* **frequency division** → 4086

4086 frequency division [multiplexing];
frequency multiplex[ing]; FDM
d Frequenzmultiplex *n*; Frequenzvielfach *n*
f multiplexage *m* [par répartition] en fréquence;
multiplexage fréquentiel
r частотное уплотнение *n*

4087 frequency modulation encoding
d Frequenzmodulationscodierung *f*
f encodage *m* par modulation de fréquence
r кодирование *n* частотной модуляцией

* **frequency multiplex** → 4086

* **frequency multiplexing** → 4086

4088 frequency shift
d Frequenzverschiebung *f*;
Frequenzumtastung *f*
f répartition *f* de fréquence
r уход *m* частоты

4089 frequency shifter
d Frequenzumtaster *m*
f répartiteur *m* de fréquence
r преобразователь *m* частоты

4090 frequently asked questions; FAQ
(a collection of questions and answers about a
particular topic)
d häufig gestellte Fragen *fpl*; oft gestellte
Fragen
f questions *fpl* fréquentes; foire *f* aux questions;
FAQ
r часто задаваемые вопросы *mpl*; ЧаВо

* **freshen** *v* **up** → 7822

4091 fringeware
d unzuverlässige Software *f*
f gratuiciel *m* à fiabilité et valeur contestables
r ненадёжное бесплатное программное
обеспечение *n*

* **front edge** → 7504

4092 front end
d Eingangsseite *f*; Vorfeld *n*
f côté *m* d'entrée
r место *n* входа; передний край *m*

4093 front-end adapter
d Front-End-Adapter *m*
f adaptateur *m* de l'acquisition de données
r адаптер *m* сбора данных

4094 front-end allocator
d Front-End-Zuordner *m*
f allocateur *m* d'entrée
r входной распределитель *m*

* **front-end amplifier** → 4882

4095 front-end application
d Vorfeldaufgabe *f*
f application *f* d'entrée
r фронтальное приложение *n*

* **front-end computer** → 8180

4096 front-end equipment
d Vorfeldeinrichtung *f*
f équipement *m* d'entrée
r оборудование *n* входа

4097 front-end multiplexer
d vorgezogener Multiplexer *m*
f multiplexeur *m* frontal; multiplexeur d'entrée
r фронтальный мультиплексор *m*

* **front-end processing** → 7223

4098 front-end processor; FEP; preprocessor
d Eingangsprozessor *m*;
Vor[arbeitungs]prozessor *m*;
Front-End-Prozessor *m*
f processeur *m* de prétraitement;
préprocesseur *m*; processeur frontal
r буферный процессор *m*; препроцессор *m*

* **frontier** → 1137

* **frontier** *adj* → 1138

* **frontier point** → 1141

* **front page** → 5314

4099 front panel
d Frontplatte *f*; Vorderseite *f*
f panneau *m* avant; plaque *f* frontale
r лицевая панель *f*

* **frozen frame** → 4079

* **frozen image** → 4080

* **FTP** → 3820

4100 FTP address
d FTP-Adresse *f*
f adresse *f* FTP
r адрес *m* протокола передачи файлов

4101 FTP client
d FTP-Client *n*

f client *m* FTP
r FTP клиент *m*

4102 FTP server
d FTP-Server *m*
f serveur *m* FTP
r сервер *m* протокола передачи файлов

4103 full
d voll; ganz
f plein; complet
r полный

4104 full adder
d Volladdierer *m*
f add[itionn]eur *m* complet; sommateur *m* complet
r полный сумматор *m*

4105 full bus
d Voll-Bit-Bus *m*
f bus *m* à pleine largeur
r полноразрядная шина *f*

* **full-color → 311**

4106 full connection diagram; overall circuit diagram
d Gesamtschaltplan *m*; Übersichtsstromlauf[plan] *m*
f schéma *m* des connexions total; diagramme *m* du câblage total
r общая схема *f* соединений; общая коммутационная схема

4107 full disjunctive normal form
d vollkommene disjunktive Normalform *f*
f forme *f* disjonctive normale complète; forme disjonctive normale parfaite
r совершенная нормальная дизъюнктивная форма *f*

* **full duplex → 3219**

4108 full IP connection
d volle IP-Verbindung *f*
f connexion *f* IP intégral
r полная IP-связь *f*

4109 full-motion digital video; animated digital video
d animiertes Digitalvideo *n*
f vidéo *m* numérique animé; animation *f* vidéo numérique intégrale
r цифровой мультипликационный фильм *m*

4110 full name
d Ganzname *m*
f nom *m* complet
r полное имя *n*

4111 full page
d Ganzseite *f*
f page *f* complète; pleine page
r полная страница *f*

4112 full-page display
d Ganzseitendisplay *n*
f écran *m* à pleine page
r полностраничный дисплей *m*

4113 full plot preview
d Ganzvorschau *f* des Plotterns
f prévisualisation *f* pleine de tracé
r полный предварительный просмотр *m* черчения

4114 full preview
d Ganzvorschau *f*
f prévisualisation *f* pleine
r полный предварительный просмотр *m*

4115 full read pulse
d voller Leseimpuls *m*
f impulsion *f* de lecture complète
r полный импульс *m* считывания

4116 full screen
d Ganzbildschirm *m*
f plein écran *m*
r полный экран *m*

4117 full-screen editor; screen editor
d Bildschirmeditor *m*
f éditeur *m* d'écran
r экранный редактор *m*

4118 full-sized keyboard
d Tastatur *f* in voller Größe; Tastatur in Originalgröße
f clavier *m* complet; clavier à pleine grandeur
r полноразмерная клавиатура *f*

4119 full text
d Volltext *m*
f texte *m* intégral; texte pleine
r полный текст *m*

4120 full-text database
d Volltextdatenbasis *f*
f base *f* de données de texte pleine
r полнотекстовая база *f* данных

4121 full-text search
d Volltextsuche *f*
f recherche *f* de texte pleine
r полнотекстовой поиск *m*

* **full tone → 2244**

4122 full transparency
d Volltransparenz *f*

f transparence *f* pleine
r полная прозрачность *f*

4123 full videocommunication
  d Bewegtbildkommunikation *f*
  f vidéocommunication *f* complète
  r полная видеосвязь *f*

4124 full video teleconference; visual conference
  d Bewegtbild-Telekonferenz *f*
  f vidéotéléconférence *f* complète
  r полная видеоконференция *f*

4125 full videotransmission
  d Bewegtbildübertragung *f*
  f vidéotransmission *f* complète
  r полная видеопередача *f*

4126 full word
  d Vollwort *n*; Ganzwort *n*
  f mot *m* entier; mot complet
  r целое слово *n*; полное слово

4127 full-word buffer
  d Vollwortpuffer *m*
  f tampon *m* [à un] mot; tampon en mot entier
  r буфер *m* на многоразрядное слово

4128 full-write pulse
  d voller Schreibimpuls *m*
  f impulsion *f* d'inscription complète
  r полный импульс *m* записи

4129 fully connected network
  d vollvermaschtes Netz *n*
  f réseau *m* à connexion complète
  r сеть *f* с топологией связанного графа;
    полностью связанная сеть

4130 fully digital processing
  d volldigitale Verarbeitung *f*
  f traitement *m* complètement numérique
  r полностью цифровая обработка *f*

4131 full zoom; zoom all
  d vollständiges Zoomen *n*
  f zoom *m* total
  r полное динамическое масштабирование *n*

4132 function
  d Funktion *f*
  f fonction *f*
  r функция *f*

4133 functional *adj*
  d funktional
  f fonctionnel
  r функциональный

4134 functional check; function[al] test
  d Funktionsprüfung *f*; Funktionstest *m*

  f test *m* fonctionnel; essai *m* fonctionnel
  r функциональная проверка *f*;
    функциональный тест *m*

4135 functional circuit
  d Funktionskreis *m*
  f circuit *m* de fonctionnement
  r функциональная схема *f*

4136 functional circuit diagram
  d Funktionsschaltungsplan *m*
  f diagramme *m* de circuit fonctionnel
  r функциональная диаграмма *f*

4137 function[al] code
  d Funktionscode *m*
  f code *m* fonctionnel; code de fonction; partie *f*
    de code d'opération
  r функциональный код *m*; код функции;
    поле *n* кода операции

4138 function[al] generator
  d Funktionsgenerator *m*; Funktionsgeber *m*;
    Funktionswandler *m*
  f générateur *m* de fonctions; traducteur *m* des
    fonctions
  r генератор *m* функций; функциональный
    преобразователь *m*

4139 functional independence
  d Funktionalunabhängigkeit *f*
  f indépendance *f* fonctionnelle
  r функциональная независимость *f*

* **functional key** → 3733

4140 functional language
  d funktionale Programmiersprache *f*
  f langage *m* fonctionnel
  r язык *m* функционального
    программирования

4141 functional protocol
  d funktionales Protokoll *n*
  f protocole *m* fonctionnel
  r функциональный протокол *m*

* **functional test** → 4134

* **function code** → 4137

* **function generator** → 4138

* **function key** → 3733

4142 function subprogram; function subroutine
  d Funktionsunterprogramm *n*
  f sous-programme *m* fonctionnel;
    sous-routine *f* fonctionnelle
  r подпрограмма-функция *f*

* **function subroutine** → 4142

4143 function table
   d Funktionstabelle *f*
   f table *f* de fonctions
   r таблица *f* функций; функциональная таблица

* **function test** → 4134

* **fundamental** → 845

4144 fundamental frequency
   d Grundfrequenz *f*
   f fréquence *f* fondamentale
   r основная частота *f*

4145 fuse
   d Schmelzsicherung *f*; Sicherung *f*
   f fusible *m*
   r [плавкий] предохранитель *m*

* **fuse link** → 4147

4146 fusible
   d schmelzbar
   f fusible
   r плавкий

4147 fusible link; fuse link
   d Schmelzverbindung *f*; aufschmelzbare Verbindung *f*; Schmelzeinsatz *m*
   f liaison *f* fusible
   r пережигаемая связь *f*; плавкая перемычка *f*

4148 fuzziness
   d Unbestimmtheit *f*
   f flou *m*
   r нечёткость *f*; нерезкость *f*; размытость *f*; расплывчатость *f*

4149 fuzzy; hazy; blurred; non sharp; unsharp
   d Fuzzy-; unscharf; unbestimmt
   f flou; non distinct
   r размытый; нечёткий; нерезкий; неясный; расплывчатый

4150 fuzzy algorithm
   d Fuzzy-Algorithmus *m*; Algorithmus *m* mit Unschärfe
   f algorithme *m* flou
   r нечёткий алгоритм *m*

4151 fuzzy graph
   d unbestimmter Graph *m*
   f graphe *m* flou
   r нечёткий граф *m*

4152 fuzzy instruction
   d Fuzzy-Instruktion *f*; unscharfe Instruktion *f*; unbestimmte Instruktion
   f instruction *f* floue
   r нечёткая инструкция *f*

4153 fuzzy logic
   d Fuzzy-Logik *f*; unbestimmte Logik; unscharfe Logik
   f logique *f* floue
   r размытая логика *f*; нечёткая логика

4154 fuzzy programming
   d Fuzzy-Programmierung *f*; Programmierung *f* mit Unschärfe
   f programmation *f* floue
   r нечёткое программирование *n*

4155 fuzzy variable
   d Fuzzy-Variable *f*; unscharfe Variable
   f variable *f* floue
   r нечёткая переменная *f*

G

* **gain constant** → **1833**

* **gain-frequency characteristics** → **370**

4156 gallery
d Galerie f
f galerie f
r галерея f

4157 game
d Spiel n
f jeu m
r игра f

4158 game-chip
d Spielchip m
f puce-jeu f
r кристалл m игры

4159 game graphics
d Spielgrafik f
f graphique m de jeu
r графика f игр

4160 game in VR
d virtuelles Spiel n
f jeu m virtuel
r игра f в виртуальной реальности

4161 game matrix
d Spielmatrix f
f matrice f de jeu
r матрица f игры

4162 game port
d Spielport m
f port m de jeu
r игровой порт m

4163 game rule
d Spielregel f
f règle f du jeu
r правило n игры

4164 game software
d Spielsoftware f
f logiciel m de jeu; ludiciel m
r программное обеспечение n игры

4165 game theory; theory of games
d Spieltheorie f
f théorie f des jeux
r теория f игр

4166 gaming
d Spielsimulierung f; Spielsimulieren n;
   Spielsimulation f
f simulation f de jeu
r моделирование n игры

4167 gap
d Abstand m; Lücke f; Spalt m
f lacune f; interstice f; fente f
r промежуток m; зазор m; щель f

4168 gap digit
d Füllziffer f
f chiffre m de remplissage
r разряд m пробела

4169 gap width
d Spaltbreite f
f largeur f d'interstice
r ширина f зазора; ширина щели

**4170 garbage; gibberish; hash; trash; junk;
     spam**
   (e-slang)
d Makulatur f; sinnlose Information f;
   Informationsmüll m; bedeutungslose
   Daten pl; unsinnige Daten; Spam n
f maculature f; ordure f; données fpl sans
   valeur
r ненужные данные pl; ненужная
   информация f; [информационный]
   мусор m

* **garbage** → **6175**

4171 garbage collection
d Sammeln n von bedeutungslosen Daten;
   Freispeichersammlung f
f collection f de maculature; collection
   d'ordures
r сбор m ненужных данных; очистка f
   памяти

4172 garbed information
d verstümmelte Information f
f information f mutilée
r искажённая информация f

4173 garbed signal
d verstümmeltes Signal n
f signal m mutilé
r зашумлённый сигнал m; искажённый
   сигнал

* **gate** → **4176, 8948**

4174 gate array
d Gatterfeld n; Universalschaltkreis m
f matrice f de portes; champ m de portes
r вентильная матрица f

4175 **gate-array approach**
 d Gatterfeldlösung *f*
 f solution *f* de champ de portes
 r реализация *f* схем на основе вентильных
       матриц

4176 **gate [circuit]**
 d Gatter *n*; Torschaltung *f*; Ausblendschaltung *f*
 f porte *f*; gate *m*; circuit *m* porte
 r вентиль *m*; стробирующая схема *f*

4177 **gated decoder**
 d gattergesteuerter Decoder *m*
 f décodeur *m* à portes
 r стробированный дешифратор *m*

4178 **gated inverter**
 d Inverter *m* mit Koinzidenzschaltung
 f inverseur *m* à circuit de coïncidence
 r инвертор *m* со схемой совпадения

4179 **gate-driver**
 d Gattertreiber *m*
 f porte *f* formateur
 r вентиль-формирователь *m*

4180 **gate extraction**
 d Gate-Extraktion *f*
 f extraction *f* de portes
 r выделение *n* вентилей

4181 **gate output**
 d Gatterausgang *m*; Torausgabe *f*
 f sortie *f* de porte
 r выход *m* вентиля

 *   **gate pulse** → 8948

4182 **gateway**
       (a device or a program which transfers data
       between networks)
 d Gateway *n*
 f écluse *f*; passerelle *f*
 r шлюз *m*

4183 **gateway computer**
 d Gateway-Computer *m*; Gateway-Rechner *m*
 f ordinateur *m* de type porte d'écluse
 r шлюзовый компьютер *m*

4184 **gather** *v*
 d [an]sammeln; anhäufen
 f saisir; accumuler; acquérir
 r собирать; накапливать; сливать

4185 **gather[ed] write**
 d sammelndes Schreiben *n*
 f enregistrement *m* à fusion
 r запись *f* со слиянием

 *   **gathering** → 122

 *   **gather write** → 4185

 *   **gauge** *v* → 1350

 *   **Gb** → 4221

4186 **general; overall; total**
 d allgemein; durchgängig; Gesamt-
 f général; total
 r общий

4187 **general [device] interface; common
       interface**
 d Mehrzweckschnittstelle *f*
 f interface *f* générale
 r общий интерфейс *m*

4188 **general information**
 d allgemeine Information *f*
 f information *f* générale
 r общая информация *f*

 *   **general interface** → 4187

 *   **general interrogation** → 4194

4189 **generalized**
 d verallgemeinert
 f généralisé
 r обобщённый

4190 **generalized Boolean algebra**
 d verallgemeinerte Boolesche Algebra *f*
 f algèbre *f* de Boole généralisée
 r обобщённая булева алгебра *f*

4191 **generalized grammar**
 d verallgemeinerte Grammatik *f*; generalisierte
       Grammatik
 f grammaire *f* généralisée
 r обобщённая грамматика *f*

4192 **generalized information management
       system**
 d verallgemeinertes
       Informationsverwaltungssystem *n*
 f système *m* de service d'information généralisé
 r универсальная информационная система *f*
       для административного управления

4193 **generalized transfer function**
 d verallgemeinerte Übertragungsfunktion *f*
 f fonction *f* de transfert généralisée
 r обобщённая передаточная функция *f*

 *   **general memory** → 5602

4194 **general poll; general interrogation**
  d allgemeine Abfrage *f*
  f interrogation *f* générale
  r общий опрос *m*

4195 **general-protection fault**
  d Verletzung *f* des allgemeinen Schutzes
  f faute *f* de protection générale
  r нарушение *n* общей защиты

4196 **general-purpose interface bus; GPIB**
  d universeller Anschlussbus *m*
  f bus *m* d'interface universel
  r универсальная интерфейсная шина *f*; шина
      общего назначения

4197 **general-purpose language**
  d universelle Sprache *f*
  f langage *m* universel
  r универсальный язык *m*

4198 **general[-purpose] register**
  d Allzweckregister *n*; Mehrzweckregister *n*;
      allgemeines Register *n*
  f registre *m* général; registre universel; registre
      banalisé
  r общий регистр *m*; регистр общего
      назначения

  * **general register** → **4198**

4199 **general utility function**
  d allgemeine Nutzenfunktion *f*
  f fonction *f* générale d'utilité
  r общая утилитная функция *f*

4200 **generate** *v*
  d generieren; erzeugen
  f générer; engendrer
  r порождать; генерировать; производить

4201 **generated information**
  d erzeugte Information *f*
  f information *f* générée
  r сгенерированная информация *f*

4202 **generated message format**
  d generiertes Nachrichtenformat *n*
  f format *m* de message engendré
  r формат *m* порождённого сообщения

4203 **generating program; generator**
  d Generierungsprogramm *n*
  f programme *m* de génération; générateur *m*
  r генерирующая программа *f*

4204 **generation**
  d Erzeugung *f*; Generierung *f*
  f génération *f*; engendrement *m*
  r порождение *n*; образование *n*

4205 **generator**
      (a circuit)
  d Generator *m*; Erzeuger *m*
  f générateur *m*
  r генератор *m*

  * **generator** → **4203**

4206 **generic**
  d generisch
  f générique; génératif
  r порождающий; родовый

4207 **generic addressing**
  d generische Adressierung *f*
  f adressage *m* générique
  r общая адресация *f*

4208 **generic frame**
  d generisches Frame *n*
  f trame *f* générative
  r родовый фрейм *m*

4209 **generic key**
  d generischer Schlüssel *m*
  f clé *f* générale; clé universelle
  r общий ключ *m*

  * **generic net** → **4210**

4210 **generic net[work]**
  d generisches Netz *n*
  f réseau *m* générique
  r порождающая сеть *f*

4211 **generic parameter**
  d Auswählbarkeitsparameter *m*; generischer
      Parameter *m*
  f paramètre *m* générique
  r видовой параметр *m*

4212 **generic word search**
  d Suche *f* mit Gattungswort
  f recherche *f* de chaîne avec troncature à droite;
      recherche de chaîne tronquée à droite
  r поиск *m* родового слова

4213 **geometric processor; geometry processor;
      GPU**
  d Geometrieprozessor *m*
  f processeur *m* géométrique; processeur de
      géométrie
  r геометрический процессор *m*; процессор
      геометрии

4214 **geometric processor chip**
  d Chip *m* des Geometrieprozessors
  f puce *f* de processeur géométrique
  r геометрический процессорный чип *m*

4215 **geometric relationship**
   d geometrischer Zusammenhang *m*
   f relation *f* mutuelle géométrique
   r геометрическая взаимосвязь *f*

   * **geometry processor** → 4213

4216 **gesture recognition**
   d Gestenerkennung *f*
   f reconnaissance *f* des gestes
   r распознавание *n* жестов

   * **ghost** → 6931

   * **ghost character** → 4218

   * **ghost image** → 6931

4217 **ghosting**
   d Geistereffekt *m*
   f linéament *m*; dédoublement *m* de l'image
   r слабое вторичное изображение *n*;
      побочное изображение; появление *n*
      ореола; "призрак" *m*

4218 **ghost[ing] character**
   d Geisterzeichen *n*
   f caractère *m* fantôme; caractère flou
   r фантомный символ *m*

   * **GHz** → 4223

   * **gibberish** → 4170

   * **GIF** → 4298

4219 **GIF file**
   d GIF-Datei *f*
   f fichier *m* GIF
   r файл *m* GIF

4220 **GIF filter**
   d GIF-Filter *m*
   f filtre *m* GIF
   r фильтр *m* GIF

4221 **gigabyte; Gb**
   d Gigabyte *n*; Gb
   f giga-octet *m*; Go
   r гигабайт *m*; Гб

   * **gigacycle** → 4223

4222 **gigaflops**
   d Gigaflops *m*
   f gigaflops *m*
   r гигафлопс *m*

4223 **gigahertz; GHz; gigacycle**
   d Gigahertz *n*; GHz

   f gigahertz *m*; GHz
   r гигагерц *m*; Ггц

4224 **gigapixel**
   d Gigapixel *n*
   f gigapixel *m*
   r гигапиксел *m*

   * **glancing** *adj* → 8663

   * **glare filter** → 445

   * **glass fiber** → 6542

   * **glass fiber LAN** → 6543

   * **glide** *v* → 8654

   * **glider** → 8661

   * **gliding** → 8664

4225 **global address**
   d Generaladresse *f*
   f adresse *f* globale
   r глобальный адрес *m*

   * **global bus** → 1919

4226 **global compatibility**
   d weltweite Kompatibilität *f*
   f compatibilité *f* globale
   r глобальная совместимость *f*

4227 **global computer network**
   d globales Rechnernetz *n*
   f réseau *m* d'ordinateurs global
   r глобальная компьютерная сеть *f*

4228 **global data**
   d globale Daten *pl*
   f données *fpl* globales
   r глобальные данные *pl*

4229 **global network navigator; GNN**
   d Gesamt-Netzwerk-Navigator *m*
   f navigateur *m* de réseau global
   r навигатор *m* глобальной сети

4230 **global realtime repeater**
   d Relaisstation *f* für globales
      Echtzeitverbindungsnetz
   f répéteur *m* pour réseau de communication
      global à temps réel
   r спутник-ретранслятор *m* для глобальной
      сети связи в реальном времени

4231 **global search**
   d Globalsuche *f*; globales Suchen *n*

f recherche *f* globale
r глобальный поиск *m*

4232 global system of mobile communications; GSM
d weltweites System *n* für mobile Kommunikation; GSM
f système *m* global de communications mobiles; groupes *mpl* systèmes mobiles; GSM
r глобальная система *f* мобильной связи

4233 global title
d globaler Name *m*
f titre *m* global
r глобальный заголовок *m*

4234 global variable
d globale Variable *f*
f variable *f* globale
r глобальная переменная *f*

4235 glossary
d Glossar *n*; Begriffserklärung *f*
f glossaire *m*
r глоссарий *m*

* **glue** *v* **together** → 6851

* **gluing** → 6852

* **GNN** → 4229

4236 goal
d Ziel *n*; Zweck *m*; Goal *n*
f but *m*; objectif *m*
r цель *f*

4237 goal seeking
d gezieltes Suchen *n*
f orientation *f* au but
r целенаправленный поиск *m*

* **going to black** → 3674

4238 good data area
d günstiger Datenbereich *m*
f zone *f* de données bonnes
r поле *n* благоприятных данных; зона *f* благоприятных данных

4239 Gopher
(an Internet service)
d Gopher *m*
f Gopher *m*
r Гофер *m*

4240 Gopher menu
d Gopher-Menü *n*
f menu *m* de Gopher

r меню *m* Гофера

4241 Gopher space
d Gopherraum *m*
f espace *m* de Gopher
r пространство *n* Гофера

4242 Gouraud shading
(Lambert or cosine shading plus the representation of specular highlighting)
d Gouraud-Schattierung *f*
f ombrage *m* Gouraud
r оттенение *n* Гуро

* **GPIB** → 4196

* **GPU** → 4213

* **grabbing** → 1431

4243 gradation
d Gradation *f*
f gradation *f*
r градация *f*

4244 gradient background
d Gradienthintergrund *m*
f fond *m* gradient
r градиентный фон *m*

4245 gradient of pulse transition
d Impuls-Flankensteilheit *f*
f gradient *m* de transition d'impulsion
r градиент *m* импульсного перехода

4246 gradient shading
d Gradientschattierung *f*
f ombrage *m* graduel
r градиентное оттенение *n*

* **grading** → 1701

* **graduate** *v* → 1350

4247 grammar
d Grammatik *f*
f grammaire *f*
r грамматика *f*

* **grand total** → 9450

4248 granulated screen raster
d granulierter Bildschirmraster *m*
f trame *f* à grains
r зернистый растр *m* экрана

* **graph** → 1641

4249 graph
d Graph *m*

f graphe *m*
r граф *m*

* **graphic** → **1641, 4251**

4250 graphic accelerator
  d grafischer Beschleuniger *m*;
    Grafikbeschleuniger *m*
  f accélérateur *m* graphique; adaptateur *m*
    graphique
  r графический ускоритель *m*; графический
    акселератор *m*

4251 graphic[al] *adj*
  d grafisch
  f graphique
  r графический

4252 graphic[al] animation
  d grafische Animation *f*
  f animation *f* graphique
  r графическая анимация *f*

4253 graphical calculation; graphical calculus
  d grafisches Rechnen *n*
  f calcul *m* graphique
  r графическое вычисление *n*

* **graphical calculus** → **4254**

4254 graphic[al] code
  d Formcode *m*; grafischer Code *m*
  f code *m* graphique
  r графический код *m*

4255 graphic[al] data
  d grafische Daten *pl*; Grafikdaten *pl*
  f données *fpl* graphiques
  r графические данные *pl*

4256 graphical [data] transmission
  d grafischer Informationsaustausch *m*
  f transmission *f* de données graphiques
  r передача *f* графической информации

4257 graphic[al] editor; graphics editor
  d Grafikeditor *m*
  f éditeur *m* graphique
  r графический редактор *m*

4258 graphical element
  d grafisches Element *n*
  f élément *m* graphique
  r графический элемент *m*

4259 graphic[al] hyperlink
  d Grafik-Hyperlink *n*; grafischer
    Querverweis *m*
  f hyperlien *m* graphique
  r графическая гиперсвязь *f*

4260 graphic[al] interface
  d Grafikinterface *n*; Grafikschnittstelle *f*
  f interface *f* graphique
  r графический интерфейс *m*

4261 graphic[al]-interface database
  d Datenbasis *f* mit grafischer Schnittstelle;
    Datenbasis mit grafischer Anfragesprache
  f base *f* de données à interface graphique
  r база *f* данных с графическим языком
    запросов

**4262 graphic[al] library; graphics library;
shape library**
  d grafische Bibliothek *f*; Bibliothek für
    grafische Grundelemente
  f bibliothèque *f* graphique; bibliothèque de
    formes
  r библиотека *f* графических фигур

4263 graphic[al] toolbar
  d grafischer Werkzeugstreifen *m*
  f barre *f* d'outils graphiques
  r графическая инструментальная лента *f*;
    панель *f* графических инструментов

* **graphical transmission** → **4256**

4264 graphic[al] user interface; GUI
  d grafische Benutzerschnittstelle *f*
  f interface *f* graphique utilisateur
  r графический пользовательский
    интерфейс *m*

* **graphic animation** → **4252**

4265 graphic area; graphics window
  d Grafikbereich *m*; Grafikfenster *n*
  f domaine *m* graphique; fenêtre *f* graphique
  r графическая область *f*; графическое окно *n*

4266 graphic bus
  d Grafikdatenbus *m*
  f bus *m* de données graphiques
  r шина *f* графических данных

4267 graphic card memory
  d Grafikkarten-Speicher *m*
  f mémoire *f* de carte graphique
  r память *f* графической карты

4268 graphic character
  d grafisches Zeichen *n*; Grafiksymbol *n*
  f caractère *m* graphique; symbole *m* graphique
  r графический символ *m*

4269 graphic chipset
  d grafischer Chipsatz *m*

f jeu *m* de circuits graphiques; jeu de composants graphiques
r набор *m* графических микросхем

4270 graphic cluster
d grafischer Cluster *m*
f grappe *f* graphique
r графический кластер *m*; графический блок *m*

* **graphic code** → 4254

4271 graphic command sequence
d grafische Kommandosequenz *f*
f séquence *f* de commandes graphiques
r последовательность *f* графических команд

4272 graphic communication
d grafische Kommunikation *f*
f communication *f* graphique
r графическая связь *f*

4273 graphic compiler
d Grafikkompilierer *m*
f compilateur *m* graphique
r графический компилятор *m*

4274 graphic computer system
d grafisches Rechnersystem *n*
f système *m* d'ordinateur graphique
r графическая компьютерная система *f*

4275 graphic [co]processor; graphics [co]processor
d Grafik[ko]prozessor *m*
f [co]processeur *m* graphique
r графический [co]процессор *m*

* **graphic data** → 4255

4276 graphic [data] input; graphic entry
d grafische Dateneingabe *f*
f entrée *f* de données graphiques
r ввод *m* графических данных

4277 graphic [data] output
d grafische Datenausgabe *f*; Grafikdatenausgabe *f*
f sortie *f* des données graphiques; émission *f* des données graphiques
r вывод *m* графических данных

4278 graphic device
d grafisches Gerät *n*
f dispositif *m* graphique
r графическое устройство *n*

4279 graphic display
d grafischer Bildschirm *m*

f afficheur *m* graphique
r графический дисплей *m*

4280 graphic display interface
d Schnittstelle *f* des grafischen Displays
f interface *f* d'afficheur graphique
r интерфейс *m* графического дисплея

* **graphic editor** → 4257

4281 graphic engine
d grafische Maschine *f*
f moteur *m* graphique
r графическая машина *f*

* **graphic entry** → 4276

4282 graphic file
d grafische Datei *f*; Grafikdatei *f*
f fichier *m* graphique
r графический файл *m*

4283 graphic font
d grafische Schrift *f*
f police *f* graphique
r графический шрифт *m*

4284 graphic format
d Grafikformat *n*
f format *m* graphique
r графический формат *m*

4285 graphic grammar
d grafische Grammatik *f*
f grammaire *f* graphique
r графическая грамматика *f*

4286 graphic hardware
d grafische Hardware *f*
f matériel *m* graphique
r графическое техническое обеспечение *n*

* **graphic hyperlink** → 4259

4287 graphic information system
d grafisches Informationssystem *n*
f système *m* informatique graphique
r графическая информационная система *f*

* **graphic input** → 4276

4288 graphic input/output error
d grafischer Eingabe/Ausgabe-Fehler *m*
f erreur *f* d'entrée/sortie graphique
r ошибка *f* графического ввода/вывода

4289 graphic interactive system
d grafisches interaktives System *n*
f système *m* interactif graphique
r графическая диалоговая система *f*

* **graphic interface** → 4260

* **graphic-interface database** → 4261

4290 graphic job processing
 d grafische Jobverarbeitung *f*
 f traitement *m* de travaux graphiques
 r обработка *f* графических заданий

* **graphic kernel system** → 4299

* **graphic language** → 4300

* **graphic library** → 4262

4291 graphic memory
 d Grafikspeicher *m*
 f mémoire *f* de données graphiques
 r память *f* графических данных

* **graphic output** → 4277

* **graphic primitive** → 7259

* **graphic print** → 4292

4292 graphic print[ing]
 d grafischer Druck *m*
 f impression *f* graphique
 r графическая печать *f*

* **graphic processor** → 4275

4293 graphics
 d Grafik *f*; grafische Mittel *npl*
 f graphique *m*
 r графика *f*; графические средства *npl*

4294 graphics adapter
 d Grafikadapter *m*
 f adaptateur *m* des unités graphiques
 r адаптер *m* графических устройств

* **graphics capability** → 4302

* **graphics card** → 9809

4295 graphics coding
 d grafische Codierung *f*
 f codage *m* graphique
 r графическое кодирование *n*

4296 graphics console
 d Grafikkonsole *f*
 f visu *m* graphique; console *m* graphique
 r графическая консоль *f*

4297 graphics controller
 d Grafikkontroller *m*
 f contrôleur *m* graphique

 r графический контроллер *m*

* **graphics coprocessor** → 4275

* **graphics designer** → 3169

* **graphics editor** → 4258

* **graphics film recorder** → 6953

4298 graphics interchange format; GIF
 d grafisches Austauschformat *n*
 f format *m* d'échange graphique
 r формат *m* графического обмена; формат обмена графикой

4299 graphic[s] kernel system
 d grafisches Kernsystem *n*
 f système *m* graphique de noyau
 r базовая графическая система *f*

4300 graphic[s] language
 d Grafiksprache *f*
 f langage *m* [de traitement] graphique
 r язык *m* обработки графической информации; язык графических символов

* **graphics library** → 4262

4301 graphic software
 d Grafiksoftware *f*
 f logiciel *m* graphique; grapheur *m*; graphiciel *m*
 r графическое программное обеспечение *n*

4302 graphics performance; graphics capability
 d Grafikfähigkeit *f*
 f productivité *f* graphique
 r графическая производительность *f*

* **graphics primitive** → 7259

4303 graphics primitives per second
 d grafische Primitivelemente *npl* pro Sekunde
 f primitives *mpl* graphiques par seconde
 r графические примитивы *mpl* в секунду

* **graphics processor** → 4275

4304 graphics printer
 d grafischer Drucker *m*
 f imprimante *f* graphique
 r графический принтер *m*

* **graphics station** → 2082

4305 graphics tablet
 d Grafiktablett *n*
 f tablette *f* graphique
 r графический планшет *m*

* **graphics window** → 4265

* **graphics workstation** → 2082

* **graphic toolbar** → 4263

4306 graphic toolbox
   d grafischer Werkzeugkasten *m*
   f boîte *f* à outils graphique
   r графический инструментальный ящик *m*

* **graphic user interface** → 4264

4307 graph loop
   d Graphschleife *f*
   f boucle *f* de graphe
   r петля *f* графа

4308 graph theory
   d Graphentheorie *f*; Theorie *f* der Graphen
   f théorie *f* des graphes
   r теория *f* графов

4309 graph with loops
   d Graph *m* mit Schleifen
   f graphe *m* avec boucles
   r граф *m* с петлями

* **graph without loops** → 156

* **grating** → 5289

4310 gray; grey
   d Grau-
   f gris
   r серый; теневой

4311 gray balance
   d Grauausgleich *m*
   f équilibre *m* pour les gris
   r баланс *m* по серому

4312 Gray code
   d Gray-Code *m*
   f code *m* de Gray
   r код *m* Грея

4313 gray component
   d Grauskomponente *f*
   f composant *m* de gris
   r компонента *f* серого

4314 grayed icon
   d abgeblendetes Symbol *n*
   f icône *f* grisée
   r икона *f* в сером

* **gray image** → 4317

4315 gray level; shade of gray; gray shade
   d Graustufe *f*
   f niveau *m* de gris
   r уровень *m* серого; уровень яркости

* **gray picture** → 4317

4316 gray scale; shading scale
   d Grau[stufen]skala *f*; Graustufung *f*
   f escalier *m* de demi-teintes gris; échelle *f* des
      gris
   r шкала *f* яркостей; шкала полутонов;
      полутоновая шкала; шкала оттенков
      серого цвета

**4317 gray[-scale] image; gray[-scale] picture;
     halftone image**
   d Graubild *n*; Halbtonbild *n*
   f image *f* de demi-teinte; image grise; image de
      niveau gris
   r полутоновое изображение *n*

* **gray-scale picture** → 4317

* **gray shade** → 4315

4318 great display
   d Großformat-Display *n*
   f écran *m* gros
   r широкоформатный дисплей *m*

* **greek** → 4319

4319 greek[ing]
   d Greeking *n*
   f symbolisation *f*; gris *m* typographique; faux
      texte *m*
   r формирование *n* строкозаменителей;
      имитирование *n* текста; процесс *m*
      представления текста в виде серых полос
      при вёрстке; грикинг *m*

4320 green-phosphor display
   d grünes Display *n*; grüner Bildschirm *m*
   f écran *m* à phosphore; écran à luminophore
      vert
   r дисплей *m* зелёного свечения

* **Greenwich meantime** → 2304

* **grey** → 4310

4321 grey *v* out
   d deaktivieren; ausgrauen
   f griser
   r становиться серым

* **grid** → 7611

4322 **grid bias**
  d Gitterverschiebung *f*
  f polarisation *f* de grille
  r смещение *n* сетки; сеточное смещение

  * **grid board** → 7613

4323 **grid button**
  d Gitterschaltfläche *f*
  f bouton *m* de grille
  r бутон *m* растра

4324 **grid coordinates**
  d Gitterkoordinaten *fpl*;
     Rechtwinkelkoordinaten *fpl*
  f coordonnées *fpl* rectangulaires
  r плоские прямоугольные координаты *fpl*

  * **grid element spacing** → 8241

  * **gridline** → 7631

  * **grid point** → 8240

  * **grid size** → 8241

  * **grid spacing** → 8241

  * **grip** *v* → 1430

4325 **grip; handle**
  d Griff *m*; Handgriff *m*
  f poignée *f*
  r захват *m*

4326 **groove; ditch**
  d Nut *f*; Rastnut *f*; Einstich *m*; Rinne *f*
  f sillon *m*; rainure *f*; rigole *f*
  r канавка *f*; жёлоб *m*

4327 **gross bit rate**
  d Gesamtbitrate *f*; Summenbitrate *f*
  f vitesse *f* de bits grosse
  r полная скорость *f* [передачи] битов

4328 **gross index; main index; master index;
       primary index**
  d Großindex *m*; Hauptindex *m*
  f index *m* gros; index maître; index principal
  r старший индекс *m*; главный индекс

4329 **gross information content**
  d Gesamtinformationsgehalt *m*
  f contenu *m* total en information
  r полное содержание *n* информации

4330 **group**
  d Gruppe *f*
  f groupe *m*
  r группа *f*

4331 **group** *v*
  d gruppieren
  f grouper
  r группировать

4332 **group addressing**
  d Gruppenadressierung *f*
  f adressage *m* de groupe
  r групповая адресация *f*

4333 **group-address message**
  d Nachricht *f* mit Gruppenadressierung
  f message *m* d'adressage de groupe
  r сообщение *n* групповой адресации

4334 **group box**
  d Gruppenkasten *m*; Gruppenfeld *n*
  f zone *f* de groupe; boîte *f* à zone
  r поле *n* группы

4335 **group carry**
  d Gruppenübertrag *m*
  f retenue *f* groupée
  r групповой перенос *m*

4336 **group code**
  d Gruppencode *m*
  f code *m* de groupe
  r код *m* группы

4337 **group counter**
  d Gruppenzähler *m*
  f compteur *m* de groupes
  r счётчик *m* групп

  * **group delay** → 4339

4338 **group-delay distortion**
  d Gruppenlaufzeitverzerrung *f*
  f distorsion *f* de retard de groupe
  r искажение *n* группового времени
     распространения

4339 **group delay [time]; group retardation;
       envelope delay**
  d Gruppenlaufzeit *f*
  f temps *m* de transit de groupe; temps de
     propagation de groupe
  r групповое время *n* распространения

4340 **grouped data**
  d gruppierte Daten *pl*
  f données *fpl* groupées
  r сгруппированные данные *pl*

4341 **group icon**
  d Gruppensymbol *n*
  f icône *f* de groupe
  r значок *m* группы

4342 grouping
  d Gruppieren *n*; Gruppierung *f*
  f groupement *m*; groupage *m*
  r группирование *n*; группировка *f*

  * **group mark → 4343**

4343 group mark[er]
  d Gruppenmarke *f*
  f marque *f* de groupe; marqueur *m* de groupe
  r метка *f* группы; маркер *m* группы

4344 group marking
  d Gruppenmarkierung *f*
  f marquage *m* de groupe
  r маркирование *n* группы

  * **group retardation → 4339**

4345 group selection
  d Gruppenwahl *f*
  f sélection *f* de groupe
  r выбор *m* группы

4346 groupware
  d Groupware *f*
  f logiciel *m* de travail en groupe; synergiciel *m*; collecticiel *m*
  r групповое [программное] обеспечение *n*

  * **GSM → 4232**

  * **guard → 7449**

4347 guard ring; protection ring
       (in a tape reel)
  d Schutzring *m*
  f bague *f* de garde; anneau *m* de garde; anneau de protection
  r защитное кольцо *n*; охранное кольцо; кольцо защиты

4348 guard signal; protection signal
  d Ausblendsignal *n*; Schutzsignal *n*
  f signal *m* de garde; signal de protection
  r сигнал *m* защиты

4349 guest administration terminal
  d Gastverwaltungsterminal *n*
  f terminal *m* de gestion-clients
  r терминал *m* администрирования гостей

4350 guest book; visitor book
  d Gästebuch *n*
  f livre *m* des visiteurs; registre *m* des visiteurs; livre des invités; livre d'hôte
  r гостевая книга *f*; книга записей

  * **GUI → 4264**

4351 guidance; guide
  d Richtlinien *npl*; Führung *f*
  f guidage *m*; guide *m*
  r управление *n*; [на]ведение *n*

4352 guide *v*; lead *v*
  d führen; leiten; lenken
  f guider; conduire
  r руководить; водить

  * **guide → 4351, 8661**

  * **guide bar → 8661**

4353 guide mark; guide score; printed register mark
  d Richtpunkt *m*; Führungsstreifen *m*
  f marque *f* de guide
  r приводочная метка *f*

  * **guide score → 4353**

4354 gulp
  d kurze Bytegruppe *f*; "Schluck" *m*
  f groupe *m* d'octets court; "gorgée" *f*
  r группа *f* байтов; галп *m*

  * **GUP → 1780**

  * **gutter → 4355**

4355 gutter [margin]
  d Bundsteg *m*; Gasse *f* im Satz
  f marge *f* de reliure; gouttière *f*
  r внутреннее корешковое поле *n*; поле переплёта

H

4356 hacker
d Hacker *m*
f hacker *m*; hackeur *m*; pirate *m*; mordu *m* de
l'informatique; bidouilleur *m*
r хэкер *m*; несанкционированный
пользователь *m*

4357 hacking
d Anzapfen *n*; Aufhacken *n*
f piratage *m* informatique
r хакерство *n*

4358 hacking call
d Zerhackenaufruf *m*
f communication *f* pirate
r несанкционированный вызов *m*

4359 hairline
(thinnest visible space or rule)
d Haarstrich *m*
f trait *m* très fin
r линия *f* с толщиной волоса; волосная
линия; линия наименьшей толщины

4360 half-adder; semi-adder
d Halbadd[ier]er *m*
f demi-add[itionn]eur *m*;
semi-add[itionn]eur *m*
r полусумматор *m*

* **half-adjust** *v* → 8124

4361 half-byte; nibble; nybble; quadbit; tetrad
d Halbbyte *n*; Tetrade *f*
f demi-octet *m*; quartet *m*; combinaison *f* de
quatre bits; tétrade *f*
r полубайт *m*; [битовая] тетрада *f*;
четырёхбитовый набор *m*; четвёрка *f*

4362 half-carry
d Halbbyte-Übertrag *m*
f retenue *f* de demi-octet
r перенос *m* из полубайта

4363 half duplex; HDX; semiduplex
d halbduplex; Semiduplex-
f semiduplex; [de]mi-duplex
r полудуплексный

4364 half-duplex channel
d Halbduplexkanal *m*
f canal *m* semiduplex
r полудуплексный канал *m*

4365 half-duplex circuit
d Halbduplexverbindung *f*;
Wechselverkehrsverbindung *f*
f circuit *m* semiduplex
r полудуплексная схема *f*

4366 half-page
d Halbseite *f*
f semi-page *m*
r полстраница *f*

4367 half router
d Halbrouter *m*
f semi-routeur *m*
r полумаршрутизатор *m*

4368 half-select pulse
d Halbwählimpuls *m*
f impulsion *f* de demi-sélection
r импульс *m* полутока выборки

4369 half-tint; halftone
d Halbton *m*
f demi-teinte *f*; demi-ton *m*
r полутон *m*; полукраска *f*

* **halftone** → 4369

4370 halftone builder
d Halbtonbilder *m*
f bâtisseur *m* de demi-tons
r программа *f* построения полутонов

* **halftone dot** → 8240

* **halftone image** → 4317

4371 halftone raster; halftone screen
d Halbtonraster *m*
f rastre *m* de demi-teinte; trame *f* simili; trame
quartilée
r полутоновый растр *m*

* **halftone screen** → 4371

4372 halftone screen frequency
d Halbtonrasterfrequenz *f*
f fréquence *f* de trame quartilée
r линиатура *f* растра

4373 halftoning
d Halbtönung *f*; Halftoning *n*
f création de demi-teintes
r образование *n* полутонов

4374 half-word; semiword
d Halbwort *n*
f demi-mot *m*; semi-mot *m*
r полуслово *n*

4375 half-write pulse
d halber Schreibimpuls *m*
f impulsion *f* de demi-inscription
r импульс *m* записи методом полутоков

4376 halt; hold; stop
d Halt *m*; Stopp *m*
f arrêt *m*; halte *f*; stop *m*
r останов *m*

4377 halt signal; hold[ing] signal
d Haltesignal *n*; Stoppsignal *n*
f signal *m* d'arrêt; signal de maintien
r сигнал *m* останова

* **handheld** → 6743

* **handheld computer** → 6743

* **handheld scanner** → 4383

* **handheld scanning** → 5627

* **hand input** → 5626

* **handle** → 4325

4378 handle; arm
d Henkel *m*; Kurbel *f*; Zeiger *m*
f anse *f*; aiguille *f*
r ручка *f*; стрелка *f* [прибора]

4379 handle *v*; manipulate *v*
d behandeln; handhaben; manipulieren
f traiter; manipuler
r обрабатывать; манипулировать

* **handler** → 4382

4380 handler; manipulator
d Händler *m*
f manipulateur *m*; gérant *m*
r манипулятор *m*

* **handler program** → 4382

4381 handling; manipulation
d Behandlung *f*; Handhabung *f*; Manipulieren *n*
f maniement *m*; traitement *m*; manipulation *f*
r обработка *f*; манипуляция *f*

4382 handling program; handler [program]
d Bearbeitungsprogramm *n*;
Handhabungsprogramm *n*
f programme *m* de traitement
r программа *f* обработки

* **hand-operated scanner** → 4383

* **hand-printed character** → 4387

* **handprinting** → 4385

4383 hand scanner; portable scanner; handheld scanner; hand-operated scanner
d Handabtaster *m*; Handscanner *m*
f scanner *m* à main; scanner manuel
r ручной сканер *m*

* **handshake** → 109

4384 handshaking; receipt operation
d Handshaking *n*; Quittungsaustausch *m*;
Quittungsbetrieb *m*
f acquittement *m* de mise de liaison;
confirmation *f* de mise de liaison; régime *m*
de quittance
r квитирование *n* установления связи;
режим *m* квитирования

4385 handwriting; handprinting
d Druckschriftschreiben *n*; Handblockschrift *f*
f écriture *f* en lettres d'imprimerie
r ручной брусковый шрифт *m*

4386 handwriting recognition
d Handschrifterkennung *f*
f reconnaissance *f* d'écriture
r распознавание *n* рукописного текста

4387 handwritten character; hand-printed character
d handgeschriebenes Zeichen *n*;
Handschriftzeichen *n*
f caractère *m* manuscrit; caractère d'écriture
r рукописный знак *m*

4388 handwritten digits
d handgeschriebene Ziffern *fpl*
f chiffres *mpl* manuscrits
r рукописные цифры *fpl*

4389 hang *v*
d aufhängen
f suspendre; pendre
r зависать

4390 hanging; pending *adj*
d hängend; überhängend; wartend
f pendant; suspendu
r висячий; ожидающий

4391 hanging; hang up; suspension; suspending
d Aussetzen *n*; Suspendierung *f*;
nichtprogrammierter Schleifenstopp *m*;
Hänger *m*
f suspension *f*
r зависание *n*; временное прекращение *n*;
приостановка *f*

* **hang up** → 4391

* **hard** *adj* → 4396

4392 hard copy
  d Hartkopie *f*; Druckkopie *f*
  f copie *f* dure; copie imprimée; copie sur
  papier; tirage *m*; facsim *m*
  r твёрдая копия *f*; бумажная копия; печатная
  копия

4393 hard disk; fixed disk; rigid disk; platter
  d Festplatte *f*; Hard-Disk *f*
  f disque *m* dur; plateau *m*
  r жёсткий [магнитный] диск *m*

4394 hard [disk] drive; HDD; drive
  d Hard-Disk-Laufwerk *n*;
  Hard-Disk-Antrieb *m*; Hard[disk]drive *n*
  f unité *f* à disque dur; dispositif *m* à disque dur;
  lecteur *m* de disque
  r запоминающее устройство *n* на жёстком
  диске; накопитель *m* на жёстком диске

* **hard drive** → 4394

* **hard error** → 4401

* **hard failure** → 4401

* **hard image** → 2256

4395 hardware
  d Hardware *f*; Gerätetechnik *f*
  f matériel *m*; équipement *m*; hardware *m*
  r аппаратные средства *npl*; техническое
  обеспечение *n*

4396 hardware; hardwired; hard *adj*
  d Hardware-; gerätetechnisch
  f [en] matériel
  r аппаратный

4397 hardware assembler
  d Hardwareassembler *m*
  f assembleur *m* hardware
  r аппаратный ассемблер *m*

* **hardware clock** → 1746

4398 hardware-compatible
  d Hardware-kompatibel
  f compatible [en] matériel
  r аппаратно-совместимый

4399 hardware cursor
  d Hardwarecursor *m*
  f curseur *m* matériel
  r аппаратный курсор *m*

4400 hardware division
  d Divisionsrealisierung *f* mittels Hardware;
  verdrahtete Division *f*
  f division *f* par matériel
  r аппаратная реализация *f* деления

**4401 hard[ware] failure; solid failure; machine
  failure; hard error**
  d harter Ausfall *m*
  f défaillance *f* du matériel; défaillance solide;
  défaillance dure
  r аппаратная неисправность *f*; аппаратный
  сбой *m*; машинный сбой; устойчивый
  отказ *m*

4402 hardware geometry processing
  d Hardwareverarbeitung *f* der Geometrie
  f traitement *m* matériel de géométrie
  r аппаратная обработка *f* геометрии

4403 hardware-implemented
  d gerätetechnisch realisiert; hardwarerealisiert
  f réalisé [en] matériel
  r аппаратно-реализованный

* **hardware interrupt** → 4404

4404 hardware interrupt[ion]
  d Hardwareunterbrechung *f*
  f interruption *f* matérielle
  r аппаратное прерывание *n*

4405 hardware profile
  d Hardwareprofil *n*
  f profil *m* matériel
  r аппаратный профиль *m*; профиль
  аппаратной конфигурации

4406 hardware program
  d Hardware-Programm *n*; festverdrahtetes
  Programm *n*
  f programme *m* matériel
  r аппаратно-реализованная программа *f*

4407 hardware-software tradeoffs
  d Hardware-Software-Abstimmung *f*;
  Abwägung *f* zwischen Hardware und
  Software Realisierung
  f accord *m* entre matériel et logiciel
  r соотношение *n* аппаратных и
  программных средств

* **hardwired** → 4396, 10010

4408 hardwired knowledge
  d festverdrahtetes Wissen *n*
  f connaissances *fpl* [incorporées] en matériel
  r жёстко-встроенные знания *npl*

* **hardwired logic** → 10011

* **hash** → 2392, 4170

4409 hash function; hashing function
  d Hash-Funktion *f*;
       Speicherabbildungsfunktion *f*
  f fonction *f* hash
  r хэш-функция *f*

* **hashing** → 7597

* **hashing function** → 4409

4410 hash search
  d Hash-Suche *f*
  f recherche *f* par hachage
  r хэш-поиск *m*

* **hash symbol** → 2392

4411 hash table
  d Hash-Tabelle *f*
  f table *f* de hash-code; table de randomisation
  r хэш-таблица *f*

* **hash total** → 1659

* **hat** → 1437

* **hazard rate** → 3684

* **hazy** → 4149

* **HDBMS** → 4470

* **HDD** → 4394

* **HDF** → 4471

* **HDX** → 4363

4412 head
  d Kopf *m*
  f tête *f*
  r головка *f*; голова *f*

4413 head address byte
  d Kopf[adresse]byte *n*
  f octet *m* d'adresse de tête
  r байт *m* адреса головки

4414 head crash
  d Kopfabsturz *m*
  f effondrement *m* de tête
  r авария *f* головки

4415 header; heading; title
  d Titel *m*; Header *m*; Kopfteil *m*; Überschrift *f*
  f header *m*; titre *m*; en-tête *m*
  r заголовок *m*; титул *m*

4416 header bit
  d Kopfbit *n*
  f bit *m* d'en-tête
  r бит *m* заголовка

4417 header label
  d Kopfetikett *n*; Anfangsetikett *n*;
       Anfangskennsatz *m*
  f étiquette *f* d'en-tête; label *m* d'en-tête
  r [за]головная метка *f*

4418 header line; headline; heading line
  d Kopfzeile *f*; Anschriftzeile *f*; Titelzeile *f*;
       Überschriftzeile *f*
  f ligne *f* d'en-tête
  r заголовный ряд *m*; строка *f* заголовка

4419 header record; head[ing] record
  d Kopfsatz *m*; Vorsatz *m*
  f enregistrement *m* [d']en-tête
  r запись *f* заголовка

4420 head gap
  d Kopfluftspalt *m*;
       Kopf-Speichermedium-Luftspalt *m*
  f interstice *m* [de tête]
  r зазор *m* [магнитной] головки [и носителя]

* **heading** → 4415

* **heading line** → 4418

* **heading record** → 4419

* **headline** → 4418

4421 head-mounted display; HMD; head-up display; HUD; head-mounted screen; videocasque
  d Kopfbildschirm *m*; Videohelm *m*
  f écran *m* monté sur la tête; visiocasque *f*;
       casque *f* de visualisation; viseur *m* tête-haute;
       visière *f* stéréoscopique; casque de vision 3D
  r головной экран *m*; видеокаска *f*

* **head-mounted screen** → 4421

* **head-per-track disk** → 3866

* **head record** → 4419

4422 head stack
  d Magnetkopfgruppe *f*; Mehrspurmagnetkopf *m*
  f groupe *m* de têtes magnétiques
  r пакет *m* [магнитных] головок

4423 head tracking
  d Kopfverfolgung *f*
  f poursuite *m* de tête
  r прослеживание *n* головой

* **head-up display** → 4421

4424 heap
 d ungeordnetes Feld *n*; Häufung *f*
 f tableau *m* non ordonné
 r неупорядоченный массив *m*; частично
   упорядоченное полное бинарное дерево *n*

* **heap** → 4425

4425 heap-allocated memory; heap
 d Häufungsspeicher *m*
 f heap *m* (constitué de blocs mémoire gérés par
   le programme)
 r память *f* с неупорядоченным хранением
   данных; память типа "куча"

4426 heapsort
 d Heapsort *m*; Gruppensortieren *n*
 f tri[age] *m* arborescent
 r пирамидальная сортировка *f*; древовидная
   сортировка

4427 heat-sensitive paper
 d wärmeempfindliches Papier *n*
 f papier *m* thermosensible
 r термочувствительная бумага *f*

4428 heat sink
 d Kühlsenke *f*
 f dissipateur *m*
 r радиатор *m*; теплоотвод *m*

4429 heavy-duty software
 d Universalsoftware *f*
 f logiciel *m* universel
 r универсальное программное
   обеспечение *n*

* **helical scan** → 4430

4430 helical scan[ning]
 d Schrägspuraufzeichnung *f*
 f balayage *m* hélicoïdal; enregistrement *m* [par
   défilement] hélicoïdal
 r спиральная развёртка *f*

4431 helical scan tape drive
 d Schrägspuraufzeichnungsbandlaufwerk *n*
 f unité *f* de bande à balayage hélicoïdal
 r ленточное устройство *n* со спиральной
   развёрткой

* **help** → 282, 7427

4432 help button
 d Hilfe-Taste *f*
 f bouton *m* d'aide
 r кнопка *f* помощной информации

4433 help desk
 d Dienstelle *f* "Betreuung"
 f assistance *f* technique; service *m* d'assistance
 r служба *f* технической помощи

* **helper** → 4434, 10019

4434 helper [application]; helper program
 d Helfer-Anwenderprogramm *n*;
   Helfer-Anwendungsprogramm *n*
 f application *f* d'assistance
 r вспомагательное приложение *n*

* **helper program** → 4434

4435 help file
 d Hilfsdatei *f*
 f fichier *m* d'aide
 r помощный файл *m*

* **help information** → 7427

4436 help menu
 d Hilfemenü *n*; Bedienungshilfemenü *n*
 f menu *m* d'aide; menu d'assistance
 r меню *n* подсказки; вспомагательное меню

4437 help request
 d Hilfsanforderung *f*
 f demande *f* d'aide
 r запрос *m* консультативной информации

4438 help screen
 d Hilfsbildschirm *m*
 f écran *m* d'aide
 r вспомагательный экран *m*

4439 help text
 d Hilfstext *m*
 f texte *m* d'aide
 r вспомагательный текст *m*

4440 help window
 d Hilfefenster *n*
 f fenêtre *f* d'aide; fenêtre assistante
 r окно *n* подсказки; окно справки

4441 heredity; inheritance
 d Vererbung *f*; Erbung *f*
 f hérédité *f*; héritage *m*
 r наследственность *f*; наследование *n*

4442 hertz; Hz
 d Hertz *m*
 f hertz *m*
 r герц *m*

**4443 heterogeneous; nonhomogeneous;
   inhomogeneous**
 d heterogen; inhomogen; nichthomogen;
   unhomogen

f hétérogène; non homogène; inhomogène
r гетерогенный; разнородный

4444 heterogeneous [computer] network
   d heterogenes Rechnernetz *n*
   f réseau *m* [d'ordinateurs] hétérogène
   r гетерогенная [компьютерная] сеть *f*

   * **heterogeneous network** → 4444

4445 heterogeneous simulation
   d heterogene Simulation *f*
   f simulation *f* hétérogène
   r гетерогенная симуляция *f*

4446 heterostructure
   d Heterostruktur *f*
   f hétérostructure *f*
   r гетероструктура *f*

4447 heuristic
   d heuristisch
   f [h]euristique ·
   r эвристический

4448 heuristic algorithm
   d heuristischer Algorithmus *m*
   f algorithme *m* heuristique
   r эвристический алгоритм *m*

4449 heuristic data
   d heuristische Daten *pl*
   f données *fpl* heuristiques
   r эвристические данные *pl*

4450 heuristic programming
   d heuristische Programmierung *f*
   f programmation *f* heuristique
   r эвристическое программирование *n*

4451 heuristic routing
   d heuristische Routenwahl *f*
   f acheminement *m* heuristique
   r эвристический выбор *m* маршрута;
      эвристическая маршрутизация *f*

4452 heuristics
   d Heuristik *f*
   f [h]euristique *f*
   r эвристика *f*

4453 heuristic seeking
   d heuristisches Suchen *n*
   f recherche *f* heuristique
   r эвристический поиск *m*

   * **hex** → 4454

4454 hex[adecimal]; sedecimal
   d hexadezimal; sedezimal

f hexadécimal; sexadécimal
r шестнадцатеричный

4455 hexadecimal coding
   d hexadezimale Codierung *f*
   f codage *m* hexadécimal
   r шестнадцатеричное кодирование *n*

4456 hexadecimal number
   d Hexadezimalzahl *f*; Hexzahl *f*
   f nombre *m* hexadécimal
   r шестнадцатеричное число *n*

4457 hexadecimal [number] system
   d Hexadezimal[zahlen]system *n*
   f système *m* hexadécimal; système de nombres
      hexadécimaux
   r шестнадцатеричная система *f* счисления

   * **hexadecimal system** → 4457

   * **hibernating process** → 558

4458 hidden; covert
   d versteckt; verdeckt
   f caché; masqué
   r скрытый

4459 hidden buffer
   d versteckter Puffer *m*
   f tampon *m* caché
   r скрытый буфер *m*

4460 hidden response
   d latente Reaktion *f*
   f réaction *f* latente
   r скрытая реакция *f*

4461 hidden variable
   d verborgene Variable *f*
   f variable *f* cachée
   r скрытая переменная *f*

4462 hide command
   d Versteckungsbefehl *m*
   f commande *f* de masquage
   r команда *f* скрытия; команда маскирования

4463 hiding
   d Versteckung *f*
   f masquage *m*
   r скрытие *n*

4464 hierarchical
   d hierarchisch
   f hiérarchique
   r иерархический

4465 hierarchical access method
   d hierarchische Zugriffsmethode *f*

f méthode f d'accès hiérarchique
r иерархический метод m доступа

4466 hierarchical classification
d hierarchische Klassifikation f
f classification f hiérarchique
r иерархическая классификация f

4467 hierarchical coding
d hierarchische Codierung f
f codage m hiérarchique
r иерархическое кодирование n

4468 hierarchical computer system;
master-slave computer system
d hierarchisches Rechnersystem n
f système m d'ordinateurs hiérarchique
r иерархическая компьютерная система f

4469 hierarchical database
d hierarchische Datenbasis f
f base f de données hiérarchique
r иерархическая база f данных

4470 hierarchical database management system;
HDBMS
d hierarchisches
Datenbasis-Managementsystem n
f système m de gestion de base de données
hiérarchique
r иерархическая система f управления баз
данных

4471 hierarchical data format; HDF
d hierarchisches Datenformat n
f format m de données hiérarchique
r иерархический формат m данных

4472 hierarchical file system
d hierarchisches Dateisystem n
f structure f arborescente des fichiers
r иерархическая файловая система f

4473 hierarchical menu
d hierarchisches Menü n
f menu m hiérarchique
r иерархическое меню n

4474 hierarchical network
d hierarchisches Netz n
f réseau m hiérarchique
r иерархическая сеть f

4475 hierarchy
d Hierarchie f; Rangordnung f; Rangfolge f
f hiérarchie f
r иерархия f

4476 hierarchy chart
d hierarchisches Ablaufdiagramm n

f organigramme m hiérarchique de programme
r иерархическая схема f программы

4477 high address
d hohe Adresse f
f adresse f haute
r высокий адрес m

4478 high bit rate
d hohe Bitrate f
f vitesse f [de transfert] de bits élevée; débit m
binaire élevé
r высокая скорость f [передачи] битов

* **high byte** → 4499

4479 high-contrast image
d Bild n mit scharfem Kontrast
f image f de contraste haute
r высококонтрастное изображение n

4480 high data rate
d hohe Datenrate f
f vitesse f [de transfert] de données élevée;
débit m de données élevé
r высокая скорость f [передачи] данных

4481 high definition
d hohe Schärfe f
f définition f haute
r высокая чёткость f

* **high-definition** adj → 4507

4482 high density
d Hochdruck m
f haute densité f
r высокое давление n; высокая плотность f

4483 high-density bipolar coding
d hochdichte Bipolarcodierung f
f codage m bipolaire à haute densité
r биполярное кодирование n с высокой
плотностью

4484 high-end computer
d High-End-Rechner m; Rechner m im oberen
Kostenbereich
f ordinateur m haut de gamme
r компьютер m старшей модели

4485 high-end scanner
d leistungsfähiger Scanner m
f scanner m haut de gamme
r сканер m высшего класса

4486 higher-level protocol
d höheres Protokoll n
f protocole m de niveau élevé
r протокол m высокого уровня

4487 highest byte
 d höchstes Byte *n*
 f octet *m* [de l'ordre] le plus haut
 r самый старший байт *m*

4488 high gain
 d hohe Verstärkung *f*
 f gain *m* élevé
 r большое усиление *n*

4489 high-level data-link control; HLDLC
 d Hochpegel-Datenleitungssteuerung *f*
 f commande *f* de liaison de données de niveau
    élevé
 r высокоуровневое управление *n* каналами
    передачи данных

4490 high-level language; high-order language
 d höhere Sprache *f*; höherwertige Sprache
 f langage *m* de niveau haut
 r язык *m* высокого уровня

4491 high-level signal
 d Signal *n* mit hohem Niveau
 f signal *m* de niveau élevé; signal supérieur
 r сигнал *m* высокого уровня

4492 highlight *v*; emphasize *v*
 d hervorheben
 f mettre en évidence
 r маркировать освещением; подсвечивать;
    высвечивать

4493 highlighted
 d hervorgehoben
 f en surbrillance; contrasté
 r высвеченный

4494 highlighted background
 d hervorgehobener Hintergrund *m*
 f fond *m* surintensifié; fond contrasté
 r подсвеченный фон *m*

4495 highlighted row
 d hervorgehobene Zeile *f*; Hochlicht-Zeile *f*;
    Spitzlicht-Zeile *f*; Glanzlicht-Zeile *f*
 f ligne *f* surintensifiée
 r подсвеченная строка *f*; высвеченная строка

4496 highlighting; emphasis
 d Hervorhebung *f*; Hervorheben *n*;
    Highlighting *n*
 f mise *f* en évidence; marquage *m* [par
    éclairage]
 r маркирование *n* [осветлением];
    выделение *n* осветлением;
    подсвечивание *n*; высвечивание *n*

4497 highlight *v* menu
 d Menü hervorheben

 f mettre en évidence de menu
 r подсвечивать меню; высвечивать меню

4498 high memory area; HMA
 d oberer Speicherbereich *m*
 f zone *f* de mémoire haute; mémoire *f* haute
 r верхняя область *f* памяти

4499 high[-order] byte
 d hohes Byte *n*
 f octet *m* [de l'ordre] haut
 r старший байт *m*

 * **high-order language** → 4490

4500 high-order system
 d System *n* mit höherer Ordnung
 f système *m* d'ordre haut
 r старшая система *f*

4501 high-order zeros; left-hand zeros
 d obere Nullen *fpl*; führende Nullen
 f zéros *mpl* supérieurs; zéros sans valeur
 r нули *mpl* в старших разрядах; незначащие
    нули

4502 high-pass filter
 d Hochpassfilter *m*
 f filtre *m* passe-haut
 r фильтр *m* верхних частот;
    высокочастотный фильтр

 * **high-performance computing** → 9046

**4503 high-performance parallel interface;
       HiPPI**
 d Hochleistungsparallelschnittstelle *f*
 f interface *f* parallèle à haute performance
 r высокоскоростный параллельный
    интерфейс *m*

4504 high-performance system
 d Hochleistungssystem *n*
 f système *m* de grande puissance; système de
    haute performance
 r система *f* высокой производительности

4505 high-redundant code
 d hochredundanter Code *m*
 f code *m* à haute redondance
 r высокоизбыточный код *m*;
    сверхизбыточный код

4506 high-resistance paper
 d elektrostatisches Papier *n*
 f papier *m* électrostatique
 r электростатическая бумага *f*

4507 high-resolution; hi-res; high-definition *adj*
 d hochauflösend

f à résolution élevée; à haute définition
r с высокой разрешающей способностью; с
высокой резкостью

4508 high-resolution screen
d hochauflösender Bildschirm *m*
f écran *m* à haute résolution
r экран *m* с высокой разрешающей
способностью

4509 highspeed; fast[-acting]
d schnell; mit hoher Geschwindigkeit;
Hochgeschwindigkeits-
f à vitesse élevée; à grande vitesse; rapide
r высокоскоростный; быстрый;
быстродействующий

* **highspeed carry** → 5497

4510 highspeed channel
d Hochleistungskanal *m*;
Hochgeschwindigkeitskanal *m*
f canal *m* de grande vitesse
r высокоскоростный канал *m*; быстрый
канал

4511 highspeed computer; fast computer
d schneller Rechner *m*
f ordinateur *m* rapide
r высокоскоростный компьютер *m*;
быстродействующий компьютер

4512 highspeed data module
d Datenmodul *m* mit hoher Geschwindigkeit
f module *m* de transmission de données à haute
vitesse
r быстродействующий модуль *m* передачи
данных

**4513 highspeed data transmission; fast data
transmission**
d Hochgeschwindigkeitsdatenübertragung *f*;
schnelle Datenübertragung *f*
f transmission *f* de données rapide
r [высоко]скоростная передача *f* данных

* **highspeed information retrieval** → 3709

4514 highspeed optical LAN
d optisches lokales Netz *n* mit hoher
Geschwindigkeit
f réseau *m* optique local à grande vitesse
r высокоскоростная оптическая местная
сеть *f*

4515 highspeed optical transmission system
d optisches Übertragungssystem *n* mit hoher
Geschwindigkeit
f système *m* de transmission optique à grande
vitesse

r высокоскоростная оптическая система *f*
передачи

* **HiPPI** → 4503

* **hi-res** → 4507

4516 history
d Geschichte *f*
f historique *m*
r предыстория *f*; хронология *f*

4517 hit
d Treffer *m*; Erfolg *m*
f impact *m*; succès *m*; coïncidence *f*
r успех *m*; попадание *n*; результативное
обращение *n*; ответная справка *f*

* **hit** *v* → 7238

4518 hitless
d erfolglos
f sans impact; sans succès
r безуспешный

4519 hit list
d Trefferliste *f*
f liste *f* d'impacts
r список *m* попаданий

4520 hit rate; hit ratio
d Trefferquote *f*; Trefferverhältnis *n*
f rapport *m* de succès; taux *m* de réussite
r коэффициент *m* эффективности [поиска]

* **hit ratio** → 4520

* **HLDLC** → 4489

* **HMA** → 4498

* **HMD** → 4421

4521 Hoare logic
d Hoare-Logik *f*
f logique *f* de Hoare
r хоаровская логика *f* (формализм для
частичного доказательства правильности
программ)

* **hold** → 4376, 4523

* **hold circuit** → 4524

4522 hold condition; hold state
d Haltezustand *m*; Haltebedingung *f*
f condition *f* de maintien
r состояние *n* блокировки; условие *n*
блокировки; состояние захвата

* holder → 9060

4523 hold[ing]
    d Halten *n*; Anhalten *n*
    f maintien *m*
    r задержка *f*; удержание *n*

* holding → 5454, 8922

4524 hold[ing] circuit
    d Warteschaltung *f*; Halteschaltung *f*;
       Haltekreis *m*
    f circuit *m* de maintien
    r схема *f* задержки; схема блокировки

* holding signal → 4377

4525 hold[ing] time
    d Haltezeit *f*
    f temps *m* de maintien; temps de stockage
    r время *n* удержания; время
       [промежуточного] сохранения

* hold signal → 4377

* hold state → 4522

* hold time → 4525

* hologram memory → 4526

4526 holographic memory; hologram memory
    d Hologrammspeicher *m*
    f hologramme-mémoire *f*
    r голографическая память *f*

4527 holographic scanner
    d holografischer Abtaster *m*
    f scanneur *m* holographique
    r голографический сканер *m*

4528 holographic storage
    d holografische Speicherung *f*
    f stockage *m* holographique
    r голографическое запоминание *n*

4529 holography
    d Holografie *f*
    f holographie *f*
    r голография *f*

4530 holy war; flame war
    (in a forum)
    d heiliger Krieg *m*
    f guerre *f* sainte; guerre d'insultes
    r бесконечный спор *m*; священная война *f* (в
       электронной переписке)

4531 home; domestic; in-house
    d heimisch; inländisch; Inland-; Haus-;
       in-house

    f domestique; propre
    r местный; домашний; собственный

4532 home address
    d Hausadresse *f*; Spuradresse *f*
    f adresse *f* domestique; adresse de piste
    r собственный адрес *m*; внутренний адрес

4533 homebanking
    d Bankgeschäfte *npl* von zu Hause;
       Homebanking *n*
    f accès *m* bancaire domestique
    r домашний доступ *m* к банковским счётам;
       локальный доступ к банковским счётам

* homebrew → 4539

* homebrew software → 4539

4534 home correction
    d manuelle Fehlerkorrektur *f* im
       Lokaldatenkanal; Fehlerkorrektur bei
       Lokalverarbeitung
    f correction *f* d'erreur du canal de données local
    r коррекция *f* ошибки в местном канале
       данных

4535 home data channel; local data channel
    d Lokaldatenkanal *m*
    f canal *m* de données local
    r местный канал *m* данных; локальный
       информационный канал

4536 home [data] register
    d Lokal[daten]register *n*
    f registre *m* [de données] local
    r локальный регистр *m* [данных]

4537 home directory; base directory; source
    directory
    d Heimatverzeichnis *n*
    f catalogue *m* de base; répertoire *m* d'origine
    r базовый каталог *m*; исходный каталог

4538 home down
    (on a screen)
    d Anfang *m* letzte Zeile
    f début *m* de dernière ligne
    r начало *n* последней строки

4539 homegrown software; homebrew
    [software]
    d hausgemachte Software *f*
    f logiciel *m* maison
    r некоммерческое программное
       обеспечение *n*; доморощённое
       программное обеспечение

4540 Home key
    d Home-Taste *f*; Rückkehrtaste *f*

f touche f de renversement; touche de remise
en position initiale
r клавиша f Home; клавиша возврата в
исходное положение

4541 home LAN; inbuilding local network
d lokales Heimnetz n; lokales Hausnetz n
f réseau m local domestique
r местная домовая сеть f

* **home location → 4543**

* **home loop → 6071**

4542 home page; welcome page; entry page
d Hauptseite f; Leitseite f
f page f propre; page personnelle; page
d'accueil
r собственная страница f

4543 home position; home location
(on a screen)
d Grundstellung f; Ausgangsstellung f;
Ausgangsposition f
f position f initiale
r исходное положение n

4544 home record; local record
d Haussatz m; Mitschreiben n
f enregistrement m domestique; enregistrement
de service; écriture f locale
r начальная запись f; служебная запись;
собственная запись

* **home register → 4536**

4545 home up
(on a screen)
d Anfang m erste Zeile
f début m de première ligne
r начало n первой строки

4546 home video market
d Heim-Videomarkt m
f vidéo-marché f domestique
r домашний видео-рынок m

4547 home video program
d Heim-Videoprogramm n
f vidéo-programme m domestique
r домашняя видео-программа f

* **homework → 9230**

4548 homogeneous network
d homogenes Netz n
f réseau m homogène
r однородная сеть f

4549 honored interrupt

d zu bearbeitender Interrupt m
f interruption f prise en compte
r прерывание n, принимаемое на обработку

* **hookup → 2377**

* **hop → 5185, 6135**

**4550 horizontal alignment; horizontal
justification**
d horizontale Ausrichtung f
f alignement m horizontal
r горизонтальное выравнивание n

4551 horizontal bar chart
d horizontales Streifendiagramm n
f diagramme m à bandes horizontaux
r горизонтальная ленточная диаграмма f

4552 horizontal data flow
d horizontaler Datenfluss m
f flux m des données horizontal
r горизонтальный поток m данных

4553 horizontal folding
d horizontale Faltung f
f plissement m horizontal
r горизонтальная свёртка f

4554 horizontal frequency
(of a screen)
d horizontale Frequenz f
f fréquence f horizontale
r горизонтальная частота f

* **horizontal justification → 4550**

4555 horizontal list box
d horizontales Listenfeld n
f zone f de liste déroulante horizontale
r горизонтальное поле n списка

4556 horizontal microprogramming
d horizontale Mikroprogrammierung f
f microprogrammation f horizontale
r горизонтальное микропрограммирование n

4557 horizontal resolution
d Horizontalauflösung f;
Horizontalauflösungsvermögen n
f résolution f horizontale
r разрешающая способность f по
горизонтали

4558 horizontal ruler
d horizontales Lineal n
f règle f horizontale
r горизонтальная измерительная линейка f

4559 **horizontal scanning; line scanning; stripe scanning**
 d horizontale Abtastung *f*; Zeilenabtastung *f*
 f balayage *m* horizontal; base *f* de temps des lignes; exploration *f* par lignes
 r горизонтальная развёртка *f*; строчная развёртка

 * **horizontal screen partitioning** → 4560

4560 **horizontal screen split; horizontal screen partitioning**
 d horizontale Teilung *f* des Bildshirms
 f splittage *m* horizontal d'écran
 r горизонтальное расщепление *n* экрана

4561 **horizontal scrollbar**
 d horizontale Bildlaufleiste *f*
 f barre *f* de défilement horizontale
 r горизонтальная линейка *f* просмотра

4562 **horizontal scrolling; left-right scrolling**
 (of screen image)
 d horizontaler Bildlauf *m*; horizontale Bild[schirmzeilen]verschiebung *f*
 f défilement *m* horizontal; déplacement *m* horizontal
 r горизонтальная прокрутка *f*

4563 **horizontal split bar**
 d horizontaler Fensterteiler *m*
 f barre *f* de fractionnement horizontale
 r горизонтальная линия *f* разбиения

 * **horizontal tab** → 4564

4564 **horizontal tab[ulation character]**
 d Horizontaleinstellung *f*; horizontaler Tabulator *m*
 f caractère *m* de tabulation horizontale
 r знак *m* горизонтальной табуляции

 * **horse** → 876

 * **host** → 4565

4565 **host [computer]; host machine; hostname computer**
 d Wirtsrechner *m*; Wirt *m*; Host[rechner] *m*; Hostcomputer *m*; Zentralrechnersystem *n*
 f ordinateur *m* hôte; hôte *m*
 r ведущий компьютер *m*; хост *m*

 * **hoster** → 9978

 * **hosting** → 4566

4566 **hosting [service]**
 d Hosting *n*
 f hébergement *m*

 r бронирование *n* памяти для размещения информации; услуга *f* по размещению информации; хостинг *m*

4567 **host interface**
 d Hostinterface *n*; Hostschnittstelle *f*
 f interface *f* de hôte
 r интерфейс *m* хоста

 * **host machine** → 4565

4568 **host mailbox**
 d Host-Briefkasten *m*; Zentralbriefkasten *m*
 f boîte *f* hôte
 r ведущий почтовый ящик *m*

 * **hostname computer** → 4565

 * **hot backup** → 4571

 * **hot image** → 1723

4569 **hot insertion; hot plugging**
 d warme Einfügung *f*; warmer Einsatz *m*; Heißeinfügung *f*
 f insertion *f* à chaud
 r горячая вставка *f*; горячее подсоединение *n* (без выключения)

 * **hotkey** → 8517

 * **hotline** → 9146

4570 **hotlist**
 d heiße Liste *f*
 f liste *f* de signets; liste de priviléguée; mémo *m* de signets
 r горячий список *m*

 * **hot plugging** → 4569

4571 **hot reserve; hot backup**
 d heißer Backup *m*
 f réservation *f* chaude
 r горячее резервирование *n*

4572 **hot site**
 d heiße Seite *f*
 f salle *f* redondante; centre *m* miroir; centre de relève immédiate
 r горячий сайт *m*

4573 **hotspot; clickable area**
 d Hotspot *m*; klickbarer Bereich *m*; heißer Fleck *m*
 f point *m* d'ancrage; point chaud; zone *f* sensible; zone cliquable
 r горячее пятно *n*; горячая точка *f*; область *f* нажатия кнопки

* housekeeping → 4574

4574 housekeeping [operation]; bookkeeping
     [operation]
  d Systemverwaltung[soperation] *f*;
     Systemorganisation[sarbeit] *f*
  f organisation *f* des opérations; actions *fpl* de
     service
  r организация *f* вычислительного процесса;
     служебные действия *npl*

* HTML → 4598

4575 HTML document
  d HTML-Dokument *n*
  f document *m* HTML
  r документ *m*, составленный
     гипертекстовым метаязыком

4576 HTML editor
  d HTML-Editor *m*
  f éditeur *m* HTML
  r редактор *m* HTML

4577 HTML file
  d HTML-Datei *f*
  f fichier *m* HTML
  r файл *m* гипертекстового метаязыка

4578 HTML tools
  d HTML-Werkzeugsatz *m*
  f outils *mpl* HTML
  r инструменты *mpl* гипертекстового
     метаязыка

* HTTP → 4599

4579 hub
  d Bandkern *m*
  f noyau *m* de bande
  r сердечник *m* для ленты

* hub → 1321, 7004

* HUD → 4421

* hull → 3451

* human language → 6041

4580 human mistake; operator error; bust
  d Bedienungsfehler *m*
  f erreur *f* humaine
  r ошибка *f* оператора

4581 hybrid
  d Hybrid-
  f hybride
  r гибридный

4582 hybrid access
  d hybrider Zugriff *m*
  f accès *m* hybride
  r гибридный доступ *m*

* hybrid circuit → 4585

4583 hybrid computer; analog-digital computer;
     digital-analog computer
  d Hybridrechner *m*
  f ordinateur *m* hybride
  r гибридный компьютер *m*

4584 hybrid data converter
  d Hybriddatenkonverter *m*
  f convertisseur *m* hybride de données
  r гибридный преобразователь *m* данных

4585 hybrid [integrated] circuit
  d [integrierte] Hybridschaltung *f*;
     Hybridschaltkreis *m*
  f circuit *m* [intégré] hybride
  r гибридная [интегральная] схема *f*

4586 hybrid language
  d Mischsprache *f*; hybride Sprache *f*
  f langage *m* hybride
  r гибридный язык *m*

* hybrid network → 4587

4587 hybrid[-type] network
  d Mischformnetz *n*
  f réseau *m* hybride
  r гибридная сеть *f*

4588 hypercycle
  d Hyperzyklus *m*; Überkreis *m*
  f hypercycle *m*
  r гиперцикл *m*

4589 hypergraph
  d Hypergraph *m*
  f hypergraphe *m*
  r гиперграф *m*

4590 hypergraphics
  d Hypergrafik *f*
  f hypergraphique *m*
  r гиперграфика *f*

4591 hyperimage
  d Hyperbild *n*
  f hyperimage *f*
  r гиперизображение *n*

4592 hyperlink
  d Hyperlink *n*
  f hyperlien *m*
  r гиперсвязь *f*; гиперссылка *f*

4593 hypermedia
 d Hypermedien *npl*; querverweisende
   Medien *npl*
 f hypermédia *m*
 r гиперсредства *npl* информации;
   гипермедиа *f*

4594 hyperspace
 d Hyperraum *m*
 f hyperespace *m*
 r гиперпространство *n*

4595 hypertext
 d Hypertext *m*; querverweisender Text *m*
 f hypertexte *m*
 r гипертекст *m*

4596 hypertext browser
 d Hypertext-Browser *m*
 f module *m* de revue hypertexte
 r гипертекстовой модуль *m* рассмотрения

4597 hypertext link
 d Hypertext-Verknüpfung *f*;
   Hypertext-Verbindung *f*
 f lien *m* hypertexte
 r гипертекстовая связь *f*

 * **hypertext markup language** → 4598

**4598 hypertext metalanguage; hypertext
   markup language; HTML**
 d Hypertext-Metasprache *f*;
   Hypertext-Markierungssprache *f*;
   Hypertext-Auszeichnungssprache *f*
 f métalangage *m* hypertexte
 r гипертекстовой метаязык *m*

4599 hypertext transfer protocol; HTTP
 d Hypertext-Übertragungsprotokoll *n*
 f protocole *m* de transfert d'hypertexte;
   protocole HTTP
 r протокол *m* гипертекстовой передачи

4600 hypervisor
 d Hypervisor *m*
 f hyperviseur *m*
 r гипервизор *m*

4601 hyphen
 d Bindestrich *m*; Trennstrich *m*; Mittelstrich *m*
 f trait *m* d'union; tiret *m*
 r дефис *m*; тире *n*; знак *m* переноса

4602 hyphenating; hyphenation
 d Silbentrennung *f*; Worttrennung *f*
 f coupage *m* de mot; coupure *f* de mot
 r разбивка *f* по слогам; расстановка *f*
   дефисов; перенос *m* слов

 * **hyphenation** → 4602

 * **hysteresis cycle** → 5572

 * **hysteresis loop** → 5572

 * **Hz** → 4442

I

* IC → 4966

4603 icon; pictogram
d Ikone f; Piktogramm n
f icône m; icone m; graphisme m;
pictogramme m
r икона f; значок m; пиктограмма f

4604 icon bar
d Ikonstreifen m
f barre f d'icônes
r полоса f икон

**4605 icon-based user interface; icon-oriented
user interface; icon-driven interface**
d bildsymbolgestützte Bedienerschnittstelle f;
symbolgesteuerte Schnittstelle f
f interface f d'utilisateur à la base d'icônes;
interface gestionnée par icônes
r иконический пользовательский
интерфейс m; пиктографический
интерфейс

* icon-driven interface → 4605

4606 iconic
d ikonisch
f iconique
r иконический; пиктографический

4607 iconic model
d ikonisches Modell n
f modèle m iconique
r портретная модель f

**4608 iconic representation; pictogram
representation**
d ikonische Darstellung f
f représentation f iconique
r иконическое представление n;
пиктографическое представление

4609 iconic technique
d ikonische Technik f
f technique f iconique
r пиктографическая техника f

4610 iconize v; stow v; shrink v
(of a window)
d ikonizieren
f icôniser
r свёртывать в пиктограмму; закрывать

4611 icon menu
d ikonisches Menü n
f menu m iconique
r пиктографическое меню n

* iconographic → 6980

* icon-oriented user interface → 4605

4612 icons arrangement
d Ikonenanordnung f
f arrangement m d'icônes
r перестановка f икон; размещение n икон;
расположение n икон

* ICW → 5055

* ID → 4618

* IDB → 4650

4613 identical
d identisch
f identique
r идентичный; тождественный

4614 identification
d Identifikation f; Identifizieren n;
Kennzeichnung f
f identification f
r идентификация f; обозначение n;
отождествление n

**4615 identification card; personality card;
badge**
d Identifikationskarte f; Ausweis m
f carte f d'identification; badge m; jeton m
r идентифицирующая карта f; жетон m

4616 identification character
d Identifikationszeichen n; Kennzeichen n
f caractère m d'identification
r идентифицирующий символ m; символ
идентификации

4617 identification protocol
d Identifizierungsprotokoll n
f protocole m d'identification
r протокол m идентификации

* identificator → 4618

4618 identifier; identificator; ID
d Identifikator m; Bezeichner m;
Identifizierer m
f identificateur m
r идентификатор m

4619 identify v
d identifizieren; gleichsetzen

f identifier
r идентифицировать; отождествлять

4620 identifying signal
   d Kennsignal *n*
   f signal *m* d'identification
   r сигнал *m* идентификации

4621 identity
   d Identität *f*
   f identité *f*
   r тождество *n*; идентитет *m*; идентичность *f*;
   тождественность *f*

   * **identity gate** → 3469

   * **idle** → 1044

4622 idle channel; free channel
   d unbelegter Kanal *m*; Ruhekanal *m*;
   Freikanal *m*
   f canal *m* disponible; canal libre; canal à
   relâche
   r незанятый канал *m*

4623 idle channel enable
   d Ruhekanalfreigabe *f*
   f activation *f* de canal disponible
   r разрешение *n* незанятого канала

4624 idle channel noise
   d Freikanalgeräusch *m*; Ruhekanalgeräusch *m*
   f bruit *m* de canal disponible
   r шум *m* незанятого канала

**4625 idle character; dummy character; nil
   symbol; null character**
   d Blindzeichen *n*; Nullzeichen *n*
   f caractère *m* inutile; caractère à vide; caractère
   nul
   r фиктивный символ *m*; псевдосимвол *m*;
   пустой символ; холостой символ;
   нуль-символ *m*

4626 idle condition; idle state
   d Ruhelage *f*; Freizustand *m*
   f état *m* libre; état à vide
   r холостое состояние *n*; состояние
   бездействия

   * **idle cycle** → 4628

4627 idle interval monitoring
   d Schreibpauseüberwachung *f*
   f monitorage *m* d'intervalle à vide
   r управление *n* холостым интервалом

**4628 idle loop; idle cycle; idling cycle; blank
   cycle; null cycle**

   d Ruheschleife *f*; Leer[lauf]gang *m*;
   Nullzyklus *m*
   f boucle *f* à vide; cycle *m* à vide; cycle blanc;
   cycle nul
   r холостой цикл *m*

4629 idle mode
   d Leermodus *m*; Leerlaufbetrieb *m*
   f mode *m* [de marche] à vide
   r режим *m* холостого хода; режим простоя

4630 idle signal
   d Leerzeichen *n*
   f signal *m* libre
   r холостой сигнал *m*; фиктивный сигнал

   * **idle state** → 4626

4631 idle time
   d Leer[lauf]zeit *f*
   f temps *m* à vide; temps mort
   r время *n* простоя

   * **idling cycle** → 4628

   * **IDN** → 4970

   * **ier** → 5995

4632 if-clause
   d Wenn-Klausel *n*
   f condition *f* "if"
   r условие *n* "если"

4633 if-statement
   d Wenn-Anweisung *f*
   f instruction *f* "if"
   r оператор *m* "если"; условный оператор

4634 ignore *v*
   d ignorieren; fortlassen
   f ignorer
   r игнорировать; пропускать

4635 ignore bit
   d Leerbit *n*
   f bit *m* à ignorer
   r пустой бит *m*

   * **ignore character** → 3825

   * **ignore sign** → 8738

   * **IIL** → 4971

   * **I²L** → 4971

4636 ill-conditioned matrix
   d schlechtkonditionierte Matrix *f*

f matrice *f* mal-conditionnée
r плохо обусловленная матрица *f*

* **illegal** → **5115**

* **illegal code** → **5118**

4637 illegal-command check;
improper-command check
d Prüfung *f* auf unzulässige Befehle
f test *m* d'instructions illégales
r контроль *m* на наличие запрещённых
команд

4638 illegal format
d illegales Format *n*; unerlaubtes Format
f format *m* illégal
r недействительный формат *m*

4639 illegal operation code
d unzulässiger Operationscode *m*; nicht
decodierbarer Operationscode *m*
f code *m* d'opération interdit
r запрещённый код *m* операции

* **illuminate** *v* → **5358**

4640 illumination; lighting
d Illumination *f*; Ausleuchtung *f*; Beleuchtung *f*
f illumination *f*; éclairement *m*; éclairage *m*
r иллюминация *f*; освещение *n*

4641 illumination data
d Beleuchtungsdaten *pl*
f données *fpl* d'illumination
r данные *pl* освещения

4642 illumination processor
d Beleuchtungsprozessor *m*
f processeur *m* d'illumination
r процессор *m* освещения

4643 illustration
d Illustration *f*
f illustration *f*
r иллюстрация *f*

* **illustrational** → **6980**

* **illustration program** → **2083**

* **illustrative** → **6980**

4644 illustrator
(a software)
d Illustrator *m*
f illustrateur *m*
r иллюстратор *m*

* **illustratory** → **6980**

4645 image; pattern; picture
d Bild *n*; Abbild *n*
f image *f*
r образ *m*; изображение *n*

4646 image analysis
d Bildanalyse *f*
f analyse *f* d'image
r анализ *m* изображения

* **image buffer** → **4037**

4647 image coding; picture coding
d Bildcodierung *f*
f codage *m* d'image
r кодирование *n* изображения

* **image communication** → **9909**

4648 image compression; image packing
d Bildkompression *f*
f compression *f* d'image
r сжатие *n* изображения; уплотнение *n*
изображения

* **image curve** → **1641**

4649 image data
d Bilddaten *pl*
f données *fpl* d'image
r данные *pl* об изображении

4650 image database; IDB
d Bilder-Datenbasis *f*
f base *f* de données d'images
r база *f* данных изображений

* **image definition** → **4676**

* **image dot** → **7015**

4651 image editing
d Bildeditieren *n*
f édition *f* d'image
r редактирование *n* изображения

4652 image editing program; image editor;
picture editor
d Bildbearbeitungsprogramm *n*; Bildeditor *m*
f programme *m* d'édition d'images; éditeur *m*
d'images
r программа *f* редактирования изображений;
редактор *m* изображений

* **image editor** → **4652**

4653 image embedding
d Bild-Einbetten *n*
f encastrement *m* d'image
r вложение *n* изображения

4654 image file
 d Bilddatei f
 f fichier m d'image
 r файл m изображения

4655 image file formats
 d Bilddatei-Formate npl
 f formats mpl de fichiers d'images
 r форматы mpl файлов изображений

4656 image format; picture format
 d Bildformat n
 f format m d'image
 r формат m изображения; формат образа

4657 image frame
 d Bildrahmen m
 f cadre m d'image
 r кадр m изображения

4658 image framing
 d Bildrahmung f
 f cadrage m d'image
 r кадрирование n изображения

4659 image generation; picture generation
 d Bildgenerierung f, Bilderzeugung f
 f génération f d'images
 r генерирование n изображений

4660 image generation frequency
 d Bildgenerierungsfrequenz f
 f fréquence f de génération d'images
 r частота f генерирования изображений

4661 image generation process
 d Bildgenerierungsprozess m
 f processus m de génération d'images
 r процесс m генерирования изображений

4662 image inserting
 d Bildeinfügung f
 f insertion f d'image
 r вставка f изображения

4663 image inverter
 d Bildinverter m
 f inverseur m d'image
 r инвертор m изображения

4664 image mailing
 d Bildsendung f, Bildeinlieferung f
 f publipostage m d'image
 r рассылка f изображения (электронной почтой)

 * **image map → 1723**

4665 image morphing
 d Bild-Morphing n

 f morphage m d'image
 r морфинг m изображения; метаморфоза f изображения

 * **image packing → 4648**

4666 image page
 d Bildseite f
 f page f d'image
 r страница f изображения

 * **image preview → 4667**

4667 image preview[ing]
 d Bildvorschau f
 f prévisualisation f d'image
 r предварительный просмотр m изображения

4668 image processing; picture processing
 d Bildbearbeitung f, Bildverarbeitung f
 f traitement m d'images
 r обработка f изображений

4669 image processing software
 d Bildbearbeitungssoftware f
 f logiciel m de traitement d'images
 r программное обеспечение n обработки изображений

4670 image processor
 d Bildprozessor m; Bildrechner m
 f processeur m d'images
 r процессор m изображений

4671 image quality; picture quality
 d Bildqualität f
 f qualité f d'image
 r качество n изображения

4672 image raster
 d Bildraster m
 f rastre m d'image
 r растр m изображения

 * **image recognition → 6864**

 * **image refreshing → 4673**

4673 image regeneration; image refreshing; display regeneration; screen redraw
 d Bildregenerierung f, Bildwiederholung f, Bildauffrischung f
 f régénération f d'image; rafraîchissement m d'image; redéfinition f d'écran
 r регенерация f изображения; обновление n изображения на экране

4674 imagery; imaging
 d Abbildung f

f imagerie *f*; présentation *f* [des données] en image
r отображение *n*

* **image scanning** → 6984

* **image scanning method** → 6985

4675 image set
 d Bildmenge *f*; Nachbereich *m*; Wertebereich *m*; Wertevorrat *m*; Wertemenge *f*
 f ensemble *m* des images
 r множество *n* образов

* **image setter** → 6962

4676 image sharpness; image definition
 d Bildschärfe *f*
 f netteté *f* de l'image; définition *f* de l'image
 r чёткость *f* изображения; резкость *f* изображения

* **image signature** → 1428

4677 image synthesis
 d Bildsynthese *f*
 f synthèse *f* d'image
 r синтез *m* изображения

4678 image [tele]transmission; picture [remote] transfer
 d Bild[fern]übertragung *f*
 f [télé]transmission *f* d'images
 r [дальняя] передача *f* изображений

* **image transmission** → 4678

4679 imaginary
 d imaginär
 f imaginaire
 r мнимый

4680 imaging
 d Bildformung *f*
 f imagination *f*; prise *f* d'images; formation *f* d'images
 r формирование *n* изображений

* **imaging** → 4674

4681 imaging characteristics
 d Abbildungseigenschaften *fpl*
 f caractéristique *f* d'imagination
 r характеристика *f* изображения

* **IMHO** → 4873

4682 immediate; instantaneous

 d unmittelbar; sofortig
 f immédiat; instantané
 r непосредственный; немедленный

4683 immediate access; instantaneous access; zero access
 d unmittelbarer Zugriff *m*; Sofortzugriff *m*; Schnellzugriff *m*; Nullzugriff *m*; Zugriff ohne Verzögerung
 f accès *m* immédiat; accès instantané; accès zéro
 r непосредственный доступ *m*; немедленный доступ; нулевой доступ; немедленная выборка *f*

4684 immediate addressing; zero-level addressing; single-level addressing
 d unmittelbare Adressierung *f*; Nullniveauadressierung *f*
 f adressage *m* immédiat; adressage à niveau zéro
 r непосредственная адресация *f*; адресация нулевого уровня

4685 immediate call termination
 d unmittelbarer Anrufabschluss *m*
 f déconnexion *f* immédiate
 r немедленное прекращние *n* вызова

4686 immediate data
 d Direktdaten *pl*
 f données *fpl* immédiates; données directes
 r непосредственно получаемые данные *pl*

4687 immiscibility analysis
 d Nichtmischbarkeitsanalyse *f*
 f analyse *f* de l'immiscibilité
 r анализ *m* несмешаемости

* **immunize** *v* → 4877

* **IMO** → 4874

* **impact** → 2352

4688 imparity; non-parity; oddness; odd parity
 d Ungeradzahligkeit *f*; Unpaarigkeit *f*; Ungeradheit *f*; ungerade Parität *f*
 f imparité *f*; non-parité *f*
 r нечётность *f*; нечётный паритет *m*

4689 imparity check; odd-parity check; parity-odd check
 d Ungeradezahligkeitsprüfung *f*
 f contrôle *m* par imparité; contrôle impair
 r контроль *m* по нечётности

4690 imperative language; procedural language
 d imperative Sprache *f*; unbedingte Sprache

    f langage *m* procédural
    r процедурный язык *m*

4691 imperative statement
    d Imperativanweisung *f*; unbedingte
       Anweisung *f*
    f instruction *f* impérative
    r повелительное высказывание *n*;
       повелительный оператор *m*

4692 imperfection
    d Störstelle *f*
    f imperfection *f*
    r несовершенство *n*; неполнота *f*;
       недостаток *m*

4693 implantation
    d Implantation *f*
    f implantation *f*
    r имплантация *f*

4694 implement *v*
    d ausführen; durchführen
    f implémenter
    r выполнять; осуществлять; претворять

4695 implementation
    d Implementierung *f*; Durchführung *f*
    f implémentation *f*; réalisation *f*
    r внедрение *n*; реализация *f*; ввод *m* в
       действие

4696 implicant
    d Implikante *f*
    f implicante *f*
    r импликанта *f*

4697 implication
    d Implikation *f*
    f implication *f*
    r импликация *f*

4698 implicator
    d Implikator *m*
    f élément *m* d'implication
    r импликатор *m*

4699 implicit; assumed
    d implizit
    f implicite
    r неявный

4700 implicit address; implied address
    d implizite Adresse *f*
    f adresse *f* implicite
    r подразумеваемый адрес *m*; неявный адрес

4701 implicit addressing; implied addressing;

inherent addressing
    d eingeschlossene Adressierung *f*; implizite
       Adressierung
    f adressage *m* implicite; adressage intrinsèque
    r неявная адресация *f*

4702 implicit model
    d implizites Modell *n*
    f modèle *m* implicite
    r неявная модель *f*

4703 implicit representation
    d implizite Darstellung *f*
    f représentation *f* implicite
    r неявное представление *n*

    * **implied address** → **4700**

    * **implied addressing** → **4701**

    * **imply** *v* → **3946**

    * **import** → **4707**

4704 import *v*
    d importieren
    f importer
    r вносить; импортировать

    * **importation** → **4707**

4705 imported image
    d importiertes Bild *n*
    f image *f* importée
    r импортированное изображение *n*

4706 importer
    d Importer *m*
    f importateur *m*
    r вноситель *m*

4707 import[ing]; importation
    d Importieren *n*
    f importation *f*
    r внесение *n*; импортирование *n*

4708 import method
    d Importmethode *f*
    f méthode *f* d'importation
    r метод *m* внесения

4709 imprecise; inexact
    d ungenau; unexakt; unpräzis[e]
    f imprécis; inexact
    r неточный; неверный

    * **improper-command check** → **4637**

4710 improved resolution
    d verbesserte Auflösung *f*

    f résolution *f* améliorée
    r улучшенная разрешающая способность *f*

    * **improvement** → **3434**

    * **impulse** → **7498**

4711 inaccessibility; unavailability;
unattainability
    d Unerreichbarkeit *f*; Unzugänglichkeit *f*
    f inaccessibilité *f*; non-disponibilité *f*
    r недостижимость *f*; недоступность *f*

4712 inaccessible; unavailable
    d unerreichbar
    f inaccessible; non accessible
    r недостижимый; недоступный

4713 inaccessible interface
    d nicht benutzbare Schnittstelle *f*
    f interface *f* inaccessible
    r недоступный интерфейс *m*

4714 inaccuracy; inexactitude
    d Ungenauigkeit *f*; Unexaktheit *f*
    f inexactitude *f*; imprécision *f*
    r неточность *f*

4715 inactive; passive
    d nichtaktiv; passiv
    f inactif; non actif
    r неактивный; пассивный

4716 inactive character
    d nichtaktives Zeichen *n*
    f caractère *m* non actif
    r неактивный знак *m*

4717 inactive node
    d nichtaktiver Knoten *m*
    f nœud *m* non actif
    r неактивный узел *m*

4718 in ascending order
    d in aufsteigender Anordnung *f*
    f dans l'ordre ascendant
    r в порядке возрастания

    * **in-betweening** → **5890**

4719 in-between task
    d Zwischenaufgabe *f*
    f tâche *f* intermédiaire
    r промежуточная задача *f*

4720 inbound mail
    d Post *f* aus dem Ausland
    f poste *f* venante de l'étranger
    r иностранная почта *f*

4721 inbox
    d Eingabekasten *m*; Posteingang *m*
    f boîte *f* de réception; corbeille *f* arrivée
    r ящик *m* для хранения входящих
       сообщений

    * **inbuilding local network** → **4541**

    * **in-built** → **6067**

4722 incalculability
    d Unzähligkeit *f*
    f incalculabilité *f*
    r неисчислимость *f*

4723 incalculable; non-computable
    d nichtberechenbar; unberechenbar
    f incalculable
    r невычислимый; неисчислимый

    * **incertainty** → **9613**

4724 incident record
    d zufällige Aufzeichnung *f*
    f enregistrement *m* imprévu; enregistrement
       d'occasion
    r случайная запись *f*

    * **incircle** → **4876**

4725 in-circuit
    d schaltungsintegriert; schaltungsintern;
       schaltkreisintegriert
    f intracircuit; interne au circuit
    r внутрисхемный

    * **in-circuit** *adj* → **6403**

4726 in-circuit emulator
    d schaltungsinterner Emulator *m*; einsteckbarer
       Mikroprozessor-Emulator *m*
    f émulateur *m* interne au circuit
    r внутрисхемный эмулятор *m*

    * **inclined** → **6360**

    * **include** *v* → **3392**

4727 inclusion
    d Inklusion *f*; Einfügen *n*; Einfügung *f*
    f inclusion *f*
    r включение *n*

4728 inclusive disjunction
    d inklusive Disjunktion *f*
    f disjonction *f* inclusive
    r неразделительная дизъюнкция *f*

    * **inclusive-OR gate** → **6572**

* **inclusive-OR operation** → 6594

4729 inclusive segments
d inklusive Segmente *npl*
f segments *mpl* inclus; segments incorporés
r совместимые сегменты *mpl*; включающие
   сегменты

4730 incoming
d ankommend; kommend; eingehend
f entrant; d'arrivée; d'entrée
r входящий

* **incoming flow** → 4899

4731 incoming mail
d eingehende Post *f*
f poste *f* entrante
r входящая почта *f*

4732 incoming message
d Eingabemeldung *f*
f message *m* entrant
r входящее сообщение *n*

* **incoming message buffer** → 4733

**4733 incoming message holding unit; incoming
   message buffer**
d Eingabemeldungspufferspeicher *m*
f tampon *m* de messages entrants
r буфер *m* входящих сообщений

* **incoming register** → 4735

4734 incoming traffic; unbound traffic
d [an]kommender Verkehr *m*
f trafic *m* entrant
r входящий трафик *m*

4735 incoming [traffic] register
d Register *n* für ankommenden Verkehr
f registre *m* de trafic entrant
r регистр *m* входящего трафика

4736 incompatibility
d Inkompatibilität *f*; Unvereinbarkeit *f*;
   Unverträglichkeit *f*
f incompatibilité *f*
r несовместимость *f*; несовместность *f*

4737 incomplete
d nichtvollständig; unvollständig
f incomplet; non complet
r неполный

* **incomplete data processing** → 4738

**4738 incomplete information processing;
   incomplete data processing**
d unvollständige Informationsverarbeitung *f*;

unvollständige Datenverarbeitung *f*
f traitement *m* d'information incomplète
r неполная обработка *f* информации;
   незавершённая обработка информации

4739 incompleteness
d Unvollständigkeit *f*
f incomplétude *f*
r неполнота *f*; незавершённость *f*

* **in-core** → 7998

4740 incorporate *v*
d einbauen; aufnehmen; einlagern; eingliedern
f incorporer
r встраивать; объединять

4741 incorporation
d Einbau *m*; Einlagerung *f*
f incorporation *f*
r встраивание *n*; объединение *n*

4742 incorrect
d unkorrekt; unakkurat
f incorrect; non correct
r некорректный

4743 incorrect inference
d unkorrekte Inferenz *f*
f inférence *f* incorrecte
r некорректный вывод *m*

4744 incorrect visualization
d unkorrekte Visualisierung *f*
f visualisation *f* non correcte
r некорректная визуализация *f*

4745 increase *v*
d wachsen
f croître; accroître
r расти; возрастать

4746 increase
d Erhöhung *f*
f augmentation *f*
r увеличение *n*

* **increasing** → 553

4747 increment
d Zuwachs *m*; Inkrement *n*
f incrément *m*; accroissement *m*
r приращение *n*; прирост *m*; инкремент *m*

4748 incremental
d inkrementell; inkremental; Inkremental-
f incrémentiel
r инкрементный; пошаговый

4749 incremental compiler
d Inkrementcompiler *m*; inkrementeller

Übersetzer *m*
f compilateur *m* incrémentiel
r инкрементный компилятор *m*; пошаговый компилятор

4750 incremental constants
d Inkrementalkonstanten *fpl*
f constantes *fpl* d'incrément
r константы *fpl* инкремента

4751 incremental data; incremental information
d Inkrementdaten *pl*
f données *fpl* incrémentielles
r данные *pl* в виде приращений

* **incremental information** → 4751

4752 incremental integrator; digital integrator
d inkrementaler Integrierer *m*; Inkrementintegrator *m*
f intégrateur *m* incrémentiel
r инкрементный интегратор *m*; дифференциальный интегратор

4753 incrustation
d Inkrustation *f*
f incrustation *f*
r врезание *n*

4754 incrustation of image
d Bildinkrustation *f*
f incrustation *f* d'image
r врезание *n* изображения

4755 incrustation of text
d Text-Inkrustation *f*
f incrustation *f* de texte
r врезание *n* текста

* **in-cut connection** → 7070

* **indefinite** → 9620

4756 indent
d Einzug *m*
f retrait *m*
r отступ *m*

4757 indentation; indenting
d Einbuchtung *f*, Einkerbung *f*, Einrückung *f*
f décrochement *m*
r отступление *n*; формирование *n* отступа

* **indenting** → 4757

4758 independence
d Unabhängigkeit *f*
f indépendance *f*
r независимость *f*

4759 independent; stand-alone
d unabhängig; selbständig
f indépendant; non dépendant
r независимый; самостоятельный

4760 independent program; stand-alone program
d unabhängiges Programm *n*
f programme *m* indépendant; programme autonome
r независимая программа *f*; автономная программа

4761 independent random variables
d unabhängige Zufallsgrößen *fpl*
f variables *fpl* aléatoires indépendantes
r независимые случайные величины *fpl*

4762 independent sampling
d unabhängige Stichprobenauswahl *f*
f échantillonnage *m* indépendant
r независимый выбор *m*

4763 independent variable; free variable
d unabhängige Veränderliche *f*; unabhängige Variable *f*; freie Variable
f variable *f* indépendante; variable libre
r независимая переменная *f*; свободная переменная

4764 indeterminacy; non-determination; undetermination
d Unbestimmtheit *f*; Indeterminiertheit *f*
f indétermination *f*; non-détermination *f*
r неопределённость *f*

4765 indeterminate system; undeterminate system
d unbestimmtes System *n*
f système *m* indéterminé
r неопределённая система *f*

4766 index
d Index *m*
f index *m*; indice *m*
r индекс *m*; показатель *m*

4767 index buffer
d Indexpuffer *m*
f tampon *m* d'index
r буферный индекс-регистр *m*

4768 indexed addressing; indexing addressing
d indizierte Adressierung *f*
f adressage *m* indexé
r индексная адресация *f*

4769 index[ed] file
d indizierte Datei *f*; Indexdatei *f*

f fichier *m* indexé; fichier d'index
r индексированный файл *m*; индексный
файл

4770 index[ed] sequential file
d indexsequentielle Datei *f*
f fichier *m* index-séquentiel; fichier séquentiel
indexé
r индексно-последовательный файл *m*

*   **index file → 4769**

4771 indexing
d Indizieren *n*; Indizierung *f*; Indexierung *f*
f indexage *m*; indexation *f*
r индексация *f*; индексирование *n*

*   **indexing addressing → 4768**

**4772 index[ing] register; B-box; B-register; base
register; modifier register**
d Indexregister *n*; B-Register *n*; Basisregister *n*;
Modifikatorregister *n*
f registre *m* d'index; registre de base
r индексный регистр *m*; базовый регистр

4773 index notation
d Indexbezeichnung *f*; Indexschreibweise *f*
f notation *f* indicielle; écriture *f* indicielle
r индексное обозначение *n*; индексная
запись *f*

*   **index register → 4772**

4774 index return
d Indexrückführung *f*
f retour *m* d'index
r возврат *m* индекса

*   **index sequential file → 4770**

*   **index word → 5229**

4775 indication; display
d Anzeichen *n*; Indikation *f*; Anzeige *f*
f indication *f*
r индикация *f*; показание *n*

4776 indication error
d Anzeigefehler *m*
f erreur *f* d'indication
r ошибка *f* индикации

4777 indicator
d Anzeiger *m*; Indikator *m*
f indicateur *m*
r индикатор *m*; указатель *m*

4778 indirect

d indirekt
f indirect
r косвенный; непрямой

4779 indirect address; deferred address
d indirekte Adresse *f*
f adresse *f* indirecte
r косвенный адрес *m*

4780 indirect addressing; deferred addressing
d indirekte Adressierung *f*
f adressage *m* indirect
r косвенная адресация *f*

4781 indirect [addressing] instruction
d indirekter Befehl *m*
f instruction *f* à adresse indirecte
r инструкция *f* с косвенной адресацией

4782 indirect input; offline input
d indirekte Eingabe *f*; Offline-Eingabe *f*
f entrée *f* indirecte; entrée hors ligne;
introduction *f* indépendante
r независимый ввод *m*; автономный ввод;
непрямой ввод

*   **indirect instruction → 4781**

4783 indirect output; offline output
d indirekte Ausgabe *f*; Offline-Ausgabe *f*
f sortie *f* indirecte; sortie indépendante; sortie
hors ligne
r независимый вывод *m*; автономный вывод;
непрямой вывод

4784 indirect scanning
d undirekte Abtastung *f*
f balayage *m* indirect
r косвенное сканирование *n*

4785 indivisible code
d unteilbarer Code *m*
f code *m* non divisible
r неразделимый код *m*

4786 indivisible element
d unteilbares Element *n*
f élément *m* non divisible
r неделимый элемент *m*

4787 induced failure
d induzierter Fehler *m*
f défaut *m* induit; défaut suggéré
r наведённый отказ *m*

4788 inductive reading head
d induktiver Lesekopf *m*
f tête *f* inductive de lecture
r индуктивная головка *f* считывания

4789 inequality
d Ungleichung f
f inéquation f; inégalité f
r неравенство n

4790 inequality sign
d Ungleichheitszeichen n
f signe m d'inégalité
r знак m неравенства

* **inert zone** → 2624

* **inexact** → 4709

* **inexactitude** → 4714

* **inexperienced user** → 6158

4791 infancy failure
d Frühausfall m
f défaillance f infantile; défaillance initiale
r приработочный отказ m

* **infection** → 9883

4792 inference engine
d Inferenzmaschine f
f moteur m d'inférence
r машина f логического вывода; механизм m логического вывода

4793 inferencing algorithm
d Inferenzalgorithmus m; Schlussfolgerungsalgorithmus m
f algorithme m d'inférence
r алгоритм m логического вывода

4794 inferential logic
d Inferenzlogik f
f logique f d'inférence
r логика f получения выводов

4795 infinite; endless
d unendlich
f infini; sans fin
r бесконечный

4796 infinite detail
(of a fractal)
d unendliches Detail n
f détail m infini
r бесконечная деталь f

* **infinite loop** → 3407

* **infinite transmission** → 9611

4797 infix
d Infix n
f infixe m

r инфикс m

4798 infix notation
d Infixnotation f; Infixschreibweise f
f notation f d'infixe
r инфиксное представление n; скобочное представление

4799 infix operator
d Infixoperator m
f opérateur m d'infixe
r инфиксный оператор m; двухместный оператор

* **infography** → 2079

4800 informatics
d Informatik f
f informatique f
r информатика f

4801 information
d Information f
f information f
r информация f

4802 information and communications technology
d Informations- und Kommunikationstechnik f
f technologie f d'information et communication
r информационная и коммуникационная технология f

4803 information bit
d Informationsbit n
f bit m d'information
r информационный бит m

4804 information burst
d Informationsburst m
f burste m d'information
r информационный взрыв m

4805 information-carrying signal
d informationsübertragendes Signal n
f signal m porteur d'information
r сигнал m, передающий информацию

* **information channel** → 2526

4806 information checking
d Informationskontrolle f
f examen m d'information; vérification f d'information
r контроль m информации

4807 information circuit
d Informationskreis m
f circuit m d'information
r информационная цепь f

* **information content** → 361

4808 information content unit
d Informationsinhaltseinheit *f*;
   Informationsgehaltseinheit *f*
f unité *f* de contenu d'information; unité de
   quantité d'information
r единица *f* количества информации

4809 information density
d Informationsflussdichte *f*; Datendurchsatz *m*
f densité *f* du flux d'information
r интенсивность *f* потока информации

* **information highway** → 4820

* **information item** → 4828

* **information loss** → 5510

4810 information overload
d Informationsüberlastung *f*
f surcharge *f* d'information
r информационная перегрузка *f*

4811 information packet
d Informationspaket *n*; Datenpaket *n*
f paquet *m* d'information; paquet de données
r информационный пакет *m*; пакет данных

4812 information processing
d Informationsverarbeitung *f*
f traitement *m* d'information
r обработка *f* информации

**4813 information provider; IP; information
     supplier**
d Informationsanbieter *m*
f fournisseur *m* d'information
r поставщик *m* информации

4814 information representation
d Informationsdarstellung *f*
f représentation *f* d'information
r представление *n* информации

4815 information retrieval
d Informationswiedergewinnung *f*;
   Informationswiederauffindung *f*
f récupération *f* d'information; recherche *f*
   d'information
r поиск *m* информации

4816 information security
d Informationssicherung *f*
f sécurité *f* d'information
r защита *f* информации

4817 information signal
d Informationssignal *n*

f signal *m* d'information
r информационный сигнал *m*

4818 information storage
d Informationsspeicherung *f*
f mise *f* en mémoire; mise d'information
r хранение *n* информации

* **information stream** → 8939

4819 information structure; data structure
d Informationsstruktur *f*; Datenstruktur *f*
f structure *f* d'information; structure de données
r структура *f* информации; структура
   данных

4820 information [super]highway
d Datenautobahn *f*; Infobahn *f*
f artère *f* d'information; autoroute *f* de
   l'information; inforoute *f*
r информационный шлюз *m*

* **information supplier** → 4813

4821 information technology; IT
d Informationstechnologie *f*
f technologie *f* [de traitement] d'information
r информационная технология *f*; технология
   обработки информации

4822 information theory
d Informationstheorie *f*
f théorie *f* de l'information
r теория *f* информации

4823 information time slot
d Informationszeitlage *f*
f tranche *f* de temps d'information
r информационный временной квант *m*

* **information transfer** → 4824

**4824 information transmission; information
     transfer**
d Informationsübertragung *f*
f transmission *f* d'information
r передача *f* информации

4825 information transmission rate
d Informationsübertragungsgeschwindigkeit *f*
f vitesse *f* de transmission de l'information
r скорость *f* передачи информации

4826 information transmitter
d Nachrichtenquelle *f*; Informationssender *m*
f transmetteur *m* d'information
r передатчик *m* информации

4827 information type
d Informationsart *f*

   f type *m* d'information
   r вид *m* информации

4828 information unit; information item
   d Informationseinheit *f*
   f unité *f* d'information
   r единица *f* информации

4829 information visualization
   d Information-Visualisierung *f*
   f visualisation *f* d'information
   r визуализация *f* информации

   * **inforouter → 2461**

   * **in gate → 4900**

4830 ingenious addressing
   d sinnreiche Adressierung *f*
   f adressage *m* ingénieux
   r смысловая адресация *f*; адресация по
      смыслу

4831 inherent; inherited
   d mitgeschleppt
   f inhérent; entraîné; hérité
   r исходный; привнесённый

   * **inherent addressing → 4701**

4832 inherent error; inherited error
   d mitgeschleppter Fehler *m*
   f erreur *f* entraînée; erreur inhérente; erreur
      héritée
   r исходная ошибка *f*; привнесённая ошибка

4833 inherent feedback
   d innere Rückkopplung *f*
   f réaction *f* propre
   r внутренняя обратная связь *f*

   * **inheritance → 4441**

   * **inherited → 4831**

   * **inherited error → 4832**

4834 inhibit *v*; disable *v*; disarm *v*; ban *v*;
   prohibit *v*
   d sperren; verhindern; unwirksam machen
   f inhiber; désactiver; bannir; anéantir
   r запрещать; предотвращать

4835 inhibit bit; disabling bit
   d Sperrbit *n*
   f bit *m* d'inhibition
   r бит *m* запрета

4836 inhibit function
   d Sperrfunktion *f*

   f fonction *f* d'inhibition
   r функция *f* запрета

4837 inhibiting input
   d Sperreingang *m*
   f entrée *f* inhibitrice; entrée d'inhibition; entrée
      d'interdiction
   r запрещающий вход *m*; вход блокировки

   * **inhibit → 4838**

   * **inhibit circuit → 4839**

4838 inhibit[ion]; disable
   d Inhibition *f*; Verhinderung *f*; Sperre *f*
   f inhibition *f*; interdiction *f*; invalidation *f*
   r запрещение *n*; запрет *m*

4839 inhibit[ory] circuit; lockout circuit
   d Sperrschaltung *f*
   f circuit *m* d'inhibition
   r схема *f* запрета

4840 inhibit signal
   d Sperrsignal *n*; Sperrzeichen *n*
   f signal *m* d'inhibition
   r сигнал *m* запрета

4841 inhomogeneity
   d Inhomogenität *f*
   f non-homogénéité *f*
   r неоднородность *f*

   * **inhomogeneous → 4443**

4842 inhomogeneous system; nonhomogeneous
   system
   d inhomogenes System *n*; nichthomogenes
      System
   f système *m* inhomogène; système non
      homogène
   r неоднородная система *f*; негомогенная
      система

   * **in-house → 4531**

   * **in-house code → 4875**

4843 in-house mail
   d Hauspost *f*
   f poste *f* interne
   r внутренняя почта *f*

   * **in-house network → 5439**

4844 in-house programming
   d In-House-Programmierung *f*
   f programmation *f* interne
   r программирование *n* собственными
      силами

4845 in inverse order
d in umgekehrter Anordnung
f en ordre inverse
r в обратном порядке

4846 initial
d Anfangs-
f initial
r начальный

4847 initial data
d Anfangsdaten *pl*
f données *fpl* initiales
r начальные данные *pl*

4848 initial error
d Anfangsfehler *m*
f erreur *f* initiale
r начальная ошибка *f*

4849 initialization; initializing
d Initialisierung *f*; Initialisieren *n*; Einleiten *n*;
   Einleitung *f*
f initialisation *f*
r инициализация *f*; задание *n* начальных
   условий

   * **initializing → 4849**

4850 initial load; preload
d Anfangsladen *n*
f chargement *m* initial; préchargement *m*
r первоначальная загрузка *f*;
   предварительная загрузка

**4851 initial load[ing] program; initial program
   loader; bootstrap[ping] loader; boot**
d Anfangsladeprogramm *n*; Anfangslader *m*;
   Selbstlader *m*; Initialisierungsprogramm *n*
f programme *m* de chargement initial;
   programme d'autochargement; programme
   d'initialisation; amorce *f*
r программа *f* начальной загрузки;
   программа самозагрузки

   * **initial load program → 4851**

4852 initial point
d Anfangspunkt *m*
f point *m* initial
r начальная точка *f*

   * **initial program load → 4853**

   * **initial program loader → 4851**

4853 initial program load[ing]
d einleitendes Programmladen *n*
f chargement *m* initial de programme
r начальная загрузка *f* программы

4854 initial reset
d Urrücksetzen *n*
f rappel *m* initial
r начальный сброс *m*

4855 initial start
d Urstart *m*
f démarrage *m* initial
r начальный запуск *m*

   * **initial state → 4856**

4856 initial status; initial state
d Anfangszustand *m*; Ausgangszustand *m*
f état *m* initial
r начальное состояние *n*

4857 initial symbol
d Anfangssymbol *n*
f symbole *m* initial
r начальный символ *m*

   * **initiate *v* → 6590**

4858 initiation
d Initiierung *f*; Initiation *f*
f initiation *f*
r инициирование *n*

4859 ink
d Tinte *f*
f encre *f*
r чернило *n*; печатная краска *f*

4860 ink cartridge
d Farbkassette *f*
f cartouche *f* d'encre
r чернильный картридж *m*

4861 ink color
d Tintenfarbe *f*
f couleur *f* d'encre
r цвет *m* чернила

4862 inker
d Farbwerk *n*
f mécanisme *m* d'encrage
r красящий механизм *m*

4863 inking
d Einfärbung *f*; Inking *n*
f encrage *m*
r закрашивание *n* [графического
   изображения]

**4864 ink-jet printer; bubble-jet printer;
   inkwriter**
d Tintenstrahldrucker *m*;
   Bubble-Jet-Drucker *m*; Tintenprinter *n*

f imprimante *f* à jet d'encre; imprimante à bulle d'encre

r струйное печатающее устройство *n*; струйный принтер *m*

4865 ink-pot; ink-well
(of ink-jet printer)
d Tintenfass *n*; Farb[en]topf *m*
f encrier *m*
r чернильница *f*

4866 ink ribbon; ribbon
d Farbband *n*
f ruban *m* encreur; ruban d'encrage
r цветная лента *f*; красящая лента; копировальная лента

* **ink-well → 4865**

* **inkwriter → 4864**

4867 inline
d mitlaufend; schritthaltend
f du même pas; concurrent; en ligne
r линейный; поточный; сопровождающий

4868 inline; aligned
d ausgerichtet; Inline-; in einer Linie
f aligné; en série
r выровненный; на одной линии

4869 inline image
d Inlinebild *n*
f image *f* alignée
r выровненное изображение *n*

4870 inline procedure
d mitlaufende Prozedur *f*
f procédure *f* immédiate
r текущая процедура *f*; оперативная процедура

4871 inline processing; online processing
d mitlaufende Verarbeitung *f*; schritthaltende Verarbeitung; Online-Verarbeitung *f*
f traitement *m* concurrent; traitement en ligne
r поточная обработка *f*; обработка в порядке поступления; неавтономная обработка; обработка в режиме "онлайн"

4872 inline program
d lineares Programm *n*
f programme *m* linéaire
r линейная программа *f*

4873 in my humble opinion; IMHO
(abbreviation in forums and e-mail)
d meiner bescheidenen Meinung nach
f à mon humble avis
r по моему скромному мнению

4874 in my opinion; IMO
(abbreviation in forums and e-mail)
d meiner Meinung nach
f à mon avis
r по моему мнению

4875 inner code; in-house code
d innerer Code *m*; interner Code
f code *m* intérieur; code interne
r внутренний код *m*

4876 inner loop; minor loop; incircle
d innerer Zyklus *m*; innere Schleife *f*
f boucle *f* inférieure; boucle mineure; cycle *m* intérieur; cycle mineur
r внутренний цикл *m*; подчинённый цикл; внутренняя петля *f*

4877 inoculate *v*; immunize *v*
d [ein]impfen
f inoculer
r прививать

4878 in-phase
d phasen[an]gleich; in Phase
f en phase
r в фазе; синфазный

4879 in-process job
d laufende Operation *f*; unvollendete Operation; unvollendeter Ablauf *m*; Rückstand *m*; Überhand *m*; unerledigte Arbeit *f*
f travail *m* inachevé; restant *m*
r незавершённое задание *n*; невыполненное задание

4880 input; entry
d Eingang *m*; Eingabe *f*
f entrée *f*; introduction *f*
r вход *m*; ввод *m*

4881 input alphabet
d Eingangsalphabet *n*; Eingabealphabet *n*
f alphabet *m* d'entrée
r входной алфавит *m*

4882 input amplifier; front-end amplifier
d Eingangsverstärker *m*
f amplificateur *m* d'entrée
r входной усилитель *m*

4883 input area
d Eingabebereich *m*
f domaine *m* d'entrée
r область *f* [памяти] ввода

4884 input buffer
d Eingabepuffer[speicher] *m*; Lesepuffer[speicher] *m*

    f tampon *m* d'entrée
    r входной буфер *m*

4885 input channel
    d Eingabekanal *m*
    f canal *m* d'entrée
    r входной канал *m*; канал ввода

    * **input character → 4918**

    * **input check → 4886**

4886 input check[ing]
    d Eingabekontrolle *f*
    f contrôle *m* d'entrée
    r контроль *m* входных данных

4887 input circuit
    d Eingangskreis *m*
    f circuit *m* d'entrée
    r входной контур *m*; входная схема *f*

    * **input clock → 4888**

4888 input clock [pulse]
    d Eingangstakt *m*
    f horloge *f* d'entrée
    r входной такт[овый импульс] *m*

4889 input code
    d Eingabecode *m*; Eingangscode *m*
    f code *m* d'entrée
    r входной код *m*

4890 input code converter
    d Eingabe-Codewandler *m*
    f convertisseur *m* de code d'entrée
    r входной кодопреобразователь *m*

4891 input data
    d Eingabedaten *pl*
    f données *fpl* d'entrée
    r входные данные *pl*

4892 input data carrier
    d Eingabedatenträger *m*
    f support *m* de données d'entrée
    r носитель *m* входных данных

4893 input data log
    d Eingabeprotokoll *n*
    f protocole *m* de données d'entrée
    r протокол *m* входных данных

4894 input data set
    d Eingangsgrößensatz *m*; Satz *m* von
        Eingangsgrößen
    f ensemble *m* de données d'entrée
    r множество *n* входных данных

4895 input enable signal
    d Eingabe-Freigabesignal *n*
    f signal *m* de déblocage d'entrée; signal de
        libération d'entrée
    r сигнал *m* разрешения ввода

4896 input end identifier
    d Eingabeschlussbezeichner *m*
    f identificateur *m* de fin d'entrée
    r идентификатор *m* конца ввода

4897 input error; error in the input data
    d Eingangsfehler *m*; Datenfehler *m*;
        Eingabefehler *m*
    f erreur *f* [des données] d'entrée
    r погрешность *f* входных данных; исходная
        погрешность; ошибка *f* ввода

4898 input filter
    d Eingangsfilter *m*
    f filtre *m* d'entrée
    r входной фильтр *m*

4899 input flow; incoming flow
    d Eingabefluss *m*; Eingabestrom *m*
    f flux *m* entrant
    r входной поток *m*

4900 in[put] gate
    d Eingangsgatter *n*; Eingangstor *n*;
        Eingabeeingang *m*
    f porte *f* d'entrée
    r входной вентиль *m*

4901 input handling
    d Eingabehandlung *f*
    f traitement *m* d'entrée
    r обработка *f* ввода

4902 input message
    d Eingabenachricht *f*
    f message *m* d'entrée
    r входное сообщение *n*

4903 input/output; I/O
    d Eingabe/Ausgabe *f*; E/A
    f entrée/sortie *f*; E/S
    r ввод/вывод *m*

4904 input/output allocation
    d Ein-/Ausgabezuordnung *f*
    f allocation *f* d'entrée/sortie
    r входно-выходное размещение *n*

4905 input/output code converter
    d Ein-/Ausgabe-Codewandler *m*
    f convertisseur *m* de code d'entrée/sortie
    r входно-выходной кодопреобразователь *m*

4906 input/output coder
    d Ein-/Ausgabe-Codierer *m*

    f codeur *m* d'entrée/sortie
    r входно-выходной шифратор *m*

4907 input/output fast channel
    d Schnellkanal *m* für Ein- und Ausgabe
    f canal *m* rapide d'entrée/sortie
    r быстродействующий канал *m* ввода/вывода

4908 input/output interface
    d Ein-/Ausgabe-Schnittstelle *f*
    f interface *f* d'entrée/sortie
    r интерфейс *m* ввода/вывода

4909 input/output interrupt; I/O interrupt
    d Eingabe/Ausgabe-Interrupt *m*; E/A-Interrupt
    f interruption *f* d'entrée/sortie; interruption E/S
    r прерывание *n* [от устройства] ввода/вывода

4910 input/output library
    d Eingabe/Ausgabe-Programmbibliothek *f*
    f bibliothèque *f* de programmes d'entrée/sortie
    r библиотека *f* программ ввода/вывода

4911 input/output procedure
    d Ein-/Ausgabe-Prozedur *f*
    f procédure *f* d'entrée/sortie
    r процедура *f* ввода/вывода

4912 input pointer
    d Eingabezeiger *m*
    f pointeur *m* d'entrée
    r входной указатель *m*

4913 input pulse
    d Eingangsimpuls *m*
    f impulsion *f* d'entrée
    r входной импульс *m*

    * **input queue** → 4920

4914 input selection
    d Eingabeauswahl *f*
    f sélection *f* d'entrée
    r входная выборка *f*; выбор *m* входа

4915 input sensitivity
    d Eingangsempfindlichkeit *f*
    f sensitivité *f* d'entrée
    r входная чувствительность *f*

4916 input sequence
    d Eingabefolge *f*
    f séquence *f* d'entrée
    r входная последовательность *f*

4917 input signal
    d Eingangssignal *n*
    f signal *m* d'entrée

    r входной сигнал *m*

    * **input stream** → 5172

4918 input symbol; input character
    d Eingabesymbol *n*
    f symbole *m* d'entrée; caractère *m* d'entrée
    r входной символ *m*; вводимый символ

4919 input word
    d Eingangswort *n*
    f mot *m* d'entrée
    r входное слово *n*

4920 input [work] queue
    d Eingabewarteschlange *f*
    f queue *f* d'entrée; file *f* d'attente d'entrée
    r входная очередь *f* [заданий]; очередь ввода; очередь на входе

    * **inquiry** → 7963

4921 inquiry character; enquiry character
    d Abfragezeichen *n*; Anfragezeichen *n*
    f caractère *m* d'interrogation
    r знак *m* поиска [ответа]

4922 inquiry method
    (of data)
    d Abfragemethode *f*
    f méthode *f* d'interrogation
    r метод *m* запроса

    * **inquiry mode** → 7099

4923 inquiry processing
    d Anfragenbearbeitung *f*
    f traitement *m* d'interrogations
    r обработка *f* запросов

4924 inquiry system
    d Auskunftssystem *n*
    f système *m* d'interrogations
    r система *f* запросов

4925 in real life; IRL
    (e-slang phrase)
    d im wirklichen Leben
    f dans le monde réel; dans la vie réelle
    r по-настоящему; в настоящей жизни

4926 insensitiveness
    d Unempfindlichkeit *f*
    f insensibilité *f*
    r нечувствительность *f*

    * **inseparable graph** → 6269

4927 insert *v*; inset *v*; paste *v*
    d einfügen; bestücken

f insérer; imbriquer
r вставлять; включать; вкладывать

4928 insert command
 d Einfügungsbefehl *m*
 f commande *f* d'insertion
 r команда *f* вставки; команда включения

 * **inserting → 4929**

4929 insertion; inserting
 d Einsetzen *n*; Einschiebung *f*
 f insertion *f*
 r вставка *f*; вставление *n*

4930 insertion gain
 d Einfügungsgewinn *m*
 f gain *m* d'insertion
 r вносимое усиление *n*

4931 insertion mode
 d Einfügungsmodus *m*
 f mode *m* d'insertion
 r режим *m* вставки

 * **insertion of data → 2546**

4932 insertion of text; text insertion
 d Texteinfügung *f*
 f saisie *f* de texte
 r вставка *f* текста

4933 insertion of toolbar
 d Hilfsmittelleiste-Einfügung *f*
 f insertion *f* de barre d'outils
 r вставка *f* панели инструментов

4934 insertion sort
 d Einfügesort *n*
 f tri[age] *m* d'insertion
 r сортировка *f* внесением

4935 Insert key; Ins key
 d Einfügetaste *f*
 f touche *f* d'insertion
 r клавиша *f* Ins

4936 insert *v* page
 d Seite einfügen
 f insérer une page
 r вставлять страницы

 * **inset *v* → 4927**

4937 insignificant
 d geringfügig; unbedeutend; unwesentlich
 f insignifiant; futile; négligeable
 r незначащий; несущественный

 * **insignificant data → 5141**

 * **Ins key → 4935**

4938 insolubility; undecidability
 d Unlösbarkeit *f*
 f insolubilité *f*
 r неразрешимость *f*

 * **inspection → 652**

4939 instability
 d Instabilität *f*
 f instabilité *f*
 r неустойчивость *f*; нестабильность *f*

4940 instable; astable; unstable
 d instabil; unbeständig
 f instable; astable
 r неустойчивый; нестабильный

4941 install *v*; setup *v*
 d einbauen; installieren; aufstellen
 f installer
 r инсталлировать; располагать

4942 installation
 d Anlage *f*; Installierung *f*; Montage *f*
 f installation *f*; montage *m*
 r инсталляция *f*; установка *f*; монтаж *m*

 * **installation program → 8479**

 * **instant → 5878**

 * **instantaneous → 4682**

 * **instantaneous access → 4683**

4943 instantiation
 d Instantiierung *f*; Umschreibung *f*
 f instanciation *f*
 r реализация *f* объекта; создание *n* объекта

 * **in-step → 9112**

4944 instruction; command
 d Instruktion *f*; Befehl *m*
 f instruction *f*; commande *f*
 r инструкция *f*; команда *f*

 * **instruction → 5319**

4945 instruction area; instruction space
 d Befehlsbereich *m*; Befehlsraum *m*
 f zone *f* d'instructions; espace *m* d'instructions
 r область *f* [хранения] инструкций

 * **instruction buffer → 1899**

4946 instruction code
d Befehlscode *m*; Befehlsschlüssel *m*
f code *m* d'instruction
r код *m* инструкции

4947 instruction counter; current address counter; program counter
d Befehlszähler *m*
f compteur *m* d'instructions
r счётчик *m* инструкций; регистр *m* [текущего] адреса

4948 instruction decoder
d Befehlsdecod[ier]er *m*
f décodeur *m* d'instructions
r дешифратор *m* инструкций

4949 instruction fetch
d Befehlsabruf *m*
f extraction *f* d'instruction
r извлечение *n* инструкции

4950 instruction initialization
d Befehlseinleitung *f*
f initialisation *f* d'instruction
r инициализация *f* инструкции

4951 instruction normalization; instruction normalizing
d Befehlsnormalisierung *f*
f normalisation *f* d'instruction
r нормализация *f* инструкции

* **instruction normalizing** → **4951**

4952 instruction number limit
d Befehlszahllimit *n*
f limite *f* de nombre d'instruction
r ограничение *n* числа инструкций

4953 instruction pointer; IP
d Instruktionszeiger *m*
f pointeur *m* des instructions
r указатель *m* команд

* **instruction register** → **1899**

4954 instruction repertoire; instruction set
d Befehlsvorrat *m*; Befehlssatz *m*
f répertoire *m* d'instructions; ensemble *m* d'instructions; jeu *m* d'instructions
r система *f* инструкций; набор *m* инструкций

4955 instruction sequence
d Befehlsfolge *f*; Anweisungsfolge *f*
f séquence *f* d'instructions
r последовательность *f* инструкций

* **instruction set** → **4954**

* **instruction space** → **4945**

4956 instructions per second; IPS
d Instruktionen *fpl* pro Sekunde
f instructions *fpl* par seconde
r инструкции *fpl* в секунде

4957 instruction tape
d Programmband *n*
f bande *f* de programme; bande d'instructions
r программная лента *f*

* **integer** → **4959, 4961, 4962**

4958 integer attribute
d Stellenattribut *n*; Ganzzahlattribut *n*
f attribut *m* entier
r описатель *m* "целое"

4959 integer [number]
d ganze Zahl *f*; Ganzzahl *f*
f entier *m*; nombre *m* entier
r целое [число] *n*

* **integer optimization** → **4960**

4960 integer programming; integer optimization
d ganzzahlige Programmierung *f*, ganzzahlige Optimierung *f*
f programmation *f* entière; optimisation *f* entière
r целочисленное программирование *n*; целочисленная оптимизация *f*

4961 integer [value]
d Ganzwert *m*
f valeur *f* entière
r целочисленное значение *n*

4962 integer[-valued]; integral; entire
d ganzzahlig; ganz[wertig]; Entier-
f entier; à valeur entière
r целочисленный; целый

4963 integer variable
d ganze Variable *f*
f variable *f* entière
r целая переменная *f*

* **integral** → **4962**

4964 integral; integrated
d integriert; Integral-
f intégré
r интегрированный; интегральный

4965 integral modem; built-in modem; integrated modem; internal modem
d integriertes Modem *n*; internes Modem

f modem *m* intégré; modem interne
r встроенный модем *m*; внутренний модем

* **integrated** → 4964

4966 integrated circuit; IC
d integrierte Schaltung *f*
f circuit *m* intégré; CI
r интегральная схема *f*; ИС

4967 integrated circuit package
d IC-Gehäuse *n*
f boîtier *m* de circuit intégré
r корпус *m* интегральной схемы

4968 integrated data network
d integriertes Datennetz *n*
f réseau *m* de données intégré
r интегрированная сеть *f* передачи данных

4969 integrated development environment
d integrierte Entwicklungsumgebung *f*
f environnement *m* de développement intégré
r интегрированная среда *f* развития

4970 integrated digital network; IDN
d integriertes digitales Netz *n*; integriertes Digitalnetz *n*; IDN
f réseau *m* numérique intégré; RNI
r интегрированная цифровая сеть *f*; ИЦС

4971 integrated injection logic; IIL; I²L
d integrierte Injektionslogik *f*; IIL; I²L
f logique *f* d'injection intégrée; IIL; I²L
r интегральная инжекционная логика *f*; ИИЛ; И²Л

4972 integrated local router
d integrierter Lokalrouter *m*; integrierter Lokalleitwegrechner *m*
f routeur *m* local intégré
r интегрированный локальный маршрутизатор *m*

* **integrated modem** → 4965

4973 integrated office communication
d integrierte Bürokommunikation *f*
f communication *f* bureautique intégrée
r интегрированная учрежденческая коммуникация *f*

4974 integrated remote router
d integrierter Fernleitwegrechner *m*; integrierter Fernrouter *m*
f routeur *m* distant intégré
r интегрированный дистанционный маршрутизатор *m*

4975 integrated resources
d integrierte Ressourcen *fpl*

f ressources *fpl* intégrées
r интегрированные ресурсы *mpl*

4976 integrated server
d integrierter Server *m*
f serveur *m* intégré
r интегрированный сервер *m*

4977 integrated services digital network; ISDN
d dienstintegriertes digitales Netz *n*; dienstintegrierendes digitales Netz
f réseau *m* numérique à intégration de services; RNIS; numéris *m*
r цифровая сеть *f* с интегрированными услугами

4978 integrated software
d integrierte Software *f*
f logiciel *m* intégré
r интегрированное программное обеспечение *n*

4979 integration
d Integration *f*
f intégration *f*
r интеграция *f*; объединение *n*

* **integration constant** → 2197

4980 integrator
d Integrator *m*; Integrierer *m*
f intégrateur *m*
r интегратор *m*

4981 integrity
d Ganzheit *f*; Integrität *f*
f intégrité *f*
r целостность *f*; сохранность *f*

4982 intelligent input-output; I²O
d intelligente Eingabe-Ausgabe *f*
f entrée/sortie *f* intelligente
r интеллектуальный ввод-вывод *m*

4983 intelligent terminal
d intelligentes Terminal *n*
f terminal *m* intelligent
r интеллектуальный терминал *m*

4984 intelligent time-division multiplexer
d intelligenter Zeitmultiplexer *m*
f multiplexeur *m* temporel intelligent
r интеллигентный мультиплексор *m* с временным уплотнением

4985 intelligent transmitter
d intelligenter Sender *m*
f transmetteur *m* intelligent
r интеллектуальный передатчик *m*

4986 intelligent vision system
d intelligentes Sehsystem *n*
f système *m* de vision intelligent
r интеллигентная система *f* визуального
 отображения

4987 intensity
d Intensität *f*
f intensité *f*
r интенсивность *f*

4988 intensity resolution
d Intensitätsauflösung *f*
f résolution *f* d'intensité
r разрешение *n* интенситета

4989 interact *v*
d zusammenwirken; wechselwirken
f interagir; collaborer; dialoguer
r взаимодействовать

* **interacting** → **4990**

4990 interaction; interacting
d interaktiver Betrieb *m*; Wechselwirkung *f*
f interaction *f*; coopération *f*
r взаимодействие *n*; взаимосвязь *f*

* **interactive** → **2283**

4991 interactive computer game
d interaktives Computerspiel *n*
f jeu *m* d'ordinateur interactif
r интерактивная компьютерная игра *f*

4992 interactive data processing
d Dialogdatenverarbeitung *f*
f traitement *m* de données interactif
r диалоговая обработка *f* данных

4993 interactive digitizing
d interaktive Digitalisierung *f*
f numérisation *f* interactive
r диалоговое дигитализирование *n*

4994 interactive display
d interaktiver Bildschirm *m*
f afficheur *m* interactif
r интерактивный дисплей *m*

* **interactive graphic** → **1723**

4995 interactive image processing
d interaktive Bildverarbeitung *f*
f traitement *m* interactif d'images
r диалоговая обработка *f* изображений

* **interactive mode** → **2850**

4996 interactive presentation

d interaktive Präsentation *f*
f présentation *f* interactive
r диалоговое представление *n*

4997 interactive television
d interaktives Fernsehen *n*
f télévision *f* interactive
r интерактивное телевидение *n*

**4998 interactive videodisk; compact
 disk-interactive; CD-I**
d interaktive Videobildplatte *f*; interaktiver
 optischer Speicher *m*
f vidéodisque *m* interactif; compact disque *m*
 interactif
r диалоговый видеодиск *m*; интерактивный
 компакт-диск *m*

4999 interactive visual browser
d interaktiver visueller Browser *m*
f butineur *m* visuel interactif
r интерактивный визуальный браузер *m*

5000 interactive visualization
d interaktive Visualisierung *f*
f visualisation *f* interactive
r диалоговая визуализация *f*

* **interblock gap** → **1069**

* **interchange** → **3561**

* **interchangeability** → **3562**

* **interchangeable** → **3563**

* **inter-character space** → **1630**

5001 interconnected board
d Verbindungskarte *f*
f plaque *f* d'interconnexion
r соединительная плата *f*

5002 interconnecting web
d Verbindungssteg *m*
f toile *f* d'araignée d'interconnexions
r сетка *f* межсоединений

5003 interconnection
d Verknüpfung *f*; Zusammenschluss *m*;
 Querverbindung *f*
f interconnexion *f*; enchaînement *m*
r взаимосвязь *f*; межсхемное соединение *n*

5004 interconnection device
d Verbindungselement *n*;
 Verbindungsvorrichtung *f*
f dispositif *m* d'interconnexion
r устройство *n* связи; элемент *m* связи

5005 interconnection process
  d Verbindungsprozess *m*
  f processus *m* d'interconnexion
  r процесс *m* взаимосвязи

5006 interconnection technique
  d Verbindungstechnik *f*
  f technique *f* d'interconnexion; connectique *f*
  r техника *f* связи

5007 interconnection topology
  d Zusammenschlusstopologie *f*;
       Zusammenschaltungstopologie *f*
  f topologie *f* d'interconnexion
  r топология *f* межсоединений

5008 interface
  d Interface *n*; Schnittstelle *f*;
       Anschlussbedingungen *fpl*
  f interface *f*; jonction *f*
  r интерфейс *m*

5009 interface cable; interface trunk
  d Schnittstellenkabel *n*
  f câble *m* d'interface
  r интерфейсный кабель *m*

5010 interface circuit
  d Schnittstellenschaltung *f*
  f circuit *m* d'interface
  r интерфейсная схема *f*

5011 interface comparator
  d Schnittstellenvergleicher *m*
  f comparateur *m* d'interface
  r интерфейсный выравнитель *m*;
       интерфейсный компаратор *m*

5012 interface compatibility
  d Scnittstellenkompatibilität *f*
  f compatibilité *f* d'interface
  r совместимость *f* с интерфейсом

5013 interface control
  d Schnittstellensteuerung *f*
  f contrôle *m* d'interface
  r управление *n* интерфейса

5014 interface controller
  d Anschlusssteuereinheit *f*
  f contrôleur *m* d'interface
  r интерфейсный контроллер *m*

5015 interface converter
  d Schnittstellenumsetzer *m*
  f convertisseur *m* d'interface
  r интерфейсный преобразователь *m*

5016 interface error

  d Schnittstellenfehler *m*
  f erreur *f* d'interface
  r ошибка *f* интерфейса

5017 interface expander
  d Schnittstellenvielfacher *m*
  f expanseur *m* d'interface
  r интерфейсный расширитель *m*

5018 interface lockout
  d Anschlusssperre *f*
  f blocage *m* d'interface
  r блокировка *f* интерфейса

5019 interface multiplier
  d Schnittstellenvervielfacher *m*
  f multiplicateur *m* d'interface
  r интерфейсный умножитель *m*

5020 interface plan
  d Schnittstellenplan *m*
  f plan *m* d'interface
  r план *m* интерфейса

5021 interface processor
  d Schnittstellenprozessor *m*
  f processeur *m* d'interface
  r интерфейсный процессор *m*

5022 interface register
  d Schnittstellenregister *n*
  f registre *m* d'interface
  r интерфейсный регистр *m*

5023 interface standard
  d Schnittstellennorm *f*
  f standard *m* d'interface
  r интерфейсный стандарт *m*

5024 interface transmitter
  d Schnittstellensender *m*
  f transmetteur *m* d'interface
  r интерфейсный передатчик *m*

* interface trunk → 5009

5025 interface unit
  d Schnittstelleneinheit *f*
  f unité *f* d'interface
  r интерфейсное устройство *n*

5026 interfacing
  d Schnittstellenrealisierung *f*
  f interfaçage *m*
  r сопряжение *n*

5027 interfere *v*
  d beeinflussen; beeinträchtigen
  f interférer
  r интерферировать; вмешиваться

* **interference immunity** → 6186

* **interference signal** → 6198

5028 interlace *v*
d [sich] verflechten; [sich] verschlingen; [sich] verweben
f entrelacer; alterner
r чередовать[ся]; переплетать[ся]; сплетать[ся]

* **interlaced image** → 5031

5029 interlaced scanning
d Zeilen[sprungs]abtastung *f*
f balayage *m* entrelacé; balayage intercalé; balayage interligne
r чересстрочная развёртка *f*; чересстрочное сканирование *n*

5030 interlaced scanning method
d Zeilensprungsverfahren *n*
f méthode *f* de balayage entrelacé; méthode d'entrelacement
r метод *m* чересстрочной развёртки

5031 interlaced [video]image
d verschlungenes Videobild *n*
f image *f* entrelacée
r зацеплённое видеоизображение *n*

5032 interlace line
d Verschlingungslinie *f*; Zwischenzeile *f*
f ligne *f* d'entrelacement
r линия *f* переплетения

5033 interlacing; intertwining; cross interlacing
d Verschlingung *f*; Verschränkung *f*
f entrelacement *m*; enlacement *m*
r переплетение *n*; сплетение *n*; зацепление *n*; скрещивание *n*

* **interlayer connection** → 9360

5034 interleaved memory; interleaving memory
d Speicher *m* mit Adressenverschränkung; Speicher mit Adressenverzahnung
f mémoire *f* à entrelaçage d'adresses; mémoire à adresses entrelacées; mémoire entrelacée
r память *f* с чередованием адресов

5035 interleaving
d Abwechseln *n*; Verzahnung *f*
f alternance *f*; imbrication *f*
r чередование *n*; перемежение *n*

5036 interleaving; bank phasing
d Speicherverschränkung *f*
f entrelaçage *m* d'adresses

r чередование *n* адресов

* **interleaving memory** → 5034

* **interline** → 4918, 5037

5037 interline [spacing]; line[-to-line] spacing; vertical line spacing; row pitch
d Zeilenabstand *m*; Zeilenschritt *m*; Abstand *m* zwischen Zeilen; Vertikalzeilenschaltung *f*
f espace[ment] *m* entre lignes; interligne *f*
r междурядие *n*; интервал *m* между строками; интерлиньяж *m*

* **interlock** → 2621

* **interlocking** → 2621

5038 intermediate
d Zwischen-
f intermédiaire
r промежуточный

5039 intermediate amplification
d Zwischenverstärkung *f*
f amplification *f* intermédiaire
r промежуточное усиление *n*

5040 intermediate calculation
d Zwischenrechnung *f*
f calcul *m* intermédiaire
r промежуточное вычисление *n*

* **intermediate memory** → 1230

* **intermediate repeater** → 7830

5041 intermediate result
d Zwischenergebnis *n*
f résultat *m* provisoire
r промежуточный результат *m*

5042 intermittent fault; transient fault
d intermittierend auftretende Störung *f*
f défaut *m* intermittent
r перемежающаяся неисправность *f*; неустойчивое повреждение *n*

5043 internal clock
d interner Takt *m*
f horloge *f* interne; horloge intérieure
r внутренний синхроимпульс *m*

* **internal clock** → 1746

5044 internal clock [pulse] supply
d interne Taktversorgung *f*
f alimentation *f* d'horloge intérieure
r подача *f* внутренних синхроимпульсов

* **internal clock supply** → 5044

5045 internal conference
 d interne Konferenz *f*
 f conférence *f* interne
 r внутренняя конференция *f*

5046 internal gain
 d innere Verstärkung *f*
 f gain *m* interne
 r внутреннее усиление *n*

5047 internal interrupt
 d innere Unterbrechung *f*; interne
     Unterbrechung
 f interruption *f* interne
 r внутреннее прерывание *n*

* **internal memory** → 5602

* **internal modem** → 4965

**5048 internal network clock; internal network
     timing**
 d netzinterner Takt *m*
 f tact *m* de réseau interne
 r внутренний такт *m* сети

* **internal network timing** → 5048

5049 internal signal
 d internes Signal *n*
 f signal *m* interne
 r внутренний сигнал *m*

5050 international settings
 d internationale Einrichtungen *fpl*
 f paramètres *mpl* internationaux
 r международные приложения *npl*

* **internaut** → 2461

5051 Internet
 d Internet *n*
 f Internet *m*; Net *m*
 r Интернет *m*

**5052 Internet access provider; Internet service
     provider; ISP**
     (firm that provides connections to a part of
     the Internet)
 d Internetverbindungsanbieter *m*;
     Internetdienstanbieter *m*;
     Internetservice-Anbieter *m*
 f fournisseur *m* d'accès Internet
 r поставщик *m* услуг Интернета

5053 Internet address
 d Internet-Adresse *f*
 f adresse *f* Internet

 r Интернет-адрес *m*

* **Internet camera** → 6087

5054 Internet citizen; net-citizen; netizen
     (citizen of the Internet)
 d Bürger *m* im Internet; Netizen *m*
 f citoyen *m* d'Internet; cítoyen de réseau
 r гражданин *m* Интернета

5055 Internet connection wizard; ICW
 d Internetverbindungsassistent *m*
 f assistant *m* de connexion Internet
 r советник *m* Интернет-связи

**5056 Internet [display tele]phone; Webphone;
     netphone; cyberphone**
 d Internet-Telefon *n*
 f téléphone *m* Internet; netphone *m*
 r телефонный номер *m* сети Internet

5057 Internet graphics
 d Internet-Grafik *f*
 f graphique *m* Internet
 r Интернет-графика *f*

**5058 Internet multicast backbone; multicast
     backbone [network]; Mbone**
 d Multicast-Backbone *n*; Mbone *n*
 f réseau *m* [de diffusion] Mbone
 r магистраль *f* многоадресной передачи;
     широковещательная магистраль

5059 Internet objects toolbar
 d Internet-Objekte-Symbolleiste *f*
 f barre *f* d'outils d'objets Internet
 r инструментальная панель *f*
     Интернет-объектов

* **Internet phone** → 5056

**5060 Internet portal; Web portal; portal page;
     portal [site]**
 d Tor *m*; Startseite *f*; Portal *n*
 f portail *m*
 r портал *m*

* **internet protocol** → 5071

5061 Internet protocol; IP
 d Internet-Protokoll *n*; IP
 f protocole *m* Internet
 r Интернет-протокол *m*

5062 Internet publish *v*
 d durch Internet publizieren
 f publier sur Internet
 r публиковать в Интернете

5063 Internet registry; IR
 d Internet Registratur *f*

f service *m* d'enregistrement de l'Internet
r Интернет-реестр *m*

5064 Internet Relay Chat; IRC
(a mechanism that allows for a number of
Internet users to connect to the same network
node and chat in real time)
d Internet-Relay-Chat *n*
f conversation *f* IRC; service *m* de bavardage
Internet
r интернетный эстафетный разговор *m*

* **Internet service provider** → **5052**

5065 Internet Society; ISOC
d Internet-Gesellschaft *f*
f Société *f* Internet
r Интернетное Общество *n*

* **Internet surfing** → **9980**

5066 Internet talk radio
d Internet-Radio *n*
f Internet-radio *m*
r интернетное радио *n*

5067 Internet telephony
d Internet-Telefonie *f*
f téléphonie *f* sur Internet; netphonie *f*
r Интернет-телефония *f*

* **Internet television** → **6078**

* **internetting** → **5069**

5068 Internet user; net user
d Internet-Anwender *m*
f utilisateur *m* d'Internet
r Интернет-пользователь *m*

**5069 internetwork communication; internetting;
internetworking; network interworking**
d netzüberschreitende Kommunikation *f*;
Wechselwirkung *f* von Netzen;
Netzübergang *m*
f interaction *f* de réseaux
r взаимодействие *n* сетей; межсетевое
взаимодействие

* **internetworking** → **5069**

**5070 internetwork interface;
network-[to-]network interface**
d Netz-Netz-Schnittstelle *f*
f interface *f* entre réseaux
r межсетевой интерфейс *m*

5071 internet[work] protocol
d Netz-Netz-Protokoll *n*
f protocole *m* entre réseaux

r межсетевой протокол *m*

5072 interoperability
d Interoperabilität *f*; Kopplungsfähigkeit *f*;
Kommunikationsfähigkeit *f*
f interopérabilité *f*; interfonctionnement *m*
r возможность *f* взаимодействия;
способность *f* к взаимодействию

* **interoperation** → **5107**

5073 inter-paragraph spacing
d Absatzabstand *m*
f espace[ment] *m* entre paragraphes
r расстояние *n* между параграфами

5074 interpolate *v*
d interpolieren
f interpoler
r интерполировать

5075 interpolated animation
d interpolierte Animation *f*
f animation *f* interpolée
r интерполированная анимация *f*

5076 interpolating function
d Interpolationsfunktion *f*
f fonction *f* d'interpolation
r интерполирующая функция *f*

5077 interpolation
d Interpolation *f*
f interpolation *f*
r интерполяция *f*

5078 interpret *v*
d interpretieren; deuten
f interpréter
r толковать; интерпретировать

5079 interpretation
d Interpretation *f*; Deutung *f*
f interprétation *f*
r интерпретация *f*; истолкование *n*;
толкование *n*

5080 interpreted language
d interpretierene Sprache *f*
f langage *m* interprété
r интерпретируемый язык *m*

* **interpreter** → **5081**

* **interpretive program** → **5081**

**5081 interpretive translator; interpret[ive]
program; interpreter**
d interpretierender Umsetzer *m*;
interpretierendes Programm *n*;
Interpret[ier]er *m*

f traducteur *m* interprétatif; programme *m*
interprét[at]eur; interpré[ta]teur *m*
r интерпретирующий транслятор *m*;
интерпретирующая программа *f*;
интерпретатор *m*

* **interpret program** → **5081**

5082 interprocess communication
d Prozesskommunikation *f*
f communication *f* entre processus
r взаимодействие *n* между процессами

5083 interprocessor communication
d Interprozessorkommunikation *f*
f communication *f* entre les processeurs
r межпроцессорная коммуникация *f*

* **interrecord gap** → **1069**

* **interrogate** *v* → **7090**

5084 interrogated information
d abgefragte Information *f*
f information *f* interrogée
r запрошенная информация *f*

* **interrogation** → **7963**

* **interrupt** *v* → **1167**

5085 interrupt call
d unterbrechungsgesteuerter Aufruf *m*
f appel *m* par interruption
r вызов *m* по прерыванию

5086 interrupt-driven I/O
d interruptgesteuerte Eingabe-Ausgabe *f*
f entrée/sortie *f* à commande par interruption;
entrée/sortie commandée par interruption
r ввод/вывод *m*, управляемый
прерываниями

5087 interrupted dialing
d abgesetzte Wahl *f*
f numérotation *f* interrompue
r прерванный вызов *m* номера

* **interrupt handler** → **5099**

5088 interruptibility
d Unterbrech[ungs]barkeit *f*
f interruptibilité *f*
r прерываемость *f*; возможность *f*
прерывания

5089 interrupt identification
d Interruptkennung *f*;
Unterbrechungsidentifizierung *f*
f identification *f* d'interruption

r идентификация *f* прерывания

5090 interrupt indication
d Unterbrechungsanzeige *f*
f indication *f* d'interruption
r обозначение *n* прерывания

5091 interrupt[ing] signal; break signal
d Interruptsignal *n*; Eingriffssignal *n*;
Anhaltesignal *n*; Breaksignal *n*
f signal *m* d'interruption
r сигнал *m* прерывания

* **interruption** → **1171**

5092 interruption-free; no-break
d unterbrechungsfrei
f sans interruption
r беспрерывный

5093 interrupt management
d Interrupt-Management *n*
f management *m* d'interruption
r управление *n* прерыванием

5094 interrupt mask
d Unterbrechungsmaske *f*
f masque *m* d'interruptions
r маска *f* прерываний

5095 interrupt procedure
d Unterbrechungsverfahren *n*;
Unterbrechungsprozedur *f*
f procédure *f* d'interruption
r процедура *f* прерывания

5096 interrupt register; breakpoint register
d Interruptregister *n*; Unterbrechungsregister *n*
f registre *m* d'interruptions
r регистр *m* прерываний

5097 interrupt request; IRQ
d Interruptanfrage *f*;
Unterbrechungsanforderung *f*
f requête *f* d'interruption; interrogation *f*
d'interruption
r запрос *m* прерывания

5098 interrupt response time
d Interruptansprechzeit *f*
f temps *m* de réponse d'interruption
r время *n* реакции на прерывание

* **interrupt routine** → **5099**

**5099 interrupt [service] routine; interrupt
handler**
d Interruptprogramm *n*;
Unterbrechungsprogramm *n*

  f programme *m* [de traitement] d'interruption
  r программа *f* [обработки] прерывания

  * **interrupt signal** → 5091

5100 interrupt system
  d Unterbrechungssystem *n*
  f système *m* d'interruption
  r система *f* прерывания

5101 interrupt vector address
  d Unterbrechungsvektoradresse *f*
  f adresse *f* de vecteur d'interruption
  r адрес *m* вектора прерывания

5102 intersect *v*
  d durchschneiden; kreuzen
  f croiser
  r пересекать

5103 intersection; crossing
  d Durchschnitt *m*
  f intersection *f*
  r пересечение *n*

  * **intertwining** → 5033

5104 interval
  d Intervall *n*
  f intervalle *m*
  r интервал *m*

  * **interval clock** → 5105

  * **interval signal** → 6871

5105 interval timer; interval clock
  d Intervallzeitgeber *m*; Zeitspanngeber *m*
  f horloge *f* à intervalles; cadenceur *m*
      d'intervalles du temps
  r интервальный таймер *m*; датчик *m*
      временных интервалов

  * **interwindow integration** → 5106

**5106 interwindow linking; interwindow
        integration**
  d Verknüpfung *f* der Fenster
  f liaison *f* entre fenêtres; liaison interfenêtre
  r связь *f* между окнами; связывание *n* окон

5107 interworking; interoperation
  d Zusammenarbeit *f*; Zusammenwirken *n*
  f travail *m* commun
  r совместная работа *f*

5108 intra-company communication
  d innerbetriebliche Kommunikation *f*
  f communication *f* à l'intérieur de la firme
  r внутрифирменная связь *f*

5109 intra-facility videoconferencing
  d Videokonferenz *f* innerhalb einer
      Unternehmenseinheit
  f vidéoconférence *f* à l'intérieur de système
  r внутрисистемная видеоконферентная
      связь *f*

5110 intranet; corporate network
  (internal systems, based on Internet
  technology, designed to connect the members
  of a specific group or single company)
  d Intranet *n*; firmeninternes Netz *n*;
      Firmennetz *n*; internes Netz *n*
  f intranet *m*
  r интранет *m*; корпоративная сеть *f*;
      внутрифирменная сеть

5111 in-transit buffering
  d In-Transit-Pufferung *f*; Transitpufferung *f*
  f tamponnage *m* de messages; tamponnage de
      communication
  r буферизация *f* при передаче сообщений

5112 intraware
  d Intranet-Software *f*
  f logiciel *m* destiné à être utilisé sur un intranet
  r интрасетевое программное обеспечение *n*

  * **introduce** *v* → 3437

5113 introduction
  d Vorstellen *n*; Vorstellung *f*
  f introduction *f*
  r введение *n*; внесение *n*

  * **intruder** → 2356

  * **intuitional logic** → 5114

5114 intuitionistic logic; intuitional logic
  d intuitionistische Logik *f*
  f logique *f* intuitionniste
  r интуиционистская логика *f*

5115 invalid; illegal
  d ungültig; unzulässig; illegal; unerlaubt
  f invalide; non valable; illégal
  r недействительный; неверный;
      недопустимый

5116 invalid call
  d unzulässiger Aufruf *m*; ungültiger Aufruf
  f appel *m* invalide
  r неверное обращение *n*

5117 invalid character
  d unzulässiges Zeichen *n*; verbotenes Zeichen
  f caractère *m* invalide
  r неверный знак *m*

5118 invalid code; illegal code; false code
  d illegaler Code *m*; ungültiger Code;
       unerlaubter Code
  f code *m* invalide; code *m* faux
  r недействительный код *m*

5119 invalid frame
  d ungültiger Datenübertragungsblock *m*
  f trame *f* invalide
  r недействительный фрейм *m* [данных]

5120 invalid message code
  d ungültiger Mitteilungscode *m*
  f code *m* de message invalide
  r недействительный код *m* сообщения

5121 invariance
  d Invarianz *f*; Unveränderlichkeit *f*
  f invariance *f*
  r инвариантность *f*

  * **inverse** *adj* → 8055

  * **inversed** *adj* → 8055

5122 inverse element
  d inverses Element *n*
  f élément *m* inverse
  r обратный элемент *m*

  * **inverse feedback** → 6057

5123 inverse function
  d Umkehrfunktion *f*; inverse Funktion *f*
  f fonction *f* inverse
  r обратная функция *f*

5124 inverse operation; reverse operation
  d inverse Operation *f*
  f opération *f* inverse
  r обратная операция *f*

  * **inverse Polish notation** → 7159

5125 inverse video; reverse video
  d inverse Bildschirmdarstellung *f*; inverses
       Video *n*
  f affichage *m* en négatif; vidéo *m* inverse
  r инверсное видеоизображение *n*

5126 inversion
  d Inversion *f*; Invertierung *f*
  f inversion *f*
  r инверсия *f*

5127 invert *v*
  d invertieren; umkehren
  f invertir; inverser
  r инвертировать; обращать

5128 inverted file
  d invertierte Datei *f*
  f fichier *m* inversé
  r инвертированный файл *m*

5129 inverted list database
  d Datenbasis *f* mit invertierter Listenstruktur
  f base *f* de données aux listes inversées
  r база *f* данных с инвертированной
       списковой структурой

  * **inverter** → 6297

  * **invertor** → 6297

  * **invoice** → 90

  * **invoke** *v* → 1354

5130 invoked procedure
  d aufgerufene Prozedur *f*
  f procédure *f* appelée; procédure demandée
  r вызванная процедура *f*; инициализируемая
       процедура

  * **I/O** → 4903

  * **I²O** → 4982

5131 I/O device
  d Eingabe/Ausgabe-Gerät *n*
  f périphérique *m* d'entrée/sortie
  r устройство *n* ввода/вывода

  * **I/O interrupt** → 4909

5132 I/O port
  d Eingabe/Ausgabe-Port *m*
  f port *m* d'entrée/sortie
  r порт *m* ввода/вывода

  * **IP** → 4813, 4953, 5061

5133 IP address
  d IP-Adresse *f*
  f adresse *f* IP
  r IP адрес *m*

5134 IP number
  d IP-Nummer *f*
  f numéro *m* IP
  r IP номер *m*

  * **IPS** → 4956

5135 IP spoofing; address spoofing
  d IP-Schwindeln *m*; IP-Hereinlegen *n*;
       Adressenschwindel *n*
  f piratage *m* [d'adresses] IP
  r подмена *f* [IP] адресов

* IR → 5063

* IRC → 5064

* IRL → 4925

* IRQ → 5097

5136 IRQ line
 d Unterbrechungsanforderungslinie *f*
 f ligne *f* d'interrogation d'interruption
 r линия *f* запроса прерывания

5137 irrecoverable; unrecoverable
 d unverbesserlich; irreparabel
 f irrémédiable; irréparable
 r неисправимый; невосстановимый

* **irrecoverable error** → 9692

5138 irreducible code
 d irreduzibler Code *m*
 f code *m* irréductible
 r неприводимый код *m*

* **irredundant** → 6259

5139 irregular
 d unregelmäßig; irregulär
 f irrégulier
 r неправильный; неравномерный; нерегулярный

5140 irregular code
 d unregelmäßiger Code *m*
 f code *m* irrégulier
 r нерегулярный код *m*

5141 irrelevant data; insignificant data
 d unwesentliche Daten *pl*
 f données *fpl* sans importance; données insignifiantes
 r несущественные данные *pl*

* **ISDN** → 4977

5142 ISDN adapter
 d ISDN-Adapter *m*
 f adaptateur *m* RNIS
 r адаптер *m* цифровой сети

5143 ISDN number
 d ISDN-Nummer *f*
 f numéro *m* RNIS
 r номер *m* цифровой сети

5144 ISDN socket
 d ISDN-Steckdose *f*
 f socle *m* RNIS
 r гнездо *n* цифровой сети

5145 ISDN-standardized message
 d ISDN-normierte Meldung *f*
 f message *m* RNIS standardisé
 r стандартиз[ир]ованное сообщение *n* цифровой сети

* **ISOC** → 5065

5146 isochronous
 d isochron
 f isochrone
 r одновременный; изохронный

5147 isolation
 d Isolation *f*
 f isolation *f*
 r изоляция *f*

5148 isolation level
 (for query transactions)
 d Isolationsniveau *n*
 f niveau *m* d'isolation
 r уровень *m* изоляции

* **ISP** → 5052

* **IT** → 4821

* **italic** → 5149

5149 italic [face]; italic typeface; obliquing text font
 d Kursiv *n*; Kursivschrift *f*; Schrägschrift *f*
 f type *m* de police italique; italique *f*; police *f* de texte incliné
 r курсив *m*

* **italic typeface** → 5149

* **item** → 7144

5150 item
 d Einzelheit *f*; Einheit *f*; Element *n*
 f unité *f*; détail *m*; élément *m*
 r отдельный предмет *m*; элемент *m*; единица *f*

5151 iterated kernel
 d iterierter Kern *m*
 f noyau *m* itéré
 r итерированное ядро *n*

5152 iteration
 d Iteration *f*
 f itération *f*
 r итерация *f*

5153 iteration factor
 d Iterationsfaktor *m*

f facteur *m* d'itération
r глубина *f* итерации

* **iteration method** → **5803**

5154 iteration process
d Iterationsprozess *m*
f processus *m* d'itération
r процесс *m* итерации

5155 iterative
d iterativ
f itératif
r итеративный; итерационный

5156 iterative coding
d Wägecodierung *f*
f codage *m* itératif
r итеративное кодирование *n*

* **iterative method** → **5803**

5157 iterative statement; repetitive statement
d Iterationsstatement *n*;
    Wiederholungsstatement *n*
f instruction *f* itérative; instruction répétitive
r оператор *m* [организации] цикла

* **iterative technique** → **5803**

5158 iterator
d Iterator *m*
f itérateur *m*; générateur *m* de simulations
    itératives
r повторитель *m*

J

* jack → 7004

* Java → 5159

5159 Java [programming language]
 d Java[-Sprache *f*]
 f [langage *m*]Java
 r [язык *m*]Ява; язык Java

* JavaScript → 5160

5160 JavaScript [scripting language]
 d Java-Skriptsprache *f*
 f langage *m* JavaScript
 r язык *m* JavaScript

* JBIG format → 5173

5161 jitter; flutter
      (of a videoimage)
 d Zittern *n*; Flattern *n*; Signalverzerrung *f*
 f perturbation *f*
 r дрожание *n*; вибрация *f*

* JM → 5192

5162 job
 d Arbeitsauftrag *m*; Auftrag *m*; Job *m*
 f travail *m*; job *m*
 r задание *n*; работа *f*

5163 job accounting system
 d Jobarbeitungssystem *n*
 f système *m* de travaux
 r система *f* учёта заданий

5164 job administration
 d Jobverwaltung *f*
 f administration *f* de travaux
 r администрирование *n* заданий

5165 job batch
 d Job-Batch *m*
 f lot *m* de travaux; lot de jobs
 r пакет *m* заданий

5166 job buffer
 d Auftragspuffer *m*
 f tampon *m* de jobs
 r буфер *m* заданий

5167 job control; job management

 d Jobsteuerung *f*; Steuerung *f* des
      Arbeitselements
 f commande *f* de travaux
 r управление *n* заданиями

5168 job control language; command language
 d Kommandosprache *f*; Jobkontrollsprache *f*
 f langage *m* de contrôle de travaux; langage de
      commandes
 r язык *m* управления заданиями; язык
      команд

5169 job definition
 d Jobdefinition *f*
 f définition *f* de travail
 r описание *n* задания

* job management → 5167

5170 job name
 d Arbeitsname *m*; Jobname *m*
 f nom *m* de travail; nom de job
 r имя *n* задания

5171 job scheduler
 d Jobprioritätssteuerprogramm *n*;
      Auftragsablaufplaner *m*
 f programme *m* de commande de travaux
 r [программа-]планировщик *m* заданий

5172 job stream; input stream; run stream
 d Jobstrom *m*
 f flux *m* de travaux; flot *m* de jobs; file *f* de
      travaux
 r поток *m* заданий

* join *v* → 585

* join → 5191

* joint → 5191

5173 joint bilevel image group format; JBIG
      format
 d JBIG-Format *n*
 f format *m* JBIG (de compression d'image fixe
      en deux tons)
 r формат *m* JBIG

5174 joint photographic expert group format;
      JP[E]G format
 d JP[E]G-Format *n*
 f format *m* JP[E]G
 r формат *m* JP[E]G

5175 journal; log[-book]; protocol
 d Journal *n*; Logbuch *n*; Protokoll *n*
 f journal *m*; procès-verbal *m*; log *m*
 r журнал *m* [регистрации]; протокол *m*

5176 journal postprocessing
d Rufdatennachverarbeitung f
f traitement m final de journal
r окончательная обработка f журнала

5177 journal recovery
d Rufdatenaufzeichnungsrestart m
f récupération f de journal
r восстановление n журнала

5178 journal roll
d Journal-Rolle f
f catalogue m de journal
r журнальный каталог m

5179 joystick
d Joystick m; Steuerknüppel m; Steuerhebel m
f manche m [à balai]; manette f; poignée f
r джойстик m; рычажный указатель m;
    координатная ручка f

5180 JP[E]G builder
d JP[E]G-Bilder m
f bâtisseur m JP[E]G
r JP[E]G-построитель m

5181 JP[E]G file
d JP[E]G-Datei f
f fichier m JP[E]G
r JP[E]G-файл m

* **JPEG format → 5174**

* **JPG builder → 5180**

* **JPG file → 5181**

* **JPG format → 5174**

* **judge → 496**

5182 judgement
d Urteil n; Aussage f
f jugement m
r суждение n; высказывание n

5183 jughead
    (a program, used in conjunction with Gopher,
    that provides the means to search all of the
    menu selections within a particular Gopher
    server)
d Jughead n
f jughead m; outil m de recherche Gopher
r служба f поиска в системе Gopher

5184 jukebox
    (a program)
d Jukebox f; Musikbox f
f logiciel m de jukebox; discothèque f
    automatique

r программа f автоматической смены

5185 jump; spring; hop
d Sprung m
f saut m
r скачок m; прыжок m; перелёт m; переход m

5186 jump effect
d Springeffekt m
f effet m de saut; effet de bond
r эффект m скока

5187 jumper; strap
d Jumper m; Kurzschlussbrücke f;
    Kontaktbrücke f; Spingler m;
    Unterbrückungsdraht m
f pont m; cavalier m; connexion f volante; fil m
    volant
r перемычка f; переходник m; переходное
    соединение n; навесной проводник m

5188 jump if overflow
d Sprung m bei Überlauf
f saut m si débordement
r переход m по переполнению

* **jump if sign → 6061**

5189 jump if zero
d Sprung m bei Null
f saut m si zéro
r переход m по нулю

**5190 jump instruction; skip instruction;
    alternate instruction**
d Sprungbefehl m; Übersprungbefehl m;
    Skipbefehl m
f instruction f de saut
r инструкция f перехода; инструкция
    пропуска

5191 junction; join[t]
d Verbindung f; Vereinigung f;
    Zusammenschaltung f; Kupplung f
f jonction f; joint m; raccord m; jointure f
r соединение n; стыковка f

* **junction capacitance → 827**

* **junk → 4170**

5192 junk mail; JM
d Müllpost f; Werbepost f; unerwünschte Post f
f poste f d'ordure
r макулатурная почта f; мусорная
    электронная почта f; незапрашиваемая
    электронная почта

5193 justifiable digit time slot
d stopfbarer Zeitabschnitt m

    f tranche *f* de temps digitale ajustable
    r выравниваемый цифровой квант *m*
      времени

    * **justification** → 308, 513

5194 **justification bit; justifying bit; match bit**
    d Anpassungsbit *n*; Stopfbit *n*
    f bit *m* de justification; bit de comparaison
    r выравнивающий бит *m*; бит совпадения;
      бит сравнения

5195 **justified text; justifying text**
    d [rechts-links-]bündiger Text *m*
    f texte *m* ajusté; texte justifié
    r двусторонне выравненный текст *m*

    * **justify** *v* → 305

    * **justifying** → 308

    * **justifying bit** → 5194

    * **justifying text** → 5195

5196 **juxtaposition**
    d Aneinanderlegung *f*; Nebeneinandersetzen *n*;
      Juxtaposition *f*
    f juxtaposition *f*
    r непосредственное соседство *n*;
      соприкосновение *n*; расположение *n*
      рядом; склеивание *n*

K

5197 Karnaugh map
  d Karnaugh-Tafel *f*
  f table *f* de Karnaugh; diagramme *m* de Karnaugh
  r карта *f* Карно

  * **KB** → 5232

  * **KBPS** → 5233

5198 kernel; nucleus
  d Kern *m*; Nukleus *m*
  f noyau *m*; nucléus *m*
  r ядро *n*

5199 kernel field; base field
  d Kernfeld *n*
  f champ *m* de noyau
  r поле *n* ядра

5200 kerning
  d Unterschneidung *f*
  f crénage *m*; réajustement *m* de l'espace entre caractères
  r кернинг *m*; согласование *n* расстояния между буквами

5201 key
  d Schlüssel *m*
  f clé *f*; clef *f*; chiffre *m*
  r ключ *m*; шифр *m*

  * **key** → 9081

5202 key; button
  d Taste *f*
  f touche *f*
  r клавиша *f*

5203 key address
  d Schlüsseladresse *f*
  f adresse *f* clé
  r ключевой адрес *m*

5204 keyboard
  d Tastatur *f*
  f clavier *m*
  r клавиатура *f*

5205 keyboard buffer
  d Zeichenspeicher *m*; Tastaturspeicher *m*
  f tampon *m* de clavier
  r буфер *m* клавиатуры

  * **keyboard coder** → 5208

5206 keyboard component
  d Tastaturbaustein *m*
  f component *m* de clavier
  r часть *f* клавиатуры

5207 keyboard customizing
  d Anpassung *f* der Tastatur
  f personnalisation *f* du clavier
  r наладка *f* заказного варианта клавиатуры

5208 keyboard [en]coder
  d Tastaturcodierer *m*
  f codeur *m* à clavier
  r шифратор *m* клавиатуры

5209 keyboard entry; keyboard-in; keyboard input
  d Tastatureingabe *f*
  f entrée *f* par clavier
  r ввод *m* с клавиатуры

  * **keyboard-in** → 5209

  * **keyboard input** → 5209

5210 keyboard inquiry; keyboard scanning
  d Tastaturabfrage *f*
  f interrogation *f* du clavier; scrutation *f* du clavier
  r опрос *m* клавиатуры; сканирование *n* клавиатуры

  * **keyboard scanning** → 5210

5211 keyboard selection; keyboard signaling
  d Tastaturwahl *f*
  f sélection *f* de clavier
  r выбор *m* клавиатуры

5212 keyboard shortcut; accelerator keyboard
  d Tastaturkürzel *n*; Tastaturkurzbefehl *m*
  f abréviation *f* clavier; raccourci-clavier *m*
  r клавишная комбинация *f* быстрого вызова; сокращённая клавиатурная команда *f*

  * **keyboard signaling** → 5211

5213 key change
  d Schlüsseländerung *f*
  f changement *m* par clé
  r изменение *n* по ключу

5214 key combination
  d Tastenkombination *f*
  f combinaison *f* de touches
  r клавишная комбинация *f*

5215 key data
  d Schlüsseldaten *pl*

f données *fpl* de clé
r ключевые данные *pl*

5216 key depression; key stroke
   d Tast[en]anschlag *m*; Tastendruck *m*
   f frappe *f* de touche
   r нажатие *n* клавиши; удар *m* клавиши

5217 key-driven
   d tastengesteuert
   f commandé par touches
   r с кнопочным управлением; с клавишным управлением

* keyed access → 64

5218 key feature
   d Schlüsseleigenschaft *f*; Hauptmerkmal *n*
   f caractéristique-clé *f*
   r ключевой признак *m*; отличительный признак

5219 key help
   d Tastenbestimmung-Information *f*
   f aide *f* pour la désignation de touches
   r консультативная информация *f* о назначении клавиш

5220 key help
   d Schlüsselhilfe *f*
   f aide *f* par clé
   r помощь *f* по ключу

5221 keylock
   d Tastensperre *f*
   f verrou *m* de touche
   r блокировка *f* клавиши

5222 keypad
   d Kleintastatur *f*; Handtastatur *f*
   f pavé *m* du clavier
   r специализированная клавиатура *f*; вспомагательная клавиатура

5223 key planes
   d Schlüsselebenen *fpl*
   f plans *mpl* clés
   r ключевые плоскости *fpl*

5224 keyset
   d Tastenfeld *n*
   f ensemble *m* de touches; panneau *m* à touches
   r ряд *m* клавиш; клавишная панель *f*

5225 keystone correction
   d Trapezentzerrung *f*
   f correction *f* de trapèze
   r коррекция *f* трапецеидального искажения

* keystone distortion → 5226

5226 keystonning; keystone distortion; trapezium distortion
   d Trapezverzerrung *f*; Trapezfehler *m*
   f raccourcissement *m* d'image avec déformation partielle; distorsion *f* trapézoïdale; distorsion de trapèze horizontale
   r трапецеидальное искажение *n*

* key stroke → 5216

5227 keystroke memory
   d Tastatur[puffer]speicher *m*
   f mémoire *f* tampon de clavier
   r буферная память *f* клавиатуры

5228 keyswitch
   d Tastenschalter *m*; Schlüsselschalter *m*
   f commutateur *m* à clé; commutateur à touches
   r кнопочный переключатель *m*; клавишный переключатель

5229 keyword; index word
   d Schlüsselwort *n*; Indexwort *n*; Stichwort *n*
   f mot *m* d'index; mot de clé; mot-clé *m*
   r ключевое слово *n*; индексное слово

5230 keyword-oriented language
   d Schlüsselwortsprache *f*
   f langage *m* orienté mot-clé
   r язык *m* ключевых слов

* kHz → 5234

5231 kill file
   (e-slang)
   d Auslöschen-Datei *f*; Filterdatei *f* gegen unerwünschte Nachrichten
   f fichier *m* filtre des messages
   r файл *m* для мусора

5232 kilobyte; KB
   d Kilobyte *n*; KB
   f kilo-octet *m*; Ko
   r килобайт *m*; Кб

5233 kilobyte per second; KBPS
   d Kilobytes *npl* pro Sekunde
   f kilo-octets *mpl* par seconde
   r килобайтов *mpl* в секунду

* kilocycles per second → 5234

5234 kilohertz; kHz; kilocycles per second
   d Kilohertz *n*
   f kilohertz *m*; kilocycles *mpl* par seconde
   r килогерц *m*; кгц

5235 kiloword
   d Kilowort *n*

    f kilomot *m*
    r килослово *n*

    * **knife plug** → 1043

    * **knob** → 1296

    * **knot** → 6165

    * **knowbot** → 5242

5236 knowledge
    d Kenntnis *f*; Wissenschaft *f*
    f savoir *m*; science *f*, connaissance *f*
    r знание *n*; познание *n*

5237 knowledge acquisition
    d Wissenserfassung *f*
    f acquisition *f* de connaissance
    r сбор *m* знаний

    * **knowledge base** → 841

5238 knowledge base system
    d Wissensbasissystem *n*
    f système *m* à base de connaissance
    r система *f* баз знаний

5239 knowledge editor
    d Wissenseditor *m*
    f éditeur *m* de connaissance
    r редактор *m* знаний

5240 knowledge engineer
    d Wisseningenieur *m*
    f ingénieur *m* cogniticien; cogniticien *m*;
    ingénieur de la connaissance; sapitaire *m*
    r инженер *m* знаний

5241 knowledge engineering
    d Wissenstechnologie *f*
    f ingénierie *f* de connaissance
    r технология *f* представления и обработки
    знаний

5242 knowledge robot; knowbot
    d Wissensroboter *m*; Knowbot *m*
    f robot *m* bibliothécaire; robot de nature
    logicielle
    r робот *m* знаний

L

5243 label; tag
   d Etikett *n*; Kennung *f*
   f étiquette *f*; label *m*
   r метка *f*; этикет *m*

5244 label cylinder
   d Kennsatzzylinder *m*
   f cylindre *m* des labels; cylindre des étiquettes
   r цилиндр *m* меток

5245 label data
   d Etikett[en]daten *pl*
   f données *fpl* du type étiquette
   r данные *pl* типа метки

   * **labeled** → 9178

   * **labeled statement** → 5246

   * **labeling** → 5247

   * **labelled** → 9178

5246 label[l]ed statement
   d markierte Anweisung *f*
   f instruction *f* étiquetée; instruction à label
   r помеченный оператор *m*

5247 label[l]ing
   d Etikettierung *f*
   f étiquetage *m*; attribution *f* de label
   r присваивание *n* меток

5248 label point
   d Etikettpunkt *m*
   f point *m* d'étiquette
   r точка *f* метки

5249 label statement
   d Kennsatzanweisung *f*
   f instruction *f* de label
   r оператор-метка *m*

5250 label style
   d Etikettstil *m*
   f style *m* d'étiquettes
   r стиль *m* меток

5251 label variable
   d Etikettvariable *f*; Label-Variable *f*
   f variable *f* [identifiante une] étiquette
   r переменная *f* типа метки

5252 labyrinth
   d Labyrinth *n*
   f labyrinthe *m*
   r лабиринт *m*

5253 ladder logic
   d Kettenlogik *f*
   f logique *f* scalaire
   r цепная логическая схема *f*; многозвенная логическая схема; многоступенчатая логика *f*

   * **lag** → 2721

   * **lagging** → 2721

   * **lag time** → 2728

5254 lag unit
   d Totzeitglied *n*
   f élément *m* de temporisation
   r звено *n* запаздывания

   * **laminated board** → 5947

   * **LAN** → 5439

5255 LAN architecture
   d Architektur *f* lokaler Netze
   f architecture *f* de réseau local
   r архитектура *f* местной сети

   * **landscape** → 5257

5256 landscape display
   d Querformat-Display *n*; Querformat-Bildschirm *m*
   f écran *m* panoramique
   r дисплей *m* с изображением, вытянутым по горизонтали

5257 landscape format; landscape [orientation]; landscape layout
   d Querformat *n*
   f format *m* horizontal; présentation *f* à l'horizontale; présentation à l'italienne
   r поперечный формат *m*

   * **landscape layout** → 5257

   * **landscape orientation** → 5257

5258 landscape paper orientation
   d Quer-Seitenausrichtung *f*
   f orientation *f* de papier paysage
   r ориентация *f* поперёк страницы

5259 language
   d Sprache *f*

f langage *m*
r [кодовый] язык *m*

5260 language driver
d Sprache-Treiber *m*
f pilote *m* de langage
r языковый драйвер *m*

5261 language identificator
d Sprachidentifikator *m*
f identificateur *m* de langage
r идентификатор *m* языка

5262 language processing
d Sprachverarbeitung *f*
f traitement *m* d'information linguistique
r обработка *f* лингвистической информации

  * **language processor → 5263**

5263 language[-specific] processor
d Sprachprozessor *m*;
   Übersetzungsprogramm *n*
f processeur *m* de langage
r языковый процессор *m*; процессор,
   ориентированный на конкретный язык

5264 language translation; translation
d Sprachübersetzung *f*
f traduction *f* de langage
r языковый перевод *m*

5265 language-understanding program
d Sprachverständnisprogramm *n*
f programme *m* de compréhension de langage
r программа *f* восприятия [естественного]
   языка

  * **laptop → 7131**

  * **laptop computer → 7131**

5266 large button
d große Taste *f*
f grand bouton *m*
r большой бутон *m*

5267 large-sample test
d Test *m* für große Stichproben
f test *m* pour les grands échantillons
r критерий *m* для больших выборок

**5268 large-scale computer; all-purpose
     computer**
d universeller Rechner *m*; Universalrechner *m*;
   Universalcomputer *m*; Allzweckrechner *m*
f ordinateur *m* universel; ordinateur
   d'utilisation générale
r универсальный компьютер *m*

5269 large-scale graphics
d Großmaßstab-Grafik *f*
f graphique *m* à grande échelle
r крупномасштабная графика *f*

5270 large-scale integrated circuit; LSI circuit
d hochintegrierte Schaltung *f*; LSI-Schaltung *f*
f circuit *m* intégré à haut degré; circuit LSI
r схема *f* с высокой степенью интеграции;
   большая интегральная схема; БИС

5271 large-scale integration; LSI
d Großintegration *f*; Hochintegration *f*; LSI
f intégration *f* à haut degré; intégration à
   grande échelle; LSI
r высокая степень *f* интеграции;
   интеграция *f* высокого уровня

5272 large-screen graphics
d Großbildgrafik *f*; Großschirmgrafik *f*
f graphique *m* à écran large
r широкоэкранная графика *f*

5273 laser[-beam] printer
d Laserdrucker *m*
f imprimante *f* [à] laser
r лазерное печатающее устройство *n*;
   лазерный принтер *m*

  * **laser disk → 1964**

  * **laser display → 5275**

5274 laser flatbed scanner
d Laser-Flachbettscanner *m*
f scanneur *m* [à] laser plat
r планшетный лазерный сканер *m*

  * **laser printer → 5273**

5275 laser[-scan] display
d Laserbildschirm *m*
f écran *m* à [rayon] laser
r лазерный экран *m*

5276 laser scanner
d Laserscanner *m*; Laserlesegerät *n*
f scanner *m* [à] laser
r лазерный сканер *m*

5277 laser scanning
d Laserabtasung *f*; Laserscannen *n*
f échantillonnage *m* [à] laser
r лазерное сканирование *n*

5278 last digit
d letzte Ziffer *f*; letzte Stelle *f*
f chiffre *m* des unités
r последняя цифра *f*

5279 last-in, first-out; LIFO
  d LIFO
  f dernier entré, premier sorti; LIFO
  r последним пришёл, первым вышел;
  магазинного типа

  * **latch → 5283, 5284**

5280 latched input; latching input
  d Eingang *m* mit Latchregister
  f entrée *f* à registre verrou; entrée tamponnée
  r вход *m* с регистром-защёлкой;
  буферизированный вход

5281 latching
  (of data)
  d Selbsthandlung *f*; Schaltzustandsfixierung *f*;
  Informationsfang *m*
  f automaintien *m* [d'état commuté];
  tamponnage *m* [d'informations]
  r фиксация *f*

5282 latching; latchup
  d Selbsthaltung *f*; Sperrung *f*; Verriegelung *f*
  f verrouillage *m*
  r защёлкивание *n*

  * **latching input → 5280**

5283 latch [register]
  d Latchregister *n*; Auffangregister *n*;
  Informationsfangregister *n*; Latch *n*;
  Auffangspeicher *m*; selbsthaltender
  Schalter *m*
  f registre *m* verrou; verrou *m*; registre de
  tampon [d'information]
  r регистр-фиксатор *m*; регистр-защёлка *m*;
  защёлка *f*

5284 latch [trigger]
  d Auffangflipflop *m*; selbsthaltender
  Schalter *m*; Latchflipflop *m*
  f bascule *f* de maintien; autocommutateur *m*;
  verrou *m*
  r фиксатор *m*; триггер-защёлка *m*;
  одноступенчатый триггер *m*

  * **latchup → 5282**

5285 latency
  d Latenz *f*
  f latence *f*
  r ожидание *n*

5286 latency time
  d Latenzzeit *f*; Wartezeit *f*
  f temps *m* de latence
  r время *n* ожидания; время латентного
  состояния

5287 latent
  d latent
  f latent
  r скрытый; латентный

5288 lateral; side
  d seitlich; lateral; Seiten-
  f latéral
  r продольный; боковой

  * **lateral parity check → 9782**

5289 lattice; grating
  d Gitterrost *m*; Rost *m*
  f lattis *m*; treillis *m*; réseau *m*
  r решётка *f*; сетка *f*

  * **launch → 8840**

5290 launcher
  d Launcher *m*; Abschussvorrichtung *f*
  f lanceur *m*
  r модуль *m* запуска; запускающий модуль

5291 law
  d Gesetz *n*; Satz *m*; Prinzip *n*
  f loi *f*; principe *m*
  r закон *m*; принцип *m*

5292 law of double negation
  d Gesetz *n* der doppelten Negation
  f loi *f* de double négation
  r закон *m* двойного отрицания; закон
  отрицания отрицания

**5293 laws of De Morgan; De Morgan['s] laws;
  De Morgan['s] formulae**
  d Gesetze *npl* von De Morgan; Formeln *fpl* von
  De Morgan
  f lois *fpl* de De Morgan; formules *fpl* de De
  Morgan
  r законы *mpl* Де Моргана; формулы *fpl* Де
  Моргана

5294 layer; level; overlay; sheet
  (in computer graphics and GIS)
  d Schicht *f*; Ebene *f*
  f couche *f*; plan *m*; calque *m*; niveau *m*
  r слой *m*

5295 layered depth image; LDI
  d Schichttiefe-Bild *n*
  f image *f* profonde en couches
  r расслоённое в глубине изображение *n*

5296 layer[ed] structure
  d Schichtstruktur *f*
  f structure *f* stratifiée
  r слоистая структура *f*

5297 layering
  d Schichtenteilung *f*; Schichtung *f*
  f division *f* en plans; division en couches
  r разбиение *n* на слои; расслоение *n*

  * **layer structure → 5296**

  * **layout → 1165**

5298 layout
  d topografische Anordnung *f*;
       Aufstellungsweise *f*; Layout *n*
  f disposition *f* [topologique]; placement *m*;
       layout *m*
  r [топологическое] расположение *n*;
       [топологическое] размещение *n*

5299 layout character; format effector
  d Anordnungszeichen *n*; Formatsteuerzeichen *n*
  f caractère *m* de disposition; caractère de mise
       en page
  r знак *m* размещения; знак спецификации
       формата

5300 layout chart; layout plan; artwork
       (sketch or plan of how a page or sheet will
       look when printed)
  d Aufstellungsplan *m*; Zeichenvorlage *f*;
       topologische Vorlage *f*
  f carte *f* de disposition; carte topologique;
       plan *m* de montage; schéma *m* topologique
  r планировка *f*; схема *f* расположения;
       топологическая схема; монтажная схема

5301 layout data
  d Layoutdaten *pl*
  f données *fpl* de disposition
  r данные *pl* о размещении

  * **layout plan → 5300**

5302 layout style
  d Layoutstil *m*
  f style *m* de layout
  r стиль *m* размещения; стиль расположения

5303 lay user
  d unprofessioneller Anwender *m*
  f utilisateur *m* non professionnel
  r непрофессиональный пользователь *m*

  * **LBA → 5465**

  * **LCD → 5409**

5304 LCD addressing
  d Adressierung *f* der Flüssigkristallbildschirme
  f adressage *m* d'afficheur à cristaux liquides
  r адресация *f* жидкокристаллического
       дисплея

5305 LCD module
  d Flüssigkristall-Anzeigemodul *n*
  f module *m* d'affichage à cristaux liquides
  r модуль *m* жидкокристоллической
       индикации

5306 LCD printer
  d Flüssigkristallanzeige-Drucker *m*
  f imprimante *f* à cristaux liquides
  r принтер *m* на жидких кристаллах;
       жидкокристаллический принтер;
       ЖК-принтер *m*

5307 LCD projector
  d Flüssigkristall-Projektor *m*
  f projecteur *m* LCD
  r проектор *m* на жидких кристаллах;
       жидкокристаллический проектор;
       ЖК-проектор *m*

  * **LDI → 5295**

  * **lead *v* → 4352**

5308 leaded carrier
  d Chipträger *m* mit vorstehenden Ausschlüssen
  f support *m* de puce avec sorties
  r кристаллодержатель *m* с выводами

  * **leader → 886**

5309 leader
  d Leiter *m*; Vorlauf *m*
  f leader *m*; directeur *m*; apériteur *m*
  r водитель *m*

5310 lead hole; mounting hole
  d Montageloch *n*
  f trou *m* de montage; trou de câblage
  r монтажное отверстие *n*; крепёжное
       отверстие

  * **leading → 5597**

  * **leading address → 8844**

5311 leading bits
  d führende Bits *npl*
  f bits *mpl* de tête; bits d'en-tête
  r ведущие биты *mpl*

5312 leading digit
  d führende Ziffer *f*
  f chiffre *m* d'en-tête
  r первая цифра *f* числа

  * **leading edge → 7504**

5313 leading edge
       (of a carrier)

d Vorderkante *f*
f bord *m* d'attaque; bord avant
r ведущий край *m*

* **leading end → 886**

5314 leading page; front page
d Leitseite *f*; Titelseite *f*
f page *f* première; page d'en-tête; page frontale
r начальная страница *f*; заголовная страница

5315 lead-lag circuit
d Vor-/Nacheilungsschaltung *f*
f circuit *m* d'antipompage
r стабилизирующая схема *f*

5316 leadless carrier; unleaded carrier
d anschlussloser Chipträger *m*
f support *m* de puce sans sorties
r безвыводный кристаллодержатель *m*

5317 leadless chip
d anschlussloser Chip *m*
f puce *f* sans sorties
r безвыводный кристалл *m*

5318 lead-out
d vorstehender Anschluss *m*; herausgeführter Anschluss
f raccordement *m* de sortie; bout *m*
r выводной провод *m*

* **lead time → 8480**

5319 learning; instruction; education
d Lernen *n*; Instruktion *f*; Ausbildung *f*
f enseignement *m*; instruction *f*; éducation *f*
r обучение *n*; наставление *n*

5320 learning automaton; learning machine
d lernender Automat *m*; lernende Maschine *f*
f automate *m* élève [autodidacte]; machine *f* enseignante
r [само]обучающийся автомат *m*

* **learning machine → 5320**

5321 learning process
d Lernprozess *m*
f processus *m* d'éducation
r процесс *m* обучения

* **learning program → 9225**

5322 leased data circuit
d Direktdatenverbindung *f*
f ligne *f* de données louée
r арендуемая линия *f* данных

5323 least significant bit; lowest order bit

d niedrigstwertiges Bit *n*; letztes signifikantes Bit
f bit *m* de l'ordre le plus bas; dernier bit significatif
r самый младший бит *m*; младший значащий бит

5324 least significant digit
d niedrigstwertige Ziffer *f*; gültige Ziffer der niedrigsten Ordnung; letzte signifikante Ziffer
f chiffre *m* de l'ordre le plus bas; dernier chiffre significatif; digit *m* du plus petit poids
r цифра *f* самого младшего разряда; [самый] младший значащий разряд *m*; младшая значащая цифра

* **LED → 5360**

5325 ledger card
d Kontokarte *f*
f carte *f* compte; fiche *f* de compte
r конто[корентная] карта *f*

5326 LED printer
d Leuchtdiodendrucker *m*
f imprimante *f* à diode électroluminiscente; imprimante à LED
r светодиодный принтер *m*

* **left-aligned → 5330**

* **left alignment → 5329**

5327 left arrow
d Linkspfeil *m*
f flèche *f* à gauche
r левая стрелка *f*

5328 left arrow key
d Linkspfeil-Taste *f*
f touche *f* de flèche à gauche
r клавиша *f* левой стрелки

5329 left[-hand] justification; left alignment
d linksbündige Justierung *f*; linksbündige Ausrichtung *f*
f justification *f* à gauche; alignement *m* à gauche
r выравнивание *n* влево; левое выравнивание

* **left-hand zeros → 4501**

* **left justification → 5329**

5330 left-justified; left-aligned
d links ausgerichtet
f aligné à gauche
r выровненный влево

5331 leftmost character
d äußerstes linkes Zeichen *n*; höchstwertiges
  Zeichen
f caractère *m* le plus à gauche; caractère
  [d'extrême] gauche
r самый левый знак *m*; крайний левый знак

5332 left mouse button; primary mouse button
d linke Maustaste *f*
f bouton *m* gauche de souris
r левый бутон *m* мыши

5333 left recursive grammar
d links rekursive Grammatik *f*
f grammaire *f* récursive gauche
r леворекурсивная грамматика *f*

* **left-right scrolling** → 4562

5334 left scroll arrow
d Bildlaufpfeil *m* links
f flèche *f* de défilement à gauche
r стрелка *f* прокрутки влево

5335 left shift
d Linksverschiebung *f*
f décalage *m* vers à gauche; déplacement *m* à
  gauche
r сдвиг *m* влево

* **lengthening** → 3355

5336 length indicator; length specifier
d Längenkennzeichen *n*; Längenangeber *m*
f indicateur *m* de longueur; spécificateur *m* de
  longueur
r показатель *m* длины; указатель *m* длины

5337 length modifier
d Längenschlüssel *m*; Längenfaktor *m*
f modificateur *m* de la longueur
r модификатор *m* длины

* **length specifier** → 5336

5338 letter
d Schreiben *n*
f lettre *f*
r письмо *n*

5339 letter; alphabetical character
d Buchstabe *m*; Schriftzeichen *n*;
  Alphabetzeichen *n*
f lettre *f*; caractère *m* alphabétique
r буква *f*; алфавитный символ *m*

5340 letterbomb; e-[mail-]bomb; mailbomb
  (in e-mail)
d E-Mail-Bombe *f*; Briefbombe *f*; Postbombe *f*
f lettre *f* bombe; bombe *f* e-mail

r [электронно-]почтовая бомба *f*;
  письмо-бомба *n*

* **lettering** → 5425

* **letter outline** → 5343

5341 letter-quality printer
d Schönschreibdrucker *m*
f imprimante *f* de qualité dactylographique
r высококачественное печатающее
  устройство *n*

5342 letter-quality printing
d Schöndruck *m*
f impression *f* de qualité dactylographique
r высококачественная печать *f*

5343 letter shape; letter outline
d Buchstabenfigur *f*
f figure *f* de lettre
r форма *f* буквы; начертание *n* буквы

* **letter slant** → 5344

5344 letter slant[ing]
d Buchtaben-Neigung *f*
f inclinaison *f* de lettres
r наклон *m* букв

* **level** → 5294

5345 level latch
d Signalpegel-Latch *n*;
  Signalpegelhaltespeicher *m*
f verrou *m* de niveau; verrou de signal
r защёлка *f* уровня сигнала

* **lexicographic** → 324

5346 lexicographic order; alphabetic[al] order
d lexikographische Ordnung *f*; alphabetische
  Anordnung *f*; alphabetische Folge *f*;
  alphabetische Reihenfolge *f*
f ordre *m* lexicographique; ordre alphabétique
r лексикографическое упорядочение *n*;
  алфавитный порядок *m*

5347 lexicon
d Lexikon *n*
f lexique *m*
r лексикон *m*

* **LF** → 5381

5348 library
d Bibliothek *f*
f bibliothèque *f*
r библиотека *f*

5349 library call
 d Bibliotheksabruf *m*
 f appel *m* de bibliothèque
 r библиотечный вызов *m*

5350 library directory
 d Bibliotheksverzeichnis *n*;
 Bibliothekkatalog *m*
 f répertoire *m* de bibliothèque; catalogue *m* de
 bibliothèque
 r справочник *m* библиотеки; каталог *m*
 библиотеки

5351 licence; license
 d Lizenz *f*
 f licence *f*
 r лиценз *m*; лицензия *f*

 * **license** → 5351

5352 license manager
 d Lizenzmanager *m*
 f gestionnaire *m* de licence
 r менажер *m* лицензии

5353 license server
 d Lizenzserver *m*
 f serveur *m* de licence
 r сервер *m* лицензии

 * **life** → 5354

 * **lifelength** → 5354

5354 life[time]; lifelength; longevity
 d Lebensdauer *f*, Nutzungsdauer *f*;
 Bindungsbereich *m*; Langlebigkeit *f*
 f temps *m* de vie; durée *f* de vie; ressource *f* de
 vie; longévité *f*
 r срок *m* службы; долговечность *f*; ресурс *m*
 долговечности

 * **LIFO** → 5279

**5355 LIFO list; LIFO stack; pushdown list;
 pushdown stack; pushdown stor[ag]e**
 d LIFO-Liste *f*
 f liste *f* LIFO; liste inverse; liste refoulée; pile *f*
 LIFO directe
 r магазинный список *m*; обёрнутый список;
 [прямой] стек *m*

5356 LIFO processing
 d LIFO-Verarbeitung *f*
 f traitement *m* de pile
 r стековая обработка *f*

 * **LIFO stack** → 5355

5357 lift *v*

 d abheben; abnehmen
 f lever; élever; hausser; dresser
 r поднимать; приподнимать

5358 light *v*; **lighten** *v*; **unblank** *v*; **illuminate** *v*
 d beleuchten; erleuchten; erhellen; aufhellen;
 illuminieren
 f éclairer; illuminer
 r освечивать; осветить; освещать

5359 light button; virtual pushbutton
 d Lichttaste *f*; Lichtknopf *m*
 f bouton *m* lumineux; touche *f* [de fonction]
 affichable
 r световая кнопка *f*

5360 light-emitting diode; LED
 d Lichtemissionsdiode *f*; Leuchtdiode *f*; LED
 f diode *f* [électro]luminescente; DEL
 r светодиод *m*

 * **lighten** *v* → 5358

 * **lightguide** → 6542

 * **lightguide fiber** → 6542

 * **lighting** → 4640

**5361 light pen; light stylus; beam pen; electronic
 pen; optical wand**
 d Lichtgriffel *m*; Lichtstift *m*; elektronischer
 Stift *m*
 f photostyle *m*; pointeur *m* optique; crayon *m*
 lumineux; crayon électronique
 r световое перо *n*; световой карандаш *m*

**5362 light-pen detection; pen detection;
 light-pen hit; light-pen strike**
 d Lichtgriffeldetektion *f*
 f détection *f* par photostyle; détection par stylet
 r указание *n* световым пером

 * **light-pen hit** → 5362

 * **light-pen strike** → 5362

5363 light source; luminous source
 d Lichtquelle *f*
 f source *f* de lumière; source lumineuse; source
 d'éclairage
 r источник *m* света; световой источник

5364 light spot; luminous spot; point of light
 d Leuchtpunkt *m*; Lichtpunkt *m*; Lichtfleck *m*;
 Leuchtfleck *m*
 f point *m* lumineux; spot *m* lumineux; repère *m*
 lumineux; tache *f* lumineuse
 r световая точка *f*; световое пятно *n*

* **light stylus** → 5361

* **lightwave communication** → 6531

* **lightwave telecommunication** → 6531

* **lightweight notebook** → 9004

* **lightweight portable** → 9004

5365 limitation
  d Begrenzung *f*
  f limitation *f*
  r ограничение *n*

* **limited** → 1142

* **limiter** → 2735

* **limiting process** → 6839

* **limitless** → 1144

* **limitless transmission** → 9611

* **limit process** → 6839

5366 line
  d Linie *f*
  f ligne *f*; droite *f*
  r линия *f*; прямая *f*

5367 line; row
  (in a text)
  d Zeile *f*; Reihe *f*
  f ligne *f*
  r строка *f*; ряд *m*

* **line advance** → 5381

* **linear array** → 6421

5368 linear code
  d linearer Code *m*
  f code *m* linéaire
  r линейный код *m*

5369 linear grammar
  d lineare Grammatik *f*
  f grammaire *f* linéaire
  r линейная грамматика *f*

5370 linear inferences per second; LIPS
  d lineare Hinderungen *fpl* pro Sekunde
  f inférences *fpl* linéaires par seconde
  r число *n* линейных логических выводов в секунду

5371 linear list
  d lineare Liste *f*

  f liste *f* linéaire
  r линейный список *m*

5372 linear logic
  d lineare Logik *f*
  f logique *f* linéaire
  r линейная логика *f*; линейная логическая схема *f*

5373 linearly independent variables
  d linear unabhängige Variablen *fpl*
  f variables *fpl* linéairement indépendantes
  r линейно независимые переменные *fpl*

* **linear memory** → 3893

5374 linear memory hierarchy
  d lineare Speicherhierarchie *f*
  f hiérarchie *f* linéaire de mémoire
  r линейная иерархия *f* памяти

* **linear raster** → 5387

5375 line caps
  d Linienenden *npl*
  f fins *mpl* de lignes
  r конечные элементы *mpl* линии

5376 line chart; line graph
  d Liniendiagramm *n*
  f diagramme *m* linéaire; graphique *m* linéaire
  r линейная диаграмма *f*

* **line clock** → 5377

5377 line clock [pulse]
  d Leitungstakt *m*
  f horloge *f* de ligne
  r тактовый импульс *m* канала

5378 line code
  d Leitungscode *m*
  f code *m* en ligne; code de transmission
  r код *m* линии

5379 line coding
  d Leitungscodierung *f*
  f codage *m* de ligne
  r кодирование *n* линии

5380 line delete character
  d Zeichen *n* für Zeilenlöschung
  f signe *m* d'effacement de ligne
  r знак *m* удаления строки

* **line discipline** → 5386

5381 linefeed; LF; line advance
  d Zeilenvorschub *m*

f avancement *m* de ligne; avancement
d'interligne; saut *m* de ligne
r перевод *m* строки

5382 linefeed character; new line character
d Zeilenvorschubzeichen *n*
f signe *m* d'avancement de ligne
r символ *m* перевода строки

5383 line finder
d Zeilenbegrenzer *m*
f limiteur *m* de ligne
r ограничитель *m* строки

5384 line generator
d Liniengenerator *m*; Zeilengenerator *m*
f générateur *m* de lignes
r генератор *m* линий; генератор строк текста

* **line graph** → **5376**

* **line group** → **1569**

* **line interface** → **1572**

* **line loop operation** → **9236**

5385 line printer; line print terminal; LPT
d Zeilendrucker *m*; Zeilendruckwerk *n*
f imprimante *f* [ligne] par ligne; imprimante en
ligne
r построчно-печатающее устройство *n*;
[по]строчный принтер *m*

* **line print terminal** → **5385**

5386 line protocol; line discipline; link protocol
d Leitungsprotokoll *n*; Leitungsdisziplin *f*;
Übermittlungsvorschrift *f*
f protocole *m* de liaison; discipline *f* de ligne
[de communication]
r протокол *m* линии [передачи]; протокол
канального уровня

* **line scanning** → **4559**

5387 line screen; linear raster
d Strichraster *m*; Linienraster *m*
f trame *f* à lignes; trame lignée; rastre *m*
linéaire
r линейный растр *m*; линиатура *f*

* **line spacing** → **5037**

5388 lines per inch; lpi
d Linien *fpl* pro Zoll
f lignes *fpl* par pouce
r линии *fpl* на дюйм

* **line splitter** → **1583**

* **line switching** → **1588**

* **line-to-line spacing** → **5037**

5389 linguistics
d Linguistik *f*
f linguistique *f*
r лингвистика *f*

* **link** *v* → **956**

* **link** → **1938, 5400, 5401, 8293**

5390 link address
d Verbindungsadresse *f*
f adresse *f* de liaison
r адрес *m* связи

5391 linkage
d Verbindungsaufbau *m*
f enchaînement *m*; établissement *m* de
communication
r связанность *f*; установление *n* связи

5392 link[age] editor; linker
d Binder *m*; Linkage-Editor *m*; Linker *m*
f éditeur *m* des liaisons; éditeur de liens
r редактор *m* связей

5393 link bit
d Verbindungsbit *n*; Link-Bit *n*
f bit *m* de liaison
r бит *m* выходного переноса; бит
расширения

5394 linked file organization
d gekettete Dateiorganisation *f*
f organisation *f* de fichiers chaînés
r организация *f* связанных файлов

5395 linked images
d verknüpfte Bilder *npl*
f images *fpl* liées
r связанные изображения *npl*

* **link editor** → **5392**

5396 linked list; chained list
d verkettete Liste *f*, verbundene Liste
f liste *f* [en]chaînée; liste liée
r связанный список *m*

5397 linked-list structure
d Struktur *f* von verbundenen Listen
f structure *f* des listes liées
r структура *f* связаннных списков

5398 linked objects
d verknüpfte Objekte *npl*

f objets *mpl* liés
r связанные объекты *mpl*

* **linker** → 5392

5399 link file
d Linkdatei *f*; Bindedatei *f*;
   Verknüpfungsdatei *f*
f fichier *m* de liens
r файл *m* связей

5400 link [indicator]
d Verbindungszeiger *m*
f indicateur *m* de liaison
r указатель *m* связи

5401 link[ing]; bind[ing]
d Verknüpfung *f*; Verbindung *f*; Verbinden *n*;
   Binden *n*; Link *n*
f liaison *f*; lien *m*; ligature *f*; embase *f*; reliure *f*
r связь *f*; связывание *n*; соединение *n*;
   привязка *f*; связка *f*

5402 link[ing] loader
d Bindelader *m*
f chargeur *m* de lien
r связывающий загрузчик *m*

5403 link interface
d Link-Leitungsschnittstelle *f*
f interface *f* de canaux de communication
r интерфейс *m* коммуникационных каналов

* **link layer** → 2573

5404 link list
d Verbindungsliste *f*
f liste *f* des liaisons
r список *m* связей

* **link loader** → 5402

* **link protocol** → 5386

5405 link resistance
d Verbindungsfestigkeit *f*
f résistance *f* de liaison
r устойчивость *f* связи

5406 links available indicator
d Anzeiger *m* der verfügbaren Verbindungen
f indicateur *m* de liaisons accessibles
r индикатор *m* доступных связей

5407 links synchronization
   (of a table)
d Verbindung-Synchronisation *f*
f synchronisation *f* de liaisons
r синхронизация *f* связей

* **link switching** → 1588

* **LIPS** → 5370

5408 liquid-crystal alphanumeric display
d alphanumerischer
   Flüssigkristallbildschirm *m*;
   alphanumerisches Flüssigkristalldisplay *n*
f afficheur *m* alphanumérique à cristaux
   liquides
r буквенно-цифровой
   жидкокристаллический дисплей *m*

**5409 liquid-crystal display; LCD; liquid-crystal
   screen**
d Flüssigkristalldisplay *n*;
   Flüssig[keits]kristallbildschirm *m*
f afficheur *m* à cristaux liquides; indicateur *m* à
   cristaux liquides; viseur *m* LCD
r жидкокристаллический дисплей *m*;
   ЖК-дисплей *m*; индикатор *m* на жидких
   кристаллах; жидкокристаллический
   экран *m*

* **liquid-crystal screen** → 5409

5410 list
d Liste *f*
f liste *f*
r список *m*

5411 list *v*
d listen
f lister
r перелистывать

5412 list box
d Listenfeld *n*
f boîte *f* de liste; zone *f* de liste déroulante
r списковое поле *n*; поле списка

5413 list data block
d Listendatenblock *m*
f bloc *m* de données en listes
r блок *m* данных списковой структуры

* **list generator** → 7952

5414 listing
d Listenform *f*; Listing *n*
f listage *m*; listing *m*
r распечатка *f*; листинг *m*

5415 listing
d Auflistung *f*
f mise *f* en liste
r составление *n* списков

5416 listing
d Ausdruck *m* in Listenform

f impression *f* de liste
r печать *f* списков

5417 list [insertion] sort
 d Folgensortieren *n* durch Einfügen
 f tri[age] *m* de liste par insertions
 r сортировка *f* списка методом вставок

5418 list processing
 d Listenverarbeitung *f*
 f traitement *m* de listes
 r обработка *f* списков

5419 list program; report program
 d Listenprogramm *n*
 f programme *m* de listes
 r программа *f* печати отчётов

5420 listserv
 (a server program)
 d automatische Mailing-Liste *f*
 f liste *f* d'envoi
 r почтовый реестр *m*

5421 list server
 d List-Server *m*
 f serveur *m* des listes
 r сервер *m* списков

* list sort → 5417

5422 list view
 d Listenansicht *f*
 f vue *f* de liste
 r списковое представление *n*

* literal → 324

5423 literal
 d Literal *n*; buchstäbliche Konstante *f*
 f littéral *m*; libellé *f*; constante *f* littérale
 r литерал *m*; литеральная константа *f*

5424 literal expression
 d Buchstabenausdruck *m*
 f expression *f* littérale
 r буквенное выражение *n*

5425 literal notation; lettering
 d buchstäbliche Bezeichnung *f*; buchstäbliche
   Darstellung *f*; Beschriftung *f*;
   Buchstabenkennzeichnung *f*
 f notation *f* littérale; notation alphabétique
 r буквенное обозначение *n*

5426 literal pool
 d Literalbereich *m*
 f zone *f* de littérals
 r область *f* литералов

* live cam → 6087

* live camera → 6087

* live video → 7711

5427 liveware; wetware
 (e-slang)
 d Datenverarbeitungspersonal *n*
 f logiciel *m* humain; logiciel vital; logiciel
   vivant
 r человеческий фактор *m*; биологический
   фактор; биофактор *m*; мозги *mpl*

* LLC → 5476

* LMI → 5443

5428 load *v*
 d laden; beladen; füllen; lasten
 f charger
 r нагружать; загружать

5429 load; charge
 d Last *f*
 f charge *f*
 r груз *m*; нагрузка *f*

5430 loadable; transient
 d ladefähig
 f chargeable
 r нерезидентный; загружаемый

5431 loadable program
 d ladefähiges Programm *n*
 f programme *m* chargeable
 r загружаемая программа *f*

5432 load address
 d Ladeadresse *f*
 f adresse *f* de chargement initial
 r начальный адрес *m* загрузки

5433 load-and-go
 d Laden *n* und Ausführen *n*
 f chargement *m* et exécution *f*; chargement
   avec lancement
 r загрузка *f* с последующим исполнением;
   исполнение *n* по загрузке

5434 load enable
 d Laderfreigabe *f*
 f validation *f* de charge
 r разрешение *n* нагрузки

* loader → 5436

* load factor → 3229

5435 loading; charging
 d Gebühren *n*; Ladung *f*; Belastung *f*

f chargement *m*
r загрузка *f*

5436 load[ing] program; loader
   d Ladeprogramm *n*; Lader *m*
   f programme *m* de charge[ment]; chargeur *m*
   r программа *f* загрузки; загрузчик *m*

   * **load mark → 887**

5437 load *v* palette
   d eine Palette laden
   f charger une palette
   r загружать палитру

   * **load program → 5436**

   * **local area broadband network → 1192**

5438 local area loop network
   d lokales Ringnetz *n*; lokales Schleifennetz *n*
   f réseau *m* local en anneau
   r местная кольцевая сеть *f*

5439 local [area] network; LAN; in-house network
   d lokales Netz[werk] *n*; LAN; hausinternes Netz; In-House-Netz *n*
   f réseau *m* local
   r локальная сеть *f*; местная сеть

   * **local area wideband network → 1192**

5440 local bus; branch bus
   d lokaler Bus *m*
   f bus *m* local
   r локалная шина *f*

   * **local data channel → 4535**

   * **local data network → 5441**

5441 local data [transfer] network
   d lokales Datenübertragungsnetz *n*
   f réseau *m* local de transfert de données
   r местная сеть *f* [передачи] данных

5442 local echo
   d lokales Echo *n*
   f écho *m* local
   r локальное эхо *n*

   * **localization → 5446**

5443 local management interface; LMI
   d lokales Management-Interface *n*; lokale Managementschnittstelle *f*
   f interface *f* de gestion locale
   r интерфейс *m* локального управления (в сети)

5444 local memory; local storage
   d lokaler Speicher *m*; Lokalspeicher *m*
   f mémoire *f* locale
   r локальная память *f*; встроенная память

   * **local network → 5439**

   * **local record → 4544**

   * **local storage → 5444**

5445 local storage address register
   d Lokalspeicher-Adressregister *n*
   f registre *m* d'adresse de mémoire locale
   r адресный регистр *m* локального запоминающего устройства

   * **location → 7150**

5446 location; localization; placement
   d Stellung *f*; Lokalisierung *f*; Ortung *f*; Plazierung *f*; Aufstellung *f*
   f localisation *f*; location *f*; [em]placement *m*
   r расположение *n*; размещение *n*; локализация *f*

5447 location address
   d Speicherzellenadresse *f*
   f adresse *f* de disposition
   r адрес *m* ячейки памяти

5448 location[al] data
   d Positionsdaten *pl*; Lagedaten *pl*
   f données *fpl* de position
   r данные *pl* о местоположении

   * **location counter → 209**

   * **location data → 5448**

   * **lock *v* → 1059**

5449 lock
   d Verriegelungsmechanismus *m*; Sperre *f*
   f verrou *m*
   r замок *m*

5450 lock-and-key protection
   d Schutz *m* vor dem Verschluss
   f protection *f* du type verrou-et-clé
   r защита *f* типа замка

5451 lock *v* an object
   d ein Objekt sperren
   f bloquer un objet
   r блокировать объект

5452 locked
   d gesperrt; verriegelt

f verrouillé; bloqué
r блокированный; запертый

5453 **lock[ed] layer**
 d blockierte Schicht *f*
 f plan *m* verrouillé; plan bloqué
 r блокированный слой *m*

 * **lock-in** → 5454, 9106

 * **locking** → 3863

5454 **locking; lockout; blocking; lock-in; holding**
 d Verriegelung *f*; Sperrung *f*; Blockierung *f*; Blockung *f*
 f verrouillage *m*; blocage *m*
 r запирание *n*; блокирование *n*; блокировка *f*

 * **locking-in** → 9106

 * **lock layer** → 5453

 * **lock-on** → 1431

 * **lockout** → 5454

5455 **lockout bit**
 d Blockierungsbit *n*
 f bit *m* de blocage
 r бит *m* блокировки

 * **lockout circuit** → 4839

 * **lock *v* up** → 1104

 * **log** → 5175, 5457

5456 **log *v*; register *v*; sign *v* on**
 d registrieren; aufzeichnen; aufschreiben
 f enregistrer; inscrire; noter
 r записывать[ся]; регистрировать[ся]

 * **log-book** → 5175

5457 **log [file]**
 (of a system activity)
 d Protokolldatei *f*
 f fichier *m* de registration; fichier d'enregistrement
 r файл *m* журнала [системы]; регистрационный файл

5458 **logger; recorder; register**
 d Registriereinrichtung *f*; Registriergerät *n*; Aufzeichnungsgerät *n*; Logger *m*; Schreiber *m*
 f dispositif *m* d'enregistrement; enregistreur *m*
 r регистрирующее устройство *n*; регистратор *m*

5459 **logging; registration; recording**
 d Erfassung *f*; Ereignisaufzeichnung *f*; Logführung *f*
 f enregistrement *m*; saisie *f*; inscription *f*
 r регистрация *f*; запись *f*; занесение *n* [в журнал]

5460 **logging cycle**
 d Protokollzyklus *m*
 f cycle *m* d'enregistrement
 r цикл *m* записи

 * **logic** → 1111, 5468

5461 **logic**
 d Logik *f*
 f logique *f*
 r логика *f*

 * **logical** → 1111

5462 **logical access control**
 d logische Zugriffskontrolle *f*
 f contrôle *m* d'accès logique
 r логическое управление *n* доступом

 * **logical add** → 2997

 * **logical addition** → 2997

5463 **logical address**
 d logische Adresse *f*
 f adresse *f* logique
 r логический адрес *m*

5464 **logic[al] array**
 d logisches Feld *n*; Logikanordnung *f*
 f tableau *m* logique; matrice *f* logique
 r логический массив *m*; логическая матрица *f*

5465 **logical block addressing; LBA**
 d logische Blockadressierung *f*
 f adressage *m* de bloc logique
 r адресование *n* логического блока

5466 **logic[al] chain**
 d logische Kette *f*
 f chaîne *f* logique
 r логическая цепочка *f*; цепочка логических схем

5467 **logical channel**
 d logischer Kanal *m*
 f canal *m* logique
 r логический канал *m*

5468 **logic[al] circuit; logic**
 d Logik[schaltung] *f*; Logikschaltkreis *m*

f circuit *m* logique; logique *f*
r логическая [цифровая] схема *f*

**5469 logical connection; logical link; logical
connective**
d logische Verbindung *f*; logische
Verknüpfung *f*; Junktor *m*
f liaison *f* logique
r логическая связка *f*

* **logical connective** → 5469

* **logical design** → 2890

5470 logical device number
d logische Gerätenummer *f*
f nombre *m* logique d'unité
r логический номер *m* устройства

5471 logical error
(in a program or in an algorithm)
d logischer Fehler *m*
f erreur *f* logique
r логическая ошибка *f*

5472 logical expression
d logischer Ausdruck *m*
f expression *f* logique
r логическое выражение *n*

5473 logical extent
d logischer Extent *m*
f étendue *f* logique
r логический экстент *m*

* **logical function** → 936

5474 logical grouping operator
d Operator *m* der logischen Gruppierung
f opérateur *m* de groupement logique
r оператор *m* логического группирования

* **logical inversion** → 5478

5475 logical level
d logische Ebene *f*
f niveau *m* logique
r логический уровень *m*

* **logical link** → 5469

5476 logical link control; LLC
d logische Verbindungssteuerung *f*
f contrôle *m* de la liaison logique
r управление *n* логической связи

5477 logical link sublayer
d logische Verbindungsteilschicht *f*
f sous-couche *f* de la liaison logique
r подуровень *m* логической связи

* **logical multiply** → 2166

5478 logic[al] negation; logic[al] inversion
d logische Negation *f*; logische Inversion *f*
f négation *f* logique; inversion *f* logique
r логическое отрицание *n*; логическая
инверсия *f*

* **logical operation** → 1117

5479 logic[al] partitioning
d logische Unterteilung *f*
f partitionnement *m* logique
r разбиение *n* на логические блоки

* **logical product** → 2166

5480 logical query
d logische Abfrage *f*
f interrogation *f* logique
r логический запрос *m*

5481 logical structure
d logische Struktur *f*
f structure *f* logique
r логическая структура *f*

* **logical sum** → 2997

* **logical unit identificator** → 5482

**5482 logical unit name; luname; logical unit
identificator**
d logischer Einheitsname *m*
f code *m* d'unité logique; nom *m* d'unité
logique
r логическое имя *n* модуля

* **logic array** → 5464

* **logic chain** → 5466

* **logic circuit** → 5468

5483 logic-enhancement memory
d logikerweiterter Speicher *m*; Speicher mit
integrierten Logikfunktionen
f mémoire *f* à fonctions intégrées
r функциональная память *f*; память со
встроенной логикой

* **logic function** → 936

5484 logic-gate redundancy
d Logikgatterredundanz *f*
f redondance *f* à porte logique
r резерв *m* с логической схемой включения

* **logic inversion** → 5478

* **logic negation** → 5478

* **logic operation** → 1117

* **logic partitioning** → 5479

* **logic sum** → 2997

5485 login; logon; sign-on
d Anmeldung *f*; Login *n*; Logon *n*
f arrivée *f*; déclenchement *m* de session;
ouverture *f* de session; démarrage *m* de
session; début *m* de session
r начало *n* сеанса; вход *m* в систему

5486 login authorization; logon authorization
d Zugangsberechtigung *f*
f autorisation *f* d'arrivée
r разрешение *n* начала сеанса

5487 login message; logon message
d Anmeldenachricht *f*
f message *m* de début de session
r сообщение *n* о начале сеанса

* **login name** → 9733

5488 login request; logon request
d Anmeldeanforderung *f*
f interrogation *f* d'arrivée
r запрос *m* на вход в систему

* **logo** → 1283

5489 logoff; logout; sign-off
d Abmeldung *f*; Logoff *n*; Logout *n*;
Austragen *n*
f fin *f* de session; sortie *f* du système session
r конец *m* сеанса; выход *m* из системы

* **logon** → 5485

* **logon authorization** → 5486

* **logon message** → 5487

* **logon request** → 5488

5490 logo screen
d Logo-Schirm *m*
f écran *m* logo
r экран *m* фирменного знака

* **logotype** → 1283

* **logout** → 5489

* **longevity** → 5354

* **long-haul network** → 9984

5491 longitudinal recording
d Längeaufzeichnung *f*
f enregistrement *m* longitudinal
r продольная запись *f*

5492 long-term memory
d Dauerspeicher *m*
f mémoire *f* à long terme
r долговременная память *f*

5493 long-time data
d Langzeitdaten *pl*
f données *fpl* de longue durée
r данные *pl* с длительным сроком хранения

5494 long-time test
d Langzeitversuch *m*
f essai *m* de longue durée
r долговременное испытание *n*

5495 lookahead; preview[ing]
d Vor[aus]schau *f*; Vorausermittlung *f*;
Vorgriff *m*
f vue *f* d'avance; prévision *f*; prévisualisation *f*;
anticipation *f*; look-ahead *m*
r предварительный просмотр *m*; просмотр
вперёд; опережение *n*

5496 lookahead buffer
d Look-Ahead-Puffer *m*
f tampon *m* de look-ahead; tampon de
présélection
r опережающий буфер *m*; буфер
предвыборки

5497 lookahead carry; highspeed carry
d vorausermittelter Übertrag *m*;
Look-Ahead-Übertrag *m*; schneller Übertrag
f retenue *f* évaluée d'avance; report *m* accéléré;
report anticipé; retenue rapide; report rapide
r ускоренный перенос *m*; транзитный
перенос

5498 look-aside buffer
d Look-Aside-Puffer *m*
f tampon *m* de look-aside; tampon
d'information précédente
r сохраняющий буфер *m*; буфер
предыстории [процесса]

5499 look-aside cache
d Look-Aside-Cache *m*
f cache *f* [en] parallèle
r кэш *m* предыстории

5500 look-through cache
d durchblickender Cache *m*
f cache *f* [en] série
r сквозной кэш *m*

5501 lookup field
 d Suchfeld *n*
 f champ *m* de recherche
 r поле *n* просмотра; просмотровое поле

5502 lookup table
 d Nachschlagtabelle *f*; Verweistabelle *f*;
    Lookup-Tabelle *f*
 f table *f* de référence; table de consultation;
    aide-mémoire *f*
 r просмотровая таблица *f*; справочная
    таблица

5503 loop
 d Zyklus *m*; Schleife *f*; Schlinge *f*
 f cycle *m*; boucle *f*; lacet *m*
 r цикл *m*; петля *f*; шлейф *m*

5504 loop button
 d Schleifenschaltfläche *f*; Umlauftaste *f*
 f bouton *m* de lacet
 r бутон *m* вращения; бутон шлейфа

 * **loopfree → 155**

5505 looping coefficient
 d Verschlingungszahl *f*
 f coefficient *m* d'entrelacements
 r коэффициент *m* зацепления

5506 loop opening
 d Schleifenöffnung *f*
 f ouverture *f* de boucle
 r прерывание *n* цикла

5507 loop structure
 d Schleifenstruktur *f*
 f structure *f* en boucle
 r шлейфовая структура *f*

5508 loose routing
 d loses Routing *n*; lose Lenkung *f*
 f routage *m* lâche
 r приближённая трассировка *f*; глобальная
    трассировка

5509 lossless compression
 d verlustfreie Kompression *f*; verlustlose
    Kompaktion *f*
 f compression *f* sans perte
 r сжатие *n* без потерь

5510 loss of information; information loss
 d Informationsverlust *m*
 f perte *f* d'information
 r потеря *f* информации

5511 lossy compression
 d Kompression *f* mit Verlust
 f compression *f* avec pertes

 r сжатие *n* с потерей

5512 lost cluster
 d verworfener Cluster *m*; unterbrochener
    Cluster
 f grappe *f* perdue
 r потерянный кластер *m*

**5513 low-bit-rate channel; low-speed-data
     channel**
 d Kanal *m* mit niedriger Bitfrequenz; langsamer
    Kanal
 f canal *m* à cadence [de bit] lente
 r низкоскоростный канал *m*

5514 low byte
 d niedriges Byte *n*
 f octet *m* faible; octet inférieur
 r младший байт *m*

5515 low contrast
 d niedriger Kontrast *m*
 f contraste *m* bas
 r низкий контраст *m*

5516 low-end computer
 d Low-End-Rechner *m*; Rechner *m* im unteren
    Kostenbereich
 f ordinateur *m* bas de gamme
 r компьютер *m* младшей модели

5517 lower case
 d Kleinschreibung *f*
 f registre *m* inférieur
 r нижний регистр *m*

5518 lowercase letters
 d Kleinbuchstaben *mpl*
 f lettres *fpl* du registre inférieur; lettres
    minuscules
 r буквы *fpl* нижнего регистра; строчные
    буквы

5519 lower data bus
 d Bus *m* für niederwertige Datenstellen
 f bus *m* de poids faible de données
 r шина *f* младших разрядов данных

 * **lower index → 9009**

5520 lowest byte
 d niedrigstes Byte *n*
 f octet *m* de l'ordre le plus bas
 r самый младший байт *m*

 * **lowest order bit → 5323**

5521 low-level language
 d Sprache *f* eines niedrigeren Niveaus

    f langage *m* à niveau inférieur; langage de bas
niveau
    r язык *m* низкого уровня

  * **low-order** → 5523

5522 low memory
    d niedriger Speicher *m*
    f mémoire *f* basse
    r младшие адреса *mpl* памяти

  * **low-order** → 5523

5523 low-order [position]
    d niedrige Stelle *f*; niederwertige Stelle;
geringste Wertigkeit *f*
    f position *f* inférieure; position la plus basse;
ordre *m* de poids bas
    r младший разряд *m*

5524 low-pass filter
    d Tiefpassfilter *m*
    f filtre *m* passe-bas
    r фильтр *m* низких частот

  * **low-profile keyboard** → 3891

5525 low quantity data
    d Kleindaten *pl*
    f données *fpl* de petite quantité
    r малое количество *n* данных

5526 low resolution
    d niedriges Auflösungsvermögen *n*
    f résolution *f* basse
    r низкая разрешающая способность *f*

5527 low-resolution monitor
    d Bildschirm *m* mit kleinem
Auflösungsvermögen
    f écran *m* à résolution basse
    r экран *m* с низкой разрешающей
способностью

**5528 low-scale integration; small-scale
integration**
    d Kleinintegration *f*
    f intégration *f* à faible échelle
    r интеграция *f* малого уровня

5529 low-speed
    d langsam; mit niedriger Geschwindigkeit
    f lent; à basse vitesse
    r низкоскоростный; медленный

  * **low-speed-data channel** → 5513

5530 low-speed transmission
    d langsame Übertragung *f*
    f transmission *f* lente
    r низкоскоростная передача *f*

  * **lpi** → 5388

  * **LPT** → 5385

  * **LSI** → 5271

  * **LSI circuit** → 5270

5531 luminance
    (the black-white portion of a video signal)
    d Luminanz *f*
    f luminance *f*; émittance *f* lumineuse
    r световое излучение *n*

5532 luminance coefficient; luminance factor
    d Luminanz-Koeffizient *m*
    f coefficient *m* de luminance; facteur *m* de
luminance
    r коэффициент *m* светового излучения

5533 luminance component
    d Luminanzkomponente *f*
    f composante *f* de luminance
    r составляющая *f* светового излучения

  * **luminance factor** → 5532

5534 luminous figure display
    d Leuchtziffernanzeige *f*
    f afficheur *m* à chiffres lumineux
    r световой индикатор *m* знаков

  * **luminous intensity** → 1183

  * **luminous source** → 5363

  * **luminous spot** → 5364

  * **luname** → 5482

5535 lurk *v*
    (e-slang)
    d lauern
    f roder; badauder
    r таиться; наблюдать

5536 lurker; observer
    (in newsgroups)
    d Lauerer *m*; Lurker *m*
    f badaud *m*; voyeur *m*
    r наблюдатель *m* (за потоком новостей)

5537 lurking
    (describe the inactivity of a subscriber who
doesn't actively participate in a mailing list or
Usenet newsgroup discussions)
    d Lauern *n*
    f badaudage *m*
    r "прослушка" *f*; тайное участие *n*
(безучастный просмотр сетевых новостей
и конференций)

  * **luser** → 7693

M

* MAC → 5708

5538 machine; engine
d Maschine *f*; Motor *m*; Engine *f*
f machine *f*; moteur *m*
r машина *f*

5539 machine check interrupt
d Maschinenfehlerunterbrechung *f*
f interruption *f* en cas de défaillance de la machine
r прерывание *n* при ошибке машины

* machine code → 5546

5540 machine-code instruction
d Maschinencodebefehl *m*
f instruction *f* en code machine
r команда *f* на машинном языке

5541 machine-dependent
d maschinenabhängig
f dépendant de machine
r машиннозависимый

* machine failure → 4401

5542 machine-independent
d maschinenunabhängig
f indépendant de machine
r машиннонезависимый

* machine intelligence → 545

5543 machine language
d Maschinensprache *f*
f langage [de] machine; langage d'ordinateur
r машинный язык *m*

5544 machine-language coding; machine-language programming; absolute coding; specific coding
d Maschinencodierung *f*; Grundcodierung *f*; einfache Codierung *f*
f codage *m* absolu; programmation *f* en langage absolu
r программирование *n* на машинном языке; программирование с применением абсолютных адресов

5545 machine-language module
d Maschinensprachemodul *n*
f module *m* en langage machine
r модуль *m* на машинном языке

5546 machine[-language] program; machine code
d Maschinen[sprach]programm *n*; Maschinencode *m*
f programme *m* [en langage] machine; code *m* [de] machine
r машинная программа *f*; программа на машинном языке; машинный код *m*

* machine-language programming → 5544

5547 machine-oriented design
d maschinenorientierter Entwurf *m*
f projet *m* orienté vers machine
r машинноориентированное проектирование *n*

* machine-oriented language → 2095

* machine program → 5546

5548 machine-readable; machine-sensible
d maschinenlesbar
f lisible par machine
r считываемый машиной; читаемый машиной

5549 machine-readable character
d maschinenlesbares Zeichen *n*
f caractère *m* lisible par ordinateur
r машинночитаемый знак *m*

5550 machine-readable medium; automated data medium
d maschinenlesbarer Datenträger *m*
f support *m* de données lisibles par machine
r машинночитаемый носитель *m*

* machine-sensible → 5548

5551 machine time; computer time
d Maschinenzeit *f*
f temps *m* de machine
r машинное время *n*

* machine translation → 694

5552 machine vision; artificial vision
d Maschinensehen *n*; künstliches Sehen *n*
f vision *f* artificielle
r машинное зрение *n*; искусственное зрение

5553 machine word
d Maschinenwort *n*
f mot *m* de machine
r машинное слово *n*

* macro → 5558, 5561

5554 macroalgorithm
d Makroalgorithmus m
f macro-algorithme m
r алгоритм m макроса

5555 macroassembler
d Makroassembler m
f macro-assembleur m
r макроассемблер m

5556 macrocell
d Makrozelle f
f macrocellule f
r макроячейка f; макроэлемент m

* macrocode → 5561

5557 macrocoding
d Makroprogrammierung f
f macroprogrammation f
r макропрограммирование n

* macrocommand → 5561

* macrodeclaration → 5558

5558 macrodefinition; macrodeclaration;
macro[s]
d Makrodefinition f;
Makrooperationsspezifikation f;
Makrodeklaration f
f macrodéfinition f; macrodéclaration f
r макроопределение n; макрообъявление n;
макродекларация f

5559 macroexpansion
d Makroexpansion f; Makroentwicklung f
f macro-expansion f
r макрорасширение n

5560 macro facility
d Makrosprachmöglichkeit f
f possibilité f de macrolangage
r возможность f макроязыка

* macrogenerator → 5566

5561 macroinstruction; macrocommand;
macrocode; macro[s]
d Makrobefehl m; Makrokommando n;
Makroinstruktion f; Makros n
f macro-instruction f; macrocommande f;
macros m
r макроинструкция f; макрокоманда f;
макрос m

5562 macroinstruction language;
macrolanguage
d Makrobefehlssprache f; Makrosprache f
f langage m de macro-instructions;

macrolangage m
r язык m макроинструкций; макроязык m

5563 macroinstruction sequence;
macrosequence
d Makro[befehls]folge f
f séquence f de macro-instructions;
macroséquence f
r последовательность f макрокоманд;
макропоследовательность f

* macrolanguage → 5562

5564 macrolibrary
d Makrobibliothek f
f macrobibliothèque f; macrolibrairie f
r макробиблиотека f

5565 macroname
d Makroname m
f macronom m
r макроимя n

5566 macroprocessor; macrogenerator
d Makroprozessor m; Makrogenerator m
f macroprocesseur m; macrogénérateur m
r макропроцессор m; макрогенератор m

* macros → 5558, 5561

* macrosequence → 5563

5567 macrostructure
d Makrostruktur f
f macrostructure f
r макроструктура f

5568 macrostructured texture
d makrostrukturierte Textur f
f texture f macrostructurée
r макроструктурированная текстура f

5569 macro virus
d Makro-Virus n
f virus m écrit dans un langage macro
r макро-вирус m; макросный вирус m

* magnetic bias → 5585

* magnetic biasing → 5585

* magnetic bubble → 5570

5570 magnetic bubble [domain]
d Magnetblase[ndomäne] f
f domaine m magnétique en bulle
r цилиндрический магнитный домен m

* magnetic card → 5580

5571 magnetic code
d magnetischer Code *m*
f code *m* magnétique
r код *m* магнитной записи

5572 magnetic cycle; hysteresis cycle; hysteresis loop
d Magnetisierungsschleife *f*; Hystereseschleife *f*
f boucle *f* de magnétisation; boucle d'hystérésis; cycle *m* d'hystérésis
r цикл *m* намагничивания; петля *f* гистерезиса; гистерезисный цикл

5573 magnetic disk
d Magnetplatte *f*; Magnetscheibe *f*
f disque *m* magnétique
r магнитный диск *m*

5574 magnetic disk memory
d Magnetscheibenspeicher *m*; Magnetplattenspeicher *m*
f mémoire *f* à disques magnétiques
r накопитель *m* на магнитных дисках; память *f* на магнитных дисках

5575 magnetic head
d Magnetkopf *m*
f tête *f* magnétique
r магнитная головка *f*

5576 magnetic-head assembly
d Magnetkopfeinheit *f*
f ensemble *m* de têtes magnétiques
r блок *m* магнитных головок

* **magnetic ink** → 5586

5577 magnetic-ink [character] reader
d Magnetschrift[zeichen]leser *m*
f lecteur *m* de badges magnétiques; lecteur d'écriture magnétique
r устройство *n* считывания магнитных знаков

* **magnetic-ink reader** → 5577

5578 magnetic inscription; magnetic recording
d magnetische Beschriftung *f*; magnetische Aufzeichnung *f*
f inscription *f* magnétique; enregistrement *m* magnétique
r магнитная запись *f*

* **magnetic recording** → 5578

5579 magnetic shift register
d magnetisches Schieberegister *n*
f registre *m* à décalages magnétiques
r сдвиговый регистр *m* на магнитных элементах

* **magnetic strip** → 5581

5580 magnetic [strip] card
d Magnet[streifen]karte *f*; magnetische Speicherkarte *f*
f carte *f* magnétique
r магнитная карта *f*; карта с магнитным кодом

5581 magnetic strip[e]
d Magnetstreifen *m*
f ruban *m* magnétique; feuillet *m* magnétique
r магнитный штрих *m*; магнитная полоска *f*

5582 mag[netic] tape; tape; band
d Magnetband *n*
f bande *f* magnétique
r магнитная лента *f*

5583 magnetic tape cartridge; tape cartridge; tape cassette; cartridge
d Magnetband-Cartridge *m*; Cartridge *m*; Magnetbandkassette *f*; Bandkassette *f*
f cartouche *f* [à bande magnétique]; cassette *f* [à bande magnétique]; cartridge *m* [à bande magnétique]
r кассеточный модуль *m*; кассета *f* [магнитной ленты]

5584 magnetic tape device; tape device; tape unit
d Magnetbandgerät *n*; Magnetbandeinheit *f*
f dispositif *m* à bande [magnétique]; unité *f* à bande
r магнитно-лентовое устройство *n*; блок *m* [магнитной] ленты

5585 magnetization; magnetic bias[ing]
d Magnetisierung *f*; Vormagnetisierung *f*
f magnétisation *f*; polarisation *f* magnétique
r намагничивание *n*; подмагничивание *n*

5586 magnetized ink; magnetic ink
d magnetisierbare Tinte *f*; Magnettinte *f*
f encre *f* magnétique
r магнитное чернило *n*

5587 magnetooptical disk
d magnetooptische Platte *f*
f disque *m* magnéto-optique
r магнитооптический диск *m*

5588 magnetooptical effect
d magnetooptischer Effekt *m*
f effet *m* magnéto-optique
r магнитооптический эффект *m*

* **magnification** → 659

* **magnifying** → 659

* **magnitude** → 9747

* **mag tape** → 5582

* **mailbomb** → 5340

* **mailbot** → 5595

* **mailbox** → 3331

5589 mailbox access
d Mailbox-Zugriff *m*
f accès *m* à la boîte aux lettres
r доступ *m* до почтового ящика

5590 mailbox menu
d Mailbox-Menü *n*
f menu *m* à la boîte aux lettres
r меню *n* почтового ящика

5591 mailbox technique
d Briefkastenverfahren *n*
f procédé *m* à boîte aux lettres
r метод *m* обмена данными при помощи
почтовых ящиков

5592 mailing; posting
d Meldung *f*; Einlieferung *f*
f publipostage *m*
r рассылка *f*

5593 mailing list; maillist
d Mailliste *f*; Verteilerliste *f*; Adressenliste *f*
f liste *f* de publipostage; liste de diffusion;
courliste *f*
r почтовый список *m*; список адресатов;
список рассылки [почты]

* **maillist** → 5593

5594 mail reflector
(a specialized address from which e-mail is
automatically forwarded to a set of other
addresses, commonly used to implement a
mail discussion group)
d Post-Reflektor *m*
f réflecteur *m* postal
r почтовый отражатель *m*

5595 mail robot; mailbot
d Postroboter *m*
f robot *m* postal; répondeur *m*
r почтовый робот *m*

5596 mail server
d Mail-Server *m*
f serveur *m* de poste
r сервер-почта *m*

5597 main; principal; master; leading
d Haupt-; Anfangs-; Leit-; Master-; führend

f principal; général; maître; dominant; premier;
initial
r главный; ведущий; старший; начальный

5598 main application window
d Hauptanwendungsfenster *n*
f fenêtre *f* d'application principale
r главное окно *n* приложения

* **main backboard** → 5599

5599 main backplane board; main backboard
d Hauptrückwandplatine *f*
f carte *f* de raccordement principale
r главная объединительная плата *f*

* **main file** → 5665

* **mainframe** → 1536, 5600

5600 mainframe [computer]
d Großrechner *m*; Großcomputer *m*
f ordinateur *m* gros; macroordinateur *m*; grand
serveur *m*; grand système *m*
r большой компьютер *m*

* **mainframe processor** → 1536

5601 mainframer
d Mainframer *m*; Hersteller *m* von
Großrechnern
f producteur *m* d'ordinateurs universels
r изготовитель *m* универсальных
компьютеров

* **main index** → 4328

**5602 main memory; general memory; internal
memory; operating memory; memory**
d Hauptspeicher *m*; Internspeicher *m*;
Operativspeicher *m*
f mémoire *f* principale; mémoire générale;
mémoire vive; mémoire interne
r основная память *f*; внутренняя память;
оперативная память

5603 main menu; root menu
d Hauptmenü *n*
f menu *m* principal; menu de racine
r главное меню *n*

5604 main program; master program
d Hauptprogramm *n*; Leitprogramm *n*
f programme *m* principal; programme maître
r главная программа *f*; основная программа;
ведущая программа

5605 mainstream
(of forums)
d Hauptströmung *f*

f ensemble *m* de forums; courant *m* major
r главный поток *m*; поточная организация *f*

* **maintainability** → 8445

5606 maintenance; attendance; servicing
  d Wartung *f*; Instandhaltung *f*; Unterhaltung *f*
  f maintenance *f*; entretien *m*; service *m*
  r поддержка *f*; [техническое]
    обслуживание *n*; уход *m*

5607 maintenance bit; service bit
  d Wartungsbit *n*; Hilfsbit *n*; Servicebit *n*;
    Hilfsschritt *m*
  f bit *m* de surveillance; bit d'entretien; bit de
    service
  r служебный бит *m*; сервисный бит

5608 main window; primary window
  d Hauptfenster *n*
  f fenêtre *f* principale
  r главное окно *n*

5609 majority
  d Majorität *f*; Mehrheit *f*
  f majorité *f*
  r большинство *n*; мажоритарность *f*

5610 majority element
  d Majoritätselement *n*
  f élément *m* majoritaire
  r мажоритарный элемент *m*

5611 make contact
  d Schließkontakt *m*; normal offener Kontakt *m*
  f contact *m* ouvert au repos; contact
    normalement ouvert
  r нормально разомкнутый контакт *m*

5612 makeup mode
  d Anlaufbetrieb *m*
  f mode *m* de mise en marche
  r режим *m* запуска

5613 makeup time
  d Ausfallzeit *f* durch Reparatur
  f temps *m* de restauration; temps de reprise
  r время *n* восстановления

5614 malfunction
  d Fehlfunktion *f*; fehlerhafter Betrieb *m*
  f fonction *f* défectueuse; fonctionnement *m*
    troublé; panne *f*
  r неправильная работа *f*; нарушение *n*
    работоспособности; сбой *m*

5615 malfunction program
  d Störungsprogramm *n*
  f programme *m* de détection des défauts
  r программа *f* обнаружения ошибок

* **MAN** → 5805

5616 management
  d Leitung *f*; Management *n*
  f direction *f*; gestion *f*; management *m*
  r управление *n*; организация *f*

* **management graphics** → 1282

5617 management information
  d Leitungsinformation *f*
  f information *f* de gestion
  r управленческая информация *f*

5618 management information base; MIB
  d Management-Informationsbasis *f*
  f base *f* d'information du gestion
  r база *f* управленческой информации

5619 management information system; MIS
  d Management-Informationssystem *n*;
    Leitungsinformationssystem *n*; MIS
  f système *m* d'information du gestion
  r управленческая информационная система *f*

5620 management science
  d Managementlehre *f*; Betriebswissenschaft *f*
  f théorie *f* de gestion; science *f* de gestion
  r теория *f* управления

* **manager** → 255, 5621

5621 manager [program]
  d Managerprogramm *n*; Manager *m*
  f programme *m* gestionnaire; gestionnaire *m*
  r управляющая программа *f*; менажер *m*

5622 mandatory attribute
  d obligatorisches Attribut *n*
  f attribut *m* obligatoire
  r обязательный атрибут *m*

* **manipulate** *v* → 4379

* **manipulation** → 4381

* **manipulator** → 4380

5623 man-machine communication
  d Mensch-Maschine-Kommunikation *f*
  f communication *f* homme-machine
  r человеко-машинное общение *n*; связь *f*
    человека с машиной

5624 man-machine interface
  d Mensch-Maschine-Schnittstelle *f*
  f interface *f* homme-machine
  r человеко-машинный интерфейс *m*

5625 man-machine system
  d Mensch-Maschine-System *n*

f système *m* homme-machine
r человеко-машинная система *f*

* **manual entry** → 5626

5626 manual input; manual entry; hand input
   d manuelle Eingabe *f*; Handeingabe *f*
   f entrée *f* manuelle; introduction *f* manuelle
   r ручной ввод *m*

5627 manual scanning; handheld scanning
   d manuelle Abtastung *f*
   f échantillonnage *m* manuel; numérisation *f* manuelle
   r ручное сканирование *n*

5628 manufacturing cell
   (composed of a number of work stations, materials, storage facilities and transport mechanisms that interconnect them)
   d Fertigungszelle *f*
   f cellule *f* de fabrication
   r производственная клетка *f*

5629 manufacturing data
   d Fabrikationsdaten *pl*
   f données *fpl* de fabrication
   r производственные данные *pl*

5630 manufacturing documentation
   d Fertigungsdokumentation *f*
   f documentation *f* de fabrication
   r производственная документация *f*

5631 many-valued; multi[ple-]valued
   d mehrwertig; mehrdeutig; vieldeutig; mehrstellig
   f polyvalent; multivalent
   r многозначный

5632 many-valued logic; multi[ple-]valued logic; multilogic
   d mehrwertige Logik *f*; mehrdeutige Logik; vieldeutige Logik; Multilogik *f*
   f logique *f* polyvalente; logique de plusieurs chiffres; multilogique *f*
   r многозначная логика *f*

5633 many-variable system
   d Mehrvariablensystem *n*
   f système *m* à plusieurs variables
   r система *f* с несколькими переменными

5634 map *v*
   d planen; abbilden
   f faire une projection; établir une correspondance
   r проецировать

5635 map; chart

d Karte *f*
f carte *f*
r карта *f*

5636 mapped buffer
   (in the display)
   d Abbildungspuffer *m*
   f tampon *m* mappé
   r буфер *m* поэлементного отображения

5637 mapped drive
   d Bildlaufwerk *n*
   f disque *m* mappé
   r подсоединённый накопитель *m*

5638 mapping
   (in memory)
   d Abbildung *f*; Einteilung *f*
   f image *f*; allocation *f*; découpage *m*
   r отображение *n*; распределение *n*

5639 margin
   d Papierrand *m*
   f marge *f*
   r поле *n* [печатной страницы]

* **marginal check** → 903

* **marginal checking** → 903

* **marginal test** → 903

* **mark** → 5644

5640 mark *v*
   d markieren
   f marquer
   r отмечать

* **mark column** → 5641

* **marked** → 9178

5641 mark[ed] column
   d markierte Spalte *f*
   f colonne *f* marquée
   r помеченная колонка *f*

5642 marked column pitch
   d Markierungsspaltenabstand *m*
   f pas *m* de colonne marquée
   r шаг *m* помеченной колонки

5643 marked zones
   d markierte Zonen *fpl*
   f zones *fpl* marquées
   r маркированные зоны *fpl*

5644 mark[er]
   d Marke *f*; Markierungszeichen *n*

f marque *f*; marqueur *m*
r пометка *f*; маркер *m*

5645 marker pulse
d Markier[ungs]impuls *m*
f impulsion *f* de marquage
r маркерный импульс *m*

5646 marking; flagging
d Markierung *f*
f marquage *m*; repérage *m*
r маркировка *f*; маркирование *n*; разметка *f*

5647 Markov chain
d Markov-Kette *f*; Markovsche Kette *f*
f chaîne *f* de Markov
r цепь *f* Маркова; марковская цепь

5648 mark position
d Markierungsstelle *f*; Markierungsposition *f*
f position *f* de marque
r позиция *f* метки

5649 mark sense reader
d Markierungsleser *m*
f lecteur *m* de marques
r устройство *n* считывания меток

5650 mask
d Maske *f*
f masque *m*
r маска *f*

5651 mask *v*
d maskieren
f masquer
r маскировать

5652 maskable interrupt
d maskierbare Unterbrechung *f*
f interruption *f* masquable
r маскируемое прерывание *n*

* **mask channel** → 329

5653 masked interrupt
d maskierte Unterbrechung *f*
f interruption *f* masquée
r маскированное прерывание *n*

* **masked search** → 9987

5654 masking
d Maskierung *f*; Maskieren *n*; Ausblenden *n*;
   Maskenvergleich *m*
f masquage *m*
r маскирование *n*; наложение *n* маски;
   выделение *n* маски; проверка *f* по маске

5655 mask-programmable

d maskenprogrammierbar
f programmable par masque
r программируемый фотошаблонами

5656 mask-programmable logic array; MPLA
d maskenprogrammierbare Logikanordnung *f*
f matrice *f* logique programmable par masque
r программируемая фотошаблонами
   матрица *f*

5657 mask register
d Maskierregister *n*
f registre *m* de masque
r регистр *m* маски

5658 mask topography
d Maskentopografie *f*
f topographie *f* de masque
r конфигурация *f* маски

* **mass** → 1244

* **mass data processing** → 1246

* **mass device** → 5659

* **mass mail** → 1247

* **mass mailing** → 1247

* **mass memory** → 5659

**5659 mass storage; mass memory; mass device;
        bulk memory**
d Massenspeicher *m*; Hintergrundspeicher *m*
f mémoire *f* massive; mémoire de masse;
   mémoire de grande taille
r массовая память *f*; память
   [сверх]большого объёма

* **master** → 5597

5660 master chip
d Master-Chip *m*; Standardchip *m*
f puce *f* de base
r базовый кристалл *m*

* **master clock** → 5662

5661 master clock
d zentraler Takt *m*; Haupttakt *m*
f horloge *f* pilote; horloge mère; rythme *m*
   pilote
r задающий импульс *m*

5662 master clock [signal generator]
d Haupttaktgeber *m*
f générateur *m* d'horloge pilote; horloge *f*
   maître
r задающий генератор *m*

5663 master data
  d Stammdaten *pl*; Hauptdaten *pl*
  f données de base; données principaux
  r основные данные *pl*; условно постоянные
      данные

5664 master disk
  d Master-Disk *f*; Hauptdisk *f*
  f disque *m* maître
  r ведущий диск *m*

5665 master file; main file
  d Hauptdatei *f*
  f fichier *m* maître; fichier principal
  r главный файл *m*; основной файл

  * **master frequency** → 7809

  * **master index** → 4328

5666 master network node
  d Master-Netzknoten *m*
  f nœud *m* de réseau maître
  r главный узел *m* сети

  * **master node** → 1535

5667 master page
  d Hauptseite *f*
  f page *f* principale
  r ведущая страница *f*; главная страница

  * **master program** → 5604

5668 master record
  d Stammeintrag *m*; Hauptsatz *m*
  f enregistrement *m* maître; article *m* permanent
  r ведущая запись *f*; эталонная запись

  * **master-slave computer system** → 4468

5669 master-slave relationship
  d Master-Slave-Verhältnis *n*
  f relation *f* maître-esclave
  r взаимодействие *n* по принципу
      "ведущий-ведомый"

5670 master-slave trigger; MS trigger
  d zweistufiger Flipflop *m*;
      Master-Slave-Flipflop *m*
  f basculeur *m* maître-esclave
  r двухступенчатый триггер *m*; триггер типа
      "главный-подчинённый"

5671 master slice
  d Stammscheibe *f*; Master-Slice *n*
  f plaque[tte] *f* maître
  r базовая пластина *f*

5672 master synchronizing pulse
  d Mastersynchronimpuls *m*
  f impulsion *f* de synchronisation pilote
  r главный импульс *m* синхронизации

5673 master tape
  d Stammband *n*
  f bande *f* maître
  r главная лента *f*; эталонная лента

5674 match *v*
  d anpassen; vergleichen; abgleichen
  f comparer; conformer
  r согласовывать; сопоставлять

  * **match** *v* → 1843

  * **match bit** → 5194

5675 match circuit; coincidence gate
  d Koinzidenzschaltung *f*
  f circuit *m* à coïncidence
  r схема *f* совпадения

  * **matching** → 1844, 2333

5676 matching
  d Paarung *f*; Matching *n*;
      Paarigkeitsvergleich *m*
  f couplage *m*; appariement *m*;
      rapprochement *m*
  r [паро]сочетание *n*; согласование *n*

5677 matching error
  d Anpassungsfehler *m*
  f erreur *f* d'adaptation
  r ошибка *f* несовпадения; ошибка
      согласования

5678 mathematical expression
  d mathematischer Ausdruck *m*
  f expression *f* mathématique
  r математическое выражение *n*

5679 mathematical formula
  d mathematische Formel *f*
  f formule *f* mathématique
  r математическая формула *f*

  * **mathematical logic** → 3972

5680 mathematical operation
  d mathematische Operation *f*
  f opération *f* mathématique
  r математическая операция *f*

5681 mathematical operator
  d mathematischer Operator *m*
  f opérateur *m* mathématique
  r математический оператор *m*

5682 mathematical symbols
d mathematische Symbole *npl*
f symboles *mpl* mathématiques
r математические символы *mpl*

5683 matrix; array
d Matrix *f*
f matrice *f*
r матрица *f*

5684 matrix adder
d Matrixaddierer *m*
f additionneur *m* matriciel
r матричный сумматор *m*

5685 matrix calculus
d Matrizenrechnung *f*; Matrizenkalkül *m*
f calcul *m* matriciel
r матричное исчисление *n*

* **matrix coder** → 5687

5686 matrix decoder
d Matrixdecodierer *m*
f décodeur *m* matriciel
r матричный дешифратор *m*

* **matrix display** → 7619

* **matrix dot** → 8240

5687 matrix [en]coder
d Matrixcodierer *m*
f codeur *m* matriciel
r матричный шифратор *m*

5688 matrix expansion
d Matrixerweiterung *f*
f expansion *f* de matrice
r расширение *n* матрицы

* **matrix font** → 7622

* **matrix image** → 7626

* **matrix line** → 5692

5689 matrix memory; coordinate store
d Matrixspeicher *m*; Koordinatenspeicher *m*
f mémoire *f* matricielle; mémoire coordonnée
r матричная память *f*; координатная память

5690 matrix processor; array processor; vector processor
d Matrixprozessor *m*; Vektorprozessor *m*; Array-Prozessor *m*
f processeur *m* de tableau; processeur vectoriel; processeur vecteur
r матричный процессор *m*; векторный процессор

5691 matrix representation
d Matrizendarstellung *f*
f représentation *f* matricielle
r матричное представление *n*

5692 matrix row; matrix line
d Matrixlinie *f*; Matrixzeile *f*
f ligne *f* de matrice
r строка *f* матрицы

5693 matrix size
d Matrixgröße *f*
f dimension *f* de matrice
r размерность *f* матрицы

5694 maximal; maximum
d maximal; Maximal-
f maximal
r максимальный

5695 maximize *v*
d maximieren
f maximaliser
r максимизировать

5696 maximize button
d Schaltfläche *f* für Maximieren
f bouton *m* de maximalisation
r кнопка *f* максимизации (окна)

5697 maximized window
d maximiertes Fenster *n*
f fenêtre *f* maximalisée
r максимизированное окно *n*

* **maximum** → 5694

5698 maximum
d Maximum *n*
f maximum *m*
r максимум *m*; максимальная величина *f*

5699 maxterm; standard sum term
d Maxterm *m*; Volldisjunktion *f*
f maxterme *m*; terme *m* disjoint
r макстерм *m*; элементарная дизъюнктивная форма *f*; совершенная дизъюнктивная форма

* **MB** → 5714

* **Mbone** → 5058

* **MCS** → 5928

* **mean** → 5703

5700 mean; average; medium; middle
d mittler

f moyen; médian; médium
r средний; умеренный

* **mean error → 736**

* **mean life → 737**

5701 mean repair time
d mittlere Wiederherstellungszeit *f*; mittlere Reparaturzeit *f*
f temps *m* moyen de dépannage; temps moyen de réparation
r среднее время *n* восстановления; среднее время простоя

5702 mean time between failures; MTBF
d mittlere Zeit *f* zwischen zwei Ausfällen
f moyenne *f* des temps de bon fonctionnement; moyen temps *m* de bon fonctionnement
r среднее время *n* безотказной работы

5703 mean [value]; average [value]
d Mittel *n*; Mittelwert *m*
f valeur *f* moyenne; moyenne *f*
r среднее [значение] *n*; средняя величина *f*

* **measuring transmitter → 9487**

5704 media
d Medien *npl*
f média *m*
r средства *npl* информации; носители *mpl*

* **media access control → 5708**

5705 media support
d Medienwartung *f*
f maintenance *f* de média
r поддержка *f* средств информации

* **medium → 5700**

5706 medium
d Medium *n*
f médium *m*; milieu *m*
r среда *f*; средство *n*

5707 medium access
d Mediumzugriff *m*
f accès *m* au médium
r доступ *m* к среде

5708 medium access control; media access control; MAC
d Mediumzugriffskontrolle *f*; Medienzugriffskontrolle *f*
f contrôle *m* de l'accès au médium; contrôle de l'accès aux supports
r управление *n* доступом к [сообщительной] среде (низшая часть канального уровня)

5709 medium duty
d mittlere Beanspruchung *f*
f charge *f* moyenne
r средняя нагрузка *f*

5710 medium information volume
d mittlere Informationsmenge *f*
f masse *f* d'information moyenne
r среднее количество *n* информации

5711 medium-scale LAN
d mittleres lokales Netz *n*; mittelgroßes lokales Netz
f réseau *m* local de taille moyenne
r средняя местная сеть *f*

5712 medium-speed data transmission
d mittelschnelle Datenübertragung *f*
f transmission *f* de données à vitesse moyenne
r передача *f* данных со средней скоростью

5713 megabit
d Megabit *n*
f mégabit *m*
r мегабит *m*

5714 megabyte; MB
d Megabyte *n*; MB
f méga-octet *m*; Mo
r мегабайт *m*; Мб

5715 megapixel
d Megapixel *n*
f mégapixel *m*
r мегапиксел *m*

5716 member; term
d Glied *n*; Member *n*; Term *m*
f membre *m*; terme *m*
r член *m*; терм *m*

5717 member record
d untergeordneter Satz *m*
f enregistrement *m* de sous-niveau
r запись *f* подчинённого уровня

5718 membrane keyboard; plastic foil keyboard
d Folientastatur *f*
f clavier *m* à diaphragme; clavier à membrane
r мембранная клавиатура *f*

* **memo file → 7808**

* **memorization → 8922**

* **memorize *v* → 8928**

* **memory → 5602**

5719 memory; storage; store
d Speicher *m*

f mémoire *f*
r память *f*; запоминающее устройство *n*

5720 memory allocation; memory assignment
  d Speicher[platz]zuordnung *f*;
      Speicherzuweisung *f*
  f allocation *f* de mémoire; répartition *f* de
      mémoire
  r распределение *n* памяти; выделение *n*
      памяти

5721 memory area; room
  d Speicherbereich *m*
  f domaine *m* de mémoire; tranche *f* de mémoire
  r область *f* памяти

  * **memory assignment** → 5720

5722 memory bank; store bank
  d Speicherbank *f*
  f banque *f* de mémoire; banc *m* de mémoire
  r банк *m* памяти

**5723 memory buffer register; memory data
       register**
  d Speicherpufferregister *n*
  f registre *m* pile de mémoire
  r буферный регистр *m* памяти

  * **memory call** → 5733

5724 memory cell; memory location
  d Speicherzelle *f*; Speicherplatz *m*
  f cellule *f* de mémoire
  r ячейка *f* памяти

5725 memory cycle
  d Speicherzyklus *m*
  f cycle *m* de mémoire
  r цикл *m* [обращения к] памяти

  * **memory data register** → 5723

5726 memory dump; dump
  d Speicherauszug *m*; Speicherabzug *m*;
      Speicherabgabe *f*
  f vidage *m* [de mémoire]; extrait *m* de mémoire
  r вывод *m* содержимого [памяти] на экран
      или печать; "снимок" *m* памяти; дамп *m*

  * **memory location** → 5724

5727 memory management; memory mapping
  d Speicherverwaltung *f*;
      Speicherbereichszuordnung *f*
  f gestion *f* de mémoire; découpage *m* de
      mémoire
  r управление *n* памятью; управление
      распределения памяти

  * **memory manager** → 5728

5728 memory manager [program]
  d Speicherverwaltungsprogramm *n*
  f programme *m* de management de la mémoire;
      gestionnaire *m* de la mémoire
  r программа *f* управления памятью

5729 memory map
  d Speicherbelegungsplan *m*;
      Speicherbelegungskarte *f*
  f carte *f* d'allocation de mémoire; plan *m*
      d'occupation de mémoire
  r карта *f* [распределения] памяти

  * **memory mapping** → 5727

5730 memory paging
  d Speicherseitenwechsel *m*
  f pagination *f* de mémoire; pageage *m* de
      mémoire
  r разбиение *n* памяти на страницы;
      листание *n* страниц памяти

5731 memory printout
  d Speicherausdruck *m*
  f sortie *f* par impression de la mémoire
  r распечатка *f* [содержимого] памяти

5732 memory protection; stor[ag]e protection
  d Speicherschutz *m*; Speicherschreibsperre *f*
  f protection *f* de mémoire
  r защита *f* памяти

  * **memory reference** → 5733

**5733 memory request; memory reference;
       memory call**
  d Speicheranforderung *f*; Speicherbezug *m*;
      Speicheraufruf *m*
  f demande *f* de mémoire; appel *m* de mémoire;
      référence *f* à la mémoire
  r запрос *m* памяти; обращение *n* к памяти

  * **memory-resident** → 7590

5734 memory sharing
  d geteilte Speichernutzung *f*
  f partage *m* de mémoire
  r совместное использование *n* памяти

**5735 memory size; stor[ag]e size; stor[ag]e
       capacity**
  d Speicherkapazität *f*; Speichergröße *f*
  f taille *f* de mémoire; capacité *f* de mémoire;
      grandeur *f* de mémoire
  r объём *m* памяти

5736 memory size unit
  d Speichergrößeneinheit *f*

f unité *f* de taille de mémoire; unité de capacité
de mémoire
r единица *f* ёмкости памяти

5737 memory space; stor[ag]e space
d Speicherraum *m*; Speicherumfang *m*
f espace *m* de mémoire; volume *m* de mémoire
r пространство *n* памяти; обьём *m* памяти

5738 memory transfer
d Speichertransfer *m*
f transfert *m* de mémoire
r передача *f* данных памяти

5739 memory word
d Speicherwort *n*
f mot *m* de mémoire
r слово *n* памяти; длина *f* ячейки памяти

5740 menu
d Menü *n*
f menu *m*
r меню *n*

5741 menu bar
d Menüleiste *f*; Menübalken *m*
f barre *f* des menus
r меню-лента *f*

5742 menu control
d Menüsteuerung *f*
f commande *f* par menu
r управление *n* с помощью меню

5743 menu customization
d Menüanpassung *f*
f personnalisation *f* de menu
r разработка *f* заказного меню

5744 menu-driven
d menügeführt; menügesteuert
f piloté par des menus; déterminé par menu; à
[base de] menu
r управляемый через меню

5745 menu file
d Menüdatei *f*
f fichier *m* de menus
r файл *m* меню

5746 menu format
d Menüformat *n*
f format *m* du type menu
r формат *m* типа меню

5747 menu group
d Menügruppe *f*
f groupe *m* de menus
r группа *f* меню

5748 menu item; menu point
d Menüelement *n*; Menüpunkt *m*
f élément *m* de menu
r элемент *m* меню

5749 menu name
d Name *m* des Menüs
f nom *m* de menu
r имя *n* меню

5750 menu option
d Menüoption *f*
f option *f* de menu
r опция *f* меню

* **menu picking** → 5751

* **menu point** → 5748

5751 menu selection; menu picking
d Menüauswahl *f*
f sélection *f* par menu
r выбор *m* на основе меню

5752 menu structure
d Menüstruktur *f*
f structure *f* du menu
r структура *f* меню

5753 merge *v*
d vermischen; verschmelzen
f interclasser; fusionner
r смешивать; сливать

5754 merge sort; sort merge
d Sortieren *n* durch Verschmelzen;
Mischsortierung *f*
f tri[age] *m* par fusion
r сортировка *f* слиянием

5755 merging; meshing
d Mischen *n*; Zusammenmischen *n*;
Verschmelzung *f*
f fusionnement *m*; interclassement *m*
r слияние *n*; смешивание *n*

5756 mesh
d Masche *f*
f filet *f*; maille *f*; réseau *m* de facettes
r [простая планарная] сеть *f*; сетка *f*

5757 meshed network; mesh[-type] network
d Maschennetz[werk] *n*; vermaschtes
Netz[werk] *n*
f réseau *m* de mailles; réseau *m* maillé
r сеть *f* с ячеистой топологией; сетчатая
схема *f*; ячеистая сеть

* **meshing** → 5755

    * **mesh network** → 5757

    * **mesh-type network** → 5757

    * **mesochronous** → 9112

5758 message
  d Nachricht *f*; Meldung *f*; Mitteilung *f*
  f message *m*
  r сообщение *n*

5759 message buffer
  d Nachrichtenverteiler *m*; Meldungspuffer *m*
  f tampon *m* de messages
  r буфер *m* сообщений

5760 message byte
  d Nachrichtenbyte *n*
  f octet *m* de message
  r байт *m* сообщения

5761 message cancellation
  d Annullierung *f* von Nachrichten
  f annulation *f* de message
  r отмена *f* сообщения; прекращение *n* сообщения

5762 message code
  d Mitteilungscode *m*; Nachrichtencode *m*
  f code *m* de message
  r код *m* сообщения

5763 message content
  d Nachrichteninhalt *m*
  f contenu *m* du message
  r содержание *n* сообщения

5764 message delay
  d Nachrichtenlaufzeit *f*
  f retard *m* de message
  r запаздывание *n* сообщения

5765 message destination
  d Bestimmungsort *m*
  f destination *f* de message
  r назначение *n* сообщения

5766 message discrimination; message dissemination
  d Meldungsverteilung *f*; Nachrichtenverteilung *f*
  f discrimination *f* de messages
  r различение *n* сообщений; разделение *n* сообщений

    * **message dissemination** → 5766

5767 message flow; message stream
  d Nachrichtenfluss *m*; Nachrichtenstrom *m*
  f flot *m* de messages; fleuve *m* de messages

  r поток *m* сообщений

5768 message format
  d Nachrichtenformat *n*; Meldungsformat *n*
  f format *m* de message
  r формат *m* сообщения

    * **message forwarding** → 5780

5769 message handling
  d Nachrichtenbehandlung *f*; Nachrichtenverwaltung *f*
  f traitement *m* des messages; messagerie *f*
  r обработка *f* сообщений

5770 message handling server
  d Mailbox-Server *m*
  f serveur *m* de traitement de messages
  r сервер *m* обработки сообщений

    * **message handling service** → 5771

5771 message handling system; message handling service; MHS
  d Mitteilungsübermittlungssystem *n*; Nachrichtenaustauschsystem *n*; Mitteilungsübermittlungsdienst
  f système *m* de messagerie
  r система *f* обработки сообщений; служба *f* обработки сообщений; протокол *m* MHS

5772 message header; message leader
  d Nachrichtenkopf *m*; Nachrichtenvorsatz *m*; Nachrichtenvorspann *m*
  f en-tête *m* de message
  r заголовок *m* сообщения

5773 message interval
  d Nachrichtenzwischenraum *m*; Nachrichtenlücke *f*
  f intervalle *m* entre messages
  r интервал *m* между сообщениями

    * **message leader** → 5772

5774 message length
  d Umfang *m* der Meldung
  f longueur *f* du message
  r длина *f* сообщения

5775 message node
  d Nachrichtenknoten *m*
  f nœud *m* de traitement de messages
  r узел *m* обработки сообщений

    * **message notification** → 5786

5776 message priority
  d Nachrichtenpriorität *f*

f priorité f de message
r приоритет m сообщения

5777 message queue; communication queue
d Meldungswarteschlange f,
Nachrichtenwarteschlange f
f queue f des messages
r очередь f сообщений

5778 message queu[e]ing
d Nachrichtenschlangenaufbau m;
Nachrichtenzwischenspeicherung f
f gestion f de la queue de messages
r буферизация f сообщений [в узлах сети]

* **message queuing → 5778**

* **message receiver → 5779**

5779 message recipient; message receiver
d Nachrichtenempfänger m
f récepteur m de messages
r приёмник m сообщений

5780 message rerouting; message forwarding; forwarding
d Nachrichten-Weiterleiten n; Weiterleitung f
f réacheminement m [des messages]; renvoi m [des messages]
r переадресация f [сообщения]; перепосылка f

5781 message routing
d Meldungslenkung f, Nachrichtenführung f
f acheminement m de messages; routage m de messages
r маршрутизация f сообщений

5782 message security labeling
d Kennzeichnung f von Nachrichten nach ihrer Sensitivität
f étiquetage m de sécurité du message
r метка f грифа сообщении

* **message start → 8851**

5783 message storage; message store
d Mitteilungsspeicher m; Nachrichtenspeicher m
f mémorisation f des messages
r банк m сообщений; хранилище n сообщений

* **message store → 5783**

* **message stream → 5767**

5784 message transfer; message transmission; messaging
d Nachrichtentransfer m; Meldungsübergabe f,

Nachrichtenübertragung f,
Mitteilungsübermittlung f
f transfert m de messages; transmission f de messages
r передача f сообщений

* **message transmission → 5784**

5785 message type
d Nachrichtentyp m
f type m de message
r тип m сообщения

5786 message [waiting] notification
d Nachrichten-Wartezeitansage f
f avis m de message en attente; avis de réception de message
r объявление n ждущего сообщения

* **messaging → 5784**

* **metacharacter → 9985**

5787 meta code
d Metacode m
f métacode m
r метакод m

5788 metacompiler
d Metacompiler m
f métacompilateur m
r метакомпилятор m

5789 metadata
d Metadaten pl
f métadonnées fpl
r метаданные pl

5790 metafile
d Metadatei f
f métafichier m
r метафайл m

5791 metagraph
d Metagraph m
f métagraphe m
r метаграф m

5792 metaknowledge
d Metawissen n
f métaconnaissances fpl
r метазнания npl

5793 metalanguage
d Metasprache f
f métalangage m
r метаязык m

5794 metamorphosis
d Metamorphose f

f métamorphose *f*
r метаморфоза *f*

5795 metamorphosis sequence; morph sequence
d Metamorphosenfolge *f*
f séquence *f* de métamorphoses
r последовательность *f* метаморфоз

5796 metanetwork
d Metanetzwerk *n*
f métaréseau *m*
r мета-сеть *f*

5797 metaoperating system
d Metabetriebssystem *n*
f métasystème *m* d'exploitation
r метаоперационная система *f*

5798 metaphor
d Metapher *f*
f métaphore *f*
r метафора *f*

5799 metasearch
d Metasuche *f*
f logiciel *m* métamoteur; métamoteur *m*;
    métarecherche *f*
r мета-поиск *m*

* **metasymbol** → 9985

5800 meta tag
d Meta-Tag *n*
f balise *f* méta; méta-tag *m*
r мета-тег *m*

* **metering pulse** → 2349

5801 method
d Methode *f*; Verfahren *n*
f méthode *f*
r метод *m*; способ *m*

* **method of comparison** → 1976

5802 method of computation
d Rechenverfahren *n*
f méthode *f* de calcul
r метод *m* вычислений; способ *m*
    вычислений

**5803 method of iteration; iteration method;
    iterative method; iterative technique**
d Iterationsmethode *f*; Iterationsverfahren *n*;
    iterative Technik *f*; iteratives Vorgehen *n*
f méthode *f* d'itération; méthode itérative;
    technique *f* itérative
r итерационный метод *m*; метод итерации

5804 metric information

d metrische Information *f*
f information *f* métrique
r метрическая информация *f*; информация в
    метрической системе

**5805 metropolitan area network; MAN; urban
    trunk network**
d Stadtbereichnetz *n*; Stadtnetz *n*
f réseau *m* métropolitain; réseau urbain
r общегородская сеть *f*

* **MHS** → 5771

* **MIB** → 5618

5806 microassembler
d Mikroassembler *m*
f micro-assembleur *m*
r микроассемблер *m*

5807 microbreak; microinterruption
d Mikrounterbrechung *f*
f micro-interruption *f*
r микропрерывание *n*

5808 microcircuit; chip; crystal
d Mikroschaltung *f*; Chip *m*
f microcircuit *m*; puce *f*; chip *m*
r микросхема *f*; чип *m*; кристалл *m*

* **microcode** → 5818

* **microcoding** → 5820

5809 microcomputer
d Mikrocomputer *m*; Mikrorechner *m*
f micro[-ordinateur] *m*
r микрокомпьютер *m*

* **microcycle** → 5814

5810 microfiche
d Mikrofiche *n/m*
f microfiche *f*
r микрофиша *f*

5811 microfilm
d Mikrofilm *m*
f microfilm *m*
r микрофильм *m*

5812 microfilm computer output; micromation
d Rechnerausgabe *f* auf Mikrofilm;
    Mikromation *f*
f sortie *f* d'ordinateur sur microfilm;
    micromation *f*
r вывод *m* из компьютера на микрофильм

5813 microframe
d Mikroframe *n*

f microtrame *f*
r микрокадр *m*; кадр *m* микрофильма

5814 microinstruction cycle; microcycle
d Mikro[befehls]zyklus *m*
f cycle *m* de micro-instruction; microcycle *m*
r цикл *m* микрокоманды; микроцикл *m*

5815 microinstruction sequence; microsequence
d Mikro[befehls]folge *f*
f séquence *f* de micro-instructions; microséquence *f*
r последовательность *f* микрокоманд; микропоследовательность *f*

* **microinterruption** → **5807**

* **micromation** → **5812**

5816 microoperation
d Mikrooperation *f*
f micro-opération *f*
r микрооперация *f*

5817 microprocessor
d Mikroprozessor *m*
f microprocesseur *m*
r микропроцессор *m*

5818 microprogram; microcode
d Mikroprogramm *n*; Mikrocode *m*
f microprogramme *m*; microcode *m*
r микропрограмма *f*; микрокод *m*

5819 microprogram memory; control store; control memory
d Mikroprogrammspeicher *m*
f mémoire *f* à microprogrammes
r [управляющая] память *f* микропрограмм

5820 microprogramming; microcoding
d Mikroprogrammierung *f*; Mikrocodierung *f*
f microprogrammation *f*; microcodage *m*
r микропрограммирование *n*

5821 microprogram unit
d Mikroprogrammsteuerwerk *n*
f unité *f* microprogrammée
r блок *m* микропрограммного управления

5822 microscanner
d Mikroscanner *m*
f microscanner *m*
r микросканер *m*

5823 microsecond
d Mikrosekunde *f*
f microseconde *f*
r микросекунда *f*

* **microsequence** → **5815**

* **middle** → **5700**

5824 middleware; connectivity software
d Middleware *f*
f logiciel *m* standard personnalisé; logiciel adapté à la configuration; interlogiciel *m*
r связующее программное обеспечение *n*; промежуточное программное обеспечение (для разнородных систем)

* **MIDI** → **6029**

5825 mid-level network; regional network
(the second level of the Internet hierarchy)
d regionales Netz[werk] *n*
f réseau *m* régional
r сеть *f* среднего уровня

5826 Millennium bug
d Jahrtausendfehler *m*; Millennium-Fehler *m*
f bogue *f* du millénaire
r ошибка *f* тысячелетия

* **millimicrosecond** → **6040**

5827 million instructions per second; MIPS
d Anzahl *f* der ausgeführten Befehle in Millionen pro Sekunde
f nombre *m* d'instructions en millions par seconde
r миллион *m* инструкций в секунду

5828 millisecond
d Millisekunde *f*
f milliseconde *f*
r миллисекунда *f*

* **MIME** → **6010**

5829 minicomputer
d Minicomputer *m*; Minirechner *m*; Kleincomputer *m*
f mini-ordinateur *m*
r миникомпьютер *m*; мини-машина *f*

5830 minimization; minimizing
d Minim[is]ierung *f*; Minimalisierung *f*
f minim[al]isation *f*
r минимизация *f*

5831 minimize *v*
d minimieren
f minimiser
r минимизировать

5832 minimize button
d Schaltfläche *f* für Minimieren

f bouton *m* de minimisation; bouton de réduction
r бутон *m* минимизирования; бутон свёртывания

5833 minimized window
d minimiertes Fenster *n*
f fenêtre *f* minimisée
r минимизированное окно *n*

* **minimizing** → 5830

5834 minimum
d Minimum *n*
f minimum *m*
r минимум *m*

5835 minimum access programming
d Programmierung *f* mit minimaler Zugriffszeit; Bestzeitprogrammierung *f*
f programmation *f* à temps d'accès minimum
r программирование *n* на минимальное время доступа

5836 minimum access routine
d Bestzeitprogramm *n*
f programme *m* optimal
r программа *f* с минимальным временем обращения

5837 minimum distance code
d Code *m* mit Mindestabstand
f code *m* à distance minimale
r код *m* с минимальным расстоянием

5838 minor
d minor; geringfügig
f mineur
r меньший; подчинённый

5839 minor hysteresis loop
d minore Hystereseschleife *f*
f boucle *f* d'hystérésis mineure
r частный гистерезисный цикл *m*

5840 minority
d Minorität *f*
f minorité *f*
r подчинённость *f*

* **minor loop** → 4876

5841 minor structure; substructure
d Unterstruktur *f*
f structure *f* mineure; structure inférieure; sous-structure *f*
r подчинённая структура *f*; внутренняя структура; подструктура *f*

5842 minterm; standard product term

d Minterm *m*; Vollkonjunktion *f*
f minterme *m*; conjonction *f* totale; terme *m* conjonctif
r минтерм *m*; элементарная конъюнктивная форма *f*

* **minus** → 8566

* **minuscule** → 8670

* **minus sign** → 8566

* **mipmap** → 5844

5843 mipmap level
d Mip-Map-Niveau *n*
f niveau *m* de mip-mapping
r уровень *m* mip-текстурирования

5844 mipmap[ping]
d Mip-Mapping *n*
f mip-mapping *m*
r множественное отображение *n* текстур одного и того же изображения; mip-текстурирование *n*

* **MIPS** → 5827

* **mirror** → 5846

5845 mirror channel
d Spiegelkanal *m*
f canal *m* spéculaire
r зеркальный канал *m*

5846 mirror [server]
d Spiegelserver *m*
f serveur *m* miroir; miroir *m*
r зеркальный сервер *m*; зеркало *n*; дублирующий сервер

* **MIS** → 5619

5847 misalignment
d Fehleinstellung *f*
f mésalignement *m*; désalignement *m*; mésajustage *m*
r погрешная выверка *f*; плохое юстирование *n*

* **miscalculation** → 2047

5848 miscellaneous
d verschieden; gemischt; vermischt; vielseitig
f divers; accessoire
r разнообразный; дополнительный

5849 misframing
d falsches Framing *n*

f décadrage m
r ошибочное кадрирование n

* **mismatch → 5850**

5850 mismatch[ing]
d Fehlanpassung f; Nichtübereinstimmung f
f déséquilibre m; discordance f;
désadaptation f; défaut m de coordination;
non-coïncidence f
r рассогласование n; несовпадение n;
несоответствие n

5851 missing data
d fehlende Daten pl; fehlende Angaben fpl
f données fpl manquantes; observation f
manquante
r недостающие данные pl

**5852 missing page interrupt; page fault
interrupt**
d Fehlseitenunterbrechung f;
Seitenfehlerunterbrechung f
f interruption f de faute de page
r прерывание n из-за отсутствия страницы

5853 missort
d Sortierfehler m
f erreur f de tri[age]
r ошибка f при сортировке

5854 misspelling
d orthografischer Fehler m
f erreur f orthographique
r орфографическая ошибка f

5855 mistiming
d Fehltaktung f; Synchronisierungsfehler m
f désynchronisation f
r рассинхронизация f

5856 misuse failure
d Ausfall m wegen des unsachgemäßen
Einsatzes
f défaut m par inadvertance
r отказ m из-за неправильного обращения

* **mix → 5859**

5857 mix v; blend v
d mischen; vermischen
f mixer; confondre; mélanger
r смешивать; сочетать[ся]

5858 mixed network
d Mischnetz n
f réseau m mixte
r смешанная сеть f

5859 mix[ing]; blend[ing]
d Mischung f; Vermischen n; Mischen n

f mixtion f; mixage m; mélange m
r смешение n; смешивание n;
перемешивание n

5860 mixing area
d Mischbereich m
f domaine m de mélange
r область f смешивания; зона f смешивания

* **MMX → 5955**

* **mnemonic → 5863**

5861 mnemonic code
d Mnemocode m; mnemonischer
Befehlscode m
f code m mnémonique
r мнемокод m; мнемонический код m

5862 mnemonic language
d Mnemoniksprache f
f langage m mnémonique
r язык m мнемосхем

5863 mnemonic[s]; mnemoscheme
d Mnemonik f; Mnemonikplan m
f mnémonique f; mnémoschème m
r мнемоника f; мнемосхема f

* **mnemoscheme → 5863**

* **mobile → 7129**

* **mobility → 7127**

5864 modal logic
d modale Logik f
f logique f modale
r модальная логика f

5865 mode
d Modus m; Betriebsweise f
f mode m; régime m
r режим m; способ m

5866 model
d Modell n
f modèle m
r модель f

* **modeler → 5868**

* **modeling → 5867**

* **modeling program → 5868**

5867 model[l]ing
d Modellierung f; Modellbildung f
f modelage m; modélisation f; création f de
modèle
r моделирование n

5868 model[l]ing program; modeler
   d Modellierer *m*
   f programme *m* de modelage; modélisateur *m*
   r моделирующая программа *f*

   * **modem** → 5875

5869 moderated conference
   d moderierte Konferenz *f*
   f conférence *f* dirigée; conférence animée
   r отредактированная конференция *f*

5870 moderator; tiebreaker
   (a person)
   d Moderator *m*; Diskussionsleiter *m*
   f modérateur *m* (personne filtrant les articles
     adressés à un groupe de discussion modéré)
   r арбитр *m*; председательствующий *m*;
     редактор *m* дискусии; модератор *m*;
     регулятор *m*

   * **modification** → 338

5871 modified address
   d modifizierte Adresse *f*
   f adresse *f* modifiée
   r модифицированный адрес *m*

5872 modifier
   d Modifikator *m*; Modifizierfaktor *m*
   f modificateur *m*
   r модификатор *m*

5873 modifier bits
   d Modifikationsbits *npl*; Änderungsbits *npl*
   f bits *mpl* de modification
   r биты *mpl* модификации;
     модифицирующие разряды *mpl*

   * **modifier register** → 4772

   * **modular counter** → 1462

5874 modulation code
   d Modulationscode *m*
   f code *f* de modulation
   r модулирующий код *m*

5875 modulator-demodulator; modem
   d Modulator-Demodulator *m*; Modem *n*
   f modulateur-démodulateur *m*; modem *m*
   r модулятор-демодулятор *m*; модем *m*

   * **module** → 1238

5876 module extender board
   d Modulverlängerungskarte *f*
   f carte *f* à extension de module
   r переходная плата *f*

   * **modulo-n check** → 8002

5877 modulo operation
   d Modulo-Operation *f*
   f opération *f* [en] modulo
   r операция *f* по модулю

   * **modulo 2 sum gate** → 3569

5878 moment; instant
   d Moment *m*; Zeitpunkt *m*
   f moment *m*; instant *m*
   r момент *m*

   * **monitor** → 3020, 3578

5879 monitor control dump
   d Monitorsteuerauszug *m*
   f vidage *m* moniteur
   r контрольная выдача *f*; контрольный
     дамп *m*

   * **monitor filter** → 9810

5880 monitoring; supervision; survey[ing]
   d Monitoren *n*; Überwachung *f*;
     Dispatcherverwaltung *f*; Supervision *f*
   f monitorage *m*; contrôle *m* [courant];
     surveillance *f*; arpentage *m*
   r [текущий] контроль *m*; диспетчерское
     управление *n*; обзор *m*; обследование *n*;
     наблюдение *n*

5881 monitoring procedure
   d Monitoring-Verfahren *n*
   f procédure *f* de monitorage
   r процедура *f* диспетчерского управления

   * **monitoring program** → 3578

5882 monitor resolution; screen resolution
   d Bildschirmauflösung *f*
   f résolution *f* d'écran
   r разрешающая способность *f* экрана

   * **monoboard** → 6412

   * **monoboard computer** → 6413

   * **monochannel** *adj* → 8600

   * **monochromatic** → 5884

5883 monochromaticity
   d Einfarbigkeit *f*
   f monochromaticité *f*
   r монохроматизм *m*; одноцветность *f*

5884 monochrome; monochromatic; one-color
   d monochrom[atisch]; einfarbig

f monochrome; monochromatique
r монохромный; монохроматический; одноцветный

5885 monochrome monitor
d Monochrom-Monitor *m*; Schwarzweißmonitor *m*
f moniteur *m* monochromatique
r монохромный экран *m*

* **monophase** → 8626

* **monopulse** → 8629

5886 monostable; one-shot
d monostabil
f monostable
r с одним устойчивым состоянием

5887 monostable multivibrator; monovibrator; univibrator; one-shot multivibrator
d monostabiler Multivibrator *m*; Monoflop *n*; Univibrator *m*
f multivibrateur *m* monostable; monovibrateur *m*
r ждущий мультивибратор *m*; моновибратор *m*

* **monovibrator** → 5887

5888 Moore automaton
d Moore-Automat *m*
f automate *m* de Moore
r автомат *m* Мура

5889 morpheme
d Morphem *n*
f morphème *m*
r морфема *f* (наименьшая неделимая значащая часть слова)

5890 morphing; in-betweening; betweening; tweening
(generating of additional smoothed frames)
d Morphing *n*
f morphage *m*
r морфинг *m*; заполнение *n* промежуточных кадров; твининг *m*

* **morph sequence** → 5795

5891 mosaic
d Mosaik-
f mosaïque
r мозаичный

5892 mosaic array
d Mosaikmatrix *f*
f matrice *f* mosaïque
r мозаичная матрица *f*

5893 mosaic graphics; block graphics
(graphical images created in character mode)
d Mosaikgrafik *f*
f graphique *m* mosaïque
r блочная графика *f*

5894 mosaic texture
d Mosaiktextur *f*
f texture *f* mosaïque
r мозаичная текстура *f*

5895 most significant bit
d höchstes signifikantes Bit *n*; höchstwertiges Bit
f bit *m* de poids supérieur; bit de l'ordre le plus haut
r [самый] старший [значащий] бит *m*; старший разряд *m*

5896 most significant digit; top digit
d höchste signifikante Ziffer *f*; höchstwertige Ziffer
f chiffre *m* de poids supérieur; digit *m* de l'ordre le plus haut
r [самая] старшая значащая цифра *f*

5897 motherboard; backboard
d Mutter[leiter]platte *f*; Hauptplatine *f*; Leiterplattenchassis *n*; Grundplatine *f*
f carte *f* mère; plaque *f* mère
r объединительная плата *f*; основная плата

5898 motion analysis system
d Bewegungsanalysis-System *n*
f système *m* d'analyse du mouvement
r система *f* анализа движения

5899 motion blur
d Bewegungsunschärfe *f*
f flou *m* dû au mouvement
r размывание *n* при движении

* **motion video** → 414

* **mount** *v* → 564

* **mounting hole** → 5310

5900 mouse
d Maus *f*; Bedienmaus *f*; Handroller *m*
f souris *f*
r манипулятор *m* типа "мышь"; мышь *f*

5901 mouse button
d Maustaste *f*
f bouton *m* de la souris
r бутон *m* мыши

5902 mouse button release *v*
d Maustaste loslassen

f dégager le bouton de la souris; lâcher le
bouton de la souris; répandre le bouton de la
souris
r отпускать клавишу мыши

5903 mouse click
d Mausklick *m*
f clic *m* de la souris
r нажатие *n* кнопки мыши

5904 mouse configuration
d Mauskonfiguration *f*
f configuration *f* de la souris
r конфигурация *f* мыши

5905 mouse dragging
d Ziehen *n* mit der Maus
f lissage *m* par bouton de souris
r перемещение *n* через мышь; буксировка *f*
через мышь

5906 mouse dropping
d Maus-Loslassen *n*
f relâchement *m* par bouton de la souris
r опускание *n* мыши

5907 mouse interface
d Mausschnittstelle *f*
f interface *f* de la souris
r интерфейс *m* мыши

5908 mouse manager
d Maus-Manager *m*
f gestionnaire *m* de la souris
r программа *f* управления мыши

5909 mouse pad
d Mausmatte *f*; Mausunterlage *f*
f tapis *m* de souris
r коврик *m* для мыши

5910 mouse pointer
d Mauszeiger *m*
f pointeur *m* de la souris; curseur *m* de la souris
r указатель *m* мыши

5911 mouse trail
(on screen)
d Mausspur *f*
f traînée *f* [du curseur] de la souris
r след *m* курсора

5912 movable
d beweglich
f mouvant
r подвижный; передвижной

5913 move *v*
d bewegen; rücken; umsetzen
f déplacer; mouvoir; remuer

r двигать[ся]; передвигать; двинуть

5914 move instruction; move statement
d Transportbefehl *m*; Überweisungsbefehl *m*
f instruction *f* de mouvement; instruction de
transport; instruction de rupture de séquence
r инструкция *f* перемещения; оператор *m*
передачи управления; оператор пересылки

* **movement file** → 9480

* **move statement** → 5914

* **move time** → 9493

* **moving-arm disk** → 5916

5915 moving head
d beweglicher Kopf *m*
f tête *f* mobile
r подвижная головка *f*

5916 moving-head disk; moving-arm disk
d Platte *f* mit bewegbaren Köpfen; Platte mit
positionierbaren Köpfen
f disque *m* à têtes mobiles
r диск *m* с подвижными головками

**5917 Moving Pictures Experts Group format;
MPEG format**
(of audiovisual files)
d MPEG-Format *n*
f format *m* MPEG
r формат *m* MPEG

* **MPEG format** → 5917

* **MPLA** → 5656

* **MS trigger** → 5670

* **MTBF** → 5702

* **MUD** → 6021

* **muldex** → 5986

* **multiaccess** → 5964

5918 multiaccess system; multiuser system
d Mehrfachzugriffssystem *n*;
Mehr[be]nutzersystem *n*
f système *m* à accès multiple; système
multiutilisateur
r система *f* с коллективным доступом;
многопользовательская система

* **multiaddress** → 5966

5919 multiaddressing
d Mehrfachadressierung *f*

f multi-adressage *m*; adressage *m* multiple
r многократное адресование *n*

5920 multiaddress instruction
    d Mehradressbefehl *m*
    f instruction *f* multi-adresse
    r многоадресная инструкция *f*

5921 multiaddress message
    d Rundschreibnachricht *f*;
    Mehradressnachricht *f*
    f message *m* multi-adresse
    r многоадресное сообщение *n*

    * **multibus → 5967**

5922 multibus architecture; multithread architecture
    d Multibusarchitektur *f*
    f architecture *f* multibus
    r многошинная архитектура *f*

    * **multicast → 5923, 5924**

5923 multicast [addressing]
    d Multicast-Adressierung *f*
    f adressage *m* multidestinaire
    r множественная адресация *f*;
    мультивещательная адресация

    * **multicast backbone → 5058**

    * **multicast backbone network → 5058**

5924 multicast[ing]
    d Multicasting *n*; Gruppenruf *m*
    f multidiffusion *f*
    r многоканальная циркулярная рассылка *f*;
    многоадресная передача *f*;
    мультивещание *n*

5925 multichannel; multiline
    d Mehrkanal-
    f multicanal; à multiples canaux; à multiples
    voies; multiligne
    r многоканальный

5926 multichannel analyzer
    d Mehrkanalanalysator *m*
    f analyseur *m* à canaux multiples
    r многоканальный анализатор *m*

5927 multichannel circuit; multitone circuit
    d Mehrkanalschaltung *f*
    f circuit *m* à canaux multiples; circuit
    multicanal
    r многоканальная схема *f*

5928 multichannel communication system; MCS
    d Mehrkanalkommunikationssystem *n*

f système *m* de communication multicanal
r многоканальная система *f* связи

5929 multichannel connection
    d Mehrkanalverbindung *f*
    f connexion *f* multicanale
    r многоканальная связь *f*

5930 multichannel LAN
    d lokales Mehrkanalnetz *n*
    f réseau *m* local multicanal
    r местная многоканальная сеть *f*

5931 multichannel modem
    d Mehrkanal-Modem *n*
    f modem *m* multicanal
    r многоканальный модем *m*

5932 multichannel protocol
    d Mehrkanalprotokoll *n*
    f protocole *m* multicanal
    r многоканальный протокол *m*

5933 multichannel signal
    d Mehrkanalsignal *n*
    f signal *m* multicanal
    r многоканальный сигнал *m*

5934 multichannel switch; multicircuit switch
    d Mehrkanalschalter *m*; Serienschalter *m*
    f commutateur *m* multicanal
    r многоканальный коммутатор *m*;
    многоканальный переключатель *m*

5935 multichannel switching
    d Mehrkanaldurchschaltung *f*
    f commutation *f* multicanale
    r многоканальная коммутация *f*

5936 multichannel system
    d Mehrkanalsystem *n*; Vielkanalsystem *n*
    f système *m* à plusieurs voies
    r многоканальная система *f*

    * **multichannel tape → 6019**

    * **multicircuit switch → 5934**

5937 multicolor plotter; color plotter
    d Mehrfarbenplotter *m*; Farbplotter *m*
    f traceur *m* en couleurs; traceur multicouleur
    r [много]цветной графопостроитель *m*

5938 multicolor printer
    d Mehrfarbendrucker *m*
    f imprimante *f* multicouleur; imprimante à
    [plusieurs] couleurs
    r многоцветное печатающее устройство *n*

5939 multicolor printing
    d Mehrfarbendruck *m*

f impression *f* multicouleur
r многоцветная печать *f*

5940 multi-column bar chart
d Mehrspalten-Streifendiagramm *n*
f diagramme *m* à barres multiples; graphique *m* à barres multiples
r многоколонная столбиковая диаграмма *f*

* **multidex** → 5986

* **multidigit shift** → 5974

5941 multidimensional array
d mehrdimensionales Datenfeld *n*
f tableau *m* multidimensionnel
r многомерный массив *m*

* **multidrop transmission** → 6002

* **multi-endpoint connection** → 6000

* **multifile volume** → 5969

5942 multiformular printer
d Mehrformulardrucker *m*
f imprimante *f* multiformulaire
r многоформулярное печатающее устройство *n*

5943 multiframe operation
d Mehrfachrahmen-Modus *m*
f opération *f* multitrame
r многокадровая работа *f*

* **multihead disk** → 3866

5944 multikey retrieval
d Suchen *n* anhand mehrerer Schlüssel
f recherche *f* multiclé
r поиск *m* по нескольким ключам

* **multilayer board** → 5947

* **multilayer card** → 5947

5945 multilayer[ed] optical disk
d Mehrschichtdisk *f*
f disque *m* optique multicouche
r многослойный оптический диск *m*

5946 multilayer[ed] structure
d Mehrschichtstruktur *f*
f structure *f* multicouche
r многослойная структура *f*

* **multilayer optical disk** → 5945

5947 multilayer [printed circuit] board; multilayer card; laminated board
d Multilagenleiterplatte *f*; Mehrebeneleiterplatte *f*; Schichtplatte *f*; Mehrschichtplatte *f*
f plaque *f* multicouche; carte *f* multicouche; plaque laminée
r многослойная [печатная] плата *f*; слоистая плата

* **multilayer structure** → 5946

5948 multilevel *adj*
d Mehrpegel-; Mehrebenen-
f multiniveau; multistage
r многоуровневый

5949 multilevel addressing
d Mehrebenenadressierung *f*
f adressage *m* multiniveau
r многоуровневая адресация *f*

* **multilevel memory** → 5950

5950 multilevel memory [system]
d mehrstufiges Speichersystem *n*
f système *m* de mémorisation multistage; système de mémorisation hiérarchisée
r многоуровневая запоминающая система *f*; иерархическая запоминающая система

* **multiline** → 5925

5951 multilink
d Mehrfach-Übermittlungsabschnitt *m*; Mehrfachanschluss *m*
f multiliaison *f*
r многопроводная связь *f*

5952 multilink procedure
d Mehrfachanschlussprozedur *f*
f procédure *f* de multiliaison
r процедура *f* многопроводной связи

5953 multilist
d Multiliste *f*
f multiliste *f*
r мультисписок *m*

* **multilogic** → 5632

* **multimedia** → 5960

5954 multimedia communications
d Multimedia-Kommunikation *f*
f communication *f* multimédia; communication multimilieu
r мультимедийная связь *f*

5955 multimedia extensions; MMX
d Multimediaerweiterungen *fpl*

f extensions *fpl* multimédia
r мультимедийные расширения *npl*

5956 multimedia file
d Multimediendatei *f*; Multimediadatei *f*
f fichier *m* multimédia
r мультимедийный файл *m*

5957 multimedia kiosk
d Multimedienkiosk *m*
f poste *m* d'informations multimédia;
kiosque *m* multimédia
r мультимедийный киоск *m*

5958 multimedia kit
d Multimedia-Bausatz *m*
f kit *m* multimédia
r набор *m* для мультимедиа

5959 multimedia streaming; streaming
d Echtzeitübertragung *f* von
Multimedia[-Dateien]
f transmission *f* [multimédia] en continu
r поточный перенос *m* мультимедийных
данных; мультимедийный поток *m*

5960 multimedia [system]
d Multimediensystem *n*; Multimedien *npl*;
Multimedia *npl*
f système *m* multimilieu; multimédia *m*
r мультимедийная система *f*

* **multinomial** *adj* → 7104

5961 multipage document
d mehrseitiges Dokument *n*
f document *m* à plusieurs pages
r многостраничный документ *m*

* **multipass compiler** → 5972

* **multipass printing** → 5973

5962 multipen plotter
d Plotter *m* mit mehreren Zeichenstiften
f traceur *m* multiplume
r многоперьевой графопостроитель *m*

5963 multiple
d Mehrfach-; mehrfach; vielfach
f multiple
r многократный; множественный

5964 multiple access; multiaccess
d Vielfachzugriff *m*; Mehrfachzugriff *m*;
Mehrfachnutzung *f*
f accès *m* multiple; multiaccès *m*
r коллективный доступ *m*; множественный
доступ; мультидоступ *m*

5965 multiple-access channel
d Mehrfachzugriffskanal *m*
f canal *m* à accès multiple
r канал *m* коллективного доступа

5966 multiple-address; multiaddress
d Mehradress-
f multi-adresse; à adresses multiples
r многоадресный

5967 multiple bus; multibus
d Mehrfachbus *m*
f multibus *m*
r мультишина *f*

5968 multiple copies
d Mehrfachkopien *fpl*
f copies *fpl* multiples
r множество *n* копий

5969 multiple-file volume; multifile volume
d Mehrdateiband *n*
f volume *m* à fichiers multiples
r многофайловый том *m*

5970 multiple firing
d Mehrfachfeuerung *f*
f déclenchement *m* multiple
r многократный запуск *m* (схемы);
множественная активация *f* (узла сети)

5971 multiple head
d Vielfachkopf *m*
f tête *f* multiple
r многосекционная головка *f*

**5972 multiple-pass compiler; multipass
compiler**
d Mehrdurchlaufübersetzer *m*
f compilateur *m* à passages multiples;
compilateur à plusieurs pas
r многопассовый компилятор *m*;
многопроходной компилятор

5973 multiple-pass printing; multipass printing
d Mehrdurchlaufdrucker *m*
f impression *f* à passages multiples
r многопассовый принтер *m*

5974 multiple-position shift; multidigit shift
d Mehrstellenverschiebung *f*
f décalage *m* de plusieurs chiffres
r многоразрядный сдвиг *m*

5975 multiple precision; multiprecision
d Mehrfachpräzision *f*
f précision *f* multiple; multiprécision *f*
r многократная точность *f*

5976 **multiple-precision arithmetic;**
       multiprecision arithmetic
   d Mehrfacharithmetik *f*
   f multi-arithmétique *f*
   r вычисления *npl* с многократной точностью

5977 **multiple print**
   d Mehrfachdruck *m*
   f impression *f* multiple
   r многократная печать *f*

5978 **multiple recursion**
   d mehrfache Rekursion *f*
   f récursion *f* multiple
   r многократная рекурсия *f*

5979 **multiple redundancy; reiterative**
       redundancy
   d mehrfache Redundanz *f*
   f redondance *f* multiple; redondance réitérative
   r многократное резервирование *n*

   * **multiple-valued** → 5631

   * **multiple-valued logic** → 5632

5980 **multiple window display; multiwindow**
       display
   d Mehrfensterdisplay *n*;
       Mehrfensterbildschirm *m*
   f écran *m* multifenêtre; écran à multifenêtrage
   r полиэкранный дисплей *m*

   * **multiplex channel** → 5985

5981 **multiplexed address-data line set**
   d multiplexbetriebener
       Adressen-Daten-Leitungssatz *m*
   f jeu *m* de lignes adresses-données
       multiplexées
   r мультиплексированная шина *f*
       "адрес-данные"

5982 **multiplexed LCD**
   d Flüssigkristall-Multiplexanzeige *f*
   f affichage *m* à cristaux liquides multiplexé
   r жидкокристаллическая мультиплексная
       индикация *f*

5983 **multiplex[ed] line**
   d Leitung *f* in Multiplexschaltung;
       Multiplexleitung *f*
   f ligne *f* multiplexée
   r мультиплексированная линия *f*

5984 **multiplexer; multiplexor**
   d Multiplexer *m*; Multiplexgerät *n*
   f multiplexeur *m*
   r мультиплексор *m*

5985 **multiplex[er] channel**
   d Multiplexkanal *m*
   f canal *m* multiplex[eur]
   r мультиплексный канал *m*

5986 **multiplexer-demultiplexer; mul[ti]dex**
   d Multiplexer-Demultiplexer *m*; Mul[ti]dex *m*
   f multiplexeur-démultiplexeur *m*; multidex *m*
   r мультиплексор-демультиплексор *m*

5987 **multiplexer logic**
   d Multiplexerlogik *f*
   f logique *f* de multiplexeur
   r логическая схема *f* мультиплексора

5988 **multiplexer subchannel**
   d Multiplexunterkanal *m*
   f sous-canal *m* de multiplexeur
   r мультиплексный подканал *m*

5989 **multiplexing**
   d Multiplexen *n*; Bündelung *f*
   f multiplexage *m*
   r мультиплексирование *n*; уплотнение *n*

5990 **multiplex interface**
   d Multiplex-Schnittstelle *f*
   f interface *f* multiplex
   r мультиплексный интерфейс *m*

   * **multiplex line** → 5983

   * **multiplexor** → 5984

5991 **multiplicand**
   d Multiplikand[us] *m*
   f multiplicande *m*
   r множимое *n*

5992 **multiplicand register**
   d Multiplikandenregister *n*
   f registre *m* de multiplicande
   r регистр *m* множимого

5993 **multiplication**
   d Multiplikation *f*; Vervielfachung *f*
   f multiplication *f*
   r умножение *n*

   * **multiplication sign** → 8565

5994 **multiplication unit; multiplier**
   d Multiplizierwerk *m*; Multiplizierer *m*
   f unité *f* multipliante; multipli[cat]eur *m*
   r устройство *n* умножения; умножитель *m*

   * **multiplier** → 5994

5995 **multiplier; factor; ier**
   d Multiplikator *m*; Multiplizierer *m*; Faktor *m*;

Vervielfacher *m*
f multipli[cat]eur *m*; facteur *m*
r [y]множитель *m*; сомножитель *m*

5996 multiplier register
d Multiplikatorregister *n*
f registre *m* de multipli[cat]eur
r регистр *m* множителя

5997 multiply *v*
d multiplizieren; malnehmen
f multiplier
r умножать

5998 multiply-accumulator
d Multiplikator-Akkumulator *m*
f multipli[cat]eur *m* accumulateur
r умножитель-аккумулятор *m*

5999 multiply-adder
d Multiplikator-Add[ier]er *m*
f multipli[cat]eur *m* add[itionn]eur
r умножитель-сумматор *m*

6000 multipoint connection; multi-endpoint connection
d Mehrpunktverbindung *f*;
Multipoint-Verbindung *f*
f connexion *f* multipointe
r многоточечное соединение *n*

* **multipoint net → 6001**

6001 multipoint net[work]
d Mehrpunktnetz[werk] *n*; Knotennetz[werk] *n*;
Multipointnetz *n*
f réseau *m* multipoint; réseau à points multiples
r многоточечная сеть *f*; многоузловая сеть

6002 multipoint transmission; multidrop transmission
d Übertragung *f* zwischen mehreren Stationen
f transmission *f* multipointe
r многоточечная передача *f*

6003 multipoint videoconferencing
d Mehrpunkt-Fernsehkonferenzsystem *n*;
Mehrpunkt-Videokonferenzsystem *n*
f système *m* de vidéoconférence multipoint
r многопозиционная система *f* видеоконференции

6004 multipole connector
d Mehrkontaktstecker *m*
f connecteur *m* multiple
r многоконтактный разъём *m*

* **multiposting → 2387**

* **multiprecision → 5975**

* **multiprecision arithmetic → 5976**

6005 multipriority
d Multipriorität *f*
f multipriorité *f*
r многоприоритетность *f*

6006 multiprocessing; multithreading
d Mehrfachverarbeitung *f*; mehrgängiger Betrieb *m*; Multithread-Betrieb *m*
f multitraitement *m*; traitement *m* multiple; mode *m* de flux multiple
r мультиобработка *f*; многократная обработка *f*; многопоточная обработка; многопоточный режим *m*

6007 multiprocessing system; multiprocessor; multiunit processor
d Multiprozessorsystem *n*; Mehrprozessor *m*; Multiprozessor *m*
f système *m* de plusieurs processeurs; multiprocesseur *m*
r мультипроцессорная система *f*; мультипроцессор *m*

* **multiprocessor → 6007**

6008 multiprogramming
d Mehrfachprogrammierung *f*
f programmation *f* multiple; multiprogrammation *f*
r мультипрограммирование *n*

6009 multi-protocol routing
d Mehrprotokoll-Routing *n*; Mehrprotokoll-Trassierung *f*
f routage *m* multiprotocole
r многопротокольная маршрутизация *f*

6010 multipurpose Internet mail extensions; MIME
(extensions to the SMTP that allow the transmittal of non-text information via e-mail)
d vielseitige Internet-Post-Erweiterungen *fpl*; MIME-Protocoll *n*
f protocole *m* MIME
r многоцелевое почтовое расширение *n* Интернета; протокол *m* MIME

6011 multiresolution
d Multiauflösung *f*; Multiresolution *f*
f résolution *f* multiple
r многократная разрешающая способность *f*

6012 multiscanning
d Vielfachscannen *n*
f multi-balayage *m*
r многократное сканирование *n*

6013 multiserver architecture
d Multiserver-Architektur *f*
f architecture *f* multi-serveur
r архитектура *f* с множеством
обслуживающих процессов

6014 multisite system
d dezentralisiertes System *n*
f système *m* multisite
r рассредоточенная система *f*

6015 multispectral scanner
d mehrspektraler Scanner *m*
f scanner *m* multispectral
r многоспектральный сканер *m*

* **multitask** → **6016**

6016 multitask[ing] [mode]
d Multitaskbetrieb *m*; Mehrprozessbetrieb *m*;
Multitasking *n*
f mode *m* [de fonctionnement] multitâche;
opération *f* multitâche
r многозадачный режим *m*; многозадачная
работа *f*

6017 multitexturing
d Multitexturieren *n*
f multi-texturation *f*
r мултитекстурирование *n*; создание *n*
множества текстур

* **multithread architecture** → **5922**

* **multithreading** → **6006**

* **multitone circuit** → **5927**

6018 multitrack head
d Mehrspur[magnet]kopf *m*
f tête *f* multipiste
r многодорожечная головка *f*

6019 multitrack tape; multichannel tape
d Mehrspurband *n*
f bande *f* multipiste
r многодорожечная лента *f*

* **multiunit processor** → **6007**

6020 multiuser access
d Mehr[be]nutzerzugriff *m*
f accès *m* multiutilisateur
r многопользовательский доступ *m*

6021 multiuser dungeon; MUD
(Internet game of type "Donjon & Dragon")
d Mehrplatzverlies *n*; Mehrplatzkerker *m*;
Rollenspiel *n*
f jeu *m* de rôle

r многопользовательское подземелье *n*;
многопользовательский замок *m*

6022 multiuser-multitasking system
d Mehr-Benutzer- und Mehr-Prozess-System *n*
f système *m* multiutilisateur et multitâche
r многопользовательская и многозадачная
система *f*

* **multiuser system** → **5918**

* **multivalued** → **5631**

* **multivalued logic** → **5632**

6023 multivibrator
d Multivibrator *m*
f multivibrateur *m*
r мультивибратор *m*

6024 multivolume file
d Mehrdatenträgerdatei *f*
f fichier *m* multivolume
r многотомный файл *m*

6025 multiway branching
d Mehrwegverzweigung *f*
f branchement *m* multivoie
r ветвление *n* на несколько путей; ветвление
на несколько ветвей

6026 multiway search tree
d Mehrwegsuchbaum *m*
f arbre *m* de recherche multivoie
r дерево *n* многоканального поиска

* **multiwindow** → **6027**

* **multiwindow display** → **5980**

6027 multiwindow[ing]
d Bildfenstertechnik *f*; Multiwindowing *n*
f multifenêtrage *m*; fenêtrage *m* multiple
r организация *f* полиэкранной работы;
многооконная работа *f*

6028 multiword operand
d Mehrwortoperand *m*
f opérande *m* à plusieurs mots
r операнд *m* из нескольких слов

6029 musical instrument digital interface; MIDI
d digitale Schnittstelle *f* für Musikinstrumente
f interface *f* numérique pour instruments de
musique
r цифровой интерфейс *m* музыкальных
инструментов

6030 mutation
d Mutation *f*

    f mutation *f*
    r мутация *f*

6031 mutual
    d wechselseitig; gegenseitig
    f mutuel
    r взаимный

N

6032 nagware
 d Nörgel-Software *f*
 f nagware *m*
 r бесплатные программные средства *npl* без
    возможности использования в пакетном
    режиме

6033 name
 d Name *m*
 f nom *m*
 r имя *n*

 * name call → 1360

 * name domain → 9427

6034 name resolution service
 d Namenauflösungsdienst *m*
 f service *m* de résolution de noms
 r сервис *m* разрешения имён

6035 name server
 d Namenserver *m*
 f serveur *m* de noms
 r сервер *m* имён

 * naming → 2752

6036 naming authority
 d Namens-Behörde; Namensautorität *f*;
    Namengeberautorität *f*
 f autorité *f* responsable de l'appellation
 r полномочия *npl* именования; полномочия
    присваивания имён

 * NAND function → 6220

 * NAND gate → 6293

6037 nanoinstruction
 d Nanoinstruktion *f*
 f nano-instruction *f*
 r наноинструкция *f*

6038 nanoprogramming
 d Nanoprogrammierung *f*
 f nanoprogrammation *f*
 r нанопрограммирование *n*

6039 nanosecond; millimicrosecond
 d Nanosekunde *f*
 f nanoseconde *f*
 r наносекунда *f*

6040 native language
    (of a microprocessor)
 d Muttersprache *f*; arteigene Sprache *f*
 f langage *m* propre; langage natif
 r собственный язык *m*

6041 natural language; human language
 d natürliche Sprache *f*
 f langage *m* naturel
 r естественный язык *m*

6042 navigate *v*
 d navigieren; befahren
 f naviguer
 r передвигаться; пилотировать

6043 navigation
 d Navigation *f*
 f navigation *f*
 r навигация *f*; передвижение *n*

6044 navigation bar
 d Navigationsstreifen *m*
 f barre *f* de navigation
 r лента *f* навигации

6045 navigation key
 d Navigationstaste *f*
 f touche *f* de navigation
 r клавиша *f* навигации

6046 navigation menu
 d Navigationsmenü *n*
 f menu *m* de navigation
 r меню *n* навигации

6047 navigation software
 d Navigationssoftware *f*
 f logiciel *m* de navigation
 r навигационное программное
    обеспечение *n*

6048 navigation tool
 d Navigationshilfsmittel *n*
 f outil *m* de navigation
 r навигационный инструмент *m*

 * navigator → 1208

6049 n-bit address
 d n-Bit-Adresse *f*
 f adresse *f* à n bits
 r n-битовый адрес *m*

6050 n-bit output
 d n-Bit-Ausgang *m*
 f sortie *f* à n bits
 r n-разрядный выход *m*

6051 n-byte data
 d n-Byte-Daten *pl*

f données *fpl* à n octets
r n-байтовые данные *pl*

* **n-channel** → 6052

6052 n-[conducting]channel
d n-Kanal *m*; n-leitender Kanal
f canal *m* n
r канал *m* n-типа

* **NDRO** → 6226

* **near-natural language** → 7535

6053 needle printer; stylus printer
d Nadeldrucker *m*
f imprimante *f* à aiguilles
r игольчатое печатающее устройство *n*

6054 negate *v*
d negieren
f nier
r отрицать; изменять знак на минус

6055 negation
d Negation *f*
f négation *f*
r отрицание *n*

* **negation element** → 6297

6056 negative
d negativ
f négatif
r отрицательный

* **negative acceleration** → 2637

* **negative disabling signal** → 6060

* **negative edge** → 6058

6057 negative feedback; degenerative feedback; inverse feedback
d Gegenkopplung *f*; negative Rückführung *f*
f [contre-]réaction *f* négative;
contre-couplage *m*; antiréaction *f*
r отрицательная обратная связь *f*

6058 negative[-going] edge
(of a pulse)
d fallende Flanke *f*; negative Taktflanke *f*
f front *m* négatif
r отрицательный фронт *m*

6059 negative[-going] pulse
d negativer Impuls *m*
f impulsion *f* négative
r отрицательный импульс *m*

6060 negative inhibit signal; negative disabling signal
d negatives Sperrsignal *n*
f signal *m* d'inhibition négatif
r отрицательный запирающий сигнал *m*

6061 negative jump; jump if sign
d Sprung *m* bei Minus
f saut *m* négatif; saut sur le [signe] moins
r переход *m* по минусу; переход по знаку минус

* **negative justification** → 6063

6062 negative logic
d negative Logik *f*
f logique *f* négative
r отрицательная логика *f*

* **negative pulse** → 6059

6063 negative [pulse] stuffing; negative justification
d Negativstopfen *n*
f justification *f* négative
r отрицательный стаффинг *m*;
выбрасывание *n* [битов или знаков]

6064 negative signal
d negatives Signal *n*
f signal *m* négatif
r отрицательный сигнал *m*

* **negative stuffing** → 6063

* **negator** → 6297

6065 neglect *v*; **disregard** *v*
d vernachlässigen
f négliger; ignorer
r пренебрегать

* **nest** → 6072

6066 nest *v*
d einfügen; einschachteln; verschachteln
f encastrer; emboîter
r вкладывать

6067 nested; in-built; built-in
d eingefügt; eingeschachtelt; verschachtelt; eingebaut
f emboîté; encastré; inséré; imbriqué;
incorporé; à bord
r гнездовой; вложенный; встроенный;
вмонтированный

6068 nested dialog
d verschachtelter Dialog *m*

f dialogue *m* imbriqué
r вложенный диалог *m*

6069 nested images
 d eingefügte Bilder *npl*
 f images *fpl* encastrées
 r вложенные изображения *npl*

6070 nested language
 d eingefügte Sprache *f*; verschachtelte Sprache
 f langage *m* imbriqué; langage à famille
 r язык *m* с гнездовой структурой

6071 nested loop; nesting loop; home loop
 d eingeschachtelte Schleife *f*;
    Einbauprogrammschleife *f*; lokaler Zyklus *m*
 f boucle *f* emboîtée; boucle d'encastrement;
    boucle locale
 r вложенный цикл *m*; местный цикл

6072 nest[ing]; embedding
 d Einbettung *f*; Einbetten *n*; Einschachtelung *f*;
    Verschachtelung *f*; Schachtelung *f*
 f encastrement *m*; imbrication *f*; emboîtage *m*;
    emboîtement *m*
 r вложение *n*; вложенность *f*; упаковка *f*;
    внедрение *n*; укладка *f*

  * **nesting loop** → **6071**

  * **nesting store** → **8803**

  * **net** → **6079**

  * **net adapter** → **6081**

  * **net administrator** → **6082**

  * **net addiction** → **2456**

  * **netaholism** → **2456**

  * **net analysis** → **6083**

  * **net architecture** → **6085**

  * **NetBEUI** → **6073**

  * **NetBIOS** → **6086**

  * **NetBIOS enhanced user interface** → **6073**

6073 NetBIOS extended user interface;
    NetBIOS enhanced user interface;
    NetBEUI
 d erweiterte BIOS-Benutzer-Schnittstelle *f*
 f protocole *m* NetBEUI
 r улучшенный интерфейс *m* пользователя
    NetBIOS; протокол *m* NetBEUI

  * **net board** → **6114**

  * **netcam** → **6087**

  * **net camera** → **6087**

  * **net circuit** → **6088**

  * **net-citizen** → **5054**

  * **net configuration** → **6093**

6074 net data
 d Nettodaten *pl*
 f données *fpl* nettes
 r чистые данные *pl*

  * **nethead** → **2461**

6075 net information content
 d Nettoinformationsgehalt *m*
 f contenu *m* net d'information
 r чистое содержание *n* информации

  * **netiquette** → **6101**

  * **netizen** → **5054**

  * **net layer** → **6117**

6076 netmail
 d Nettomeldung *f*
 f poste *f* nette
 r личная почта *f*

  * **net model** → **6120**

  * **net operating system** → **6125**

  * **net operation** → **6126**

  * **net optimization** → **6127**

  * **netphone** → **5056**

6077 net police
 d Netzpolizei *f*
 f police *f* Internet
 r полиция *f* сетевых нравов; интернетная
    полиция (самозванная)

  * **net security** → **6134**

  * **net server** → **6136**

  * **net software** → **6138**

  * **netsurfer** → **2461**

  * **netsurfing** → **9980**

* **net synthesis** → 6141

* **net termination unit** → 6143

6078 **net TV; Internet television**
  d Netzfernsehen *n*
  f télévision *f* Internet
  r сетевое телевидение *n*

* **net user** → 5068

* **netware** → 6138

* **net watcher** → 6150

* **network** → 1670

6079 **net[work]**
  d Netz[werk] *n*
  f réseau *m*
  r сеть *f*

6080 **network access**
  d Netzzugang *m*; Netz[werk]zugriff *m*
  f accès *m* au réseau
  r сетевой доступ *m*

6081 **net[work] adapter**
  d Netzadapter *m*
  f adaptateur *m* [de] réseau
  r сетевой адаптер *m*

6082 **net[work] administrator; supervisor**
  d Netzadministrator *m*
  f administrateur *m* [de] réseau
  r сетевой администратор *m*

* **network analogue** → 6120

6083 **net[work] analysis**
  d Netzwerkanalyse *f*
  f analyse *f* de réseau
  r анализ *m* сети; сетевой анализ

6084 **network analyzer**
  d Netzwerkanalysator *m*
  f analyseur *m* des réseaux
  r анализатор *m* сетей

6085 **net[work] architecture**
  d Netzarchitektur *f*; Netzgestaltung *f*
  f architecture *f* de réseau
  r архитектура *f* сети

6086 **network basic input/output system; NetBIOS**
  d grundlegendes Netz-Ein-/Ausgabesystem *n*; NetBIOS-Protokoll *n*
  f système *m* base d'entrée/sortie pour réseaux; protocole *m* NetBIOS
  r сетевая базовая система *f* ввода/вывода

* **network board** → 6114

6087 **net[work] camera; netcam; Internet camera; Web camera; Webcam; live camera; live cam**
  d Netzkamera *f*; Webkamera *f*
  f caméra *f* de réseau; caméra reliée à l'Internet; caméra *f* Web; Webcaméra *f*
  r сетевая камера *f*; Web-камера *f*

* **network card** → 6114

6088 **net[work] circuit**
  d Netzschaltbild *n*; Netzschaltung *f*
  f circuit *m* de réseau
  r сетевая схема *f*

6089 **network client**
  d Netzclient *n*
  f client *m* réseau
  r сетевой клиент *m*

* **network clock** → 6090

6090 **network clock [pulse]; network timing [pulse]**
  d Netztakt *m*; Netztakteinheit *f*
  f impulsion *f* d'horloge de réseau; horloge *f* de réseau
  r тактовый импульс *m* сети

6091 **network communication**
  d Netzwerkkommunikation *f*
  f communication *f* des réseaux
  r сетевая связь *f*

6092 **network computer**
  d Netzcomputer *m*
  f ordinateur *m* en réseau
  r сетевой компьютер *m*

6093 **net[work] configuration**
  d Netzkonfiguration *f*
  f configuration *f* de réseau
  r конфигурация *f* сети; структура *f* сети

6094 **network congestion**
  d Netzüberlastung *f*
  f surcharge *f* de réseau
  r перегруженность *f* сети

6095 **network database**
  d Netzdatenbasis *f*
  f base *f* de données de réseau
  r сетевая база *f* данных

6096 **network definition language**
  d Netzwerkdefinitionssprache *f*

f langage *m* de définition des réseaux
r язык *m* описания сетей

* **network delay** → 6148

6097 network design
d Netzwerkentwurf *m*
f conception *f* de réseau
r проект *m* сети

* **network diagram** → 6104

6098 network drive
d Netzantrieb *m*
f lecteur *m* réseau
r сетевой диск *m*; сетевой накопитель *m*; сетевой дисковод *m*

6099 network[ed] environment; network neighborhood
d Netz[werk]umgebung *f*
f environnement *m* de réseau; voisinage *m* réseau
r сетевая [операционная] среда *f*; сетевое окружение *n*; доступные узлы *mpl* сети

6100 network endpoint
d Verbindungsendpunkt *m*
f point *m* final de réseau
r оконечная точка *f* сети

* **network environment** → 6099

6101 network etiquette; netiquette
(guidelines to good manners on the Internet)
d Netikette *f*
f netiquette *f*
r сетевой этикет *m*; сетикет *m*

6102 network failure; network fault
d Netzstörung *f*; Netzfehler *m*
f défaut *m* de réseau
r сбой *m* в сети; повреждение *n* в сети

* **network fault** → 6102

6103 network file system; NFS
d Netzwerk-Dateisystem *n*
f système *m* de partage de fichiers
r сетевая система *f* файлов

6104 network graph; network diagram
d Netzwerkdiagramm *n*
f diagramme *m* de réseau; graphique *m* de réseau
r сетевой график *m*; сетевая модель *f*

6105 network identification
d Netzkennung *f*
f identification *f* de réseau

r обозначение *n* сети

6106 network identity
d Netzidentität *f*
f identité *f* de réseau
r идентичность *f* сети

6107 network independence
d Netzunabhängigkeit *f*
f indépendance *f* de réseau
r независимость *f* сети

6108 network-independent interface
d netzunabhängige Schnittstelle *f*
f interface *f* indépendante de réseau
r универсальный сетевой интерфейс *m*

6109 network information center; NIC
(an electronic site where users can hunt down information about specific capabilities of a network)
d Netzwerkinformationszentrum *n*
f centre *m* d'information sur le réseau
r информационный центр *m* сети

* **network information service** → 6455

6110 networking
d Vernetzung *f*
f mise *f* en réseau; réseautique *f*
r подключение *n* к сети; объединение *n* в сеть

* **networking server** → 6136

6111 network integration
d Netzintegration *f*
f intégration *f* de réseaux
r объединение *n* сетей

6112 network integrator
d Netzintegrator *m*
f intégrateur *m* de réseau
r сетевой интегратор *m*

6113 network interface
d Netzschnittstelle *f*
f interface *f* de réseau
r сетевой интерфейс *m*

6114 network interface card; NIC; net[work] board; network card
(the hardware that connects an individual computer to a network)
d Netzanschlusskarte *f*; Netz[werk]karte *f*
f carte *f* réseau
r плата *f* сетевого интерфейса; сетевая плата

6115 network interface technology
d Netzanschlusstechnik *f*

f technologie *f* d'interface de réseau
r технология *f* сетевого интерфейса

6116 network internal protocol
d netz[werk]internes Protokoll *n*
f protocole *m* de réseau interne
r внутренний протокол *m* управления сетью

* **network interworking** → 5069

6117 net[work] layer; network level
d Netz[werk]schicht *f*; Netzebene *f*;
Vermittlungsschicht *f*
f couche *f* réseau; niveau *m* de réseau
r сетевой слой *m*; сетевой уровень *m*

* **network level** → 6117

6118 network links
d Netzverbindungen *fpl*
f liaisons *fpl* de réseau
r сетевые связи *fpl*

**6119 network management; network
supervision; network monitoring**
d Netzführung *f*; Netzwerkverwaltung *f*;
Netzüberwachung *f*
f gestion *f* de réseau; management *m* de réseau;
monitorage *m* de réseau
r управление *n* сетью

6120 net[work] model; network analogue
d Netzwerknachbildung *f*
f modèle *m* de réseau; imitation *f* de réseau
r модель *f* сети

* **network monitoring** → 6119

* **network neighborhood** → 6099

* **network-network interface** → 5070

6121 network news transfer protocol; NNTP
(the protocol used to transfer Usenet pieces
on the Internet)
d NNTP-Protokoll *n*
f protocole *m* Internet d'accès aux serveurs de
news
r сетевой протокол *m* передачи новостей;
протокол NNTP

6122 network node; network point; node
(computer or other peripheral within a
network)
d Netz[werk]knoten *m*; Knoten *m*
f nœud *m* [de réseau]
r узел *m* [сети]

* **network node clock** → 6124

* **network node clock pulse** → 6124

**6123 network node configuration; node
configuration**
d Netzknotenkonfiguration *f*
f configuration *f* des nœuds de réseau
r конфигурация *f* узлов сети

**6124 network node frame clock; node frame
clock; network node timing; network node
clock [pulse]**
d Rahmentakt *m* des Netzknotens;
Netzknotentakt *m*
f horloge *f* des nœuds de réseau
r тактовый импульс *m* узлов сети

* **network node timing** → 6124

6125 net[work] operating system; NOS
d Netzwerk-Betriebssystem *n*
f système *m* opérationnel de réseau; système
d'exploitation de réseau
r сетевая операционная система *f*

6126 net[work] operation
d Netzoperation *f*
f opération *f* de réseau
r сетевая операция *f*

6127 net[work] optimization
d Netzoptimierung *f*
f optimisation *f* de réseau
r оптимизация *f* сети

**6128 network parameters; network utility;
network settings**
d Netzmerkmal *n*
f paramètres *mpl* de réseau
r параметры *mpl* сети

6129 network planning
d Netzplanung *f*
f planification *f* de réseau
r сетевое планирование *n*

* **network point** → 6122

6130 network processor
d Netzwerkprocessor *m*
f processeur *m* de réseau
r сетевой процессор *m*

6131 network protocol
d Netz[vermittlungs]protokoll *n*;
Netzwerkprotokoll *n*
f protocole *m* de réseau
r сетевой протокол *m*

6132 network protocol layer
d Netzprotokollschicht *f*

f couche *f* de protocole de réseau
r уровень *f* сетевого протокола

6133 network relay; relay
d Netzwerkbinder *m*
f connecteur *m* de réseaux
r активный узел *m* сети

6134 net[work] security
d Netzsicherung *f*; Netzwerksicherheit *f*
f sécurité *f* de réseau
r защита *f* сети

6135 network segment; hop
d Teilstrecke *f*; Etappe *f*
f segment *m* de réseau
r сетевой сегмент *m*; интервал *m* связи;
транзитный участок *m* [линии связи]

6136 net[work] server; networking server;
server
d Netz[werk]-Zubringer *m*;
Netz[werk]-Server *m*; Server *m*; Zubringer *m*
f serveur *m* [de réseau]
r [сетевой] сервер *m*

6137 network service; online data service
d Netzdienst *m*
f service *m* de réseau
r сетевая услуга *f*; сетевая служба *f*

    * **network settings → 6128**

6138 net[work] software; netware
d Netzsoftware *f*
f logiciel *m* de réseau
r сетевое программное обеспечение *n*

6139 network stability
d Netzstabilität *f*
f stabilité *f* de réseau
r устойчивость *f* сети

    * **network supervision → 6119**

    * **network surfer → 2461**

6140 network synchronization; network timing
d Netzsynchronisation *f*
f synchronisation *f* des réseaux
r синхронизация *f* сети

6141 net[work] synthesis
d Netzwerksynthese *f*
f synthèse *f* des réseaux
r синтез *m* сетей

6142 network technique
d Netzwerktechnik *f*;
Netzentwicklungstechnik *f*

f technique *f* des réseaux
r техника *f* [создания] сетей

    * **network terminal → 9262**

6143 net[work] termination unit; network
terminator; NT[U]
d Netzabschlussgerät *n*;
Nachrichtenfernschaltgerät *n*; NGF
f terminateur *m* de réseau
r терминатор *m* сети; сетевой терминатор

    * **network terminator → 6143**

6144 network theory
d Netzwerktheorie *f*
f théorie *f* des réseaux
r теория *f* сетей

6145 network throughput
d Netzdurchsatz *m*
f débit *m* de réseau
r пропускная способность *f* сети

6146 network time protocol; NTP
(a protocol used to synchronize time between
computers on the Internet)
d Netzsynchronisationsprotokoll *n*
f protocole *m* de synchronisation des réseaux
r сетевой протокол *m* времени; сетевой
протокол синхронизации; протокол NTP

    * **network timing → 6090, 6140**

    * **network timing pulse → 6090**

    * **network-to-network interface → 5070**

6147 network topology
d Netz[werk]topologie *f*
f topologie *f* de réseau
r топология *f* сети

6148 network [transfer] delay
d Netzverzögerung *f*; Netztransportzeit *f*;
Netztransferverzug *m*
f retard *m* [de transfert] dans un réseau
r сетевая задержка *f*; задержка переноса в
сети

6149 network user identification; NUI
d Netzbenutzerkennung *f*
f identification *f* d'utilisateur dans un réseau
r идентификация *n* пользователя в сети

    * **network utility → 6128**

6150 net[work] watcher
d Netzüberwacher *m*

f surveilleur *m* de réseau
r наблюдатель *m* сети

    * **neural net → 6151**

6151 neural net[work]; neuronic net[work]
d neuronales Netz *n*
f réseau *m* neurone; réseau neuronal
r нейронная сеть *f*

6152 neurocomputer
d Neurocomputer *m*
f neuro-ordinateur *m*; ordinateur *m* à neurones formels
r нейрокомпьютер *m*

    * **neuronic net → 6151**

    * **neuronic network → 6151**

    * **newbie → 6158**

    * **newcomer → 6158**

    * **new line character → 5382**

    * **newsgroup → 2996**

    * **news mailing → 6155**

6153 newspaper
d Zeitung *f*
f journal *m*
r газета *f*

6154 newspaper [page] transmission
d Zeitungs[seiten]übertragung *f*
f transmission *f* [de page] de journaux
r [постраничная] передача *f* газет

    * **newspaper transmission → 6154**

6155 news posting; news mailing
d Nachrichtenbuchung *f*; Nachrichtenpostsendung *f*
f article *m* de forum; contribution *f*
r рассылка *f* новостей

6156 newsreader
(a program)
d Nachrichtenleser *m*
f lecteur *m* de news
r программа *f* чтения новостей

6157 news server
d Nachrichtenserver *m*
f serveur *m* de news
r сервер *m* новостей

6158 new user; inexperienced user; novice;

newcomer; newbie
d [Internet-]Neuling *n*
f utilisateur *m* sans expérience
r начинающий пользователь *m*; неопытный пользователь; новичок *m*; чайник *m*

    * **NFS → 6103**

    * **N-group → 2996**

    * **nibble → 4361**

    * **NIC → 6109, 6114**

6159 nil
d Nichts *n*; Leere *f*
f vide *m*
r пустота *f*

6160 nil report
d Fehlanzeige *f*
f rapport *m* nul
r пустое сообщение *n*; ложная индикация *f*

    * **nil symbol → 4625**

6161 nine's complement; complement on nine
d Neunerkomplement *n*
f complément *m* à neuf
r дополнение *n* до девяти

6162 nine's complement number
d neunerkomplemente Zahl *f*
f nombre *m* complément à neuf
r число *n* в обратном десятичном коде

6163 n-input gate
d Gatter *n* mit n Eingängen
f porte *f* à n entrées
r вентиль *m* с n входами

    * **NNTP → 6121**

    * **no-break → 5092**

    * **no-break power supply → 9659**

    * **no-current period → 6870**

6164 nodal point
d Knotenpunkt *m*
f point *m* nodal
r узловая точка *f*

    * **node → 6122**

6165 node; knot; vertex
d Knoten *m*; Ecke *f*
f nœud *m*
r узел *m*; вершина *f*

6166 node address
    d Knotenadresse *f*
    f adresse *f* de nœud
    r адрес *m* узла

6167 node addressing
    d Knotenadressierung *f*
    f adressage *m* de nœud
    r адресование *n* узла

6168 node computer
    d Knotenrechner *m*
    f ordinateur *m* de nœud
    r узловой компьютер *m*

    * node configuration → 6123

    * node edit → 6169

6169 node edit[ing]
    d Knotenbearbeitung *f*
    f édition *f* de nœuds
    r редактирование *n* узлов

    * node frame clock → 6124

6170 node of a graph; vertex of a graph
    d Knoten[punkt] *m* eines Graphs
    f sommet *m* d'un graphe; nœud *m* d'un graphe
    r вершина *f* графа

6171 node ordering
    d Knotenanordnung *f*
    f ordre *m* des nœuds
    r расположение *n* узлов

6172 node processor
    d Knotenprozessor *m*
    f processeur *m* de nœud
    r процессор *m* узла; узловой процессор

6173 node topology
    d Knoten-Topologie *f*
    f topologie *f* des nœuds
    r топология *f* узлов

6174 noise *v*
    d rauschen; stören
    f bruiter
    r шуметь

6175 noise; garbage; perturbation
    d Rauschen *n*; Geräusch *n*; Störung *f*
    f bruit *m*; brouillage *m*; parasitage *m*; perturbation *f*
    r шум *m*; помеха *f*; возмущение *n*; искажение *n*

6176 noise-balancing circuit
    d Rauschunterdrückungsschaltung *f*
    f circuit *m* d'élimination des bruits
    r схема *f* для подавления шумов

6177 noise block
    d Störblock *m*
    f bloc *m* de bruit
    r шумовой блок *m*

6178 noise burst
    d Störungsbündel *n*
    f paquet *m* de bruit
    r шумовой пакет *m*

6179 noise channel; noisy channel
    d Rauschkanal *m*; verrauschter Kanal *m*; rauschbehafteter Kanal
    f canal *m* à bruit; canal avec bruits
    r шумящий канал *m*; канал с помехами

    * noise characteristics → 6193

6180 noise compensation
    d Rauschkompensation *f*
    f compensation *f* du bruit
    r компенсация *f* шума

6181 noise component
    d Rauschanteil *m*
    f composante *f* de bruit
    r шумовая составляющая *f*; компонента *f* шума

6182 noise estimation
    d Rauschbewertung *f*
    f évaluation *f* du bruit
    r оценка *f* искажения

6183 noise factor; noise figure
    d Rauschfaktor *m*; Rauschzahl *f*; Rauschmaß *n*; Ballastquote *f*
    f facteur *m* de bruit; coefficient *m* de bruit
    r фактор *m* шума; шум-фактор *m*; коэффициент *m* шума

    * noise figure → 6183

6184 noise filter
    d Rauschfilter *m*
    f filtre *m* de bruit
    r фильтр *m* шума

6185 noise-free; noiseless
    d rauschfrei; störungsfrei
    f sans bruit
    r безшумовой; без шума

6186 noise immunity; noise resistance; interference immunity
    d Rauschfestigkeit *f*; Rauschunempfindlichkeit *f*; Störsicherheit *f*

f immunité *f* au bruit; résistance *f* au
brouillage; immunité contre les parasites
r нечувствительность *f* к шуму;
помехоустойчивость *f*;
помехозащищённость *f*

6187 noise interference
d Rauscheinmischung *f*
f interférence *f* de bruit
r шумовое возмущение *n*; шумовое
вмешательство *n*

* **noise killer** → 6191

* **noiseless** → 6185

6188 noiseless channel
d rauschfreier Kanal *m*
f canal *m* sans bruits
r канал *m* без помех

6189 noise level
d Rauschpegel *m*; Störpegel *m*; Rauschniveau *n*
f niveau *m* de bruit
r уровень *m* шума

6190 noise-limited
d rauschbegrenzt
f limité par le bruit
r с ограничением шума

6191 noise limiter; noise killer
d Störbegrenzer *m*
f limiteur *m* de bruit
r ограничитель *m* шума

6192 noise margin
d Störabstand *m*; Störspannungsspanne *f*
f marge *f* de bruit
r запас *m* помехоустойчивости

6193 noise properties; noise characteristics
d Rauscheigenschaften *fpl*
f caractéristiques *fpl* du bruit
r свойства *npl* шума

6194 noise pulse; disturb pulse
d Störimpuls *m*
f impulsion *f* de bruit; impulsion perturbatrice
r шумовой импульс *m*; импульс помехи;
мешающий импульс

6195 noise pulse counter
d Störungszähler *m*
f compteur *m* d'impulsions de bruit
r счётчик *m* шумовых импульсов

6196 noise pulse generator
d Störsender *m*
f générateur *m* d'impulsions de bruit

r генератор *m* шумовых импульсов

6197 noise removal and filtering
d Entfernung *f* und Filtrierung *f* des Rauschens
f élimination *f* et filtrage *m* du bruit
r устранение *n* и фильтрирование *n*
искажения

* **noise resistance** → 6186

**6198 noise signal; parasitic signal; spurious
signal; drop-in [signal]; disturb signal;
interference signal**
d Störsignal *n*; Interferenzsignal *n*
f signal *m* de bruit; signal-bruit *m*; signal
parasite; signal perturbateur
r шумовой сигнал *m*; паразитный сигнал;
сигнал помехи; ложный сигнал

6199 noise source
d Rauschquelle *f*
f source *f* de bruit
r источник *m* шума

6200 noise spectrum
d Rauschspektrum *n*; Störspektrum *n*
f spectre *m* de bruit
r спектр *m* шума

6201 noise suppression
d Rauschunterdrückung *f*;
Geräuschunterdrückung *f*
f suppression *f* de bruit
r подавление *n* шума

6202 noise threshold
d Rauschgrenze *f*
f seuil *m* de bruit
r порог *m* шума

6203 noisy
d rauschend; mit Rauschen; verrauscht;
rauschbehaftet
f bruyant; avec bruits
r шумящий; с помехами; с высоким уровнем
шумов

* **noisy channel** → 6179

6204 noisy digit
d Störziffer *f*
f chiffre *m* de bruit
r шумовой разряд *m*

6205 noisy image
d rauschendes Bild *n*; verrauschtes Bild
f image *f* bruyante
r изображение *n* с высоким уровнем шумов

6206 noisy signal
d Rauschsignal *n*; verrauschtes Signal *n*

f signal *m* brouillé
r сигнал *m* с шумами

6207 nomenclature
   d Nomenklatur *f*; Namensregister *n*;
     Fachbezeichnung *f*
   f nomenclature *f*
   r номенклатура *f*

6208 nomenclature language software
   d Fachsprachensoftware *f*
   f logiciel *m* d'un langage de nomenclature
   r терминологическое программное
     обеспечение *n*

6209 nominal; rated
   d nominell; nominal; Nominal-; Soll-; Nenn-
   f nominal
   r номинальный; расчётный

6210 nominal bit rate
   d Nennbitrate *f*
   f vitesse *f* de bits nominale
   r номинальная скорость *f* [передачи] битов

   * **nominal load** → 7643

6211 nominal pulse length
   d Sollschrittlänge *f*
   f longueur *f* d'impulsion nominale
   r номинальная длина *f* импульса

   * **nominal rating** → 7644

6212 nominal value; rated value; rating
   d Nennwert *m*; Sollwert *m*
   f valeur *f* nominale
   r номинальное значение *n*

   * **nominal white** → 549

   * **nomogram** → 309

   * **nonaddressable memory** → 8489

6213 non-antagonistic game; zero-sum game
   d Nichtantagonistenspiel *n*; Nullsummenspiel *n*
   f jeu *m* non antagoniste; jeu de somme zéro
   r неантагонистическая игра *f*; игра с
     нулевой суммой

6214 nonarithmetic shift
   d nichtarithmetische Verschiebung *f*
   f décalage *m* non arithmétique
   r неарифметический сдвиг *m*

6215 non-binary code
   d nichtbinärer Code *m*
   f code *m* non binaire
   r недвоичный код *m*

6216 non-binary error correcting code
   d nichtbinärer Fehlerkorrekturcode *m*
   f code *m* de correction d'erreur non binaire
   r недвоичный код *m* с исправлением
     ошибок

6217 nonblocking
   d blockierungsfrei
   f non bloque; sans blocage
   r неблокированный

   * **non-cascade code** → 6218

6218 non-cascading code; non-cascade code
   d nichtkaskadierender Code *m*
   f code *m* non cascade; code de diffusion unique
   r некаскадный код *m*

   * **non-computable** → 4723

6219 nonconcurrency
   d Konkurrenzfehlen *n*
   f non-concurrence *f*
   r непараллельность *f*

6220 nonconjunction; NAND function;
     stroke-function; Sheffer['s] stroke
     [operation]
   d Nichtkonjunktion *f*; NAND-Funktion *f*;
     Schefferscher Strich *m*
   f non-conjonction *f*; fonction *f* ET NON;
     fonction de trait; trait *m* de Sheffer
   r отрицание *n* конъюнкции; функция *f*
     НЕ-И; штрих *m* Шеффера

6221 non-connected in Internet; offline
   d nicht verbunden; aus der Leitung
   f horli
   r выключенный

6222 noncontact recording
   d kontaktlose Aufzeichnung *f*
   f enregistrement *m* sans contact; écriture *f* sans
     contact
   r бесконтактная запись *f*

6223 non-contrast image; soft image
   d nichtkontrastes Bild *n*
   f image *f* sans contraste; image grisâtre
   r неконтрастное изображение *n*

6224 non-cooperative game; coalitionless game
   d nichtkooperatives Spiel *n*
   f jeu *m* sans alliances
   r некооперативная игра *f*; некоалиционная
     игра

6225 non-denumerability; uncountability;
     non-enumerability
   d Überabzählbarkeit *f*; Unabzählbarkeit *f*;
     Nichtabzahlbarkeit *f*

    f non-dénombrabilité *f*; innumérabilité *f*
    r несчётность *f*; неперечислимость *f*

6226 nondestructive reading; nondestructive readout; NDRO
    d nichtzerstörendes Lesen *n*; zerstörungsfreies Auslesen *n*
    f lecture *f* non destructive
    r считывание *n* без разрушения [информации]

    * **nondestructive readout** → 6226

    * **non-determination** → 4764

6227 nondeterministic algorithm
    d nichtdeterministischer Algorithmus *m*
    f algorithme *m* non déterminatif
    r недетерминированный алгоритм *m*

6228 non-digital information; non-numerical information
    d nichtdigitale Information *f*; nichtnumerische Information
    f information *f* non digitale; information non numérique
    r нецифровая информация *f*; нечисловая информация

    * **non-directed graph** → 6252

6229 nondisjunction; NOR function; Peirce function
    d negierte Disjunktion *f*; NOR-Funktion *f*; Peirce-Funktion *f*; Antialternative *f*
    f non-disjonction *f*; fonction *f* ON; fonction de Peirce
    r отрицание *n* дизъюнкции; функция *f* НЕ-ИЛИ; функция Пирса; стрелка *f* Пирса

6230 non-emissive display
    d Display *n* ohne Emission
    f afficheur *m* non émissif
    r дисплей *m* без эмиссии

    * **non-enumerability** → 6225

6231 non-equilibrium
    d Ungleichgewicht *n*; Nichtgleichgewicht *n*
    f déséquilibre *m*
    r неравновесие *n*

6232 non-equivalence
    d Nichtäquivalenz *f*
    f non-équivalence *f*
    r неэквивалентность *f*; неравнозначность *f*

    * **non-equivalence gate** → 3569

6233 nonerasable memory

    d nichtlöschbarer Speicher *m*
    f mémoire *f* inaltérable
    r нестираемая память *f*; постоянная память

6234 nonexpanded memory
    d nichterweiterter Speicher *m*
    f mémoire *f* non paginée
    r нерасширяемая память *f*

    * **non-feeding character** → 6272

6235 nonflickering
    d flimmerfrei
    f sans scintillement
    r немерцающий

    * **nonflickering screen** → 3899

6236 nonformatted; unformatted
    d nichtformatiert; unformatiert; formatfrei
    f non formaté
    r неформатированный; свободного формата

6237 nonformatted data; unformatted data
    d nichtformatierte Daten *pl*; unformatierte Daten
    f données *fpl* non formatées
    r неформатированные данные *pl*

6238 nonformatted record; unformatted record
    d nichtformatierter Satz *m*; formatfreier Satz
    f enregistrement *m* non formaté
    r неформатированная запись *f*; запись свободного формата

6239 nonglare screen
    d blendfreier Bildschirm *m*
    f écran *m* sans taches de lumière
    r безбликовый экран *m*

6240 non-hierarchical network
    d nichthierarchisches Netz *n*
    f réseau *m* non-hiérarchique
    r неиерархическая сеть *f*

    * **nonhomogeneous** → 4443

    * **nonhomogeneous system** → 4842

6241 non-iconic model
    d nichtbildhaftes Modell *n*
    f modèle *m* non imagé
    r неиконическая модель *f*

6242 nonimpact printer; nonmechanical printer
    d anschlagfreier Drucker *m*; nichtmechanischer Drucker
    f imprimante *f* non impacte; imprimante non mécanique
    r безударное печатающее устройство *n*; немеханическое печатающее устройство

6243 non-interlaced mode
      (of a monitor)
      d unverschachtelte Betriebsweise *f*
      f mode *m* non entrelacé
      r режим *m* без чередования строк; режим с
      прогрессивной развёрткой

6244 noninterruption discipline; nonpreemptive
      discipline
      d Bedienungsdisziplin *f*
      f discipline *f* sans interruption
      r дисциплина *f* без прерывания
      обслуживания

6245 non-Latin alphabet
      d nichtlateinisches Alphabet *n*
      f alphabet *m* non latin
      r нелатинский алфавит *m*

6246 nonlinear animation
      d nichtlineare Animation *f*
      f animation *f* non linéaire
      r нелинейная анимация *f*

6247 nonlinear interaction
      d nichtlineare Wechselwirkung *f*
      f interaction *f* non linéaire
      r нелинейное взаимодействие *n*

6248 nonlinear medium
      d nichtlineares Medium *n*
      f milieu *m* non linéaire
      r нелинейная среда *f*

6249 nonlinear quantizing; nonuniform
      quantizing
      d nichtlineare Quantisierung *f*;
      nichtgleichmäßige Quantisierung
      f quantification *f* non linéaire; quantification
      non uniforme
      r нелинейное квантование *n*; неравномерное
      квантование

6250 nonlinear Z buffer
      d nichtlineare Z-Buffer *m*
      f Z-buffer *m* non linéaire
      r нелинейный Z-буфер *m*

   * nonmechanical printer → 6242

6251 nonmemory reference instruction
      d nichtspeicherbezogener Befehl *m*;
      speicherbezugsfreier Befehl
      f instruction *f* non relative à la mémoire
      r инструкция *f* [, выполняемая] без
      обращения к памяти

   * non-numerical information → 6228

6252 non-oriented graph; non-directed graph;

undirected graph
      d ungerichteter Graph *m*
      f graphe *m* non orienté; graphe non dirigé
      r неориентированный граф *m*

6253 nonpacked format
      d ungepacktes Format *n*
      f format *m* non condensé; format dilaté
      r неупакованный формат *m*

   * non-parity → 4688

   * nonpreemptive discipline → 6244

6254 non-printing characters
      d nichtdruckbare Zeichen *npl*
      f caractères *mpl* non imprimables
      r непечатаемые символы *mpl*

6255 nonprint key
      d nichtschreibende Taste *f*
      f touche *f* de non-impression
      r непечатаемая клавиша *f*

6256 nonpriority interrupt
      d nichtvorrangige Unterbrechung *f*
      f interruption *f* non prioritaire
      r неприоритетное прерывание *n*

6257 nonprocedural language; declarative
      language
      d nichtprozedurale Sprache *f*
      f langage *m* non procédural; langage déclaratif
      r непроцедурный язык *m*; декларативный
      язык

6258 nonredundancy
      d Nichtredundanz *f*
      f non-redondance *f*
      r безызбыточность *f*

6259 nonredundant; irredundant
      d nichtredundant
      f non redondant
      r безызбыточный; незарезервированный

6260 nonredundant code; unprotected code
      d nichtredundanter Code *m*
      f code *m* sans redondance; code non redondant
      r код *m* без избытка; незащищённый код

6261 non-registered access
      d nicht registrierter Zugriff *m*; nicht registrierter
      Zugang *m*
      f accès *m* non homologué
      r незарегистрированный доступ *m*

6262 nonrelocatable program
      d unverschiebliches Programm *n*

    f programme *m* irrelogeable
    r неперемещаемая программа *f*

6263 nonremovable disk
    d feststehende Platte *f*; unbewegliche Platte
    f disque *m* non amovible; disque inaltérable;
    disque fixe
    r бессменный диск *m*; фиксированный диск

6264 nonresident program
    d nichtresidentes Programm *n*
    f programme *m* non résident
    r нерезидентная программа *f*

6265 non-return-to-change recording
    d Ohne-Rückkehr-zu-Aufzeichung *f*
    f enregistrement *m* monopolaire
    r однополярная запись *f*

6266 non-return-to-zero; NRZ
    d ohne Rückkehr zu Null
    f sans retour à zéro; de non-retour à zéro
    r без возврата к нулю; без возвращения к
    нулю

6267 nonsegmented addressing
    d nichtsegmentierte Adressierung *f*
    f adressage *m* sans segmentation
    r несегментная адресация *f*

6268 nonselective printout
    d nichtselektiver Ausdruck *m*
    f impression *f* non sélective
    r сплошная распечатка *f*

6269 nonseparable graph; inseparable graph
    d artikulationsfreier Graph *m*; inseparabler
    Graph
    f graphe *m* inarticulé; graphe inséparable;
    graphe non divisible
    r граф *m* без сочленений; несепарабельный
    граф; неразложимый граф

**6270 non-shared subchannel; unshared
    subchannel**
    d nicht gemeinsambenutzer Unterkanal *m*
    f sous-canal *m* non partagé
    r неразделяемый подканал *m*; монопольный
    подканал

    * **non sharp → 4149**

6271 nonsignificant digit; nonsignificant zero
    d nichtsignifikante Stelle *f*; nichtsignifikante
    Null *f*
    f digit *m* non significatif; zéro *m* non
    significatif
    r незначащий разряд *m*; незначащий нуль *m*

    * **nonsignificant zero → 6271**

**6272 non-spacing character; non-feeding
    character**
    d Zeichen *n* ohne Vorschub
    f caractère *m* non espace
    r неинтервальный знак *m*

6273 non-square pixel
    d nichtquadratisches Pixel *n*
    f pixel *m* non carré
    r неквадратный пиксел *m*

6274 non-square pixel geometry
    d Geometrie *f* der nichtquadratischen Pixel
    f géométrie *f* de pixels non carrés
    r геометрия *f* неквадратных пикселов

6275 nonstandard information
    d nichtstandardisierte Information *f*
    f information *f* non standard
    r нестандартная информация *f*

6276 non-stationary input
    d nichtstationärer Eingang *m*
    f entrée *f* non stationnaire
    r нестационарный вход *m*

6277 nonstorage display
    d Bildschirm *m* ohne Speicherung
    f écran *m* sans mémoire
    r дисплей *m* без [блока] памяти

6278 non-transparent texture
    d nichttransparente Textur *f*
    f texture *f* non transparente
    r непрозрачная текстура *f*

6279 nonuniform network
    d ungleichartiges Netz *n*
    f réseau *m* non uniforme
    r неоднородная сеть *f*

    * **nonuniform quantizing → 6249**

6280 non-vectored interrupt
    d nichtvektorisierte Unterbrechung *f*
    f interruption *f* non vectorisée
    r невекторное прерывание *n*; прерывание
    без запоминания вектора прерывания

6281 non-voice communication
    d nichtsprachliche Kommunikation *f*
    f communication *f* non vocale
    r неречевая связь *f*

6282 non-voice information
    d Nonvoice-Information *f*
    f information *f* non vocale
    r неречевая информация *f*

    * **non-volatile memory → 3426**

6283 **no-op[eration] instruction; do-nothing instruction; null instruction; pass instruction; dummy instruction**
  d Befehl *m* "keine Operation"; Leerbefehl *m*; Scheinbefehl *m*
  f instruction *f* nulle; instruction vide; instruction fictive; instruction factice
  r холостая инструкция *f*; фиктивная инструкция; пустая инструкция

  * **no-op instruction → 6283**

  * **NOR function → 6229**

  * **NOR gate → 6304**

  * **norm** *v* → **6287**

6284 **normal**
  d normal; Normal-
  f normal
  r нормальный

6285 **normal algorithm**
  d Normalalgorithmus *m*
  f algorithme *m* normal
  r нормальный алгоритм *m*

6286 **normalization; normalizing; third normal form**
  d Norm[alis]ierung *f*
  f normalisation *f*; homologation *f*
  r нормализование *n*; нормализация *f*

6287 **normalize** *v*; **norm** *v*
  d normalisieren; normieren
  f normaliser; normer
  r нормализовать; нормировать

6288 **normalized**
  d normalisiert
  f normalisé
  r нормализованный

6289 **normalized data**
  d normalisierte Daten *pl*
  f données *fpl* normalisées
  r нормализованные данные *pl*

6290 **normalized form**
  d normalisierte Form *f*
  f forme *f* normalisée
  r нормализованная форма *f*

  * **normalizing → 6286**

  * **normal-vector interpolation shading → 6937**

6291 **normative logic**
  d normative Logik *f*
  f logique *f* normative
  r нормативная логика *f*

  * **NOS → 6125**

6292 **no-signal**
  d Signallosigkeit *f*; signalloser Zustand *m*
  f non-signal *m*; absence *f* de signal
  r отсутствие *n* сигнала

6293 **NOT-AND gate; NAND gate**
  d UND-NICHT-Gatter *n*; NAND-Gatter *n*
  f porte *f* ET-NON
  r схема *f* НЕ-И

  * **notation → 6325**

6294 **notation; designation**
  d Bezeichnung *f*; Schreibweise *f*; Notation *f*
  f notation *f*; signification *f*
  r обозначение *n*; означение *n*

  * **notation of a number → 6325**

6295 **not-busy interrupt**
  d Freigabeunterbrechung *f*
  f interruption *f* de non occupation; interruption de libération d'un accès
  r прерывание *n* по освобождению

6296 **not-carry**
  d negierter Übertrag *m*
  f non-report *m*
  r отрицание *n* переноса

  * **notch** *v* → **2753**

6297 **NOT circuit; NOT gate; inverter; invertor; negator; negation element**
  d Neinschaltung *f*; NICHT-Schaltung *f*; NICHT-Gatter *n*; NICHT-Tor *m*; Inverter *m*; Negationsschaltung *f*; Umkehrschaltung *f*; Negator *m*
  f circuit *m* NON; porte *f* NON; circuit de négation; inverseur *m*; négateur *m*
  r схема *f* НЕ; схема инверсии; инвертор *m*; элемент *m* НЕ

6298 **note; remark**
  d Bemerkung *f*
  f note *f*; remarque *f*
  r примечание *n*

  * **notebook → 6299**

6299 **notebook [computer]**
  d Notebook *n*
  f ordinateur *m* bloc-notes; ordinateur notebook; notebook *m*
  r компьютер-блокнот *m*; блокнотный компьютер; ноутбук *m*

* notepad → 6300, 6301

6300 notepad [computer]; clipboard computer
d Notizblatt *n*
f ardoise *f* électronique
r записная книжка *f*; [планшет-]блокнот *m*

6301 notepad [memory]
d Zusatzspeicher *m*
f mémoire *f* notepad
r память *f* для сохранения содержимого
регистров

* NOT gate → 6297

* notification → 427

6302 notion
d Begriff *m*
f notion *f*
r понятие *n*

6303 NOT operation
d NICHT-Operation *f*
f opération *f* NON
r операция *f* HE

6304 NOT-OR gate; NOR gate; zero-match gate
d NOR-Gatter *n*; NICHT-ODER-Gatter *n*
f porte *f* OU-NON; porte ON
r схема *f* HE-ИЛИ

6305 not-sum
d Summennegation *f*
f non-somme *f*; inversion *f* de somme
r инверсия *f* суммы

* novice → 6158

* no-wait memory → 6306

6306 no-wait [state] memory
d Speicher *m* ohne Wartezeit
f mémoire *f* sans état d'attente
r память *f* с нулевым временем ожидания

* NRZ → 6266

6307 NRZ coding
d Codierung *f* ohne Rückkehr zu Null;
NRZ-Codierung *f*
f codage *m* sans retour à zéro; codage NRZ
r кодирование *n* без возврата к нулю

* NT → 6143

* NTP → 6146

* NTU → 6143

* nucleus → 5198

* NUI → 6149

* nuke *v* → 1709

* null → 6310, 10087

* null character → 4625

* null cycle → 4628

* null data → 6310

6308 null device
d Pseudogerät *n*
f dispositif *m* nul
r фиктивное устройство *n*

6309 null hypothesis
d Nullhypothese *f*
f hypothèse *f* nulle
r нуль-гипотеза *f*; нулевая гипотеза *f*

6310 null [information]; null data
d Leerinformation *f*; Nullinformation *f*;
Nulldaten *pl*
f information *f* vide; information manquante;
valeur *f* non définie
r отсутствие *n* информации; отстутствие
данных; неопределённое значение *n*

* null instruction → 6283

6311 nullmodem
d Nullmodem *n*
f câble *m* liant directement deux ordinateurs;
éliminateur *m* de modem
r нуль-модем *m*; безмодемная связь *f*

6312 null object; zero object
d Nullobjekt *n*
f objet *m* nul
r нулевой объект *m*

6313 null value
d Nullwert *m*
f valeur *f* zéro
r нулевое значение *n*

6314 number
d Nummer *f*
f numéro *m*
r номер *m*

6315 number
d Zahl *f*; Anzahl *f*
f nombre *m*
r число *n*

6316 **number cruncher; cruncher**
   d Arithmetikschaltkreis m; "Zahlenknacker" m
   f circuit m arithmétique; "casseur m de
      nombres"
   r сверхбыстродействующий вычислитель m

6317 **numbered information frame**
   d numerierter Informationsrahmen m;
      numerierter Informationsblock m
   f trame f d'information numérotée
   r нумерованный информационный блок m

6318 **number generator**
   d Zahlengenerator m
   f générateur m de nombres
   r генератор m чисел

6319 **numbering; numeration**
   d Numerierung f
   f numér[ot]ation f; numérotage m
   r нумерация f; нумерование n

6320 **number of copies**
   d Kopienzahl f; Zahl f der Kopien
   f nombre f de copies
   r число n копий

6321 **number of partitions**
   d Partitionszahl f; Zahl f der Zerlegungen
   f nombre m de partitions
   r число n разбиений

6322 **number of repetitions**
   d Wiederholungszahl f; Zahl f der
      Wiederholungen
   f nombre m de répétitions
   r число n повторений

6323 **number of rows; row number**
      (of a rectangular array or of a table)
   d Zeilenzahl f; Zeilenanzahl f; Zahl f der Zeilen
   f nombre m de lignes; nombre de rangées
   r число n строк

6324 **number register**
   d Zahlenregister n
   f registre m de nombre
   r регистр m числа

6325 **number representation; notation [of a
      number]**
   d Zahlendarstellung f
   f représentation f des nombres; notation f des
      nombres
   r представление n чисел

6326 **number sign**
   d Vorzeichen n
   f signe m de nombre
   r знак m числа

 *   **number symbol** → 6329

6327 **number system; numeral system**
   d Zahlensystem n
   f système m de nombres
   r числовая система f; система счисления

6328 **numeral** adj
   d numeral
   f numéral
   r числовой

6329 **numeral; number symbol**
   d Numerale n; Zahlsymbol n
   f numéral m; symbole m numérique
   r нумерал m; числительное [имя] n;
      числовой символ m

 *   **numeral system** → 6327

 *   **numeration** → 6319

 *   **numeric** → 6330

6330 **numeric[al]; digital**
   d numerisch; digital
   f numérique; digital
   r численный; цифровой

6331 **numerical analysis**
   d numerische Analyse f
   f analyse f numérique
   r численный анализ m

6332 **numeric[al] chain data**
   d numerische Kettendaten pl
   f données fpl d'enchaînement numériques
   r данные pl типа цифровых строк; числовые
      строковые данные

 *   **numerical code** → 2880

6333 **numeric[al] control**
   d numerische Steuerung f
   f commande f numérique
   r числовое [программное] управление n

 *   **numerical data** → 2889

6334 **numeric[al] database**
   d numerische Datenbasis f
   f base f de données numérique
   r цифровая база f данных

 *   **numerical display** → 2892

 *   **numerical image** → 2900

 *   **numerical keyboard** → 6344

6335 **numerical operator**
d Zahlenoperator *m*
f opérateur *m* numérique
r числовой оператор *m*

* **numerical pulse** → **2919**

* **numerical signal** → **2920**

6336 **numerical value**
d Zahlenwert *m*
f valeur *f* numérique
r числовое значение *n*; численное значение

6337 **numeric attribute**
d Zahlenattribut *n*
f attribut *m* numérique
r числовой атрибут *m*

6338 **numeric box**
d numerischer Kasten *m*
f boîte *f* numérique
r числовой ящик *m*

6339 **numeric calculation**
d numerische Berechnung *f*
f calcul *m* numérique
r численный расчёт *m*; численное
вычисление *n*

* **numeric chain data** → **6332**

6340 **numeric characteristic**
d Kennziffer *f*; Kennummer *f*
f caractéristique *f* numérique
r числовая характеристика *f*

* **numeric control** → **6333**

* **numeric database** → **6334**

* **numeric display** → **2892**

6341 **numeric expression**
d numerischer Ausdruck *m*
f expression *f* numérique
r цифровое выражение *n*

6342 **numeric format; digital format**
d numerisches Format *n*
f format *m* numérique
r цифровой формат *m*

6343 **numeric function**
d numerische Funktion *f*
f fonction *f* numérique
r цифровая функция *f*

* **numeric image** → **2900**

* **numeric input** → **2905**

6344 **numeric keypad; numerical keyboard**
d numerische Tastatur *f*
f pavé *m* numérique; clavier *m* numérique
r цифровая клавиатура *f*

* **numeric output** → **2913**

* **numeric pulse** → **2919**

* **nybble** → **4361**

O

*   OBB → 6585

6345 obelisk
  d Obelisk *m*
  f obélisque *m*
  r крестик *m*; кинжал *m*; обелиск *m*

6346 object
  d Objekt *n*
  f objet *m*
  r объект *m*

6347 object class
  d Objektklasse *f*; Klasse *f* des Objekts
  f classe *f* d'objet
  r класс *m* объекта

*   object code → 6358

6348 object instruction
  d Objektbefehl *m*; übersetzter Befehl *m*
  f instruction *f* d'objet
  r инструкция *f* на выходном языке

6349 object language; target language
  d Objektsprache *f*; Zielsprache *f*
  f langage *m* d'objet; langage de destination
  r объектный язык *m*; выходной язык

6350 object linking and embedding; OLE
  (a capability that gives all Windows
  applications a standard way of incorporating
  objects)
  d Einbetten *n* und Verknüpfen *n* von Objekten
  f liaison *f* et imbrication *f* d'objets
  r связывание *n* и встраивание *n* объектов;
  связывание и внедрение *n* объектов

6351 object-oriented database; OODB
  d objektorientierte Datenbasis *f*
  f base *f* de données orientée objets
  r объектно-ориентированная база *f* данных

6352 object-oriented graphical language
  d objektorientierte grafische Sprache *f*
  f langage *m* graphique orienté objets; langage
  graphique à objets
  r объектно-ориентированный графический
  язык *m*

6353 object-oriented graphics
  d objektorientierte Grafik *f*
  f graphique *m* orienté objets
  r объектно-ориентированная графика *f*

6354 object-oriented language
  d objektorientierte Sprache *f*
  f langage *m* orienté objets; langage à objets
  r объектно-ориентированный язык *m*

6355 object-oriented platform
  d objektorientierte Plattform *f*
  f plate-forme *f* orientée objets
  r объектно-ориентированная платформа *f*

6356 object[-oriented] programming; OOP
  d objektorientierte Programmierung *f*;
  Objektprogrammierung *f*
  f programmation *f* par objets
  r объектно-ориентированное
  программирование *n*; объектовое
  программирование

6357 object-oriented rendering system
  d objektorientiertes Rendering-System *n*
  f système *m* rendu orienté objets
  r объектно-ориентированная система *f*
  тонирования

*   object phase → 6359

**6358 object program; object code; target
  program; target code**
  d übersetztes Programm *n*; Objektprogramm *n*;
  Zielprogramm *n*; Objektcode *m*
  f programme *m* [en langage] d'objet;
  programme de destination; code *m* d'objet
  r объектная программа *f*; целевая
  программа; объектный код *m*

*   object programming → 6356

6359 object time; object phase
  d Objektzeit *f*; Objektphase *f*
  f temps *m* d'objet; phase *f* d'objet
  r время *n* объектной программы; фаза *f*
  объектной программы

6360 oblique; inclined; slanted; sloping; tilting
  d schief; geneigt; schräg; kippbar
  f oblique; incliné
  r наклонный; косой

6361 oblique font; slanted font
  d schräge Schrift *f*
  f police *f* oblique
  r наклонный шрифт *m*

*   obliquing text font → 5149

*   observer → 5536

* **occupancy** → 6365

6362 occupancy probability
d Besetzungswahrscheinlichkeit *f*
f probabilité *f* d'occupation
r вероятность *f* размещения

6363 occupancy problem
d Besetzungsproblem *n*; Belegungsproblem *n*
f problème *m* d'occupation
r задача *f* о размещении

6364 occupancy rate
d Besetzungsgrad *m*
f cote *f* d'occupation
r степень *f* занятости

6365 occupation; occupancy; seizure; seizing
d Besetzung *f*; Belegung *f*; Ausnutzung *f*; Nutzung *f*
f occupation *f*; encombrement *m*; engagement *m*; prise *f*
r занятие *n*; занятость *f*

* **OCIS** → 6387

* **OCR** → 6529

6366 OCR font
d OCR-Schrift *f*
f fonte *f* à lecture optique; police *f* OCR
r оптически распознаваемый шрифт *m*

6367 octal
d oktal
f octal
r восьмеричный

6368 octal arithmetic
d oktale Arithmetik *f*
f arithmétique *f* octale
r восьмеричная арифметика *f*

* **octal coder** → 6371

6369 octal decoder
d Oktaldecodierer *m*
f décodeur *m* octal
r восьмеричный дешифратор *m*

6370 octal digit
d oktale Ziffer *f*
f chiffre *m* octal
r цифра *f* в восьмеричной системы [счисления]

6371 octal [en]coder
d Oktalcodierer *m*
f codeur *m* octal

r восьмеричный шифратор *m*

6372 octal notation; octal representation
d Oktaldarstellung *f*
f notation *f* octale; représentation *f* octale
r восьмеричное представление *n*

6373 octal number
d Oktalzahl *f*
f nombre *m* octal
r восьмеричное число *n*

6374 octal [number] system
d Oktal[zahlen]system *n*
f système *m* [de numération] octal
r восьмеричная система *f* [счисления]

* **octal representation** → 6372

* **octal system** → 6374

* **ODBC** → 6479

6375 odd
d ungerade; ungeradzahlig
f impair
r нечётный

6376 odd-even
d ungerade-gerade
f impair-pair
r нечётно-чётный

6377 odd-even check; even-odd check
d Ungerade-Gerade-Prüfung *f*
f vérification *f* impair-pair
r контроль *m* [по] нечётности-чётности

6378 odd index
d ungerader Index *m*
f index *m* impair
r нечётный индекс *m*

* **oddness** → 4688

6379 odd number
d ungerade Zahl *f*
f nombre *m* impair
r нечётное число *n*

* **odd parity** → 4688

* **odd-parity check** → 4689

* **OEM** → 6589

6380 off; out of circuit *adj*
d aus; off
f hors; off
r выключенный

6381 off-chip
    d außerhalb des Schaltkreises
    f en-dehors du circuit; hors puce
    r внешний по отношению к [микро]схеме

6382 off condition; off state
    d Aus-Zustand *m*
    f état *m* au repos
    r выключенное состояние *n*

6383 offering signal
    d Aufschaltezeichen *n*
    f signal *m* d'intrusion
    r сигнал *m* включения; предупредительный
       сигнал

    * office automater → 6384

    * office automation → 6385

6384 office automation expert; office systems
       expert; office automater
    d Büroautomatisierungsexperte *m*
    f bureauticien *m*
    r эксперт *m* автоматизации учрежденческой
       деятельности

6385 office automati|zati|on
    d Büroautomatisierung *f*
    f automatisation *f* bureautique
    r автоматизация *f* учрежденческой
       деятельности

    * office code → 2846

6386 office communication
    d Bürokommunikation *f*
    f communication *f* bureautique;
       communication de bureau
    r учрежденческая коммуникация *f*;
       учрежденческая связь *f*

6387 office communication and information
       system; OCIS
    d Bürokommunikation- und
       Informationssystem *n*
    f système *m* bureautique de communication et
       d'information
    r учрежденческая коммуникационная и
       информационная система *f*

6388 office communication system
    d Bürokommunikationssystem *n*
    f système *m* de communication bureautique
    r учрежденческая система *f* связи

6389 office computer
    d Bürocomputer *m*; Bürorechner *m*
    f ordinateur *m* bureautique
    r учрежденческий компьютер *m*

6390 office information system
    d Büroinformationssystem *n*
    f système *m* d'information de bureau
    r учрежденческая информационная
       система *f*

6391 office network
    d Büronetzwerk *n*
    f réseau *m* de bureau
    r учрежденческая сеть *f*

    * office on the go → 7134

    * office systems expert → 6384

6392 office technique
    d Bürotechnik *f*
    f technique *f* de bureau; bureautique *f*
    r бюротехника *f*

    * offline → 6221

6393 offline; autonomous
    d abgetrennt; getrennt; autonom; Offline-
    f hors ligne; autonome; offline
    r автономный; независимый; офлайн

    * offline data acquisition → 6394

6394 offline data collection; offline data
       acquisition
    d Offline-Datenerfassung *f*
    f saisie *f* offline des données
    r автономный сбор *m* данных

    * offline input → 4782

6395 offline mode
    d getrennte Arbeitsweise *f*; ungekoppelter
       Betrieb *m*; Offline-Modus *m*
    f mode *m* autonome; mode hors ligne
    r автономный режим *m*

    * offline output → 4783

    * off-normal contact → 1168

6396 off position
    d Ausschaltstellung *f*; Ruhestellung *f*
    f position *f* d'arrêt; position de coupure;
       position de repos
    r выключенное положение *n*

    * off-screen memory → 4037

    * offset → 8507

6397 offset
    d Versatz *m*; Offset *n*

f offset *m*
r оффсет *m*

* **offset address** → 3011

6398 offset carrier
d versetzter Träger *m*
f porteuse *f* décalée
r смещённая несущая *f*

* **off state** → 6382

6399 off-the-shelf hardware
d konfektioniertes Hardware *n*
f matériel *m* confectionné; matériel commercialisé
r покупное аппаратное обеспечение *n*

6400 off time
d Ausschaltzeit *f*; Ruhezeit *f*
f temps *m* d'état d'arrêt
r время *n* пребывания в выключенном состоянии

* **OLE** → 6350

6401 OLE automation
d OLE-Automation *f*
f automation *f* OLE
r OLE-автоматизация *f*

6402 OLE object
d OLE-Objekt *n*
f objet *m* OLE
r OLE-объект *m*

6403 on; in-circuit *adj*
d Ein-; auf
f en marche
r включённый

6404 on-board
d auf der Steckeinheit
f [intégré] à la plaque
r размещённый на плате

* **on-board computer** → 1091

6405 on-board logic
d eingebaute Logik *f*; plattenintegrierte Logik
f logique *f* à bord; logique intégrée; logique incorporée
r встроенная логика *f* платы

6406 on-chip
d auf dem Chip; chipintern
f [intégré] à la puce
r внутрикристаллический; размещённый на кристалле

6407 on-chip memory
d schaltkreisintegrierter Speicher *m*
f mémoire *f* intégrée
r память *f*, интегрированная в кристалле

6408 on-chip redundancy
d chipinterne Redundanz *f*
f redondance *f* [interne] de circuit sur puce
r избыточность *f* схемы кристалла

6409 on condition; on state
d Ein-Zustand *m*; Einschaltzustand *m*
f état *m* [de mise] en marche
r включённое состояние *n*

* **on-demand processing** → 2741

* **on-demand video** → 9824

6410 one-address; single-address
d Ein-Adress-
f à adresse unique
r одноадресный

6411 one-address instruction; single-address instruction
d Ein-Adress-Befehl *m*; 1-Adress-Befehl *m*
f instruction *f* à une adresse; instruction à adresse unique
r одноадресная инструкция *f*

* **one-address message** → 8592

* **one-address point** → 8593

* **one-at-a-time mode** → 8431

6412 one-board; single-board; monoboard
d Einplatinen-; Einkarten-
f à carte unique
r одноплатый

6413 one-board computer; monoboard computer
d Einplatinenrechner *m*
f ordinateur *m* à carte unique
r одноплатый компьютер *m*

* **one-bus structure** → 8596

6414 one-byte
d mit einem Byte
f à un octet
r однобайтовый

6415 one-cell buffer
d Einzellenpuffer *m*
f tampon *m* à cellule unique
r одноклеточный буфер *m*

* **one-channel** → 8600

6416 one-chip; single-chip
d Einchip-; auf einem Chip integriert
f à puce unique; à une seule puce
r однокристаллический; однокристалльный; одночиповый

6417 one-chip codec
d Einchip-Codec *m*
f codec *m* à puce unique; codec à une seule puce
r однокристалльный кодек *m*

* **one-chip computer** → 2094

6418 one-chip rendering processor
d Einchip-Rendering-Prozessor *m*
f processeur *m* rendu à puce unique
r одночиповый процессор *m* тонирования

* **one-color** → 5884

6419 one-column bar chart
d Einzelspalte-Streifendiagramm *n*
f diagramme *m* à barre unique
r одноколонная столбиковая диаграмма *f*

6420 one-digit adder; single-digit adder
d einstelliges Addierwerk *n*
f add[itionn]eur *m* monodigit
r одноразрядный сумматор *m*

6421 one-dimensional array; linear array
d eindimensionales Feld *n*; lineares Feld
f tableau *m* à une dimension; tableau linéaire
r одноразмерный массив *m*; линейный массив

* **one-directional** → 9643

6422 one input
d Einereingang *m*; "1"-Eingang *m*
f entrée *f* d'un; entrée de "1"
r вход *m* единицы

6423 one-level code
d Direktcode *m*; Ein-Niveau-Code *m*
f code *m* à un niveau
r одноуровневый код *m*

6424 one-level store
d Ein-Niveau-Speicher *m*
f mémoire *f* à un niveau
r одноуровневая память *f*

6425 one-line assembler
d Zeilenassembler *m*
f assembleur *m* par ligne
r построчный ассемблер *m*

6426 one-line text box; text box; text-entry field
d einlineares Textfeld *n*
f zone *f* de texte [simple ligne]; champ *m* de texte monoligne; case *f* de saisie simple; boîte *f* de saisie monoligne
r однолинейное поле *n* текста

6427 one-pass compiler; single-pass compiler
d Einpassübersetzer *m*; Einschritt-Compiler *m*
f compilateur *m* à passage unique; compilateur à évolution unique
r однопроходной компилятор *m*

6428 one-sample method
d Einstichprobenverfahren *n*
f méthode *f* à un seul échantillon
r метод *m* одной выборки

6429 one's complement; complement on one
d Einserkomplement *n*; Komplement *n* zu 1
f complément *m* à un
r дополнение *n* до единицы; обратный двоичный код *m*

* **one-shot** → 5886

* **one-shot job** → 6430

* **one-shot multivibrator** → 5887

* **one-shot operation** → 6431

* **one-sided** → 8633

6430 one-step job; one-shot job
d nur einmal ausgeführter Job *m*; One-shot-Job *m*
f travail *m* à une fois
r разовое задание *n*

6431 one-step operation; single-step operation; one-shot operation; step-by-step operation
d Schrittbetrieb *m*; Einzelschrittbetrieb *m*; schrittweise Operation *f*
f opération *f* [pas] à pas
r работа *f* в пошаговом режиме

6432 one-to-many correspondence
d einmehrdeutige Korrespondenz *f*; einmehrdeutige Zuordnung *f*
f correspondance *f* multivoque
r многозначное соответствие *n*

6433 one-to-one
d eineindeutig; Eins-zu-Eins-
f un à un; biunivoque
r взаимно-однозначный

6434 one-to-one assembler
d Eins-zu-Eins-Assembler *m*

  f assembleur *m* un à un
  r инъективный ассемблер *m*

6435 one-to-one communication
  d Eins-zu-Eins-Kommunikation *f*
  f communication *f* un à un
  r взаимно-однозначная связь *f*; связь один к
    одному

**6436 one-to-one correspondence; univalent
    correspondence**
  d eineindeutige Zuordnung *f*; bijektive
    Zuordnung
  f correspondance *f* biunivoque; correspondance
    bijective
  r взаимно-однозначное соответствие *n*;
    биективное соответствие

6437 one-valued; single-valued
  d einwertig; eindeutig
  f univoque; monovalent; univalent
  r однозначный

  * **one-way** → **9643**

  * **one-way channel** → **8575**

6438 one-way classification
  d Einwegklassifikation *f*
  f classification *f* selon une entrée; classification
    selon un caractère
  r группировка *f* по одному признаку;
    классификация *f* по одному признаку

6439 one-way communication
  d einseitige Kommunikation *f*
  f communication *f* unilatérale; communication
    unidirectionnelle
  r односторонняя коммуникация *f*

6440 one-way interaction
  d einseitige Wechselwirkung *f*
  f interaction *f* unilatérale
  r одностороннее взаимодействие *n*

6441 one-way logical channel
  d gerichteter logischer Kanal *m*; einseitiger
    logischer Kanal
  f canal *m* logique unilatéral
  r односторонний логический канал *m*

6442 one-way mode
  d Einwegbetrieb *m*
  f mode *m* unidirectionnel
  r однонаправленный режим *m*

  * **online** → **2170, 2283**

6443 online
  d mitlaufend; [prozess]gekoppelt;

rechnerverbunden; Online-
  f en ligne; direct
  r неавтономный; управляемый; зависимый

6444 online adapter
  d Online-Adapter *m*
  f adaptateur *m* de communication
    interprocesseur
  r адаптер *m* межпроцессорной связи

6445 online backup
  d mitlaufende Reserve *f*; aktive Reserve
  f sauvegarde *f* en ligne
  r горячий резерв *m*

6446 online computing
  d mitlaufendes Rechnen *n*; Online-Rechnen *n*
  f calcul *m* en ligne
  r вычисление *n* в темпе поступления данных

6447 online data
  d Online-Daten *pl*
  f données *fpl* en ligne
  r оперативные данные *pl*

  * **online data acquisition** → **6448**

**6448 online data collection; online data
    acquisition**
  d Online-Datenerfassung *f*; prozessgekoppelte
    Datenerfassung *f*
  f acquisition *f* de données en ligne
  r неавтономный сбор *m* данных

  * **online data service** → **6137**

6449 online data transmission
  d Datendirektübertragung *f*
  f transmission *f* de données en ligne
  r непосредственная передача *f* данных

6450 online dialog
  d prozessgekoppelter Dialog *m*
  f dialogue *m* [en] direct
  r непосредственный диалог *m*

6451 online discussion
  d Online-Diskussion *f*
  f discussion *f* en ligne
  r непосредственная дискуссия *f*

6452 online documentation
  d Online-Dokumentation *f*
  f documentation *f* en ligne
  r интерактивная документация *f*

6453 online file
  d Online-Datei *f*
  f fichier *m* en ligne
  r оперативно-доступный файл *m*

6454 online help
 d Online-Hilfe f
 f aide f directe; aide en ligne
 r непосредственная помощь f;
  интерактивная помощь

6455 online information service; network
  information service
 d Online-Informationsdienst m;
  Netzwerkinformationsdienst m
 f service m d'information en ligne
 r сетевая информационная служба f; сетевая
  информационная услуга f

6456 online operation
 d Leitungsbetrieb m; Online-Betrieb m
 f exploitation f en ligne; travail m en ligne
 r неавтономная работа f; работа в режиме
  "онлайн"

 * online processing → 4871

6457 online service
 d abrufbereiter Dienst m
 f service m en ligne
 r интерактивная услуга f; непосредственная
  услуга

6458 online transaction processing
 d Online-Transaktionsverarbeitung f
 f traitement m de transactions en ligne
 r неавтономная обработка f транзакций;
  обработка регистрации событий в режиме
  "онлайн"

6459 on-off
 d auf-zu; ein-aus
 f par tout ou rien; marche-arrêt
 r включённый-выключенный;
  двухпозиционный

6460 on-off control
 d Zweipunktregelung f; Ein-Aus-Steuerung f
 f réglage m à deux positions; commande f
  marche-arrêt
 r двухпозиционное управление n

6461 on-off-switch
 d Ein-Aus-Schalter m
 f commutateur m marche-arrêt
 r двухпозиционный переключатель m

6462 on position
 d Einschaltstellung f; Arbeitsstellung f;
  Betriebsstellung f
 f position f [de mise] en marche; position de
  travail
 r включённое положение n; рабочее
  положение

6463 on-screen graphics
 d Bildschirmgrafik f
 f infographie f sur l'écran
 r экранная графика f

6464 on-screen log
 d bildschirmorientiertes Journal n
 f journal m sur l'écran
 r экранный журнал m

 * on-screen menu → 8249

6465 on-site data processing
 d Datenverarbeitung f am Ort
 f traitement m de données sur le site
 r обработка f данных на месте

6466 on-site test
 d Test m am Einsatzort
 f test m in situ; test sur lien
 r проверка f на месте [эксплуатации]

 * on state → 6409

6467 on-the-fly printer
 d Drucker m mit dynamischer Schreibung
 f imprimante f à la volée
 r печатающее устройство n с беспрерывной
  печатью; печатающее устройство с
  "летающей" головкой

6468 on time
 d Einschaltzeit f
 f temps m d'état en circuit
 r время f пребывания во включённом
  состоянии

 * OODB → 6351

 * OOP → 6356

 * op-amp → 6506

 * opcode → 6511

6469 open v
 d öffnen; eröffnen
 f ouvrir
 r открыть

6470 open architecture
 d offene Architektur f
 f architecture f ouverte
 r открытая архитектура f

6471 open-architecture network
 d offene Netzwerkarchitektur f
 f réseau m d'architecture ouverte
 r сеть f с открытой архитектурой

6472 **open channel**
d offener Kanal *m*
f canal *m* ouvert
r открытый канал *m*

6473 **open circuit**
d offener Stromkreis *m*; offener
Wirkungskreis *m*; offener Schaltkreis *m*
f circuit *m* ouvert; chaîne *f* ouverte
r разомкнутая цепь *f*; разомкнутый контур *m*

6474 **open-circuited**
d leerlaufend
f à marche vide
r разомкнутый; работающий вхолостую

6475 **open code**
d offener Code *m*
f code *m* ouvert
r открытый код *m*

6476 **open communication**
d offene Kommunikation *f*
f communication *f* ouverte
r открытая связь *f*

6477 **open communication network**
d offene Kommunikations[zug]verbindung *f*
f réseau *m* de communication ouverte
r сеть *f* открытой связи

6478 **open cycle; open loop**
d offener Zyklus *m*; offene Schleife *f*; geöffnete
Schleife
f cycle *m* ouvert; boucle *f* ouverte
r разомкнутый цикл *m*; открытый цикл

6479 **open database connectivity; ODBC**
(DLL file that Microsoft Query and Microsoft
Excel can use to connect to a particular
database)
d offene Datenbankschnittstelle *f*
f connexion *f* aux bases de données ouverte
r открытая связь *f* с базами данных;
интерфейс *m* ODBC

6480 **opening**
d Eröffnung *f*
f ouverture *f*
r открытие *n*

6481 **opening flag**
d Beginnflagge *f*
f flag *m* d'ouverture
r флаг *m* открытия

6482 **open LAN**
d offenes lokales Netz *n*; offenes LAN
f réseau *m* local ouvert
r открытая локальная сеть *f*

* **open loop** → 6478

6483 **open-loop control**
d rückführungslose Regelung *f*;
rückführungsfreie Steuerung *f*
f réglage *m* à la boucle ouverte; commande *f*
sans réaction
r управление *n* по разомкнутому контуру;
регулирование *n* без обратной связи

6484 **open network**
d offenes Netz *n*
f réseau *m* ouvert
r открытая сеть *f*

6485 **open statement**
d Eröffnungsanweisung *f*
f opérateur *m* d'ouverture
r оператор *m* открытия

6486 **open system**
d offenes System *n*
f système *m* ouvert
r открытая система *f*

6487 **open system architecture**
d offenes Systemarchitektur *f*
f architecture *f* du système ouverte
r открытая системная архитектура *f*

6488 **open systems interconnection; OSI**
(a conceptual model and set of protocols for
networks, promulgated by the ISO)
d Verknüpfung *f* offener Systeme
f interconnexion *f* entre systèmes ouverte
r открытое взаимодействие *n* систем

6489 **open telecommunication**
d offene Telekommunikation *f*
f télécommunication *f* ouverte
r открытая дистанционная связь *f*

6490 **operand**
d Operand *m*; Rechengröße *f*
f opérande *m*
r операнд *m*

6491 **operand vector**
d Operandenvektor *m*
f vecteur *m* opérande
r вектор-операнд *m*

6492 **operate** *v*
d betreiben; arbeiten; bedienen
f opérer; travailler; asservir
r оперировать; действовать; работать

6493 **operating; operation**
d Betrieb *m*; Betriebsführung *f*

f exploitation *f*; fonctionnement *m*
r эксплуатация *f*; работа *f*; оперирование *n*

6494 operating; operational *adj*
  d Betriebs-; Arbeits-
  f opérationnel
  r операционный

6495 operating characteristics; operational factor
  d Betriebskennlinie *f*; Arbeitskennlinie *f*
  f caractéristique *f* d'opération; facteur *m* opérationnel
  r эксплуатационная характеристика *f*; рабочая характеристика

  * **operating data** → **3428**

6496 operating delay
  d Ansprechverzögerung *f*
  f retard *m* opérationnel
  r операционная задержка *f*; задержка выполнения

6497 operating information system
  d Betriebsinformationssystem *n*
  f système *m* d'information d'exploitation
  r информационная система *f* обеспечения эксплуатации

6498 operating life
  d Betriebsdauer *f*
  f vie *f* en exploitation
  r эксплуатационный ресурс *m*; эксплуатационный срок *m*

  * **operating memory** → **5602**

6499 operating mode
  d Arbeitsmodus *m*; Betriebsart *f*
  f mode *m* d'exploitation; mode de travail
  r режим *m* эксплуатации; рабочий режим

6500 operating ratio
  d Nutzungsgrad *m*; effektiver Betriebsfaktor *m*
  f coefficient *m* d'efficacité
  r коэффициент *m* использования

6501 operating sequence
  d Bediensequenz *f*
  f séquence *f* opérationnelle
  r последовательность *f* оперирования

6502 operating speed
  d Arbeitsgeschwindigkeit *f*
  f vitesse *f* de fonctionnement
  r скорость *f* оперирования

6503 operating system; OS
  (of a computer)

d Operationssystem *n*; Betriebssystem *n*
f système *m* opérationnel; système *m* d'exploitation; sysdex *m*
r операционная система *f*; ОС; система эксплуатации

6504 operating time
  d Betriebszeit *f*
  f temps *m* d'opération
  r рабочее время *n* машины; оперативное время

  * **operation** → **6493**

6505 operation
  d Operation *f*
  f opération *f*
  r операция *f*

  * **operational** *adj* → **6494**

6506 operational amplifier; op-amp
  d Operationsverstärker *m*
  f amplificateur *m* opérationnel
  r операционный усилитель *m*

  * **operational factor** → **6495**

6507 operational reliability
  d Betriebssicherheit *f*
  f fiabilité *f* opérationnelle; fiabilité de l'exploitation
  r эксплуатационная надёжность *f*

6508 operational research; operations research
  d Operationsforschung *f*; Betriebsforschung *f*
  f recherche *f* opérationnelle; recherche d'opérations
  r исследование *n* операций

  * **operational sign** → **6509**

  * **operational software** → **9154**

6509 operation[al] symbol; operation[al] sign; operator
  d Operationssymbol *n*; Operationszeichen *n*; Operator *m*
  f symbole *m* d'opération; opérateur *m*
  r символ *m* операции; знак *m* операции; оператор *m*

6510 operational unit
  d Funktionsbaustein *m*
  f unité *f* opérationnelle; bloc *m* fonctionnel
  r операционный автомат *m*; функциональный блок *m*

6511 operation code; opcode
  d Operationscode *m*; Operationsschlüssel *m*; Opcode *m*

f code *m* d'opération
r код *m* операции

6512 operation inhibit signal
d Betriebssperrsignal *n*
f signal *m* d'inhibition de l'opération
r сигнал *m* запрета операции

* **operation limiter** → **6513**

6513 operation limiting signal; operation limiter
d Operationsabschlusssignal *n*
f signal *m* de limitation de l'opération
r сигнал *m* ограничения операции

6514 operation logic
d Operationslogik *f*; Operationsverknüpfung *f*
f logique *f* d'opération
r операционная логика *f*

6515 operation loop
d Operationsschleife *f*
f cycle *m* opératoire; cycle de travail
r рабочий цикл *m*

6516 operation mode register
d Operationsmodusregister *n*
f registre *m* de mode d'opération
r регистр *m* режима оперирования

6517 operation on a set; operation with a set
d Operation *f* auf einer Menge
f opération *f* sur un ensemble
r операция *f* над множеством

6518 operations decoder
d Operationsdecoder *m*
f décodeur *m* d'opérations
r дешифратор *m* операций

* **operation sign** → **6509**

* **operations research** → **6508**

* **operation symbol** → **6509**

6519 operation table
d Operationstabelle *f*
f table *f* d'opérations
r таблица *f* операций

* **operation with a set** → **6517**

* **operator** → **6509, 8863**

6520 operator
(a person)
d Operator *m*; Bediener *m*
f opérateur *m*
r оператор *m*

6521 operator equation
d Operatorengleichung *f*
f équation *f* opératorielle
r операторное уравнение *n*

* **operator error** → **4580**

6522 operator interrupt
d Unterbrechung *f* durch den Operateur;
Eingriff *m* durch den Operateur
f interruption *f* par [le pupitre de] l'opérateur
r прерывание *n* с пульта оператора

* **operator notation** → **7209**

6523 operator time
d Bedienzeit *f*
f temps *m* d'opérateur
r время *n* обслуживания оператором

6524 optical bus structure
d optische Busstruktur *f*
f structure *f* de bus optique
r структура *f* оптической шины

6525 optical bus system
d optisches Bussystem *n*
f système *m* de bus optique
r система *f* оптических шин

6526 optical cable link
d optische Kabelstrecke *f*
f liaison *f* par câble optique
r связь *f* оптическим кабелем

6527 optical channel
d optischer Kanal *m*
f canal *m* optique; voie *f* optique
r оптический канал *m*

6528 optical character reader
d optischer Klarschriftleser *m*
f lecteur *m* optique de caractères
r оптический считыватель *m* знаков

6529 optical character recognition; OCR
d optische Zeichenerkennung *f*;
Mustererkennung *f* von Schriften
f reconnaissance *f* optique de caractères
r оптическое распознавание *n* символов

6530 optical code
d optischer Code *m*
f code *m* optique
r оптический код *m*

* **optical coding** → **6541**

**6531 optical communication; lightwave
[tele]communication**
d optische Kommunikation *f*; optische

Telekommunikation *f*

f [télé]communication *f* optique;
[télé]communication par ondes lumineuses

r оптическая связь *f*; оптическая
[теле]коммуникация *f*

**6532 optical communication channel; optical
communication line**

d optischer Kommunikationskanal *m*; optischer
Nachrichtenkanal *m*

f canal *m* de communication optique; ligne *f* de
communication optique

r оптический канал *m* связи; оптическая
линия *f* связи

* **optical communication line** → 6532

6533 optical communication system

d optisches Nachrichtensystem *n*; optisches
Kommunikationssystem *n*

f système *m* de communication optique

r оптическая система *f* связи

6534 optical coupler; optocoupler; optron

d optischer Koppler *m*; Optokoppler *m*

f coupleur *m* optique; optocoupleur *m*;
optron *m*

r оптический соединитель *m*; оптрон *m*

6535 optical coupling

d optische Kopplung *f*

f couplage *m* optique

r оптическая стыковка *f*; оптическое
соединение *n*

6536 optical data bus

d optischer Datenbus *m*

f bus *m* de données optique

r оптическая шина *f* данных

6537 optical data converter

d optischer Datenkonverter *m*

f convertisseur *m* de données optique

r оптический преобразователь *m* данных

**6538 optical data processing; optical
information processing**

d optische Datenverarbeitung *f*; optische
Informationsverarbeitung *f*

f traitement *m* optique de données;
traitement *m* optique d'information

r оптическая обработка *f* данных;
оптическая обработка информации

6539 optical density

d Schwärzungsdichte *f*

f densité *f* optique

r плотность *f* почернения

* **optical disk** → 1964

**6540 optical document reader; videoscan
document reader**

d optischer Dokumentleser *m*; optischer
Belegleser *m*

f lecteur *m* optique de documents

r оптический считыватель *m* документов

6541 optical [en]coding

d optische Codierung *f*; optische
Verschlüsselung *f*

f codage *m* optique; codification *f* optique

r оптическое кодирование *n*

**6542 optical fiber; optical waveguide; OWG;
lightguide [fiber]; glass fiber**

d Lichtwellenleiter *m*; LWL; optische Faser *f*;
Lichtleitfaser *f*; Optikfaser *f*; Glasfaser *f*

f fibre *f* optique; fibre de verre; guide *m*
[d'onde] optique; guide de lumière

r световод *m*; оптическое волокно *n*;
световолокно *n*; стекловолокно *n*;
оптический волновод *m*

**6543 optical fiber LAN; glass fiber LAN; fiber
optic LAN**

d lokales Lichtwellenleiternetz *n*; lokales
Glasfasernetz *n*

f réseau *m* local à fibres optiques; réseau local
à fibres de verre

r местная световодная сеть *f*; локальная
световодная сеть

* **optical fiber transmission** → 3760

6544 optical font

d optische Schriftart *f*; optisch auswertbare
Schrift *f*

f fonte *f* optique

r шрифт *m* для оптического распознавания

* **optical information processing** → 6538

6545 optically-sensed document

d optisch lesbarer Beleg *m*

f document *m* à lecture optique

r оптически считываемый документ *m*

6546 optical mark reader

d optischer Markierungsleser *m*; optischer
Markierbelegleser *m*

f lecteur *m* de marquages optiques

r устройство *n* оптического считывания
меток

6547 optical memory

d optischer Speicher *m*

f mémoire *f* optique

r оптическая память *f*

6548 optical processor

d optischer Prozessor *m*

 f processeur *m* optique
 r оптический процессор *m*

6549 optical reader; photoelectric[al] reader
 d optischer Leser *m*; fotoelektrischer Leser;
  Klarschriftleser *m*
 f lecteur *m* optique; balayeur *m* optique; lecteur
  photoélectrique
 r оптическое считывающее устройство *n*;
  оптический сканер *m*; фотосчитыватель *m*

**6550 optical reading; optical sensing; optical
 scanning**
 d optisches Lesen *n*
 f lecture *f* optique
 r оптическое считывание *n*

 * **optical scanning** → **6550**

 * **optical sensing** → **6550**

6551 optical signal; visual signal; visible signal
 d optisches Signal *n*
 f signal *m* optique
 r оптический сигнал *m*

6552 optical signal processor
 d optischer Signalprozessor *m*
 f processeur *m* de signaux optiques
 r процессор *m* оптических сигналов

6553 optical tape
 d optisches Band *n*
 f bande *f* optique
 r оптическая лента *f*

 * **optical wand** → **5361**

 * **optical waveguide** → **6542**

6554 optimal resolution; optimum resolution
 d optimales Auflösungsvermögen *n*
 f résolution *f* optimale
 r оптимальная разрешающая способность *f*

6555 optimal value; optimum [value]
 d Optimalwert *m*; Optimum *n*
 f valeur *f* optimum; valeur optimale;
  optimum *m*
 r оптимальное значение *n*; оптимальная
  величина *f*; оптимум *m*

 * **optimation** → **6556**

6556 optimization; optimation
 d Optimierung *f*; Optimisierung *f*;
  Optimalisierung *f*
 f optimisation *f*
 r оптимизация *f*

6557 optimization problem
 d Optimierungsproblem *n*
 f problème *m* d'optimisation
 r задача *f* оптимизации

6558 optimization theory
 d Optimierungstheorie *f*
 f théorie *f* d'optimisation
 r теория *f* оптимизации

6559 optimize *v*
 d optimieren
 f optimiser
 r оптимизировать

 * **optimizer** → **6560**

6560 optimizer [software]
 d Optimisator *m*
 f optimisateur *m*; logiciel d'optimisation
 r оптимизатор *m*

 * **optimum** → **6555**

 * **optimum resolution** → **6554**

6561 optimum scanner resolution
 d optimales Scannerauflösungsvermögen *n*
 f résolution *f* de scanner optimale
 r оптимальная разрешающая способность *f*
  сканера

 * **optimum value** → **6555**

6562 option
 d Option *f*; Angebot *n*; wahlfreie Möglichkeit *f*
 f option *f*
 r опция *f*

6563 optional
 d wahlfrei; wahlweise; optional; willkürlich
 f optionnel; aux choix; facultatif
 r необязательный; факультативный;
  выборочный; выбираемый

6564 optional facility
 d wahlweise Zusatzeinrichtung *f*; wahlweiser
  Zusatz *m*
 f supplément *m* par option
 r выборочное средство *n*

 * **optional sampling** → **6565**

**6565 optional selection; optional sampling;
 random sampling**
 d willkürliche Auswahl *f*; Zufallsauswahl *f*
 f choix *m* arbitraire; sélection *f* arbitraire;
  échantillonnage *m* aléatoire
 r произвольный выбор *m*; случайный выбор

6566 option byte
  d Wahlbyte *n*; Auswahlbyte *n*
  f octet *m* optionnel
  r выбираемый байт *m*

6567 options dialog box
  d Dialogfeld *n* "Optionen"
  f boîte *f* de dialogue d'options
  r диалоговый ящик *m* выбора

  * optocoupler → 6534

6568 optoelectronic; optronic
  d optronisch
  f optoélectronique; optronique
  r оптоэлектронный

6569 optoelectronic digital logic
  d optoelektronische Digitallogik *f*
  f logique *f* numérique optoélectronique
  r оптоэлектронная цифровая логическая
     схема *f*

6570 optoelectronic interface
  d optoelektronische Schnittstelle *f*
  f interface *f* optoélectronique
  r оптоэлектронный интерфейс *m*

6571 optoelectronics
  d Optoelektronik *f*
  f optoélectronique *f*
  r оптоэлектроника *f*

  * optron → 6534

  * optronic → 6568

**6572 OR circuit; OR gate; inclusive-OR gate;
     union gate**
  d ODER-Schaltung *f*; [inklusives]
     ODER-Gatter *n*
  f circuit *m* OU; porte *f* OU [inclusif]; porte
     d'union
  r схема *f* ИЛИ; схема объединения

  * order → 2718, 2959

6573 order
  d Ordnung *f*
  f ordre *m*
  r порядок *m*

6574 order *v*
  d ordnen; anordnen
  f ordonner
  r упорядочивать; располагать в
     определённом порядке

6575 order; place; position; rank
     (of a digit)

  d Zifferstelle *f*; Position *f*
  f position *f* [de chiffre]; rang *m*
  r [цифровой] разряд *m*; позиция *f*

6576 ordered information
  d geordnete Information *f*
  f information *f* classée
  r упорядоченная информация *f*

6577 order handling
  d Auftragsbearbeitung *f*
  f travail *m* d'ordre
  r обработка *f* директивой

6578 ordering
  d Ordnung *f*; Anordnung *f*; Ordnen *n*;
     Anordnen *n*
  f ordonnance *f*; ordonnancement *m*
  r упорядочение *n*; упорядоченность *f*

6579 order[ing] relation
  d Ordnungsrelation *f*; Ordnungsbeziehung *f*
  f relation *f* d'ordre
  r отношение *n* порядка

6580 orderly closedown
  d betriebsvorschriftsmäßiges Abschalten *n*
  f mise *f* au repos ordonnée
  r правильный останов *m*; останов по
     указанию

  * order of precedence → 6581

6581 order of priority; order of precedence
  d Prioritätsordnung *f*
  f ordre *m* de priorité
  r порядок *m* приоритета; приоритетность *f*
     [действий]

6582 order range
  d Ordnungsbereich *m*
  f plage *f* d'exposants; région *f* d'exposants
  r диапазон *m* порядков

  * order relation → 6579

  * OR function → 2997

  * organization chart → 3920

6583 organizer
  d Organisator *m*; Organizer *m*
  f agenda *m* électronique; organiseur *m*
  r организатор *m*

  * OR gate → 6572

  * orgraph → 2955

6584 oriented; directed
  d orientiert; gerichtet

   f orienté; dirigé
   r ориентированный; направленный

6585 oriented bounded box; OBB
   d orientiertes begrenztes Kästchen *n*
   f boîte *f* délimitée orientée
   r ориентированный ограничивающий ящик *m*

   * **oriented graph** → **2955**

   * **origin** → **6587, 6591**

   * **original** → **7249**

6586 original
   d Original *n*
   f original *m*
   r оригинал *m*; подлинник *m*

6587 origin[al address]
   d ursprüngliche Adresse *f*; Originaladresse *f*;
      absolute Programmanfangsadresse *f*
   f adresse *f* d'origine; adresse *f* absolue
      originelle
   r [абсолютный] начальный адрес *m*;
      исходный адрес

6588 original data
   d Ausgangsdaten *pl*; Ursprungsdaten *pl*
   f données *fpl* originaux; données d'origine
   r исходные данные *pl*; оригинальные
      данные

6589 original equipment manufacturer; OEM
   d Hersteller *m* von Originalteilen
   f fabricant *m* de matériel vendant directement
   r подлинный изготовитель *m* оборудования

6590 originate *v*; initiate *v*; begin *v*
   d beginnen; einleiten
   f commencer; initier
   r начинать; инициировать

   * **originating code** → **8736**

6591 origin[ation]
   d Ursprung *m*; Entstehung *f*
   f origine *f*
   r источник *m*; исход *m*

6592 originator
   (the user who creates, addresses, and usually
   sends a message)
   d Verursacher *m*; Auftraggeber *m*
   f expéditeur *m*
   r создатель *m*; автор *m*; инициатор *m*

6593 Oring
   d Verbinden *n* durch ODER
   f exécution *f* d'opération OU

   r осуществление *n* операции ИЛИ

6594 OR operation; inclusive-OR operation
   d ODER-Operation *f*;
      Inklusiv-ODER-Operation *f*
   f opération *f* OU [inclusif]
   r операция *f* [включающее] ИЛИ

6595 orthogonal; perpendicular *adj*
   d orthogonal; perpendikulär
   f orthogonal; perpendiculaire
   r ортогональный; перпендикулярный

6596 orthogonal memory
   d orthogonaler Speicher *m*
   f mémoire *f* orthogonale
   r ортогональная память *f*

   * **orthogonal window** → **7752**

6597 orthographic corrector; spell[ing] checker
   d orthografischer Korrektor *m*;
      Rechtschreibkorrektor *m*
   f correcteur *m* orthographique
   r корректор *m* правописания;
      грамматический корректор; правописный
      словарь *m*

6598 orthography; spelling
   d Orthographie *f*; Rechtschreibung *f*
   f orthographie *f*
   r правописание *n*; орфография *f*

   * **OS** → **6503**

6599 oscillate *v*
   d oszillieren; schwanken
   f osciller
   r осциллировать; колебаться

6600 oscillating circuit; oscillator [circuit]; tank [circuit]
   d Oszillatorschaltung *f*; Oszillator *m*
   f circuit *m* oscillant; circuit oscillateur;
      oscillateur *m*
   r колебательная схема *f*; схема генератора;
      осциллятор *m*

6601 oscillation
   d Oszillation *f*
   f oscillation *f*
   r осцилляция *f*

   * **oscillator** → **6600**

   * **oscillator circuit** → **6600**

   * **OSI** → **6488**

   * **outage** → **3679**

* **outage time** → 2623

6602 outbound transmission
d ausstrahlende Transmission *f*
f transmission *f* sortante
r исходящая передача *f*

6603 outbox
d Postausgang *m*; Ausgangskasten *m*;
  ausgehende Post *f*
f boîte *f* d'envoi
r ящик *m* для исходящих сообщений

* **outcome** → 8029

6604 outcoming group
d Ausgangsgruppe *f*
f groupe *m* de sortie
r группа *f* вывода

* **outer** → 3629

6605 outer macroinstruction
d äußerer Makrobefehl *m*
f macro-instruction *f* externe
r внешняя макроинструкция *f*

6606 outer tape face
d Bandaußenfläche *f*
f surface *f* externe de bande
r внешняя сторона *f* ленты

6607 outgoing
d [ab]gehend; ausgehend
f de sortie; sortant; de départ; partant
r исходящий

6608 outgoing line
d abgehende Leitung *f*; Abgangsleitung *f*;
  Abnehmerleitung *f*
f ligne *f* sortante; ligne partante
r исходящая линия *f* [связи]

6609 outgoing mail
d ausgehende Post *f*
f poste *f* sortante
r исходящая почта *f*

* **outlet** → 8690

6610 outlier; ejection
d Ausschlag *m*; Ausreißer *m*
f éjection *f*; expulsion *f*
r выброс *m*; выбраковка *f*

* **outline** → 2249

6611 outline font
d Konturschrift *f*
f police *f* de contour

r контурный шрифт *m*

6612 outline symbol
d konturiertes Symbol *n*
f symbole *m* de contour
r контурный символ *m*

6613 out-of-balance packet
d Paket *n* mit fehlerhafte Prüfsumme
f paquet *m* à somme de contrôle erronée
r пакет *m* с неверной контрольной суммой

* **out of circuit** *adj* → 6380

6614 out-of-range address
d Adresse *f* außerhalb des Adressraums
f adresse *f* hors de l'espace adressable
r адрес *m* за пределами адресного
  пространства

6615 out-of-service time
d für Benutzer nicht geeignete Rechnerzeit *f*
f temps *m* hors service
r время *n*, не предназначенное для
  пользователей

* **output** → 3582, 6630

6616 output
  (of data)
d Ausgabe *f*
f extraction *f*; émission *f*; sortie *f*
r вывод *m*; выход *m*

6617 output alphabet; set of output symbols
d Ausgangsalphabet *n*; Ausgangsmenge *f*
f alphabet *m* de sortie
r выходной алфавит *m*; множество *n*
  выходных символов

6618 output area
d Ausgabebereich *m*; Pufferausgabebereich *m*
f domaine *m* de sortie
r область *f* вывода; буферная зона *f* вывода

6619 output channel
d Ausgabekanal *m*
f canal *m* de sortie
r выходной канал *m*; канал вывода

6620 output connection
d Ausgangsverbindung *f*
f connexion *f* de sortie
r выходное соединение *n*

6621 output control
d Ausgabesteuerung *f*
f contrôle *m* de sortie; commande *f* de sortie
r управление *n* выводом

6622 **output data**
 d Ausgabedaten *pl*
 f données *fpl* de sortie
 r выходные данные *pl*

6623 **output data carrier; output information carrier**
 d Ausgabedatenträger *m*;
   Ausgabeinformationsträger *m*
 f porteur *m* de données de sortie; porteur
   d'information de sortie
 r носитель *m* выходных данных; носитель
   выводимой информации

6624 **output delay**
 d Ausgangs[signal]verzögerung *f*
 f retardement *m* de sortie
 r задержка *f* вывода; задержка выходного
   сигнала

6625 **output device**
 d Ausgabeeinheit *f*; Ausgabegerät *n*
 f dispositif *m* de sortie
 r выходное устройство *n*

6626 **output disabling; output lockout**
 d Ausgabesperre *f*; Ausgabeblockierung *f*
 f inhibition *f* du sortie; blocage *m* du sortie
 r запрещение *n* вывода; блокировка *f* выхода

 * **output enable** → 6627

6627 **output enabling; output enable**
 d Ausgangsfreigabe *f*
 f libération *f* du sortie; validation *f* du sortie
 r разблокировка *f* выхода; открытие *n*
   выхода; деблокирование *n* выхода

6628 **output function**
 d Ausgabefunktion *f*
 f fonction *f* de sortie
 r функция *f* выхода; функция выходов

 * **output information carrier** → 6623

6629 **output level**
 d Ausgangspegel *m*
 f niveau *m* de sortie
 r уровень *m* выходного сигнала

 * **output lockout** → 6626

 * **output primitive** → 7259

6630 **output [result]; computing result**
 d Rechenergebnis *n*
 f résultat *m* de calcul
 r результат *m* вычислений; выходной
   результат

6631 **output signal**
 d Ausgangssignal *n*
 f signal *m* de sortie
 r выходной сигнал *m*

6632 **output value**
 d Ausgabewert *m*; Ausgabegröße *f*
 f grandeur *f* de sortie
 r выходная величина *f*

6633 **output variable**
 d Ausgabevariable *f*
 f variable *f* de sortie
 r выходная переменная [величина] *f*

 * **outside** → 3629

6634 **outsourcing**
 d Ausgliederung *f*
 f externalisation *f*; sous-traitance *f*
 r отдавание *n* работы на сторону

 * **outward** *adj* → 3629

 * **overall** → 4186

 * **overall circuit diagram** → 4106

6635 **overflow**
 d Überlauf *m*; Bereichsüberschreitung *f*
 f dépassement *m* [de capacité]; débordement *m*
 r переполнение *n*

6636 **overflow data**
 d Überlaufdaten *pl*
 f données *fpl* de dépassement
 r данные *pl* переполнения

6637 **overflow error**
 d Überlauffehler *m*
 f erreur *f* de dépassement
 r ошибка *f* из-за переполнения

6638 **overflow flag**
 d Überlaufkennzeichen *n*
 f marque *f* de dépassement
 r флаг *m* переполнения; флажок *m*
   переполнения

6639 **overflow record**
 d Überlaufsatz *m*
 f enregistrement *m* de dépassement
 r переполняющая запись *f*

 * **overhead** → 6642

6640 **overhead**
 d Organizationsaufwand *m*;
   Systemleistungsanteil *m* für
   Eigenorganisation; Mehraufwand *m*

f effort *m* d'organisation
r затраты *fpl* на вспомогательные операции

6641 overhead bit; extra bit
d zusätzliches Bit *n*; Zusatzbit *n*
f bit *m* supplémentaire
r дополнительный [служебный] бит *m*;
   экстрабит *m*

6642 overhead[s]
d Verwaltungsaufwand *m*;
   Organisationsaufwand *m*; Gemeinkosten *pl*
f dépenses *fpl* [improductives]; frais *mpl*;
   effort *m* d'organisation
r непроизводительные затраты *fpl*;
   издержки *fpl*

* overlap → 6646

6643 overlap *v*
d überlappen
f recouvrir; chevaucher
r налагать; перекрывать; совмещать; иметь
   общую внутреннюю часть; покрывать

6644 overlapped access
d überlappter Zugriff *m*
f accès *m* chevauché; accès *m* avec
   chevauchement; accès superposé
r доступ *m* с перекрытием; выборка *f* с
   перекрытием

6645 overlapped processing
d überlappte Verarbeitung *f*
f traitement *m* à chevauchement
r совмещённая обработка *f*

6646 overlap[ping]
d Überlappung *f*
f chevauchement *m*; recouvrement *m*
r перекрытие *n*; совмещение *n*; наложение *n*

6647 overlapping channels
d überlappende Kanäle *mpl*
f canaux *mpl* superposés
r перекрывающиеся каналы *mpl*

* overlay → 5294

6648 overlay
d Überlagerung *f*; Overlay *n*
f recouvrement *m*; superposition *f*; overlay *m*
r наложение *n*; перекрытие *n*; оверлей *m*

6649 overlay network
d Overlaynetz *n*
f réseau *m* de recouvrement
r оверлейная сеть *f*

6650 overlay program

d Überlagerungsprogramm *n*
f programme *m* de recouvrement
r программа *f* с перекрываемой структурой

6651 overlay structure
d Überlagerungsstruktur *f*
f structure *f* de recouvrement
r перекрываемая структура *f*; оверлейная
   структура

6652 overload *v*
d über[be]lasten; überbeanspruchen; überlagern
f surcharger
r перегружать

6653 overload; congestion
d Über[be]lastung *f*; Überbeanspruchung *f*;
   Flattern *n*
f surcharge *f*
r перегрузка *f*; перегруженность *f*

6654 overload protection
d Überlastungsschutz *m*
f protection *f* contre une surcharge
r защита *f* от перегрузки

* overprint → 6656

6655 overprint *v*
d überdrucken
f surimprimer
r надпечатывать; печатать поверх [текста]

6656 overprint[ing]
d Überdruckung *f*; Doppeldruck *m*
f surimpression *f*
r надпечатание *n*; надпечатка *f*; забивка *f*

6657 override *v*
d aufheben; überschreiben
f casser; abolir; abroger
r подменять; игнорировать

6658 overriding
d Aufhebung *f*
f asservissement *m*
r подмена *f*; отмена *f*

* overrun → 6661

6659 overrun bit
d Informationsverlustbit *n*; Leerlaufbit *n*
f bit *m* de dépassement; bit de perte
   d'information
r бит *m* потери информации; бит выхода за
   допустимые пределы

* overrun check signal → 6660

6660 overrun control signal; overrun check
     signal
    d Überlaufkontrollsignal *n*
    f signal *m* de contrôle de dépassement
    r сигнал *m* контроля переполнения

6661 overrun[ning]
    d Überlauf *m*; Überlaufen *n*;
    Aufnahmekapazitätsüberschreitung *f*
    f engorgement *m* [de canal]; excédent *m* de
    rendement; dépassement *m*
    r выход *m* за границы (памяти); перегрузка *f*
    [канала передачи]; переполнение *n*

6662 overrun of data; data overrun
    d Datenverlust *m*
    f perte *f* de données
    r потеря *f* данных [из-за переполнения]

6663 oversampling
    d Überabtastung *f*
    f suréchantillonnage *m*
    r сверхразвёртка *f*; сверхсканирование *n*

    *   overshoot → 6664

6664 overshoot[ing]
    d Überregelung *f*; Überoszillation *f*;
    Überschwingen *n*; Übersteuerung *f*
    f surréglage *m*; surrégulation *f*; dépassement *m*
    [de niveau] de réglage; suroscillation *f*
    r перерегулирование *n*; отклонение *n* от
    заданного значения; выброс *m* сигнала

6665 overstrike *v*
    d überdrucken
    f superposer
    r набирать лишние символы; налагать знаки

6666 oversynchronization
    d Übersynchronisierung *f*
    f sursynchronisation *f*
    r пересинхронизация *f*

6667 overview
    d Überblick *m*; Übersicht *f*
    f vue *f* synoptique; survol *m*; aperçu *m*
    r обзор *m*

6668 overwriting
    d Überschreiben *n*; Überschreibung *f*
    f superposition *f* d'enregistrement
    r перезапись *f*; наложение *n* записей

    *   OWG → 6542

P

* **pack** → 3007, 6670

6669 pack *v*
  d verdichten; konzentrieren; packen
  f empaqueter; emballer; condenser; concentrer
  r уплотнять; упаковывать; упаковать

* **package** → 472, 3393

6670 package; pack; packet; bundle; batch
  d Paket *n*; Stapel *m*
  f paquet *m*; pile *f*
  r пакет *m*

* **packaging** → 6689

6671 packaging style
  d Gehäusentyp *m*; Verpackungsart *f*
  f type *m* de boîtier; type de paquetage
  r тип *m* корпуса; тип упаковки

6672 packed data
  d gepackte Daten *pl*
  f données *fpl* paquetées
  r данные *pl* в упакованном формате

* **packed file** → 2036

6673 packed format
  d gepacktes Format *n*
  f format *m* condensé; format groupé
  r упакованный формат *m*

6674 packed message
  d gepackte Nachricht *f*
  f message *m* condensé
  r упакованное сообщение *n*

* **packet** → 6670

* **packet assembler/disassembler** → 6675

* **packet assembly** → 6689

**6675 packet assembly/disassembly facility;
        packet assembler/disassembler; PAD**
  d Paketierer/Depaketierer *m*;
       PAD-Einrichtung *f*
  f assembleur/désassembleur *m* des paquets
  r ассемблер/дисассемблер *m* пакетов

* **packet commutator** → 6682

6676 packet delay
  d Paket[übertragungs]verzögerung *f*
  f retard *m* des paquets; délai *m* de transmission
       des paquets
  r задержка *f* [передачи] пакетов; задержка
       транзита

6677 packet disassembly; depackaging
  d Depaketierung *f*; Entpaketierung *f*
  f désassemblage *m* de paquets
  r распакование *n*; разборка *f* пакетов

6678 packet Internet groper; PING
  (a protocol that determines whether a remote
  computer is active and where it can be
  contacted)
  d Ping *m*
  f utilitaire *m* Ping; Ping *m*
  r пакетный интернетный искатель *m*;
       пакетный "ощупыватель" *m* Интернета;
       пинг *m*

* **packetization** → 6689

6679 packet mode
  d Paketmodus *m*
  f mode *m* condensé
  r режим *m* работы с упакованными данными

6680 packet-oriented
  d paketorientiert; paketweise
  f orienté sur le paquet
  r пакетноориентированный

6681 packet-oriented access procedure
  d paketorientierte Zugangsprozedur *f*
  f procédure *f* d'accès orientée sur le paquet
  r пакетная процедура *f* доступа

* **packet protocol** → 6684

6682 packet switch; packet commutator
  d Paketvermittler *m*
  f commutateur *m* de paquets
  r коммутатор *m* пакетов

6683 packet-switched connection
  d paketvermittelte Nachricht *f*
  f message *m* commuté en paquets
  r сообщение *n*, передаваемое по сети с
       коммутацией пакетов

6684 packet-switched data exchange; DATEX-P
  d paketvermittelte Datenübertragung *f*
  f échange *m* de données commuté en paquets
  r передача *f* данных с коммутацией пакетов

6685 packet-switched data network; PSDN
  d paketvermitteltes Datennetz *n*
  f réseau *m* de commutation de données par
       paquets
  r сеть *f* передачи данных с коммутацией
       пакетов

6686 packet switching
d Paketvermittlung *f*
f commutation *f* de paquets
r коммутация *f* пакетов

6687 packet[-switching] protocol
d Paketvermittlungsprotokoll *n*;
Paketübertragungsprotokoll *n*
f protocole *m* de communication par paquets
r протокол *m* коммутации пакетов;
протокол *m* пакетной связи

**6688 packet transmission; batch
communication**
d Paketübertragung *f*
f communication *f* par lots
r пакетная передача *f*; пакетная связь *f*

**6689 packing; packaging; packetization; packet
assembly; batching; encapsulation**
d Paketierung *f*; Paketbildung *f*; Packung *f*;
Verpackung *f*
f [em]paquetage *m*; empilement *m*
r пакетирование *n*; формирование *n* пакета;
упаковка *f*

**6690 packing density; packing fraction; packing
factor**
d Packungsdichte *f*; Verdichtungsfaktor *m*
f densité *f* de paquetage; facteur *m* de
paquetage
r плотность *f* упаковки; коэффициент *m*
уплотнения

* **packing factor** → **6690**

* **packing fraction** → **6690**

* **packing into boxes** → **1150**

* **packing program** → **2714**

* **pad** → **2173, 6691**

* **PAD** → **6675**

* **pad** *v* → **3823**

* **pad character** → **3825**

6691 pad[ding]; filling
d Auffüllen *n*; Auffüllung *f*
f remplissage *m*; garnissage *m*
r дополнение *n*; заполнение *n*; набивка *f*

* **padding character** → **3825**

6692 page
d Seite *f*
f page *f*
r страница *f*

6693 pageable
d seitenorganisierte; seitenwechselbar
f paginé
r странируемый

6694 pageable partitioning
d seitenorganisierte Unterteilung *f*
f partitionnement *m* paginé
r разбиение *n* по страницам

6695 page address
d Seitenadresse *f*
f adresse *f* de page
r адрес *m* страницы

6696 page [at-a-time] printer
d Seitendrucker *m*; Blattdrucker *m*
f imprimante *f* à pages
r постранично-печатающее устройство *n*

* **page backward** → **6705**

6697 page border
d Seitenrahmen *m*
f bordure *f* de page
r кайма *f* страницы

6698 page break
d Seitenabbruch *m*
f interruption *f* de page; saut *m* de page
r прерывание *n* страницы

6699 page chaining
d Seitenkettung *f*
f chaînage *m* de page; enchaînement *m* de
pages
r сцепление *n* страниц

6700 page change; paging
d Seitenwechsel *m*
f changement *m* de pages; échange *m* de pages
r замещение *n* страниц; обмен *m*
страницами

6701 page curl
d Seiteaufrollen *n*
f roulage *m* de page; tuilage *m* de page;
ondulation *f* de page
r завиток *m* страницы

6702 page cut
d Seitenschnitt *m*
f coupe *f* de page
r срез *m* страницы

6703 page cut effect
d Effekt *m* des Seitenschnitts
f effet *m* de coupe de page
r эффект *m* среза страницы

6704 paged memory; paging device; page mode RAM; paged RAM
d seitenorganisierter Speicher *m*; Seitenspeicher *m*
f mémoire *f* en pages; mémoire en mode page; mémoire paginée
r [оперативная] память *f* со страничной организацией; память с постраничным отображением

6705 page-down; page backward
d Rück[wärts]blättern *n*
f pageage *m* en arrière; défilement *m* en arrière
r листание *n* назад; возврат *m* на предыдущую страницу

6706 Page Down key; PgDn key
d Bild-nach-unten-Taste *f*
f touche *f* de pageage en arrière
r клавиша *f* листания назад

* **paged RAM** → 6704

6707 page exporting
d Seite-Exportieren *n*
f exportation *f* de page
r экспортирование *n* страницы

* **page fault interrupt** → 5852

* **page fixing** → 6717

6708 page footing
d Seitenfuß *m*
f total *m* final de page
r суммарная информация *f* в конце страницы

6709 page format
d Seitenformat *n*
f format *m* de page
r формат *m* страницы

6710 page format selection
d Seitenformatauswahl *f*
f sélection *f* de format de page
r выбор *m* формата страницы

6711 page frame
d Seitenrahmen *m*; Seitenfach *n*
f cadre *m* de page; trame *f* de page
r блок *m* страницы; страничный блок

6712 page header
d Seitentitel *m*
f en-tête *f* de page
r заголовок *m* страницы

6713 page home line
d Seitenanfang *m*
f début *m* de page; première ligne *f* de page
r первый ряд *m* страницы; начало *n* страницы

6714 page image format; PIF
d Seitendarstellung-Format *n*
f format *m* d'image de page
r формат *m* изображения страницы

6715 page-in
d Seiteneinlagerung *f*
f chargement *m* de page
r загрузка *f* страницы; подкачка *f* страницы

6716 page-layout
d Seitenanordnung *f*; Seitentopologie *f*
f disposition *f* de pages; topologie *f* de pages
r макет *m* страницы; топология *f* страницы

6717 page locking; page fixing
d Seitenfixieren *n*; Residentmachen *n* von Seiten
f fixation *f* de page
r фиксация *f* страниц

6718 page-makeup
d Seitenumbruch *m*
f maquettage *m* de page
r макетирование *n* страницы

6719 page migration
d Seitenwanderung *f*
f migration *f* de pages
r пересылка *f* страниц

6720 page mode
d Seiten[zugriffs]modus *m*
f mode *m* de page
r режим *m* доступа до страницы

* **page mode RAM** → 6704

6721 page number
d Seitennummer *f*
f numéro *m* de page
r номер *m* страницы

6722 page numbering
d Seitennumerierung *f*
f numération *f* de pages
r нумерация *f* страниц

6723 page-on demand system
d Seitenanforderungssystem *n*
f système *m* de requête de pages
r система *f* заказа страницы

6724 page-out
d Seitenauslagerung *f*

f renvoi *m* de page; évacuage *m* de page
r удаление *n* страницы; откачка *f* страницы

* **page printer** → 6696

6725 pager
d Anrufmelder *m*; Pager *m*; Taschenpiepser *m*;
Piepser *m*
f pager *m*
r пейджер *m*

6726 page reader
d Seitenleser *m*; Blattleser *m*
f lecteur *m* de pages
r устройство *n* считывания страниц

6727 page setting
d Seiteneinrichtung *f*
f établissement *m* de page; mise *f* en page
r установление *n* параметров страницы

6728 page setup *v*
d die Seite einrichten
f mettre en page
r установлять параметы страницы

6729 page size
d Seitengröße *f*
f taille *f* de page
r размер *m* страницы

6730 page template
d Seitenschablone *f*
f maquette *f* de page
r шаблон *m* страницы; маска *f* страницы

6731 page turning
d Seitenblättern *n*; Durchblättern *n*
f transfert *m* de pages; pageage *m*;
feuilletage *m*
r смена *f* страниц; листание *n*

6732 page-up
d Vorwärtsblättern *n*
f pageage *m* en avant
r листание *n* вперёд

6733 Page Up key; PgUp key
d Bild-nach-oben-Taste *f*
f touche *f* de pageage en avant; touche de page
précédente
r клавиша *f* листания вперёд; клавиша PgUp

6734 page waiting
d Warten *n* auf einen Seitenwechsel
f attente *f* de [chargement de] page
r ожидание *n* страницы [при подкачке]

* **pagination** → 6735

6735 paging; pagination
d Seitenbildung *f*; Paginierung *f*
f pagination *f*
r разбиение *n* на страницы; разбивка *f* на
страницы; страничная организация *f*

* **paging** → 6700

6736 paging algorithm
d Seitenwechselalgorithmus *m*
f algorithme *m* de substitution de pages
r алгоритм *m* замещения страниц

* **paging device** → 6704

6737 paging rate
d Seitenwechselrate *f*
f densité *f* d'échange de pages; rythme *m*
d'échange de pages; cadence *f* de pagination
r интенсивность *f* обмена страниц; частота *f*
обмена страниц

6738 paint box; paint system
d Malkasten *m*
f palette *f* graphique; palette électronique
r система *f* рисования

6739 paint brush; brush
d Paint-Brush *n*; Pinsel *m*
f pinceau *m*; brosse *f*
r кисть *f* (для рисования); кисточка *f*

* **paint bucket** → 3913

* **paint program** → 2083

* **paint system** → 6738

6740 pair; couple
d Paar *n*
f paire *f*; couple *m*
r пара *f*

6741 paired cable
d paarverteiltes Kabel *n*
f câble *m* en paire
r сдвоенный кабель *m*

6742 palette
d Palette *f*
f palette *f*
r палитра *f*

* **palm-size computer** → 6743

* **palmtop** → 6743

**6743 palmtop [computer]; palm-size computer;
pocket computer; handheld [computer]**
d Palmtop *m*; Kleinstcomputer *m*;
Handheld-Computer *m*; Handmikrorechner *m*

f ordinateur *m* de poche; ordinateur qui tient
  dans la main
r карманный компьютер *m*

* **pan** → **6747**

6744 pan *v*
  d bildverschieben
  f faire un pan[oramique]; effectuer un
    panoramique; panoramiquer
  r панорамировать

* **pane** → **9032**

6745 panel
  d Armaturentafel *f*; Schalttafel *f*;
    Bedienungsfeld *n*
  f panneau *m*; pupitre *m*
  r панель *f*

6746 pan function
  d Bildverschiebenfunktion *f*; Funktion *f* zur
    punktweisen Bildverschiebung
  f fonction *f* de panoramique
  r функция *f* для перемещения изображения

6747 pan[ning]
  d Verschieben *n*; Schwenken *n*
  f mouvement *m* panoramique; panoramique *m*;
    pan *m*
  r панорамирование *n*

* **panorama** → **6748**

* **panoramic picture** → **6748**

6748 pan[oramic] view; panoramic picture;
  panorama
  d Panoramaansicht *f*; Rundbildaufnahme *f*;
    Panoramabild *n*; Panorama *n*
  f vue *f* panoramique; panorama *m*
  r панорамное изображение *n*; панорамный
    вид *m*; панорама *f*

6749 pan[oramic] zoom
  d Panorama-Zoomen *n*
  f zoom *m* panoramique
  r панорамное динамическое
    масштабирование *n*

* **pan view** → **6748**

* **pan zoom** → **6749**

6750 paper
  d Papier *n*
  f papier *m*
  r бумага *f*

* **paper advance** → **6751**

6751 paper feed; paper advance
  d Papierzuführung *f*; Papiervorschub *m*
  f avancement *m* de papier; acheminement *m* de
    papier
  r подача *f* бумаги; протяжка *f* бумаги

* **paper holder** → **6758**

6752 paperless
  d papierlos
  f sans papier
  r безбумажный

* **paper mount** → **6758**

6753 paper orientation
  d Papierorientierung *f*
  f orientation *f* de papier
  r ориентация *f* бумаги

6754 paper release
  d Papierauslösung *f*
  f libération *f* de papier
  r освобождение *n* бумаги; разблокировка *f*
    бумаги

6755 paper roller
  d Papiervorschubrolle *f*; Papierführungsrolle *f*
  f rouleau *m* d'entraînement de papier
  r ролик *m* для протяжки бумаги

6756 paper size
  d Papierformat *n*
  f taille *f* de papier
  r размер *m* бумаги

6757 paper skip
  d Papiersprung *m*
  f saut *m* de papier
  r холостой прогон *m* бумаги

* **paper slew** → **6759**

6758 paper support; paper mount; paper holder
  d Papierhalter *m*; Papierstütze *f*
  f support *m* de papier; réglette *f* de papier
  r бумагодержатель *m*; стойка *f* для бумаги

6759 paper throw; paper slew; paper transport
  d Papiertransport *m*
  f transport *m* de papier
  r прогон *m* бумаги; транспорт *m* бумаги

* **paper transport** → **6759**

6760 paragraph
  d Absatz *m*; Paragraph *m*
  f paragraphe *m*
  r параграф *m*; абзац *m*

6761 paragraph aligning; paragraph justifying
d Absatzausrichtung f
f alignement m de paragraphe; justification f de paragraphe
r выравнивание n параграфа [по обеим границам]

6762 paragraph beginning
d Absatzbeginn m
f début m de paragraphe
r начало n параграфа

6763 paragraph editing
d Absatzbearbeitung f
f édition f de paragraphe
r редактирование n параграфа

6764 paragraph [end] mark
d Absatzendmarke f
f marque f de fin de paragraphe
r маркер m конца параграфа

6765 paragraph formatting
d Absatzformatierung f
f formatage m de paragraphe
r форматирование n параграфа

6766 paragraphing
d Paragrapheneintragen n
f découpage m en paragraphes
r введение n параграфов

* **paragraph justifying** → 6761

* **paragraph mark** → 6764

6767 paragraph properties
d Absatzeigenschaften fpl
f propriétés fpl de paragraphe
r свойства npl параграфа

6768 paragraph sign
d Paragraphenzeichen n
f marque f de paragraphe
r символ m параграфа

6769 paragraph text
d Absatztext m
f texte m courant
r текст m параграфа

6770 parallel
d parallel
f parallèle
r параллельный

6771 parallel access
d Parallelzugriff m; gleichlaufender Zugriff m
f accès m parallèle
r параллельный доступ m

* **parallel-by-bit interface** → 1016

* **parallel-by-byte data** → 1310

6772 parallel cable
d Parallelkabel n
f câble m parallèle
r параллельный кабель m

6773 parallel channel
d Parallelkanal m
f canal m parallèle
r параллельный канал m

6774 parallel coding
d Parallelcodierung f
f codage m parallèle
r параллельное кодирование n

6775 parallel computer; concurrent computer; simultaneous computer
d Parallelrechner m; Konkurrenzrechner m
f ordinateur m parallèle; ordinateur concurrent
r параллельный компьютер m

6776 parallel control
d parallele Kontrolle f; parallele Steuerung f
f contrôle m parallèle
r параллельное управление n

6777 parallel data channel
d Paralleldatenkanal m
f canal m de données parallèle
r параллельный информационный канал m

6778 parallel data transmission
d parallele Datenübertragung f
f transmission f de données parallèle
r параллельная передача f данных

6779 parallel graphic processor
d Parallelgrafikprozessor m
f processeur m graphique parallèle
r параллельный графический процессор m

6780 paralleling
d Parallellauf m
f parallélisation f
r распараллеливание n

6781 parallel input/output; PIO
d Parallel-Ein-/Ausgabe f; Parallel-E/A f
f entrée/sortie f parallèle; E/S parallèle
r параллельный ввод/вывод m

6782 parallel interface
d parallele Schnittstelle f; Parallelschnittstelle f
f interface f parallèle
r параллельный интерфейс m

6783 parallelism
 d Parallelität *f*
 f parallélisme *m*
 r параллелизм *m*

6784 parallel microprogramming
 d Parallelmikroprogrammierung *f*
 f microprogrammation *f* parallèle
 r параллельное микропрограммирование *n*

   * **parallel mode** → 8586

6785 parallel modem
 d Parallelmodem *n*
 f modem *m* parallèle
 r параллельный модем *m*

6786 parallel operation
 d parallele Operation *f*; parallele Arbeitsweise *f*;
   Parallelbetrieb *m*
 f opération *f* [en] parallèle
 r параллельная операция *f*; параллельное
   действие *n*

6787 parallel-operation bit
 d Parallellaufbit *n*
 f bit *m* d'opération parallèle
 r бит *m* параллельной работы

6788 parallel-operation decoder
 d paralleler Decodierer *m*
 f décodeur *m* d'opération parallèle
 r дешифратор *m* параллельного действия

6789 parallel-operation recognition
 d Parallellaufauswahl *f*
 f reconnaissance *f* d'opération parallèle
 r распознавание *n* параллельного действия

6790 parallel output
 d Parallelausgabe *f*
 f sortie *f* parallèle
 r параллельная выдача *f*; параллельный
   выход *m*

6791 parallel-parallel method
 d Parallel-Parallel-Verfahren *n*
 f méthode *f* parallèle-parallèle
 r параллельный метод *m*

6792 parallel port
 d parallele Anschlussstelle *f*
 f port *m* parallèle
 r параллельный порт *m*

6793 parallel printer
 d Paralleldrucker *m*
 f imprimante *f* parallèle
 r параллельный принтер *m*

6794 parallel search
 d Parallelsuche *f*; Parallelabfrage *f*
 f recherche *f* parallèle
 r параллельный поиск *m*

6795 parallel-serial
 d Parallel-Seriell-
 f parallèle-sériel
 r параллельно-последовательный

**6796 parallel-serial conversion; parallel series
   conversion; serialization**
 d Parallel-Seriell-Umsetzung *f*
 f conversion *f* parallèle-sérielle
 r параллельно-последовательное
   преобразование *n*

**6797 parallel-serial converter; parallel series
   converter; serializer; dynamicizer**
 d Parallel-Seriell-Umsetzer *m*;
   Seriellumsetzer *m*
 f convertisseur *m* parallèle-sériel
 r преобразователь *m* из параллельной
   формы в последовательную

   * **parallel series conversion** → 6796

   * **parallel series converter** → 6797

   * **parallel transmission** → 8589

6798 parameter
 d Parameter *m*; Bestimmungsgröße *f*
 f paramètre *m*
 r параметр *m*

6799 parametric programming
 d parametrische Programmierung *f*
 f programmation *f* paramétrique
 r параметрическое программирование *n*

6800 parametric rasterization
 d parametrische Rasterung *f*
 f rastérisation *f* paramétrique
 r параметрическая растеризация *f*;
   параметрическое растрирование *n*

6801 parametrization
 d Parametrisierung *f*
 f paramétrisation *f*; paramétrage *m*
 r параметризация *f*

   * **parasitic signal** → 6198

6802 parent
 d Eltern-; übergeordnet; Stamm-
 f parent
 r родительский

6803 parent directory
 d Stammverzeichnis *n*; übergeordnetes

Verzeichnis *n*
f répertoire *m* parent
r родительский каталог *m*; каталог-предок *m*

6804 parentheses; round brackets
d runde Klammern *fpl*
f parenthèses *fpl* [rondes]
r круглые скобки *fpl*

* **parenthesis free notation → 7209**

6805 parity
d Parität *f*
f parité *f*
r паритет *m*; чётность *f*

6806 parity bit
d Paritätsbit *n*
f bit *m* de parité
r бит *m* [контроля] по чётности

6807 parity check; even parity check
d [gerade] Paritätskontrolle *f*; geradzahlige Gleichheitskontrolle *f*; Paritätsprüfung *f*
f contrôle *m* de parité [paire]; vérification *f* de parité
r контроль *m* по чётности; проверка *f* на чётность

6808 parity-checking code
d Paritätsprüfungscode *m*
f code *m* à essai de parité
r код *m* с контролем по чётности

6809 parity digit
d Paritätsziffer *f*
f chiffre *m* de parité; digit *m* parité
r разряд [контроля] *m* чётности

6810 parity flag; P-flag
d Paritätskennzeichen *n*; P-Bit *n*; Paritätsmarker *m*; Paritätsflag *n*
f flag *m* de parité; marque *f* de parité; bit *m* P
r флаг *m* [контроля] чётности; P-бит *m*

6811 parity function
d Paritätsfunktion *f*
f fonction *f* de parité
r чётная функция *f*

6812 parity interrupt
d Paritätsunterbrechung *f*; Paritätsinterrupt
f interruption *f* de parité
r прерывание *n* из-за нарушения чётности

* **parity-odd check → 4689**

6813 park *v*
d parken; abstellen
f bloquer

r парковать

* **parody page → 8787**

* **parole → 6848**

6814 parole circuit
d Wortschaltkreis *m*
f circuit *m* de parole
r схема *f* для обработки пароля

6815 parole processing
d Parolenverarbeitung *f*
f traitement *m* de parole
r обработка *f* пароля

6816 parser; syntax analyzer
d Parser *m*; Syntaxanalysator *m*; Syntaxanalysierer *m*
f analyseur *m* syntaxique
r синтаксический анализатор *m*

* **parse tree → 9128**

6817 parsing; syntax analysis
d Parsing *n*; syntaktische Analyse *f*; Syntaxanalyse *f*
f analyse *f* lexicale; analyse syntaxique
r параметрический анализ *m*; синтаксический анализ; синтаксический разбор *m*

6818 parsing algorithm
d Algorithmus *m* der syntaktischen Analyse; Parseralgorithmus *m*
f algorithme *m* d'analyse lexicale
r алгоритм *m* синтаксического анализа

6819 part; portion
d Teil *m*; Anteil *m*
f partie *f*; part *f*
r часть *f*

6820 part coding
d Teilcodierung *f*
f codage *m* en partie
r частичное кодирование *n*

6821 part-failure rate; partial failure rate
d Teilausfallrate *f*
f cote *f* de manques partiels
r интенсивность *f* частичных отказов

6822 partial carry
d Teilübertrag *m*
f report *m* partiel; retenue *f* partielle
r частичный перенос *m*

6823 partial decoder
d partieller Decodierer *m*

f décodeur *m* partiel
r неполный дешифратор *m*

* **partial failure rate** → 6821

* **partial solution** → 6827

6824 partial storage
d Teilspeicherung *f*
f mémorisation *f* partielle
r частичное запоминание *n*; частичное хранение *n*

* **partial sum** → 9027

6825 partial sum register
d Teilsummenregister *n*
f registre *m* de somme partielle
r регистр *m* частичной суммы

* **partial total** → 9027

* **participant** → 9007

6826 particular; special
d partikulär; speziell
f particulier
r частный; отдельный; конкретный

6827 particular solution; partial solution
d partikuläre Lösung *f*; Teillösung *f*; spezielle Lösung
f solution *f* particulière
r частное решение *n*

* **partition** → 6832

6828 partition *v*
d aufteilen; unterteilen; untergliedern
f partager; segmenter
r разделять; расчленять; разбивать

6829 partition
(of the memory)
d Speicherzone *f*; Partition *f*; Bereich *m*
f zone *f* de mémoire
r раздел *m*; сегмент *m*

6830 partitioned
d aufgeteilt; untergliedert; unterteilt
f partagé; divisé
r разделённый; расчленённый; секционированный

6831 partitioned access method
d untergliederte Zugriffsmethode *f*
f méthode *f* d'accès par partition; méthode d'accès subdivisé
r библиотечный метод *m* доступа

6832 partition[ing]
d Zerlegung *f*; Einteilung *f*; Aufteilung *f*; Teilung *f*; Partition *f*
f partition *f*; partage *m*; partitionnement *m*
r разбиение *n*; расчленение *n*; разделение *n*

* **part list** → 6834

6833 part number
d Teilnummer *f*
f numéro *m* de pièce; numéro d'identification
r номер *m* части; номер детали

6834 part[s] list
d Stückliste *f*; Teilliste *f*
f liste *f* des pièces détachées
r спецификация *f*; список *m* деталей

6835 partword
d Teilwort *n*
f mot *m* partiel
r частичное слово *n*; часть *f* слова

6836 partword addressing
d Teilwortadressierung *f*
f adressage *m* de mot partiel
r адресование *n* к части слова

* **party** → 7053

6837 party line
d Gemeinschaftsleitung *f*; Gemeinschaftsanschluss *m*; Partylinie *f*
f ligne *f* commune
r линия *f* коллективного пользования; групповая линия

6838 pass; passage; run
d Durchlauf *m*; Lauf *m*; Arbeitsgang *m*
f passage *m*; cours *m*; pas *m*
r проход *m*; прогон *m*

* **passage** → 6838

6839 passage to the limit; limit[ing] process
d Grenzübergang *m*
f passage *m* à la limite
r переход *m* к пределу; предельный переход

* **pass instruction** → 6283

* **passive** → 4715

6840 passive bus
d passiver Bus *m*
f bus *m* passif
r пассивная шина *f*

6841 passive [computer] graphics
d passive Rechnergrafik *f*

f infographie *f* passive
r пассивная компьютерная графика *f*

6842 passive distribution system
d passives Verzweigungssystem *n*
f système *m* de distribution passif
r пассивная разветвительная система *f*

6843 passive element
d passiver Baustein *m*
f élément *m* passif
r пассивный элемент *m*

* **passive graphics** → **6841**

6844 passive matrix
d Passivmatrix *f*
f matrice *f* passive
r пассивная матрица *f*

6845 passive-matrix color display
d Passivmatrix-Farbdisplay *n*
f écran *m* couleur à matrice passive
r [жидкокристаллический] цветной
дисплей *m* с пассивной матрицей

6846 passive-matrix display
d Passivmatrix-Display *n*
f écran *m* à matrice passive
r дисплей *m* с пассивной матрицей

6847 passive redundancy
d passive Redundanz *f*; funktionsbeteiligte
Redundanz
f redondance *f* passive
r постоянное резервирование *n*

6848 password; parole
d Kennwort *n*; Passwort *n*
f mot *m* de passe; [passe-]parole *f*
r пароль *m*

* **password protection** → **6849**

6849 password security; password protection
d Passwortschutz *m*; Kennwortschutz *m*
f sécurité *f* de mot-clé; sécurité de mot de passe
r защита *f* ключевого слова

* **paste** *v* → **4927**

6850 paste *v* special
d speziell einfügen
f insérer spécialement
r вкладывать специально

**6851 paste *v* together; patch *v* together; piece *v*
together; glue *v* together; sew *v***
d zusammenkleben
f coller

r склеи[ва]ть; приклеивать; клеить

6852 pasting together; gluing
d Zusammenkleben *n*; Kleben *n*
f collage *m*; recollement *m*
r склеивание *n*

* **PAT** → **6906**

* **patch** → **1236**

6853 patch *v*
d flicken; ausflicken; einsetzen
f corriger; rapiécer
r ставить заплаты (в программе)

6854 patch *v*
d anschließen; [ein]stöpseln; rangieren
f enficher
r подключать; подсоединять

* **patching** → **6855**

6855 patching [a program]
d [Programm-]Direktkorrektur *f*
f correction *f* de bogue [d'un programme]
r внесение *n* "заплат" [в программу]

* **patchtip** → **7067**

* **patch *v* together** → **6851**

* **path** → **8135**

* **pathological Internet use** → **2456**

* **pathologically eclectic rubbish lister** →
7188

* **pattern** → **4645, 9245**

6856 pattern
d Motiv *n*
f motif *m*; forme *f* [géométrique régulière]
r мотив *m*; узор *m*; рисунок *m*

6857 pattern block
d Motivblock *m*
f bloc *m* mosaïque; bloc de formes
r блок *m* рисунка

6858 pattern feature
d Schablonengestaltung *f*; Schablonenraster *m*
f aspect *m* de modèle; rastre *m* de modèle
r вид *m* шаблона; растр *m* шаблона

6859 pattern file
(.pat)
d Musterdatei *f*

f fichier *m* de modèles
r файл *m* шаблонов

6860 pattern generator
(in the pattern recognition)
d Mustergenerator *m*
f générateur *m* d'images; générateur des
configurations
r генератор *m* изображений; генератор
образов

6861 pattern generator
(in the coding)
d Codemustergenerator *m*
f générateur *m* de combinaisons codées
r генератор *m* кодовых комбинаций

* **pattern match → 6862**

6862 pattern match[ing]
d Musteranpassung *f*
f appariement *m* de formes
r соответствие *n* изображений

6863 pattern plane
d Leiter[zug]ebene *f*
f face *f* à conducteurs
r слой *m* сигнальных проводников; слой
межсоединений

6864 pattern recognition; image recognition; PR
d Bilderkennung *f*; Mustererkennung *f*;
Gestalterkennung *f*
f reconnaissance *f* d'images; reconnaissance de
modèles; reconnaissance de formes
r распознавание *n* образов; распознавание
изображений; распознавание формы

6865 pattern regularity
(of a texture)
d Motivregelmäßigung *f*
f régularité *f* de motif
r регулярность *f* мотива

6866 pause
d Pause *f*
f pause *f*
r пауза *f*

6867 pause indication
d Pausenmeldung *f*
f indication *f* de pause
r обозначение *n* паузы

6868 pause instruction
d Pausebefehl *m*
f instruction *f* de pause
r инструкция *f* паузы

6869 pause key

d Pausentaste *f*
f touche *f* de pause
r клавиша *f* "пауза"

6870 pause period; no-current period
d Pausenschritt *m*
f temps *m* de pause; période *f* de pause
r период *m* паузы; длительность *f* паузы

6871 pause signal; interval signal
d Pausenzeichen *n*
f signal *m* de pause
r сигнал *m* паузы

6872 pausing
d Pausieren *n*
f mise *f* en pause
r установление *n* паузы

* **paving → 9377**

* **PB → 6927**

* **Pbyte → 6927**

* **PC → 6923**

* **PCD → 6940**

6873 PCD file
d PCD-Datei *f*
f fichier *m* PCD
r файл *m* PCD

* **PD → 7486**

* **PDF → 7133**

* **peak factor → 368**

6874 pecker
d Abfühlstift *m*
f poinçon *m*
r считывающий штифт *m*

6875 peer *adj*
d seinesgleichen; gleichberechtigt
f égal
r равноправный

6876 peer code review
d Experteneinschätzung *f* eines Programms
f évaluation *f* d'expertise d'un programme
r экспертная оценка *f* программы

6877 peer modules
d gleichberechtigte Module *npl*
f modules *mpl* égaux
r равноправные модули *mpl*

6878 **peer-to-peer architecture**
  d Architektur *f* mit gleichberechtigtem Zugriff
  f architecture *f* par accès égal
  r одноранговая архитектура *f*; архитектура
    равноправных узлов

6879 **peer-to-peer LAN**
  d lokales Netz *n* mit gleichberechtigtem Zugriff
  f réseau *m* [local] par accès égal
  r [локальная] сеть *f* с равноправным
    доступом

  * **peer-to-peer protocol** → 7088

  * **peg count** → 9466

  * **peg counter** → 9467

  * **peg meter** → 9467

  * **Peirce decomposition** → 6880

  * **Peirce function** → 6229

6880 **Peirce['s] decomposition**
  d Peircesche Zerlegung *f*
  f décomposition *f* de Peirce
  r разложение *n* Пирса

  * **pel** → 7015

  * **PEM** → 7326

6881 **pen; stylus**
  d Schreibfeder *f*; Stift *m*; Griffel *m*
  f stylo *m*; plume *f*
  r перо *n*

  * **pen-based computer** → 6891

6882 **pen-based data entry**
  d Stift-basierte Dateneingabe *f*
  f entrée *f* de données sans clavier
  r перьевой ввод *m* данных

6883 **pen carriage; pen holder**
  d Stiftträger *m*
  f porte-plume *f*; support *m* de plume
  r перьевой держатель *m*; перьевая каретка *f*

6884 **pencil; sheaf; bundle; bunch**
  d Büschel *n*; Bündel *n*; Garbe *f*
  f faisceau *m*; pinceau *m*; gerbe *f*
  r пучок *m*; связка *f*; сноп *m*; жгут *m*; ствол *m*

  * **pen detection** → 5362

  * **pending** *adj* → 4390

6885 **pending message**
  d wartende Nachricht *f*

  f message *m* pendant; message suspendu
  r ожидающее сообщение *n*; "подвешенное"
    сообщение

6886 **pen down** *v*
  d den Stift untergehen
  f baisser de plume
  r снимать перо

6887 **penetration**
  d Eindringen *n*; Eindringtiefe *f*;
    Durchdringung *f*
  f pénétration *f*
  r проникновение *n*; проницаемость *f*

  * **pen holder** → 6883

6888 **pen icon**
  d Stiftikone *f*
  f icône *f* de stylo
  r икона *f* пера

6889 **penless plotter**
  d Plotter *m* ohne Stifte; stiftfreier Plotter
  f traceur *m* sans plumes
  r безперьевой графопостроитель *m*

6890 **pen plotter**
  d Zeichnenstift-Plotter *m*; Stiftplotter *m*
  f traceur *m* à plumes
  r перьевой графопостроитель *m*

6891 **pentop computer; pen-based computer**
  d Pentop-Computer *m*
  f ordinateur *m* sans clavier; tablette *f*
    électronique
  r компьютер *m* с рукописным вводом
    данных; компьютер с перьевым вводом
    данных

6892 **pen** *v* **up**
  d den Stift anheben
  f lever de plume
  r поднимать перо

  * **per cent** → 6893

  * **percent** → 6894

6893 **percent; per cent**
  d Prozent *n*
  f pourcentage *m*; pour-cent *m*
  r процент *m*

6894 **percent [sign]; percent symbol**
    (%)
  d Prozentzeichen *n*
  f signe *m* de pourcentage; symbole *m* de
    pourcentage
  r символ *m* процента

* **percent symbol** → 6894

6895 percept
d Wahrnehmungsobjekt n
f objet m de perception
r объект m восприятия

6896 perception
d Perzeption f; Wahrnehmung f
f perception f
r перцепция f; восприятие n; ощущение n

6897 perfect
d perfekt; vollkommen
f parfait; idéal
r совершенный; полный

6898 perfect information
d vollständige Information f
f information f complète; information parfaite
r полная информация f

6899 perfect information game
d Spiel n mit vollständiger Information
f jeu m d'information parfaite
r игра f с полной информацией

6900 perforate v; **punch** v
d lochen; stanzen; perforieren
f perforer; poinçonner
r перфорировать; пробивать

6901 perforation
d Perforation f
f perforation f
r пробивка f отверстий

6902 performance
d Leistung f; Leistungsvermögen n
f performance f; productivité f
r производительность f

6903 performance chart; performance curve
d Arbeitsdiagramm n
f diagramme m de marche; courbe f de réponse
r рабочая диаграмма f

* **performance curve** → 6903

6904 period
d Periode f; Zeitraum m
f période f
r период m

* **periodic decimal fraction** → 1688

* **peripheral** → 6908

6905 peripheral
d peripher

f périphérique
r периферийный; внешний

6906 peripheral allocation table; peripheral assignment table; PAT
d periphere Zuordnungstafel f
f table f d'affectation des périphériques
r таблица f размещения периферийных устройств

* **peripheral assignment table** → 6906

6907 peripheral data transfer
d periphere Datenübertragung f
f transfert m périphérique de données
r периферийная передача f данных

6908 peripheral device; peripheral [unit]
d periphere Einheit f; Peripheriegerät n; Anschlussgerät n
f dispositif m périphérique; unité f périphérique; périphérique m
r периферийное устройство n; внешнее устройство

6909 peripheral interface adapter; PIA
d Peripherieschnittstellen-Anpassungsbaustein m; PIA-Schaltkreis m
f adaptateur m d'interface périphérique
r периферийный интерфейсный адаптер m; ПИА

6910 peripheral slot
d Steckplatz m für Peripheriebausteine
f jack m de raccordement extérieur
r гнездо n для внешних соединений

* **peripheral unit** → 6908

6911 periphery
d Peripherie f
f périphérie f
r периферия f

* **PERL** → 7188

* **PERL scripting language** → 7188

* **permanent** → 3864

6912 permanent data; fixed data
d permanente Daten pl
f données fpl permanentes; données fixes; données constantes
r постоянные данные pl; фиксированные данные

6913 permanent failure; stuck-at fault
d Dauerfehler m; permanenter Fehler m

f défaut *m* persistant; défaut permanent
r устойчивая неисправность *f*; устойчивая ошибка *f*

6914 permanent format
d Fixformat *n*; permanentes Format *n*
f format *m* permanent
r постоянный формат *m*

6915 permanent joint; fixed joint
d nichtlösbare Verbindung *f*
f jonction *f* fixe
r неразъёмное соединение *n*

* **permanent memory** → 7671

6916 permanent one
d Dauer-Eins *f*
f un *m* permanent; une *f* permanente
r постоянная единица *f*

* **permissibility** → 256

* **permissible solution** → 258

* **permissible value** → 259

6917 permission; allowance
d Erlaubnis *f*
f permission *f*
r разрешение *n*; позволение *n*

* **permittivity** → 2862

6918 permutation
d Permutation *f*
f permutation *f*
r перестановка *f*; пермутация *f*

6919 permutation code
d Permutationscode *m*
f code *m* de permutation
r перестановочный код *m*

* **perpendicular** *adj* → 6595

6920 persistence; persistency
d Stetigkeit *f*
f persistance *f*
r устойчивость *f*

6921 persistence; retention
(of a screen)
d Nachleuchtdauer *f*
f persistance *f*; traînage *m*; rémanence *f*
r послесвечение *n*

* **persistency** → 6920

* **persistent screen** → 271

6922 personal authorization
d personenbezogener Berechtigungsnachweis *m*; personenbezogene Berechtigung *f*
f autorisation *f* personnelle
r персональное разрешение *n* на доступ

6923 personal computer; PC
d persönlicher Rechner *m*; Personalcomputer *m*; PC
f ordinateur *m* personnel
r персональный компьютер *m*

6924 personal data
d personenbezogene Daten *pl*; Personendaten *pl*; Personeninformation *f*
f données *fpl* personnelles
r личные данные *pl*

* **personality card** → 4615

6925 personalizing
d Personifizierung *f*
f personnification *f*
r олицетворение *n*

* **PERT** → 7398

* **perturbation** → 6175

6926 perturbation coefficient
d Störungskoeffizient *m*
f coefficient *m* de perturbation
r коэффициент *m* возмущений

6927 petabyte; Pbyte; PB
d Petabyte *n*
f péta-octet *m*
r петабайт *m*

6928 Petri net
d Petri-Netz *n*
f réseau *m* de Petri
r сетка *f* Петри

* **P-flag** → 6810

* **PgDn key** → 6706

* **PgUp key** → 6733

6929 phantom
d Phantom *n*
f fantôme *m*
r фантом *m*

6930 phantom circuit
d Phantomleitung *f*; Phantomkreis *m*
f circuit *m* fantôme; circuit combiné
r фантомная цепь *f*; искусственная цепь

6931 phantom image; ghost [image]
  d Phantombild *n*; Geisterbild *n*; Nebenbild *n*
  f image *f* fantôme
  r фантомное изображение *n*

6932 phantom view
  d Phantomdarstellung *f*
  f vue *f* fantôme
  r фантомный вид *m*

6933 phase
  d Phase *f*
  f phase *f*
  r фаза *f*

6934 phase-encoded recording
  d phasencodierte Aufzeichnung *f*;
    Aufzeichnung mit Richtungstaktschrift
  f enregistrement *m* en modulation de phase
  r запись *f* с фазовым кодированием

  * **phaser** → **4066**

  * **phasing** → **4068**

  * **philoxenic** → **9727**

6935 phoneme
  d Phonem *n*
  f phonème *m*
  r фонема *f*

6936 phonemic analysis
  d phonemische Analyse *f*
  f analyse *f* phonémique
  r фонемический анализ *m*

  * **Phong rendering** → **6937**

6937 Phong shading; Phong rendering;
    normal-vector interpolation shading
    (Lambert or cosine shading plus smoothing
    and specularity of faceted surfaces)
  d Phong-Schattierung *f*; Phong-Rendering *n*
  f ombrage *m* de Phong; ombrage par
    interpolation de vecteurs de la normale
  r затенение *n* методом Фонга; рендеринг *m*
    Фонга

6938 Phong-shading processor
  d Phong-Schading-Prozessor *m*
  f processeur *m* d'ombrage de Phong
  r процессор *m* затенения методом Фонга

  * **phonic** → **114**

6939 phonocode
  d Phonocode *m*
  f phonocode *m*
  r фонокод *m*

  * **photo** → **6948**

6940 photo-CD; PCD
  d Foto-Kompaktdisk *f*; Foto-CD *f*
  f disque *m* optique photo
  r фото-компактдиск *m*

6941 photocomposition; phototypesetting
  d Fotosatz *m*; Lichtsatz *m*
  f photocomposition *f*
  r фотонабор *m*

6942 photocomposition system
  d Fotosatzsystem *n*; Lichtsatzsystem *n*
  f système *m* de photocomposition
  r фотонаборная система *f*

6943 photocopier
  d Fotokopierer *m*
  f photocopieur *m*; photocopieuse *f*
  r фотокопирующее устройство *n*

6944 photodiode
  d Fotodiode *f*
  f photodiode *f*
  r фотодиод *m*

  * **photoelectrical reader** → **6549**

  * **photoelectric reader** → **6549**

6945 photoelectric scanner
  d fotoelektrischer Abtaster *m*
  f scanneur *m* photoélectrique
  r фотоэлектрический сканер *m*

6946 photoelectric scanning
  d fotoelektrische Abtastung *f*
  f exploration *f* photoélectrique
  r фотоэлектрическое сканирование *n*

6947 photographic memory
  d fotografischer Speicher *m*
  f mémoire *f* photographique
  r фотографическая память *f*

6948 photo[graphy]
  d Foto *n*; Lichtbild *n*
  f photo[graphie] *f*
  r фотография *f*; фотосъёмка *f*; снимок *m*

6949 photography importing
  d Foto-Importieren *n*
  f importation *f* de photo[graphie]
  r импортирование *n* фотографии

6950 photolithographic mask; photomask;
    photo pattern
  d fotolithografische Maske *f*; Fotoschablone *f*

f masque *m* photolithographique;
photomasque *m*; modèle *m* photographique
r фотолитографическая маска *f*;
фотомаска *f*; фотошаблон *m*

* **photomask** → 6950

6951 photomasking
d Fotomaskierung *f*; Fotolithografie *f*
f photomasquage *m*; photolithographie *f*
r фотолитография *f*

6952 photonumeric
d fotonumerisch
f photonumérique
r фотоцифровой

* **photo pattern** → 6950

6953 photoplotter; graphics film recorder; film recorder; video hard copy unit
d Fotoplotter *m*
f phototraceur *m*; système *m* de phototraçage
r фотоплоттер *m*; фотопостроитель *m*

6954 photorealistic
d fotorealistisch
f photoréaliste
r фотореалистический

* **photorealistic render** → 6955

6955 photorealistic render[ing]
d fotorealistisches Rendering *n*
f rendu *m* photoréaliste
r фотореалистическое тонирование *n*; фотореалистический рендеринг *m*

6956 photorealistic representation
d fotorealistische Darstellung *f*
f représentation *f* photoréaliste
r фотореалистическое представление *n*

6957 photorealistic texture
d fotorealistische Textur *f*
f texture *f* photoréaliste
r фотореалистическая текстура *f*

6958 photoscanner
d Fotoscanner *m*
f scanner *m* d'images photo; photoscanner *m*
r фото-сканер *m*

6959 photosensing mark
d optisch lesbare Markierung *f*; Fotofühlmarke *f*
f marque *f* photosensible
r метка *f* для оптического считывания

6960 photosensor

d Fotosensor *m*
f capteur *m* photoélectrique
r фотодатчик *m*

6961 photos scrapbook
d Fotoskizzenbuch *n*
f classeur *m* de photos
r буферный файл *m* фотографий

6962 phototypesetter; image setter
d Fotosatzmaschine *f*
f photocomposeuse *f*
r фотонаборная машина *f*

* **phototypesetting** → 6941

6963 phrase
d Phrase *f*
f phrase *f*
r фраза *f*; словосочетание *n*

6964 phrase structure grammar; transformational grammar
d Satzstrukturgrammatik *f*; Transformationsgrammatik *f*
f grammaire *f* de composants immédiats; grammaire transformationnelle
r трансформационная грамматика *f*

* **physical address** → 16

6965 physical channel
d physischer Kanal *m*
f canal *m* physique
r физический канал *m*

6966 physical interface
d physische Schnittstelle *f*
f interface *f* physique
r физический интерфейс *m*

6967 physical layer
d Bitübertragungsschicht *f*
f couche *f* physique
r физический уровень *m*

6968 physical memory; physical storage; real memory; real storage
d Realspeicher *m*
f mémoire *f* physique
r физическая память *f*; имеющаяся память

6969 physical protocol
d Bitübertragungsprotokoll *n*
f protocole *m* physique
r протокол *m* физического слоя

6970 physical record
d physischer Satz *m*

f enregistrement *m* physique
r физическая запись *f*

* **physical storage** → 6968

* **PIA** → 6909

6971 **pica**
    (1/6 inch or 1/72 foot)
    d Pica
    f pica
    r пика

6972 **pick** *v*
    d auswählen
    f désigner
    r отбирать; выбирать

6973 **pickbox; selection box**
    d Auswahlkasten *m*; Auswahlfeld *n*
    f boîte *f* de sélection; boîte de désignation
    r ящик *m* отбора

6974 **pick button**
    d Auswahl-Schaltfläche *f*
    f bouton *m* de désignation; bouton sélecteur
    r кнопка *f* выбора; бутон *m* выбора

6975 **pick device; picker**
    d Abzugvorrichtung *f*; Picker *m*
    f dispositif *m* de désignation; dispositif
       d'identification
    r устройство *n* указания; подборщик *m*

* **picker** → 6975

6976 **picking**
    (the elements on the screen)
    d Identifizierung *f*
    f désignation *f*
    r указание *n*; отбор *m*; подбор *m*

* **pickup** → 8381

6977 **picoprocessor**
    d Picoprozessor *m*
    f picoprocesseur *m*
    r пикопроцессор *m*

6978 **picoprogramming**
    d Picoprogrammierung *f*
    f picoprogrammation *f*
    r пикопрограммирование *n*

6979 **picosecond**
    d Pikosekunde *f*
    f picoseconde *f*
    r пикосекунда *f*

* **pictogram** → 4603

* **pictogram representation** → 4608

6980 **pictorial; pictoric; iconographic;**
    illustrational; illustrative; illustratory
    d piktografisch; bildlich; bildhaft; malerisch
    f pictural
    r наглядный; изобразительный;
       иллюстрированный

6981 **pictorial representation**
    d bildliche Darstellung *f*
    f représentation *f* picturale
    r картинное представление *n*

* **pictoric** → 6980

* **picture** → 4645

6982 **picture box**
    d Bildkasten *m*
    f zone *f* d'image
    r ящик *m* изображения

* **picture catalog** → 1490

* **picture cell** → 7015

* **picture coding** → 4647

* **picture communication** → 9909

* **picture dot** → 7015

* **picture editor** → 4652

* **picture element** → 7015

* **picture format** → 4656

6983 **picture frequency**
    d Bild[wechsel]frequenz *f*;
       Bildergeschwindigkeit *f*
    f fréquence *f* d'images; cadence *f* d'images
    r частота *f* смены изображений

* **picture generation** → 4659

* **picture processing** → 4668

* **picture quality** → 4671

* **picture remote transfer** → 4678

6984 **picture scanning; image scanning**
    d Bildabtastung *f*; Bildscannen *n*
    f exploration *f* d'image; balayage *m* d'image;
       échantillonnage *m* d'image
    r сканирование *n* изображения

6985 **picture scanning method; image scanning
method**
  d Bildabtastungsmethode *f*
  f méthode *f* d'exploration d'images
  r метод *m* сканирования изображений

  *   **picture setting** → **6986**

6986 **picture setup; picture setting**
  d Bildaufbau *m*
  f établissement *m* d'image
  r установка *f* изображения

  *   **picture slip** → **4061**

6987 **picture symbol**
  d Abbildungssymbol *n*
  f symbole *m* d'image
  r символ *m* изображения

  *   **picture transfer** → **4678**

  *   **piece *v* together** → **6851**

  *   **PIF** → **6714**

  *   **piggyback** → **6988**

6988 **piggyback [card]**
  d Schaltkreis *m* in Huckepack-Montage
  f plaque *f* en montage à califourchon;
      carte-fille *f*
  r плата *f* с микросхемами, установленными
      в контактных панелях

6989 **piggyback memory**
  d Piggyback-Speicher *m*
  f mémoire *f* à accès partagé en réception et en
      émission
  r память *f* правых и обратных пакетов
      [сообщений]

6990 **piggyback socket**
  d Huckepack-Soskel *m*; Fassung *f* auf
      Schaltkreisgehäuse
  f socle *m* à califourchon
  r контактная панель *f* для установки
      микросхем

6991 **piling-up**
  d Aufeinandertürmen *n* der Zeichen
  f empilement *m* de signes; heurt *m* de signes
  r набегание *n* знаков при печатании

6992 **pilot *v***
  d vorsteuern
  f piloter
  r управлять

6993 **pilot carrier**
  d Pilotträger *m*
  f porteuse-pilote *f*
  r контрольная несущая частота *f*

6994 **pilot code**
  d Vorcode *m*
  f code *m* pilote
  r контрольный код *m*

6995 **pilot receiver**
  d Pilotempfänger *m*
  f récepteur *m* pilote
  r контрольный приёмник *m*

6996 **pilot run**
  d Piloteinsatz *m*; Ersteinsatz *m*
  f application *f* pilote
  r опытное применение *n*

6997 **pilot signal**
  d Schlüsselzeichen *n*
  f signal *m* pilote
  r контрольный сигнал *m*

6998 **pin**
  d Pin *m*; Stift *m*
  f fiche *f*; cheville *f*; broche *f*; patte *f*; picot *m*
  r [контактный] вывод *m*; штифт *m*;
      штырёк *m*; шип *m*

  *   **pinch roller** → **1697**

6999 **pin compatibility**
  d Pinkompatibilität *f*
  f compatibilité *f* par broches
  r совместимость *f* по выводам

7000 **pin connect**
  d Pinanschluss *m*
  f connexion *f* à broches
  r штекерное соединение *n*

7001 **pin count**
  d Anschlussstiftzahl *f*
  f nombre *m* de broches
  r число *n* выводов

7002 **pin-feed paper**
  d Papier *n* mit Führungslochrand
  f papier *m* à perforation pour transport
  r бумага *f* с ведущими отверстиями

  *   **PING** → **6678**

7003 **pinhole**
  d Pinloch *n*
  f trou *m* de pointe
  r точечное отверстие *n*

7004 pin jack; jack; hub; bush; female connector
- *d* Klinke *f*; Steck[er]buchse *f*; Buchse *f*; Fassung *f*
- *f* cliquet *m*; jack *m* de broche; nid *m*; douille *f* [à contact]; alvéole *m*
- *r* [контактное] гнездо *n*; [штепсельная] розетка *f*; фишка *f*

7005 pinout
- *d* Pinausgang *m*; Anschlussstiftausgang *m*
- *f* broche *f* de microcircuit; sortie *f* de fiches
- *r* наружный вывод *m* [микросхемы]; штекерный вывод; штырьковый вывод

*   **PIO → 6781**

7006 pipeline
- *d* Pipeline *f*; Fließband *n*
- *f* pipeline *m*; chaîne *f*; conveyor *m*
- *r* конвейер *m*

7007 pipeline chip
- *d* Pipelinechip *m*
- *f* puce *f* de pipeline
- *r* кристалл *m* конвейерного процессора

7008 pipeline[d] processor
- *d* Pipelineprozessor *m*
- *f* processeur *m* pipeline
- *r* процессор *m* конвейерной обработки; конвейерный процессор

7009 pipeline processing; pipelining
- *d* Pipelineverarbeitung *f*; Fließbandarbeitsweise *f*; Fließbandarbeit *f*; Befehlsverknüpfung *f*
- *f* traitement *m* pipeline; pipelinage *m*
- *r* конвейерная обработка *f*; конвейеризация *f*

*   **pipeline processor → 7008**

*   **pipelining → 7009**

*   **pitch → 8241**

7010 pitch
- *d* Ganghöhe *f*; Gang *m*; Stufe *f*
- *f* pas *m* [polaire]; entraxe *m*
- *r* шаг *m*; ход *m*

*   **pivot → 7012**

7011 pivot
- *d* Pivot *n*
- *f* pivot *m*
- *r* поворот *m*

7012 pivot[al]
- *d* Pivot-

- *f* pivotant
- *r* ведущий; направляющий

7013 pivotal column
- *d* Pivotspalte *f*
- *f* colonne-pivot *f*
- *r* направляющий столбец *m*

7014 pivoting window; single-action window
- *d* Pivotfenster *n*; Fenster *n* mit einfacher Bewegung
- *f* fenêtre *f* pivotante
- *r* направляющее окно *n*

7015 pixel; picture element; pel; picture cell; image dot; picture dot
- *d* Pixel *n*; Bildpunkt *m*; Bildelement *n*
- *f* pixel *m*; élément *m* pictural; élément d'image
- *r* пиксел *m*; элемент *m* изображения

7016 pixel address; pixel position
- *d* Pixel-Adresse *f*; Pixelposition *f*
- *f* adresse *f* de pixel; position *f* de pixel
- *r* адрес *m* пиксела

*   **pixel arithmetic → 7017**

7017 pixel arithmetic[s]
- *d* Pixel-Arithmetik *f*
- *f* arithmétique *f* de pixel
- *r* пиксельная арифметика *f*

7018 pixel block
- *d* Pixel-Block *m*
- *f* trame *f* de pixels
- *r* блок *m* пикселов

7019 pixel bus
- *d* Bildelementübertragungsbus *m*; Pixel-Bus *m*
- *f* bus *m* de pixel
- *r* шина *f* передачи элементов изображения

7020 pixel-by-pixel panning
- *d* bildpunktweises Verschieben *n*
- *f* faisant *m* panoramique
- *r* поэлементная прокрутка *f*; прокрутка пиксел за пикселом

7021 pixel cache
- *d* Pixel-Cache *m*
- *f* cache *f* de pixels
- *r* кэш-память *f* пикселов

7022 pixel caching
- *d* Pixel-Schreiben *n* im Cache
- *f* mise *f* en cache de pixels
- *r* кэширование *n* пикселов

*   **pixel clock → 7026**

7023 **pixel color**
d Pixel-Farbe *f*
f couleur *f* de pixel
r цвет *m* пиксела

7024 **pixel color values**
d Farbwerte *mpl* eines Pixels
f valeurs *fpl* des couleurs de pixel
r коды *mpl* цветов пиксела

* **pixel depth** → 1870

7025 **pixel engine**
d Pixel-Maschine *f*
f moteur *m* pixel
r пиксельная машина *f*

7026 **pixel frequency; pixel clock**
(number of pixels drawn per second in MHz)
d Pixelfrequenz *f*; Pixeluhr *f*
f fréquence *f* de pixels
r частота *f* пикселов

* **pixel graphics** → 7623

7027 **pixel intensity**
d Pixel-Intensität *f*
f intensité *f* de pixel
r интенситет *m* пиксела

7028 **pixel interpolator**
d Pixel-Interpolator *m*
f interpolateur *m* de pixels
r интерполятор *m* пикселов

7029 **pixelization; space quantization**
d Bildpunktverarbeitung *f*
f pixélisation *f*
r разбиение *n* на пикселы; пространственное
квантование *n* [изображения];
разложение *n* изображения на
(минимальные) элементы; пикселизация *f*

7030 **pixel matrix**
d Pixelmatrix *f*
f matrice *f* de pixels
r пиксельная матрица *f*

7031 **pixel node**
d Pixel-Knoten *m*
f nœud *m* de pixel
r узел *m* пиксела

7032 **pixel pattern**
d Pixelmuster *n*
f modèle de pixel
r шаблон *m* пиксела; образец *m* пиксела;
модель *f* пиксела

7033 **pixel-phasing**

d Pixel-Phasing *n*
f phasage *m* de pixels
r фазировка *f* пикселов; фазирование *n*
пикселов

7034 **pixel plane**
d Pixel-Ebene *f*
f plan *m* de pixel
r плоскость *f* пиксела

* **pixel position** → 7016

7035 **pixel processor**
d Pixel-Prozessor *m*; Grafikprozessor *m*
f processeur *m* de pixels
r процессор *m* элементов изображения

7036 **pixel processor pipeline**
d Pixel-Prozessor-Pipeline *f*
f pipeline *m* de processeur de pixels
r конвейер *m* процессора обработки
пикселов

7037 **pixel rendering**
d Pixel-Rendering *n*
f rendu *m* pixel
r пиксельное тонирование *n*; пиксельный
рендеринг *m*

7038 **pixel resolution**
d Pixel-Auflösungsvermögen *n*
f résolution *f* de pixel; nombre *m* de pixels
r пиксельная разрешающая способность *f*

7039 **pixel set**
d Pixelmenge *f*
f ensemble *m* de pixels
r множество *n* пикселов

* **pixel shading** → 3053

7040 **pixels per inch; PPI**
d Pixels *npl* pro Zoll
f pixels *mpl* par pouce
r пикселы *mpl* на дюйм

7041 **pixel value**
d Pixelwert *m*
f valeur *f* de pixel
r значение *n* пиксела

* **PLA** → 7407

* **place** → 6575

7042 **place; point**
d Platz *m*; Stelle *f*; Ort *m*
f place *f*; endroit *m*
r пункт *m*; место *n*

7043 placeholder
d Stellenhalter *m*; Platzhalter *m*
f zéro *m* structurel; zéro teneur de place
r структурный нуль *m*

* **placement** → **5446**

7044 plain-copy correction
d Klarschriftkorrektur *f*
f correction *f* de copie en clair
r корректура *f* открытой копии

7045 plain-copy log
d Klarschriftprotokoll *n*
f protocole *m* de copie en clair
r протокол *m* открытого копия

7046 plain text
d Klarschrift *f*; Klartext *m*
f texte *m* plan; texte en clair; texte en format ASCII
r незашифрованный текст *m*; гладкий текст; открытый текст; простой текст

* **planar patch** → **3149**

7047 plane
d Ebene *f*
f plan *m*
r плоскость *f*

* **planner** → **8221**

7048 plasma display
d Plasmadisplay *n*; Plasmabildschirm *m*
f afficheur *m* à plasma; écran *m* à plasma
r плазменный экран *m*

* **plastic foil keyboard** → **5718**

* **plate** → **1090**

7049 plate
d Platine *f*
f platine *f*; plat *m*
r пластина *f*; пластинка *f*

7050 platen
d Schreibwalze *f*
f cylindre *m* [porte-cliché]; rouleau *m*
r валик *m* [печатающего устройства]; печатающий валик

7051 platform
d Plattform *f*
f plate[-]forme *f*
r платформа *f*

* **plating** → **1796**

* **platter** → **4393**

7052 plausibility check; reasonableness check
d Plausibilitätskontrolle *f*; Plausibilitätsprüfung *f*
f contrôle *m* de vraisemblance
r проверка *f* [данных] на достоверность

7053 play; party
d Spiel *n*; Partie *f*
f jeu *m*; partie *f*
r игра *f*; партия *f*

7054 playback
d Playback *n*; Wiedergabe *f*
f reproduction *f*; play-back *m*
r воспроизведение *n*; проигрывание *n*

* **plot** → **1641, 7065**

7055 plot *v*
d plotten; grafisch darstellen; maschinell zeichnen; mit einem Kurvenschreiber aufzeichnen
f tracer
r представлять графически; чертить; вычерчивать; строить

7056 plot file; drawing file
d Zeichnungsdatei *f*
f fichier *m* de trace; fichier de dessin
r файл *m* чертежа; чертёжный файл

7057 plot layout
d Plotter-Layout *n*
f maquette *f* de traçage
r макет *m* вычерчивания

7058 plot orientation
d Plottern-Orientierung *f*
f orientation *f* de traçage
r ориентация *f* вычерчивания

* **plot program** → **7066**

7059 plot spooling
d Plottern-Spulung *f*; Plottern-Spulen *n*
f spoulage *m* de traçage
r спулинг *m* черчения; буферизированный выход *m* на графопостроитель

7060 plotter
d Plotter *m*; Kurvenschreiber *m*
f traceur *m* [de courbes]; traceur graphique
r графопостроитель *m*

7061 plotter configuration
d Plotterkonfiguration *f*
f configuration *f* de traceur
r конфигурация *f* графопостроителя

7062 **plotter manager**
d Plotter-Manager *m*
f gestionnaire *m* de traçage
r менажер *m* графопостроителя

7063 **plotter name**
d Plottername *m*
f nom *m* de traceur
r имя *n* графопостроителя

7064 **plotter speed**
d Plotter-Geschwindigkeit *f*
f vitesse *f* de traceur
r скорость *f* графопостроителя

7065 **plot[ting]**
d Plottern *n*; maschinelles Zeichnen *n*;
Ausdruck *m* des Kurvenschreibers
f traçage *m*; tracement *m*
r машинное нанесение *n*; [машинное]
вычерчивание *n*; вывод *m* на
графопостроитель

7066 **plot[ting] program**
d Plotternprogramm *n*
f programme *m* de traçage; programme de
tracement
r программа *f* машинного вычерчивания

7067 **plug; patchtip**
d Stecker *m*; Steckkontakt *m*; Stöpsel *m*
f connecteur *m*; fiche *f*; prise *f* mâle
r штепсель *m*; разъём *m*; штекер *m*;
контактный штырёк *m*

* **plug-and-go** *adj* → 7069

7068 **plug *v* and play *v*; plug *v* & play *v***
d einstecken und einschalten;
einstecken&einschalten; anschließen und
benutzen
f branchez et ça marchez
r подключай и работай

7069 **plug-and-play; plugplay; plug-and-go** *adj*
d Plug-and-Play-
f immédiatement utilisable; prêt à tourner; prêt
à l'emploi
r готовый к [немедленному] применению

* **plug compatibility** → 7077

7070 **plug connection; in-cut connection**
d Steckverbindung *f*; Steckvorrichtung *f*
f connexion *f* à fiches
r штепсельное соединение *n*

* **plug connector** → 3283

7071 **plug-ended cord**

d Schnurstecker *m*
f corde *f* à fiche; corde à connecteur
r шнур *m* с штепселем; шнур с разъёмом

7072 **pluggable; plug-in; plug-type; removable**
d austauschbar; steckbar
f enfichable; changeable; remplaçable; à fiches
r сменный; съёмный; вставной

7073 **plugging chart**
d Steckschema *n*; Schalttafeldiagramm *n*;
Steckplan *m*
f schéma *m* des fiches
r схема *f* коммутаций; коммутационная
диаграмма *f*

7074 **plugging list**
d Steckliste *f*
f liste *f* des connexions; liste des fiches
r список *m* разъёмных соединений

* **plug-in** → 7072

7075 **plug-in board; plug-in card; plug-in
circuitry**
d steckbare Leiterplatte *f*; Steckeinheit *f*;
steckbare Schaltungskarte *f*;
Einsteckleiterplatte *f*
f plaque *f* enfichable; carte *f* enfichable
r сменная плата *f* [с разъёмом]; съёмная
плата

7076 **plug-in cabling**
d Steckkabeltechnik *f*; Einschubverkabelung *f*
f câblage *m* à fiches
r техника *f* разводки кабелей

* **plug-in card** → 7075

* **plug-in circuitry** → 7075

* **plug-in module** → 176

* **plug *v* & play *v*** → 7068

* **plugplay** → 7069

7077 **plug[-to-plug] compatibility**
d Steckerkompatibilität *f*; Steckverträglichkeit *f*
f compatibilité *f* par connecteur; compatibilité
de fiches
r совместимость *f* по разъёму;
совместимость на уровне разъёмов

* **plug-type** → 7072

* **plus** → 181

* **plus sign** → 181

* pocket computer → 6743

7078 pocket size
  d Taschenformat n
  f taille f de poche
  r карманный размер m

* pocket sorting → 7586

* point → 7042

* point v → 3109

7079 point
  (a sign)
  d Punkt m
  f point m
  r точка f

7080 point v
  d indizieren
  f montrer; indiquer
  r указать; направлять

7081 point contact
  d Spitzenkontakt m
  f contact m de point
  r точечный контакт m

7082 pointer
  d Zeiger m; Hinweis m; Pointer m
  f pointeur m; aiguille f
  r указатель m

* pointer stack register → 8811

7083 pointer variable
  d Zeigervariable f
  f variable f d'indicateur
  r переменная f типа указателя

* point of light → 5364

7084 point of presence; PoP
  (used in the context of telecommunications
  between companies and ISPs)
  d Anschlusspunkt m eines Dienstanbieters im
  Nahbereich; Gegenwartsort m;
  Anwesenheitsstelle f
  f point m de connexion
  r точка f присутствия

7085 point-to-multipoint communication
  d Punkt-zu-Mehrpunkt-Verbindung f
  f communication f point à multipoint
  r связь f точки с множеством точек

* point-to-point circuit → 7086

7086 point-to-point communication;

point-to-point link; point-to-point circuit
  d Punkt-[zu-Punkt-]Verbindung f
  f liaison f point à point; connexion f de sections
  r прямая связь f между [двумя] точками;
  двухточечная связь

7087 point-to-point communication channel
  d Standleitungsübertragungskanal m
  f voie f de transmission entre deux points
  r двухточечный канал m связи

* point-to-point link → 7086

* point-to-point protocol → 7088

7088 point-to-point [serial line] protocol;
  peer-to-peer protocol; PPP
  d Punkt-zu-Punkt-Protokoll n
  f protocole m point à point; protocole PPP
  r протокол m точка-точка

7089 poke v
  d stoßen; stecken; stöbern
  f écrire en mémoire vive
  r засовывать; записывать в память

* Polish notation → 7209

* poll → 7093

7090 poll v; interrogate v
  d [zyklisch] abfragen; [zyklisch] abrufen;
  ausgewählt abfragen
  f interroger; sonder
  r опрашивать; запрашивать

7091 polled circuit operation; polling circuit
  operation
  d Leitungsabrufbetrieb m
  f opération f d'interrogation de ligne; opération
  de sondage de circuit
  r операция f опроса линии

7092 polled environment
  d auswählend abzufragende Systemumgebung f
  f environnement m interrogeant
  r опрашиваемое оборудование n

7093 poll[ing]
  d [zyklische] Abfrage f; [zyklisches]
  Abrufen n; Sendeaufruf m; Sendeabruf m
  f appel m [sélectif]; invitation f à émettre;
  interrogation f
  r [упорядоченный] опрос m; запрос m;
  вызов m

7094 polling character
  d Sendeabrufzeichen n; Abrufzeichen n
  f caractère m d'invitation [à émettre]
  r символ m опроса

* **polling circuit operation** → 7091

* **polling interrupt** → 7095

7095 polling interrupt[ion]
 d Abrufunterbrechung *f*;
 Anforderungsunterbrechung *f*;
 Abfrageunterbrechung *f*
 f interruption *f* d'interrogation; interruption par
 appel
 r прерывание *n* по вызову

7096 polling interval
 d Abfrageintervall *n*; Abrufintervall *n*
 f intervalle *m* entre requêtes; intervalle
 d'interrogation
 r интервал *m* опроса; интервал запроса

7097 polling list
 d Aufrufliste *f*
 f liste *f* d'interrogations
 r список *m* запросов; список опросов

7098 polling method
 (of a channel)
 d Aufrufverfahren *n*
 f méthode *f* d'interrogation
 r метод *m* опроса

7099 polling mode; inquiry mode
 d Abrufbetrieb *m*; Abfragemodus *m*
 f mode *m* d'interrogation
 r режим *m* опроса; режим вызова; режим
 запроса

7100 polling multiple access
 d Mehrfachzugriff *m* durch Abfrage;
 Mehrfachzugriff durch Sendeaufruf
 f accès *m* multiple par interrogation [préalable]
 r коллективный доступ *m* опросом

7101 polling phase
 d Abrufphase *f*
 f phase *f* d'interrogation
 r фаза *f* опроса; фаза вызова

7102 polling signal
 d Abrufsignal *n*
 f signal *m* d'interrogation
 r опрашивающий сигнал *m*; сигнал опроса

7103 polymorphism
 d Polymorphismus *m*
 f polymorphisme *m*
 r полиморфизм *m*

7104 polynomial; multinomial *adj*
 d polynomisch; multinomial
 f polynomial; multinomial
 r полиномиальный; мультиномиальный

7105 polynomial code
 d polynomischer Code *m*
 f code *m* polynôme
 r полиномиальный код *m*

7106 polynomial time algorithm
 d Polynomialzeitalgorithmus *m*; Algorithmus *m*
 mit polynomiellem Zeitaufwand
 f algorithme *m* à temps polynomial
 r полиномиальный алгоритм *m*

* **pool** → 1230

7107 pool
 d Pool *m*; Ansammlung *f*
 f pool *m*
 r пул *m*; накопитель *m*

* **pooled data** → 278

7108 pooling
 d Sammelbetrieb *m*; Gemeinschaftsbetrieb *m*;
 Zusammenfassen *n*
 f mise *f* en pool; réunion *f*
 r буферизация *f*; организация *f* пула

7109 pooling of data; data pooling
 d Zusammenfassen *n* von Daten;
 Datengruppierung *f*; Gesamtheit *f* an Daten;
 Datenverbund *m*
 f réunion *f* de données
 r объединение *n* данных; группировка *f*
 данных

* **pool memory** → 1230

* **PoP** → 7084

* **POP** → 7166

7110 pop
 d Auskellern *n*; Entkellern *n*
 f dépilage *m*; dépilement *m*
 r извлечение *n*; выталкивание *n*

7111 pop instruction; pull instruction
 d Kellerdatenholbefehl *m*;
 Auskellerungsbefehl *m*
 f instruction *f* de sortie de pile
 r инструкция *f* извлечения из стека

7112 populated board; chip card
 d Leiterplatte *f* mit integrierten Schaltkreisen;
 Chipkarte *f*
 f plaque *f* de circuits intégrés; carte à puce
 r плата *f* с интегральными схемами

7113 populated database
 d geladene Datenbasis *f*; besetzte Datenbasis

f base *f* de données remplie
r наполненная база *f* данных

7114 population
d Population *f*; Gesamtheit *f*
f population *f*
r популяция *f*; совокупность *f*; заполнение *n* [файла]

7115 population statistics
d Populationsstatistik *f*
f statistique *f* de populations
r статистика *f* популяций

7116 popup
d Popup-
f relevant
r всплывающий

7117 pop *v* up
d hervorholen
f relever; surgir
r доставать; извлекать

7118 popup button
d Popup-Taste *f*
f bouton *m* flash; bouton relevant
r всплывающая кнопка *f*

7119 popup help
d Popup-Hilfe *f*
f aide *f* relevante
r всплывающая помощная информация *f*

7120 popup menu
d Popup-Menü *n*; Auftauch-Menü *n*
f menu *m* relevant; menu à liste directe; menu superposable; menu en incrustation
r всплывающее меню *n*

7121 popup palette
d Popup-Palette *f*
f palette *f* relevante
r всплывающая палитра *f*

7122 popup program
d Popup-Programm *n*
f programme *m* résidant en mode fenêtre
r всплывающая программа *f*

7123 popup slider
d Popup-Schieber *m*
f règle *f* en incrustation
r всплывающий ползунок *m*

7124 popup window
d Aufspringfenster *n*
f fenêtre *f* à liste directe; fenêtre flash; fenêtre en incrustation
r всплывающее окно *n*

7125 port
d Anschluss *m*; Anschlussstelle *f*
f port *m*
r порт *m*; место *n* подключения

7126 port
(in Internet)
d Port *m*; Pforte *f*; Tor *n*
f porte *f*; point *m* d'accès; accès *m*
r порт *m*

7127 portability; transportability; relocatability; mobility
d Portabilität *f*; Transportierbarkeit *f*; Übertragbarkeit *f*; Verschieblichkeit *f*
f portabilité *f*; transportabilité *f*; relogeabilité *f*; mobilité *f*
r переносимость *f*; перемещаемость *f*; мобильность *f*

7128 portable
d tragbar
f portatif
r портативный

7129 portable; transportable; relocatable; mobile
d übertragbar; portierbar; verschiebbar; versetzbar; mobil
f portable; relogeable; translatable; déplaçable; transportable; mobile
r переносной; переносимый; перемещаемый; мобильный

7130 portable code
d portierbarer Code *m*
f code *m* mobile
r мобильный код *m*

7131 portable computer; laptop [computer]
d tragbarer Rechner *m*; Laptop-Computer *m*
f ordinateur *m* portatif; ordinateur portable; ordinateur laptop
r портативный компьютер *m*; дорожный компьютер

7132 portable database system
d portierbares Datenbasissystem *n*
f système *m* portable de base de données
r мобильная система *f* баз данных

7133 portable document format; PDF
(of Acrobat reader)
d PDF-Format *n*
f format *m* de documents portatifs; format *m* PDF
r формат *m* переносимых документов; формат PDF

7134 portable office; office on the go
d tragbares Büro *n*; portables Büro

f bureau *m* portatif; bureau portable
r мобильный офис *m*

7135 portable program; relocatable program
d tragbares Programm *n*; verschiebbares Programm
f programme *m* portable; programme réallocable; programme translatable; programme relogeable
r перемещаемая программа *f*

* **portable scanner** → 4383

* **port address** → 7139

* **portal** → 5060

* **portal page** → 5060

* **portal site** → 5060

7136 portation
d Portierung *f*
f portage *m*
r перенос *m*

* **portion** → 6819

7137 port-mapped input/output
d portzugeordnete Ein-/Ausgabe *f*
f entrée/sortie *f* avec répartition entre des ports
r ввод/вывод *m* с распределением по портам

7138 portmapper
d Portspiegel *m*
f miroir *m* de ports
r зеркало *n* портов

7139 port number; port address
d Einlassnummer *f*
f adresse *f* de port
r номер *m* порта

7140 portrait display
d Hochformat-Display *n*; Hochformatbildschirm *m*
f écran *m* de portrait
r дисплей *m* с изображением, вытянутым по вертикали

* **portrait format** → 7141

* **portrait layout** → 7141

* **portrait orientation** → 7141

7141 portrait [paper] orientation; portrait format; portrait layout; vertical format; upright format
d Hochformat-Orientierung *f*

f orientation *f* [de papier] portrait; orientation verticale; format *m* vertical; présentation *f* à verticale; présentation à la française
r ориентация *f* вдоль страницы

7142 port selection
d Port-Auswahl *f*; Tor-Auswahl *f*
f sélection *f* de porte
r выбор *m* порта

7143 port-to-port protocol
d Port-Zu-Port-Protokoll *n*
f protocole *m* port à port
r протокол *m* межпортового обмена информацией

* **position** → 6575

7144 position; item
d Position *f*; Lage *f*
f position *f*
r позиция *f*; положение *n*

7145 position[al] code
d Stellencode *m*; Positionscode *m*
f code *m* pondéré; code positionnel
r позиционный код *m*

7146 position[al] key
d Positionsschlüssel *m*
f clé *f* positionnelle
r позиционный ключ *m*

* **positional notation** → 7147

7147 positional number system; positional notation; radix number system
d Positionssystem *n*; Stellen[wert]system *n*
f système *m* pondéré; système de numération de position
r позиционная система *f* счисления

* **position code** → 7145

7148 positioned text
d positionierter Text *m*
f texte *m* positionné
r позиционированный текст *m*

7149 position encoder
d Positionscodierer *m*; Stellungscodierer *m*
f codeur *m* de position
r шифратор *m* положения

7150 positioning; location
d Positionierung *f*; Positionieren *n*
f positionnement *m*
r позиционирование *n*

* **position key** → 7146

* positive delivery notification → 2156

* positive disabling signal → 7154

7151 positive flag
   d Gutkennung *f*; Gutkennzeichen *n*
   f flag *m* positif
   r положительный флаг *m*

7152 positive-going edge
      (of a pulse)
   d positive Flanke *f*
   f front *m* positif
   r положительный фронт *m*

7153 positive-going pulse
   d positiver Impuls *m*
   f impulsion *f* positive
   r положительный импульс *m*

7154 positive inhibiting signal; positive disabling
      signal
   d positives Sperrsignal *n*
   f signal *m* d'inhibition positif
   r положительный сигнал *m* запрета

7155 positive jump
   d Sprung *m* bei Plus
   f saut *m* positif; saut sur le plus
   r переход *m* по плюсу

* positive justification → 7157

* positive/negative justification → 7156

7156 positive/negative [pulse] stuffing;
      positive/negative justification
   d Positiv-Negativ-Stopfen *n*
   f justification *f* positive-négative
   r положительно-отрицательное импульсное
      выравнивание *n*

* positive/negative stuffing → 7156

7157 positive [pulse] stuffing; positive
      justification
   d Positivstopfen *n*; positives Stopfen *n*
   f justification *f* positive
   r положительное выравнивание *n*

* positive stuffing → 7157

* postedit → 7158

7158 postedit[ing]
   d Nacheditieren *n*
   f édition *f* postérieure
   r постредактирование *n*; заключительное
      редактирование *n*

7159 postfix notation; inverse Polish notation
   d Postfixnotation *f*; inverse polnische
      Schreibweise *f*
   f notation *f* postfixée; notation suffixée;
      notation polonaise inverse
   r постфиксная запись *f*; обратная польская
      запись

7160 postindexing
   d Nachindizierung *f*
   f postindexage *m*
   r постиндексация *f*

* posting → 5592

7161 posting
   d Buchen *n*
   f passation *f*
   r регистрация *f*; запись *f* [единицы
      информации]

7162 postmaster
   d Postmeister *m*
   f maître *m* de poste; postier *m*; chef *m* de poste
   r ответственный *m* за почту; почтмейстер *m*

* post-mortem → 7163

7163 post-mortem [program]
   d Post-mortem-Programm *n*
   f programme *m* post-mortem
   r программа *f* постоперационного контроля;
      программа пост-мортем

* postmultiplication → 7164

7164 postmultiplying; postmultiplication
   d Multiplikation *f* von rechts
   f multiplication *f* à droite
   r умножение *n* справа

7165 postnormalization
   d Nachnormalisierung *f*
   f normalisation *f* subséquente
   r последующая нормализация *f*;
      нормализация результата

7166 post office protocol; POP
   d Postamtsprotokoll *n*
   f protocole *m* POP; protocole postal
   r протокол *m* отделения связи; почтовый
      протокол; протокол POP

7167 post office server
   d Postamtsserver *m*
   f serveur *m* de messagerie; serveur de bureau
      postal
   r сервер *m* отделения связи; почтовый
      сервер

7168 postprocessing
- *d* Nachverarbeitung *f*
- *f* traitement *m* final
- *r* окончательная обработка *f*

7169 postprocessor; backend processor
- *d* Postprozessor *m*; Back-End-Prozessor *m*
- *f* postprocesseur *m*
- *r* постпроцессор *m*

7170 post-run output
- *d* Ausgabe *f* nach Anschluss eines Programmlaufs
- *f* sortie *f* de résultats d'exécution
- *r* вывод *m* результатов прогона

* **PostScript → 7177**

7171 PostScript file
- *d* PostScript-Datei *f*
- *f* fichier *m* PostScript
- *r* Postscript файл *m*

* **PostScript fill → 7172**

7172 PostScript fill[ing]
- *d* PostScript-Füllung *f*
- *f* remplissage *m* de texture PostScript
- *r* заполнение *n* с PostScript-текстурой

7173 PostScript fill pattern
- *d* PostScript-Füllmuster *n*
- *f* motif *m* de remplissage PostScript
- *r* PostScript-шаблон *m* закраски

7174 PostScript font
- *d* PostScript-Schrift *f*
- *f* police *f* PostScript
- *r* PostScript-шрифт *m*

7175 PostScript halftone screen
- *d* PostScript-Halbtonbildschirm *m*
- *f* écran *m* demi-teinte PostScript
- *r* полутоновый PostScript-экран *m*

7176 PostScript image
- *d* PostScript-Bild *n*
- *f* image *f* PostScript
- *r* PostScript-изображение *n*

7177 PostScript [language]
- *d* PostScript-Sprache *f*
- *f* langage *m* PostScript
- *r* язык *m* Postscript; язык *m* описания страниц

7178 PostScript pattern
- *d* PostScript-Muster *m*; PostScript-Motiv *n*
- *f* motif *m* PostScript
- *r* PostScript-шаблон *m*; PostScript-мотив *m*

7179 PostScript printer
- *d* PostScript-Drucker *m*
- *f* imprimante *f* [dotée de] PostScript
- *r* PostScript-принтер *m*

7180 PostScript texture
- *d* PostScript-Textur *f*
- *f* texture *f* PostScript
- *r* PostScript-текстура *f*

7181 pot
- *d* reservierter Speicherbereich *m*
- *f* espace *m* de mémoire réservé
- *r* зарезервированная область *f* памяти

* **power → 9058**

7182 power
- *d* Potenz *f*; Leistung *f*
- *f* puissance *f*
- *r* мощность *f*

7183 power amplifier
- *d* Leistungsverstärker *m*
- *f* amplificateur *m* de puissance
- *r* усилитель *m* мощности

* **power conservation → 267**

* **power management → 267**

7184 power module; power pack
- *d* Versorgungseinheit *f*; Netzgerät *n*
- *f* bloc *m* d'alimentation; unité *f* d'alimentation
- *r* блок *m* питания

* **power outlet → 8690**

7185 power output
- *d* Ausgangsleistung *f*; Strahlungsleistung *f*
- *f* puissance *f* de sortie; puissance d'émission
- *r* выходная мощность *f*; мощность излучения

* **power pack → 7184**

* **power rating → 7644**

* **power saving → 267**

7186 power set; set of all subsets; Boolean
- *d* Potenzmenge *f*; Menge *f* aller Mengen
- *f* ensemble *m* de tous les sous-ensembles; ensemble des parties d'un ensemble; booléan *m*
- *r* множество *n* всех подмножеств; булеан *m* [множества]

7187 power user
- *d* Potenzbenutzer *m*

f utilisateur *m* averti
r квалифицированный пользователь *m*;
  опытный пользователь

* **PPI** → **7040**

* **PPP** → **7088**

* **PR** → **6864**

**7188 practical extraction and report language;
       pathologically eclectic rubbish lister;
       PERL [scripting language]**
d Praktische Erweiterungs- und
  Berichtssprache *f*; PERL[-Sprache *f*]
f [langage *m*] PERL
r язык *m* практичного извлечения и отчётов;
  [язык] ПЕРЛ

7189 preamplifier
d Vorverstärker *m*
f préamplificateur *m*
r предусилитель *m*

7190 precede *v*
d vorangehen; vorausgehen
f précéder
r предшествовать

* **precedence** → **7313**

7191 precedence
d Vorhergehen *n*; Präzedenz *f*
f précédence *f*
r предшествование *n*

7192 precedence grammar
d Grammatik *f* mit Vorgängerbeziehungen
f grammaire *f* de précédence
r грамматика *f* с предшествованием

* **precedence indicator** → **7319**

7193 precedence relation
d Präzedenzrelation *f*
f relation *f* de précédence
r отношение *n* предшествования

7194 precedence table
d Präzedenztabelle *f*
f table *f* de précédence
r таблица *f* предшествования

* **precision** → **103**

7195 precondition
d Vorbedingung *f*
f précondition *f*
r предусловие *n*

7196 predecessor
d Vorgänger *m*
f prédécesseur *m*; précédent *m*; antécédent *m*
r предшественник *m*; предшествующий
  элемент *m*

7197 predefined variable
d im voraus definierte Variable *f*
f variable *f* prédéfinie
r предварительно дефинированная
  переменная *f*

7198 predicted response
d vorhersehbare Reaktion *f*; voraussagbare
  Reaktion
f réponse *f* prédicable
r ожидаемый отклик *m*

7199 prediction; prognosis; forecasting
d Vorhersage *f*; Prognostizierung *f*; Prediktion *f*
f prédiction *f*; prévision *f*
r предсказание *n*; прогнозирование *n*;
  предварительный расчёт *m*

7200 pre-editing
d Voreditieren *n*
f préédition *f*
r предварительное редактирование *n*;
  предредактирование *n*

7201 pre-emphasis
d Preemphase *f*
f préaccentuation *f*; préemphase *f*;
  préemphasage *m*; précorrection *f*
r предварительная коррекция *f*

7202 preemptive strategy
d verdrängende Strategie *f*
f stratégie *f* prédominante; stratégie de
  préemption
r стратегия *f* абсолютного приоритета

7203 preference
d Präferenz *f*; Vorzug *m*; Bevorzugung *f*
f préférence *f*
r преференция *f*; предпочтение *n*

7204 preference relation
d Vorzugsrelation *f*
f relation *f* de préférence
r отношение *n* предпочтения

* **preferred** → **3724**

7205 preferred value
d Vorzugswert *m*
f valeur *f* de préférence
r стандартный номинал *m*

* **prefetch** → **7206**

7206 prefetch[ing]
d Vorausholen *n*; Vorlaufendholen *n*
f prélecture *f*; appel *m* préalable
r предварительное извлечение *n*;
предварительный вызов *m*

7207 prefix
d Präfix *n*
f préfixe *m*
r приставка *f*; префикс *m*

7208 prefix address
d Vorsatzadresse *f*
f adresse *f* préfixe
r префиксный адрес *m*

* **prefix code → 2846**

**7209 prefix notation; Polish notation;
parenthesis free notation; operator
notation**
d Präfixschreibweise *f*; polnische
Schreibweise *f*; klammerfreie Notation *f*
f notation *f* préfixée; notation polonaise;
notation sans parenthèses
r префиксная запись *f*; польская запись;
бесскобочная запись

7210 prefix operator
d Präfixoperator *m*
f opérateur *m* préfixe
r префиксный оператор *m*; одноместный
оператор

* **preformat → 7211**

7211 preformat[ting]
d Vorformatieren *n*
f préformatage *m*
r предварительное форматирование *n*

7212 pre-image; before-image
d Urbild *n*; vorheriges Bild *n*
f image *f* anticipée; pré-image *f*
r праобраз *m*; первообраз *m*;
предварительное изображение *n*

7213 preindexing
d Vorindizierung *f*
f préindexage *m*
r предварительная индексация *m*

**7214 preliminary data processing; data
preparation**
d vorbereitende Datenverarbeitung *f*;
Datenaufbereitung *f*
f traitement *m* préliminaire de données;
prétraitement *m* de données; préparation *f* de
données

r предварительная обработка *f* данных;
подготовка *f* данных

7215 preliminary logic
d vorläufige Logik[schaltung] *f*
f logique *f* préliminaire
r логические схемы *fpl* предварительной
обработки

* **preload → 4850**

7216 preloaded
d im voraus eingerichtet
f préchargé
r предварительно загруженный

7217 preloaded font
d im voraus eingerichtetes Font *n*
f fonte *f* préchargée
r предварительно загруженный шрифт *m*

* **premature cleardown → 7218**

* **premature connection release → 7218**

* **premature disconnect → 7218**

**7218 premature disconnect[ion]; premature
cleardown; premature connection release**
d vorzeitige Verbindungsauslösung *f*;
vorzeitige Trennung *f*
f déconnexion *f* prématurée
r преждевременное прерывание *n* [связи]

7219 premultiplication
d Multiplikation *f* von links nach rechts
f multiplication *f* à gauche
r умножение *n* слева

7220 prenormalization
d Vornormalisierung *f*
f prénormalisation *f*
r преднормализация *f*

7221 preparation; preparing
d Vorbereitung *f*
f préparation *f*
r подготовка *f*

* **preparation time → 8480**

* **preparing → 7221**

7222 preprinted form
d Vorabdruck *m*
f prétirage *m*; formulaire *m* préimprimé
r предпечатный формуляр *m*

7223 preprocessing; front-end processing
d Vorverarbeitung *f*; Front-End-Verarbeitung *f*

f traitement *m* préliminaire; traitement
préalable; prétraitement *m*
r предварительная обработка *f*; первичная
обработка

* **preprocessor** → **4098**

7224 prescription
d Vorschrift *f*
f prescription *f*
r предписание *n*

7225 prescriptive knowledge
d Wissen *n* in Form von Vorschriften
f connaissances *fpl* prescriptibles
r знания *npl* в форме предписаний

7226 preselection
d Vor[aus]wahl *f*
f présélection *f*
r предварительная выборка *f*

7227 preselection stage
d Vorwahlstufe *f*
f étage *m* de présélection
r ступень *f* предварительной выборки

7228 presence
d Präsenz *f*; Anwesenheit *f*
f présence *f*
r присутствие *n*; наличие *n*

7229 presentation
d Präsentation *f*; Darstellung *f*
f présentation *f*
r представление *n*

* **presentation graphics** → **1282**

**7230 presentation graphics software; desktop
presentation**
d Präsentationsgrafik-Software *f*
f logiciel *m* de présentation assistée par
ordinateur; présentation *f* assistée par
ordinateur; présentatique *f*; PRéAO
r программное обеспечение *n* деловой
графики

7231 presentation layer
d Datendarstellungschicht *f*;
Darstellungsschicht *f*
f couche *f* de présentation
r представительный уровень *m*

* **preset** → **7235**

7232 preset *v*
d voreinstellen
f ajuster d'avance; présélectionner; prérégler;
prépositionner

r предварительно установлять

7233 preset counter
d Vorwahlzähler *m*
f compteur *m* à présélection
r счётчик *m* с предварительной установкой

7234 preset parameter
d voreingestellter Parameter *m*; vorgegebener
Parameter
f paramètre *m* prédéfini; paramètre établi
r заданный параметр *m*; предварительно
установленный параметр

7235 preset[ting]
d Voreinstellung *f*; Voreinstellen *n*; Festlegen *n*
von Anfangsbedingungen
f forçage *m*; établissement *m* d'avance;
prédéfinition *f*; fixation *f* d'une condition
initiale
r предварительная установка *f*

7236 presort *v*
d vorsortieren
f trier d'avance
r предварительно сортировать

7237 presorting
d Vorsortierung *f*
f prétri[age] *m*
r предварительная сортировка *f*;
предсортировка *f*

7238 press *v*; **hit** *v*
d pressen; drücken
f presser; serrer
r нажимать

7239 pressed button
d gedrückte Schaltfläche *f*
f bouton *m* enfoncé
r нажатый бутон *m*

7240 prestore *v*
d vorspeichern
f mettre en mémoire d'avance; mémoriser
d'avance
r предварительно запоминать

7241 presubscript
d vorgestellter unterer Index *m*
f pré-sous-index *m*
r преднижний индекс *m*

* **presumptive address** → **830**

7242 presuperscript
d vorgestellter oberer Index *m*
f pré-superindex *m*
r предверхний индекс *m*

7243 preventive maintenance
d vorbeugende Wartung *f*
f maintenance *f* préventive
r профилактическое обслуживание *n*;
профилактика *f*

* **preview → 5495**

7244 preview *v*
d im voraus besichtigen
f prévisualiser
r предварительно просматривать

7245 preview area; preview zone
d Vorschauzone *f*
f zone *f* d'aperçu; zone de prévisualisation
r зона *f* предварительного просмотра

* **previewing → 5495**

* **preview zone → 7245**

7246 previous carry
d Übertrag *m* aus der nächsthöheren Position
f report *m* de rang précédent
r перенос *m* из предыдущего разряда

7247 previous contents
d vorhergehender Inhalt *m*; vorheriger Inhalt
f contenu *m* précédent
r предыдущее содержимое *n*;
предшествующее содержимое

7248 prewarping
d vorherige Verbiegung *f*
f gauchissement *m* d'avance; gauchissement
préalable
r предварительное искажение *n*

7249 primary; prime; original
d primär; ursprünglich
f primaire; originel
r первичный; первоначальный; исходный;
примарный

7250 primary data
d Primärdaten *pl*
f données *fpl* primaires
r первоначальные данные *pl*; первичные
данные

7251 primary display
d Erstmonitor *m*
f afficheur *m* primaire
r первичный дисплей *m*

* **primary index → 4328**

7252 primary key
d primärer Schlüssel *m*

f clé *m* primaire
r первичный ключ *m*; главный ключ

7253 primary memory
d primärer Speicher *m*
f mémoire *f* primaire
r первичная память *f*

* **primary mouse button → 5332**

* **primary window → 5608**

* **prime → 7249, 7257**

7254 prime divisor
d Primteiler *m*; Primdivisor *m*
f diviseur *m* premier
r простой делитель *m*

7255 prime element
d Primelement *n*
f élément *m* premier
r простой элемент *m*

7256 prime implicant
d normale Implikante *f*
f implicante *m* simple
r простая импликанта *f*

7257 prime [sign]; prime symbol
(')
d Strich *m*; Strichsymbol *n*
f prime *f*
r прим *m*; штрих *m*

* **prime symbol → 7257**

7258 primitive data type
d Primitivdatentyp *m*
f type *m* primitif de données
r базисный тип *m* данных

* **primitive → 7259**

**7259 primitive [element]; graphic[s] primitive;
output primitive**
d primitives Element *n*; Primitiv *n*;
Grafikgrundelement *n*; Grundelement *n*
f élément *m* primitif; primitive *f* [graphique]
r примитивный элемент *m*; базисный
элемент; [графический] примитив *m*

7260 primitive recursion
d primitive Rekursion *f*
f récursion *f* primitive
r примитивная рекурсия *f*

7261 primitive recursive function
d primitiv rekursive Funktion *f*

f fonction *f* primitive récursive
r примитивно-рекурсивная функция *f*

7262 primitive root
 d primitive Wurzel *f*
 f racine *f* primitive
 r первообразный корень *m*; примитивный
    корень

 * **principal** → **5597**

 * **print** → **7296**

7263 print *v*
 d drucken
 f imprimer
 r печатать

7264 printable area
 d druckbarer Bereich *m*
 f zone *f* imprimable
 r печатаемая зона *f*; печатаемая область *f*;
    область печати

7265 printable background
 d druckbarer Hintergrund *m*
 f fond *m* imprimable
 r печатаемый фон *m*

7266 printable page
 d druckbare Seite *f*
 f page *f* imprimable
 r печатаемая страница *f*

7267 print band
 d Druckband *n*
 f bande *f* d'imprimante
 r лента *f* печатающего устройства

7268 print bar; type bar
 d Typenstange *f*; Typenstab *m*; Druckstange *f*
 f barre *f* d'impression; barre à caractères; tige *f*
    à caractères
 r литерный стержень *m*; литерный рычаг *m*;
    печатающая штанга *f*

7269 print buffer
 d Druckpuffer *m*
 f tampon *m* d'impression
 r буфер *m* печати

7270 print [column] spacing; character pitch
 d Druckspaltenteilung *f*;
    Druckspaltenabstand *m*
 f partage *m* de colonne d'impression
 r расстояние *n* между столбцами печати

7271 print cycle
 d Druckzyklus *m*
 f cycle *m* d'impression

r цикл *m* печати

 * **print driver** → **7284**

 * **printed board** → **7273**

 * **printed card** → **7273**

7272 printed circuit
 d gedruckter Schaltkreis *m*; gedruckte
    Schaltung *f*
 f circuit *m* imprimé
 r печатная схема *f*

7273 printed [circuit] board; printed card
 d Printplatte *f*; gedruckte Leiterplatte *f*
 f plaque *f* à câblage imprimé
 r печатная плата *f*

7274 printed circuit master
 d Leiterplattenoriginal *n*
 f circuit *m* imprimé maître
 r чертёж *m* печатной платы;
    фотооригинал *m* печатной платы

7275 printed form
 d gedruckte Form *f*
 f forme *f* imprimée
 r отпечатанная форма *f*

7276 print[ed] page copy
 d Blattkopie *f*; Druckseitkopie *f*
 f copie *f* de page imprimée
 r копия *f* печатной страницы

 * **printed register mark** → **4353**

7277 printed wiring
 d gedruckte Verdrahtung *f*
 f câblage *m* [à circuit] imprimé
 r печатный монтаж *m*

7278 printer
 d Drucker *m*; Printer *n*
 f imprimante *f*; imprimeur *m*
 r печатающее устройство *n*; принтер *m*

7279 printer adjustment
 d Druckereinstellung *f*
 f ajustement *m* d'imprimante
 r настраивание *n* принтера

7280 printer calibration
 d Druckerkalibrierung *f*
 f calibrage *m* d'imprimante
 r калибровка *f* принтера

7281 printer color profile
 d Druckerfarbprofil *n*

f profil *m* de couleurs d'imprimante
r цветовой профиль *m* принтера

7282 printer colors
d Druckerfarben *fpl*
f couleurs *fpl* d'imprimante
r цвета *mpl* принтера

7283 printer configuration
d Druckerkonfiguration *f*
f configuration *f* d'imprimante
r конфигурация *f* принтера

7284 print[er] driver
d Druck[er]treiber *m*
f excitateur *m* d'impression; gestionnaire *m*
d'impression; pilote *m* d'imprimante
r драйвер *m* принтера; драйвер печати

7285 printer font
d Druckerschrift *f*
f police *f* d'imprimante
r шрифт *m* принтера; принтерный шрифт

7286 print[er] format; printer layout
d Druckformat *n*; Druckform *f*; Druckbild *n*
f format *m* d'impression
r формат *m* печати; макет *m* печати

7287 printer gamut
d Drucker-Gamut *n*
f gamme *f* d'imprimante
r цветовой диапазон *m* принтера

7288 printer icon
d Druckersymbol *n*
f icône *f* d'imprimante
r икона *f* принтера

7289 printer interface
d Druckerschnittstelle *f*
f interface *f* d'imprimante
r интерфейс *m* принтера

* **printer layout** → 7286

7290 printer model
d Druckermodell *n*
f modèle *m* d'imprimante
r модель *f* принтера

7291 printer resolution
d Druckerauflösung *f*
f résolution *f* d'imprimante
r разрешающая способность *f* принтера

7292 printer's mark
d Druckermarke *f*; Druckerzeichen *n*
f marque *f* d'imprimante
r маркер *m* принтера

7293 print[er] spooler
d Druckspooler *m*
f spouleur *m* d'impression
r программа *f* для печати; блок *m* подкачки
[информации] для печати

7294 printer virtual memory
d virtueller Speicher *m* von Druckern
f mémoire *f* virtuelle de l'imprimante
r виртуальная память *f* принтера

7295 print file
d Druckdatei *f*
f fichier *m* d'impression
r файл *m* печати

* **print format** → 7286

7296 print[ing]
d Druck *m*; Drucken *n*
f impression *f*
r печатание *n*

7297 print[ing] quality
d Druckqualität *f*
f qualité *f* d'impression
r качество *n* печати

7298 printing speed
d Druckgeschwindigkeit *f*
f vitesse *f* d'impression
r скорость *f* печати

7299 printing system
d Drucksystem *n*
f système *m* d'impression
r система *f* печатания

7300 print job
d Druckauftrag *m*
f job *m* d'impression
r задание *n* о печати

7301 print member
d Druckglied *n*; Typenträger *m*
f élément *m* d'impression
r печатающий элемент *m*

7302 print merge
d Druckvereinigung *f*
f fusionnement *m* d'impression
r слияние *n* печати; объединение *n* печати

7303 printout
d Ausdruck *m*; Druck[er]ausgabe *f*
f impression *f*; aspect *m* d'impression; sortie *f*
par impression
r распечатка *f*; отпечаток *m*; вывод *m* на
печать

* **print page copy** → 7276

7304 print preview
d Druckvorschau *f*
f aperçu *m* avant l'impression; vision *f* avant l'impression
r предпечатное представление *n*

* **print quality** → 7297

7305 print report
d Druckbericht *m*
f rapport *m* d'impression
r отчёт *m* о печати; отчёт печатания

7306 print script
d Druckskript *m*
f script *m* d'impression
r принтерный скрипт *m*

7307 print server
d Druck-Server *m*
f serveur *m* d'impression
r сервер *m* печати; станция *f* печати

7308 print setting; print setup
d Druckeinrichtung *f*
f établissement *m* d'impression; paramètre *m* d'imprimante
r установка *f* печати; наладка *f* печати

* **print setup** → 7308

* **print spacing** → 7270

* **print spooler** → 7293

7309 print spool file
d Druckspoolerdatei *f*
f fichier *m* de spoule d'impression
r файл *m* спулера печатания

7310 print style
d Druckstil *m*
f style *m* d'impression
r стиль *m* печатания

7311 print *v* to a file
d in einer Datei drucken
f imprimer dans un fichier
r печатать в файле

7312 prioritization
d Priorisierung *f*; Prioritätszuordnung *f*; Vorrangszuteilung *f*
f attribution *f* de priorités; affectation *f* de priorités
r присваивание *n* приоритетов; назначение *n* приоритетов

7313 priority; precedence
d Priorität *f*; Vorrang *m*
f priorité *f*
r приоритет *m*; приоритетность *f*; преимущество *n*; первенство *n*

7314 priority acceptance
d Prioritätsübernahme *f*
f acceptation *f* prioritaire
r приоритетный приём *m*

7315 priority connection
d Vorrangverbindung *f*
f connexion *f* prioritaire
r приоритетное соединение *n*

* **priority degree** → 7318

7316 priority flag
d Bevorrechtigungskennzeichen *n*; Prioritätskennzeichen *n*
f flag *m* de priorité
r флаг *m* приоритета

7317 priority function
d Vorrangfunktion *f*
f fonction *f* prioritaire
r приоритетная функция *f*

7318 priority grading; priority degree
d Prioritätsstufe *f*; Grad *m* der Vorrangigkeit; Prioritätsgrad *m*
f grade *m* de priorité; degré *m* de priorité
r степень *f* приоритета; уровень *m* приоритета

7319 priority indicator; precedence indicator
d Vorranganzeiger *m*; Prioritätsanzeiger *m*
f indicateur *m* de priorité
r указатель *m* приоритета

7320 priority list
d Prioritätsreihe *f*
f liste *f* des priorités
r список *m* приоритетов

7321 priority program
d Prioritätsprogramm *n*
f programme *m* de priorité
r программа *f* с приоритетом

7322 priority queue
d prioritätsgeordnete Warteschlange *f*
f queue *f* de priorité
r очередь *f* по приоритету

7323 priority resolution
d Prioritätsauflösung *f*; Prioritätsentschlüsselung *f*

f résolution *f* de priorité
r разрешение *n* приоритета

7324 priority-shifted interrupt
d Unterbrechung *f* mit änderbarer Priorität;
Interrupt *m* mit Wechselpriorität
f interruption *f* à priorité variable
r прерывание *n* с изменяемым приоритетом

7325 privacy
d Geheimhaltung *f*
f confidentialité *f*; sécurité *f*
r секретность *f*; конфиденциальность *f*;
сохранение *n* тайны

7326 privacy enhanced mail; PEM
(an encryption standard generally used to
secure Internet mail)
d PEM-Norm *f*
f courrier *m* à sécurité renforcée; courrier
sécurisé; courrier à confidentialité ajoutée
r почта *f* повышенной секретности;
закодированная почта; протокол *m* PEM

7327 privacy language
d Schutzsprache *f*
f langage *m* de secret
r язык *m* защиты

7328 privacy lock
d Schutzsperre *f* für personenbezogene Daten
f verrou *m* de confidentialité
r замок *m* секретности

7329 privacy protection
d Geheimnisschutz *m*
f protection *f* de confidentialité
r защита *f* секретности

7330 private domain name
d Name *m* eines privaten Versorgungsbereiches
f nom *m* de domaine privé
r имя *n* личного домена

7331 private key
d privater Schlüssel *m*
f clé *f* secrète; clef *m* secret
r личный ключ *m*; секретный ключ

7332 private library
d Privatbibliothek *f*
f bibliothèque *f* privée
r личная библиотека *f*; частная библиотека

7333 private network
d privates Netz[werk] *n*
f réseau *m* privé
r частная сеть *f*

7334 privileged user

d privilegierter Anwender *m*
f utilisateur *m* privilégié
r привилегированный пользователь *m*

7335 privilege level
d Privilegierungsebene *f*
f niveau *m* privilégié
r уровень *m* привилегированности

7336 probabilistic
d probabilistisch
f probabilistique
r вероятностный

7337 probabilistic decoding
d Wahrscheinlichkeitsdecodierung *f*
f décodage *m* probabilistique
r вероятностное дешифрирование *n*

7338 problem; task
d Problem *n*; Task *f*; Aufgabe *f*
f problème *m*; tâche *f*; devoir *m*
r задача *f*

7339 problem data; task data
d Problemdaten *pl*; Aufgabedaten *pl*
f données *fpl* de problème
r данные *pl* задачи

* **problem of coloration → 1873**

* **problem of coloring maps in four colors →
4009**

7340 problem-oriented language
d problemorientierte Programmiersprache *f*
f langage *m* orienté [vers un] problème
r проблемно-ориентированный язык *m*

7341 problem solving
d Problemlösung *f*
f solution *f* de problème
r решение *n* задачи

* **problem-solving environment → 7416**

7342 problem-solving knowledge
d Problemlösungswissen *n*
f connaissances *fpl* des méthodes de solutions
de problèmes
r знания *npl* о методах решения задач

7343 problem-statement language
d Problemstellungssprache *f*
f langage *m* de définition de problèmes
r язык *m* постановки задач

7344 procedural
d prozedural; Prozedural-

f procédural
r процедурный

* **procedural language** → 4690

7345 procedural reasoning
  d prozedurales Reasoning *n*
  f raisonnement *m* procédural
  r рассуждение *n* с использованием процедур

7346 procedural textures
  d prozedurale Texturen *fpl*
  f textures *fpl* procéduraux
  r процедурные текстуры *fpl*

7347 procedure
  d Prozedur *f*
  f procédure *f*; procédé *m*
  r процедура *f*

7348 procedure call
  d Prozeduraufruf *m*
  f appel *m* d'une procédure
  r вызов *m* процедуры

7349 procedure deactivation
  d Deaktivieren *n* einer Prozedur
  f déactivation *f* de procédure
  r деактивизация *f* процедуры

7350 procedure declaration
  d Prozedurbeschreibung *f*;
    Prozedurvereinbarung *f*
  f déclaration *f* de procédure; description *f* de
    procédure
  r описание *n* процедуры

7351 procedure-oriented language
  d prozedurorientierte Programmiersprache *f*;
    verfahrensorientierte Programmiersprache
  f langage *m* orienté [vers une] procédure
  r процедурно-ориентированный язык *m*

7352 procedure reference
  d Prozedurreferenz *f*
  f référence *f* à une procédure
  r обращение *n* к процедуре

7353 procedure statement
  d Prozeduranweisung *f*
  f opérateur *m* de procédure
  r оператор *m* процедуры

7354 process
  d Prozess *m*
  f processus *m*
  r процесс *m*

7355 process algorithm
  d Prozessalgorithmus *m*

  f algorithme *m* de processus
  r алгоритм *m* управления процессом

7356 process automation
  d Prozessautomatisierung *f*
  f automat[isat]ion *f* de processus
  r автоматизация *f* [технологических]
    процессов

7357 process control; process management
  d Prozesssteuerung *f*; Prozessführung *f*
  f management *m* de processus; commande *f* de
    processus
  r управление *n* процессом

7358 process control computer
  d Prozessrechner *m*
  f ordinateur *m* de commande de processus;
    ordinateur de commande industriel
  r компьютер *m* для управления
    технологическими процессами

7359 process data; process information
  d Prozessdaten *pl*; Prozessinformation *f*
  f données *fpl* de processus; information *f* de
    processus
  r данные *pl* о процессе; информация *f* о
    процессе

7360 process-data transmission
  d Prozessdatenübermittlung *f*
  f transmission *f* de données de processus
  r передача *f* данных о процессе

7361 processed image
  d verarbeitetes Bild *n*
  f image *f* traitée; image dépouillée
  r обработанное изображение *n*

* **process information** → 7359

7362 processing; treatment
  d Verarbeitung *f*; Bearbeitung *f*
  f traitement *m*
  r обработка *f*

7363 processing block
    (in a block scheme)
  d Verarbeitungsblock *m*
  f bloc *m* de traitement
  r блок *m* обработки; операторный блок

7364 processing element
  d Verarbeitungselement *n*
  f élément *m* de traitement
  r процессорный элемент *m*; элементарный
    процессор *m*

7365 processing transparency
  d Verarbeitungstransparenz *f*

f transparence *f* de traitement
r прозрачность *f* обработки

* **processing unit** → 7370

* **process management** → 7357

7366 process node
d Prozessknoten *m*
f nœud *m* fonctionnel
r функциональный узел *m*

* **processor** → 7370

7367 processor node
d Prozessorknoten *m*
f nœud *m* de processeur
r процессорный узел *m*

7368 processor power
d Prozessorleistung *f*
f performance *f* de processeur
r производительность *f* процессора

7369 processor status word; PSW
d Prozessorstatuswort *n*
f mot *m* d'état de processeur
r слово *n* состояния процессора

7370 processor [unit]; processing unit
d Prozessor *m*; Verarbeitungseinheit *f*
f processeur *m*; unité *f* de traitement
r процессор *m*; процессорный блок *m*

7371 process queue
d Bearbeitungs[warte]schlange *f*
f queue *f* de traitement
r очередь *f* на обработку

7372 producer process
d produzierender Prozess *m*; Quellenprozess *m*
f processus *m* producteur
r процесс-источник *m*

7373 product-identification code
d Erzeugnis-Kennzeichencode *m*
f code *m* d'identification du produit
r идентификационный код *m* продукта

7374 production control automation
d Automatisierung *f* der Fertigungssteuerung
f automa[tisa]tion *f* de la gestion industrielle
r автоматизация *f* управления производством

7375 production control computer
d Produktionssteuerrechner *m*
f ordinateur *m* de la gestion de production
r компьютер *m* управления производством

7376 production language
d Produktionssprache *f*
f langage *m* des productions
r язык *m* продукций; продукционный язык

7377 production rule
d Produktionsregel *f*
f règle *f* de production
r правило *n* продукции; продукционное правило

7378 production run
d produktiver Lauf *m*; Arbeitslauf *m*
f cours *m* de fonctionnement
r рабочий прогон *m*

7379 product kernel
d Produktkern *m*
f noyau *m* de produit
r ядро-произведение *n*

7380 product register
d Produktregister *n*
f registre *m* de produit
r регистр *m* произведения

7381 product sign
d Produktzeichen *n*
f signe *m* de produit
r знак *m* произведения

7382 profile
d Profil *n*
f profil *m*
r профиль *m*

7383 profile deleting
d Profillöschung *f*
f effacement *m* de profil
r стирание *n* профиля

7384 profile file
d Anwenderparameterdatei *f*
f fichier *m* de profil
r файл *m* параметров пользователя

7385 profile image
d Profilbild *n*
f image *f* de profil
r изображение *n* профиля

7386 profile importing
d Profilimportieren *n*
f importation *f* de profil
r внесение *n* профиля

7387 profile parameter
d Profilparameter *m*
f paramètre *m* de profil
r параметр *m* профиля

7388 profitable data processing
   d wirtschaftliche Datenverarbeitung *f*
   f traitement *m* de données rentable
   r прибыльная обработка *f* данных;
     экономичная обработка данных

  * **prognosis** → 7199

7389 program
   d Programm *n*
   f programme *m*
   r программа *f*

7390 program block; code block
   d Programmblock *m*; Programmeinheit *f*
   f bloc *m* de programme; bloc de code
   r блок *m* программы

7391 program body
   d Programmrumpf *m*
   f corps *m* de programme
   r тело *n* программы

7392 program-controlled data channel
   d programmgesteuerter Datenkanal *m*
   f canal *m* de données commandé par
     programme
   r программно-управляемый
     информационный канал *m*

  * **program counter** → 4947

7393 program counter addressing
   d Befehlszähleradressierung *f*
   f adressage *m* par le compteur d'instructions
   r адресация *f* по счётчику команд

7394 program credit
   (on the screen)
   d Programmkredit *m*
   f titre *m* de programme
   r программный кредит *m*; программный
     титр *m*

7395 program division
   d Programmabschnitt *m*; Programmteil *m*
   f division *f* de programme
   r раздел *m* программы

7396 program entry
   d Programmeingang *m*; Programmeintritt *m*
   f entrée *f* de programme
   r вход *m* в программу; точка *f* входа в
     программу

7397 program error; program fault
   d Programmfehler *m*
   f erreur *f* de programme; défaut *m* de
     programme
   r ошибка *f* программы; программная ошибка

**7398 program evaluation and review technique;
PERT**
   d PERT[-Verfahren *n*]
   f technique *f* de révision et d'estimation de
     programmes
   r метод *m* просмотра и оценки программ

  * **program fault** → 7397

7399 program folder
   d Programmmappe *f*
   f dossier *m* de programme
   r программная папка *f*

7400 program generator
   d Programmgenerator *m*
   f générateur *m* de programmes
   r программный генератор *m*; генератор
     программ

7401 program interrupt
   d Programmunterbrechung *f*
   f interruption *f* de programme
   r прерывание *n* программы

7402 program library; software library
   d Programmbibliothek *f*; Programmothek *f*
   f bibliothèque *f* de programmes
   r библиотека *f* программ

  * **program link** → 7403

7403 program link[age]
   d Programmverbindung *f*
   f liaison *f* de programme
   r компоновка *f* программы;
     межпрограммные связи *fpl*

7404 program loop
   d Programmschleife *f*
   f boucle *f* de programme
   r петля *f* программы

7405 programmable communication interface
   d programmierbares
     Kommunikationsinterface *n*;
     programmierbare
     Kommunikationsschnittstelle *f*
   f interface *f* de communication programmable
   r программируемый интерфейс *m* системы
     связи

7406 programmable logic; programmed logic
   d programmierbare Logik *f*
   f logique *f* programmable
   r программируемая логика *f*; схема *f* с
     программируемой логикой

7407 programmable logic array; PLA
   d programmierbare Logikanordnung *f*;

programmierbares Logikgatterfeld *n*; PLA
f matrice *f* logique programmable; champ *m* logique programmable; PLA
r программируемая логическая матрица *f*; ПЛМ

7408 programmable multiplexer
d programmierbarer Multiplexer *m*
f multiplexeur *m* programmable
r программируемый мультиплексор *m*

7409 programmable read-only memory; PROM
d programmierbarer Festwertspeicher *m*; PROM
f mémoire *f* permanente programmable
r программируемая постоянная память *f*; ППЗУ

7410 programmable wait loop
d programmierbare Warteschleife *f*
f boucle *f* d'attente programmable
r программируемый цикл *m* ожидания

7411 program manager
d Programm-Manager *m*
f gestionnaire *m* de programme
r диспетчер *m* программы

7412 programmed clock raster
d programmierter Taktraster *m*
f grille *f* d'horloge programmée
r запрограммированная тактовая сетка *f*

* **programmed logic → 7406**

7413 programmer
(a person)
d Programmierer *m*
f programmeur *m*
r программист *m*

7414 programming
d Programmierung *f*; Programmieren *n*
f programmation *f*
r программирование *n*

7415 programming language
d Programmiersprache *f*
f langage *m* de programmation
r язык *m* программирования

7416 programming support environment; problem-solving environment
d Programmierungsunterlagen *fpl*
f environnement *m* de programmation
r среда *f* программирования; средства *npl* поддержки программирования

7417 program parameter
d Programmparameter *m*

f paramètre *m* de programme
r программный параметр *m*

* **program resident → 7418**

7418 program resident [part]; resident
d residenter Programmteil *m*; speicherresidenter Programmteil; Resident *m*; residenter Teil *m*
f résident *m* [d'un programme]; partie *f* résidente [d'un programme]
r резидентная часть *f* программы; резидент *m*

7419 program status word; PSW
d Programmzustandswort *n*; Programmstatuswort *n*
f mot *m* d'état de programme
r слово *n* состояния программы

7420 program step
d Programmschritt *m*
f pas *m* de programme
r шаг *m* программы

7421 program testing; program verification
d Programm[über]prüfung *f*; Programmrichtigkeitsprüfung *f*
f essai *m* de programme; vérification *f* de programme
r тестирование *n* программы; отладка *f* программы

* **program verification → 7421**

7422 program window
d Programmfenster *n*
f fenêtre *f* de programme
r окно *n* программы

7423 progress bar
d Fortschrittsbalken *m*
f barre *f* de progression
r полоса *f* продвижения; полоса движения вперёд

* **prohibit *v* → 4834**

* **project → 2777**

* **project *v* → 2778**

7424 prolog section
d Prologsektion *f*
f section *f* de prologue
r вводная секция *f*

7425 prologue
(of a program)
d Prolog *m*; Einleitungsteil *m*

f prologue *m*
r вводная часть *f*

* prolongation → 3355

* PROM → 7409

* PROM burner → 7426

* PROM programmator → 7426

* PROM programmer → 7426

7426 PROM programmer [unit]; PROM programmator; PROM burner; blaster
d Programmator *m*; Programmierer *m*; Programmiergerät *n*
f programmateur *m*; unité *f* de programmation
r программатор *m* [ПЗУ]; программирующее устройство *n*

* prompt → 7428, 7432

7427 prompt; help [information]
d Prompt *n*; Hinweis *m*; Hilfsinformation *f*
f consigne *f*; prompt *m*; invite *f*; information *f* d'aide
r подсказка *f*; указание *n*; вспомагательная информация *f*; консультативная информация

7428 prompt [character]
d Aufforderungszeichen *n*; Bereitschaftszeichen *n*; Hinweiszeichen *n*
f caractère *m* de consigne; caractère de sollicitation
r знак *m* подсказки

7429 prompted dialog
d Dialog *m* mit Bedienerhinweis; Dialog mit Prompt
f dialogue *m* à souffler; dialogue suggéré
r диалог *m* с подсказками

7430 prompting
d Bedienerführung *f* [mittels Hinweiszeichen]
f incitation *f*; guidage *m*
r выдача *f* подсказки

7431 prompting query
d Anfrage *f* mit einem Hinweis
f demande *f* à suggestion
r запрос *m* с подсказкой

7432 prompt [text]
d Führungstext *m*; Bedienerführungstext *m*
f texte *m* de suggestion
r текст *m* подсказки

* proof → 1646

7433 proof listing
d Prüfliste *f*
f listage *m* d'épreuve
r контрольный листинг *m*

7434 proof reading
d Prüflesen *n*; Überprüfungslesen *n*
f lecture *f* d'épreuve
r проверочное считывание *n*

* propagated error → 7435

7435 propagating error; propagated error
d sich fortpflanzender Fehler *m*; mitlaufender Fehler
f erreur *f* propagée
r распространяющаяся ошибка *f*

7436 propagation
d Ausbreitung *f*; Verbreitung *f*; Fortpflanzung *f*
f propagation *f*
r распространение *n*

7437 propagation delay
d Ausbreitungsverzögerung *f*
f délai *m* de propagation
r задержка *f* распространения

* property → 3732

7438 property setting
d Eigenschaft-Einrichtung *f*
f établissement *m* de propriété
r установление *n* признака

7439 property sort
d Sortierung *f* nach Eigenschaften
f tri[age] *m* propre; tri[age] par attribut
r сортировка *f* по признаку

7440 proportion
d Proportion *f*
f proportion *f*
r пропорция *f*

7441 proportional
d proportional; proportionell
f proportionnel
r пропорциональный

* proportional font → 7442

* proportionally spaced font → 7442

7442 proportional [spacing] font; proportionally spaced font
d Proportionalschriftsatz *m*
f police *f* à espacement proportionnel; police proportionnelle
r шрифт *m* с пропорциональной разрядкой; пропорциональный шрифт

7443 **propositional variable; sentential variable**
  d Aussagenveränderliche *f*; Aussagenvariable *f*
  f variable *f* propositionnelle
  r пропозициональная переменная *f*;
       высказывательная переменная

7444 **proprietary system**
  d Markensystem *n*
  f système *m* exclusif [constructeur]; système
       propriétaire
  r патентованная система *f*

7445 **protected code**
  d geschützter Code *m*
  f code *m* protégé
  r защищённый код *m*

7446 **protected data**
  d geschützte Daten *pl*
  f données *fpl* protégées
  r защищённые данные *pl*

7447 **protected data field**
  d geschütztes Datenfeld *n*
  f champ *m* de données protégé
  r защищённое поле *n* данных

7448 **protected mode**
  d geschützter Modus *m*
  f mode *m* protégé
  r защищённый режим *m*

7449 **protection; guard**
  d Schutz *m*
  f protection *f*; garde *f*
  r защита *f*

7450 **protection key**
  d Schutzschlüssel *m*
  f clé *f* de protection
  r ключ *m* защиты

7451 **protection method**
  d Sicherungsverfahren *n*
  f méthode *f* de protection
  r метод *m* защиты

7452 **protection operation**
  d Sicherungsoperation *f*
  f opération *f* de protection
  r защитная операция *f*

  *   **protection ring** → 4347

  *   **protection signal** → 4348

  *   **protocol** → 5175

7453 **protocol**
       (of communication)

7454 **protocol architecture**
  d Protokollarchitektur *f*
  f architecture *f* de protocole
  r архитектура *f* протокола

7455 **protocol circuit**
  d Protokollteil *m*
  f circuit *m* de protocole
  r схема *f* протокола

7456 **protocol conversion**
  d Protokoll[um]wandlung *f*;
       Protokollkonvertierung *f*
  f conversion *f* de protocole
  r преобразование *n* протокола

7457 **protocol converter**
  d Protokollwandler *m*; Protokollkonverter *m*
  f convertisseur *m* de protocole
  r преобразователь *m* протокола

7458 **protocol data unit**
  d Protokoll-Dateneinheit *f*
  f unité *f* de données de protocole
  r элемент *m* данных протокола

7459 **protocol element**
  d Protokollelement *n*
  f élément *m* de protocole
  r элемент *m* протокола

7460 **protocol element definition**
  d Protokollelementdefinition *f*
  f définition *f* d'élément de protocole
  r определение *n* элемента протокола

7461 **protocol group; protocol stack**
  d Protokollgruppe *f*; Protokollstapel *m*
  f groupe *m* de protocoles; pile *f* de protocoles
  r группа *f* протоколов; стек *m* протоколов;
       комплект *m* протоколов; набор *m*
       протоколов

  *   **protocol stack** → 7461

7462 **protocol standard**
  d Protokollnorm *f*
  f standard *m* de protocole; norme *f* de protocole
  r стандарт *m* протокола

7463 **prototype**
  d Prototyp *m*
  f prototype *m*
  r прототип *m*; [опытный] образец *m*

  *   **prototyping board** → 1165

*   provider → 9057

7464 proximity search
d   Annäherungssuche f
f   recherche f [par opérateurs] de proximité
r   поиск m близости

*   proxy → 7467

7465 proxy graphics
d   Proxy-Grafik f
f   graphique m proximal; graphique de serveur
     mandaté
r   графика f прокси-сервера

7466 proxy object
d   Proxy-Objekt n
f   objet m proximal
r   объект m прокси-сервера

7467 proxy [server]
d   Proxy-Server m; Stellvertreter m
f   serveur m proxy; serveur mandaté
r   прокси-сервер m

*   PSDN → 6685

*   pseudo- → 3212

7468 pseudoaddress
d   Pseudoadresse f
f   pseudo-adresse f
r   псевдоадрес m

*   pseudocode → 31

7469 pseudocolor
d   Pseudofarbe f; Falschfarbe f
f   pseudocouleur f
r   псевдоцвет m

7470 pseudocompiler
d   Pseudocompiler m
f   pseudo-compilateur m
r   псевдокомпилятор m

7471 pseudocomplement
d   Pseudokomplement n
f   pseudocomplément m
r   псевдодополнение n

7472 pseudographics; quasi graphics; character graphics
d   Pseudografik f; Quasi-Grafik f;
     Zeichengrafik f; Symbolgrafik f
f   pseudographique m; graphique m par
     caractères
r   псевдографика f

7473 pseudo-image

d   Pseudobild n
f   pseudo-image f
r   псевдоизображение n; псевдообраз m

7474 pseudoinstruction
d   Pseudobefehl m
f   pseudo-instruction f
r   псевдоинструкция f

7475 pseudolanguage
d   Pseudosprache f
f   pseudolangage m
r   псевдоязык m

7476 pseudomachine
d   Pseudomaschine f
f   pseudomachine f
r   псевдомашина f; псевдопроцессор m

7477 pseudomachine language
d   Pseudomaschinensprache f
f   langage m pseudomachine
r   псевдомашинный язык m

7478 pseudooperation
d   Pseudooperation f
f   pseudo-opération f
r   псевдооперация f

7479 pseudopage
d   Pseudoseite f
f   pseudo-page f
r   псевдостраница f

7480 pseudorandom number
d   pseudozufällige Zahl f
f   nombre m pseudo-aléatoire
r   псевдослучайное число n

7481 pseudorandom number sequence
d   pseudozufällige Zahlenfolge f;
     pseudozufällige Zahlenreihe f
f   suite f de nombres pseudo-aléatoires
r   последовательность f псевдослучайных
     чисел

7482 pseudorandom sequence
d   Pseudozufallsfolge f
f   séquence f pseudo-aléatoire; suite f
     pseudo-aléatoire
r   псевдослучайная последовательность f

*   PSW → 7369, 7419

7483 public
d   allgemein; öffentlich; Gemeinschaft-
f   public; publique
r   общедоступный; общего пользования;
     опубликованный

7484 **public[-access] data network**
 d öffentliches Datennetz *n*
 f réseau *m* publique de données
 r сеть *f* [передачи] общедоступных данных

 * **publication** → 7490

7485 **public data**
 d allgemein zugängliche Daten *pl*
 f données *fpl* publiques
 r общедоступные данные *pl*; данные общего
  пользования

 * **public data carrier** → 7489

 * **public data network** → 7484

7486 **public domain; PD**
 d Gemeingut *m*; Public-Domain *f*
 f domaine *m* public
 r общая область *f*

7487 **public key**
 d öffentlicher Schlüssel *m*; allgemeiner
  Schlüssel
 f clé *f* publique; clef *m* publique
 r открытый ключ *m*; общедоступный ключ;
  опубликованный ключ

7488 **public site**
 d allgemeine Site *f*; öffentliche Site
 f site *m* public
 r общедоступный сайт *m*

7489 **public volume; public data carrier**
 d Gemeinschaftsdatenträger *m*
 f volume *m* publique; porteur *m* publique de
  données
 r общий том *m*; том для общесистемных
  функций

7490 **publishing; publication**
 d Verlegung *f*; Publizieren *n*; Publishing *n*;
  Verlagsgewerbe *f*; Veröffentlichung *f*
 f publication *f*
 r публикование *n*; публикация *f*; издание *n*

7491 **puck**
 d Scheibe *f*
 f palet *m*
 r шайба *f*; координатно-указательное
  устройство *n* для ввода с планшета

7492 **pullback; fibered product**
 d Pullback *n*; Faserprodukt *n*
 f produit *m* fibré
 r расслоённое произведение *n*

7493 **pulldown list**
 d Pulldown-Liste *f*

 f liste *f* déroulante
 r падающий список *m*

7494 **pulldown menu; dropdown menu; tear-off
  menu**
 d Pulldown-Menü *n*; Dropdown-Menü *n*;
  Rollomenü *n*
 f menu *m* déroulant
 r развёрнутое меню *n*; падающее меню;
  спускающееся меню

7495 **pulldown window**
 d Pulldown-Fenster *n*; Rollofenster *n*
 f fenêtre *f* déroulante
 r раскрывающееся [вниз] окно *n*; падающее
  окно

7496 **pulled position**
  (of a button)
 d Arbeitsstellung *f*
 f position *f* retirée; position lâchée
 r отжатое положение *n*

 * **pull instruction** → 7111

7497 **pull** *v* **up**
 d hochziehen
 f tirer en haut
 r повышать [в уровень]

 * **pulsation** → 881

7498 **pulse; impulse**
 d Impuls *m*; Puls *m*
 f impulsion *f*
 r импульс *m*

7499 **pulse code**
 d Pulscode *m*; Impulscode *m*
 f code *m* [de modulation] d'impulsion
 r импульсный код *m*

7500 **pulse counter**
 d Impulszähler *m*
 f compteur *m* d'impulsions
 r счётчик *m* импульсов

 * **pulse edge** → 7502

7501 **pulse enable**
 d Impulsfreigabe *f*
 f validation *f* d'impulsion
 r разрешение *n* импульса;
  разблокирование *n* импульса

7502 **pulse front; pulse edge; edge**
 d Impulsflanke *f*; Flanke *f*
 f flanc *m* [d'impulsion]; front *m* [d'impulsion]
 r фронт *m* [импульса]

7503 pulse generation
d Impulserzeugung *f*
f génération *f* d'impulsions
r генерация *f* импульсов

7504 pulse leading edge; leading edge; pulse leading front; front edge; forward edge; rising edge
d Impulsvorderflanke *f*; Anstiegsflanke *f*; Vorderflanke *f* [eines Impulses]; steigende Flanke *f*
f flanc *m* avant [d'impulsion]; flanc frontal; flanc montant
r передний фронт *m* [импульса]; фронт нарастания

* **pulse leading front** → **7504**

7505 pulse rise time
d Impulsanstiegszeit *f*
f durée *f* de montée d'impulsion
r время *n* нарастания импульса

7506 pulse sequence; pulse train
d Impulsfolge *f*; Impulszug *m*
f séquence *f* d'impulsions; train *m* d'impulsions
r импульсная последовательность *f*

* **pulse train** → **7506**

* **pulsing** → **881**

* **pump** → **7507**

7507 pump[ing]
d Pumpen *n*
f pompage *m*
r накачка *f*

7508 pump pulse
d Pumpimpuls *m*
f impulsion *f* de pompage
r импульс *m* накачки

* **punch** *v* → **6900**

* **punctuate** *v* → **3109**

7509 punctuation
d Zeichensetzung *f*; Interpunktion *f*
f ponctuation *f*
r пунктуация *f*

7510 punctuation character; punctuation mark
d Satzzeichen *n*
f signe *m* de ponctuation
r знак *m* пунктуации; символ *m* пунктуации

* **punctuation mark** → **7510**

7511 purge date
d Löschdatum *n*; Verfalldatum *n*
f date *f* de nettoyage
r дата *f* чистки

* **purging** → **1715, 7512**

7512 purification; purging; clean[ing]; clear[ing]; clearance (of errors)
d Reinigung *f*
f purification *f*; nettoyage *m*
r очистка *f*; очищение *n*

7513 push *v*
d hinzufügen
f pousser; ajouter
r толкать; прибавлять

7514 push-button entry
d Drucktasteneingabe *f*
f entrée *f* par bouton
r кнопочный ввод *m*

* **push** *v* **down** → **7517**

7515 pushdown automaton; pushdown machine
d Kellerautomat *m*
f automate *m* pile; automate avec mémoire-cave
r автомат *m* с магазинной памятью

* **pushdown list** → **5355**

* **pushdown machine** → **7515**

* **pushdown stack** → **5355**

* **pushdown storage** → **5355**

* **pushdown store** → **5355**

7516 push instruction
d Kellerspeicherungsbefehl *m*; Einkellerungsbefehl *m*
f instruction *f* en pile; instruction en mémoire-cave
r инструкция *f* обращения к стеку; инструкция записи в стек

7517 push *v* **onto stack; push** *v* **down**
d in den Kellerspeicher bringen; einkellern
f mettre en pile; mettre en mémoire-cave
r проталкивать в стек; поместить в стек

7518 pushout; fibered sum
d Pushout *n*; Fasersumme *f*; Kofaserprodukt *n*
f somme *f* fibrée
r расслоённая сумма *f*

    * **push-pop memory → 8803**

7519 push-pull output
  d Gegentaktausgang *m*
  f sortie *f* push-pull
  r двухтактный выход *m*

    * **pushup list → 3777**

    * **pushup stack → 3777**

Q

* QBIC → 7538

* Q bit → 7525

* QIL package → 7521

* quadbit → 4361

7520 **quad gate**
  d Vierfachgatter *n*
  f porte *f* quadruple
  r счетверённый вентиль *m*

7521 **quad-in-line package; QIL package**
  d Quad-In-Line-Gehäuse *n*
  f boîtier *m* à quatre rangées de broches
  r корпус *m* с четырёхрядным
     расположением выводов

* quadrichromatic → 4007

* quadricolor → 4007

* quadricolor print process → 4008

7522 **quadruple phantom circuit**
  d Duplex-Doppelphantomkreis *m*
  f circuit *m* fantôme quadruple
  r четвёрно-фантомный контур *m*

7523 **qualified name**
  d qualifizierter Name *m*; gekennzeichneter
     Name
  f nom *m* qualifié; nom qualificatif
  r уточнённое имя *n*; выбранное имя

7524 **qualifier**
  d Qualifikationsbegriff *m*; Kennzeichner *m*
  f qualificateur *m*
  r квалификатор *m*; уточнитель *m*

* qualifier bit → 7525

7525 **qualifying bit; qualifier bit; Q bit**
  d Qualifikationsbit *n*; Unterscheidungsbit *n*
  f bit *m* de qualification
  r указательный бит *m*

7526 **quality**
  d Güte *f*; Qualität *f*
  f qualité *f*
  r качество *n*; добротность *f*

* quantifier → 2936

* quantization → 2993

* quantization distortion → 7530

* quantization noise → 7530

7527 **quantization step; quantizing step;
     quantizing value**
  d Quantisierungsschritt *m*;
     Quantisierungswert *m*
  f pas *m* de quantification
  r шаг *m* квантования

7528 **quantized signal**
  d quantisiertes Signal *n*
  f signal *m* quantifié
  r квантованный сигнал *m*;
     дискретизированный сигнал

7529 **quantizer**
  d Quantisierer *m*; Quantifikator *m*;
     Größenwandler *m*
  f quantificateur *m*
  r квантователь *m*; квантующее устройство *n*

* quantizing → 2993

7530 **quantizing distortion; quantizing noise;
     quantization distortion; quantization noise**
  d Quantisierungsverzerrung *f*;
     Quantisierungsgeräusch *n*;
     Quantisierungsrauschen *n*
  f distorsion *f* de quantification; bruit *m* de
     quantification
  r искажение *n* квантования

* quantizing noise → 7530

* quantizing step → 7527

* quantizing value → 7527

7531 **quantum**
  d Quantum *n*; Betrag *m*
  f quantum *m*
  r квант *m*; квантованное значение *n*

7532 **quartz oscillator; crystal oscillator; crystal
     resonator**
  d Quarzoszillator *m*; Quarzschwinger *m*
  f oscillateur *m* à quartz
  r кварцевый осциллятор *m*; кварцевый
     резонатор *m*

* quasi graphics → 7472

7533 **quasilinear**
  d quasilinear

f quasi-linéaire
r квазилинейный

7534 quasi-monochromatic
d quasimonochromatisch
f quasi-monochromatique
r квазимонохроматический

7535 quasi-natural language; near-natural language
d quasinatürliche Sprache *f*; natürlichnahe Sprache
f langage *m* quasi-naturel
r квазиестественный язык *m*; язык, близкий к естественному

* **quenching pulse** → 1047

* **query** → 7963

7536 query builder
d Abfragegenerator *m*
f créateur *m* d'interrogations
r создатель *m* запросов; инструмент *m* генерирования запросов

7537 query by example
d Anfrage *f* mit Hilfe von Beispielen
f interrogation *f* par des exemples
r запрос *m* на примерах

7538 query by image content; QBIC
d bildinhaltliche Abfrage *f*
f interrogation *f* par le contenu d'image
r запрос *m* содержанием изображения

7539 query criteria
d Abfrage-Kriterium *n*
f critère *m* d'interrogation
r критерий *m* запроса

7540 query enhancement
d Abfrageerweiterung *f*
f extension *f* d'interrogation
r расширение *n* запроса

7541 query language
d Abfragesprache *f*; Anfragesprache *f*
f langage *m* de requête
r язык *m* запросов

7542 query optimizer
d Abfrageoptimisator *m*
f optimisateur *m* d'interrogations
r оптимизатор *m* запросов

7543 query server
d Abfrage-Server *m*
f serveur *m* d'interrogation
r сервер *m* запросов

7544 query system; question system
d Frage-System *n*
f système *m* de questions
r запросная система *f*

7545 query transaction
d Abfrage-Transaktion *f*
f transaction *f* d'interrogation
r транзакция *f* запроса

7546 question-answer dialog
d Frage-Antwort-Dialog *m*
f dialogue *m* par question-réponse
r диалог *m* в запросно-ответном режиме

* **question system** → 7544

* **queue** → 3777

7547 queue; waiting line
d Schlange *f*; Warteschlange *f*
f queue *f*; file *f* d'attente
r очередь *f*

7548 queued access method
d Warteschlangen-Zugriffsverfahren *n*; erweiterte Zugriffsmethode *f*
f méthode *f* d'accès par queues
r метод *m* доступа с очередями

7549 queue entry
d Warteschlangeneintragung *f*
f inscription *f* de queue
r вхождение *n* в очередь

7550 queu[e]ing
d Einreihen *n* in Warteschlange; Bilden *n* der Warteschlangen; Warteschlangenorganisation *f*
f mise *f* en queue; création *f* de queues
r образование *n* очереди; организация *f* очередей; очередизация *f*

7551 queu[e]ing circuit
d Warteschlangen-Schaltung *f*
f circuit *m* de mise en queue
r схема *f* образования очереди

7552 queu[e]ing condition
d Warteschlangen-Zustand *m*
f condition *f* de mise en queue
r состояние *n* очередизации

7553 queu[e]ing delay
d Warteschlangen-Verzugszeit *f*
f délai *m* de mise en queue
r задержка *f* очередизации

7554 queu[e]ing field
d Schlangebereich *m*; Schlangefeld *n*

f champ *m* de queue
r поле *n* очереди

7555 queu[e]ing list
  d Warteschlangenliste *f*
  f liste *f* de queue
  r список *m* очереди

7556 queu[e]ing model; waiting-line model
  d Warteschlangenmodell *n*
  f modèle *m* de queue; modèle de file d'attente
  r модель *f* очереди

7557 queu[e]ing principle
  d Wartezeitprinzip *n*
  f principe *m* de mise en queue
  r принцип *m* очередизации

7558 queu[e]ing probability
  d Wartewahrscheinlichkeit *f*
  f probabilité *f* de mise en queue
  r вероятность *f* образования очереди

7559 queu[e]ing problem
  d Warteschlangenproblem *n*
  f problème *m* de queue
  r проблема *f* очереди

7560 queu[e]ing theory; theory of queues; waiting-line theory
  d Bedienungstheorie *f*; Warteschlangentheorie *f*; Theorie *f* der Massenbedienung
  f théorie *f* de files d'attente; théorie des queues
  r теория *f* очередей; теория [массового] обслуживания

7561 queue interface
  d Warteschlangenschnittstelle *f*
  f interface *f* de queue
  r интерфейс *m* очереди

7562 queue length
  d Warteschlangenlänge *f*
  f longueur *f* de queue
  r длина *f* очереди

7563 queue length indicator
  d Warteschlangenlängenanzeige *f*
  f indicateur *m* de longueur de queue
  r указатель *m* длины очереди

  * queuing → 7550

  * queuing circuit → 7551

  * queuing condition → 7552

  * queuing delay → 7553

  * queuing field → 7554

  * queuing list → 7555

  * queuing model → 7556

  * queuing principle → 7557

  * queuing probability → 7558

  * queuing problem → 7559

  * queuing theory → 7560

7564 quick digitalization
  d Schnelldigitalisierung *f*
  f digitalisation *f* rapide
  r быстрое оцифрование *n*

7565 quick format
  d Schnellformatierung *f*
  f formatage *m* rapide
  r быстрое форматирование *n*

7566 quick reference
  d schneller Verweis *m*
  f référence *f* rapide
  r быстрая ссылка *f*

7567 quick-start modem
  d Schnellstart-Modem *n*; Anfahr-Modem *n*
  f modem *m* à connexion rapide
  r модем *m* быстрого доступа

7568 quiescent state
  d Ruhezustand *m*
  f état *m* de repos
  r состояние *n* покоя

7569 quiescing
  d Zurückweisungshalt *m*
  f arrêt *m* de refus; "quiescing" *m*
  r "замораживание" *n*; останов *m* из-за отказа

7570 quinary
  d quinär
  f quinaire
  r пятеричный

7571 quinary number
  d quinäre Zahl *f*
  f nombre *m* quinaire
  r пятеричное число *n*

  * quit → 3582

  * quittance → 109

7572 quota
  d Quote *f*

    f quota *m*
    r процентная часть *f*; доля *f*; квота *f*

7573 quota method
    d Leitungssuchverfahren *n* nach prozentualer
       Verkehrsaufteilung
    f méthode *f* de quotas
    r метод *m* квот

    * **quotation mark → 453**

    * **quotation marks → 3139**

    * **quote marks → 3139**

    * **quotes → 3139**

7574 qwerty keyboard
    d Qwerty-Tastatur *f*
    f clavier *m* qwerty
    r клавиатура *f* qwerty

R

* **rack** → 876

* **radial configuration** → 8837

* **radial network** → 8860

* **radiant** → 3372

7575 radiator; cooler
   d Kühler *m*; Heizkörper *m*; Kühlkörper *m*
   f radiateur *m*; dissipateur *m* thermique
   r излучатель *m*; радиатор *m*

7576 radio button
   d Radioschaltfläche *f*; rundes Optionsfeld *n*;
     Optionsschaltfläche *f*; Schaltknopf *m*
   f bouton *m* radio; bouton d'option; cercle *m*
     d'option; case *f* radio
   r радиокнопка *f*; зависимая кнопка *f*

7577 radio card
   d Funkkarte *f*; Radiokarte *f*
   f carte *f* radio
   r радио-плата *f*

7578 radiosity; adaptive meshing
     (of global illumination model)
   d Radiosity *n*
   f radiosité *f*
   r диффузное отражение *n*; излучательность *f*

7579 radiosity algorithm
   d Radiosity-Algorithmus *m*
   f algorithme *m* de radiosité
   r алгоритм *m* диффузного отражения

7580 radiosity model
   d Radiosity-Modell *n*
   f modèle *m* de radiosité
   r модель *f* излучательности; модель
     диффузного отражения

7581 radix; base [number]; count base
     (of a number system)
   d Zahlenbasis *f*; Grundzahl *f*; Grundbasis *f*;
     Radix *f*
   f base *f* [de numération]; nombre *m* de base
   r основание *n* системы счисления

7582 radix complement; complement on n; true
     complement
   d Radixkomplement *n*; n-Komplement *n*;
     wahres Komplement *n*; Basiskomplement *n*

   f complément *m* à la base; complément vrai;
     complément juste
   r дополнение *n* до основания системы
     счисления; дополнение до n; точное
     дополнение

7583 radix-minus-one complement; diminished
     radix complement; complement on n-1
   d (n-1)-Komplement *n*
   f complément *m* à la base minus un;
     complément faux
   r поразрядное дополнение *n*; обратный
     код *m*; дополнение до (n-1)

7584 radix notation; base notation; radix scale;
     scale notation
   d Basisschreibweise *f*; Radixschreibweise *f*
   f notation *f* de base; notation de racine;
     notation positionnelle
   r позиционное представление *n*

* **radix number system** → 7147

7585 radix point
   d Radixpunkt *m*; Zahlenkomma *n*;
     Basiskomma *n*
   f point *m* de base; virgule *f* numérique
   r точка *f* в позиционном представлении;
     запятая *f* в позиционном представлении

* **radix scale** → 7584

* **radix sort** → 7586

7586 radix sort[ing]; digital sorting; pocket
     sorting
   d · digitales Sortierverfahren *n*;
     Ziffernsortiermethode *f*
   f tri[age] *m* digital; tri[age] numérique
   r цифровая сортировка *f*; поразрядная
     сортировка

* **RAM** → 7593

* **RAMDAC** → 7587

7587 RAM digital/analog converter; RAMDAC
   d RAM-Digital-Analog-Konverter *m*;
     RAM-Digital-Analog-Wandler *m*
   f convertisseur *m* numérique-analogique RAM
   r цифрово-аналоговый преобразователь *m*
     памяти с произвольным доступом

* **RAM disk** → 9861

* **ramification** → 1157

* **ramification point** → 1163

7588 ramified algorithm
   d verzweigter Algorithmus *m*

f algorithme *m* ramifié
r разветвлённый алгоритм *m*

7589 ramp-load head
d Kopf *m* mit veränderbarem Andruck
f tête *f* à pression variable
r головка *f* с переменным усилием прижима

* **ramp time → 8478**

7590 RAM-resident program; memory-resident; terminate-and-stay resident program; TSR program; resident program
d residentes Programm *n*
f programme *m* résident
r резидентная программа *f*

7591 random; aleatory; stochastic; accidental; arbitrary
d zufällig; Zufalls-; willkürlich; stochastisch
f aléatoire; arbitraire; accidentel; fortuit; stochastique
r случайный; стохастический; произвольный

7592 random access
d wahlfreier Zugriff *m*; beliebiger Zugriff; Zufallszugriff *m*
f accès *m* m aléatoire; accès arbitraire
r произвольный доступ *m*; случайный доступ

7593 random-access memory; RAM; read-write memory
d Speicher *m* mit wahlfreiem Zugriff; Lese-Schreib-Speicher *m*; RAM
f mémoire *f* à accès aléatoire; mémoire [de] lecture-écriture; RAM
r память *f* с произвольным доступом; память для чтения-записи

7594 random-access network
d Netz *n* mit Zufallszugriff
f réseau *m* à accès aléatoire
r сеть *f* со случайным доступом

* **random data → 497**

7595 random error; accidental error
d Zufallsfehler *m*; statistischer Fehler *m*
f erreur *f* aléatoire; erreur accidentelle
r случайная ошибка *f*

7596 random event; chance event
d zufälliges Ereignis *n*
f événement *m* aléatoire; événement fortuit
r случайное событие *n*

* **randomization → 7597**

7597 randomizing; randomization; hashing
d willkürliche Verteilung *f*; Randomisierung *f*; Hashing *n*
f randomisation *f*; arrangement *m* au hasard; hashing *m*; transformation *f* aléatoire
r рандомизация *f*; хэширование *n*; расположение *n* в случайном порядке

7598 random logic
d frei gestaltete Logik *f*; willkürlich angeordnete Logik
f logique *f* de structure libre
r логические схемы *fpl* с нерегулярной структурой

7599 randomness
d Wahllosigkeit *f*
f aspect *m* aléatoire; caractère *m* aléatoire
r стохастичность *f*; случайность *f*

7600 random number
d Zufallszahl *f*
f nombre *m* aléatoire
r случайное число *n*

7601 random number generator
d Zufallsgenerator *m*
f générateur *m* de nombres aléatoires
r генератор *m* случайных чисел

7602 random order
d zufällige Ordnung *f*
f ordre *m* aléatoire
r случайный порядок *m*; произвольный порядок

7603 random sample
d Zufallsstichprobe *f*
f échantillon *m* aléatoire
r случайная выборка *f*; произвольная выборка

* **random sampling → 6565**

7604 random variable; aleatory variable
d Zufallsvariable *f*; Zufallsgröße *f*
f variable *f* aléatoire; grandeur *f* aléatoire
r случайная переменная *f*; случайная величина *f*

7606 range; span
d Spannweite *f*; Variationsbreite *f*
f étendue *f*
r размах *m*; амплитуда *f*

* **range → 10103**

7605 range
d Umfang *m*; Reichweite *f*; Wertebereich *m*; Diapason *m*

f plage *f*; rangée *f*
r охват *m*; область *f* значений; диапазон *m*

7607 range of a sample
d Stichproben[variations]breite *f*
f étendue *f* d'un échantillon
r размах *m* выборки

* **rank** → 6575

7608 rank
d Rang *m*
f rang *m*
r ранг *m*

7609 ranking
d Rangierung *f*
f rangement *m*
r ранжирование *n*; упорядочение *n*

7610 rapid recording
d Schnellaufzeichnung *f*
f enregistrement *m* rapide
r ускоренная запись *f*

* **RARP** → 8054

7611 raster; scan pattern; grid
(of a screen)
d Raster *m*; Grid *n*
f trame *f*; rastre *m*; grille *f*
r растр *m*; решётка *f*; сетка *f*

7612 raster angle; screen angle
d Rasterwinkel *m*
f angle *m* de rastre; angle de trame
r угол *m* [поворота] растра; угол установки растра

* **raster blaster** → 1058

7613 raster board; grid board
d Raster[leiter]platte *f*
f plaque *f* à trame; plaque à grille
r плата *f* с координатной сеткой

7614 raster conversion
d Rasterkonvertierung *f*
f conversion *f* en rastre
r растровое преобразование *n*

7615 raster count
d Rasterzahl[ung] *f*
f nombre *m* de pixels de trame; comptage *m* de grilles; définition *f* de trame
r число *n* элементов растра; отсчёт *m* адресуемых координат

* **raster data** → 1005

7616 raster data model
d Modell *n* der Rasterdaten
f modèle *m* de données de trame
r модель *f* данных растра

7617 raster density
d Rasterdichte *f*
f densité *f* de rastre; densité de trame
r плотность *f* растра

7618 raster direction
d Rasterrichtung *f*
f direction *f* de rastre
r направление *n* растра

7619 raster display; matrix display; raster monitor
d Rasterbildschirm *m*; Rasterdisplay *n*; Rastermonitor *m*; Matrixanzeige *f*
f écran *m* dot-matrice; écran à balayage [tramé]; écran à balayage récurrent; visu *m* matriciel; visu à quadrillage
r растровый дисплей *m*; матричный дисплей; мозаичный индикатор *m*

7620 raster file
d Rasterdatei *f*
f fichier *m* rastre; fichier trame
r растровый файл *m*

7621 raster file format
d Format *n* der Rasterdatei
f format *m* de fichier rastre
r формат *m* растрового файла

7622 raster font; matrix font; bitmap font
d Rasterschrift *f*; Matrixschrift *f*
f police *f* de caractères tramés; police de caractères en mode points; police de trame; police matricielle
r растровый шрифт *m*; матричный шрифт *m*

7623 raster graphics; bitmap[ped] graphics; pixel graphics; scan graphics
d Rastergrafik *f*; Bitmap-Grafik *f*; Pixel-Grafik *f*; Punktgrafik *f*
f graphique *m* rastre; graphique trame; infographie *f* par quadrillage; infographie par balayage tramé; graphique bitmap; graphique de visualisation par bits; graphique à pixels
r растровая графика *f*; графика с растровым отображением; точечная графика

7624 raster graphics system
d rastergrafische System *f*
f système *m* de graphique trame
r растровая графическая система *f*

7625 raster grid
d Rastergitter *n*

f grille *f* rastre
r растровая сетка *f*

7626 raster image; matrix image; bitmap [image]
d Rasterbild *n*; Bitmap *n*; Bitmap-Bild *n*
f image *f* matricielle; image rastre; image pixélisée; image à points; bitmap *m*
r растровое изображение *n*; побитовое отображение *n*; поразрядное отображение; точечное изображение

7627 raster image memory
d Rasterbildspeicher *m*
f mémoire *f* d'images rastres; mémoire d'images matricielles
r память *f* растровых изображений

7628 raster image processor
d Raster-Image-Prozessor *m*
f processeur *m* d'images matricielles
r процессор *m* растровых изображений

7629 rasterization
d Rasterung *f*
f rastérisation *f*
r растеризация *f*; растрирование *n*

7630 rasterize *v*
d rastern
f rastériser
r растеризовать; преобразовывать в растровый формат

7631 raster line; gridline
d Rasterlinie *f*
f ligne *f* de rastre; ligne de trame; ligne de grille
r линия *f* растра; растровая линия; линия сетки

* **raster monitor → 7619**

* **raster overlay → 7633**

7632 raster pattern
d Rastermuster *n*
f modèle *m* trame
r растровая модель *f*

7633 raster[-pattern] overlay
d Rastermuster-Overlay *n*
f recouvrement *m* de [modèle] trame
r перекрытие *n* растровой модели

7634 raster plotter
d Rasterplotter *m*
f traceur *m* par ligne; traceur à trame
r растровый графопостроитель *m*

7635 raster plotting
d Rasterplottern *n*
f traçage *m* par ligne; traçage à trame
r растровое вычерчивание *n*

* **raster point → 8240**

7636 raster printer
d Rasterdrucker *m*
f imprimante *f* rastre
r растровый принтер *m*

7637 raster-scan device
d Rasterscan-Gerät *n*; Rasterscan-Einrichtung *f*
f dispositif *m* à balayage de trame
r растровое сканирующее устройство *n*

* **raster scan → 7638**

7638 raster scan[ning]
d Rasterscannen *n*; Rasterabtastung *f*
f balayage *m* ligne par ligne; balayage récurrent; balayage de trame
r растровое сканирование *n*

7639 raster-scan writing
d Rasterscan-Schreiben *n*
f enregistrement *m* trame
r растровая запись *f*

7640 raster-[to-]vector conversion
d Raster-Vertor-Konvertierung *f*
f conversion *f* de rastre en vecteur
r растрово-векторное преобразование *n*

7641 raster unit
d Rastereinheit *f*
f unité *f* de trame
r растровая единица *f*

* **raster-vector conversion → 7640**

* **rate → 1639, 1831, 8774**

* **rated → 6209**

7642 rated life
d Nennlebensdauer *f*
f durée *f* de vie nominale
r номинальный срок *m* службы

7643 rated load; nominal load
d Nennlast *f*; Nennbelastung *f*
f charge *f* nominale
r номинальная нагрузка *f*; расчётная нагрузка

* **rated output → 7644**

**7644 rated power; power rating; nominal
       rating; rated output**
   d Nennleistung *f*
   f puissance *f* nominale
   r номинальная мощность *f*

  * **rated value** → 6212

  * **rating** → 6212

7645 rating chart
   d Leistungsdiagramm *n*
   f diagramme *m* de charge
   r нагрузочная способность *f*

  * **rational language** → 7847

7646 raw data
   d Rohdaten *pl*; unbehandelte Daten *pl*
   f données *fpl* brutes; données crues
   r необработанные данные *pl*

  * **raw tape** → 1048

  * **ray** → 878

7647 ray casting
   d Ray-Casting *n*
   f transtypage *m* de rayons
   r отслеживание *n* лучей

7648 ray-casting technique
   d Ray-Casting-Technik *f*
   f technique *f* de transtypage
   r техника *f* отслеживания лучей

7649 raytrace rendering
   d Ray-Trace-Rendering *n*
   f rendu *m* lancé de rayons
   r тонирование *n* трассировкой лучей;
      рендеринг *m* трассировкой лучей

7650 raytracing
   d Ray-Tracing *n*; Strahlverfolgung *f*
   f raytracing *m*; lancé *m* de rayons
   r трассировка *f* лучей

7651 raytracing application
   d Ray-Tracing-Anwendung *f*
   f application *f* de raytracing
   r приложение *n* трассировки лучей

7652 raytracing method
   d Ray-Tracing-Methode *f*
   f méthode *f* de raytracing
   r метод *m* трассировки лучей

  * **RCTL** → 8005

  * **RDBMS** → 7859

  * **reachability** → 74

  * **reach-through** → 2302

7653 reach-through hole
   d Durchgangsloch *n*
   f trou *m* à travers
   r сквозное отверстие *n*

  * **read** → 7665

7654 read *v*; sense *v*
   d lesen; ablesen
   f lire
   r читать; считывать

7655 readability
   d Lesbarkeit *f*
   f lisibilité *f*
   r удобочитаемость *f*

7656 read-back
   d Rücklesen *n*; Echolesen *n*
   f lecture *f* arrière; écho-lecture *f*
   r обратное считывание *n*; эхосчитывание *n*

  * **read-back check** → 3266

7657 read buffer
   d Lesepuffer *m*
   f tampon *m* de lecture
   r буфер *m* считывания

7658 read bus
   d Lesebus *m*
   f bus *m* de lecture
   r шина *f* чтения

7659 read data
   d Lesedaten *pl*
   f données *fpl* de lecture
   r считываемые данные *pl*

7660 readdressing
   d Umadressierung *f*; Neuadressierung *f*
   f réadressage *m*
   r переадресация *f*; переадресование *n*

7661 read driver
   d Leseleitungstreiber *m*
   f formateur *m* [de signaux] de lecture
   r формирователь *m* [сигналов] считывания

7662 reader
     (a program)
   d Eingabeprogramm *n*
   f programme *m* d'entrée
   r программа *f* ввода

7663 reader; reading unit
   d Leser *m*; Leseeinheit *f*

f lecteur *m*; unité *f* de lecture
r считыватель *m*; считывающее
устройство *n*

* **read head** → 7666

7664 read-in *v*
d einlesen
f lire dans; introduire
r считать в; записывать

7665 read[ing]; sensing
d Lesen *n*; Ablesen *n*; Ablesung *f*
f lecture *f*
r чтение *n*; считывание *n*

7666 read[ing] head; sensing head
d Lesekopf *m*
f tête *f* lectrice; tête de lecture
r считывающая головка *f*

7667 reading line
d Ablesestrich *m*
f division *f* de lecture; trait *m* de repère
r отсчётный штрих *m*

7668 read[ing] rate; read[ing] speed
d Lesegeschwindigkeit *f*; Leserate *f*
f vitesse *f* de lecture
r скорость *f* чтения; скорость считывания

* **reading speed** → 7668

7669 read[ing] time; readout time; sensing time
d Lesezeit *f*; Auslesezeit *f*
f temps *m* de lecture
r время *n* чтения; время считывания

* **reading unit** → 7663

7670 read-mostly memory; RMM
d Meist-Lese-Speicher *m*
f mémoire *f* surtout à lire; mémoire RMM
r память *f* преимущественно для чтения;
репрограммируемая память

**7671 read-only memory; ROM; fixed memory;
permanent memory**
d Nurlesespeicher *m*; Festwertspeicher *m*;
Permanentspeicher *m*; ROM
f mémoire *f* à lecture seulement; mémoire fixe;
mémoire permanente; mémoire morte
r память *f* только для чтения; постоянная
память; ПЗУ

7672 readout
d Auslesen *n*; Sichtanzeige *f*; Anzeige *f*
f lecture *f*; affichage *m*; relevé *m*
r считывание *n*; вывод *m* считываемой
информации; снятие *n* показаний; отсчёт *m*

7673 read-out *v*
(from memory)
d auslesen; ausgeben; herauslesen
f lire; extraire
r считывать [из памяти]; извлекать

7674 read[out] pulse; readout strobe
d Auslesetakt *m*
f impulsion *f* de lecture
r импульс *m* считывания

* **readout strobe** → 7674

* **read pulse** → 7674

* **read rate** → 7668

7675 readset
d zu lesender Satz *m*
f ensemble *m* à lire
r считываемый набор *m*

* **read speed** → 7668

* **read time** → 7669

7676 read time slot
d Auslesezeitlage *f*
f tranche *f* de temps de lecture
r квант *m* времени считывания

7677 read-write channel
d Lese-Schreib-Kanal *m*
f canal *m* de lecture-écriture
r канал *m* записи-считывания

7678 read-write conflict
d Lese-Schreib-Konflikt *m*
f collision *f* lecture-écriture
r конфликт *m* [по совпадению обращений
для] чтения и записи

7679 read-write head; combined head
·d Lese-Schreib-Kopf *m*; kombinierter Kopf *m*
f tête *f* de lecture-écriture; tête combinée
r головка *f* чтения-записи; универсальная
головка

* **read-write memory** → 7593

7680 ready
d fertig; bereit
f prêt; fait
r готовый

* **ready condition** → 7681

7681 ready criterion; ready condition
d Bereitschaftskriterium *m*

f critère m d'empressement; condition f
d'empressement
r критерий m готовности

7682 ready flag; done flag
d Fertigkennzeichen n; Ready-Flag n
f flag m fait; drapeau m prêt
r флаг m готовности

7683 ready for data
d Datenempfangsbereitschaft m;
Übertragungsbereitschaft m
f empressement m de [réception de] données
r готовность f приёма данных

7684 ready state; ready status
d Bereitzustand m
f état m prêt
r состояние n готовности

* **ready status** → 7684

* **ready-to-receive condition** → 7685

**7685 ready-to-receive state; ready-to-receive
condition**
d Empfangsbereitschaft m
f état m prêt de réception
r состояние n готовности приёма

7686 ready-to-transmit state
d Sendebereitschaft m
f état m prêt de transmission
r состояние n готовности к передаче

7687 real
d real; Real-; reell; Echt-
f réel
r реальный; вещественный

* **RealAudio** → 7688

7688 RealAudio [technology]
(a software application that lets you hear
sound over the Web)
d echtes Audio n
f technologie f RealAudio
r RealAudio-технология f

7689 realism
d Realismus m
f réalisme m
r реализм m

7690 realistic computer graphics
d realistische Computergrafik f
f graphique m d'ordinateur réaliste
r реалистическая компьютерная графика f

7691 realistic image

d realistisches Bild n
f image f réaliste
r реалистическое изображение n

7692 realistic image synthesis
d Synthese f des realistischen Bilds
f synthèse f d'image réaliste
r синтез m реалистического изображения

* **realizability** → 3730

7693 real luser; luser
(loser + user)
d Luser m; naives Gemüt n (Verlierer +
PC/Internet-Benutzer)
f internouille m; nultilisateur m; nultilisatrice f
r неумелый пользователь m

7694 RealMedia architecture; RMA
(audio, video and animation)
d RealMedia-Technologie f
f technologie f RealMedia
r RealMedia-технология f

7695 RealMedia encoder
d RealMedia-Encoder m
f encodeur m RealMedia
r RealMedia-шифратор m

* **real memory** → 6968

* **real storage** → 6968

7696 realtime adj
d Echtzeit-; Realzeit-
f en temps réel; live
r в реальном времени; в реальном масштабе
времени

7697 realtime animation
d Realzeitanimation f
f animation f en temps réel
r мультипликация f в реальном времени;
анимация f в реальном времени

7698 realtime buffer
d Echtzeitpuffer m
f tampon m [de mode] de temps réel
r буфер m [режима] реального времени

7699 realtime clock
d Echtzeituhr f; Echtzeittakt m
f horloge f en temps réel
r часы pl реального времени; датчик m
реального времени

7700 realtime [computer] graphics
d Realzeitgrafik f; Echtzeit-Computer-Grafik f
f graphique m en temps réel
r графика f в реальном времени

* realtime counter → 7713

7701 realtime data
  d Echtzeitdaten pl
  f données fpl en temps réel
  r данные pl в системах реального времени

7702 realtime 3D virtual world
  d Realzeit-3D-Virtualwelt f
  f monde m virtuel 3D en temps réel
  r трёхмерный виртуальный мир m в реальном времени

7703 realtime 3D visualization
  d Realzeit-3D-Visualisierung f
  f visualisation f tridimensionnelle en temps réel
  r трёхмерная визуализация f в реальном времени

7704 realtime gesture recognition system
  d Realzeit-Gestenerkennungssystem n
  f système m de reconnaissance des gestes en temps réel
  r система f распознавания жестов в реальном времени

* realtime graphics → 7700

7705 realtime mode
  d Echtzeitarbeitsmodus m; Echtzeitbetrieb m
  f régime m en temps réel; mode m en temps réel
  r режим m [работы] в реальном времени

7706 realtime-oriented 3D graphics toolkit
  d Realtime-orientierte 3D-Grafikwerkzeugsatz m
  f kit m d'instruments de graphique 3D en temps réel
  r инструментальный набор m трёхмерной графики в реальном времени

7707 realtime output
  d Echtzeitausgabe f; Echtzeitausgang m
  f sortie f en temps réel
  r вывод m в реальном времени

7708 realtime processing
  d Echtzeitverarbeitung f; Realzeitverarbeitung f
  f traitement m en temps réel
  r обработка f в реальном времени

7709 realtime rendering
  d Realzeitrendering n
  f rendu m en temps réel
  r тонирование n в реальном времени; рендеринг m в реальном времени

7710 realtime sampling
  d Realzeit-Stichprobenauswahl f

  f échantillonnage m en temps réel
  r выборка f в реальном времени

7711 realtime video; live video
  d Realzeit-Video n
  f vidéo m en temps réel
  r реальное видео n; видео в реальном [масштабе] времени; "живое" видео

7712 realtime visual simulation
  d visuelle Simulation f in Realzeit
  f simulation f visuelle en temps réel
  r визуальная симуляция f в реальном времени

7713 realtime [working] counter
  d Realzeitzähler m; Echtzeitzähler m
  f compteur m en temps réel
  r счётчик m[, работающий] в реальном времени

7714 realtime zooming
  d Realzeitzoomen n
  f zoom m en temps réel
  r масштабирование n в реальном времени

* rearrangement → 7930

* reasonableness check → 7052

* reassembler → 2975

7715 reassembling; disassembling
  d Reassemblierung f; Disassemblierung f
  f réassemblage m; désassemblage m
  r обратное ассемблирование n

7716 reassignment
  d Neuzuweisung f
  f réattribution f
  r переназначение n

7717 reboot v
  d neu booten
  f réamorcer
  r повторно загружать

7718 reboot
  d Wiederselbstladen n
  f rechargement m initial
  r повторная начальная загрузка f; перезагрузка f

7720 recall v
  d wiederaufrufen; zurückrufen
  f rappeler; appeler de nouveau
  r вызывать снова

7719 recall; ringback; callback
  d Wiederherbeiruf m; Rückruf m; Rückfrage f

f rappel *m*; appel *m* répété; appel par retour;
appel double
r повторный вызов *m*; обходной вызов;
двойной вызов

* **receipt operation** → **4384**

7721 **receive** *v*
d empfangen; aufnehmen
f recevoir; acquérir; obtenir
r получать; принимать

7722 **receive buffer**
d Empfangspuffer *m*
f tampon *m* de réception
r буфер *m* приёма

7723 **receive buffer register**
d Empfangspufferregister *n*
f registre *m* de tampon de réception
r буферный регистр *m* приёма

7724 **receive control**
d Empfangssteuerung *f*
f contrôle *m* de réception
r управление *n* приёмом ·

* **receive data** → **7729**

7725 **received backward channel data**
d Hilfskanal-Empfangsdaten *pl*
f données *fpl* reçues par canal inverse
r данные *pl*, принимаемые обратным
каналом

7726 **received-bit timing**
d Empfangsbittakt *m*
f synchronisation *f* des bits reçus
r синхронизация *f* принимаемых битов

7727 **received-byte timing**
d Empfangsbytetakt *m*
f synchronisation *f* des octets reçus
r синхронизация *f* принимаемых байтов

7728 **received-character timing**
d Empfangszeichentakt *m*
f synchronisation *f* des caractères reçus
r синхронизация *f* принимаемых символов

7729 **receive[d] data**
d Empfangsdaten *pl*
f données *fpl* reçues
r принимаемые данные *pl*

7730 **receiver; recipient**
d Empfänger *m*
f récepteur *m*; destinataire *m*
r приёмник *m*; получатель *m*; реципиент *m*;
адресат *m*

* **recept** → **53**

* **reception** → **53**

7731 **receptor**
d Rezeptor *m*
f récepteur *m*
r рецептор *m*

* **recipient** → **7730**

* **reciprocation** → **3205**

* **reciprocity** → **3205**

* **recirculating shift register** → **1691**

* **reckon** *v* → **1345**

7732 **recognition**
d Erkennung *f*
f reconnaissance *f*
r распознавание *n*; различение *n*

7733 **recognition logic**
d Erkennungslogik *f*
f logique *f* de reconnaissance
r логика *f* распознавания

7734 **recognition matrix**
d Erkennungsmatrix *f*
f matrice *f* de reconnaissance
r распознающая матрица *f*

7735 **recognize** *v*
d erkennen
f reconnaître
r распознавать

7736 **recognizer**
d Erkennungseinrichtung *f*
f reconnaisseur *m*
r устройство *n* распознавания

7737 **recognizing grammar**
d identifizierende Grammatik *f*
f grammaire *f* de reconnaissance
r распознающая грамматика *f*

7738 **recompile** *v*
d neu übersetzen
f recompiler
r перекомпилировать; повторно
компилировать

7739 **reconfiguration; reconfiguring**
d Rekonfigurierung *f*
f reconfiguration *f*
r реконфигурация *f*

*   **reconfiguring** → 7739

7740 reconnect *v*
  d umklemmen; umkoppeln
  f réconnaître
  r распознавать

*   **record** *v* → 10060

*   **record** → 2589

7741 record address
  d Satzadresse *f*
  f adresse *f* d'enregistrement
  r адрес *m* записи

*   **recorder** → 5458, 9205

*   **record gap** → 1069

*   **record head** → 10064

*   **recording** → 5459

*   **recording head** → 10064

*   **recording rate** → 10072

*   **recording speed** → 10072

7742 record layout; record structure
  d Satzstruktur *f*; Datensatz-Layout *n*;
    Satzaufbau *m*
  f disposition *f* d'enregistrement; structure *f*
    d'enregistrement
  r структура *f* записи

*   **record lock** → 7743

7743 record lock[ing]
  d Satzsperre *f*; Satzverriegelung *f*
  f verrou *m* [au niveau] d'enregistrement;
    verrouillage *m* d'enregistrement
  r замок *m* [на уровне] записи; захват *m*
    записи; блокировка *f* записи

*   **record rate** → 10072

7744 record separator
  d Satztrennzeichen *n*;
    Aufzeichnungsseparator *m*
  f séparateur *m* d'enregistrements
  r разделитель *m* записей

*   **record speed** → 10072

*   **record structure** → 7742

7745 recover *v*; **restore** *v*
  d wiederherstellen; wiedereinsetzen

  f récupérer; regagner; restaurer; restituer;
    remettre
  r восстанавливать

7746 recoverable abend
  d Abnormalhalt *m* mit Wiederaufbau
  f arrêt *m* anormal restaurable
  r аварийный останов *m* с восстановлением

7747 recoverable error
  d heilbarer Fehler *m*; wiedergutzumachender
    Fehler
  f erreur *f* remédiable
  r ошибка *f*, допускающая восстановление;
    исправимая ошибка

*   **recovery** → 8024

7748 rectangular array
  d rechteckiges Feld *n*
  f réseau *m* rectangulaire; tableau *m*
    rectangulaire
  r прямоугольный массив *m*

7749 rectangular cell
  d rechtwinklige Zelle *f*
  f cellule *f* rectangulaire
  r прямоугольная клетка *f*

7750 rectangular loop
    (of hysteresis)
  d Rechteckschleife *f*
  f boucle *f* rectangulaire
  r прямоугольная петля *f*

7751 rectangular pulse
  d Rechteckimpuls *m*
  f impulsion *f* rectangulaire
  r прямоугольный импульс *m*

7752 rectangular window; orthogonal window
  d rechtwinkliges Fenster *n*
  f fenêtre *f* rectangulaire; fenêtre orthogonale
  r прямоугольное окно *n*

*   **rectification** → 2808

*   **rectifier** → 2811

7753 rectify *v*
  d rektifizieren
  f rectifier; redresser
  r спрямлять; ректифицировать

7754 recursion
  d Rekursion *f*
  f récursion *f*; récurrence *f*
  r рекурсия *f*

7755 recursive algorithm
  d rekursiver Algorithmus *m*

f algorithme *m* récursif
r рекурсивный алгоритм *m*

7756 recursive descendant method
d rekursive Absteigemethode *f*
f méthode *f* récurrente décroissante
r метод *m* рекурсивного спуска

7757 recursive function
d rekursive Funktion *f*
f fonction *f* récursive
r рекурсивная функция *f*

7758 recursive list; self-referent list
d rekursive Liste *f*
f liste *f* récursive
r рекурсивный список *m*

7759 recursive raytracing
d rekursives Ray-Tracing *n*
f raytracing *m* récursif
r рекурсивная трассировка *f* лучей

7760 recursivity
d Rekursivität *f*
f récursivité *f*
r рекурсивность *f*

7761 recycle bin; waste basket; trash [bin]
d Mülleimer *m*
f boîte *f* de recyclage
r корзина *f* для мусора; мусорная корзина

7762 recycling
d Rückführung *f*; Recycling *n*
f recyclage *m*
r рециркуляция *f*; рециклирование *n*;
возврат *m*

7763 recycling program
d Rückführungsprogramm *n*
f programme *m* de recyclage
r программа *f* возврата

7764 redefinition
d Umdefinieren *n*; Neufestlegung *f*
f rédéfinition *f*
r переопределение *n*

7765 red, green and blue; RGB
d Rot, Grün und Blau; RGB
f rouge, vert et bleu; RVB
r красный, зелёный и синий

* **redirect** *v* → **4002**

7766 redirect[ion] page
d umleitende Seite *f*
f page *f* de redirection
r перенаправленная страница *f*;

переадресованная страница

* **redirect page** → **7766**

7767 redisplay *v*
d wiederdarstellen
f réafficher
r повторно изображать

7768 redistribution
d Umverteilung *f*; Neuverteilung *f*
f redistribution *f*
r перераспределение *n*

7769 redo *v*
d wiederherstellen
f rétablir (la dernière opération annulée)
r переделывать

7770 redo command
d Wiederherstellungsbefehl *m*
f commande *f* de rétablissement
r команда *f* переделывания

7771 reduce *v*
d reduzieren; verringern
f réduire
r приводить; сокращать; редуцировать

* **reduced** → **2**

7772 reduced data
d reduzierte Daten *pl*; verdichtete Daten *pl*
f données *fpl* réduites
r сжатые данные *pl*

7773 reduced grammar
d reduzierte Grammatik *f*
f grammaire *f* réduite
r ограниченная грамматика *f*

7774 reduced input
d reduzierte Eingabe *f*
f entrée *f* réduite
r ввод *m* уплотнённой информации

7775 reduced instruction set computer; RISC
d Rechner *m* mit reduziertem Befehlsatz
f ordinateur *m* à jeu d'instructions réduit
r компьютер *m* с сокращённым набором
команд

7776 reduced reservation
d reduzierte Reservation *f*
f réservation *f* réduite
r сокращённое резервирование *n*; сжатое
резервирование

7777 reduced view
d reduzierte Ansicht *f*

f vue *f* réduite
r уменьшенный вид *m*

* **reducing** → 7778

7778 reduction; reducing; foreshortening
d Reduktion *f*; Reduzierung *f*; Verkleinerung *f*;
   Verringerung *f*
f réduction *f*
r редукция *f*; понижение *n*; приведение *n*;
   сокращение *n*

7779 reduction of contrast
d Kontrastminderung *f*; Schwärzungsabfall *m*
f réduction *f* du contraste
r понижение *n* контраста

7780 reduction of data; data reduction
d Reduktion *f* der Daten; Datenreduktion *f*
f réduction *f* des données
r сокращение *n* данных; приведение *n*
   данных

7781 reduction of gray value
d Reduktion *f* des Grauwerts
f réduction *f* de valeur de gris
r уменьшение *n* оттенка серого

7782 redundancy; superabundance;
   excessiveness
d Redundanz *f*; Reserve *f*
f redondance *f*; excédent *m*; réserve *f*
r избыточность *f*; резерв *m*

7783 redundancy check; redundant [digit] check
d Redundanzprüfung *f*; Redundanzkontrolle *f*
f contrôle *m* par redondance; essai *m* de
   redondance
r контроль *m* [с введением] избыточности

7784 redundancy of language
d Redundanz *f* der Sprache
f redondance *f* de langage
r избыточность *f* языка

7785 redundancy rate
d Redundanzrate *f*
f degré *m* de redondance
r кратность *f* резервирования

7786 redundant; abundant; excessive
d redundant; überschießend; abundant;
   überflüssig; übervollständig
f redondant; abondant; excessif
r избыточный; резервный; резервированный

7787 redundant bit
d redundantes Bit *n*
f bit *m* redondant
r избыточный бит *m*

7788 redundant character
d redundantes Zeichen *n*
f caractère *m* redondant
r избыточный знак *m*

* **redundant check** → 7783

7789 redundant code
d redundanter Code *m*
f code *m* redondant
r избыточный код *m*

* **redundant digit check** → 7783

7790 redundant failure
d Redundanzausfall *m*
f défaillance *f* de système redondant
r отказ *m* резервной системы

* **redundant replica** → 3225

7791 redundant system
d redundantes System *n*
f système *m* redondant
r избыточная система *f*

* **reenterability** → 7793

7792 reenterable; reentrant
d wiedereintrittsfähig; eintrittsinvariant;
   ablaufinvariant
f réentrable; réentrant; réutilisable
r многократно используемый; многократно
   входимый

* **reenterable program** → 7796

7793 reentrance; reenterability
d Wiedereintrittsinvarianz *f*; Ablaufinvarianz *f*;
   Reenterabilität *f*
f réentrance *f*
r повторная входимость *f*

7794 reentrance feature
d Wiedereintrittsfähigkeit *f*
f facilité *f* de réentrance
r возможность *f* многократного входа

* **reentrant** → 7792

7795 reentrant data
d Wiedereintrittsdaten *pl*
f données *fpl* de réentrance
r повторно входимые данные *pl*

7796 reentrant program; reenterable program
d wiedereintrittsfähiges Programm *n*;
   eintrittsinvariantes Programm

f programme *m* réentrant; programme
réentrable
r многократно используемая программа *f*

* **reentry** → 7851

7797 reexecution
d Wiederausführung *f*
f réexécution *f*
r повторное выполнение *n*

7798 reference
d Referenz *f*; Verweis *m*
f référence *f*
r ссылка *f*; обращение *n*

7799 reference
d Bezug *m*
f référence *f*
r эталон *m*; опора *f*

* **reference address** → 830

7800 reference beam
d Referenzstrahl *m*
f faisceau *m* de référence
r опорный луч *m*; эталонный луч

7801 reference by meaning
d Referenz *f* nach dem semantischen Inhalt
f référence *f* par signification
r обращение *n* по смыслу

7802 reference circuit
d Bezugskreis *m*
f circuit *m* de référence
r эталонная цепь *f*

* **reference clock** → 7803

7803 reference clock [generator]
d Bezugstaktgeber *m*
f générateur *m* d'horloge de référence
r опорный тактовый датчик *m*

7804 reference clock pulse
d Bezugstakt *m*
f tact *m* de référence; horloge *f* de référence
r опорный тактовый импульс *m*

7805 reference data
d Bezugsdaten *pl*
f données *fpl* de référence
r справочные данные *pl*; эталонные данные

7806 reference data system
d Bezugsdatensystem *n*
f système *m* de données de référence
r справочно-информационная система *f*

7807 reference edge
d Bezugskante *f*; Bezugsrand *m*
f marge *f* de référence
r опорный край *m*

7808 reference file; memo file
d Referenzdatei *f*; Bezugsdatei *f*
f fichier *m* de référence; fichier étalon
r эталонный файл *m*; справочный файл

* **reference frame** → 4045

7809 reference frequency; master frequency
d Bezugsfrequenz *f*; Referenzfrequenz *f*
f fréquence *f* de référence
r опорная частота *f*; задающая частота;
ведущая частота

7810 reference instruction
d Referenzbefehl *m*
f instruction *f* de référence
r инструкция *f* обращения

7811 reference language
d Bezugssprache *f*
f langage *m* de référence
r эталонный язык *m*

* **reference mark** → 2409

7812 reference recording
d Bezugsaufzeichnung *f*
f écriture *f* de référence
r контрольная запись *f*

7813 reference signal
d Bezugssignal *n*
f signal *m* de référence
r опорный сигнал *m*; эталонный сигнал

* **reference system** → 9150

7814 reference toolbar
d Referenz-Hilfsmittelstreifen *m*
f barre *f* d'outils de référence
r инструментальная панель *f* ссылок

7815 reference voxel
d Referenz-Voxel *n*
f voxel *m* de référence
r эталонный трёхмерный пиксел *m*

7816 refined data
d verfeinerte Daten *pl*
f données *fpl* raffinées
r уточнённые данные *pl*

* **refinement operation** → 2591

* **reflected binary code** → 2476

7817 **reflecting software; reflector**
(a program)
d Reflektor *m*
f réflecteur *m*
r программа-отражатель *f*

7818 **reflective LCD**
d reflektiver Flüssigkristallbildschirm *m*
f écran *m* à cristaux liquides réfléchissant
r отражающий жидкокристаллический
дисплей *m*; отражающий ЖК-дисплей *m*

* **reflector** → 7817

* **reformat** → 7819

7819 **reformat[ting]**
d Umformatieren *n*; Formatänderung *f*
f reformatage *m*; modification *f* du format
r переформатирование *n*; изменение *n*
формата

7820 **reframe** *v*
d Aufnahmen wiederherstellen
f recadrer
r повторно кадрировать

7821 **reframing**
d Aufnahmen-Wiederherstellung *f*;
Rahmenänderung *f*
f retramage *m*; recadrage *m*
r повторное формирование *n* кадра;
повтор *m* кадрирования

* **refresh** → 7825

7822 **refresh** *v*; **freshen** *v* **up**
d auffrischen; erneuern
f rafraîchir
r обновлять; освежать

7823 **refresh buffer**
d Refresh-Puffer *m*; Auffrischungspuffer *m*
f tampon *m* de rafraîchissement
r буфер *m* регенерации

7824 **refresh display**
d Bildschirm *m* mit Bildwiederholung;
Refresh-Display *n*
f écran *m* à rafraîchissement d'image
r дисплей *m* с регенерацией изображения

7825 **refresh[ing]; refreshment**
d Auffrischung *f*; Refresh *n*
f rafraîchissement *m*
r обновление *n*; регенерация *f*

* **refreshment** → 7825

7826 **refresh rate**

(of an image)
d Auffrischrate *f*; Refresh-Rate *f*;
Wiederholfrequenz *f*; Wiederholrate *f*
f fréquence *f* de rafraîchissement
r частота *f* регенерации

7827 **regenerate** *v*
d regenerieren
f régénérer
r регенерировать

7828 **regenerate** *v* **texture**
d Füllmuster regenerieren
f régénérer une texture
r регенерировать текстуру

7829 **regeneration**
d Regenerierung *f*; Regeneration *f*
f régénération *f*
r регенерация *f*; повторная генерация *f*

7830 **regenerative repeater; intermediate
repeater; regenerator; repeater [circuit]**
d Zwischenregenerator *m*;
Zwischenverstärker *m*; Regenerator *m*;
Wiederholer *m*; Repeater *m*
f répéteur *m* [régénérateur]; répéteur
intermédiaire; régénérateur *m*;
amplificateur *m* intermédiaire
r промежуточный повторитель *m*;
промежуточный усилитель *m*;
регенератор *m*

* **regenerator** → 7830

* **regional network** → 5825

* **register** *v* → 5456

* **register** → 5458

7831 **register**
(a digital circuit)
d Register *n*
f registre *m*
r регистр *m*

7832 **register addressing**
d Registeradressierung *f*
f adressage *m* par registre
r регистровая адресация *f*

* **register array** → 7834

* **register capacity** → 7835

7833 **registered application**
d registrierte Anwendung *f*
f application *f* enregistrée
r регистрированное приложение *n*

7834 register file; register set; register array
 d Registerfeld *n*; Registersatz *m*;
    Registerblock *m*
 f fichier *m* de registres; jeu *m* de registres;
    champ *m* de registres
 r регистровый файл *m*; блок *m* регистров

7835 register length; register capacity
 d Registerlänge *f*; Registerkapazität *f*
 f longueur *f* de registre; capacité *f* de registre
 r длина *f* регистра; разрядность *f* регистра

7836 register operand
 d Registeroperand *m*
 f opérande *m* de registre
 r регистровый операнд *m*

7837 register printout
 d Registerausdruck *m*
 f impression *f* de registres
 r распечатка *f* содержимого регистров

7838 register rotation
 d Registerumlauf *m*
 f rotation *f* de registre
 r кольцевой сдвиг *m* регистра

 * **register set → 7834**

7839 register stack
 d Registerkeller *m*
 f pile *f* de registres
 r стек *m* регистров

 * **register switching system → 7841**

7840 register-to-register instruction
 d Register-zu-Register-Befehl *m*
 f instruction *f* d'échange registre-registre;
    instruction entre registres
 r инструкция *f* межрегистровой пересылки

7841 register[-type] switching system
 d Registerkoppelsystem *n*
 f système *m* de commutation de registres
 r регистровая система *f* коммутации

 * **registration → 5459**

7842 registration problem
 d Registrierproblem *n*
 f problème *m* d'enregistrement
 r проблема *f* регистрации

7843 regression
 d Regression *f*
 f régression *f*
 r регрессия *f*

7844 regular cell structure
 d reguläre Zellenstruktur *f*; regelmäßige
    Zellenstruktur
 f structure *f* de cellule régulière
 r регулярная клеточная структура *f*;
    однородная структура

7845 regular data transfer
 d regulärer Datentransfer *m*; normaler
    Datentransfer
 f transfert *m* de données régulier
 r регулярный перенос *m* данных

 * **regular error → 9134**

7846 regular font
 d regelmäßige Schrift *f*
 f police *f* régulière
 r нормальный шрифт *m*

7847 regular language; rational language
 d reguläre Sprache *f*
 f langage *m* régulier; langage rationnel
 r регулярный язык *m*

 * **regulate *v* → 246**

7848 regulation
 d Regelung *f*; Regulierung *f*
 f régulation *f*; réglage *m*
 r регулирование *n*

7849 regulator
 d Regler *m*; Regelgerät *n*
 f régulateur *m*
 r регулятор *m*

 * **reinitialization → 8019**

7850 reinitialize *v*; reinitiate *v*
 d neu starten; neu einleiten; neu einrichten; neu
    vorbereiten
 f réinitialiser
 r повторно инициализировать

 * **reinitiate *v* → 7850**

7851 reinput; reinsertion; reentry
 d Wiedereingabe *f*; Wiedereintritt *m*
 f réintroduction *f*; réinsertion *f*; entrée *f* de
    retour
 r повторный вход *m*; повторный ввод *m*;
    повторное внесение *n*

 * **reinsertion → 7851**

 * **reinstall → 7852**

7852 reinstall[ation]
 d Wiedereinsetzen *n*

f réinstallation *f*
r переинсталлирование *n*

7853 reiteration
d Wiederholung *f*
f réitération *f*
r повторная итерация *f*

* **reiterative redundancy** → **5979**

7854 reject *v*; **discard** *v*; **throw** *v* **off**
d beseitigen; verwerfen; ablehnen
f rejeter; repousser; refuser; décliner
r отбрасывать; выбрасывать; отклонять

* **reject** → **7855**

7855 reject[ion]
d Verwerfen *n*; Rückweisung *f*; Ablehnung *f*
f rejet *m*
r отбрасывание *n*; отказ *m*; непринятие *n*

7856 rekeying
d Tastaturwiedereingabe *f*
f réentrée *f* par clavier
r повторный ввод *m* с клавиатуры

7857 relation
d Relation *f*; Beziehung *f*
f relation *f*; rapport *m*
r реляция *f*; отношение *n*

7858 relational database
d Relationsdatenbasis *f*
f base *f* de données relationnelle
r реляционная база *f* данных

7859 relational database management system; RDBMS
d relationales Datenbasis-Managementsystem *n*
f système *m* de gestion de bases de données relationnelles; SGDBR
r система *f* управления реляционных баз данных

7860 relation[al] operator
d relationale Operator *m*
f opérateur *m* de relation
r реляционный оператор *m*; оператор отношения

7861 relation character; relation symbol
d Relationszeichen *n*
f caractère *m* de relation; symbole *m* relationnel
r знак *m* отношения; символ *m* [операции] отношения

* **relation operator** → **7860**

7862 relationship
d Zusammenhang *m*
f relation *f* [mutuelle]
r взаимоотношение *n*; взаимосвязь *f*

* **relation symbol** → **7861**

7863 relative address
d relative Adresse *f*
f adresse *f* relative
r относительный адрес *m*

7864 relative programming
d relative Programmierung *f*
f programmation *f* relative
r программирование *n* в относительных адресах

7865 relative redundancy
d relative Redundanz *f*
f redondance *f* relative
r относительная избыточность *f*

7866 relay
d Relais *n*
f relais *m*
r реле *n*

* **relay** → **6133, 9502**

* **relaying** → **9502**

7867 relay set
d Relaissatz *m*
f ensemble *m* de relais
r релейный набор *m*; набор реле

* **release** → **9776**

7868 release; enable
(of a resource)
d Auslösen *n*; Auslösung *f*; Freigabe *f*
f relâchement *m*; déclenchement *m*; libération *f*
r разблокировка *f*; освобождение *n*

7869 release circuit
d Freigabeschaltung *f*
f circuit *m* de déclenchement
r схема *f* разблокировки

* **release pulse** → **9554**

7870 release signal
d Freigabesignal *n*
f signal *m* de déclenchement
r сигнал *m* отключения; сигнал *m* разблокировки

7871 relevance feedback
(documents retrieved in a search that are used to further refine the search)

d Bedeutungsrückkopplung *f*
f rétroaction *f* de pertinence; pertinence *f* rétroactive; contrôle *m* de pertinence
r релевантная обратная связь *f*

7872 **relevance logic**
(in knowledge base)
d Bedeutung-Logik *f*
f logique *f* [de définition] de pertinence
r логика *f* определения релевантности; механизм *m* определения релевантности

7873 **reliability**
d Zuverlässigkeit *f*
f fiabilité *f*
r надёжность *f*; безотказность *f*

7874 **reliability data**
d Zuverlässigkeitsdaten *pl*
f données *fpl* de fiabilité
r показатели *mpl* надёжности

7875 **reliability test**
d Zuverlässigkeitstest *m*
f essai *m* de fiabilité
r испытания *npl* на надёжность

7876 **reliability theory; theory of reliability**
d Zuverlässigkeitstheorie *f*
f théorie *f* de fiabilité
r теория *f* надёжности

7877 **reliable**
d zuverlässig; betriebssicher
f fiable
r надёжный; достоверный

*   **relief effect → 3362**

*   **reload → 7879**

7878 **reload** *v*
d nachfüllen
f recharger; réamorcer
r перезагружать

7879 **reload[ing]**
d Neuladung *f*; Neuladen *n*
f rechargement *m*
r повторная загрузка *f*; перезагрузка *f*

7880 **reload state**
d Neuladung-Zustand *m*
f état *m* de rechargement
r состояние *n* перезагрузки

*   **relocatability → 7127**

*   **relocatable → 7129**

7881 **relocatable address**
d verschiebbare Adresse *f*
f adresse *f* relocatable
r перемещаемый адрес *m*; настраиваемый адрес

7882 **relocatable library**
d verschiebbare Bibliothek *f*; Bibliothek von Objektmodulen; Modulbibliothek *f*
f bibliothèque *f* de programmes relogeables; bibliothèque de modules d'objets
r перемещаемая библиотека *f*; библиотека объектных модулей

7883 **relocatable module**
d verschiebbarer Modul *m*
f module *m* relocatable
r перемещаемый модуль *m*; настраиваемый модуль

*   **relocatable program → 7135**

7884 **relocating loader**
d verschieblicher Lader *m*
f chargeur *m* translatant; chargeur à décalage
r перемещающий загрузчик *m*

7885 **relocation**
d Umsiedlung *f*; Versetzung *f*
f relocation *f*; relogement *m*
r перемещение *n*; настройка *f* по месту

*   **remainder → 7887**

7886 **remainder register**
d Restregister *n*
f registre *m* de reste
r регистр *m* остатка

7887 **remainder [term]; rest**
d Rest *m*; Restglied *n*
f reste *m*; terme *m* résiduel
r остаток *m*; остаточный член *m*

*   **remark → 6298**

7888 **remote**
d Remote-; entfernt; Fern-
f distant; à distance; éloigné
r дистанционный; удалённый

7889 **remote access**
d Fernzugriff *m*
f accès *m* à distance; accès distant; accès éloigné
r дистанционный доступ *m*

*   **remote access method → 9228**

7890 **remote-access server**
  d Fernzugriff-Server *m*
  f serveur *m* d'accès distant
  r сервер *m* дистанционного доступа

7891 **remote adjustment**
  d Ferneinstellen *n*
  f ajustement *m* éloigné
  r удалённая настройка *f*

7892 **remote administration**
  d Fernadministration *f*
  f administration *f* éloignée
  r удалённое администрирование *n*

7893 **remote batch**
  d Remote-Batch *m*
  f pile *f* à distance; pile éloignée
  r дистанционный пакет *m*

7894 **remote batch teleprocessing**
  d Remote-Batch-Fernverarbeitung *f*
  f télétraitement *m* par lots
  r телеобработка *f* в пакетном режиме

  * **remote communication** → 9229

7895 **remote control; distance control;**
      telecontrol; telecommand; teleguidance;
      supervisory control
  d Fernsteuerung *f*; Fernwirken *n*;
      Fernkontrolle *f*
  f télécontrôle *m*; télécommande *f*;
      téléguidage *m*
  r телеуправление *n*; дистанционное
      управление *n*; телеконтроль *m*

7896 **remote data**
  d Ferndaten *pl*
  f données *fpl* à distance; données éloignées
  r данные *pl*, поступающие дистанционно

  * **remote data entry** → 7897

7897 **remote data input; remote data entry**
  d Datenferneingabe *f*
  f entrée *f* de données éloignée
  r дистанционный ввод *m* данных;
      удалённый ввод данных

7898 **remote data output**
  d Datenfernausgabe *f*
  f sortie *f* de données éloignée
  r дистанционный вывод *m* данных

  * **remote data processing** → 2598

  * **remote data transmission** → 2597

7899 **remote device**

  d Ferngerät *n*
  f dispositif *m* éloigné
  r удалённое устройство *n*; дистанционное
      устройство

7900 **remote diagnostic**
  d Ferndiagnose *f*
  f diagnostic *m* éloigné; télédiagnostic *m*
  r дистанционная диагностика *f*

7901 **remote diagnostic system**
  d Ferndiagnosesystem *n*
  f système *m* de diagnostic éloigné
  r система *f* дистанционной диагностики

7902 **remote dialog processing**
  d Dialogfernverarbeitung *f*
  f traitement *m* dialogue éloigné
  r диалоговая дистанционная обработка *f*

  * **remote load** → 3143

  * **remote loading** → 3143

7903 **remote maintenance; remote support**
  d Fernwartung *f*
  f télémaintenance *f*
  r дистанционная поддержка *f*

7904 **remote output**
  d Fernausgabe *f*
  f sortie *f* éloignée
  r дистанционный выход *m*

7905 **remote procedure call; RPC**
  d Fernprozeduraufruf *m*;
      Fernverfahrensaufruf *m*
  f invocation *f* de procédures à distance
  r удалённый вызов *m* процедур

  * **remote processing** → 9236

7906 **remote sensing**
  d Fernerkundung *f*; Fernablesung *f*;
      Fernabtastung *f*
  f télédétection *f*; détection *f* à distance
  r дистанционное зондирование *n*

  * **remote support** → 7903

7907 **remote terminal**
  d Fernterminal *n*
  f terminal *m* distant
  r удалённый терминал *m*; дистанционный
      терминал

7908 **remote user**
  d Remote-Benutzer *m*
  f utilisateur *m* éloigné
  r удалённый пользователь *m*

* **remote vote** → 9242

* **removable** → 7072

* **removable disk** → 3564

7909 **removable disk pack store**
  d Wechselplattenspeicher *m*
  f dispositif *m* à disque interchangeable
  r запоминающее устройство *n* со сменным
  диском

7910 **removal; removing**
  d Entfernung *f*; Aussonderung *f*; Beseitigung *f*
  f enlèvement *m*; dégagement *m*
  r удаление *n*; устранение *n*

* **remove** *v* → 1709

* **removing** → 7910

7911 **rename** *v*
  d neubenennen; umbenennen
  f changer de nom; renommer
  r переименовать

7912 **rename** *v* **page**
  d die Seite umbenennen
  f renommer une page
  r переименовать страницу

7913 **renaming**
  d Umbenennung *f*
  f renomination *f*
  r переименование *n*

7914 **render** *v*
  d rendern; wiedergeben
  f rendre
  r тонировать

7915 **render background color**
  d Hintergrundfarbe *f* des Renderings
  f couleur *f* de fond de rendu
  r фоновый цвет *m* тонирования

7916 **render [display] window**
  d Rendering-Fenster *n*
  f fenêtre *f* [d'affichage] de rendu
  r окно *n* тонирования; окно рендеринга

7917 **rendered object**
  d gerendertes Objekt *n*
  f objet *m* rendu
  r тонированный объект *m*

7918 **rendered texture**
  d gerenderte Textur *f*
  f texture *f* rendue
  r тонированная текстура *f*

7919 **render effects**
  d Rendering-Effekte *mpl*
  f effets *mpl* de rendu
  r эффекты *mpl* тонирования; эффекты
  рендеринга

7920 **renderer**
  (a program)
  d Rendering-Programm *n*
  f fournisseur *m*; moteur *m* de rendu
  r программа *f* рендеринга

7921 **render file**
  d Rendering-Datei *f*
  f fichier *m* de rendu
  r рендеринг-файл *m*

7922 **rendering**
  d Rendering *n*; Rendern *n*
  f rendu *m*
  r тонирование *n*; рендеринг *m*

7923 **rendering algorithm**
  d Rendering-Algorithmus *m*
  f algorithme *m* de rendu
  r алгоритм *m* тонирования; алгоритм
  рендеринга

7924 **rendering equation**
  d Rendering-Gleichung *f*
  f équation *f* de rendu
  r уравнение *n* тонирования; уравнение
  рендеринга

7925 **rendering pipeline**
  (a series of 2D views, separated from 3D
  model)
  d Rendering-Fließband *n*
  f conveyor *m* de rendu
  r конвейер *m* тонирования; конвейер
  рендеринга

7926 **rendering process**
  d Rendering-Prozess *m*
  f processus *m* de rendu
  r процесс *m* тонирования; процесс
  рендеринга

7927 **rendering processor**
  d Rendering-Prozessor *m*
  f processeur *m* rendu
  r тонирующий процессор *m*;
  рендеринг-процессор *m*

7928 **render toolbar**
  d Rendering-Hilfsmittelstreifen *m*
  f barre *f* d'outils de rendu
  r инструментальная панель *f* тонирования

* **render window** → 7916

* **reorder** → 7930

7929 reorder *v*
d neuordnen; umordnen
f réarranger
r переупорядочивать

7930 reorder[ing]; rearrangement
d Umordnung *f*; Neuordnung *f*
f reclassement *m*; réarrangement *m*
r переупорядочение *n*; перестройка *f*

7931 repaginate *v*
d neupaginieren
f repaginer
r перевёрстывать; повторно разбивать на
страницы; перенумеровать страницы

7932 repair *v*
d reparieren
f réformer; remédier
r исправлять; восстанавливать

7933 repeat *v*
d wiederholen
f répéter
r повторять[ся]

7934 repeatability
d Wiederholbarkeit *f*
f répétitivité *f*
r повторяемость *f*

* **repeat counter** → 7936

* **repeater** → 7830

* **repeater circuit** → 7830

* **repeat reading** → 7975

7935 repeat scanning; rescanning
d wiederholte Abtastung *f*;
Abfühlwiederholung *f*; Wiederabfühlung *f*
f exploration *f* répétée; balayage *m* répétitif;
exploration répétitive
r повторное сканирование *n*; повторный
отсчёт *m*

7936 repeat [time] counter; repetition counter
d Wiederhol[ungs]zeitzähler *m*
f compteur *m* de répétitions
r счётчик *m* повторений

* **repertoire** → 7937

7937 repertory; repertoire
d Vorrat *m*; Menge *f*
f répertoire *m*; stock *m*
r набор *m*; перечень *m*; реестр *m*; опись *m*

* **repertory** → 2962

7938 repertory code
d Kurz[ruf]nummer *f*; Kurzwahlzeichen *n*
f code *m* de répertoire
r код *m* справочника

7939 repetition
d Repetition *f*; Wiederholung *f*
f répétition *f*
r повторение *n*

* **repetition counter** → 7936

7940 repetition instruction
d Wiederholungsbefehl *m*
f instruction *f* de répétition
r инструкция *f* повторения; инструкция
организации цикла

7941 repetitive mode
d repetierender Betrieb *m*
f mode *m* de répétition
r циклический режим *m*; режим повторения

* **repetitive statement** → 5157

7942 replace *v*
d ersetzen
f remplacer; substituer
r подставлять; заменять

7943 replace *v* **color**
d eine Farbe ersetzen
f remplacer une couleur
r замещать цвет

7944 replacement
d Ersetzung *f*; Ersatz *m*
f remplacement *m*
r замена *f*

**7945 replacement redundancy; standby
redundancy**
d Redundanz *f* durch Ersetzen;
Standby-Redundanz *f*;
nichtfunktionsbeteiligte Redundanz
f redondance *f* par remplacement; redondance à
substitution
r резервирование *n* замещением;
резервирование путём дублирования

7946 replacer
d Umsetzgerät *n*; Austauscher *m*
f substitueur *m*
r устройство *n* замещения; заменитель *m*

7947 replace *v* **text**
d einen Text ersetzen

f remplacer un texte
r замещать текст

* **replication** → 3141

7948 replication of code
d Programmvervielfältigung *f*;
Programmreplikation *f*
f duplication *f* de code; duplication de
programme
r тиражирование *n* программы

7949 reply message
d Antwortmeldung *f*; Antwortnachricht *f*
f message *m* de réponse
r ответное сообщение *n*

7950 report
d Report *m*; Liste *f*; Bericht *m*
f rapport *m*; liste *f*
r отчёт *m*

* **reporter** → 7952

7951 report format
d Listenformat *n*
f format *m* de rapport
r формат *m* отчёта

**7952 report generator; report writer; reporter;
list generator**
d Reportgenerator *m*; Listengenerator *m*
f générateur *m* de rapports; générateur de listes
r генератор *m* отчётов

7953 report heading
d Listenkopf *m*
f titre *m* de rapport
r заголовок *m* отчёта

* **reporting** → 9508

* **report program** → 5419

7954 report section
d Listenkapitel *n*
f section *f* de rapport; section de liste
r раздел *m* отчёта; глава *f* отчёта

* **report writer** → 7952

7955 repository
d Behälter *m*; Aufbewahrungsort *m*;
Repository *n*; Lager *m*
f référentiel *m*
r репозиторий *m*; архив *m*; хранилище *n*

7956 representation
d Repräsentation *f*
f représentation *f*

r представление *n*

7957 reprocessing
d Aufarbeitung *f*
f retraitement; remaniement *m*
r переработка *f*

7958 reproducer; reproductor
d Dubliziergerät *n*; Vervielfältiger *m*;
Doppler *m*
f reproducteur *m*; reproductrice *f*
r дубликатор *m*; репродуктор *m*

7959 reproducibility
d Reproduzierbarkeit *f*
f reproductibilité *f*
r воспроизводимость *f*

7960 reproducing channel
d Wiedergabekanal *m*
f canal *m* de reproduction
r канал *m* воспроизведения

7961 reproduction
d Reproduktion *f*
f reproduction *f*
r воспроизведение *n*; репродукция *f*

* **reproductor** → 7958

7962 reprogramming
d Umprogrammieren *n*; Neuprogrammieren *n*
f reprogrammation *f*
r перепрограммирование *n*

**7963 request; interrogation; demand; inquiry;
enquiry; query**
d Anforderung *f*; Abfrage *f*; Anfrage *f*
f requête *f*; interrogation *f*; question *f*;
demande *f*
r запрос *m*; опрос *m*; заказ *m*; справка *f*

7964 request chain
d Anforderungskette *f*
f chaîne *f* de demandes
r цепочка *f* запросов

**7965 requested information; wanted
information**
d angeforderte Information *f*
f information *f* demandée
r потребованная информация *f*

7966 request for comments; RFC
(the documents that contain the standards and
other information for the TCP/IP protocols
and the Internet in general)
d Abfrage *f* für Bemerkungen; Anforderung *f*
für Bemerkungen

f demande *f* de commentaires
r запрос *m* на комментарии

7967 request for discussion; RFD
d Abfrage *f* für Diskussion; Anforderung *f* für Konferenz
f demande *f* de discussion
r запрос *m* на обсуждение

7968 request initiator
d Anforderungsinitiator *m*
f initiateur *m* de requête
r инициатор *m* запроса

* request response time → 88

7969 request to send; RTS
d Sendeaufforderung *f*
f demande *f* d'envoyer
r запрос *m* на передачу

7970 request word
d Anforderungswort *n*
f mot *m* de requête
r слово *n* запроса

7971 required; desired; sought for; wanted
d gesucht; verlangt
f cherché; désiré
r искомый; запрашиваемый

7972 requirement; demand
d Forderung *f*; Anforderung *f*; Bedarf *m*; Erfordernis *n*
f nécessité *f*; exigence *f*
r требование *n*; потребность *f*

7973 requirement description
d Bedarfsdeskription *f*
f description *f* des nécessités
r описание *n* требований; техническое задание *n*

7974 requirements tracer
(a program)
d Anforderungsverfolger *m*; Anforderungsfolge-Prüfprogramm *n*
f traceur *m* de demandes; programme *m* de poursuite de demandes
r программа *f* прослеживания требований

7975 rereading; repeat reading
d wiederholte Lesung *f*
f lecture *f* répétée; relecture *f*
r повторное считывание *n*

* rerecording → 8068

7976 rerun
d Wiederholungslauf *m*; Wiederanlauf *m*

f repassage *m*
r повторный прогон *m*

7977 rerun *v*; rollback *v*
d wiederholen
f réexécuter; reprendre
r повторять прогон; повторять запуск

7978 rerun point
d Wiederholungspunkt *m*
f point *m* de reprise; point de repassage
r точка *f* перезапуска

7979 resample *v*
d wieder abfragen; wieder abtasten; wieder probieren
f rééchantillonner
r делать повторную выборку [изображения]; сделать перевыборку

7980 resampling
d wiederholte Stichprobenauswahl *f*
f rééchantillonnage *m*
r повторная выборка *f*

* rescanning → 7935

7981 rescue dump
d Rettungsumspeicherung *f*
f vidage *m* de sauvegarde; vidage protecteur
r защитный дамп *m*

7982 research
d Forschung *f*; Suche *f*
f recherche *f*
r исследование *n*; поиск *m*

7983 research-oriented processing
d forschungsorientierte Verarbeitung *f*
f traitement *m* orienté recherche
r обработка *f* экспериментальных данных

7984 reselection
d wiederholte Selektion *f*
f resélection *f*
r повторный выбор *m*

7985 reservation
d Reservation *f*; Reservierung *f*
f réservation *f*
r резервирование *n*

7986 reservation data
d Reservierungsdaten *pl*
f données *fpl* de réservation
r данные *pl* резервирования

* reserve → 780

7987 reserved word
d reserviertes Wort *n*

f mot m réservé
r зарезервированное слово n; служебное
слово

* **reset** v → **428, 10095**

* **reset** → **7993, 8024, 8037**

7988 reset v; **back** v **out**
d zurücksetzen; rücksetzen; zurückbringen
f remettre; retourner; rappeler
r возвращать [в исходное состояние];
сбрасывать; переустановлять

7989 reset collision
d Rücksetzzusammenstoß m
f collision f de remise
r конфликт m сброса; конфликт возврата в
исходное состояние

7990 reset input
d Rücksetzeingang m
f entrée f de remise à zéro; entrée à l'état initial
r вход m сброса; вход установки в исходное
состояние

7991 reset mode
d Betriebsart f "Rücksetzen"
f mode m de remise
r режим m задания начальных условий

7992 reset signal
d Rückstellsignal n; Rückstellzeichen n
f signal m de remise à zéro
r сигнал m сброса; сигнал возврата в
исходное состояние

* **reset time** → **7994**

* **resetting** → **8024, 10096**

7993 reset[ting]
d Rückkehr f im Wiederanlaufpunkt
f relance f au point de reprise
r сброс m; возврат m в точку рестарта

7994 reset[ting] time
d Rücksetzzeit f
f temps m de retour; temps de remise [à zéro]
r время n возврата [в исходное состояние];
время сброса

7995 reshape v
d wieder formieren
f remettre en forme; reconstruire
r повторно формировать

7996 residence
d Aufenthalt m
f résidence f

r пребывание n; простой m

7997 residence time
d Verweilzeit f
f temps m de résidence; temps de blocage;
temps d'achèvement
r длительность f [программируемого]
останова

* **resident** → **7418**

7998 resident; in-core
d resident; speicherresident; systemeigen
f résident
r резидентный

7999 resident fonts
d Residentschriften fpl
f polices fpl résidentes
r резидентные шрифты mpl

* **resident program** → **7590**

8000 residual [class] code
d Restklassencode m
f code m de classe résiduelle; code résidu
r код m в остаточных классах; код в
остатках

* **residual code** → **8000**

8001 residual distortion
d Restverzerrung f
f distorsion f résiduelle
r остаточное искажение n

8002 residue check; modulo-n check
d Restprüfung f; Modulo-n-Kontrolle f;
Modulo-n-Prüfung f
f essai m résiduel; essai modulo n; contrôle m
modulo n
r контроль m по остатку; контроль по
модулю n

8003 resistance
d Widerstand m
f résistance f
r сопротивление n

8004 resistor
d Resistor m; Widerstand m
f résistance f; résistor m
r резистор m

8005 resistor-capacitor-transistor logic; RCTL
d Widerstand-Kondensator-Transistor-Logik f
f logique f résistor-condensateur-transistor
r резисторно-ёмкостно-транзисторная
логика f; РЭТЛ-схемы fpl

8006 resize *v*
  d in der Größe anpassen
  f redimensionner
  r переоразмерять

  * **resolution** → 2657, 8007

8007 **resolution [capability]; resolution power;
  resolving power**
  d Auflösungsvermögen *n*
  f pouvoir *m* de résolution; puissance *f* de
  résolution; résolution *f*
  r разрешающая способность *f*

8008 **resolution cell**
  d Auflösungsraumelement *n*; Rasterzelle *f*
  f point *m* de trame; point de résolution
  r клетка *f* растра

  * **resolution power** → 8007

8009 **resolver**
  d Auflöser *m*; Resolver *m*
  f [ré]solveur *m*
  r решающее устройство *n*

  * **resolving power** → 8007

8010 **resonator**
  d Schwinger *m*
  f résonateur *m*
  r резонатор *m*

8011 **resource**
  d Ressource *f*; Systemmittel *n*
  f ressource *f*
  r ресурс *m*

  * **resource administrator** → 8014

8012 **resource allocation**
  d Ressourcenzuordnung *f*;
  Systemmittelzuordnung *f*
  f allocation *f* des ressources
  r распределение *n* ресурсов

8013 **resource contention**
  d Ressourcenkonflikt *m*;
  Betriebsmittelanforderungskonflikt *m*
  f conflit *m* de ressources
  r конфликт *m* при доступе к ресурсам

8014 **resource manager; resource administrator**
  d Ressourcenmanager *m*;
  Ressourcenverwalter *m*
  f gestionnaire *m* de ressources
  r администратор *m* ресурсов;
  распорядитель *m* ресурсов

  * **response** → 434, 1614

  * **response curve** → 1614

8015 **response frame**
  d Antwortseite *f*; Antwortseitenrahmen *m*
  f page *f* exigeant une réponse; cadre *m* de
  réponse
  r кадр *m* ответа

8016 **response function**
  d Antwortfunktion *f*; Ansprechfunktion *f*
  f fonction *f* de réponse
  r функция-ответ *f*

8017 **response rate**
  d Antwortrate *f*; Ansprechrate *f*
  f cote *f* de réponse
  r коэффициент *m* [времени] ответа

  * **response signal** → 435

  * **responsivity** → 8379

  * **rest** → 7887

8018 **restart** *v*
  d aufsetzen; wiederanlaufen lassen
  f redémarrer; relancer; recommencer
  r повторно запускать; рестартировать

8019 **restart; reinitialization**
  d Wiederanlauf *m*; Restart *m*
  f reprise *f*; redémarrage *m*;
  recommencement *m*; réamorçage *m*
  r повторный [за]пуск *m*; рестарт *m*

8020 **restart collision**
  d Zusammenstoß *m* beim Restart
  f collision *f* de reprise
  r конфликт *m* рестарта; нарушение *n*
  рестарта

8021 **restart indication**
  d Restart-Anzeige *f*
  f indication *f* de reprise; indication de
  redémarrage
  r индикация *f* рестарта

8022 **restart priority**
  d Restartpriorität *f*
  f priorité *f* de reprise; priorité de redémarrage
  r приоритет *m* рестарта

8023 **restart request**
  d Restart-Anforderung *f*
  f requête *f* de reprise
  r запрос *m* на рестарт

  * **restoration** → 8024

  * **restore** *v* → 7745

8024 **restore; restoration; reset[ting]; recovery**
    d Wiederherstellung *f*; Wiederaufbau *m*;
      Erholung *f*; Rückgewinnung *f*
    f restauration *f*; restitution *f*; récupération *f*
    r восстановление *n*

8025 **restore; restoring**
    d Rückspeichern *n*
    f remémorisation *f*
    r повторное запоминание *n*

    * **restoring** → 8025

    * **restricted** → 1142

8026 **restricted access**
    d eingeschränkter Zugriff *m*; beschränkter
      Zugriff
    f accès *m* restreint
    r ограниченный доступ *m*

8027 **restriction; constraint**
    d Restriktion *f*; Einschränkung *f*;
      Beschränkung *f*; Nebenbedingung *f*
    f restriction *f*; contrainte *f*
    r ограничение *n*; рестрикция *f*

8028 **restructurable chip**
    d restrukturierbarer Chip *m*
    f puce *f* restructurable
    r кристалл *m* с изменяемой структурой

8029 **result; outcome**
    d Resultat *n*; Ergebnis *n*; Ausgang *m*
    f résultat *m*; issue *f*
    r результат *m*; исход *m*; итог *m*

8030 **resultant**
    d Resultante *f*
    f résultant *m*
    r результант *m*

    * **retardation** → 2721

    * **retention** → 6921

    * **retrace** → 3929

8031 **retransmission**
    d nochmalige Übertragung *f*; erneutes
      Senden *n*; Weitersendung *f*
    f retransmission *f*; retransfert *m*
    r повторная передача *f*; промежуточная
      передача

8032 **retransmitter**
    d Weiterbeförderer *m*
    f retransmetteur *m*
    r промежуточный передатчик *m*;
      ретранслятор *m*

    * **retrieval** → 8037, 8278

8033 **retrieval**
    d Wiederauffinden *n*; Wiederauffindung *f*
    f retrouvement *m*
    r повторный поиск *m*

8034 **retrieval code**
    d Informationssuchcode *m*
    f code *m* de recherche
    r код *m* поиска

    * **retrieval query** → 8035

8035 **retrieval request; retrieval query**
    d Suchanfrage *f*; Retrieval-Anforderung *f*;
      Rechercheanfrage *f*
    f requête *f* de recherche; interrogation *f* de
      recherche
    r поисковый запрос *m*; запрос на поиск

8036 **retrieve** *v*
    d nachholen; zugreifen; abrufen
    f rechercher; retrouver
    r искать; отыскать

8037 **return; reset; retrieval; backout**
    d Rückkehr *f*; Rücksetzen *n*; Rückstellen *n*;
      Backout *n*; Zurücksetzen *n*
    f retour *m*; remise *f* [en état]; rétablissement *m*;
      reprise *f*; rappel *m*
    r возврат *m*; возвращение *n*

8038 **return address**
    d Rückkehradresse *f*; Rücksprungadresse *f*
    f adresse *f* de retour
    r адрес *m* возврата

8039 **return buffer**
    d Rücksprungpuffer *m*
    f tampon *m* de retour
    r буфер *m* возврата

8040 **return button; return key**
    d Rückrichtung-Taste *f*
    f bouton *m* de retour; touche *f* de retour
    r кнопка *f* возврата

    * **return channel** → 785

8041 **return circuit**
    d Rückleitung *f*
    f circuit *m* de retour
    r схема *f* возврата

8042 **return code**
    d Rückkehrcode *m*
    f code *m* de retour
    r код *m* возврата

* **return instruction** → 775

* **return key** → 8040

8043 **return loss**
  d Rückflussdämpfung *f*; Fehlerdämpfung *f*
  f affaiblissement *m* de retour
  r затухание *n* при возврате; потери *fpl* из-за
     возврата

* **return path** → 3737

8044 **return pulse**
  d Rückimpuls *m*
  f impulsion *f* inverse
  r обратный импульс *m*

8045 **return switching circuit**
  d Rückkehrschaltkreis *m*
  f circuit *m* de commutation de retour
  r цепь *f* коммутации возврата

8046 **return-to-zero**
  d Rückkehr *f* zu Null
  f retour *m* à zéro
  r возвращение *n* к нулю; возврат *m* к нулю

8047 **return-to-zero coding**
  d Rückkehr-zu-Null-Codierung *f*
  f codage *m* de type retour à zéro
  r кодирование *n* типа возвращения к нулю

8048 **reusability**
  d Wiederverwendbarkeit *f*;
     Wiederbenutzbarkeit *f*
  f réutilisabilité *f*
  r возможность *f* многократного
     использования

8049 **reusable resource**
  d wiederverwendbare Ressource *f*;
     mehrfachnutzbares Betriebsmittel *n*
  f ressource *f* réutilisable
  r повторно используемый ресурс *m*;
     многократно используемый ресурс

8050 **reuse**
  d Wiederverwendung *f*
  f réusage *m*
  r многократное использование *n*; повторное
     использование

8051 **reversal**
  d Umkehrung *f*; Wendung *f*
  f retournement *m*; redressement *m*
  r реверсирование *n*; изменение *n*
     направления на обратное

8052 **reversal finder**
  d Umkehr[ungs]finder *m*;

     Umschwung-Finder *m*
  f viseur-redresseur *m*
  r реверсивный визир *m*

* **reversal time** → 9583

* **reverse** → 8056

8053 **reverse** *v*
  d umkehren; umdrehen
  f reverser
  r обращать; реверсировать

8054 **reverse ARP; RARP**
  d inverses Adressauflösungsprotokoll *n*
  f protocole *m* RARP
  r протокол *m* определения обратного адреса

* **reverse bias** → 745

* **reverse channel** → 785

8055 **reverse counter; up-down counter**
  d umgekehrter Zähler *m*
  f compteur *m* reverse
  r обратный счётчик *m*

8056 **reverse[d]; inverse[d]** *adj*
  d umgekehrt; umkehrt; invers
  f reverse; inverse; renversé; rétroactif
  r обратный; инверсный; перевёрнутый;
     реверсивный; противоположный

* **reverse operation** → 5124

8057 **reverse quote**
  (`)
  d Gegenquote *f*; Rückwärtsquote *f*
  f guillemet *m* renversé
  r обратная кавычка *f*

* **reverse scan** → 8058

8058 **reverse scan[ning]**
  d umgekehrte Abtastung *f*
  f balayage *m* inverse
  r обратное сканирование *n*; сканирование с
     возвратом

* **reverse video** → 5125

8059 **reversible**
  d umkehrbar
  f réversible
  r обратимый

* **reversible counter** → 914

8060 **reversible process**
  d umkehrbarer Prozess *m*

f processus *m* réversible
r обратимый процесс *m*

8061 reversion
 d Reversion *f*; Rücklauf *m*
 f réversion *f*; renversement *m*
 r перевращение *n*; обращение *n*

8062 revert *v*
 d zurückgeben; zurückkehren
 f retourner; revenir
 r возвращаться

8063 review
 d Rundschau *f*
 f revue *f*
 r просмотр *m*

 * **review article method → 909**

 * **revision → 652**

8064 revision number
 d Revisionsnummer *f*
 f numéro *m* de révision
 r номер *m* ревизии

8065 revision tracking
 d Revisionsverfolgung *f*
 f poursuite *m* de révision
 r прослеживание *n* ревизии

 * **revolve** *v* → **1687**

8066 rewind
 d Rückspulen *n*; Umspulen *n*
 f rembobinage *m*
 r перемотка *f*

8067 rewrite *v*
 d rückschreiben; wieder[ein]schreiben
 f ré[é]crire; réinscrire; réenregistrer
 r перезаписывать

8068 rewrite; rerecording
 d Wieder[ein]schreiben *n*; Umschnitt *m*
 f réécriture *f*; réenregistrement *m*
 r перезапись *f*

 * **RFC → 7966**

 * **RFD → 7967**

 * **RGB → 7765**

8069 RGB color
 d RGB-Farbe *f*
 f couleur *f* RVB
 r цвет *m* RGB

8070 RGB color format
 d RGB-Farbformat *n*
 f format *m* de couleurs RVB
 r цветной формат *m* RGB

8071 RGB color mode
 d RGB-Farbmodus *m*
 f régime *m* de couleurs RVB
 r цветной режим *m* RGB

8072 RGB image
 d RGB-Bild *n*
 f image *f* RVB
 r изображение *n* RGB

8073 RGB slider
 d RGB-Schieber *m*
 f curseur *m* RVB
 r ползунок *m* RGB

8074 RGB/XYZ matrix
 d RGB/XYZ-Matrix *f*
 f matrice RGB/XYZ
 r матрица *f* RGB/XYZ

 * **ribbon → 802, 4866**

 * **ribbon cable → 3889**

8075 ribbon cartridge
 d Farbbandkassette *f*
 f cartouche *f* de ruban
 r кассета *f* с красящей лентой

8076 rich text
 d erweiterter Text *m*
 f texte *m* enrichi
 r обогащённый текст *m*

8077 rich text format; RTF
 d erweitertes Textformat *n*; RTF-Format *n*
 f format *m* RTF
 r формат *m* RTF; формат обогащённого текста

8078 right
 d recht; gerade
 f droit
 r правый; прямой

 * **right address → 8082**

 * **right-aligned → 8084**

 * **right alignment → 8083**

8079 right arrow
 d Rechtspfeil *m*
 f flèche *f* droite
 r правая стрелка *f*

8080 **right arrow key**
   d Rechtspfeil-Taste *f*
   f touche *f* à flèche droite
   r клавиша *f* правой стрелки

8081 **right-click**
   (of the mouse)
   d Klick *m* auf der rechten Maustaste
   f clic *m* sur le bouton droit
   r щелчок *m* правой кнопки

8083 **right[-hand] justification; right alignment**
   d rechtsbündige Justierung *f*; rechtsbündige Ausrichtung *f*
   f justification *f* à droit; alignement *m* à droit
   r выравнивание *n* вправо; выравнение *n* по правому краю; выравнивание по самому правому знаку

8082 **right[-hand end] address; rightmost address**
   d rechte Adresse *f*
   f adresse *f* droite
   r правый адрес *m*

   * **right justification** → 8083

8084 **right-justified; right-aligned**
   d rechts ausgerichtet; rechtsbündig
   f serré à droit; aligné à droit
   r выровненный вправо

   * **rightmost address** → 8082

8085 **right mouse button**
   d rechte Maustaste *f*
   f bouton *m* droit de souris
   r правый бутон *m* мыши

8086 **right-of-access code**
   d Berechtigungszeichen *n*; Berechtigungsschlüssel *m*
   f code *m* de droit d'accès
   r код *m* права доступа

8087 **right scroll arrow**
   d Bildlaufpfeil *m* rechts
   f flèche *f* de défilement à droit
   r стрелка *f* прокрутки вправо

8088 **right shift; shift right**
   d Rechtsverschiebung *f*
   f décalage *m* à droit
   r сдвиг *m* вправо

   * **rightsizing** → 3146

8089 **rightsizing; downsizing**
   d Tendenz *f* zu kleineren Einheiten
   f migration *f* vers les systèmes petits; migration

vers le tout micro
   r выбор *m* оптимальной платформы; перенос *m* (прикладных систем) с больших компьютеров на малые

   * **rigid disk** → 4393

   * **ringback** → 7719

8090 **ring bus**
   d Ringbus *m*
   f bus *m* en anneau
   r кольцевая шина *f*

8091 **ring-bus transmission**
   d Ringbusübertragung *f*
   f transmission *f* par bus en anneau
   r передача *f* по кольцевой шине

8092 **ring configuration**
   d Ringstruktur *f*
   f configuration *f* en anneau
   r кольцевая конфигурация *f*

8093 **ring counter**
   d Ringzähler *m*
   f compteur *m* en anneau; compteur annulaire; compteur circulaire
   r кольцевой счётчик *m*

8094 **ring database**
   d Datenbasis *f* mit Ringstruktur
   f base *f* de données en anneau
   r база *f* данных с кольцевой структурой

   * **ring network** → 8097

8095 **ring port**
   d Ringport *m*
   f port *m* de réseau bouclé
   r порт *m* кольцевой сети

   * **ring shift** → 1685

8096 **ring topology**
   d Ringtopologie *f*
   f topologie *f* d'anneau
   r кольцевая топология *f*

8097 **ring[-type] network**
   d Ringnetz[werk] *n*; ringförmiges Netz *n*
   f réseau *m* en anneau; réseau bouclé
   r кольцевая сеть *f*; сеть кольцевого типа

8098 **ripple carry**
   d durchrieselnder Übertrag *m*
   f retenue *f* ruisselante; report *m* en travers
   r [последовательно] распространяющийся перенос *m*; сквозной перенос

8099 ripple-carry adder
   d Schnellübertragsaddierer *m*
   f add[itionn]eur *m* à report en travers
   r сумматор *m* со сквозным переносом

8100 ripple counter
   d durchlaufender Zähler *m*; Asynchronzähler *m*
   f compteur *m* courant; compteur d'ondulations;
      compteur d'oscillations
   r счётчик *m* со сквозным переносом;
      счётчик числа колебаний

8101 ripple delay
   d Schnellübertragsverzögerung *f*
   f délai *m* de report; délai de retenue
   r задержка *f* в цепи переноса

   * **RISC** → 7775

8102 rise delay; rising delay
     (of a signal)
   d Anstiegsverzögerung[szeit] *f*
   f délai *m* de la montée
   r задержка *f* нарастания

   * **rise time** → 8478

   * **rising delay** → 8102

   * **rising edge** → 7504

   * **RMA** → 7694

   * **RMM** → 7670

8103 roaming
   d Roaming *n*; Herumstreifen *n*
   f itinérance *f*; trafic *m* de long portée; suivi *m*
   r роуминг *m*; автоматическое
      подключение *n* к местной сети связи

   * **robot** → 9716

   * **roll** → 2962

   * **rollback** *v* → 7977

8104 rollback
   d Rückkehr *f*
   f recul *m*; roulement *m* en arrière
   r откат *m*; отмена *f*

8105 rollback-and-retry
   d Rückkehr *f* mit Wiederholung
   f recul *m* avec reprise de traitement
   r откат *m* с повторением обработки

8106 roll *v* down
   d Bildschirmzeilen abwärts verschieben
   f décaler des lignes de l'écran vers le bas

   r сдвигать строки [текста на экране] в
      обратном направлении

8107 rollin
     (in memory)
   d Einspeichern *n*; Rollin *n*
   f enroulement *m*; chargement *m*; rollin *m*
   r развёртывание *n*; загрузка *f*; подкачка *f*

8108 rolling
   d Rundbiegen *n*; Wälzen *n*; Rollen *n*
   f roulage *m*; roulement *m*; défilement *m*;
      déroulement *m*; cintrage *m*; cylindrage *m*;
      laminage *m*
   r прокрутка *f*; качание *n*; ролинг *m*

8109 rolling ball; trackball [mouse]; tracker
      ball; control ball
   d Trackball *n*; Rollkugel *f*
   f trackball *m*; souris *f* trackball; boule *f*
      roulante; boule de commande
   r [ко́ординатный] шар *m*; шаровой
      указатель *m*; трекбол *m*

8110 rolling mouse
   d Rollmaus *f*
   f souris *f* roulante
   r вращающаяся мышь *f*

8111 rollout
     (from memory)
   d Ausspeichern *n*; Rollout *n*
   f déroulement *m*; rejet *m*; rollout *m*
   r разгрузка *f*; откачка *f*

8112 rollover
   d Drüberrollen *n*
   f renversement *m*
   r перебор *m*; одновременное нажатие *n*
      [нескольких] клавиш

8113 rollup
   d Roll[-]up *n*
   f déroulement *m* séquentiel ascendant;
      cumul *m*
   r свёртывание *n* строк (на экране дисплея)

8114 roll *v* up
   d Bildschirmzeilen aufwärts verschieben
   f décaler des lignes de l'écran vers le haut
   r сдвигать строки [текста на экране] в
      прямом направлении

8115 rollup group
   d Rollup-Gruppe *f*
   f groupe *m* déroulant
   r закатывающаяся группа *f*; поднимающаяся
      группа

   * **ROM** → 7671

8116 Roman number system
d römische Zahlensystem f
f système m de numération romaine
r римская система f счисления

8117 Roman numeral
d römisches Numerale n; römisches Zahlsymbol n
f chiffre m romaine; symbole m numérique romaine; numéral m romaine
r римская цифра f

8118 ROM emulator
d ROM-Emulator m
f émulateur m ROM
r ROM-эмулятор m

* **room → 5721**

8119 root account
d Hauptaccount n; Grundaccount n
f compte m de racine
r счёт m администратора

8120 root directory
d Wurzel-Direktory n; Wurzelverzeichnis n
f répertoire m [de] racine
r корневой справочник m; корневой каталог m

* **root menu → 5603**

8121 root record
d Ausgangssatz m
f écriture f d'appui
r исходная запись f; запись-прототип f

8122 root server
d Hauptserver m
f serveur m de domaine principal
r корневой сервер m

* **rotate v → 1687**

* **rotating → 1692**

* **rotation → 1692**

8123 rotation[al] speed; rotation rate
d Rotationsgeschwindigkeit f; Umlaufgeschwindigkeit f
f vitesse f de rotation; vitesse de circulation
r скорость f вращения

* **rotation rate → 8123**

* **rotation speed → 8123**

* **rough sketch → 9363**

8124 round v; half-adjust v
d runden
f arrondir
r округлять

* **round brackets → 6804**

* **round dots → 1683**

8125 round function
d Rundungsfunktion f
f fonction f d'arrondissement
r функция f округления

8126 rounding; roundness; round-off
d Rundung f; Runden n; Abrundung f
f arrondissement m
r округление n

8127 rounding error
d Rundungsfehler m
f erreur f d'arrondissement
r ошибка f округления

* **roundness → 8126**

* **round-off → 8126**

8128 roundoff accumulator
d Akkumulator m mit Abrundung; abrundender Akkumulator
f accumulateur m à arrondissement [par excès]
r накапливающий сумматор m с округлением

8129 round-robin discipline
d zyklische Bedienungsdisziplin f
f discipline f de priorités tournantes
r циклическая дисциплина f обслуживания

8130 round-robin[-like] scheduling
d Ablauffolgesteuerung f nach Rundgangschema
f ordonnancement m à tour de rôle
r циклическая диспетчеризация f

* **round-robin scheduling → 8130**

* **round screen → 1683**

8131 round trip
(of the search tree)
d Round-Trip m
f cycle m de rotation; tour m
r полный обход m

8132 round-trip delay; round-trip time; RTT
d Verzögerung f wegen der Empfangsbestätigung

f délai *m* à attendre un acquittement
r задержка *f* из-за подтверждения приёма; время *n* поездки туда и обратно

8133 round-trip time
d Round-Trip-Zeit *f*
f temps *m* de transmission et d'accusé de réception
r время *n* на передачу и подтверждение приёма

* **round-trip time → 8132**

8134 route *v*
d leiten
f router
r маршрутизировать; направлять

8135 route; path; way
d Leitweg *m*; Route *f*; Weg *m*; Bahn *f*; Pfad *m*
f route *f*; chemin *m*; voie *f*; cours *m*
r маршрут *m*; путь *m*; дорога *f*; курс *m*

8136 route channel
d Streckenkanal *m*
f canal *m* de route
r канал *m* маршрута

* **route clock → 8137**

8137 route clock [pulse]
d Streckentakt *m*
f horloge *f* de route
r тактовый импульс *m* маршрута

8138 route code; routing code
d Streckencode *m*; Leitwegcode *m*
f code *m* d'acheminement
r код *m* маршрута; код направления

8139 router
d Router *m*; Lotser *m*; Wegrechner *m*
f routeur *m*; traceur *m*; détoureuse *f*; poste *f* d'acheminement
r трассировщик *m*; маршрутизатор *m*

8140 routine *adj*
d Routine-; Standard-
f routinier
r рутинный; стандартный

8141 routine
d Routine *f*; Standardprogramm *n*
f routine *f*; programme *m* standard
r стандартная программа *f*

8142 routine library
d Routinebibliothek *f*
f bibliothèque *f* des routines
r библиотека *f* стандартных программ

8143 routing
d Leitweglenkung *f*; Leitwegsuchen *n*; Wegewahl *f*; Lenkung *f*; Weiterleiten *n*; Routing *n*
f acheminement *m*; choix *m* d'itinéraire; routage *m*
r маршрутизация *f*; выбор *m* пути

* **routing code → 8138**

8144 routing table
d Leitwegtabelle *f*
f table *f* de routage
r таблица *f* маршрутизации; таблица маршрутов

* **row → 5367**

8145 row buffer
d Einzeilenpuffer *m*; Zeilenpuffer *m*
f tampon *m* [de] ligne
r буфер *m* на одну строку

8146 row decoder
d Zeilenentschlüsseler *m*; Zeilendecoder *m*; X-Decoder *m*; Reihendecoder *m*
f décodeur *m* de ligne
r дешифратор *m* строки

* **row edit → 8147**

8147 row edit[ing]
d Zeilenbearbeitung *f*
f édition *f* de rangée
r редактирование *n* строки

* **row length → 8150**

* **row number → 6323**

8148 row numbering
d Zeilennumerierung *f*
f numération *f* de lignes
r нумерация *f* строк

8149 row offset
d Zeilenverschiebung *f*
f décalage *m* de lignes
r смещение *n* строк

* **row pitch → 5037**

8150 row size; row length
d Zeilenlänge *f*
f longueur *f* de ligne
r длина *f* строки

* **row sum → 9040**

* **RPC → 7905**

* **R-S trigger** → 8473

* **RTF** → 8077

* **RTS** → 7969

* **RTT** → 8132

8151 rubber-band graphics
 d Gummibandgrafik *f*
 f graphique *m* à fil élastique
 r эластичная графика *f*; графика с резиновой
 нитью

8152 rubber-band selection
 d Gummiband-Auswahl *f*
 f sélection *f* par fil élastique
 r выбор *m* методом резиновой нити

8153 rubric
 (a subarea of dialog box)
 d Rubrik *f*
 f rubrique *f*
 r рубрика *f*

8154 rule
 d Regel *f*
 f règle *f*
 r правило *n*

8155 rule base
 d Basis *f* von Regeln; Regelbasis *f*
 f base *f* de règles
 r база *f* правил

8156 rule of thumb
 d empirische Regel *f*; Faustregel *f*;
 Faustformel *f*
 f règle *f* empirique
 r эмпирическое правило *n*; практическое
 правило

8157 ruler
 d Zeilenlineal *n*; Lineal *n*
 f ruleur *m*; règle *f*
 r [измерительная] линейка *f*

8158 ruler crosshair
 d Lineal-Fadenkreuz *n*
 f viseur *m* de réticule en croix
 r крест *m* нитей измерительной линейки

* **run** → 3574, 6838

8159 run *v* a script
 d einen Skript ausführen
 f exécuter un script
 r выполнять скрипт

8160 runaway

 d Weglaufen *n*
 f passage *m* hors contrôle
 r выход *m* из-под контроля

* **runner** → 8661

* **running** → 3574

* **running index** → 9755

8161 running point; variable point
 d laufender Punkt *m*
 f point *m* courant
 r текущая точка *f*

8162 run[ning] time; execution time
 d Durchlaufzeit *f*; Laufzeit *f*
 f temps *m* de marche [continue]; temps de
 déroulement
 r время *n* прогона; время выполнения

* **run stream** → 5172

* **run time** → 8162

8163 runtime output
 d Laufzeitausgabe *f*
 f sortie *f* pendant le passage [du programme]
 r вывод *m* данных при прогоне [программы]

8164 runtime software
 d Laufzeitsoftware *f*
 f exécuteur *m*; moteur *m* d'exécution
 r оттранслированное программное
 обеспечение *n*; исполняемое программное
 обеспечение

S

8165 safe mode
 d Sichere Betriebsart *f*; unversehrter Modus *m*
 f mode *m* sans échec
 r безопасный режим *m* (загрузки)

 * **safety** → 8301

 * **sagittal** → 539

8166 sample
 d Muster *n*; Stichprobe *f*; Probe *f*; Abtastwert *m*
 f échantillon *m* [d'essai]; modèle *m* d'essai; étalon *m*
 r образец *m*; выборка *f*; проба *f*; отсчёт *m*

8167 sample code
 d Stichprobencode *m*
 f code *m* d'échantillon
 r код *m* выборки

8168 sampled data
 d Stichprobendaten *pl*; Abtastwerte *mpl*
 f données *fpl* échantillonnées; données d'exploration
 r выборочные данные *pl*

8169 sampled-data control
 d Abtastregelung *f*
 f commande *f* de balayage; commande d'échantillonnage
 r дискретное управление *n*; импульсное управление

8170 sampled signal
 d abgetastetes Signal *n*
 f signal *m* échantillonné
 r сканируемый сигнал *m*

8171 sample program
 d Typenprogramm *n*
 f programme *m* type
 r эталонная программа *f*

 * **sample pulse** → 8948

 * **sample rate** → 8174

8172 samples per second
 d Stichproben *fpl* pro Sekunde
 f échantillons *fpl* par seconde
 r выборки *fpl* в секунде

8173 sampling

 d Stichprobenauswahl *f*; Stichprobenerhebung *f*; Abtastung *f*
 f échantillonnage *m*; prélèvement *m* d'échantillons
 r процесс *m* выборки; опробирование *n*; отбор *m* выборок

8174 sampling rate; sample rate; scan[ning] frequency; scanning rate; sensing rate
 d Abtastrate *f*; Scanrate *f*; Abtastfrequenz *f*
 f taux *m* d'échantillonnage; fréquence *f* d'échantillonnage; fréquence de balayage; fréquence d'exploration; cote *f* de scrutation
 r частота *f* взятия отсчётов; частота развёртки; скорость *f* выборки

8175 sampling synthesizer
 d Stichproben-Sprachgenerator *m*
 f synthétiseur *m* de prélèvement d'échantillons
 r синтезатор *m* звуковых образцов

8176 sampling window
 d Abtastfenster *n*
 f fenêtre *f* d'échantillonnage
 r окно *n* выборки

8177 sandwich tape
 d Mehrschichtband *n*
 f bande *f* multicouche
 r многослойная лента *f*

8178 sanitizer
 (a software)
 d Desinfizierer *m*
 f désinfectant *m*
 r программа *f* очистки (памяти)

8179 sanity
 d Intaktheit *f*
 f état *m* sain; état de marche
 r исправность *f*

 * **SAPI** → 8763

8180 satellite computer; front-end computer
 d Satellitenrechner *m*; Front-End-Rechner *m*
 f ordinateur *m* satellite
 r сателлитный компьютер *m*; периферийный компьютер

8181 satellite data exchange; DATEX-S
 d Datenübertragung *f* per Satelliten
 f échange *m* de données satellite
 r сателлитный обмен *m* данными

 * **satellite net** → 8182

8182 satellite net[work]
 d Satellitennetz *n*

f réseau *m* satellite
r спутниковая сеть *f*

8183 saturated; saturating
  d saturiert; gesättigt
  f saturé
  r насыщенный

  * **saturating** → 8183

8184 saturating trigger
  d gesättigter Flipflop *m*
  f basculeur *m* saturé
  r насыщенный триггер *m*

8185 saturation
  d Sättigung *f*; Saturation *f*
  f saturation *f*
  r насыщение *n*; насыщенность *f*

8186 saturation current
  d Sättigungsstrom *m*
  f courant *m* de saturation
  r ток *m* насыщения

8187 save *v*
  d aufbewahren; sicherstellen
  f conserver; sauvegarder
  r сохранять

8188 save area
  d Sicherstellungsbereich *m*; Rettungsbereich *m*
  f zone *f* de sauvegarde; champ *m* de sauvegarde
  r область *f* сохранения

8189 save-carry logic
  d Save-Carry-Logik *f*
  f logique *f* de conservation de retenue
  r логика *f* сохранения переноса

8190 save command
  d Speichern-Befehl *m*
  f commande *f* de sauvegarde
  r команда *f* сохранения

8191 saving
  d Sicherstellung *f*; Rettung *f*
  f sauvegarde *f*
  r сохранение *n*

  * **scaffold** → 4067

  * **SCAI** → 9083

8192 scalable font; vector font
  d vektorielle Schrift *f*; Vektorschrift *f*
  f police *f* vectorisée; police de taille variable; police vectorielle
  r векторный шрифт *m*; масштабируемый шрифт *m*

  * **scalable graphics** → 9770

8193 scalable rendering processor
  d skalierbarer Vektorrendering-Prozessor *m*
  f processeur *m* de rendu vectorisé
  r процессор *m* масштабируемого оттенения

8194 scalar *adj*
  d skalar
  f scalaire
  r скалярный

  * **scalar** → 8195

8195 scalar [quantity]
  d Skalar *n*; skalare Größe *f*
  f scalaire *m*; grandeur *f* scalaire
  r скаляр *m*; скалярная величина *f*

8196 scale *v*; size *v*
  d skalieren; maßstabsgerecht ändern
  f modifier à l'échelle
  r масштабировать

8197 scale factor; scaling factor; scaling multiplier
  d Skalenfaktor *m*; Maßstabsfaktor *m*
  f facteur *m* d'échelle
  r масштабный коэффициент *m*; масштабный множитель *m*

  * **scale notation** → 7584

8198 scaling
  d Skalierung *f*; Maßstabsänderung *f*
  f mise *f* à l'échelle; choix *m* d'échelle
  r масштабирование *n*; выбор *m* масштаба; пересчёт *m*

  * **scaling factor** → 8197

  * **scaling multiplier** → 8197

  * **scan** → 8209

8199 scan *v*
  d abfühlen; abtasten; ablesen
  f balayer; explorer; scannériser
  r сканировать; развёртывать; считывать

8200 scan area
  d Abtastbereich *m*
  f zone *f* de balayage
  r область *f* сканирования

8201 scan converter
  d Scankonverter *m*
  f convertisseur *m* de balayage
  r сканирующий преобразователь *m*

* **scan frequency** → 8174

* **scan graphics** → 7623

8202 scanner
  d Abtaster *m*; Scanner *m*
  f scanner *m*; scanneur *m*
  r сканер *m*; сканирующее устройство *n*

8203 scanner calibration
  d Scanner-Kalibrierung *f*
  f calibrage *m* de scanner
  r калибровка *f* сканера

8204 scanner characteristics
  d Scanner-Merkmale *npl*
  f caractéristiques *fpl* de scanner
  r характеристики *fpl* сканера

8205 scanner configuration
  d Scanner-Konfiguration *f*
  f configuration *f* de scanner
  r конфигурация *f* сканера

8206 scanner file
  d Scanner-Datei *f*
  f fichier *m* de scanner
  r файл *m* сканера

8207 scanner resolution
  d Scannerauflösungsvermögen *n*
  f résolution *f* de scanner
  r разрешающая способность *f* сканера

8208 scanner software
  d Scannersoftware *f*; Programmierhilfen *fpl* des Scanners
  f logiciel *m* de scanner
  r программное обеспечение *n* сканера

8209 scan[ning]; exploration; exploring
  d Abtastung *f*; Abtasten *n*; Scanning *n*; Scannen *n*; Scan *n*
  f balayage *m*; scrutation *f*; exploration *f*; scannérisation *f*
  r сканирование *n*; развёртка *f*

* **scanning frequency** → 8174

8210 scanning input
  d Abtasteingang *m*
  f entrée *f* de balayage
  r сканирующий вход *m*

* **scanning method** → 8212

* **scanning rate** → 8174

8211 scanning speed; sensing speed
  d Abtastgeschwindigkeit *f*

  f vitesse *f* d'exploration
  r скорость *f* сканирования

8212 scanning technique; scanning method
  d Abtastverfahren *n*
  f méthode *f* de balayage
  r метод *m* сканирования

* **scan pattern** → 7611

* **scatter** *v* → 2872

* **scattering** → 3010

* **scatter read** → 8213

8213 scatter read[ing]
  d Streulesung *f*; gestreutes Lesen *n*
  f lecture *f* dispersée; lecture diffusée
  r чтение *n* вразброс

8214 scene
  d Szene *f*
  f scène *f*
  r сцена *f*

8215 scene analysis
  d Szenenanalyse *f*
  f analyse *f* de scène
  r анализ *m* сцены

8216 scene builder
  d Szenenbilder *m*
  f bâtisseur *m* de scène
  r компоновщик *m* сцен; разработчик *m* сцен; построитель *m* сцен

8217 scene digitalization
  d Szenendigitalisierung *f*
  f numérisation *f* de scène
  r оцифрование *n* сцены

8218 scene graph
  (directed acyclic graph whose nodes contain geometry and texture information for scene components)
  d Szenengraph *m*
  f graphe *m* de scène
  r граф *m* сцены

8219 scene synthesis
  d Szenensynthese *f*
  f synthèse *f* de scène
  r синтез *m* сцены

8220 schedule; timetable
  d Ablaufplan *m*; Zeitplan *m*
  f table *f* de temps; plan *m* [de déroulement]; horaire *m*
  r расписание *n*; график *m*

8221 scheduler; planner
 d Ablauflister *m*; Disponent *m*; Scheduler *m*;
 Zeitplaner *m*
 f planificateur *m*; distributeur *m*
 r планировщик *m*

8222 scheduling
 d Ablauf[folge]planung *f*
 f planification *f* [de séquence]; établissement *m*
 d'un plan
 r планирование *n*; составление *n* графика

8223 scheduling algorithm
 d Reihenfolgealgorithmus *m*
 f algorithme *m* de planification; algorithme
 d'ordonnancement
 r алгоритм *m* планирования

8224 scheduling problem
 d Ablaufplanungsproblem *n*;
 Reihenfolgeproblem *n*
 f problème *m* de planification
 r задача *f* о составлении расписаний

8225 schema; scheme
 d Schema *n*
 f schéma *m*; schème *m*
 r схема *f*; план *m*

8226 schematic design
 d Schaltungsentwurf *m*
 f conception *f* de circuiterie
 r схемотехническое проектирование *n*

8227 schematic visualization
 d schematische Visualisierung *f*
 f visualisation *f* schématique
 r схематическая визуализация *f*

 * **scheme → 8225**

8228 scientific computer
 d wissenschaftlicher Rechner *m*
 f ordinateur *m* scientifique
 r компьютер *m* для научных расчётов

 * **scissoring → 1742**

8229 scope
 d Spielraum *m*; Gültigkeitsbereich *m*;
 Wirkungsbereich *m*
 f domaine *m* d'action; champ *m* de validité
 r область *f* действия; диапазон *m* действия

8230 score
 d Note *f*
 f score *m*; note *f*
 r оценка *f*

 * **score → 1652**

 * **SCP → 8459**

 * **scrambled virus → 3399**

 * **scrambler → 8231**

8231 scrambler [circuit]
 d Verwürfler *m*; Scrambler *m*
 f embrouilleur *m*; circuit *m* brouilleur;
 brasseur *m*
 r скрэмблер *m*

8232 scrambling
 d Verwürfelung *f*
 f embrouillage *m*; mélange *m*
 r запутывание *n*; размешивание *n*;
 перемешивание *n*; зашумление *n*

8233 scrapbook
 d Skizzenbuch *n*
 f classeur *m*
 r текстографический буферный файл *m*

 * **scratch *v* → 1709**

 * **scratch area → 10040**

 * **scratch file → 10042**

8234 scratch [magnetic] tape
 d Arbeitsband *n*
 f bande *f* de manœuvre
 r оперативная лента *f*

8235 scratchpad register
 d Notizregister *n*; Zwischenregister *n*
 f registre *m* de bloc-notes
 r оперативный запоминающий регистр *m*;
 быстрый регистр; регистр
 сверхоперативной памяти

 * **scratch tape → 8234**

8236 screen
 d Bildschirm *m*
 f écran *m*
 r экран *m*

 * **screen angle → 7612**

 * **screen buffer → 3015**

8237 screen capture; screen dump; screenshot
 d Bildschirm-Sammeln *n*; Momentaufnahme *f*
 der aktuellen Darstellung auf dem Monitor
 f capture *f* d'écran; copie *f* d'écran
 r снимок *m* экрана; скриншот *m*

8238 screen capturer
 d Bildschirmsammler *m*

f capteur *m* d'écran
r экранный уловитель *m*

8239 screen diagonal
d Bildschirmdiagonale *f*
f diagonale *f* d'écran
r диагональ *m* экрана

**8240 screen dot; matrix dot; halftone dot; dot;
grid point; raster point**
d Rasterpunkt *m*; Halbtonpunkt *m*;
Gitterpunkt *m*
f point *m* rastre; point d'écran; point de grille
r точка *f* растра; растровая точка; элемент *m*
растра

**8241 screen dot pitch; dot pitch; array pitch;
pitch; grid [element] spacing; grid size**
d Bildschirmpunktabstand *m*; Pixelabstand *m*;
Punktabstand *m*; Rastermaß *n*;
Raster[element]abstand *m*; Pitch *m*
f pas *m* de masque; espacement *m* entre pixels;
distance *f* entre points; espacement *m* de
grille; pas *m* de grille; pitch *m*
r расстояние *n* между точками изображения
на экране; расстояние между элементами
растра; шаг *m* расположения [растровых]
точек; шаг растра; шаг сетки

* **screen driver** → 3021

* **screen dump** → 8237

* **screen editor** → 4117

8242 screen factor
d Schirmfaktor *m*
f facteur *m* d'écran
r коэффициент *m* экранирования

* **screen flicker** → 8243

8243 screen flicker[ing]
d Bildschirmblinken *n*
f scintillement *m* d'écran
r мигание *n* экрана

8244 screen formatting
d Bildschirmformattierung *f*
f formatage *m* d'écran
r форматирование *n* изображения на экране

8245 screen frequency
d Bildschirmfrequenz *f*
f fréquence *f* d'écran
r частота *f* экрана

8246 screen function
d Bildschirmfunktion *f*
f fonction *f* d'écran

r экранная функция *f*

8247 screen grid
d Bildschirmgitter *n*
f grille-écran *f*
r экранная решётка *f*

8248 screening
d Vorrecherche *f*; Screening *n*
f filtrage *m*; premier tri[age] *m*; blindage *m*
r отсеивание *n*; первичная сортировка *f*

* **screening** → 8503

* **screen memory** → 4037

8249 screen menu; on-screen menu
d Bildschirmmenü *n*
f menu *m* d'écran
r экранное меню *n*

8250 screen mode
d Bildschirmmodus *m*
f mode *m* d'écran
r экранный режим *m*

* **screen name** → 9733

8251 screen overlay
d Bildschirm-Overlay *n*
f recouvrement *m* d'écran
r перекрытие *n* экрана

8252 screen painter
d Bildschirmmaler *m*
f unité *f* de coloriage de l'écran
r экранный оформитель *m*; блок *m*
раскраски изображения на экране

8253 screen phone
d Bildschirmtelefon *n*
f téléphone *m* écran
r экранный телефон *m*

* **screen redraw** → 4673

* **screen resolution** → 5882

* **screen saver** → 8254

8254 screen saver [program]
d Bildschirmschoner *m*; Bildschirmsparer *m*
f programme *m* de protection d'écran;
économiseur *m* d'écran; écran *m* de vieille
r экранный сберегатель *m*

* **screenshot** → 8237

8255 screen size
d Bildschirmgröße *f*

f taille *f* d'écran
r размер *m* экрана

8256 screen snapshot
d Bildschirm-Schnappschuss *m*
f image *f* instantanée sur l'écran
r моментальный снимок *m* экрана

* **screen split** → 8257

8257 screen split[ting]
d Teilung *f* des Bildshirms
f splittage *m* d'écran
r расщепление *n* экрана

8258 screen view; display view
d Bildschirmansicht *f*
f vue *f* d'écran
r экранный вид *m*

8259 screen window
d Bildfenster *n*
f fenêtre *f* d'écran
r экранное окно *n*

* **script** → 1388, 1909

8260 script file
d Skriptdatei *f*
f fichier *m* de scripts
r скрипт-файл *m*; файл сценария

8261 script language
d Skriptsprache *f*
f langage *m* de scripts
r язык *m* [описания] сценариев; язык
подготовки сценариев; сценарный язык

8262 script manager
d Skript-Manager *m*
f gestionnaire *m* de scripts
r программа *f* управления скриптов

8263 scriptware
d Skriptware *f*
f scripticiel *m*
r сценарное программное обеспечение *n*

8264 scrollable window
d rollbares Bildfenster *n*
f fenêtre *f* défilable
r прокручиваемое окно *n*

8265 scroll arrow
d Bildlaufpfeil *m*
f flèche *f* de défilement
r стрелка *f* прокрутки

8266 scrollbar; elevator
d Rollbalken *n*; Bildlaufleiste *f*

f barre *f* de défilement; ascenseur *m*
r лента *f* прокручивания; линейка *f*
просмотра

8267 scroll box
d Bildlauffeld *n*
f boite *f* de défilement; curseur *m* de défilement
r бегунок *m*

* **scroll** → 8268

8268 scroll[ing]
(of a screen image)
d Rollen *n*; Blättern *n*;
Bild[schirmzeilen]verschiebung *f*; Bildlauf *m*;
Bildrollen *n*
f défilement *m*; décalage *m* vertical
r прокрутка *f*; прокручивание *n*;
скроллинг *m*

8269 scrolling text box
d Durchlauftextfeld *n*
f champ *m* de texte déroulant; zone *f* de texte
multiligne; case *f* de saisie multiple
r ящик *m* прокручивания [многострочного]
текста

* **SCSI** → 8668

8270 SCSI identifier
d SCSI-Bezeichner *m*
f numéro *m* SCSI
r идентификатор *m* интерфейса SCSI

8271 sculptor program
d Bildhauerprogramm *n*
f programme *m* sculpteur
r программа *f* скульптор

8272 sculptured key
d gestaltete Taste *f*
f touche *f* en relief
r рельефная клавиша *f*

* **SDF** → 8740

* **SDRAM** → 9119

8273 seam *v*
d nähen
f joindre
r набороздить; сшить; сшивать

8274 seamless
d spaltfrei; nachtlos
f sans soudure
r без шва; из одного куска; цельнотянутый;
цельнокроенный

8275 seamless background
d spaltfreier Hintergrund *m*

f fond *m* sans soudure
r непрерывный фон *m*; цельнокроенный фон

8276 seamless interface
  d nahtloses Interface *n*; integrierte Schnittstelle *f*
  f liaison *f* transparente
  r цельнокроенный интерфейс *m*

* search → 8278

8277 search algorithm
  d Suchalgorithmus *m*
  f algorithme *m* de recherche
  r алгоритм *m* поиска

* search engine → 9976

8278 search[ing]; seek[ing]; retrieval
  d Suche *f*; Suchen *n*; Untersuchung *f*
  f recherche *f*
  r поиск *m*; искание *n*

8279 searching strategy
  d Suchstrategie *f*
  f stratégie *f* de recherche
  r стратегия *f* искания

8280 search key
  d Suchschlüssel *m*
  f clé *f* de recherche
  r ключ *m* поиска

8281 search mask
  d Suchmaske *f*
  f masque *m* de recherche
  r маска *f* поиска

8282 search procedure
  d Suchverfahren *n*
  f procédure *f* de recherche
  r процедура *f* отыскания; процедура поиска

8283 search process
  d Suchprozess *m*
  f processus *m* de recherche
  r процесс *m* отыскания; процесс поиска

8284 search register
  d Suchwortregister *n*
  f registre *m* de recherche
  r регистр *m* признака

8285 search string; finder chain
  d Such[zeichen]kette *f*
  f chaîne *f* de recherche
  r строка *f* поиска; цепочка *f* поиска

8286 search tree
  d Suchbaum *m*
  f arbre *m* de recherche

r дерево *n* поиска

8287 second
  d Sekunde *f*
  f seconde *f*
  r секунда *f*

8288 secondary
  d sekundär; zweit
  f secondaire; deuxième
  r вторичный; второстепенный; второй

8289 secondary channel; co-channel
  d Zweitkanal *m*
  f canal *m* secondaire
  r вторичный канал *m*; вспомагательный канал

8290 secondary memory
  d Sekundärspeicher *m*
  f mémoire *f* secondaire
  r вторичная память *f*

* secondary recipient → 2313

8291 second order logic
  d Prädikatenlogik *f* zweiter Stufe
  f logique *f* de second ordre; logique de deuxième ordre
  r логика *f* предикатов второго порядка

8292 section
  (of a document)
  d Abschnitt *m*
  f section *f*
  r раздел *m*

8293 section; link
  d Sektion *f*; Abschnitt *m*; Schnitt *m*; Strecke *f*
  f section *f*; coupe *f*
  r секция *f*; отсек *m* [линии]; участок *m*; отрезок *m*; звено *n*

8294 section header
  d Abschnittskopf *m*
  f tête *f* de section
  r заголовок *m* секции; заголовок раздела

8295 sectioning
  d Sektionierung *f*
  f sectionnement *m*
  r секционирование *n*

8296 sector
  d Sektor *m*
  f secteur *m*
  r сектор *m*

8297 sector interleave
  (of a magnetic disk)
  d Plattensektorauslassung *f*

f entrelacement *m* de secteurs
r чередование *n* секторов

8298 secure site
d gesicherte Site *f*
f site *m* sécurisé
r защищённый сайт *m*; защищённый узел *m*

8299 secure socket layer; SSL
(an open protocol for securing data
communications across computer networks)
d SSL-Protokoll *n*
f protocole *m* SSL; couche *f* de "réceptacles"
sécurisés; couche d'échange protégée
r протокол *m* защищённых сокетов;
протокол SSL

8300 secure wide area network; SWAN
d gesichertes weiträumiges Netzwerk *n*
f réseau *m* étendu sécurisé
r защищённая глобальная сеть *f*; надёжная
глобальная сеть

8301 security; safety
d Sicherheit *f*; Schutz *m*
f sécurité *f*; sûreté *f*
r безопасность *f*; защита *f*

8302 security bit
d Schutzbit *n*
f bit *m* de protection
r бит *m* защиты

8303 security category; security clearance
d Sicherheitskategorie *f*
f catégorie *f* de sécurité; clairance *f* de sécurité
r категория *f* допуска; уровень *m* защиты

* **security clearance → 8303**

8304 security declaration
d Berechtigungserklärung *f*
f déclaration *f* de sécurité
r объявление *n* прав доступа

* **sedecimal → 4454**

* **seek → 8278**

8305 seek check bit
d Suchprüfbit *n*
f bit *m* de contrôle de recherche
r контрольный бит *m* поиска

8306 seek command
d Suchbefehl *m*
f commande *f* de recherche
r команда *f* поиска

* **seeking → 8278**

8307 seek time
d Suchzeit *f*; Einstellzeit *f*
f temps *m* de recherche
r время *n* установки; время поиска

8308 segment
d Segment *n*; Strecke *f*
f segment *m*
r сегмент *m*; отрезок *m*

8309 segmentation
d Segmentierung *f*; Unterteilung *f*
f segmentation *f*
r сегментирование *n*; сегментация *f*

8310 segmentation and block formation
d Segmentierung *f* und Blockbildung *f*
f segmentation *f* et formation *f* de blocs
r сегментирование *n* и формирование *n*
блоков

8311 segmented encoding law
d segmentierte Codierungskennlinie *f*
f loi *f* de codage à segments
r линейно-ломанная характеристика *f*
кодирования

8312 seize *v*
d belegen
f occuper
r занять; занимать; захватывать

* **seizing → 6365**

* **seizure → 6365**

* **select → 8319**

8313 select *v*; choose *v*
d auswählen; wählen; selektieren
f sélectionner; choisir
r выбирать; отбирать; избирать

8314 select *v* all
d alles auswählen
f tout sélectionner
r выбирать всё

8315 selected read data
d ausgewählte Lesedaten *pl*
f données *fpl* de lecture sélectionnées
r выборочные данные *pl* считывания

8316 selected text characters
d Zeichen *npl* des markierten Texts
f caractères *mpl* de texte sélectionné
r символы *mpl* выбранного текста

* **selecting → 8319**

8317 **selecting bar**
d Auswahlbalken *n*
f barre *f* de sélection
r полоса *f* выбора

* **selecting circuit** → 8322

8318 **select input**
d Auswahleingang *m*
f entrée *f* de sélection
r вход *m* выбора

* **selection** → 2845

8319 **selection; select[ing]; choice**
d Auswahl *f*; Wahl *f*; Selektion *f*
f sélection *f*; choix *m*
r выбор *m*; выборка *f*; отбор *m*; селекция *f*

* **selection box** → 6973

* **selection code** → 2846

8320 **selection cursor; element cursor**
d Auswahlkursor *m*
f curseur *m* de sélection
r курсор *m* выбора

8321 **selection cycling**
d zyklische Wiederholung *f* der Auswahl
f bouclage *m* de sélection
r зацикливание *n* выбора

* **selection frame** → 8329

8322 **selection logic; selecting circuit**
d Auswahllogik *f*; Auswahlschaltung *f*
f logique *f* de sélection; circuit *m* de sélection
r логика *f* выбора; логическая схема *f* селекции; селективный контур *m*

8323 **selection method**
d Selektionsmethode *f*
f méthode *f* de sélection
r селективный метод *m*; метод выборки

8324 **selection mode**
d Anforderungsbetriebsart *f*
f mode *m* de sélection
r режим *m* выборки

8325 **selection process**
d Auswahlprozess *m*; Auswahlvorgang *m*
f processus *m* de sélection
r процесс *m* выбора

8326 **selection register**
d Auswahlregister *n*
f registre *m* de sélection
r регистр *m* выбора

8327 **selection signal**
d Auswahlsignal *n*; Wählzeichen *n*
f signal *m* de sélection
r сигнал *m* выборки

8328 **selection signal buffer**
d Wählzeichenpuffer *m*
f tampon *m* d'impulsion de sélection
r буфер *m* импульса выборки

8329 **selection window; selection frame**
d Auswahlfenster *n*
f fenêtre *f* de sélection; cadre *f* de sélection
r окно *n* выбора

8330 **selective booting**
d selektives Starten *n*
f séquence *f* de lancement personnalisable
r селективная загрузка *f*

* **selective dump** → 8684

* **selective pulse** → 8948

8331 **selectivity**
d Selektivität *f*; Trennvermögen *n*; Trennschärfe *f*
f sélectivité *f*
r селективность *f*; избирательность *f*

* **selector** → 8335

8332 **selector; choice device**
d Selektor *m*; Auswähler *m*; Wähler *m*
f sélecteur *m*
r селектор *m*; искатель *m*

8333 **selector channel**
d Selektorkanal *m*; Wählerkanal *m*
f canal *m* sélectif; canal sélecteur
r селекторный канал *m*

8334 **selector setting signal**
d Wählereinstellzeichen *n*
f signal *m* d'établissement de sélecteur
r сигнал *m* установки селектора

8335 **selector [switch]**
d Selektor *m*; Wähler *m*; Auswahlschalter *m*
f sélecteur *m*; commutateur *m* de sélection
r селектор *m*; [селекторный] переключатель *m*

8336 **select statement; case statement**
d Auswahlanweisung *f*; Fachstatement *n*; Wählanweisung *f*
f instruction *f* de sélection; opérateur *m* de choix; opérateur de cas
r оператор *m* отбора; оператор выбора

* **select time** → 88

* **self-acting** → 685

8337 **self-adapting; auto-adapting**
d selbsteinstellend
f auto-adaptatif
r самоадаптирующийся;
самоприспосабливающийся

8338 **self-adjusting**
d selbstanpassend
f auto-ajustable; autoréglable
r самонастраивающийся

8339 **self-aligning; auto-aligning**
d selbstausrichtend
f auto-alignant
r самовыравнивающийся

* **self-aligning system** → 3945

* **self-alignment** → 673

* **self-call** → 676

8340 **self-channeling; auto-channeling**
d Eigenkanalbildung f
f autocanalisation f
r образование n собственного канала

* **self-check** → 684

* **self-checking** → 684

8341 **self-checking; self-testing; auto-checking;**
auto-testing adj
d selbstprüfend
f autocontrôlé
r самопроверяющийся;
самоконтролирующийся

8342 **self-checking code**
d selbstprüfender Code m
f code m de autovérification; code autocontrôlé
r самоконтролирующийся код m; код с
самопроверкой

8343 **self-checking device**
d selbstüberwachte Einheit f
f unité f autocontrôlée
r самоконтролирующееся устройство n

* **self-clocking** adj → 8354

8344 **self-clocking**
d Selbsttaktierung f
f rythme m propre; autosynchronisation f
r самосинхронизация f; автосинхронизация f

8345 **self-correcting code**
d selbstkorrigierender Code m
f code m autocorrecteur
r самокорректирующийся код m

8346 **self-documented**
d selbstdokumentiert
f autodocumenté
r самодокументируемый

8347 **self-extracting file**
d selbst
f fichier m auto-extractible
r саморазворачивающийся [архивный]
файл m

8348 **self-holding circuit**
d Selbsthaltestromkreis m
f circuit m d'automaintien
r схема f автоблокировки

8349 **self-learning system**
d selbstlernendes System n
f système m à auto-apprentissage; système
autodidactique
r самообучающаяся система f

8350 **self-loading; bootstrapping**
d Selbstladen n; Bootstrapping n
f autochargement m; amorce f
r самозагрузка f; начальная загрузка f

8351 **self-loading program**
d selbstladendes Programm n
f programme m autochargeur
r самозагружающаяся программа f

* **self-programming** → 698

* **self-referent list** → 7758

* **self-regulation** → 688

8352 **self-relocatable**
d selbstverschiebbar
f autotransportable
r самоперемещаемый

* **self-replication** → 8353

8353 **self-reproduction; self-replication**
d Selbstreproduktion f
f autoreproduction f
r самовоспроизведение n

8354 **self-synchronized; self-timed;**
self-clocking adj
d selbstablaufsteuernd; selbsttaktierend
f à propre synchronisation; autohorlogique
r самосинхронизирующийся; с внутренней
синхронизацией

* **self-testing** → 8341

* **self-timed** → 8354

8355 semantic
  d semantisch
  f sémantique
  r семантический

8356 semantic node
  d semantischer Knoten m
  f nœud m sémantique
  r узел m семантической сети

8357 semantics
  d Semantik f
  f sémantique f
  r семантика f

* **semaphore** → 8358

8358 semaphore [variable]
  d Semaphor m; Semaphorvariable f
  f sémaphore m; variable f sémaphore
  r семафор m; семафорная переменная f

* **semi-adder** → 4360

8359 semianalytic code
  d halbanalytischer Befehlscode m
  f code m semi-analytique
  r полуаналитический код m

8360 semi-automated digitizing
  d halbautomatische Digitalisierung f
  f numérisation f demi-auto
  r полуавтоматизированное оцифрование n

8361 semicircular array
  d halbkreisförmige Anordnung f
  f réseau m semi-circulaire
  r полуциклическая сетка f

8362 semicolon
  (;)
  d Semikolon n
  f point-virgule m
  r точка f с запятой

8363 semicompiling
  d Halbkompilierung f
  f demi-compilation f
  r полукомпиляция f

8364 semiconductor
  d Halbleiter m
  f semiconducteur m
  r полупроводник m

* **semiduplex** → 4363

* **semilogarithmic representation** → 3907

8365 semipermanent
  d semipermanent
  f semi-permanent
  r полупостоянный; полуустойчивый

8366 semipermanent data
  d semipermanente Daten pl
  f données fpl semi-permanentes
  r полупостоянные данные pl

8367 semipermanently connected channel
  d semipermanent durchgeschalteter Kanal m
  f canal m connecté à mi-temps
  r полупостоянно связанный канал m

8368 semipermanent memory
  d Halbfestspeicher m
  f mémoire f semi-permanente
  r полупостоянная память f

* **semiword** → 4374

8369 send v
  d senden; aussenden; abgeben
  f envoyer; émettre
  r отправлять; посылать

8370 send amplifier
  d Sendeverstärker m
  f amplificateur m de transfert
  r усилитель m пересылки

8371 send buffer
  d Sendepuffer m
  f tampon m de transfert
  r пересылочный буфер m

* **send device** → 9524

* **sender** → 9524

8372 sending
  d Sendung f
  f émission f
  r пересылка f

8373 sending sequence
  d Sendeablauf m
  f séquence f d'émission
  r последовательность f передачи;
     последовательность излучения

* **send unit** → 9524

* **sense** v → 7654

* **sense** → 2956

8374 **sense** *v*
   d abtasten
   f palper; explorer
   r воспринимать; опознавать

8375 **sense amplifier**
   d Abfühlverstärker *m*; Abtastverstärker *m*
   f amplificateur *m* d'exploration
   r усилитель *m* считывания

8376 **sense bit**
   d Lesebit *n*; Abtastbit *n*
   f bit *m* de lecture
   r бит *m* считывания

8377 **sensed signal**
   d abgenommenes Signal *n*
   f signal *m* détecté
   r принятый сигнал *m*

8378 **sense signal**
   d Abfühlsignal *n*; Lesesignal *n*
   f signal *m* de lecture; signal d'exploration
   r сигнал *m* считывания

8379 **sensibility; sensitivity; responsivity**
   d Empfindlichkeit *f*
   f sensibilité *f*
   r чувствительность *f*

   * **sensing** → 7665

8380 **sensing**
   d Abfühlen *n*; Wahrnehmung *f*
   f palpation *f*; saisie *f*
   r ощущение *n*; опознавание *n*

   * **sensing device** → 8381

8381 **sensing element; sensing device; sensor;
     pickup**
   d Fühlelement *n*; Messfühler *m*; Geber *m*;
     Sensor *m*; Aufnehmer *m*;
     Messwertaufnehmer *m*
   f élément *m* sensible; capteur *m* [de mesure];
     senseur *m*
   r чувствительный элемент *m*; считывающий
     элемент; сенсор *m*; датчик *m*

   * **sensing head** → 7666

   * **sensing rate** → 8174

   * **sensing speed** → 8211

   * **sensing time** → 7669

   * **sensitive screen** → 9454

   * **sensitivity** → 8379

   * **sensor** → 8381

8382 **sensor-based computer**
   d auf Sensoren basierender Rechner *m*; Rechner
     mit Sensoren
   f ordinateur *m* à senseurs
   r управляющий компьютер *m* с датчиками

   * **sensor glove** → 2563

   * **sentence** → 570

8383 **sentence**
   d Satz *m*; Anweisungssatz *m*
   f sentence *f*
   r предложение *n*

8384 **sentential language**
   d sententielle Sprache *f*
   f langage *m* de sentence
   r сентенциальный язык *m*

   * **sentential variable** → 7443

   * **sentinel** → 3875

8385 **sent mail**
   d gesandte Post *f*
   f poste *f* envoyée
   r отправленная почта *f*

8386 **separable programming**
   d separable Programmierung *f*
   f programmation *f* séparable
   r сепарабельное программирование *n*

8387 **separate** *v*
   d trennen
   f séparer
   r отделять

8388 **separate bit**
   d getrenntes Bit *n*
   f bit *m* séparé
   r отдельный бит *m*

8389 **separate network**
   d Einzelnetz *n*
   f réseau *m* séparé
   r разделительная сеть *f*

   * **separating** → 8391

8390 **separating filter**
   d Trennungsfilter *m*
   f filtre *m* de séparation
   r разделительный фильтр *m*

8391 **separation; separating**
   d Auszug *m*; Trennung *f*; Separation *f*

f séparation *f*
r разделение *n*; отделение *n*; сепарация *f*

8392 separation bit
d Separationsbit *n*
f bit *m* de séparation; bit séparateur
r бит *m* разделения; разделительный бит

8393 separation of variables
d Trennung *f* der Variablen; Trennung der Veränderlichen
f séparation *f* des variables
r разделение *n* переменных

8394 separation signal
d Trennungszeichen *n*; Trennungssignal *n*
f signal *m* de séparation
r сигнал *m* разделения

* **separation symbol** → 8395

* **separator** → 8395

8395 separator [symbol]; separation symbol; delimiter sign
d Trennzeichen *n*; Trennsymbol *n*; Endezeichen *n*; Begrenzungssymbol *n*
f signe *m* séparateur; symbole *m* délimiteur
r знак *m* ограничения; разделительный символ *m*

8396 sequence
d Folge *f*; Reihenfolge *f*; Sequenz *f*
f séquence *f*; suite *f*
r последовательность *f*; порядок *m* [следования]

* **sequence check** → 8398

8397 sequence check bit
d Reihungsprüfbit *n*
f bit *m* de contrôle de séquence
r бит *m* проверки последовательности

8398 sequence check[ing]
d Folgeprüfung *f*; Reihungsprüfung *f*
f contrôle *m* de séquence
r проверка *f* последовательности

8399 sequence control marker
d Reihungssteuermarke *f*; Einsteller *m*
f marqueur *m* de contrôle de séquence
r маркер *m* управления последовательностью

8400 sequence counter
d Folgezähler *m*
f compteur *m* de séquence
r счётчик *m* последовательности

8401 sequence number
d Folgenummer *f*
f numéro *m* de séquence; numéro d'ordre
r порядковый номер *m*

8402 sequence of iterations
d Iterationsfolge *f*
f suite *f* des itérations
r последовательность *f* итераций

8403 sequencer
d Sequenzer *m*; Ablauffolgesteuereinrichtung *f*; Befehlsabwicklungsfolgesteuerung *f*
f séquenceur *m*
r устройство *n*, задающее последовательность; микропрограммный автомат *m*

8404 sequence symbol
d Folgesymbol *n*
f symbole *m* de séquence
r символ *m* последовательности

8405 sequence timer
d Folgezeitgeber *m*
f générateur *m* de séquence; générateur de suite
r генератор *m* последовательности [импульсов]; последовательный таймер *m*

8406 sequencing
d Reihenfolgebestimmung *f*; Sequentialisieren *n*
f détermination *f* de séquence
r установление *n* последовательности

* **sequential** → 8414

8407 sequential access; serial access; consecutive access
d sequentieller Zugriff *m*; serieller Zugriff; aufeinanderfolgender Zugriff
f accès *m* séquentiel; accès en série; accès consécutif
r последовательный доступ *m*

8408 sequential addressing
d sequentielle Adressierung *f*
f adressage *m* séquentiel
r последовательное адресование *n*; магазинное адресование

8409 sequential circuit
d Schaltwerk *n*; sequentielle Schaltung *f*; Folgeschaltung *f*
f circuit *m* séquentiel
r последовательностная схема *f*; схема с памятью

8410 sequential data stripping
d Auswerten *n* von sequentielle Daten

f étalement *m* des données séquentielles
r изъятие *n* последовательных данных

8411 sequential depth
(of a logic circuit)
d sequentielle Tiefe *f*
f profondeur *f* séquentielle
r последовательностная глубина *f*

8412 sequential file
d sequentielle Datei *f*
f fichier *m* séquentiel
r последовательный файл *m*

* **sequential mode → 8431**

8413 sequential sampling
d sequentielle Stichprobennahme *f*
f échantillonnage *m* séquentiel
r последовательный выбор *m*

8414 serial; sequential; consecutive
d seriell; sequentiell; aufeinanderfolgend;
konsequent
f sériel; séquentiel; consécutif
r последовательный; серийный; следующий
один за другим

8415 serial acceptance
d serielle Akzeptanz *f*
f acceptance *f* sérielle
r последовательный приём *m*

* **serial access → 8407**

8416 serial adder
d Serielladd[ier]er *m*; Serielladdierwerk *n*
f add[itionn]eur *m* sériel
r последовательный сумматор *m*

8417 serial asynchronous interface
d serielle asynchrone Schnittstelle *f*
f interface *f* asynchrone sérielle
r серийный асинхронный интерфейс *m*

8418 serial by bit
d bitseriell
f sériel par bit
r последовательный по битам

* **serial-by-bit interface → 1025**

8419 serial by character
d zeichenseriell
f sériel par caractère
r последовательный по символам

8420 serial cable
d serielles Kabel *n*
f câble *m* sériel

r серийный кабель *m*

* **serial carry → 9035**

8421 serial channel
d serieller Kanal *m*
f canal *m* sériel; voie *f* sérielle
r последовательный канал *m*

8422 serial computer
d seriell arbeitender Rechner *m*;
Seriellrechner *m*
f ordinateur *m* sériel
r компьютер *m* последовательного действия

* **serial configuration → 8436**

8423 serial data line
d serielle Datenleitung *f*
f ligne *f* de données sérielle
r линия *f* последовательного обмена
данными

8424 serial equipment
d Serienausrüstung *f*; Seriengeräte *npl*
f équipement *m* sériel
r серийное оборудование *n*

8425 serial format
d serielles Format *n*
f format *m* sériel
r последовательный формат *m*

8426 serial input/output
d serielle Eingabe/Ausgabe *f*
f entrée/sortie *f* sérielle
r последовательный ввод/вывод *m*

* **serial interface → 8428**

* **serialization → 6796**

* **serializer → 6797**

8427 serial job
d serieller Job *m*
f job *m* sériel
r последовательное задание *n*

8428 serial [line] interface
d serielle Schnittstelle *f*; Schnittstelle für
serielle Datenübertragung
f interface *f* [de ligne] sérielle
r серийный интерфейс *m* линии;
последовательный интерфейс

8429 serial line Internet protocol; SLIP
d serielles Internet-Protokoll *n*;
SLIP-Protokoll *n*

f protocole m Internet de ligne sérielle;
protocole SLIP
r Интернет-протокол m серийной линии

8430 serial link
d serielle Verbindung f
f liaison f sérielle
r последовательная связь f

8431 serial mode; sequential mode;
one-at-a-time mode
d sequentielle Betriebsweise f
f mode m sériel; mode séquentiel
r последовательный режим m

* **serial-parallel conversion** → **8437**

* **serial-parallel converter** → **8438**

8432 serial-parallel operation
d Serien-Parallel-Betrieb m
f opération f série-parallèle
r серийно-параллельная работа f

8433 serial-parallel system
d Serien-Parallelsystem n
f système m série-parallèle
r серийно-параллельная система f

8434 serial port
d serieller Port m; serielle Anschlussstelle f
f port m sériel
r серийный порт m

8435 serial printer
d serieller Drucker m
f imprimante f sérielle
r принтер m последовательного действия

8436 serial representation; serial configuration
d Seriendarstellung f
f représentation f sérielle
r последовательное представление n

8437 serial-[to-]parallel conversion
d Serien-Parallel-Umsetzung f
f conversion f série-parallèle
r серийно-параллельное преобразование n

8438 serial-[to-]parallel converter; deserializer;
staticizer
d Serien-Parallel-Umsetzer m;
Serien-Parallel-Wandler m
f convertisseur m série-parallèle
r серийно-параллельный преобразователь m;
последовательно-параллельный
преобразователь

* **serial transfer** → **8439**

8439 serial transmission; serial transfer
d serielle Übertragung f; Serienübertragung f;
serieller Transfer m; Serientransfer m
f transmission f sérielle; transfert m sériel
r последовательная передача f

8440 series; train
d Reihe f
f série f; train m
r ряд m

8441 series connection
d Reihenschaltung f; Serienschaltung f
f connexion f en série; montage m en série
r последовательное включение n

* **server** → **6136**

8442 server common control
d Server-Zentralsteuerung f
f contrôle m commun de serveur
r общее управление n сервером

8443 server manager
d Serververwalter m
f gestionnaire m de serveur
r управитель m сервера

8444 service
d Bedienung f
f entretien m; service m
r обслуживание n; услуга f

8445 serviceability; maintainability
d Servicefreundlichkeit f;
Betriebsfreundlichkeit f
f serviabilité f; utilisabilité f; maintenabilité f
r обслуживаемость f; удобство n
эксплуатации

* **service bit** → **5607**

* **service check** → **8446**

8446 service check[ing]
d Wartungskontrolle f
f contrôle m d'entretien
r профилактический контроль m

8447 service disk
d Dienstplatte f
f disque m de service
r служебный диск m

8448 service interruption
d Betriebsunterbrechung f
f interruption f de service
r служебное прерывание n

8449 service layer
d Dienstschicht f

f couche *f* service
r служебный слой *m*

* **service processor** → 2192

8450 service program; service routine; utility [program]
d Dienstprogramm *n*
f programme *m* de service; programme *m* utilitaire; utilitaire *m*
r обслуживающая программа *f*; сервисная программа; вспомогательная программа; служебная программа; утилит *m*

8451 service provider
d Dienstanbieter *m*; Dienstgeber *m*
f fournisseur *m* de services
r поставщик *m* услуг

* **service routine** → 8450

* **servicing** → 5606

8452 serving channel address
d Abnehmeradresse *f*
f adresse *f* de canal d'abonné
r адрес *m* абонентской линии

8453 servosurface
d Servofläche *f*; Sitzfläche *f*
f servosurface *f*
r рабочая поверхность *f*

8454 servosystem
d Servosystem *n*
f système *m* d'asservissement
r сервосистема *f*

8455 session
d Session *f*; Sitzung *f*
f session *f*; séance *f*
r сессия *f*; сеанс *m*

8456 session access
d Sessionszugriff *m*
f accès *m* pendant une session
r доступ *m* в сеансе связи

8457 session connection
d Sitzung[verbindung] *f*
f connexion *f* de session
r сеансовая связь *f*

8458 session-connection synchronization
d Sitzung-Synchronisation *f*
f synchronisation *f* de connexion de session
r синхронизация *f* сеансовой связи

8459 session [control] protocol; SCP
d Sitzungs[steuer]protokoll *n*;

Sessionprotokoll *n*
f protocole *m* [de commande] de session
r протокол *m* обслуживания сеансов; протокол сеансового уровня сети

8460 session entity
d Sitzungsinstanz *f*; Kommunikationssteuerungsinstanz *f*
f entité *f* de session
r целостность *f* сессии

8461 session key
d Sitzungsschlüssel *m*
f clé *f* de session
r ключ *m* сеанса

8462 session layer
(of network protocol)
d Sitzungsschicht *f*; Kommunikationssteuerungsschicht *f*; Verbindungsschicht *f*
f niveau *m* de session
r сеансовый уровень *m*

8463 session node
d Sitzungsknoten *m*
f nœud *m* de session
r узел *m* сетевого соединения; узел формирования сети

* **session protocol** → 8459

8464 session reliability
d Sitzungszuverlässigkeit *f*
f fiabilité *f* de session
r надёжность *f* сеанса

* **set** → 8474

* **set** *v* → 2021

8465 set *v*
d setzen; einstellen
f établir
r установлять

8466 set; ensemble
d Menge *f*; Satz *m*
f ensemble *m*
r множество *n*; комплект *m*

8467 set command
d Einstellenbefehl *m*
f commande *f* d'établissement
r команда *f* установления

* **set device** → 8471

8468 set [im]pulse
d Setzimpuls *m*

f impulsion *f* de mise à un
r импульс *m* установки в единицу

8469 set input
d Setzeingang *m*
f entrée *f* du signal de mise à un
r вход *m* сигнала установки в единицу

* **set of all subsets** → 7186

* **set of output symbols** → 6617

8470 set point; set value
d Einstellwert *m*
f valeur *f* de consigne; grandeur *f* de consigne;
valeur établie; valeur prescrite
r заданная величина *f*; заданное значение *n*

**8471 set [point] device; set [point] transmitter;
setting device**
d Sollwertgeber *m*; Einsteller *m*
f excitateur *m*; consignateur *m*
r задающее устройство *n*; задатчик *m*

8472 set point output
d Sollwertausgabe *f*
f sortie *f* d'excitateur
r выход *m* задающего устройства

* **set point transmitter** → 8471

* **set pulse** → 8468, 8477

8473 set-reset trigger; R-S trigger
d Setz-Rücksetz-Flipflop *m*; Flipflop *m*
mit R-S-Tastung; R-S-Flipflop *m*
f basculeur *m* asymétrique; basculeur de
service; basculeur R-S
r триггер *m* с раздельными входами;
дежурный триггер

* **set time** → 8478

8474 set[ting]; setup; establishment
d Einstellung *f*; Einstellen *n*; Einrichtung *f*
f établissement *m*; mise *f* au point
r установление *n*; установка *f*; настройка *f*

* **setting device** → 8471

8475 setting equipment
d Einstelleinrichtung *f*
f équipement *m* d'ajustage
r оборудование *n* настройки

8476 setting function
d Einstellfunktion *f*
f fonction *f* d'établissement
r функция *f* установления

8477 set[ting] pulse
d Einstellimpuls *m*
f impulsion *f* d'ajustage
r установочный импульс *m*

**8478 set[ting] time; build[ing]-up time; rise
time; ramp time**
(of a signal)
d Einstellungszeit *f*; Einschwingzeit *f*;
Regelzeit *f*; Anlaufzeit *f*; Anstiegszeit *f*
f temps *m* d'accroissement; temps de montée;
temps de réponse; temps *m* d'établissement;
durée *f* de mise en régime permanent
r время *n* установления [режима]; время
нарастания; характеристическое время;
длительность *f* переднего фронта

* **set transmitter** → 8471

* **setup** → 563. 8474

* **setup** *v* → 4941

8479 setup program; installation program
d Installationsprogramm *n*
f programme *m* d'installation
r программа *f* установки; программа
настройки; инсталляционная программа

**8480 setup time; formative time; preparation
time; lead time**
d Aufstellzeit *f*; Vorbereitungszeit *f*;
Aufbauzeit *f*
f temps *m* d'établissement; temps de
préparation [au travail]
r время *n* установления; время подготовки
[к работе]

* **set value** → 8470

8481 severity code
d Sicherheitscode *m*
f code *m* significatif
r код *m* серьёзности [уровня] ошибки

* **sew** *v* → 6851

* **SGML** → 8816

8482 SGML entity
d SGML-Instanz *f*
f entité *f* SGML
r SGML примитив *m*

* **SGRAM** → 9120

* **shade** → 8486

* **shade of gray** → 4315

8483 shader; shadow software
d Schattierungsprogramm *n*;
Schattierung-Software *f*
f programme *m* d'ombrage; logiciel *m*
d'ombrage
r программа *f* построения теней;
программное обеспечение *n* затенения

8484 shading
d Schattierung *f*; Schattieren *n*; Abschattung *f*
f ombrage *m*
r оттенение *n*; затенение *n*

8485 shading processor
d Schattierung-Prozessor *m*
f processeur *m* d'ombrage
r процессор *m* оттенения; процессор
затенения

* **shading scale** → 4316

8486 shadow; shade
d Schatten *m*
f ombre *f*
r тень *f*

8487 shadow generation
d Schattengenerierung *f*
f génération *f* d'ombre
r генерирование *n* тени

8488 shadow mask; aperture mask
d Schattenmaske *f*; Lochmaske *f*
f masque *m* perforé; masque à trous
r теневая маска *f*

8489 shadow memory; nonaddressable memory
d Schattenspeicher *m*
f mémoire *f* fantôme
r теневая память *f*

* **shadow recording** → 3005

* **shadow software** → 8483

* **shape** → 3967

* **shape library** → 4262

8490 share *v*
d teilen; gemeinsam benutzen
f partager; utiliser en commun
r разделять; совместно использовать

* **shareable file** → 8492

8491 shared control
d gemeinsame Steuerung *f*
f gestion *f* partagée; gestion mixte; gestion
collective

r коллективное управление *n*

8492 shared file; shareable file
d gemeinsam genutzte Datei *f*;
gemeinschaftliche Datei
f fichier *m* [utilisé en] commun; fichier partagé
r коллективный файл *m*; файл совместного
пользования

8493 shared resource
d gemeinsame Ressource *f*; anteilig genutzte
Einrichtung *f*
f ressource *f* partagée
r совместно используемый ресурс *m*;
разделённый ресурс

8494 shared-resource system
d verteiltes System *n*
f système *m* de ressources partagées
r система *f* совместно используемых
ресурсов

* **sharer** → 9007

8495 shareware
d Shareware *f*
f shareware *m*; logiciel *m* contributif; logiciel à
contribution volontaire; partagiciel *m*
r некоммерсиальное программное
обеспечение *n*; шеруер *m*

* **sharpen effect** → 8498

8496 sharpening
d Schärfeeinstellung *f*; Scharfschleifen *n*
f affûtage *m*; retaillage *m*; émouture *f*
r увеличение *n* резкости

* **sharpening effect** → 8498

8497 sharpness; definition
d Schärfe *f*
f netteté *f*; définition *f*
r чёткость *f*; резкость *f*; ясность *f*

8498 sharpness effect; sharpen[ing] effect
d Schärfeeffekt *m*
f effet *m* de netteté
r эффект *m* чёткости; эффект резкости

* **sheaf** → 6884

* **sheet** → 3451, 5294

8499 sheet
d Blatt *n*; Vordruck *m*
f feuille *f*; formulaire *m*
r лист *m*; бланк *m*; перечень *m* [документов]

8500 sheet-feed plotter
d Plotter *m* mit Blattzuführung

f traceur *m* en feuilles
r графопостроитель *m* с полистовой
подачей

8501 sheet-feed scanner
d Scanner *m* mit Blattzuführung
f scanner *m* feuille à feuille; scanner en feuilles
r сканер *m* с полистовой подачей

8502 sheet size
d Blattgröße *f*
f taille *f* de feuille
r размер *m* листа

* **Sheffer stroke → 6220**

* **Sheffer's stroke operation → 6220**

* **shell → 3451**

* **shield → 826**

8503 shielding; screening
d Schirmung *f*; Abschirmung *f*
f blindage *m*
r экранирование *n*

* **shift → 8507**

8504 shift code
d Umschaltecode *m*
f code *m* de décalage
r код *m* смещения

* **shift counter → 8509**

8505 shifted text
d verschobener Text *m*
f texte *m* décalé
r перемещенный текст *m*; сдвинутый текст

* **shifter → 8510, 8514**

8506 shift indexing
d Schrägindizierung *f*
f indexage *m* de décalage
r смещённое индексирование *n*

8507 shift[ing]; displacement; offset
d Verschiebung *f*; Schieben *n*; Schiftung *f*;
Verlagerung *f*
f décalage *m*; déplacement *m*
r сдвиг *m*; смещение *n*; рассогласование *n*

8508 shifting character
d Verschiebungszeichen *n*
f caractère *m* de décalage
r символ *m* сдвига; знак *m* смещения

8509 shift[ing] counter

d Schiftzähler *m*; Verschiebezähler *m*
f compteur *m* de décalage
r счётчик *m* числа сдвигов; сдвигающий
счётчик

8510 shift[ing] register; shifter
d Schieberegister *n*; Verschiebungsregister *n*
f registre *m* de décalage; décaleur *m*
r регистр *m* сдвига; сдвиговый регистр

8511 shift instruction
d Schiebebefehl *m*; Verschiebebefehl *m*
f instruction *f* de décalage
r инструкция *f* сдвига

8512 Shift key
d Schift-Taste *f*; Umschalttaste *f*
f touche *f* Maj; touche de commutation; touche
de décalage des registres
r клавиша *f* Shift; клавиша переключения
[регистров]

**8513 shift operator; displacement operator;
translation operator**
d Verschiebungsoperator *m*;
Translationsoperator *m*
f opérateur *m* de déplacement; opérateur de
translation
r оператор *m* сдвига

* **shift register → 8510**

* **shift right → 8088**

8514 shift unit; shifter
d Schiebeeinrichtung *f*;
Verschiebeeinrichtung *f*
f dispositif *m* de décalage; unité *f* de décalage;
décaleur *m*
r схема *f* сдвига; сдвигающее устройство *n*;
сдвигатель *m*

8515 short
d kurz; verkürzt; gekürzt
f court; écourté; bref
r короткий; укороченный

8516 shortcut
d Shortcut *n*; schneller Zugang *m*; Kürzel *n*
f raccourci *m*; accès *m* rapide
r сокращение *n*; сокращённое
наименование *n*; укорачивание *n*; краткая
форма *f*; быстрый вызов *m*

* **shortcut division → 8**

8517 shortcut key; accelerator [key]; hotkey
d Hotkey; Shortcut-Taste *f*;
Beschleunigungstaste *f*

f touche *f* raccourci; touche directe; touche [d'accès] rapide; clé *f* accélératrice
r горячая клавиша *f*; клавиша быстрого вызова; клавиша быстрого выбора команд; быстрая клавиша

* **shortcut menu** → 2227

8518 shortcut operation
d abgekürzte Operation *f*
f opération *f* abrégée; opération accélérée
r укороченная операция *f*; ускоренная операция

8519 shortcut test
d Kurztest *m*
f test *m* rapide
r скоростное испытание *n*

8520 shorten *v*; **cancel** *v*
d kürzen; wegkürzen
f simplifier; réduire
r сокращать; упрощать

8521 short message service; SMS
d Kurznachrichtendienst *m*; Dienst *m* das Versenden von kurzen Nachrichten
f service *m* de messages courts
r обслуживание *n* коротких сообщений

* **short multiplication** → 9

8522 short precision
d niedrige Genauigkeit *f*
f précision *f* écourtée; précision limitée
r ограниченная точность *f*

* **short subtraction** → 11

* **short-term** → 8525

8523 short-term filing
d Kurzzeitarchivierung *f*
f archivage *m* de courte durée
r краткосрочное архивирование *n*

8524 short-term performance
d Kurzzeitverhalten *n*; Kurzzeitcharakteristik *f*
f caractéristique *f* à court terme
r кратковременная характеристика *f*

8525 short-time; short-term
d Kurzzeit-
f de courte durée; à court terme
r краткосрочный; кратковременный

8526 short-time data
d Kurzzeitdaten *pl*
f données *fpl* de courte durée
r краткосрочные данные *pl*

8527 short-time interrupt
d Kurzzeitunterbrechung *f*
f interruption *f* temporaire
r кратковременное прерывание *n*

* **shrink** *v* → 4610

8528 shrink *v*
d schrumpfen; kleiner werden
f contracter; déformer
r сжимать

* **shrinkage** → 8529

8529 shrinking; shrinkage; contraction
d Schrumpfung *f*; Schwinden *n*; Schwund *m*; Kontraktion *f*
f retrait *m*; rétrécissement *m*; contraction *f*
r сокращение *n*; свёртывание *n*; контракция *f*

* **shunt** → 1180

8530 shutdown
d Zwischenstopp *m*
f arrêt *m*
r закрытие *n*

8531 shut *v* **down**
d herunterfahren
f arrêter
r выключать; закрыть; остановить; отключать

8532 shuttle carriage
d hin- und herbewegbarer Wagen *m*
f chariot *m* [à mouvement de] navette
r челночная каретка *f*

* **side** → 5288

8533 side-mounted keyboard
d getrennt montierte Tastatur *f*; seitenmontierte Tastatur
f clavier *m* séparé mécaniquement
r выносная клавиатура *f*

* **sigma notation** → 9042

* **sign** → 1593

* **@ sign** → 607

8534 signal
d Signal *n*; Zeichen *n*; Zeichenträger *m*
f signal *m*
r сигнал *m*

8535 signal buffer
d Signalpuffer *m*; Zeichenpuffer *m*

f tampon *m* de signaux
r буфер *m* сигналов

8536 signal carrier
d Signalträger *m*
f porteuse *f* de signal
r несущая *f* сигнала

8537 signal coding
d Signalcodierung *f*
f codage *m* de signaux
r кодирование *n* сигналов

8538 signal conditioner; signal shaper
d Signalformer *m*
f [con]formateur *m* de signaux
r формирователь *m* сигналов

8539 signal conditioning; signal shaping
d Signalaufbereitung *f*; Signalformung *f*
f formatage *m* de signal; formation *f* de signal
r формирование *n* сигнала; образование *n* сигнала; поддержка *f* сигнала

8540 signal decoding
d Signalentschlüsselung *f*; Signaldecodierung *f*
f décodage *m* de signal
r дешифрирование *n* сигнала

8541 signal delay
d Signalverzögerung *f*
f retard *m* du signal
r задержка *f* сигнала

8542 signal detection; signal recognition
d Signalerkennung *f*
f reconnaissance *f* de signaux
r распознавание *n* сигналов

8543 signal generator; signalizer
d Signalgenerator *m*; Signalgeber *m*; Wechselsender *m*; Prüfsender *m*
f générateur *m* de signaux
r сигнальный генератор *m*; генератор сигналов

8544 signaling
d Signalübertragung *f*
f transmission *f* de signaux
r передача *f* сигналов

8545 signaling protocol
d Signalisierungsprotokoll *n*; Signalaustauschprotokoll *n*
f protocole *m* d'échange de signaux
r протокол *m* обмена сигналами

8546 signal interrupt; signal splitting
d Zeichenunterbrechung *f*
f interruption *f* de signal

r прерывание *n* сигнала

* **signalizer** → 8543

8547 signal processing
d Signalverarbeitung *f*
f traitement *m* de signaux
r обработка *f* сигналов

8548 signal processor
d Signalprozessor *m*
f processeur *m* de signaux
r сигнальный процессор *m*

* **signal recognition** → 8542

* **signal shaper** → 8538

* **signal shaping** → 8539

* **signal splitting** → 8546

8549 signal-to-noise ratio
d Signal-Rausch-Verhältnis *n*; Rauschabstand *m*
f rapport *m* signal-bruit
r отношение *n* сигнал-шум

8550 signal valid bit
d Signalgültigkeitsbit *n*
f bit *m* de validation de signal
r бит *m* достоверности сигнала

8551 signature
(used to identify the sender of an e-mail message or Usenet article, that appears at the end of either communication)
d Signatur *f*; Unterschrift *f*
f signature *f*; empreinte *f*
r сигнатура *f*; подпись *f*

8552 signature file
d Unterschriftendatei *f*; Signatur-Datei *f*
f fichier *m* de signatures
r сигнатурный файл *m* (с информацией о пользователе)

8553 signature layout
d Signaturaufstellung *f*
f disposition *f* de la signature
r размещение *n* сигнатуры

8554 sign bit
d Vorzeichen[bit] *n*; Zeichenbit *n*
f bit *m* de signe
r знаковый бит *m*; знаковый разряд *m*

8555 sign changer; sign reverser
d Vorzeichenumkehrer *m*

f changeur *m* de signe; inverseur *m* de signe
r знакоинвертор *m*

8556 sign digit; signed field
   d Vorzeichenziffer *f*
   f chiffre *m* de signe
   r цифра *f* [алгебраического] знака

8557 signed complement
   d vorzeichenbehaftetes Komplement *n*
   f complément *m* avec signe
   r дополнение *n* со знаком

   * **signed field** → **8556**

8558 signed number
   d vorzeichenbehaftete Zahl *f*; Zahl mit
      Vorzeichen
   f nombre *m* muni de signe; nombre signé
   r число *n* со знаком

8559 significance
   d Signifikanz *f*; Bedeutsamkeit *f*; Wertigkeit *f*
   f signification *f*; importance *f*
   r значимость *f*

8560 significant digit; significant figure
   d signifikante Stelle *f*; bedeutsame Ziffer *f*;
      wesentliche Ziffer
   f digit *m* significatif; digit révélateur; chiffre *m*
      significatif
   r значащий разряд *m*; значащая цифра *f*

   * **significant figure** → **8560**

   * **sign of addition** → **181**

8561 sign of disjunction
   d Disjunktionszeichen *n*; Adjugat *n*
   f signe *m* de disjonction
   r знак *m* дизъюнкции

**8562 sign of division; division sign; divider;
divisor**
   d Divisionszeichen *n*; Teiler *m*; Divisor *m*
   f signe *m* de division; diviseur *m*;
      démultiplicateur *m*
   r знак *m* деления; делитель *m*

   * **sign-off** → **5489**

8563 sign of implication
   d Implikationszeichen *n*; Subjugat *n*
   f signe *m* d'implication
   r знак *m* импликации

8564 sign of inclusion
   d Enthaltenszeichen *n*
   f signe *m* d'inclusion
   r знак *m* включения

8565 sign of multiplication; multiplication sign
   d Multiplikationszeichen *n*; Malzeichen *n*
   f signe *m* de multiplication
   r знак *m* умножения

**8566 sign of subtraction; subtraction sign;
minus [sign]**
   d Subtraktionszeichen *n*; Minuszeichen *n*;
      Differenzzeichen *n*; Minus *n*
   f signe *m* de soustraction; moins *m*
   r знак *m* вычитания; знак минус; минус *m*

   * **sign-on** → **5485**

   * **sign *v* on** → **5456**

8567 sign register
   d Vorzeichenregister *n*
   f registre *m* de signe
   r регистр *m* знака

   * **sign reverser** → **8555**

8568 silicon chip
   d Siliziumchip *m*
   f puce *f* de silicium
   r кремниевый кристалл *m*

8569 silicon compiler
   d Silicon-Compiler *m*
   f compilateur *m* de silicium
   r кремниевый компилятор *m*; компилятор
      кремниевых ИС

   * **similarity** → **2161**

   * **similitude** → **2161**

   * **SIMM** → **8617**

   * **simple** → **8591**

8570 simple branch point
   d einfacher Verzweigungspunkt *m*
   f point *m* de ramification simple
   r простая точка *f* ветвления

8571 simple grammar
   d einfache Grammatik *f*
   f grammaire *f* simple
   r простая грамматика *f*

8572 simple mail transfer protocol; SMTP
   d einfaches Mail-Übertragungsprotokoll *n*;
      Mailpostprotokoll *n* SMTP
   f protocole *m* habituel de messagerie de
      l'Internet; protocole SMTP
   r простой протокол *m* передачи почты;
      протокол SMTP

8573 simple ratio channel
 d Zeitvielfachkanal m mit Periodenverteilung
   nach einfachen Teilverhältnissen
 f voie f multiple à partage du temps dans des
   rapports simples
 r канал m с простыми соотношениями
   разделения времени

8574 simplex
 d Simplex n
 f simplex m
 r симплекс m

8575 simplex channel; simplex circuit;
     single-ended channel; one-way channel
 d Simplexkanal m; Einwegkanal m
 f canal m simplex; canal unilatéral
 r симплексный канал m; односторонний
   канал

 * simplex circuit → 8575

8576 simplex transmission
 d Simplexübertragung f
 f transmission f simplex
 r симплексная передача f

8577 simplification
 d Vereinfachung f
 f simplification f
 r упрощение n

8578 simplification strategies
 d Vereinfachungsstrategien fpl
 f stratégies fpl de simplification
 r стратегии fpl упрощения

8579 simplified data transmission
 d vereinfachte Datenübermittlung f
 f transmission f simplifiée des données
 r упрощённая передача f данных

8580 simply connected
 d einfach zusammenhängend
 f simplement connecté
 r односвязный

8581 simulation
 d Simulation f; Simulierung f
 f simulation f; imitation f
 r [имитационное] моделирование n;
   имитация f

8582 simulation pass; simulation run
 d Simulationslauf m
 f passage m de simulation; passage [de]
   simulateur
 r имитационный прогон m; прогон модели

 * simulation run → 8582

8583 simulator
 d Simulator m; Simulationseinrichtung f
 f simulateur m; imitateur m
 r симулятор m; имитатор m

8584 simultaneity
 d Gleichzeitigkeit f; Simultaneität f
 f simultanéité f
 r одновременность f; совместность f

 * simultaneous → 2121

8585 simultaneous access
 d simultaner Zugriff m; gleichzeitiger Zugriff
 f accès m simultané
 r одновременный доступ m

 * simultaneous computer → 6775

8586 simultaneous mode; parallel mode
 d Simultanbetrieb m
 f mode m parallèle
 r режим m параллельной обработки

8587 simultaneous peripheral operation on line;
     SPOOL; spooling
 d simultaner peripherer Direktbetrieb m;
   SPOOL-Betrieb m; Spooling n; Spulen n;
   Spulung f
 f exécution f de SPOOL; spoulage m
 r подкачка f; откачка f; буферирование n;
   дебуферирование n; спулинг m

8588 simultaneous translation system
 d Simultanübersetzungssystem n
 f système m de traduction simultanée
 r система f синхронного перевода

8589 simultaneous transmission; parallel
     transmission
 d simultane Übertragung f;
   Simultanübertragung f; parallele Übertragung
 f transmission f simultanée; transmission
   parallèle
 r одновременная передача f; встречная
   передача

8590 single
 d einzeln; Einzel-; allein
 f seul; unique; singulier
 r один; отдельный; единственный;
   самостоятельный

8591 single; simple
 d einfach
 f simple; unique
 r однократный; одинарный

 * single-action window → 7014

* **single-address** → 6410

* **single-address instruction** → 6411

8592 single-address message; one-address message
d Einfachadressnachricht *f*
f message *m* à adresse unique
r одноадресное сообщение *n*

8593 single-address point; one-address point
d Einfachergebnispunkt *m*
f point *m* à adresse unique
r одноадресный пункт *m*

8594 single-bit fault correction
d Einbitfehlerkorrektur *f*
f correction *f* de défaut d'un bit
r исправление *n* однобитовых ошибок

8595 single-bit fault detection
d Einbitfehlererkennung *f*
f détection *f* de défaut d'un bit
r обнаружение *n* однобитовых ошибок

* **single-board** → 6412

8596 single-bus structure; one-bus structure
d Einzelbusstruktur *f*
f structure *f* à bus unique
r одношинная структура *f*

8597 single-bus-transfer mode
d Einzelübertragungsbusbetriebsweise *f*
f mode *m* de bus à transfert unique
r обмен *m* данными по одной общей шине

8598 single-byte transfer
d Einzel-Byte-Übertragung *f*
f transfert *m* d'octets uniques
r передача *f* отдельных байтов

8599 single channel
d Einfachkanal *m*
f canal *m* unique; monocanal *m*
r одиночный канал *m*; отдельный канал

8600 single-channel; one-channel; monochannel *adj*
d Einkanal-; Einzelkanal-
f monocanal; monovoie
r одноканальный

8601 single-channel codec
d Einkanalcodec *m*; Einzelkanalcodec *m*
f codec *m* monocanal
r одноканальный кодек *m*

8602 single-channel communication
d Einkanalübertragung *f*
f communication *f* à une voie; communication monocanale
r одноканальная коммуникация *f*

8603 single-channel communication controller
d Einkanal-Datenübertragungskontroller *m*
f contrôleur *m* de communication à canal unique
r одноканальный коммуникационный контроллер *m*

8604 single-channel connection
d Einkanalverbindung *f*; Einzelkanalverbindung *f*
f connexion *f* à une voie; connexion monocanale
r одноканальная связь *f*

8605 single-channel controller
d Einkanalkontroller *m*
f contrôleur *m* monocanal
r одноканальный контроллер *m*

8606 single-channel data transmission
d Einkanal-Datenübertragung *f*
f transmission *f* de données monocanale
r одноканальная передача *f* данных

8607 single-channel input
d Einkanaleingabe *f*
f entrée *f* monocanale
r одноканальный ввод *m*

8608 single-channel interface
d Einkanalschnittstelle *f*
f interface *f* monocanale
r одноканальный интерфейс *m*

8609 single-channel output
d Einkanalausgabe *f*
f sortie *f* monocanale
r одноканальный вывод *m*

8610 single-channel signal
d Einzelkanalsignal *n*
f signal *m* monocanal
r одноканальный сигнал *m*

8611 single-channel through connection
d Einzelkanaldurchschaltung *f*
f connexion *f* entière monocanale
r одноканальное сквозное соединение *n*

* **single-chip** → 6416

8612 single-circuit
d Einkreis-; einschleifig
f à circuit unique
r одноконтурный; односхемный

8613 single click
  d Einzelklick *m*
  f clic *m* unique
  r одиночное нажатие *n* кнопки

  * **single clock** → 8627

8614 single clock pulse; single timing pulse
  d Einzeltakt *m*
  f horloge *f* simple; horloge unique
  r одиночный тактовый импульс *m*

8615 single clock pulse control
  d Einzeltaktsteuerung *f*
  f contrôle *m* par horloges simples
  r однофазное управление *n*

  * **single-digit adder** → 6420

  * **single-ended channel** → 8575

8616 single error
  d einfacher Fehler *m*
  f erreur *f* simple
  r одиночная ошибка *f*

8617 single inline memory module; SIMM
  d einreihiges Speichermodul *n*
  f barrette *f* de mémoire vive
  r модуль *m* памяти с однорядным
    расположением выводов

  * **single-layer board** → 8618

8618 single-layer [printed] board
  d Einebenenleiterplatte *f*; Einlagenleiterplatte *f*
  f circuit *m* imprimé à couche unique
  r однослойная [печатная] плата *f*

  * **single-level addressing** → 4684

  * **single-operand operation** → 9603

8619 single-pass
  d Einschritt-; Einweg-
  f à pas unique
  r однопассовый; одношаговый

8620 single-pass algorithm
  d Einwegalgorithmus *m*
  f algorithme *m* à pas unique
  r однопассовый алгоритм *m*

  * **single-pass compiler** → 6427

8621 single-pass multitexturing
  d Einweg-Multitexturieren *n*
  f multi-texturation *f* simple-passe;
    multi-texturation à pas unique
  r создание *n* множества текстур за один шаг

8622 single-pass segmentation
  d Einwegsegmentierung *f*
  f segmentation *f* à pas unique
  r однопассовое сегментирование *n*

**8623 single-pass segmentation of 3D
         pseudo-manifolds**
  d Einwegsegmentierung *f* der
    3D-Pseudo-Kopien
  f segmentation *f* à pas unique de pseudo-copies
    3D
  r однопассовое сегментирование *n*
    трёхмерных псевдо-копий

8624 single-pass trilinear filtering
  d Einweg-Trilinear-Filtering *n*
  f filtrage *m* trilinéaire simple-passe
  r одношаговое трилинейное
    фильтрирование *n*

8625 single-pen plotter
  d Plotter *m* mit einfachem Zeichenstift
  f traceur *m* à plume unique
  r одноперьевой графопостроитель *m*

8626 single-phase; monophase
  d einphasig; Einphasen-
  f à phase unique; monophase
  r однофазный

8627 single[-phase] clock
  d Einphasentakt *m*
  f rythme *m* à phase unique
  r однотактная синхронизация *f*; однофазная
    синхронизация

8628 single precision
  d einfache Genauigkeit *f*
  f précision *f* simple
  r одинарная точность *f*

8629 single pulse; monopulse
  d Einzelimpuls *m*; Mono[im]puls *m*
  f impulsion *f* unique; monoimpulsion *f*
  r одиночный импульс *m*; моноимпульс *m*

8630 single-pulse generator
  d Einzelimpulsgeber *m*
  f générateur *m* d'impulsions uniques
  r генератор *m* одиночных импульсов

8631 single redundancy
  d einfache Redundanz *f*
  f redondance *f* unique
  r однократное резервирование *n*

8632 single-sheet feed
  d Einzelblattzuführung *f*;
    Einzelformularzuführung *f*
  f alimentation *f* de papier en feuilles

r полистовая подача *f* бумаги

8633 single-sided; one-sided; unilateral
d einseitig; unilateral
f unilatéral; à un seul côté; à une face
r односторонний

8634 single-sided board
d einseitige Leiterplatte *f*
f plaque *f* à une face
r односторонняя плата *f*

* single-step operation → 6431

8635 single-task mode
d Einzelprogrammbetrieb *m*
f régime *m* à une tâche
r однозадачный режим *m*

* single timing pulse → 8614

* single-valued → 6437

8636 single-word transfer
d Einzelwortübertragung *f*
f transfert *m* de mots individuels
r перенос *m* отдельными словами

* sinistrorse → 444

* sinistrorsum → 444

* site → 9977

* size *v* → 8196

8637 skeletal code
d Skelettcode *m*; Rahmencode *m*
f code *m* squelette
r скелетный код *m*

8638 skeletal grammar
d Skelettgrammatik *f*
f grammaire *f* squelettique
r остовная грамматика *f*

8639 skip
d Übersprung *m*; Auslassung *f*
f saut *m*; manque *m*; omission *f*
r проскок *m*; пропуск *m*; перескок *m*

* skip instruction → 5190

* skip key → 9160

8640 slab
d Halbleiterkristall *m*; Tafel *f*
f cristal *m* semi-conducteur; plaque *f*
r кристалл *m* полупроводника

8641 slack
d Rückstand *m*; Schlupf *m*
f écart *m*
r остаток *m*

8642 slack bits
d Schlupf-Bits *npl*
f bits *mpl* de remplissage
r заполняющие биты *mpl*; дополняющие биты

8643 slack variable; dummy variable
d Schlupfvariable *f*
f variable *f* d'écart; variable fictive
r слабая переменная *f*; дополнительная переменная; фиктивная переменная; мнимая переменная

* slanted → 6360

* slanted font → 6361

8644 slash; forward slash
d Schrägstrich *m*; Slash *n*
f barre *f* oblique; barre penchée
r [прямая] косая черта *f*

8645 slave
d untergeordnet; Slave-
f esclave; asservi
r подчинённый; ведомый

8646 slave computer
d Nebenrechner *m*
f ordinateur *m* esclave
r подчинённый компьютер *m*

8647 slave disk
d Slave-Disk *f*
f disque *m* esclave
r ведомый диск *m*

8648 slave node
d Slave-Knoten *m*
f nœud *m* esclave
r подчинённый узел *m*

8649 slave store
d Slave-Speicher *m*
f mémoire *f* esclave
r подчинённая память *f*

* sleeping process → 558

8650 slice
d Scheibe *f*; Scheibenteil *m*
f tranche *f*
r слой *m*; вырезка *f*; разрез *m*

8651 slice architecture
d Scheibenarchitektur *f*

f architecture *f* en tranches
r секционированная архитектура *f*; слоистая
архитектура

8652 slice handling
d Teil[wort]verarbeitung *f*
f traitement *m* en tranches
r обработка *f* по частям

8653 slicing
d Aufschneiden *n*; Schneiden *n*
f mise *f* en tranches
r расслоение *n*; секционирование *n*

8654 slide *v*; glide *v*; slip *v*; drag *v*
d gleiten; abgleiten; rutschen
f glisser; lisser
r скользить; глиссировать

* slide → **8661**

8655 slide; diapositive
d Schlitten *m*; Diapositiv *n*
f diapositive *f*
r диапозитив *m*; слайд *m*; прозрачная
плёнка *f*

* **slide bar** → **8661**

8656 slide file
d Diapositivdatei *f*
f fichier *m* de diapositive
r файл *m* слайда; диапозитивный файл

8657 slide file format
d Diapositivdateiformat *n*
f format *m* de fichiers de diapositives
r формат *m* диапозитивных файлов

8658 slide-in chassis
d Einschub *m*
f châssis *m* glissant; tiroir *m* avec éléments de
montage
r съёмный блок *m*; сменный блок; вставной
блок

8659 slide library
d Diapositivbibliothek *f*
f bibliothèque *f* de diapositives
r библиотека *f* слайдов

8660 slide master
d Diapositiv-Meister *m*
f maître *m* de diapositives
r мастер *m* диапозитивов

**8661 slide[r]; slide bar; runner; guide [bar];
glider; slipper**
d Schieber *m*; Läufer *m*; Gleiter *m*
f glissière *f*; glisseur *m*; curseur *m* [de réglage];

coulisseau *m*; réglette *f*; coulisse *f*
r ползунок *m*; движок *m*; слайдер *m*;
скользящий элемент *m*

8662 slide show
d Diavorführung *f*
f diaporama *m*; projection *f* de diapositives
r проигрывание *n* слайдов

8663 sliding; slipping; glancing *adj*
d gleitend; verschieblich
f glissant
r скользящий

8664 sliding; gliding; slipping[-down]
d Gleiten *n*; Gleitung *f*; Rutschen *n*;
Rutschung *f*; Schleifen *n*
f glissement *m*; glissage *m*; dérapage *m*
r скольжение *n*; соскальзывание *n*; плавное
движение *n*

8665 slim calculator
d Flachrechner *m*
f calculateur *m* flat
r плоский калькулятор *m*

* slip *v* → **8654**

* SLIP → **8429**

* slipper → **8661**

* slipping → **8663, 8664**

* slipping-down → **8664**

* sloping → **6360**

8666 slot; throat
d Schlitz *m*; Einsteckschlitz *m*; Steckplatz *m*
f prise *f* femelle; place *f* à enficher; jack *m*;
fente *f*; créneau *m*; logement *m*;
emplacement *m*
r [щелевое] отверстие *n*; канал *m*; гнездо *n*

* **slow-time scale** → **3623**

8667 small capitals; small caps
d Kapitälchen *n*
f petite capitaux *mpl*
r уменьшенные заглавные буквы *fpl*; малые
прописные буквы

* **small caps** → **8667**

8668 small computer system interface; SCSI
d Schnittstelle *f* für Kleincomputersystem
f interface *f* aux petits systèmes d'ordinateur
r интерфейс *m* малых вычислительных
систем; интерфейс SCSI

8669 small icon
(representing a folder or a file)
d kleine Ikone *f*; kleines Symbol *n*
f miniature *f*
r малая пиктограмма *f*

8670 small letter; minuscule
d Kleinbuchstabe *m*
f lettre *f* minuscule; minuscule *f*
r строчная буква *f*

* **small-scale integration** → **5528**

8671 small-scale LAN
d kleines lokales Netz *n*
f réseau *m* local de taille réduite; réseau local de petite taille
r небольшая местная сеть *f*

8672 smart card
d Smart-Card *f*
f carte *f* à mémoire
r интеллектуальная карточка *f*

8673 smart interface
d intelligente Schnittstelle *f*
f interface *f* intelligente
r интеллигентный интерфейс *m*

8674 smart memory
d intelligenter Speicher *m*
f mémoire *f* intelligente
r интеллектуальная память *f*

8675 smiley; emoticon
d Emoticon *n*
f émoticône *m*; binette *f*; sourire *m*; mimique *f*; rictus *m*; faciès *m*; grimace *f*
r смайлик *m*; ухмылочка *f*; эмограмма *f*; пиктограмма *f* для передачи эмоций

8676 smoothing filter
d Glättungsfilter *m*
f filtre *m* de lissage
r сглаживающий фильтр *m*

8677 smooth scrolling
d stetiger Schriftbildlauf *m*; stetige Bildverschiebung *f*; ununterbrochenes Rollen *n*
f évolution *f* continue d'écriture; défilement *m* lent
r непрерывное изображение *n* в рулонном режиме; плавное изображение

8678 smooth shading
d glatte Schattierung *f*
f ombrage *m* lisse
r гладкое оттенение *n*; плавное оттенение

* **SMP** → **9105**

* **SMS** → **8521**

* **SMT** → **9066**

* **SMTP** → **8572**

* **SNA** → **9149**

8679 SnailMail; snail mail
(regular postal service mail, which is slower than electronic mail)
d "Schneckenpost" *f*
f courrier *m* escargot
r обычная почта *f*; улиточная почта; почта улитки; медленная почта

* **snail mail** → **8679**

8680 snap *v*
(on the screen grid)
d fangen; schnappen; ausrichten
f attirer; accrocher
r привязывать; запирать; ухватываться; защёлкивать; прыгать; перепрыгивать

* **snap** → **8682**

8681 snap
d Fang *m*
f magnétisme *m*
r привязка *f*; защёлка *f*; прыжок *m*

8682 snap[ping]
d Ausrichten *n*
f accrochage *m*; croquage *m*
r привязывание *n*

8683 snapshot
(of the screen or the memory)
d Schnappschuss *m*; Momentaufnahme *f*
f instantané *m*
r моментный снимок *m*; мгновенное состояние *n*

8684 snapshot dump; selective dump
d Momentausdruck *m*; Momentanspeicherauszug *m*; Schnappschussspeicherauszug *m*; selektiver Speicherauszug *m*
f vidage *m* [dynamique] sélectif; vidage instantané [de la mémoire]; vidage à la demande
r выборочный дамп *m*; моментальный дамп

8685 snapshot file
d Speicherauszugsdatei *f*
f fichier *m* d'images instantanées
r файл *m* моментных снимков

8686 snapshot key
d Momentanspeicherauszug-Taste f
f touche f d'images instantanées
r клавиша f фиксирования мгновенного
  состояния [экрана]

8687 sniffer
(a person or a program)
d Schnüffler m
f mouchard m; renifleur m
r анализатор m пакетов

8688 sniffer file
d Schnüfflerdatei f
f fichier m de renifleur
r файл m анализатора пакетов

8689 socket
d Sockel m; Fassung f; Buchse f
f socle m; culot m
r гнездо n; цоколь m; сокет m

8690 socket outlet; power outlet; outlet
d Steckdose f; Anschlussdose f; Auslass m
f sortie f [de puissance]
r входная точка f [сети]; розетка f
  соединителя; вылет m

8691 soft copy; transient copy
d nichtdauerhafte Kopie f; Bildschirmkopie f;
  Softcopy n
f copie f non dure; copie sur écran
r недокументальная копия f; экранная
  копия; мягкая копия

8692 soft error
d nichtdauerhafter Fehler m
f erreur f non dure
r кратковременная ошибка f

* **soft image** → **6223**

* **soft patch** → **1236**

8693 soft return
d weicher Zeilenumbruch m
f retour m non dur
r мягкий возврат m; программный возврат (в
  начало следующей строки)

* **soft robot** → **9716**

8694 soft-sectored disk
d softsektorierte Platte f
f disque m découpé en secteurs par logiciel
r программно-секционированный диск m

8695 software
d Software f; Programmierhilfen fpl
f logiciel m; software m

r программное обеспечение n; программные
  системы fpl

* **software bundle** → **8704**

**8696 software copy services; software
     replication services**
d Software-Reproduktionsdienste mpl
f services mpl de reproduction de logiciel
r службы fpl копирования программного
  обеспечения

8697 software counter
d programmierbarer Zähler m
f compteur m logiciel
r программно-реализованный счётчик m;
  программный счётчик

8698 software database
d Datenbasis f der Software
f base f de données de logiciels
r база f данных с описанием программ

8699 software engineering; software technology
d Software-Engineering n; Softwaretechnik f;
  Softwaretechnologie f; Programmiertechnik f
f technique f logicielle; ingénierie f logicielle
r техника f [разработки] программного
  обеспечения; программотехника f

* **software firm** → **8705**

8700 software house
d Softwarehaus n;
  Software-Dienstleistungsfirma f
f entreprise f de services logiciels; société f
  logicielle
r программотехническая фирма f

8701 software interrupt
d Software-Interrupt m; programmierte
  Unterbrechung f
f interruption f de logiciel
r программное прерывание n

8702 software layer
d Softwareschicht f
f couche f de logiciel
r уровень m программного обеспечения

* **software library** → **7402**

8703 software metrics
d Softwaremetrik f
f métrique f de logiciel
r метрика f программного обеспечения

**8704 software package; software suite; software
     bundle**
d Softwarepaket n

f paquet *m* logiciel; suite *f* logicielle
r комплект *m* программных средств;
комплект программного обеспечения

8705 software publisher; software firm
d Softwarefirma *f*
f éditeur *m* de logiciel
r издатель *m* программного обеспечения;
фирма-производитель *f* программного
обеспечения

* **software replication services → 8696**

8706 software stack
d Software-Stapelspeicher *m*
f empilage *m* logiciel
r программный стек *m*

8707 software strategy
d Softwarestrategie *f*
f stratégie *f* logicielle
r стратегия *f* программного обеспечения

* **software suite → 8704**

* **software technology → 8699**

* **solid failure → 4401**

8708 solid font
d Festschrift *f*
f police *f* solide
r монолитный шрифт *m*

8709 solid-ink printer
d Festtinte-Drucker *m*
f imprimante *f* à encre solide
r принтер *m* с твёрдым или
термопластичным красителем

8710 solid texture
d kompakte Textur *f*
f texture *f* solide
r текстура *f* твёрдого тела; текстура
объёмного объекта

* **solution → 2657**

8711 solvability
d Lösbarkeit *f*; Auflösbarkeit *f*
f résolubilité *f*
r разрешимость *f*

* **SONET → 9123**

8712 son tape
d Sohnband *n*; Datenband *n* dritter Generation
f bande *f* fils; bande de troisième génération
r лента *f* третьего поколения

* **sort → 8716**

8713 sort v
d sortieren
f trier
r сортировать

* **sorter → 8717**

8714 sort file
d Sortierdatei *f*
f fichier *m* de tri[age]
r файл *m* сортировки

8715 sort function
d Sortierfunktion *f*
f fonction *f* de triage
r функция *f* сортировки

8716 sort[ing]
d Sortierung *f*; Sortieren *n*
f tri[age] *m*
r сортировка *f*; сортирование *n*

8717 sorting program; sorter
d Sortierprogramm *n*; Sortierer *m*
f programme *m* de tri[age]; trieur *m*
r программа *f* сортировки

8718 sortkey
d Sortierschlüssel *m*
f clé *f* de tri[age]
r ключ *m* сортировки

* **sort merge → 5754**

8719 sort/merge program
d Mischsortierungsprogramm *n*
f programme *m* de triage par fusion
r программа *f* сортировки слиянием

8720 sort order
d Sortierungsordnung *f*; Ordnung *f* der
Sortierung
f ordre *m* de triage
r порядок *m* сортировки

8721 sort pass
d Sortierdurchlauf *m*
f passage *m* de tri[age]
r проход *m* сортировки

* **sought for → 7971**

* **sound → 114**

8722 sound and video options
d Schall- und Videooptionen *fpl*
f options *fpl* vidéo et son
r звуковые и видео опции *fpl*

* **sound board** → 8723

8723 sound card; sound board
  d Soundkarte *f*; Schallkarte *f*
  f carte *f* sonore; carte son
  r звуковая плата *f*

8724 sound data; speech data; vocal data
  d Klangdaten *pl*; Sprachdaten *pl*
  f données *fpl* phoniques; données vocales; données de la parole
  r звуковые данные *pl*; речевые данные; речевая информация *f*

8725 sound file; voice file
  d Klangdatei *f*
  f fichier *m* sonore; fichier vocal
  r звуковой файл *m*

8726 sound font
  d Schallschrift *f*
  f fonte *f* sonore
  r звуковой шрифт *m*

* **sound recognition** → 8769

8727 sound recognition software
  d Schallerkennungssoftware *f*
  f logiciel *m* de reconnaissance vocale
  r софтуер *m* распознавания звука

8728 sound synthesis
  d Klangerzeugung *f*; Klangsynthese *f*
  f synthèse *f* de son
  r синтез *m* звука

8729 source
  d Quelle *f*
  f source *f*
  r источник *m*; исток *m*

* **source code** → 8736

* **source directory** → 4537

8730 source document
  d Ursprungsbeleg *m*; Primärbeleg *m*
  f document *m* d'origine; document de base
  r исходный документ *m*; первичный документ

* **source editor** → 8731

8731 source editor [program]
  d Quellencode-Editorprogramm *n*
  f éditeur *m* source
  r редактор *m* исходного текста

8732 source grammar
  d Quell[en]grammatik *f*

  f grammaire *f* source; grammaire initiale
  r исходная грамматика *f*

8733 source language
  d Quell[en]sprache *f*
  f langage *m* source
  r входной язык *m* транслятора

8734 source library
  d Quellen[programm]bibliothek *f*; Bibliothek *f* für Quellenmodule
  f bibliothèque *f* des programmes d'origine; bibliothèque des modules d'origine
  r библиотека *f* исходных модулей

8735 source of clock pulses
  d Taktimpulsquelle *f*
  f source *f* d'impulsions d'horloge
  r источник *m* тактовых импульсов

* **source of error** → 3516

8736 source program; source code; originating code
  d Quellprogramm *n*; Originalprogramm *n*; Quellcode *m*; Ursprungscode *m*
  f programme *m* [de] source; programme d'origine; code *m* d'origine; code [de] source
  r исходная программа *f*; первичная программа; исходный код *m*; порождающий код

8737 source statement
  d Quellenanweisung *f*; Anweisung *f* in Quellsprache
  f instruction *f* source
  r оператор *m* на входном языке

* **space** → 8738

* **space bar** → 8741

* **spaceborne computer** → 284

8738 space [character]; blank [character]; ignore sign
  (in a text)
  d Leerzeichen *n*; Zwischenraumzeichen *n*; Lückenzeichen *n*
  f caractère *m* d'espace[ment]; caractère vide; caractère blanc; blanc *m*
  r знак *m* пробела; пробел *m*; знак пропуска; интервал *m*

8739 space code
  d Abstandscode *m*; Pausencode *m*
  f code *m* d'espace
  r код *m* интервала

8740 **space-delimited format; SDF**
    d räumlich begrenztes Format *n*;
       Platz-abgegrenztes Format
    f format *m* délimité en espace
    r пространственно-ограниченый формат *m*

8741 **space key; space bar**
    d Leertaste *f*; Space-Taste *f*;
       Zwischenraumtaste *f*
    f touche *f* de vide; touche d'espacement
    r клавиша *f* пробела; кнопка *f* пропуска

    * **space quantization** → 7029

8742 **spacing**
    d Abstandsbestimmung *f*; Anordnung *f* mit
       Zwischenraumzeichen
    f espacement *m*; allocation *f* espacée
    r расположение *n* с интервалами

8743 **spacing after paragraphs**
    d Abstand *m* nach Absätzen
    f espacement *m* devant les paragraphes
    r расстояние *n* за параграфами

8744 **spacing before paragraphs**
    d Abstand *m* vor Absätzen
    f espacement *m* après les paragraphes
    r расстояние *n* перед параграфами

    * **spam** → 4170, 8745

8745 **spam[ming]**
    (in Internet)
    d Versenden *n* von Spam; Sülze *f*
    f inondation *f*; arrosage *m*; multipostage *m*
       [abusif]; spamme *f*; publicité *f*
    r рассылка *f* практически бесполезной
       информации большому числу абонентов
       электронной почтой

    * **span** → 7606

8746 **spanned record**
    d segmentierter Satz *m*
    f enregistrement *m* à chaînage; enregistrement
       chaîné
    r связанная запись *f*

8747 **spare**
    d leer; Reserve-
    f de réserve
    r свободный; лишний

8748 **spare bit**
    d unbelegtes Bit *n*
    f bit *m* de réserve
    r резервный бит *m*

8749 **spare channel**

    d Reservekanal *m*
    f canal *m* de réserve
    r свободный канал *m*

8750 **speaker**
    d Sprecher *m*
    f parleur *m*; speaker *m*
    r динамик *m*; громкоговоритель *m*;
       акустическая колонка *f*

8751 **speaking circuit; talking circuit**
    d Sprechstromkreis *m*
    f circuit *m* de conversation
    r схема *f* разговора

    * **special** → 6826

8752 **special character**
    d Sonderzeichen *n*
    f caractère *m* spécial
    r специальный символ *m*

8753 **special character sequence**
    d Sonderzeichenfolge *f*
    f séquence *f* de caractères spéciaux
    r последовательность *f* специальных
       символов

8754 **special character sequence decoder**
    d Sonderzeichenfolgedecodierer *m*
    f décodeur *m* de séquence de caractères
       spéciaux
    r дешифратор *m* последовательности
       специальных символов

8755 **special character sequence detection**
    d Sonderzeichenfolgeerkennung *f*
    f détection *f* de séquence de caractères
       spéciaux
    r обнаружение *n* последовательности
       специальных символов

8756 **special-purpose computer; dedicated
     computer**
    d Spezial[zweck]rechner *m*; spezialisierter
       Rechner *m*; zweckorientierter Rechner
    f ordinateur *m* spécialisé
    r специализированный компьютер *m*

8757 **specification**
    d Spezifikation *f*
    f spécification *f*
    r спецификация *f*

8758 **specification language**
    d Spezifikationssprache *f*
    f langage *m* de spécifications
    r язык *m* спецификаций

8759 **specificator; specifier**
    d Spezifikator *m*

f spécificateur *m*
r спецификатор *m*

* **specific code** → 18

* **specific coding** → 5544

8760 specific poll
d Einzelaufruf *m*
f interrogation *f* spécifique; appel *m* sélectif spécifique
r специальный [упорядоченный] опрос *m*

* **specifier** → 8759

8761 speech; verbal
d Sprach-; verbal
f verbal; de la parole; de langage
r языковый; устный; речевой

8762 speech-accompanying document transmission
d gesprächsbegleitende Unterlagenübermittlung *f*
f transmission *f* de documents accompagnée de parole
r передача *f* документов при помощи речи

8763 speech application programming interface; SAPI
d Softwareschnittstelle *f* für Sprachdaten; SAPI-Standard *m*
f interface *f* vocale de programmation d'application; standard *m* SAPI
r интерфейс *m* [прикладного программирования] речевой информации

8764 speech coding; voice encoding; speech encryption; voice encryption
d Sprachcodierung *f*; Sprachverschlüsselung *f*
f codage *m* de la parole; chiffrage *m* de la parole
r кодирование *n* речи; шифрование *n* речи

8765 speech connection with accompanying text transmission
d textbegleitete Sprechverbindung *f*
f connexion *f* vocale avec transmission *f* de texte
r речевая связь *f*, сопровождаемая передачей текста

* **speech data** → 8724

* **speech digitalization** → 9912

* **speech encryption** → 8764

* **speech generator** → 8773

8766 speech input; verbal input; voice input
d Spracheingabe *f*
f entrée *f* parlée; entrée verbale; entrée vocale
r речевой ввод *m*

8767 speech memory
d Sprachspeicher *m*
f mémoire *f* vocale; mémoire de langage
r память *f* для записи речи

8768 speech output; verbal output; voice output
d Sprachausgabe *f*
f sortie *f* de parole; sortie verbale; sortie vocale
r речевой вывод *m*; вывод данных голосом

8769 speech recognition; sound recognition; voice recognition
d Sprach[laut]erkennung *f*
f reconnaissance *f* de la parole; reconnaissance vocale
r распознавание *n* речи

8770 speech response; voice response
d Sprachreaktion *f*; Sprachantwort *f*
f réponse *f* vocale
r ответ *m* в речевой форме

8771 speech synthesis; voice synthesis
d Sprachsynthese *f*
f synthèse *f* de la parole
r синтез *m* речи

8772 speech synthesis card
d Sprachsynthese[leiter]platte *f*
f carte *f* de synthèse de la parole
r печатная плата *f* синтезатора речи

* **speech-synthesis chip** → 9916

8773 speech synthesizer; speech generator; VF generator
d Sprachsynthetisator *m*; Sprachgenerator *m*; Sprachlauterzeuger *m*
f synthétiseur *m* de la parole; générateur *m* de la parole; générateur de signaux vocaux
r синтезатор *m* речи; генератор *m* речи

8774 speed; rate; velocity
d Geschwindigkeit *f*
f vitesse *f*; rapidité *f*
r скорость *f*; быстрота *f*

* **spell checker** → 6597

* **spelling** → 6598

* **spelling checker** → 6597

* **spider** → 2461

* **spin lock** → 2621

* **split** → 8782

8775 split *v*
d [zer]spalten; zersplittern; zerteilen
f scinder; fractionner
r расщеплять; дробить; разделять

8776 split bar; splitter bar
(of the window)
d Fensterteiler *m*; Aufteilungsleiste *f*
f barre *f* de fractionnement; barre de splittage
r разделительная линейка *f*; лента *f* разбиения

8777 split box
d Teilungsfeld *n*
f curseur *m* de fractionnement
r маркер *m* разбиения

8778 split field
d geteiltes Feld *n*
f champ *m* divisé
r разделённое поле *n*

8779 split line
d Aufteilungslinie *f*
f ligne *f* de séparation
r линия *f* разбиения

8780 split screen; divided screen
d geteilter Bildschirm *m*
f écran *m* partagé; écran divisé; écran dédoublé; écran fractionné
r разделённый экран *m*; полиэкран *m*

8781 split-screen format
d geteiltes Bildschirmformat *n*
f format *m* multifenêtre
r полиэкранный формат *m*; многооконный формат

* **splitter bar** → 8776

8782 split[ting]
d Aufteilung *f*; Aufteilen *n*; Spaltung *f*; Splitting *n*; Splitten *n*
f splittage *m*; scindement *m*; fractionnement *m*; scission *f*
r расщепление *n*; дробление *n*; разбиение *n*

* **spoke** → 9057

8783 spontaneous request
d spontane Anforderung *f*
f interrogation *f* spontanée
r случайный запрос *m*

* **spoof** → 8786

8784 spoof *v*
(in Internet)
d schwindeln
f pirater; mystifier
r имитировать соединение; получать доступ путём обмана

8785 spoofing
d Hereinlegen *n*; Schwindeln *n*; Austricksen *n*
f usurpation *f*; piratage *m*; mystification *f* [sur un réseau]; arnaque *f*; tromperie *f* (action de bombarder à nombreuses listes des diffusion)
r имитация *f* соединения; получение *n* доступа путём обмана; спуфинг *m*

8786 spoofing program; spoof
d Schwindelprogramm *n*
f programme *m* espion; usurpateur *m*
r программа *f* подмены (адресов)

* **spoof page** → 8787

8787 spoof [Web] page; parody page
d Schwindelseite *f*
f site *m* pastiche; site parodique; contre-site *m*
r ложная [Web-]страница *f*

* **SPOOL** → 8587

8788 spooled plotting
d spulendes Plottern *n*
f traçage *m* tamponné
r буферизированное вычерчивание *n*

8789 spooler
(a program)
d Spool-Programm *n*
f programme *m* de spool; spoule *m*
r программа *f* подкачки; программа откачки

8790 spooler
(a device)
d Spooler *m*
f bobineuse *f*
r устройство *n* перемотки [катушки]

* **spooling** → 8587

8791 spot
d Loch *n*; Fleck *m*
f tache *f*; spot *m*
r пятно *n*

8792 spotlight
d Spotlight *n*; Streiflicht *n*
f projecteur *m* à faisceau concentré; projecteur spot; projecteur convergent; projecteur intensif
r прожектор *m* для подсветки

* spread → 8793

8793 spread[ing]
  d Ausdehnung f; Spreizung f
  f étalement m; propagation f
  r протягивание n; распространение n;
    разброс m

* spreadsheet → 3337

8794 spreadsheet
  d Rechenblatt n
  f feuille f de calcul [électronique]
  r [крупноформатная] электронная таблица f

* spring → 5185

8795 sprite
  (small pictogram, used in games; graphical
  image that can move within a larger graphic)
  d Geist m
  f sprite m; lutin m; démon m
  r динамический графический элемент m;
    спрайт m

8796 sprocked paper
  d Zahnradpapier n
  f papier m perforé
  r перфорированная бумага f

* spurious signal → 6198

* SQL → 8964

8797 SQL driver
  d SQL-Treiber m
  f driver m SQL
  r SQL-драйвер m

8798 SQL editor
  d SQL-Editor m
  f éditeur m SQL
  r SQL-редактор m

8799 SQL file
  d SQL-Datei f
  f fichier m SQL
  r SQL-файл m

8800 SQL query
  d SQL-Abfrage f
  f interrogation f SQL
  r SQL-запрос m

8801 square brackets
  ([ ])
  d eckige Klammern fpl
  f crochets mpl
  r квадратные скобки fpl

* squeezed file → 2036

* SRAM → 8870

* SSL → 8299

8802 stable coalition
  (a mutual support group of high potential
  units that keep each other active during the
  stable state)
  d stabile Koalition f; feste Vereinigung f
  f coalition f stable
  r устойчивая коалиция f

8803 stack; nesting store; push-pop memory
  d Stapel[speicher] m; Keller[speicher] m
  f pile f; [mémoire-]cave f; mémoire f
    d'empilage
  r стек m; магазин m; магазинная память f

8804 stack architecture
  d Kellerspeicherstruktur f;
    Kellerspeicheraufbau m
  f architecture f de pile
  r стековая архитектура f

8805 stack depth
  d Kellerspeichertiefe f; Kellerungstiefe f
  f profondeur f de pile
  r глубина f стека

* stacked data processing → 867

8806 stacker
  d Ablagefach n; Streifenablage f
  f stockeur m; mémoris[at]eur m
  r накопитель m; укладчик m

8807 stack frame
  d Stackrahmen m; Kellerspeichersprosse f
  f échelon m de pile
  r граница f стека

* stack indicator → 8811

8808 stacking
  d Kellerung f; Stapelung f
  f mise f en cave; empilage m
  r запись f в стек; помещение n в стек

8809 stacking order
  d Aufstapeln-Ordnung f
  f ordre m d'empilage
  r порядок m записи в стек

8810 stack instruction
  d Stackbefehl m; Kellerbefehl m
  f instruction f de pile
  r инструкция f работы со стеком

8811 stack pointer; stack indicator; pointer stack register
  d Stapel[an]zeiger *m*; Kellerzeiger *m*; Stackadressregister *n*
  f pointeur *m* de cave; registre *m* de pile
  r указатель *m* стека; регистр *m* указателя стека

8812 stack-to-stack paper
  d gestapeltes Papier *n*
  f papier *m* en feuilles
  r бумага *f*, сложенная стопкой

* **stage** → 1464

* **stairstepping** → 301

8813 stale link
  d schale Verbindung *f*
  f hyperlien *m* détruit; hyperlien déplacé
  r устаревшая связь *f*; гиперсвязь *f* на несуществующий адрес

* **stand** → 876

* **stand-alone** → 4759

* **stand-alone program** → 4760

* **standard** *adj* → 2694

8814 standard
  d Standard *m*; Norm *f*
  f standard *m*; norme *f*
  r стандарт *m*

8815 standard code
  d Standardcode *m*
  f code *m* standard
  r стандартный код *m*

8816 standard generalized markup language; SGML
  d standardisierte generalisierte Aufzeichnungssprache *f*
  f langage *m* standard généralisé de balisage; langage normalisé de balisage généralisé; langage SGML
  r стандартный обобщённый язык *m* разметки; язык SGML

8817 standard interface
  d Standardschnittstelle *f*; Standardinterface *n*; genormte Schnittstelle *f*
  f interface *f* standard[isée]; interface normalisée
  r стандартный интерфейс *m*

8818 standard interface lockout
  d Normanschlusssperre *f*
  f blocage *m* d'interface standard[isée]
  r блокировка *f* стандартного интерфейса

8819 standard interface number
  d Normanschlussnummer *f*
  f numéro *m* d'interface standard[isée]
  r номер *m* стандартного интерфейса

8820 standard interface register
  d Normanschlussregister *n*
  f registre *m* d'interface standard[isée]
  r регистр *m* стандартного интерфейса

8821 standard interface switch
  d Standardanschlussschalter *m*
  f commutateur *m* d'interface standard[isée]
  r переключатель *m* стандартного интерфейса

8822 standard keyboard
  d Standardtastatur *f*
  f clavier *m* standard
  r стандартная клавиатура *f*

8823 standard library; building block library
  d Standardbibliothek *f*; Bausteinbibliothek *f*
  f bibliothèque *f* des modules standardisés; bibliothèque standard
  r библиотека *f* стандартных модулей

8824 standard library file
  d standardmäßige Bibliothekdatei *f*
  f fichier *m* de bibliothèque standard
  r стандартный библиотечный файл *m*

8825 standard model
  d Standardmodell *n*
  f modèle *m* standard
  r стандартная модель *f*

8826 standard paper size
  d Papier-Normalformat *n*
  f format *m* de papier standard
  r стандартный формат *m* бумаги

* **standard product term** → 5842

8827 standard profile
  d Standardprofil *n*
  f profil *m* standard
  r стандартный профиль *m*

8828 standard protocol
  d Standardprotokoll *n*
  f protocole *m* standard
  r стандартный протокол *m*

8829 standard representation
  d Standarddarstellung *f*

f représentation *f* standard
r стандартное представление *n*

* **standard sum of products** → 2999

* **standard sum term** → 5699

* **standard text style** → 2702

8830 standard toolbar
d Standardhilfsmittelstreifen *m*
f barre *f* d'outils standard
r стандартная инструментальная лента *f*;
   стандартная панель *f* инструментов

* **standby** → 780

8831 standby assembly
d Reserveaggregat *n*
f assemblage *m* de réserve
r резервная установка *f*

8832 standby block
d Reserveblock *m*; Standby-Block *m*
f bloc *m* de réserve
r резервный блок *m*

8833 standby channel
d Ersatzkanal *m*
f canal *m* de réserve
r резервный канал *m*

8834 standby mode
d Bereitschaftsbetrieb *m*; Standby-Betrieb *m*;
   Ersatzmodus *m*
f mode *m* à réservation; mode de réserve
r режим *m* с резервированием; режим
   резерва

* **standby redundancy** → 7945

8835 star bus
d Sternbus *m*
f bus *m* en étoile
r шина *f* типа "звезда"

8836 star-bus transmission
d Sternbusübertragung *f*
f transmission *f* par bus en étoile
r передача *f* по шине типа "звезда"

8837 star configuration; radial configuration
d Sternkonfiguration *f*
f configuration *f* en étoile
r звездообразная конфигурация *f*

* **star network** → 8860

* **star-shaped network** → 8860

8838 star structure
d Sternstruktur *f*
f structure *f* en étoile
r звездообразная структура *f*

8839 start *v*
d starten; lassen
f démarrer; lancer
r запускать; стартировать

8840 start; startup; launch
d Start *m*; Starten *n*
f démarrage *m*; départ *m*
r запуск *m*; старт *m*; пуск *m*

* **start address** → 8844

8841 start bit
d Startbit *n*; Einschaltbit *n*
f bit *m* de départ
r начальный бит *m*; бит стартовой посылки

* **start character** → 8852

8842 start code
d Startcode *m*
f code *m* de départ
r код *m* начала; стартовый код

8843 start edge
d Startflanke *f*
f flanc *m* de démarrage
r фронт *m* запуска

* **start head character** → 8850

8844 start[ing] address; leading address
d Startadresse *f*; Leitadresse *f*
f adresse *f* initiale; adresse de commencement
r начальный адрес *m*

8845 starting chain
d Anlasskette *f*
f chaîne *f* de démarrage
r запускающая цепь *f*

8846 start key
d Starttaste *f*
f touche *f* de marche
r пусковая клавиша *f*

8847 start level
d Anlaufebene *f*
f niveau *m* de démarrage
r пусковой уровень *m*

8848 start-of-block signal
d Blockbeginnsignal *n*; Blockanfangssignal *n*
f signal *m* de début de bloc
r сигнал *m* начала блока

8849 start of frame; frame start
 d Rahmenbeginn *m*
 f démarrage *m* de trame; démarrage de cadre
 r старт *m* фрейма; старт кадра

8850 start-of-heading character; start head character
 d Kopfanfangszeichen *n*; Startkopfzeichen *n*
 f caractère *m* de début d'en-tête
 r символ *m* начала заголовка

8851 start of message; message start
 d Nachrichtenbeginn *m*
 f début *m* de message
 r начало *n* сообщения

8852 start[-of-message] character
 d Nachrichtenbeginnzeichen *n*; Beginnzeichen *n*
 f caractère *m* de début de message
 r символ *m* начала сообщения

8853 start of text
 d Textanfang *m*; Textbeginn *m*
 f début *m* de texte
 r начало *n* текста; старт *m* текста

8854 start-of-text character
 d Starttextzeichen *n*; Textanfangszeichen *n*; Textbeginnzeichen *n*
 f caractère *m* de début de texte
 r знак *m* начала текста

8855 star topology
 d Sterntopologie *f*
 f topologie *f* en étoile
 r звездообразная топология *f*

 * **start-stop blockout → 1069**

8856 start-stop mode
 d Start-Stopp-Betrieb *m*
 f mode *m* marche-arrêt
 r стартстопный режим *m*

8857 start-stop terminal
 d Start-Stopp-Endstelle *f*
 f terminal *m* start-stop; terminal arythmique
 r стартстопный терминал *m*

8858 start-stop transmission
 d Start-Stopp-Übertragung *f*
 f transmission *f* start-stop; transmission marche-arrêt
 r стартстопная передача *f*

8859 start time
 d Startzeit *f*
 f temps *m* de démarrage
 r время *n* старта

 * **startup → 8840**

8860 star[-wired] network; star-shaped network; radial network
 d Sternnetz *n*; Netz *n* mit Sternstruktur
 f réseau *m* en étoile; réseau radial
 r звездообразная сеть *f*; радиальная сеть

8861 state; status
 d Zustand *m*; Status *m*
 f état *m*; statut *m*
 r состояние *n*

8862 state diagram
 d Zustandsdiagramm *n*
 f diagramme *m* d'états
 r диаграмма *f* состояний

 * **statement → 570**

8863 statement; operator
  (as an instruction)
 d Statement *n*; Anweisung *f*
 f instruction *f*; opérateur *m*
 r инструкция *f*; оператор *m*

8864 state processing
 d Zustandsverarbeitung *f*
 f traitement *m* d'états
 r обработка *f* состояний

8865 state transition diagram
 d Diagramm *n* der Zustandsübergange
 f diagramme *m* de transitions d'états; diagramme de passages
 r диаграмма *f* переходов между состояниями

8866 static; stationary; steady-state
 d statisch; stationär; stehend; ortsfest
 f statique; stationnaire; établi; permanent
 r статический; постоянный; стационарный; стоячий; установленный

8867 static binding
 d statische Bindung *f*
 f lien *m* statique
 r статическая связка *f*

 * **static error → 8874**

8868 static image; static picture; static pattern; still[-frame] image; still picture; fixed image; freeze-frame image; freezing frame
 d Standbild *n*; Stehbild *n*; statisches Bild *n*; stehendes Bild
 f image *f* statique; image fixe
 r статичное изображение *n*; фиксированное изображение; неподвижное изображение

8869 static information
   d statische Information *f*
   f information *f* fixe; information statique
   r постоянная информация *f*; установленная
      информация

    * **staticizer** → **8438**

8870 static memory; static RAM; SRAM
   d statischer Speicher *m*
   f mémoire *f* statique
   r статическая [оперативная] память *f*

    * **static pattern** → **8868**

**8871 static-pattern compression; still-image
     compression**
   d Kompression *f* der statischen Bilder
   f compression *f* d'images statiques
   r сжатие *n* статичных изображений

    * **static picture** → **8868**

**8872 static-picture transmission; still-image
     transmission**
   d Standbildübertragung *f*; Stehbildübertragung *f*
   f transmission *f* d'images statiques;
      transmission d'images fixes
   r передача *f* статичных изображений

    * **static RAM** → **8870**

8873 static routing
   d statisches Routing *n*
   f routage *m* statique
   r статическая маршрутизация *f*

    * **stationary** → **8866**

**8874 stationary error; steady-state error; static
     error**
   d stationärer Fehler *m*; statischer Fehler
   f erreur *f* stationnaire; erreur statique
   r статическая ошибка *f*

8875 statistical analysis
   d statistische Analyse *f*
   f analyse *f* statistique
   r статистический анализ *m*

8876 statistical databank
   d statistische Datenbank *f*
   f banque *f* de données statistiques
   r банк *m* статистических данных

8877 statistical decision theory
   d statistische Entscheidungstheorie *f*
   f théorie *f* de la décision statistique
   r статистическая теория *f* разрешения

8878 statistical pattern
   d statistische Bilder *npl*
   f images *fpl* statistiques
   r статистические изображения *npl*

8879 statistics
   d Statistik *f*
   f statistique *f*
   r статистика *f*

    * **status** → **8861**

8880 status bar
   d Statusleiste *f*
   f barre *f* d'état
   r лента *f* состояния; строка *f* статуса; строка
      состояния

8881 status block
   d Zustandsblock *m*
   f bloc *m* d'état
   r блок *m* состояния

8882 status buffer
   d Zustandspuffer *m*
   f tampon *m* d'état
   r буфер *m* состояния

8883 status character
   d Zustandszeichen *n*
   f caractère *m* d'état
   r знак *m* состояния

**8884 status code; condition code; status
     identifier**
   d Zustandskennzeichen *n*; Zustandscode *m*
   f code *m* d'état; identificateur *m* d'état;
      indicateur *m* d'état
   r код *m* состояния; идентификатор *m*
      состояния

8885 status flag
   d Zustandsflag *n*; Statusflag *n*
   f drapeau *m* d'état; signe *m* d'état
   r флаг *m* состояния

    * **status identifier** → **8884**

8886 status information
   d Zustandsinformation *f*; Statusinformation *f*
   f information *f* d'état
   r информация *f* о состоянии

8887 status line
   d Statuslinie *f*
   f ligne *f* d'état
   r линия *f* состояния

8888 status poll
   d Statusabfrage *f*

f interrogation *f* d'état
r опрос *m* состояния

8889 status register
  d Zustandsregister *n*; Statusregister *n*
  f registre *m* d'état
  r регистр *m* состояния

8890 status table
  d Zustandstabelle *f*
  f table *f* d'états
  r таблица *f* состояний

8891 status triggering
  d Zustandstriggerung *f*; zustandsgesteuerte
    Triggerung *f*
  f déclenchement *m* par état
  r запуск *m* по состоянию

8892 status vector
  d Zustandsvektor *m*
  f vecteur *m* d'état
  r вектор *m* состояния

  *   **steady-state** → 8866, 8893

  *   **steady-state error** → 8874

8893 steady-state [mode]; steady-state regime
  d Beharrungszustand *m*; stationärer Zustand *m*
  f mode *m* permanent; régime *m* stationnaire
  r установившееся состояние *n*;
    стационарный режим *m*

  *   **steady-state regime** → 8893

8894 steered latch
  d steuerbares Latch *n*
  f verrou *m* conduit
  r управляемая защёлка *f*

  *   **steering circuit** → 2264

8895 steganography
  (a method of cryptography - hiding a secret
  message within a large one)
  d Steganografie *f*
  f stéganographie *f*
  r стеганография *f*

8896 stem indexing; stemming
  d Stammindizierung *f*
  f indexation *f* par radicaux; indexation par
    racines
  r корневая индексация *f*

  *   **stemming** → 8896, 8897

8897 stem search; stemming
  d Stammsuche *f*

f recherche *f* de radical
r поиск *m* корня; корневой поиск

  *   **stencil** → 9245

8898 stencil
  (special information for each pixel, whether
  and how it is drawn and redrawn)
  d Matrize *f*; Stencil *n*
  f stencil *m*
  r узор *m*

8899 stencil buffer
  d Stencil-Puffer *m*
  f tampon *m* de stencil
  r буфер *m* шаблонов

8900 step
  d Schritt *m*
  f pas *m*
  r шаг *m*

8901 step-by-step; stepped; stepwise
  d schrittweise; stufenweise
  f pas à pas
  r пошаговый

  *   **step-by-step carry** → 1466

8902 step-by-step control; stepping control
  d Einzelschrittsteuerung *f*
  f contrôle *m* pas à pas
  r пошаговое управление *n*

  *   **step-by-step operation** → 6431

8903 step-by-step selection
  d schrittweise Wegesuche *f*
  f sélection *f* pas à pas
  r пошаговый выбор *m*

8904 step counter
  d Schrittzähler *m*
  f compteur *m* à pas
  r пошаговый счётчик *m*; счётчик шагов

8905 step-down
  d Abwärtsübersetzung *f*
  f démultiplication *f*
  r понижение *n*; преобразование *n* с
    понижением

8906 step of iteration
  d Iterationsschritt *m*
  f pas *m* d'itération
  r шаг *m* итерации

  *   **stepped** → 8901

  *   **stepping control** → 8902

* stepwise → 8901

8907 **stereographic**
d stereografisch
f stéréographique
r стереографический

8908 **stereographic image**
d stereografisches Bild *n*
f image *f* stéréographique
r стереографическое изображение *n*

8909 **stereoscopic**
d stereoskopisch
f stéréoscopique
r стереоскопический

8910 **stereoscopic casque**
d stereoskopischer Helm *m*
f casque *f* stéréoscopique
r стереоскопическая каска *f*

8911 **stereoscopic plotter**
d stereoskopischer Plotter *m*
f traceur *m* stéréoscopique
r стереоскопический графопостроитель *m*

8912 **stereoscopic vision**
d stereoskopische Vision *f*; stereoskopisches Sehen *n*
f vision *f* stéréoscopique
r стереоскопическое зрение *n*

8913 **stereoscopy**
d Stereoskopie *f*
f stéréoscopie *f*
r стереоскопия *f*

8914 **stereo sound card**
d Stereoschallkarte *f*
f carte *f* son[ore] stéréo
r стереозвуковая карта *f*

8915 **stereo speaker**
d Stereosprecher *m*
f speaker *m* stéréo
r стереогромкоговоритель *m*; стереорепродуктор *m*

8916 **stereoview**
d Stereosicht *f*
f stéréovue *f*
r стереопредставление *n*; стереовид *m*

* **still-frame image** → 8868

* **still image** → 8868

* **still-image compression** → 8871

* **still-image transmission** → 8872

* **still picture** → 8868

* **stochastic** → 7591

8917 **stochastic algorithm**
d stochastischer Algorithmus *m*
f algorithme *m* stochastique
r вероятностный алгоритм *m*; стохастический алгоритм

8918 **stochastic modeling**
d stochastisches Modellierung *f*
f modelage *m* stochastique
r стохастическое моделирование *n*

8919 **stochastic optimization; stochastic programming**
d stochastische Optimierung *f*; stochastische Programmierung *f*
f optimisation *f* stochastique; programmation *f* stochastique
r стохастическое программирование *n*

8920 **stochastic process**
d stochastischer Prozess *m*
f processus *m* stochastique
r стохастический процесс *m*

* **stochastic programming** → 8919

* **stop** → 4376

8921 **stop bit**
d Stoppbit *n*
f bit *m* d'arrêt; bit de stop
r стоповый бит *m*

* **storage** → 5719

8922 **storage; storing; store; holding; memorization**
d Speichern *n*; Speicherung *f*
f stockage *m*; mémorisation *f*; emmagasinage *m*; maintien *m*
r хранение *n*; запоминание *n*

8923 **storage bit**
d Speicherbit *n*
f bit *m* de la mémoire
r бит *m* памяти

* **storage capacity** → 5735

8924 **storage decoder**
d Decoder *m* mit Speicherung
f décodeur *m* à mémoire
r декодер *m* с памятью; запоминающий декодер; дешифратор *m* с памятью; запоминающий дешифратор

8925 storage display
d Bildschirmgerät *n* mit Speicherung
f écran *m* à mémoire
r дисплей *m* с блоком памяти

8926 stor[ag]e duration
d Speicherdauer *f*
f durée *f* de mise en mémoire; durée de mémorisation
r длительность *f* хранения

* **storage protection** → 5732

8927 storage register
d Speicherregister *n*
f registre *m* de mémoire
r запоминающий регистр *m*

* **storage size** → 5735

* **storage space** → 5737

* **store** → 5719, 8922

8928 store *v*; memorize *v*
d [ein]speichern; merken
f mémoriser; stocker; emmagasiner
r запоминать; хранить; сохранять

8929 store address
d Speicheradresse *f*
f adresse *f* de stockage
r адрес *m* хранения

8930 store and forward transfer
d Ausspeichertransfer *m*
f transfert *m* avec stockage intermédiaire
r передача *f* данных с промежуточным хранением

* **store bank** → 5722

* **store capacity** → 5735

8931 stored carry
d speicherbarer Übertrag *m*
f report *m* stocké; report mémorisé
r запоминаемый перенос *m*

* **stored error** → 96

8932 stored message
d gespeicherte Nachricht *f*; gespeicherte Mitteilung *f*
f message *m* en mémoire
r архивированное сообщение *n*

8933 stored message listing; stored message summary
d gespeicherter Nachrichtenausdruck *m*

f listage *m* des messages en mémoire; résumé *m* des messages en mémoire
r листинг *m* архивированных сообщений; резюме *n* архивированных сообщений

* **stored message summary** → 8933

* **store duration** → 8926

* **store protection** → 5732

* **store size** → 5735

* **store space** → 5737

* **store *v* through** → 10071

* **storing** → 8922

* **stow *v*** → 4610

* **strap** → 5187, 8934

8934 strap[ping]
d Drahtbügelkopplung *f*; Koppelleitung *f*
f jumelage *m*
r спарение *n*; сдвоение *n*

8935 strategy
d Strategie *f*
f stratégie *f*
r стратегия *f*

8936 stray
d Irrfahrt *f*
f errance *f*
r блуждание *n*; возмущение *n*; паразитная ёмкость *f*

* **stream** → 3919

* **streamer** → 8938

* **streaming** → 5959

8937 streaming tape
d Streamer-Band *n*
f bande *f* mobile
r бегущая лента *f*

8938 streaming tape drive; streamer; cartridge tape driver; tape cartridge unit
d Streamer-Magnetbandlaufwerk *n*; Streamer-Laufwerk *n*; [Cartridge-]Streamer *m*; Kassetten-Streaminggerät *n*; Kassetenlaufwerk *n*; Bandkassetteneinheit *f*
f dérouleur *m* de bande mobile; dispositif *m* de stockage dévideur; dévideur *m*;

[cartouche-]streamer *m*; dérouleur *m* [en
continu] à cassette; dérouleur de bande
[magnétique] à cartouche
r накопитель *m* на бегущей ленте;
кассетный накопитель на магнитной
ленте; стример *m*; кассеточное лентовое
запоминающее устройство *n*

*   **stream mode** → 1271

8939 stream of information; information stream
d Informationsstrom *m*
f flux *m* d'information
r поток *m* информации; информационный
поток

8940 strict implication
d strikte Implikation *f*
f implication *f* stricte
r строгая импликация *f*

*   **strike *v* out** → 8941

8941 strike *v* through; strike *v* out; expunge *v*
d durchstreichen
f barrer; rayer
r зачёркивать; удалять

8942 strikethrough text
d durchgestrichener Text *m*
f texte *m* barré
r зачёркнутый текст *m*

*   **string** → 1631

8943 string conversion
d Stringkonvertierung *f*; Kettekonvertierung *f*
f conversion *f* de chaîne
r преобразование *n* строки

8944 string data
d Stringdaten *pl*
f données *fpl* de [type de] chaîne
r строковые данные *pl*

8945 string quotes
d Kettenanführungszeichen *npl*
f guillemets *mpl* de chaîne
r ведущие кавычки *fpl* строки

8946 string value
d Wert *m* der Kette
f valeur *f* de chaîne
r значение *n* строки; строковое значение

8947 strip *v*
d abstreifen; abisolieren
f retirer; dénuder
r зачищать; снимать изоляцию

*   **strip code** → 819

*   **stripe scanning** → 4559

*   **strip printed cable** → 3889

*   **strobe** → 8948

**8948 strobe [pulse]; sample pulse; selective
pulse; gate [pulse]**
d Strobe[impuls] *m*; Abtastimpuls *m*;
Tastimpuls *m*; Auswahlimpuls *m*;
Torimpuls *m*; Auftastimpuls *m*
f impulsion *f* d'encastrement; impulsion
d'échantillonnage; impulsion de porte;
impulsion de sélection
r стробирующий импульс *m*;
строб-импульс *m*; импульс выборки;
импульс совпадения

8949 strobe signal
d Übernahmesignal *n*
f signal *m* stroboscopique; strobe *m*
r стробоскопический сигнал *m*; строб *m*

*   **stroke** → 2352

8950 stroke; bar; dash
d Gedankenstrich *m*; Strich *m*; Stab *m*
f trait *m*; raie *f*; hachure *f*
r черта *f*; штрих *m*; тире *n*

8951 stroke device
d Liniengeber *m*
f lecteur *m* de courbes
r устройство *n* ввода последовательности
позиций

8952 stroked writing
d Strichschreiben *n*
f écriture *f* hachurée
r штриховая запись *f*

*   **stroke-function** → 6220

8953 stroke generator
d Strich[zeichen]generator *m*
f générateur *m* de traits
r генератор *m* штрихов

*   **stroke marking** → 2496

8954 strong conjunction
d starke Konjunktion *f*
f conjonction *f* forte
r сильная конъюнкция *f*

8955 strong disjunction
d starke Disjunktion *f*

f disjonction *f* forte
r сильная дизъюнкция *f*

8956 strong lockout
  d Vollsperre *f*
  f verrouillage *m* fort
  r полная блокировка *f*

8957 strongly connected; strongly coupled; tightly coupled
  d fest zusammenhängend; stark zusammenhängend; fest gekoppelt
  f fortement connecté; à couplage fort
  r сильно связанный; наглухо связанный

  * **strongly coupled → 8957**

8958 structural parameter
  d Strukturparameter *m*
  f paramètre *m* de structure
  r параметр *m* структуры

8959 structure
  d Struktur *f*
  f structure *f*
  r структура *f*

8960 structured data
  d strukturierte Daten *pl*
  f données *fpl* structurées
  r структурированные данные *pl*

8961 structured program
  d strukturiertes Programm *n*
  f programme *m* structuré
  r структурированная программа *f*

8962 structured programming
  d strukturierte Programmierung *f*
  f programmation *f* structurée
  r структурное программирование *n*

8963 structured query
  d strukturierte Abfrage *f*
  f interrogation *f* structurée
  r структурированный запрос *m*

8964 structured query language; SQL
  d Sprache *f* der strukturierten Abfragen
  f langage *m* de requête structurée
  r язык *m* структурированных запросов

  * **stuck-at → 3864**

  * **stuck-at fault → 6913**

8965 stuck-at one
  d haftende Eins *f*
  f unité *f* constante; un *m* constant
  r константная единица *f*

8966 stuck-at-one fault
  d Haftfehler *m* an Logikpegel "1"
  f défaut *m* de type un constant
  r неисправность *f* типа "константная единица"

8967 stuck-at-X fault
  d Haftfehler *m* an Logikpegel "X"
  f défaut *m* de type incertitude constante
  r неисправность *f* типа константного неопределённого состояния

8968 stuck-at-zero
  d haftende Null *f*
  f zéro *m* constant
  r константный нуль *m*

8969 stuck-at-zero fault
  d Haftfehler *m* an Logikpegel "0"
  f défaut *m* de type zéro constant
  r неисправность *f* типа "константный нуль"

8970 stuck-open fault
  d Stuck-Open-Fehler *m*; Haftfehler *m* "Leiterunterbrechung"
  f défaut *m* de type coupure constante
  r неисправность *f* типа константного обрыва

  * **stuff** *v* **→ 3823**

  * **stuff → 8971**

8971 stuff[ing]
  d Auffüllen *n*; Stopfen *n*
  f intercalation *f*; interlude *m*; bourrage *m*
  r заполнение *n*; вставка *f*; вставление *n*; стаффинг *m*

8972 stuffing bit channel
  d Stopfbitkanal *m*
  f canal *m* de bits d'intercalation
  r канал *m* битов заполнения

8973 stuffing procedure
  d Stopfverfahren *n*
  f procédure *f* d'intercalation
  r процедура *f* заполнения

8974 style
  d Stil *m*
  f style *m*
  r стиль *m*

8975 style deleting
  d Stillöschung *f*
  f effacement *m* de style
  r устранение *n* стиля

8976 style gallery
  d Stilgalerie *f*

f galerie *f* de styles
r галерея *f* стилей

8977 style library
d Stilbibliothek *f*
f bibliothèque *f* de styles
r библиотека *f* стилей

8978 style list
d Stilliste *f*
f liste *f* de styles
r список *m* стилей

8979 style manager
d Stilmanager *m*
f gestionnaire *m* de styles
r стилевой менажер *m*

8980 style name
d Stilname *m*
f nom *m* de style
r имя *n* стиля

8981 style properties
d Stileigenschaften *fpl*
f propriétés *fpl* de style
r характеристики *fpl* стиля; свойства стиля

* **style selection** → 1666

8982 styles page
d Stilseite *f*
f page *f* de styles
r страница *f* стилей

8983 style template
d Stilschablone *f*
f modèle *m* de style
r шаблон *m* стиля; стилевой макет *m*

* **stylus** → 6881

* **stylus printer** → 6053

8984 subaccess
d Subzugriff *m*
f sous-accès *m*
r подвыборка *f*; выборка *f* из выборки

8985 sub-address
d Subadresse *f*
f sous-adresse *f*
r подадрес *m*

8986 sub-addressing
d Subadressierung *f*
f sous-adressage *m*
r частичное адресование *n*

* **subarea** → 8994

8987 subarray
d Unterfeld *n*
f sous-tableau *m*
r подмассив *m*; часть *f* массива

8988 subassembly
d Untereinheit *f*
f sous-ensemble *m*
r компоновочный узел *m*

8989 subblock; blockette
d Teilblock *m*
f sous-bloc *m*
r подблок *m*

* **subchain** → 9024

8990 subchannel; tributary channel
d Subkanal *m*; Unterkanal *m*; abgeleiteter Kanal *m*
f sous-canal *m*
r подканал *m*; дополнительный канал *m*

8991 subcircuit
d Teilschaltung *f*; Nebenstromkreis *m*
f sous-circuit *m*
r подсхема *f*; часть *f* схемы

8992 subdirectory
d Unterkatalog *m*; Teilverzeichnis *n*
f sous-catalogue *m*; sous-répertoire *m*; sous-dossier *m*
r подкаталог *m*; подсправочник *m*

8993 subdivision
d Unterteilung *f*
f subdivision *f*
r подразделение *n*; подразбиение *n*

8994 subdomain; subregion; subarea
d Unterbereich *m*; Teilbereich *m*; Teilgebiet *n*
f sous-domaine *m*
r подобласть *f*

8995 subfield
d Unterkörper *m*; Teilkörper *m*
f sous-corps *m*
r подполе *n*; подтело *n*

8996 subframe
d Unteraufnahme *f*; Subframe *n*
f sous-trame *f*; sous-cadre *m*
r подкадр *m*

8997 subgroup
d Untergruppe *f*; Baugruppe *f*
f sous-groupe *m*
r подгруппа *f*

* **subheading** → 9026

8998 subimage
d Teilbild *n*
f sous-image *f*
r часть *f* изображения

8999 subinterval
d Teilintervall *n*
f sous-intervalle *m*
r подинтервал *m*

9000 sublanguage
d Untersprache *f*
f sous-langage *m*
r подмножество *n* языка

9001 sublist
d Unterliste *f*
f sous-liste *f*
r подсписок *m*

9002 submenu
d Untermenü *n*
f sous-menu *m*
r подменю *n*

* **subnet → 9003**

9003 subnet[work]
d Teilnetz *n*; Subnetz *n*
f sous-réseau *m*
r подсеть *f*

* **subnotebook → 9004**

9004 subnotebook [computer]; ultraportable notebook; lightweight notebook; lightweight portable
d Leichtnotebook *m*
f pico-ordinateur *m*; ordinateur *m* ultraportatif; ultraportable *m*; portable *m* ultraléger
r субблокнотный компьютер *m*

9005 subprogram; subroutine
d Unterprogramm *n*
f sous-programme *m*; sous-routine *f*
r подпрограмма *f*

* **subrack → 1643**

* **subregion → 8994**

* **subroutine → 9005**

9006 subroutine jump
d Unterprogrammsprung *f*
f saut *m* à sous-programme
r переход *m* к подпрограмме

9007 subscriber; abonent; participant; sharer
d Teilnehmer *m*; Abonnent *n*;

Anschlussinhaber *m*
f abonné *m*; participant *m*
r абонент *m*; участник *m*; подписчик *m*

* **subscriber's meter → 1367**

9008 subscript *v*
d tiefstellen
f indicer
r индицировать

9009 subscript; lower index
d unterer Index *m*; tiefgestellter Index
f indice *m* inférieur; indice en bas
r нижний индекс *m*; подстрочный индекс

9010 subscript brackets
d Indexklammern *fpl*
f accolades *fpl* indiquées; crochets *mpl* indiqués
r индексные скобки *fpl*

9011 subscripted variable
d Variable *f* mit unterem Index; indizierte Variable
f variable *f* à indice inférieur; variable indexée; variable indicée
r переменная *f* с нижним индексом; индексированная переменная

9012 subscript expression
d Indexausdruck *m*
f expression *f* indiquée; expression indexée
r выражение *n* с индексами; индексное выражение

9013 subscripting
d Tiefstellen *n*
f indexation *f*
r индицирование *n*

9014 subscription
d Abonnement *n*
f abonnement *m*
r абонемент *m*

9015 subsection
d Teilabschnitt *m*
f sous-section *f*
r подраздел *m*

9016 subsequence
d Teilfolge *f*
f sous-suite *f*
r подпоследовательность *f*

9017 subsequence counter
d Zähler *m* der Mikrotakte

f compteur *m* de sous-séquence; compteur de
microtemps
r счётчик *m* микрокоманд

9018 subsequent; consequent
d folgend; nachfolgend; konsequent
f subséquent; conséquent; postérieur; ultérieur
r следующий; последующий

9019 subset
d Untermenge *f*; Teilmenge *f*
f sous-ensemble *m*; sous-multitude *f*
r подмножество *n*

9020 substitution
d Substitution *f*; Ersetzung *f*
f substitution *f*
r подстановка *f*; субституция *f*; замена *f*

9021 substitution list
d Substitutionsliste *f*
f liste *f* de substitutions
r список *m* подстановок

9022 substitution list address
d Substitutionslistenadresse *f*
f adresse *f* de liste de substitutions
r адрес *m* списка подстановок

9023 substrate
d Substrat *n*; Trägerschicht *f*; Unterlage *f*
f substrat *m*; galette *f*
r подставка *f*; основание *n*

9024 substring; subchain
d Teil[zeichen]kette *f*; Teilstring *n*
f sous-chaîne *f*; sous-ligne *f*
r подцепочка *f*; подстрока *f*

* **substructure → 5841**

9025 subsystem
d Teilsystem *n*; Untersystem *n*; Subsystem *n*
f sous-système *m*
r подсистема *f*

9026 subtitle; subheading
d Zwischenüberschrift *f*; Untertitel *m*
f sous-titre *m*
r подзаголовок *m*

9027 subtotal; partial sum; partial total
d Zwischensumme *f*; Partialsumme *f*;
Teilsumme *f*
f sous-total *m*; somme *f* partielle
r промежуточная сумма *f*; частичная сумма

* **subtracter → 9029**

9028 subtracting; subtraction

d Subtraktion *f*; Subtrahieren *n*
f soustraction *f*
r вычитание *n*

* **subtraction → 9028**

* **subtraction sign → 8566**

9029 subtraction unit; subtracter; subtractor
d Subtrahierwerk *n*; Subtrahierer *m*;
Subtraktor *m*
f soustracteur *m*
r субтрактор *m*; вычитатель *m*

9030 subtractive
d subtraktiv
f soustractif
r вычитаемый

* **subtractor → 9029**

9031 subtype
d Untertyp *m*
f sous-type *m*
r подтип *m*

9032 subwindow; pane
d Unterfenster *n*; Fensterausschnitt *m*
f sous-fenêtre *f*
r подокно *n*

9033 subword
d Unterwort *n*
f sous-mot *m*
r подслово *n*

9034 succession
d Nachfolge *f*
f succession *f*
r последовательность *f*; приемственность *f*;
наследование *n*

9035 successive carry; serial carry
d sukzessiver Übertrag *m*; fortlaufender
Übertrag; Seriellübertrag *m*
f report *m* successif; report séquentiel; report
sériel
r последовательный перенос *m*

9036 suffix
d Suffix *n*
f suffixe *m*
r суффикс *m*

9037 suffixing
d Suffigierung *f*
f suffixation *f*
r суффиксация *f*

9038 sum
d Summe *f*

f somme *f*
r сумма *f*

9039 sum by columns; column sum
    d Spaltensumme *f*
    f somme *f* par colonnes
    r сумма *f* по столбцам

9040 sum by row; row sum
    d Zeilensumme *f*
    f somme *f* par lignes
    r сумма *f* по строкам

    * **sum check** → 9041

    * **sum index** → 3213

    * **summand** → 169

    * **summary** → 29

    * **summation** → 178

9041 sum[mation] check; sum test
    d Summenkontrolle *f*; Summenprüfung *f*
    f contrôle *m* par somme; contrôle par
       sommation; test *m* de somme
    r контроль *m* по сумме; контроль по
       суммированию

    * **summation sign** → 9042

9042 summation symbol; summation sign;
    sigma notation
    d Summenzeichen *n*
    f signe *m* de sommation
    r знак *m* суммирования; знак суммы

    * **summator** → 171

9043 sum modulo 2
    d Summe *f* modulo 2
    f somme *f* modulo 2
    r сумма *f* по модулю 2

    * **sum-out gate** → 9044

    * **sum output** → 188

9044 sum-[read]out gate
    d Summenausgabegatter *n*
    f porte *f* de lecture de somme; porte de total
    r вентиль *m* выдачи суммы

    * **sum test** → 9041

    * **sum total** → 9450

    * **superabundance** → 7782

9045 supercomputer
    d Superrechner *m*; Supercomputer *m*
    f superordinateur *m*
    r суперкомпьютер *m*

9046 supercomputing; high-performance
    computing
    d Hochleistungsrechnung *f*
    f calcul *m* intensif
    r организация *f* вычислений на
       суперкомпьютерах

    * **super index** → 9052

9047 superlanguage
    d superhöhere Sprache *f*; ultrahöhere Sprache
    f superlangage *m*; langage *m* de très haut
       niveau
    r язык *m* сверхвысокого уровня

9048 supernet
    d Supernetz *n*
    f superréseau *m*
    r суперсеть *f*

9049 superpipelining
    d Superpipelineverarbeitung *f*
    f superpipelinage *m*
    r суперконвейеризация *f*.

9050 superposed code
    d Überlagerungscode *m*
    f code *m* superposé
    r суперпозиционный код *m*

9051 superposition
    d Superposition *f*
    f superposition *f*
    r суперпозиция *f*

9052 superscript; super index
    d Index *m* rechts oben; oberer Index;
       hochgestellter Index
    f index *m* supérieur
    r верхний индекс *m*

9053 superstructure
    d Superstruktur *f*
    f superstructure *f*
    r сверхструктура *f*

9054 supervise *v*
    d überwachen
    f superviser
    r администрировать

    * **supervision** → 5880

    * **supervisor** → 3578, 6082

9055 supervisory circuit
   d Überwachungsschaltung *f*
   f circuit *m* de supervision
   r схема *f* текущего контроля

   * **supervisory control** → 7895

9056 supplement
   d Supplement *n*; Zusatz *m*
   f supplément *m*
   r добавление *n*

9057 supplier; provider; vendor; spoke
   d Versorger *m*; Ernährer *m*; Anbieter *m*;
      Provider *m*
   f fournisseur *m*
   r поставщик *m*

9058 supply; power
   d Versorgung *f*
   f alimentation *f*
   r питание *n*

   * **supply length** → 2739

9059 support *v*
   d unterstützen
   f supporter; soutenir; appuyer
   r поддерживать; обеспечивать

   * **support** → 1443

9060 support; holder
   d Stütze *f*; Halter *m*
   f appui *m*; support *m*
   r опора *m*; поддержка *f*; держатель *m*

9061 support equipment
   d Hilfsausrüstung *f*; Hilfsanlagen *fpl*
   f équipement *m* auxiliaire; équipement support
   r вспомагательное оборудование *n*

9062 suppose *v*; **assume** *v*
   d annehmen; voraussetzen; vermuten
   f supposer; admettre
   r допускать; предполагать

9063 suppression
   d Unterdrückung *f*
   f suppression *f*
   r подавление *n*

9064 suppression of data
   d Datenunterdrückung *f*
   f blocage *m* des données
   r блокировка *f* данных

9065 surf *v*; **cruise** *v*; **wander** *v*
   (in Internet)
   d [umher]wandern; herumfahren

   f surfer
   r бродить; путешествовать; странствовать

   * **surface in relief** → 3363

9066 surface mounting technology; SMT
   d Oberflächenmontagetechnik *f*
   f technologie *f* de montage en surface
   r технология *f* поверхностного монтажа

9067 surface texture
   d Flächentextur *f*; Oberflächentextur *f*
   f texture *f* de surface
   r текстура *f* поверхности

   * **surfer** → 2461

   * **surfing** → 9980

   * **surround** → 9069

9068 surround *v*
   d umgeben
   f entourer
   r окружать

9069 surround[ing]
   d Umgebung *f*
   f entourage *m*
   r окружение *n*

   * **survey** → 5880

   * **surveying** → 5880

9070 susceptibility
   d Suszeptibilität *f*
   f susceptibilité *f*
   r восприимчивость *f*; чувствительность *f*

   * **suspending** → 4391

   * **suspend state** → 9953

   * **suspension** → 4391

   * **SWAN** → 8300

   * **swap** → 9077

9071 swap area
   d Austauschbereich *m*; Swapping-Bereich *m*
   f domaine *m* d'échange; domaine de swapping
   r область *f* взаимного обмена; область
      свопинга

9072 swap file
   d Auslagerungsdatei *f*
   f fichier *m* d'échange
   r файл *m* свопинга; файл подкачки

9073 swap gate
 d Datenaustauschgatter *n*; Datentransfergatter *n*
 f porte *f* d'échange d'information; porte d'échange de données
 r вентиль *m* обмена информации

9074 swap-in
 d Einlagern *n*; Einlagerung *f*; Swap-in *n*
 f chargement *m* [par permutation]; swap-in *m*
 r загрузка *f*; подкачка *f*

9075 swap-out
 d Auslagern *n*; Auslagerung *f*; Swap-out *n*
 f vidage *m* [par permutation]; renvoi *m*; swap-out *m*
 r разгрузка *f*; откачка *f*

9076 swapper
 d Austauscher *m*
 f échangeur *m*
 r обменник *m*

9077 swap[ping]
 d Austausch *m*; Wechsel *m*; Swapping *n*; Prozess-Ein-/Auslagerung *f*
 f échange *m*; permutation *f*; swapping *m*
 r перекачка *f*; [взаимный] обмен *m*; своппинг *m*

9078 swatch
 (a square containing color in color palette)
 d Musterstreifen *m*; Probenstreifen *m*
 f coupon *m*; échantillon *m*; swatch *m*
 r образчик *m*

9079 sweep generator
 d Kippgenerator *m*; Ablenkgenerator *m*
 f générateur *m* de balayage
 r генератор *m* развёртки

* **sweep rate** → 9080

9080 sweep speed; sweep rate
 d Ablenkgeschwindigkeit *f*
 f vitesse *f* de balayage
 r скорость *f* развёртки

9081 switch; key; commutator
 d Schalter *m*; Kommutator *m*
 f commutateur *m*; aiguilleur *m*
 r ключ *m*; переключатель *m*; коммутатор *m*

9082 switch board; switch panel
 d Schalttafel *f*
 f panneau *m* à commutateurs
 r коммутаторная панель *f*; распределительный щит *m*

9083 switch-computer application interface; SCAI
 d Kommutator-Computer-Benutzungsschnittstelle *f*
 f interface *f* commutateur-ordinateur
 r прикладной интерфейс *m* коммутатор-компьютер

9084 switched access
 (a network connection that can be created and eliminated as necessary)
 d [um]geschalteter Zugriff *m*
 f accès *m* commuté
 r коммутируемый доступ *m*

* **switched line** → 2844

9085 switched network; switching network; dialed network; dialup network
 d Wähl[vermittlungs]netz *n*; Koppelnetz *n*; Koppeleinrichtung *f*; Vermittlungsnetz *n*
 f réseau *m* commuté
 r коммутируемая сеть *f*

9086 switching; commutation
 d Schalten *n*; Durchschalten *n*; Durchschaltung *f*; Kommutierung *f*
 f commutation *f*
 r переключение *n*; коммутация *f*

* **switching behaviour** → 9088

9087 switching channel group
 d Durchschaltekanalgruppe *f*
 f groupe *m* de canaux de commutation
 r переключательная группа *f* каналов

9088 switching characteristics; switching behaviour
 d Schaltenverhalten *n*
 f caractéristiques *fpl* de commutation; comportement *m* en commutation
 r характеристики *fpl* переключения; режим *m* коммутации

9089 switching circuit
 d Umschaltnetzwerk *n*; Schaltkreis *m*
 f circuit *m* de commutation
 r переключательная схема *f*

9090 switching delay
 d Schaltverzögerung *f*
 f retard *m* de commutation
 r задержка *f* коммутации

* **switching key** → 9429

* **switching network** → 9085

* **switching-off** → 2979

9091 switching processor
 d Vermittlungsprozessor *m*

f processeur *m* de commutation
r коммутационный процессор *m*

9092 switch[ing] variable
d Schaltvariable *f*
f variable-aiguillage *f*; variable *f* de type
"commutateur"
r переменная *f* типа "переключатель"

9093 switch *v* off; turn *v* off
d abschalten; ausschalten
f couper; déclencher
r выключать

9094 switch *v* on; turn *v* on
d einschalten
f enclencher; brancher
r включать

* **switchover → 1557**

* **switch panel → 9082**

9095 switch register
d Schalterregister *n*
f registre *m* de commutateurs
r тумблерный регистр *m*

* **switch variable → 9092**

* **symbol → 1593**

* **symbol addressing → 325**

* **symbol bar → 1595**

* **symbol font → 1610**

* **symbol generator → 1612**

9096 symbolic
d symbolisch
f symbolique
r символический

* **symbolic addressing → 325**

9097 symbolic description
d symbolische Beschreibung *f*
f description *f* symbolique
r символьное описание *n*

9098 symbolic language
d symbolische Sprache *f*
f langage *m* symbolique
r символический язык *m*

9099 symbolic layout
d symbolische Anordnung *f*
f disposition *f* symbolique

r символическое расположение *n*

* **symbolic logic → 3972**

9100 symbolic notation
d symbolische Bezeichnung *f*
f notation *f* symbolique
r символическое обозначение *n*

9101 symbolic processing
d Symbolverarbeitung *f*
f traitement *m* symbolique
r обработка *f* символьной информации

9102 symbol library
d Symbolbibliothek *f*
f bibliothèque *f* de symboles
r библиотека *f* символов

* **symbol of equivalence → 3470**

* **symbol table → 1618**

9103 symmetrical channel
d symmetrischer Kanal *m*
f canal *m* symétrique
r симметрический канал *m*

9104 symmetrical interface
d symmetrische Schnittstelle *f*
f interface *f* symétrique
r симметрический интерфейс *m*

* **symmetric list → 3133**

9105 symmetric multiprocessing; SMP
d symmetrische Mehrfachverarbeitung *f*
f multitraitement *m* symétrique
r симметрическая мультиобработка *f*

* **sync byte → 9110**

9106 synchronism; lock[ing]-in
d Synchronismus *m*; Synchronität *f*;
Gleichlauf[zwang] *m*
f synchronisme *m*; mise *f* au pas
r синхронизм *m*; синхронность *f*

9107 synchronization; synchronizing
d Synchronisation *f*; Gleichlaufsteuerung *f*
f synchronisation *f*
r синхронизация *f*

9108 synchronize *v*
d synchronisieren
f synchroniser
r синхронизировать

9109 synchronizer
d Synchronisiereinrichtung *f*; Synchronisator *m*

f synchroniseur *m*
r синхронизирующее устройство *n*;
синхронизатор *m*

* **synchronizing** → **9107**

9110 sync[hronizing] byte
d Gleichlaufbyte *n*; Synchronisierbyte *n*
f octet *m* synchroniseur
r синхронизирующий байт *m*

9111 synchronizing interface
d Synchronisierschnittstelle *f*
f interface *f* de synchronisation
r синхронизирующий интерфейс *m*

9112 synchronous; in-step; mesochronous
d synchron; gleichlaufend
f synchrone; au pas
r синхронный

9113 synchronous buffer
d Synchronpuffer *m*
f tampon *m* synchrone
r синхронный буфер *m*

9114 synchronous character
d Synchronzeichen *n*
f caractère *m* synchrone
r синхронный символ *m*

9115 synchronous communications interface
d synchrone Übertragungsschnittstelle *f*
f interface *f* de communication synchrone
r синхронный связной интерфейс *m*

9116 synchronous data network
d Synchrondatennetz *n*
f réseau *m* de données synchrone
r синхронная сеть *f* данных

* **synchronous data transfer** → **9117**

**9117 synchronous data transmission;
synchronous data transfer**
d synchrone Datenübertragung *f*
f transmission *f* synchrone de données
r синхронная передача *f* данных

9118 synchronous digital hierarchy
d synchrone digitale Hierarchie *f*
f hiérarchie *f* synchrone digitale
r синхронная цифровая иерархия *f*

9119 synchronous dynamic RAM; SDRAM
d synchroner dynamischer RAM-Speicher *m*;
synchroner dynamischer
Schreib-/Lesespeicher *m*
f mémoire *f* vive dynamique synchrone;
mémoire RAM dynamique synchrone

r синхронная динамическая [оперативная]
память *f*

9120 synchronous graphics RAM; SGRAM
d synchroner grafischer RAM-Speicher *m*
f mémoire *f* synchrone dédiée à l'affichage
r синхронная память *f* графических данных

9121 synchronous input
d Synchroneingabe *f*
f entrée *f* synchrone
r синхронный ввод *m*

9122 synchronous logic
d synchrone Logik *f*
f logique *f* synchrone
r синхронная логика *f*

9123 synchronous optical network; SONET
d synchrones optisches Netzwerk *n*
f réseau *m* optique synchrone
r синхронная оптическая сеть *f*; синхронная
сеть оптической связи

9124 syntactic graph; syntax graph
d syntaktischer Graph *m*
f graphe *m* syntaxique
r синтаксический граф *m*

9125 syntax
d Syntax *f*
f syntaxe *f*
r синтаксис *m*

* **syntax analysis** → **6817**

* **syntax analyzer** → **6816**

9126 syntax error
d Syntaxfehler *m*
f erreur *f* syntaxique
r синтаксическая ошибка *f*

* **syntax graph** → **9124**

9127 syntax selection
d Syntaxauswahl *f*
f sélection *f* syntaxique
r синтаксический выбор *m*

9128 syntax tree; parse tree
d Syntaxbaum *m*
f arbre *m* syntaxique
r дерево *n* синтаксического анализа; дерево
грамматического разбора

9129 synthesis
d Synthese *f*
f synthèse *f*
r синтез *m*

9130 **synthesizer**
  d Synthetisator *m*
  f synthétiseur *m*
  r синтетизатор *m*

9131 **synthetic actor; actor**
  d Akteur *m*
  f actor *m*; acteur *m*
  r синтетический действующий субъект *m*;
    актор *m*

  * **synthetic image** → 2077

9132 **system**
  d System *n*
  f système *m*
  r система *f*

9133 **system administrator**
  d Systemadministrator *m*; Systemverwalter *m*
  f administrateur *m* système
  r системный администратор *m*

  * **system analyst** → 9153

9134 **systematic error; error constant; fixed
    error; regular error**
  d systematischer Fehler *m*; konstanter Fehler;
    fester Fehler; regelmäßiger Fehler
  f erreur *f* systématique; erreur constante; erreur
    fixe; erreur régulière
  r систематическая ошибка *f*; постоянная
    ошибка; регулярная ошибка

9135 **system breakdown; system failure; system
    error**
  d Systemausfall *m*; Systemfehler *m*;
    Systemstörung *f*
  f défaut *m* de système; défaillance *f* de
    système; erreur *f* système
  r системный отказ *m*; системная ошибка *f*

9136 **system bus**
  d System-Bus *m*
  f bus *m* système
  r системная шина *f*

9137 **system-call interrupt**
  d Systemaufrufunterbrechung *f*;
    Systemaufrufinterrupt *m*
  f interruption *f* système
  r системное прерывание *n*

  * **system clock** → 9138

9138 **system clock [pulse]**
  d Systemtakt *m*
  f rythme *m* [de] système
  r такт *m* системы

9139 **system compatibility**
  d Systemkompatibilität *f*
  f compatibilité *f* [au niveau] de système
  r совместимость *f* на системном уровне;
    совместимость систем

  * **system crash** → 6

9140 **system data**
  d Systemdaten *pl*
  f données *fpl* de système
  r системные данные *pl*

9141 **system directory**
  d Systemkatalog *m*
  f catalogue *m* [de] système
  r системная директория *f*

9142 **system disk**
  d systemresidente Platte *f*
  f disque *m* système
  r системный диск *m*

  * **system error** → 9135

  * **system failure** → 9135

9143 **system file**
  d Systemdatei *f*
  f fichier *m* système
  r системный файл *m*

9144 **system for data transfer; transmission data
    system**
  d System *n* für Datenübertragung;
    Datenübertragungssystem *n*
  f système *m* de transmission des données;
    système de transfert des données
  r система *f* передачи данных

9145 **system generation**
  d Systemgenerierung *f*
  f génération *f* de système
  r генерация *f* системы

9146 **system hotline; hotline**
  d heißer Draht *m*; direkter Telefonservice *m*
  f support *m* technique; assistance *f*
    téléphonique; numéro *m* d'urgence; hotline *f*
  r горячая линия *f*

9147 **system log**
  d Systemnachweis *m*; Systcmprotokoll *n*
  f journal *m* de bord; procès-verbal *m* de
    machine
  r системный журнал *m*

9148 **system menu**
  d Systemmenü *n*

    f menu *m* système
    r системное меню *n*

9149 system network architecture; SNA
    d Systemnetzarchitektur *f*
    f architecture *f* système de réseau
    r системная сетевая архитектура *f*; сетевая
    архитектура систем

9150 system of reference; reference system
    d Bezugssystem *n*; Referenzsystem *n*
    f système *m* de référence
    r система *f* отсчёта

9151 system partition
    d Systempartition *f*
    f partition *f* système
    r системный раздел *m*

9152 system printer
    d Systemdrucker *m*
    f imprimante *f* système
    r системный принтер *m*

9153 system[s] analyst
    d Systemanalytiker *m*; Systemberater *m*
    f analyste *m/f* système
    r системный аналитик *m*

9154 system software; operational software
    d Betrieb-Software *f*; Betriebsprogramme *npl*;
    Systemsoftware *f*; Basissoftware *f*
    f logiciel *m* [de] système; logiciel opérationnel
    r системное программное обеспечение *n*

9155 system tables
    d Systemtabellen *fpl*
    f tables *fpl* de système
    r системные таблицы *fpl*

9156 system variable
    d Systemvariable *f*
    f variable *f* système
    r системная переменная *f*

9157 systolic algorithm
    d systolischer Algorithmus *m*
    f algorithme *m* systolique
    r систолический алгоритм *m*

9158 systolic array
    d systolisches Feld *n*
    f tableau *m* systolique; matrice *f* systolique
    r систолическая матрица *f*

9159 systolic chip
    d Systolic-Chip *m*
    f puce *f* systolique
    r кристалл *m* систолической матрицы

T

* tab → 9173

9160 Tab key; skip key
d Tabulatortaste *f*
f touche *f* Tab
r клавиша *f* Tab

9161 table
d Tabelle *f*; Tafel *f*
f table *f*; tableau *m*
r таблица *f*

9162 table calculation
d Tabellenkalkulation *f*
f calcul *m* tabulaire
r табличное вычисление *n*

9163 table cell
d Tabellenfeld *n*
f case *f* d'un tableau
r клетка *f* таблицы; ячейка *f* таблицы

9164 table column
d Tabellenspalte *f*
f colonne *f* de table
r колонка *f* таблицы

9165 table data
d Tabellendaten *pl*
f données *fpl* de tableau
r табличные данные *pl*

9166 table look-up; table searching
d Tabellensuchen *n*; Tabellenlesen *n*
f recherche *f* dans une table; consultation *f* de
    table
r просмотр *m* таблицы; табличный поиск *m*

9167 table memory
d Tabellenspeicher *m*
f mémoire *f* organisée en tableaux
r память *f* табличного типа

9168 table row
d Tabellenzeile *f*
f ligne *f* de table
r строка *f* таблицы

* table searching → 9166

9169 table synchronization
d Tabellensynchronisation *f*
f synchronisation *f* de table
r синхронизация *f* таблицы

* tablet → 2941

* table-top → 2784

9170 tabular
d tabellarisch; tafelmäßig
f tabulaire
r табличный

9171 tabulate *v*
d tabulieren
f tabuler
r табулировать

* tabulating → 9172

9172 tabulation; tabulating
d Tabulierung *f*; Darstellung *f* in Tabellenform;
    tabellarische Darstellung
f tabulation *f*; mise *f* en table
r табулирование *n*; табуляция *f*; составление
    n таблицы

9173 tabulator; tab
d Tabulator *m*
f tabulateur *m*
r табулятор *m*

* tact → 1755

* tactile display → 9455

* tactile-type sensor → 9456

9174 tag
(of HTML)
d Tag *n*; HTML-Befehl *m*
f balise *f*
r тег *m*

* tag → 2175, 5243

9175 tag
(of the message blocs in the network)
d Anhänger *m*; Schildchen *n*; Trennzeichen *n*;
    Öse *f*
f tag *m*
r ярлык *m*; этикетка *f*; бирка *f*

9176 tag array
d Etikettenfeld *n*
f tableau *m* d'étiquettes
r массив *m* тегов; память *f* тегов

9177 tag bit
d Etikettbit *n*; Anhängerbit *n*
f bit *m* marqueur
r теговый бит *m*

9178 tagged; label[l]ed; marked
d gekennzeichnet; markiert

f libellé; marqué; étiqueté
r помеченный; отмеченный

9179 tagged architecture
d gekennzeichnete Architektur *f*
f architecture *f* par étiquette; architecture marquée
r теговая архитектура *f*

9180 tagged computer
d Computer *m* mit gekennzeichneter Architektur
f ordinateur *m* à architecture par étiquette
r компьютер *m* с теговой организацей

9181 tagged data
d markierte Daten *pl*
f données *fpl* marquées; données libellées
r тегированные данные *pl*; помеченные данные; отмеченные данные

9182 tagged grammar
d gekennzeichnete Grammatik *f*
f grammaire *f* à étiquettes; grammaire libellée
r грамматика *f* с индикаторами

9183 tagged image
d gekennzeichnetes Bild *n*
f image *f* libellée; image marquée
r отмеченное изображение *n*; помеченное изображение

9184 tagged image file format; TIFF
d TIFF-Format *m*
f format *m* TIFF
r формат *m* TIFF

9185 tag memory
d Etikettenspeicher *m*
f mémoire à étiquettes; mémoire à tags
r тегированная память *f*; признаковая память

9186 tag number
d Tag-Nummer *f*
f numéro *m* étiqueté; numéro marqué
r кодовая метка *f*

9187 tag reader
d Etikettenleser *m*
f lecteur *m* d'étiquettes
r считыватель *m* меток

9188 tag sort
d Tag-Sortieren *n*
f triage *m* d'étiquettes
r сортировка *f* признаков

* **talk** → 1645

* **talking circuit** → 8751

9189 tally; count
d Zahleinheit *f*; Gesamtbetrag *m*; Gesamtergebnis *n*
f unité *f* de comptage; total *m*
r единица *f* счёта; итог *m*

* **tandem circuit** → 1467

9190 tandem computer; double computer
d Doppelrechner *m*
f ordinateur *m* double
r двойной компьютер *m*

* **tank** → 6600

* **tank circuit** → 6600

* **tap** → 9209

9191 tap
d Abgreif *m*
f prise *f*
r отвод *m*

9192 tape
d Band *n*; Streifen *m*
f bande *f*; ruban *m*
r лента *f*

* **tape** → 5582

9193 tape-break stop
d Bandriss-Stopp *m*
f arrêt *m* par rupture de bande
r останов *m* при обрыве ленты

* **tape cable** → 3889

9194 tape capacity
d Bandkapazität *f*
f capacité *f* de bande
r ёмкость *f* ленты

* **tape cartridge** → 5583

* **tape cartridge unit** → 8938

* **tape cassette** → 5583

* **tape controller** → 9195

9195 tape control unit; tape controller
d Bandsteuereinheit *f*; Bandkontroller *m*
f unité *f* de commande à bande
r контроллер *m* запоминающего устройства на магнитной ленте

* **tape device** → 5584

9196 tape drive
 d Bandlaufwerk *n*; Bandantrieb *m*;
   Bandvorschubeinrichtung *f*
 f mécanisme *m* d'entraînement de bande;
   transporteur *m* de bande
 r лентопротяжный механизм *m*

9197 tape feed
 d Bandvorschub *m*; Lochstreifentransport *m*
 f avancement *m* de bande; entraînement *m* de
   bande
 r протяжка *f* ленты

 * **tape-feed roll** → 9198

9198 tape-feed roll[er]
 d Bandvorschubrolle *f*; Streifenvorschubrolle *f*
 f rouleau *m* d'entraînement de bande
 r лентопротяжный валик *m*

9199 tape file
 d Banddatei *f*; Magnetbanddatei *f*
 f fichier *m* de bande [magnétique]
 r файл *m* на ленте; ленточный файл

9200 tape format
 d Bandformat *n*
 f format *m* de bande
 r формат *m* ленты

 * **tape label** → 9203

9201 tape library
 d Bandbibliothek *f*
 f bibliothèque *f* de bandes; magnétothèque *f*
 r библиотека *f* магнитных лент

9202 tape loading
 d Bandladen *n*
 f chargement *m* de bande
 r заправка *f* ленты

 * **tape mark** → 9203

9203 tape mark[er]; tape label
 d Bandmarke *f*
 f marque *f* de bande; étiquette *f* de bande
 r маркер *m* ленты; метка *f* ленты

 * **tapeoff** → 9204

 * **taper** → 9204

**9204 taper [coupler]; T-coupler; T-connector;
   tee-coupler; tapping element; tapeoff**
 d T-Koppler *m*; Taper *m*; konischer Koppler *m*;
   Koppler mit verändertem Querschnitt
 f coupleur *m* [à configuration] en T; coupleur à
   raccord progressif
 r соединитель *m* формы T; коническое

согласующее устройство *n*; соединитель с
плавным изменением сечения

9205 tape recorder; recorder
 d Bandgerät *n*
 f magnétoscope *m*
 r магнитофон *m*

9206 tape trailer
 d Band-Trailer *m*; Bandnachlauf *m*
 f fin *f* arrière de bande
 r хвост *m* ленты

9207 tape transport
 d Bandtransport *m*
 f transport *m* de bande
 r передвижка *f* ленты; транспорт *m* ленты

 * **tape unit** → 5584

9208 tape winder
 d Bandwickler *m*
 f enrouleur *m* de bande
 r устройство *n* лентонамотки

 * **TAPI** → 9234

9209 tap[ping]
 d Abzweigung *f*
 f branchement *m*
 r ответвление *n* [от линии]

 * **tapping element** → 9204

 * **target** → 2797

9210 target
 d Zielscheibe *f*
 f cible *f*
 r мишень *f*

 * **target address** → 2798

 * **target code** → 6358

 * **target language** → 6349

 * **target program** → 6358

 * **task** → 7338

9211 task abnormal end
 d Taskabnormalhalt *m*
 f arrêt *m* anormal de tâche
 r аварийное завершение *n* задачи

9212 task administration
 d Taskverwaltung *f*
 f administration *f* de tâches
 r администрирование *n* задач

9213 **taskbar**
  d Taskstreifen *m*; Taskleiste *f*;
    Anwendungsleiste *f*
  f barre *f* de tâches
  r лента *f* задач

9214 **taskbar button**
  d Taskstreifentaste *f*
  f bouton *m* d'outil de tâches
  r кнопка *f* ленты задач

  * **task data** → 7339

9215 **task description**
  d Aufgabenbeschreibung *f*
  f description *f* de tâche
  r описание *n* задачи

9216 **tasking**
  d Aufgabenzuweisung *f*
  f création *f* de tâches
  r организация *f* прохождения задач;
    размещение *n* задач

9217 **task management**
  d Aufgabensteuerung *f*; Aufgabenverwaltung *f*
  f gestion *f* des tâches
  r управление *n* задачами

9218 **task queue**
  d Aufgabenwarteschlange *f*
  f queue *f* de tâches
  r очередь *f* задач

  * **task swapper** → 9219

9219 **task switcher; task swapper**
  d Aufgabenschalter *m*
  f sélectionneur *m* de tâches
  r переключатель *m* заданий

  * **tattooing algorithm** → 9962

  * **tax** → 1639

9220 **taxonomy**
  d Taxonomie *f*
  f taxonomie *f*
  r таксономия *f*

9221 **taxonomy formation**
    (in AI)
  d Taxonomie-Formation *f*; taxonomische
    Formation
  f formation *f* de taxinomie
  r классификационное образование *n*;
    таксономическое образование

  * **TB** → 9253

  * **T-connector** → 9204

  * **T-coupler** → 9204

  * **TCP/IP** → 9514

9222 **TCP/IP address**
  d TCP/IP-Adresse *f*
  f adresse *f* TCP/IP
  r адрес *m* протокола TCP/IP

9223 **TCP/IP domain**
  d TCP/IP-Domain *f*
  f domaine *m* TCP/IP
  r область *f* протокола TCP/IP

9224 **TCP/IP name**
  d TCP/IP-Name *m*
  f nom *m* TCP/IP
  r имя *n* TCP/IP

9225 **teaching program; learning program;
    tutor**
  d lehrendes Programm *n*; Lehrprogramm *n*
  f programme *m* enseignant; programme
    didactique; programme de formation
  r обучающая программа *f*

  * **teachware** → 2354

  * **teardrop** → 800

  * **tear-off menu** → 7494

9226 **technology**
  d Technologie *f*
  f technologie *f*
  r технология *f*

  * **tee-coupler** → 9204

9227 **telecharge** *v*
  d fernladen
  f télécharger
  r загружать дистанционно

  * **telecharging** → 3143

  * **telecommand** → 7895

  * **telecommunication** → 9229

9228 **telecommunication access method; remote
    access method**
  d Fernverarbeitungszugriffsmethode *f*
  f méthode *f* d'accès à distance
  r дистанционный метод *m* доступа

  * **telecommunication network** → 1947

9229 telecommunication[s]; remote
communication
d Fernübertragung *f*; Telekommunikation *f*
f télécommunication *f*; communication *f* à
distance
r дистанционная связь *f*; дистанционная
передача *f*; телекоммуникация *f*

9230 telecommuting; flexiplace; homework
d Telearbeit *f*
f télétravail *m*
r дистанционное использование *n*
[компьютера]

9231 teleconference
d Telekonferenz *f*
f téléconférence *f*
r телеконференция *f*

9232 teleconferencing; conferencing
d Telekonferenz-Kommunikation *f*
f communication *f* par téléconférence
r [теле]конферентная связь *f*

* telecontrol → 7895

* teleguidance → 7895

9233 teleinformatics; telematics; compunication
d Teleinformatik *f*; Telematik *f*
f téléinformatique *f*; télématique *f*
r телеинформатика *f*; телематика *f*

* telematics → 9233

9234 telephony application programming
interface; TAPI
d TAPI-Standard *m*;
Telefonie-Zugriffschnittstelle *f*
f interface *f* de programmation d'application de
transfert téléphonique; norme *f* TAPI;
standard *m* TAPI
r интерфейс *m* прикладного
программирования для передачи данных,
факсов и голосовых сообщений

9235 teleprinter; teletype[writer]; typewriter
terminal; teletype printer; TTY; ticker
d Ferndrucker *m*; Fernschreiber *m*;
Fernschreibgerät *n*; Ticker *m*
f téléimprimeur *m*; téléscripteur *m*; télétype *m*;
téléautographe *m*
r дистанционное печатающее устройство *n*;
телетайп *m*; телеграфный аппарат *m*

9236 teleprocessing; remote processing; line
loop operation
d Fernverarbeitung *f*; Remote-Processing *n*
f télétraitement *m*; traitement *m* à distance
r телеобработка *f*; дистанционная

обработка *f*

9237 teleprocessing monitor
d Fernverarbeitungsmonitor *m*; TP-Monitor *m*
f moniteur *m* de télétraitement
r монитор *m* для телеобработки

9238 teleprocessing system
d Fernverarbeitungssystem *n*
f système *m* de télétraitement
r система *f* телеобработки

* telescript → 9243

* teletype → 9235

9239 teletype *v*
d fernschreiben
f téléimprimer
r печатать дистанционно

9240 teletype code
d Fernschreibcode *m*
f code *m* de télétype
r телетайпный код *m*

* teletype printer → 9235

9241 teletypesetting
d Fernsetzen *n*
f position *f* à distance
r абонентский телетайпный пункт *m*

* teletypewriter → 9235

9242 televote; remote vote
d Televotum *m*
f télévote *m*
r телеголосование *n*; дистанционное
голосование *n*

9243 telewriting; telescript
d Bildfernschreiben *n*; Fernschreiben *n* mit
Schreibstift
f télé-écriture *f*
r телекопирование *n*

9244 Telnet
(a program that lets you log onto a remote
computer)
d Telnet *n*
f Telnet *m*
r протокол *m* Telnet; программа *f* Telnet

9245 template; stencil; pattern
d Schablone *f*; Schrittschablone *f*; Vorlage *f*;
Formatbild *n*
f maquette *f*; modèle *m*
r шаблон *m*; трафарет *m*; макет *m*;
образец *m*; модель *f*

9246 **template file**
  d Datei *f* der Schablone
  f fichier *m* de maquettes
  r макетный файл *m*

9247 **template wizard**
  d Schablone-Assistent *m*
  f assistant *m* de maquettes
  r советник *m* создания шаблона

9248 **temporal; temporary**
  d zeitlich; zeitweilig
  f temporel; temporaire
  r временной

9249 **temporal compression**
  d zeitliche Kompression *f*
  f compression *f* temporelle
  r временное сжатие *n*

9250 **temporal database**
  d zeitliche Datenbasis *f*
  f base *f* de données temporelle
  r временная база *f* данных

9251 **temporal extent**
  d zeitlicher Extent *m*
  f étendue *f* temporelle
  r временное расширение *n*

  * **temporary** → **9248**

9252 **temporary file**
  d zeitliche Datei *f*
  f fichier *m* temporaire
  r временной файл *m*

  * **temporary memory** → **1230**

9253 **terabyte; TB**
  d Tera-Byte *n*
  f téra-octet *m*
  r терабайт *m*

9254 **teraflops**
  d Teraflops *m*
  f téraflops *m*
  r терафлопс *m*

  * **term** → **5716**

  * **terminal** *adj* → **3831**

  * **terminal** → **9266**

9255 **terminal**
  d Endstelle *f*; Anschlussklemme *f*; Klemme *f*;
    Anschlusspunkt *m*; Terminal *n*
  f borne *f*; terminal *m*
  r зажим *m*; клемма *f*

9256 **terminal adapter**
  d Endgerätanpassung *f*; Terminaladapter *m*
  f adaptateur *m* terminal
  r терминальный адаптер *m*

9257 **terminal addressing**
  d Endgerätadressierung *f*;
    Terminaladressierung *f*
  f adressage *m* de terminal
  r адресование *n* терминала

9258 **terminal computer**
  d Endstellenrechner *m*; Terminalrechner *m*
  f ordinateur *m* terminal
  r терминальный компьютер *m*

  * **terminal device** → **9266**

9259 **terminal emulation**
    (a technique in which one computer imitates a
    terminal while communicating with another
    computer, such as a mainframe, by using
    special software)
  d Terminalemulation *f*
  f émulation *f* de terminal
  r эмуляция *f* терминала

9260 **terminal emulator**
  d Terminalemulator *m*
  f émulateur *m* de terminal
  r терминальный эмулятор *m*

9261 **terminal identifier**
  d Terminalbezeichner *m*;
    Terminalidentifikator *m*
  f identificateur *m* de terminal
  r идентификатор *m* терминала

9262 **terminal of network; network terminal**
  d Endgerät *n* des Netzwerkes; Terminal *n* des
    Netzwerkes
  f terminal *m* de réseau
  r сетевой терминал *m*

  * **terminal point** → **3419**

9263 **terminal server**
  d Terminalserver *m*
  f serveur *m* de terminaux
  r сервер *m* терминалов; терминальный
    сервер

9264 **terminal server software**
  d Terminalserver-Software *f*
  f logiciel *m* de serveur de terminaux
  r программное обеспечение *n*
    терминального сервера

9265 **terminal session**
  d Terminalsitzung *f*

f session *f* à terminal
r сеанс *m* работы на терминале

9266 terminal [unit]; terminal device; end device
d Terminal *n*; Endgerät *n*
f. terminal *m*; appareil *m* terminal
r терминал *m*; оконечное устройство *n*

9267 terminate *v*
d beenden
f terminer
r завершить

* **terminate-and-stay resident program** →
7590

* **terminate flag** → 2007

9268 terminating circuit; termination circuit; terminator
d Endschaltung *f*; Abschlussschaltung *f*;
Terminator *m*; Nachbereiter *m*
f circuit *m* de terminaison; circuit final;
terminateur *m*
r схема *f* окончания; оконечный каскад *m*
[схемы]

9269 termination; finishing; completion
d Beendigung *f*; Termination *f*; Vollendung *f*;
Fertigbearbeitung *f*
f terminaison *f*; achèvement *m*; finissage *m*
r окончание *n*; завершение *n*

* **termination circuit** → 9268

* **terminator** → 2007, 9268

9270 terminator
(a sign)
d Beendigungszeichen *n*; Beendigungssymbol *n*
f symbole *m* de terminaison; signe *m* de fin
r символ *m* окончания; знак *m* завершения

9271 ternary
d ternär
f ternaire
r троичный

9272 ternary code
d Ternärcode *m*
f code *m* ternaire
r троичный код *m*

9273 ternary logic; three-value logic; three-state logic; tristate logic
d Ternärlogik *f*; Tri-State-Logik *f*
f logique *f* ternaire
r троичная логика *f*; трёхзначная логика

9274 ternary number notation; ternary representation
d ternäre Zahlendarstellung *f*; ternäre
Schreibweise *f*
f notation *f* de nombres ternaire
r троичное представление *n*; представление
чисел в троичной системе

* **ternary representation** → 9274

9275 ternary symbol
d Ternärschritt *m*
f symbole *m* ternaire
r троичный символ *m*

* **tessellation** → 9377

* **tessellation automaton** → 1518

* **test *v*** → 1647

* **test** → 1646

* **test bit** → 1648

9276 test data
d Testdaten *pl*
f données *fpl* de test
r тестовые данные *pl*; результаты *mpl* теста

9277 test equipment; testing device; tester; exercizer
d Prüfgerät *n*; Prüfeinrichtung *f*;
Prüfvorrichtung *f*; Tester *m*
f équipement *m* d'essai; dispositif *m* d'essai;
testeur *m*; essayeur *m*
r устройство испытания; тестер *m*

* **tester** → 9277

9278 tester interface; testing interface
d Prüfeinrichtungsschnittstelle *f*
f interface *f* de testeur
r интерфейс *m* тестера

* **testing device** → 9277

* **testing interface** → 9278

9279 test job; test request
d Prüfauftrag *m*; Testanforderung *f*
f job *m* de test; requête *f* d'essai
r тестовое задание *n*; запрос *m* теста

9280 test log; test protocol
d Testprotokoll *n*
f protocole *m* d'essai
r протокол *m* испытания

9281 test loop
d Prüfschleife *f*

f boucle *f* d'essai
r тестовая петля *f*

9282 test method
d Prüfmethode *f*; Prüfverfahren *n*
f méthode *f* d'essai
r метод *m* испытания

* **testpoint** → **1655**

9283 test program
d Testprogramm *n*; Prüfprogramm *n*
f programme *m* d'essai; programme de test
r тестовая программа *f*; программа
испытаний

* **test protocol** → **9280**

* **test request** → **9279**

9284 test signal
d Testsignal *n*; Prüfsignal *n*; Kontrollsignal *n*
f signal *m* d'essai; signal de contrôle
r сигнал *m* проверки

9285 test-state bit
d Prüfzustandsbit *n*
f bit *m* d'état de test
r бит *m* состояния теста

9286 test-state decoder
d Prüfzustandsauswerter *m*
f décodeur *m* d'état de test
r дешифратор *m* состояния теста

9287 test transaction
d Testtransaktion *f*
f transaction *f* de test
r групповая операция *f* контроля

* **tetrad** → **4361**

9288 text
d Text *m*
f texte *m*
r текст *m*

9289 text alignment; text justification
d Textausrichtung *f*
f alignement *m* de texte
r выравнивание *n* текста

* **text area** → **9290**

9290 text block; text area
d Textblock *m*
f bloc *m* de texte
r текстовой блок *m*; текстовое поле *n*

9291 text boundaries

d Textgrenzen *fpl*
f limites *fpl* de texte
r границы *fpl* текста

* **text box** → **6426**

9292 text carrier
d Textträger *m*
f porteur *m* de texte
r носитель *m* текста

9293 text color
d Textfarbe *f*
f couleur *f* de texte
r цвет *m* текста

9294 text composition; composition
d Textgestaltung *f*; Textzusammensetzung *f*
f composition *f* [de texte]
r набор *m* текста; составление *n* текста;
компоновка *f* текста

9295 text data
d Textdaten *pl*
f données *fpl* de texte
r текстовые данные *pl*

9296 text-display mode
d Textanzeigemodus *m*;Textanzeigebetriebsart *f*
f mode *m* d'affichage de texte
r режим *m* отображения текста

9297 text editing
d Textbearbeitung *f*
f édition *f* de texte
r редактирование *n* текста

9298 text editor
d Texteditor *m*; Textbearbeitungsprogramm *n*;
Textaufbereiter *m*
f éditeur *m* de texte
r текстовой редактор *m*

* **text-entry field** → **6426**

9299 text envelope
d Texthülle *f*
f enveloppe *f* de texte
r оболочка *f* текста

9300 text exploding
d Text-Explodieren *n*
f décomposition *f* de texte
r развязывание *n* текста

9301 text field
d Textfeld *n*
f champ *m* de texte
r поле *n* текста

9302 text file
 d Textdatei *f*
 f fichier *m* de texte
 r текстовой файл *m*

9303 text fitting
 d Textanpassung *f*
 f ajustage *m* de texte
 r налаживание *n* текста

 * **text flow → 9341**

9304 text font
 d Textschrift *f*
 f police *f* de texte
 r текстовой шрифт *m*

9305 text formatting
 d Textformatierung *f*; Textformatieren *n*
 f formatage *m* de texte
 r форматирование *n* текста

9306 text frame
 d Textrahmen *m*
 f cadre *m* de texte
 r текстовой кадр *m*; рамка *f* текста

9307 text generation flag
 d Textgenerierung-Kennzeichen *n*
 f repérage *m* de génération de texte
 r флаг *m* генерирования текста

 * **text insertion → 4932**

9308 text insertion point
 d Texteinfügungspunkt *m*
 f point *m* d'insertion de texte
 r точка *f* вставки текста

 * **text justification → 9289**

 * **text mode → 1619**

 * **text-numeric database → 9322**

 * **terminal → 9266**

9309 text obliquing angle
 d Schrägwinkel *m* des Textes
 f angle *m* d'inclinaison de texte
 r угол *m* наклона текста

9310 text orientation
 d Textorientierung *f*
 f orientation *f* de texte
 r ориентация *f* текста

9311 text page
 d Textseite *f*
 f page *f* de texte

 r текстовая страница *f*; страница текста

9312 text position
 d Textposition *f*
 f position *f* de texte
 r позиция *f* текста; расположение *n* текста

9313 text processing; word processing; alpha processing
 d Textverarbeitung *f*; Wortverarbeitung *f*; Alphaverarbeitung *f*
 f traitement *m* de texte; traitement de mots
 r обработка *f* текста; обработка слов

9314 text processor; word processor
 d Wortprozessor *m*
 f texteur *m*
 r текстовой процессор *m*; система *f* текстообработки

9315 text record
 d Textsatz *m*
 f phrase *f* du texte
 r текстовая запись *f*

9316 text resizing
 d Text-Größenänderung *f*
 f changement *m* de taille de texte
 r изменение *n* размера текста

9317 text rotation
 d Textdrehung *f*
 f rotation *f* de texte
 r ротация *f* текста; поворот *m* текста

9318 text selecting
 d Textauswahl *f*
 f sélection *f* de texte
 r выбор *m* текста

9319 text size
 d Textgröße *f*
 f taille *f* de texte
 r размер *m* текста

9320 text style
 d Textstil *m*
 f style *m* de texte
 r текстовой стиль *m*

9321 text template
 d Textschablone *f*
 f maquette *f* de texte
 r текстовой шаблон *m*

9322 text[ual]-numeric[al] database
 d text- und numerische Datenbasis *f*
 f base *f* de données textuelle numérique
 r текстово-цифровая база *f* данных

9323 **textual selection**
d textuelle Auswahl f
f sélection f textuelle
r текстовой выбор m

9324 **texture**
d Textur f; Füllmuster n
f texture f
r текстура f; побитовая ткань f

9325 **texture analysis**
d Textur-Analyse f
f analyse f de texture
r анализ f текстуры

9326 **texture blend**
d Textur-Überblendung f
f dégradé m de texture
r переливание n текстуры

9327 **texture characteristics**
d Texturmerkmale npl
f caractéristiques fpl de la texture
r характеристики fpl текстуры

9328 **texture compression**
d Textur-Kompression f;
Texturenkomprimierung f
f compression f de texture
r сжатие n текстуры

9329 **texture library**
d Füllmusterbibliothek f; Texturbibliothek f
f bibliothèque f de textures
r библиотека f текстур

9330 **texture list**
d Texturliste f
f liste f de textures
r список m текстур

* **texture map → 9331**

9331 **texture map[ping]**
d Texturenabbildung f
f mappage m de texture
r отображение n текстуры; наложение n
текстуры

9332 **texture mapping hardware**
d Texturenabbildungshardware f
f matériel m de mappage de texture
r аппаратное обеспечение n отображения
текстуры

9333 **texture memory**
d Texturspeicher m
f mémoire f de textures
r память f текстур

9334 **texture mipmapping**
d Textur-Mip-Mapping n
f mip-mapping m de texture
r множественное отображение n текстуры

9335 **texture modulation**
d Textur-Modulation f
f modulation f de textures
r модуляция f текстур

9336 **texture morphing**
d Textur-Morphing n
f morphage m de texture
r морфинг m текстуры

9337 **texture swapping**
d Texture-Swapping n
f swapping m de texture
r своппинг m текстуры

9338 **texture transparency**
d Textur-Transparenz f
f transparence f de texture
r прозрачность f текстуры

9339 **texturing**
d Texturieren n; Texturierung f
f texturation f
r текстурирование n

9340 **text window**
d Textfenster n
f fenêtre f de texte
r текстовое окно n

* **text wrap → 9341**

9341 **text wrap[ping]; text flow**
d Text-Umhüllung f
f habillage m de texte
r размещение n текста вокруг
[изображения]; завёрстывание n текста;
заворачивание n текста

* **theory of algorithms → 299**

* **theory of games → 4165**

* **theory of queues → 7560**

* **theory of reliability → 7876**

9342 **thermal printer; thermoprinter;
electrothermic printer**
d Thermodrucker m; elektrothermischer
Drucker m
f imprimante f thermique; imprimante
thermographique
r термографический принтер m;
устройство n термопечати

9343 thermal wax-transfer printer
 d Thermowachsdrucker *m*
 f imprimante *f* à transfert thermique
 r термографический принтер *m* с подачей
    воскового красителя; термопринтер *m* с
    подачей красителя; термовосковой
    принтер

 * **thermoprinter** → **9342**

9344 thesaurus
 d Thesaurus *m*; Sprachthesaurus *m*
 f thésaurus *m*
 r тезаурус *m*

 * **the Web** → **10054**

9345 thin-film electroluminescent display
 d Dünnschicht-Elektrolumineszenzdisplay *n*;
    Dünnschicht-Elektrolumineszenzanzeige *f*
 f afficheur *m* électroluminescent à couche
    mince
 r тонкослойный электролюминесцентный
    индикатор *m*

 * **thinker** → **2658**

9346 thin-window display
 d Kleinformat-Display *n*
 f écran *m* à fenêtre mince
 r узкоформатный дисплей *m*

 * **third normal form** → **6286**

 * **thrash** → **9347**

9347 thrash[ing]
 d Thrashing *n*
 f écroulement *m*; tassage *m*; battage *m*
 r пробуксовка *f*

9348 thread
    (a message and its responses in a newsgroup)
 d Faden *m*; Netzfaden *m*
 f fil *m* de discussion
 r нить *f*

9349 thread testing
 d Testen *n* von Funktionsmöglichkeiten
 f test *m* de possibilités fonctionnelles
 r тестирование *n* функциональных
    возможностей

9350 three-address instruction
 d Dreiadressbefehl *m*
 f instruction *f* à trois adresses
 r трёхадресная инструкция *f*

9351 three-dimensional; tri-dimensional; 3D
 d dreidimensional; 3D

 f tridimensionnel; à trois dimensions; 3D
 r трёхмерный; 3D

 * **three-excess code** → **3560**

9352 three-level code
 d gleichstromfreier dreistufiger Code *m*
 f code *m* à trois niveaux
 r трёхуровневый код *m*

9353 three-party conference; add-on conference
 d Dreierkonferenz *f*
 f conférence *f* à trois participants
 r конференция *f* из трёх участников

 * **three-state logic** → **9273**

9354 three-state output; tristate output
 d Ausgang *m* mit drei Zuständen;
    Tri-State-Ausgang *m*
 f sortie *f* à trois états
 r выход *m* с тремя [устойчивыми]
    состояниями

9355 three-tuple; triplet
 d Tripel *n*; Drilling *m*
 f triplet *m*
 r тройка *f*; триплет *m*

 * **three-value logic** → **9273**

 * **threshold** → **9357**

9356 threshold logic
 d Schwellen[wert]logik *f*;
    Schwellwertlogik *f*
 f logique *f* à seuil
 r пороговая логика *f*

9357 threshold [value]
 d Schwell[en]wert *m*; Schwelle *f*
 f valeur *f* de seuil; seuil *m*
 r пороговая величина *f*; порог *m*

 * **throat** → **8666**

9358 through-connect bit
 d Durchschaltbit *n*
 f bit *m* de connexion en transit
 r бит *m* транзитной связи

9359 through-connect command
 d Durchschaltenbefehl *m*
 f commande *f* de connexion en transit
 r команда *f* транзитной связи

9360 through-connection; interlayer connection
 d Durchschalten *n*; Durchschaltung *f*;
    Durchkontaktierung *f*

f connexion *f* entière
r сквозное соединение *n*; межслойное
соединение

9361 throughput
d Durchlässigkeit *f*; Durchlassfähigkeit *f*
f rendement *m*; débit *m*
r пропускная способность *f*; прохождение *n*

* **throw** *v* **off** → 7854

9362 thumb
d Thumb *n*; Daumen *m*
f pouce *m*
r перст *m* (курсор с вытянутым
указательным пальцем)

* **thumbnail** → 9363

**9363 thumbnail [image]; thumbnail
representation; rough sketch**
d Thumbnail *n*; Umrissskizze *f*; Kennsatz *m*;
Daumennagel *m*; Minibild *n*
f onglet *m*; croquis *m* [minuscule]; image *f*
timbre poste; image miniature; image
vignette; imagette *f*
r набросок *m*; свёрнутое [в пиктограмму]
изображение *n*

* **thumbnail representation** → 9363

9364 thumbnail review
d Thumbnail-Übersicht *f*
f revue *f* de croquis minuscules; revue d'images
miniatures; revue d'images vignettes
r просмотр *m* свёрнутых изображений

9365 thumbscanner
d Thumbscanner *m*
f scanner *m* dactyloscopique
r дактилоскопический сканер *m*

* **tick** → 1755

* **ticker** → 9235

* **tiebreaker** → 5870

* **TIFF** → 9184

* **tight coupling** → 1775

* **tightly coupled** → 8957

9366 tightly-coupled processors
d eng gekoppelte Prozessoren *mpl*
f processeurs *mpl* à couplage rigide
r сильно связанные процессоры *mpl*;
процессоры с непосредственной связью

9367 tilde; wave
(~)
d Tilde *f*
f tilde *m*
r тильда[-эллипсис] *f*

9368 tile; tiled pattern
d nebeneinander angeordnetes Muster *m*;
Musterkachel *m*
f mosaïque *m*
r неперекрывающийся образец *m*;
мозаичный шаблон *m*; мозаика *f*

9369 tiled horizontally
d nebeneinander angeordnet
f disposé horizontalement en mosaïque
r горизонтально неперекрывающийся

9370 tiled pages
d nebeneinander angeordnete Seiten *fpl*
f pages *fpl* en mosaïque
r неперекрывающиеся страницы *fpl*

* **tiled pattern** → 9368

9371 tiled vertically
d untereinander angeordnet
f disposé verticalement en mosaïque
r вертикально непекрывающийся

9372 tiled viewports
d nebeneinander angeordnete
Ansichtfenster *npl*
f clôtures *fpl* en mosaïque
r неперекрывающиеся области *fpl*
просмотра; неперекрывающиеся окна *npl*
просмотра

9373 tiled wallpaper
d nebeneinander angeordnete Tapeten *fpl*
f image *f* de fond en mosaïque
r неперекрывающийся экранный фон *m*;
неперекрывающиеся обои *pl*

9374 tiled windows
d nebeneinander angeordnete Fenster *npl*
f fenêtres *fpl* [disposées] en mosaïque
r неперекрывающиеся окна *npl*; окна
мозаикой

9375 tile size
d Kachelgröße *f*
f taille *f* de mosaïque
r размер *m* мозаичного шаблона

9376 tile width
d Kachelbreite *f*
f largeur *f* de mosaïque
r ширина *f* мозаичного шаблона

9377 tiling; tessellation; paving; covering of the plane with tiles
d Nebeneinander-Anordnung *f*; Musterkachelung *f*; Parkettierung *f*
f pavage *m*; dallage *m*; tessellation *f*; disposition *f* en mosaïque
r разбиение *n* плоскости на многоугольники; покрытие *n* плоскости многоугольниками; мозаичное размещение *n*; неперекрывающееся размещение; тасселяция *f*

* **tilting** → 6360

9378 time
d Zeit *f*
f temps *m*
r время *n*; период *m* времени; момент *m* времени

9379 time-addressed signal
d zeitlagenadressiertes Signal *n*
f signal *m* à adressage temporaire
r сигнал *m* с адресацией по времени передачи; сигнал с временной привязкой

9380 time-averaged
d zeitgemittelt; über die Zeit gemittelt
f moyenné dans le temps
r усреднённый по времени

9381 time base; time scale
d Zeitbasis *f*; Zeitskala *f*
f base *f* de temps
r линия *f* развёртки во времени; шкала *f* времени; масштаб *m* [по оси] времени

9382 time-base circuit
d Kippschaltung *f*
f circuit *m* de base de temps
r цепь *f* развёртки; схема *f* развёртки

9383 time chart; timing chart; timing sheet; timing diagram
d Zeitdiagramm *n*
f diagramme *m* de temps; chronogramme *m*
r времедиаграмма *f*; временная диаграмма *f*

9384 time code; timing code
d Zeitcode *m*; Timecode *m*
f code *m* temporel; code horaire; temps-code *m*
r временной код *m*

9385 time control byte
d Zeitsteuerbyte *n*
f octet *m* de commande de temps
r байт *m* синхронизации

9386 timed; clocked
d synchron; zeitlich festgelegt; getaktet

f synchrone; à temps fixe; rythmé
r синхронизированный; с заданной длительности

9387 timed-access register
d Zugriffszeitsteuerregister *n*
f registre *m* de synchronisation d'accès
r регистр *m* синхронизации доступа

* **time-date generator** → 9388

9388 time-date generator [program]
d Zeit-Datum-Geberprogramm *n*
f programme *m* générateur d'heure et date
r программа-генератор *f* часа и даты

9389 timed delay
d feste Zeitverzögerung *f*
f délai *m* de temps fixe; temps de transit
r фиксированная временная задержка *f*

9390 time-dependent; time-varying
d zeitabhängig; zeitvariant
f dépendant du temps; non stationnaire
r зависимый от времени; нестационарный

* **time-derived channel** → 9393

9391 time division; timesharing
d Zeit[auf]teilung *f*; Time-Sharing *n*
f répartition *f* temporelle; partage *m* de temps; découpage *m* de temps
r разделение *n* времени

* **time-division method** → 9399

9392 time-division multiple access
d zeitüberlapper Mehrfachzugriff *m*; Mehrfachzugriff im Zeitmultiplex
f accès *m* multiple par répartition temporelle
r коллективный доступ *m* с временным уплотнением

9393 time-division multiplex channel; time-derived channel; timesharing link
d Zeitmultiplexkanal *m*
f canal *m* multiplexé dans le temps
r [мультиплексный] канал *m* с разделением по времени; [мультиплексный] канал с времеделением; канал с временным уплотнением

9394 time-division multiplex connection
d Zeitmultiplexkanalverbindung *f*; Zeitvielfachverbindung *f*
f connexion *f* multiplexée dans le temps
r связь *f* с временным мультиплексированием

9395 time[-division] multiplex[ing]
d Zeitvielfach *n*; Zeitmultiplexen *n*

f multiplexage *m* [à répartition] dans le temps
r мультиплексирование *n* с временным уплотнением; временное мультиплексирование

9396 time-division multiplex network
d Zeitmultiplex-Durchschaltenetz *n*
f réseau *m* multiplexé dans le temps
r сеть *f* с временным мультиплексированием

9397 time-division multiplex switch unit
d Zeitmultiplex-Koppeleinrichtung *f*
f commutateur *m* multiplexé dans le temps
r коммутатор *m* с временным мультиплексированием

9398 time-division multiplex system
d Zeitmultiplexsystem *n*; Zeitvielfachsystem *n*
f système *m* multiplexé dans le temps
r система *f* с временным мультиплексированием

**9399 time[-division] multiplex technique;
time-division method**
d Zeitmultiplexverfahren *n*;
Zeitvielfachverfahren *n*
f procédé *m* multiplex [de division de temps]
r метод *m* временного мультиплексирования; метод времеделения

9400 timed loop
d zeitlich festgelegte Schleife *f*
f boucle *f* fixée en durée
r цикл *m* заданной длительности

   *   **time equalizer → 3269**

9401 time interrupt
d Zeitunterbrechung *f*
f interruption *f* par le temps
r прерывание *n* по времени

9402 time logic
d zeitliche Logik *f*
f logique *f* temporaire
r временная логика *f*

   *   **time-multiplex → 9395**

   *   **time-multiplex technique → 9399**

9403 timeout
d Zeitsperre *f*; Auszeit *f*; Timeout *n*
f temps *m* inexploitable; temps de suspension; temporisation *f*
r превышение *n* лимита времени; блокировка *f* по времени; тайм-аут *m*

9404 timeout mode

d Timeout-Betrieb *m*
f mode *m* de limitation de temps
r режим *m* ограничения по времени

9405 timeout test
d Zeitablaufprüfung *f*
f essai *m* de temps inexploitable
r проверка *f* лимита времени

9406 time-pulse code
d Zeit-Impuls-Code *m*
f code *m* d'impulsions à déplacement dans le temps
r время-импульсный код *m*

**9407 time-pulse generator; timing circuit;
timing [pulse] generator; timer**
d Zeit[takt]geber *m*; Zeitglied *n*;
Zeitsignalgenerator *m*; Zeitgeberschaltung *f*
f générateur *m* d'impulsions d'horloge;
horloge *f*; rythmeur *m*; minuteur *m*;
minuterie *f*
r генератор *m* хронирующих импульсов;
генератор *m* синхросигналов; таймер *m*;
датчик *m* времени

**9408 time quantization; time sampling; time
slicing; time slotting**
d Zeitquantisierung *f*; Zeitquantelung *f*;
Time-Slicing *n*
f quantification *f* dans le temps;
échantillonnage *m* dans le temps; tranchage *m*
de temps
r квантование *n* [по] времени; нарезание *n*
[машинного] времени

   *   **timer → 9407**

9409 timer allocation
d Taktzuordnung *f*
f allocation *f* de rythmeur
r размещение *n* таймера

   *   **timer-counter → 2346**

9410 timer table
d Zeitgebertabelle *f*; Zeitgliedtabelle *f*
f table *f* de rythmeur
r таблица *f* таймера

   *   **time sampling → 9408**

   *   **time scale → 9382**

9411 time-schedule document
d zeitbestimmende Unterlage *f*
f document *m* de déroulement de temps
r документ *m* распределения времени

   *   **timesharing → 9392**

* **timesharing link** → 9393

9412 timesharing operation
 d Teilnehmerbetrieb *m*;
    Time-Sharing-Operation *f*
 f opération *f* en temps partagé
 r работа *f* с разделением времени

9413 timesharing system
 d Time-Sharing-System *n*
 f système *m* à temps partagé
 r система *f* с разделением времени

9414 time slice; time slot
 d Zeitscheibe *f*; Zeitschlitz *m*; Zeitlage *f*
 f tranche *f* de temps; créneau *m* temporel
 r квант *m* времени; отрезок *m* времени;
    временной канал *m*; интервал *m*
    временного канала

9415 time-slice access
 d Zeitlagenzugriff *m*
 f accès *m* par tranche de temps
 r доступ *m* в отрезке времени

9416 time-slice code
 d Zeitschlitzcode *m*
 f code *m* de tranche de temps
 r код *m* кванта времени

9417 time-slice comparator
 d Zeitlagenvergleicher *m*
 f comparateur *m* de tranches de temps
 r компаратор *m* квантов времени

9418 time-slice counter
 d Zeitlagenzähler *m*
 f compteur *m* de tranches de temps
 r счётчик *m* квантов времени

* **time slicing** → 9408

* **time slot** → 9414

9419 time-slot register
 d Zeitlagenregister *n*
 f registre *m* de tranche de temps
 r регистр *m* канала времени

* **time slotting** → 9408

* **timetable** → 8220

* **time-varying** → 9391

9420 timing; clocking
 d Takt[ier]ung *f*; Zeitablauf *m*; Zeitmessung *f*;
    Zeitsteuerung *f*
 f minutage *m*; horloge *f*; commande *f* de temps;
    rythme *m*

 r [календарная] синхронизация *f*;
    тактирование *n*

* **timing channel** → 1748

* **timing chart** → 9384

* **timing circuit** → 9407

* **timing code** → 9385

9421 timing control
 d Taktregelung *f*
 f contrôle *m* de minutage; contrôle de
    synchronisation
 r управление *n* синхронизацией

* **timing diagram** → 9384

* **timing edge** → 1756

* **timing failure** → 1757

9422 timing generation
 d Takterzeugung *f*
 f génération *f* d'impulsions d'horloge
 r генерирование *n* синхроимпульсов

* **timing generator** → 9407

* **timing phase** → 1760

* **timing phase synchronization** → 1761

* **timing pulse** → 1755

* **timing pulse edge** → 1756

* **timing pulse failure** → 1757

* **timing pulse generator** → 9407

* **timing pulse rate** → 1762

* **timing pulse train** → 1764

* **timing rate** → 1762

* **timing sheet** → 9384

* **timing train** → 1764

9423 timing verification
 d Zeitablaufverifizierung *f*
 f vérification *f* de relations temporelles
 r верификация *f* временных соотношений

* **tip** → 9442

* **title** → 4415

9424 **title bar**
 d Titelleiste *f*; Titelbalken *m*
 f barre *f* de têtes; barre d'en-têtes; barre de titre
 r полоса *f* заголовка

9425 **title bar text**
 d Titelleistetext *m*
 f texte *m* de barre de têtes
 r текст *m* полосы заголовка

9426 **title block**
 d Titelblock *m*
 f bloc *m* de têtes
 r блок *m* заголовков

9427 **title domain; name domain**
 d Titelbereich *m*; Gültigkeitsbereich *m* der Namen
 f domaine *m* de noms
 r область *f* заголовков; область названий

 * **toggle** → 9550

9428 **toggle** *v*
 d kippen
 f basculer
 r генерировать релаксационные колебания

9429 **toggle button; toggle switch; toggle key; tumbler; switching key**
 d Kippschalter *m*; doppelpoliger Umschalter *m*
 f bouton *m* bascule; commutateur *m* basculeur; inverseur *m* à bascule; interrupteur *m* à bascule; touche *f* à bascule
 r тумблерный переключатель *m*; тумблер *m*

 * **toggle circuit** → 9550

 * **toggle key** → 9429

 * **toggle switch** → 9429

 * **token** → 869

9430 **token-access protocol**
 d Token-Passing-Protokoll *n*
 f protocole *m* d'accès par jeton
 r протокол *m* эстафетного доступа

9431 **token bus**
 d Token-Bus *m*
 f bus *m* à jeton
 r эстафетная шина *f*

9432 **token bus network**
 d Token-Bus-Netz *n*
 f réseau *m* en bus à jeton
 r сеть *f* с маркерным доступом; сеть с эстафетным доступом

9433 **token passing**
 d Token-Passing *n*
 f passage *m* de jeton
 r передача *f* маркера

 * **token ring** → 9434

9434 **token ring [network]**
 d Ringnetzwerk *n* mit "Token-Access"-Mechanismus; Token-Ring-Netz[werk] *n*
 f réseau *m* en anneau à jeton
 r кольцевая сеть *f* с передачей маркера; кольцевая сеть с эстафетным доступом; эстафетная кольцевая сеть

 * **tone** → 114

9435 **toner**
 d Toner *m*
 f toner *m*
 r тонер *m*

9436 **tool**
 d Werkzeug *n*; Hilfsmittel *n*; Instrument *n*
 f outil *m*; instrument *m*
 r средство *n*; инструмент *m*

9437 **toolbar**
 d Werkzeugstreifen *m*; Hilfsmittelsleiste *f*
 f barre *f* d'outils
 r инструментальная лента *f*; панель *f* инструментов

9438 **toolbar button; toolbar item**
 d Hilfsmittelschaltfläche *f*; Hilfsmittelsstreifenelement *n*
 f bouton *m* de barre d'outils
 r кнопка *f* панели инструментов

 * **toolbar item** → 9438

9439 **toolbox**
 d Werkzeugkasten *m*
 f boîte *f* à outils
 r инструментальный ящик *m*; меню *n* операций

9440 **tool icon**
 d Hilfsmittelsymbol *n*
 f icône *f* d'outil
 r икона *f* инструмента

9441 **toolkit**
 d Werkzeugsatz *m*
 f kit *m* d'instruments
 r инструментальный пакет *m*; инструментальный набор *m*

9442 **tooltip; tip**
 d Tip *m*

f info-bulle *f*
r сведение *n* для инструментальной кнопки

* **top → 1437**

* **top digit → 5896**

9443 topic
(of a newsgroup, e-mail, etc)
d Thema *n*; Gesprächsthema *n*
f topique *m*; sujet *m*; thème *f*
r тематический раздел *m*; тема *f*; раздел описания

9444 top key
d Top-Taste *f*
f touche *f* de registre supérieur
r клавиша *f* верхнего регистра

9445 toplevel domain
(in Internet)
d höchste Domain *f*; höchste Hierarchiestufe *f* bei den Domains
f domaine *m* de tête; domaine de premier niveau; domaine principal
r главный домен *m*; домен высшего уровня

9446 top of file; beginning of file
d Dateianfang *m*
f début *m* de fichier
r начало *n* файла

9447 topological analysis
d topologische Analyse *f*
f analyse *f* topologique
r топологический анализ *m*

9448 topological arrangement
(of a network)
d topologische Anordnung *f*
f arrangement *m* topologique
r топологическая компоновка *f*

9449 topology
d Topologie *f*
f topologie *f*
r топология *f*

* **total → 4186, 9450**

9450 total [amount]; grand total; final total; sum total
d Gesamtbetrag *m*; Gesamtsumme *f*; Endsumme *f*
f somme *f* totale; total *m* général; montant *m* total
r общая сумма *f*; конечная сумма

9451 total bit stream
d Gesamtbitfluss *m*

f flot *m* de bits total
r полный поток *m* битов

* **touch device → 9454**

* **touch display → 9455**

9452 touchpad; touch-sensitive tablet; trackpad
d Touchpad *n*
f pavé *m* tactile; trackpad *m*
r сенсорная панель *f*

9453 touch scanner
d Berührungsscanner *m*
f scanner *m* tactile
r сенсорный сканер *m*

* **touch screen → 9455**

9454 touch[-sensitive] device
d Gerät *n* mit Berührungseingabe; Sensor-Gerät *n*
f unité *f* sensorielle; unité tactile; élément *m* sensitif
r сенсорное устройство *n*; сенсорный элемент *m*

* **touch-sensitive display → 9455**

9455 touch[-sensitive] screen; sensitive screen; touch[-sensitive] display; tactile display
d Berührungsbildschirm *m*; Sensor-Bildschirm *m*; empfindlicher Bildschirm *m*; Touchscreen *n*
f écran *m* sensoriel; écran sensitif; écran tactile
r сенсорный экран *m*; тактильный экран

* **touch-sensitive tablet → 9452**

9456 touch sensor; tactile-type sensor
d Berührungssensor *m*; taktiler Sensor *m*
f capteur *m* [du type] tactile; senseur *m* tactile
r тактильный датчик *m*

9457 tower
d Turm *m*
f bloc *m* vertical
r вертикальный блок *m*

* **trace *v* → 3158, 9463**

9458 trace; trail
d Spur *f*; Ablauffolge *f*
f trace *f*; poursuite *f* de déroulement; droite *f* de suite
r след *m*; трасса *f*

9459 trace; tracing
d Trassieren *n*; Tracing *n*; Trassierung *f*; Aufzeichnung *f*; Durchzeichnung *f*

f traçage *m*; tracement *m*
r трассирование *n*; трассировка *f*

9460 trace command
d Tracing-Befehl *m*
f commande *f* de traçage
r команда *f* трассировки

9461 trace device; tracer
d Folgeeinrichtung *f*; Nachlaufeinrichtung *f*
f unité *f* de traçage; dispositif *m*
d'asservissement; localisateur *m* de la trace
r следящее устройство *n*

9462 trace program; tracing program; tracer
d Folgeprüfprogramm *n*;
Ablaufverfolgungsprogramm *n*;
Trace-Programm *n*
f programme *m* de traçage; programme de
poursuite; programme de dépistage
r программа *f* трассировки

* **tracer** → 9461, 9462

* **tracing** → 9459

* **tracing program** → 9462

9463 track *v*; trace *v*
d folgen; verfolgen
f suivre; tracer
r следить

9464 track; channel
d Spur *f*; Bahn *f*
f piste *f*; trace *f*
r дорожка *f*; тракт *m*

* **trackball** → 8109

* **trackball mouse** → 8109

* **tracker ball** → 8109

* **trackpad** → 9452

9465 traffic
d Verkehr *m*; Trafik *n*
f trafic *m*
r трафик *m*; поток *m* [информационного]
обмена

* **traffic analysis** → 9470

**9466 traffic count; traffic metering; traffic
measurement; peg count**
d Verkehrszählung *f*; Verkehrsmessung *f*
f comptage *m* de trafic; mesure *f* de trafic
r счёт *m* трафика; измерение *n* трафика

**9467 traffic counter; peg counter; peg meter;
traffic meter**
d Verkehrszähler *m*
f mesureur *m* de trafic; compteur *m* de trafic
r счётчик *m* трафика

9468 traffic data
d Verkehrsdaten *pl*
f données *fpl* de trafic
r данные *pl* трафика

9469 traffic data administration
d Verkehrsdatenverwaltung *f*
f administration *f* de données de trafic
r администрирование *n* данных трафика

9470 traffic [data] analysis
d Verkehrs[daten]analyse *f*;
Verkehrsauswertung *f*
f analyse *f* [de données] de trafic
r анализ *m* [данных] трафика

**9471 traffic data collection; traffic data
recording**
d Verkehrsdatenerfassung *f*
f collection *f* de données de trafic;
enregistrement *m* de données de trafic
r совокупность *f* данных трафика; набор *m*
данных трафика

* **traffic data recording** → 9471

* **traffic measurement** → 9466

* **traffic meter** → 9467

* **traffic metering** → 9466

9472 traffic routing
d Verkehrslenkung *f*
f routage *m* de trafic
r маршрутизация *f* трафика

9473 traffic routing data
d Verkehrslenkdaten *pl*
f données *fpl* de routage de trafic
r данные *pl* для маршрутизации трафика

9474 traffic simulation
d Verkehrssimulation *f*
f simulation *f* de trafic
r моделирование *n* трафика

9475 traffic statistics
d Verkehrsstatistik *f*
f statistique *f* de trafic
r статистика *f* трафика

9476 traffic trace diagram
d Verkehrsverlaufdiagramm *n*

f diagramme *m* de traçage de trafic
r диаграмма *f* слежения трафика

* **trail** → **9458**

9477 trailer label
  d Nachsatz *m*; Traileretikett *n*
  f label *m* de fin; label traîneur; étiquette *f*
     d'arrière
  r концевая метка *f*; конечная метка

* **trailing edge** → **752**

* **train** → **8440**

9478 transaction
  d Vorgang *m*; Transaktion *f*; Scheingeschäft *n*;
     Schwindelgeschäft *n*
  f transaction *f*
  r информационный обмен *m*; транзакция *f*

9479 transaction code
  d Transaktionscode *m*
  f code *m* de transaction
  r код *m* транзакции

9480 transaction file; detail file; movement file
  d Vorgangsdatei *f*; Bewegungsdatei *f*
  f fichier *m* de transactions; fichier de détails;
     fichier de mouvements
  r файл *m* транзакций; файл сообщений

9481 transaction language
  d Transaktionssprache *f*
  f langage *m* de transactions
  r язык *m* транзакций

* **transaction log** → **9483**

* **transaction management** → **9482**

9482 transaction processing; transaction
     management
  d Vorgangsverarbeitung *f*
  f traitement *m* de transactions; management *m*
     de transactions
  r обработка *f* транзакций; управление *n*
     транзакций

9483 transaction protocol; transaction log
  d Transaktionsprotokoll *n*
  f protocole *m* de transactions
  r протокол *m* транзакций

* **transceiver** → **9525**

* **transcoder** → **1805**

9484 transcoding; code conversion
  d Transcodierung *f*; Umcodierung *f*;

Codeumsetzung *f*; Kennzahlumrechnung *f*
  f transcodage *m*
  r перекодирование *n*

9485 transcribe *v*
  d umschreiben; eintragen
  f transcrire
  r перезаписывать; описывать

* **transcribing** → **9486**

9486 transcription; transcribing
  d Umschreibung *f*
  f transcription *f*
  r перезапись *f*; транскрипция *f*

9487 transducer; measuring transmitter
  d Wandler *m*; Messwandler *m*;
     Messumformer *m*
  f transducteur *m*; convertisseur *m* de mesure
  r [измерительный] преобразователь *m*;
     измерительный датчик *m*

* **transfer** → **9508**

9488 transfer *v*; **transmit** *v*
  d übertragen; senden; übermitteln
  f transférer; transmettre; lancer
  r переносить; передавать; пересылать

* **transfer channel** → **9510**

* **transfer characteristics** → **9511**

9489 transfer code
  d Übergabezeichen *n*; Übernahmecode *m*
  f code *m* de transfert
  r код *m* переноса

9490 transfer command; transfer instruction;
     transmission command
  d Übertragungsbefehl *m*; Transferbefehl *m*;
     Sendebefehl *m*
  f instruction *f* de transfert; commande *f* de
     transmission
  r команда *f* пересылки; команда передачи

9491 transfer format
  d Übertragungsformat *n*
  f format *m* de transfert
  r формат *m* переноса

* **transfer function** → **9517**

* **transfering** → **9508**

* **transfer instruction** → **9490**

* **transfer protocol** → **1957**

* **transfer rate** → 9519

9492 transfer register
 d Übernahmeregister *n*
 f registre *m* de transfert
 r регистр *m* переноса

* **transfer speed** → 9519

9493 transfer time; move time
 d Übertragungszeit *f*; Transferzeit *f*
 f temps *m* de transfert
 r время *n* передачи

* **transform** → 9496

9494 transform *v*
 d transformieren; umwandeln; umformen
 f transformer
 r преобразовывать; трансформировать

9495 transformability
 d Transformiertbarkeit *f*
 f transformabilité *f*
 r преобразуемость *f*

9496 transform[ation]
 d Umwandlung *f*; Umsetzung *f*;
   Transformation *f*
 f transformation *f*
 r преобразование *n*; трансформация *f*

* **transformational grammar** → 6964

9497 transformer
 d Transformator *m*; Umformer *m*; Übertrager *m*
 f transformateur *m*
 r преобразователь *m*; трансформатор *m*

* **transient** → 5430

9498 transient *adj*
 d vorübergehend; Einschwing-; transient
 f transitoire
 r переходный; транзитный; неустойчивый

* **transient copy** → 8691

* **transient fault** → 5042

* **transient phenomenon** → 9499

9499 transient process; transient phenomenon
 d Umschaltvorgang *m*; Einschwingvorgang *m*
 f processus *m* transitoire; phénomène *m*
   transitoire
 r переходный процесс *m*

* **transinformation** → 9523

9500 transistor
 d Transistor *m*; Halbleitertriode *f*
 f transistor *m*; triode *f* à cristal
 r транзистор *m*

9501 transistor-transistor logic; TTL
 d Transistor-Transistor-Logik *f*; TTL
 f logique *f* transistor-transistor; TTL
 r транзисторно-транзисторная логика *f*; ТТЛ

9502 transit; relay[ing]; hop
 d Transit *m*; Weiterleitung *f*
 f transit *m*
 r транзит *m*; ретрансляция *f*

9503 transition
 d Transition *f*; Übergang *m*
 f transition *f*
 r переход *m*

9504 transit network
 (a network which passes traffic between other
  networks in addition to carrying traffic for its
  own hosts)
 d Transitnetz *n*
 f réseau *m* de transit
 r транзитная сеть *f*

* **translating** → 9505

* **translating program** → 9506

* **translation** → 5264

9505 translation; translating
 d Translation *f*; Übersetzung *f*
 f translation *f*
 r трансляция *f*; сдвиг *m*

* **translation operator** → 8513

**9506 translation program; translating program;
    translator**
 d Übersetzungsprogramm *n*; Translator *m*
 f programme *m* de translation; translateur *m*
 r транслирующая программа *f*; транслятор *m*

* **translator** → 9506

9507 transliteration
 d Transliteration *f*
 f translittération *f*
 r транслитерация *f*

9508 transmission; transfer[ing]; reporting
 d Übertragung *f*; Transmission *f*; Übergabe *f*
 f transmission *f*; transfert *m*
 r передача *f*; перенос *m*

9509 transmission accuracy
 d Übertragungsgenauigkeit *f*

f précision f de transmission
r точность f передачи

9510 transmission channel; transmission link; transmission line; transfer channel; transmission path
d Übertragungskanal m; Übertragungsleitung f; Übertragungsweg m
f canal m de transmission; voie f de transmission; canal de transfert
r канал m передачи; линия f передачи

9511 transmission characteristics; transfer characteristics
d Übertragungscharakteristik f
f caractéristique f de transmission; caractéristique de transfert
r характеристика f передачи; передаточная характеристика

* **transmission command → 9490**

9512 transmission command queue
d Sendebefehlswarteschlange f
f queue f d'instructions de transmission
r очередь f команд передачи

* **transmission control → 1939**

* **transmission control character → 1940**

9513 transmission control code
d Übertragungssteuercode m
f code m de commande de transmission
r код m управления передачи

9514 transmission control protocol/Internet protocol; TCP/IP
d TCP/IP-Protokoll n
f protocole m TCP/IP
r протокол m TCP/IP

9515 transmission data; transmit[tal] data
d Sendedaten pl
f données fpl de transmission
r передаваемые данные pl

* **transmission data network → 2532**

* **transmission data system → 9144**

* **transmission delay → 1941**

9516 transmission device
d Übertragungsbaustein m; Übertragungsgerät n
f dispositif m de transmission
r устройство n передачи

* **transmission end → 3417**

9517 transmission function; transfer function
d Übertragungsfunktion f; übertragungstechnische Funktion f
f fonction f de transmission; fonction de transfert
r функция f передачи; передаточная функция

* **transmission line → 9510**

* **transmission link → 9510**

9518 transmission method
d Übertragungsverfahren n
f méthode f de transmission
r метод m передачи

* **transmission path → 9510**

* **transmission protocol → 1957**

9519 transmission rate; transmission speed; transfer speed; transfer rate
d Übertragungsgeschwindigkeit f; Übertragungsrate f; Transfergeschwindigkeit f; Transferrate f
f débit m de transmission; vitesse f de transfert; taux m de transfert
r скорость f передачи

* **transmission speed → 9519**

9520 transmission system interface
d Übertragungsschnittstelle f
f interface f de système de transmission
r интерфейс m системы передачи

* **transmit v → 9488**

9521 transmit bit timing
d Sendebittakt[ier]ung f
f synchronisation f des bits de transmission
r синхронизация f передаваемых битов

9522 transmit byte timing
d Sendebytetakt[ier]ung f
f synchronisation f des octets de transmission
r синхронизация f передаваемых байтов

* **transmit data → 9515**

* **transmittal data → 9515**

9523 transmitted information; transinformation
d übertragene Information f; Transinformation f
f information f transférée; transinformation f
r переданная информация f; трансинформация f

9524 **transmitter; sender; send device; send unit**
  d Transmitter *m*; Sender *m*; Absender *m*;
    Sendeteil *n*; Adressant *m*
  f transmetteur *m*; émetteur *m*; partie *f* émetteur;
    expéditeur *m*
  r передатчик *m*; трансмиттер *m*;
    излучатель *m*; передаточный элемент *m*

9525 **transmitter-receiver; transceiver**
  d Sender *m* und Empfänger *m*;
    Sendeempfänger *m*; Transceiver *m*
  f émetteur-récepteur *m*; transceiveur *m*
  r приёмопередатчик *m*

9526 **transparency**
  d Transparenz *f*; Durchsichtigkeit *f*
  f transparence *f*
  r прозрачность *f*

9527 **transparent**
  d transparent
  f transparent
  r прозрачный

9528 **transparent background**
  d transparenter Hintergrund *m*
  f fond *m* transparent
  r прозрачный фон *m*

9529 **transparent command**
  d transparenter Befehl *m*
  f commande *f* transparente
  r прозрачная команда *f*

9530 **transparent data**
  d transparente Daten *pl*
  f données *fpl* transparentes
  r прозрачные данные *pl*

9531 **transparent mode**
  (of data transfer)
  d Transparenzmodus *m*; transparente
    Betriebsweise *f*
  f mode *m* transparent
  r прозрачный режим *m*

9532 **transparent texture**
  d transparente Textur *f*
  f texture *f* transparente
  r прозрачная текстура *f*

9533 **transponder**
  d Transponder *m*
  f transpondeur *m*
  r транспондер *m*; преобразователь *m*
    непрерывных данных в цифровые

  * **transport** → 9534

  * **transportability** → 7127

  * **transportable** → 7129

9534 **transport[ation]; dispatch; conveyance**
  d Transport *m*; Beförderung *f*
  f transport *m*
  r транспортировка *f*; перевоз *m*

9535 **transport layer**
  d Transportschicht *f*
  f couche *f* de transport
  r транспортный уровень *m*

9536 **transport protocol**
  d Transport[schicht]protokoll *n*
  f protocole *m* [de couche] de transport
  r транспортный протокол *m*; протокол
    транспортного уровня

9537 **transputer**
  d Transputer *m*
  f transputer *m*
  r транспьютер *m*

  * **transversal** → 9538

9538 **transverse; transversal; cross**
  d transversal; Quer-
  f transversal; croisé
  r поперечный; перекрёстный

  * **trap** *v* → 1430

  * **trapezium distortion** → 5226

9539 **trap setting**
  (in a program)
  d Trap-Setzen *n*
  f création *f* de trappes
  r установка *f* ловушек

  * **trash** → 4170, 7761

  * **trash bin** → 7761

  * **traversal** → 1301

  * **treatment** → 7362

9540 **tree**
  d Baum *m*
  f arbre *m*
  r дерево *n*

9541 **tree chart**
  d Baumdiagramm *n*
  f diagramme *m* arborescent
  r древовидная диаграмма *f*

9542 **tree[-coded] menu**
  d baumförmiges Menü *n*

f menu *m* arborescent
r древовидное меню *n*

9543 tree grammar
d Baumgrammatik *f*
f grammaire *f* arborescente
r древовидная грамматика *f*

9544 tree index
d Baumindex *m*
f index *m* d'arbre
r древовидный индекс *m*

* **tree menu → 9542**

9545 tree structure
d Baumstruktur *f*
f structure *f* d'arbre; structure arborescente
r древовидная структура *f*

9546 tree-structured network
d Netz *n* mit Baumstruktur
f réseau *m* arborescent; réseau d'arbre
r сеть *f* с древовидной структурой

9547 tree view
d Baumansicht *f*
f vue *f* d'arbre; vue arborescente
r древовидное представление *n*

* **trial → 616**

9548 trial-and-error method
d Versuch-und-Irrtum-Methode *f*;
   Trial-and-Error-Methode *f*
f méthode *f* d'essais et d'erreurs
r метод *m* проб и ошибок

9549 trial pass; trial run
d Probelauf *m*; Versuchslauf *m*
f passage *m* d'essai
r пробный прогон *m*; тестовой прогон

* **trial run → 9549**

* **tributary channel → 8990**

* **tri-dimensional → 9351**

9550 trigger; flip-flop; bistable multivibrator; toggle [circuit]
d Trigger *m*; Flipflop *m*; Auslöser *m*;
   Kippstufe *f*; bistabiler Multivibrator *m*
f basculeur *m*; bascule *f*; trigger *m*;
   multivibrateur *m* bistable
r триггер *m*; триггерная схема *f*;
   мультивибратор *m* с двумя устойчивыми
   состояниями

9551 trigger button

d Auslösetaste *f*
f bouton *m* de démarrage
r кнопка *f* пуска

9552 trigger decoder
d Triggerdecod[ier]er *m*
f décodeur *m* à bascules
r триггерный дешифратор *m*

9553 triggering
d Triggerung *f*
f mise *f* en marche; lancement *m*
r запуск *m*

9554 triggering pulse; firing pulse; release pulse
d Triggerimpuls *m*
f impulsion *f* de déclenchement; impulsion de
   démarrage
r запускающий импульс *m*; пусковой
   импульс

9555 trigger level
d Triggerebene *f*
f niveau *m* du basculeur
r уровень *m* переключения

9556 trilinear filtering
d Trilinear-Filtering *n*
f filtrage *m* trilinéaire
r трилинейное фильтрирование *n*;
   трилинейная фильтрация *f*

9557 trilinear interpolator
d Trilinear-Interpolator *m*
f interpolateur *m* trilinéaire
r трилинейный интерполятор *m*

9558 trilinear mipmapping
d Trilinear-Mip-Mapping *n*
f mip-mapping *m* trilinéaire
r трилинейное mip-текстурирование *n*

9559 trilinear texture
d Trilinear-Textur *f*
f texture *f* trilinéaire
r трилинейная текстура *f*

9560 trilinear texture filtering
d Trilinear-Textur-Filtering *n*
f filtrage *m* de texture trilinéaire
r фильтрирование *n* трилинейной текстуры

* **trimmer → 9561**

9561 trimming capacitor; trimmer
d Abgleichkondensator *m*;
   Trimmer[kondensator] *m*
f trimmer *m*
r [до]настроивающий конденсатор *m*;
   триммер *m*

* **trip computer** → 284

9562 **triple buffering**
  d dreifache Pufferung *f*
  f tamponnage *m* triple
  r тройное буферирование *n*; тройная
     буферизация *f*

* **triplet** → 9355

* **tristate logic** → 9273

* **tristate output** → 9354

* **Trojan horse** → 9563

9563 **Trojan horse [program]**
     (a virus)
  d Trojanisches Pferd *n*
  f cheval *m* de Troie; programme *m* de Troie
  r троянский кон *m*

* **trouble** → 3679

* **trouble indicator** → 3498

9564 **troubleshooting**
  d Störungssuche *f*
  f recherche *f* de pannes
  r поиск *m* неисправностей

* **trouble signal** → 3687

9565 **true**
     (as logical one)
  d Wahre *n*
  f vrai *m*
  r "истина" *f*; логическая единица *f*

* **true complement** → 7582

9566 **true error**
  d wahrer Fehler *m*
  f erreur *f* vraie
  r истинная ошибка *f*

9567 **true gate**
  d Direktcodegatter *n*
  f porte *f* de code droit
  r вентиль *m* прямого кода

9568 **true proposition**
  d wahre Aussage *f*
  f proposition *f* vraie
  r истинное высказывание *n*

* **true representation** → 3689

9569 **true representation**
  d direktes Codieren *n*; Direktcodedarstellung *f*

  f représentation *f* à code droit
  r представление *n* в прямом коде

9570 **TrueType font**
  d TrueType-Schrift *f*
  f police *f* TrueType
  r TrueType-шрифт *m*

9571 **true value**
  d wahrer Wert *m*
  f valeur *f* vraie
  r истинное значение *n*

9572 **truncation**
  d Abschneiden *n*
  f tronquage *m*; troncature *f*
  r усечение *n*; отбрасывание *n*

9573 **truncation error; error of truncation**
  d Abbrechfehler *m*; Abbruchfehler *m*
  f erreur *f* de troncature
  r ошибка *f* при отбрасывании [членов];
     погрешность *f* обрыва

9574 **trunk group**
  d Leitungsbündel *m*
  f groupe *m* de voies magistral
  r магистральная группа *f* каналов связи

9575 **truth**
  d Wahrheit *f*
  f vérité *f*; véracité *f*
  r истинность *f*

9576 **truth function**
  d Wahrheitsfunktion *f*
  f fonction *f* de vérité
  r функция *f* истинности

9577 **truth table**
  d Wahrheits[werte]tabelle *f*
  f table *f* de vérité; table de valeurs vraies
  r таблица *f* истинности

9578 **truth value**
  d Wahrheitswert *m*
  f valeur *f* de vérité
  r значение *n* истинности

* **TSR program** → 7590

* **TTL** → 9501

* **TTY** → 9235

* **tumbler** → 9429

9579 **tuple**
  d Tupel *n*; Cortege *n*

f cortège *m*
r кортеж *m*

9580 tuple-structured data
d tupelstrukturierte Daten *pl*
f données *fpl* sous forme de cortèges
r данные *pl* в форме кортежей

9581 Turing computability
d Turing-Berechenbarkeit *f*
f calculabilité *f* au sens de Turing
r вычислимость *f* по Тьюрингу

* **Turing machine → 9582**

9582 Turing['s] machine
d Turing-Maschine *f*
f machine *f* de Turing
r машина *f* Тьюринга

* **turn-about time → 9583**

**9583 turnaround time; turn-about time;
reversal time**
d Umschaltzeit *f*; Umsteuerzeit *f*;
Gesamtlaufzeit *f*
f temps *m* de rotation; temps de retournement;
délai *m* de propagation aller-retour
r время *n* оборота; оборотное время; полное
время (передачи и приёма сигнала); время
реверсирования направления

9584 turnkey network
d schlüsselfertiges Netz *n*; Turnkey-Netz *n*
f réseau *m* clés en main
r сеть *f* "под ключ"

9585 turnkey system
d schlüsselfertiges System *n*;
Turnkey-System *n*
f système *m* clés en main; système disponible
pour utilisation immédiate
r система *f* "под ключ"; система, готовая к
непосредственному использованию

* **turn *v* off → 9093**

* **turn *v* on → 9094**

9586 turtle graphics
d Turtle-Grafik *f*
f graphique *m* de la tortue
r "черепашья" графика *f*

* **tutor → 9225**

* **tweening → 5890**

9587 twin screen mode
d Doppelbildschirmmodus *m*

f mode *m* double écran
r режим сдвоённого экрана

* **twisted pair → 9588**

9588 twisted pair [cable]
d Kupferdrahtleitung *f*
f câble *m* à paires torsadées
r витая пара *f*; скрученный двухжильный
провод *m*; телефонный провод

9589 two-address instruction
d Zweiadressbefehl *m*
f instruction *f* à deux adresses
r двухадресная инструкция *f*

9590 two-dimensional; bidimensional; 2D
d zweidimensional
f à deux dimensions; bidimensionnel; [en] 2D
r двумерный; двудимензионный; плоский

* **two-directional → 912**

9591 two-level memory
d Zweiebenenspeicher *m*
f mémoire *f* à deux niveaux
r двухуровневая память *f*

* **two-party line → 3220**

9592 two-pass assembler
d Zwei-Schritt-Assembler *m*
f assembleur *m* à deux passages
r двухпроходной ассемблер *m*

* **two scale → 947**

9593 two's complement; complement on two
d Zweierkomplement *n*
f complément *m* à deux; code *m*
complémentaire à deux
r дополнение *n* до двух; дополнительный
код *m* двоичного числа

* **two-sided → 920**

* **two-way → 912**

* **two-way linked list → 3133**

* **two-way mode → 3223**

* **two-way-simultaneous communication →
3221**

* **type → 1610**

9594 type
d Typ *m*

    f type *m*
    r тип *m*; вид *m*

    * **type bar → 7268**

9595 typecast
    d Typisierung *f*
    f typage *m*
    r приведение *n* типов (данных)

9596 type declaration; type specification
    d Typvereinbarung *f*
    f déclaration *f* de type
    r описание *n* типа

    * **typeface → 9598**

    * **type font → 1610**

9597 type of error
    d Fehlerart *f*
    f type *m* d'erreur
    r вид *m* ошибки; род *m* ошибки

9598 type of [font] style; typeface; font style
    d Schrifttyp *m*; Schriftform *f*; Typenart *f*
    f type *m* de caractères; œil *m* de caractère;
       espèce *f* de caractère; style *m* de jeu de
       caractères; genre *m* de caractères; relief *m* de
       caractères
    r вид *m* шрифта; начертание *n* шрифта;
       рисунок *m* шрифта

    * **type of style → 9598**

    * **type specification → 9596**

    * **type style → 1610**

    * **typewriter terminal → 9235**

U

9599 ultimate load
  d Höchstbelastung *f*; Höchstbeanspruchung *f*;
     Grenzbelastung *f*
  f charge *f* limite
  r предельная нагрузка *f*; максимально
     допустимая нагрузка

9600 ultrahigh-access memory
  d ultraschneller Speicher *m*
  f mémoire *f* [à accès] ultrarapide
  r сверхбыстродействующая память *f*

9601 ultralarge-scale integration
  d Ultrahochintegration *f*
  f intégration *f* à ultragrande échelle
  r интеграция *f* ультравысокого уровня

9602 unambiguous grammar
  d eindeutige Grammatik *f*
  f grammaire *f* non ambiguë
  r однозначная грамматика *f*

9603 unary operation; single-operand operation
  d unäre Operation *f*; unäre Verknüpfung *f*;
     Einoperanden-Operation *f*
  f opération *f* unaire; opération à opérande
     unique
  r унарная операция *f*; одноместная операция

9604 unassigned
  d nicht zugeordnet; nicht zugewiesen
  f non assigné
  r незакреплённый; неназначенный

9605 unassigned device
  d freies Gerät *n*
  f dispositif *m* non assigné
  r неназначенное устройство *n*

9606 unattended operation
  d unbediente Operation *f*; bedienungsfreier
     Betrieb *m*
  f opération *f* sans surveillance d'opérateur
  r работа *f* без надзора оператора

9607 unauthorized
  d unbefugt; unberechtigt
  f non autorisé
  r несанкционированный

9608 unauthorized access
  d unbefugter Zugriff *m*; unberechtigter Zugriff
  f accès *m* non autorisé
  r несанкционированный доступ *m*

9609 unauthorized user
  d unberechtigter Benutzer *m*; Unbefugter *m*
  f utilisateur *m* non autorisé
  r незарегистрированный пользователь *m*

9610 unavailable node
  d unerreichbarer Knoten *m*
  f nœud *m* inaccessible
  r недоступный узел *m*

**9611 unbound transmission; limitless
     transmission; infinite transmission**
  d ungebundene Transmission *f*; ungebundene
     Übertragung *f*
  f transmission *f* non limitée
  r несвязная передача *f*; неограниченная
     передача

9612 uncertain information processing
  d entkettene Informationsverarbeitung *f*;
     unsichere Datenverarbeitung *f*

f traitement *m* de l'information incertaine
r неопределённая *f* обработка информации; сомнительная обработка данных

9613 uncertainty; incertainty
d Unwahrhaftigkeit *f*; Ungewissheit *f*
f incertitude *f*
r недостоверность *f*

9614 uncertainty factor
d Ungewissheitsfaktor *f*
f coefficient *m* d'incertitude
r коэффициент *m* недостоверности

9615 uncoded input
d uncodierte Eingabe *f*
f entrée *f* non codée
r некодированный ввод *m*

9616 uncommitted logic array; ULA
d unverdrahtete Logikanordnung *f*; ULA-Baustein *m*
f assemblage *m* logique non commuté; module *m* ULA
r несвязная логическая матрица *f*

9617 uncomplemented input
d nichtinvertierender Eingang *m*
f entrée *f* non inversante
r неинвертирующий вход *m*

* **uncompress** *v* → 2679

9618 unconditional branch; unconditional jump
d unbedingte Verzweigung *f*; unbedingter Sprung *m*
f branchement *m* inconditionnel; saut *m* inconditionnel
r безусловный переход *m*

* **unconditional jump** → 9618

* **uncorrectable error** → 9692

* **uncountability** → 6225

* **undecidability** → 4938

9619 undeclared variable
d unvereinbare Variable *f*
f variable *f* non déclarée
r необъявленная переменная *f*

9620 undefined; undetermined; unidentifiable; indefinite
d undefiniert; undeterminiert
f non défini; indéfini; non déterminé; indéterminé
r недефинированный; неопределённый

9621 undefined variable
d undefinierte Variable *f*
f variable *f* non définie; variable indéfinie
r неопределённая переменная *f*

9622 undelete *v*; **unerase** *v*
d ungelöschen
f restaurer; rétablir
r отменять удаление; восстанавливать (после удаления)

9623 underflow
(of significant bits)
d Unterlauf *m*; Unterschreitung *f*
f dépassement *m* vers le bas; sous-passement *m*
r исчезновение *n*; потеря *f*

9624 underline *v*; **underscore** *v*; **emphasize** *v*
d unterstreichen
f souligner
r подчёркивать

9625 underlined text
d unterstrichener Text *m*
f texte *m* souligné
r подчёркнутый текст *m*

* **underlining** → 9627

9626 underload
d Unterlast *f*; Unterlastung *f*
f sous-charge *f*
r недогрузка *f*; неполная нагрузка *f*

* **underscore** *v* → 9624

* **underscore** → 9628

9627 underscore; underscoring; underlining
d Unterstreichung *f*; Unterstreichen *n*
f soulignement *m*
r подчёркивание *n*

9628 underscore [sign]
d Unterstreichungszeichen *n*
f signe *m* de soulignement
r знак *m* подчёркивания

* **underscoring** → 9627

* **undeterminate system** → 4765

* **undetermination** → 4764

* **undetermined** → 9620

9629 undirected
d ungerichtet
f non orienté
r ненаправленный; неориентированный

* undirected graph → 6252

9630 undisturbed one
d Lesespannung f der ungestörten Eins
f un m non perturbé
r неразрушенная единица f

9631 undisturbed zero
d Lesespannung f der ungestörten Null
f zéro m non perturbé
r неразрушенный нуль m

* undo → 9633

9632 undo v
d rückgängig machen; rückgängig erstellen;
den vorherigen Zustand wiederherstellen
f annuler; défaire
r отменять последнее действие

9633 undo[ing]
d Rückgang m
f annulation f
r возврат m; откат m; отмена f последнего
действия

9634 undoing actions
d rückgängige Wirkungen fpl
f actions fpl d'annulation
r отменяющие действия npl; возвратные
действия

* unerase v → 9622

* unformatted → 6236

* unformatted data → 6237

* unformatted record → 6238

9635 unfreeze v
d auftauen; Fixierung aufheben
f dégeler; décongeler; débloquer
r размораживать; разфиксировать; отменить
фиксацию

9636 ungroup v
d Gruppierung aufheben
f dégrouper
r разгруппировать

9637 unibus
d Unibus m; Unileitung f
f unibus m
r шинная структура f с одной шиной

9638 unicity; uniqueness
d Unität f; Eindeutigkeit f
f unicité f

r единственность f

* Unicode → 9672

9639 Unicode character
d Unicode-Zeichen n; Universalcode-Zeichen n
f caractère m Unicode
r уникодовый символ m

9640 Unicode character map
d Unicode-Zeichentabelle f
f table f de caractères Unicode
r таблица f уникодовых символов; таблица
символов шрифта Unicode

9641 Unicode character string
d Unicode-Zeichenkette f
f chaîne f de caractères Unicode
r цепочка f уникодовых символов

9642 Unicode font
d Universalcode-Schrift f
f police f Unicode
r уникодовый шрифт m

* unidentifiable → 9620

9643 unidirectional; one-directional; one-way
d unidirektional; einseitig gerichtet; Einweg-;
einfach gerichtet
f à une direction; unidirectionnel
r однонаправленный; однопроходный

9644 unidirectional bus
d Einzelrichtungsbus m
f bus m unidirectionnel
r однонаправленная шина f

9645 unidirectional dimensioning
d einseitig gerichtete Dimensionierung f
f cotation f à une direction
r однонаправленное оразмерение n

9646 unidirectional LAN
d unidirektionales lokales Netz n
f réseau m local unidirectionnel
r однонаправленная местная сеть f

9647 unidirectional printing
d unidirektionales Drucken n
f impression f unidirectionnelle
r печать f в одном направлении

9648 unification
d Unifikation f
f unification f
r унификация f

* unified bus → 1919

9649 unified messaging
d vereinheitlichte Mitteilungsübermittlung *f*
f messagerie *f* unifiée
r унифицированная передача *f* сообщений

9650 uniform
d gleichmäßig; gleichförmig; uniform
f uniforme
r равномерный; однородный; однообразный

9651 uniform code
d gleichmäßiger Code *m*; gleichförmiger Code;
   uniformer Code
f code *m* uniforme
r равномерный код *m*

9652 uniform continuity of mapping
d gleichmäßige Stetigkeit *f* einer Abbildung
f continuité *f* uniforme d'une application
r однородная непрерывность *f* отображения

9653 uniform resource locator; URL
d Adresszeile *f* für jedes beliebige
   Internet-Angebot; einheitlicher
   Quellenlokalisierer *m*
f localisateur *m* uniforme de ressource (sur
   l'Internet); repère *m* uniforme de ressource;
   adresse *f* [URL]; adresse réticulaire
r унифицированный указатель *m* ресурсов;
   единообразный определитель *m* ресурса;
   указатель URL

9654 uniform scaling
d gleichmäßige Skalierung *f*
f mise *f* à l'échelle uniforme
r однородное масштабирование *n*

9655 uniform transparency
d gleichmäßige Transparenz *f*
f transparence *f* uniforme
r равномерная прозрачность *f*

* **unilateral → 8633**

9656 uninitialized variable; unassigned variable
d nichtinitialisierte Variable *f*
f variable *f* non initialisée; variable non
   assignée
r неинициализированная переменная *f*

9657 uninstall *v*
d deinstallieren
f désinstaller
r деинсталлировать

9658 unintentional access
d unbeabsichtigter Zugriff *m*
f accès *m* non intentionnel
r непреднамеренный доступ *m*

**9659 uninterruptible power supply; UPS;
no-break power supply**
d unterbrechungsfreie Stromversorgung *f*; USV
f alimentation *f* en car de manque d'électricité;
   onduleur *m*
r беспрерывное питание *n*

9660 union
d Vereinigung *f*
f [ré]union *f*
r объединение *n*

9661 union command
d Vereinigungsbefehl *m*
f commande *f* d'union
r команда *f* объединения

* **union gate → 6572**

9662 unipolar
d unipolar; Einfachstrom-
f unipolaire
r униполярный; однополярный

9663 unipolar logic signal
d Einfachstrom-Logiksignal *n*
f signal *m* logique unipolaire
r однополярный логический сигнал *m*

9664 uniprocessing
d Univerarbeitung *f*
f unitraitement *m*; traitement *m* à un processeur
r однопроцессорная обработка *f*

9665 uniprocessor configuration
d Einprozessorkonfiguration *f*
f configuration *f* uniprocesseur
r однопроцессорная конфигурация *f*

9666 unique address
d eindeutige Adresse *f*
f adresse *f* unique
r однозначный адрес *m*

* **uniqueness → 9638**

9667 unit
   (as a measure)
d Einheit *f*; Einer *m*
f unité *f*
r единица *f*

9668 unit; block
   (as a part of construction)
d Geräteeinheit *f*; Block *m*; Baustein *m*
f unité *f*; bloc *m*; module *m*
r устройство *n*; блок *m*; модуль *m*

9669 unit digit
d Einerziffer *f*

f chiffre *m* des uns
r цифра *f* разряда единиц

9670 unity operator
   d Einsoperator *m*
   f opérateur *m* unité
   r единичный оператор *m*

   * **univalent correspondence** → 6436

**9671 universal asynchronous
      receiver/transmitter; UART**
   d universeller asynchroner
      Empfänger/Sender *m*
   f récepteur/émetteur *m* asynchrone universel
   r универсальный асинхронный
      приёмопередатчик *m*; УАПП

9672 universal code; Unicode
   d Universalcode *m*; Unicode *m*
   f code *m* universel; Unicode *m*
   r универсальный код *m*; уникод *m*
      (двухбайтовая кодировка всех алфавитов
      мира)

   * **universal filter** → 320

9673 universal serial bus; USB
   d universeller serieller Bus *m*
   f bus *m* universel sériel
   r универсальная последовательная шина *f*

   * **universal time coordinated** → 2304

   * **univibrator** → 5887

9674 Unix-to-Unix decoding; uudecoding
   d Uudecodierung *f*
   f uudécodage *m* (logiciel de décodage)
   r декодирование *n* Unix-Unix

9675 Unix-to-Unix encoding; uuencoding
      (a common Internet formatting standard for
      encoding files attached to electronic mail
      messages)
   d Uuencodierung *f*
   f uuencodage *m* (logiciel de codage)
   r кодирование *n* Unix-Unix

   * **unlabeled** → 9676

   * **unlabeled file** → 9677

   * **unlabeled statement** → 9678

9676 unlabel[l]ed
   d nichtetikettiert
   f sans label; non étiqueté
   r непомеченный

9677 unlabel[l]ed file
   d Datei *f* ohne Kennsätze
   f fichier *m* sans labels; fichier sans étiquettes
   r файл *m* без меток

9678 unlabel[l]ed statement
   d nichtmarkierte Anweisung *f*
   f instruction *f* non étiquetée
   r непомеченный оператор *m*

9679 unlatched output
   d Ausgang *m* ohne Latch[register]
   f sortie *f* sans registre verrou
   r выход *m* без [регистра-]защёлки

   * **unleaded carrier** → 5316

   * **unlimited** → 1144

9680 unload; discharge
   d Entladung *f*; Entlastung *f*
   f décharge[ment] *m*
   r разгрузка *f*; разряд *m*

   * **unlock** → 9683

9681 unlock *v*; unblock *v*; deblock *v*
   d freigeben; befreien; entsperren; entblocken
   f déverrouiller; débloquer; libérer; ouvrir
   r разблокировать; деблокировать

9682 unlocked
   d freigegeben; entsperrt
   f unverrouillé; débloqué
   r разблокированный

9683 unlock[ing]; unblock[ing]
   d Entsperrung *f*; Entsperren *n*; Entblockung *f*
   f déverrouillage *m*; déblocage *m*
   r снятие *n* блокировки; разблокирование *n*;
      деблокирование *n*

9684 unmarked
   d nichtmarkiert; unbezeichnet; nicht
      gekennzeichnet
   f sans marque; non marqué
   r немаркированный

9685 unmoved
   d unbeweglich; unbewegt; ungerührt
   f non mouvant
   r неперемещаемый

   * **unpack** → 9691

9686 unpack *v*; depacketize *v*
   d auspacken; entpacken; entpaketieren
   f déballer; dépaqueter
   r распаковывать; распаковать

9687 unpack[ag]ed; uncased
d ungepackt; ungekapselt; gehäuselos
f sans corpus; sans boîtier
r бескорпусный

9688 unpack[ag]ed circuit; uncased circuit
d ungepackte Schaltung f
f circuit m non condensé
r бескорпусная схема f

9689 unpacked
d entpackt
f dépaqueté
r распакованный

* **unpacked → 9687**

* **unpacked chip → 821**

* **unpacked circuit → 9688**

9690 unpacked format
d entpackte Form f
f format m dégroupé
r распакованный формат m

9691 unpack[ing]
d Entpacken n
f dépaquetage m
r распаковка f

* **unprotected code → 6260**

* **unrecoverable → 5137**

9692 unrecoverable error; irrecoverable error; uncorrectable error
d nichtbehebbarer Fehler m; unkorrigierbarer Fehler; unverbesserlicher Fehler
f erreur f incorrigible; erreur non éliminable; erreur irrémédiable; erreur irréparable
r невосстановляемая ошибка f; неисправимая ошибка

9693 unrestricted grammar
d unbeschränkte Grammatik f
f grammaire f sans contraintes
r грамматика f общего вида; грамматика без ограничений

* **unshared subchannel → 6270**

* **unsharp → 4149**

* **unsharped mask → 440**

* **unsharp mask → 440**

9694 unsigned number
d vorzeichenlose Zahl f

f nombre m sans signe
r число n без знака

* **unstable → 4940**

9695 unsubscribe v
d Abonnement abbestellen
f désabonner
r отказаться от подписки

9696 untestable fault
d unprüfbarer Fehler m
f défaut m non testable; défaut non vérifiable
r непроверяемый дефект m

* **unzip v → 2679**

* **unzoom → 10115**

* **unzoom v → 10114**

9697 up counter
d Aufwärtszähler m
f compteur m additif; compteur totalisateur
r суммирующий счётчик m; накапливающий счётчик

9698 updatable
d aktualisierbar; veränderlich; änderbar
f actualisable
r обновляемый; скорректированный; регенерируемый

9699 updatable data
d Änderungsdaten pl
f données fpl de renouvellement
r обновляемые данные pl

* **update → 9703**

9700 update v
d aktualisieren; ändern
f actualiser
r обновлять; актуализировать; модернизировать

9701 update cursor
d Aktualisierungscursor m
f curseur m d'actualisation
r курсор m обновления

9702 update method
d Aktualisierungsmethode f
f méthode f d'actualisation
r метод m обновления

9703 updating; update
d Aktualisierung f; Änderung f; Bugfix n
f mise f au jour; mise au niveau; actualisation f
r корректировка f; обновление n; актуализация f; модернизация f

* **up-down counter** → 8054

9704 upgrade
d Steig[er]ung *f*
f montée *f*; évolution *f* [d'un système]; mise *f* à
niveau
r надстройка *f*; подъём *m*; повышение *n*

9705 upgrade *v*
d ausbauen; aufstocken; steigern; aufrüsten;
erneuen
f augmenter
r поднимать; повышать; надстраивать

9706 upload *v*
(to send or transmit a file from one computer
to a server)
d heraufladen; hochladen
f transférer [de fichier] ver un serveur
r загружать в главную систему

9707 upper case
d Großbuchstabenregister *n*
f registre *m* supérieur
r верхний регистр *m*

9708 uppercase alphabet
d Großbuchstabenalphabet *n*
f alphabet *m* du registre supérieur
r алфавит *m* верхнего регистра

9709 uppercase letters; capital letters; caps
d Großbuchstaben *mpl*
f lettres *fpl* du registre supérieur; lettres
majuscules; majuscules *mpl*; capitales *fpl*
r буквы *fpl* верхнего регистра; прописные
буквы; большие буквы; заглавные буквы

9710 upper data bus
d Bus *m* für höherwertige Datenstellen
f bus *m* de poids forts de données
r шина *f* старших разрядов данных

9711 upper memory block; UMB
d oberer Speicherblock *m*
f bloc *m* de zone de mémoire supérieure
r блок *m* верхней памяти

* **upright format** → 7141

* **UPS** → 9659

9712 upstream
(e-slang)
d flussaufwärts; stromaufwärts
f en amont
r выше по течению; вверх по течению (о
передаче информации по цепочке
серверов)

* **uptime** → 3313

* **urban trunk network** → 5805

* **URL** → 9653

* **usage** → 9713

* **USB** → 9673

9713 use; utilization; usage; using
d Benutzung *f*; Nutzung *f*; Auslastung *f*
f usage *m*; utilisation *f*
r пользование *n*; употребление *n*

* **Usenet** → 9738

9714 user; consumer
d Benutzer *m*; Anwender *m*; Nutzer *m*
f utilisateur *m*; usager *m*
r пользователь *m*

* **user access** → 9734

**9715 user account; account; accounting
information**
d Benutzerkonto *n*; Account *m*
f compte *m* [utilisateur]
r счёт *m*; учётная информация *f* [о
пользователе]

9716 user agent; agent; soft robot; robot; bot
d Agent *m*; Bot *m*; Roboter *m*; Handelnde *m*
f agent *m*; bot *m*; robot *m*; logiciel *m*
automatique
r агент *m* [пользователя]; программный
агент; программа-агент *f*

9717 user-available memory
d nutzerorientierter Speicher *m*
f mémoire *f* à la portée d'utilisateur
r память *f*, доступная пользователю

9718 user configuration
d Teilnehmerkonfiguration *f*
f configuration *f* d'utilisateur
r конфигурация *f* пользователя

9719 user data conversion
d Benutzerdatenkonvertierung *f*
f conversion *f* de données d'utilisateur
r преобразование *n* данных пользователя

9720 user datagram protocol; UDP
d Teilnehmerdatagramm-Protokoll *n*;
Benutzerdatagramm-Protokoll *n*
f protocole *m* de datagrammes d'utilisateur;
protocole UDP
r протокол *m* пользовательских дейтаграмм;
протокол UDP

9721 user data packet
d Benutzerdatenpaket n
f paquet m de données d'utilisateur
r пакет m данных пользователя

9722 user-defined
d benutzerdefiniert; benutzerbestimmt
f défini par l'utilisateur
r определяемый пользователем

9723 user[-defined] library
d Anwenderbibliothek f
f bibliothèque f de l'utilisateur
r библиотека f пользователя

9724 user-dependent
d benutzerabhängig
f dépendant par l'utilisateur
r зависимый от пользователя

9725 user-dependent parameter
d benutzerabhängiger Parameter m
f paramètre m dépendant par l'utilisateur
r параметр m, зависимый от пользователя

9726 user-friendliness
d Anwenderfreundlichkeit f;
Benutzerfreundlichkeit f
f commodité f pour l'utilisateur
r удобство n для пользователя

9727 user-friendly; easy-to-use; philoxenic
d benutzerfreundlich
f amical [pour l'utilisateur]
r ориентированный на пользователя;
дружественный [к пользователю];
удобный для пользователя

9728 user-friendly interface
d benutzerfreundliche Schnittstelle f
f interface f amicale pour l'utilisateur
r дружественный интерфейс m

9729 user group
d Benutzergruppe f; Anwendergruppe f
f groupe m d'utilisateurs
r группа f пользователей

* **userid** → 9730

* **user ID** → 9730

9730 user identificator; userid; user ID
d Benutzerkennzeichen n;
Benutzeridentifizierer m; Benutzerkennung f
f identificateur m d'utilisateur
r идентификатор m пользователя

9731 user-input function
d Benutzereingangsfunktion f

f fonction f d'entrée de l'utilisateur
r функция f пользовательского ввода

9732 user interface
d Benutzerschnittstelle f;
Anwenderschnittstelle f
f interface f de l'utilisateur
r пользовательский интерфейс m

* **user library** → 9723

9733 user name; login name; screen name
(an address that designates a personal
account)
d Benutzername m; Benutzeridentität f;
registrierter Name m
f nom m d'utilisateur; nom enregistré; nom de
log; nom de connexion
r имя n пользователя; учётное имя;
зарегистрированное имя

9734 user [network] access
d Anwenderzugriff m
f accès m d'utilisateur au réseau
r доступ m пользователя сети

9735 user options
d Anwenderoptionen fpl
f options fpl d'utilisateur
r возможности fpl, доступные пользователю

9736 user-positioned text
d vom Benutzer positionierter Text m
f texte m positionné par l'utilisateur
r текст m, позиционированный
пользователем

9737 user-programmable product
d anwenderprogrammierbares Produkt n
f produit m programmable par l'utilisateur
r изделие n, программируемое
пользователем

9738 user's network; Usenet
(network for discussions)
d Netz n für Benutzer; Usenet n
f Usenet m (réseau offrant un service de
discussion asynchrone mondial appelé Usenet
News)
r пользовательская сеть f; сеть Usenet

9739 user-visible register
d für einen Anwender zugängliches Register n
f registre m accessible par l'utilisateur
r регистр m, доступный пользователю

* **using** → 9713

* **UTC** → 2304

* **utility** → **8450**

9740 utility code
d Merkmalcode *m*
f code *m* utilitaire
r вспомагательный код *m*

9741 utility function
d Nutzenfunktion *f*; Dienstfunktion *f*
f fonction *f* d'utilité
r утилитная функция *f*; служебная функция

* **utility program** → **8450**

9742 utility theory
d Utilitytheorie *f*
f théorie *f* de l'utilité
r теория *f* выгоды

* **utilization** → **9713**

* **utilization layer** → **469**

* **uudecoding** → **9674**

* **uuencoding** → **9675**

V

*   vacant → 1044

9743 **vacant register**
    d Unbesetztregister *n*
    f registre *m* vacant
    r регистр *m* занятости

*   **vagueness** → 355

*   **validate** *v* → 2154

*   **validation** → 666

9744 **valid data; clean data**
    d gültige Daten *pl*; fehlerlose Daten
    f données *fpl* valables; données valides
    r правильные данные *pl*; достоверные
         данные

9745 **validity**
    d Gültigkeit *f*; Echtheit *f*; Validität *f*
    f validité *f*
    r достоверность *f*; справедливость *f*

*   **valuation** → 3528

*   **valuator** → 9746

9746 **valuator [device]**
    d Wertgeber *m*
    f comparateur *m*
    r блок *m* вычисления или ввода значений;
         блок присваивания значений

9747 **value; magnitude**
    d Wert *m*; Größe *f*
    f valeur *f*; grandeur *f*
    r величина *f*; значение *n*

9748 **value-added network; VAN**
    d Netz *n* mit gesteigertem Gebrauchswerk;
         Netz mit erweiterten
         Übertragungsmöglichkeiten
    f réseau *m* aux services complémentaires;
         réseau à valeur ajoutée; RVA
    r сеть *f* с дополнительными услугами

*   **VAN** → 9748

9749 **variability**
    d Variabilität *f*
    f variabilité *f*
    r изменчивость *f*; разнообразие *n*

9750 **variable**
    d Variable *f*; Veränderliche *f*
    f variable *f*
    r переменная *f*

9751 **variable attribute**
    d veränderliches Attribut *n*
    f attribut *m* variable
    r переменный атрибут *m*

9752 **variable block**
    d veränderlicher Block *m*
    f bloc *m* de variables
    r блок *m* переменных

9753 **variable coefficient**
    d veränderlicher Faktor *m*
    f coefficient *m* variable
    r переменный коэффициент *m*

9754 **variable frequency display; VFD**
    d Variable-Frequenz-Monitor *m*; VFD
    f afficheur *m* de fréquence variable
    r дисплей *m* с переменной частотой

9755 **variable index; running index**
    d variabler Index *m*
    f indice *m* variable; indice courant
    r переменный индекс *m*; текущий индекс;
         пробегающий индекс

9756 **variable length block**
    d Block *m* veränderlicher Länge
    f bloc *m* de longueur variable
    r блок *m* переменной длины

9757 **variable-length code**
    d Code *m* mit variabler Länge
    f code *m* à longueur variable
    r неравномерный код *m*

9758 **variable-length operation**
    d Operation *f* mit Wörtern variabler Länge
    f opération *f* en longueur variable
    r операция *f* со словами переменной длины

*   **variable point** → 8161

9759 **variable range**
    d Variablenbereich *m*
    f domaine *m* des valeurs de variable
    r область *f* значений переменной

9760 **variable units**
    d veränderliche Einheiten *fpl*
    f unités *fpl* variables
    r переменные единицы *fpl*

9761 variant
d Variante *f*
f variante *f*
r вариант *m*

9762 variation
d Variation *f*
f variation *f*
r вариация *f*

* **VC → 9854**

* **VDU → 9894**

* **VE → 9862**

9763 vector
d Vektor *m*
f vecteur *m*
r вектор *m*

9764 vector address
d Einsprungsadresse *f*; Vektoradresse *f*
f adresse *f* vectorielle
r адрес *m* вектора

9765 vector[-based] image; vector pattern
d vektorisiertes Bild *n*; Vektorbild *n*
f image *f* vectorielle
r векторное изображение *n*

9766 vector calculus
d Vektorrechnung *f*
f calcul *m* vectoriel
r векторное исчисление *n*

9767 vector computer
d Feldrechner *m*; Vektorrechner *m*
f ordinateur *m* vectoriel
r векторный компьютер *m*

9768 vector display
d Vektor-Display *n*
f écran *m* vectoriel
r векторный дисплей *m*

9769 vector[ed] interrupt
d Vektorinterrupt *m*; gerichtete Unterbrechung *f*
f interruption *f* vectorisée; interruption à vecteur
r векторное прерывание *n*

* **vector font → 8192**

9770 vector graphics; scalable graphics
d Vektorgrafik *f*
f graphique *m* vectoriel
r векторная графика *f*

* **vector image → 9765**

* **vector interrupt → 9769**

9771 vector memory
d Vektorspeicher *m*
f mémoire *f* vectoriel
r векторная память *f*

* **vector pattern → 9765**

* **vector processor → 5690**

9772 Veitch diagram
d Veitch-Diagramm *n*
f diagramme *m* de Veitch
r диаграмма *f* Вейча

* **velocity → 8774**

* **vendor → 9057**

9773 Venn diagram
d Venn-Diagramm *n*
f diagramme *m* d'Euler-Venn
r диаграмма *f* Венна

* **ventilation unit → 2301**

* **ventilator → 2301**

* **verb → 1912**

* **verbal → 8761**

* **verbal input → 8766**

* **verbal output → 8768**

9774 verbal request
d verbale Anforderung *f*
f interrogation *f* verbale
r устный запрос *m*

* **verification → 1646**

9775 verifier
d Prüfer *m*; Lochprüfer *m*
f vérificatrice *f*; vérificateur *m*
r контрольник *m*; верификатор *m*

* **verify *v* → 1647**

9776 version; release
(a variant)
d Ausgabe *f*; Herausgabe *f*; Freigabeversion *f*; Version *f*
f version *f*; livraison *f*; révision *f*
r выпуск *m*; версия *f*; редакция *f*

9777 version number
d Versionsnummer *f*

f numéro *m* de version
r номер *m* версии

* **vertex** → 6165

* **vertex of a graph** → 6170

9778 vertical bar
(|)
d vertikaler Strich *m*
f barre *f* verticale
r вертикальная черта *f*

* **vertical format** → 7141

* **vertical line spacing** → 5037

9779 vertical list box
d vertikales Listenfeld *n*
f zone *f* de liste déroulante verticale
r вертикальное поле *n* списка

9780 vertical microprogramming
d vertikale Mikroprogrammierung *f*
f microprogrammation *f* verticale
r вертикальное микропрограммирование *n*

9781 vertical parity
d Querparität *f*
f parité *f* verticale
r вертикальная чётность *f*

9782 vertical parity check; lateral parity check
d vertikale Paritätskontrolle *f*;
Querparitätsprüfung *f*
f contrôle *m* de parité vertical
r вертикальный контроль *m* по чётности

9783 vertical parity error
d Querparitätsfehler *m*
f erreur *f* de parité verticale
r вертикальная ошибка *f* по чётности

9784 vertical redundancy check; VRC
d Querredundanzprüfung *f*
f contrôle *m* de redondance vertical
r вертикальный контроль *m* избыточности

* **vertical resolution** → 9785

9785 vertical resolution [capability]
d vertikales Auflösungsvermögen *n*;
Vertikalauflösungsvermögen *n*
f résolution *f* verticale
r разрешающая способность *f* по вертикали;
вертикальная разрешающая способность

9786 vertical ruler
d vertikales Lineal *n*
f règle *f* verticale

r вертикальная измерительная линейка *f*

9787 vertical scanning
d vertikale Abtastung *f*
f balayage *m* vertical
r вертикальная развёртка *f*; кадровая
развёртка

* **vertical screen partitioning** → 9788

9788 vertical screen split; vertical screen partitioning
d vertikale Teilung *f* des Bildshirms
f splittage *m* d'écran vertical
r вертикальное расщепление *n* экрана

9789 vertical scroll bar; vertical scroll line
d vertikale Bildlaufleiste *f*; vertikaler
Rollbalken *m*; vertikaler
Verschiebenbalken *m*
f barre *f* de défilement verticale; barre de
déplacement verticale
r вертикальная линейка *f* просмотра

* **vertical scroll** → 9790

9790 vertical scroll[ing]
(of screen image)
d vertikale Bild[schirmzeilen]verschiebung *f*
f défilement *m* vertical; déroulement *m* vertical
r вертикальная прокрутка *f*; вертикальное
прокручивание *n*; вертикальное
перемещение *n*

* **vertical scroll line** → 9789

9791 vertical split bar
d vertikaler Fensterteiler *m*
f barre *f* de fractionnement verticale
r вертикальная линейка *f* разбиения;
вертикальная разделительная линейка

* **vertical tab** → 9792

9792 vertical tab[ulation character]
d Vertikaleinstellungszeichen *n*; vertikaler
Tabulator *m*
f caractère *m* de tabulation verticale
r знак *m* вертикальной табуляции

9793 vertical toolbar
d vertikaler Werkzeugstreifen *m*
f barre *f* d'outils verticale
r вертикальная панель *f* инструментов

9794 vertical visual selector
d vertikales visuelles Auswahlfeld *n*
f sélecteur *m* visuel vertical
r вертикальный визуальный селектор *m*

9795 very large-scale integration; VLSI
  d Großbereichsintegration *f*; VLSI
  f intégration *f* à très grande échelle; intégration
       extrême
  r интеграция *f* сверхвысокого уровня;
       сверхбольшая интеграция

  *   **VESA → 9813**

  *   **VFAT → 9864**

  *   **VFD → 9754**

  *   **VF generator → 8773**

  *   **VGA → 9820**

  *   **VGA output connector → 3734**

9796 video acceleration
  d Videobeschleunigung *f*
  f accélération *f* vidéo
  r видеоускорение *n*

  *   **video accelerator → 9797**

9797 video accelerator [card]
  d Videobeschleuniger *m*
  f carte *f* vidéo accélérée; accélérateur *m* vidéo
  r видеоускоритель *m*; видео-акселератор *m*;
       плата *f* видеоускорителя

9798 videoamplifier
  d Videoverstärker *m*
  f amplificateur *m* vidéo
  r видеоусилитель *m*

9799 video applications
  d Videoanwendungen *fpl*
  f vidéo-applications *fpl*
  r видео-приложения *npl*

9800 video buffer
  d Bildpuffer *m*
  f tampon *m* vidéo
  r видео-буфер *m*

9801 videobus
  d Videobus *m*
  f bus *m* vidéo
  r шина *f* видеосигналов

9802 video camera
  d Videokamera *f*
  f vidéocaméra *f*
  r видеокамера *f*

9803 videocapture
  d Videoerfassung *f*

  f capture *f* vidéo; acquisition *f* vidéo
  r видеозахват *m*; видеоулавливание *n*

  *   **videocard → 9809**

  *   **videocasque → 4421**

9804 videoclip
  d Videoclip *n*
  f vidéoclip *m*; clip *m* vidéo
  r видеоклип *m*

  *   **video coding → 9814**

  *   **videocommunication → 9909**

9805 video compatibility
  d Videoverträglichkeit *f*
  f vidéo-compatibilité *f*
  r видеосовместимость *f*

9806 video conference
  d Videokonferenz *f*
  f vidéoconférence *f*
  r видеоконференция *f*

  *   **video configuration → 9815**

  *   **videodata → 9838**

9807 video digitizer
  d Video-Digitalisierer *m*
  f numériseur *m* vidéo; digitalisateur *m* vidéo
  r устройство *n* оцифровки
       видеоизображений

9808 videodisk
  d Videodisk *f*
  f vidéodisque *m*
  r видеодиск *m*

  *   **video display → 3020**

  *   **video display board → 9809**

**9809 video display card; video display board;
       display card; videocard; graphics card**
  d Videokarte *f*; Grabber-Karte *f*;
       Bildschirmadapter *m*
  f carte *f* vidéo; carte graphique
  r видеокарта *f*; видеоплата *f*; графическая
       плата *f*; графическая карта *f*

9810 video display filter; monitor filter
  d Gewebefilter *m*; Bildschirmfilter *m*
  f filtre *m* d'écran
  r экранный фильтр *m*

9811 video display processor; display processor
  d Bildschirmprozessor *m*; Displayprozessor *m*

    f processeur *m* de gestion de l'affichage;
    processeur d'afficheur
    r дисплейный процессор *m*

9812 video driver
    d Videotreiber *m*
    f pilote *m* vidéo
    r видеодрайвер *m*

9813 Video Electronics Standards Association;
    VESA
    d Zusammenschluss *m* von
    Grafik-Standard-Herstellen
    f Association *f* des standards en
    vidéo-électronique
    r Ассоциация *f* стандартов по
    видеоэлектронике; Ассоциация VESA

9814 video [en]coding
    d Videocodierung *f*
    f vidéocodage *m*; codage *m* vidéo
    r видеокодирование *n*

9815 video equipment; video configuration
    d Video-Ausrüstung *f*; Videogeräte *npl*
    f équipement *m* vidéo
    r видео-оборудование *n*

9816 video file
    d Videodatei *f*
    f fichier *m* vidéo
    r видео-файл *m*

9817 videogame
    d Videospiel *n*
    f jeu *m* vidéo
    r видеоигра *f*

9818 videogenerator
    d Video[signal]generator *m*
    f générateur *m* vidéo
    r генератор *m* видеосигналов

    * **videogram** → **651**

9819 videographics
    d Videografik *f*
    f graphique *m* vidéo
    r видеографика *f*

9820 videographics adapter; videographics
    array; VGA
    d VGA-Standard *m*
    f carte *f* graphique vidéo; norme *f* VGA
    r видеографическая матрица *f*; стандарт *m*
    VGA

    * **videographics array** → **9820**

    * **video hard copy unit** → **6953**

    * **videoimage** → **9827**

9821 video input
    d Videoeingang *m*
    f entrée *f* vidéo
    r вход *m* видеоданных

9822 video logic
    d Videologik *f*
    f logique *f* vidéo
    r видео-логика *f*

9823 video memory
    d Videospeicher *m*
    f mémoire *f* vidéo
    r видео-память *f*; память *f* видеоданных

9824 video on demand; on-demand video
    d Video *n* auf Abruf; Video auf Nachforderung;
    mitlaufendes Video
    f vidéo *m* par requête; vidéo à la demande
    r заказное видео *n*

9825 video on the Web
    d Video *n* auf Web
    f vidéo *m* sur le Web
    r видео *n* в Web

9826 video output
    d Videoausgang *m*
    f sortie *f* vidéo
    r выход *m* видеоданных

9827 video picture; videoimage
    d Fernsehbild *n*; Videobild *n*
    f image *f* vidéo
    r видеоизображение *n*

9828 video printer
    d Videodrucker *m*
    f vidéo-imprimante *f*; imprimante *f* vidéo
    r видеопринтер *m*

9829 videorecord
    d Videosatz *m*
    f vidéo-écriture *f*
    r видеозапись *f*

9830 video recorder
    d Videorecorder *m*; Videoaufzeichnungsgerät *n*
    f enregistreur *m* vidéo
    r устройство *n*, записывающее
    видеосигналы

    * **videoscan document reader** → **6540**

9831 video scanner
    d Bildscanner *m*
    f scanner *m* vidéo
    r видео-сканер *m*

9832 video signal
  d Videosignal *n*; Bildsignal *n*
  f signal *m* vidéo; vidéosignal *m*
  r видеосигнал *m*

9833 video telephone
  d Bildtelefon *n*
  f vidéotéléphone *m*
  r видеотелефон *m*

9834 videotexture
  d Videotextur *f*
  f vidéo-texture *f*
  r видео-текстура *f*

9835 video wall
  d Videowand *f*
  f mur *m* vidéo
  r видеостена *f*

9836 videoware
  d Videosoftware *f*
  f vidéociel *m*; logiciel *m* vidéo
  r видео-софтуер *m*

9837 view
  d Ansicht *f*
  f vue *f*
  r вид *m*

9838 viewdata; videodata
  d Videodaten *pl*
  f vidéodonnées *fpl*
  r видеоданные *pl*

  * **viewer → 1208**

  * **viewing → 9897**

9839 view manager
  d Ansicht-Manager *m*
  f gestionnaire *m* de vues
  r менажер *m* представлений

9840 view menu
  d Ansichtmenü *n*
  f menu *m* de représentation
  r меню *n* представления

9841 view menu items
  d Ansichtmenüelemente *npl*
  f éléments *mpl* de menu de représentation
  r элементы *mpl* меню представления

9842 viewport
  d Ansichtfenster *n*; Darstellungsfeld *n*
  f clôture *f*
  r область *f* просмотра; окно *n* просмотра;
     видовой экран *m*

9843 vignetting
  d Vignetten *n*; Vignettierung *f*
  f vignettage *m*
  r образование *n* виньеток

  * **violation → 2491**

  * **viral infection → 9883**

9844 virgin medium
  d unvorbereiteter Datenträger *m*
  f porteur *m* [de données] vierge; support *m* non
     formaté
  r чистый носитель *m*; неформатированный
     носитель

9845 virtual
  d virtuell
  f virtuel
  r виртуальный

9846 virtual actor
  d virtueller Akteur *m*
  f acteur *m* virtuel
  r виртуальный актор *m*

9847 virtual addressing
  d virtuelle Adressierung *f*
  f adressage *m* virtuel
  r виртуальная адресация *f*

9848 virtual address space
  d virtueller Adressraum *m*
  f espace *m* d'adresses virtuelles
  r пространство *n* виртуальных адресов

9849 virtual agent
  d virtueller Agent *m*
  f agent *m* virtuel
  r виртуальный агент *m*

9850 virtual architecture
  d virtuelle Architektur *f*
  f architecture *f* virtuelle
  r виртуальная архитектура *f*

9851 virtual art
  d virtuelle Kunst *f*
  f art *m* virtuel
  r виртуальное искусство *n*

9852 virtual camera
  d virtuelle Kamera *f*
  f caméra *f* virtuelle
  r виртуальная камера *f*

9853 virtual channel
  d virtueller Kanal *m*
  f canal *m* virtuel
  r виртуальный канал *m*

9854 virtual circuit; VC
  d virtuelle Schaltung *f*
  f circuit *m* virtuel
  r виртуальная схема *f* [связи потребителей]

9855 virtual circuit protocol
  d Protokoll *n* der virtuellen Verbindung
  f protocole *m* de circuit virtuel
  r протокол *m* виртуальной схемы [связи]

9856 virtual community
  d virtuelle Gemeinschaft *f*; virtuelle Gemeinde *f*
  f communauté *f* virtuelle
  r виртуальное общество *n*

  * **virtual computer** → 9868

9857 virtual connection
  d virtuelle Verbindung *f*
  f connexion *f* virtuelle
  r виртуальное соединение *n*

9858 virtual corporation
  d virtuelle Firma *f*
  f firme *f* virtuelle
  r виртуальная фирма *f*

9859 virtual creatures
  d virtuelle Schöpfungen *fpl*
  f créatures *fpl* virtuelles
  r виртуальные создания *npl*

9860 virtual 3D environment
  d virtuelle 3D-Umgebung *f*
  f environnement *m* virtuel 3D
  r виртуальное 3D пространство *n*

9861 virtual disk; RAM disk
  d virtuelle Disk *f*; virtuelles Laufwerk *n*
  f disque *m* virtuel
  r виртуальный диск *m*; псевдодиск *m*

9862 virtual environment; VE
  d virtuelle Umgebung *f*
  f environnement *m* virtuel
  r виртуальная среда *f*

9863 virtual environment interface
  d Schnittstelle *f* der virtuellen Umgebung
  f interface *f* d'environnement virtuel
  r интерфейс *m* виртуального пространства

9864 virtual file allocation table; VFAT
  d virtuelle Tabelle *f* der Dateizuweisungen
  f table *f* d'allocation de fichiers virtuelle
  r виртуальная таблица *f* размещения файлов

9865 virtual imagery
  d virtuelle Abbildung *f*
  f imagerie *f* virtuelle
  r виртуальные изображения *npl*

9866 virtuality
  d Virtualität *f*
  f virtualité *f*
  r виртуальность *f*

9867 virtualization
  d Virtualisierung *f*
  f virtualisation *f*
  r виртуализация *f*

9868 virtual machine; virtual computer
  d virtueller Computer *m*
  f machine *f* virtuelle
  r виртуальная [вычислительная] машина *f*

9869 virtual mark
  d virtuelle Marke *f*
  f marque *f* virtuelle
  r виртуальная метка *f*

9870 virtual memory; virtual stor[ag]e
  d virtueller Speicher *m*
  f mémoire *f* virtuelle
  r виртуальная память *f*

9871 virtual network
  d virtuelles Netz *n*
  f réseau *m* virtuel
  r виртуальная сеть *f*

9872 virtual partition
  d virtuelle Zerlegung *f*
  f partition *f* virtuelle
  r виртуальный раздел *m*

9873 virtual printer
  d virtueller Drucker *m*
  f imprimante *f* virtuelle
  r виртуальный принтер *m*

  * **virtual pushbutton** → 5359

9874 virtual reality; VR
  d virtuelle Realität *f*
  f réalité *f* virtuelle; RV
  r виртуальная реальность *f*

  * **virtual reality language** → 9875

9875 virtual reality [modeling] language; VRML
  d Sprache *f* der Modellierung der virtuellen Realität
  f langage *m* de modélisation de la réalité virtuelle
  r язык *m* моделирования виртуальной реальности; язык VRML

9876 virtual representation
  d virtuelle Darstellung f
  f représentation f virtuelle
  r виртуальное представление n

9877 virtual ring topology
  d virtuelle Ringtopologie f
  f topologie f en anneau virtuelle
  r виртуальная кольцевая топология f

9878 virtual screen
  d virtueller Bildschirm m
  f écran m virtuel
  r виртуальный экран m

9879 virtual server
  d virtueller Server m
  f serveur m virtuel
  r виртуальный сервер m

  * virtual storage → 9870

  * virtual store → 9870

9880 virtual telecommunication access method;
       VTAM
  d virtuelle
       Telekommunikation-Zugriffsmethode f
  f méthode f d'accès de télécommunication
       virtuelle
  r виртуальный телекоммуникационный
       метод m доступа

9881 virtual vision
  d virtuelle Vision f; virtuelles Sehen n
  f vision f virtuelle
  r виртуальное зрение n

9882 virtual world
  d virtuelle Welt f
  f monde m virtuel; univers m virtuel
  r виртуальный мир m

  * virus → 2106

9883 virus contamination; virus infection; viral
       infection; infection
  d Virusverletzung f; Viruskontamination f
  f contamination f par virus; infection f virale;
       infection par virus
  r заражение n [вирусом]

  * virus-detection program → 447

9884 virus hoax
  d Virusfehlalarm m; Virusfalschmeldung f
  f virus m canular; canular m
  r подделка f вируса

  * virus infection → 9883

  * virus-protection program → 447

9885 virus-removal software; virus remover
  d Virus-Entfernungssoftware f
  f logiciel m de suppression de virus; logiciel
       d'élimination de virus
  r программное обеспечение n уничтожения
       вирусов; уничтожитель m вирусов

  * virus remover → 9885

9886 virus-specific detection program
  d spezifisches Antivirusprogramm n
  f programme m de détection de virus
       spécifique; antivirus m spécifique
  r программа f обнаруживания конкретного
       вируса

9887 visibility
  d Visibilität f; Sicht f; Anschaulichkeit f
  f visibilité f
  r видимость f; наглядность f

9888 visibility system; vision system; visual
       system
  d Visionssystem n; Computervisionssystem n;
       visuelles Erkennungssystem n; Sehsystem n;
       visuelles System n
  f système m de vision; système visuel
  r система f машинного зрения; визуальная
       система

9889 visible
  d sichtbar
  f visible
  r видимый

  * visible signal → 6551

9890 vision
  d Vision f; Sehen n
  f vision f
  r [техническое] зрение n

  * vision system → 9888

9891 vision test
  d Sehprüfung f
  f essai m de vision
  r проверка f машинного зрения

  * visitor book → 4350

9892 visual
  d visuell; anschaulich
  f visuel
  r визуальный; наглядный

  * visual communication → 9909

* **visual conference** → 4124

9893 visual database
d visuelle Datenbasis *f*
f base *f* de données visuelles
r база *f* визуальных данных;
визуализационная база данных

9894 visual display unit; VDU
(dumb terminals and intelligent terminals)
d visuelles Darstellungsgerät *n*
f unité *f* d'affichage visuel
r устройство *n* визуального представления

9895 visual element
d visuelles Element *n*
f élément *m* visuel
r визуальный элемент *m*

9896 visual interpretation; visual representation
d anschauliche Deutung *f*; Veranschaulichung *f*
f représentation *f* visuelle
r наглядное представление *n*; наглядное
истолкование *n*

9897 visualization; viewing
d Visualisierung *f*; Sichtbarmachung *f*;
Besichtigung *f*
f visualisation *f*; prise *f* de vue; visionnement *m*
r визуализация *f*; выдавливание *n*

9898 visualization algorithm
d Visualisierungsalgorithmus *m*
f algorithme *m* de visualisation
r алгоритм *m* визуализации

9899 visualization application
d Visualisierungsanwendung *f*
f application *f* de visualisation
r визуализационное приложение *n*

9900 visualization clock
d Anzeigetakt *m*
f horloge *f* de visualisation
r такт *m* визуализации

9901 visualization hardware
d Visualisierungshardware *f*
f matériel *m* de visualisation
r аппаратное обеспечение *n* визуализации

9902 visualization system
d Visualisierungssystem *n*
f système *m* de visualisation
r визуализационная система *f*

9903 visualization task
d Visualisierungsaufgabe *f*
f tâche *f* de visualisation
r задача *f* визуализации

9904 visualization toolkit; VTK
d Visualisierung-Werkzeugsatz *m*
f kit *m* d'instruments de visualisation
r инструментальный набор *m* визуализации

9905 visual realism
d visueller Realismus *m*
f réalisme *m* visuel
r визуальный реализм *m*

9906 visual reality
d visuelle Realität *f*
f réalité *f* visuelle
r визуальная реальность *f*

* **visual representation** → 9896

9907 visual selector
d visuelles Auswahlfeld *n*
f sélecteur *m* visuel
r визуальный селектор *m*

* **visual signal** → 6551

9908 visual simulation
d visuelle Simulation *f*
f simulation *f* visuelle
r визуальная симуляция *f*

* **visual system** → 9888

**9909 visual [tele]communication;
videocommunication; image
communication; picture communication**
d Bild[tele]kommunikation *f*; visuelle
Kommunikation *f*; Video-Kommunikation *f*
f [télé]communication *f* visuelle;
communication d'images;
vidéocommunication *f*
r видеосвязь *f*; визуальная связь *f*;
визуальная коммуникация *f*;
видеокоммуникация *f*

* **VLSI** → 9795

* **vocal data** → 8724

* **vocoder** → 9911

9910 voice analyzer
d Sprachanalysator *m*
f analyseur *m* de la parole
r анализатор *m* речи

9911 voice coder; vocoder
d Sprachcodierer *m*; Vocoder *m*;
Sprachverschlüsseler *m*
f vocodeur *m*
r устройство *n* речевого вывода; вокодер *m*

9912 voice digitalization; speech digitalization
  d Sprachdigitalisierung *f*
  f digitalisation *f* d'un signal vocal
  r цифровое преобразование *n* звукового
      сигнала

  * **voice encoding** → **8764**

  * **voice encryption** → **8764**

  * **voice file** → **8725**

  * **voice input** → **8766**

9913 voice-mail
  d Sprachpost
  f messagerie *f* vocale; courrier *m* vocal
  r речевая почта *f*; голосовая почта;
      телефонный автоответчик *m*

  * **voice output** → **8768**

  * **voice port adapter** → **9914**

9914 voice port card; voice port adapter
  d Sprachportkarte *f*
  f carte *f* d'accès de diffuseur d'annonces
  r плата *f* речевого порта

  * **voice recognition** → **8769**

  * **voice response** → **8770**

9915 voice server
  d Sprachserver *m*
  f serveur *m* vocal
  r сервер *m* речевых сообщений

  * **voice synthesis** → **8771**

9916 voice-synthesis chip; speech-synthesis chip
  d Sprachsynthetisatorchip *m*
  f circuit *m* de synthèse de la parole
  r микросхема *f* синтезатора речи

  * **void** → **1044**

9917 volatile
  d flüchtig; energieabhängig
  f volatil
  r энергозависимый; непостоянный;
      изменчивый

9918 volatile information
  d flüchtige Information *f*; unbeständige
      Information
  f information *f* volatile
  r энергозависимая информация *f*

  * **volatile memory** → **3425**

9919 volatility
  d Flüchtigkeit *f*; Energieabhängigkeit *f*
  f volatilité *f*
  r энергозависимость *f*

9920 voltage-to-digital converter
  d Spannung-Code-Wandler *m*;
      Spannung-Code-Umsetzer *m*
  f convertisseur *m* de tension en code
      numérique
  r преобразователь *m* напряжения в код

9921 volume
      (of a book, a catalog or a memory)
  d Volumen *n*
  f volume *m*; tome *m*
  r том *m*

9922 volume; bulk
  d Volumen *n*; Rauminhalt *m*
  f volume *m*
  r объём *m*

9923 volume [cell] element; voxel; 3D pixel
  d Voxel *n*
  f élément *m* de volume; pixel *m* 3D; voxel *m*
  r элемент *m* объёма; воксел *m*

  * **volume data** → **9925**

  * **volume element** → **9923**

9924 volume label
  d Datenträgerkennsatz *m*; Datenträgeretikett *n*
  f étiquette *f* de volume
  r метка *f* тома

  * **volume of computation** → **360**

  * **volume rendering** → **9926**

9925 volumetric data; volume data
  d räumliche Daten *pl*
  f données *fpl* volumétriques
  r объёмные данные *pl*; пространственные
      данные

9926 volumetric rendering; volume rendering
  d räumliches Rendering *n*
  f rendu *m* volumétrique
  r объёмное тонирование *m*; объёмный
      рендеринг *m*

9927 voluntary interrupt
  d beabsichtigte Unterbrechung *f*;
      programmierter Interrupt *m*
  f interruption *f* volontaire
  r запрограммированное прерывание *n*

9928 voted redundancy
   d Auswahlredundanz *f*; Redundanz *f* nach dem Votierungsprinzip
   f redondance *f* à votation
   r резервирование *n* по схеме голосования

9929 voter
   d Votierschaltung *f*; Voter *m*
   f schéma *m* de vote
   r схема *f* голосования

9930 voting
   d Votierung *f*; Voting *n*
   f votation *f*; vote *m*
   r голосование *n*

9931 voucher
   d Quittung *f*; Quittungsbeleg *m*
   f quittance *f*
   r квитанция *f*

   * **voxel** → **9923**

9932 voxel array
   d Voxel-Feld *n*
   f tableau *m* de voxels
   r массив *m* элементов объёма

9933 voxel detection
   d Voxel-Detektion *f*
   f détection *f* de voxel
   r обнаруживание *n* элемента объёма

9934 voxel-detection processor
   d Voxel-Detektion-Prozessor *m*
   f processeur *m* de détection de voxels
   r процессор *m* обнаруживания *n* элементов объёма

9935 voxel memory
   d Voxel-Speicher *m*
   f mémoire *m* de voxels
   r память *f* элементов объёма

9936 VP locked to page
   d Fluchtpunkt *m* gesperrt an der Seite
   f point *m* de fuite verrouillé sur la page
   r нейтральная точка *f*, фиксированная к странице

   * **VR** → **9874**

9937 VR applications
   d Anwendungen *fpl* der virtuellen Realität
   f applications *fpl* de réalité virtuelle
   r приложения *npl* виртуальной реальности

   * **VRC** → **9784**

9938 VR design
   d Design *n* der virtuellen Realität
   f conception *f* de réalité virtuelle
   r проектирование *n* виртуальной реальности

9939 VR design system
   d Projektierungssystem *n* der virtuellen Realität
   f système *m* de conception de réalité virtuelle
   r система *f* проектирования виртуальной реальности

9940 VR dynamic simulator
   d dynamischer Simulator der virtuellen Realität
   f simulateur *m* de réalité virtuelle dynamique
   r динамический симулятор *m* виртуальной реальности

   * **VRML** → **9875**

9941 VR model
   d Modell *n* der virtuellen Realität
   f modèle *m* de réalité virtuelle
   r модель *f* виртуальной реальности

   * **VR protocol** → **9944**

9942 VR system
   d System *n* der virtuellen Realität
   f système *m* à réalité virtuelle
   r система *f* виртуальной реальности

9943 VR technology
   d Technologie *f* der virtuellen Realität
   f technologie *f* de réalité virtuelle
   r технология *f* виртуальной реальности

9944 VR [transfer] protocol
   d Übertragungsprotokoll *n* der virtuellen Realität; Protokoll *n* der virtuellen Realität
   f protocole *m* de transfert de réalité virtuelle
   r протокол *m* [связи] виртуальной реальности

   * **VTAM** → **9880**

   * **VTK** → **9904**

W

* 3W → 10054

9945 wafer
d Halbleiterscheibe *f*; Unterlage *f*; Wafer *m*;
Kristallplättchen *n*
f plaque[tte] *f* semiconductrice; galette *f*
r полупроводниковая пластина *f*; подложка *f*

9946 wafer-scale integration
d Gesamtwaferintegration *f*
f intégration *f* à l'échelle de la galette
r интеграция *f* в масштабе пластины

* WAIS → 9983

* wait → 9947

* wait condition → 9953

* wait cycle → 9950

9947 wait[ing]; expectation
d Warten *n*; Erwartung *f*
f attente *f*; expectative *f*
r ожидание *n*

* waiting condition → 9953

* waiting cycle → 9950

9948 waiting flag
d Wartekennzeichen *n*
f drapeau *m* d'attente
r флаг *m* ожидания

* waiting line → 7547

* waiting-line model → 7556

* waiting-line theory → 7560

9949 wait[ing] list
d Warteliste *f*
f liste *f* d'attente
r список *m* очерёдности

9950 wait[ing] loop; wait[ing] cycle
d Wartezyklus *m*; Warteschleife *f*
f cycle *m* d'attente
r цикл *m* ожидания

9951 waiting mode
d Wartemodus *m*

f mode *m* d'attente
r режим *m* ожидания

9952 waiting queue field
d Warteschlangebereich *m*; Wartefeld *n*
f champ *m* de queue d'attente
r поле *n* очереди ожидания

**9953 wait[ing] state; wait[ing] condition;
suspend state**
d Wartezustand *m*; Wartebedingung *f*
f état *m* d'attente; condition *f* d'attente
r состояние *n* ожидания

* wait list → 9949

* wait loop → 9950

* wait state → 9953

9954 wallpaper
d Tapete *f*; Hintergrundmotiv *n*
f papier *m* peint; fond *m* d'écran
r [экранный] фон *m*; обои *pl*

* WAN → 9984

* wander *v* → 9065

* wanderer → 2461

* wanted → 7971

* wanted information → 7965

* warm boot → 9955

* warm reboot → 9955

9955 warm [re]start; warm [re]boot
d warmer Wiederanlauf *m*; Warmstarten *n*;
Warmstart *m*
f [re]démarrage *m* à chaud
r тёплый рестарт *m*

* warm start → 9955

9956 warning flag; warning mark
d Warnmarke *f*
f marque *f* d'alarme
r флаг *m* тревоги

* warning mark → 9956

9957 warp *v*
d verbiegen
f gondoler; gaucher
r искажать; деформировать

9958 warpage; warping
d Verbiegung *f*; Verkrümmung *f*

f gauchissement *m*; déformation *f* [non
uniforme]
r деформирование *n*; [неоднородное]
искажение *n*

9959 warp filter
d Warp-Filter *m*
f filtre *m* de gauchissement
r фильтр *m* деформирования

* **warping** → **9958**

9960 warping tools
d verwerfende Hilfsmittel *npl*
f outils *mpl* de déformation
r средства *npl* деформирования
изображений

* **waste basket** → **7761**

9961 watermark generation
d Wasserzeichengenerierung *f*
f génération *f* de filigrane
r генерирование *n* водяного знака

**9962 watermarking algorithm; tattooing
algorithm**
d Wasserzeichenalgorithmus *m*
f algorithme *m* de création de filigrane;
algorithme de tatouage numérique
r алгоритм *m* изготовления водяного знака

* **wave** → **9367**

9963 wave form digitizer
d Signaldigitalisierer *m*
f digitaliseur *m* de signaux analogiques
r дискретизатор *m* [аналоговых] сигналов

9964 wavefront computations
d Wellenfrontrechnen *n*
f calcul *m* ondulatoire
r волновые исчисления *npl*

* **way** → **2956, 8135**

9965 weak precedence grammar
d Grammatik *f* mit schwachen
Vorgängerbeziehungen
f grammaire *f* à prédécession faible
r грамматика *f* со слабым
предшествованием

9966 wear-out failure
d Ermüdungsausfall *m*; Erschöpfungsausfall *m*;
Alterungsausfall *m*
f défaillance *f* de fatigue; défaillance d'usure
r отказ *m* за счёт износа; износовый отказ

9967 Web authoring program

d Web-Autorenprogramm *n*
f programme *m* de création de document Web;
outil *m* de composition de pages Web
r авторская программа *f* Web-документов

9968 Web[-based] training
d Web-basierte Wissenvermittlung *f*
f formation *f* [par le] Web
r образование *n* в Web

9969 Web browser
d Webbrowser *m*; Netzbummer *m*
f butineur *m* Web
r Web-браузер *m*

* **Webcam** → **6087**

* **Web camera** → **6087**

9970 Web chat room; chat room
d Plauschecke *f*
f bavardoir *m*
r место *n* для киберобщения; электронные
кулуары *mpl*

9971 Webdesigner; Web publisher
d Webdesigner *m*; Grafiker *m* und Hersteller *m*
von Websites
f concepteur *m* [de pages] HTML; créateur *m*
[de pages] HTML; développeur *m* [de pages]
HTML
r Web-дизайнер *m*; проектировщик *m*
Web-страниц

9972 Web document
d Webdokument *n*
f document *m* Web
r Web-документ *m*

9973 Web graphics
d Webgrafik *f*
f graphique *m* Web
r Web-графика *f*

* **Web hoster** → **9978**

* **Web magazine** → **3329**

9974 Webmaster
d Webmaster *m*
f Webmaître *m*; maître *m* de la toile
r Web-мастер *m*

9975 Web page
d Webseite *f*; Netzseite *f*
f page *f* Web
r Web-страница *f*

* **Web page hoster** → **9978**

* **Webphone** → 5056

* **Web portal** → 5060

* **Web publisher** → 9971

9976 **Web search engine; search engine; Web search tool**
(a WWW site that serves as an index to other sites on the Web)
d Searchengine *f*; Suchmaschine *f*
f moteur *m* de recherche; chercheur *m*; outil *m* de recherche; morche *m*; araignée *f*
r поисковый механизм *m*; искалка *f*

* **Web search tool** → 9976

9977 **Web site; site**
d Website *f*; Site *f*; Web-Angebot *n*; [Web-]Standort *m*
f site *m* Web
r узел *m* всемирной паутины; узел WWW; [Web-]сайт *m*

9978 **Web [site] hoster; Web page hoster; hoster**
d Webbetreiber *m*
f hébergeur *m* [de sites Web]; hébergeur de pages Web; fournisseur *m* d'hébergement
r приёмник *m* Web-страниц; хозяин *m* Web-страниц

9979 **Web space**
d Webraum *m*
f espace *m* Web
r Web-пространство *n*

9980 **Websurfing; Internet surfing; cybersurfing; netsurfing; surfing**
d Surfen *n*; ungezieltes Stöbern *n* im WWW
f surf *m* [sur le Net]; cybersurf *m*; balade *f* [sur Internet]
r [Web-]серфинг *m*

* **Web training** → 9968

9981 **Web-TV**
d Webfernsehen *n*; Internet-Zugang *m* über den Fernseher
f télévision *f* Web
r Web-телевидение *n*

* **Webzine** → 3329

* **welcome page** → 4542

* **wetware** → 5427

9982 **whiffletree multiplier**
d Kaskadenvervielfacher *m*
f multipli[cat]eur *m* arborescent

r каскадный умножитель *m*

9983 **wide area information servers; WAIS**
(an Internet multimedia search-and-retrieve tool offering more than 500 databases)
d Weltdatenserver *mpl*
f serveurs *m* d'information globaux; serveurs d'information déporté
r глобальные информационные серверы *mpl*

9984 **wide area network; WAN; long-haul network**
d Weltdatennetz *n*; flächendeckendes Computernetz *n*; Weitverkehrsnetz *n*; weiträumiges Netzwerk *n*
f réseau *m* global; grand réseau; réseau étendu
r мировая сеть *f*; глобальная сеть

* **wideband** → 1185

* **wideband bus** → 1186

* **wideband channel** → 1188

* **wideband characteristics** → 1189

* **wideband communication network** → 1190

* **wideband information retrieval** → 1191

* **wideband LAN** → 1192

* **wideband line** → 1193

* **wideband signal** → 1194

* **wideband source** → 1195

* **wideband transmission** → 1196

* **wildcard** → 9985

9985 **wildcard [character]; wildcard symbol; metasymbol; metacharacter**
d Wildcardzeichen *n*; Wildcard *f*; Stellvertreterzeichen *n*; Joker *m*; Jokerzeichen *n*; Ersatzzeichen *n*; Metasymbol *n*
f caractère *m* générique; caractère de remplacement; caractère de substitution; métacaractère *m*; métasymbole *m*
r подстановочный символ *m*; шаблон *m* подстановки; безразличный символ; групповой символ; метасимвол *m*; метазнак *m*; джокерный символ; джокер *m*

9986 **wildcard designation**
d Wildcard-Benennung *f*; Ersatzzeichen-Bestimmung *f*
f désignation *f* par métacaractère
r обозначение *n* любых символов

9987 **wildcard search; masked search**
  d Wildcard-Suche *f*; Suche *f* mit einer Maske
  f recherche *f* approximative; recherche avec
     caractère de remplacement; recherche avec
     masque
  r поиск *m* безразличными символами;
     маскированный [безразличными
     символами] поиск

  * **wildcard symbol** → 9985

9988 **window**
  d Fenster *n*; Ausschnitt *m*
  f fenêtre *f*
  r окно *n*

9989 **window border**
  d Fensterrand *m*
  f bordure *f* de fenêtre
  r граница *f* окна

9990 **window commutation**
  d Fensterkommutierung *f*
  f commutation *f* de fenêtres
  r переключение *n* окон

9991 **windowed environment**
  d Fensterumgebung *f*
  f environnement *m* à fenêtres
  r оконная среда *f*

9992 **window elements**
  d Fensterelemente *npl*
  f éléments *m* de fenêtre
  r элементы *mpl* окна

9993 **window frame**
  d Fensterrahmen *m*
  f filet *m* de fenêtre
  r рамка *f* окна

9994 **window function**
  d Windowfunktion *f*
  f fonction *f* fenêtre
  r функция-окно *f*

9995 **windowing; fenestration**
  d Fensterung *f*; Fenstertechnik *f*;
     Ausschnittsdarstellung *f*
  f fenêtrage *m*
  r кадрирование *n* [изображения];
     организация *f* окон

9996 **window list**
  d Fenstersliste *f*
  f liste *f* de fenêtres
  r список *m* окон

9997 **window manager**
  d Fenstermanager *m*; Window-Manager *m*
  f gestionnaire *m* des fenêtres
  r администратор *m* полиэкранного режима

9998 **window menu**
  d Fenstermenü *n*
  f menu *m* fenêtre
  r оконное меню *n*

9999 **window object**
  d Fensterobjekt *n*
  f objet *m* fenêtre
  r объект *m* типа окна

10000 **window selection**
  d Fensterauswahl *f*
  f sélection *f* de fenêtre
  r выбор *m* окна

10001 **window selection mode**
  d Fensterauswahl-Modus *m*
  f mode *m* de sélection de fenêtre
  r режим *m* выбора окна

10002 **window size**
  d Fenstergröße *f*
  f taille *f* de fenêtre
  r размер *m* окна

10003 **windows layout**
  d Fensteranordnung *f*; Fensterlayout *n*
  f disposition *f* des fenêtres
  r схема *f* организации окон; конфигурация *f*
     окон

10004 **Windows metafile; WMF**
  d Windows-Metadatei *f*; WMF
  f métafichier *m* Windows; WMF
  r Windows метафайл *m*; WMF-файл *m*

10005 **windows programming**
  d Programmierung *f* der Fenster
  f programmation *f* de fenêtres
  r программирование *n* окон

10006 **windows system**
  d Fenstersystem *n*
  f système *m* de fenêtres
  r оконная система *f*

10007 **window tree**
  d Baum *m* der Fenster
  f arbre *m* de fenêtres
  r дерево *n* окон

10008 **wire** *v*
  d verdrahten
  f enfiler
  r соединять проводами

10009 **wire**
  d Draht *m*; Leiter *m*

f fil *m*
r провод[ник] *m*; жила *f*; проволока *f*

10010 wired; hardwired
    d festverdrahtet; verkabelt; verdrahtet
    f à montage fixe; câblé
    r жёстко замонтированный; проводной;
    запаянный

    * **wired glove** → 2563

10011 wired logic; hardwired logic
    d verdrahtete Logik *f*; festverdrahtete Logik
    f logique *f* câblée; logique matérielle
    r проводная логика *f*; "монтажная" логика;
    жёсткая логика; аппаратная логика

10012 wired program
    d verdrahtetes Programm *n*; Festprogramm *n*
    f programme *m* câblé
    r зашитая программа *f*; коммутируемая
    программа

10013 wireframe
    d Drahtrahmen *m*; Wire-Frame *n*; Drahtgitter *n*
    f fil *m* de fer
    r каркас *m*

10014 wireframe representation
    d Drahtrahmendarstellung *f*;
    Wire-Frame-Darstellung *f*
    f représentation *f* fil de fer; représentation
    filaire
    r каркасное представление *n*

10015 wireframe view
    d Drahtrahmen-Ansicht *f*
    f vue *f* fil de fer; vue filaire
    r каркасный вид *m*

10016 wirehead
    d Drahtkopf (Internet-Techniker oder
    -Experten)
    f technicien *m* spécialisé dans les technologies
    de l'Internet
    r специалист *m* по Интернет-технологиям

    * **wireless communication** → 10017

10017 wireless [tele]communication
    d drahtfreie Fernkommunikation *f*
    f [télé]communication *f* sans fil
    r беспроводная связь *f*

10018 wiring
    d Verdrahtung *f*
    f filerie *f*; canalisation *f* électrique
    r прокладка *f*; проводка *f*;
    межсоединения *npl*

    * **with graceful degradation** → 3678

10019 wizard; helper
    d Assistent *m*; Zauberer *m*; Genie *n*
    f assistant *m*
    r советник *m*; помощник *m*

    * **WMF** → 10004

10020 WMF graphics
    d WMF-Grafik *f*
    f graphique *m* WMF
    r графика *f* формата WMF

10021 word
    d Wort *n*
    f mot *m*
    r слово *n*

10022 word bit
    d Wortbit *n*
    f bit *m* de mot
    r бит *m* слова

10023 word count
    d Wortzählung *f*
    f compte *m* de mots
    r счёт *m* слов

10024 word counter
    d Wortzähler *m*
    f compteur *m* de mots
    r счётчик *m* слов

10025 word displacement
    d wortweise Distanz *f*
    f déplacement *m* de mot
    r смещение *n* слова

10026 word generator
    d Wortgenerator *m*
    f générateur *m* de mots
    r генератор *m* машинных слов

10027 word input decoder
    d Worteingabebewerter *m*
    f décodeur *m* de mots d'entrée
    r дешифратор *m* входных слов

10028 word interleaving
    d Wortverschaltung *f*
    f entrelaçage *m* de mots
    r чередование *n* слов

10029 word length; word size
    d Wortlänge *f*; Wortgröße *f*
    f longueur *f* du mot; grandeur *f* du mot
    r длина *f* слова; размер *m* слова

    * **word memory** → 10030

10030 word[-organized] memory
 d Wortspeicher *m*; wortorganisierter
     Speicher *m*
 f mémoire *f* à [accès par] mots
 r память *f* с пословной организацией

10031 word output buffer control
 d Wortausgabepuffersteuerung *f*
 f contrôle *m* de mots de sortie par tampon
 r буферное управление *n* выходными
     словами

10032 word output register
 d Wortausgaberegister *n*
 f registre *m* de sortie de mot
 r выходной регистр *m* слова

 * **word period** → 10038

 * **word processing** → 9313

 * **word processor** → 9314

10033 word processor network
 d Wortprozessornetz *n*
 f réseau *m* de texteur
 r сеть *f* с системой текстообработки

10034 word pulse
 d Wortimpuls *m*
 f impulsion *f* de mots
 r импульс *m* в числовой шине

10035 word section
 d Wortteil *m*
 f section *f* de mot
 r отрезок *m* слова

 * **word size** → 10029

10036 word space; word spacing
 d Wortraum *m*
 f intervalle *m* entre les mots; espace *m* entre les
     mots
 r пробел *m* между словами; расстояние *n*
     между словами

 * **word spacing** → 10036

10037 word structure
 d Wortstruktur *f*
 f structure *f* de mot; format *m* de mot
 r структура *f* слова

10038 word time; word period
 d Wort[takt]zeit *f*
 f temps *m* de mot; période *f* de mot
 r время *n* [вывода] слова; период *m* слова

10039 word wrap
 d Wortumbruch *m*
 f habillage *m* de mot; retour *m* automatique de
     mot à la ligne
 r завёртывание *n* слова

10040 work area; workspace; scratch area
     (of a memory)
 d Arbeitsbereich *m*; Arbeitsfeld *n*;
     Notizenbereich *m*
 f espace *m* de travail; zone *f* de travail;
     domaine *m* de travail
 r рабочая область *f*; рабочая зона *f*

10041 workbook
 d Arbeitsheft *n*
 f livre *f* de travail
 r рабочий журнал *m*

10042 work file; scratch file
 d Arbeitsfile *n*; Arbeitsdatei *f*; Notizdatei *f*
 f fichier *m* de travail
 r рабочий файл *m*; вспомагательный файл

 * **working page** → 2420

10043 working storage
 d Arbeitsspeicher *m*
 f mémoire *f* de travail
 r рабочая память *f*

10044 working window
 d Arbeitsfenster *n*
 f fenêtre *f* de travail
 r рабочее окно *n*

10045 work-in-process queue
 d Warteschlange *f* der laufenden Nachrichten
 f queue *f* de messages en [état de] traitement
 r очередь *f* частично обработанных
     сообщений

10046 work session
 d Arbeitssitzung *f*
 f session *f* de travail
 r рабочая сессия *f*

10047 worksheet
 d Arbeitsblatt *n*
 f feuille *f* de travail
 r рабочий лист *m*

10048 worksheet formatting
 d Arbeitsblatt-Formatierung *f*
 f formatage *m* de feuille de travail
 r форматирование *n* рабочего листа

10049 worksheet orientation
 d Arbeitsblatt-Orientierung *f*
 f orientation *f* de feuille de travail
 r ориентация *f* рабочего листа

10050 worksheet splitting
d Arbeitsblatt-Aufteilung f
f splittage m de feuille de travail
r разделение n рабочего листа

10051 worksheet switching
d Durchschaltung f der Arbeitsblätter
f commutation f de feuilles de travail
r переключение n рабочих листов

* **workspace** → **10040**

10052 workstation videoconference
d Arbeitsplatz-Bildkonferenz f
f vidéoconférence f par stations de travail
r видеоконференция f рабочих станций

10053 worldwide switched data network
d Weltdatenwählnetz n
f réseau m mondial de commutation de
données
r мировая сеть f коммутации данных

10054 World Wide Web; WWW; 3W; the Web
d weltweites Gewebe n; WWW; 3W
f [World Wide] Web m; WWW; 3W; Toile f
r всемирная [компьютерная] сеть f;
всемирная паутина f; сеть WWW; веб m

10055 worm
(a virus)
d Wurm m
f ver m
r программа-червь f; червь m

* **WORM optical disk** → **10065**

10056 worst-case code
d Worst-Case-Code m
f code m du cas le plus défavorable
r тяжёлый код m

* **wraparound** → **1694**

10057 wrapped image
d Wickelbild n; gewickeltes Bild n; umhülltes
Bild
f image f habillée; image vêtue; image
entourée; image enveloppée; image enroulée
r окутанное изображение n; охваченное
изображение

10058 wrapping
d Umhüllung f; Umbruch m;
Drahtwickeltechnik f
f habillage m; emballage m; enroulement m
r окутывание n; завёртывание n;
охватывание n; обёртка f

10059 writable memory
d überschreibbarer Speicher m
f mémoire f réinscriptible
r перезаписываемая память f

10060 write v; record v
d schreiben; einschreiben
f écrire; enregistrer
r писать; записывать

10061 write; writing
d Schreiben n
f écriture f
r записывание n; запись f

10062 write counter
d Einlesezähler m
f compteur m de signaux d'écriture
r счётчик m сигналов записи

10063 write driver
d Schreibleitungstreiber m
f formateur m de signaux d'écriture
r формирователь m сигналов записи

* **write-enable notch** → **10068**

10064 write head; writing head; record[ing] head
d Schreibkopf m; Aufzeichnungskopf m;
Aufnahmekopf m
f tête f d'écriture; tête d'enregistrement
r записывающая головка f; головка записи

**10065 write-once read-many optical disk;
WORM optical disk**
d einmalig beschreibbare optische
Spreicherplatte f
f disque m optique numérique non effaçable
r оптический диск m с однократной
записью; запоминающее устройство n без
возможности перезаписи

10066 write-protected memory
d schreibgeschützter Speicher m
f mémoire f protégée en écriture
r память f с защитой от записи

10067 write protection
d Schreibschutz m
f protection f en écriture
r защита f от записи

10068 write-protect notch; write-enable notch
d Schreibschutzbezeichnung f
f encoche f de protection d'écriture; encoche
d'interdiction d'écriture; découpure f de
protection
r обозначение n защиты от записи

10069 write pulse
d Schreibimpuls m

f impulsion *f* d'écriture

r импульс *m* записи

10070 writeset

d zu schreibender Zeichenvorrat *m*

f ensemble *m* à écriture

r записываемый набор *m*

10071 write *v* through; store *v* through

d durchschreiben; durchspeichern

f mémoriser avec écriture dans un tampon intermédiaire

r записывать через промежуточный буфер

* **writing** → **10061**

* **writing head** → **10064**

* **writing rate** → **10072**

10072 writing speed; writing rate; record[ing] speed; record[ing] rate

d Schreibgeschwindigkeit *f*

f vitesse *f* d'écriture

r скорость *f* записи

10073 writing tools

d Schreibhilfsmittel *npl*

f outils *mpl* d'enregistrement

r инструменты *mpl* регистрирования

* **WWW** → **10054**

10074 wysiwyg

d Was du siehst, bekommst du; Wysiwyg *n*

f tel écran-tel écrit; tel-tel

r что видишь, то и получишь (при печати)

10075 wysiwyg program

d Wysiwyg-Programm *n*

f programme *m* tel-tel

r программа *f* wysiwyg

X

10076 xerocopy
 d Xerokopie *f*
 f xérocopie *f*
 r ксерокопия *f*

 * **XML** → **3618**

 * **Xmodem** → **3640**

 * **XOR** → **3570**

 * **X terminal** → **3646**

10077 XY [coordinate] plotter
 d XY-Koordinatenplotter *m*; XY-Plotter *m*
 f traceur *m* XY; traceur à deux coordonnées;
    traceur sur axes X et Y
 r двухкоординатный графопостроитель *m*

 * **XY plotter** → **10077**

10078 XYZ/RGB matrix
 d XYZ/RGB-Matrix *f*
 f matrice *f* XYZ/RGB
 r матрица *f* XYZ/RGB

Y

10079 Y-address counter
  d Y-Adress[en]zähler *m*
  f compteur *m* d'adresses Y
  r счётчик *m* адресов Y

10080 Y-component
  d Y-Komponente *f*
  f composante *f* Y
  r Y-компонента *f*; яркостная компонента *f* видеосигнала

10081 yellow pages
  d gelbe Seiten *fpl*
  f pages *fpl* jaunes
  r жёлтые страницы *fpl*

10082 Ymodem
  (a file transfer protocol, faster than Xmodem, but not as advanced as Zmodem)
  d Y-Modem *n*
  f modem *m* Y
  r Y-модем *m*

10083 yoke
  d Joch *m*; Gabel *f*; Bügel *m*
  f déflecteur *m*; fourche *f*
  r скоба *f*; зажим *m*; стыковочный узел *m*

10084 Y-register
  d Y-Register *n*
  f registre *m* Y
  r Y-регистр *m* (для хранения значения координаты Y графопостроителя); регистр *m* хранения подинтегральной функции в ЦДА

Z

* **Z-bit** → **10090**

10085 Z-buffer; depth buffer
(of 3D graphics subsystem)
d Z-Puffer *m*; Puffer *m* der Tiefe
f mémoire *f* de la troisième dimension;
Z-buffer *m*; buffer *m* de profondeur
r Z-буфер *m*; буфер *m* глубины

10086 Z-buffer algorithm
d Z-Puffer-Algorithmus *m*
f algorithme *m* de Z-buffer
r алгоритм *m* Z-буфера

10087 zero; null
d Null *f*; Nullstelle *f*
f zéro *m*
r нуль *m*

* **zero access** → **4683**

10088 zero access memory
d zugriffszeitfreier Speicher *m*
f mémoire *f* d'accès zéro
r память *f* с нулевым доступом

10089 zero-address instruction
d adressenloser Befehl *m*
f instruction *f* sans adresse
r безадресная инструкция *f*

10090 zero bit; Z-bit
d Nullbit *n*
f bit *m* zéro
r разряд *m* нуля; Z-бит *m*

* **zero compression** → **10098**

* **zero division** → **3062**

* **zero fill** → **10091**

10091 zero fill[ing]; zero padding; zeroizing
d Auffüllen *n* mit Nullen
f garnissage *m* de zéros; remplissage *m* par zéros
r заполнение *n* нулями; дополнение *n* нулями

10092 zero gate
d Nullsetzgatter *n*
f porte *f* zéro
r вентиль *m* установки на нуль

* **zeroizing** → **10091**

* **zero-level addressing** → **4684**

* **zero-match gate** → **6304**

* **zero object** → **6312**

10093 zero offset indexed addressing
d indizierte Nullversatzadressierung *f*
f adressage *m* indexé au déplacement nul
r индексная адресация *f* с нулевым смещением

* **zero padding** → **10091**

10094 zero-page addressing
d Page-Null-Adressierung *f*; indirekte Adressierung *f* über Speicherseite Null
f adressage *m* sur page zéro
r адресация *f* в режим нулевой страницы

10095 zero *v* reset; reset *v*; clear *v*; annul *v*
d nullsetzen; annullieren
f annuler
r устанавливать в нуль; аннулировать

* **zero reset** → **10096**

10096 zero reset[ting]; resetting; clearing
d Nullsetzen *n*
f [re]mise *f* à zéro
r установка *f* в нуль; сброс *m*

10097 zero state
d Nullzustand *m*
f état *m* zéro
r нулевое состояние *n*

* **zero-sum game** → **6213**

10098 zero suppression; zero compression
d Nullenunterdrückung *f*
f suppression *f* des zéros
r подавление *n* [незначащих] нулей

10099 Z filter
d Z-Filter *m*
f filtre *m* Z
r Z-фильтр *m*

* **zip *v*** → **2033**

10100 zip drive
d Zip-Laufwerk *n*
f lecteur *m* zip
r zip-дисковод *m*; переносной дисковод

10101 zip file
d Zip-Datei *f*

f fichier *m* zip; fichier comprimé
r архивный файл *m*, сжатый с помощью
архиватора zip

10102 Zmodem
(a file transfer protocol which transmits data
between modems in blocks of 512 bytes)
d Z-Modem *n*
f Z-modem *m*
r Z-модем *m*

10103 zone; area; range
d Zone *f*; Bereich *m*; Gebiet *n*
f zone *f*; domaine *m*
r зона *f*; область *f*; участок *m*

10104 zoned format
d gezontes Format *n*
f format *m* en zones
r зонный формат *m*

* zoom → 10112

* zoom all → 4131

10105 zoom box
d Zoomfeld *n*
f boîte *f* de zoom
r рамка *f* трансфокации

10106 zoom center
d Zoom-Zentrum *n*
f centre *m* de zoom
r центр *m* динамического масштабирования

10107 zoom coefficient
d Zoomkoeffizient *m*
f coefficient *m* de zoom
r коэффициент *m* динамического
масштабирования

10108 zoom extent
d Zoomumfang *m*
f étendu *m* de zoom
r охват *m* динамического масштабирования

10109 zoom function
d Zoom-Funktion *f*
f fonction *f* de zoom
r функция *f* динамического
масштабирования

10110 zoom *v* in
d die Gummilinse zuziehen
f faire un zoom vers gros plan
r раскрывать; распахивать (окно);
приближать (изображение); увеличить
масштаб

10111 zoom in

d Vergrößerung *f*
f zoom *m* [d'accompagnement] avant
r наезд *m*; приближение *n* (изображения)

10112 zoom[ing]
d Zoomen *n*; dynamisches Skalieren *n*
f variation *f* de focale; effet *m* de loupe;
zooming *m*; zoom *m*
r масштабирование *n*; изменение *n*
масштаба изображения; трансфокация *f*;
наводка *f* на резкость

10113 zoom-in limit
d Grenze *f* der Vergrößerung
f limite *f* de zoom avant
r граница *f* приближения

10114 zoom *v* out; unzoom *v*
d die Gummilinse aufziehen
f faire un zoom vers plan général
r отдалять (изображение); запахивать
(окно); уменьшить масштаб

10115 zoom out; unzoom
d Verkleinerung *f*
f zoom *m* [d'accompagnement] arrière
r отъезд *m* (от изображения)

10116 zoom-out limit
d Grenze *f* der Verkleinerung
f limite *f* de zoom arrière
r граница *f* отъезда (от изображения)

10117 zoom previous
d vorhergehendes Zoomen *n*
f zoom *m* précédent
r предыдущее динамическое
масштабирование *n*

10118 zoom range
d Zoomumfang *m*
f domaine *m* de zoom
r охват *m* масштабирования

10119 zoom window
d Zoomfenster *n*
f fenêtre *m* de zoom
r окно *n* масштабирования

10120 zoom zone
(on toolbar)
d Zoom-Bereich *m*
f zone *f* de zoom
r зона *f* масштабирования

Deutsch

Blocklänge 1077
Blocklücke 1069
Blockmarke 1074
Blockmarkierer 1074
blockmultiplex 1075
Blockmultiplexkanal 1076
Blockprüfzeichen 1062
Blockprüfzeichenfolge 4038
Blockrückweisung 4055
Blockschaltbild 3920
Blockschema 3920
Blocksortieren 1078
Blocktransfer 1079
Blockübertragung 1079
Blockumschaltung 815
Blockung 5454
Blockungsfaktor 1072
Block veränderlicher Länge 9756
blockweiser Datentransfer 1079
blockweiser Modus 1061
blockweise Sortierung 1078
blockweise Übertragung 1079
blockweise Verarbeitung 867
Blockzähler 1064
Blue-Screen 1081
Bookmark 1109
Boolesch 1111
Boolesche Funktion 936
Boolesche Matrix 1114
Boolesche Methode 1115
Boolesche Modellierung 1116
Boolesche Operation 1117
Boolescher Ausdruck 1113
Boolescher Operator 1118
Boolesches Polynom 1119
Boolesche Sprache 1112
Boolesche Variable 1120
Boot-Diskette 1122
booten 1126
Boot-Laufwerk 1123
Boot-Partition 1121
Bootsektor 1125
Bootstrapping 8350
Bootstrap-Protokoll 1128
Boot-Zerlegung 1121
Bordcomputer 1091
Bordrechner 1091
Borgen 1130
Bot 9716
Bottom-up-Entwurf 1135
Box 1147
Boxplot 3920
Brandmauer 3851
Brandschutzmauer 3851
Breaksignal 5091
Brechpunkt 1173
B-Register 4772
Breitband 1185
Breitband-Bus 1186
breitbandige Quelle 1195

Breitbandigkeit 1189
Breitband-Informationsabruf 1191
Breitbandkabel 1187
Breitbandkanal 1188
Breitbandkommunikationsnetz 1190
Breitbandleitung 1193
Breitbandquelle 1195
Breitbandsignal 1194
Breitbandübertragung 1196
Brenner 1267
Brett 1090
Brettschaltung 1165
Briefbombe 5340
Briefkasten 3331
Briefkastenverfahren 5591
bringen 1184
    in den Kellerspeicher ~ 7517
Bringephase 3755
Browser 1208
Browser-basierte Anwendung 1209
Browser-Dialogbox 1207
Browser-Fenster 1210
Browsing 1212
Bruch 2358, 4023
Brücke 1177
Brückenfilter 1179
Brückenprogramme 1182
Brückenschaltung 1178
Bubble-Jet-Drucker 4864
Bubblesort 1216
Buchen 7161
Büchermappe 1456
Buchführung 91
Buchhaltungssoftware 94
Buchhaltungssoftwarepaket 94
Buchse 7004, 8689
Buchstabe 5339
Buchstabe mit Akzent 46
Buchstaben- 324
Buchstabenausdruck 5424
Buchstabenfigur 5343
Buchstabenkennzeichnung 5425
buchstäblich 324
buchstäbliche Bezeichnung 5425
buchstäbliche Darstellung 5425
buchstäbliche Konstante 5423
Bucht 875
Buchtaben-Neigung 5344
Buchung 1108
Buck 869
Buck-Passing-Protokoll 1219
Buckübertragungsverzögerung 1217
Budget 1220
Bügel 10083
Bugfix 9703
Bump-Map 1257

Bump-Map-Bild 1258
Bump-Mapping 1259
Bump-Mapping-Fläche 1261
Bump-Mapping-Prozessor 1260
Bündel 6884
Bündelader 848
Bündelkabel 1265
Bündelung 5989
bündiger Text 5195
Bundsteg 4355
Bürger im Internet 5054
Büroautomatisierung 6385
Büroautomatisierungsexperte 6384
Bürocomputer 6389
Büroinformationssystem 6390
Bürokommunikation 6386
Bürokommunikationssystem 6388
Bürokommunikation- und Informationssystem 6387
Büronetzwerk 6391
Bürorechner 6389
Bürotechnik 6392
Burst 1268
Bürste 1214
Bürstenwähler 1215
Burster 1269
Burstmodus 1271
Bus 1273
Busadressregister 1274
Busarbiter 1275
Bus auf der Rückwandplatine 766
Büschel 6884
Busfreigabe 1279
Bus für höherwertige Datenstellen 9710
Bus für niederwertige Datenstellen 5519
Businterface 1285
Buskonflikt 1277
Busleitung 1287
Bus mit zweifacher Redundanz 3207
Busnetz 1291
Busnetzwerk 1291
Busschnittstelle 1285
Busstruktur 1288
Busstruktur mit Steuersignalkaskadierung 2488
Busterminator 1289
Bustopologie 1290
Bustreiber 1278
Busverkehr 1281
Busvermittlung 1281
Buszähler 1280
Buszuteiler 1275
Bypass 1302
Bypasskanal 1303

Français

aperture 451
apostrophe 453
appareil 2819
appareil à cassettes pour bande
    magnétique 1485
appareil à copier 2306
appareil de restitution
    stéréoscopique 3136
appareil de secours 782
appareil du bureau 2785
appareillage 3467
appareil photonumérique 2877
appareil terminal 9266
apparence 456
apparent 454
appariement 5676
appariement de formes 6862
apparition graduelle 3673
apparition graduelle de caractères
    1608
apparition progressive 3673
appel 1383, 7093
appel au discussion 1374
appel automatique 676
appel au vote 1376
appel d'administration 251
appel de bibliothèque 5349
appel de mémoire 5733
appel de report 1454
appel de retenue 1454
appel diffusé 1204
appel double 7719
appel d'une procédure 7348
appeler 1354
appeler de nouveau 7720
appel invalide 5116
appel nominal 1360
appel par interruption 5085
appel par nom 1360
appel par numéro 2845
appel par référence 1361
appel par retour 7719
appel par valeur 1362
appel pour l'opinion 1375
appel préalable 7206
appel répété 7719
appel sélectif 7093
appel sélectif spécifique 8760
appel suspendu 1405
appendice 458
applet 460
applicabilité 461
applicable 462
application 463
application basée à butineur 1209
application bureautique 2783
application d'acheteur 1728
application d'acquéreur 1728
application d'assistance 4434
application de bureau 2783

application d'effet 3301
application d'entrée 4095
application de raytracing 7651
application de visualisation 9899
application enregistrée 7833
application pilote 6996
applications de réalité virtuelle
    9937
appliquer 480
appliquer l'option 481
appliquette 460
apport de contrôle 654
apporter 1184, 3650
appréciation 3528
approchable 485
approche 482
approché 486
approcher 483
approvisionnement d'information
    2602
approximabilité 484
approximable 485
approximatif 486
approximation 491
approximation vraisemblable 893
approximer 487
appui 1152, 9060
appui d'appel 1395
appuyer 1695, 9059
araignée 9976
arbitrage 498
arbitraire 7591
arbitre 496
arbitre de bus 1275
arbitreur 496
arbre 9540
arbre binaire 955
arbre binaire sélecteur 949
arbre de fenêtres 10007
arbre de recherche 8286
arbre de recherche binaire 949
arbre de recherche multivoie 6026
arbre de répertoire 2969
arbre des défaillances 3721
arbres fractals 4022
arbre syntaxique 9128
architecture 501
architecture de pile 8804
architecture de protocole 7454
architecture de réseau 6085
architecture de réseau de
    communication 1948
architecture de réseau local 5255
architecture du système ouverte
    6487
architecture EISA 3617
architecture en tranches 8651
architecture marquée 9179
architecture multibus 5922
architecture multi-serveur 6013

architecture ouverte 6470
architecture par accès égal 6878
architecture par étiquette 9179
architecture plane 3885
architecture système de réseau
    9149
architecture virtuelle 9850
archivage 508
archivage automatique 675
archivage de courte durée 8523
archives 505
ardoise électronique 6300
arête 3280
argument 512
argumentation 513
arithmétique 514
arithmétique binaire 926
arithmétique d'adresse 200
arithmétique de pixel 7017
arithmétique octale 6368
armoire 1643
arnaque 8785
arobas 607
arobase 607
arpentage 5880
arrangement 526
arrangement au hasard 7597
arrangement de contacts 2208
arrangement d'icônes 4612
arrangement topologique 9448
arranger 524
arranger tout 525
arrêt 4376, 8530
arrêt anormal 5
arrêt anormal de tâche 9211
arrêt anormal restaurable 7746
arrêt de canal 1585
arrêt de fin de papier 3999
arrêt de formulaires 3999
arrêt de refus 7569
arrêter 8531
arrêt par rupture de bande 9193
arrêt sur adresse 233
arrière-plan 751, 754
arrière-plan bitmap 995
arrivée 533, 5485
    d'~ 4730
arrondir 8124
arrondissement 8126
arrosage 8745
artère d'information 4820
artère sérielle par octet 1314
article 540, 2589
article de forum 6155
article permanent 5668
articulation 541
artificiel 542
arts graphiques assistés par
    ordinateur 2058
art virtuel 9851

complément 1991
complément à deux 9593
complémentaire 1992
complément à la base 7582
complément à la base minus un 7583
complément à neuf 6161
complémentation 1997
complément à un 6429
complément avec signe 8557
complémenteur 1999
complément faux 7583
complément juste 7582
complément vrai 7582
complet 2003, 4103
complètement 2011
compléter 2002, 3823
complétion 2011
complétude 2009
complexe 2013, 2014
complexité 2015
component de clavier 5206
comportement 891
comportement en commutation 9088
composant 2019
composant conventionnel 2279
composant de gris 4313
composante 2019
composante basique 849
composante de bruit 6181
composante de luminance 5533
composantes de document 3077
composante Y 10080
composé 2022
composer 2021
composite 2022
composition 2028, 9294
composition de texte 9294
composition par ordinateur 2070
compresser 2033, 2391
compressibilité 2038
compression 2040
compression asynchrone 598
compression avec pertes 5511
compression de bits 984
compression de caractères 1622
compression de codes 1804
compression de données 2533
compression de fichier 3787
compression de fractale 4013
compression de texture 9328
compression de vidéo numérique 2931
compression d'image 4648
compression d'images statiques 8871
compression sans perte 5509
compression temporelle 9249
comprimer 2033

comptabilité 91
comptage 1347, 2338
comptage de cycles 2464
comptage de grilles 7615
comptage de trafic 9466
comptage en arrière 2342
comptant 2341
compte 90
compte 2338, 9715
compte de mots 10023
compte de racine 8119
compter 1345, 2339
compte régressif 2342
compteur 2343
compteur additif 9697
compteur à décades 2648
compteur annulaire 8093
compteur à pas 8904
compteur à présélection 7233
compteur à retard 2723
compteur avant-arrière 914
compteur bidirectionnel 914
compteur cascade 1462
compteur circulaire 8093
compteur courant 8100
compteur d'abonné 1367
compteur d'adresses 209
compteur d'adresses Y 10079
compteur de blocs 1064
compteur décadique 2648
compteur décimal 2648
compteur de conversations 1367
compteur de cycles 2465
compteur de décalage 8509
compteur de documents 3078
compteur de groupes 4337
compteur de microtemps 9017
compteur de mots 10024
compteur de paquets 864
compteur de points 3110
compteur de porteurs 1446
compteur de répétitions 7936
compteur d'erreurs 3488
compteur descendant 3142
compteur de séquence 8400
compteur de signaux d'écriture 10062
compteur de sous-séquence 9017
compteur de soustraction 3142
compteur de trafic 9467
compteur de tranches de temps 9418
compteur d'impulsions 7500
compteur d'impulsions de bruit 6195
compteur d'instructions 4947
compteur d'ondulations 8100
compteur d'oscillations 8100
compteur en anneau 8093
compteur en temps réel 7713

compteur horaire 2346
compteur logiciel 8697
compteur ordinal 1700
compteur reverse 8055
compteur réversible 914
compteur totalisateur 9697
compte utilisateur 9715
computation 1347
computationnel 2045
concaténation 2112
concentrateur 1321
concentrateur de données 2534
concentrateur digital 2886
concentration 2115
concentration de données 2533
concentrer 6669
concept 2117
concepteur 2659, 3169
concepteur de pages HTML 9971
concepteur de puces 1663
concepteur HTML 9971
conception 2777, 2780
conception assistée par ordinateur 2053
conception de bas en haut 1135
conception de circuiterie 8226
conception de réalité virtuelle 9938
conception de réseau 6097
conception géométrique assistée par ordinateur 2057
conception technique 3429
concevoir 2778
concordance 2120
concurrence 1985
concurrent 2121, 4867
condensateur 1419
condensation de données 2586
condenser 6669
condition 2124
condition "if" 4632
condition aux limites 1139
condition d'attente 9953
condition de chaîne 1543
condition de compatibilité 1978
condition de maintien 4522
condition de mise en queue 7552
condition d'empressement 7681
condition exceptionnelle 3554
condition occupée 1293
conditions sur chantier 3768
conductance 2128
conductance électrique 2133
conducteur 2134
conducteur composite 2024
conducteur nu 822
conductibilité active 2128
conductibilité électrique 3316
conductivité 2133
conduire 4352

écran graphique par points 1006
écran gros 4318
écran logo 5490
écran matriciel
    électroluminescent 3319
écran monté sur la tête 4421
écran multifenêtre 5980
écran noir 1041
écran noir et blanc 1037
écran panoramique 5256
écran par points 1006
écran partagé 8780
écran pixel 1006
écran pixélisé 1006
écran plat 3896
écran rétroéclairé 763
écran sans clignotement 3899
écran sans mémoire 6277
écran sans scintillement 3899
écran sans taches de lumière 6239
écran sensitif 9455
écran sensoriel 9455
écran tactile 9455
écran vectoriel 9768
écran virtuel 9878
écraser 1744
écrêtage 1742
écrêteur 1741, 1743
écrire 10060
écrire en mémoire vive 7089
écriture 10061
écriture consécutive 2184
écriture d'appui 8121
écriture de référence 7812
écriture en lettres d'imprimerie
    4385
écriture hachurée 8952
écriture indicielle 4773
écriture locale 4544
écriture miroir 3005
écriture sans contact 6222
écroulement 9347
EDI 3323
éditer 3287
éditeur 3294
éditeur de connaissance 5239
éditeur d'écran 4117
éditeur de formulaires 3995
éditeur de liens 5392
éditeur de logiciel 8705
éditeur des liaisons 5392
éditeur de texte 9298
éditeur d'images 4652
éditeur graphique 4257
éditeur HTML 4576
éditeur par boutons 1298
éditeur source 8731
éditeur SQL 8798
édition 3290
édition de nœuds 6169

édition de paragraphe 6763
édition de rangée 8147
édition de texte 9297
édition d'image 4651
édition finale 1708
édition postérieure 7158
éditique 2060
éducation 5319
effaçage 1715
effaçage de connexion 2176
effaçage en arrière 1714
effacement 1045, 1715
effacement de profil 7383
effacement de style 8975
effacement de zones 510
effacement de zones d'image 510
effacer 1709
    tout ~ 1710
effacer l'écran 1720
effacer une page 2730
effecteur 3308
effectif 3302
effectuer un panoramique 6744
efférence 3309
effet 3300
effet acousto-optique 121
effet de bande 804
effet de bond 5186
effet de brouillard 3938
effet de coupe de page 6703
effet de crénelage 302
effet de loupe 10112
effet d'embrumer 1085
effet d'embuer 1085
effet de netteté 8498
effet de saut 5186
effet de voile 3938
effet flou 1085
effet magnéto-optique 5588
effet relief 3362
effets de rendu 7919
efficace 3302
efficacité 3311
efficience 3311
efflorescence 1080
effondrement de système 6
effondrement de tête 4414
effort d'organisation 6640, 6642
égal 6875
égalisateur 1984
égalisation 308, 796
égaliser 305
égalité 3459
éjecter 3312
éjection 6610
élaboration 2814
élargir 3615
élargissement 3591
électron 3320
électronique 3322, 3335

élément 1503, 3346, 5150
élément binaire 932
élément constitutif 1238
élément d'adaptation pour clients
    2435
élément d'affichage 3023
élément de champ 529
élément de code 1814
élément de comparaison 1975
élément de données 2568
élément de menu 5748
élément de protocole 7459
élément de tableau 529
élément de temporisation 5254
élément de traitement 7364
élément de volume 9923
élément d'image 7015
élément d'implication 4698
élément d'impression 7301
élément dual 3203
élément graphique 4258
élément inverse 5122
élément majoritaire 5610
élément matriciel 528
élément non divisible 4786
élément passif 6843
élément pictural 7015
élément premier 7255
élément primitif 7259
éléments constitutifs 2020
éléments de fenêtre 9992
éléments de menu de
    représentation 9841
élément sensible 8381
élément sensitif 9454
élément visuel 9895
élever 5357
éliminateur de modem 6311
élimination 1410, 3349
élimination et filtrage du bruit
    6197
éliminer 2733
elliptique 3352
éloigné 7888
élongation 3355
emballage 3393, 10058
emballage de données 2542
emballer 6669
embase 5401
emboîtage 6072
emboîté 6067
emboîtement 6072
emboîter 6066
embouchure 451
embouteillage 2162
embranchement 1157
embrassement mort 2621
embrassement mortel 2621
embrouillage 8232
embrouilleur 8231

embrumer 1084
émetteur 3370, 9524
émetteur de données 2594
émetteur d'impulsion de
    caractères 1612
émetteur-récepteur 9525
émettre 8369
émission 3367, 6616, 8372
émission de données 2584
émission des données graphiques
    4277
émissivité 3369
émittance lumineuse 5531
emmagasinage 8922
emmagasiner 8928
émoticône 8675
émouture 8496
empaquetage 6689
empaquetage compact 2756
empaqueter 6669
empilage 8808
empilage automatique 704
empilage logiciel 8706
empilement 6689
empilement de signes 6991
empirique 3373
emplacement 5446, 8666
emplacement libre 3594
employer 480
empoigner 1430
empreinte 8551
empreinte digitale 3841
empressement de données 7683
empressement de réception de
    données 7683
emprunt 1130
emprunt circulaire 2471
émulateur 3380
émulateur de terminal 9260
émulateur interne au circuit 4726
émulateur ROM 8118
émulation 3379
émulation de terminal 9259
encadreur 4052
encapsulage 1427
encapsulation 1427
encapsuler 3388
encastré 6067
encastrement 6072
encastrement d'image 4653
encastrer 6066
enchaînement 1550, 5003, 5391
enchaînement de données 2570
enchaînement de pages 6699
enclenchement 2452
enclencher 9094
enclore 3392
encoche de protection d'écriture
    10068
encoche d'interdiction d'écriture

10068
encodage par modulation de
    fréquence 4087
encodeur RealMedia 7695
encombrement 2162, 6365
encrage 4863
encre 4859
encre conductrice 2131
encre magnétique 5586
encrier 4865
encryptage 3400
encryption entière 3421
endommager 2335
endroit 7042
énergie 3424
enfichable 7072
enficher 6854
enfiler 10008
engagement 6365
engendrement 4204
engendrer 4200
engorgement 6661
engorgement de canal 6661
enlacement 5033
enlèvement 7910
enli 2170
enregistrement 1108, 2589, 5459
enregistrement à chaînage 8746
enregistrement à deux niveaux
    978
enregistrement à fusion 4185
enregistrement audio 643
enregistrement automatique 702
enregistrement bloqué 1066
enregistrement chaîné 8746
enregistrement d'en-tête 4419
enregistrement de base 854
enregistrement de capacité 1423
enregistrement de catalogue de
    données 1489
enregistrement de dépassement
    6639
enregistrement de données 2575,
    2589
enregistrement de données
    d'appels 1369
enregistrement de données de
    trafic 9471
enregistrement de piste 1579
enregistrement d'erreurs 3501
enregistrement des défauts 3686
enregistrement de service 4544
enregistrement de sous-niveau
    5717
enregistrement d'occasion 4724
enregistrement domestique 4544
enregistrement en modulation de
    phase 6934
enregistrement en-tête 4419
enregistrement fils 1660

enregistrement hélicoïdal 4430
enregistrement imprévu 4724
enregistrement longitudinal 5491
enregistrement magnétique 5578
enregistrement maître 5668
enregistrement monopolaire 6265
enregistrement non formaté 6238
enregistrement par défilement
    hélicoïdal 4430
enregistrement physique 6970
enregistrement rapide 7610
enregistrement sans contact 6222
enregistrement trame 7639
enregistrer 5456, 10060
enregistreur 5458
enregistreur du temps utilisé
    3315
enregistreur vidéo 9830
enrichissement 3434
enrobage 1427, 1796
enroulement 8107, 10058
enrouleur de bande 9208
enseignement 5319
enseignement assisté par
    ordinateur 2071
ensemble 8466
ensemble à écriture 10070
ensemble à lire 7675
ensemble de caractères ASCII
    557
ensemble de cartes 1093
ensemble de circuits 1675
ensemble de connecteurs externes
    3631
ensemble de construction
    supplémentaire 187
ensemble de données 2595
ensemble de données d'entrée
    4894
ensemble de forums 5605
ensemble de pixels 7039
ensemble de plaques 1093
ensemble de relais 7867
ensemble de sélection active 142
ensemble des images 4675
ensemble des parties d'un
    ensemble 7186
ensemble de têtes magnétiques
    5576
ensemble de touches 5224
ensemble de tous les sous-
    ensembles 7186
ensemble d'instructions 4954
en-tête 4415
en-tête de colonne 1886
en-tête de message 5772
en-tête de page 6712
entier 4959, 4962
entité 3441, 3442
entité de données 2545

entité de session 8460
entité géométrique 3442
entité SGML 8482
entourage 9069
entourer 9068
entraîné 4831
entraînement 154, 3157
entraînement de bande 9197
entraînement dynamique 3248
entraîner 3735
entrance 3704
entrant 4730
entraxe 7010
entrée 3444, 4880
   d'~ 4730
entrée à l'état initial 7990
entrée à registre verrou 5280
entrée commune 1929
entrée d'autorisation 3386
entrée de "1" 6422
entrée de balayage 8210
entrée de basculement 2001
entrée de commande 2269
entrée de données 2546
entrée de données éloignée 7897
entrée de données graphiques
   4276
entrée de données sans clavier
   6882
entrée de programme 7396
entrée de remise à zéro 7990
entrée de retour 7851
entrée de sélection 8318
entrée de signal de basculement
   2001
entrée de validation 3386
entrée d'inhibition 4837
entrée d'interdiction 4837
entrée d'un 6422
entrée du signal de mise à un
   8469
entrée en communication
   automatique 680
entrée fausse d'information 3701
entrée formatée 3988
entrée hors ligne 4782
entrée indirecte 4782
entrée inhibitrice 4837
entrée manuelle 5626
entrée monocanale 8607
entrée non codée 9615
entrée non formatée 3982
entrée non inversante 9617
entrée non stationnaire 6276
entrée numérique 2905
entrée par bouton 7514
entrée par clavier 5209
entrée parlée 8766
entrée réduite 7774
entrée sans format 3982

entrée/sortie 4903
entrée/sortie à commande par
   interruption 5086
entrée/sortie analogique 376
entrée/sortie avec répartition entre
   des ports 7137
entrée/sortie commandée par
   interruption 5086
entrée/sortie intelligente 4982
entrée/sortie parallèle 6781
entrée/sortie sérielle 8426
entrée symétrique 794
entrée synchrone 9121
entrée tamponnée 5280
entrée unité 905
entrée verbale 8766
entrée vidéo 9821
entrée vocale 8766
entrée zéro 906
entrelaçage d'adresses 5036
entrelaçage de bits 991
entrelaçage de mots 10028
entrelacement 5033
entrelacement d'audio et vidéo
   647
entrelacement de secteurs 8297
entrelacer 5028
entreprise de services logiciels
   8700
entrer 3437
entretien 5606, 8444
entropie 3443
énumérabilité 2340
énumérateur 3450
énumérateur de bus 1280
énumérateur du BIOS 964
énumération 3447
enveloppe 3451
enveloppe de câble 1327
enveloppe de texte 9299
envelopper 2297
environnement 3454
environnement à fenêtres 9991
environnement client/serveur
   1730
environnement de développement
   intégré 4969
environnement de programmation
   7416
environnement de réseau 6099
environnement interrogeant 7092
environnement virtuel 9862
environnement virtuel 3D 9860
environnement virtuel distribué
   3048
envoi de courrier en lots 1247
envoi en BCC 1052
envoi en nombre 1247
envoyer 8369
épine dorsal 746

épreuve 616, 1646
épreuve d'appel 1357
EPROM 3476
épurateur 1707
équation 3466
équation de rendu 7924
équation opératorielle 6521
équerres 399
équilibrage 796
équilibrage de câble 1320
équilibre 793
équilibre pour les gris 4311
équilibreur 797, 1983
équipement 3467, 4395
équipement auxiliaire 9061
équipement cryptographique 2401
équipement cryptologique 2406
équipement d'ajustage 8475
équipement d'entrée 4096
équipement d'essai 9277
équipement sériel 8424
équipement support 9061
équipement vidéo 9815
équivalence 3468
équivalent 3471
errance 8936
erreur 3480
erreur absolue 19
erreur accidentelle 7595
erreur accumulée 96
erreur admissible 257
erreur aléatoire 7595
erreur constante 9134
erreur cumulée 96
erreur d'accumulation 96
erreur d'adaptation 5677
erreur d'arrondissement 8127
erreur de calcul 2047
erreur de coïncidence 1845
erreur de déclaration 2668
erreur de dépassement 6637
erreur de la méthode 3505
erreur d'entrée 4897
erreur d'entrée/sortie graphique
   4288
erreur de parité verticale 9783
erreur de programme 7397
erreur des données d'entrée 4897
erreur de tri 5853
erreur de triage 5853
erreur de troncature 9573
erreur d'exploitation 37
erreur d'indication 4776
erreur d'interface 5016
erreur double 3128
erreur entraînée 4832
erreur fatale 3713
erreur fixe 9134
erreur héritée 4832
erreur humaine 4580

Русский

биокулярный 957
биологический фактор 5427
биометрические
    идентификационные
    системы 962
бионическая сеть 963
биофактор 5427
биполярное кодирование с
    высокой плотностью 4483
биполярный 969
биполярный микропроцессор
    970
бирка 9175
БИС 5270
бистабильность 975
бистабильный 976
бистабильный жидкий
    кристалл 977
бит 979
    P-~ 6810
    Z-~ 10090
бит адреса 203
бита/ов в секунду 1030
бит блокировки 5455
бит в секунду 1030
бит выравнивания 3460
бит выхода за допустимые
    пределы 6659
бит выходного переноса 5393
бит достоверности сигнала
    8550
бит заголовка 4416
бит запрета 4835
бит защиты 8302
бит индикации перепосылки
    4005
бит кадра 4036
бит контроля ошибок 3482
бит контроля по чётности 6806
битовая глубина 986
битовая комбинация 1018
битовая строка 983
битовая тетрада 4361
бит памяти 8923
бит параллельной работы 6787
бит переноса 1453
бит потери информации 6659
бит по чётности 6806
бит проверки 1648
бит проверки
    последовательности 8397
бит разделения 8392
бит разрешения 3382
бит расширения 5393
бит/сек 1030
бит слова 10022
бит совпадения 5194
бит состояния теста 9285
бит сравнения 5194
бит стартовой посылки 8841

бит считывания 8376
бит транзитной связи 9358
биты модификации 5873
бифуркация 918
бланк 8499
бланкирование 1045
блеск 1183
бликоподавляющая панель 446
блиттер 1058
"блоб" 93
блок 1786, 9668
блок баннера 817
блок верхней памяти 9711
блок ветвления 2658
блок вызова 1358
блок вычисления или ввода
    значений 9746
блок данных 1218, 4028
блок данных списковой
    структуры 5413
блок заголовков 9426
блокирование 5454
блокированное прерывание
    2972
блокированный 5452
блокированный слой 5453
блокировать 1059
блокировать объект 5451
блокировка 5454
блокировка выхода 6626
блокировка данных 9064
блокировка записи 7743
блокировка интерфейса 5018
блокировка клавиши 5221
блокировка по времени 9403
блокировка стандартного
    интерфейса 8818
блок клавиатуры
    редактирования 3293
блок ленты 5584
блок магнитной ленты 5584
блок магнитных головок 5576
блок микропрограммного
    управления 5821
блок-мультиплексный 1075
блок-мультиплексный канал
    1076
блокнот 2941, 6300
блокнотный компьютер 6299
блок обработки 7363
блок объяснения 3600
блок оценки 3535
блок переменной длины 9756
блок переменных 9752
блок пикселов 7018
блок питания 7184
блок подкачки для печати 7293
блок подкачки информации для
    печати 7293
блок предварительного

изображения 883
блок присваивания значений
    9746
блок программы 7390
блок раскраски изображения на
    экране 8252
блок регистров 7834
блок решения 2658
блок рисунка 6857
блок сбора данных 1218
блок состояния 8881
блок сравнения 1970
блок страницы 6711
блок-схема 3920
блок-схема обработки данных
    2559
блок управления выборкой
    команд 1901
блок управления доступом 67
блок функциональных клавиш
    468
блочная графика 5893
блочная конструкция 1065
блочная сортировка 1078
блочный код 1063
блочный комментарий 1149
блочный принцип 1239
блочный счётчик 1064
блуждание 8936
бод 872
боковой 5288
болтовня 1645
большая интегральная схема
    5270
большая стилизованная первая
    буква 3186
большие буквы 9709
большинство 5609
большого объёма 1244
большое усиление 4488
большой бутон 5266
большой двоичный объект 938
большой компьютер 5600
большой массив данных 2520
большой объём данных 2520
большой шрифт 919
бонус-инструменты 1107
бортовой компьютер 1091
брандмауэр 3851
брань 3879
браузер 1208
    Web-~ 9969
браузер чертежей 3162
бродилка 1208
бродить 9065
бродяга 2461
брокер 1205
бронирование памяти для
    размещения информации
    4566